PLACE IN RETURN BOX to remove this checkout from your record.
TO AVOID FINES return on or before date due.
MAY BE RECALLED with earlier due date if requested.

DATE DUE	DATE DUE	DATE DUE

5/08 K:/Proj/Acc&Pres/CIRC/DateDue.indd

WETLAND HABITATS OF NORTH AMERICA

THE STEPHEN BECHTEL FUND

IMPRINT IN ECOLOGY AND THE ENVIRONMENT

The Stephen Bechtel Fund has

established this imprint to promote

understanding and conservation of

our natural environment.

Wetland Habitats of North America

ECOLOGY AND CONSERVATION CONCERNS

Edited by

DAROLD P. BATZER

ANDREW H. BALDWIN

UNIVERSITY OF CALIFORNIA PRESS

Berkeley Los Angeles London

The publisher gratefully acknowledges the generous contribution to this book provided by the Stephen Bechtel Fund.

University of California Press, one of the most distinguished university presses in the United States, enriches lives around the world by advancing scholarship in the humanities, social sciences, and natural sciences. Its activities are supported by the UC Press Foundation and by philanthropic contributions from individuals and institutions. For more information, visit www.ucpress.edu.

University of California Press
Berkeley and Los Angeles, California

University of California Press, Ltd.
London, England

Library of Congress Cataloging-in-Publication Data

Wetland habitats of North America : ecology and conservation concerns / edited by Darold P. Batzer and Andrew H. Baldwin.
    p.   cm.
    ISBN 978-0-520-27164-7 (cloth : alk. paper)
    1. Wetlands—North America.   2. Wetland ecology—North America.   3. Wetland conservation—North America.   I. Batzer, Darold P.   II. Baldwin, Andrew H.
    QH102.W48   2012
    577.68097—dc23   2011035545

Manufactured in China

19   18   17   16   15   14   13   12
10   9   8   7   6   5   4   3   2   1

The paper used in this publication meets the minimum requirements of ANSI/NISO Z39.48–1992 (R 1997) *(Permanence of Paper).* ♾

Cover photograph: Tidal freshwater marsh, Patuxent River, Anne Arundel County, Maryland. Photo by Andrew H. Baldwin.

This book is dedicated to Linda, Brant, and Ross (D. P. B.)

and to

Virginia, Paula, Catherine, and Elizabeth (A. H. B.).

In memory of Charles C. Baldwin, Joan G. Ehrenfeld, and Robert L. Jefferies

CONTENTS

ADDITIONAL MATERIALS ARE AVAILABLE ONLINE AT
WWW.UCPRESS.EDU/GO/WETLANDHABITATS.

CONTRIBUTORS

MERRYL ALBER, Department of Marine Sciences, University of Georgia, Athens, GA 30602

CLARK R. ALEXANDER, Skidaway Institute of Oceanography, Savannah, GA 31411

DOUGLAS C. ANDERSEN, U.S. Geological Survey, Fort Collins Science Center, c/o U.S. Bureau of Reclamation, MS 86-68220, PO Box 25007, Denver, CO 80225

ANDREW H. BALDWIN, Department of Environmental Science and Technology, 1423 Animal Science Building, University of Maryland, College Park, MD 20742, baldwin@umd.edu

ROBERT F. BALDWIN, Department of Forestry and Natural Resources, Lehotsky Hall, Clemson University, Clemson, SC 29631

LORETTA L. BATTAGLIA, Department of Plant Biology and Center for Ecology, Southern Illinois University Carbondale, Mailcode 6509, Carbondale, IL 62901, lbattaglia@plant.siu.edu

DAROLD P. BATZER, Department of Entomology, University of Georgia, Athens, GA 30602, dbatzer@uga.edu

MELISSA BOOTH, University of Georgia Marine Institute, Sapelo Island, GA 31327

AMY B. BORDE, Pacific Northwest National Laboratory, Marine Sciences Laboratory, 1529 West Sequim Bay Road, Sequim, WA 98382

ADRIAN BURD, Department of Marine Sciences, University of Georgia, Athens, GA 30602

WEI-JUN CAI, Department of Marine Sciences, University of Georgia, Athens, GA 30602

ARAM J. K. CALHOUN, Department of Wildlife Ecology, University of Maine, Orono, ME 04469, calhoun@maine.edu

JOHN C. CALLAWAY, Department of Environmental Science, University of San Francisco, 2130 Fulton Street, San Francisco, CA 94117, callaway@usfca.edu

RODNEY A. CHIMNER, School of Forest Resources and Environmental Science, Michigan Tech University, 1400 Townsend Drive, Houghton, MI 49931

DAVID J. COOPER, Department of Forest, Rangeland and Watershed Stewardship, Forestry Room 200, Colorado State University, Fort Collins, CO 80523, David.Cooper@warnercnr.colostate.edu

CHRISTOPHER CRAFT, School of Public and Environmental Affairs, Indiana University, Bloomington, IN 47405

FRANK DAY, Department of Biological Sciences, Old Dominion University, Norfolk, VA 23529

JOHN W. DAY, Jr., Coastal Ecology Institute, Louisiana State University, 2237 Energy Coast and Environment Building, Baton Rouge, LA 70803

CHESTER B. DEPRATTER, South Carolina Institute of Archaeology and Anthropology, University of South Carolina, Columbia, SC 29208

ANDRÉ DESROCHERS, Peatland Ecology Research Group, Pavillon Paul-Comtois, Université Laval 2425, rue de l'Agriculture, Québec, Québec G1V 0A6, Canada

HEIDA L. DIEFENDERFER, Pacific Northwest National Laboratory, Marine Sciences Laboratory, 1529 West Sequim Bay Road, Sequim, WA 98382

DANIELA DI IORIO, Department of Marine Sciences, University of Georgia, Athens, GA 30602

KEVIN S. DILLON, Department of Coastal Sciences, University of Southern Mississippi, 703 East Beach Drive, Ocean Springs, MS 39564

JOAN EHRENFELD, Department of Ecology, Evolution, and Natural Resources, SEBS, 14 College Farm Road, New Brunswick, NJ 08901

JOSEPH P. FLESKES, U.S. Geological Survey–Western Ecological Research Center, 6924 Tremont Road, Dixon, CA 95620, joe_fleskes@usgs.gov

MEGAN K. GAHL, Department of Biology, Canadian Rivers Institute, University of New Brunswick, 100 Tucker Park Boulevard, Saint John, New Brunswick E2L 4L5, Canada

EVELYN E. GAISER, Department of Biological Sciences and Southeast Environmental Research Center, Florida International University, Miami, FL 33199, gaisere@fiu.edu

SUSAN GALATOWITSCH, University of Minnesota, Department of Horticultural Science, 305 Alderman Hall, St. Paul, MN 55108, galat001@umn.edu

STEPHEN W. GOLLADAY, J. W. Jones Ecological Research Center, Route 2, Box 2324, Newton, GA 39870

LAURA GOUGH, Department of Biology, University of Texas at Arlington, Arlington, TX 76019, gough@uta.edu

MARTHA GRAF, Peatland Ecology Research Group, Pavillon Paul-Comtois, Université Laval 2425, rue de l'Agriculture, Québec, Québec G1V 0A6, Canada

DAVID A. HAUKOS, Kansas Cooperative Fish and Wildlife Research Unit, Kansas State University, Manhattan, KS 66506

MARK W. HESTER, Department of Biology, University of Louisiana at Lafayette, PO Box 42451, Lafayette, LA 70504

CHARLES S. HOPKINSON, Department of Marine Sciences, University of Georgia, Athens, GA 30602

CLIFF R. HUPP, U.S. Geological Survey, 430 National Center, 12201 Sunrise Valley Drive, Reston, VA 20192

DULCE INFANTE MATA, Instituto de Ecología, A.C., Red de Ecología Funcional, Carretera Antigua a Coatepec no. 351, El Haya, Xalapa 91070, Veracruz, México

CAROL A. JOHNSTON, Department of Biology and Microbiology, Box 2207B, South Dakota State University, Brookings, SD 57007–0896, carol.johnston@sdstate.edu

SAMANTHA B. JOYE, Department of Marine Sciences, University of Georgia, Athens, GA 30602

PATRICK J. KANGAS, Department of Environmental Science and Technology, 1426 Animal Science Building, University of Maryland, College Park, MD 20742

RICHARD F. KEIM, 227 School of Renewable Natural Resources, Louisiana State University Agricultural Center, Baton Rouge, LA 70803

MARY JANE KELEHER, Salt Lake Community College, Biology Department, 4600 Redwood Road, Salt Lake City, UT 84130, MaryJane.Keleher@slcc.edu

SAMMY L. KING, Louisiana Cooperative Fish and Wildlife Research Unit, U.S. Geological Survey, 124 School of Renewable Natural Resources, Baton Rouge, LA 70803, sking16@lsu.edu

L. KATHERINE KIRKMAN, J. W. Jones Ecological Research Center, Route 2, Box 2324, Newton, GA 39870, kkirkman@jonesctr.org

CLAUDE LAVOIE, Peatland Ecology Research Group, Pavillon Paul-Comtois, Université Laval 2425, rue de l'Agriculture, Québec, Québec G1V 0A6, Canada

B. GRAEME LOCKABY, School of Forestry and Wildlife Sciences, Auburn University, Auburn, AL 36849

HUGO LÓPEZ ROSAS, Instituto de Genética, Universidad del Mar, Puerto Escondido 71980, Oaxaca, México

KAREN L. MCKEE, U.S. Geological Survey, National Wetlands Research Center, 700 Cajundome Boulevard, Lafayette, LA 70506, mckeek@usgs.gov

SCOTT T. MCMURRY, Department of Zoology, Oklahoma State University, Stillwater, OK 74078

J. PATRICK MEGONIGAL, Smithsonian Environmental Research Center, 647 Contees Wharf Road, Edgewater, MD 21037

CHRISTOF D. MEILE, Department of Marine Sciences, University of Georgia, Athens, GA 30602

DAVID M. MERRITT, U.S. Forest Service Watershed, Fish, and Wildlife, and Colorado State University Natural Resource Ecology Laboratory, Natural Resources Research Center, 2150 Centre Avenue, Building A, Suite 368, Fort Collins, CO 80526

WILLARD S. MOORE, Department of Earth and Ocean Sciences, University of South Carolina, Columbia, SC 29208

PATRICIA MORENO-CASASOLA, Instituto de Ecología, A.C., Red de Ecología Funcional, Carretera Antigua a Coatepec no. 351, El Haya, Xalapa 91070, Veracruz, México, patricia.moreno@inecol.edu.mx

V. THOMAS PARKER, Department of Biology, 449 Hensill Hall, 1600 Holloway Avenue, San Francisco State University, San Francisco, CA 94132

STEVEN C. PENNINGS, Department of Biology and Biochemistry, University of Houston, Houston, TX 77204, scpennin@Central.UH.EDU

MATTHEW C. PERRY, U.S. Geological Survey, Patuxent Wildlife Research Center, 12100 Beech Forest Road, Laurel, MD 20708

MARK S. PETERSON, Department of Coastal Sciences, University of Southern Mississippi, 703 East Beach Drive, Ocean Springs, MS 39564

MONIQUE POULIN, Peatland Ecology Research Group, Pavillon Paul-Comtois, Université Laval 2425, rue de l'Agriculture, Québec, Québec G1V 0A6, Canada

JONATHAN S. PRICE, Peatland Ecology Research Group, Pavillon Paul-Comtois, Université Laval 2425, rue de l'Agriculture, Québec, Québec G1V 0A6, Canada

CURTIS J. RICHARDSON, Wetland Center, Nicholas School of the Environment and Earth Science, Duke University, Durham, NC 27708, curtr12@gmail.com

LINE ROCHEFORT, Peatland Ecology Research Group, Pavillon Paul-Comtois, Université Laval 2425, rue de l'Agriculture, Québec, Québec G1V 0A6, Canada, Line.Rochefort@fsaa.ulaval.ca

CHARLES T. ROMAN, National Park Service, North Atlantic Coast Cooperative Ecosystem Studies Unit, University of Rhode Island, Narragansett, RI 02882

JOHN M. RYBCZYK, Department of Environmental Science, ES437, Huxley College, Western Washington University, 516 High Street, Bellingham, WA 98225

DON SADA, Desert Research Institute, Division of Hydrological Sciences, 2215 Raggio Parkway, Reno, NV 89512

MICHAEL L. SCOTT, U.S. Geological Survey, Fort Collins Science Center, Fort Collins, CO 80526

GARY P. SHAFFER, Department of Biological Sciences, 405 Biology Building, Southeastern Louisiana University, Box 10736, Hammond, LA 70402

BRIAN R. SILLIMAN, Department of Biology, University of Florida, Gainesville, FL 32611

LORA L. SMITH, J. W. Jones Ecological Research Center, Route 2, Box 2324, Newton, GA 39870

LOREN M. SMITH, Department of Zoology, Oklahoma State University, Stillwater, OK 74078, loren.smith@okstate.edu

MARIA STRACK, Peatland Ecology Research Group, Pavillon Paul-Comtois, Université Laval 2425, rue de l'Agriculture, Québec, Québec G1V 0A6, Canada

JULIET C. STROMBERG, School of Life Sciences, Arizona State University, Tempe, AZ 85287–4501,jstrom@asu.edu

RONALD M. THOM, Pacific Northwest National Laboratory, Marine Sciences Laboratory, 1529 West Sequim Bay Road, Sequim, WA 98382

VICTOR THOMPSON, Department of Anthropology, The Ohio State University, Columbus, OH 43210

JOEL C. TREXLER, Department of Biological Science, Florida International University, 3000 NE 151st Street, Miami, FL 33199

JENNEKE M. VISSER, Institute for Coastal Ecology and Engineering and School of Geoscience, University of Louisiana at Lafayette, PO Box 44650, Lafayette, LA 70504, jvisser@louisiana.edu

JOHN P. WARES, Department of Genetics, University of Georgia, Athens, GA 30602

PAUL R. WETZEL, Center for the Environment, Ecological Design and Sustainability, Smith College, Northampton, MA 01063

DENNIS F. WHIGHAM, Smithsonian Environmental Research Center, 647 Contees Wharf Road, Edgewater, MD 21037

CATHLEEN WIGAND, U.S. Environmental Protection Agency, Office of Research and Development, National Health and Environmental Effects Research Lab, Atlantic Ecology Division, Narragansett, RI 02882, wigand.cathleen@epa.gov

DOUGLAS A. WILCOX, Department of Environmental Science and Biology, The College at Brockport, State University of New York, 350 New Campus Drive, Brockport, NY 14420, dwilcox@brockport.edu

MARK S. WOODREY, Coastal Research and Extension Center, Mississippi State University, 1815 Popps Ferry Road, Biloxi, MS 39532

PREFACE

Wetlands are a prominent landscape feature throughout the North American continent. While the general characteristics of wetlands are well understood, there has not been a systematic assessment of the scientific literature on the ecology of different wetland habitat types in various parts of North America, or a compendium of the threats to their conservation. We were inspired by the robust and incredibly detailed series "Community Profiles" and "Estuarine Profiles," published by the U.S. Fish and Wildlife Service primarily in the 1980s, with a few in the early 1990s. There are 56 of these profiles, each of which focuses on a particular wetland type or estuary in a specific part of the USA. We have adopted a similar geographic and habitat approach in this book, in which experts familiar with wetlands from many parts of North America provide analyses of current and classic literature on studies collected in, or directly relevant to, their particular region of study.

In editing this book, we have kept the needs of a fairly broad audience in mind: students, scientists, engineers, environmental managers, policymakers, and the general public. Our goal is to provide reviews of recent, scientifically rigorous literature directly relevant to understanding, managing, protecting, and restoring wetland ecosystems in various regions of North America. This book should be useful as a textbook in graduate and undergraduate courses in ecology and environmental science programs, but also should be a valuable reference for researchers in academic and governmental institutions. We hope it will foster improved understanding of variation in ecological processes and threats to conservation across the regions of North America, and that it will point the way toward future research and collaborations. The habitat approach used here also lends itself to application in managing and restoring different types of wetlands in a wide range of geomorphic and hydrologic settings. The broad geographic coverage and habitat format are also well suited to developing environmental policy relevant to wetland regulation over large areas. And, finally, the text and layout of the chapters, while grounded in rigorous science, are accessible to anyone interested in learning more about the great diversity and variability of the types of wetlands in their own region or in other parts of North America.

We extend our deepest thanks and appreciation to the contributors to this book and to our anonymous reviewers, who volunteered their time, knowledge, and enthusiasm toward the creation of this book, and to our families, who put up with our late nights and celebrated our successes.

Andy Baldwin
Darold Batzer

CHAPTER 1

Wetland Habitats of North America

An Introduction

ANDREW H. BALDWIN and DAROLD P. BATZER

The goal of this book is to summarize recent literature and current perspectives on the ecology of wetland habitats of the North American continent and primary concerns regarding their conservation. All wetlands, by definition, share certain characteristics, notably the seasonal or permanent saturation or inundation of soils. This waterlogging of soils and the presence of standing water impose ecological constraints on organisms and a geomorphological environment very different from those of nonwetland ecosystems. Beyond the broad umbrella of inundation and soil saturation, however, wetlands differ dramatically between and within climatic and geomorphic zones due to myriad interacting physical, chemical, and biological processes. Environmental studies or restoration projects conducted in one type of wetland in one part of North America may have outcomes that are broadly or narrowly applicable to wetlands elsewhere. This creates a dilemma for wetland scientists, students, managers, and policymakers, who must identify research projects, implement management or restoration, and develop environmental policy based on limited information.

In this book, we chose a habitat and geographical approach to highlight differences among the most important ecological characteristics and threats to the major types of North American wetlands. This book is a companion volume to *Ecology of Freshwater and Estuarine Wetlands* (Batzer and Sharitz 2006), which addresses ecosystem processes and structural attributes of wetlands in general, across many types of wetlands. Other recent books that provide general information include *Wetlands* (Mitsch and Gosselink 2007), *Wetland Ecology: Principles and Conservation* (Keddy 2010), and *The Biology of Freshwater Wetlands* (van der Valk 2006). The earlier edition of *Wetlands* (Mitsch and Gosselink 2000) included seven chapters on individual coastal and inland wetland habitats, which were updated and expanded in a separate volume, *Wetland Ecosystems* (Mitsch, Gosselink, et al. 2009). Individual habitats were also treated in *Coastal Wetlands: An Integrated Ecosystem Approach* (Perillo, Wolanski, et al. 2009) and in *Ecology of Tidal Freshwater Forested Wetlands of the Southeastern United States* (Conner, Doyle, et al. 2007). Our book differs from these

works in that it takes a systematic, geographic approach to capture a similar set of ecosystem characteristics and conservation concerns for all major wetland habitat types within different regions of North America. In this, our approach is similar to the "Community Profiles" series published by the U.S. Fish and Wildlife Service.

The wetlands of North America are wonderfully diverse. They range from the tropics to the Arctic and are widespread in Canada, the United States, Mexico, and Central America. The chapters in this book are written by experts with deep knowledge and experience in most of the major types of wetlands in different regions of North America (Fig. 1.1). Our coverage is complete, with one important exception: Arctic coastal wetlands. Robert Jefferies, a leader in this area, had agreed to author a chapter on this topic, but, to our great sadness, he passed away before he could do so. We refer the reader to a chapter he coauthored in another book (Martini, Jefferies, et al. 2009). To provide a framework, we asked authors to address several main aspects of the wetlands in their region:

- Geology, hydrology, and biogeochemistry
- Plant communities
- Animal communities
- Key ecological processes and controls
- Conservation concerns or threats

To reduce repetition between chapters, we specifically asked authors not to include general information on wetlands, but to focus only on studies or information collected in their region. Chapters on coastal wetlands are included in part I of the book. They are grouped separately from nontidal wetlands because of the overriding influence of tidal hydrology on their structure and functioning. Inland wetlands are grouped in part II. There are many more habitat types of inland wetlands than coastal wetlands due to great variation in relative inputs of precipitation, surface water, and groundwater, as well as their greater surface area and richness of plant and animal taxa. Wetlands of the temperate zone have received more scientific attention than those of the tropics and Arctic, and hence we

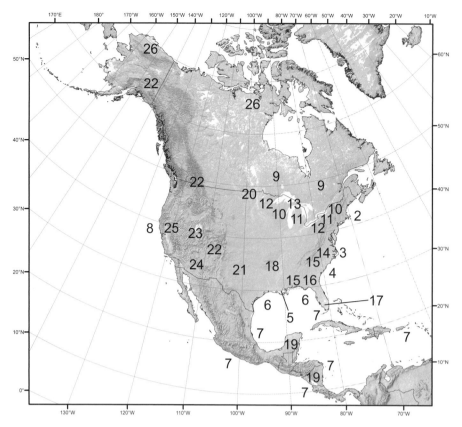

FIG. 1.1. Location of wetlands covered in this book within the North American continent. Numbers correspond to the chapter covering those wetlands. Coastal wetland chapters have numbers in the ocean adjacent to their position on the coast. Map prepared by A. H. Baldwin.

include more chapters on those wetlands, which primarily occur in the USA. The vast areas of wetlands in northern North America and biologically rich tropical wetlands are nonetheless important and ecologically interesting ecosystems deserving of greater study.

In this introductory chapter, we summarize important differences and similarities between wetland habitats in different regions of North America, separating discussion of coastal and inland wetlands and focusing on key ecological processes and conservation concerns. To assess the generality of processes and concerns, as well as their regional importance, we list their occurrence in each chapter in Tables 1.1 (coastal wetlands) and 1.2 (inland wetlands). This approach does not mean that some processes are not important in regions elsewhere, but may reflect a lack of literature on the topic. Differences among the relative importance of dominant or unique plant or animal taxa are also discussed here.

Coastal Wetlands

Key Ecological Processes and Controls

The development of coastal wetlands is fundamentally a result of geomorphology and climate, which together create hydrologic characteristics that exert an overriding influence on wetland ecosystem structure and function. All authors of coastal chapters in this book explicitly or implicitly identify these factors as fundamental controls on wetland ecosystems (Table 1.1a). The hydrology of coastal wetlands differs considerably

from that of inland wetlands in being dominated by tides and, to a lesser extent, surface water inflows (which control salinity, nutrient supply, and sediment deposition). Groundwater and precipitation are rarely mentioned in the coastal chapters. Because coastal wetlands are located in the depositional zone of rivers in estuaries, it is not surprising that sedimentation and salinity are also uniformly recognized as important. However, several biotic processes are mentioned in all of the coastal chapters, including productivity, peat accumulation, predation, outwelling, and vegetation zonation, which are discussed in more detail in this section.

High primary productivity, coupled with slow decomposition rates due to anaerobic conditions, favors the accumulation of peat in soils, providing a mechanism important for the maintenance of wetland surface elevation relative to sea level. Primary productivity and peat accumulation are highlighted in all of the coastal chapters, and decomposition and anaerobiosis are featured in a majority of them (Table 1.1a). Elevation and salinity gradients within individual wetlands and across estuaries lead to horizontal zonation of emergent and submergent plants, another ubiquitous topic in the coastal chapters. Stress-tolerant species occur where salinity or depth and duration of inundation are greater (and hypoxia more pronounced), such as the lower elevations of salt marshes, but studies have demonstrated that these species are often poor competitors in fresher or higher-elevation sites, such as the higher elevations of tidal freshwater wetlands. Under stressful conditions, one species may facilitate the growth of others by, for example, aerating the soil or shading to reduce salinity. Competition and facilitation are recognized as important pro-

TABLE I.I

A. Key ecological processes and controls

B. Conservation concerns highlighted by authors of seven chapters addressing coastal wetlands

Processes/controls and concerns are sorted first in decreasing order of
the number of chapters in which they are noted and then alphabetically.
A triangle (▲) indicates the process or concern is discussed in a chapter.

	No. of chapters	Chapter number						
		2	3	4	5	6	7	8
A. KEY ECOLOGICAL PROCESSES AND CONTROLS								
Climatic variation (El Niño, drought, latitude, elevation)	7	▲	▲	▲	▲	▲	▲	▲
Geomorphic variation (topography, soils, glaciation)	7	▲	▲	▲	▲	▲	▲	▲
Hydrologic variation (hydroperiod, flows, groundwater inputs, evapotranspiration)	7	▲	▲	▲	▲	▲	▲	▲
Nutrient supplies (phosphorus/nitrogen limitation and cycling)	7	▲	▲	▲	▲	▲	▲	▲
Outwelling and external trophic support	7	▲	▲	▲	▲	▲	▲	▲
Peat accumulation	7	▲	▲	▲	▲	▲	▲	▲
Predation	7	▲	▲	▲	▲	▲	▲	▲
Primary productivity	7	▲	▲	▲	▲	▲	▲	▲
Salinity/conductivity	7	▲	▲	▲	▲	▲	▲	▲
Sedimentation	7	▲	▲	▲	▲	▲	▲	▲
Vegetation gradients and zonation	7	▲	▲	▲	▲	▲	▲	▲
Decomposition	6	▲	▲	▲	▲	▲	▲	
Plant-animal interactions (herbivory, detritivory, plants/wood as habitat)	6	▲	▲	▲	▲	▲	▲	
Anoxia/oxygen	5	▲		▲	▲	▲	▲	
Seed dispersal/rain, seed predation, seed banks, and seedling recruitment	5		▲		▲	▲	▲	▲
Competition (food, light, nutrients)	4	▲		▲			▲	▲
Habitat connectivity (isolation, upland-wetland interaction, patchiness)	4	▲			▲	▲		▲
Storms (hurricanes, floods)	4			▲	▲	▲	▲	
Endemism	3					▲	▲	▲
Facilitation	3	▲					▲	▲
Fire	3		▲		▲	▲		
Keystone species (ecosystem engineers, beavers)	3		▲	▲				▲
Mutualism (N-fixation, mycorrhizae)	3	▲		▲				▲
pH (acidity, alkalinity)	2	▲		▲				

(continued)

TABLE 1.1 *(continued)*

	No. of chapters	Chapter number						
		2	3	4	5	6	7	8
B. CONSERVATION CONCERNS								
Sea-level rise	7	▲	▲	▲	▲	▲	▲	▲
Restoration/mitigation practices	6	▲	▲		▲	▲	▲	▲
Eutrophication (point and nonpoint sources)	5	▲	▲	▲		▲	▲	
Hydrologic alteration (ditches, dikes, filling, tidal restrictions, groundwater withdrawal, flow regulations)	5	▲	▲		▲	▲	▲	
Invasive/exotic species	5	▲	▲		▲	▲		▲
Climate shifts (precipitation, temperature)	4	▲		▲			▲	▲
Watershed imperviousness, development, and land-use change	4	▲		▲		▲	▲	
Drought	3			▲	▲	▲		
Population increase	3	▲		▲				▲
Subsidence	3		▲		▲			▲
Sudden die-back	3	▲		▲	▲			
Elevated CO_2	2	▲						▲
Freshwater delivery to coastal wetlands/excess salinity	2			▲				▲

NOTE: Only those processes or concerns addressed in at least two chapters are listed. Chapter numbers refer to North American coastal wetlands of the 2. North Atlantic, 3. Chesapeake Bay, 4. South Atlantic, 5. Mississippi River Delta, 6. Gulf of Mexico, 7. Neotropics, and 8. Pacific.

cesses in about half the coastal chapters. Some salt-marsh soils become acidic when drained (acid-sulfate soils, mentioned in two coastal chapters), but coastal wetland soils are generally pH-circumneutral.

High rates of primary productivity and, in many wetlands, structural, spatial, and species diversity of plants, result in high rates of secondary production. Coastal wetlands support estuarine food webs not only by providing in situ habitat and food sources, but also by exporting or "outwelling" organic matter to estuaries, forming an important foundation of coastal food webs that is emphasized in all of the coastal chapters. Coastal wetlands often serve as nurseries for larval and juvenile stages of aquatic organisms, providing refuge from predation, an ecological process mentioned in all of the coastal chapters. Plant-animal interactions are also a major process in most coastal wetlands; herbivory is most frequently mentioned, both for its role in food-web support and as a disturbance process affecting plant community dynamics. Seed-related processes, including dispersal, predation, seed banks, and seedling recruitment, mentioned in a majority of the coastal chapters, are often important to the regeneration of plant communities following disturbance and are critical to diversity maintenance in wetlands containing a large proportion of annual species, such as tidal freshwater marshes. The particular importance of storms and hurricanes is recognized for those regions experiencing regular major hurricanes, i.e., the southeastern U.S. coasts and parts of the Neotropics. Some plants and animals function as ecosystem engineers, altering the geomorphology and hydrology of coastal

wetlands; examples include beavers, crabs, and dominant clonal plants. Thus, the vegetation of coastal wetlands is dynamic, in large part due to continued natural disturbance, seed and seedling-recruitment processes, and competitive interactions.

Conservation Concerns

It is not a surprise that sea-level rise is identified as a major threat to coastal wetlands in all parts of North America (Table 1.1b). Increases in the rate of eustatic sea-level rise, coupled with land subsidence in many regions, will challenge the capacity of coastal wetlands to keep pace with rising sea levels. Eutrophication due to inputs of nitrogen or phosphorus from point and nonpoint sources is also identified as important in all regions except the Pacific coast. Excess nutrients are important in shifting plant species composition and have been implicated as a potential factor in marsh die-back.

Many wetlands have been hydrologically altered since European colonization, but despite environmental statutes regulating activities in wetlands, hydrologic alterations continue to threaten coastal wetlands in many regions of North America. Notably, these are not mentioned as being of overriding importance for south Atlantic wetlands, which are relatively unimpacted physically relative to other parts of the North American coast (except for widespread historic conversion of tidal freshwater wetlands to rice fields), or for Pacific coast wetlands, where the vast majority of coastal wetlands historically were lost due to diking, but which are currently closely protected and restoration efforts are ongoing (Table 1.1b). Neotropical coastal wetlands, in contrast, were primarily used for sustainable harvest of vegetation and animal products until recent decades, when many mangrove forests have been converted to aquaculture ponds or tourist resorts.

Nonnative or invasive species of plants or animals are also identified as a major conservation concern in a majority of coastal wetland chapters (Table 1.1b). Exceptions are the south Atlantic coastal wetlands and the Neotropics. South Atlantic wetlands may not face the invasive species problems of other regions due to lower ongoing physical alteration of coastal wetlands, perhaps due to lower population densities. In the Neotropics, temperate-zone plants and animals may not be able to tolerate elevated temperatures or to compete with tropical plants, reducing their threat to tropical ecosystems.

In addition to causing increases in eustatic sea levels, changes in precipitation and temperature may impact wetlands in several ways and are mentioned in a majority of the coastal chapters. Lower precipitation may result in salinity increases in some regions where flow of freshwater to the coast is already insufficient or decreasing due to human alteration of hydrology, for example in the Pacific coast and south Atlantic watersheds. Similarly, climate change may cause widespread drought, a likely factor in die-back of coastal wetlands. Higher temperatures will differentially affect the growth of plant and animal species, as well as speed up processes such as decomposition that are fundamental to wetland ecosystem function. Increases in atmospheric CO_2 (mentioned in only two chapters but likely to be important in all wetlands) are not only a cause of climate change, but also will alter plant community dynamics and potentially other ecosystem processes. Increasing human population density (identified in three coastal chapters) continues to threaten coastal wetlands via watershed development, land-use changes, harvesting of plant and animal resources, and further hydrologic alteration.

These and other conservation concerns are related and linked in complex ways that require novel research approaches to untangle. Manipulative experiments that examine multiple processes together can provide insights into how factors such as CO_2, nutrients, salinity, and temperature interact. Such experiments, coupled with observational studies and system modeling, can help us progress toward greater understanding and better prediction of how human activities are affecting coastal wetlands. However, the chapters in this book highlight that coastal wetland research must be multidisciplinary so that interactions between hydrology, climate, geomorphology, biogeochemistry, and organisms can be explored.

Inland Wetlands

Key Ecological Processes and Controls

As for coastal systems, hydrologic variation is identified as an important control on ecology by every author addressing inland wetlands (Table 1.2a). Given that inland wetlands can be fed by various sources of water (precipitation, groundwater, riverine flows), and that water budgets can vary greatly—either spatially among and within wetlands, or temporally among and within seasons, years, and decades—the importance given to hydrology is to be expected. Geomorphic and climatic variation are also identified as being important con-

trols by most authors, primarily because these are the factors that most influence the hydrology of inland wetlands. The chemical nature of the water, including nutrient levels (phosphorus and, to a lesser extent, nitrogen), pH, oxygen level, and salinity (especially in western wetlands), is also considered important. It is clear from Table 1.2a that the abiotic template dictated by the physico-chemical conditions of water is considered *the* major control on the ecology of inland wetlands.

However, biotic interactions in inland wetlands are also considered important influences by most authors (Table 1.2a). Bottom-up controls are most frequently discussed. Nutrient limitation on plants from P and N, as well as competition for light and space, are common themes. Mutualism, especially in relation to nitrogen fixation by plants/microbes, is discussed in five chapters. Plants as food (herbivory or detritivory) or as habitat are considered crucial bottom-up controls on wetland animals by most authors. Top-down control from predation, either on other animals or on plants, is identified as an important control by about half of the authors of inland wetland chapters. Control of wetlands by keystone animal species is another important top-down impact, with beavers being by far the most influential animal.

The impact of disturbance is a third general theme developed by authors of inland wetland chapters. Fire is identified as an important control in half of the chapters, particularly those focusing on the southeastern USA. Storms (primarily hurricanes in the Southeast and the tropics) floods, and droughts are other important disturbances. With the general importance of disturbance in inland wetlands, successional processes are identified as important controls by half of the authors.

Landscape features as controls on inland wetlands is the final major theme developed by authors. As mentioned, geomorphic variation is considered a crucial impact on wetlands by most authors, and besides the impacts on hydrology, direct impacts of soils and topography are often identified as being important. Habitat connectivity across landscapes (e.g., isolation or patchiness) and interactions between uplands and embedded wetlands is a major theme, particularly for depressional habitats.

Conservation Concerns

Since hydrology is considered the major ecological control on inland wetlands, it follows that any impacts on water budgets for wetlands are of particular concern (see Table 1.2b). Many of the authors of inland wetland chapters highlight threats from climate change, primarily because of concerns about potential hydroperiod alteration. Other concerns included under the umbrella of hydrology are impacts of flow regulation of rivers by dams and levees on riparian floodplain wetlands, impacts of groundwater pumping on assorted wetlands, and continued concern about any management that drains wetlands. While most author concern focuses on the threats posed by making wetlands drier, some chapters point out that factors that increase hydroperiods also need to be considered. For northeastern seasonal wetlands (see chapter 10), the authors point out that past mitigation efforts that have focused on developing long-hydroperiod ponds may actually pose a threat to seasonal wetland pools, as important functions associated with seasonal flooding are not being replaced. The theme of restoration is developed by several authors, again with the overriding theme focusing on restoration of natural hydrology.

TABLE 1.2

A. Key ecological controls
B. Conservation concerns as highlighted by authors of 18 chapters
addressing inland wetlands of North America

Processes/controls and concerns are sorted first in decreasing order of
number of chapters in which they are noted and then alphabetically.
A triangle (▲) indicates the process or concern was discussed in a chapter.

	No. of chapters	Chapter number			
		9	10	11	12
A. KEY ECOLOGICAL PROCESSES AND CONTROLS					
Hydrologic variation (hydroperiod, flows, groundwater inputs, evapotranspiration)	18	▲	▲	▲	▲
Geomorphic variation (topography, soils, glaciation, karstic landscapes)	17	▲	▲	▲	▲
Nutrient supplies (phosphorus/nitrogen limitation and cycling)	13	▲		▲	
Plant-animal interactions (herbivory, detritivory, plants/wood as habitat)	11		▲		▲
Climatic variation (El Niño, drought, latitude, elevation)	10				
Anoxia/oxygen	9	▲	▲		▲
Fire	9	▲			
Habitat connectivity (isolation, upland-wetland interaction, patchiness)	9	▲	▲	▲	▲
pH (acidity, alkalinity)	9	▲		▲	▲
Predation	9		▲		▲
Succession	9	▲		▲	▲
Keystone species (ecosystem engineers, beavers)	8	▲			▲
Salinity/conductivity	7				
Storms (hurricanes, floods)	7				
Competition (food, light, nutrients)	6	▲			
Decomposition	6	▲			
Endemism	5	▲			
Mutualism (N-fixation, mycorrhizae)	5	▲			▲
Primary productivity	5	▲			
Peat accumulation	4	▲			
Sedimentation	4				▲
Vegetation gradients and zonation	4	▲			

Authors writing about conservation of inland wetlands focus on another major theme: biodiversity issues, primarily threatened or endangered species. Because many inland wetlands exist as isolated patches on the landscape, it is not surprising that endemic species, or at least species that occur across a restricted area, can be common. As these habitats are destroyed or degraded, resident species may become threatened. Because wetlands support biota unique from that of uplands, the value of embedded wetlands in buttressing overall regional diversity is frequently mentioned. Several authors point out that connectivity among wetland patches and between wetlands and surrounding uplands all need to be considered when assessing the integrity of overall wetland systems.

A group of conservation threats to inland wetlands receives a similar level of attention from authors. Agriculture and water pollution have long been associated with the decline of inland wetlands, and both themes are still highlighted by the authors of this book. However, threats from urbanization and other development, and from climate change, are now receiving a similar level of focus. The threat from invasive species, particu-

13	14	15	16	17	18	19	20	21	22	23	24	25	26
▲	▲	▲	▲	▲	▲	▲	▲	▲	▲	▲	▲	▲	▲
	▲	▲	▲	▲	▲	▲	▲	▲	▲	▲	▲	▲	▲
	▲	▲	▲	▲	▲	▲	▲		▲		▲	▲	▲
▲		▲			▲	▲	▲	▲	▲		▲		▲
▲	▲			▲	▲	▲	▲	▲	▲		▲		▲
▲		▲			▲		▲			▲			▲
	▲	▲	▲	▲	▲	▲					▲		▲
		▲					▲	▲		▲	▲		
	▲		▲		▲	▲	▲						▲
▲		▲	▲	▲		▲		▲					▲
▲			▲		▲		▲				▲		▲
				▲	▲		▲		▲		▲	▲	
					▲		▲	▲	▲	▲	▲	▲	
▲	▲		▲	▲	▲	▲					▲		
▲				▲	▲	▲							▲
			▲	▲	▲		▲	▲					
		▲								▲	▲	▲	
									▲		▲		▲
			▲	▲	▲								▲
			▲	▲					▲				
▲					▲						▲		
							▲		▲	▲			

(continued)

larly plants, is another pervasive theme (similar to coastal wetlands). Threats from livestock grazing are mentioned by nearly every author addressing western North American habitats.

Because many "isolated" inland wetlands have recently lost legal protections from the U.S. government (e.g., Downing, Winer, et al. 2003), concern over wetland regulation in the USA is another important theme for many authors. However, concerns are not limited to recent statutory changes; instead a general angst exists about the adequacy of current laws protecting inland wetlands. Several authors express concerns over the effectiveness of wetland monitoring programs, and also about declining appreciation of wetland virtues among the general public.

Conclusions

This synthesis suggests some interesting ecological differences between coastal and inland wetlands. To some extent, this reflects the perspectives of the researchers working in each

TABLE 1.2 *(continued)*

	No. of chapters	Chapter number			
		9	10	11	12
B. CONSERVATION CONCERNS					
Hydrologic alteration (flow regulation, groundwater pumping, ditching, drainage)	17	▲		▲	▲
Biodiversity threats (endangered/threatened species, beta or alpha diversity)	13		▲	▲	▲
Invasive/exotic species	12			▲	▲
Threats from urbanization	12	▲	▲	▲	
Threats from climate change	10	▲	▲		
Restoration/mitigation practices	9	▲	▲	▲	
Threats from agriculture	9				
Water-quality issues (pollution, eutrophication)	9			▲	
Regulatory issues	7		▲		
Grazing impacts	6				
Connectivity issues (habitat fragmentation, upland-wetland interaction)	5	▲	▲		
Mining impacts (peat mining, gas/oil extraction)	5	▲			
Logging	4				
Mercury contamination	4	▲			▲
Monitoring issues	4	▲	▲		
Sedimentation	4				▲

NOTE: Only those processes or concerns addressed in at least four chapters are listed. If a specific topic is not highlighted for a specific habitat type, readers should not assume a lack of relevance, but simply that authors do not prioritize the topic in their review. Chapter numbers refer to 9. northern peatlands, 10. northeastern seasonal woodland pools, 11. northern red maple and black ash swamps, 12. beaver wetlands, 13. Great Lakes coastal marshes, 14. pocosins, 15. southeastern depressional wetlands, 16. southeastern swamp complexes, 17. Florida Everglades, 18. floodplain wetlands of the southeastern Coastal Plain, 19. tropical freshwater swamps and marshes, 20. northern Great Plains wetlands, 21. High Plains playas, 22. western mountain wetlands, 23. desert spring wetlands of the Great Basin, 24. riparian floodplain wetlands of the arid and semiarid Southwest, 25. wetlands of the Central Valley of California and Klamath Basin, and 26. freshwater Arctic tundra wetlands.

type of wetland, but ecological controls are probably unique in many ways. In general, abiotic factors, hydrology, geomorphic variation, and climate are identified as important controls in most inland chapters. Only two biotic processes or controls, nutrient supplies and plant-animal interactions, are featured in more than half of these chapters. Similar abiotic processes and the additional abiotic factors of salinity and sedimentation are recognized in all coastal wetlands chapters. However, biotic controls and processes are mentioned more frequently in coastal than in inland wetlands discussions. In particular, outwelling and trophic support, primary production, plant-animal interactions, decomposition, seed and seedling processes, competition, and habitat connectivity all feature in more than half of the coastal chapters. This difference in the relative importance of biotic versus abiotic ecological controls and processes may reflect the highly variable nature of hydrology in inland wetlands as compared to the relatively constant hydrologic regime of tides in coastal habitats. Given the more stable environment of coastal habitats, biotic interaction may be permitted to become particularly influential. Biotic interaction is likely also important in inland wetlands, but outcomes

may be hard to predict because the abiotic foundation is constantly changing.

In coastal wetlands, the trophic connection between the wetlands and the open waters of the ocean through outwelling is considered one of the most important ecological controls or processes. Except perhaps in Great Lakes and floodplain wetlands, this kind of relationship does not exist in inland wetlands. On the other hand, because inland wetlands are often embedded in uplands, the interaction between wetlands and surrounding landscapes is frequently highlighted by authors addressing those habitats.

Despite some differences in ecological interactions, perceived threats to both coastal and inland wetlands are remarkably similar. In all wetlands, concerns about human-induced hydrologic change (whether from development or climate change) seem paramount. Climate change, invasive species, and land-use changes are clearly among the most serious threats to the persistence of all wetlands. Regulatory policy that promotes conservation and sound management needs to be strengthened for all wetlands, and wetland-restoration practices need to be improved overall. These actions can mod-

13	14	15	16	17	18	19	20	21	22	23	24	25	26
▲	▲	▲	▲	▲	▲	▲	▲	▲	▲	▲	▲	▲	▲
▲	▲	▲	▲	▲	▲	▲				▲	▲	▲	
▲			▲	▲	▲	▲	▲	▲		▲	▲	▲	
▲	▲	▲	▲	▲		▲			▲		▲	▲	
▲		▲	▲	▲			▲				▲	▲	▲
	▲	▲	▲	▲	▲		▲				▲		
▲	▲	▲		▲	▲		▲	▲			▲	▲	
▲	▲	▲		▲		▲	▲	▲			▲		
▲	▲	▲				▲		▲			▲		
						▲	▲	▲	▲	▲	▲		
			▲	▲		▲							
	▲							▲	▲				▲
	▲	▲	▲		▲								
			▲		▲								
		▲						▲					
					▲		▲	▲					

erate the effects of human population growth and activities on wetlands so that their ecological and socioeconomic functions and benefits can be maintained.

References

Batzer DP, Sharitz RR, editors. 2006. *Ecology of freshwater and estuarine wetlands.* Berkeley: University of California Press.

Conner WH, Doyle TW, Krauss KW, editors. 2007. *Ecology of tidal freshwater forested wetlands of the southeastern United States.* Dordrecht, The Netherlands: Springer.

Downing DM, Winer C, Wood LD. 2003. Navigating through the Clean Water Act jurisdiction: a legal review. *Wetlands* 23:475–93.

Keddy PA. 2010. *Wetland ecology: principles and conservation,* 2nd ed. Cambridge: Cambridge University Press.

Martini IP, Jeffries RL, et al. 2009. Polar coastal wetlands: development, structure, and land use. In *Coastal wetlands: an integrated ecosystem approach,* Perillo GME, Wolanski E, et al., editors. Amsterdam: Elsevier, pp. 119–55.

Mitsch WJ, Gosselink JG. 2000. *Wetlands,* 3rd ed. New York: Wiley.

Mitsch WJ, Gosselink JG. 2007. *Wetlands,* 4th ed. New York: Wiley.

Mitsch WJ, Gosselink JG, et al. 2009. *Wetland ecosystems.* New York: Wiley.

Perillo GME, Wolanski E, et al. 2009. *Coastal wetlands: an integrated ecosystem approach.* Amsterdam: Elsevier.

van der Valk AG 2006. *The biology of freshwater wetlands.* Oxford: Oxford University Press.

PART I

COASTAL WETLANDS

CHAPTER 2

North Atlantic Coastal Tidal Wetlands

CATHLEEN WIGAND and CHARLES T. ROMAN

North Atlantic tidal wetlands are found behind barrier islands and sand spits, in sheltered bays, and throughout the region's drowned-river valley estuaries, areas protected from direct wave action of the sea. They are primarily driven and sustained by the rise and fall of tides and bounded on the land side by the high water of the monthly spring tide cycle. Tidal wetlands include freshwater, brackish-water, and salt-marsh ecosystems and within the North Atlantic region can collectively be termed coastal wetlands. Coastal wetlands provide numerous ecosystem services, including fish, shellfish, and wildlife habitat; flood abatement and erosion control; water quality maintenance; and carbon sequestration (e.g., Odum, Smith, et al. 1984; Rabenhorst 1995; Teal and Howes 2000; Millenium Ecosystem Assessment 2005). With a worldwide estimate of 75% of the human population living in coastal regions (Emeis, Benoit, et al. 2001), coastal tidal wetlands are located in areas of intense commercial and residential activities. Urbanization is particularly relevant within the northeastern U.S., with coastal wetlands subjected to extensive physical alterations to the landscape, introduction of nonnative species, nitrogen (N) overenrichment, contaminants, and other stresses (Fig. 2.1) (Tiner 2005; Bertness, Ewanchuk, et al. 2002; Bertness, Silliman, et al. 2009; Gedan, Silliman, et al. 2009; Crain, Gedan, et al. 2009). Conservation efforts are required to restore and sustain the structure and function of North Atlantic coastal wetlands and associated ecosystem services (Fig. 2.1) (Gedan, Silliman, et al. 2009; Bertness, Silliman, et al. 2009).

The North Atlantic coast can be divided into three regions with differing geomorphology: the Gulf of Maine region, including the Bay of Fundy; the coast from Cape Cod to the Hudson River; and the New Jersey Atlantic coast and Delaware Bay. In the Gulf of Maine region, the tidal range is large, especially in the Bay of Fundy (4+ m), leading to wetlands only in protected areas with considerable depths of deposited sediments. River and tidal erosion is high in the soft rocks of the Bay of Fundy area, producing an abundance of reddish silt. Throughout the remainder of the Gulf of Maine, salt marshes are built mainly on marine sediments and wetland peat, and there is less transport of sediment from the hard-rock watersheds. Fringing wetlands (narrow in width and small in size) are present along the Gulf of Maine coast (Morgan, Burdick, et al. 2009), although broad expanses of coastal wetlands also exist (e.g., Scarborough Marsh, Maine; Great Marsh, Massachusetts).

Coastal wetlands along the southern New England shore, including Cape Cod and southern Massachusetts, Rhode Island, Connecticut, and Long Island, also have extensive wetland peat accumulations and are often characterized by sandy to hard-rock watersheds. From New Jersey south, including Delaware Bay, individual tidal wetlands are more extensive than along the glaciated coast to the north (Teal and Teal 1969; Roman, Jaworski, et al. 2000). The size of individual salt marshes averages about 27 ha in Delaware Bay, and they are about 5 times greater in size than salt marshes farther north along the coast (Table 2.1). Using the U.S. Fish and Wildlife National Wetland Inventory (NWI) data for the northeastern U.S. states and taking into account estuarine intertidal emergent (i.e., salt marshes), estuarine intertidal scrub-shrub, and riverine tidal emergent (i.e., freshwater and brackish tidal marshes), there are about 159,131 ha of coastal wetlands from Maine to Delaware Bay (Table 2.1). Wetlands of the New Jersey and Delaware coasts of the Delaware Bay Estuary account for 38% of this total area. Jacobson, Jacobson, et al. (1987) estimated the areal extent of Maine coastal tidal marshes as 7,890 ha using planimetry studies and Maine Geological Survey coastal maps, and their estimate is similar to the estimate of 8,723 ha based on NWI data of estuarine intertidal emergent wetlands (Table 2.1).

The areal extent (82,578 ha) of the coastal tidal wetlands in the state of New Jersey is the largest among the northeastern U.S. states. Extensive back-barrier salt marshes occur along the New Jersey Atlantic coast to Cape May, with extensive tidal wetlands, ranging from salt to freshwater tidal, along the New Jersey, Delaware, and Pennsylvania shores of the Delaware Bay and River (Chapman 1960; Daiber and Roman 1988). The Delaware Bay wetlands consist of 59,515 ha of salt marsh, 457 ha of scrub-shrub marsh, and 334 ha of freshwater and brackish tidal marshes among the states of New Jersey, Delaware, and Pennsylvania. About 54% of the Delaware Bay wetlands are in New Jersey and 46% in Delaware.

In the northeastern U.S., there is a wide range of development pressure and land-use history, with some watersheds exposed to almost three centuries of intense urbanization (e.g., the lower Hudson River), while others have endured less development

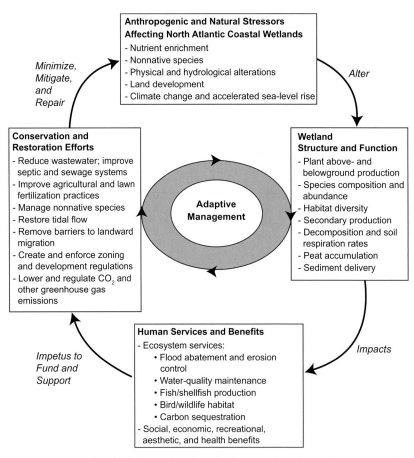

FIG. 2.1. Conceptual model depicting the effect of anthropogenic and natural stressors on the structure and function of North Atlantic coastal wetlands and the role of conservation and restoration efforts in mitigating stressors and promoting human services and benefits.

(e.g., the Maine estuaries) (Roman, Jaworski, et al. 2000). With urbanization, there have been many physical changes (e.g., filling, ditching, diking, and fragmentation) along the North Atlantic coasts that have had adverse effects on tidal wetlands (Bertness, Silliman, et al. 2009; Crain, Gedan, et al. 2009). Nitrogen overenrichment associated with human activities and wastewater is common in the Northeast and is linked to changes in the community structure and ecosystem processes of coastal wetlands (Lerberg, Holland, et al. 2000; Cloern 2001; Deegan 2002; Wigand 2008; Fitch, Theodose, et al. 2009). The flux of bioactive N as ammonium or nitrate from New England rivers is currently 5 to 20 times higher than during preindustrial times (Howarth, Billen, et al. 1996; Jaworski, Howarth, et al. 1997). In addition, global climate change and associated alterations such as accelerated sea-level rise, habitat fragmentation, and increases in severity of storms, precipitation, droughts, and air temperatures are predicted to affect tidal wetland structure and function (IPCC 2007; Frumhoff, McCarthy, et al. 2007). In this chapter, coastal tidal wetlands from the Bay of Fundy and Gulf of Maine to Delaware Bay will be characterized and current conservation concerns and restoration practices examined.

Geology, Soils, and Tidal Wetland Development Processes

During the last glacial period (Wisconsin), about 20,000 years before present (ybp), a large ice sheet (Laurentide) covered much of North America, extending as far south as the lower Hudson River and Long Island (Sirkin and Bokuniewicz 2006). Glacial activity shaped river valleys and estuaries by carving or scouring bedrock and delivered large amounts of sediment that is the foundation for many current geomorphological shoreline features, such as barrier beaches. A rapid retreat of the ice sheet occurred due to a natural global warming trend between 17,000 and 13,000 ybp. The global warming caused thermal expansion of the ocean. Subsequently, sea levels began to rise, flooding the North Atlantic coast by about 100 m, resulting in the present-day shoreline. During this period, incised river valleys became drowned (e.g., Hudson River, Narragansett Bay) and low-lying basins became flooded (Rabenhorst 1995). The Gulf of Maine shoreline, Cape Cod (Massachusetts) and the offshore islands, along with Block Island (Rhode Island) and Long Island (New York), owe their present landscape to the actions of the last continental glacier (e.g., scouring, sediment deposition, and outwash) and the rise in sea level that followed (Kraft 1988; Oldale 1992).

Salt marshes in the North Atlantic developed within protected embayments as the rise in sea level slowed and stabilized 4,000–6,000 ybp (Oldale 1992). Prior to that time, the submergence of the region may have been too rapid for extensive wetlands to form (Oldale 1992). Redfield's (1965) classic study describes growth of a spit and the Sandy Neck/Barnstable Marsh about 4,000 years ago. In southern Maine a basal radiocarbon date of 4,220 ybp is reported for peat collected from a back-barrier salt marsh, while on the northern coast of

TABLE 2.1

Northeastern U.S. state	Estuarine intertidal emergent (ha)	Average size (ha)	Estuarine intertidal scrub-shrub (ha)	Average size (ha)	Riverine tidal emergent (ha)	Average size (ha)	Total areal extent (ha)
Delaware[a]	27,471	27.3	236	4.1	4	3.5	27,711
New Jersey	81,665	19.6	646	1.7	267	10.7	82,578
Pennsylvania	0	na	0	na	64	7.1	64
New York	12,319	4.5	346	1.1	4	1.0	12,669
Connecticut	4,846	4.8	23	2.6	68	3.1	4,936
Rhode Island	1,370	1.3	90	0.7	0	na	1,460
Massachusetts	18,176	4.7	412	1.5	2	1.2	18,590
New Hampshire	2,340	7.9	0	na	0	na	2,340
Maine	8,723	2.7	39	0.9	21	1.3	8,783

NOTE: Classification of the wetlands are based on Cowardin, Carter, et al. (1979). The areal extents of the wetlands are based on available National Wetland Inventory (NWI)b collected from 1977 to 1982 (Tiner 1985a,b, 1989). For a specific state, when a class of wetlands has no acreage (0) reported in the NWI database, the average size is reported as not applicable (na).

[a] Only tidal wetlands located in Delaware Bay are reported for the state of Delaware.

[b] The source data are aerial photographs, and metadata for the NWI are available at www.fws.gov/wetlands/Data/metadata/conus_wet_poly_metadata.htm.

Maine salt marsh peat dates to 4,095 ybp, with salt marsh peat overlying freshwater peat (Kelley, Belknap, et al. 1988; Kelley, Gehrels, et al. 1995). Orson, Warren, et al. (1987) describe a scenario of marsh development beginning about 3,800–4,000 years ago on Long Island Sound (Connecticut), with freshwater marsh replaced by salt marsh as the river valley drowned with sea-level rise, similar to the Maine example. As wetlands developed, the soils accrued mineral and organic materials and underwent vertical accretion at rates approximately equal to those of sea-level rise (Rabenhorst 1995).

In light of predictions of accelerated sea-level rise in the North Atlantic over the next century, recent research has focused on which factors contribute to vertical elevation and the maintenance of the wetland platform (e.g., Bricker-Urso, Nixon, et al. 1989; Morris, Sundareshwar, et al. 2002; Turner, Howes, et al. 2009; Cahoon and Guntenspergen 2010). When tidal wetland soils are inundated with seawater, anaerobic conditions usually result. In many tidal wetlands in the North Atlantic, subsurface processes such as peat accumulation and decomposition can affect surface elevation. In contrast, freshwater tidal wetlands in the Delaware Bay estuary are generally not characterized by dense peat substrates; thus these tidal systems are more dependent on sediment delivery and inorganic sediments to maintain elevation in response to sea-level rise (Orson, Warren, et al. 1998). At sites in the Northeast, researchers have noted changes in vegetation from high marsh species (e.g., *Spartina patens*) to more flood-tolerant species (e.g., *Spartina alterniflora*), perhaps a response to wetter conditions related to accelerated rates of sea-level rise (Warren and Niering 1993; Donnelly and Bertness 2001; Smith 2009).

Sulfate reduction is common in North Atlantic salt marshes. For many marsh plants (e.g., *S. alterniflora*), high concentrations of sulfide (> 1 mM) can be detrimental to growth and are sometimes toxic (Mendelssohn, McKee, et al. 1981; Koch, Men-

delssohn, et al. 1990; Mendelssohn and Morris 2000). It is suspected that frequent exposure to high sulfide levels (2–4 mM) in Jamaica Bay (New York) salt marshes contributes to the loss of belowground roots and rhizomes, making these marshes more susceptible to erosion and subsidence (Kolker 2005).

Jamaica Bay marshes, with just 355 ha of salt marsh islands remaining in 2003, are reported to be disappearing at rates as high as 22 ha per year for the period 2003–05 (NPS 2007). In a Jamaica Bay study comparing belowground roots and rhizomes at shallow (0–10 cm) and deep (10–20 cm) depths, between a rapidly deteriorating marsh (Black Bank) and a more stable one (JoCo marsh), it is clear that the deteriorating marsh had significantly (P < 0.05) less belowground biomass (Davey, Wigand, et al. 2011; Table 2.2). Black Bank marsh had significantly (P < 0.05) less fine root mass (diameter < 1 mm) at shallow and deep depths in the high marsh zone. The mass of the coarse roots and rhizomes (≥ 1 mm diameter) at depth were significantly (P < 0.05) greater at JoCothan Black Bank marsh, but there was no statistical difference in the shallow coarse root mass between the sites (Table 2.2). The densities of the rhizomes at both depths, and the densities of the coarse roots at the shallow depths, were significantly (P < 0.05) greater in the stable marsh. However, the rhizome diameters in the deteriorating marsh were significantly greater at both depths (Table 2.2, Fig. 2.2). The finding of larger-diameter rhizomes at the deteriorating marsh suggest that this morphological change may assist the plant in adapting to stressed conditions such as nutrient-enriched and low redox soils (Darby and Turner 2008). Larger-diameter rhizomes may aid in transporting oxygen to the rhizosphere and increase structural support for the taller aboveground shoots and increased aboveground biomass reported for marsh plants subject to nutrient enrichment (e.g., Sullivan and Daiber 1974; Gallagher 1975; Valiela, Teal, et al. 1975), and furthermore may provide a conduit for release

TABLE 2.2

Belowground biomass,[a] densities, and diameters of roots and rhizomes comparing
deteriorating (Black Bank) and stable (JoCo) marshes at Jamaica Bay, New York

Soil depth	Roots and rhizomes	Marsh type		P
		Stable	Deteriorating	
0–10 cm	Fine root mass (g m^{-2})	3,975 ± 461	1,697 ± 129	*
	Coarse root and rhizome mass (g m^{-2})	2,757 ± 689	2,858 ± 557	ns
	Rhizome density (# m^{-2})	8,935 ± 654	6,087 ± 387	*
	Coarse root density (# m^{-2})	16,669 ± 1840	6,524 ± 537	*
	Rhizome diameter (mm)	3.59 ± 0.22	4.55 ± 0.14	*
	Coarse root diameter (mm)	1.37 ± 0.004	1.37 ± 0.007	ns
10–20 cm	Fine root mass (g m^{-2})	2,874 ± 373	1,631 ± 206	*
	Coarse root and rhizome mass (g m^{-2})	1,893 ± 56	1,001 ± 128	*
	Rhizome density (# m^{-2})	6,586 ± 914	3,968 ± 352	ns
	Coarse root density (# m^{-2})	17,918 ± 731	3,569 ± 273	*
	Rhizome diameter (mm)	3.00 ± 0.06	4.22 ± 0.07	*
	Coarse root diameter (mm)	1.38 ± 0.005	1.41 ± 0.004	*

NOTE: Data source: Davey, Wigand, et al. 2011. Data are provided for two depths (shallow 0–10 cm, deep 10–20 cm), with samples sorted by fine (< 1 mm) and coarse (≥ 1 mm) roots/rhizomes for biomass, coarse roots (≥ 1 mm < 2 mm), and rhizomes (≥ 2 mm) for density and diameter comparisons. Significance (P < 0.05) is indicated with (*), nonsignificant with ns.

[a] Belowground biomass was estimated with a 15 cm diameter PVC corer, and samples were hand-sieved (1.0 mm).

[b] Densities and diameters of roots and rhizomes were estimated using images sampled with computer-aided tomography coupled with image analyzer software.

of excess organic acids that might accumulate due to fermentative respiratory processes (Mendelssohn, McKee, et al. 1981; DeLaune, Smith, et al. 1984; Naido, McKee, et al. 1992).

Biogeochemistry

Organic matter at the base of many North Atlantic coastal wetland food webs includes both in situ wetland production and detritus derived from the surrounding watershed and coastal waters (Odum, Smith, et al. 1984; Valiela, Teal, et al. 1985; Howes, Dacey, et al. 1985; Findlay, Nieder, et al. 2009). Primary production of tidal freshwater wetlands in the Northeast is high, and estimates for some individual species are over 2,000 g m^{-2} yr^{-1} (e.g., *Zizania aquatica,* wild rice), likely because of the tidal subsidy, which includes the delivery of nutrient-rich waters on the flood tide and the removal of metabolic by-products on the ebb tide (Whigham 2009). As reported for tidal freshwater wetlands, primary productivity in North Atlantic salt marshes is high, and *Spartina alterniflora* belowground productivity is usually at least twice as great, and sometimes as much as 20 times greater, than aboveground productivity (e.g., Delaware above: 1,487 g m^{-2}, below: 6.5 kg m^{-2}, Roman and Daiber 1984; New Jersey above: 429–525 g m^{-2}, below: 11 kg m^{-2}, Smith, Good, et al. 1979; Rhode Island above: 500–2,400 g m^{-2}, below: 3.5–17 kg m^{-2}, Wigand 2008; Massachusetts above: 424 g m^{-2}, below: 3.5 kg m^{-2}, Valiela, Teal, et al. 1975, 1976). When belowground roots and rhizomes die, they form peat, are exported out of the system, or are decomposed (Teal and Howes 1996 ; Howes, Dacey, et al. 1985). Annually, about 80% of the belowground roots and rhizomes at the Great Sippewis-

sett Marsh (Massachusetts) were decomposed (Howes, Dacey, et al. 1985; Teal and Howes 1996). Most of the sediment in the salt marsh was anoxic, so sulfate reduction accounted for a large part of the decomposition, with carbon dioxide either released into the atmosphere or reabsorbed by growing plants. Only approximately 1% of the reduced carbon was exported in the Great Sippiwissett to the atmosphere as methane or dimethyl sulfide (Howes, Dacey, et al. 1985).

Belowground bacterial transformations have other consequences in North Atlantic coastal wetland soils besides decomposing organic matter. The decomposition of organic matter using nitrate as the electron acceptor results in the loss of nitrogen gas from the wetland system (i.e., denitrification). This is an important process in North Atlantic wetlands associated with urbanized watersheds, because it transforms land-derived N loads into nitrogen gas (Howes, Weiskel, et al. 1996; Valiela, Cole, et al. 2000). Denitrification in salt marshes receiving low watershed N loadings (≤ 10 kg N ha^{-1}y^{-1}) in Narragansett Bay (Rhode Island) was estimated to transform 100% of incoming N (Davis, Nowicki, et al. 2004). However, in an impacted salt marsh receiving a high watershed N load (6,037 kg N ha^{-1}y^{-1}), there were substantially lower denitrification rates. In fact, net N fixation rather than denitrification was measured, suggesting that the salt marsh had switched from being an N sink to an N source (Davis, Nowicki, et al. 2004). Similarly, in an ecosystem-scale manipulative experiment in salt marshes of Plum Island Sound (Massachusetts), Drake, Peterson, et al. (2009) demonstrated how N fertilization (increase from < 4 umol L^{-1} to 70–90 umol L^{-1} nitrate) caused a considerable increase in the export of unprocessed nitrate to coastal waters. While the reference marsh in the Plum Island study was able to process

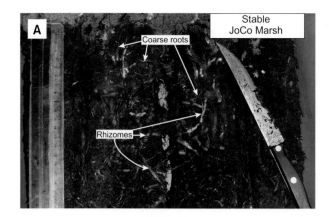
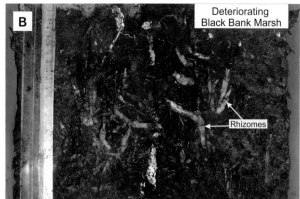

FIG. 2.2. Belowground roots and rhizomes in marsh soils collected from Jamaica Bay, New York. A. JoCo marsh. B. Black Bank marsh. Approximately 20 cm depth of soil is shown, as indicated by the metric ruler. Note the larger diameter of rhizomes in the deteriorating marsh. (Photo courtesy of C. Wigand.)

100% of the added nitrate through assimilation, dissimilation, sorption, or sedimentation processes, the fertilized marsh was able to process only 50–60%.

In a global estimate, salt marshes were reported to sequester carbon at an average rate of 210 g C m^{-2} y^{-1}, and, along with mangroves in the U.S., they are estimated to sequester about 5 Tg C y^{-1}, accounting for 1–2% of the carbon sink for the conterminous U.S. (Chmura, Anisfield, et al. 2003). Using the salt marsh carbon sequestration rate (210 g C m^{-2} y^{-1}) and NWI areal estimates (Table 2.1) for estuarine intertidal wetlands in the northeastern U.S., an estimated 0.33 Tg C y^{-1} is sequestered, which is equivalent to CO$_2$ emissions from approximately 136 million gallons of gasoline consumed (USEPA 2005). The northeastern estuarine intertidal wetland carbon sequestration amounts to approximately 0.7% of the total North American wetland soils sink (49 Tg C y^{-1}) (Bridgham, Megonigal, et al. 2006) or 0.1% of the conterminous U.S. carbon sink (300–580 Tg C y^{-1}) (Pacala, Hurtt, et al. 2001). Regions of the U.S. with extensive areas of coastal saline and brackish wetlands (e.g., the southeast Atlantic and Gulf of Mexico) would be expected to contribute a greater percentage of the carbon sequestration than wetlands along the northeastern coast of the U.S.

Plant Communities and Key Ecological Controls

The vegetation of North Atlantic brackish and saline tidal wetlands is primarily composed of salt-tolerant grasses and rushes. Micro- and macroalgae are also often important components of the autotrophic community of tidal wetlands (Nixon and Oviatt 1973; Brinkhuis 1977; Roman, Able, et al. 1990). Tidal freshwater wetlands are more species rich than wetlands located downstream in the estuary. Herbaceous-dominated tidal freshwater wetlands are characterized by *Schoenoplectus* spp. (bulrushes), *Typha* spp. (cattails), *Impatiens capensis* (jewelweed), and the nonnatives *Lythrum salicaria* (purple loosestrife) and *Phragmites australis,* as well as many other species (Baldwin, Barendregt, et al. 2009; Leck, Baldwin, et al. 2009). Tidal freshwater wetlands dominated by shrubs or tree species (e.g., *Acer rubrum,* red maple) are often referred to as swamps.

Brackish-water tidal wetlands dominated by *Typha angustifolia* (narrow-leaved cattail) and freshwater tidal wetlands with *Zizania aquatica, Pontederia cordata* (pickerelweed), and *Schoenoplectus pungens* (common three-square) are common along tidal reaches of the Connecticut River (Metzler and Tiner 1992) and Hudson River (Kiviat, Findlay, et al. 2006).

However, many rivers throughout the Northeast have been dammed, limiting the extent of tidal riverine wetlands. In addition, nonnative plant species are increasingly a problem in tidal freshwater and brackish waters and in some areas can include nearly homogenous stands of *L. salicaria* and *P. australis* (Templer, Findlay, et al. 1998; Kiviat 2009).

In the estuarine subtidal waters adjacent to tidal freshwater wetlands in the Hudson River, there are more than 20 submersed aquatic plant species, including *Vallisneria americana* (wild celery), *Potamogeton* spp., *Najas* spp., *Elodea* spp., and widespread occurrence of the nonnative *Trapa natans* (water chestnut). In almost all subtidal vegetated areas in the Hudson River, *V. americana* is the predominant plant; however the nonnative *T. natans* accounts for roughly 25% of the coverage (Findlay, Wigand, et al. 2006).

The physiography and vegetation of tidal wetlands have been described in detail for southern New England salt marshes (Miller and Egler 1950; Redfield 1972; Niering and Warren 1980; Nixon 1982). Distinct vegetation zones are often present, with a narrow band of tall *S. alterniflora* occupying the low marsh along creek and ditch banks, flooded twice daily by tides (Fig. 2.3). The high marsh zone is flooded less frequently and often is characterized by a mosaic of vegetation including *S. patens, Distichlis spicata,* short form *S. alterniflora,* and *Juncus gerardii.* Salt marsh pannes, shallow depressions on the wetland surface, are often vegetated with a variety of forbs (e.g., *Triglochin maritimum, Plantago maritima, Suaeda maritima*). The forb panne assemblage can consist of over a dozen plant species and is considered one of the most diverse salt marsh associations (Miller and Egler 1950; Chmura, Chase, et al. 1997; Gedan and Bertness 2009). Salt marsh pools can be present throughout the high marsh mosaic, with some containing the submerged aquatic plant *Ruppia maritima* (widgeon grass) (Adamowicz and Roman 2005; Wilson, Kelley, et al. 2009).

In protected coastal waters adjacent to salt marshes, rooted submerged aquatic vegetation is often found, *Zostera marina* (eelgrass) in more saline habitats and *R. maritima* in less saline areas. However, in the nutrient-enriched coastal waters found in many northeastern subestuaries, macroalgal species such as *Ulva lactuca* and *Enteromorpha* spp. have replaced submerged aquatic vegetation (Short, Burdick, et al. 1995; Short and Burdick 1996; Kinney and Roman 1998; Deegan 2002). Valiela, Cole, et al. (2000) propose that the maintenance of *Z. marina* in many subestuaries in New England may depend upon the condition of fringing salt marshes and their ability to intercept land-derived N.

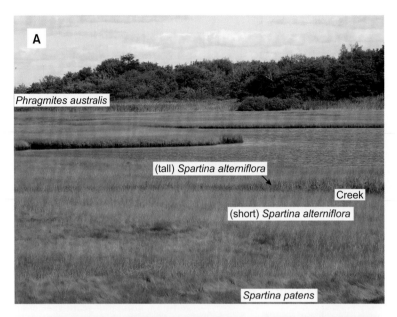

FIG. 2.3. Typical North Atlantic salt marshes. A. Southern New England (photo courtesy of R. McKinney). B. Bay of Fundy (photo courtesy of G. Chmura).

The low marsh along the Maine coast, north and east of Penobscot Bay, is dominated by *S. alterniflora,* but the high marsh has a wide diversity of plant species (Calhoun, Cormier, et al. 1993). In addition to *S. patens* and *J. gerardii,* the mosaic pattern of northern Maine salt marshes may include *J. balticus, Festuca rubra, Agrostis gigantea,* and *Carex paleacea,* among others. Along the upland border of salt marshes throughout southern New England and extending into southern Maine, the nonnative and invasive reed *P. australis* commonly occurs and may be expanding in salt, brackish, and freshwater tidal wetlands throughout the North Atlantic region (Hellings and Gallagher 1992; Chambers, Meyerson, et al. 1999; Bertness, Ewanchuk, et al. 2002; Bertness, Silliman, et al. 2009; Lathrop, Windham, et al. 2003; League, Colbert, et al. 2006). The Maine coastline may represent a transition to Bay of Fundy salt marshes, where vegetation zones of *S. alterniflora, Plantago maritima, S. patens, C. paleacea,* and *J. balticus* are reported (Fig. 2.3) (Pielou and Routledge 1976; Chmura, Chase, et al. 1997).

In the Delaware–New Jersey area, the sequence of tidal salt marsh to brackish-water wetlands occurs as a progression up the Delaware estuary from the mouth at Cape Henlopen and Cape May to the farthest limits of tidal influence near Trenton, New Jersey (Daiber and Roman 1988). Vast expanses of salt marsh are found in Sussex County, Delaware, and Cape May County, New Jersey. Typical brackish-water wetlands include wetlands associated with the Maurice River (Cumberland County, New Jersey), and examples of tidal freshwater wetlands are found upstream of Philadelphia, especially near Trenton (Good and Good 1975; Leck, Simpson, et al. 1988).

The salt-marsh plant zonation in the New Jersey Atlantic coast back-barrier systems and the Delaware Bay estuary is similar to New England salt marshes, with *S. alterniflora* dominating in the low marsh, and the tall form of this species fringing the lower intertidal areas, along creeks and ditch banks (Good 1965; Daiber and Roman 1988). Moving from the intertidal creek toward the upland is a transition area, a salt-marsh border community composed of *J. gerardii* (black grass) and *Iva frutescens* (marsh elder). Finally, approaching the upland is a marsh border community composed of *Baccharis halimifolia* (groundsel tree), *P. australis,* and often *Toxicodendron radicans* (poison ivy). Most Delaware Bay salt marshes such as those throughout the Northeast region are dissected by a network of

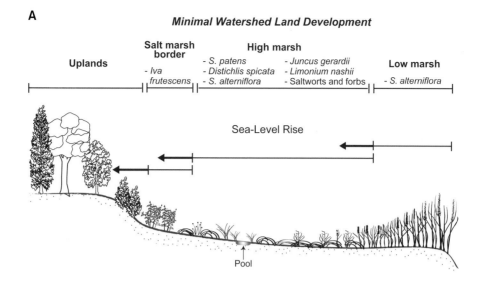

A

Minimal Watershed Land Development

Uplands | Salt marsh border | High marsh | Low marsh

- *Iva frutescens*

- *S. patens*
- *Distichlis spicata*
- *S. alterniflora*

- *Juncus gerardii*
- *Limonium nashii*
- Saltworts and forbs

- *S. alterniflora*

Sea-Level Rise

Pool

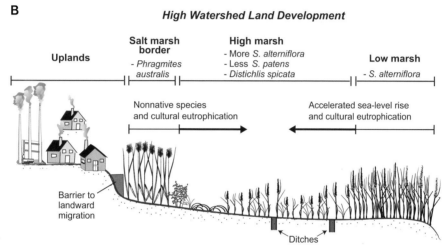

B

High Watershed Land Development

Uplands | Salt marsh border | High marsh | Low marsh

- *Phragmites australis*

- More *S. alterniflora*
- Less *S. patens*
- *Distichlis spicata*

- *S. alterniflora*

Nonnative species and cultural eutrophication

Accelerated sea-level rise and cultural eutrophication

Barrier to landward migration

Ditches

FIG. 2.4. A schematic depicting effects of accelerated sea-level rise and cultural eutrophication on plant zonation in salt marshes subject to (A) minimal watershed land development and (B) high watershed land development. (Warren and Niering 1993; Bertness 1999; Wigand, McKinney, et al. 2003; Silliman and Bertness 2004.)

mosquito ditches. Old spoil piles from these ditches are often elevated enough so that tidal flooding is less frequent, thereby allowing marsh elder to colonize along the ditches (Bourn and Cottam 1950).

The high marsh community of freshwater tidal wetlands in the Delaware estuary are often composed of a mix of emergent species including *Peltandra virginica* (arrow arum), *T. angustifolia, Polygonum* spp. (tearthumbs), *Acornus calamus* (sweet flag), and *Bidens laevis* (bur marigolds). Shrubs such as *Rosa palustris* (swamp rose), *Cephalanthus occidentalis* (buttonbush), *Salix* spp. (willow), and *Cornus amomum* (silky dogwood) and saplings of red maple may be scattered within these marshes or occur along the upland edge (Tiner 1987). *Morella cerifera L.* (wax myrtle) may form a dense shrub thicket along the landward edge. Many tidal fresh marshes grade naturally into freshwater tidal swamps consisting of overstory species of red maple, green ash, and black gum; understory shrubs of southern arrowwood, alders, sweet pepperbush, and others; and emergent plants such as tussock sedge, skunk cabbage, jewelweed, and cardinal flower.

Brackish wetlands in the Delaware Bay estuary are transi-

tional, occurring in areas where salinity ranges from < 5 to 20 ppt. The vegetation mosaic is variable, with some typical saltmarsh species intermixed with common freshwater plants. Brackish wetlands in more seaward locations are sometimes dominated by *S. alterniflora* or *S. cynosuroides* (big cordgrass). If the locations are only slightly brackish, then many freshwater wetland plants and *T. angustifolia* are common. Dominant plants in the brackish high marsh are *S. patens* and *Schoenoplectus americanus* (common three-square sedge). Plants bordering the upland may include *Panicum virgatum L* (switchgrass), *L. salicaria,* and *P. australis.*

In plant transplant studies in Narragansett Bay, Rhode Island, tidal wetlands, Crain, Silliman, et al. (2004) demonstrated that spatial segregation across estuarine salinity gradients was primarily driven by competitively superior freshwater plants displacing salt-tolerant plants to physically harsh saltmarsh habitats, whereas freshwater wetland plants were limited from living in salt marshes by physical factors (e.g., high salinities and sulfides). In northeastern salt marshes, the classic plant zonation patterns are currently changing, perhaps in response to accelerated sea-level rise, global warming, and nutrient enrichment (e.g., Niering and Warren 1980; Levine, Brewer, et al. 1998; Emery, Ewanchuk, et al. 2001; Pennings and Bertness 2001; Bertness, Ewanchuk, et al. 2002; Wigand, McKinney, et al. 2003; Silliman and Bertness 2004; Gedan and Bertness 2009).

In some New England salt marshes, many of the salt-tolerant forbs and *S. patens* have been displaced by more efficient N competitors, such as *S. alterniflora* and the nonnative *P. australis* (Fig. 2.4). Under N-enriched conditions, there is sometimes less allocation of carbon to the roots and rhizomes and greater decomposition of N-rich organic matter (Turner, Swenson, et al. 2004, 2009; Wigand, Brennan, et al. 2009). Furthermore, the soil strength is reduced and more susceptible to erosional processes from natural events and human activities (Turner, Swenson, et al. 2004; Turner, Howes, et al. 2009). In addition, less belowground accumulation can affect marsh elevation in organic-rich soils in the Northeast, making them more susceptible to sea-level rise and submergence.

Gedan and Bertness (2009) used warming chambers (increase of 0.33 to 3.28°C) to simulate global warming in forb panne/*S. patens* communities in New England salt marshes. It was found that the warming treatment reduced forb panne cover, reduced plant diversity, and favored *S. patens* at all sites. With a warming trend, it is expected that the structure and function of Northeast salt marshes will be altered.

Some recent research has supported the hypothesis that top-down control of coastal wetland vegetation by consumers (e.g., snails, crabs, and insects) has been greatly underestimated and that human disturbance is triggering intensified consumer control (Silliman, Bertness, et al. 2009). For wetland plants, it has been observed that grazing by snails and other consumers might be enhanced when plants are stressed (e.g., under drought conditions or N-enrichment) (Silliman, Van de Koppel, et al. 2005). In addition, Bertness, Silliman, et al. (2009) report that in large fertilized plots (4 m × 4 m) in New England, grasshoppers and leafhoppers had damaged over 90% of the *S. alterniflora* in fertilized plots, suggesting that nutrient enrichment in urbanized coastal wetlands may increase insect herbivory.

Over the past decade, a rather sudden wetland die-back has been observed at several sites in New England, with studies on Cape Cod strongly indicating that grazing by herbivorous crabs, *Sesarma reticulatum,* is a major cause (Holdredge, Bertness, et al. 2008). However, other factors, such as fungal pathogens, drought conditions, and sulfide toxicity, may be tied to sudden die-back events noted throughout the Atlantic and Gulf of Mexico U.S. coasts (Alber, Swenson, et al. 2008).

Animal Communities

Fishes and Decapod Crustaceans

North Atlantic coastal wetlands, as well as submerged aquatic vegetation habitats, support commercially harvested estuarine fauna, but also serve an important role by providing habitat for forage species in support of commercial and recreational fishes and coastal bird populations. Resident fishes, such as mummichogs *(Fundulus heteroclitus)* and sticklebacks (e.g., *Gasterosteus aculeatus, Apeltes quadracus*), and seasonal residents such as silversides *(Menidia menidia),* tend to numerically dominate the fish fauna of Northeast coastal wetlands (Ayvazian, Deegan, et al. 1992; Dionne, Dochtermann, et al. 2006; Able, Fahay, et al. 2002; Targett and McCleave 1974; Fell, Weissbach,

et al. 1998; Mulkana 1966; Roundtree and Able 1992; Able and Fahay 2010). In more southern coastal latitudes—the southeast Atlantic and Gulf of Mexico—fish with life history strategies classified as nursery, marine, or transient visitor often represent a greater proportion of total fish fauna within shallow estuarine systems (see review by McIvor and Rozas 1996; Roman, Jaworski, et al. 2000). However, it is important to note that although resident species dominate northeastern coastal wetlands, these habitats support a rich fish fauna of diverse life histories, including diadromous species (e.g., alewife, *Alosa pseudoharengus;* American eel, *Anguilla rostrata*), marine (e.g., pollock, *Pollachius virens;* white hake, *Urophycis tenuis*), freshwater (e.g., white sucker, *Catostomus commersonii*), and nursery species (e.g., menhaden, *Brevoortia tyrannus;* bay anchovy, *Anchoa mitchilli*). In fish surveys of shallow estuarine–salt marsh systems from Maine to southern New Jersey, species richness is high (York River, Maine, 23 species, Dionne, Dochtermann, et al. 2006; Nauset Marsh, Massachusetts, 35 species, Able, Fahay, et al. 2002; Bissel Cove, Rhode Island, 20 species, Nixon and Oviatt 1973; Great Bay–Little Egg Harbor, New Jersey, 60 species, Roundtree and Able 1992).

The forage species of Northeast tidal wetlands, the mummichogs, silversides, and others, provide essential prey resources for larger marine species such as adult striped bass *(Morone saxatilis)* and bluefish *(Pomatomus saltatrix)* (Fay, Neves, et al. 1983; Abraham 1985), and groundfish such as pollack and hake (Dionne, Dochtermann, et al. 2006). Striped bass caught in marsh creeks often have guts full of mummichogs (Teal and Howes 2000). The edges between open water and wetland vegetation are often frequented by transient fish species that prey on smaller fish (Cicchetti and Diaz 2000).

Anadromous fish, such as alewife, blueback herring *(Alosa awstivalis),* rainbow smelt *(Osmerus mordax),* American shad *(A. sapidissima),* and striped bass, among others, and the catadromous American eel are well represented in the small Northeast tidal wetlands (Able and Fahay 1998), as well as the region's major estuarine and tidal freshwater systems (e.g., the Hudson River estuary; Waldman 2006; Able and Fahay 2010). The fish fauna of fresh and brackish-water tidal wetlands are less studied than in more saline marshes in the northeastern U.S., but some typical species include banded killifish *(Fundulus diaphanous),* pumpkinseed *(Lepomis gibbosus),* bluegill *(Lepomis macrochirus),* and crevalle jack *(Cranx hippos),* among others (e.g., Fell, Weissbach, et al. 1998; Schmidt and Lake 2006; Swarth and Kiviat 2009).

Regarding decapods, sand shrimp *(Crangon septemspinosa)* and grass shrimp *(Palaemonetes pugio)* tend to dominate catches within Northeast coastal wetlands, including seagrass beds (Raposa and Roman 2001; Able, Fahay, et al. 2002; Fell et al. 1998; Roundtree and Able 1992). The nonnative green crab *(Carcinus maenas),* a predatory species, is often a conspicuous component of the salt-marsh decapod community (e.g., Dionne, Dochtermann, et al. 2006; Raposa 2002; Able, Fahay, et al. 2002). The Asian shore crab *(Hemigrapsis sanguineus),* first noted in New Jersey in 1988 and now extending north to Maine, is becoming common on hard-bottom intertidal habitats (Ledesma and O'Conner 2001) and has been observed in salt marshes.

Benthic and Terrestrial Invertebrates

Invertebrates are important food for fish and avifauna in coastal wetlands. On the Delaware River, Crumb (1977) identified a total of 70 taxa, including tubificid oligochaetes, chironomids, and the introduced Asiatic clam *(Corbicula fluminea).* In the Hudson River tidal freshwater wetlands, chironomids, oligochaetes, and copepods composed 90% or greater of the total sample, and species richness was positively correlated with soil organic matter (Findlay, Schoeberl, et al. 1989; Mihocko, Kiviat, et al. 2003).

Changes in native vegetation by an invasive plant (e.g., *P. australis*) can dramatically alter the resource base for native consumers, altering trophic structure and food web interactions (Gratton and Denno 2005, 2006). Gratton and Denno (2006) examined the arthropod assemblages associated with a restored *Spartina* marsh and a *Phragmites*-invaded marsh in the Alloway Creek Watershed (New Jersey) using stable isotope approaches. The dominant arthropod primary consumers present on the marsh surface in the *Phragmites* marsh were those capable of consuming algae, phytoplankton, and, to a lesser extent, detritus such as Collembola (springtails, saprovores/fungal feeders) and chironomids (midges, algal filter feeders). In contrast, in the restored *Spartina* marshes, the assemblages were characterized by a diverse and abundant guild of free-living, externally feeding herbivores such as planthoppers and mirid bugs as well as predators such as spiders. These results suggest that the arthropod food webs shifted from dependence on the native *Spartina* plant to a mostly detritus-based food web in the *Phragmites*-invaded marsh.

In surveys of Narragansett Bay, Rhode Island, salt marshes, a significantly higher percentage of deposit-feeders were reported in marshes with the highest watershed N loads, but there were no detectable relationships of N loading with the total number of infaunal individuals or taxa richness among the marshes (Wigand 2008). However, significant positive relationships were reported between N loads and the number of infaunal species and taxa richness in the mudflats adjacent (within 1 m) to the salt-marsh bank. Some deposit-feeders in the samples included *Capitella capitata, Heteromastus filiformis, Leitoscoloplos fragilis, Mediomastus ambiseta,* and other oligochaetes. In addition, the density and biomass of ribbed mussels *(Geukensia demissa)* significantly increased with increasing N loads among the salt marshes (Chintala, Wigand, et al. 2006). Extremely high densities (5,700 per m²) of ribbed mussels have also been reported in the nutrient-enriched salt marshes of Jamaica Bay, New York (Franz 1993).

Avifauna and Wildlife

In a USEPA (2006) review of avifauna and wildlife associated with New England salt marshes, 79 bird, 20 mammal, and 6 amphibian and reptile species that utilize coastal wetlands at some point in their life history were reported. Of the 79 birds, 15 species were identified as species that have been observed to nest in some part of the salt-marsh ecosystem. Among the species were salt marsh sharp-tailed sparrow, seaside sparrow, clapper rail, mallard, marsh wren, red-winged blackbird, and willet. Other bird species associated with New England marshes are year-round and seasonal foragers (USEPA 2006). In general, dabbling ducks (e.g., mallard, black, greenwinged teal, wood duck), Canada geese, and whistling swans appear to prefer tidal freshwater habitat, while diving ducks, mergansers, snow geese, and sea ducks prefer salt marsh–associated habitat (Odum 1988).

Coastal bird species are reported to be some of the species most vulnerable to climate change because of the adverse effects of accelerated sea-level rise, increased air and water temperatures, and storms on habitat and prey items (North American Bird Conservation Initiative, US Committee 2010). Loss of suitable nesting habitat due to alterations in flooding and hydrological regimes, as well as changes in plant zonation patterns, is known to threaten tidal wetland sparrow species (DiQuinzio, Paton, et al. 2002; Gjerdrum, Elphick, et al. 2005; Shriver, Vickery, et al. 2007).

In New Jersey, the Cape May marshes are well known for the hundreds of thousands of shorebirds attracted during migrations, and therefore Delaware Bay is known as one of the most important stopovers in the eastern U.S. for shorebirds (Teal and Teal 1969; Clark, Niles, et al. 1993; Niles, Bart, et al. 2009). Northbound migrant shorebirds are often observed in the spring in Delaware Bay, and most abundant species are the semi-palmated sandpiper *(Calidris pusilla),* ruddy turnstone *(Aremaria interpres),* red knot *(Calidris canutus),* and sanderling *(Calidris alba)* (Clark, Niles, et al. 1993; Niles, Bart, et al. 2009).

Accelerated sea-level rise is linked with habitat fragmentation, and rising temperatures are linked with changes in the timing of invertebrate spawnings (e.g., horseshoe crabs) and bird migrations. These climate changes and effects, along with other anthropogenic pressures such as horseshoe crab overharvesting, are reported to be contributing to the decline of the red knot in Delaware Bay (Niles, Bart, et al. 2009; Faurby, King, et al. 2010).

In addition to Delaware Bay, two sections of the Upper Bay of Fundy, Shepody Bay (New Brunswick) and Minas Basin (Nova Scotia), together totaling 62,000 ha, are recognized as hemispheric sites of importance by the Western Hemispheric Shorebird Reserve Network (www.whsrn.org). The Bay of Fundy provides diverse habitat for between 1 and 2.5 million semi-palmated sandpipers, which in any one year is up to 75% of the world population. There are numerous other protected coastal ecosystems throughout the Northeast, including USFWS National Wildlife Refuges and National Park Service seashores, as well as lands protected and managed by state and local agencies and conservation organizations that provide an outstanding diversity of tidal wetland ecosystems and essential habitat for fish, birds, and other wildlife.

The USEPA (2006) describes six mammals (meadow jumping mouse, meadow vole, muskrat, New England cottontail, Norway rat, and woodland vole) that sometimes nest in northeastern salt marshes and several species of amphibians and reptiles (e.g., common snapping turtle, eastern painted turtle, northern water snake) known to be inhabitants. In addition, there are a number of mammals that forage on plants and animals in salt marshes (e.g., coyote, fisher, fox, shrew, raccoon, and deer).

Tidal freshwater wetlands in the Northeast support a high diversity of invertebrate and vertebrate species. The diversity of fishes and birds is especially high, but no species is found exclusively in tidal freshwater habitat (Swarth and Kiviat 2009). For example, the great blue heron *(Ardea herodias)* is common in tidal freshwater habitats, yet it also occurs in a wide variety of other aquatic habitats. Raptors are attracted to tidal freshwater wetlands by abundant prey, and it is common to see osprey *(Pandion haliaetus)* and northern harriers *(Circus cyaneus)* in these wetlands (Swarth and Kiviat 2009). Probably because of salt stress, tidal freshwater wetlands have many more species of reptiles and amphibians than do salt marshes. Salamanders, frogs and toads, turtles, and snakes thrive in most tidal freshwater wetlands, but only a few can tolerate the osmotic problems presented by saltwater (Odum 1988). Along the upper edges of tidal freshwater wetlands in the Northeast, the green frog *(Rana clamitans),* green treefrog *(Hyla cinerea),* spring peeper *(Pseudacris crucifer),* Fowler's toad *(Bufo fowleri),* and American toad *(B. americanus)* are found (Swarth and Kiviat 2009). Along with a small number of frogs and toads, the spotted salamander *(Ambystoma maculatum)* lays eggs in tidal freshwater wetlands on the Hudson and Connecticut Rivers (Mihocko, Kiviat, et al. 2003).

Conservation Concerns and Restoration Alternatives

Sea-Level Rise and Wetland Sustainability

Coastal wetlands are dynamic environments, increasing in vertical elevation and migrating, often landward, as sea level rises (Redfield 1965). However, under a predicted regime of greatly accelerated rates of sea-level rise (Meehl, Stocker, et al. 2007; Rahmstorf 2007), the potential for submergence or loss of vegetated tidal wetland habitat increases (Orson, Panageotou, et al, 1985; Stevenson and Kearney 2009). When sea-level rise is greater than increases in wetland elevation, wetlands can become submerged, soils become waterlogged, and plant growth becomes stressed, often contributing to conversion of vegetated wetlands to mudflat or open-water habitats. Based on observed vegetation changes and estimates of accretion rates using radiometric dating techniques, there is evidence that some Northeast salt marshes may be in the early stages of submergence (e.g., Connecticut, Warren and Niering 1993, Orson, Warren, et al. 1998; Rhode Island, Donnelly and Bertness 2001; Massachusetts, Roman, Peck, et al. 1997), while some sites are currently experiencing rapid conversion from vegetated wetland to mudflats or open water, with sea-level rise identified as one of several contributing factors (e.g., Jamaica Bay, New York, Hartig, Gornitz, et al. 2002). There are numerous salt-marsh sites along the North Atlantic coast with surface elevation tables and horizon markers, a method designed to monitor marsh elevation and evaluate accretion and belowground processes related to surface elevation changes (e.g., Cahoon, Day, et al. 1999), but none of these data have been published yet, and long-term data are required to elucidate trends.

With sea-level rise, the more flood-tolerant *S. alterniflora* may migrate landward and invade the high marsh (Fig. 2.4), as noted in the Northeast by Donnelly and Bertness (2001), resulting in a more homogenous marsh landscape that could subsequently reduce available niches for other organisms (Warren and Niering 1993; Deegan 2002; Silliman and Bertness 2002). Additionally, in the developed northeastern U.S., there are often human-made barriers to landward migration by coastal wetlands (e.g., bulkheads, walls, buildings) (Fig. 2.4). An effective climate change adaptation strategy would be to restore human-impacted shorelines where appropriate to facilitate the migration and resilience of tidal marshes.

Another adaptation strategy that some agencies are experimenting with involves the placement of sediment on deteriorating wetlands, raising the elevation (i.e., gaining elevation capital; Cahoon and Guntenspergen 2010). In Jamaica Bay, New York, a 0.8-ha deteriorating wetland was supplemented with sediment using a thin-layer sediment spray technique, as applied in Louisiana (Cahoon and Cowan 1988). Also in Jamaica Bay, a larger (14-ha) restoration program conducted by the U.S. Army Corp of Engineers (USACE) is ongoing, with additional sites proposed, using dredge material placed on the wetland surface. Monitoring, being conducted cooperatively by the USACE and the National Park Service, is ongoing to evaluate the sustainability of these sediment-supplemented marshes and to quantify environmental responses.

Hydrologic Alterations

Hydrology is the fundamental factor that defines the structure and function of tidal wetlands, and in the highly urbanized northeastern U.S., there has been widespread alteration of hydrologic regimes from ditching, tidal restrictions (e.g., bridges, causeways, dikes, tide gates), channelization and drainage, impoundments, and other human alterations (Crain, Gedan, et al. 2009). Bourn and Cottam (1950) estimated that 90% of all salt marshes from Maine to Virginia have been ditched for mosquito-control purposes and confirmed by a more recent survey indicating that 94% of marshes from Maine to Connecticut had been ditched (Crain, Gedan, et al. 2009). A majority of the ditches were dug in the 1930s and create a very conspicuous gridlike feature. The effects of ditching include a lowering of the marsh water table level, shifts in vegetation, draining of marsh pools and pannes, and subsequent loss of fish and wildlife support functions (see reviews; Daiber 1986; Crain, Gedan, et al. 2009).

There are ongoing efforts in the northeastern U.S. to restore hydrologic processes and ecological functions that have been altered by ditching, including ditch filling (e.g., Assateague Island National Seashore, Maryland), ditch plugging and pool creation (e.g., Rachel Carson National Wildlife Refuge, Maine; Adamowicz, Roman, et al. 2004), but these are currently at a small scale and experimental, with ongoing monitoring. However, state and county mosquito-control agencies have adopted "open marsh water management" (OMWM) as a physical mosquito-control technique, with widespread application in many areas. Instead of the indiscriminate grid ditching of the 1930s, conducted without regard to mosquito breeding areas, OMWM focuses on breeding areas and integrates the OMWM with the existing grid-ditched marsh. OMWM was developed in New Jersey in the mid-1960s (Ferrigno and Jobbins 1968), and the technique continues to be modified and evaluated (Wolfe 1996; Lathrop, Cole, et al. 2000; Meredith and Lesser 2007; Rochlin, Iwanejko, et al. 2009).

Tidal restrictions are prevalent throughout the Northeast. Roads and railroads that cross wetlands often have undersized culverts or bridges, and tidal flow is restricted. Impoundments have been built to create waterbird habitat and dikes established for flood protection and mosquito control or to facilitate salt hay farming. With tidal restrictions, water levels can be drained or impounded, depending on the restricting structure; vegetation often changes from *Spartina*-dominated to the invasive *Phragmites* (Roman, Niering, et al. 1984; Kiviat 2009); fish and bird communities are altered (e.g., Raposa 2008; Benoit and Askins 1999); and wetland porewater biogeochemistry is altered, sometimes leading to acid-sulfate conditions (Portnoy 1999; Anisfeld and Benoit 1997; Findlay, Nieder, et al. 2009). Although tidal restrictions are widespread in the coastal northeastern U.S. and impacts can be severe, restoration of tidal flow is a highly successful practice that has been ongoing throughout the region for over two decades. Successful projects range from the 4,000-ha restoration of former impounded salt hay areas along the New Jersey shore of Delaware Bay (e.g., Weinstein, Teal, et al. 2001; Able, Grothues, et al. 2008), to restoration of portions of the degraded Hackensack Meadowlands, New Jersey (Kiviat and MacDonald

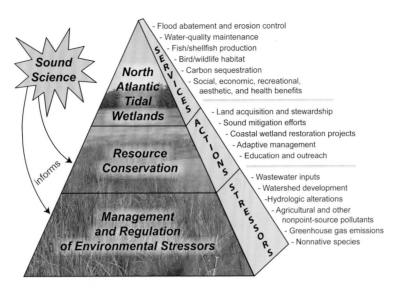

FIG. 2.5. Societal practices and actions necessary for sustaining North Atlantic tidal wetlands and the services that they provide.

2004), to numerous smaller restored systems throughout New England and Atlantic Canada (Burdick, Dionne, et al. 1997; Roman, Raposa, et al. 2002; Buchsbaum, Catena, et al. 2006; Wozniak, Roman, et al. 2006; Byers and Chmura 2007; Raposa 2008; Smith, Roman, et al. 2009). Warren, Fell, et al. (2002) reviewed two decades of tidal restoration projects in Connecticut. Although site responses are variable, these studies clearly document that with restoration of hydrologic regimes, *Phragmites* marsh returns to *Spartina*-dominated marsh, nekton and bird communities as well as trophic interactions are restored, and water quality is improved.

Watershed Development and Increases in Nutrients

Wastewater (e.g., sewage treatment effluent, septic systems, cesspools) and other nonpoint-source (e.g., fertilizers, pesticides) pollution inputs to North Atlantic coastal wetlands increase with watershed development and human activities (Valiela, Collins, et al. 1997; Bertness, Ewanchuk, et al. 2002). Using stable nitrogen isotopes, researchers have found direct relationships between the rise in human population in the northeastern U.S., coastal watershed development, and stable nitrogen isotope ratios in plants (*Spartina* spp., macroalgae) and animals (ribbed mussels, mummichogs) in coastal tidal wetlands (McClelland, Valiela, et al. 1997; McClelland and Valiela 1998; McKinney, Nelson, et al. 2001; Wigand, Comeleo, et al. 2001; Wigand, McKinney, et al. 2007; Cole, Valiela, et al. 2004; Cole, Kroeger, et al. 2005; Bannon and Roman 2008). Alongside these increases in wastewater delivery to North Atlantic coastal wetlands are changes in plant communities, species diversity (Fig. 2.4) (Bertness, Ewanchuk, et al. 2002; Bertness, Silliman, et al. 2009; Wigand, McKinney, et al. 2003; Silliman and Bertness 2004; Crain 2007), and soil processes (e.g., denitrification potential, soil respiration) (Davis, Nowicki, et al. 2004; Wigand, McKinney, et al. 2004; Wigand, Brennan, et al. 2009). For example, Crain (2007) demonstrated in fertilization experiments how wetland plants in tidal, oligohaline marshes in southern Maine were colimited by both N and phosphorus, and that this limitation was essential for maintaining high plant species diversity. In addition, wastewater associated with urbanization, and nonpoint-source pollution associated with agriculture in the northeastern U.S., promotes the invasion of nonnative *P. australis* along the upland borders of coastal wetlands (Chambers, Meyerson, et al. 1999; Silliman and Bertness 2004). These findings support the hypothesis that wastewater nutrients (N and phosphorus) are altering the structure and function of coastal wetlands (Crain 2007; Wigand 2008; Bertness, Silliman, et al. 2009; Turner, Howes, et al. 2009). Management and conservation of watershed natural lands to act as sinks for wastewater before it reaches coastal habitats in the North Atlantic, reduction of fertilizer application, buffer creation to reduce agricultural runoff, and societal conservation efforts to reduce human wastewater can all help sustain coastal wetlands.

Sustaining North Atlantic Coastal Wetlands

There are multiple stressors in the North Atlantic, including wastewater inputs, hydrologic alterations, nonpoint-source pollutants, nonnative species, and greenhouse gas emissions, which alter the structure and function of coastal tidal wetlands and need to be effectively managed to sustain the wetlands and the services that they provide (Fig. 2.5). These stressors act independently and interactively, often resulting in adverse effects on wetland communities, system processes, and the delivery of ecosystem services.

Effective regulation, informed by sound science, is needed to manage stressors in the North Atlantic. In addition, conservation actions to sustain coastal wetlands include land acquisition and stewardship, mitigation efforts, and wetland restoration projects using an adaptive management approach (Fig. 2.5). An excellent example of how adaptive management has been successfully used in salt marsh restoration projects is a 4,000-ha salt marsh restoration on Delaware Bay carried out by Public Service Enterprise Group (PSEG) as mitigation for a discharge permit (Teal and Weishar 2005). The degraded marshes that were targeted for restoration included old salt hay farms enclosed by dikes and brackish areas dominated by *P. australis*. Initial stakeholder meetings were organized to set restoration goals and monitoring priorities. Stakeholders included regulators, scientists, staff from PSEG, and local residents. Formal targets with timelines were set for the restoration of the wetland. Leaders of the monitoring program typically met twice a year with stakeholders and a committee of regulators and external scientists to review the monitoring data and to suggest further management actions as needed. The PSEG restoration project has successfully met its targets thus far (Teal and Weishar 2005). There are numerous other examples of science and monitoring, adaptive management, regulation, partnerships, management actions, and environmental education intersecting for effective restoration and conservation of North Atlantic coastal wetlands, and beyond any doubt, these conservation practices are critical to sustain North Atlantic coastal tidal wetlands and their associated services (e.g., flood abatement, water quality maintenance, fish/shellfish production, carbon sequestration, and recreational benefits).

Acknowledgments

Dennis Whigham and an anonymous reviewer provided very helpful reviews of the manuscript. We thank Mike Charpentier for analyzing the NWI data for the northeastern U.S. states, and Patricia DeCastro for assisting in the creation of the graphics. Julia Hyman, a University of Rhode Island Coastal Institute IGERT Fellow, supported by NSF grant #0504103, assisted with the carbon sequestration calculations. Mention of trade names or commercial products does not constitute endorsement or recommendation for use by the U.S. Environmental Protection Agency. This chapter, contribution number AED-10-067, has been technically reviewed by the US EPA-ORD-NHEERL, and approved for publication. Approval does not signify that the contents necessarily reflect the views and policies of the Agency.

References

Able KW, Fahay MP. 1998. The first year in the life of estuarine fishes in the middle Atlantic Bight. New Brunswick, NJ: Rutgers Univ. Press.

Able KW, Fahay MP, et al. 2002. Seasonal distribution and abundance of fishes and decapod crustaceans in a Cape Cod estuary. *Northeast. Nat.* 9:285–302.

Able KW, Fahay MP, et al. 2010. Ecology of estuarine fishes: temperate waters of the Western North Atlantic. Baltimore, MD: John Hopkins Univ. Press.

Able KW, Grothues TM, et al. 2008. Long term response of fishes and other fauna to restoration of former salt hay farms: multiple measures of restoration success. *Rev. Fish Biol. Fish.* 18:65–97.

Abraham BJ. 1985. Species profiles: life histories and environmental requirements of coastal fishes and invertebrates (Mid-Atlantic) mummichog and striped killifish. *USFWS Biol. Rpt.* 82(11). USACOE, TR EL-82-4.

Adamowicz SC, Roman CT. 2005. New England salt marsh pools: a quantitative analysis of geomorphic and geographic features. *Wetlands* 25:279–88.

Adamowicz SC, Roman CT, et al. 2004. Initial response of salt marshes to ditch plugging and pool creation (ME). *Ecol. Restor.* 22:53–54.

Alber M, Swenson EM, et al. 2008. Salt marsh dieback: an overview of recent events in the US. *Estuar. Coast. Shelf Sci.* 80:1–11.

Anisfeld SC, Benoit G. 1997. Impacts of flow restrictions on salt marshes: an instance of acidification. *Env. Sci. Technol.* 31:1650–57.

Ayvazian SG, Deegan LA, Finn JT. 1992. Comparison of habitat use by estuarine fish assemblages in the Acadian and Virginian zoogeographic provinces. *Estuaries* 15:368–83.

Baldwin AH, Barendregt A, Whigham DF. 2009. Tidal freshwater wetlands—an introduction to the ecosystem. In *Tidal freshwater wetlands,* Baldwin AH, Barendregt A, Whigham DF, editors. Leiden: Backhuys Publ., pp. 1–10.

Bannon RO, Roman CT. 2008. Using stable isotopes to monitor anthropogenic nitrogen inputs to estuaries. *Ecol. Appl.* 18:22–30.

Benoit LK, Askins RA. 1999. Impact of spread of *Phragmites* on the distribution of birds in Connecticut tidal marshes. *Wetlands* 19:194–208.

Bertness MD. 1999. *The ecology of Atlantic shorelines.* Sunderland, MA: Sinauer Assoc.

Bertness MD, Ewanchuk P, Silliman BR. 2002. Anthropogenic modification of New England salt marsh landscapes. *Proc. Natl. Acad. Sci. USA* 99:1395–98.

Bertness MD, Silliman BR, Holdredge C. 2009. Shoreline development and the future of New England salt marsh landscapes. In *Human impacts on salt marshes: a global perspective,* Silliman BR, Grosholz ED, Bertness MD, editors. Berkeley: Univ. Calif. Press, pp. 137–48.

Bourn WS, Cottam C. 1950. *Some biological effects of ditching tidewater marshes.* Res. Rpt. 19. Washington, DC: USFWS.

Bricker-Urso S, Nixon SW, et al. 1989. Accretion rates and sediment accumulation in Rhode Island salt marshes. *Estuaries* 12:300–17.

Bridgham SD, Megonigal JP, et al. 2006. The carbon balance of North American wetlands. *Wetlands* 26:889–916.

Brinkhuis BH. 1977. Comparisons of salt-marsh fucoid production estimated from three different indices. *J. Phycol.* 13:328–35.

Buchsbaum RN, Catena J, et al. 2006. Changes in salt marsh vegetation, *Phragmites australis,* and nekton in response to increased tidal flushing in a New England salt marsh. *Wetlands* 26:544–57.

Burdick DM, Dionne M, et al. 1997. Ecological responses to tidal restorations of two northern New England salt marshes. *Wetl. Ecol. Manag.* 4:129–44.

Byers SE, Chmura GL. 2007. Salt marsh vegetation recovery on the Bay of Fundy. *Estuar. Coasts* 30:869–77.

Cahoon DR, Cowan JH Jr. 1988. Environmental impacts and environmental policy implications of spray disposal of dredged material in Louisiana wetlands. *Coast. Manage.* 16:341–62.

Cahoon DR, Guntenspergen GR. 2010. Climate change, sea-level rise, and coastal wetlands. *Natl. Wetl. Newsl.* 32:8–12.

Cahoon DR, Day JW, Reed DJ. 1999. The influence of surface and shallow subsurface soil processes on wetland elevation: a synthesis. *Curr. Top. Wetl. Biogeochem.* 3:72–88.

Calhoun AJK, Cormier JE, et al. 1993. *The wetlands of Acadia National Park and vicinity.* Orono, ME: Maine Agric. For. Exper. Sta. Misc. Publ. 721.

Chambers RM, Meyerson LA, Saltonstall K. 1999. Expansion of *Phragmites australis* into tidal wetlands of North America. *Aquat. Bot.* 64:261–73.

Chapman VJ. 1960. *Salt marshes and salt deserts of the world.* New York: Interscience Publ.

Chintala MM, Wigand C, Thursby G. 2006. *Comparison of Geukensia demissa* populations in Rhode Island fringe salt marshes with varying nitrogen loads. *Mar. Ecol. Prog. Ser.* 320:101–108.

Chmura GL, Chase P, Bercovitch J. 1997. Climatic controls of the middle marsh zone in the Bay of Fundy. *Estuaries* 20:689–99.

Chmura GL, Anisfeld SC, et al. 2003. Global carbon sequestration in tidal, saline wetland soils. *Glob. Biogeochem. Cycles* 17(4):1111, doi:10.1029/2002GB001917.

Cicchetti G, Diaz RJ. 2000. Types of salt marsh edge and export of trophic energy from marshes to deeper habitats. In *Concepts and controversies in tidal marsh ecology,* Weinstein M, Kreeger J, editors. Netherlands: Kluwer Academic, pp. 515–42.

Clark KE, Niles LJ, Burger J. 1993. Abundance and distribution of migrant shorebirds in Delaware Bay. *Condor* 95:694–705.

Cloern JE. 2001. Our evolving conceptual model of the coastal eutrophication problem. *Mar. Ecol. Prog. Ser.* 210:223–53.

Cole ML, Kroeger KD, et al. 2005. Macrophytes as indicators of land-derived wastewater: application of a $\delta^{15}N$ method in aquatic systems. *Water Resour. Res.* 41:W01014.

Cole ML, Valiela I, et al. 2004. Assessment of a $\delta^{15}N$ method to indicate anthropogenic eutrophication in aquatic systems. *J. Env. Qual.* 33:124–32.

Cowardin LM, Carter V, et al. 1979. Classification of wetlands and deepwater habitats of the United States. FWS/OBS-79/31. Washington, DC: USFWS.

Crain CM. 2007. Shifting nutrient limitation and eutrophication effects in marsh vegetation across estuarine salinity gradients. *Estuar. Coasts* 30:26–34.

Crain CM, Gedan KB, Dionne M. 2009. Tidal restrictions and mosquito ditching in New England marshes: case studies of the biotic evidence, physical extent, and potential for restoration of altered hydrology. In *Human impacts on salt marshes: a global perspective,* Silliman BR, Grosholz ED, Bertness MR, editors. Berkeley: Univ. Calif. Press, pp. 149–70.

Crain CM, Silliman BR, et al. 2004. Physical and biotic drivers of plant distribution across estuarine salinity gradients. *Ecology* 85:2539–49.

Crumb SE. 1977. Macrobenthos of the tidal Delaware River between Trenton and Burlington, New Jersey. *Chesap. Sci.* 18:253–65.

Daiber FC. 1986. *Conservation of tidal marshes.* New York: Van Nostrand Reinhold.

Daiber FC, Roman CT. 1988. Tidal marshes. In *The Delaware Estuary: rediscovering a forgotten resource,* Bryant TL, Pennock JR, editors. Newark: Univ. Delaware Sea Grant College Prog., pp. 95–113.

Darby FA, Turner RE. 2008. Effects of eutrophication to salt marsh roots, rhizomes, and soils. *Mar. Ecol. Prog. Ser.* 363:63–70.

Davey E, Wigand C, et al. 2011. Use of computed tomography imaging for quantifying coarse roots, rhizomes, peat, and particle densities in marsh soils. *Ecol Appl.* 21:2156–2171.

Davis JL, Nowicki B, Wigand C. 2004. Denitrification in fringing salt marshes of Narragansett Bay, RI, USA. *Wetlands* 24:870–78.

Deegan LA. 2002. Lessons learned: the effects of nutrient enrichment on the support of nekton by seagrass and salt marsh ecosystems. *Estuaries* 25:727–42.

DeLaune C, Smith J, Tolley MD. 1984. The effect of sediment redox potential on nitrogen uptake, anaerobic root respiration and growth of *Spartina alterniflora* Loisel. *Aquat. Bot.* 18:223–30.

Dionne M, Dochtermann J, Leonard A. 2006. Fish communities and habitats of the York River watershed. Wells, ME: Wells National Estuarine Research Reserve.

DiQuinzio DA, Paton PWC, Eddleman WR. 2002. Nesting ecology of salt marsh sharp-tailed sparrows in a tidally restricted salt marsh. *Wetlands* 22:179–85.

Donnelly JP, Bertness MD. 2001. Rapid shoreward encroachment of salt marsh cordgrass in response to accelerated sea-level rise. *Proc. Natl. Acad. Sci. USA* 98:14218–23.

Drake DC, Peterson BJ, et al. 2009. Salt marsh ecosystem biogeochemical responses to nutrient enrichment: a paired ^{15}N tracer study. *Ecology* 90:2535–46.

Emeis KC, Benoit JR, et al. 2001. Unifying concepts for integrated coastal management. In *Science and integrated coastal management,* von Bodungen B, Turner RK, editors. Berlin: Dahlem Univ. Press, 341–64.

Emery NC, Ewanchuk PJ, Bertness MD. 2001. Competition and salt-marsh plant zonation: stress tolerators may be dominant competitors. *Ecology* 82:2471–85.

Faurby S, King, TL, et al. 2010. Population dynamics of American horseshoe crabs—historic climatic events and recent anthropogenic pressures. *Molec. Ecol.* 19:3088–3100.

Fay CW, Neves R, Pardue GB. 1983. Species profiles: life histories and environmental requirements of coastal fishes and invertebrates (Mid-Atlantic). USFWS Div. Biol. Serv. FWS/OBS-82/11.10. USACE, TR EL-82-4.

Fell PE, Weissbach SP, et al. 1998. Does invasion of oligohaline tidal marshes by reed grass, *Phragmites australis* (Cav.) Trin. Ex Steud., affect the availability of prey resources for the mummichog, *Fundulus heteroclitus* L.? *J. Exp. Mar. Biol. Ecol.* 222:59–77.

Ferrigno F, Jobbins DM, 1968. Open marsh water management. Proc. 55th Annu. Meeting NJ Mosq. Exterm. Assoc. 55:104–15.

Findlay SEG, Nieder WC, Ciparis S. 2009. Carbon flows, nutrient cycling, and food webs in tidal freshwater wetlands. In *Tidal freshwater wetlands,* AH Baldwin, Barendregt A, Whigham DF, editors. Leiden: Backhuys Publ., pp. 137–44

Findlay S, Schoeberl K, Wagner B, 1989. Abundance, composition and dynamics of the invertebrate fauna of a tidal freshwater wetland. *J. N. Am. Benthol. Soc.* 8: 140–148.

Findlay S, Wigand C, Nieder WC. 2006. Submersed macrophyte distribution and function in the tidal freshwater Hudson River. In *The Hudson River estuary,* Levinton JS, Waldman J, editors. New York: Cambridge Univ. Press, pp. 230–41.

Fitch R, Theodose T, Dionne M. 2009. Relationships among upland development, nitrogen, and plant community composition in a Maine salt marsh. *Wetlands* 29:1179–88.

Franz DR. 1993. Allometry of shell and body growth in ribbed mussels *(Geukensia demissa)* in relation to shore level. *J. Exp. Mar. Biol. Ecol.* 174:193–207.

Frumhoff PC, McCarthy JJ, et al. 2007. Confronting climate change in the US Northeast: science, impacts, and solutions. Syn. Rep. NE Climate Impacts Assess. (NECIA). Cambridge, MA: Union of Concerned Scientists.

Gallagher J. 1975. Effect of an ammonium nitrate pulse on growth and elemental composition of natural stands of *Spartina alterniflora* and *Juncus roemerianus. Am. J. Bot.* 62:644–48.

Gedan KB, Bertness MD. 2009. Experimental warming causes rapid loss of plant diversity in New England salt marshes. *Ecol. Letters* 12:842–44.

Gedan KB, Silliman BR, Bertness MD. 2009. Centuries of human-driven change in salt marsh ecosystems. *Annu. Rev. Mar. Sci.* 1:117–41.

Gjerdrum C, Elphick CS, Rubega M. 2005. Nest site selection and nesting success in salt marsh breeding sparrows: the importance of nest habitat, timing, and study site differences. *Condor* 107:849–62.

Good, RE. 1965. Salt marsh vegetation, Cape May, New Jersey. *Bull. NJ Acad. Sci.* 10:1–11.

Good RE, Good NF. 1975. Vegetation and production of the Woodbury Creek–Hessian Run freshwater tidal marshes. *Bartonia* 43:38–45.

Gratton C, Denno R. 2005. Restoration of arthropod assemblages in *Spartina* salt marsh following removal of the invasive plant *Phragmites australis. Restor. Ecol.* 13:358–72.

Gratton C, Denno R. 2006. Arthropod food web restoration following removal of an invasive wetland plant. *Ecol. Appl.* 16:622–31.

Hartig EK, Gornitz V, et al. 2002. Anthropogenic and climate-change impacts on salt marshes of Jamaica Bay, NY City. *Wetlands* 22:71–89.

Hellings SE, Gallagher JL. 1992. The effects of salinity and flooding on *Phragmites australis. J. Appl. Ecol.* 29:41–49.

Holdredge C, Bertness MD, Altieri AH. 2008. Role of crab herbivory in die-off of New England marshes. *Conserv. Biol.* 23:672–79.

Howarth RW, Billen G, et al. 1996. Regional nitrogen budgets and riverine N and P fluxes for the drainages to the North Atlantic Ocean: natural and human influences. *Biogeochem.* 35:75–139.

Howes BL, Dacey WH, Teal JM. 1985. Annual carbon mineralization and belowground production of *Spartina alterniflora* in a New England salt marsh. *Ecology* 66:595–605.

Howes BL, Weiskel PK, et al. 1996. Interception of freshwater and nitrogen transport from uplands to coastal waters: the role of saltmarshes. In *Estuarine shores,* Nordstrom KF, Roman CT, editors. Chichester, UK: John Wiley and Sons, pp. 287–310.

IPCC (Intergovernmental Panel on Climate Change). 2007. *Climate change 2007: the physical science basis.* Cambridge: Cambridge Univ. Press.

Jacobson HA, Jacobson GL Jr, Kelley JT. 1987. Distribution and abundance of tidal marshes along the coast of Maine. *Estuaries* 10:126–31.

Jaworski NA, Howarth RW, Hetling LJ. 1997. Atmospheric deposition of nitrogen oxides onto the landscape contributes to coastal eutrophication in the northeast United States. *Env. Sci. Technol.* 31:1995–2004.

Kelley JT, Belknap DF, et al. 1988. The morphology and origin of salt marshes along the glaciated coastline of Maine, USA. *J. Coast. Res.* 4:649–65.

Kelley JT, Gehrels WR, Belknap DF. 1995. The geological development of tidal marshes at Wells, Maine. *J. Coast. Res.* 11:136–53.

Kinney EH, Roman CT. 1998. Response of primary producers to nutrient enrichment in a shallow estuary. *Mar. Ecol. Prog. Ser.* 163:89–98.

Kiviat E. 2009. Invasive plants in tidal freshwater wetlands of the USA east coast. In *Tidal freshwater wetlands,* Baldwin AH, Barendregt A, Whigham DF, editors. Leiden: Backhuys Publ., pp. 105–14.

Kiviat E, MacDonald K. 2004. Biodiversity patterns and conservation in the Hackensack Meadowlands, New Jersey: history, ecology, and restoration of a degraded urban wetland. *Urban Habitats* 2:28–61.

Kiviat E, Findlay SEG, Nieder WC. 2006. Tidal wetlands of the Hudson River estuary. In *The Hudson River estuary,* Levinton JS, Waldman JR, editors. New York: Cambridge Univ. Press, pp. 279–95.

Koch MS, Mendelssohn IA, et al. 1990. Mechanism for the hydrogen-sulfide-induced growth limitation in wetland macrophytes. *Limnol. Oceanogr.* 35:399–408.

Kolker AS. 2005. The impacts of climate variability and anthropogenic activities on salt marsh accretion and loss on Long Island. Ph.D. diss., Mar. Sci. Res. Ctr., Stony Brook Univ., NY.

Kraft JC. 1988. Geology. In *The Delaware Estuary: rediscovering a forgotten resource,* Bryant TL, Pennock JR, editors. Newark: Univ. Delaware Sea Grant College Prog., pp. 31–42.

Lathrop RG, Cole MB, Showalter RD 2000. Quantifying the habitat structure and spatial pattern of New Jersey USA salt marshes under different management regimes. *Wetl. Ecol. Manag.* 8:163–72.

Lathrop RG, Windham L, Montesano P. 2003. Does *Phragmites* expansion alter the structure and function of marsh landscapes? Patterns and processes revisited. *Estuaries* 26:423–35.

League MT, Colbert EP, et al. 2006. Rhizome growth dynamics of native and exotic haplotypes of *Phragmites australis* (common reed). *Estuar. Coasts* 29:269–76.

Leck MA, Baldwin AH, et al. 2009. Plant communities of tidal freshwater wetlands of the continental USA and Canada. In *Tidal freshwater wetlands,* Baldwin AH, Barendregt A, Whigham DF, editors. Leiden: Backhuys Publ., pp. 41–58.

Leck MA, Simpson RL, et al. 1988. Plants of the Hamilton marshes: a Delaware River freshwater tidal wetland. *Bartonia* 54:1–17.

Ledesma ME, O'Connor NJ. 2001. Habitat and diet of the non-native crab *Hemigrapsus sanguineus* in southern New England. *Northeast. Nat.* 8:63–74.

Lerberg SB, Holland AF, Sanger DM. 2000. Responses of tidal creek macro-benthic communities to the effects of watershed development. *Estuaries* 23:838–53.

Levine J, Brewer S, Bertness M. 1998. Nutrients, competition and plant zonation in a New England salt marsh. *J. Ecol.* 86:285–92.

McClelland JW, Valiela I. 1998. Linking nitrogen in estuarine producers to land derived sources. *Limnol. Oceanogr.* 43:577–85.

McClelland JW, Valiela I, Michener RH. 1997. Nitrogen stable isotope signatures in estuarine food webs: a record of increasing urbanization in coastal watersheds. *Limnol. Oceanogr.* 42:930–37.

McIvor CC, Rozas LP. 1996. Direct nekton use of intertidal salt-marsh habitat and linkage with adjacent habitats: a review from the southeastern United States. In *Estuarine shores,* Nordstrom KF, Roman CT, editors. Chichester, UK: J. Wiley and Sons, pp. 311–34.

McKinney R, Nelson WG, et al. 2001. Ribbed mussel nitrogen isotope signatures reflect nitrogen sources in coastal salt marshes. *Ecol. Appl.* 11:203–14.

Meehl GA, Stocker TF, et al. 2007. Global climate projections. In *Climate change 2007: the physical science basis: contribution of working group I to the 4th Assessment Report of the Intergovernmental Panel on Climate Change,* Solomon S, Qin D, et al., editors. Cambridge: Cambridge Univ. Press, pp. 747–822.

Mendelssohn IA, Morris JT. 2000. Eco-physiological controls on the productivity of *Spartina alterniflora* Loisel. In *Concepts and controversies in tidal marsh ecology,* Weinstein M, Kreeger K, editors. The Netherlands: Kluwer Academic, pp. 59–80.

Mendelssohn IA, McKee KL, Patrick WH Jr. 1981. Oxygen deficiency in *Spartina alterniflora* roots: metabolic adaptation to anoxia. *Science* 214:439–41.

Meredith WH, Lesser CR. 2007. An overview of Open Marsh Water Management (OMWM) in Delaware, 1979–2007. *Proc. NJ Mosq. Contr. Assoc.* 94:55–69.

Metzler KJ, Tiner RW. 1992. *Wetlands of Connecticut.* State Geol. Nat. Hist. Surv., Hartford, CT: DEP and USFWS, Nat. Wetl. Invent.

Mihocko G, Kiviat E, et al. 2003. Assessing ecological functions of Hudson River fresh-tidal marshes: reference data and a modified hydrogeomorphic (HGM) approach. New Paltz: NY State Dept. Env. Conserv., Hudson River Estuary Prog.

Millennium Ecosystem Assessment. 2005. *Ecosystems and human well-being: wetlands and water synthesis.* Washington, DC: World Resour. Inst.

Miller WB, Egler FE. 1950. Vegetation of the Wequetequok-Pawcatuck tidal-marshes, Connecticut. *Ecol. Monogr.* 20:143–72.

Morgan PA, Burdick DM, Short FT. 2009. The functions and values of fringing salt marshes in northern New England, USA. *Estuar. Coasts* 32:483–95.

Morris JT, Sundareshwar PV, et al. 2002. Responses of coastal wetlands to rising sea levels. *Ecology* 83:2869–77.

Mulkana MS. 1966. The growth and feeding habits of juvenile fishes in two Rhode Island estuaries. *Gulf Res. Rpts.* 2:97–167.

Naidoo GK, McKee L, Mendelssohn IA. 1992. Anatomical and metabolic responses to waterlogging and salinity in *Spartina alterniflora* and *S. patens* (Poaceae). *Am. J. Bot.* 79:765–70.

Niering WA, RS Warren. 1980. Vegetation patterns and processes on New England salt marshes. *BioScience* 30:301–07.

Niles LJ, Bart J, et al. 2009. Effects of horseshoe crab harvest in Delaware Bay on red knots: are harvest restrictions working? *BioScience* 59:153–64.

Nixon SW. 1982. The ecology of New England high salt marshes: a community profile. FWS/OBS-81/55. Washington, DC: USFWS.

Nixon SW, Oviatt CA. 1973. Ecology of a New England salt marsh. *Ecol. Monogr.* 43:463–98

North American Bird Conservation Initiative, US Committee. 2010. The state of the birds 2010: report on climate change, USA. Washington, DC: USDI, www.stateofthebirds.org.

NPS (National Park Service). 2007. *An update on the disappearing salt marshes of Jamaica Bay, New York.* Gateway Nat. Rec. Area, NPS, USDI, Jamaica Bay Watershed Protection Plan Advisory Com.

Odum WE. 1988. Comparative ecology of tidal freshwater and salt marshes. *Annu. Rev. Ecol. Syst.* 19:147–76.

Odum WE, Smith TJ III, et al. 1984. The ecology of tidal freshwater marshes of the United States east coast: a community profile. USFWS. FWS/OBS-83/17.

Oldale RN. 1992. *Cape Cod and the islands: the geologic story.* East Orleans, MA: Parnassus Imprints.

Orson R, Panageotou W, Leatherman SP. 1985. Response of tidal salt marshes of the US Atlantic and Gulf coasts to rising sea levels. *J. Coast. Res.* 1:29–37.

Orson RA, Warren RS, Niering WA. 1987. Development of a tidal marsh in a New England river valley. *Estuaries* 10:20–27.

Orson RA, Warren RS, Niering WA. 1998. Interpreting sea level rise and rates of vertical marsh accretion in a southern New England tidal marsh. *Estuar. Coast. Shelf Sci.* 47:419–29.

Pacala SW, Hurtt GC, et al. 2001. Consistent land- and atmosphere-based U.S. carbon sink estimates. *Science* 292:2316–20.

Pennings SC, Bertness MD. 2001. Salt marsh communities. In *Marine community ecology,* Bertness MD, Gaines SD, Hay M, editors. Sunderland, MA: Sinauer, pp. 289–316.

Pielou EC, Routledge RD. 1976. Salt marsh vegetation: latitudinal gradients in the zonation patterns. *Oecologia* 24:311–21.

Portnoy JW. 1999. Salt marsh diking and restoration: biogeochemical implications of altered wetland hydrology. *Env. Manage.* 24:111–20.

Rabenhorst MC. 1995. Carbon storage in tidal marsh soils. In *Advances in soil science, soils and global change,* Lal R, Kimble J, et al., editors. Boca Raton, FL: CRC Lewis Publ., pp. 93–103.

Rahmstorf S. 2007. A semi-empirical approach to projecting future sea-level rise. *Science* 315:368–70.

Raposa KB. 2002. Early responses of fishes and crustaceans to restoration of a tidally restricted New England salt marsh. *Restor. Ecol.* 10:665–76.

Raposa KB. 2008. Early ecological responses to hydrologic restoration of a tidal pond and salt marsh complex in Narragansett Bay, Rhode Island. *J. Coast. Res.* 55:180–92.

Raposa KB, Roman CT. 2001. Seasonal habitat-use patterns of nekton in a tide restricted and unrestricted New England salt marsh. *Wetlands* 21:451–61.

Redfield AC. 1965. The ontogeny of a salt marsh estuary. *Science* 147:50–55.

Redfield AC. 1972. Development of a New England salt marsh. *Ecol. Monogr.* 42:201–37.

Rochlin I, Iwanejko T, et al. 2009. Geostatistical evaluation of integrated marsh management impact on mosquito vectors using before-after-control-impact (BACI) design. *Internat. J. Hlth. Geographics* 8:35–55.

Roman CT, Daiber FC. 1984. Aboveground and belowground primary production dynamics of two Delaware Bay tidal marshes. *Bull. Torrey Bot. Club* 3:34–41.

Roman CT, Able KW, et al. 1990. Primary productivity of angiosperm and macroalgae dominated habitats in a New England salt marsh: a comparative analysis. *Estuar. Coast. Shelf Sci.* 30:35–45.

Roman CT, Jaworski N, et al. 2000. Estuaries of the northeastern US: habitat and land use signatures. *Estuaries* 23:743–64.

Roman CT, Niering WA, Warren RS. 1984. Salt marsh vegetation change in response to tidal restriction. *Env. Manage.* 8:141–50.

Roman CT, Peck JA, et al. 1997. Accretion of a New England (USA) salt marsh in response to inlet migration, storms, and sea-level rise. *Estuar. Coast. Shelf Sci.* 45:717–27.

Roman CT, Raposa KB, et al. 2002. Quantifying vegetation and nekton response to tidal restoration of a New England salt marsh. *Restor. Ecol.* 10:450–60.

Roundtree RA, Able KW. 1992. Fauna of polyhaline subtidal marsh creeks in southern New Jersey: composition, abundance and biomass. *Estuaries* 15:171–85.

Schmidt RE, Lake TR. 2006. The role of tributaries in the biology of Hudson River fishes. In *The Hudson River estuary,* Levinton JS, Waldman J, editors. New York: Cambridge Univ. Press, pp. 205–16.

Short FT, Burdick DM. 1996. Quantifying eelgrass habitat loss in relation to housing development and nitrogen loading in Waquoit Bay, Massachusetts. *Estuaries* 19:730–39.

Short FT, Burdick DM, Kaldy JE III. 1995. Mesocosm experiments quantify the effects of eutrophication on eelgrass, *Zostera marina* L. *Limnol. Oceanogr.* 40:740–49.

Shriver WG, Vickery PD, et al. 2007. Flood tides affect breeding ecology of two sympatric sharp-tailed sparrows. *Auk* 124:552–60.

Silliman BR, Bertness MD. 2002. A trophic cascade regulates salt marsh primary productivity. *Proc. Natl. Acad. Sci. USA* 99:10500–05.

Silliman BR, Bertness MD 2004. Shoreline development drives invasion of *Phragmites australis* and the loss of plant diversity on New England salt marshes. *Conserv. Biol.* 18:1424–34.

Silliman BR, Bertness MD, Thomsen MS 2009. Top-down control and human intensification of consumer pressure in southern US salt marshes. In *Human impacts on salt marshes: a global perspective,* Silliman BR, Grosholz ED, Bertness MD, editors. Berkeley: Univ. Calif. Press, pp. 103–14.

Silliman BR, Van de Koppel J, et al. 2005. Drought, snails, and large-scale die-off of southern US salt marshes. *Science* 310:1803–06.

Sirkin L, Bokuniewicz H. 2006. The Hudson River Valley: geological history, landforms, and resources. In *The Hudson River estuary,* Levinton JS, Waldman JR, editors. New York: Cambridge Univ. Press, pp. 13–23.

Smith KK, Good RE, Good NF. 1979. Production dynamics for above and belowground components of a New Jersey *Spartina alterniflora* tidal marsh. *Estuar. Coast. Mar. Sci.* 9:189–201.

Smith S, Roman CT, et al. 2009. Responses of plant communities to incremental hydrologic restoration of a tide-restricted salt marsh in southern New England (MA USA). *Restor. Ecol.* 17:606–18.

Smith SM. 2009. Multi-decadal changes in salt marshes of Cape Cod, MA: photographic analyses of vegetation loss, species shifts, and geomorphic changes. *Northeast Nat.* 16:183–208.

Stevenson JC, Kearney MS. 2009. Impacts of global climate change and sea-level rise on tidal wetlands. In *Human impacts on salt marshes: a global perspective,* Silliman BR, Grosholz ED, Bertness MD, editors. Berkeley: Univ. Calif. Press, pp. 171–206.

Sullivan MJ, Daiber FC. 1974. Response in production of cord grass, *Spartina alterniflora,* to inorganic nitrogen and phosphorus fertilizer. *Chesapeake Sci.* 15:12–123.

Swarth CW, Kiviat E. 2009. Animal communities in North American tidal freshwater wetlands. In *Tidal freshwater wetlands,* Baldwin AH, Barendregt A, Whigham DF, editors. Leiden: Backhuys Publ., pp. 71–88.

Target TE, McCleave JD. 1974. Summer abundance of fishes in a

Maine tidal cove with special reference to temperature. *Trans. Amer. Fish. Soc.* 2:325–30.

Teal J, Teal M. 1969. *Life and death of the salt marsh.* New York: Ballantine Books.

Teal JM, Howes BL. 1996. Long-term stability in a salt marsh ecosystem. *Limnol. Oceanogr.* 41:802–809.

Teal JM, Howes BL. 2000. Salt marsh values: retrospection from the end of the century. In *Concepts and controversies in tidal marsh ecology,* Weinstein MP, Kreeger DA, editors. Netherlands: Kluwer Publ., pp. 9–22.

Teal JM, Weishar L. 2005. Ecological engineering, adaptive management, and restoration management in Delaware Bay salt marsh restoration. *Ecol. Eng.* 25:304–14.

Templer P, Findlay SEG, Wigand C. 1998. Sediment chemistry associated with native and non-native emergent macrophytes of a Hudson River Ecosystem. *Wetlands* 18:70–78.

Tiner RW Jr. 1985a. *Wetlands of New Jersey.* Newton Corner, MA: USFWS, Nat. Wetl. Invent.

Tiner RW Jr. 1985b. *Wetlands of Delaware.* Newton Corner, MA: USFWS, Nat. Wetl. Invent. Dover: Delaware Dept. Nat. Resour. Env. Contr., Wetl. Sec.

Tiner RW. 1987. *A field guide to coastal wetland plants of the northeastern United States.* Amherst: Univ. MA Press.

Tiner RW Jr. 1989. *Wetlands of Rhode Island.* Newton Corner, MA: USFWS, Nat. Wetl. Invent.

Tiner RW. 2005. Assessing cumulative loss of wetland functions in the Nanticoke River watersheds using enhanced national wetlands inventory data. *Wetlands* 25:405–19.

Turner RE, Howes BL, et al. 2009. Salt marshes and eutrophication: an unsustainable outcome. *Limnol. Oceanogr.* 54:1634–42.

Turner RE, Swenson EM, et al. 2004. Below-ground biomass in healthy and impaired salt marshes. *Ecol. Res.* 19:29–35.

USEPA. 2005. Emission facts: average carbon dioxide emissions resulting from gasoline and diesel fuel. EPA420-F-05-001. Washington, DC.

USEPA. 2006. A framework for the assessment of the wildlife habitat value of New England salt marshes. Washington, DC: EPA/600/R-06/132 ORD.

Valiela I, Cole ML, et al. 2000. Role of salt marshes as part of coastal landscapes. In *Concepts and controversies in tidal marsh ecology,* Weinstein M, Kreeger K, editors. Netherlands: Kluwer Academic, pp. 23–28.

Valiela I, Collins G, et al. 1997. Nitrogen loading from coastal watersheds to receiving estuaries: new method and application. *Ecol. Appl.* 7:358–80.

Valiela I, Teal JM, Persson NY. 1976. Production and dynamics of experimentally enriched salt marsh vegetation: belowground biomass. *Limnol. Oceanogr.* 21:245–52.

Valiela I, Teal JM, Sass WJ. 1975. Production and dynamics of salt marsh vegetation and the effects of experimental treatment with sewage sludge. *J. Appl. Ecol.* 12:973–81.

Valiela I, Teal JM, et al. 1985. Decomposition in salt marsh ecosystems: the phases and major factors affecting disappearance of above-ground organic matter. *J. Exp. Mar. Biol. Ecol.* 89:29–54.

Waldman JR. 2006. The diadromous fish fauna of the Hudson River: life histories, conservation concerns, and research avenues. In *The Hudson River estuary,* Levinton JS, Waldman JR, editors. New York: Cambridge Univ. Press, pp. 171–88.

Warren RS, Niering WA. 1993. Vegetation change on a northeast tidal marsh: interaction of sea-level rise and marsh accretion. *Ecology* 74:96–103.

Warren RS, Fell PE, et al. 2002. Salt marsh restoration in Connecticut: 20 years of science and management. *Restor. Ecol.* 10:497–513.

Weinstein MP, Teal JM, et al. 2001. Restoration principles emerging from one of the world's largest tidal marsh restoration projects. *Wetl. Ecol. Manag.* 9:387–407.

Whigham DF 2009. Primary production in tidal freshwater wetlands. In *Tidal freshwater wetlands,* Baldwin AH, Barendregt A, Whigham DF, editors. Leiden: Backhuys Publ., pp. 115–22.

Wigand C. 2008. Coastal salt marsh community change in Narragansett Bay in response to cultural eutrophication. In *Science for ecosystem-based management,* Desbonett A, Costa-Pierce BA, editors. New York: Springer, pp. 499–522.

Wigand C, Brennan P, et al. 2009. Soil respiration rates in coastal marshes subject to increasing watershed nitrogen loads in southern New England, USA. *Wetlands* 29:952–63.

Wigand C, Comeleo R, et al. 2001. Outline of a new approach to evaluate ecological integrity of salt marshes. *Human Ecol. Risk Assess.* 7:1541–54.

Wigand C, McKinney R, et al. 2003. Relationships of nitrogen loadings, residential development, and physical characteristics with plant structure in New England salt marshes. *Estuaries* 26:1494–1504.

Wigand C, McKinney R, et al. 2004. Denitrification enzyme activity of fringe salt marshes in New England, USA. *J. Env. Qual.* 33:1144–51.

Wigand C, McKinney R, et al. 2007. Varying stable nitrogen iso-

tope ratios of different coastal marsh plants and their relationships with wastewater nitrogen and land use in New England USA. *Env. Monitor. Assess.* 131:71–81.

Wilson KR, Kelley JT, et al. 2009. Stratigraphic and ecophysical characterization of salt marsh pools: dynamic landforms of the Webhannet salt marsh, Wells ME. *Estuar. Coasts* 32:855–70.

Wolfe RJ. 1996. Effects of open marsh water management on selected tidal marsh resources: a review. *J. Am. Mosq. Contr. Assoc.* 12:701–12.

Wozniak AS, Roman CT, et al. 2006. Monitoring food web changes in tide-restored salt marshes: a carbon stable isotope approach. *Estuar. Coasts* 29:568–78.

CHAPTER 3

Coastal Wetlands of Chesapeake Bay

ANDREW H. BALDWIN, PATRICK J. KANGAS, J. PATRICK MEGONIGAL,
MATTHEW C. PERRY, and DENNIS F. WHIGHAM

Chesapeake Bay is the largest estuary in the United States. It occupies 5,700 km², has 6,400 km of shoreline, and is fed by about 50 major and thousands of minor tributaries (Fig. 3.1) (US EPA 1982, 2004; White 1989). Its location entirely within the flat topography of the Atlantic Coastal Plain has favored the development of vast areas of wetlands, including tidal freshwater, oligohaline (intermediate), and brackish (mesohaline) marshes (dominated by herbaceous plants), tidal freshwater swamps (dominated by woody plants), submersed macrophyte ("seagrass") beds, and tidal mudflats lacking vascular plants (Fig. 3.2a–g). We estimate that about 160,000 ha of these types of coastal wetlands occur in the Bay, based on several sources (Wass and Wright 1969; McCormick and Somes 1982; Tiner and Burke 1995; Tiner, Berquist, et al. 2001).

Coastal wetlands of Chesapeake Bay experience a range of tidal amplitudes and salinity regimes. Mean amplitude is 0.9 m at the Bay mouth and generally lower along major subestuaries such as the Patuxent (0.37–0.73 m), Potomac (0.43–0.85 m), Rappahannock (0.37–0.79 m), and Nanticoke (0.67–0.73 m), but can be higher, for example, up to 1.16 m on the upper tidal reaches of the York River (Fig. 3.1) (Hicks 1964). Although tidal amplitude decreases moving north across the Bay proper, within subestuaries the maximum amplitude often occurs near the upper reach of tidal influence, i.e., in the tidal freshwater zone (Hicks 1964). Tidal amplitude of Bay wetlands is small relative to those of the rest of the East Coast (WWW Tide and Current Predictor, http://tbone.biol.sc.edu/tide), and in this respect Bay wetlands are more similar to Gulf Coast than to other Atlantic Coast wetlands. Salinity regimes range from tidal freshwater (< 0.5 ppt salinity) at the upper reaches of the Bay and its subestuaries to polyhaline (18–30 ppt) near the mouth, although most of the Bay is below 20 ppt and brackish water predominates (US EPA 2004). During summer months, particularly during droughts, salinity in typically freshwater areas may increase to 5–7 ppt (Baldwin 2007). Salinity can also fluctuate daily at a given location by as much as 5 ppt due to tidal exchange (White 1989). The diversity and size of Chesapeake Bay coastal wetlands provide a unique natural laboratory to examine the influence of global, regional, and local changes caused by humans on estuarine structure and function.

Hydrogeology and Biogeochemistry

Chesapeake Bay is a drowned river valley that formed in the late Pliocene (Hobbs 2004) and began filling with water 10,000 years ago as sea level rose due to Holocene warming. Sediment originating in both the 166,500-km² catchment and the continental shelf has since filled the Bay (Hobbs, Halka, et al. 1992) to an average depth of about 7 m. Soil erosion and subsequent sediment deposition in streams and estuaries accelerated dramatically in the 17th century as European settlers converted forests to agriculture (Brush 1984), with consequences for both tidal and nontidal wetlands.

Prior to the 17th century, Chesapeake Bay streams supported extensive nontidal wetlands with relatively organic-rich soils (Walter and Merritts 2008), reflecting their low rates of sediment deposition and capacity to accumulate carbon. Many of these fluvial presettlement wetlands were buried in the 17th and 18th centuries by fine upland sediments deposited behind tens of thousands of mill dams constructed for water power (Walter and Merritts 2008). The 17th-century spike in soil erosion is also apparent in sediment cores from Bay tidal wetlands (Pasternack, Brush, et al. 2001). For example, sediment deposition at Jug Bay on the Patuxent River, Maryland, increased fivefold from an apparent pre-European rate of < 1 mm yr⁻¹ to a 19th-century rate of 5 mm yr⁻¹ (Khan and Brush 1994). Because of this sharp increase in sediment loading, it is possible that European settlement initially increased the area of Bay tidal wetlands, particularly the area of tidal freshwater wetlands at the head of tide, where the channel is relatively narrow and shallow. The high suspended sediment loads of the present-day Chesapeake Bay and its tributaries are a legacy of soil erosion that began with European settlement and is ongoing today (Schenk and Hupp 2009).

Rates and patterns of sediment deposition influence wetland ecosystem attributes such as soil organic matter content, nutrient availability, and soil surface elevation, and spatiotemporal variation in sediment deposition is the source of structural and functional differences among and within wetlands (Pasternack 2009). Deposition rates in both tidal (Jordan, Pierce, et al. 1986) and nontidal (Noe and Hupp 2009) fluvial

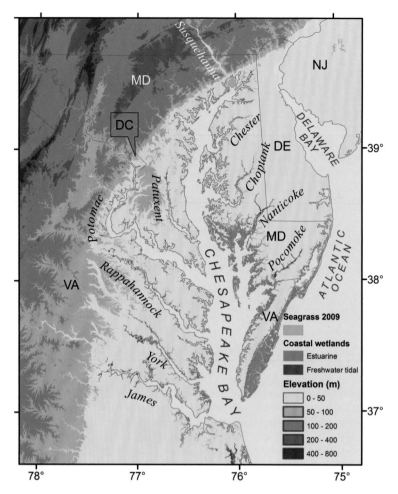

FIG. 3.1. Major tributaries and coastal wetlands of Chesapeake Bay. The location of estuarine and freshwater tidal wetlands is based on U.S. Fish and Wildlife National Wetlands Inventory geospatial data and includes wetlands with emergent vegetation, unvegetated intertidal areas (mudflats), and vegetated shallow-water areas (seagrasses or algae). "Seagrass 2009" is the distribution of submersed aquatic vegetation (SAV) beds determined in 2009 by the Virginia Institute of Marine Science Submerged Aquatic Vegetation program (http://web.vims.edu/bio/sav/sav09/). Map prepared by A. H. Baldwin.

Chesapeake Bay wetlands are related to the suspended sediment load of the floodwater. In a comparison of two sites separated by 19 km on the Mattaponi River, Virginia, rates of sediment deposition were up to tenfold higher at the site farthest downstream and closest to the turbidity maximum (Darke and Megonigal 2003). The turbidity maximum is a dynamic feature of Chesapeake Bay that coincides roughly with the freshwater-saltwater interface (Schubel 1968) and responds to variation in the discharge of the Susquehanna River (Schubel and Prichard 1986). At the site scale, deposition rates in both tidal and nontidal wetlands (Ross, Hupp, et al. 2004) decline rapidly with distance from the fluvial source and increasing elevation (i.e., decreasing frequency of inundation). Such factors contribute to the observation that tidal low-marsh soils near fluvial sources are relatively low in organic matter and mineral rich compared to high-marsh or interior marsh soils (A. Bald-

win pers. obs.). Many Bay tidal high marshes have peat soils (sapric histosols) with profiles up to 5 m deep composed of > 70% soil organic matter (P. Megonigal pers. obs.).

The productivity and composition of vegetation can regulate sediment deposition rates in tidal wetlands, provided that suspended sediment does not limit the process. Plant density and height were highly correlated with sediment deposition rates in a tidal freshwater wetland located near the turbidity maximum of the Mattaponi River, but not at a site 19 km upstream, where sediment concentrations were much lower (Darke and Megonigal 2003). In other Chesapeake Bay tidal freshwater wetlands, sediment deposition was strongly correlated to plant community type (Pasternack and Brush 2001) and creek bank deposition was higher in vegetated than in unvegetated areas (Neubauer, Anderson, et al. 2002). The seasonal dynamics of vegetation contribute to intra-annual varia-

FIG. 3.2. *(opposite)* Examples of Chesapeake Bay wetland ecosystems. A. Jug Bay in the freshwater tidal portion of the Patuxent River subestuary. B. Freshwater tidal marsh, showing zonation into low and high marsh plant communities. C. Brackish marsh, showing *Spartina cynosuroides* (foreground), *S. patens* (middle), and *Juncus roemerianus* (background). D. Chambers for the CO_2 elevation experiment at the Smithsonian Environment Research Center. E. Freshwater tidal swamp. F. Landsat mosaic of the Choptank and Nanticoke River subestuaries and adjacent eastern Chesapeake Bay shoreline. G. Restored freshwater tidal marsh on the Anacostia River, Washington, DC. (Photo credits: A: A. Luckenbach; B, C, E, G: A. H. Baldwin; D: J. P. Megonigal. Used with permission.)

tion in sedimentation, with peak deposition coinciding with peak plant biomass (Leonard 1997; Pasternack and Brush 2001; Neubauer, Anderson, et al. 2002; Darke and Megonigal 2003); however, there are exceptions (Kastler and Wiberg 1996).

Chesapeake Bay tidal wetlands must periodically increase soil mass in order to rise in elevation at a pace coincident with sea-level rise, a process that many extant Bay wetlands have maintained for the past 6,000 years over an approximately 5 m increase in sea level. Plant-enhanced sediment deposition is one mechanism for adding soil mass, but many Bay wetland soils are composed almost entirely of decaying plant matter. In comparison to sediment deposition, there is relatively little known about how organic processes such as wetland plant productivity and decomposition govern the gain or loss of soil organic matter and elevation in tidal wetland soils.

Wetlands are sinks, sources, and transformers of matter that cross the upland-aquatic interface. Sediment deposition is an important vehicle for importing allochthonous particulate organic carbon and nutrients into wetland soils (Morse, Megonigal, et al. 2004). For example, at Sweet Hall Marsh, a Chesapeake Bay tidal freshwater wetland, one-third of organic carbon inputs are imported with sediment, with the remainder from in situ production (Neubauer, Anderson, et al. 2002). Seven nontidal Bay Coastal Plain rivers deposit a large fraction of their annual load of nitrogen (24%) and phosphorus (59%) in the adjacent floodplain (Noe and Hupp 2009). Tidal wetlands also appear to be efficient nutrient traps, sequestering 35% of the nitrogen and 81% of the phosphorus load in the upper reaches of the Patuxent River by one rough estimate (Merrill and Cornwell 2000).

Tidal wetlands can be either sources or sinks of particulate and dissolved matter, depending on factors such as tidal range, subsystem area, and distance to the ocean (Childers, Day, et al. 2000), all of which vary across Chesapeake Bay. There has been relatively little work on energy and nutrient exchange in the Bay. Studies of the brackish Rhode River subsestuary concluded that brackish tidal wetlands acted mainly to transform nutrients from particulate to dissolved forms, and identified mudflats as the most important nutrient sink (Jordan, Correll, et al. 1983). Net export of ammonium has been observed in both brackish and tidal freshwater wetlands (Jordan and Correll 1991; Neubauer, Anderson, et al. 2005), but the direction of nitrate exchange differed between the low marshes at these sites. Both denitrification (Hopfensperger, Kaushal, et al. 2009) and dissimilatory nitrate reduction to ammonium (Tobias, Macko, et al. 2001) are sinks for nitrate in Bay tidal wetlands.

Early work on carbon export in tidal marshes was motivated by the hypothesis that these systems export energy (as carbon) to aquatic food webs. Recent work on dissolved organic carbon (DOC) has been motivated by the effects of light-adsorbing forms of DOC (i.e., chromophoric dissolved organic matter, or CDOM) on ultraviolet light penetration and the possibility of using the CDOM signature to trace the flux of estuarine compounds into coastal oceans. Both brackish and freshwater tidal wetlands of the Bay are net sources of CDOM to the estuary (Tzortziou, Neale, et al. 2008; Megonigal and Neubauer 2009). There is limited evidence that tidal wetlands are dominant sources of dissolved inorganic carbon to Chesapeake Bay (Neubauer and Anderson 2003).

The biogeochemical factors that control specific pathways of microbial respiration are important for understanding the wetlands as simultaneous sinks of carbon dioxide (CO_2) and sources of methane (CH_4), a powerful greenhouse gas. Methane emissions are typically higher in nontidal than tidal wetlands (Bridgham, Megonigal, et al. 2006) because sulfate-reducing microbes outcompete methanogens for organic carbon, an effect that varies predictably with salinity (Poffenbarger, Needelman, et al. 2011). Methane production in Chesapeake Bay wetlands is also regulated by iron availability (Neubauer, Givler, et al. 2005) and possibly humic acid availability (Keller, Weisenhorn, et al. 2009).

Plant Communities

Wetland plant communities of Chesapeake Bay are species rich; a total of 286 emergent vascular plant species were recorded at 9 tidal wetland sites spanning salinities of about 0.5–22 ppt in the James River estuary (Fig. 3.1) (Atkinson, Bodkin, et al. 1990). *Emergent plants,* as used in this chapter, means those having stems or leaves protruding above the water. Furthermore, benthic microalgae are important primary producers in emergent marshes, seagrass beds, and mudflats, and macroalgae are also common in shallow open water where attachment substrate occurs (White 1989).

Emergent Plants

Salinity is the most important environmental variable controlling emergent plant species composition across estuaries. In general, the number of plant species within plots or distinct wetlands increases as average salinity decreases, proceeding from areas near the confluence of Chesapeake Bay and the Atlantic Ocean and the upper reaches of the tide, where the Susquehanna River discharges into the Bay. Within individual subestuaries, salinity also varies from the confluence with the Bay to the upper extent of the tide (Anderson, Brown, et al. 1968). Oligohaline wetlands may have species richness similar to or higher than that of tidal freshwater wetlands farther upstream (Anderson, Brown, et al. 1968; Sharpe and Baldwin 2009), possibly due in part to periodic salinity intrusions that promote coexistence of brackish and freshwater species.

Only a few species can establish and grow in the brackish wetlands and salt marshes that occur at the downstream end of the salinity gradient (see estuarine wetlands in Figs. 3.1 and 3.2c), including the graminoids *Spartina alterniflora, S. patens, S. cynosuroides* (Fig. 3.3h), *Juncus roemerianus, Schoenoplectus americanus,* and *Distichlis spicata* and the shrub *Iva frutescens* (Anderson 1972; Sharpe and Baldwin 2009). A few forbs also occur in higher-salinity wetlands, such as the annual *Pluchea purpurascens.* At the most saline sites, near the mouth of the Bay, obligate halophytes such as *Salicornia virginica* and *Limonium carolinianum* occur (Perry and Atkinson 1997). Within a given brackish wetland, spatial patterns in plant community composition are due primarily to elevation-related differences in inundation.

The tidal freshwater and oligohaline wetlands of Chesapeake Bay (tidal freshwater wetlands are shown in Figs. 3.1 and 3.2a–b) include many species common in nontidal wetlands, but often at different relative abundances. Although a given wetland site may contain 50 or more species, among the most widespread and dominant perennials are *Peltandra virginica, Leersia oryzoides, Acorus calamus,* and *Nuphar lutea* (Fig. 3.3e) (Doumlele 1981; Perry, Bilcovic, et al. 2009; Sharpe and Baldwin 2009). These low-salinity wetlands differ considerably from brackish and salt marshes in that annuals, such as *Polygonum arifolium* (Fig. 3.3j), *P. sagittatum, Impatiens capensis,*

FIG. 3.3. Plant species of Chesapeake Bay wetlands. A. Royal fern, *Osmunda regalis*. B. River bulrush, *Schoenoplectus fluviatilis*. C. Purple-stemmed aster, *Symphyotrichum puniceum*. D. Saltmarsh mallow, *Kosteletzkya virginica*. E. Spatterdock, *Nuphar lutea*. F. Bur-marigold, *Bidens laevis*. G. Pickerelweed, *Pontederia cordata*. H. Big cordgrass, *Spartina cynosuroides*. I. Ground nut, *Apios americana*. J. Halberd-leaved tearthumb, *Polygonum arifolium*. K. Swamp tupelo, *Nyssa biflora*. (Photo credits: A–F, H, J–K: A. H. Baldwin; G, I: K. Jensen. Used with permission.)

and *Bidens laevis* (Fig. 3.3f), may make up half of the species in the community and, in some cases, most of the biomass (Baldwin, Egnotovich, et al. 2001; Baldwin and Pendleton 2003; Whigham 2009). These wetlands exhibit horizontal zonation, with the frequently flooded low marsh often a monoculture of *N. lutea* (Perry and Atkinson 2009) and most other species occurring in the high marsh (Leck, Baldwin, et al. 2009). Species composition varies seasonally, with *A. calamus* and *P. virginica* reaching their maximum abundance early in the growing season and annuals peaking later (Baldwin 2004; Perry, Bilcovic, et al. 2009; Whigham 2009). Saltwater intrusion may cause interannual variation in species composition: salt-tolerant species were abundant in a tidal freshwater wetland during low-flow, higher-salinity conditions, but freshwater species became dominant during wetter, fresher years (Davies 2004 in Perry, Bilcovic, et al. 2009).

Tidal freshwater and oligohaline swamps (Fig. 3.2e) are probably the most species-rich type of coastal wetland in the Bay, but also the least studied (Conner, Doyle, et al. 2007; Leck, Baldwin, et al. 2009). Although a few species of woody plants dominate the canopy, including *Fraxinus pennsylvanica, Acer rubrum,* and *Nyssa sylvatica* (Kroes, Hupp, et al. 2007), in plots at 24 sites along the Nanticoke River (Fig. 3.1), more than 40 species of trees and shrubs and over 100 herbaceous species were observed (Baldwin 2007). Similarly, on the Pamunkey River, a tributary of the York River, 20 canopy, 23 subcanopy, and 69 herbaceous species were recorded at 23 sites (Rheinhardt 1992). The diversity of herbaceous plants is due in part to the hummock-hollow microtopography typical of these wetlands. Periodic salinity intrusions during droughts may also be a cause of high plant diversity in some swamps (Peterson and Baldwin 2004; Baldwin 2007).

Seagrass Beds

Seagrasses are abundant in shallow waters across the Bay (Fig. 3.1), but species richness is higher in freshwater than in saline areas (Moore, Wilcox, et al. 2000). The spatial distribution of seagrass beds is also related to variables controlling light (depth, water turbidity, epiphytes on leaves, nutrients) and physiochemical factors including sediment grain size and organic matter content, porewater sulfide concentration, water currents (minimum need and maximum tolerance), and tolerance of individual species to waves (Koch 2001; Kemp, Batiuk, et al. 2004). Lower abundance of seagrasses is associated with higher agricultural and urban development (Li, Weller, et al. 2007).

About 20 species of submersed macrophytes occur in Chesapeake Bay, which can be divided into 4 species associations (Moore, Wilcox, et al. 2000; Moore 2009). An association dominated by *Zostera marina* predominates in the lower, most saline parts of the Bay, while an association dominated by *Ruppia maritima* is most widespread in the middle parts of the Bay. Farther upstream along the Bay and subestuaries is an association dominated by *Potamogeton pectinatus* and *P. perfoliatus,* and in the freshest parts of the Bay the most abundant type is a "freshwater mixed" association dominated by *Vallisneria americana* and two nonnative species, *Myriophyllum spicatum* and *Hydrilla verticillata;* this association contains more species (12) than the others (4 each for the *Ruppia* and *Potamogeton* associations and 2 for the *Zostera* association).

Changes in the abundance of seagrass beds in Chesapeake Bay over time have been both dramatic and well documented. In the 1930s, eelgrass *(Zostera marina)* populations, predomi-

nant in the lower, more saline parts of the Bay, were damaged by eelgrass wasting disease, a pandemic caused by the protist *Labyrinthula zosterae* (Orth and Moore 1984; Moore 2009). Another major change in Bay seagrass beds was an increase in the Eurasian water milfoil *(Myriophyllum spicatum)* in the fresher parts of the Bay in the late 1950s and 1960s (Orth and Moore 1984). Subsequent to these changes, an "unprecedented decline" in seagrass beds began (Orth and Moore 1983), perhaps exacerbated by high sediment and freshwater loading from Hurricane Agnes in 1972, but largely due to increases in nutrient concentrations associated with human population growth in the watershed, which promoted phytoplankton and epiphyte growth, shading leaves and reducing plant growth (Kemp, Boynton, et al. 2005). There has been a modest recovery of seagrasses in the Bay since about 1985, particularly in subestuaries where nutrient loading has decreased (Kemp, Boynton, et al. 2005).

Micro- and Macroalgae

Benthic microalgae, or microphytobenthos, occur on the surface of marsh soils, mudflats, leaves and stems of emergent and submergent plants, and sediment surface in shallow waters, habitats that are widespread and abundant in Chesapeake Bay (Rizzo and Wetzel 1985).

Microalgal communities in Atlantic coastal wetlands are dominated by pennate diatoms, green algae (Chlorophytes) and blue-green algae (Cyanobacteria) (Pinckney and Zingmark 1993; Mitsch and Gosselink 2000). Subtidal oyster bars in the upper Bay supported 22 taxa of benthic algae (12 Chlorophyta, 2 Phaeophyta, and 8 Rhodophyta; Connor 1978). In the York River subestuary, no significant differences in benthic soil/sediment community metabolism and chlorophyll concentrations among habitats (marsh, mudflat, sandflat, eelgrass, and subtidal sand) were observed when data for the whole study were pooled (Rizzo and Wetzel 1985). The chlorophyll *a* concentration observed (16–23 mg m^{-2}) was lower than that in marshes dominated by *Spartina alterniflora* or *Phragmites australis* on Kent Island, farther north in the Bay (Posey, Alphin, et al. 2003). Based on stable isotope measurements, benthic diatoms, C$_3$ plants, phytoplankton, and *S. alterniflora* together were important in supporting consumers in a low-salinity marsh system in the Bay (Stribling and Cornwell 1997).

Macroalgae are not normally observed in marshes, mudflats, or tidal forested wetlands of Chesapeake Bay because they require a hard substrate on which to attach via a holdfast, such as oyster shells, generally in shallow open waters (White 1989). However, they may also attach to fleshy sessile animals such as sponges and tunicates, submersed and emergent plants, and manmade structures including docks and rip-rap (Wulff and Webb 1969). Four classes of macroalgae occur in the Bay: Rhodophyceae, Phaeophyceae, Xanthophyceae, and Chlorophyceae (Orris 1980). Macroalgae have been observed to exhibit vertical zonation on pilings spanning the intertidal and shallow subtidal zones (Wulff and Webb 1969).

Animal Communities

Fish and Invertebrates

Tidal wetlands, seagrass beds, and adjacent shallow waters of Chesapeake Bay support diverse and productive fish and invertebrate communities (Fig. 3.4a–l). Invertebrate production in a 140-ha seagrass bed in Virginia was estimated at 200 g dry weight m^{-2} yr^{-1}, or 4.8 metric tons (t) dry weight of invertebrates and 56 t of invertebrate production over the year for the whole seagrass bed (Fredette, Diaz, et al. 1990). Fish that rely on these habitats for spawning or nurseries include economically important species such as striped bass *(Morone saxatilis)* and yellow perch *(Perca flavescens),* while small fish such as killifishes *(Fundulus* spp.) and mosquitofish *(Gambusia affinis)* are abundant and important ecological links between benthic and pelagic species (Lippson 1973; White 1989). Crabs, shrimp, amphipods, snails, polychaete worms, clams, zooplankton, terrestrial insects and spiders, and a diverse array of other taxa vary widely between marsh, swamp, seagrass, and tidal-flat habitats and across salinity gradients (Lippson 1973; Odum, Smith, et al. 1984; White 1989; Swarth and Kiviat 2009).

Some of the most widespread and abundant wetland-dependent species are mummichog *(Fundulus heteroclitus),* naked goby *(Gobiosoma bosci),* grass shrimp *(Palaemonetes pugio),* and blue crab *(Callinectes sapidus)* (Fig. 3.4g), which occur in both fresh and saline habitats and use the surface of emergent wetlands (during tides or remaining in surface pools), seagrass beds, and near-shore shallow water devoid of vegetation (Ruiz, Hines, et al. 1993; Yozzo and Smith 1998). Use of the wetland surface during low tide may be promoted by microtopography resulting from dominant emergent vegetation such as *Peltandra virginica* or reduced if dense beds of seagrasses occur in the lower intertidal zone (Yozzo and Smith 1998). Historically, small species such as mummichog and grass shrimp were abundant in deeper seagrass beds, but the decline in area of seagrasses may have led to a restriction of these fish and crustaceans to shallow, unvegetated waters near shore (Ruiz, Hines, et al. 1993). Killifish were more abundant in Bay marshes dominated by *Spartina alterniflora* than those dominated by *Phragmites australis,* while the opposite was true for grass shrimp (Meyer, Johnson, et al. 2001). No significant difference in number of nekton species between habitats was observed, however. Colonization by *Phragmites* may ultimately greatly reduce killifish use of the wetland surface due to large increases in biomass and litter deposition, resulting in less standing water (Hunter, Fox, et al. 2006).

Terrestrial Vertebrates

The coastal wetlands of Chesapeake Bay support hundreds of species of turtles, frogs, snakes, waterfowl, songbirds, birds of prey, and aquatic and terrestrial mammals (Fig. 3.4a–l; Odum, Smith et al. 1984; White 1989; Swarth and Kiviat 2009). The terrestrial fauna of tidal swamps and marshes is similar to that of nontidal freshwater wetlands and more diverse than that of brackish and salt marshes, seagrass beds, and mudflats (Odum, Smith et al. 1984). Fauna of these latter habitats are adapted for feeding, growth, or reproduction in saline or continuously flooded conditions (Mendelssohn and Batzer 2006). A few Bay species, such as diamondback terrapin *(Malaclemys terrapin),* swamp sparrow *(Melospiza georgiana),* clapper rail *(Rallus longirostris),* marsh wren *(Cistothorus palustris),* and meadow vole *(Microtus pennsylvanicus),* are restricted to coastal wetland habitats (Mitchell 1994; Robbins 1996; Greenberg and Maldonado 2006).

Nutria *(Myocastor coypus),* an exotic species introduced to Chesapeake Bay, has played an important ecological role via high grazing pressure in some brackish wetlands, as has been demonstrated using exclosures (Mitchell, Gabrey, et al. 2006; Whigham, Baldwin, et al. 2009; G. M. Haramis pers. comm.). Nutria herbivory has positive effects on waterfowl and open-water species but negative effects on rails and marsh sparrows (Mitchell, Gabrey, et al. 2006). The removal of nutria has improved habitat for the native herbivore muskrat *(Ondatra zibethicus).* Nutria and muskrats feed extensively on three-square sedge *(Schoenoplectus americanus)* as well as the starch-rich tubers of cattail *(Typha latifolia* and *T. angustifolia).* Muskrat populations have traditionally been largest in the wetlands of Dorchester County, Maryland, especially during the 1920s to 1930s (Smith 1938; Harris 1952). In contrast with nutria, smaller muskrat "eat-outs" of vegetation can provide excellent habitat for rails (Meanley 1978), although larger eat-outs will result in habitat changes similar to that of nutria herbivory (Mitchell, Gabrey, et al. 2006).

American black duck *(Anas rubripes),* which historically has been the most numerous duck on the Bay (Perry 1988; Perry and Deller 1995), also benefit from limited nutria and muskrat eat-outs, where they feed on a variety of invertebrates and submersed macrophyte species. Seagrasses were important in the diet of black ducks in the past (Stewart 1962), but in more recent years seagrasses have declined and these ducks have moved into emergent plant habitats. Large numbers of black ducks nested on Bay islands in the 1950s (Stotts and Davis 1960). When these sites were resurveyed in the 1980s, many of the islands had disappeared or were greatly reduced in size by erosion (Stotts 1986). For example, Poplar Island was reduced from 400 ha in 1847 to only 2 ha in recent years. A major project by the Corps of Engineers is the restoration of wetland and upland habitats on Poplar Island with dredge material from the Baltimore Harbor shipping channel. Restoration of Poplar Island and other Bay islands should benefit the black duck by providing tidal brackish marshes for nesting habitat with minimal exposure to predators (Haramis, Jorde, et al. 2002; Erwin, Brinker, et al. 2010).

The Canada goose *(Branta canadensis;* fig. 3.4f) is a native species that occurs in Bay wetlands as a migratory bird and also as a resident nonmigratory species. Wintering populations of migratory Canada geese have historically occurred in the Chesapeake Bay region but actually increased with the decline of seagrasses, which led geese to become consumers of residue from the harvest of agricultural crops (e.g., corn). Exclosure studies demonstrated that expanding populations of nonmigrating Canada geese significantly reduced the populations of wild rice *(Zizania aquatica)* and other annual species in tidal freshwater wetlands in the Patuxent River (Baldwin and Pendleton 2003; Haramis and Kearns 2007). The negative impacts of goose grazing on seedling establishment occur in the spring, when juveniles and molting adults eat or trample seedlings. Effective management of goose populations and efforts to restore populations of wild rice have been successful on the Patuxent River (Haramis and Kearns 2007). Feeding by nonmigrating geese has also hindered tidal wetland restoration efforts on the Anacostia River (Hammerschlag, Baldwin, et al. 2006). Possible negative effects of exclosures include debris and sediment accumulation, animal exclusion and entrapment, and aesthetics (C. Swarth pers. comm.). Although four of the six species of North American rails can be found in Bay tidal freshwater wetlands (Meanley 1965), the sora *(Porzana carolina)* is the species most common in the Patuxent rice marshes and the species most impacted by loss of wild rice to goose grazing. Their migratory stopover occurs shortly after the wild rice and other seeds fall to the water, and these seeds form the bulk of their diet (Meanley 1965).

FIG. 3.4. Examples of Chesapeake Bay wetland fauna. A. Virginia rail, *Rallus limicola*. B. Least bittern, *Ixobrychus exilis*. C. Young osprey, *Pandion haliaetus,* in nest. D. Bald eagle, *Haliaeetus leucocephalus*. E. Den of muskrat, *Ondatra zibethicus*. F. Canada geese, *Branta canadensis*. G. Blue crabs, *Callinectes sapidus*. H. Praying mantis, Insecta: Mantodea. I. Fishing spider, *Dolomedes* sp. J. Green sunfish, *Lepomis cyanellus*. K: Striped killifish, *Fundulus majalis*. L. American eel, *Anguilla rostrata*. (Photo credits: A–D, F: G. Kearns; E, H–I: A. H. Baldwin; G: A. Young; J: R. Aguilar; K, I: M. Kramer. Used with permission.)

Although the species and life-history traits of reptiles and amphibians inhabiting Chesapeake Bay coastal wetlands are generally known (Harris 1975; White 1989; Mitchell 1994), few ecological studies or recent surveys exist. Diversity is much lower in saline than in tidal freshwater wetlands (Odum, Smith, et al. 1984), and the most common groups restricted to tidal marshes and estuaries are colubrid snakes and emydid turtles, for example northern water snake *(Nerodia sipedon)*

and diamondback terrapin (Greenberg and Maldonado 2006). In the Patuxent River, smaller terrapins, primarily males, were more abundant in shallow water than in deeper water, making them vulnerable to drowning in crab pots and susceptible to coastal development, while larger, primarily female, terrapins were more abundant in deeper water, where they are vulnerable to speedboats (Roosenburg, Haley, et al. 1999). Bycatch reduction devices on crab pots reduced terrapin bycatch but had no effect on the size and number of crabs caught (Roosenberg and Green 2000). The Poplar Island restoration site provides excellent terrapin nesting habitat, due largely to a lack of nest predators such as foxes, raccoons *(Procyon lotor),* and otters *(Lutra canadensis);* 68 nests and 565 hatchlings were recorded during one year (Roosenburg, Allman, et al. 2003). These results suggest that island restoration will help offset nesting site losses due to development.

Key Ecological Processes

Productivity and Decomposition

Aboveground net primary production measurements for Chesapeake Bay wetlands generally range from about 1,000 to 1,500 g dry weight m^{-2} yr^{-1}, and the values fall within those expected for the East Coast (Turner 1976). However, aboveground productivity of a tidal freshwater marsh dominated by *Peltandra virginica* on the Pamunkey River in Virginia was only 780 g m^{-2} over one growing season (Doumlele 1981). Oligohaline and mesohaline marshes on tributaries to the York River had even lower aboveground production (560–570 g m^{-2} yr^{-1}; Mendelssohn and Marcellus 1976). In contrast, net aboveground productivity of *Hibiscus moscheutos* in a brackish marsh on the Choptank River was 1,210–1,220 g m^{-2} yr^{-1} over a two-year period, with peak aboveground standing crop of 550–590 g m^{-2} (Cahoon and Stevenson 1986). Belowground biomass of *H. moscheutos* was 1,060–1,320 g m^{-2}, about double the aboveground biomass. Mean live standing biomass in Patuxent River marshes varied across sites with different communities types, ranging on the low end from sites dominated by *P. virginica* and *Polygonum arifolium* (990 g m^{-2}) up to sites dominated by *Phragmites australis* (1,990 g m^{-2}), *Spartina cynosuroides* (2,160 g m^{-2}), and *Typha* spp. (2,340 g m^{-2}) (Flemer, Heinle, et al. 1978). Thus, Chesapeake Bay marshes demonstrate large variation in biomass production across plant communities, salinity regimes, and river systems.

The aboveground biomass of seagrass communities is lower than that of marshes: for example, in the range of 100–250 g m^{-2} in the York River (Moore 2009) and 60–100 g m^{-2} in unfertilized plots and 210–340 g m^{-2} in fertilized plots in seagrass beds near the Virginia portion of the Delmarva Peninsula (Orth 1977). Root and rhizome biomass in the unfertilized plots was higher (160–170 g m^{-2}) than leaf biomass, and fertilization resulted in no significant effect on belowground biomass. Estimates of seagrass biomass across the entire Chesapeake Bay are that maximum summer biomass increased from 15,000 t (about 0.7 t ha^{-1}) in 1985 and 1986 up to almost 25,000 t (0.9 t ha^{-1}) from 1991 through 1993 (Moore, Wilcox, et al. 2000). Minimum biomass occurred in December and January 1996 (< 5,000 t).

Rapid rates of decomposition were reported for tidal freshwater wetland vegetation in a tributary of the York River in which 70 to 80% of plant mass was lost within two months (Odum and Heywood 1978). Other studies of decomposition have shown more typical loss rates of about 80% over an annual cycle (Kassner 2001; P. Kangas unpub.). Slower decomposition rates were observed in stems of *Hibiscus moscheutos,* which are somewhat woody: only 45% decomposed within two years (Cahoon and Stevenson 1986).

In a brackish marsh community on the western shore of Chesapeake Bay dominated by *Schoenoplectus americanus,* annual net ecosystem production (NEP) was estimated at 1.45–1.59 kg C m^{-2} during two years based on measurements of carbon (C) fluxes for gross primary production (GPP; 1.89–2.08 kg C m^{-2}) and ecosystem respiration (R$_e$; 0.44–0.49 kg C m^{-2}) (Drake, Muehe, et al. 1996). Elevating atmospheric CO$_2$ increased GPP by 30% and decreased R$_e$ by 36–57%, resulting in an overall increase in NEP by 50–58% up to 2.17–2.51 kg C m^{-2}.

Herbivory

Grazing by birds and mammals is important in some Bay coastal wetlands and seagrass beds. In a tidal freshwater wetland on the Patuxent River, low-marsh plots fenced to exclude Canada geese and other large animals had significantly higher peak total biomass (940 g m^{-2}) than unfenced plots (350 g m^{-2}), although biomass in high-marsh plots was not significantly affected (Baldwin and Pendleton 2003). In another study in the same part of the river, stalk density of *Zizania aquatica* was about 97 stalks m^{-2} but only 2.7 stalks m^{-2} in unfenced plots (Haramis and Kearns 2007). Herbivorous insects are also important in some Bay wetlands: they consumed about 15% of annual aboveground production of *Hibiscus moscheutos,* or about 30% of peak biomass (Cahoon and Stevenson 1986). The periwinkle snail, *Littoraria irrorata,* is an important grazer on *Spartina alterniflora* leaf tissue and fungal biomass, and snail density was found to be negatively related to stem density of *S. alterniflora* in a York River salt marsh (Long and Burke 2007). In experimental seagrass ecosystems, grazers have been found to reduce growth of epiphytic algae on macrophyte leaves, increasing macrophyte production (Neckles, Wetzel, et al. 1993). Some taxa also graze on macrophyte leaves, and grazing response varies between grazing organisms (Duffy, MacDonald, et al. 2001).

Ecosystem Experiments

Global change experiments have been performed since 1986 at the Smithsonian's Global Change Research Wetland, a brackish marsh located on the Rhode River (on the western shore of the Bay, due east of Washington, DC). The site is operated by the Smithsonian Environmental Research Center. One of the experiments, which has been ongoing for more than 25 years, has reported that elevated atmospheric CO$_2$ significantly increases the net primary productivity (NPP) of the C$_3$ sedge *Schoenoplectus americanus* in both monoculture and mixed plots, but not the NPP of the C$_4$ grasses *Spartina patens* and *Distichlis spicata* (Curtis, Drake, et al. 1989; Curtis, Drake, and Whigham 1989; Drake 1992; Erickson, Megonigal, et al. 2007). In a second ongoing experiment, which began in 2006 (Fig. 3.2d), the well-documented stimulation of ecosystem-level NPP by elevated CO$_2$ added as a single factor was significantly reduced in treatments that crossed elevated CO$_2$ and added nitrogen, simulating eutrophication (Langley and Megonigal 2010). This reduction in CO$_2$ stimulation of NPP was caused by a nitrogen-induced shift in plant community composition that favored CO$_2$-indifferent C$_4$ species. Collectively, these studies highlight the important role that plant community composition will play in determining ecosystem responses to multiple, interacting global change variables.

Another ecosystem tidal wetland experiment was conducted as part of a 10-year EPA-supported project entitled the Multiscale Experimental Ecosystem Research Center (Petersen, Kennedy, et al. 2009). As part of the study, experimental 6-m² salt marsh ecosystems containing a tidal inundation gradient were seeded with wetland plant species (high and low plant diversity) and several representative macroinvertebrates. Studies of nutrient fertilization and fire were also conducted in the mesocosms, and effects of fire in the small-scale mesocosms were similar to those observed in the field (Schmitz 2000). No significant differences in primary production or nutrient removal were found between high- and low-diversity mesocosms (Petersen, Kennedy, et al. 2009).

Conservation Concerns

Wetlands in Chesapeake Bay, as in the rest of the country, suffered considerable losses between the late 1700s and 1980s (Tiner 1985; Baldwin 2009). Maryland lost more than 60% of its wetlands (Hayes 1996a), losses in Virginia were between 40–50% (Hayes 1996b), and only 10% of the original wetland area remained in the District of Columbia (Hayes 1996a). Losses have decreased, but efforts to restore and mitigate wetlands have offset only a small percentage of past wetland losses (Boesch and Greer 2003). Historically, intertidal wetland losses in the Bay were mostly due to direct human activities (dredging, filling, draining), but many current and future impacts are indirect, such as the effects of rising sea level in response to global warming, continued degradation of water quality, and invasive species. Sudden marsh die-back has not been widespread in the Bay but is plausible in the future, given the potential for increased temperatures as a result of global warming and changes in precipitation patterns (Alber et al. 2008).

Sea-Level Rise

Sea-level rise arguably poses the single greatest threat to Bay intertidal wetlands. The rate of sea-level rise is projected to increase significantly in the Bay (Boesch and Greer 2003), resulting in an increased rate of erosion of coastal margins (Wood, Boesch, et al. 2002) and subsequent wetland loss. Significant wetland losses have already been documented, particularly in brackish marshes on the eastern shore of the Bay (Kearney, Grace, et al. 1988; Wray, Leatherman, et al. 1995). In low-lying areas where intertidal wetlands cannot migrate landward, losses of brackish and oligohaline wetlands are projected to be significant over the next half century (Larsen, Clark, et al. 2004).

Extensive tidal freshwater wetlands still occur in some Bay subestuaries (e.g., Nanticoke, Pocomoke, York, Patuxent), and tidal freshwater wetlands experienced less deterioration than did brackish wetlands in the Nanticoke subestuary (Kearney, Grace, et al. 1988). These wetlands are, however, likely to suffer significantly in response to increased rates of sea-level rise due to intrusion of brackish water (e.g., Perry and Hershner 1999). Tidal freshwater wetlands will also be threatened because they occur in geomorphic settings where there are limitations to upstream and horizontal migration due to steep slopes (western shore) and steep river gradients at the Fall Line between the Coastal Plain and Piedmont (Neubauer and Craft 2009; Whigham, Baldwin, et al. 2009).

Some Bay wetlands may not succumb as rapidly as others to sea-level rise. Wray, Leatherman, et al. (1995) projected that the three Bay upland islands they studied (Poplar, James,

and Barren) would disappear by 2010. However, Poplar Island is being restored using dredge material, and James and Barren Islands still exist and are also slated for restoration or shoreline protection (www.nab.usace.army.mil/Factsheets/PDFs/Civil/MD-MidBayIsland-GI.pdf). Wetlands dominated by the nonnative genotype of *Phragmites australis* (Rooth and Stevenson 2000) have the potential to keep pace with sea-level rise due to high rates of root and rhizome production and a network of dense stems and litter that increase sediment accumulation.

Eutrophication

Excess nutrients have been a persistent problem in Chesapeake Bay for decades, and most of the past, current, and future restoration efforts focus on a reduction of nutrient inputs from point and nonpoint sources (Boesch and Greer 2003). A primary impact of excess nutrients on Bay subtidal wetlands has been the decline in seagrasses (Orth 1994), but effects on intertidal wetlands may be no less important. One potential effect of increased nitrogen (N) is the rapid expansion of the nonnative genotype of *Phragmites australis* since the 1980s (King, Deluca, et al. 2007; McCormick, Kettenring, et al. 2010a). The expansion of *Phragmites* subsequent to the onset of eutrophic conditions is likely an example of a lag effect that has been shown to be common for invasive species (Crooks and Soule 1999) and a threshold response associated with a critical change in the nutrient status of the Bay (King, Deluca, et al. 2007). Furthermore, seed production was greater in cross-pollinated plants fertilized with N (Kettenring, McCormick, et al. 2011), and the nonnative genotype was more productive than the native genotype under elevated N conditions (T. Mozder unpub.).

Increased N may exacerbate the effects of sea-level rise. The surface elevation of brackish wetlands increased at a rate that was almost twice the current rate of sea-level rise under conditions of elevated CO_2 (Langley, McKee, et al. 2009). However, N addition resulted in a smaller increase in substrate elevation, about equal to the current rate of sea-level rise, and was correlated with a decrease in belowground production. The observed decrease in belowground biomass was probably due partly to a shift in allocation from belowground to aboveground tissues and a shift from C_3 to C_4 species (Langley and Megonigal 2010).

Invasive Plants

NONNATIVE STRAIN OF *PHRAGMITES AUSTRALIS*

The nonnative strain has been responsible for a relatively recent expansion of *P. australis* in Chesapeake Bay intertidal wetlands (Saltonstall 2002; King, Deluca, et al. 2007) associated with human activities (development) at or near the shoreline (King, Deluca, et al. 2007; Chambers, Havens, et al. 2008). Recent research in Bay subestuaries has provided insight into the proximate causes for its expansion. McCormick, Kettenring, et al. (2010a,b) and Kettenring and Whigham (2009) sampled patches of *Phragmites* in Bay subestuaries that had upland watersheds dominated by different land uses (forests versus varying amounts of development). Their results indicate that patches with multiple genotypes produce more viable seeds than patches with lower genetic diversity and suggest that disturbance in developed watersheds promotes colonization from seed, leading to multiple-genotype patches that cross-pollinate and produce more viable seed than low-diversity patches. Furthermore, *Phragmites* seeds occurred in the seed bank at much higher densities in patches producing viable seeds than patches that did not (Baldwin, Kettenring, et al. 2010).

The importance of seed dispersal and seedling recruitment may explain the observed invasion and expansion of *Phragmites* in part of the Rhode River subestuary where there has been no development in recent years (Kettenring, McCormick, et al. 2009). The potential consequences of the continued spread, primarily by seeds into wetlands that have not had any anthropogenic disturbances, of the nonnative strain are dramatic. All Bay brackish intertidal wetlands, other than low marshes dominated by *Spartina alterniflora,* potentially will be invaded, and *Phragmites* is also expanding in Bay freshwater intertidal wetlands. Although replacement of native plant communities and reduction of plant diversity (Chambers, Meyerson, et al. 1999) will result from continued expansion of the nonnative strain in Chesapeake Bay intertidal wetlands, effects on diversity of fauna and ecosystem function are complex and may not be disastrous (e.g., Findlay, Groffman, et al. 2003; Weis and Weis 2003).

OTHER NONNATIVE PLANTS

Hydrilla verticillata and *Myriophyllum spicata* are dominant in vast seagrass beds where the Susquehanna River flows into the upper Bay (Fig. 3.1). These species have shallower roots than the native species *Vallisneria americana,* which, when codominant with the two nonnative species, resulted in lower sediment porewater concentrations of phosphate than when it was absent (Wigand, Stevenson, et al. 1997). The leaves of *V. americana* may physically capture *H. verticillata* fragments, promoting colonization of the nonnative species, and *V. americana* does not inhibit growth unless nutrient supply is limited (Chadwell and Engelhardt 2008). The nonnative submersed macrophyte *Trapa natans* (water chestnut) is not widespread in Chesapeake Bay. but is common in other East Coast estuaries (Whigham, Baldwin, et al. 2009). The emergent herb *Lythum salicaria* (purple loosestrife) is also not widespread in Bay coastal wetlands, although it does occur in some tidal freshwater marshes (Neff, Rusello, et al. 2009). *Murdannia keisak* (marsh dewflower) is locally abundant in some tidal freshwater marshes (Baldwin and Pendleton 2003).

Native and Nonnative Animals

In addition to nutria and nonmigrating Canada geese, snow geese *(Chen caerulescens)* eat-outs have been documented for wetlands on the Delmarva Peninsula (Sherfy and Kirkpatrick 2003). Mute swan *(Cygnus olor),* which increased from 5 to about 4,000 animals between 1962 and 1999, can have a significant and detrimental impact on seagrasses (Hindman and Harvey 2004; Tatu, Anderson, et al. 2007). However, mute swan numbers now have been reduced to under 500, and management plans will attempt to maintain the population near zero on public waters. Beaver activities in tidal wetlands appear to be restricted to the tidal freshwater portion of tidal rivers (Swarth and Kiviat 2009), where they can create non-

tidal ponds containing submersed macrophytes (A. Baldwin pers. obs.).

Wetland Restoration

A goal of the 2009 Chesapeake Bay Executive Order (http://executiveorder.chesapeakebay.net/) is to restore 10,000 ha of tidal and nontidal wetlands. Current efforts in estuarine habitats are focused on living shorelines, tidal wetlands, seagrasses, and remote island habitats (www.ngs.noaa.gov/PROJECTS/Wetlands/). Sediments that are used in the restoration of brackish tidal wetlands in at least two projects are dredged materials from Baltimore Harbor. Restoration of the Poplar Island complex includes approximately 220 ha of intertidal wetlands (Miller and Murphy 2002), and 4,500 ha of wetlands are proposed for Blackwater National Wildlife Refuge (http://library.fws.gov/CCPs/CMC/cmc_index_final.html). Sediments dredged from the Anacostia River also have been used in efforts to restore tidal freshwater wetlands (Fig. 3.2g) (Hammerschlag, Baldwin, et al. 2006). There have been numerous efforts to restore eroded shorelines and wetlands throughout Chesapeake Bay (e.g., Garbisch and Garbisch 1994; Hardaway, Varnell, et al. 2002; Havens, Varnell, et al. 2002), and there are companies that specialize in wetland and shoreline restoration. Most restoration efforts are relatively small in scale, and although data on the area of intertidal wetlands restored in the Bay are lacking, the total is only a minor component of the area lost. For example, wetland losses in the Virginia portion of Chesapeake Bay between 1988 and 1998 were 124 ha per year compared to 0.07 ha of compensatory mitigation (Hardaway, Varnell, et al. 2002).

Conclusions

Chesapeake Bay supports one of the greatest concentrations of coastal wetlands in North America. Hydrogeomorphic conditions that have developed since the last ice age have led to the formation of a diversity of coastal wetland types, including tidal freshwater wetlands, tidal brackish and salt marshes, mudflats, and submersed aquatic vegetation beds. These wetlands have high primary productivity and support a diverse array of vegetation types, algae, fish and invertebrates, and terrestrial wildlife.

However, the future of Chesapeake Bay wetlands is uncertain. Rising relative sea level has the greatest potential to reduce the area of Bay tidal wetlands. The second most important process affecting coastal wetlands is likely to be the spread of the nonnative genotype of *Phragmites australis*. The invasion of *Phragmites* has accelerated in recent years, and its spread, primarily from seed, appears to be self-perpetuating once patches with multiple genotypes have become established. Submersed aquatic vegetation beds, which have been impacted to a greater degree than emergent wetlands, will continue to be threatened by eutrophication, which reduces light available for photosynthesis. Restoration of coastal wetlands in Chesapeake Bay has had some success, but the area of restored wetlands is less than that lost and the persistence of restored wetlands under future sea-level and eutrophication scenarios is unknown.

The audience addressed in this chapter, which includes students, researchers, environmental managers and engineers, and policymakers, is critical to sustaining the wetlands of

Chesapeake Bay. Students and researchers must continue scientific discovery of the processes and actions that underlie changes in Bay ecosystems because ecological knowledge is the foundation for environmental management and policy-making. As noted in this chapter, many of the Bay's wetland habitats, their species interactions, and their hydrological and biogeochemical processes are poorly understood. Environmental managers and engineers need to base restoration activities on this ecological knowledge to avoid wasting resources on unsustainable or underperforming wetlands. Managers and engineers must also bear in mind the dynamic nature of these ecosystems and potential future changes due to sea-level rise, elevated CO_2, invasive plants and animals, and eutrophication. Wetland restoration is a particularly challenging activity that has produced many failures; adopting an adaptive restoration approach based on monitoring and building knowledge of restoration techniques will lead to more successful restoration outcomes. Engineers and managers should also continue to explore and develop new techniques, such as thin-layer sediment application, to help wetlands keep pace with sea-level rise and accept nonnative species such as *Phragmites australis* if that is the only wetland plant community that will persist in, for example, a eutrophic environment with high rates of relative sea-level rise and nonresident herbivores. Finally, by introducing legislation and developing regulations and guidelines, policymakers at the local, state, and national levels can have a great positive impact on the sustainability of Chesapeake Bay wetlands. Locally, land use (for ecotourism, recreation, agriculture, or other activities that do not pose barriers to migration) in the flat Coastal Plain adjacent to coastal wetlands can be regulated to provide space for wetlands to migrate inland as sea level continues to rise. At the local and state level, improved management of runoff from agricultural and urban lands can be required to reduce nutrient and sediment loading; "living shorelines" (constructed wetlands) can be used to stabilize shores instead of rip-rap, bulkheads, and other erosion-control structures; and more wildlife sanctuaries can be created (Erwin, Haramis, et al. 1993). Requiring more stringency in avoiding wetland impacts in development projects and, if there is no realistic way to avoid such impacts, longer-term monitoring of mitigation sites are necessary to reduce the rate of net wetland loss and improve restoration techniques. Finally, at the national level, efforts to regulate greenhouse gas emissions should be expanded, not only because of their role in climate warming, but also because of their strong influence on plant community composition. Furthermore, the Chesapeake Bay Program, established by Congress in the 1980s to restore and protect the Bay, should be fully supported and expanded.

Impacts to Chesapeake Bay wetlands will continue, an unavoidable outcome due to the increasing human population density in the Bay watershed. Efforts to protect, manage, and restore Bay wetlands must be weighed against other pressing socioeconomic needs. Focusing on important wetlands or wetland-rich regions that are amenable to conservation, management, or restoration will ensure that humans and other organisms will continue to benefit from the ecosystem services provided by Bay wetlands into the foreseeable future.

Acknowledgments

We are grateful to Greg Kearns of Patuxent Wetland Park for bird photos and to Margaret Kramer and other members of the Fish and Invertebrate Ecology Lab at the Smithsonian Environmental Research Center for photos of fish and invertebrates.

References

Alber M, Swenson EM, Adamowicz SC, Mendelssohn IA. 2008. Salt marsh dieback: an overview of recent events in the US. *Estuar. Coast. Shelf Sci.* 80:1–11.

Anderson RR. 1972. Submersed vascular plants of the Chesapeake Bay and tributaries. *Chesap. Sci.* 13 Supplement:S87–S89.

Anderson RR, Brown RG, Rappleye RD. 1968. Water quality and plant distribution along the upper Patuxent River, Maryland. *Chesap. Sci.* 9:145–56.

Atkinson RB, Bodkin NL, Perry JE. 1990. New county records collected in tidal wetlands of four coastal plain counties along the James River, Virginia. *Castanea* 55:56–64.

Baldwin AH. 2004. Restoring complex vegetation in urban settings: the case of tidal freshwater marshes. *Urban Ecosyst.* 7:137.

Baldwin AH. 2007. Vegetation and seed bank studies of salt-pulsed swamps of the Nanticoke River, Chesapeake Bay. In *Ecology of tidal freshwater forested wetlands of the southeastern United States,* Conner WH, Doyle TW, Krauss KW, editors. Dordrecht, The Netherlands: Springer, pp. 139–60.

Baldwin AH. 2009. Restoration of tidal freshwater wetlands in North America. In *Tidal freshwater wetlands,* Barendregt A, Whigham DF, Baldwin AH, editors. Leiden, The Netherlands: Backhuys, pp. 207–22.

Baldwin AH, Egnotovich MS, Clarke E. 2001. Hydrologic change and vegetation of tidal freshwater marshes: field, greenhouse, and seed-bank experiments. *Wetlands* 21:519–31.

Baldwin AH, Kettenring KM, Whigham DF. 2010. Seed banks of *Phragmites australis*–dominated brackish wetlands: relationships to seed viability, inundation, and land cover. *Aquat. Bot.* 93:163–69.

Baldwin AH, Pendleton FN. 2003. Interactive effects of animal disturbance and elevation on vegetation of a tidal freshwater marsh. *Estuaries* 26:905–15.

Boesch, DF, Greer J. 2003. *Chesapeake futures choices for the 21st century.* Edgewater, MD: Chesapeake Research Consortium.

Bridgham SD, Megonigal JP, et al. 2006. The carbon storage of North American wetlands. *Wetlands* 26:889–916.

Brush GS. 1984. Patterns of recent sediment accumulation in Chesapeake Bay. *Chem. Geol.* 44:227–42.

Cahoon DR, Stevenson JC. 1986. Production, predation, and decomposition in a low-salinity *Hibiscus* marsh. *Ecology* 67:1341–50.

Chadwell TB, Engelhardt KAM. 2008. Effects of pre-existing submersed vegetation and propagule pressure on the invasion success of *Hydrilla verticillata*. *J. Appl. Ecol.* 45:515–23.

Chambers RM, Havens KJ, et al. 2008. Common reed *Phragmites australis* occurrence and adjacent land use along estuarine shoreline in Chesapeake Bay. *Wetlands* 28:1097–103.

Chambers RM, Meyerson LA, Saltonstall K. 1999. Expansion of *Phragmites australis* into tidal wetlands of North America. *Aquat. Bot.* 64:261–73.

Childers DL, Day JW Jr, McKellar HN Jr. 2000. Twenty more years of marsh and estuarine flux studies: revisiting Nixon (1980). In *Concepts and controversies in tidal marsh ecology,* Weinstein MP, Kreeger DA, editors. Dordrecht, The Netherlands: Kluwer, pp. 391–423.

Conner WH, Doyle TW, Krauss KW, editors. 2007. *Ecology of tidal freshwater forested wetlands of the southeastern United States.* Dordrecht, The Netherlands: Springer.

Connor JL. 1978. Benthic algae in Chesapeake Bay, Maryland. *J. Phycol.* 14:20.

Crooks JA, Soule ME. 1999. Lag times in population explosions of invasive species: causes and implications. In *Invasive species and biodiversity management,* Sandlund OT, Schei PJ, Viken A, editors. Dordrecht, The Netherlands: Kluwer, pp. 103–25.

Curtis PS, Drake BG, et al. 1989. Growth and senescence in plant communities exposed to elevated CO_2 concentrations on an estuarine marsh. *Oecologia* 78:20–26.

Curtis PS, Drake BG, Whigham DF. 1989. Nitrogen and carbon

dynamics in C_3 and C_4 estuarine marsh plants grown under elevated CO_2 in situ. *Oecologia* 78:297–301.

Darke AK, Megonigal JP. 2003. Control of sediment deposition rates in two mid-Atlantic coast tidal freshwater wetlands. *Estuar. Coast. Shelf Sci.* 57:255–68.

Davies, SB. 2004. Vegetation dynamics of a tidal freshwater marsh: long-term and inter-annual variability and their relation to salinity. MS Thesis. Gloucester Point, VA: Virginia Institute of Marine Science, College of William and Mary.

Doumlele DG. 1981. Primary production and seasonal aspects of emergent plants in a tidal freshwater marsh. *Estuaries* 4:139–42.

Drake BG. 1992. A field study of the effects of elevated CO_2 on ecosystem processes in a Chesapeake Bay wetland. *Aust. J. Bot.* 40:579–95.

Drake BG, Muehe MS, et al. 1996. Acclimation of photosynthesis, respiration and ecosystem carbon flux of a wetland on Chesapeake Bay, Maryland, to elevated atmospheric CO_2 concentration. *Plant Soil* 187:111–18.

Duffy JE, MacDonald KS, et al. 2001. Grazer diversity, functional redundancy, and productivity in seagrass beds: an experimental test. *Ecology* 82:2417–34.

Erickson JE, Megonigal JP, et al. 2007. Salinity and sea level mediate elevated CO_2 effects on C_3–C_4 plant interactions and tissue nitrogen in a Chesapeake Bay tidal wetland. *Glob. Change Biol.* 13:202–15.

Erwin RM, Brinker DF, et al. 2010. Islands at bay: rising seas, eroding islands, and waterbird habitat loss in Chesapeake Bay (USA). *J. Coast. Conserv.* 15:51–60.

Erwin RM, Haramis GM, et al. 1993. Resource protection for waterbirds in Chesapeake Bay. *Env. Manage.* 17:613–69.

Findlay S, Groffman P, Dye S. 2003. Effects of *Phragmites australis* on marsh nutrient cycling. *Wetl. Ecol. Manag.* 11:157–65.

Flemer DA, Heinle DR, et al. 1978. Standing crops of marsh vegetation of two tributaries of Chesapeake Bay. *Estuaries* 1:157–63.

Fredette TJ, Diaz RJ, et al. 1990. Secondary production within a seagrass bed (*Zostera marina* and *Ruppia maritima*) in lower Chesapeake Bay. *Estuaries* 13:431–40.

Garbisch EW, Garbisch JL. 1994. Control of upland bank erosion through tidal marsh construction on restored shores: application in the Maryland portion of Chesapeake Bay. *Env. Manage.* 18:677–91.

Greenberg R, Maldonado JE. 2006. Diversity and endemism in tidal-marsh vertebrates. In *Terrestrial vertebrates of tidal marshes: evolution, ecology, and conservation,* Greenberg R, Maldonado JE, et al., editors. Camarillo, CA: Cooper Ornithological Society, pp. 32–53.

Hammerschlag RS, Baldwin AH, et al. 2006. Five years of monitoring reconstructed freshwater tidal wetlands in the urban Anacostia River (2000–2004). Laurel and College Park, MD: USGS Patuxent Wildlife Research Center and University of Maryland.

Haramis GM, Jorde DG, et al. 2002. Breeding performance of Smith Island black ducks. In *Black ducks and their Chesapeake Bay habitats: proceedings of a symposium,* Perry MC, editor. Report USGS/BRD/ITR-2002-0005. Washington, DC: USGS, pp. 22–30.

Haramis GM, Kearns GD. 2007. Herbivory by resident geese: the loss and recovery of wild rice along the tidal Patuxent River. *J. Wildl. Manag.* 71:788–94.

Hardaway CS, Varnell LM, et al. 2002. An integrated habitat enhancement approach to shoreline stabilization for a Chesapeake Bay island community. *Wetl. Ecol. Manag.* 10:289–302.

Harris HS Jr. 1975. Distributional survey (Amphibia/Reptilia): Maryland and the District of Columbia. *Bull. Maryland Herp. Soc.* 11:73–167.

Harris VT. 1952. Muskrats on tidal marshes of Dorchester County. Publ. no. 91. Solomons Island, MD: Chesapeake Biological Laboratory.

Havens KJ, Varnell LM, Watts BD. 2002. Maturation of a constructed tidal marsh relative to two natural reference tidal marshes over 12 years. *Ecol. Eng.* 18:305–15.

Hayes MA. 1996a. Maryland and the District of Columbia wetland resources. In *National water summary on wetland resources* (Water-Supply paper 2425), Fretwell JD, Williams JS, Redman PJ, compilers. Reston, VA: USGS, pp. 219–24.

Hayes MA. 1996b. Virginia wetland resources. In *National water summary on wetland resources* (Water-Supply paper 2425),

Fretwell JD, Williams JS, Redman PJ, compilers. Reston, VA: USGS, pp. 387–92.

Hicks SD. 1964. Tidal wave characteristics of Chesapeake Bay. *Chesap. Sci.* 5:103–13.

Hindman LJ, Harvey WF. 2004. Status and management of mute swans in Maryland. In *Mute swans and their Chesapeake Bay habitats: proceedings of a symposium,* Perry MC, editor. USGS/BRD/ITR-2004-0005. Reston, VA: USGS, pp. 11–7.

Hobbs CH III. 2004. Geological history of Chesapeake Bay, USA. In *Quat. Sci. Rev.* 23:641–61.

Hobbs CH III, Halka JP, et al. 1992. Chesapeake Bay sediment budget. In *J. Coast. Res.* 8:292–300.

Hopfensperger KN, Kaushal SS, et al. 2009. Influence of plant communities on denitrification in a tidal freshwater marsh of the Potomac River, United States. *J. Env. Qual.* 38:618–26.

Hunter KL, Fox DA, et al. 2006. Responses of resident marsh fishes to stages of *Phragmites australis* invasion in three mid Atlantic estuaries. *Estuar. Coast.* 29:487–98.

Jordan TE, Correll DL. 1991. Continuous automated sampling of tidal exchanges of nutrients by brackish marshes. *Estuar. Coast. Shelf Sci.* 35:527–45.

Jordan TE, Correll DL, Whigham DF. 1983. Nutrient flux in the Rhode River: tidal exchange of nutrients by brackish marshes. *Estuar. Coast. Shelf Sci.* 17:651–67.

Jordan TE, Pierce JW, Correll DL. 1986. Flux of particulate matter in the tidal marshes and subtidal shallows of the Rhode River estuary. *Estuaries* 9:310–19.

Kassner SL. 2001. Soil development as a functional indicator of a reconstructed freshwater tidal marsh. MS thesis, University of Maryland, College Park.

Kastler J, Wiberg PL. 1996. Sedimentation and boundary changes of Virginia salt marshes. *Estuar. Coast. Shelf Sci.* 42:683–700.

Kearney MS, Grace RE, Stevenson JC. 1988. Marsh loss in the Nanticoke estuary, Chesapeake Bay. *Geogr. Rev.* 78:205–20.

Keller JK, Weisenhorn PB, Megonigal JP. 2009. Humic acids as electron acceptors in wetland decomposition. *Soil Biol. Biochem.* 41:1518–22.

Kemp WM, Batiuk R, et al. 2004. Habitat requirements for submersed aquatic vegetation in Chesapeake Bay: water quality, light regime, and physical-chemical factors. *Estuaries* 27:363–77.

Kemp WM, Boynton WR, et al. 2005. Eutrophication of Chesapeake Bay: historical trends and ecological interactions. *Mar. Ecol. Prog. Ser.* 303:1–29.

Kettenring KM, McCormick MK, et al. 2009. *Phragmites australis* (common reed) invasion in the Rhode River subestuary of the Chesapeake Bay: disentangling the effects of foliar nutrients, genetic diversity, patch size, and seed viability *Estuar. Coast.* 33:118–26.

Kettenring KM, McCormick MK, et al. 2011. Mechanisms of *Phragmites australis* invasion in the Chesapeake Bay: feedbacks among genetic diversity, nutrients, and sexual reproduction. *J. Appl. Ecol.* 48:1305–1313.

Kettenring KM, Whigham DF. 2009. Seed viability and seed dormancy of non-native *Phragmites australis* in suburbanized and forested watersheds of the Chesapeake Bay, USA. *Aquat. Bot.* 91:199–204.

Khan H, Brush GS. 1994. Nutrient and metal accumulation in a freshwater tidal marsh. *Estuaries* 17:345–60.

King RS, Deluca WV, et al. 2007. Threshold effects of coastal urbanization on *Phragmites australis* (common reed) abundance and foliar nitrogen in Chesapeake Bay. *Estuar. Coast.* 30:1–13.

Koch EM. 2001. Beyond light: physical, geological, and geochemical parameters as possible submersed aquatic vegetation habitat requirements. *Estuaries* 24:1–17.

Kroes DE, Hupp CR, Noe GB. 2007. Sediment, nutrient, and vegetation trends along the tidal, forested Pocomoke River, Maryland. In *Ecology of tidal freshwater forested wetlands of the southeastern United States,* Conner WH, Doyle TW, Krauss KW, editors. Dordrecht, The Netherlands: Springer, pp. 113–37.

Langley JA, McKee KL, et al. 2009. Elevated CO_2 stimulates marsh elevation gain, counterbalancing sea-level rise. *PNAS* 106:6182–86.

Langley JA, Megonigal JP. 2010. Ecosystem response to elevated CO_2 levels limited by nitrogen-induced plant species shift. *Nature* 466:96–99.

Larsen C, Clark I, et al. 2004. The Blackwater NWR inundation model: rising sea level on a low-lying coast: land planning for wetlands. Open file report 04-1302. http://pubs.usgs.gov/of/2004/1302/. Reston, VA: USGS.

Leck MA, Baldwin AH, et al. 2009. Plant communities of tidal freshwater wetlands of the continental USA and southeastern Canada. In *Tidal freshwater wetlands,* Barendregt A, Whigham DF, Baldwin AH, editors. Leiden, The Netherlands: Backhuys, pp. 41–58.

Leonard LA. 1997. Controls of sediment transport and deposition in an incised mainland marsh basin, southeastern North Carolina. *Wetlands* 17:263–74.

Li XY, Weller DE, et al. 2007. Effects of watershed and estuarine characteristics on the abundance of submersed aquatic vegetation in Chesapeake Bay subestuaries. *Estuar. Coast.* 30:840–54.

Lippson AJ. 1973. *The Chesapeake Bay in Maryland: an atlas of natural resources.* Baltimore: Johns Hopkins University Press.

Long CW, Burke RP. 2007. Habitat size, flora, and fauna: interactions in a tidal saltwater marsh. *J. Exp. Mar. Biol. Ecol.* 353:80–88.

McCormick J, Somes HA Jr. 1982. *The coastal wetlands of Maryland.* Chevy Chase: MD DNR, Coastal Zone Management, Jack McCormick and Associates.

McCormick MK, Kettenring KM, et al. 2010a. Extent and reproductive mechanisms of *Phragmites australis* spread in brackish wetlands in Chesapeake Bay, Maryland (USA). *Wetlands* 30:67–74.

McCormick MK, Kettenring KM, et al. 2010b. Spread of invasive *Phragmites australis* in estuaries with differing degrees of development: genetic patterns, Allee effects and interpretation. *J. Ecol.* 98:1369–1378.

Meanley B. 1965. Early-fall food and habitat of the sora in the Patuxent River Marsh, Maryland. *Chesap. Sci.* 6:235–37.

Meanley B. 1978. *Blackwater.* Cambridge, MD: Tidewater.

Megonigal JP, Neubauer SC. 2009. Biogeochemistry of tidal freshwater wetlands. In *Coastal wetlands: an integrated ecosystem approach,* Perillo GME, Wolanski E, et al.editors. The Netherlands: Elsevier, pp. 535–63.

Mendelssohn IA, Batzer DP. 2006. Abiotic constraints for wetland plants and animals. In *Ecology of freshwater and estuarine wetlands,* Batzer DP, Sharitz RR, editors. Berkeley: University of California Press, pp. 82–114.

Mendelssohn IA, Marcellus KL. 1976. Angiosperm production of three Virginia marshes in various salinity and soil nutrient regimes. *Chesap. Sci.* 17:15–23.

Merrill JZ, Cornwell JC. 2000. The role of oligohaline marshes in estuarine nutrient cycling. In *Concepts and controversies in tidal marsh ecology,* Weinstein MP, Kreeger DA, editors. Dordrecht, The Netherlands: Kluwer, pp. 425–41.

Meyer DL, Johnson JM, Gill JW. 2001. Comparison of nekton use of *Phragmites australis* and *Spartina alterniflora* marshes in the Chesapeake Bay, USA. *Mar. Ecol. Prog. Ser.* 209:71–84.

Miller JK, Murphy D. 2002. 2001 Baseline wetland vegetation and monitoring for the Poplar Island restoration project. CBFO-FAO2-02. Annapolis, MD: USFWS.

Mitchell JC. 1994. *The reptiles of Virginia.* Washington, DC: Smithsonian Institution Press.

Mitchell LR, Gabrey S, et al. 2006. Impacts of marsh management on coastal-marsh bird habitats. In *Terrestrial vertebrates of tidal marshes: evolution, ecology, and conservation,* Greenberg R, Maldonado JE, et al., editors. Camarillo, CA: Cooper Ornithological Society, pp. 32–53.

Mitsch WJ, Gosselink JG. 2000. *Wetlands,* 3rd edition. New York: Wiley.

Moore KA. 2009. Submersed aquatic vegetation of the York River. *J. Coast. Res.* SI57:50–58.

Moore KA, Wilcox DJ, Orth RJ. 2000. Analysis of the abundance of submersed aquatic vegetation communities in the Chesapeake Bay. *Estuaries* 23:115–27.

Morse JL, Megonigal JP, Walbridge MR. 2004. Sediment nutrient accumulation and nutrient availability in two tidal freshwater marshes along the Mattaponi River, Virginia, USA. *Biogeochem.* 69:165–206.

Neckles HA, Wetzel RL, Orth RJ. 1993. Effects of nutrient enrichment and grazing on epiphyte-macrophyte (*Zostera marina* L.) dynamics. *Oecologia* 93:285–95.

Neff KP, Rusello K, Baldwin AH. 2009. Rapid seed bank development in restored tidal freshwater wetlands. *Restor. Ecol.* 17:539–48.

Neubauer SC, Anderson IC. 2003. Transport of dissolved inorganic carbon from a tidal freshwater marsh to the York River estuary. *Limnol. Oceanogr.* 48:299–307.

Neubauer SC, Anderson IC. 2002. Sediment deposition and accretion in a mid-Atlantic (U.S.A.) tidal freshwater marsh. *Estuar. Coast. Shelf Sci.* 54:713–27.

Neubauer SC, Anderson IC, Neikirk BB. 2005. Nitrogen cycling and ecosystem exchanges in a Virginia tidal freshwater marsh. *Estuaries* 28:909–22.

Neubauer SC, Craft CB. 2009. Global change and tidal freshwater wetlands: scenarios and impacts. In *Tidal freshwater wetlands,* Barendregt A, Whigham DF, Baldwin AH, editors. Leiden, The Netherlands: Backhuys, pp. 253–66.

Neubauer SC, Givler K, et al. 2005. Seasonal patterns and plant-mediated controls of subsurface wetland biogeochemistry. *Ecology* 86:3334–44.

Noe GB, Hupp CR. 2009. Retention of riverine sediment and nutrient loads by coastal plain floodplains. *Ecosystems* 12:728–46.

Odum WE, Heywood MA. 1978. Decomposition of intertidal freshwater marsh plants. In *Freshwater wetlands: ecological processes and management potential,* Good RE, Whigham DF, Simpson RL, editors. New York: Academic Press, pp. 89–97.

Odum WE, Smith TJ III, et al. 1984. The ecology of tidal freshwater marshes of the United States East Coast: a community profile. FWS/OBS-83/17. Washington, DC: USFWS.

Orris PK. 1980. A revised species list and commentary on the macroalgae of the Chesapeake Bay in Maryland. *Estuaries* 3:200–06.

Orth RJ. 1977. Effect of nutrient enrichment on growth of the eelgrass *Zostera marina* in the Chesapeake Bay, Virginia, USA. *Mar. Biol.* 44:187–94.

Orth RJ. 1994. Chesapeake Bay submersed aquatic vegetation: water quality relationships. *Lake Reserv. Manage.* 10:49–52.

Orth RJ, Moore KA. 1983. Chesapeake Bay: an unpredented decline in submersed aquatic vegetation. *Science* 222:51–53.

Orth RJ, Moore KA. 1984. Distribution and abundance of submersed aquatic vegetation in Chesapeake Bay: an historical perspective. *Estuaries* 7:531–40.

Pasternack GB. 2009. Hydrogeomorphology and sedimentation in tidal freshwater wetlands. In *Tidal freshwater wetlands,* Barendregt A, Whigham D, Baldwin A, editors. Leiden, The Netherlands: Backhuys, pp. 31–40.

Pasternack GB, Brush GS. 2001. Seasonal variations in sedimentation and organic content in five plant associations on a Chesapeake Bay tidal freshwater delta. *Estuar. Coast. Shelf Sci.* 53:93–106.

Pasternack GB, Brush GS, Hilgartner WB. 2001. Impact of historic land-use change on sediment delivery to a Chesapeake Bay sub-estuarine delta. *Earth Surf. Process. Landf.* 26:409–27.

Perry JE, Atkinson RB. 1997. Plant diversity along a salinity gradient of four marshes on the York and Pamunkey Rivers in Virginia. *Castanea* 62:112–18.

Perry JE, Atkinson RB. 2009. York River tidal marshes. *J. Coast. Res.* SI57:40–49.

Perry JE, Bilcovic DM, et al. 2009. Tidal freshwater wetlands of the mid-Atlantic and southeastern United States. In *Tidal freshwater wetlands,* Barendregt A, Whigham DF, Baldwin AH, editors. Leiden, The Netherlands: Backhuys, pp. 157–66.

Perry JE, Hershner CH. 1999. Temporal changes in the vegetation pattern in a tidal freshwater marsh. *Wetlands* 19:90–99.

Perry MC. 1998. Wetland habitats for wildlife of the Chesapeake Bay. In *Ecology of wetlands and associated systems,* Majumdar SK, Miller EW, Brenner FJ, editors. Easton: Pennsylvania Academy of Science, pp. 332–49.

Perry MC, Deller AS. 1995. Waterfowl population trends in the Chesapeake Bay area. In *Toward a sustainable watershed: the Chesapeake experiment* (Proceedings of the 1994 Chesapeake Research Conference, CRC Pub. 149), Hill P, Nelson S, editors. Edgewater, MD: Chesapeake Research Consortium, pp. 490–504.

Peterson JE, Baldwin AH. 2004. Variation in wetland seed banks across a tidal freshwater landscape. *Am. J. Bot.* 91:1251–59.

Petersen JE, Kennedy VS, et al., editors. 2009. *Enclosed experimental ecosystems and scale: tools for understanding and managing coastal ecosystems.* New York: Springer.

Pinckney J, Zingmark RG. 1993. Biomass and production of benthic microalgal communities in estuarine habitats. *Estuaries* 16:887–97.

Poffenbarger H, Needelman B, Megonigal JP. 2011. Salinity influence on methane emissions from tidal marshes. *Wetlands* 31:831–842.

Posey MH, Alphin TD, et al. 2003. Benthic communities of common reed *Phragmites australis* and marsh cordgrass *Spartina alterniflora* marshes in Chesapeake Bay. *Mar. Ecol. Prog. Ser.* 261:51–61.

Rheinhardt R. 1992. A multivariate analysis of vegetation patterns in tidal freshwater swamps of lower Chesapeake Bay, U.S.A. *Bull. Torrey Bot. Club* 119:192–207.

Rizzo WM, Wetzel RL. 1985. Intertidal and shoal benthic community metabolism in a temperate estuary: studies of spatial and temporal scales of variability. *Estuaries* 8:342–51.

Robbins CS. 1996. *Atlas of the breeding birds of Maryland and the District of Columbia.* Pittsburgh, PA: University of Pittsburgh Press.

Roosenburg WM, Allman PE, Fruh BJ. 2003. Diamondback terrapin nesting on the Poplar Island environmental restoration project. In *Proceedings of the 13th Biennial Coastal Zone Conference.* Baltimore, MD: NOAA.

Roosenburg WM, Green JP. 2000. Impact of a bycatch reduction device on diamondback terrapin and blue crab capture in crab pots. *Ecol. Appl.* 10:882–89.

Roosenburg WM, Haley KL, McGuire S. 1999. Habitat selection and movements of diamondback terrapins, *Malaclemys terrapin,* in a Maryland estuary. *Chelonian Conserv. Biol.* 3:425–29.

Rooth JE, Stevenson JC. 2000. Sediment deposition patterns in *Phragmites australis* communities: implications for coastal areas threatened by rising sea-level. *Wetl. Ecol. Manag.* 8:173–83.

Ross KM, Hupp CR, Howard AD. 2004. Sedimentation in floodplains of selected tributaries of the Chesapeake Bay. In *Riparian vegetation and fluvial geomorphology,* Bennett SJ, Simon A, editors. Washington, DC: American Geophysical Union, pp. 187–214.

Ruiz GM, Hines AH, Posey MH. 1993. Shallow water as a refuge habitat for fish and crustaceans in nonvegetated estuaries—an example from Chesapeake Bay. *Mar. Ecol. Prog. Ser.* 99:1–16.

Saltonstall K. 2002. Cryptic invasion by a non-native genotype of the common reed, *Phragmites australis,* into North America. *PNAS* 99:2445–49.

Schenk ER, Hupp CR. 2009. Legacy effects of colonial millponds on floodplain sedimentation, bank erosion, and channel morphology, mid-Atlantic, USA. *J. Am. Water Resourc. Assoc.* 45:597–606.

Schmitz JP. 2000. Meso-scale community organization and response to burning in mesocosms and a field salt marsh. MS thesis, University of Maryland, College Park.

Schubel JR. 1968. Turbidity maximum of the northern Chesapeake Bay. *Science* 161:1013–15.

Schubel JR, Prichard DW. 1986. Responses of upper Chesapeake Bay to variations in discharge of the Susquehanna River. *Estuaries* 9:236–49.

Sharpe PJ, Baldwin AH. 2009. Patterns of wetland plant species richness across estuarine gradients of Chesapeake Bay. *Wetlands* 29:225–35.

Sherfy MH, Kirkpatrick RL. 2003. Invertebrate response to snow goose herbivory on moist-soil vegetation. *Wetlands* 23:236–49.

Smith FR. 1938. Muskrat investigations in Dorchester County, MD, 1930–34. Circular no. 474. Washington, DC: USDA.

Stewart RE. 1962. Waterfowl populations in the upper Chesapeake region. Special Scientific Report—Wildlife, no. 65. Washington, DC: USFWS.

Stotts VD. 1986. A survey of breeding American black ducks in the Eastern Bay region of Maryland in 1986. Annapolis, MD: USFWS.

Stotts VD, Davis DE. 1960. The black duck in Chesapeake Bay of Maryland: breeding behavior and biology. *Chesap. Sci.* 1:127–54.

Stribling JM, Cornwell JC. 1997. Identification of important primary producers in a Chesapeake Bay tidal creek system using stable isotopes of carbon and sulfur. *Estuaries* 20:77–85.

Swarth CW, Kiviat E. 2009. Animal communities in North American tidal freshwater wetlands. In *Tidal freshwater wetlands,* Barendregt A, Whigham DF, Baldwin AH, editors. Leiden, The Netherlands: Backhuys, pp. 71–88.

Tatu KS, Anderson JT, et al. 2007. Mute swans' impact on submersed aquatic vegetation in Chesapeake Bay. *J. Wildl. Manag.* 71:1431–39.

Tiner RE. 1985. Wetlands of the Chesapeake Bay watershed: an overview. In *Proceedings of the Conference—Wetlands of the Chesapeake,* Groman HA, Henderson TR, et al., editors. Washington, DC: Environmental Law Institute, pp. 16–29.

Tiner RW, Bergquist HC, et al. 2001. Watershed-based wetland characterization for Delaware's Nanticoke River watershed: a preliminary assessment report. Newton Corner, MA: USFWS.

Tiner RW, Burke DG. 1995. Wetlands of Maryland. Hadley, MA, and Annapolis, MD: USFWS and MD DNR.

Tobias CR, Macko SA, et al. 2001. Tracking the fate of a high concentration groundwater nitrate plume through a fringing marsh: a combined groundwater tracer and in situ isotope enrichment study. *Limnol. Oceanogr.* 46:1977–89.

Turner RE. 1976. Geographic variations in salt marsh macrophyte production: a review. *Contrib. Mar. Sci.* 20:47–68.

Tzortziou M, Neale PJ, et al. 2008. Tidal marshes as a source of optically and chemically distinctive colored dissolved organic matter in the Chesapeake Bay. *Limnol. Oceanogr.* 53:148–59.

US EPA. 1982. Chesapeake Bay: introduction to an ecosystem. Washington, DC.

US EPA. 2004. Chesapeake Bay: introduction to an ecosystem. EPA 903-R-04-003. Washington, DC.

Walter RC, Merritts DJ. 2008. Natural streams and the legacy of water-powered mills. *Science* 319:299–304.

Wass ML, Wright TD. 1969. Coastal wetlands of Virginia. Special Report in Applied Marine Science and Ocean Engineering, no. 10. Gloucester Point: Virginia Institute of Marine Science.

Weis JS, Weis P. 2003. Is the invasion of the common reed, *Phragmites australis,* into tidal marshes of the eastern US an ecological disaster? *Mar. Poll. Bull.* 46:816–20.

Whigham DF. 2009. Primary production in tidal freshwater wetlands. In *Tidal freshwater wetlands,* Barendregt A, Whigham DF, Baldwin AH, editors. Leiden, The Netherlands: Backhuys, pp. 115–22.

Whigham DF, Baldwin AH, Swarth CW. 2009. Conservation of tidal freshwater wetlands in North America. In *Tidal freshwater wetlands,* Barendregt A, Whigham DF, Baldwin AH, editors. Leiden, The Netherlands: Backhuys, pp. 233–40.

White CP. 1989. *Chesapeake Bay: nature of the estuary: a field guide.* Centreville, MD: Tidewater.

Wigand C, Stevenson JC, Cornwell JC. 1997. Effects of different submersed macrophytes on sediment biogeochemistry. *Aquat. Bot.* 56:233–44.

Wood RJ, Boesch DF, Kennedy VS. 2002. Future consequences of climate change for the Chesapeake Bay ecosystem and its fisheries. *Am. Fish. Soc. Symp.* 32:171–84.

Wray RD, Leatherman SP, Nicholls RJ. 1995. Historic and future land loss for upland and marsh islands in the Chesapeake Bay, Maryland, U.S.A. *J. Coast. Res.* 11:1195–203.

Wulff BL, Webb KL. 1969. Intertidal zonation of marine algae at Gloucester Point, Virginia. *Chesap. Sci.* 10:29–35.

Yozzo DJ, Smith DE. 1998. Composition and abundance of resident marsh-surface nekton: comparison between tidal freshwater and salt marshes in Virginia, USA. *Hydrobiologia* 362:9–19.

CHAPTER 4

South Atlantic Tidal Wetlands

STEVEN C. PENNINGS, MERRYL ALBER,
CLARK R. ALEXANDER, MELISSA BOOTH, ADRIAN BURD,
WEI-JUN CAI, CHRISTOPHER CRAFT, CHESTER B. DEPRATTER,
DANIELA DI IORIO, CHARLES S. HOPKINSON, SAMANTHA B. JOYE,
CHRISTOF D. MEILE, WILLARD S. MOORE, BRIAN R. SILLIMAN,
VICTOR THOMPSON, and JOHN P. WARES

This chapter reviews tidal wetlands that occur along the Atlantic coast of the United States from the northern border of North Carolina to the northern distribution limit of mangroves in central Florida. The South Atlantic coast has a warm climate, a wide tidal range, and fewer anthropogenic impacts than the North and Central Atlantic coasts. It is a gently sloping coast that supports extensive tidal salt marshes. Tidal brackish marshes are common where rivers provide a source of freshwater. Rivers upstream of estuaries are bordered by tidal freshwater marshes and swamps. Below, we discuss the historical human use of the area. Then, building on Pomeroy and Wiegert (1981), Wiegert and Freeman (1990), and Dame, Alber, et al. (2000), we review the ecology of South Atlantic tidal wetlands and discuss regional conservation concerns.

Historic Human Use of the Landscape

Around 2200 B.C., coastal populations of Native Americans in the South Atlantic began intensively harvesting oysters, *Crassostrea virginica,* and other shellfish (DePratter 1979; Thomas 2008), leaving thick shell deposits, including shell rings up to 150 m across, on barrier and back-barrier islands (Crusoe and DePratter 1976; Thompson 2007). When Europeans arrived, Native American populations were at their peak (DePratter 1978; Thomas 2008; Thompson and Turck 2009). By the late 1600s, however, Native American populations were severely reduced by Old World diseases and forced relocation by Europeans (Worth 1995). The shell deposits that they left behind, however, were so extensive that European inhabitants mined them for road fill and construction material (Sullivan 2001).

After 1600, human use of coastal wetlands shifted in focus. Rice was farmed in diked tidal marshes in Georgia and South Carolina from the mid-1700s to circa 1900 (Coclanis 1989, 1993). Some former rice fields are currently maintained as habitat for waterfowl. Cypress and other wetland trees were harvested in coastal wetlands, and pine and hardwoods on coastal highlands, and they were floated downstream to coastal docks during the late 19th and early 20th centuries

(Sullivan 2001). Ballast stone offloaded into coastal wetlands by ships receiving timber formed novel back-barrier islands. Dredging of channels began in the late 1800s to accommodate shipping and continues today. Dredge spoil was deposited onto adjacent marshes, forming another type of novel island (Sullivan 2001). Finally, commercial and recreational harvesting of oyster, crab, shrimp, and fish expanded in the 20th century. How these various impacts affect the current functioning of tidal wetlands in the South Atlantic is largely unknown.

The Physical Setting

Geology

The South Atlantic coastline receives sediment from erosion of the Appalachian Mountains, the deeply weathered soils and bedrock hills of the Piedmont, and the thick, sandy soils of the Coastal Plain (Fig. 4.1) (Kennedy 1964). Rivers draining the Piedmont typically transport more water and an order of magnitude more sediment than those draining the Coastal Plain (Meade 1982). Early farming practices increased sediment loads, but this effect has decreased since the 1940s (Trimble 1974). Most transported sediment is trapped behind dams or in estuarine wetlands, and little reaches the continental shelf (Milliman, Pilkey, et al. 1972; Meade 1982).

Coastal marshes (Fig. 4.2) formed several thousand years ago behind developing barrier islands that moderated wave action (Alexander and Henry 2007; Mallinson, Burdette, et al. 2008). Barrier islands in North Carolina, northern South Carolina, and Florida are composed of unconsolidated sands (Hayes 1994). In contrast, barrier islands in southern South Carolina and Georgia are compound, with younger, sandy components on their eastern sides and older, stratigraphically variable deposits on their western sides. Back-barrier islands (= hammocks) occur between barrier islands and the mainland, and were created either by erosion of uplands, progradation of the shoreline, or anthropogenic deposition of dredge-spoil, ballast stone, or oyster shell.

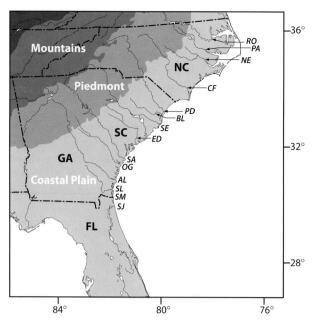

FIG. 4.1. Physiographic regions of the southeastern U.S., and major southeastern rivers, from north to south: RO, Roanoke; PA, Pamlico; NE, Neuse; CF, Cape Fear; PD, Pee Dee; BL, Black; SE, Santee; ED, Edisto; SA, Savannah; OG, Ogeechee; AL, Altamaha; SL, Satilla; SM, St. Marys; SJ, St. Johns.

Climate and Oceanographic Context

The southeastern United States has a generally warm and wet climate, driven by the interaction between marine tropical and continental polar air masses. Tropical air is unstable and is driven into the region by clockwise circulation around the subtropical Atlantic high-pressure cell (the Bermuda High), giving rise to thunderstorm activity during the summer. The continental polar air mass interacts with the marine tropical air mass during winter, forming baroclinic instabilities that promote cyclogenesis, leading to the bulk of the winter precipitation. South Florida, however, has drier winters than the rest of the region because the Atlantic high-pressure cell tends to move toward the equator during winter, leading to sinking air and inhibiting convective storm activity (Soulé 1998). The strength and location of the Bermuda High are major factors determining the supply of freshwater to Georgia coastal systems (Sheldon and Burd unpublished) and historic patterns of rainfall in the Southeast (Stahle and Cleaveland 1992).

Tidal patterns in the South Atlantic are primarily driven by the semidiurnal lunar tide (M2) and the solar tide (S2). The tidal range varies from 1 to 3 m depending on location and M2–S2 interactions. When the dominant M2 tidal wave enters bays and estuaries, nonlinear interactions with irregular creek geometries and bottom topography produce overtides (harmonics) and more complicated tidal cycles (Huang, Chen, et al. 2008). These overtides generally produce asymmetric tidal currents, with the ebb current stronger and shorter than the flood current. Water stored in intertidal marshes also contributes to ebb dominance in the channel.

River flow, precipitation, and groundwater discharge create an along-channel salinity gradient as high as 1 PSU km⁻¹ (Blanton, Alber, et al. 2001). Because the estuaries are shallow, vertical stratification is easily destroyed by tidal stirring (vertical mixing) (McKay and Di Iorio 2010). Ocean inputs are mediated by seasonal wind patterns that cause sea level to fall or rise by up to 0.4 m in the summer versus fall and winter, respectively (Di Iorio unpublished).

Land Use and Freshwater Inputs

Rivers are a major source of nutrients and freshwater to coastal wetlands, and estuarine salinity is well predicted by river discharge (Sheldon and Alber 2002; Di Iorio unpublished). Nutrient delivery varies with flow within a river: nitrate+nitrite dominates dissolved nitrogen (N) loading of the Altamaha River during periods of low flow, whereas dissolved organic nitrogen increases in importance during high flow (Weston, Hollibaugh, et al. 2003). The 12 largest watersheds are dominated by forest (33 to 70%) and agriculture (18 to 43.5%). The most important watershed N inputs are fertilizer (33%), net import of food and livestock feed (31%), and agricultural N fixation (26%) (Schaefer and Alber 2007a). Riverine N export is correlated with watershed N input (Schaefer and Alber 2007a), but the proportion of N exported to the estuary is only 9% (Table 4.1), less than half of global estimates of ~25% (Boyer, Goodale, et al. 2002; Galloway, Dentener, et al. 2004), possibly due to temperature-driven differences in denitrification (Schaefer and Alber 2007a).

Another source of freshwater and nutrients to coastal wetlands is submarine groundwater discharge (Moore 1999). Groundwater fluxes of nutrients, metals, and dissolved inorganic and organic carbon (C) can rival or exceed riverine fluxes (Krest, Moore, et al. 2000; Moore, Krest, et al. 2002; Crotwell and Moore 2003). The nature of groundwater discharge has been altered by dredging, which can breach underlying confining layers (Duncan 1972), and by groundwater use, which can lower potentiometric surfaces in aquifers, causing seawater infiltration (Landmeyer and Stone 1995).

Soils and Biogeochemistry

Tidal salt and brackish marshes of the Southeast generally have sandy, mineral soils, with higher bulk density and less organic C and N than marshes of the North Atlantic and Gulf coasts (Coultas and Calhoun 1976; Daniels, Kleiss, et al. 1984; Gardner, Smith, et al. 1992; Craft 2007). Soils are typically high in sulfides and have poorly developed horizons or layers. Porosity is high, ranging from > 50% in mineral soils to 90% in organic soils (Craft, Seneca, et al. 1991). The pH of moist salt and brackish marsh soils is neutral to slightly basic, but some soils become acidic upon drying as sulfide is oxidized to sulfate (Daniels, Kleiss, et al. 1984). Cation exchange capacity varies depending on clay and organic content, but exchange sites are dominated by base cations, Na, K, Ca, and Mg. Brackish and fresh marshes and swamps tend to have organic or organic-rich mineral soils (Daniels, Kleiss, et al. 1984; Loomis and Craft 2010). Tidal freshwater marshes and swamps contain little sulfide and are slightly more acidic than brackish and salt marshes (Loomis and Craft 2010).

Within the Southeast, tidal-marsh soil properties vary depending on salinity, geomorphic position, tide range, vegetation type, and other factors (Table 4.2). Barrier-island salt marshes have very sandy soils, with high bulk density and low nitrogen compared with lagoonal salt marshes (Table 4.2).

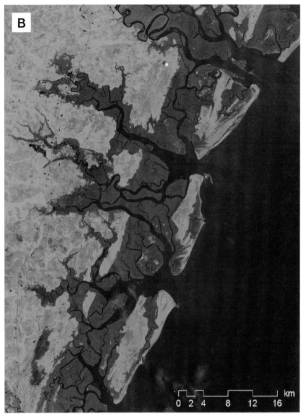

FIG. 4.2. A. Aerial view of creek network permeating *Spartina alterniflora* salt marsh, Georgia. B. Aerial view of part of the Georgia coast, with light-green barrier islands to right, mainland to left, and dark green tidal wetlands between. C. Creekbank of *S. alterniflora* salt marsh at high tide. D. Wrack disturbance in upper levels of salt marsh, with *S. alterniflora* in foreground and *Juncus roemerianus* behind. E. Creekbank of *S. alterniflora* salt marsh at low tide, with oyster reef at water's edge. (Photo credits: A: Clark Alexander; B: 2000 Landsat ETM+ produced by the U.S. Geological Survey; C: K. Więski; D: C. Hladik; E: S. Pennings. Used by permission.)

TABLE 4.1

Watershed area, land use, N budgets, and N export for major watersheds of the southeastern U.S.

Watershed	Watershed Area (km²)	Forest (%)	Agriculture (%)	Urban (%)	Wetlands (%)	Water (%)	Other (%)	Watershed N input (kg N km⁻² yr⁻¹)	Specific runoff (mm yr⁻¹)	Riverine N export (kg N km⁻² yr⁻¹)	Percent N export (%)
Roanoke (NC)	21,984	69.6	22.2	2.8	1.7	2.5	1.4	2,889	352	197	7
Pamlico (NC)	5,748	58.8	26.5	2.7	10.3	0.6	1.0	4,118	334	446	11
Neuse (NC)	7,033	51.0	29.3	7.6	9.8	1.5	0.7	4,884	341	446	9
Cape Fear (NC)	13,599	62.8	20.8	7.0	6.0	1.5	1.8	3,604	355	248	7
Pee Dee (NC)	21,448	61.2	27.0	5.5	3.8	1.1	1.4	4,039	467	390	10
Santee (SC)	32,017	69.7	18.1	7.0	0.8	2.2	2.1	2,676	433	312	12
Black (SC)	3,274	33.3	43.5	3.0	18.1	0.2	1.9	3,282	286	158	5
Edisto (SC)	6,944	45.0	32.3	1.6	15.2	0.7	5.3	2,913	337	228	8
Savannah (GA)	25,488	65.9	18.0	2.8	4.7	3.6	4.9	2,762	418	272	10
Ogeechee (GA)	8,415	44.9	33.6	0.7	14.2	0.6	5.9	3,098	330	283	9
Altamaha (GA)	35,112	57.9	24.5	3.5	7.3	1.2	5.7	3,099	339	273	9
Satilla (GA)	7,348	45.9	30.4	1.0	14.4	0.6	7.7	3,203	275	365	11
Area-weighted average		59.7	24.5	3.9	6.6	1.7	3.5	3,199	379	294	9

NOTE: Watershed N input was obtained by summing all inputs (net atmospheric deposition, fertilizer, N fixation, and net food and feed import) and subtracting non–food crop export. Adapted from Schaefer and Alber (2007a). Specific runoff is calculated as annual river flow divided by watershed area, thus allowing comparisons among watersheds of different sizes.

TABLE 4.2

Selected properties of tidal marsh soils (0–30 cm) of the southeast Atlantic coast
(North Carolina, South Carolina, Georgia, and Florida)
as a function of geomorphic position and location on the salinity gradient

	Sand (%)	Silt (%)	Clay (%)	Bulk density (g cm⁻³)	Organic matter (%)	Total N (%)	Total P (ug g⁻¹)
BARRIER/SEA ISLAND							
Salt marsh[a,b,c,d]	65 ± 8	16 ± 2	13 ± 2	0.94 ± 0.14	4 ± 1	0.19 ± 0.04	690 ± 240
RIVERINE							
Salt marsh[b,c,e–l]	57 ± 10	20 ± 7	11 ± 4	0.56 ± 0.09	12 ± 2	0.36 ± 0.05	530 ± 100
Brackish marsh[e,f,g,k,m]	16 ± 16	29 ± 16	27 ± 27	0.33 ± 0.07	28 ± 7	0.81 ± 0.26	620 ± 10
Tidal freshwater marsh[e,k]	32	41	2	0.23 ± 0.02	25 ± 4	0.73 ± 0.05	740 ± 190
Tidal forest[n]	66	7	1	0.45	26	0.64	490
LAGOONAL							
Brackish marsh[a,b,o,p]	13	30	6	0.17 ± 0.02	51 ± 3	1.58 ± 0.12	860 ± 60

[a] Craft, Seneca, and Broome 1993.
[b] Craft, Broome, and Seneca 1988.
[c] Four barrier-island salt marshes and one riverine salt marsh (Craft unpublished data).
[d] Two marshes (Sapelo River estuary) (Craft 2007). Sand, silt, and clay content (Craft unpublished data).
[e] Two salt marshes, one brackish marsh, and one tidal freshwater marsh (Paludan and Morris 1999).
[f] Three salt marshes and one brackish marsh (Bradley and Morris 1990).
[g] One salt marsh (Goni and Thomas 2000).
[h] Two salt marshes. Silt content is silt plus clay (Gardner, Smith, Michener 1992).
[i] Two salt marshes (Sharma, Gardner, et al. 1987).
[j] One salt marsh (Vogel, Kjerfve, and Gardner 1996).
[k] Three rivers (Ogeechee, Altamaha, Satilla) (Loomis and Craft 2010). Sand, silt, and clay content (Craft unpublished data).
[l] N from Haines, Chalmers, et al. (1977), P from Nixon (1980).
[m] Coultas and Calhoun 1976.
[n] Craft unpublished data.
[o] Craft, Broome, and Seneca 1986.
[p] Craft, Seneca, and Broome 1991.

Some tidal freshwater and brackish marshes (i.e., those in the Albemarle-Pamlico estuaries) are underlain by several meters of peat, due to the microtidal tide regime, low sediment inputs, and low salinity relative to marshes elsewhere (Craft, Seneca, et al. 1993). Phosphorus content does not vary strongly among barrier-island, riverine, and lagoonal marshes (Table 4.2).

As in all wetlands, biogeochemical conditions in sediments vary as a function of plant production, microbial processes, macrofauna, and hydrology. The relative importance of these factors varies spatially, driving variation in biogeochemical zonation in both horizontal (across the marsh) and vertical (over depth) directions. Bioturbation and plant roots affect vertical structure, creating fine-scale spatial variation in redox conditions (Bull and Taillefert 2001; Kostka, Gribsholt, et al. 2002; Gribsholt, Kostka, et al. 2003). Large-scale horizontal zonation occurs along the salinity gradient in estuaries. In salt marshes, inundation with seawater rich in sulfate favors organic matter decomposition and mineralization via microbially mediated sulfate reduction, whereas in tidal fresh marshes, decomposition of organic matter is limited by the availability of terminal electron acceptors, and methanogenesis is of more pronounced importance (Weston and Joye 2005; Weston, Dixon, et al. 2006). Soil biogeochemical conditions vary seasonally (Bull and Taillefert 2001), driven by variation in availability of labile dissolved organic carbon more than

by variation in temperature (Weston and Joye 2005; Weston, Porubsky, et al. 2006).

Microbial, Plant, and Animal Communities

Microbial Communities

Microbes drive the detritus-based food webs of South Atlantic wetlands and surrounding waters through their activities in mineralizing plant biomass and processing carbon. Four or five species of ascomycetous fungi are the primary decomposers of *Spartina alterniflora* along the entire U.S. Atlantic coast, complemented by seven major bacterial taxa (Newell, Blum, et al. 2000; Newell 2001; Buchan, Newell, et al. 2003). *Spartina patens* hosts a higher diversity of ascomycete species than *S. alterniflora* (Lyons, Alber, et al. 2009). A different suite of ascomycetous fungi are the major decomposers of black needlerush, *Juncus roemerianus* (Newell 2003). Less work has been done on the microbial decomposers of tidal brackish and fresh marshes.

Recent studies using molecular techniques have shown that the sediment bacterial communities of *Spartina*-dominated salt marshes in the South Atlantic Bight are quite diverse, with estimates of "species" richness comparable to those in terrestrial soil (Caffrey, Bano, et al. 2007; Lasher, Dyzszynski, et al. 2009). A variety of protist species consume bacteria but may not control their densities (First and Hollibaugh 2008).

Benthic Algae

Benthic microalgae (diatoms and cyanobacteria) are abundant in South Atlantic salt marshes compared with Central and North Atlantic sites, but are less abundant than in some Gulf coast marshes (Joye unpublished data). Macroalgae are rare in South Atlantic marshes due to the combination of turbid water, which limits photosynthesis when algae are submerged, and hot temperatures, which cause desiccation when algae are exposed. Microalgal biomass is often greatest on mudflats, because these areas are fully exposed to sunlight and constantly moist. Water stress at higher elevations favors cyanobacteria at the expense of diatoms. Microalgae are also common in lower-salinity marshes, though data are limited (Neubauer, Miller, et al. 2000; Neubauer, Givler, et al. 2005).

Microalgae production can rival that of angiosperms in coastal marshes (Tyler, Mastronicola, et al. 2003; Porubsky, Velasquez, et al. 2008), and enters the food web more directly (Currin, Newell, et al. 1995). Benthic microalgae account for 10 to 60% of gross primary production (Pinckney and Zingmark 1993a,b; Sullivan and Currin 2000) and 20 to 25% of net vascular plant production (Tobias and Neubauer 2009). Cyanobacteria are an important source of fixed nitrogen during periods of nitrogen limitation (Tyler, McGlathery, et al. 2003), whereas benthic microalgae can release copious dissolved organic carbon to the water under nutrient-replete conditions (Porubsky, Velasquez, et al. 2008).

Angiosperms

The dominant salt-marsh plant in the South Atlantic is the grass *Spartina alterniflora* (Fig. 4.2a–e), which occurs in monospecific stands at low to intermediate elevations, sometimes mixed with *Salicornia virginica* or other species at intermediate elevations (Wiegert and Freeman 1990). High marsh elevations are dominated by *Juncus roemerianus* (Pennings, Grant, et al. 2005) and *Borrichia frutescens* (Pennings and Moore 2001). This zonation pattern is driven by competition and varying sensitivities of the different plants to flooding and salinity stress. In some marshes, the border between *S. alterniflora* and high-marsh vegetation is interrupted by an unvegetated salt pan with porewater salinities several times those of seawater (Pennings and Bertness 1999) that is surrounded by a group of highly salt-tolerant plant species (Wiegert and Freeman 1990).

Latitudinal variation in climate drives variation in plant ecology. North of Virginia, aboveground parts of grasses and rushes senesce in the fall, but plants south of Virginia grow year-round (Gallagher, Reimold, et al. 1980). Due to this difference in phenology and warmer temperatures, primary production is greater at low than at high latitudes (Turner 1976). A number of low-latitude plants, such as *J. roemerianus* and *B. frutescens*, do not occur north of Virginia (Pennings and Bertness 1999), likely because they cannot tolerate harsh winters. Because salt-marsh plants can benefit each other by shading the soil and ameliorating high soil salinities, and because low-latitude marshes are hotter than high-latitude marshes, it is reasonable to hypothesize that low-latitude plant communities would be strongly structured by positive interactions (Pennings and Bertness 1999). This hypothesis, however, is false. Instead, competitive interactions predominate among salt-marsh plants in the South Atlantic, in part because the more salt-sensitive plant species are rare at low latitudes and in part because low-latitude species are stronger competitors due to their larger size (Pennings, Selig, et al. 2003).

Brackish marshes are dominated by *Spartina cynosuroides* and *Juncus roemerianus* (Higinbotham, Alber, et al. 2004). The distribution of *S. cynosuroides* and *S. alterniflora* on creekbanks shifts depending on river discharge and estuarine salinity (White and Alber 2009). The dominant plant in tidal fresh marshes is the grass *Zizaniopsis milacea* (Higinbotham, Alber, et al. 2004), and tidal swamps are dominated by the trees *Taxodium distichum* (bald cypress) and *Nyssa aquatica* (tupelo gum) (Conner, Doyle, et al. 2007). Several aspects of the marsh-plant community vary systematically along the estuarine salinity gradient. Species richness increases fivefold from saline to fresh sites (Więski, Guo, et al. 2010). Plants are tallest, and nitrogen stocks in plants greatest, at fresh sites, but standing biomass and carbon stocks in vegetation are greatest at brackish sites.

Marine and Terrestrial Invertebrates

Southeastern salt marshes support dense populations of mollusks and crustaceans (Fig. 4.3a–g). The mud snail *Illyanassa obsoleta* occurs in the low marsh and feeds on carrion and algae (Currin, Newell, et al. 1995). The periwinkle *Littoraria irrorata* occurs in the mid-marsh and feeds on fungal decomposers of *Spartina alterniflora* (Silliman and Newell 2003). The pulmonate *Melampus bidentatus* occurs at high elevations, especially in areas not frequented by *Littoraria* (Lee and Silliman 2006), and feeds on biofilms and fungi. The oyster *Crassostrea virginica* is the dominant bivalve, forming low-lying reefs. The ribbed mussel, *Geukensia demissa*, forms mounds in the mid-marsh (Smith and Frey 1985; Stiven and Gardner 1992). The Carolina marsh clam *Polymesoda caroliniana* occurs at low densities in the high marsh.

Eight crab and several shrimp species are common. Predatory mud crabs, *Panopeus herbstii* and *Euritium limosum*, occur throughout all *Spartina* zones (Silliman, Layman, et al. 2004). Predatory blue crabs, *Callinectus sapidus*, enter and leave marshes with the tides. The deposit-feeding sand fiddler, *Uca pugilator*, and mud fiddler, *U. pugnax*, occur in sandy and muddy salt habitats, respectively, while the larger *U. minax* occurs in brackish habitats. Finally, the omnivorous wharf crab, *Armases cinereum*, and the herbivorous purple marsh crab, *Sesarma reticulatum*, occur, respectively, at the terrestrial border and lower edge of the marsh. The commercial brown, white, and pink shrimp and the smaller grass shrimp use salt marshes for feeding and nursery habitats. Finally, a variety of meso- and microinvertebrates occupy marshes, living in association with plants or in marsh soils. These taxa represent an important trophic link between detritus or microalgae and larger consumers, but only a few have been well studied (Haines and Montague 1979; Kneib 1986; Kneib, Newell, et al. 1997; Graça, Newell, et al. 2000; Griffin and Silliman 2011).

The marshes are also populated by "terrestrial" invertebrates (Fig. 4.4a–e), most notably insects and spiders (Davis and Gray 1966; Pfeiffer and Wiegert 1981). More is known about arthropod food webs in salt marshes than about those in low-salinity marshes. *Spartina alterniflora* supports several herbivores including the planthoppers *Prokelisia marginata* and *P. dolus*, the bug *Trigonotylus uhleri*, several stem borers, and the tettigoniid *Orche-*

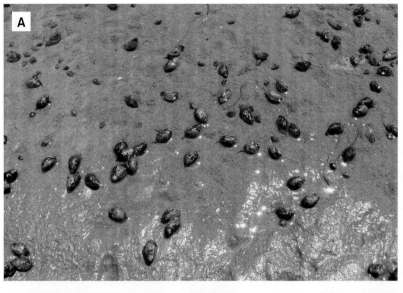

FIG. 4.3. A. Mud snail, *Illyanassa obsoleta*. B. Mussel, *Geukensia demissa*. C. Littorine snail, *Littoraria irrorata,* at high densities on *Spartina alterniflora.* D. *Alligator mississippiensis* at marsh edge. E. Mud fiddler crab, *Uca pugnax*. F. Herbivorous crab, *Sesarma reticulatum.* G. Predatory crab, *Eurytium limosum.* (Photo credits: A–C, E, G: S. Pennings; D: J Nifong; F: K. Więski. Used by permission.)

FIG. 4.4. A. Tettigoniid grasshopper, *Orchelimum fidicinium*. B. *Prokelisia* spp. planthopper on *Spartina alterniflora*. C. Aphids, *Uroleucon ambrosiae,* on *Iva frutescens*. D. Succulent plant, *Batis maritima*. E. Forb, *Solidago sempervirens*. (Photo credits: A, D, E: S. Pennings; B–C: C.-K. Ho. Used by permission.)

limum fidicinium (Smalley 1960; Stiling and Strong 1984). These are fed on by a variety of parasitoids and predatory insects and spiders (Pfeiffer and Wiegert 1981; Stiling and Bowdish 2000).

The shrub *Borrichia frutescens* supports several herbivores, including the planthopper *Pissonotus quadripustulatus,* the gall fly *Asphondylia borrichiae,* and the lepidopteran *Argyresthia* sp. (Moon and Stiling 2004), all of which are attacked by hymenopteran parasitoids (Moon, Rossi, et al. 2000). The shrub *Iva frutescens* supports several herbivores, including leaf-galling mites, the aphid *Uroleucon ambrosiae,* the beetles

Ophraella notulata and *Paria aterrima,* and the grasshoppers *Paroxya clavuliger* and *Hesperotettix floridensis* (Ho and Pennings 2008; Pennings, Ho, et al. 2009). Predators include ladybugs, spiders, and the crab *Armases cinereum.*

Vertebrates

Vertebrate utilization of marsh habitat for feeding, foraging, and reproduction is one of the most understudied aspects of tidal-marsh ecology. The list of vertebrates that utilize tidal marshes is extensive, including feral hogs and horses, deer, raccoons, otters, bobcats, dolphins, sharks, teleost fish, birds, lizards, snakes, turtles, and alligators (Fig. 4.3d). Most of these are not full-time residents of marshes, but instead visit from terrestrial or marine habitats to forage on wetland plants, invertebrates, and fish. For example, although large alligators on barrier islands may spend up to 80% of their time in the marine waters of salt marshes, and consume a diet composed of up to 88% marine organisms by weight, they periodically return to freshwater wetlands to reduce osmotic stress and reproduce (J. Nifong and B. Silliman unpublished data).

The degree to which vertebrates depend on marshes is in general poorly documented, but it certainly varies among taxa. The fish mullet and mummichog inhabit marsh creeks in huge numbers and feed on marsh detritus and small invertebrates in creeks and on the marsh surface. Mummichogs occur rarely in habitats besides marshes, and while mullet occur across a range of ecosystem types, their numbers are highest near wetlands (Kneib 1986). Other vertebrates, such as raccoons and hogs, are opportunistic foragers in tidal wetlands (Nifong and Silliman pers. observation), but some individuals may feed extensively in these habitats.

The effects that vertebrates have on marsh structure and function are, with a few exceptions, poorly understood. Top-down effects are likely to be large but localized for many vertebrates, such as feral hogs and horses, nondetectable for some, such as otters, and huge and widespread for a few, such as mummichogs. Mummichogs have been relatively well studied, and play critical roles in controlling invertebrate densities. They also play a key role in cross-ecosystem subsidies because they are trophic intermediates that relay C and N from marsh invertebrates to estuarine habitats when they are consumed by larger fishes (Kneib 1986, 1997).

Biogeography of Wetland Communities

The biogeographic paradigm for Atlantic coast marine communities involves transitions at Cape Cod, Cape Hatteras, and Cape Canaveral (Fig. 4.5). These boundaries, however, may not apply to wetland communities. For example, the strong transition zone at Cape Hatteras, where the Gulf Stream diverges from the coastal shelf (Briggs 1974), primarily affects species with low dispersal ability and those distributed far out on the continental shelf (Fischer 1960; Briggs 1974; Schwartz 1989; Roy, Jablonski et al. 1998). In contrast, estuarine invertebrates show other biogeographic transitions associated with temperature gradients (Engle and Summers 1999) (Fig. 4.5). Similarly, phylogeographic surveys along the Florida coast indicate that the canonical transition zone at Cape Canaveral is strongest for species with restricted dispersal (Pelc, Warner, et al. 2009), although the Florida peninsula does act as a barrier for many species (Avise 1992).

Phylogeographic studies of *Spartina alterniflora* show genetic transitions across Chesapeake Bay (Blum, Bando, et al. 2007), reflecting the transition between the Upper and Lower Virginian provinces documented by Engle and Summers (1999). Similarly, the planthopper *Prokelisia marginata* is divided into a mid-Atlantic and a South Atlantic–Gulf coast clade, with a boundary in Virginia (Denno, Peterson, et al. 2008). A number of other wetland animals, including fiddler crabs, bivalves, and sheepshead minnow, also display a transition between the Upper and Lower Virginian provinces (Díaz-Ferguson, Rob-

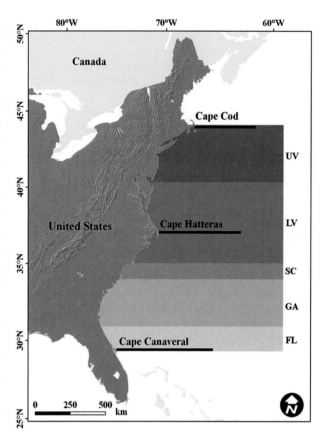

FIG. 4.5. "Classic" marine biogeographic transitions at Cape Cod, Cape Hatteras, and Cape Canaveral. Biogeographic regions that may be more appropriate to estuarine habitats (Engle and Summers 1999) are indicated by shading; UV, Upper Virginian; LV, Lower Virginian; SC, South Carolinian; GA, Georgian; FL, Floridian.

inson, et al. 2009). The transition from high to low latitudes across the mid-Atlantic region is associated with changes in climate that affect the life history and productivity of *Spartina* (Turner 1976; Kirwan, Guntenspergen, et al. 2009), a large increase in wetland habitat (Bertness 1999), a transition from dominance by *S. patens* to *Juncus romerianus* in the middle elevations of salt marshes, an increased abundance of salt-tolerant plant species such as *Salicornia* spp. (Pennings and Bertness 1999), and turnover in dominant insect herbivore species (Wason and Pennings 2008). These transitions lead to variation in ecological interactions at different latitudes (Pennings and Silliman 2005; Pennings, Selig, et al. 2003; Pennings, Ho, et al. 2009).

Key Ecological Processes

Disturbance

The primary disturbance in South Atlantic tidal marshes is the deposition of floating mats of dead vegetation (wrack) onto the marsh by high tides (Fig. 4.2d). Wrack disturbance is more common in North Atlantic than South Atlantic tidal marshes because the aboveground biomass of plants at high latitudes completely dies back in the winter (Turner 1976) and is vulnerable to erosion by ice. In contrast, plants at low latitudes grow year-round, and tend to decompose in place (Newell 1993). Wrack tends to be moved by wind and currents into predictable locations that are regularly disturbed (Fischer, Klug, et al. 2000). Although heavy mats of wrack harm vegetation, thin layers may benefit it by shading the soil and ameliorating salinities or by leaching nutrients (Pennings and Richards 1998). In addition, wrack creates habitat for spiders and is a major food source for detritivores (Zimmer, Pennings, et al. 2004). Wrack exported from estuaries can trap sand and nucleate the formation of dunes on beaches. Little is known about wrack in tidal brackish or fresh marshes, but the tall vegetation in these marshes probably limits effects to the marsh edge.

Microbial Decomposition

Angiosperm production of South Atlantic wetlands enters the food web primarily through decomposition rather than herbivory. In salt marshes, the dominant grasses decay in a standing position, and initial decomposition of dead stalks and leaves occurs in the air, with periodic wetting by rain and tides. Ascomycetous fungi are the predominant mediators of this phase of decomposition, and production of fungal organic mass is on the order of 535 g m^{-2} y^{-1} (Newell 2003). Fungi-laden decaying leaves are attractive foods for a variety of consumers, including snails and amphipods (Graça 2000; Kneib, Newell, et al. 1997; Silliman and Newell 2003). These detritivores fragment leaves, which fall into sediments alongside collapsing stalks. Bacteria replace fungi as the dominant decomposers in salt-marsh sediments, but fungal activity remains high in low-salinity sediments (Newell 2003). Fungal biomass is low, but fungal activity per unit of biomass is high, in low-salinity systems (Newell 2003), and detritivorous periwinkles, amphipods, and crabs are less abundant in fresh than in salty marshes (Graça, Newell, et al. 2000; Newell and Porter 2000). The bulk of angiosperm biomass enters the sediments and water column as detritus composed primarily of lignocellulose (Benner, Newell, et al. 1984), which is highly recalcitrant to decomposition. Microbial decomposition of lignocellulose in the sediments is highest during the summer, and is primarily mediated by bacteria (Benner, Maccubbin, et al. 1986).

Ecosystem Engineering

Several species in South Atlantic salt marshes are ecosystem engineers, changing the physical environment through non-trophic mechanisms. *Spartina alterniflora* creates the marsh platform by trapping sediment and producing peat (Grosholz, Levin, et al. 2009). Emergent plants also ameliorate desiccation at low tide and hinder access by predators, benefitting small animals that live in the marsh. Burrowing by fiddler crabs, *Uca* spp., oxygenates salt-marsh soils, and crabs excrete wastes in burrows, transporting nutrients from the marsh surface to plant root zones; consequently, crabs stimulate plant growth (Montague 1982). Patches of mussels, *Geukensia demissa,* on the marsh platform engineer mounds capped with vigorous plant growth (Kuenzler 1961; Smith and Frey 1985). Mussels bind sediments and deposit nutrient-rich feces and pseudofeces onto the marsh surface (Kraeuter 1976; Newell and Krambeck 1995). Because mussels are largely absent from marsh edges in the South Atlantic due to predation (see below), they are less important engineers than in New England (Bertness 1984), but oyster reefs at the lower edge of South Atlantic salt marshes (Fig. 4.2e) may play a similar role. Ecosystem engineers are likely also important in tidal brackish and fresh marshes, but this has not been studied.

Herbivory and Predation

Early studies in the South Atlantic found that most of the carbon flow from *Spartina alterniflora* to the ecosystem was through detrital processing rather than herbivory (Teal 1962). From this arose the conclusion that herbivory was unimportant in marsh processes. In fact, herbivory rates in salt marshes are similar to those in most terrestrial ecosystems (Cebrian 1999). As described above, herbivores in salt marshes include insects, crabs, and snails. Most of these can suppress plants when common (Denno, Peterson, et al. 2000; Silliman and Zieman 2001; Stiling and Moon 2005; Ho and Pennings 2008), and two, the snail *Littoraria irrorata* and the crab *Sesarma reticulatum,* have been implicated in contributing to localized dieback of vegetation (Silliman et al. 2005; Hughes, Fitzgerald, et al. 2009). Herbivory in salt marshes is affected by the abiotic gradients across which the plants grow (Denno, Lewis, et al. 2005). For example, *Littoraria* caged at 600 m^{-2} reduced *S. alterniflora* biomass by 90% in creekbank plots, versus 65% in mid-marsh plots (Silliman and Bertness 2002). How stress affects herbivory differs as a function of plant and herbivore species (Moon and Stiling 2002a,b; Goranson, Ho, et al. 2004; Stiling and Moon 2005). Little is known about herbivore communities and impacts in tidal brackish and fresh marshes.

Herbivores are more abundant and do more damage to salt-marsh plants in the South than in the North Atlantic (Pennings, Ho, et al. 2009). This pattern, which is probably driven by cold climates limiting herbivore growth rates and densities at high latitudes, may be an important selective factor on plant traits. Salt-marsh plants are tougher, less nutritious, and more chemically defended at low versus high latitudes (Siska, Pennings, et al. 2002). As a result, high-latitude plants support better herbivore growth (Ho, Pennings, et al. 2010).

Predation rates vary with elevation, and are usually highest at the creekbank (Lin 1989; Silliman and Bertness 2002). Predation rates are probably higher in South than in North Atlantic salt marshes, but the evidence is largely anecdotal. For example, the ribbed mussel occurs along creekbanks in the North Atlantic but is relegated to higher elevations in the South Atlantic. Mussels transplanted to lower elevations were quickly eaten (Stiven and Gardner 1992), suggesting that southern marshes experience higher predation rates than northern ones; however, this hypothesis has not been tested with rigorous comparative studies. Similarly, predation rates in arthropod food webs are probably higher in South than in North Atlantic salt marshes (Pennings pers. observation), but again rigorous comparisons are lacking. Herbivorous arthropod food webs are strongly structured by top-down control from parasites and predators (Ho and Pennings 2008; Marczak, Ho, et al. 2010).

Ecosystem Metabolism

The metabolism of South Atlantic estuaries has long been of interest due to their high productivity and potential role in subsidizing marine food webs (Odum 1961, 1968; Schelske and Odum 1962). The simplest depiction of the C cycle of an estuary includes production, respiration, organic C storage and burial, and exchanges with the atmosphere, uplands,

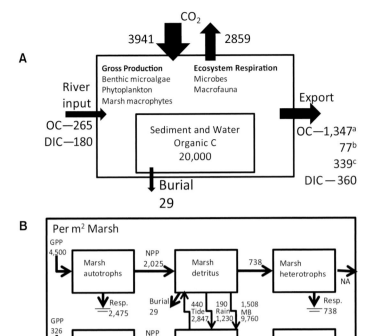

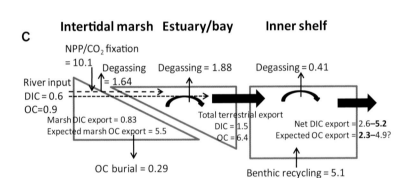

FIG. 4.6. Three ecosystem views of South Atlantic marshes. A. Simplified carbon budget. Units are either gC m^{-2}yr^{-1} or gC m^{-2}. Export fluxes with superscripts refer to: [a] mass balance of estuarine system; [b] mass balance of nearshore heterotrophy; and [c] measured export from North Inlet marshes in South Carolina. Abbreviations: OC: organic carbon; DIC: dissolved inorganic carbon. B. Carbon budgets for linked marsh and aquatic estuarine subsystems. Fluxes between marsh and aquatic systems are shown relative to both marsh and aquatic areas (because there is more marsh than water, an output from each square meter of marsh becomes a much larger input to each square meter of water). Units are gC m^{-2}yr^{-1}. Abbreviations: MB: mass balance; Resp.: respiration; NPP: net primary production; GPP: gross primary production; NA: unknown. C. Conceptual carbon transport model and mass balance analysis for a marsh-estuary–inner shelf continuum scaled up to the entire South Atlantic Bight. Units are in 10^{12} gC yr^{-1}. Estimates are based on a total marsh area of 5.0×10^9 m^2.

and ocean (Fig. 4.6a). Few of these processes are easily measured. Consequently, most attempts to quantify C fluxes have employed indirect measures, such as mass balance of offshore C budgets (Hopkinson 1985) or mass balance of all the producer and consumer communities (Wiegert, Christian, et al. 1981; Hopkinson and Hoffman 1984; Hopkinson 1988). Organic C fluxes associated with rivers are well documented (Mulholland and Kuenzler 1979; Hopkinson and Hoffman 1984), but those associated with groundwater fluxes are just beginning to be defined (Moore, Blanton, et al. 2006).

Ecosystem metabolism (production and respiration) dominates the coastal C cycle, exceeding riverine inputs by an order of magnitude (Fig. 4.6a). Approximately two-thirds of fixed C inputs are returned to the atmosphere by respiration. Considerable C is exported offshore; however, direct measures are rare, and C export is usually estimated based on mass balance of the estuary (Hopkinson 1988) or heterotrophic demands of the nearshore ocean (Hopkinson and Hoffman 1984; Hopkinson 1988; Cai, Pomeroy, et al. 1999; Cai, Wang, et al. 2003).

Estimates of production and respiration are similar throughout the South Atlantic and Gulf coasts, but are considerably reduced in the North Atlantic (Hopkinson 1988). Estimates of export to the ocean are considerably higher on the South Atlantic (up to 59%) than on the Gulf and Northeast coasts (1 to 38%), probably reflecting both high primary production and the high tidal range in the South Atlantic.

Salt-marsh estuaries are often conceptualized as separate marsh and aquatic systems with linked C budgets (Fig. 4.6b). This approach indicates that the salt marsh is autotrophic (P/R = 4,500/3,213 = 1.4:1) while the aquatic system is heterotrophic (P/R = 326/574 = 0.56:1), and that each square meter of marsh exports 1,500 gC yr^{-1} to estuarine creeks and bays. This is equivalent to an input of almost 10,000 gC to each square meter of water. Mass balance for the aquatic portion (tidal creeks and bays) suggests a flux in excess of 5,000 gC m^{-2} of water surface yr^{-1} to the ocean. In addition, rivers contribute 1,852 kgC m^{-1} shoreline yr^{-1} to the coastal zone, much of which passes to the ocean with little alteration or loss during estuarine transit.

Cai and coworkers (Cai, Pomeroy, et al. 1999; Cai, Wang, et al. 2003; Wang, Cai, et al. 2005; Cai 2011) conceptualized southeastern estuaries as a benthic subsystem and an aquatic subsystem (Fig. 4.6c). They used free water measurements of dissolved O_2 and CO_2 to document metabolism of both aquatic components and those portions of the benthic subsystem flooded at any time. This was a significant advance, as it did not rely solely on transport of organic C to tidal creeks to satisfy heterotrophic demands; instead, the water subsystem moves onto the marsh and there integrates some aspects of respiration occurring on the marsh. This approach indicated that the estuarine, bay, and inner-shelf waters of the Georgia Bight are heterotrophic and respire large quantities of organic C exported from intertidal marshes.

Conservation Concerns

Between 1980 and 2003, coastal counties of the Southeast Atlantic had the largest rate of population increase (58%) of any coastal region in the coterminous United States. Most of this growth occurred in Florida (EPA 2008), but tourists and retirees are also placing pressure on the Carolinas and Georgia, which are projected to gain 11 million residents by 2025 (U.S. Census Bureau 2000). These human population changes will drive changes in land use and increase demand for water supply, wastewater disposal, and coastal resources. Conservation concerns for the region include freshwater delivery, eutrophication, management of top consumers, climate change, and marsh die-back.

Freshwater Delivery to the Coast

Changes in industrial and human demand for water are likely to affect freshwater delivery to the coast. Because nutrients, pollutants, sediment, and organic material are all carried along with freshwater, changes in freshwater delivery will affect the delivery of these materials as well (Alber 2002). Similarly, changes in land cover, such as clearing and draining land for agriculture, will also affect the delivery of freshwater and associated materials to the coast. Anthropogenic impacts on freshwater delivery will be layered on top of natural variability in freshwater discharge to estuaries. All five Georgia riverine estuaries exhibit at least a 29-fold interannual difference between minimum and maximum discharge (GCRC 2002). For example, the onset of drought led to increasing salinities in the Satilla River as freshwater discharge declined from almost $150 \, m^3 s^{-1}$ in February 1999 to below $10 \, m^3 s^{-1}$ in May and June 1999 (Blanton, Alber, et al. 2001). Freshwater inflow also undergoes a regular annual cycle, with seasonal maxima in discharge during the spring and minima in the fall.

Potential changes in freshwater inflow are of concern because they will affect estuarine resources (Alber 2002). For example, a tide gate and diversion canal near the Savannah River National Wildlife Refuge displaced the salt wedge 6 to 8 miles upstream, causing a shift toward salt-tolerant marsh vegetation and changes in fauna (Pearlstine, Kitchens, et al. 1993). When the tide gate and canal were later removed, there was a shift back toward a tidal freshwater community. Similarly, natural variation in freshwater inflow in the Altamaha River estuary between drought and wet years altered the distribution of *Spartina cynosuroides* (White and Alber 2009) and affected sediment deposition on the marsh surface (Craft unpublished) and

productivity of *Spartina alterniflora* (Pennings unpublished). Finally, drought promotes marsh die-back (below).

Eutrophication

Eutrophication is increasing on the South Atlantic coast. Nitrogen and phosphorus inputs to watersheds have increased over the last 50 years, reflecting fertilizer input and an increase in the human population (Schaefer and Alber 2007b). Dissolved oxygen levels at the Skidaway Institute of Oceanography in Georgia show a steady drop over 19 years (Verity, Alber, et al. 2006). Symptoms of eutrophication (nuisance and toxic algal blooms, hypoxia/anoxia, fish and shellfish mortality) exist in nearly half of the major southeastern estuaries, with future deterioration predicted (Bricker, Longstaff, et al. 2007). In the recent National Coastal Condition Report (EPA 2008), 54% of the water-quality index ratings in the South Atlantic were fair or poor, and 59% of chlorophyll *a* concentrations were fair. Eutrophication would be expected to stimulate microbial activity (Sundareshwar, Morris, et al. 2003), increase plant productivity (Gallagher 1975), and favor some plant species, especially *Spartina alterniflora*, over others (Pennings, Stanton, et al. 2002). Moreover, because plants commonly respond to eutrophication by investing more biomass aboveground and less below, eutrophication may reduce belowground production and thereby reduce the ability of marshes to keep pace with rising sea levels (Darby and Turner 2008). In addition, fertilization may increase the palatability of plants to herbivores by increasing plant nitrogen content (Silliman and Zieman 2001; Moon, Rossi, et al. 2000; Moon and Stiling 2002a,b).

Management of Top Consumers

Humans have markedly affected the densities of many top consumers in southeastern estuarine systems. Alligator densities are rebounding from historic hunting, but landings of commercially important fish and shellfish are declining (EPA 2008). Impacts of recreational anglers are difficult to assess but will likely increase as population densities rise. We lack good data on anthropogenic impacts on most top consumers in southeastern wetlands; however, humans typically reduce the populations of large marine predators to a fraction of their natural densities (Jackson, Kirby, et al. 2001; Myers, Baum, et al. 2007), and so it is likely that populations of many predators in southeastern coastal wetlands have been similarly depressed. The consequences of depressed predator densities for southeastern marsh food webs remain largely unexplored.

Climate Change

Changing climate probably will lead to accelerated sea-level rise and increased storm activity in the South Atlantic. The contemporary rate of relative sea-level rise (RSLR) along the South Atlantic is 2–3 mm yr^{-1} (Craft, Clough, et al. 2009), and vertical accretion rates in the region range from 2 mm yr^{-1} for salt marshes to 4–6 mm yr^{-1} for brackish and tidal freshwater marshes (Craft 2007), indicating that they are able to keep pace with RSLR by trapping sediment and accumulating soil organic matter. Climate projections suggest that SLR will accelerate in the coming century. Although marsh accretion rates increase with greater sea level (Morris, Sundareshwar, et al. 2002), accelerated RSLR is likely to lead to some losses of tidal marshes, with losses unequal among tidal fresh, brackish, and salt marshes (Craft, Clough, et al. 2009). Rising sea levels will also move saltwater farther into estuaries, which will likely accelerate decomposition of soil organic matter (Weston, Dixon, et al. 2006; Craft 2007), further limiting the ability of low-salinity marshes to keep pace with RSLR.

Hurricanes and storms can drive saltwater upstream, uproot vegetation, and either deposit or erode sediments (Nyman, Crozier, et al. 1995; Cahoon 2006). Hurricane effects on Gulf coast wetlands have been severe (Chabreck and Palmisano 1973). In North Carolina, heavy rainfall from hurricanes lowered salinity and increased N and organic C loadings to estuaries, with cascading effects on estuarine food webs (Paerl, Bales, et al. 2001). Georgia and South Carolina receive relatively few hurricanes (Hopkinson, Lugo, et al. 2008); however, the frequency of storms in the South Atlantic is projected to increase in the future (Hayden and Hayden 2003).

Marsh Die-Back

In 2001–02, salt marshes in Georgia and South Carolina experienced a sudden die-back event that left bare patches in multiple parts of marshes and affected both *Spartina alterniflora* and *Juncus roemerianus* (Ogburn and Alber 2006). Many areas were naturally revegetating by 2009. Sudden die-back has also been observed in other years in the Southeast and in other areas of the country (Alber, Swenson, et al. 2008; Osgood and Silliman 2009). In the South Atlantic, die-back was associated with low rainfall and low river inflow. In 2001–02, the Palmer Drought Severity Index for Georgia and South Carolina was characterized as "extreme drought," and soils at several sites were cracked and desiccated. Die-back was also associated with drought in Louisiana but not in other areas of the country (Alber, Swenson, et al. 2008).

The variety of die-back patterns makes it difficult to come up with a single explanation for these events. When present at high densities, the snail *Littoraria irrorata* can strongly suppress *Spartina alterniflora,* and drought may increase plant vulnerability to grazing (Silliman and Bertness 2002; Silliman, van de Koppel, et al. 2005). An interaction between snail grazing and drought may explain die-back events on barrier islands, where snail densities are often high, but is less likely to explain die-back at inland locations, where snail densities are generally low. Other possibilities include drought-induced changes in soil chemistry or the presence of fungal pathogens (McKee, Mendelssohn, et al. 2004; Osgood and Silliman 2009). Rigorous evaluation of the various hypotheses is difficult because transient die-back events are often not noticed until they are well developed, at which point the factor causing die-back may no longer be present.

Conclusions

The warm climate, high sediment supply, and high tidal range of the South Atlantic have combined to produce geologically resilient, biogeochemically dynamic, and biologically productive wetlands. Gaps in our scientific understanding include a paucity of research on lower-salinity tidal marshes and swamps (but see Conner, Doyle, et al. 2007), a weak but rapidly emerging understanding of microbial diversity, and a poor understanding of the ecology of top consumers. South Atlantic coastal wetlands are not pristine, but have been less affected by anthropogenic impacts and climate change than coastal marshes elsewhere in the U.S.; however, they are likely to deteriorate in coming decades as sea levels and human populations rise unless they are protected by proactive and strong management policies that regulate land use, freshwater delivery to the coast, eutrophication, and harvesting of top consumers.

Acknowledgments

We thank the National Science Foundation for ongoing funding to the Georgia Coastal Ecosystems Long-Term Ecological Research Program (OCE06-20959).

References

Alber M. 2002. A conceptual model of estuarine inflow management. *Estuaries* 25:1246–61.

Alber M, Swenson EM, et al. 2008. Salt marsh dieback: an overview of recent events in the US. *Estuar. Coast. Shelf Sci.* 80:1–11.

Alexander CR, Henry VJ. 2007. Wassaw and Tybee Islands—comparing undeveloped and developed barrier islands. In *Guide to fieldtrips: 56th annual meeting, southeastern section of the Geological Society of America,* Rich F, editor. Statesboro: Geological Society of America, pp. 187–98.

Avise JC. 1992. Molecular population structure and the biogeographic history of a regional fauna: a case history with lessons for conservation biology. *Oikos* 63:62–76.

Benner R, Maccubbin AE, Hodson RE. 1986. Temporal relationship between the deposition and microbial degradation of lignocellulosic detritus in a Georgia salt marsh and the Okefenokee Swamp. *Microb. Ecol.* 12:291–98.

Benner R, Newell SY, et al. 1984. Relative contributions of bacteria and fungi to rates of degradation of lignocellulosic detritus in salt-marsh sediments. *Appl. Env. Microbiol.* 48:36–40.

Bertness MD. 1984. Ribbed mussels and *Spartina alterniflora* production in a New England salt marsh. *Ecology* 65:1794–807.

Bertness MD. 1999. *The ecology of Atlantic shorelines.* Sunderland, MA: Sinauer.

Blanton J, Alber M, Sheldon J. 2001. Salinity response of the Satilla river estuary to seasonal changes in freshwater discharge. In *Proceedings of the 2001 Georgia Water Resources Conference,* Hatcher KJ, editor. Athens, GA, pp. 619–22.

Blum MJ, Bando KJ, et al. 2007. Geographic structure, genetic diversity and source tracking of *Spartina alterniflora*. *J. Biogeogr.* 34:2055–69.

Boyer EW, Goodale CL, et al. 2002. Anthropogenic nitrogen sources and relationships to riverine nitrogen export in the northeastern U.S.A. *Biogeochem.* 57/58:137–69.

Bradley PM, Morris JT. 1990. Physical characteristics of salt marsh sediments: ecological implications. *Mar. Ecol. Prog. Ser.* 61:245–52.

Bricker S, Longstaff B, et al. 2007. Effects of nutrient enrichment in the nation's estuaries: a decade of change. NOAA Coastal Ocean Program Decision Analysis Series No. 26, 328. National Centers for Coastal Ocean Science, Silver Spring, MD.

Briggs JC. 1974. *Marine zoogeography.* New York: McGraw Hill.

Buchan A, Newell SY, et al. 2003. Dynamics of bacterial and fungal communities on decaying salt marsh grass. *Appl. Env. Microbiol.* 69:6676–87.

Bull DC, Taillefert M. 2001. Seasonal and topographic variations in porewaters of a southeastern USA salt marsh as revealed by voltammetric profiling. *Geochem. Trans.* 13:1–8.

Caffrey JM, Bano N, et al. 2007. Ammonia oxidation and ammonia-oxidizing bacteria and archaea from estuaries with differing histories of hypoxia. *ISME Journal* 1:660–62.

Cahoon DR. 2006. A review of major storm impacts on coastal wetland elevations. *Estuar. Coasts* 29:889–98.

Cai W-J. 2011. Estuarine and coastal ocean carbon paradox: CO_2 sinks or sites of terrestrial carbon incineration? *Annu Rev. Mar. Sci.* 3:123–145.

Cai W-J, Pomeroy LR, et al. 1999. Oxygen and carbon dioxide mass balance for the estuarine-intertidal marsh complex of five rivers in the southeastern U.S. *Limnol. Oceanogr.* 44:639–49.

Cai W-J, Wang Z, Wang Y. 2003. The role of marsh-dominated heterotrophic continental margins in transport of CO_2 between the atmosphere, the land-sea interface and the ocean. *Geophys. Res. Lett.* 30:1849, doi:10.1029/2003GL017633.

Cebrian J. 1999. Patterns in the fate of production in plant communities. *Am. Nat.* 154:449–68.

Chabreck RH, Palmisano AW. 1973. The effects of Hurricane Camille on the marshes of the Mississippi River delta. *Ecology* 54:1118–23.

Coclanis PA. 1989. *The shadow of a dream: economic life and death in the South Carolina low country, 1670–1920.* New York: Oxford Univ. Press.

Coclanis PA. 1993. Distant thunder: the creation of a world market in rice and the transformations it wrought. *Am. Hist. Rev.* 98:1050–78.

Conner WH, Doyle TW, Drauss KW. 2007. Ecology of tidal freshwater forested wetlands of the southeastern United States. Dordrecht: Springer.

Coultas CL, Calhoun FG. 1976. Properties of some tidal marsh soils of Florida. *Soil Sci. Soc. Am. J.* 40:72–76.

Craft CB. 2007. Freshwater input structures soil properties, vertical accretion, and nutrient accumulation of Georgia and U.S. tidal marshes. *Limnol. Oceanogr.* 52:1220–30.

Craft CB, Broome SW, Seneca ED. 1986. Carbon, nitrogen and phosphorus accumulation in man-initiated marsh soils. In *Proceedings of the 29th annual meeting of the Soil Science Society of North Carolina, Raleigh, NC, USA,* Amoozegar A, editor, pp. 117–31.

Craft CB, Broome SW, Seneca ED. 1988. Nitrogen, phosphorus and organic carbon pools in natural and transplanted marsh soils. *Estuar. Coasts* 11:272–80.

Craft C, Clough J, et al. 2009. Forecasting the effects of accelerated sea-level rise on tidal marsh ecosystem services. *Front. Ecol. Env.* 7:73–78.

Craft CB, Seneca ED, Broome SW. 1991. Porewater chemistry of natural and created marsh soils. *J. Exp. Mar. Biol. Ecol.* 152:187–200.

Craft CB, Seneca ED, Broome SW. 1993. Vertical accretion in microtidal regularly and irregularly flooded estuarine marshes. *Estuar. Coast. Shelf Sci.* 37:371–86.

Crotwell AM, Moore WS. 2003. Nutrient and radium fluxes from submarine groundwater discharge to Port Royal Sound, South Carolina. *Aquat. Geochem.* 9:191–208.

Crusoe D, DePratter CB. 1976. A new look at the Georgia coastal Shell Mound Archaic. *Fla. Anthropol.* 29:1–23.

Currin CA, Newell SY, Paerl HW. 1995. The role of standing dead and *Spartina alterniflora* and benthic microalgae in salt marsh food webs: considerations based on multiple stable isotope analysis. *Mar. Ecol. Prog. Ser.* 121:99–116.

Dame R, Alber M, et al. 2000. Estuaries of the south Atlantic coast of North America: their geographical signatures. *Estuaries* 23:793–819.

Daniels RB, Kleiss HJ, et al. 1984. Soil systems in North Carolina. North Carolina Agricultural Research Service, Bulletin no. 467. Raleigh: NC State Univ.

Darby FA, Turner RE. 2008. Below- and aboveground biomass of *Spartina alterniflora:* response to nutrient addition in a Louisiana salt marsh. *Estuaries and Coasts* 31:326–34.

Davis LV, Gray IE. 1966. Zonal and seasonal distribution of insects in North Carolina salt marshes. *Ecol. Monogr.* 36:275–95.

Denno RF, Lewis D, Gratton C. 2005. Spatial variation in the relative strength of top-down and bottom-up forces: causes and consequences for phytophagous insect populations. *Ann. Zool. Fenn.* 42:295–311.

Denno RF, Peterson MA, et al. 2000. Feeding-induced changes in plant quality mediate interspecific competition between sap-feeding herbivores. *Ecology* 81:1814–27.

Denno RF, Peterson MA, et al. 2008. Life-history evolution in native and introduced populations. In *Specialization, speciation, and radiation: the evolutionary biology of herbivorous insects,* Tilmon KJ, editor. Berkeley: Univ. Calif. Press, pp. 296–310.

DePratter CB. 1978. Prehistoric settlement and subsistence systems, Skidaway Island, Georgia. *Early Ga.* 6:65–80.

DePratter CB. 1979. Shellmound Archaic on the Georgia coast. *S.C. Antiq.* 11:1–69.

Díaz-Ferguson E, Robinson JD, et al. 2009. Comparative phylogeography of North American Atlantic salt marsh communities. *Estuar. Coasts* 33:828–39.

Duncan DA. 1972. High resolution seismic survey. In *Port Royal Sound environmental study,* 85–106. Columbia: SC Water Resources Commission.

Engle VD, Summers JK. 1999. Latitudinal gradients in benthic community composition in Western Atlantic estuaries. *J. Biogeogr.* 26:1007–23.

EPA. 2008. National coastal condition report III. Office of Research and Development/Office of Water, EPA, Washington, DC. EPA-620/R-03/002.

First MR, Hollibaugh JT. 2008. Protistan bacterivory and benthic microbial biomass in an intertidal creek mudflat. *Mar. Ecol. Prog. Ser.* 361:59–68.

Fischer AG. 1960. Latitudinal variations in organic diversity. *Evolution* 14:64–81.

Fischer JM, Klug JL, et al. 2000. Spatial pattern of localized disturbance along a southeastern salt marsh tidal creek. *Estuaries* 23:565–71.

Gallagher JL. 1975. Effect of an ammonium nitrate pulse on the growth and elemental composition of natural stands of *Spartina alterniflora* and *Juncus roemerianus. Am. J. Bot.* 62:644–48.

Gallagher JL, Reimold RJ, et al. 1980. Aerial production, mortality, and mineral accumulation-export dynamics in *Spartina alterniflora* and *Juncus roemerianus* plant stands in a Georgia salt marsh. *Ecology* 61:303–12.

Galloway JN, Dentener FJ, et al. 2004. Nitrogen cycles: past, present, and future. *Biogeochem.* 70:153–226.

Gardner LR, Smith BR, Michener WK. 1992. Soil evolution along a forest-salt marsh transect under a regime of slowly rising sea level, southeastern United States. *Geoderma* 55:141–57.

GCRC. 2002. The effects of changing freshwater inflow to estuaries: a Georgia perspective. Georgia Coastal Research Council. www.gcrc.uga.edu/PDFs/inflow1119.pdf.

Goni CA, Thomas KA. 2000. Sources and transformations of organic matter in surface soils and sediments from a tidal estuary (North Inlet, South Carolina, USA). *Estuar. Coasts* 23:548–64.

Goranson CE, Ho C-K, Pennings SC. 2004. Environmental gradients and herbivore feeding preferences in coastal salt marshes. *Oecologia* 140:591–600.

Graça MA, Newell SY, Kneib RT. 2000. Grazing rates of organic matter and living fungal biomass of decaying *Spartina alterniflora* by three species of salt-marsh invertebrates. *Mar. Biol.* 136:281–89.

Gribsholt B, Kostka JE, Kristensen E. 2003. Impact of fiddler crabs and plant roots on sediment biogeochemistry in a Georgia saltmarsh. *Mar. Ecol. Prog. Ser.* 259:237–51.

Griffin, J, Silliman BR. 2011. Predator diversity stabilizes and strengthens trophic control of a keystone grazer. *Biol. Letters* 7:79–82.

Grosholz ED, Levin LA, et al. 2009. Changes in community structure and ecosystem function following *Spartina alterniflora* invasion of Pacific estuaries. In *Human impacts on salt marshes: a global perspective,* Silliman BR, Grosholz ED, Bertness MD, editors. Berkeley: Univ. Calif. Press, pp. 23–40.

Haines E, Chalmers A, et al. 1977. Nitrogen pools and fluxes in a Georgia salt marsh. In *Estuarine processes,* vol. 2: *Circulation, sediments, and transfer of material in the estuary,* Wiley M, editor. New York: Academic Press, pp. 241–54.

Haines EB, Montague CL. 1979. Food sources of estuarine invertebrates analyzed using $^{13}C/^{12}C$ ratios. *Ecology* 60:48–56.

Hayden BP, Hayden NR. 2003. Decadal and century-long changes in storminess at long-term ecological research sites. In *Climate variability and ecosystem response at long-term ecological research sites,* Greenland D, Goodin DG, Smith RC, editors. New York: Oxford Univ. Press, pp. 262–85.

Hayes M. 1994. Georgia Bight. In *Barrier Islands,* RA Davis Jr., editor. New York: Springer-Verlag, pp. 233–304.

Higinbotham CB, Alber M, Chalmers AG. 2004. Analysis of tidal marsh vegetation patterns in two Georgia estuaries using aerial photography and GIS. *Estuaries* 27:670–83.

Ho C-K, Pennings SC. 2008. Consequences of omnivory for trophic interactions on a salt marsh shrub. *Ecology* 89:1714–22.

Ho, CK, Pennings SC, Carefoot TH. 2010. Is diet quality an overlooked mechanism for Bergmann's Rule? *Am. Nat.* 175:269–76.

Hopkinson CS. 1985. Shallow-water benthic and pelagic metabolism: evidence of heterotrophy in the nearshore Georgia Bight. *Mar. Biol.* 87:19–32.

Hopkinson CS. 1988. Patterns of organic carbon exchange between coastal ecosystems: the mass balance approach in salt marsh ecosystems. In *Coastal-offshore ecosystem interactions,* Jansson B-O, editor. Berlin: Springer-Verlag, pp. 122–54.

Hopkinson CS, Hoffman FA. 1984. The estuary extended—a recipient-system study of estuarine outwelling in Georgia. In *The estuary as a filter,* VS Kennedy, editor. New York: Academic Press, pp. 313–30.

Hopkinson CS, Lugo AE, et al. 2008. Forecasting effects of sealevel rise and windstorms on coastal and inland ecosystems. *Front. Ecol. Env.* 6:255–63.

Huang H, Chen C, et al. 2008. A numerical study of tidal asymmetry in Okatee Creek, South Carolina. *Estuar. Coast. Shelf Sci.* 78:190–202.

Hughes ZJ, FitzGerald DM, et al. 2009. Rapid headward erosion of marsh creeks in response to relative sea level rise. *Geophys. Res. Lett.* 36, L03602, doi:10.1029/2008GL036000.

Jackson JB, Kirby MX, et al. 2001. Historical overfishing and the recent collapse of coastal ecosystems. *Science* 293:629–37.

Kennedy VC. 1964. Sediment transported by Georgia streams. USGS Water-Supply Paper 1668.

Kirwan ML, Guntenspergen GR, Morris JT. 2009. Latitudinal trends in *Spartina alterniflora* productivity and the response of coastal marshes to global change. *Glob. Chang. Biol.* 15:1982–89.

Kneib RT. 1986. The role of *Fundulus heteroclitus* in salt marsh trophic dynamics. *Am. Zool.* 26:259–69.

Kneib RT. 1997. The role of tidal marshes in the ecology of estuarine nekton. *Oceanogr. Mar. Biol. Ann. Rev.* 35:163–220.

KneibRT, Newell SY, Hermeno ET. 1997. Survival, growth and reproduction of the salt-marsh amphipod *Uhlorchestia spartinophila* reared on natural diets of senescent and dead *Spartina alterniflora* leaves. *Mar. Biol.* 128:423–31.

Kostka JE, Gribsholt B, et al. 2002. The rates and pathways of carbon oxidation in bioturbated saltmarsh sediments. *Limnol. Oceanogr.* 47:230–40.

Kraeuter JN. 1976. Biodeposition by salt-marsh invertebrates. *Mar. Biol.* 35:215–23.

Krest JM, Moore WS, et al. 2000. Marsh nutrient export supplied by groundwater discharge: evidence from radium measurements. *Glob. Biogeochem. Cycles* 14:167–76.

Kuenzler EJ. 1961. Structure and energy flow of a mussel population in a Georgia salt marsh. *Limnol. Oceanogr.* 6:191–204.

Landmeyer JE, Stone PA. 1995. Radiocarbon and δ^{13}C values related to ground-water recharge and mixing. *Ground Water* 33:227–34.

Lasher C, Dyszynski G, et al. 2009. The diverse bacterial community in intertidal, anaerobic sediments at Sapelo Island, Georgia. *Microb. Ecol.* 58:244–61.

Lee S, Silliman B. 2006. Competitive displacement of a detritivorous salt marsh snail. *J. Exp. Mar. Biol. Ecol.* 339:75–85.

Lin J. 1989. Influence of location in a salt marsh on survivorship of ribbed mussels. *Mar. Ecol. Prog. Ser.* 56:105–10.

Loomis MJ, Craft CB. 2010. Carbon sequestration and nutrient (nitrogen, phosphorus) accumulation in river-dominated tidal marshes, Georgia, USA. *Soil Sci. Soc. Am. J.* 74:1028–36.

Lyons JI, Alber M, Hollibaugh JT. 2009. Ascomycete fungal communities associated with early decay leaf blades of three *Spartina* species and a *Spartina* hybrid in the San Francisco Bay. *Oecologia* 162:435–42.

Mallinson D, Burdette K, et al. 2008. Optically stimulated luminescence age controls on late Pleistocene and Holocene coastal lithosomes. North Carolina, USA. *Quaternary Res.* 69:97–109.

Marczak LB, Ho C-K, et al. 2010. Latitudinal variation in topdown and bottom-up control of a salt marsh food web. *Ecology* 92:276–81.

McKay P, Di Iorio D. 2010. Cycle of vertical and horizontal mixing in a shallow tidal creek. *J. Geophys. Res.* 115, C01004, doi:10.1029/2008JC005204.

McKee KL, Mendelssohn IA, Materne MD. 2004. Acute salt marsh dieback in the Mississippi River deltaic plain: a drought induced phenomenon? *Glob. Ecol. Biogeogr.* 13:65–73.

Meade RH. 1982. Sources, sinks, and storage of river sediment in the Atlantic drainage of the United States. *J. Geol.* 90:235–52.

Milliman JD, Pilkey OH, Ross DA. 1972. Sediments of the continental margin of the eastern United States. *Geol. Soc. Am. Bull.* 83:1315–34.

Montague CL. 1982. The influence of fiddler crab burrows and burrowing on metabolic processes in salt marsh sediments. In *Estuarine comparisons,* VS Kennedy, editor. New York: Academic Press, pp. 283–301.

Moon DC, Rossi AM, Stiling P. 2000. The effects of abiotically induced changes in host plant quality (and morphology) on a salt marsh planthopper and its parasitoid. *Ecol. Ent.* 25:325–31.

Moon DC, Stiling P. 2002a. The effects of salinity and nutrients on a tritrophic salt-marsh system. *Ecology* 83:2465–76.

Moon DC, Stiling P. 2002b. Top-down, bottom-up, or side to side? Within-trophic-level interactions modify trophic dynamics of a salt marsh herbivore. *Oikos* 98:480–90.

Moon DC, Stiling P. 2004. The influence of a salinity and nutrient gradient on coastal vs. upland tritrophic complexes. *Ecology* 85:2709–16.

Moore WS. 1999. The subterranean estuary: a reaction zone of ground water and sea water. *Mar. Chem.* 65:111–25.

Moore WS, Blanton JO, Joye S. 2006. Estimates of flushing times, submarine groundwater discharge, and nutrient fluxes to Okatee River, South Carolina. *J. Geophys. Res.* 111, doi:10.1029/2005JC003041.

Moore WS, Krest J, et al. 2002. Thermal evidence of water exchange through a coastal aquifer: implications for nutrient fluxes. *Geophys. Res. Lett.* 29:1–49.

Morris JT, Sundareshwar PV, et al. 2002. Responses of coastal wetlands to rising sea level. *Ecology* 83:2869–77.

Mulholland PJ, Kuenzler EJ. 1979. Organic carbon export from upland and forested wetland watersheds. *Limnol. Oceanogr.* 24:960–66.

Myers RA, Baum JK, Shepherd TD, et al. 2007. Cascading effects of the loss of apex predatory sharks from a coastal ocean. *Science* 315:1846–50.

Neubauer SC, Givler K, et al. 2005. Seasonal patterns and plantmediated controls of subsurface wetland biogeochemistry. *Ecology* 86:3334–44.

Neubauer SC, Miller WD, Anderson IC. 2000. Carbon cycling in a tidal freshwater marsh ecosystem: a carbon gas flux study. *Mar. Ecol. Prog. Ser.* 199:13–31.

Newell SY. 1993. Decomposition of shoots of a salt-marsh grass: methodology and dynamics of microbial assemblages. *Adv. Microb. Ecol.* 13:301–26.

Newell SY. 2001. Spore-expulsion rates and extents of blade occupation by ascomycetes of the smooth-cordgrass standing-decay system. *Bot. Mar.* 44:277–85.

Newell SY. 2003. Fungal content and activities in standing-decaying leaf blades of plants of the Georgia Coastal Ecosystems research area. *Aquat. Microb. Ecol.* 32:95–103.

Newell SY, Blum LK, et al. 2000. Autumnal biomass and potential productivity of salt marsh fungi from 29 to 43 north latitude along the United States Atlantic coast. *Appl. Env. Microbiol.* 66:180–85.

Newell SY, Krambeck C. 1995. Responses of bacterioplankton to tidal inundations of a saltmarsh in a flume and adjacent mussel enclosures. *J. Exp. Mar. Biol. Ecol.* 190:79–95.

Newell SY, Porter D. 2000. Microbial secondary production from saltmarsh-grass shoots, and its known and potential fates. In *Concepts and controversies in tidal marsh ecology,* Weinstein MP, Kreeger DA, editors. Dordrecht: Kluwer, pp. 159–85.

Nixon SW. 1980. Between coastal marshes and coastal waters: a review of twenty years of speculation and research on the role of salt marshes in estuarine productivity and water chemistry. In *Estuarine and wetland processes with emphasis on modeling,* Hamilton P, McDonald KB, editors. New York: Plenum, pp. 437–525.

Nyman JA, Crozier CR, DeLaune RD. 1995. Roles and patterns of hurricane sedimentation in an estuarine marsh landscape. *Estuar. Coast. Shelf Sci.* 40:665–79.

Odum EP. 1961. The role of tidal marshes in estuarine production. In *The Conservationist.* Albany: NY State Conservation Department, pp. 12–15.

Odum EP. 1968. A research challenge: evaluating the productivity of coastal and estuarine water. In *Proceedings of the Second Sea Grant Conference.* Kingston: Univ. RI.

Ogburn MB, Alber M. 2006. An investigation of salt marsh dieback in Georgia using field transplants. *Estuar. Coasts* 29:54–62.

Osgood DT, Silliman BR. 2009. From climate change to snails: potential causes of salt marsh dieback along the U.S. eastern seaboard and Gulf coasts. In *Human impacts on salt marshes: a global perspective,* Silliman BR, Grosholz ED, Bertness MD, editors. Berkeley: Univ. Calif. Press, pp. 231–54.

Paerl HW, Bales JD, et al. 2001. Ecosystem impacts of three sequential hurricanes (Dennis, Floyd, and Irene) on the United States' largest lagoonal estuary, Pamlico Sound, NC. *Proc. Natl. Acad. Sci. USA* 98:5655–60.

Paludan C, Morris JT. 1999. Distribution and speciation of phosphorus along a salinity gradient in intertidal marsh sediments. *Biogeochem.* 45:197–221.

Pearlstine LG, Kitchens WM, et al. 1993. Tide gate influences on a tidal marsh. *Water Res. Bull.* 29:1009–19.

Pelc RA, Warner RR, Gaines SD. 2009. Geographical patterns of genetic structure in marine species with contrasting life histories. *J. Biogeogr.* 36:1881–90.

Pennings SC, Bertness MD. 1999. Using latitudinal variation to examine effects of climate on coastal salt marsh pattern and process. *Curr. Top. Wetl. Biogeochem.* 3:100–11.

Pennings SC, Grant M-B, Bertness MD. 2005. Plant zonation in low-latitude salt marshes: disentangling the roles of flooding, salinity and competition. *J. Ecol.* 93:159–67.

Pennings SC, Ho C-K, et al. 2009. Latitudinal variation in herbivore pressure in Atlantic coast salt marshes. *Ecology* 90:183–95.

Pennings SC, Moore DJ. 2001. Zonation of shrubs in western Atlantic salt marshes. *Oecologia* 126:587–94.

Pennings SC, Richards CL. 1998. Effects of wrack burial in salt-stressed habitats: *Batis maritima* in a southwest Atlantic salt marsh. *Ecography* 21:630–38.

Pennings SC, Selig ER, et al. 2003. Geographic variation in positive and negative interactions among salt marsh plants. *Ecology* 84:1527–38.

Pennings SC, Silliman BR. 2005. Linking biogeography and community ecology: latitudinal variation in plant-herbivore interaction strength. *Ecology* 86:2310–19.

Pennings SC, Stanton LE, Brewer JS. 2002. Nutrient effects on the composition of salt marsh plant communities along the southern Atlantic and Gulf coasts of the United States. *Estuaries* 25:1164–73.

Pfeiffer WJ, Wiegert RG. 1981. Grazers on *Spartina* and their predators. In *The ecology of a salt marsh,* Pomeroy LR, Wiegert RG, editors. New York: Springer-Verlag, pp. 87–112.

Pinckney J, Zingmark R. 1993a. Biomass and production of benthic microalgal communities in five typical estuarine environments. *Estuaries* 16:887–97.

Pinckney J, Zingmark R. 1993b. Modelling intertidal benthic microalgal annual production in estuarine ecosystems. *J. Phycol.* 29:396–407.

Pomeroy LR, Wiegert RG, editors. 1981. *The ecology of a salt marsh.* New York: Springer-Verlag.

Porubsky WP, Velasquez L, Joye SB. 2008. Nutrient-replete benthic microalgae as a source of dissolved organic carbon to coastal waters. *Estuar. Coasts* 31:860–76.

Roy K, Jablonski D, et al. 1998. Marine latitudinal diversity gradients: tests of causal hypotheses. *Proc. Natl. Acad. Sci. USA* 95:3699–702.

Schaefer SC, Alber M. 2007a. Temperature controls a latitudinal gradient in the proportion of watershed nitrogen exported to coastal ecosystems. *Biogeochem.* 85:333–46.

Schaefer SC, Alber M. 2007b. Temporal and spatial trends in nitrogen and phosphorus inputs to the watershed of the Altamaha River, Georgia, USA. *Biogeochem.* 86:231–49.

Schelske CL, Odum EP. 1962. Mechanisms maintaining high productivity in Georgia estuaries. *Proc. Gulf and Caribbean Fish. Inst.* 14:75–80.

Schwartz FJ. 1989. Zoogeography and ecology of fishes inhabiting North Carolina's marine waters to depths of 600 meters. In *North Carolina coastal oceanography symposium,* George RY, Hulbert AW, editors. Rockville, MD: NOAA, pp. 335–74.

Sharma P, Gardner LR, et al. 1987. Sedimentation and bioturbation in a salt marsh as revealed by ^{210}Pb, ^{137}Cs and ^{7}Be studies. *Limnol. Oceanogr.* 32:313–26.

Sheldon JE, Alber M. 2002. A comparison of residence time calculations using simple compartment models of the Altamaha River Estuary, Georgia. *Estuaries* 25:1304–17.

Silliman BR, Bertness MD. 2002. A trophic cascade regulates salt marsh primary production. *Proc. Natl. Acad. Sci. USA* 99:10500–505.

Silliman BR, Layman CA, et al. 2004. Predation by the black-clawed mud crab, *Panopeus herbstii,* in mid-Atlantic salt marshes: further evidence for top-down control of marsh grass production. *Estuaries* 27:188–96.

Silliman BR, Newell SY. 2003. Fungal farming in a snail. *Proc. Natl. Acad. Sci. USA* 100:15643–48.

Silliman BR, van de Koppel J, et al. 2005. Drought, snails, and large-scale die-off of southern U.S. salt marshes. *Science* 310:1803–06.

Silliman BR, Zieman JC. 2001. Top-down control of *Spartina alterniflora* by periwinkle grazing in a Virginia salt marsh. *Ecology* 82:2830–45.

Siska EL, Pennings SC, et al. 2002. Latitudinal variation in palatability of salt-marsh plants: which traits are responsible? *Ecology* 83:3369–81.

Smalley AE. 1960. Energy flow of a salt marsh grasshopper population. *Ecology* 41:672–77.

Smith JM, Frey RW. 1985. Biodeposition by the ribbed mussel *Geukensia demissa* in a salt marsh, Sapelo Island, Georgia. *J. Sed. Res.* 55:817–28.

Soulé PT. 1998. Some spatial aspects of southeastern United States climatology. *J. Geogr.* 97:142–50.

Stahle DW, Cleaveland MK. 1992. Reconstruction and analysis of spring rainfall over the southeastern U.S. for the past 1000 years. *Bull. Am. Meteorol. Soc.* 73:1947–61.

Stiling P, Bowdish TI. 2000. Direct and indirect effects of plant clone and local environment on herbivore abundance. *Ecology* 81:281–85.

Stiling P, Moon D. 2005. Are trophodynamic models worth their salt? Top-down and bottom-up effects along a salinity gradient. *Ecology* 86:1730–36.

Stiling PD, Strong DR. 1984. Weak competition among *Spartina* stem borers, by means of murder. *Ecology* 64:770–78.

Stiven AE, Gardner SA. 1992. Population processes in the ribbed mussel *Geukensia demissa* (Dillwyn) in a North Carolina salt marsh tidal gradient: spatial pattern, predation, growth and mortality. *J. Exp. Mar. Biol. Ecol.* 160:81–102.

Sullivan B. 2001. *Early days on the Georgia tidewater: the story of McIntosh County and Sapelo,* 6th ed. Darien, GA: Darien Printing.

Sullivan MJ, Currin CA. 2000. Community structure and functional dynamics of benthic microalgae in salt marshes. In *Concepts and controversies in tidal marsh ecology,* Weinstein MP, Kreeger DA, editors. Dordrecht: Kluwer, pp. 81–106.

Sundareshwar PV, Morris JT, et al. 2003. Phosphorus limitation of coastal ecosystem processes. *Science* 299:563–65.

Teal JM. 1962. Energy flow in the salt marsh ecosystem of Georgia. *Ecology* 43:614–24.

Thomas DH. 2008. *Native American landscapes of St. Catherines Island, Georgia.* American Museum of Natural History, Anthropological Papers, no. 88, 1–1136.

Thompson VD. 2007. Articulating activity areas and formation processes at the Sapelo Island shell ring complex. *Southeast. Archaeol.* 26:91–107.

Thompson V, Turck JA. 2009. Adaptive cycles of coastal hunter-gatherers. *Am. Antiq.* 74:255–78.

Tobias C, Neubauer SC. 2009. Salt marsh biogeochemistry—an overview. In *Coastal wetlands: an integrated ecosystem approach,* Perillo GME, Wolanski E, et al., editors. Amsterdam: Elsevier, pp. 445–92.

Trimble SW. 1974. Man-induced soil erosion on the southern Piedmont, 1700–1970. Ankeny, IA: Soil Conserv. Soc. Am.

Turner RE. 1976. Geographic variations in salt marsh macrophyte production: a review. *Contrib. Mar. Sci.* 20:47–68.

Tyler AC, Mastronicola TA, McGlathery KJ. 2003. Nitrogen fixation and nitrogen limitation of primary production along a natural marsh chronosequence. *Oecologia* 136:431–38.

Tyler AC, McGlathery KJ, Anderson IC. 2003. Benthic algae control sediment-water column fluxes of organic and inorganic nitrogen compounds in a temperate lagoon. *Limnol. Oceanogr.* 48:2125–37.

U.S. Census Bureau. 2000. *Population projections for South Carolina.* Washington, DC.

Verity PG, Alber M, Bricker SB. 2006. Development of hypoxia in well-mixed estuaries. *Estuar. Coasts* 29:665–73.

Vogel RL, Kjerfve B, Gardner LR. 1996. Inorganic sediment budget for the North Inlet salt marsh, South Carolina, U.S.A. *Mangroves & Salt Marshes* 1:23–35.

Wang AZ, Cai W-J, et al. 2005. The southeastern continental shelf of the United States as an atmospheric CO_2 source and an exporter of inorganic carbon to the ocean. *Cont. Shelf Res.* 25:1917–41.

Wason EL, Pennings SC. 2008. Grasshopper (Orthoptera: Tettigoniidae) species composition and size across latitude in Atlantic coast salt marshes. *Estuar. Coasts* 31:335–43.

Weston NB, Dixon RE, Joye SB. 2006. Ramifications of increased salinity in tidal freshwater sediments: geochemistry and microbial pathways of organic matter mineralization. *J. Geophys. Res., Biogeosci.* 111, G01009, doi:10.1029/2005JG000071.

Weston NB, Hollibaugh J, et al. 2003. Nutrients and dissolved organic matter in the Altamaha River and loading to the coastal zone. In *Proc. 2003 Ga. Water Resource Conf.,* Hatcher KJ, editor. Athens: Univ. Georgia.

Weston NB, Joye SB. 2005. Temperature-driven decoupling of key phases of organic matter degradation in marine sediments. *Proc. Natl. Acad. Sci. USA* 102:17036–40.

Weston NB, Porubsky WP, et al. 2006. Porewater stoichiometry of terminal metabolic products, sulfate, and dissolved organic carbon and nitrogen in estuarine intertidal creek-bank sediments. *Biogeochem.* 77:375–408.

White SN, Alber M. 2009. Drought-associated shifts in *Spartina alterniflora* and *S. cynosuroides* in the Altamaha River estuary. *Wetlands* 29:215–24.

Wiegert RG, Christian RR, Wetzel RL. 1981. A model view of the marsh. In *The ecology of a salt marsh,* 184–218. Pomeroy LR, Wiegert RG, editors. New York: Springer-Verlag.

Wiegert RG, Freeman BJ. 1990. Tidal salt marshes of the southeast Atlantic coast: a community profile. Biological Report 85 (7.29). Washington, DC: USFWS.

Więski K, Guo H, et al. 2010. Ecosystem functions of tidal fresh, brackish, and salt marshes on the Georgia coast. *Estuar. Coasts* 33:161–69.

Worth JE. 1995. *The struggle for the Georgia coast: an eighteenth-century Spanish retrospective on Guale and Mocama.* Am. Museum Natural Hist., Anthropol. Papers no. 75.

Zimmer M, Pennings SC, et al. 2004. Salt marsh litter and detritivores: a closer look at redundancy. *Estuaries* 27:753–69.

CHAPTER 5

Mississippi River Delta Wetlands

JENNEKE M. VISSER, JOHN W. DAY, JR., LORETTA L. BATTAGLIA,
GARY P. SHAFFER, and MARK W. HESTER

Coastal wetlands of the Mississippi River Delta consist of two physiographic units: the Deltaic Plain to the east and the Chenier Plain to the west (Roberts 1997). Chapter 5 focuses on the Deltaic Plain. The Chenier Plain marshes are described in chapter 6. During the 20th century, a massive loss of coastal wetlands (Barras, Bernier, et al. 2008), mostly marshes, occurred in this area. Most research has focused on marsh loss (i.e., Day, Schaffer, et al. 2000; Day, Boesch, et al. 2007), but recently more attention has been given to the issue of coastal forested wetland loss (Conner and Tolliver 1990; Chambers, Conner, et al. 2005; Chambers, Fisher, et al. 2007; Shaffer, Wood, et al. 2009). At present, there are plans for a large-scale effort to restore the delta, including its forested wetlands. To do this, it is necessary to understand both the processes that formed the delta and the forces that led to its deterioration.

The delta is generally divided into areas of growth (active delta lobes) and areas of deterioration (abandoned lobes) that represent different stages of the transgressive phase of the delta cycle (Penland, Boyd, et al. 1988). The abandoned lobes are characterized by a series of vegetation zones, first described by Penfound and Hathaway (1938), that run roughly parallel to the coast and have different salinity, hydrology, and soil conditions (Table 5.1, Fig. 5.1). These vegetation zones range from saline marshes along the coast to tidal freshwater forested wetlands in the upper parts of the basins.

Geology

Development of the Missisissippi Delta

The Mississippi Delta formed over the past 6,000 to 7,000 years as a series of overlapping delta lobes (Roberts 1997) as sea level stabilized near its present level after rising more than 100 m from the low reached at the height of the last glacial period, about 15,000 years ago. Areas of the Delta that receive river water and associated sediments (active lobes) increased wetland extents, while areas where river input ceased as the river switched to other channels (abandoned lobes) decreased in wetland extent. Overall there was a net increase in the area of wetlands over the past several thousand years, until the 20th century.

A number of factors served to enhance the growth of the delta and retard its deterioration. With the exception of the first delta lobe, significant parts of all subsequent lobes have been incorporated into the current delta as a system of overlapping and interwoven distributary systems (Gosselink, Coleman, et al. 1998). Functioning distributaries, overbank flooding, crevasse splays (i.e., breaks in a natural levee that form smaller delta splays inland from the mouth of the river), and reworking of sands formed a skeletal framework of natural levee ridges and barrier islands within which the delta formed (Kesel 1989; Kesel, Yodis, et al. 1992). The distributary network was very efficient in sediment retention, and about 25% of sediment flux was retained in the delta (Kesel, Yodis, et al. 1992; Törnqvist, Paola, et al. 2007). Riverine input is important to deltaic wetlands for several reasons. Freshwater input provides a buffer against saltwater intrusion, nutrients increase productivity, mineral sediments strengthen soils and help build up the elevation of the land. Under anaerobic conditions, sulfate-reducing bacteria can generate hydrogen sulfide, which is soluble in water and toxic to plants. Minerals in the river water, such as iron, can react with sulfide, making insoluble metal sulfides, which are not toxic. The input of materials to deltas, which is so important to their survival, is not constant over time but occurs in hierarchical pulses that produce both benefits and negative impacts that vary spatially and temporally (Table 5.2). These pulsing events range from daily tides to switching of river channels, which occur at intervals from hundreds to greater than 1,000 years and include crevasses; regular storms such as those associated with frontal passages; annual river floods; strong storms such as hurricanes; and great river floods.

Delta Deterioration

Over the past half century there has been an enormous loss of coastal wetlands in the delta, with a total loss of about 2,551 km² between 1956 and 2006 (Barras, Bernier, et al. 2008). The current loss rate for the delta is between 38.9 ± 5.6 km² y⁻¹ (Barras, Bernier, et al. 2008). Understanding the causes of this loss is important not only for a scientific appreciation of the mech-

TABLE 5.1

Habitat type	Present area[a] (ha)	Soil salinity[b] (ppt)	Soil bulk sensity[c] (g cm^{-3})	Soil organic matter[d] (%)
Deltaic marsh	95,862	1.7	1.10	11
Forested wetlands	140,000		0.21	23
Fresh marsh	210,538	1.2	0.09	67
Oligohaline marsh	139,819	4.1	0.08	60
Mesohaline marsh	169,293	7.4	0.14	37
Saline marsh	248,188	10.5	0.29	19

[a] Marsh based on Sasser, Visser, et al. (2008); forested wetlands from Conner and Tolliver (1990).
[b] From Chabreck 1972.
[c] Marsh from Hatton, DeLaune, and Patrick (1983); forested wetlands from Myers, Shaffer, and Llewellyn (1995); deltaic marsh from Faulkner and Poach (1996).
[d] Deltaic marsh from Johnson, Sasser, and Gosselink (1995); forested wetlands from Myers, Shaffer, and Llewellyn (1995); other marshes from Chabreck (1972).

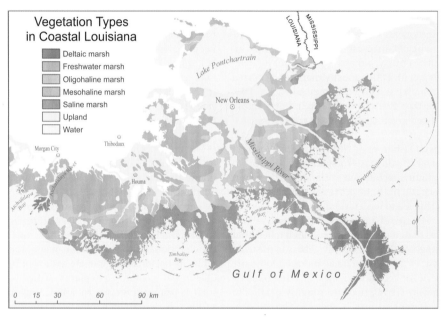

FIG. 5.1. Distribution of marsh types over the deltaic plain. (Adapted from Sasser, Visser, et al. 2008.)

anisms involved, but also so that effective management plans can be developed to restore the Mississippi Delta (see Boesch, Josselyn, et al. 1994; Boesch, Shabman, et al. 2006; Day, Schaffer, et al. 2000; Day, Boesch, et al. 2007; Shaffer, Hoeppner, et al. 2005; Törnqvist, Paola, et al. 2007; and Galloway, Boesch, et al. 2009 for reviews of these issues).

Erosion along large water bodies and along the Gulf of Mexico accounts for approximately 30% of the loss (Penland, Wayne, et al. 2000). Most (57%) of the wetland loss is due to elevation deficits (Penland, Wayne, et al. 2000). Wetlands in the area experience relative sea-level rise (RSLR), a combination of subsidence plus eustatic sea-level rise (ESLR). Subsidence in the area is driven by many processes that occur at different spatial and temporal scales (Table 5.3). Wetlands must grow vertically at a rate equal to the rate of RSLR if they are to survive in the

long term. If there is an elevation deficit (surface elevation gain < RSLR), the site will become progressively more waterlogged and vegetation will become stressed and eventually die (Mendelssohn and Morris 2000). The elevation deficit is increasing as sediment delivery to the delta has decreased due to:

- a reduction of the suspended sediment load in the Mississippi River caused by dam construction upstream (Kesel 1988, 1989). The suspended sediment load carried by the Mississippi River has decreased by about half since 1700 (Meade 1995). The greatest decrease occurred after 1950 with the completion of large dams on the Missouri River and its tributaries.
- flood-control levees along the Mississippi River, resulting in the elimination of riverine input to most

TABLE 5.2
A hierarchy of forcing or pulsing events affecting the
formation and sustainability of deltas

Event	Time scale	Effect
Major changes in river channels	500–1,000 years	New delta lobe formation Major deposition
Major river floods	50–100 years	Channel switching Major deposition
Major storms	5–20 years	Major deposition Enhanced production Erosion
Average river floods	Annual	Enhanced deposition Freshening (lower salinity) Nutrient input Enhanced 1° and 2° production
Normal storm events (frontal passage)	Weekly	Enhanced deposition Organism transport Net transport Erosion
Tides	Daily	Drainage/marsh production Low net transport

NOTE: After Day, Martin, et al. 1997.

TABLE 5.3
Processes affecting subsidence in the Mississippi River Delta

Process	Subsidence (mm/year)	Time scale	Area affected
Tectonic faulting	15–20 0.14–0.18	Decade Millennia	Coastal region
Fluid withdrawal	8–12	Decade	Local
Sediment loading	1–8	Century	Holocene Delta
Holocene sediment compaction	1–5	Century	Holocene Delta
Glacial isostatic adjustment	0.6–2	Millennia	Gulf Region

NOTE: After Yuill, Lavoie, and Feed 2009

of the delta (Boesch, Josselyn, et al. 1994; Day, Schaffer, et al. 2000; Day, Boesch, et al. 2007). Most active distributaries were closed. Crevasses have been mostly eliminated, and the river mouth was made more efficient for navigation. This has resulted in the loss of river sediments directly to deep waters of the Gulf of Mexico.

Within the delta, pervasive altered wetland hydrology, mostly caused by canals and navigation channels, is another important factor contributing to wetland loss. Drilling access canals, pipeline canals, and deep-draft navigation channels have left a dense network of about 15,000 km of canals in the coastal wetlands of Louisiana. Although canals are estimated to compose about 15% of the direct loss, their indirect destructive impact has been much greater (Turner, Costanza,

et al. 1982; Turner 1997; Day, Shaffer, et al. 2000). Spoil banks, composed of the material dredged from the canals, interrupt sheet flow, impound water, and cause deterioration of wetlands (Shirley and Battaglia 2006, 2008). Long, deep navigation channels that connect saline and freshwater areas tend to lessen freshwater retention time and allow greater inland penetration of saltwater (Shaffer, Day, et al. 2009).

In summary, there is a broad consensus that wetland loss is a complex interaction of a number of factors acting at different spatial and temporal scales (e.g., Day and Templet 1989; Boesch, Josselyn, et al. 1994; Day, Pont, et al. 1995; Day, Martin, et al. 1997). Day, Shaffer, et al. (2000) and Day, Boesch, et al. (2007) conclude that isolation of the delta from the Mississippi River by levees is perhaps the most important factor for the delta as a whole.

Hydrology and Soils

Deltaic Marshes

Areas with active river inputs of sediment and water include the active delta at the mouth of the Mississippi River and the Atchafalaya Delta complex in Atchafalaya Bay. These areas are highly influenced by the physical forcing of annual floods. The approximately 500-year-old Balize Delta (at the Mississippi River mouth) appears to have reached its maximum expansion and is starting to decline in wetland area (Gosselink, Coleman, et al. 1998). In contrast, the Atchafalaya Delta complex is less than 100 years old and continues to expand, especially during high river discharge years. Soils of the recently colonized mudflats are highly mineral, with little organic matter (Table 5.1), and the most recent splays have very little organic matter (0.5%; Johnson, Sasser, et al. 1985).

The hydrology of the active delta is in large part driven by the seasonal changes in discharge from the Mississippi and Atchafalaya rivers. The highest discharges usually occur from late winter to early spring, and low flows generally occur during September and October (Holm and Sasser 2001). Salinity incursions can occur during the low-discharge months and are generally associated with tropic disturbances and the passage of cold fronts (Holm and Sasser 2001).

Saline Marshes and Mangroves

Tides in the Gulf of Mexico have an astronomical range of approximately 0.5 m, are of the diurnal type, and are affected by biweekly and seasonal cycles. Seasonal water levels have a bimodal distribution; lowest water levels occur in January and February; water rises to a first peak in May and June, declines in July, and then rises to the highest levels in September and October (Swenson and Swarzenski 1995). Frontal passages can significantly affect water movement (1 m range) and explain water-level variations approximately one-third of the time (Swenson and Swarzenski 1995). Areas dominated by *Spartina alterniflora* or *Juncus roemerianus* on average have more frequent flooding events (190 events y⁻¹) and a longer duration (50% of the year) than areas with *Distichlis spicata* (140 events y⁻¹, 40% of the year) (Sasser 1977). Sites dominated by *Avicennia germinans* are slightly less frequently flooded than *Spartina alterniflora* sites (Patterson, Mendelssohn, et al. 1993).

Salinity fluctuates seasonally and follows the water-level pattern (Swenson and Swarzenski 1995). Salinity in coastal Louisiana is influenced by the freshwater discharge of the Mississippi River, with higher salinity associated with lower river discharges (Wiseman, Swenson, et al. 1990). Over an 18-year period, salinity at the coast fluctuated between 2 and 34 ppt and averaged around 19 ppt (Visser, Sasser, et al. 2006).

Saline wetland soils have a high mineral content, with soil density ranging from 0.14 to 0.49 g cm⁻³ (DeLaune, Buresh, et al. 1979; Patterson and Mendelssohn 1991; DeLaune, Devai, et al. 2002) and low organic matter (averaging between 10 and 25%; Chabreck 1972; DeLaune, Devai, et al. 2002). Mangroves tend to occur in areas at the higher end of the bulk density range along creekbanks and tend to have higher soil salinities than adjacent herbaceous salt marshes (Patterson and Mendelssohn 1991). The high mineral content of saline marsh soils is partially due to deposition of sediments from adjacent bays during the regular tides as well as during high-energy events such as cold front passages and tropical storms (Reed, Peter-

son, et al. 2006; Turner, Milan, et al. 2006; Nyman, Walters, et al. 2006). The low organic matter content may be related to increased decomposition due to high sulfate availability (DeLaune, Devai, et al. 2002), as well as the high export of dead aboveground material by the tides.

Mesohaline Marshes

Mesohaline marshes tend to be flooded less frequently than saline marshes (Sasser 1977; Childers and Day 1990), explaining the dominance of *Spartina patens*, which has relatively low flood tolerance (Broome, Mendelssohn, et al. 1995; Lessmann, Mendelssohn, et al. 1997; Spalding and Hester 2007; Visser and Sandy 2009). Mesohaline marsh soils have characteristics that are intermediate between saline and fresh marsh soils (Table 5.1) and reflect the general trend of increasing organic matter in the soil with distance from the coast (Palmisano 1970; Hatton, DeLaune, et al. 1983).

Fresh and Oligohaline Marshes

Fresh and oligohaline marshes develop after the initial delta prograding and natural levee formation along the major distributary channels limits the input to the oldest part of the prograding delta (Frazier 1967; Gosselink, Coleman, et al. 1998). As these marshes become hydrologically separated from the river, soil formation becomes more and more driven by organic matter from plants. Therefore, fresh and oligohaline marshes outside the active delta have highly organic soils averaging 67% organic matter (Chabreck 1972). Approximately 75% of these marshes are floating marshes (Evers, Holm, et al. 1996). Floating marsh soils consist of an organic mat made from mostly living roots and rhizomes interspersed with more or less decomposed organic matter derived from dead plants (Sasser, Gosselink, et al. 1995; Sasser, Gosselink, et al. 1996). These floating mats move up and down with changing water levels and therefore have limited natural sedimentation, and most sediment deposited moves through the mat (Sasser, Visser, et al. 1995; Carpenter, Sasser, et al. 2007). As a result, floating marshes have peat soils (> 65% organic matter) and very low mineral density, resulting in very low bulk density (< 0.08 g cm⁻³) (Hatton, DeLaune, et al. 1983; Sasser, Gosselink, et al. 1995; Sasser, Gosselink, et al. 1996). Floating marshes have variable mat thicknesses. Some are thick (approximately 30 cm) and strong (with thick rhizomes) enough to support the weight of a human, while others have thin root-mats (approximately 10 cm) that can support the weight of smaller animals (Sasser, Gosselink, et al. 1995). Attached fresh and oligohaline marshes have slightly higher bulk density (0.1–0.2 g cm⁻³) and lower organic matter content (40–60%), especially when receiving some sediment input (Holm, Sasser, et al. 2000; DeLaune, Jugsujinda, et al. 2003). In floating marshes, nutrient availability is related to the movement of water in the mat and may be driven by evaporation, precipitation, and runoff from adjacent uplands (Sasser, Gosselink, et al. 1991; Visser and Sasser 2009).

Fresh and oligohaline marshes are located near the upper extent of tidal influence, and water fluctuation due to tides is very small (~5 cm); wind-driven and seasonal water level fluctuation, however, can be as high as 80 cm (Sasser, Gosselink, et al. 1995; Swenson and Swarzenski 1995). Due to the driving forces of water-level fluctuation, flooding duration in attached fresh and oligohaline marshes tends to be on the order of weeks and sometimes months (Swarzenski 1992).

Salinity in the fresh marshes is generally low and rarely exceeds 2 ppt (Swenson and Swarzenski 1995). Salinity in oligohaline marshes is also low on average, but these marshes receive regular incursions of higher-salinity water during wind events (tropical and winter storms) that push saline water inland (Swenson and Swarzenski 1995). These salinity pulses regularly exceed 10 ppt. As a result, oligohaline marshes have soil salinities that average between 2 and 5 ppt (Swenson and Swarzenski 1995).

Forested Wetlands

Forested wetlands are located adjacent to the interdistributary ridges and historically received sediment input from flooding during high river stages. Currently, sediment input in these systems is limited and restricted to flooding events associated with storms. Forested wetland soils are lower in organic matter and have a higher bulk density than freshwater marshes (Table 5.1). However, soil profiles show dramatic changes, with lower bulk density and higher organic matter in the top 15 cm of the soil (Rybczyk, Callaway, et al. 1998). Coastal floodplain forests are subject to tidal influence at the seaward edge of their distribution and generally occur no lower than the uppermost landward location of the tidal interface (Doyle, Krauss, et al. 2010). The fluvial and deltaic forces that shaped this wetland ecosystem have created spatiotemporal heterogeneity in habitat across the floodplain. The structure and function of floodplain ecosystems are primarily driven by hydroperiod, which is itself shaped by these processes (Hupp and Osterkamp 1996). Flood pulses provide exchanges of nutrients, water, organic matter, sediments (Junk, Bayley, et al. 1989), and propagules. Although flooding can impose abiotic stresses on floodplain plant species, many of them are highly adapted to and dependent upon these processes and exchange of materials. The timing, periodicity, duration, and extent of flooding influence nutrient cycling (Lockaby and Walbridge 1998), dispersal avenues (Schneider and Sharitz 1988), regeneration opportunities (Sharitz and Mitsch 1993), tree growth (Keeland and Sharitz 1995), and productivity (Conner and Day 1976; Megonigal, Conner, et al. 1997). The flooding that maintains riverfloodplain connectivity is crucial for maintaining a dynamic environmental template that supports high biodiversity and thus the ecological integrity of the wetland ecosystem. Unfortunately, this landscape has a long history of anthropogenic modification that has broken or damaged these ecological connections (Blanton and Marcus 2009). In the modern landscape, the hydrologic regime is highly modified, and many floodplains are isolated from channels.

Plant Communities and Key Ecological Controls

Deltaic Marshes

The vegetation of the two active systems is very different. In the active delta at the Mississippi river mouth, the vegetation on the outer fringe consists of virtually monospecific stands of 4–5-m-tall *Phragmites australis* (White, Hauber, et al. 2004). These areas are dominated by the Eurasian strain of *P. australis* that is likely to have been introduced to Louisiana ship packing materials or ballast, perhaps as early as the late 19th century (Howard, Travis, et al. 2008). In contrast, most of the *P. australis* found outside the active delta belongs to the native Gulf coast strain (Howard, Travis, et al. 2008). *Schoenoplectus deltarum* dominates the highly diverse crevasse splays of the inner delta (White 1993). The only similarity with the Atchafalaya Delta is the *Salix nigra*–dominated vegetation that occurs on the highest elevations on the upstream end of the splay islands. In the early 1980s, large areas of the Atchafalaya Delta splays were dominated by *Sagittaria latifolia* (Johnson, Sasser, et al. 1985). By the late 1980s, these areas had converted to mudflats with patches of *Justicia ovata* (Shaffer, Sasser, et al. 1992). In the Atchafalaya Delta, the decrease in *Sagittaria* flats has been attributed to the combined stresses of grazing and salinity-intrusion events (Evers, Sasser, et al. 1998; Holm and Sasser 2001), with both mammals and waterfowl contributing to the grazing pressure. At the same time, species diversity at the higher elevations has increased (Shaffer, Sasser, et al. 1992). The *Sagittaria* flats were a highly productive system (aboveground production estimated between 465 and 4,056 g m^{-2} y^{-1} and belowground production between 233 and 1,199 g m^{-2} y^{-1}), with production positively related to elevation (Visser 1989).

Saline Marshes and Mangroves

The vegetation in the saline zone of the inactive delta has low species richness and is dominated by *Spartina alterniflora,* with patches of *Juncus roemerianus* (Visser, Sasser, et al. 1998). *Avicennia germinans* reaches its northern distribution in Louisiana and may be expanding due to global warming (McKee and Rooth 2008; Perry and Mendelssohn 2009; see also chapter 6). The last time the population was killed by frost occurred in 1989, after which the population reestablished from seeds. Some individuals exceeded 2 m tall by 2000.

Primary production of *Spartina alterniflora,* estimated at 2,658 g m^{-2} y^{-1}, is lower than that of the other dominant plant species, while *Juncus roemerianus,* at 3,416 g m^{-2} y^{-1}, has the second highest primary production after *Spartina patens* (Hopkinson, Gosselink, et al. 1978). Interannual variation in fall aboveground biomass of *S. alterniflora* is significantly related to nitrogen availability in the surface waters and was highest during years with intermediate levels of nitrogen (TKN of ~120 μg at l^{-1}) (Visser, Sasser, et al. 2006). Muskrat density is highly positively correlated with nitrogen availability in the Mississippi River Delta and may explain declining biomass at the highest nitrogen levels (Visser, Sasser, et al. 2006). The site with a higher level of flooding had smaller peak biomass during optimal nitrogen conditions (Visser, Sasser, et al. 2006). In contrast, belowground biomass is reduced when marsh plots were fertilized with nitrogen and phosphorus (Darby and Turner 2008a). Belowground biomass in *S. alterniflora* marshes is dominated by rhizomes, with decreasing belowground biomass in the spring, when mass is used for aboveground growth, and in the late summer, when mass is used for flowering (Darby and Turner 2008b). Significant variation exists in the response of different *S. alterniflora* populations to hypersalinity (Pezeshki and DeLaune 1995; Hester, Mendelssohn, et al. 1998, 2001). Salinity in these polyhaline marshes rarely exceeds the salinity tolerance of even the most sensitive populations.

Saline wetlands are in a constant struggle to maintain their elevation in the face of RSLR (Reed and Cahoon 1992). In 2000, the delta experienced a sudden and acute dieback event that affected over 100,000 ha of *Spartina alterniflora*–dominated salt marsh (McKee, Mendelssohn, et al. 2004). This event is distinct from the more gradual die-back in waterlogged salt marshes (Mendelssohn and McKee 1988). Between May and October 2000, affected areas showed a progression from yellow to brown leaves to bare mud as *S. alterniflora* and, to a lesser extent, *Spartina patens* died and decomposed, usually in interior portions of the marsh. Other cooccuring species *(Juncus roemerianus, Avicennia germinans)* were visually unaffected. In the case of salt marsh die-back, drought or other stressors could make plants more susceptible to conditions that are normally tolerated. *S. alterniflora* is susceptible to the combined effects of drought, reduced pH, and bioavailable metals— all of which are sublethal when taken individually (Twilley, Klerks, et al. 2005). In the case of sudden salt marsh die-back, it could be that a combination of changes in soil chemistry and pathogens interact with plants in different stages of vulnerability. Alternatively, ongoing stressors such as eutrophication and/or sea-level rise may have made marsh plants susceptible to drought, which may explain why sudden die-back has not been reported previously (Alber, Swenson, et al. 2008).

Mesohaline Marshes

The vegetation in mesohaline marshes can be divided into two major types. The slightly more common mesohaline wiregrass is dominated by *Spartina patens* and often contains some *Distichlis spicata* (Visser, Sasser, et al. 1998). The mesohaline mixture vegetation type does not have a clear dominant and is a mixture of *S. alterniflora, S. patens,* and *D. spicata.* Transitions between oligohaline and mesohaline marsh types can be subtle and often can be punctuated by disturbance events, such as tropical storms and hurricanes (Brewer and Grace 1990; Meert and Hester 2010). For example, oligohaline marshes that receive occasional salt pulses (e.g., from storm surges) often have *S. patens* as part of the plant community; dominance may shift away from typical oligohaline community composition toward *S. patens* with salt pulses and toward *Schoenoplectus americanus* with burn events or loss of marsh surface elevation (Brewer and Grace 1990; Gough and Grace 1998; Meert and Hester 2010).

Primary production of *Spartina patens* (6,043 g m^{-2} y^{-1}) can be the highest of any plant in the delta; *Distichlis spicata* production (3,237 g m^{-2} y^{-1}) is closer to the average (Hopkinson, Gosselink, et al. 1978). It is, however, important to note that Hopkinson, Gosselink, et al. (1978) used an *S. patens* site located in an oligohaline marsh, which may explain its very high production. *S. patens* productivity in brackish marshes can be substantially lower (1,342–1,428 g m^{-2} y^{-1}; White, Weiss, et al. 1978). Although *S. patens* productivity does decrease with increasing salinity, it is very productive in the range of salinity levels encountered in the mesohaline coastal marshes, and is capable of tolerating, albeit with decreased productivity, salinity levels even greater than those encountered in tidal salt marshes (Hester, Mendelssohn, et al. 2001). The sensitivity of *S. patens* to the effects of increased flooding is much more important in understanding what is driving the high rates of *S. patens* mesohaline marsh loss, as well as constraining its distribution lower in the estuary, where frequency, depth, and duration of flooding increase (Burdick, Mendelssohn, et al. 1989; Lessmann, Mendelssohn, et al. 1997; Spalding and Hester 2007; Meert and Hester 2010; Merino, Huval, et al. 2010).

Spalding and Hester (2007) reported that *Spartina patens* displayed much greater sensitivity to increased flooding than oligohaline *(Sagitarria lancifolia)* or freshwater *(P. hemitomon)* plant species. Total *S. patens* biomass decreased > 50% with a change in mean water level from –10 cm below the marsh surface to +20 cm above the marsh surface, whereas the range of salinity levels assessed (0 to 6 ppt) had no effect on productivity (Spalding and Hester 2007). Merino, Huval, et al. (2010) reported that *S. patens* productivity was not affected by nutrients when productivity was limited by elevated salinity (18 ppt), whereas at lower salinities (2–6 ppt) *S. patens* productivity peaked at 2.43 mg N cm^{-3}. Meert and Hester (2010) reported that although *S. patens* leaf N increased in response to increased N loading, the codominant, *Schoenoplectus americanus,* consistently assimilated 25 to 31% more N in leaf tissue under all N-loading conditions. Interestingly, *S. americanus* also had consistently higher leaf tissue P concentrations than *S. patens* across all P loadings.

Fresh and Oligohaline Marshes

The vegetation of fresh and oligohaline marshes is quite diverse and changed in species composition over the second half of the 20th century. Penfound and Hathaway (1938) described the fresh attached marshes near the swamp-forest edge as codominated by *Typha latifolia* and *Schoenoplectus californicus,* with *P. hemitomon* as a common other species, and oligohaline marshes near the swamp forest edge as dominated by *Phragmites australis* or *Cladium mariscus.* O'Neill (1949) described the majority of the fresh marsh in the delta as dominated by floating *P. hemitomon,* whereas floating *Schoenoplectus pungens* marshes dominated the areas between *P. hemitomon*–dominated fresh marshes and brackish marshes. However, O'Neill (1949) provided no detailed description of the floating *S. pungens* vegetation type. The first truly extensive vegetation survey was performed in 1968 (Chabreck 1972). Analysis of these data revealed three fresh vegetation types and two oligohaline vegetation types (Visser, Sasser, et al. 1998). Fresh marsh dominated by *P. hemitomon* was slightly more common (53% of the fresh sites) than fresh marsh dominated by *Sagittaria lancifolia* (40% of the fresh sites). The remaining fresh sites were dominated by *Zizaniopsis miliacea.* In the last four decades, some *P. hemitomon* floating marshes have converted to thin-mat floating marshes codominated by *Eleocharis baldwinii* and *Hydrocotyle umbellata* (Sasser, Gosselink, et al. 1995; Evers, Holm, et al. 1996; Visser, Sasser, et al. 1999). The first oligohaline marsh vegetation type is a mixture that is dominated by *S. lancifolia* in the spring, but becomes a mixture of spikerushes (*Eleocharis* spp.), sedges (*Cyperus* spp.), and *Bacopa monnieri* in the fall. An analysis of the 1997 vegetation survey data split this vegetation type into two: marshes dominated by *S. lancifolia* and those codominated by *Eleocharis* spp. and *S. lancifolia* (Visser and Sasser 1998). The second oligohaline vegetation type is dominated by *Spartina patens.* Some of the thick-mat floating marshes have been invaded by woody species, including *Morella cerifera,* the exotic *Triadica sebifera, Ilex cassine,* and *Acer rubrum* (Battaglia, Denslow, et al. 2007). The shaded ground layer of shrub thickets can have markedly lower herbaceous cover and even compositional differences relative to the surrounding emergent marsh vegetation (Battaglia, Denslow, et al. 2007).

Although primary production of freshwater marshes is generally considered to be phosphorus limited (e.g., Verhoeven, Koerselman, et al. 1996; Chiang, Craft, et al. 2000), Louisiana's fresh and oligohaline marshes are primarily nitrogen limited (DeLaune, Smith, et al. 1986; Visser and Sasser 2009; Mayence and Hester 2010). However, high nitrogen availability may decrease aboveground biomass, presumably due to increased grazing pressure (Visser and Sasser 2009). Grazers in fresh and oligohaline marshes are nutria *(Myocastor coypus)*, white-tailed deer *(Odocoileus virginianus)*, and muskrat *(Ondatra zibethicus)*. Conversion of the *P. hemitomon*–dominated marsh to spikerush-dominated marshes is most likely due to increased nutria populations (Visser, Sasser, et al. 1999).

Although the majority of wetland loss occurs in the brackish and saline marsh zones (Hartley 2009), some wetland loss occurs in fresh and oligohaline marshes (Howes, FitzGerald, et al. 2010). Fresh marsh species are highly tolerant of submergence (Willis and Hester 2004; Visser and Sandy 2009), and a large percentage of these marshes float. Therefore, loss due to submergence is highly unlikely. Highly organic soils may be more sensitive to shear forces during wind and high water-flow events, and some loss may occur as pieces of mat break off and are transported away (Howes, FitzGerald, et al. 2010). Floating marsh fragments are often seen in adjacent water bodies, but this does not always result in marsh loss (Sasser, Visser, et al. 1995). Fresh and oligohaline marsh plants are highly sensitive to salinity, especially when salinity increases rapidly (Webb and Mendelssohn 1996; Hester, Mendelssohn, et al. 1998; Howard and Mendelssohn 1999; Willis and Hester 2004; Spalding and Hester 2007). Occasionally salinity pulses kill vegetation; sometimes these denuded marshes recover, and sometimes they do not (Flynn et al. 1989; Visser, Sasser, et al. 2002; Steyer 2008). An experimental removal of grazing pressure from a marsh that had turned to open water after a hurricane showed that the effect of hurricanes can be exacerbated by grazing pressure (Visser, Franken, et al. 1999). Plants reestablished naturally in ungrazed plots, and transplanted plants survived when protected from grazing. Nutria can also contribute to hurricane damage. Heavily grazed areas converted to open water after an intensive hurricane season (Scarborough and Mouton 2007). Recently eutrophication has been postulated as a factor in the loss of fresh and oligohaline marshes in an area affected by river reintroduction (Swarzenski, Doyle, et al. 2008).

Forested Wetlands

Similar in structure and function to other forested floodplain communities in the southeastern U.S., these coastal floodplains, when healthy and functioning, are characterized by high productivity and biodiversity. Where saltwater intrusion has occurred, however, these stands can be heavily degraded (Krauss, Duberstein, et al. 2009; Shaffer, Day, et al. 2009), as evidenced by "skeleton forests" of standing dead bald cypress *(Taxodium distichum)* trees that remain in many parts of coastal Louisiana.

As stressors such as saltwater intrusion increase, all tree species except for bald cypress suffer complete mortality (Shaffer, Day, et al. 2009). Given their position, where the floodplain forest and marsh communities meet and intermingle, large changes in composition are expected to occur within and across these ecotones with changing climate. Despite their ecological significance, they are poorly understood and understudied, perhaps due to the difficulties in accessing and working in them.

Community structure and function are closely linked to salinity and flooding gradients across the heterogeneous forested wetland landscape (Krauss, Duberstein, et al. 2009). These strong abiotic gradients vary with subtle changes in microtopography and generate dramatic gradients in vegetation over sometimes small spatial scales (Wall and Darwin

1999). Compositional turnover depends in part on species-specific physiological tolerances to the two environmental gradients. Although we discuss below the dominant plant species that typify different parts of the floodplain, it is important to note that the boundaries between these are gradual.

The natural levees that parallel distributary channels are the driest and constitute the most "upland" portions of the floodplain. They support species in the system that are the least tolerant of flooding, such as the evergreen *Quercus virginiana* (live oak), a tree that is largely restricted to this part of the floodplain (White, Darwin, et al. 1983; Denslow and Battaglia 2002). Other typical canopy species include *Celtis laevigata* (hackberry), *Q. nigra* (water oak), *Ulmus americana* (American elm), *Fraxinus pennsylvanica* (green ash), *Liquidambar styraciflua* (sweetgum), and *Acer rubrum* (red maple). Midstory small trees include *Crataegus* spp. (hawthorn), *Ilex decidua* (deciduous holly), and *Carpinus caroliniana* (musclewood). The understories of bottomland hardwood forests are generally sparse. In some forests, however, the dwarf palmetto *(Sabal minor)* can be very abundant.

With the exception of live oak, the other species that occupy levee forests also occur further downslope in areas prone to more frequent inundation. With increasing flood frequency and duration, these species typically increase in basal area before declining in abundance and giving way to more flood-tolerant species such as *Fraxinus profunda* (pumpkin ash) and *Carya aquatica* (water hickory). Red maple is the most widespread of the bottomland hardwood species, occurring in the driest levees and flooded backswamps and forest-marsh ecotone habitats (Denslow and Battaglia 2002; Battaglia, Denslow, et al. 2007).

The backswamps and sloughs, which are the most inundated but still forested parts of the floodplain, are dominated by bald cypress and water tupelo *(Nyssa aquatica)*. Depending on site history, some areas may have one or the other or be codominated by the two. The understory is mostly depauperate of emergent species, but in some places exotic floating aquatic species have colonized and now dominate this stratum. Submerged aquatic vegetation also thrives in flooded backswamps where the canopy is relatively open and light availability in the water column is adequate.

Animal Communities

Active Delta Lobes

The active deltas create important habitat for 14 species of wintering waterfowl, with an average of 13,700 birds observed during winter surveys in the Atchafalaya Delta complex (Fuller et al. 1988). Waterfowl were more numerous on the *Sagittaria* flats. Most of the mammalian grazing pressure in the Atchafalaya complex is from nutria *(Myocastor coypus)*, an introduced rodent. White-tailed deer *(Odocoileus virginianus)* are common in the deltaic and fresh marshes. Both the emergent marsh and the submerged aquatic vegetation of the delta provide important habitat for estuarine nekton, especially during the summer and fall (Castellanos and Rozas 2001).

Saline Marshes and Mangroves

The use of saline wetlands by birds, mammals, reptiles, and amphibians is limited because most of these species require fresh drinking water. Most of these species have higher densities in the fresher part of the system and only occasionally use the saline part of the system (Condrey, Kemp, et al. 1995). A few species, including diamondback terrapin *(Malaclemys terrapin),* salt marsh snake *(Nerodia clarkii),* seaside sparrow *(Ammodramus maritimus),* and salt marsh sharp-tailed sparrow *(Ammodramus caudacutus),* have adapted to this environment (Condrey, Kemp, et al. 1995). Brown pelicans *(Pelecanus occidentalis)* prefer to nest in the mangroves (Visser, Vermilion, et al. 2005).

Although tidal saline and mesohaline marshes probably function in a variety of ways to enhance growth and survival of particular nekton species, the relative importance of food versus refuge from predation is poorly understood (Boesch and Turner 1984) and probably varies across species and life-history stages (Jones, Baltz, et al. 2002). Twenty-four species of fish spent their full life cycle in the saline and mesohaline marshes (Condrey, Kemp, et al. 1995); these included killifishes *(Fundulus* spp.) and gobies *(Gobioides* spp.). Twenty-six species spent the early part of their life cycle in the marsh and the later part offshore (Condrey, Kemp, et al. 1995); these include fisheries species such as menhaden *(Brevoortia patronus),* drum *(Sciaeops ocellatus),* and flounder *(Paralichthys lethostigma).* The interface between the marsh and tidal creeks may provide the highest habitat value (Peterson and Turner 1994; Minello and Rozas 2002). Growth of fishes may be controlled by temperature, salinity, and dissolved oxygen (Baltz, Fleeger, et al. 1998).

Louisiana's extensive fishery production seems unaffected by the extensive land loss, and there are several hypotheses to explain this (Chesney, Baltz, et al. 2000):

1. The relationship between fishery landings and marsh loss may be complicated. Suitable habitat may not be directly related to total marsh area:
   a. Marsh edge may be more important;
   b. Increased abundance of aquatic macrophytes may partially offset marsh loss.
2. Turbidity of Louisiana estuarine waters is high and may provide an alternative form of refuge for early life-history stages.
3. Fish production may have shifted from species requiring marsh habitat to open-water forms.
4. Some of the impact associated with lost habitat may be offset by increased production associated with eutrophication.
5. Marsh habitat may not be essential to many of the organisms typically captured in trawls; hence, no relationship with marsh loss would be expected for those species.

Mesohaline Marshes

Mesohaline marshes are an integral part of the greater estuarine food web and the nursery services it provides. Mesohaline marsh edges are extensively used by small fishes and are an important habitat for crabs *(Callinectes sapidus)* and shrimp *(Farfantepenaeus aztecus* and *Litopenaeus setiferus)* (Thom, LaPeyre, et al. 2004). Mesohaline marshes provide important habitat for wintering waterfowl, especially gadwall *(Anas strepera).* Muskrat *(Ondatra zibethicus)* and river otters *(Lontra canadensis)* are found in greatest densities in the mesohaline marshes (Condrey, Kemp, et al. 1995).

Fresh and Oligohaline Marshes

Animal diversity reaches its peak in the fresh to oligohaline marshes, with extensive populations of mammals, birds, reptiles, amphibians, and fishes. Fresh and oligohaline marshes are an important breeding habitat for alligators *(Alligator mississippiensis)* and mottled ducks *(Anas fulvigula)* (Condrey, Kemp, et al. 1995). The introduced nutria reaches its highest population densities in the fresh marshes. Thirty-seven species of freshwater fish occur in the delta (Condrey, Kemp, et al. 1995), such as catfishes *(Ictalurus* spp.), gars *(Lepisoteus* spp.), sunfishes *(Lepomis* spp.), and bass *(Morone* spp.).

Forested Wetlands

Forested wetlands provide important habitat for a diverse group of animals. Virtually all of the eastern land bird species in the United States and numerous species from the western USA migrate through the coastal forests of Louisiana and utilize the forest canopy (Lowery 1974). The resident avifauna of these forested wetlands can be characterized by the presence and relative abundance of several wading and/or waterbirds, woodpeckers, and songbirds (Burdick, Cushman, et al. 1989). With respect to neotropical migratory birds, it has been shown that swamps with intact overstory canopies are more diverse than degraded swamps (Zoller 2004). The lower species diversity in degraded swamps is believed to be a result of a reduction of the vertical structure of the forest. The bald eagle *(Haliaeetus leucocephalus)* and swallow-tailed kite *(Elanoides forficatus),* which nest in the wetland forests of coastal Louisiana, require very tall overstory trees for nesting. Louisiana black bear *(Ursus americanus luteolus)* and Rafinesque's big-eared bat *(Plecotus rafinesquii)* frequently use hollows of large trees for nesting (Weaver, Tabberer, et al. 1990; Hightower, Wagner, et al. 2002; Gooding and Langford 2004). Large hollow water tupelo, characteristic of older swamp forests, appear particularly important to Rafinesque's big-eared bat (Lance, Hardcastle, et al. 2001; Gooding and Langford 2004).

Wetland and aquatic invertebrates are a major link in food-web dynamics of the coastal forest and are critical for the maintenance of fish and wildlife populations (Chambers, Conner, et al. 2005). Impounded, stagnant water can reduce invertebrate production as well as diversity (Sklar 1985; Batzer, Rader, et al. 1999) and therefore negatively affect the fish and wildlife that depend on them as a food source. Furthermore, impoundments have detrimental effects on mature trees through reduced net production, crown die-back, increased susceptibility to insects and pathogens, and increased mortality (Conner, Gosselink, et al. 1981; King 1995; Keeland, Conner, et al. 1997). Both bald cypress and water tupelo can be heavily grazed by caterpillars. Complete defoliation during the spring can be widespread and seems to be a more recent development (Chambers, Conner, et al. 2005).

Conservation Concerns

Restoration Options

The loss of wetlands as they convert to open water is the primary conservation concern in the delta. Major restoration efforts include the Coastal Wetlands Planning, Protection, and Restoration Act (CWPPRA) and the Water Resources Development Act (WRDA). WRDA has constructed two major freshwater reintroduction structures: Caernarvon and Davis Pond. CWPPRA has constructed over 80 projects from 1990 to the present (see http://lacoast.gov). The most common restoration techniques used by CWPPRA in the first decade of the program were hydrologic restoration and shoreline protection, but wetland creation with dredged sediments has been more common in recent years. Most of the restoration projects in the active delta consist of maximizing sediment capture by creating new crevasses that allow water to flow into areas that have been cut off from the main river flow. Llewellyn and Shafer (1993) proposed using the emergent macrophyte *Justicia lanceolata* as a facilitator of land building. This native species is not grazed and is highly effective at trapping sediment, increasing elevation, and facilitating the establishment of a diverse plant community.

Some promising restoration techniques rehabilitate deteriorating marshes before they are lost using sediment enhancement with slurries (Slocum et al. 2005; LaPeyre, Gossman, et al. 2009; Stagg and Mendelssohn 2010) or with spray applications (Ford et al. 1999). These techniques restore elevations that increase primary production and accretion processes, rehabilitating the marsh and increasing its survival length by several decades.

Marsh loss in fresh and oligohaline marshes has been substantially reduced and in some instances reversed through a CWPPRA project that provides an incentive payment for the harvesting of the exotic grazer nutria (see http://nutria.com).

Climate Change

Global climate change will strongly impact the delta. Average ESLR for the 20th century was 1 to 2 mm yr^{-1} (Gornitz, Lebedeff, et al. 1982) and is currently between 3 and 4 mm yr^{-1} (FitzGerald, Penland, et al. 2008). The Intergovernmental Panel on Climate Change (IPCC) forecasts a mean rise of about 40 cm by 2100, but recent reports indicate that ESLR will be a meter or more by 2100 (Rahmstorf 2007; Pfeffer, Harper, et al. 2008; Vermeer and Rahmstorf 2009). Recent evidence suggests that tropical storm activity has increased in frequency and intensity (e.g., Hoyos, Agudelo, et al. 2006). After the barrier islands, the coastal marshes and forested wetlands bear the brunt of these storms as they make landfall. In the forests, wind damage, including uprooting, bole snapping, branch falls, and defoliation, are common (Keeland and Gorham 2009). In addition, the IPCC indicates that the northern Gulf of Mexico will experience more frequent droughts.

The northern Gulf of Mexico is particularly vulnerable to sea-level rise, flooding, and erosion from storms (Hammar-Klose and Thieler 2001). The combined impacts of climate change have important implications for coastal wetlands of the Mississippi Delta (Day, Boesch, et al. 2007; Day, Christian, et al. 2008). Blum and Roberts (2009) concluded that most of the delta plain will disappear by 2100 due to accelerated sea-level rise and a reduction of sediment input from the basin. Shaffer, Wood, et al. (2009) reported that most forested wetlands in the upper Pontchartrain basin will disappear in the 21st century. Clearly, coastal restoration efforts will have to be more intensive to offset the impacts of climate change. It seems clear that even the most ambitious restoration plans can restore or maintain only a portion of the coast in this century.

References

Alber M, Swenson EM, et al. 2008. Salt marsh dieback: an overview of recent events in the US. *Estuar. Coast. Shelf Sci.* 80:1–11.

Baltz DM, Fleeger JW, et al. 1998. Food, density, and microhabitat: factors affecting growth and recruitment potential of juvenile saltmarsh fishes. *Env. Biol. Fish.* 53:89–103.

Barras JA, Bernier JC, Morton RA. 2008. *Land area change in coastal Louisiana—a multidecadal perspective (from 1956 to 2006).* Scientific Investigations Map 3019. Reston, VA: USGS.

Battaglia LL, Denslow JS, Hargis TG. 2007. Does woody species establishment alter herbaceous community composition of freshwater floating marshes? *J. Coast. Res.* 23:1580–87.

Batzer DP, Rader RB, Wissinger SA. 1999. *Invertebrates in freshwater wetlands of North America: ecology and management.* New York: Wiley.

Blanton P, Marcus WA. 2009. Railroads, roads and lateral disconnection in the river landscapes of the continental United States. *Geomorphology* 112:212–27.

Blum MD, Roberts HH. 2009. Drowning of the Mississippi Delta due to insufficient sediment supply and global sea-level rise. *Nat. Geosci.* 2:488–91.

Boesch DF, Josselyn MN, et al. 1994. Scientific assessment of coastal wetland loss, restoration and management in Louisiana. *J. Coast. Res.* SI20.

Boesch DF, Shabman L, et al. 2006. *A new framework for planning the future of coastal Louisiana after the hurricanes of 2005.* Cambridge,MA: Univ. Maryland Cntr. Environ. Sci.

Boesch DF, Turner RE. 1984. Dependence of fishery species on salt marshes: the role of food and refuge. *Estuaries* 7:460–68.

Brewer JS, Grace JB. 1990. Plant community structure in an oligohaline tidal marsh. *Plant Ecol.* 90:93–107.

Broome SW, Mendelssohn IA, McKee KL. 1995. Relative growth of *Spartina patens* (Ait.) Muhl., and *Scirpus olneyi* Gray occurring in a mixed stand as affected by salinity and flooding depth. *Wetlands* 15:20–30.

Burdick DM, Cushman D, et al. 1989. Faunal changes due to bottomland hardwood forest loss in the Tensas watershed, Louisiana. *Conserv. Biol.* 3:282–92.

Burdick DM, Mendelssohn IA, McKee KL. 1989. Live standing crop and metabolism of the marsh grass *Spartina patens* as related to edaphic factors in a brackish, mixed marsh community in Louisiana. *Estuaries* 12:195–204.

Carpenter K, Sasser CE, et al. 2007. Sediment input into a floating freshwater marsh: effects on soil properties, buoyancy, and plant biomass. *Wetlands* 27:1016–24.

Castellanos DL, Rozas LP. 2001. Nekton use of submerged aquatic vegetation, marsh, shallow unvegetated bottom in the Atchafalaya River, Louisiana, tidal freshwater ecosystem. *Estuaries* 24:184–97.

Chabreck RH. 1972. Vegetation, water, and soil characteristics of the Louisiana coastal region. *La. State Univ. Agric. Exp. Station Bull.* 664.

Chambers JL, Conner WH, et al. 2005. *Conservation, protection and utilization of Louisiana's coastal wetland forests.* Baton Rouge: Louisiana Governor's Office of Coastal Activities. www.coastalforestswg.lsu.edu/.

Chambers JQ, Fisher JI, et al. 2007. Hurricane Katrina's carbon footprint on U.S. Gulf coast forests. *Science* 318:1107.

Chesney EJ, Baltz DM, Thomas RG. 2000. Louisiana estuarine coastal fisheries and habitats: perspectives from a fish's eye view. *Ecol. Appl.* 10:350–66.

Chiang C, Craft CB, et al. 2000. Effects of four years of N and P additions on Everglades plant communities. *Aquat. Bot.* 68:61–78.

Childers DL, Day JW. 1990. Marsh-water column interactions in two Louisiana estuaries. I. Sediment dynamics. *Estuaries* 13:393–403.

Condrey R, Kemp P, et al. 1995. *Characterization of the current status, trends, and probable causes of change in living resources in the Barataria-Terrebonne estuarine system.* BTNEP Publ. 21. Thibodaux, LA: Barataria-Terrebonne National Estuary Program.

Conner WH, Day JW. 1976. Productivity and composition of a

baldcypress–water tupelo site and a bottomland hardwood site in a Louisiana swamp. *Am. J. Bot.* 63:1354–64.

Conner WH, Tolliver JR. 1990. Long-term trends in the baldcypress *(Taxodium distichum)* resource in Louisiana (U.S.A.). *For. Ecol. Manag.* 33/34:543–57.

Conner WH, Gosselink JG, Parrando RT. 1981. Comparison of the vegetation of three Louisiana swamp sites with different flooding regimes. *Am. J. Bot.* 68:320–31.

Darby FA, Turner RE. 2008a. Effects of eutrophication on salt marsh root and rhizome biomass accumulation. *Mar. Ecol. Prog. Ser.* 363:63–70.

Darby FA, Turner RE. 2008b. Below- and aboveground *Spartina alterniflora* production in a Louisiana salt marsh. *Estuar. Coasts* 31:223–231.

Day JW, Templet P. 1989. Consequences of sea level rise: implications from the Mississippi Delta. *Coast. Manage.* 17:241–57.

Day JW, Pont D, et al. 1995. Impacts of sea-level rise on deltas in the Gulf of Mexico and the Mediterranean: the importance of pulsing events to sustainability. *Estuaries* 18:636–47.

Day J, Martin J, et al. 1997. System functioning as a basis for sustainable management of deltaic ecosystems. *Coast. Manage.* 25:115–54.

Day J, Shaffer G, et al. 2000. Pattern and process of land loss in the Mississippi delta: a spatial and temporal analysis of wetland habitat change. *Estuaries* 23:425–38.

Day JW, Boesch DF, et al. 2007. Restoration of the Mississippi Delta: lessons learned from hurricanes Katrina and Rita. *Science* 315:1679–84.

Day JW, Christian RR, et al. 2008. Consequences of climate change on the ecogeomorphology of coastal wetlands. *Estuar. Coasts* 31:477–91.

DeLaune RD, Buresh RJ, Patrick WH. 1979. Relationship of soil properties to standing crop biomass of *Spartina alterniflora* in a Louisiana marsh. *Estuar. Coast. Mar. Sci.* 8:477–87.

DeLaune RD, Smith CJ, Sarafyan MN. 1986. Nitrogen cycling in a freshwater marsh of *Panicum hemitomon* on the Deltaic Plain of the Mississippi River. *J. Ecol.* 74:249–56.

DeLaune RD, Devai I, et al. 2002. Sulfate reduction in Louisiana marsh soils of varying salinities. *Commun. Soil Sci. Plant Anal.* 33:79–94.

DeLaune RD, Jugsujinda A, et al. 2003. Impact of Mississippi River freshwater reintroduction on enhancing marsh accretionary processes in a Louisiana estuary. *Estuar. Coast. Mar. Sci.* 58:653–62.

Denslow JS, Battaglia LL. 2002. Stand composition and structure across a changing hydrologic gradient: Jean Lafitte National Park, Louisiana, USA. *Wetlands* 22:738–52.

Doyle TW, Krauss KW, et al. 2010. Predicting the retreat and migration of tidal forests along the northern Gulf of Mexico under sea-level rise. *For. Ecol. Manag.* 259:770–77.

Evers DE, Holm GO, Sasser CE. 1996. *Digitization of the floating marsh maps in the Barataria and Terrebonne basins, Louisiana.* BTNEP Publ. 28. Thibodaux, LA: Barataria-Terrebonne National Estuary Program.

Evers DE, Sasser CE, et al. 1998. The impact of vertebrate herbivores on wetland vegetation in Atchafalaya Bay, Louisiana. *Estuaries* 21:1–13.

Faulkner SP, Poach ME. 1996. *Functional comparison of created and natural wetlands in the Atchafalaya Delta, Louisiana.* WRP-RE-16. Vicksburg, MS: USACE Waterways Exper. Sta.

FitzGerald D, Penland S, et al. 2008. *The impact of the Mississippi River Gulf Outlet (MR-GO): geology and geomorphology.* Expert Report. Denham Springs, LA.

Flynn KM, McKee KL, Mendelssohn IA. 1995. Recovery of freshwater marsh vegetation after a saltwater intrusion event. *Oecologia* 103:63–72.

Ford MA, Cahoon DR, Lynch JC. 1999. Restoring marsh elevation in a rapidly subsiding salt marsh by thin-layer deposition of dredged material. *Ecological Engineering* 12:189–205.

Frazier DE. 1967. Recent deltaic deposits of the Mississippi River: their development and chronology. *Gulf Coast Assoc. Geol. Soc. Trans.* 17:287–315.

Fuller DA, Peterson GW, et al. 1988. The distribution and habitat use of waterfowl in Atchafalaya Bay, Louisiana. In *Vegetation and waterfowl use of islands in Atchafalaya Bay,* Sasser CE, Fuller DA, editors. Baton Rouge: Louisiana Board of Regents, pp. 73–103.

Galloway GE, Boesch DF, Twilley RR. 2009. Restoring and protecting coastal Louisiana. *Issues Sci. Technol.* 25:29–38.

Gooding G, Langford JR. 2004. Characteristics of tree roosts of Rafinesque's big-eared bat and southeastern bat in northeastern Louisiana. *Southwest. Nat.* 49:61–67.

Gornitz V, Lebedeff S, Hansen J. 1982. Global sea level trend in the past century. *Science* 215:1611–14.

Gosselink JG, Coleman JM, Stewart RE. 1998. Coastal Louisiana. In *Status and trends of the nation's biological resources,* vol. 1, Mac MJ, Opler PA, et al., editors. Reston, VA: USGS, pp. 385–436.

Gough L, Grace JB. 1998. Effects of flooding, salinity, and herbivory on coastal plant communities, Louisiana, United States. *Oecologia* 117:527–35.

Hammar-Klose ES, Thieler ER. 2001. *Coastal vulnerability to sea-level rise: a preliminary database for the U.S. Atlantic, Pacific and Gulf of Mexico coasts.* USGS Digital Data Ser. 68. http://pubs.usgs.gov/dds/dds68/htmldocs/project.htm.

Hartley SB. 2009. *Modified methodology for projecting coastal Louisiana land changes over the next 50 years.* Scientific Investigations Map 3098. Reston, VA: USGS.

Hatton RS, DeLaune RD, Patrick WH. 1983. Sedimentation, accretion, and subsidence in the marshes of Barataria Basin, Louisiana. *Limnol. Oceanogr.* 28:494–502.

Hester MW, Mendelssohn IA, McKee KL. 1998. Intraspecific variation in salt tolerance and morphology in *Panicum hemitomon* and *Spartina alterniflora* (Poaceae). *Int. J. Plant Sci.* 159:127–38.

Hester MW, Mendelssohn IA, McKee KL. 2001. Species and population variation to salinity stress in *Panicum hemitomon, Spartina patens,* and *Spartina alterniflora:* morphological and physiological constraints. *Env. Exp. Bot.* 46:277–97.

Hightower DA, Wagner RO, Pace RM. 2002. Denning ecology of female American black bears in south central Louisiana. *Ursus* 13:11–17.

Holm GO, Sasser CE. 2001. Differential salinity response between two Mississippi River subdeltas: implications for changes in plant composition. *Estuaries* 24:78–89.

Holm GO, Sasser CE, et al. 2000. Vertical movement and substrate characteristics of oligohaline marshes near a high-sediment, riverine system. *J. Coast. Res.* 16:164–71.

Hopkinson CS, Gosselink JG, Parrondo RT. 1978. Aboveground production of seven marsh plant species in coastal Louisiana. *Ecology* 59:760–69.

Howard RJ, Mendelssohn IA. 1999. Salinity as a growth constraint on growth of oligohaline marsh macrophytes. II. Salt pulses and recovery potential. *Am. J. Bot.* 86:795–806.

Howard RJ, Travis SE, Sikes BA. 2008. Rapid growth of a Eurasian haplotype of *Phragmites australis* in a restored brackish marsh in Louisiana, USA. *Biol. Invasions* 10:369–79.

Howes NC, FitzGerald DM, et al. 2010. Hurricane-induced failure of low salinity wetlands. *Proc. Nat. Acad. Sci.* 107:14014–19.

Hoyos CD, Agudelo PA, et al. 2006. Deconvolution of the factors contributing to the increase in global hurricane intensity. *Science* 312:94–97.

Hupp CF, Osterkamp WR. 1996. Riparian vegetation and fluvial geomorphic processes. *Geomorphology* 14:277–95.

Johnson WB, Sasser CE, Gosselink JG. 1985. Succession of vegetation in an evolving delta, Atchafalaya Bay, Louisiana. *J. Ecol.* 73:973–86.

Jones RF, Baltz DM, Allen RL. 2002. Patterns of resource use by fishes and macroinvertebrates in Barataria Bay, Louisiana. *Mar. Ecol. Prog. Ser.* 237:271–89.

Junk WJ, Bayley PB, Sparks RE. 1989. The flood pulse concept in river-floodplain systems. In *Proceedings of the International Large River symposium,* Dodge DP, editor. Can. Special Publ. Fish Aquat. Sc. 106, pp. 110–27.

Keeland BD, Gorham LE. 2009. Delayed tree mortality in the Atchafalaya Basin of southern Louisiana following Hurricane Andrew. *Wetlands* 29:101–11.

Keeland BD, Sharitz RR. 1995. Season growth patterns of *Nyssa sylvatica* var *biflora, Nyssa aquatica,* and *Taxodium distichum* as affected by hydrologic regime. *Can. J. For. Res.* 25:1084–96.

Keeland BD, Conner WH, Sharitz RR. 1997. A comparison of wetland tree growth response to hydrologic regime in Louisiana and South Carolina. *For. Ecol. Manag.* 90:237–50.

Kesel RH. 1988. The decline of the suspended load of the lower

Mississippi River and its influence on adjacent wetlands. *Env. Geol. Water Sci.* 11:271–81.

Kesel RH. 1989. The role of the Mississippi River in wetland loss in southeastern Louisiana, U.S.A. *Env. Geol. Water Sci.* 13:183–93.

Kesel RH, Yodis E, McCraw D. 1992. An approximation of the sediment budget of the lower Mississippi River prior to major human modification. *Earth Surf. Process. Landf.* 17:711–22.

King SL. 1995. Effects of flooding regime on two impounded bottomland hardwood stands. *Wetlands* 15:272–84.

Krauss KW, Duberstein JA, et al. 2009. Site condition, structure, and growth of baldcypress along tidal/non-tidal salinity gradients. *Wetlands* 29:505–19.

Lance RF, Hardcastle BT, et al. 2001. Day-roost selection by Rafinesque's big-eared bats *(Corynorhinus rafinesquii)* in Louisiana forests. *J. Mammal.* 82:166–72.

LaPeyre MK, Gossman B, Piazza BP. 2009. Short- and long-term response of deteriorating brackish marshes and open-water ponds to sediment enhancement by thin-layer dredge disposal. *Estuar. Coasts* 32:390–402.

Lessmann JM, Mendelssohn IA, et al. 1997. Population variation in growth response to flooding in three marsh species. *Ecol. Eng.* 8:31–47.

Llewellyn DW, Shaffer GP. 1993. Marsh restoration in the presence of intense herbivory: the role of *Justicia lanceolata* (Chapm.) Small. *Wetlands* 13:176–84.

Lockaby BG, Walbridge MR. 1998. Biogeochemistry. In *Southern forested wetlands: ecology and management,* Messina MG, Conner WH, editors. New York: Lewis, pp. 149–72.

Lowery GH. 1974. *Louisiana birds.* Baton Rouge: LSU Press.

Mayence CE, Hester MW. 2010. Growth and allocation by a keystone wetland plant, *Panicum hemitomon,* and implications for managing and rehabilitating coastal freshwater marshes, Louisiana, USA. *Wetl. Ecol. Manag.* 18:149–63.

McKee KL, Rooth JE. 2008. Where temperate meets tropical: multi-factorial effects of elevated CO_2, nitrogen enrichment, and competition on a mangrove-salt marsh community. *Glob. Change Biol.* 14:971–84.

McKee KL, Mendelssohn IA, Materne MD. 2004. Acute salt marsh dieback in the Mississippi River deltaic plain: a drought-induced phenomenon? *Glob. Ecol. Biogeogr.* 13:65–73.

Meade RH. 1995. Setting: geology, hydrology, sediments, and engineering of the Mississippi River. In *Contaminants in the Mississippi River,* Meade RH, editor. Reston, VA: USGS Circular 1133. http://pubs.usgs.gov/circ/circ1133/geosetting.html.

Meert DR, Hester MW. 2010. Response of a Louisiana oligohaline marsh plant community to nutrient availability and disturbance. *J. Coast. Res.* 54:174–85.

Megonigal JP, Conner WH, et al. 1997. Aboveground production in southeastern floodplain forests: a test of the subsidy-stress hypothesis. *Ecology* 78:370–84.

Mendelssohn IA, McKee KL. 1988. *Spartina alterniflora* die-back in Louisiana: time-course investigation of soil waterlogging effects. *J. Ecol.* 76:509–21.

Mendelssohn IA, Morris JT. 2000. Eco-physiological constraints on the primary productivity of *Spartina alterniflora.* In *Concepts and controversities of tidal marsh ecology,* Weinstein MP, Kreeger DA, editors. New York: Kluwer, pp. 59–80.

Merino JH, Huval D, Nyman AJ. 2010. Implication of nutrient and salinity interaction on the productivity of *Spartina patens. Wetl. Ecol. Manag.* 18:111–17.

Minello TJ, Rozas LP. 2002. Nekton in Gulf Coast wetlands: fine-scale distributions, landscape patterns, and restoration implications. *Ecol. Appl.* 12:441–55.

Myers RS, Shaffer GP, Llewellyn DW. 1995. Baldcypress (*Taxodium distichum* (L.) Rich.) restoration in southeast Louisiana: the relative effects of herbivory, flooding, competition, and macronutrients. *Wetlands* 15:141–48.

Nyman JA, Walters RJ, et al. 2006. Marsh vertical accretion via vegetative growth. *Estuar. Coast. Shelf Sci.* 69:370–80.

O'Neill T. 1949. *The muskrat in the Louisiana coastal marshes.* New Orleans: LA Wildl. Fish. Comm.

Palmisano AW. 1970. *Plant community-soil relationships in Louisiana coastal marshes.* Ph.D. diss., Louisiana State Univ., Baton Rouge.

Patterson CS, Mendelssohn IA. 1991. A comparison of physico-

chemical variables across plant zones in a mangal/salt marsh community in Louisiana. *Wetlands* 11:139–61.

Patterson CS, Mendelssohn IA, Swenson EM. 1993. Growth and survival of *Avicennia germinans* seedlings in a mangal/salt marsh community in Louisiana, U.S.A. *J. Coast. Res.* 9:801–10.

Penfound WT, Hathaway ES. 1938. Plant communities in the marshlands of southeastern Louisiana. *Ecol. Monogr.* 8:1–56.

Penland S, Boyd R, Suter JR. 1988. Transgressive depositional systems of the Mississippi Delta plain: a model for barrier shoreline and shelf sand development. *J. Sed. Res.* 58:932–49.

Penland S, Wayne L, et al. 2000. Process classification of coastal land loss between 1932 and 1990 in the Mississippi River deltaic plain. U.S. Geological Survey Open File Report 00-418.

Perry CL, Mendelssohn IA. 2009. Ecosystem effects of expanding populations of *Avicennia germinans* in a Louisiana salt marsh. *Wetlands* 29:396–406.

Peterson GW, Turner RE. 1994. The value of salt marsh edge vs. interior as a habitat for fish and decapod crustaceans in a Louisiana tidal marsh. *Estuaries* 17:235–62.

Pezeshki SR, DeLaune RD. 1995. Variations in the response of two US Gulf coast populations of *Spartina alterniflora* to hypersalinity. *J. Coast. Res.* 11:89–95.

Pfeffer WT, Harper JT, O'Neel S. 2008. Kinematic constraints on glacier contributions to 21st-century sea-level rise. *Science* 321:1340–43.

Rahmstorf S. 2007. A semi-empirical approach to projecting future sea-level rise. *Science* 315:368–70.

Reed DJ, Cahoon DR. 1992. The relationship between marsh surface topography, hydroperiod, and growth of *Spartina alterniflora* in a deteriorating Louisiana salt marsh. *J. Coast. Res.* 8:77–87.

Reed DJ, Peterson MS, Lezina BJ. 2006. Reducing the effects of dredged material levees on coastal marsh function: sediment deposition and nekton utilization. *Env. Manage.* 37:671–85.

Roberts HH. 1997. Dynamic changes of the Holocene Mississippi River Delta plain: the delta cycle. *J. Coast. Res.* 13:605–27.

Rybczyk JM, Callaway JC, Day, JW. 1998. A relative elevation model for a subsiding coastal forested wetland receiving wastewater effluent. *Ecol. Model.* 112:23–44.

Sasser CE. 1977. *Distribution of vegetation in Louisiana coastal marshes as response to tidal flooding.* MS thesis, Louisiana State Univ., Baton Rouge.

Sasser CE, Gosselink JG, Shaffer GP. 1991. Distribution of nitrogen and phosphorus in a Louisiana freshwater floating marsh. *Aquat. Bot.* 41:317–31.

Sasser CE, Gosselink JG, et al. 1995. Hydrologic, vegetation, and substrate characteristics of floating marshes in sediment-rich wetlands of the Mississippi river delta plain, Louisiana, USA. *Wetl. Ecol. Manag.* 3:171–87.

Sasser CE, Gosselink JG, et al. 1996. Vegetation substrate and hydrology in floating marshes in the Mississippi River Delta plain wetlands, USA. *Plant Ecol.* 122:129–42.

Sasser CE, Visser JM, et al. 1995. The role of environmental variables in interannual variation in species composition and biomass in a sub-tropical minerotrophic floating marsh. *Can. J. Bot.* 73:413–24.

Sasser CE, Visser JM, et al. 2008. *Vegetation types in coastal Louisiana in 2007.* USGS Open-File Report 2008-1224. http://pubs.usgs.gov/of/2008/1224/.

Scarborough J, Mouton E. 2007. *Nutria harvest distribution 2006–2007 and a survey of nutria herbivory damage in coastal Louisiana in 2007.* Baton Rouge: Louisiana DNR.

Schneider RL, Sharitz RR. 1988. Hydrochory and regeneration in a bald cypress water tupelo swamp forest. *Ecology* 69:1055–63.

Shaffer GP, Day JW, et al. 2009. The MRGO navigation project: a massive human-induced environmental, economic, and storm disaster. *J. Coast. Res.* 54:206–24.

Shaffer GP, Hoeppner SS, Gosselink JG. 2005. The Mississippi River alluvial plain: characterization, degradation, and restoration. In *The world's largest wetlands,* Fraser LH, Keddy PA, editors. Cambridge: Cambridge Univ. Press, pp. 272–315.

Shaffer GP, Sasser CE, et al. 1992. Vegetation dynamics in the emerging Atchafalaya Delta, Louisiana, USA. *J. Ecol.* 80:677–87.

Shaffer GP, Wood WB, et al. 2009. Degradation of baldcypress-water tupelo swamp to marsh and open water in southeastern Louisiana, USA: an irreversible trajectory? *J. Coast. Res.* 54:152–65.

Sharitz RR, Mitsch WJ. 1993. Southern floodplain forests. In *Biodiversity of the southeastern United States: lowland terrestrial communities*, Martin WH, Boyce SG, Echternacht AC, editors. New York: Wiley, pp. 311–71.

Shirley LJ, Battaglia LL. 2006. Assessing vegetation change in coastal marsh-forest transitions along the northern Gulf of Mexico using National Wetlands Inventory data. *Wetlands* 26:1057–70.

Shirley LJ, Battaglia LL. 2008. Projecting fine resolution landcover dynamics in a rapidly changing coastal landscape. *J. Coast. Res.* 24:1545–54.

Sklar FH. 1985. Seasonality and community structure of the backswamp invertebrates in a Louisiana cypress-tupelo swamp. *Wetlands* 5:69–86.

Spalding EA, Hester MW. 2007. Interactive effects of hydrology and salinity on oligohaline plant species productivity: implications of relative sea-level rise. *Estuar. Coast.* 30:214–25.

Stagg CL, Mendelssohn IA. 2010. Restoring function to a submerged salt marsh. *Restor. Ecol.* 18:10–17.

Steyer GD. 2008. *Landscape analysis of vegetation change in coastal Louisiana following hurricanes Katrina and Rita.* Ph.D. diss., Louisiana State Univ., Baton Rouge.

Swarzenski CM. 1992. *Mat movement in coastal Louisiana marshes: effect of salinity and inundation on vegetation and nutrient levels.* Ph.D. diss., Old Dominion Univ., Norfolk, VA.

Swarzenski CM, Doyle TW, et al. 2008. Biogeochemical response of organic-rich freshwater marshes in the Louisiana delta plain to chronic river water influx. *Biogeochem.* 90:49–63.

Swenson EM, Swarzenski CM. 1995. Water levels and salinity in the Barataria-Terrebonne estuarine system. In *Status and trends of hydrologic modification, reduction in sediment availability, and habitat loss/modification in the Barataria-Terrebonne estuarine system,* Reed DJ, editor. Thibodaux, LA: Barataria-Terrebonne National Estuary Program, pp. 129–201.

Thom CSB, LaPeyre MKG, Nyman JA. 2004. Evaluation of nekton use and habitat characteristics of restored Louisiana marsh. *Ecol. Eng.* 23:61–75.

Törnqvist TE, Paola C, et al. 2007. Comment on "Wetland sedimentation from Hurricanes Katrina and Rita." *Science* 316:201.

Turner RE. 1997. Wetland loss in the northern Gulf of Mexico: multiple working hypotheses. *Estuaries* 29:1–13.

Turner RE, Costanza R, Schaife W. 1982. Canals and wetland erosion rates in coastal Louisiana. In *Proceedings of the Conference on Coastal Erosion and Wetland Modification in Louisiana: Causes, Consequences, and Options,* Boesch DF, editor. Slidell, LA: USFWS, pp. 73–84.

Turner RE, Milan CS, Swenson EM. 2006. Recent volumetric changes in salt marsh soils. *Estuar. Coast. Shelf Sci.* 69:352–59.

Twilley RR, Klerks PL, et al. 2005. Integrative approach to understanding the causes of salt marsh dieback: experimental manipulations of hydrology and soil biogeochemistry (Task II.2). Baton Rouge: Louisiana DNR. http://brownmarsh.com/data/II-2/bmII-2_final.pdf.

Verhoeven JTA, Koerselman W, Meuleman AFM. 1996. Nitrogen- or phosphorus-limited growth in herbaceous, wet vegetation: relations with atmospheric inputs and management. *Trends Ecol. Evol.* 11:494–97.

Vermeer M, Rahmstorf S. 2009. Global sea level linked to global temperature. *Proc. Nat. Acad. Sci. USA* 106:21527–32.

Visser JM. 1989. *The impact of vertebrate herbivores on primary production of *Sagittaria *marshes in the Wax Lake Delta, Atchafalaya Bay, Louisiana.* Ph.D. diss., Louisiana State Univ., Baton Rouge.

Visser JM, Sandy ER. 2009. The effects of flooding on four common Louisiana marsh plants. *Gulf of Mexico Sci.* 27:21–29.

Visser JM, Sasser CE. 1998. *1997 coastal vegetation analysis.* Baton Rouge: Louisiana DNR.

Visser JM, Sasser CE. 2009. The effect of environmental factors on floating fresh marsh end-of-season biomass. *Aquat. Bot.* 91:205–12.

Visser JM, Sasser CE, et al. 1998. Marsh vegetation types of the Mississippi River deltaic plain. *Estuaries* 21:818–28.

Visser JM, Sasser CE, et al. 1999. Long-term vegetation change in Louisiana tidal marshes, 1968–92. *Wetlands* 19:168–75.

Visser JM, Sasser CE, et al. 2002. The impact of a severe drought on the vegetation of a subtropical estuary. *Estuaries* 25:1184–96.

Visser JM, Sasser CE, Cade BS. 2006. The effect of multiple stressors on salt marsh end-of-season biomass. *Estuar. Coast.* 29:328–39.

Visser JM, Franken F, Sasser CE. 1999. Effects of grazing on the recovery of oligohaline marshes impacted by Hurricane Andrew. In *Recent research in coastal Louisiana,* Rozas LP, Nyman JA, et al., editors. Baton Rouge: Louisiana SeaGrant, pp. 295–304.

Visser JM, Vermilion WG, et al. 2005. Nesting habitat requirements for brown pelican and their management implications. *J. Coast. Res.* 21:e27–e35.

Wall DP, Darwin SP. 1999. Vegetation and elevational gradients within a bottomland hardwood forest of southeastern Louisiana. *Am. Midl. Nat.* 142:17–30.

Weaver KM, Tabberer DK, et al. 1990. Bottomland hardwood forest management for black bears in Louisiana. *Proc. Ann. Southeast. Assoc. Fish Wildl. Agen.* 44:342–50.

Webb EC, Mendelssohn IA. 1996. Factors affecting vegetation dieback of an oligohaline marsh in coastal Louisiana: field manipulation of salinity and submergence. *Am. J. Bot.* 83:1429–34.

White DA. 1993. Vascular plant community development on mudflats in the Mississippi River Delta, Louisiana, USA. *Aquat. Bot.* 45:171–94.

White DA, Darwin SP, Thien LB. 1983. Plants and plant communities of Jean Lafitte National Historic Park, Louisiana. *Tulane Stud. Zool. Bot.* 24:100–29.

White DA, Hauber DP, Hood CS. 2004. Clonal differences in *Phragmites australis* from the Mississippi River Delta. *Southeast. Nat.* 3:531–44.

White DA, Weiss TA, et al. 1978. Productivity and decomposition of the dominant salt marsh plants in Louisiana. *Ecology* 59:751–59.

Willis JM, Hester MW. 2004. Interactive effects of salinity, flooding, and soil type on *Panicum hemitomon*. *Wetlands* 24:43–50.

Wiseman WJ, Swenson EM, Kelly FJ. 1990. Control of estuarine salinities by coastal ocean salinity. In *Residual currents and long-term transport,* Cheng RT, editor. New York: Springer, pp. 184–93.

Yuill B, Lavoie D, Feed DJ. 2009. Understanding subsidence processes in coastal Louisiana. *J. Coast. Res.* 54:23–36.

Zoller JA. 2004. *Seasonal differences in bird communities of a Louisiana swamp and manipulation of the breeding densities of prothonotary warblers.* Master's thesis, Southeastern Louisiana Univ., Hammond.

CHAPTER 6

Wetlands of the Northern Gulf Coast

LORETTA L. BATTAGLIA, MARK S. WOODREY, MARK S. PETERSON,
KEVIN S. DILLON, and JENNEKE M. VISSER

Coastal ecosystems of the Gulf Coastal Plain spanning the northern Gulf of Mexico (GOM) are ecotonal in nature, in that they occupy the terrestrial-marine interface and are influenced bidirectionally from forces at their seaward and landward sides (Dardeau, Modlin, et al. 1992). Across this interface, species that characterize the transition are arrayed primarily according to their physiological tolerances to gradients of salinity and flooding, as well as sulfide concentrations and substrate stability (Baldwin and Mendelssohn 1998). Differential and individualistic responses of coastal species to these conditions result in rapid compositional turnover and narrow, sometimes distinct, zonation patterns oriented perpendicular to the coast. Although some zones, particularly those closer to the seaward end of the transition, are low in richness, the *cumulative* diversity across the subtle topographic gradients that characterize these low-lying ecosystems is very high. Coastal transitions typically encompass salt marsh, brackish marsh, fresh marsh, an ecotone between the marsh and vegetation adapted to drier conditions, and upland vegetation that may be dominated by forest or coastal prairie species. Intrusion of the marine environment into the terrestrial parts of the gradient occurs at different temporal and spatial scales, with chronic but relatively slow changes in sea level (Parry, Canziani, et al. 2007), relatively infrequent but sometimes extensive tropical storm–generated surges (Blood, Anderson, et al. 1991), and frequent but spatially restricted inundation with tides.

The objectives of this chapter are (1) to summarize compositional trends in the flora and fauna; (2) to describe the key ecological processes; and (3) to synthesize the major conservation threats in coastal wetland ecosystems of the northern GOM. The geographic boundaries extend from Matagorda Bay, Texas, along the northern Gulf of Mexico to Tampa Bay, Florida (Fig. 6.1). The Louisiana Deltaic Plain, which is covered in chapter 5 (Visser et al.), is omitted from this discussion.

Biogeochemistry

The gentle sloping of the Coastal Plain from the panhandle of Florida to west Texas lends itself to extensive coastal wetlands that span a salinity gradient from fresh to hypersaline condi-

tions. Many of the estuaries in this region are influenced by freshwater inputs, but also have an influential salinity gradient extending from their marine side (Peterson, Weber, et al. 2007). These estuaries are also some of the most productive and diverse systems (Gunter 1967; Day et al. 1989; Lowe, DeVries, et al. 2009). In contrast, some estuaries are marine dominated, with little freshwater input, as illustrated by Grand Bay in Mississippi (Peterson, Waggy, et al. 2007), and systems farther east into the Florida panhandle, such as Perdido Bay. However, other large systems appear to be a patchwork, with some areas that are markedly influenced by freshwater inflow and other areas that are more marine dominated.

To the east of the Mississippi River, barrier island–lagoon complexes and well-developed drowned river valleys dominate the coastal landscape. The geomorphology of western Louisiana to the Trinity–San Jacinto River Valley in Galveston, Texas, is classified as strand plain/Chenier Plain systems that host extensive wetlands, although a few drowned river valleys are also present. Sediment types in all of these areas are highly dependent on wave energy and hydrodynamics, with larger-grained sand being found on barrier islands, passes, and shallow coastal edges and finer-grained sediments found in the deeper estuaries and low-energy environments (Schroeder and Wiseman 1999).

Due to the wide variety of hydrodynamic conditions, sediment texture is quite variable along the northern GOM. Kaolinite, illite, and montmorillonite are common clays in the region that can have a large impact on the geochemical and biogeochemical cycling of nutrients and metals (Schroeder and Wiseman 1999); however, no published studies to date have investigated these processes in the region. Preliminary studies in Mississippi coastal and freshwater marshes have shown that large amounts of phosphate are readily adsorbed to sediment; the mechanisms are poorly understood, but may have dramatic impacts on water-column phosphate concentrations in these shallow coastal systems (K Dillon unpublished).

Sulfur (S) and iron (Fe) redox reactions appear to be major pathways for carbon cycling in some salt-marsh systems. Some of the highest rates of sulfate reduction found in the salt-marsh literature have been measured in a *Juncus roemerianus* (black needle rush) marsh in coastal Alabama (22.0 mol SO_4 $m^{-2}y^{-1}$;

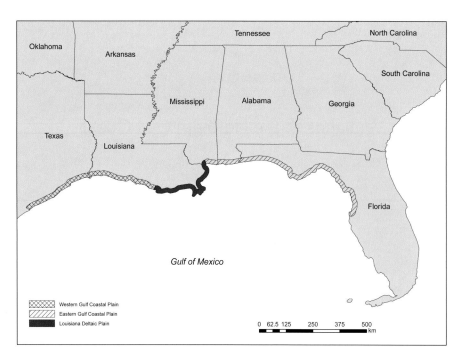

FIG. 6.1. This map illustrates the geographic extent of coastal habitat in the northern GOM. The western and eastern Gulf Coastal Plains are interrupted in southeastern Louisiana by the Louisiana Deltaic Plain (see Visser et al., chapter 5). We gratefully acknowledge Guy Schmale for producing this figure.

Miley and Kiene 2004). In terms of carbon, sulfate reduction in this system consumed between 11 and 38% of the total marsh primary production, which is equivalent to 16 to 90% of the annual belowground production. Despite these high rates, H_2S concentrations were relatively low due to sulfide oxidation or precipitation reactions with iron to produce pyrite. Hsieh and Yang (1997) found that pyrite concentrations in a St. Marks, Florida, *J. roemerianus* marsh were high, as were dissolved iron concentrations, suggesting that these marsh systems have a high potential for H_2S removal via pyrite formation. The high Fe content in sediments is thought to remove the reduced H_2S product of sulfate reduction in these sediments via pyrite precipitation, thereby preventing hydrogen sulfide accumulation and subsequent toxicity to plants (Hsieh and Yang 1997).

Disturbances by animals that churn or mix sediments (i.e., bioturbation) can have dramatic effects on sediment chemistry where iron is abundant. Increased aeration of sediments can allow rapid cycling between reduced and oxidized forms of iron. While bioturbation effects have yet to be quantified in the northern GOM, and in *J. roemerianus*–dominated marshes in particular, high iron and sulfide concentrations are found in many of these systems, suggesting that this process may be biogeochemically important in areas with high bioturbation. Clearly, S and Fe redox reactions are important anaerobic respiration pathways for carbon cycling for *J. roemerianus* marshes along the northern GOM; however, to date, these processes have been only sparsely quantified in northern GOM salt marshes.

Primary Productivity

Marsh Macrophytes

Juncus roemerianus is the dominant marsh species along the northern GOM, and these marshes have very high above-

ground production rates (1,000–4,000 g C m^{-2}yr^{-1}). *Spartina alterniflora* (eastern cordgrass) has similar productivity (Stout 1978), but these stands are generally spatially restricted to narrow bands at the marine-terrestrial interface. Production in areas dominated by other species such as *S. patens* (salt meadow hay) is often much lower and similar to adjacent forests, which range from 200 to 400 g C m^{-2}yr^{-1} (Hsieh 1996). Apart from inherent species-specific production capacity, another primary driver of productivity patterns along the northern GOM is elevation. Nutrient availability, porewater chemistry, redox potential, sediment type, sedimentation rates, and salinity often parallel changes in elevation such that it is often used as a surrogate for these other factors. Changes in primary productivity along these gradients can lead to differences in the amount of organic matter that accumulates belowground or reaches the marsh floor, and structural differences in shoots can influence the fraction of detrital matter that is held within the marsh for burial and the fraction that is exported out of the marsh as particulate organic matter. There are also potential differences in peat formation due to differences in nutrient availability and species-specific differences in productivity and decomposition rates between marsh macrophytes. Greenhouse fertilization experiments indicate a noticeable increase in peat formation with fertilization of *J. roemerianus* over time scales of a few months (Biber pers. comm.) and suggest that nutrient availability could have dramatic impacts on rates of carbon sequestration in some marshes.

Sea-level rise in the last 5,000 to 10,000 years has led to the formation of present-day coastal wetlands around the globe. Increased carbon sequestration by marsh sediments is one of the many ecological consequences of sea-level rise (Rabenhorst 1995). Studies in Florida marshes have shown that coastal marsh soils have accumulated 30 to 100 kg m^{-2} of soil organic carbon, while adjacent forest soils have accumulated only 5 to 10 kg m^{-2} of organic carbon (Coultas 1996). Another study, conducted in the St. Marks Wildlife Refuge, showed that C, N, and P inventories were higher in low marsh communities and correlated with aboveground productivity rates. The higher C inventory in the low marsh (~29 kg m^{-2}) relative to the middle and upper marsh (15–16 kg m^{-2}) indicates that C sequestration increases significantly as coastal wetlands mature (Choi, Wang, et al. 2001). These results imply that the landward expansion of coastal marshes into forested regions could increase C sequestration by an order of magnitude if marsh accretion rates can keep pace with the rate of sea-level rise. Loss of accumulated marsh C by erosional processes in retrograding marshes (such as Grand Bay in eastern Mississippi Sound) can be a source of CO_2 to the atmosphere as previously sequestered peat is oxidized; however, little is currently known about these processes along the northern GOM, and thus the topic warrants investigation.

In the St. Marks marshes, historical changes in vegetation, as determined by stable carbon isotopes, occurred in upper marsh regions with a transition from C_4 vegetation (likely *Spartina patens*) to the current C_3 marsh vegetation dominated by *Juncus roemerianus* (Choi, Wang, et al. 2001). Based on radiocarbon measurements, this change occurred in the past century and is attributable to sea-level rise and the landward retreat of marsh vegetation. As forests became inundated from sea-level rise, the high marsh plant *S. patens* moved into the area initially and was then replaced with the more salt-tolerant *J. roemerianus* as the water level and salinity increased. These results suggest that changes in dominance patterns in these plant communities, concomitant with environmental changes from high-marsh to low-marsh conditions, are likely to drive shifts in productivity and associated carbon sequestration.

Microbenthos

Benthic microalgae are a functional group of primary producers that includes diatoms, cyanobacteria, and green algae. The dominant component of this functional group in the GOM is the diatom community (Sullivan 1978). Species diversity of diatoms may be higher than initially believed and can depend on species of marsh macrophytes present, sedimentary characteristics, and proximity to high-salinity waters (Cook and Whipple 1982; Sullivan and Currin 2000).

Microphytobenthos production rates in a Mississippi *Juncus* marsh were low (28 g C m^{-2} y^{-1}) compared to rates measured beneath nearby stands of *Spartina alterniflora* (57 g C m^{-2} y^{-1}), *Distichlis spicata* (salt grass; 88 g C m^{-2} y^{-1}), and *Schoenoplectus americanus* (chairmaker's bulrush; 115 g C m^{-2} y^{-1}) (Sullivan and Moncreif 1988). The best predictor of benthic microalgal production in this system appeared to be soil moisture (higher production in drier sediments). Sullivan and Moncreif (1990) showed that benthic microalgae had a much lower rate of primary productivity (21–151 g C m^{-2} y^{-1}) relative to marsh plants (248–742 g C m^{-2} y^{-1}). However, the more easily assimilated benthic microalgae were preferentially grazed upon by consumers and, based on a dual stable isotope analysis, appeared to serve as a more important C source than the more abundant and refractory marsh macrophytes. Despite the large disparity of biomass between the marsh plants and the microphytobenthos, isotopic studies reveal that over 50% of the carbon assimilated by invertebrates and Gulf killifish in Mississippi and Louisiana marshes was derived from the microphytobenthos (Deegan and Garritt 1997). At this time, it appears unclear whether organic matter derived from microphytobenthos is exported from salt marshes to any large degree.

Vegetation

Eastern Gulf Coastal Plain

Coastal ecosystems in the Gulf have microtidal hydroperiods (Rozas 1995). The tidal regime, as well as the history of tropical storm surge and other saltwater intrusion events, creates a dynamic soil salinity gradient that drives and underlies trends in community composition as species are arrayed, in part, according to their salinity tolerances (Fig. 6.2). Thus, coastal transition communities of the eastern Gulf of Mexico have high overlap in terms of species composition, particularly at their seaward edge.

At their seaward edge, intact coastal transitions of the northern GOM typically have a relatively narrow band of salt marsh dominated by salt-tolerant graminoids. *Spartina alterniflora* is the most abundant, with *Distichlis spicata* and *Spartina patens* commonly co-occurring. Tidal creeks and bayous interrupt the salt and brackish marshes, linking them intimately with the sea. Although not nearly as common as the other two *Spartina* species, *S. cynosuroides* (big cordgrass) can be found at some sites flanking the creeks. Some areas near these waterways are unvegetated and consist of exposed mudflats, an important habitat for many bird and invertebrate species. Because the most seaward salt marsh experiences regular and frequent tidal flushing, soils are generally less saline than those farther inland and have less buildup of toxic sulfides; here the "tall form" of *S. alterniflora* is often found.

Hypersaline conditions may develop in low and high marshes that experience irregular tidal flooding and high evapotranspiration. In those areas, salt and brackish marsh species are found at reduced densities and sometimes in their "short form." Salt pannes occur in the most extreme hypersaline conditions. These communities are composed of sparse cover of the "short forms" and halophytes such as *Distichlis spicata* and the succulent *Salicornia bigelovii* (glasswort) (Hunter, Morris, et al. 2008). Salt pannes tend to have a high percentage of bare ground and coincide with peak soil water salinities across the transition (Paudel and Battaglia unpublished).

With decreases in salinity and length of hydroperiod at more inland locations, salt marsh transitions into brackish marsh (Moody and Aronson 2007). Brackish marshes are often expansive and dominated by *Juncus roemerianus*. Plant diversity is remarkably low, and many of these stands are dense monocultures of this species. Despite the low plant diversity in salt and brackish marshes, these communities provide essential functions to marine and terrestrial ecosystems. Their high net primary productivity fuels the detrital food web (Pennings, Siska, et al. 2001), and the structure of the vegetation is closely linked to the life-history requirements of many wildlife species. Finally, these communities bear the brunt of tropical storms as they make landfall, and thus shelter the more interior and sensitive portions of the ecosystem.

With reduced salinity stress farther inland, more species from the regional species pool can cope physiologically, and species diversity increases (Dardeau, Modlin, et al. 1992). Freshwater marsh species that dominate these areas include *Cladium mariscus* (Jamaica swamp sawgrass) and *Panicum virgatum* (switchgrass). Many other graminoids can occur here, along with small forbs such as *Sabatia stellaris* (rose of Plym-

FIG. 6.2. Coastal transition typical of the eastern Gulf Coastal Plain. A thin band of *Spartina alterniflora* occurs at the water's edge and gives way to often expansive stands of *Juncus roemerianus,* the dominant species in northern GOM marshes. A maritime pine island with *Pinus elliottii* in the overstory can be seen in the background. Eglin Air Force Base, East Bay, Florida. (Photo credit: Loretta Battaglia.)

FIG. 6.3. Coastal transition typical of the western Gulf Coastal Plain. The zonation sequence (right to left) is *Juncus roemerianus* marsh giving way to a salt panne to a *Spartina alterniflora* marsh and to the open bay. Central Texas coast. (Photo credit: Jenneke Visser.)

outh) and *Agalinis maritima* (saltmarsh false foxglove), and even broad-leaved wetland macrophytes such as *Sagittaria lancifolia* (fresh bulltongue) and *Pontederia cordata* (pickerelweed) (Clark, Brown, et al. 2008). Freshwater marshes of this region generally occupy relatively narrow zones (Shirley and Battaglia 2006).

With increasing elevation and distance from the sea, freshwater marshes transition quickly to wetland hardwood forest or maritime pine savanna, depending on edaphic characteristics and topographic configuration of the landward transition. Often, the marsh-forest ecotone has the appearance of a wetland savanna, with scattered flood-tolerant woody species and freshwater marsh vegetation in the groundcover. Where fire and other disturbances that reduce woody species are infrequent, the ecotone typically has dense shrub cover. *Morella cerifera* (wax myrtle) is common and often dominates the community. Other common species include *Ilex vomitoria* (yaupon), *Baccharis halimifolia* (saltbush), *Hypericum* spp. (St. Johnswort), and *Iva frutescens* (Jesuit's bark) (Kalk and Battaglia in review).

In general, facultative and upland species increase in abundance along these coastal transitions with decreasing flood frequency and exposure to elevated salinity conditions. Often, the ecotone gives way to a fringing wetland forest dominated by wetland hardwood species such as *Acer rubrum* (red maple), *Nyssa biflora* (swamp tupelo), *Persea borbonia* (redbay), and *Magnolia virginiana* (sweet bay magnolia). Other areas support wet pine flatwoods with *Pinus elliottii* (slash pine) in the canopy and rich understories composed of carnivorous plants (e.g., *Sarracenia leucophylla*), numerous graminoids (e.g., *Scleria* spp., *Rhynchospora* spp.), and other indicator species such as *Eriocaulon decangulare* (pipewort), *Xyris difformis* (yelloweyed grass), and *Polygala cruciata* (drumheads) (Brewer 2006). Where the adjacent upland is undisturbed, longleaf pine/wiregrass *(Pinus palustris/Aristida stricta)* savannas are typical.

Western Gulf Coast Plain

The western Gulf coast vegetation zones also change from saline marshes near the coast to freshwater tidal marshes in the interior (Fig. 6.3). In addition, coastal salinity is higher at the arid western end (Alexander and Dunton 2002) and fresher at the eastern end, with higher local precipitation and greater influence of the Mississippi River, whose waters are transported westward by the prevailing currents. Salinity is strongly correlated with many other environmental factors as well as vegetation composition (Visser, Sasser, et al. 2000).

Along the western Louisiana and eastern Texas coast, vegetation zonation follows the stranded beach ridges, or Cheniers, that generally are oriented parallel to the coast. *Cheniere* is a French word that indicates the natural vegetation on these beach ridges is dominated by oaks such as *Quercus virginiana* (live oak). Although Chenier woodlands were once extensive, most have now been converted to rangeland, roads, or homesites, and remnant forest is often invaded by the aggressive exotic *Triadica sebifera* (Chinese tallow tree), which leads to reduced native diversity, especially in smaller patches of fragmented forests (Neyland and Meyer 1997).

Most of the coastal marshes along the central Texas coast formed on the edge of river valleys that flooded when sea levels rose during the Holocene and therefore have highly mineral soils (White, Morton, et al. 2002). In many areas, water delivery to the coast is limited. This limitation, coupled with relatively high elevations of the marsh platform, limiting tidal inundation and high evapotranspiration, leads to development of hypersaline marshes (Heinsch, Heilman, et al. 2004). *Salicornia bigelovii* and *Batis maritima* (turtleweed) are the dominant plants in these marshes (Alexander and Dunton 2002). In areas with more freshwater input, *Spartina alterniflora, Distichlis spicata,* and *Borrichia frutescens* dominate along the coast.

Along the Chenier Plain, the marshes closest to the coast are primarily mesohaline marsh and are codominated by *Spartina patens* and *Schoenoplectus americanus* (Visser, Sasser, et al. 2000). Grazing by waterfowl and mammals can affect the relative dominance of these species (Taylor, Grace, et al. 1994). Oligohaline marshes in the Chenier Plain are mostly dominated by *S. patens* and are increasingly invaded by *Phragmites australis* (common reed) and *Typha* spp. (cattail) (Visser, Sasser, et al. 2002). Farther inland in the Chenier Plain, the vegetation consists of extensive freshwater marshes dominated by *Panicum hemitomon* (fresh maidencane) and *Sagittaria lancifolia* (Visser, Sasser, et al. 2002).

The presence of water in an oligohaline marsh in the late summer is an important factor linked to increased aboveground biomass (Bhattacharjee, Haukos, et al. 2009). Thus, drought episodes can have dramatically negative effects on these marshes. Heinsch, Heilman, et al. (2004) showed that saline marshes in the mid-Texas region release carbon dioxide to the atmosphere during drought, while carbon is sequestered during periods in which freshwater is introduced from local rivers.

Seagrass Communities

Many estuaries and coastal lagoons found west of Apalachicola Bay have little salt-marsh vegetation but considerable seagrass beds (Durako, Browder, et al. 1985). *Thalassia testudinum* (turtlegrass) is the dominant from Perdido Bay eastward, with some stands of *Cymodocea filiformis* (manatee grass) and *Halodule wrightii* (shoalweed). In contrast, west of Perdido Bay through the Louisiana state line, *H. wrightii* dominates with *Ruppia maritima* (widgeongrass) and, rarely, *Syringodium filiforme*. This distribution pattern is mainly driven by water clarity and substrate characteristics (Durako, Browder, et al. 1985) and suggests that habitat diversity increases east of Mobile Bay, Alabama, because of the addition of many structurally complex seagrass communities. Cedar Key appears to be the dividing line between temperate fauna to the north and subtropical/tropical to the south (Kilby 1955).

An east-west transition in seagrass habitats occurs along the northern GOM near Mobile Bay, Alabama (Byron and Heck 2006). East of Mobile Bay, seagrass habitats were more similar to the sites in Apalachee Bay, Florida, with higher water clarity and *T. testudinum* dominating the community. West of Mobile Bay, sites appeared more temperate, with water clarity being much lower, sediments muddier, and *H. wrightii* as the most abundant seagrass species. Apparently, increased water temperature due to global climate change has allowed northward movement of subtropical and tropical fish species into habitat with noncoevolved temperate species. Comparisons between seagrass-fish assemblages based on 1970s and 2006–07 data sets revealed 11 new taxa that were completely absent in the 1970s in the northern GOM (Fodrie, Heck, et al. 2010). Three species showed large increases in abundance during the ~30-year interval, and all of these tropical or subtropical species now make up a greater percentage of seagrass-associated fish assemblages in the northern GOM than in the past. The observed regional increases in air and sea surface temperatures (> 3 °C) were correlated with shifts in the distribution of these species into the northern GOM (Fodrie, Heck, et al. 2010).

Invertebrate and Fish Communities

The fisheries (and shellfish) production of the northern GOM is a large percentage of the total fisheries production in the United States (NMFS Fisheries Statistics Division, www.st.nmfs.noaa.gov/st1/commercial/index.html). The area from Port Arthur, Texas, to Pascagoula, Mississippi, has been recognized for over four decades as the Fertile Fisheries Crescent (Gunter 1963). The vast expanses of coastal wetland habitat and river subsidies are now definitively linked with this historically high fish productivity (Day et al. 1989).

Invertebrate Communities

Numerous meiofauna and macroinvertebrate species play key functional roles in the regeneration of nutrients and movement of energy in northern GOM estuarine ecosystems (Twilley, Cowan, et al. 1999). They provide important biogeochemical linkages between the benthic and pelagic components of these detrital-based estuarine ecosystems (Hansen and Kristensen 1997). The trophic connections they form are particularly important to fisheries production. Thus, the health and integrity of these assemblages have both ecological and economic implications. Their sedentary nature and residence within or upon coastal sediments that concentrate pollutants make macroinfaunal communities informative as indicators of estuarine health and anthropogenic impacts (Rakocinski, Brown, et al. 1997; Brown, Gaston, et al. 2000).

Crassostrea virginica (eastern oyster) is a filter-feeder that is considered to be a keystone species in this system. It filters sediment and pollutants from the water column, and the reefs it creates provide habitat for other species. Two of the important foragers in northern GOM marsh communities are *Uca* spp. (fiddler crabs) and *Callinectes sapidus* (blue crab). These crustaceans and other foraging species consume algae, bacteria, fungi, detritus, and meiofauna from the sediment surface. Blue crabs also consume oysters and clams and occasionally feed upon plant material. Fiddler crabs are very abundant marsh dwellers that provide abundant food resources to marsh birds (Rush, Soehren, et al. 2009) and other wildlife species, e.g., raccoons. Predators of blue crabs include marsh birds, estuarine fish, and sea turtles. Blue crabs and oysters are also consumed by humans and are considered to be highly valuable fishery species.

Fish and Nekton Assemblages

Many estuaries of the GOM are dynamic transitional systems (sensu Schiemer, Zalewski, et al. 1995) in that they link fresh and salt habitats and are driven by freshwater inputs that vary with rainfall events and drought cycles. For example, Beckett, Viskup, et al. (1992) reported that freshwater fishes in freshwater ponds on Horn Island, Mississippi, likely colonized when coastal rivers adjacent to the Mississippi Sound flooded. In this case, opening of this dispersal avenue resulted in established, persistent populations. In contrast, the effects of drought on the trophic organization of a river-dominated GOM estuary, albeit pronounced, were ephemeral (Livingston, Niu, et al. 1997). Based on a long-term study (9.5 years), they found that the system experienced a major state change during a natural two-year natural drought when an important threshold was exceeded. They suggested that the drought reduced turbidity in the water, which led to rapid changes in primary production and subsequent shifts in the trophic structure of the community; the shifts were reversed to predrought assemblages when normal rainfall returned (Livingston, Niu, et al. 1997).

The fish assemblages associated with these different systems vary in composition and diversity, in part because of the different degree of connectivity to riverine versus marine assemblages (Durako, Browder, et al. 1985; O'Connell, Cashner, et al. 2004). Freshwater inflows are an important element of static and dynamic habitat components (Peterson 2003) and are part of the complex habitat template (Gibson 1994) upon which fish (and other nekton) population and community dynamics operate. This driver is clearly associated with the pulsing of estuarine-dependent fishes (and other nekton) into and out of estuaries (Rozas 1995).

Within estuarine systems, the structure of nekton assemblages varies depending upon the freshwater input and the spatial and temporal extent of available habitat along the salinity gradient (Durako, Browder, et al. 1985; Peterson 2003; Peterson, Weber, et al. 2007). In early work on estuarine systems (papers reviewed in Gunter 1967), many studies illustrated these patterns by quantifying the integration of fresh- and saltwater fishes (and other nekton), many of which use salt marsh exclusively. Recently, studies have shown that physiological capabilities of fishes (and other nekton) underpin use of these estuaries from the freshwater side (Lowe, DeVries, et al. 2009) and the estuarine/marine side (Peterson, Comyns, et al. 2004). Because these systems are hierarchical in nature (Peterson, Weber, et al. 2007), the physiological basis of distribution and abundance (Wikelski and Cooke 2006) is modified by habitat availability and the food and spawning sites this habitat provides (Peterson 2003). Finally, across freshwater-dominated tidal estuaries, assemblages often have high beta diversity due to habitat diversity (Stout 1984), and the associated fishes and other nekton (Jelbart, Ross, et al. 2007) utilize multiple habitat types, contributing to higher growth rates.

Terrestrial Vertebrates

Terrestrial vertebrates found in northern GOM coastal ecosystems are taxonomically diverse, with abundance varying seasonally (Chabreck 1988). In addition, some of the higher vertebrates, including reptiles, birds, and mammals, are among the organisms most commonly observed by humans and are highly sought after by photographers, bird-watchers, hunters, and trappers. The objectives of this section are as follows: (1) to highlight taxa of ecological importance, and (2) to discuss the significance of these species or communities to our understanding of the ecology of northern GOM ecosystems. Among the groups highlighted in this section are amphibians such as the oak toad *(Bufo quercicus)* and green treefrog *(Hyla cinerea)*; reptiles such as the diamondback terrapin *(Malaclemys terrapin)*; birds such as waterfowl, herons, egrets, and marsh birds; and mammals, including muskrat *(Ondatra zibethicus)* and raccoon *(Procyon lotor)*. We have chosen to highlight these species or groups because of their ecological importance in Gulf coast tidal marshes and/or adjacent landward communities that are part of the broader coastal transition ecosystem. Several of the species are endemic to Gulf coast marshes, some are of high concern from a conservation perspective, and others are important because of the functional role they play in these ecosystems.

Environmental Conditions Affecting Distribution of Terrestrial Vertebrates

The abundance of individuals constituting coastal vertebrate animal communities varies widely across Gulf coast ecosystems and is influenced by prevailing environmental conditions such as moisture, salinity regime, water depth and tidal fluctuations, and vegetation communities (Chabreck 1988). These environmental conditions vary regionally and locally to produce quite distinct animal communities at a variety of geographic scales. Although most estuarine animals exhibit distributions or behaviors related to salinity patterns (Day et al. 1989), the literature directly linking their populations with

this and other factors is limited. Some species that occur in the broader landscape are physiologically restricted by salinity. Salamanders, for example, are not typically found in areas subject to saline flooding (Pough, Andrews, et al. 2003).

Daily and seasonal tidal fluctuations affect access to resources and the safety of estuarine wildlife (Day et al. 1989). High water levels can have both positive and negative impacts: high tides provide protection from predators, but also can destroy the nests, eggs, and young of terrestrial vertebrates. Low water levels allow "terrestrial" species to use the intertidal zone, yet also can expose them to predators while they are utilizing open mudflat habitats.

The spatial and temporal characteristics of vascular plant communities are particularly important to wildlife. Seasonal and interannual changes in species composition, vertical structure, plant form and texture, and presence of litter or standing dead vegetation are features of vegetation that strongly influence wildlife distributions (Day et al. 1989). With the exception of amphibians, vertebrates in coastal marshes often have broad habitat affinities. Linkages between plant communities and wildlife are perhaps best exemplified by coastal birds. Although species composition may differ in the marsh-nesting bird communities, the same pattern of horizontal and vertical stratification reported in a New Jersey salt marsh (Burger 1985) can be observed in the extensive marshes along the Gulf coast. In general terms, clapper rails nest in low marsh areas (i.e., close to tidal creeks and guts), whereas various species of terns and gulls will nest throughout the marsh but select the highest spots. Marsh-dwelling sparrows tend to occupy mid-marsh areas, while marsh wrens and red-winged blackbirds are associated with high marsh vegetation, including *Iva* spp., *Baccharis* spp., and *Phragmites* spp.

Endemism

Tidal marshes are among the most productive ecosystems in the world, with abundant plant and animal food resources throughout the emergent marsh and marine food chains, yet the terrestrial vertebrate communities associated with these habitats are depauperate in species (Greenberg 2006). Despite low diversity, these fauna exhibit a high proportion of endemic taxa. There are approximately 25 species of terrestrial vertebrates that are either wholly restricted to, or have recognized subspecies restricted to, coastal marshes of the region (Greenberg, Maldonado, et al. 2006). Of these species, 4 are reptiles, 12 are birds, and 9 are mammals. Surprisingly, 24 of the 25 taxa exhibiting complete or partial endemism were found in North America (Greenberg and Maldonado 2006). Thirteen, or 52%, of these species or recognized subspecies are restricted to northern GOM tidal marshes (online appendix 6.1), highlighting the importance and need to better understand their ecology and role in these ecosystems. Given the many threats facing coastal marshes worldwide, it is not surprising that all 13 endemic marsh species are at some heightened level of conservation concern (online appendix 6.1).

Amphibians

With few exceptions, amphibians are largely restricted to areas outside of the saline environment that characterizes coastal-marsh communities of the northern GOM. Communities such as nontidal freshwater marshes and wet pine flatwoods that are part of the broader coastal transition ecosystem, but rarely impacted by saltwater intrusion, provide habitat for numerous amphibian species (Langford, Borden, et al. 2007). Given trends in land use, habitat fragmentation, and global amphibian declines, these habitats are especially critical and valuable in the modern coastal landscape.

In these interior parts of the coastal landscape, amphibian diversity increases sharply, particularly in areas that contain shallow depressions and freshwater ponds. Amphibians are major predators of numerous invertebrate species and thus constitute important trophic linkages in the coastal food web. *Amphiuma means* (two-toed amphiuma) and *Siren intermedia* (lesser siren) exploit mostly aquatic habitat but can burrow into the mud and utilize tunnels excavated by crayfish during drought periods. Anuran species are most commonly found in or around these ephemeral wetland habitats. *Hyla cinerea* is abundant and often found in microsites that hold standing water, including the PVC pipes that are commonly used to mark ecological field sites. This species is actually one of the few that is tolerant of brackish conditions (Mitchell and Anderson 1994) and whose distribution can extend farther seaward. *Bufo quercicus* occurs in mixed pine/oak communities and appears to favor areas that have been recently burned (Langford, Borden, et al. 2007). *Rana utricularia* (southern leopard frog) is also quite common and utilizes more upland habitat for feeding in the summer (Johnson 1992). Terrestrial salamanders such as *Desmognathus auriculatus* (southern dusky salamander) may be found underneath downed logs and other woody debris. Widespread and unexplained declines in populations have been reported for this species in recent years, even in undisturbed habitats, and it is therefore of conservation concern (Means and Travis 2007).

Reptiles

Diamondback terrapins are the only turtle species specialized to salt-marsh and estuarine habitats in the temperate zone (Hart and Lee 2006). Three of the seven subspecies of diamondback terrapins are found in the coastal marshes of the GOM (online appendix 6.1). In addition to their salt-marsh endemic status, terrapins historically were economically and culturally important. Terrapins supported a multimillion-dollar industry catering to the gourmet restaurant trade until population reductions reduced harvest to unsustainable levels. Lazell (1979) noted that terrapins were virtually eliminated in the late 1800s and early 1900s due to overharvest and habitat modification. Because of their reduced numbers and specific habitat requirements, diamondback terrapins are listed as a species of conservation concern throughout the GOM (online appendix 6.1).

Few published studies have focused on Gulf coast diamondback terrapin populations. Mann (1995) undertook a coastwide survey to assess the presence and abundance of diamondback terrapins in Mississippi. Using depredated nests as a proxy for nesting females, he estimated a coastwide population of 535 nesting terrapins. He documented terrapin nesting activity across the Mississippi coast, locating nests at 9 of the 10 sites he surveyed. Trapping efforts also confirmed terrapins to be widespread across the Mississippi Gulf coast, although the number documented was relatively low when compared with the Atlantic coast. Mann (1995) suggested that terrapin numbers have declined in Mississippi since the 1940s and that crab pots, which inadvertently trap them, are likely responsible.

The most recent survey for diamondback terrapins was conducted in Galveston Bay, Texas (Hogan 2003). Occurrence surveys, conducted over two nesting seasons, indicated terrapins were captured most frequently in April and May. Terrapin habitat use in this area—shell hash areas, salt marshes, and oyster-shell reefs—were similar to habitats documented in previous studies of Texas coastal areas (Hogan 2003).

Birds

The vastness of the Gulf coast marshes is matched by the diversity and sheer numbers of birds found in these coastal habitats. Ninety percent of all bird species of eastern North America have been observed in them (Lowery and Newman 1954). Stout (1984) noted that *Juncus*-dominated marshes of the northeastern GOM support year-round residents such as *Rallus longirostris* (clapper rail) and *Ardea herodias* (great blue heron), summer-nesting species such as *Ixobrychus exilis* (least bittern), migrants such as *Cistothorus platensis* (sedge wren), and winter residents such as *Aythya affinis* (lesser scaup).

Birds are perhaps the most studied wildlife species in the northern GOM. More than 40 species of waterfowl frequent these marshes, with each species having its own set of environmental requirements (Lynch 1968). They can be significant herbivores in coastal marshes and help disperse propagules of marsh plants (Weller 1999). Predatory birds, such as osprey, are also major carnivores and play an important role in the upper trophic levels of marsh and estuarine food chains (Stout 1984).

In spite of numerous published studies focused on birds utilizing Gulf coast marshes, only two specifically focused on marsh bird community assemblages. Weller (1994a) conducted surveys in all months of the year and recorded 121 bird species in a coastal Texas wetland complex. Despite the large number of species recorded, only 23 species used the site regularly, although their pattern of wetland use varied by species and season. Although the wetlands provided different resources for different species, most species used the area either for migration stopover sites or as wintering habitat. Avian species richness varied by vegetation type, being generally lowest in the drier areas dominated by *Spartina spartinae* (Gulf cordgrass) and highest in *Distichlis spicata* and mudflat areas. The vegetation zone dominated by *Schoenoplectus americanus* had the deepest and most regularly flooded water conditions, tallest vegetation, and consistently high usage by birds. Weller (1994b) examined only the summer bird community and, noting similar patterns of species richness in relation to vegetation zones, suggested wetland species–habitat relationships are consistent across seasons.

Gulf coast marshes provide critical habitat for millions of wintering waterfowl, predominantly ducks and geese. Southern coastal marshes of the Mississippi flyway along the GOM provide habitat for over 400,000 geese, 4 million ducks, 1.5 million *Fulica americana* (American coots), hundreds of thousands of shorebirds, and other migratory birds that utilize these areas at some stage of their annual cycle (Chabreck, Joanen, et al. 1989). Although waterfowl are commonly seen in winter in these coastal marshes, their numbers increase from the eastern portion of the Gulf coast toward the west. Presumably, this pattern is related to the gradient of coastal marsh habitat availability from east to west along the Gulf. Of the 1,024,700 ha of marsh found along the north-central Gulf coast, 986,700 ha (96%) are found in Louisiana, followed by 27,800 ha (3%) in Mississippi and 10,200 ha (1%) in Alabama

(Chabreck, Joanen, et al. 1989). Freshwater and intermediate marshes associated with the GOM represent the most valuable waterfowl habitats in this area. Brackish marshes are the most extensive habitat and represent the traditional wintering grounds for *Chen caerulescens* (snow geese), provide year-round habitat for *Anas fulvigula* (mottled ducks), and are also of high value to *Anas strepera* (gadwalls) and lesser scaup (Chabreck, Joanen, et al. 1989). Salt-marsh habitats play only a minor role and are generally considered to be of low value to waterfowl (Williams and Chabreck 1986).

Waterfowl associated with the central flyway winter in the "rice prairies" (former coastal prairies now cultivated for rice production), wet prairies, coastal marshes, and bays found along the Texas coast (Hobaugh, Stutzenbaker, et al. 1989). In coastal Texas, geese make extensive use of rice prairie habitats (Hobaugh, Stutzenbaker, et al. 1989). Dabbling ducks, including *Anas acuta* (northern pintail), gadwall, *A. america* (American widgeon), *A. crecca* (green-winged teal), and *A. clypeata* (northern shovelers) use estuarine vegetated wetlands and inland palustrine areas. Diving ducks such as *Aythya collaris* (redheads), lesser scaup, *A. marila* (greater scaup), *A. valisineria* (canvasbacks), and *Oxyura jamaicensis* (ruddy ducks) are dispersed widely along the coast, with many using freshwater ponds and marshes just inland from the coast. Redheads are most common in the Laguna Madre, where over 75% of the U.S. population winters (Woodin and Michot 1996).

Of all the various groups of birds associated with coastal marshes, wading birds, including herons, egrets, and ibises, are probably the most visible to and most watched by the casual observer. At least some species in this group can be found in marshes throughout the year, with species composition and numbers fluctuating seasonally (Day, Smith, et al. 1973). In addition, some species utilize coastal marshes for breeding, some winter in these productive habitats, and others use these habitats during the spring and fall as they move between their breeding and wintering areas. Clearly, these birds play an important role in the trophic dynamics of estuarine-based food webs (Stout 1984).

Several studies have investigated the effects of prescribed fire, a primary management tool, on marsh bird communities (Nyman and Chabreck 1995; Gabrey, Afton, et al. 2001). Gabrey, Afton, et al. (2001) noted that vegetation did not differ between the burned and unburned plots by the first summer postburn and that bird species composition was not affected by winter burns. However, surveys of all bird species and of sparrows were two times greater in burned than in unburned marshes during the second summer postburn only (Gabrey, Afton, et al. 2001). Thus, winter marsh burning for waterfowl appears to be compatible with management for other marsh birds, provided that sufficient winter cover for passerines is included in management plans. Further, they noted that sparrows were generally more abundant in unimpounded marshes.

Two studies, focused specifically on fire effects on breeding seaside sparrows in Louisiana (Gabrey and Afton 2000) and along the upper Texas coast (Whitbeck 2002), found similar patterns of abundance of breeding male seaside sparrows. In both studies, sparrow abundance was highest on the study plots in the second breeding season postburn. Further, the authors noted a positive relationship between sparrow abundance and cover of dead vegetation. The authors suggest that dead vegetation may serve several ecological functions for marsh-nesting sparrows. First, both studies noted that dead vegetation is the primary material used for nest building. Second, Gabrey and Afton (2000) hypothesized that dead vegetation may serve as a substrate for invertebrate prey, which are a primary food source for seaside sparrows during the nesting season (Post and Greenlaw 1994). Third, Whitbeck (2002) suggested that dead vegetation may provide elevated nesting substrate that keeps nests above fluctuating water levels.

In addition to breeding birds, Gabrey, Afton, et al. (2001) also evaluated the effects of burning on winter marsh bird populations in Louisiana. Winter bird surveys were conducted immediately after burns, and a second time one year postburn. Wintering seaside sparrows were absent immediately following burns, but were present in unburned marshes and also in burn treatment plots one year postburn. *Ammodramus nelsoni* (Nelson's sharp-tailed sparrows), a migratory winter endemic to Gulf coast marshes, were recorded in burned marshes during the first winter but were found only in scattered patches of unburned vegetation. However, this species was observed frequently in unburned plots during both survey periods and in burn treatment plots one year postburn. Gabrey, Afton, et al. (2001) concluded that winter burning reduces the suitability of marshes as winter habitat, but only for a few months immediately following burns.

"Secretive" marsh birds, including species such as clapper rail and least bittern, which are not often seen and call infrequently, were the focus of a recent study conducted along the marshes of the Alabama-Mississippi coastline. Utilizing standardized marsh bird monitoring data, Rush, Soehren, et al. (2009) used species occupancy modeling to assess the impacts of human-induced and natural processes on populations of marsh birds found along the northern GOM. Modeling efforts suggested that predicted change in habitat characteristics of northern GOM marshes could impact the distribution of marsh bird species. However, for most species, the direction of the effect on occupancy was not clear until the magnitude of habitat change exceeded 20% of present conditions. For example, an increase in the extent of *Juncus roemerianus*–dominated marsh would lead to higher occupancy rates by both clapper rail and seaside sparrow. However, the potential for continued development and loss of habitat interspersion could reduce the presence of these species. For least bittern, *Cistothorus palustris* (marsh wren), and *Geothlypis trichas* (common yellowthroat), marsh loss and alteration may ultimately lead to reduced occupancy.

Mammals

Muskrats are among the most efficient herbivores of Gulf coast marshes (Bhattacharjee, Haukos, et al. 2007). Under ideal conditions, when their abundances are high (Chabreck 1988), they can have dramatic effects on coastal marsh vegetation through massive eat-outs. Various factors can influence muskrat populations in marshes along the GOM. Palmisano (1973) studied habitat preferences for muskrats by looking at the interaction between vegetation types, salinity, extent of flooding, and drought on distribution and abundance of muskrat in Louisiana marshes. Although muskrats occurred in all plant communities, population densities varied greatly; brackish marshes composed of a mixed community of *Schoenoplectus americanus* and *Spartina patens* were the preferred habitat. However, muskrat colonies can rapidly develop in less-preferred habitats when conditions are favorable. These colonies may remain in these suboptimal habitats for one or two years and then disappear, whereas populations remain stable in *S. americanus* habitats as long as they are healthy. Kinler (1986) noted that water depth is a critical factor affecting muskrat populations; high tides can cover lodges, drown young animals, and displace or even kill adults. Severe drought conditions can have the biggest impact on muskrat populations, with animals of all ages often dying from lack of water while the marsh is dry (O'Neil 1949). Drought impacts are further exacerbated by the development of hypersaline soil conditions that often lead to a die-off of *S. americanus,* a primary food plant for muskrats.

Raccoons occupy a wide range of habitats in Gulf coast marshes and are opportunistic feeders, consuming both animal and plant material (Chabreck 1988). Their diet is flexible, reflecting their opportunistic foraging behavior. When crayfish are abundant, raccoons feed almost exclusively on them; when birds are nesting, they feed on eggs and young birds; when fruit ripens on marsh ridges and spoil banks, they feed on fruit.

Fleming (1975) used radio telemetry to study the movement patterns of raccoons in the coastal marshes of Louisiana. He found that although raccoons are primarily nocturnal, feeding activity during daylight hours was frequently observed in areas with pronounced tidal fluctuations. Habitat use was not equal among various marsh habitat types; levee berms were used more intensively during the summer, impounded areas and bayous during the fall, and extensive open-water areas during the winter. He also noted that raccoon movements were affected by seasonal fluctuations of marsh water levels.

Hunting and Wildlife Viewing

Estuaries and coastal wetlands are important from an economic perspective because they have large, readily observable faunas that attract hunters and wildlife-watchers. For example, 268 bird species have been documented on the Grand Bay Estuary, located along the Mississippi- Alabama border. This number represents 69% of the 387 species documented in the Birds of the Mississippi Coastal Counties Checklist for the six southernmost counties in Mississippi (Woodrey and Walker 2009). Mammals of the Gulf coast marshes are also important for meat and fur (Palmisano 1973).

Socioeconomic surveys conducted on a regular basis clearly demonstrate the economic value of wilderness in the United States. The National Survey on Recreation and the Environment, conducted by the U.S. Forest Service, noted that from 1999–2003, 157.5 million people 16 years and older participated in wildlife viewing and photographing activities, while 23.7 million participated in hunting-related activities (NSRE 2010). Nationally, the U.S. Fish and Wildlife Service reports that 517 million sportspersons participated in hunting activities, spending $42.0 billion (USFWS and US Census Bureau 2006). Wildlife-watchers, including bird-watchers, numbered 71.1 million participants who spent an estimated $45.7 billion. For the five Gulf coast states, over 16.4 million people participated in wildlife-associated recreation and spent over $22.5 billion on these activities.

Key Ecological Processes

Carbon Sequestration

The high productivity of marshes in this region makes them more valuable CO_2 sinks per unit area than most other terrestrial systems. Choi and Wang (2004) used bomb ^{14}C to inves-

tigate short- and long-term C sequestration rates in a Florida *J. roemerianus* marsh. They found that short-term C accumulation rates varied across the marsh, being highest in the low marsh (117 g C m^{-2}yr^{-1}), slightly lower in the middle marsh (101 g C m^{-2}yr^{-1}), and lowest in the high marsh (65 g C m^{-2}yr^{-1}). In other coastal regions, mangroves and *Spartina alterniflora* marshes have been shown to lock up 210 ± 20 g C m^{-2}yr^{-1} (Chmura, Anisfield, et al. 2003). The difference in long-term and short-term rates was attributed to the anaerobic decomposition of peat organic matter over long time scales (100–1,000 years), higher rates of primary productivity in more recent years due to sea-level rise (Morris, Sundareshwar, et al. 2002), fertilization effects of increased atmospheric CO_2 concentrations (Cherry, McKee, et al. 2009), and increased atmospheric deposition of nitrogen due to anthropogenic air pollution (Hungate, Holland, et al. 1997). Loss of accumulated marsh C by erosional processes can be a source of CO_2 to the atmosphere as previously sequestered peat is oxidized to CO_2; however, little is currently known about these processes along the northern GOM.

Trophic Relay and Outwelling

The movement of production within the estuary and among habitat types, as well as between the estuarine watershed and coastal ocean, is important to the functioning of this ecosystem. The former occurs when different species and life stages of estuarine nekton move biomass from the intertidal marsh across the landscape to the subtidal habitat (Kneib 1997). This production movement is facilitated by small juvenile and adult residents (e.g., cyprinodontids, fundulids, palaemonids) that are consumed by transient predators in the subtidal zone at low tide. The resulting chain of predator-prey interactions (young residents to adult residents to juvenile transient predators) establishes a "trophic relay" that moves marsh production in a horizontal direction across the landscape and toward the open estuary. By accumulating biomass during their juvenile stages in tidal estuaries and migrating offshore as adults, transients can transfer production from the intertidal marsh directly to the coastal ocean. Forage species whose life histories involve large-scale migrations of young from spawning grounds to the estuary and back (estuarine-dependent nekton) run a gauntlet of predators along the way. During the time they spend within the tidal marsh nurseries, transient species such as prawns and silversides (i.e., penaeids, atherinids) are as susceptible to estuarine predators as permanent marsh residents, and so also contribute to the trophic relay in much the same way during this stage in their life.

The latter scale of production movement can occur as larval or older-stage transient fishes (and other nekton) use estuaries as nurseries and then move back offshore as subadults or adults (Dame and Allen 1996). For example, Deegan (1993), working on gulf menhaden, *Brevoortia patronus,* found that this species exported from Fourleague Bay, Louisiana, roughly 5–10% of the total primary production of the estuary, with nitrogen and phosphorus export of the same magnitude as waterborne export. From these estimates of material flux, exported adult fishes are clearly important, high-quality sources of estuarine productivity in the coastal ocean.

Although estuaries are generally considered ecological "pumps" that fuel adjacent ecosystems, the rates of transfers and quantity of exchanges can vary between systems depending on age and distance from the ocean. Some systems appear to inwell and others outwell materials. More mature estuarine systems that are closer to the ocean are more likely to fit the outwelling hypothesis (Dame and Allen 1996). Additionally, these systems are highly dynamic and prone to disturbances that can alter spatial and temporal patterns of production and export.

Disturbances

Tropical storms are large-scale, frequent disturbances in the northern GOM that interrupt the chronic background "creeping" stress of sea-level rise. Furthermore, the intensity of category 4 and 5 hurricanes appears to be on the rise (Bender, Knutson, et al. 2010). Coastal ecosystems are some of the first ecosystems directly impacted by tropical storms and associated incursions of the sea as the storms make landfall. Concomitant with strong winds, coastal marshes and forests are enveloped by a surge of saline water of variable depth, salinity, and duration, depending on characteristics of the storm and location of the site relative to the eye of the storm. Deposition of sediment and wrack can accompany floodwaters, leading to burial of vegetation (Tate 2010). Even short-term surges can produce lasting ecological effects, particularly those involving lingering increases in salinity. Many species experience mortality at the seaward end of their distributions after storm surge recedes, but expansion at the landward end can be delayed in species that are dispersal-limited (L Battaglia and W Platt unpublished).

The frequent tropical storms have important influences on species distributions along coastal elevation gradients, independently and in conjunction with sea-level rise. For example, in the western Gulf, due to the many artificial levees, saline water enters with storm surge and is often trapped in normally freshwater marshes. In some areas this has turned *Panicum hemitomon*–dominated fresh marshes into *Spartina patens*– and *Typha domingensis*–codominated marshes (Steyer, Perez, et al. 2007). In addition, the shear forces of wind and water may remove vegetation from large tracts, reducing the species diversity in these marshes (Neyland 2007).

Fire is an important driver of marsh and upland communities across the broader coastal transition. In marshes, it is associated with higher biomass of some species such as *Spartina patens* (Gabrey and Afton 2001), but it may also have negative effects on soil organic accumulation, organic matter export to the estuary, and wildlife use (Nyman and Chabreck 1995). At the landward end of the coastal gradient, periodic fires maintain biodiversity of understory communities within wet pine flatwoods and longleaf pine savannas by reducing cover of encroaching shrubs and hardwoods.

Wetland Management and Restoration

Many marshes in this region are managed through a combination of fall or winter burning and structural marsh management (i.e., levees and water control structures) (Day, Holz, et al. 1990). These management practices are intended to (1) improve waterfowl and furbearer habitat, (2) maintain historic isohaline lines, and (3) create and maintain emergent wetlands. They do not always function similarly to natural systems, however. For example, belowground biomass was higher in natural than in managed marshes (Gabrey and Afton 2001). Large root mass may be a response to the high salinity and low

water potential conditions of natural marshes, enabling plants to maintain water uptake and reduce internal salt concentrations (Smith, Good, et al. 1979). In addition, belowground productivity in managed marshes can be inhibited because of persistent anaerobic conditions associated with limited drainage (Gabrey and Afton 2001).

The loss of coastal marshes in the region has been partially offset by the creation of often large (> 40–200 ha) salt marshes using dredged sediments from shipping channels (Elsey-Quirk, Middleton, et al. 2009). Establishment of plants in these marshes is mostly through wind dispersal of seeds from adjacent natural marshes, and establishment of seedlings is increased adjacent to established vegetation. However, created marshes seldom have the topographic variability found in natural marshes and take many years of maturation before they provide the same habitat quality as natural marshes (Edwards and Proffit 2003).

With each tropical storm that makes landfall, there are tremendous social and economic costs. In some of the heavily damaged areas of the northern GOM, people have elected not to rebuild, to take advantage of buyout opportunities presented by state and federal agencies, and to relocate out of the immediate area (Perch-Nielsen, Bättig, et al. 2008). Buyouts of coastal homesteads, predominantly at the landward end of these coastal transitions, provide unprecedented potential for research and development of appropriate restoration and management plans. Shifting ownership of coastal properties currently accounts for relatively small changes in land use but is likely to become more common as buyout efforts are ramped up in the wake of recent hurricanes (USACE 2010). Restored buyout properties could provide critical habitat and play a role in provision of stepping-stone corridors for landward migration of species affected by climate change. Such a dynamic habitat network could enhance landscape fluidity such that species could move around in response to climate change (Manning, Fischer, et al. 2009). Planning for management of these properties is still in the early stages, but there is growing interest in restoring native vegetation and developing an adaptive restoration framework for these coastal sites.

Conservation Concerns

The integrity of these complex coastal landscape features is essential for maintaining ecological functioning and the goods and services they provide. Keeping these productive near-shore environments intact under continued developmental pressure is imperative to meet ecologic and economic sustainability goals (Peterson and Lowe 2009). For example, the probability of attaining similar landings values in 2050 as in the 2004 *Callinectes sapidus* fishery, based on five scenarios of habitat loss, was only 26% when blue crab landings were simulated with only 20% submerged aquatic vegetation loss in Mobile Bay. Moreover, there was only a 4% chance of obtaining 2004 landings values in 2050 with only a 10% shoreline hardening scenario (Jordan, Smith, et al. 2008). These projections suggest that small habitat losses or changes can be linked to large ecologic and economic losses over time. Finally, it is apparent that even the smallest patch of natural marsh habitat supports a larger diversity of fauna than nearby altered habitat, suggesting that it matters where a salt-marsh habitat patch is located in the landscape because it will influence habitat quality, connectivity, and the composition of infauna and epifauna nekton assemblages (Partyka and Peterson 2008).

Sea-Level Rise

Given their location at the land-water interface, coastal transitions of this region are directly influenced by global climate change, in particular sea-level rise and changing tropical storm regimes. Despite the fact that coastal species have evolved with changing sea level, recent and rapid relative sea-level rise (Parry, Canziani, et al. 2007) in some areas and projected intensification of tropical storms in the region (Bender, Knutson, et al. 2010) threaten these vulnerable ecosystems. In places where the rate of relative sea-level rise is greater than accretion, land loss is inevitable (Scavia, Field, et al. 2002). Because land loss generally occurs on the seaward end of coastal transitions (Shirley and Battaglia 2006), species eventually must adapt, migrating inland and replacing more upland species, or disappear from the landscape (Brinson, Christian, et al. 1995). That is not to say that coastal plant species are merely passive members of ecosystems subject to the inexorable toll of sea-level rise, as predicted by some simple digital elevation models. The importance of vegetation in trapping sediment and organic accretion is becoming increasingly apparent (Day, Boesch, et al. 2007), suggesting that under some scenarios coastal species can keep pace with sea-level rise (Morris, Sundareshwar, et al. 2002; McKee and Cherry 2009). However, anthropogenic changes in land use and development fragment coastal landscapes, increasing ecosystem fragility and limiting the ability of species to migrate in response to climate change.

Few published studies directly address the potential impacts of sea-level rise on coastal marsh wildlife. However, Inkley, Anderson, et al. (2004) suggested that new coastlines farther inland from existing ones may eventually create wildlife habitats if various impediments do not impede landward migration of wetlands and the wildlife species associated with them. Without assistance, this landward migration will be limited by human development. Sea-level rise will likely affect tidal and salinity regimes in estuaries and adjacent habitats, thereby altering vegetation communities and zonation, which in turn will affect associated biota. Some wildlife species could be displaced inland or disappear entirely if coastal marshes are rapidly inundated (Inkley, Anderson, et al. 2004). Loss of Gulf coast wetlands and their associated ecosystem functions essential for wintering waterfowl will continue (Inkley, Anderson, et al. 2004). Rush, Soehren, et al. (2009) suggested that sea-level rise and natural as well as human-induced habitat change will lead to reductions in marsh area, loss of freshwater marsh habitat, and an increase in the extent of mesohaline and polyhaline salt marsh.

Hydrologic Modifications and Land-Use Changes

Modification of river systems draining into the GOM by channelization and levees (reviewed in Gunter 1967) has changed the manner in which nutrients, sediments, and freshwater are delivered to these coastal ecosystems. These modifications and others have influenced the associated estuaries that serve as ecotones between fresh and saltwater and provide structural habitat for many ecologically and economically important nekton (Peterson and Lowe 2009; see online appendix 6.2). Development pressure has led to massive habitat loss and fragmentation of this fragile landscape. At a broader scale, changing land use in these coastal watersheds has resulted in eutrophication, pollution, and degradation of water quality (Singh 2010).

Invasive Species

Frequent disturbances make this landscape highly vulnerable to establishment and proliferation of invasive species. Common invasive plants in this region include *Triadica sebifera* (Chinese tallow), *Imperata cylindrica* (cogongrass), *Ligustrum sinense* (Chinese privet), and *Lygodium japonicum* (Japanese climbing fern). Laurel wilt disease (LWD), vectored by an exotic ambrosia beetle from Asia, was recently introduced to coastal Mississippi. Fraedrich, Harrington, et al. (2008) found high LWD-induced mortality (92%) in *Persea borbonia* (redbay), the primary host. The impacts of LWD on northern GOM coastal forests are likely to be devastating, as this species is a subcanopy dominant. There are also invasive fishes in these systems. For example, Adams and Wolfe (2007) reported that the northward range expansion by the Mayan cichlid *Cichlosoma urophthalmus* is likely facilitated by the connectivity between altered freshwater and tidal estuarine habitats.

Summary

Coastal ecosystems of the northern Gulf of Mexico are ecologically complex and economically valuable. Uninterrupted coastal transitions provide habitat that supports high levels of biodiversity and numerous ecosystems goods and services, including buffering of tropical storm impacts. These ecosystems are increasingly threatened by land-use changes in their coastal watersheds, development, invasive species, intensified tropical storms, and sea-level rise. Their resilience capacity to these cumulative stressors will continue to be increasingly tested. Careful management and adaptive restoration that is responsive to climate change impacts will be required to maintain the structure and function of these precious but vulnerable communities.

References

Adams AJ, Wolfe RK. 2007. Occurrence and persistence of nonnative *Cichlasoma urophthalmus* (family Cichlidae) in estuarine habitats of south-west Florida (USA): environmental controls and movement patterns. *Mar. Freshw. Res.* 58:921–30.

Alexander HD, Dunton KH. 2002. Freshwater inundation effects on emergent vegetation of a hypersaline salt marsh. *Estuaries* 25:1426–35.

Baldwin AH, Mendelssohn IA. 1998. Effects of salinity and water level on coastal marshes: an experimental test of disturbance as a catalyst for vegetation change. *Aquat. Bot.* 61:255–68.

Beckett DC, Viskup BJ, Ross ST. 1992. Occurrence of *Lepomis* (Osteichthyes: Centrarchidae) in Horn Island ponds. *Northeast Gulf Sci.* 12:129–33.

Bender MA, Knutson TR, et al. 2010. Modeled impact of anthropogenic warming on the frequency of intense Atlantic hurricanes. *Science* 327:454–58.

Bhattacharjee JD, Haukos D, Neaville J. 2007. Vegetation response to disturbance in a coastal marsh in Texas. *Comm. Ecol.* 8:14–24.

Bhattacharjee JD, Haukos DA, Neaville J. 2009. Influence of biotic and abiotic factors on annual aboveground biomass of an intermediate coastal marsh. *Wetlands* 29:690–96.

Blood ER, Anderson P, et al. 1991. Effects of Hurricane Hugo on coastal soil solution chemistry in South Carolina. *Biotropica* 23:348–55.

Brewer JS. 2006. Resource competition and fire-regulated nutrient demand in carnivorous plants of wet pine savannas. *Appl. Veg. Sci.* 9:11–16.

Brinson MM, Christian RR, Blum LK. 1995. Multiple states in the sea level-induced transition from terrestrial forest to estuary. *Estuaries* 18:648–59.

Brown SS, Gaston GR, et al. 2000. Macrobenthic trophic structure responses to environmental factors and sediment contaminants in northern Gulf of Mexico estuaries. *Estuaries* 23:411–24.

Burger J. 1985. Habitat selection in temperate marsh-nesting birds. In *Habitat selection in birds,* Cody ML, editor. San Diego: Academic Press, pp. 253–81.

Byron D, Heck KL Jr. 2006. Hurricane effects on seagrasses along Alabama's Gulf coast. *Estuar. Coast.* 29:939–42.

Chabreck RA. 1988. *Coastal marshes: ecology and wildlife management.* Minneapolis: Univ. Minnesota Press.

Chabreck RH, Joanen T, Paulus SL. 1989. Southern coastal marshes and lakes. In *Habitat management for migrating and wintering waterfowl in North America,* Smith LM, Pederson RL, Kaminski RM, editors. Lubbock: Texas Tech Univ. Press, pp. 249–77.

Cherry JA, McKee KL, Grace JB. 2009. Elevated CO_2 enhances biological contributions to elevation change in coastal wetlands by offsetting stressors associated with sea-level rise. *J. Ecol.* 97:67–77.

Chmura GL, Anisfeld SC, et al. 2003. Global carbon sequestration in tidal, saline wetland soils. *Glob. Biogeochem. Cycles* 17:1111.

Choi Y, Wang Y. 2004. Dynamics of carbon sequestration in a coastal wetland using radiocarbon measurements. *Glob. Biogeochem. Cycles* 18:GB4016.

Choi Y, Wang Y, Hsieh YP, Robinson L. 2001. Vegetation succession and carbon sequestration in a coastal wetland in northwest Florida: evidence from carbon isotopes. *Glob. Biogeochem. Cycles* 15:311–19.

Clark J, Brown SA, et al. 2008. *Selected plants of coastal Mississippi and Alabama: Grand Bay National Estuarine Research Reserve and Weeks Bay National Estuarine Research Reserve 2008.* Moss Point, MS: Grand Bay NERR and Mississippi Department of Marine Resources.

Cook LL, Whipple SA. 1982. The distribution of edaphic diatoms along environmental gradients of a Louisiana salt marsh. *J. Phycology* 18:64–71.

Coultas CL. 1996. Soils of the intertidal marshes of Florida's Gulf Coast. In *Ecology and management of tidal marshes,* Coultas CL, Hsieh YP, editors. Delray, FL: St. Lucie Press, pp. 53–75.

Dame RF, Allen DM. 1996. Between estuaries and the sea. *J. Exp. Marine Biol. Ecol.* 200:169–85.

Dardeau MR, Modlin RF, et al. 1992. Estuaries. In *Biodiversity of the southeastern United States: quatic communities,* Hackney CT, Adams SM, Martin WH, editors. New York: Wiley, pp. 615–744.

Day JW Jr., Smith W, et al. 1973. Community structure and carbon budget of a salt marsh and shallow bay estuarine system in Louisiana. LSU-SG-72-04. Baton Rouge: Center for Wetland Resources, Louisiana State University.

Day JW Jr., Hall CS, et al. 1989. *Estuarine ecology.* New York: Wiley.

Day JW Jr., Boesch DF, et al. 2007. Restoration of the Mississippi Delta: lessons from hurricanes Katrina and Rita. *Science* 315:1679–84.

Day RH, Holz RK, Day JW Jr. 1990. An inventory of wetland impoundments in the coastal zone of Louisiana, USA: historical trends. *Env. Manag.* 14:229–40.

Deegan LA. 1993. Nutrient and energy transport between estuaries and coastal marine ecosystems by fish migration. *Can. J. Fish. Aquat. Sci.* 50:74–79.

Deegan LA, Garritt RH. 1997. Evidence for spatial variability in estuarine food webs. *Mar. Ecol. Prog. Ser.* 147:31–47.

Durako MJ, Browder JA, et al. 1985. Salt marsh habitat and fishery resources of Florida. In *Florida aquatic habitat and fishery resources,* Seaman W Jr., editor. Kissimmee: Florida Chapter of the American Fisheries Society, pp. 189–280.

Edwards KR, Proffitt CE. 2003. Comparison of wetland structural characteristics between created and natural salt marshes in southwest Louisiana, USA. *Wetlands* 23:344–56.

Elsey-Quirk TBA, Middleton BA, Proffitt CE. 2009. Seed dispersal and seedling emergence in a created and a natural salt marsh on the Gulf of Mexico coast in southwest Louisiana, U.S.A. *Restor. Ecol.* 17:422–32.

Fleming DM. 1975. Movement patterns of the coastal marsh raccoon in Louisiana and notes on its life history. M.S. thesis, Louisiana State University, Baton Rouge.

Fodrie FJ, Heck KL, et al. 2010. Climate-related, decadal-scale assemblage changes of seagrass-associated fishes in the northern Gulf of Mexico. *Glob. Clim. Biol.* 16:48–59.

Fraedrich SW, Harrington TC, et al. 2008. A fungal symbiont of the redbay ambrosia beetle causes a lethal wilt in redbay and other Lauraceae in the southeastern United States. *Plant Dis.* 92:215–24.

Gabrey SW, Afton AD. 2000. Effects of winter marsh burning on abundance and nesting activity of Louisiana seaside sparrows in the Gulf Coast Chenier Plain. *Wilson Bull.* 112:365–72.

Gabrey SW, Afton AD. 2001. Plant community composition and biomass in Gulf Coast Chenier Plain marshes: responses to winter burning and structural marsh management. *Env. Manag.* 27:281–93.

Gabrey SW, Afton AD, Wilson BC. 2001. Effects of structural marsh management and winter burning on plant and bird communities during summer in the Gulf Coast Chenier Plain, USA. *Wildl. Soc. Bull.* 29:218–31.

Gibson RN. 1994. Impact of habitat quality and quantity on the recruitment of juvenile flatfishes. *Neth. J. Sea Res.* 32:191–206.

Greenberg R. 2006. Tidal marshes: home for the few and highly selected. In *Terrestrial vertebrates of tidal marshes: evolution, ecology, and conservation,* Greenberg R, Maldonado JE, et al., editors. Studies in Avian Biology 32. Camarillo, CA: Cooper Ornithological Society, pp. 2–9.

Greenberg R, Maldonado JE. 2006. Diversity and endemism in tidal-marsh vertebrates. In *Terrestrial vertebrates of tidal marshes: evolution, ecology, and conservation,* Greenberg R, Maldonado JE, et al., editors. Studies in Avian Biology 32. Camarillo, CA: Cooper Ornithological Society, pp. 32–53.

Greenberg R, Maldonado J, et al. 2006. Tidal marshes: a global perspective on the evolution and conservation of their terrestrial vertebrates. *Bioscience* 56:675–85.

Gunter G. 1963. The fertile fisheries crescent. *J. Miss. Acad. Sci.* 9:286–90.

Gunter G. 1967. Some relationships of estuaries to fisheries of the Gulf of Mexico. In *Estuaries,* Lauff GH, editor. Washington, DC: American Association for the Advancement of Science, pp. 621–38.

Hansen K, Kristensen E. 1997. Impact of macrofaunal recolonization on benthic metabolism and nutrient fluxes in a shallow marine sediment previously overgrown with macroalgal mats. *Estuar. Coast. Shelf Sci.* 45:613–28.

Hart KM, Lee DS. 2006. The diamondback terrapin: the biology, ecology, cultural history, and conservation status of an obligate estuarine turtle. In *Terrestrial vertebrates of tidal marshes: evolution, ecology, and conservation,* Greenberg R, Maldonado JE, et al., editors. Studies in Avian Biology 32. Camarillo, CA: Cooper Ornithological Society, pp. 206–13.

Heinsch FA, Heilman JL, et al. 2004. Carbon dioxide exchange in a high marsh on the Texas Gulf coast: effects of freshwater availability. *Agric. For. Meteorol.* 125:159–72.

Hobaugh WC, Stutzenbaker CD, Flickinger EL. 1989. The rice prairies. In *Habitat management for migrating and wintering waterfowl in North America,* Smith LM, Pederson RL, Kaminski RM, editors. Lubbock: Texas Tech Univ. Press, pp. 367–83.

Hogan JL. 2003. Occurrence of the diamondback terrapin *(Malaclemys terrapin littoralis)* at South Deer Island in Galveston Bay, Texas, April 2001–May 2002. Open-File Report 03-022. Austin, TX: USGS.

Hsieh YEP. 1996. Assessing aboveground and net primary production of vascular plants in marshes. *Estuaries* 19:82–85.

Hsieh YP, Yang CH. 1997. Pyrite accumulation and sulfate depletion as affected by root distribution in a *Juncus* (needle rush) salt marsh. *Estuar. Coast.* 20:640–45.

Hungate BA, Holland EA, et al. 1997. The fate of carbon in grasslands under carbon dioxide enrichment. *Nature* 388:576–79.

Hunter A, Morris NMB, et al. 2008. Effects of nutrient enrichment on *Distichlis spicata* and *Salicornia bigelovii* in a marsh pan. *Wetlands* 28:760–75.

Inkley DB, Anderson MG, et al. 2004. *Global climate change and wildlife in North America.* Wildlife Society Technical Review 04-2. Bethesda, MD: Wildlife Society.

Jelbart JE, Ross PM, Connolly RM. 2007. Fish assemblages in seagrass beds are influenced by the proximity of mangrove forests. *Mar. Biol.* 150:993–1002.

Johnson AS, Hale PE. 1992. The historical foundations of pre-scribed burning for wildlife: a southeastern perspective. In *The role of fire in nongame wildlife management and community restoration: traditional uses and new directions: proceedings of a workshop (Sept. 15, 2000),* Ford WM, Russell KR, Moorman CE, editors. Report NE-288. Parsons, WV: USDA Forest Serv. Northeast. Res. Sta., pp. 11–23.

Johnson TR. 1992. *The amphibians and reptiles of Missouri.* Missouri Department of Conservation, Jefferson City, MIssouri.

Jordan SJ, Smith LM, Nestlerode JA. 2008. Cumulative effects of coastal habitat alterations on fishery resources: toward prediction at regional scales. *Ecol. Soc.* 14:16: www.ecologyandsociety.org.

Kilby JD. 1955. The fishes of two Gulf coastal marsh areas of Florida. *Tulane Stud. Zool.* 2:175–247.

Kinler QJ. 1986. Muskrat reproduction and the effects of tidal flooding in Louisiana. MS thesis, Louisiana State Univ., Baton Rouge.

Kneib RT. 1997. The role of tidal marshes in the ecology of estuarine nekton. *Oceanogr. Mar. Biol. Annu. Rev.* 35:163–220.

Langford GJ, Borden JA, et al. 2007. Effects of prescribed fire on the herpetofauna of a southern Mississippi pine savanna. *Herp. Cons. Biol.* 2:135–43.

Lazell JD Jr. 1979. Diamondback terrapins at Sandy Neck aqua-sphere. *New England Aquar.* 13:28–31.

Livingston RJ, Niu X, et al. 1997. Freshwater input to a gulf estuary: long-term control of trophic organization. *Ecol. Appl.* 7:277–99.

Lowe MR, DeVries DR, et al. 2009. Coastal largemouth bass (*Micropterus salmoides*) movement in response to changing salinity. *Can. J. Fish. Aquat. Sci.* 66:2174–88.

Lowery GH Jr., Newman RJ. 1954. The birds of the Gulf of Mexico. In *Gulf of Mexico: its origin, waters, and marine life,* Galtsoff PS, editor. Washington, DC: USFWS, pp. 519–40.

Lynch JJ. 1968. Values of the south Atlantic and Gulf coast marshes and estuaries to waterfowl. In *Proceedings of the coastal marsh and estuary management symposium,* Newson JD, editor. Baton Rouge: Louisiana State Univ., pp. 51–63.

Mann TM. 1995. Population surveys for diamondback terrapin (*Malaclemys terrapin*) and Gulf salt marsh snake (*Nerodia clarkii clarkii*) in Mississippi. Report no. 37. Jackson: Museum of Natural Science, Mississippi Dept. Wildlife, Fisheries, Parks.

Manning AD, Fischer J, et al. 2009. Landscape fluidity—a unifying perspective for understanding and adapting to global change. *J. Biogeog.* 36:193–99.

McKee KL, Cherry JA. 2009. Hurricane Katrina sediment slowed elevation loss in subsiding brackish marshes of the Mississippi River Delta. *Wetlands* 29:2–15.

Means DB, Travis J. 2007. Declines in ravine-inhabiting dusky salamanders of the southeastern US coastal plain. *Southeast. Nat.* 6:83–96.

Miley GA, Kiene RP. 2004. Sulfate reduction and porewater chemistry in a Gulf coast *Juncus roemerianus* (needlerush) marsh. *Estuar. Coast.* 27:472–81.

Mitchell JC, Anderson JM. 1994. *Amphibians and reptiles of Assateague and Chincoteague Islands.* Special pub. no. 2. Martinsville: Virginia Museum of Natural History.

Moody RM, Aronson RB. 2007. Trophic heterogeneity in salt marshes of the northern Gulf of Mexico. *Mar. Ecol. Prog. Ser.* 331:49–65.

Morris JT, Sundareshwar PV, et al. 2002. Response of coastal wetlands to rising sea level. *Ecology* 83:2869–77.

NSRE (National Survey on Recreation and the Environment). 2010. America's participation in outdoor recreation: results from NSRE (with weighted data) (versions 1 to 13). www.srs.fs.usda.gov/trends/Nsre/nsre2.html; accessed February 28, 2010.

Neyland R. 2007. The effects of Hurricane Rita on the aquatic vascular flora in a large fresh-water marsh in Cameron Parish, Louisiana. *Castanea* 72:1–7.

Neyland R, Meyer HA. 1997. Species diversity of Louisiana chenier woody vegetation remnants. *J. Torrey Bot. Soc.* 124:254–61.

Nyman JA, Chabreck RH. 1995. Fire in coastal marshes: history and recent observations. *Proc. Tall Timbers Fire Ecol. Conf.* 19:134–41.

O'Connell MT, Cashner RC, Schieble CS. 2004. Fish assemblage stability over fifty years in the Lake Pontchartrain estuary: comparisons among habitats using canonical correspondence analysis. *Estuaries* 27:807–17.

O'Neil T. 1949. *The muskrat in the Louisiana coastal marsh.* New Orleans: LA Dept. Wildl. Fish.

Palmisano AW Jr. 1973. Habitat preference of waterfowl and fur animals in the northern Gulf coast marshes. In *Proceedings of the coastal marsh and estuary management symposium,* Chabreck RH, editor. Baton Rouge: Louisiana State Univ., pp. 163–90.

Partyka ML, Peterson MS. 2008. Habitat quality and salt marsh species assemblages along an anthropogenic estuarine landscape. *J. Coast. Res.* 24:1570–82.

Parry ML, Canziani OF, et al., editors. 2007. *Climate change 2007: impacts, adaptation and vulnerability.* Contribution of Working Group II to the Fourth Assessment Report of the Intergovernmental Panel on Climate Change. Cambridge: Cambridge Univ. Press.

Pennings SC, Siska EL, Bertness MD. 2001. Latitudinal differences in plant palatability in Atlantic coast salt marshes. *Ecology* 82:1344–59.

Perch-Nielsen SL, Bättig MB, Imboden D. 2008. Exploring the link between climate change and migration. *Clim. Chang.* 91:375–93.

Peterson MS. 2003. A conceptual view of environment-habitat-production linkages in tidal-river estuaries. *Rev. Fish. Sci.* 11:291–313.

Peterson MS, Comyns BH, et al. 2004. Defining the fundamental physiological niche of young estuarine fishes and its relationship to understanding distribution, vital metrics, and optimal nursery conditions. *Env. Biol. Fishes* 71:143–49.

Peterson MS, Weber MR, et al. 2007. Integrating in situ quantitative geographic information tools and size-specific laboratory-based growth zones in a dynamic river-mouth estuary. *Aquat. Cons. Mar. Freshw. Ecosyst.* 17:602–18.

Peterson MS, Waggy GL, Woodrey MS. 2007. *Grand Bay National Estuarine Research Reserve: an ecological characterization.* Moss Point, MS: Grand Bay NERR.

Peterson MS, Lowe MR. 2009. Implications of cumulative impacts to estuarine and marine habitat quality for fish and invertebrate resources. *Rev. Fish. Sci.*17:505–23.

Post W, Greenlaw JS. 2009. Seaside sparrow (*Ammodramus maritimus*). In *The birds of North America online,* Poole, A, editor. Ithaca: Cornell Lab of Ornithology; retrieved from *The Birds of North American online:* http://bna.birds.cornell.edu.bna/species/127HYPERLINK.

Pough FH, Andrews RM, et al. 2003. *Herpetology,* 3rd ed. Boston: Benjamin Cummings.

Rabenhorst M. 1995. Carbon storage in tidal marsh soils. In *Soils and global change,* Lal R, Kimble J, et al., editors. Boca Raton, FL: Lewis, pp. 93–104.

Rakocinski CF, Brown SS, et al. 1997. Macrobenthic responses to natural and contaminant-related gradients in northern Gulf of Mexico estuaries. *Ecol. Appl.* 7:1278–16.

Rozas LP. 1995. Hydroperiod and its influence on nekton use of the salt marsh: a pulsing ecosystem. *Estuaries* 18:579–90.

Rush SA, Soehren EC, et al. 2009. Occupancy of select marsh birds within northern Gulf of Mexico tidal marsh: current estimates and projected change. *Wetlands* 29:798–808.

Scavia D, Field JC, et al. 2002. Climate change impacts on US coastal and marine ecosystems. *Estuaries* 25:149–64.

Schiemer F, Zalewski M, Thorpe JE. 1995. Land/inland water ecotones: intermediate habitats critical for conservation and management. *Hydrobiologia* 303:259–64.

Schroeder WW, Wiseman WJ. 1999. Geology and hydrodynamics of Gulf of Mexico estuaries. In *Biogeochemistry of Gulf of Mexico estuaries,* Bianchi TS, Pennock JR, Twilley RR, editors. New York: Wiley, pp. 3–28.

Shirley LJ, Battaglia LL. 2006. Assessing vegetation change in coastal landscapes of the northern Gulf of Mexico. *Wetlands* 26:1057–70.

Singh H. 2010. Modeling impact of land use/cover changes on water quality and quantity of Fish River watershed. MS thesis, Auburn University, AL.

Smith KK, Good RE, Good NF. 1979. Production dynamics for above and belowground components of a New Jersey *Spartina alterniflora* tidal marsh. *Estuar. Coast. Mar. Sci.* 9:189–201.

Steyer GD, Perez BC, et al. 2007. *Potential consequences of saltwater intrusion associated with Hurricanes Katrina and Rita.* Lafayette, LA: USGS National Wetlands Research Center.

Stout JP. 1978. An analysis of annual growth and productivity of *Juncus roemerianus* Scheele and *Spartina alterniflora* Loisel in coastal Alabama. Ph.D. diss., NC State Univ., Raleigh.

Stout JP. 1984. The ecology of irregularly flooded salt marshes of the northeastern Gulf of Mexico: a community profile. Biological Report 85(7.1). Washington, DC: USFWS.

Sullivan MJ. 1978. Diatom community structure: taxonomic and statistical analyses of a Mississippi salt marsh. *J. Phycol.* 14:468–75.

Sullivan MJ, Currin CA. 2000. Community structure and functional dynamics of benthic microalgae in salt marshes. In *Concepts and controversies in tidal marsh ecology,* Weinstein MP, Kreeger DA, editors. Dordrecht, The Netherlands: Kluwer, pp. 81–106.

Sullivan MJ, Moncreif CA. 1988. Primary production of edaphic algal communities in a Mississippi salt marsh. *J. Phycol.* 24:49–58.

Sullivan MJ, Moncreif CA. 1990. Edaphic algae are important components of salt marsh food webs: evidence from multiple stable isotope analysis. *Mar. Ecol. Prog. Ser.* 62:149–59.

Tate AS. 2010. Short-term response of coastal vegetation in northwestern Florida to experimental storm surge and wrack application. M.S. thesis, Southern Illinois University, Carbondale.

Taylor KL, Grace JB, et al. 1994. The interactive effects of herbivory and fire on an oligohaline marsh, Little Lake, Louisiana, USA. *Wetlands* 14:82–87.

Twilley RR, Cowan J, et al. 1999. Benthic nutrient fluxes in selected estuaries in the Gulf of Mexico. In *Biogeochemistry of Gulf of Mexico estuaries,* Bianchi TS, Pennock JR, Twilley RR, editors. New York: Wiley, pp. 163–209.

USACE. 2010. Mississippi coastal improvement program, Hancock, Harrison, and Jackson Counties, Mississippi. Comprehensive plan and integrated programmatic environmental impact statement. www.sam.usace.army.mil/mscip/default .htm. Mobile, AL: USACE.

USFWS and US Census Bureau. 2006. 2006 national survey of fishing, hunting, and wildlife-associated recreation. Washington, DC: USFWS.

Visser JM, Sasser CE, et al. 2000. Marsh vegetation types of the Chenier Plain, Louisiana, USA. *Estuaries* 23:318–27.

Visser M, Sasser CE, et al. 2002. The impact of a severe drought on the vegetation of a subtropical estuary. *Estuaries* 25:1184–95.

Weller MW. 1994a. Seasonal dynamics of bird assemblages in a Texas estuarine wetland. *J. Field Ornithol.* 65:388–401.

Weller MW. 1994b. Bird-habitat relationships in a Texas estuarine marsh during summer. *Wetlands* 14:293–300.

Weller MW. 1999. *Wetland birds: habitat resources and conservation implications.* Cambridge: Cambridge Univ. Press.

Whitbeck MW. 2002. Response of breeding seaside sparrows to fire on the upper Texas coast. MS thesis, Texas A&M Univ., College Station.

White WA, Morton RA, Holmes CW. 2002. A comparison of factors controlling sedimentation rates and wetland loss in fluvial–deltaic systems, Texas Gulf coast. *Geomorphology* 44:47–66.

Wikelski M, Cooke SJ. 2006. Conservation physiology. *Trends Ecol. Evol.* 21:38–46.

Williams SO III, Chabreck RH. 1986. *Quantity and quality of waterfowl habitat in Louisiana.* Report no. 8. Baton Rouge: Louisiana State Univ. School of Forestry, Wildlife, and Fisheries.

Woodin MC, Michot TC. 1996. Foraging behavior of redheads (*Aythya americana*) wintering in Texas and Louisiana. *Hydrobiologia* 567:129–41.

Woodrey MS, Walker J. 2009. *Selected birds of the Grand Bay National Estuarine Research Reserve and vicinity.* Moss Point, MS: Grand Bay NERR, Mississippi Dept. Marine Resources.

CHAPTER 7

Neotropical Coastal Wetlands

KAREN L. MCKEE

The Neotropical region, which includes the tropical Americas, is one of the world's eight biogeographic zones. It contains some of the most diverse and unique wetlands in the world, some of which are still relatively undisturbed by humans. This chapter focuses on the northern segment of the Neotropics (south Florida, the Caribbean islands, Mexico, and Central America), an area that spans a latitudinal gradient from about 7°N to 29°N and 60°W to 112°W. Examples of coastal wetlands in this realm include the Everglades (Florida, USA), Ten Thousand Islands (Florida, USA), Laguna de Términos (Mexico), Twin Cays (Belize), and Zapata Swamp (Cuba). Coastal wetlands are dominated by mangroves, which will be emphasized here, but also include freshwater swamps and marshes, saline marshes, and seagrass beds. Several reviews and books have included information about Neotropical wetlands (Seeliger 1992; Rejmankova, Pope, et al. 1995; Mendelssohn and McKee 2000; Ellison 2004). In-depth information about the biology, distribution, structure, function, and conservation of mangroves can be found in several texts (Tomlinson 1994; Yáñez-Arancibia and Lara-Domínguez 1999; Saenger 2002; Spaulding, Kainuma, et al. 2010). Considerable research has been conducted on the geomorphology, biogeochemistry, ecological processes, and human impacts in specific ecosystems such as the Everglades, but less is known about other Neotropical wetlands.

Mangroves, which are an ecological group of tropical and subtropical trees, have been studied throughout the Neotropics. In the coastal plain, mangroves occupy the low- to mid-intertidal zone, often forming near-impenetrable barriers along shorelines. Salt-marsh vegetation tolerant of hypersaline conditions may occur landward of mangroves where rainfall and freshwater from upland runoff and groundwater are low and evapotranspiration rates are high. Where freshwater inputs are more plentiful and create brackish or oligohaline conditions, herbaceous marshes containing grasses, sedges, and rushes develop. Freshwater systems contain emergent herbaceous vegetation and periphyton (a complex mixture of algae, bacteria, and plant detritus) in continually flooded coastal plains such as in the Everglades and the coastal plain of northern Belize. Known human impacts to Neotropical coastal wetlands date at least to the time of the Mayan civili-

zation (Pre-Classic to Late Classic Maya: 2000 B.C. to 900 A.D.) (Pohl 1990; McKillop 2005). Removal of natural resources (fuelwood, bark) and use of mangrove forests for fishing, hunting, and salt production in Central America have been confirmed by archaeological evidence. Modern civilizations have exploited wetlands for economic benefit: coastal agriculture, salt production, intensive aqua/mariculture, urban and industrial expansion, tourism, mosquito control, and flood control.

The aim of this chapter is to provide a broad overview of Neotropical coastal wetlands of the North American continent, with an emphasis on mangroves, since this is the dominant vegetation type and because in-depth coverage of all wetland types is impossible here. Instead, the goal is to describe the environmental settings, plant and animal communities, key ecological controls, and some conservation concerns, with specific examples. Because this book deals with wetlands of North America, this chapter excludes coastal wetlands of South America. However, much of the information is applicable to mangrove, marsh, and seagrass communities of other tropical regions.

Environmental Setting

Climate

The climate in the northern portion of the Neotropics ranges from subtropical wet (Florida) to tropical-equatorial (Panama) (Oliver 2005). Occasional cold fronts during December to January may bring strong northwest winds and cooler temperatures as far south as Honduras. Frost prevents mangrove survival above about 29°N in North America. However, mangrove distribution intersects that of temperate salt marsh at these northern latitudes, creating an important ecotone where species dominance fluctuates between tropical and temperate vegetation types (Stevens, Fox, et al. 2006). Rainfall varies from relatively arid conditions (< 1 m) to wetter conditions in other areas (5–6 m/yr). Neotropical latitudes on both the Pacific and Caribbean coasts of Mexico and Central America experience wet and dry seasons: February to May (dry) and June to January (wet). On the Pacific coast, the dry season is more pronounced, with greater differences in rainfall between wet and dry seasons. The northern Neotropics lies within the hurricane belt and is vulnerable to tropical storms and hurricanes that move inland from the Caribbean Sea. Many major hurricanes have passed through this region from 1893 to present (www.nhc.noaa.gov/pastall.shtml, accessed March 19, 2010). Some of the most destructive to mangroves and other coastal systems include Donna (1960), Hattie (1961), Gilbert (1988), Andrew (1992), and Mitch (1998).

Geology

GEOMORPHOLOGY, SOILS, AND SEDIMENTARY PROCESSES

The geomorphological settings of Neotropical coastal wetlands are quite varied, ranging from alluvial plains to oceanic islands built on carbonate platforms. A striking contrast occurs between the Caribbean and Pacific coasts of Mexico and Central America in terms of hydrogeology and biogeochemistry. On the Pacific coast, the topography leads to narrow platforms, which abut mountains, limiting development of coastal wetlands. On the Caribbean side of the isthmus, there are wide coastal plains with relief of a few centimeters over several kilometers. Mangroves occur in river deltas, estuaries, and coastal lagoons; along open coastlines; and on carbonate platforms (Thom 1984). An example of a deltaic setting with many distributary channels and deposition of terrigenous sands, silts, and clays is the Grijalva-Usumacinta Delta in the states of Tabasco and Campeche, Mexico. Here, mangroves and other coastal marsh plants occur in lagoons, abandoned river channels, interdistributary basins and swales (Thom 1967). Laguna de Términos (Mexico) is a large lagoon-estuarine system protected from wave energy and separated from the Gulf of Mexico by Isla del Carmen. It contains large stands of mangroves as well as extensive seagrass beds (Rivera-Arriaga, Lara-Domínguez, et al. 2003). The many mangrove-dominated islands in the MesoAmerican Barrier Reef System (Belize) are examples of low-energy carbonate platforms occurring in shallow, oligotrophic waters. In this setting, mangroves grow atop coral or limestone platforms and are protected by offshore reefs (Macintyre, Toscano, et al. 2004).

The different geomorphic settings found in this region engender dramatic variation in soils and sediments. Two basic types of sediments are found: (1) allochthonous sediments, which originate outside the system and are carried into the wetland by various processes. Terrigenous sediments may be transported by rivers, whereas marine sediments such as calcareous sands are carried by tides, currents and storm surge; (2) autochthonous sediments, produced and deposited in place, primarily peats derived from wetland plants. Thick peat deposits are common beneath Caribbean mangroves where terrigenous sediment is in low supply; some deposits are over 10 m thick. Mangroves and other wetlands on the Caribbean coast may accumulate carbonate sand or marl (fine-grained deposit). Detritus and root matter contribute to the organic proportion. The flooded, low-oxygen environment of wetlands limits decomposition of organic matter, so, depending on inundation frequency and duration, different soil textures may occur: peat (> 40%), organic (20–40%) or mineral (< 20%).

Mangroves are often referred to as "land-builders," a concept based on observations of mangrove prop roots extending in a seaward direction along with an advancing front of seedlings. The progradation (lateral extension of the landform) of the shoreline was thought to occur as sediment deposition was encouraged by the presence of aerial roots. The idea of mangroves as primary land-builders was challenged by geomorphologists who argued that mangroves (and their vegetation structure) were instead influenced by geomorphic processes (Egler 1948). Mangroves become established only once soil elevations are suitable. Thereafter, however, mangroves can contribute directly to accretion through organic matter deposition by trapping sediment and by preventing erosion.

ACCRETION AND ELEVATION DYNAMICS

Sea level has risen and fallen many meters over geologic time (in concert with ice ages), and the persistence of mangroves and other coastal wetlands depends upon maintenance of soil elevation and salinity regime within tolerance limits of the emergent vegetation. As explained above, these wetlands occur over a range of geomorphic settings, but can occupy extremes along a sedimentary gradient from minerogenic (built by mineral sediment deposition) to organogenic (built by organic matter accumulation). Mineral sediment, plant litter, and microbial-algal matter accumulate on the soil surface and contribute to vertical accretion of the wetland (McKee 2011). Other physical processes include scouring by currents and daily tides or storms (Whelan, Smith, et al. 2009) and shrink-swell of soils and groundwater movement (Whelan, Smith, et al. 2005). In addition, belowground accumulation of plant roots and rhizomes adds to soil volume and upward expansion of soil surfaces (McKee, Cahoon, et al. 2007; McKee 2011). Because decomposition rates are very slow in mangrove and marsh wetlands, organic matter often accrues, especially in oligotrophic settings. The rate of elevation change in a peat-forming mangrove system (Belize) was altered by adding nitrogen or phosphorus to different stands of red mangrove, which influenced root matter accumulation (McKee, Cahoon, et al. 2007).

Peat deposits beneath mangroves in the Neotropics attest to the importance of organic matter to soil building relative to sea-level rise (McKee, Cahoon, et al. 2007). Cores collected through these peat deposits show that mangroves in Belize (online appendix, Fig. 7.1) and elsewhere in the Caribbean have kept up with sea-level rise throughout the Holocene (10,000 years) by accumulation of refractory mangrove roots. In fact, radiocarbon dating of mangrove peat (along with coral reef dates) has been used to reconstruct a sea-level curve for the Caribbean and Western Atlantic region. These examples illustrate the importance of biological processes such as production and decomposition to maintenance of soil elevations in peat-forming mangroves throughout the Neotropics.

Hydrology and Biogeochemistry

A major factor influencing mangroves and other coastal vegetation is the tides. There is a dramatic variation in tide range along Caribbean and Pacific coasts. On the Caribbean side, tides vary from microtidal (Belize = 0.2 m) to mesotidal (Panama = 3 m). On the Pacific coast, tide ranges vary from 1.5 to 5 m. Variation in tides has consequences for the vertical extent of the intertidal zone and for organisms adapted to periodic submergence and exposure to the air. A greater tidal extent also leads to greater incursion of saltwater inland and the lateral extent of estuarine wetlands, but the reach of saline waters is modified by the topography and width of the coastal plain. For example, mangrove fringes are relatively narrow along parts of the Panamanian coast (Caribbean) where the steep relief leads to a narrow platform for low-lying coastal vegetation.

Another consequence of the topography, tides, and climate is salinity regime. In the more arid, microtidal settings of the Yucatán and Caribbean islands, salinity varies from sea-strength (35–36 practical salinity unity, or psu) along regularly flooded shorelines to hypersaline conditions (60–100 psu) in upper intertidal zones that are flushed infrequently by spring tides (Cintron, Lugo, et al. 1978; McKee 1995b). With high evapotranspiration combined with low rainfall and infrequent tidal flushing, interior coastal wetlands develop saltpans or are vegetated by halophytes such as succulents and grasses that can tolerate hypersaline conditions (Costa and Davy 1992). In the Gulf of Fonseca, extensive saltpans (13,000 ha) occur at the landward margin of mangrove forests (Jimenez 1992). Although saltpans appear to be unvegetated, they often contain a surface crust or biofilm composed of algal and microbial communities. At the other extreme are areas characterized by high annual rainfall (> 3 m) or by freshwater inflow from rivers or groundwater. In these settings, salinity can vary from sea-strength along tidal creeks to freshwater at the upland border where oligohaline or freshwater marsh species predominate (Lovelock, Feller, et al. 2005).

Carbon cycling through Neotropical coastal wetlands derives from autochthonous production or is imported by tides or rivers. The most important sources of autochthonous carbon are plant litter and benthic and epiphytic algae. Depending upon the landscape position of the wetland, it may receive subsidies of carbon (and nutrients) in the form of wrack from adjacent areas (e.g., seagrass wrack transported into a mangrove fringe), nekton, and phytoplankton. Depending on their productivity, connectivity, and hydrology, mangroves and marshes may export substantial amounts of dissolved organic carbon (DOC) and nitrogen (DON). Microbial mats commonly found in mangrove scrub forests and ponds may be important sources of DOC and DON to tidal creeks (Joye and Lee 2004). Microbial mats also fix nitrogen, which provides a subsidy for mangroves. seagrasses, and benthic communities, whereas denitrification lowers inorganic nitrogen concentrations (Lee and Joye 2006). Addition of excess nutrients to these systems can alter patterns of carbon and nutrient cycling. The Florida Everglades is an oligotrophic system, particularly with respect to phosphorus, and enrichment has caused changes in nitrification and denitrification rates (White and Reddy 2003) and turnover rates of carbon, nitrogen, and phosphorus (Corstanje, Reddy, et al. 2007). Increases in nutrient availability caused a decrease in nutrient resorption efficiency of mangroves in Belize so that the chemical composition of the leaf litter was altered (Feller, Whigham, et al. 1999). Nutrient enrichment similarly affected oligotrophic marshes, causing changes in decomposition rates (Rejmankova and Houdkova 2006) and composition and productivity of cyanobacterial mats (Rejmankova and Komarkova 2005).

Plant Communities

Floristics

Mangrove forests and saline marshes in the Neotropics are not very diverse floristically and can be dominated by a single plant species. In total, there are eight core species of mangrove occurring in the Neotropics, but their occurrence differs on the Caribbean and Pacific coasts (Spaulding, Kainuma, et al. 2010). Dominant mangrove species on the Caribbean side include red mangrove *(Rhizophora mangle)* (Fig. 7.1a), black mangrove *(Avicennia germinans),* and white mangrove *(Laguncularia racemosa).* Buttonwood *(Conocarpus erectus)* occurs as scattered trees or bushes, particularly in disturbed areas where the soil is less flooded. *Avicennia schaueriana* can be found in the Lesser Antilles, Trinidad and Tobago, and the Turks and Caicos. *Rhizophora racemosa harrisonii* (thought to be a hybrid by some researchers) has been reported in Trinidad and Tobago, but is more common on the Pacific coast of Central America. Also found on the Pacific coast are *A. bicolor* and *Pelliciera rhizophoreae* (small populations of this species also occur on the Caribbean coast) (Fig. 7.1b).

Various herbaceous species also occur in association with mangroves or as coastal strand communities (Fig. 7.2). Widespread throughout salt marshes of the Neotropics are succulent forbs such as *Batis maritima, Sesuvium portulacastrum,* and *Salicornia virginica* and grasses such as *Distichlis spicata, Sporobolus virginicus, Spartina alterniflora,* and *S. spartinae* (Lopez-Portillo and Ezcurra 1989; Davy and Costa 1992). These species can occur as patches in the mid- to upper-intertidal zone where mangroves are sparse or canopy openings develop, and in narrow fringes seaward of mangroves (Florida Bay, Tampa Bay, and Ten Thousand Islands), but can also create extensive stands, as in Belize (West 1977). The mangrove fern *Acrostichum aureum* can be found in greater abundance in disturbed mangrove areas. Perennially flooded wetlands found in karstic settings (Florida Everglades, northern Belize, Cuba's Zapata Swamp) typically contain mixtures of emergent macrophytes *(Cladium mariscus* ssp. *jamaicense, Eleocharis* spp., *Typha domingensis,* floating algal mats and submersed macrophytes (Ross, O'Brien, et al. 1992; Rejmankova, Pope, et al. 1995).

Also associated with mangroves is a diverse macroalgal community known collectively as Bostrychietum and includes such genera as *Bostrychia, Caloglossa,* and *Catenella.* Macroalgae grow attached to aerial roots and bark of mangroves as well as to the soil surface and are particularly well developed in the Caribbean due to high water transparency and stable salinity (Por 1984). Also closely linked to mangroves are seagrass communities, which can form extensive beds, particularly in the clear, shallow waters of the Caribbean. Common species include *Thalassia testudinum, Syringodium isoetifolium, Halodule beaudettei,* and *Kolerupia maritima.*

Structural Characteristics

GENERAL FEATURES

Structural characteristics of coastal wetlands such as canopy height, stem density, species composition, and biomass are influenced by hydrology, nutrient input, and climatic factors such as temperature and rainfall. Lugo and Snedaker (1974) described six forest types based on attributes of mangrove forests in Florida (tree size, productivity, and species composition): riverine, overwash, fringe, basin, scrub, and hammock. These forest types reflect differences in geomorphology and hydrology and are generally applicable to mangroves throughout the northern Neotropics. Species richness in mangroves and other coastal wetlands is influenced by temperature, tidal amplitude, rainfall, catchment area, freshwater seepage, and frequency of disturbance (Lugo and Snedaker 1974; Tomlin-

FIG. 7.1. Mangroves are the dominant coastal plant community in the Neotropics. A. The red mangrove *(Rhizophora mangle)* is a widespread species, typically forming the most seaward vegetation zone. B. The tea mangrove *(Pelliciera rhizophorae)* occurs mainly on the Pacific coast of Central America, but small populations, such as the one depicted here, also occur on the Caribbean coast. Photos by K. L. McKee.

son 1994). Mangroves are often described as lacking an understory, as found in rainforests, due to the combination of salinity, flooding, and shading stresses (Lugo 1986). An understory may develop, however, where the canopy is more open (Fig. 7.2a) or where rainfall or freshwater runoff lowers salinity levels. Canopy gaps may result from natural events, such as lightning strikes, wind damage, frost, wood-boring insects, and dieback (Smith, Robblee, et al. 1994; Feller and McKee 1999).

Coastal salt marshes occur on low sandflats and are dominated by species with a high salt tolerance. Canopy height and other structural features vary depending on species. Succulent forbs include prostrate growth forms such as *S. portulacastrum* and *B. maritima.* Short grasses such as *D. spicata* and *S. virginicus* form dense patches, whereas *S. spartinae,* another grass, is taller and has a more bunchlike growth. Canopy height and stem density vary with hydroedaphic conditions and where they extend into mangrove stands (Lopez-Portillo and Ezcurra 1989).

Species Zonation

Spatial variation in species occurrence and abundance is observed across environmental gradients in both mangrove and marsh communities where strong environmental gradients exist. For example, patterns for mangrove communities in Florida and the Caribbean often show *R. mangle* occupying the seaward zone, followed by *A. germinans,* and *L. racemosa* in more landward positions. Although zonation patterns are usually depicted as a rigid sequence proceeding from the shoreline to landward, many patterns resemble a mosaic, with species occurring repeatedly where the land mass is interrupted by watercourses or other variations in topography. Although zonation typically refers to patterns created by different species, variation in stature and productivity of plants across environmental gradients may also cause distinct spatial patterns. Zones may be composed of different architectural forms that represent variations in height and vigor. Such height-form

zonation in mangroves and their causes have been extensively studied (McKee, Feller, et al. 2002; Feller, Whigham, et al. 2003; Lovelock, Feller, et al. 2005). A particular focus has been on the "dwarf" height form of *R. mangle,* which forms extensive stands in south Florida, Belize, and Panama. These stunted trees are mature, but reach only a meter or less in height (online appendix, Fig. 7.2). The cause of spatial variation in tree stature and productivity can be traced to stress gradients (flooding, salinity, and/or nutrients). In a series of studies conducted in several geographic locations, investigators have stimulated growth of stunted mangroves by additions of fertilizer. In Belize, for example, dwarf trees fertilized with phosphorus attained heights similar to that of "normal" trees (4–5 m) within five years (online appendix, Fig. 7.2).

Few studies have examined species zonation in Neotropical salt marshes. One study described variation in marsh and mangrove vegetation across transects in Laguna de Mecoacán, Mexico (Lopez-Portillo and Ezcurra 1989). The low intertidal zone had a narrow *R. mangle* fringe, followed by *A. germinans* in the lowest elevations. At landward, low-relief positions, *B. maritima* and dwarf *A. germinans* occurred. The high intertidal positions were occupied by *S. spartinae* and blackbead *(Pithecellobium).*

Vertical Stratification

In addition to horizontal spatial patterns, Neotropical mangroves also exhibit vertical stratification. The three main strata are readily observed along shorelines and tidal creekbanks: supratidal, intertidal, and subtidal. Each stratum is occupied by a unique assemblage of organisms associated with different mangrove vegetative structures. The supratidal includes all the arboreal portions of the forest and is occupied by birds, reptiles, crabs, snails, insects, and spiders. In humid, wet regions, mangroves also support a diverse assemblage of arboreal epiphytes, including orchids, bromeliads, ferns, vines, and cacti (online appendix, Fig. 7.3). The intertidal stratum is associated with the aerial root system and extends from high- to low-tide

FIG. 7.2. Coastal marsh vegetation often occurs in association with mangroves or in disturbed areas. A. Black mangrove forest with an understory of herbaceous halophytes. B. Salt marsh that has developed in a former mangrove forest cleared for construction of a fishing camp. Examples of common saltmarsh species: C. saltwort *(Batis maritima),* D. sea purselane *(Sesuvium portulacastrum),* E. spikegrass *(Distichlis spicata).* Photos by K. L. McKee.

levels, where organisms (barnacles, isopods, crabs, oysters, amphipods, snails, and macroalgae) experience periodic submergence and drying. The subtidal stratum occurs below low-tide level, where mangrove aerial roots dangle into the water and provide substrate for a variety of organisms. In addition to sessile epibionts, various species of fish, shrimp, polychaetes, brittlestars, nudibranchs, and jellyfish are found in the subtidal environment. Vertical strata are especially well developed in Caribbean mangrove systems, where the tropical climate and clear waters allow development of a rich and diverse intertidal and subtidal community (Ellison and Farnsworth 1992).

Animal Communities

Structural features, both vertical and horizontal, of marshes and mangroves determine the diversity and composition of animal communities. Mangrove forests, with their arboreal structure and unique root systems, offer greater variety and space for support of birds, reptiles, invertebrates, and mammals. However, marshes and mangroves share many of the same fauna.

Invertebrates

MARINE MACROFAUNA

Common invertebrates found in Neotropical coastal wetlands are mollusks, crabs, worms, and insects. Gastropods typically seen in Neotropical mangrove forests include the mangrove periwinkle *(Littoraria angulifera),* which occurs in different colors and shell shapes associated with local environmental conditions (Merkt and Ellison 1998) and feeds on fungi present on mangrove aerial roots and bark. The coffee bean snail *(Melampus coffeus)* feeds on fallen leaf litter at low tide, then moves onto tree trunks and prop roots as the tide floods the forest (Proffitt and Devlin 2005). The ladder hornsnail *(Cerithidea scalariformis)* occurs in mangrove forests as well as saline marshes and exhibits plasticity in its demographic traits. When populations were exposed in a reciprocal transplant experiment to mangrove forest and exposed marsh habitats, those maintained in the exposed marsh (regardless of source) showed faster growth, earlier maturation, greater size, and higher rates of parasitism (Smith and Ruiz 2004). The mangrove tree crab *(Aratus pisonii),* which is common throughout the Neotropics, feeds on mangrove leaves and propagules in the canopy and on detritus and algae in the intertidal zone; it also has been observed feeding on insect larvae (McKeon and Feller 2004). Another omnivorous tree crab *(Goniopsis cruentata)* ventures onto the forest floor, where it scavenges for food, including fallen mangrove propagules (McKee 1995a). The hairy land crab *(Ucides cordatus)* is an herbivore that pulls fallen leaves into its large burrows, where they decompose. The most abundant decapod is the fiddler crab *(Uca* spp.), which favors mudflats and saltpans, where it builds burrows and feeds on benthic bacteria and microalgae.

In the Caribbean, a diverse epibiont community can develop on mangrove prop roots and peat banks (Ellison and Farnsworth 1992). In this type of habitat, few hard substrates occur for settlement of sessile organisms. Consequently, the prop roots of the red mangrove, which extend into the subtidal stratum, become encrusted with an abundant community of sponges, tunicates, anemones, algae, corals, shrimp, brittlestars, and other invertebrates. The mangrove oyster *(Crassostrea rhizophorae)* grows attached to the prop roots of red mangrove throughout the Neotropics. Similarly, the blades of turtlegrass, *T. testudinum,* serve as substrate for a diverse assemblage of microscopic and macroscopic organisms such as tiny, stinging anemones *(Bunodeopsis* sp.*)* and numerous bryozoans, hydroids, sponges, ascidians, and setpulid worms. On the Pacific coast of Central America, where sediment muddies the water, the biodiversity of subtidal and intertidal communities is lower.

INSECTS

Although early scientific records suggested that the insect fauna in mangroves was as depauperate as the flora, later work showed that they are the most abundant and species-rich group of animals in some Neotropical mangroves (Feller 1995; Feller and Mathis 1997). Aquatic and semiaquatic insects (Diptera, Hemiptera, Odonata, and Coleoptera) are abundant in mangroves due to the extensive mudflats, ponds, and detritus. The shore-fly family (Ephydridae) is one of the most species rich in Belizean mangroves, with 55 species collected so far. Wood-feeding insects have also been studied in Belize, with more than 35 species of wood-boring beetles and moths. The most conspicuous wood-feeding insect is the termite *(Nasutitermes* sp.), which builds large nests constructed of chewed wood. A diverse guild of leaf-feeding insects includes the mangrove puss moth *(Megalopyge* sp.), leaf miners *(Marmara* spp.), io moth *(Automeris* sp.), bagworm (Oiketicinae), and mangrove buckeye *(Junonia* spp.). Other mangrove-dwelling arthropods include ants, spiders, isopods, scorpions, crickets, scale insects, mites, roaches, and thrips. After dark, the mangrove forest twinkles with bioluminescent light from fireflies (Lampyridae).

Vertebrates

Many aquatic and terrestrial vertebrate species, such as fish, lizards, snakes, birds, rodents, bats, monkeys, and deer, may be observed in mangrove forests, but relatively few reside in or reproduce there (Luther and Greenberg 2009). Only 24 species of terrestrial vertebrates are reported to be endemic to mangroves in the Neotropics, and a similar number (25) are restricted to tidal marshes (Greenberg, Maldonado, et al. 2006).

In the Neotropics, mangroves and seagrasses are important feeding and nursery grounds for many commercially important or reef-dependent fish species such as snapper *(Lutjanus* spp.), tarpon *(Megalops atlanticus),* barracuda *(Sphyraena barracuda),* jack *(Caranx* spp.), sheepshead *(Archosargus probatocephalus),* and red drum *(Sciaenops ocellatus).* An unusual species of fish has adapted to life in microhabitats of mangroves and salt marshes of Florida, Central America, and Caribbean islands (Davis, Taylor, et al. 1990). The habitat preference of the Neotropical killifish *(Kryptolebias* [previously *Rivulus*] *marmoratus)* is stagnant pools, leaf litter, and the burrows of land crabs, *Cardisoma guanhumi* (Florida) or *U. cordatus* (Belize). This fish is hermaphroditic and self-fertilizes, a useful adaptation for isolated animals.

Birds are typically the most visible and colorful vertebrates found in Neotropical coastal wetlands. Many transient species use these wetlands as wintering grounds, but there are also a number of resident species. In mangroves, some of the more common residents include the mangrove warbler *(Dendroica petechia erithachorides),* Yucatán vireo *(Vireo magister),* osprey *(Pandion haliaetus),* white-crowned pigeon *(Patagioenas leucocephala),* and green-breasted mango *(Anthracothorax prevostii).* Birds also use mangrove stands for nesting: magnificent frigatebird *(Fregata magnificens),* brown booby *(Sula leucogaster),* and brown pelican *(Pelecanus occidentalis).* These large birds, which feed offshore, can be found in large colonies in the mangrove canopy, often using the same location year after year as rookeries. Wading birds common to both mangrove and marsh habitats include the clapper rail *(Rallus longirostris),* great blue heron *(Ardea herodias),* green-backed heron *(Butorides striata),* and little blue heron *(Egretta caerulea).* The clapper rail, which often builds nests in the marsh grass, feeds on crabs and other small invertebrates. Many Neotropical and Nearctic migratory land and wading birds use mangrove forests on Caribbean islands as stopovers: ruddy turnstone *(Arenaria interpres),* sanderling *(Calidris alba),* and black-bellied plover *(Pluvialis squatarola).*

A few reptiles are found in the mangrove habitat, where they are commonly seen on tree trunks, limbs, and aerial roots (Campbell 1998; McKeon and Feller 2004). The Mayan coastal anole *(Anolis sagrei)* is a ubiquitous resident, often seen on tree branches, where it feeds on small insects such as ants and termites. Other reptiles include iguanas *(Ctenosaura similis),* geckos *(Thecadactylus rapicauda* and *Aristelliger georgeensis),* and snakes such as the boa constrictor *(Boa constrictor).* Coastal scrub communities adjacent to mangroves provide habitat for other types of snakes (vine snake, *Oxybelis* sp.), turtles (furrowed wood turtle, *Rhinoclemmys areolata),* and terrapins (diamondback terrapin, *Malaclemys terrapin rhizophorarum).* The largest reptiles inhabiting coastal wetlands in the Neotropics are the American crocodile *(Crocodylus acutus),* Morelet's crocodile *(C. moreletii),* and caiman *(Caiman crocodilus).* The American crocodile is found in south Florida, the Caribbean islands, and throughout Central America, where it inhabits mangrove forests, saline lakes, and river mouths. The caiman, which can also tolerate a range of salinities, occurs from southern Mexico to Panama and into South America. Morelet's crocodile is reported on the Yucatán Peninsula (Campbell 1998). Both the crocodile and caiman feed on aquatic invertebrates (as juveniles), fish, amphibians, reptiles, and waterbirds.

Little information exists about terrestrial mammals in mangroves or in coastal marshes of the Neotropics. The smallest mammals found in mangrove and marsh habitats include rodents, rabbits, and bats. Although most abundant in South America, the Neotropical river otter *(Lontra longicaudis)* can be spotted in wetlands, streams, lagoons, and lakes in Mexico and Central America. Its habitats range from intermittent freshwater to permanent saltwater marshes and swamps. It feeds mostly on mollusks and fish, but also eats the occasional bird or small reptile. The whitetail deer *(Odocoileus virginianus)* and the Florida Key deer *(O. virginianus clavium),* which is endangered, also spend time in mangroves and coastal marshes. The largest mammal found in Neotropical coastal wetlands is the West Indian manatee *(Trichechus manatus),* which feeds on seagrass and other submerged aquatic vegetation. There are at least two distinct subspecies, the Florida manatee *(T. m. latirostris)* and the Antillean or Caribbean manatee *(T. m. mantanus)* (Domning and Yayek 1986), but possibly more based on molecular genetics (Garcia-Rodriguez, Bowen, et al. 1998). They occur throughout the Caribbean in shallow rivers and estuaries.

Key Ecological Processes

Primary Productivity

Data on net primary production in Neotropical coastal wetlands are not extensive. Table 7.1 summarizes above- and belowground production measured in mangrove, freshwater marsh, and seagrass communities from Florida to Panama. Most studies of primary production have mainly focused on aboveground components, and in most cases, these measures are crude estimates of productivity, especially for mangroves. The most commonly used approach (for mangroves) is to measure litterfall rates, which involves monthly collection of plant litter (leaves, woody twigs, and reproductive parts) accumulated in litter traps. The values for annual litterfall range from 34 to 2,208 g m^{-2} yr^{-1}, with an average of 965 for maximum values reported for each location (Table 7.1). Mangrove litterfall rates provide an idea of the amount of organic matter and carbon available for turnover and export, but do not include production of all wood, aerial roots, or belowground biomass. The ratio of wood production to litterfall in Neotropical mangroves ranges from 0.37 to 1.5, with an average of 0.8 (Bouillon, Borges, et al. 2008). Thus, a crude estimate for total aboveground production, including wood, would be 2,200 g m^{-2} yr^{-1}. Based on the few data available, belowground production by mangroves ranges from 18 to 1,146, with an average maximum of 712 g m^{-2} yr^{-1}, which is about one-third the estimate for aboveground production. Spatial and temporal variation in mangrove productivity has been attributed to differences in hydrology, which controls salinity level, nutrient inputs, and sulfide concentrations (Day, Coronado-Molina, et al. 1996; McKee and Faulkner 2000).

In comparison, annual aboveground production for marsh and seagrass communities (average of maximum values reported) is, respectively, 2,003 and 639 g m^{-2} yr^{-1}. Although the most conspicuous photosynthetic organisms in Neotropical wetlands are macrophytes, algae are major contributors to food webs in coastal waters via both detrital and grazing pathways. Some estimates suggest that the algal biomass in Neotropical mangroves is equal to the annual biomass of leaf litterfall from *R. mangle* (Puerto Rico; Rodriguez and Stoner 1990), and, with a four to five times greater turnover rate, algal productivity may easily exceed aboveground production of mangroves. In a Bahamian lagoon, the net primary production of algal epiphytes on seagrasses and mangrove prop roots was 5.22 and 8.54 g C kg^{-1} d^{-1} (Koch and Madden 2001).

Decomposition

The detrital pathway is a major route through which carbon and energy flow in mangrove and other coastal wetlands. Information about the mechanisms controlling rates of organic matter degradation provides insight into carbon storage potential, nutrient cycling, and soil accretion. However, surprisingly few studies have been conducted in Neotropical mangrove systems to determine rates of decomposition (McKee and Faulkner 2000; Middleton and McKee 2001; Romero, Smith, et al. 2005; Poret, Twilley, et al. 2007). In addition to insights into carbon and nutrient dynamics, an understanding of the processes leading to peat formation is particularly important for Neotropical systems, many of which are characterized by substantial peat deposits and thereby dependent upon organic matter buildup to maintain surface elevations relative to sea level.

Studies have investigated rates of herbaceous plant decomposition in the Everglades and Belize, much of it focused on the effects of nutrients (Davis 1991; Rejmankova and Houdkova 2006). Unlike salt marshes, mangrove litter is composed of woody and nonwoody materials, which decompose at dramatically different rates. The mass loss of leaves was four times faster than wood or roots in a Belizean mangrove system (Middleton and McKee 2001). Mangrove tissue degradation is accelerated by macrofauna such as crabs and snails, which fragment leaves into smaller particles (Middleton and McKee 2001; Proffitt and Devlin 2005).

Competition and Facilitation

Distribution and relative abundance of plant species growing in stressful and variable habitats are regulated in part by species-specific tolerances to flooding, salinity, shading, low nutrients, and other factors (Mendelssohn, McKee, et al. 1982; McKee 1995b). In addition to interspecific differences, there may also be intraspecific (within species) variation in plant stress tolerance (Hester, Mendelssohn, et al. 2001). However, plants are additionally influenced by competitive interactions whereby co-occurring species differ in ability to acquire resources such as nutrients or light. Species-specific attributes, such as inherent growth rate, shade tolerance, and nutrient-use efficiency, interact to determine the outcome of plant-plant interactions. Although stress tolerance of some Neotropical wetland species has been studied in monoculture, species responses in mixed culture have not been examined. A study of three herbaceous species *(Spartina patens, Sagittaria lancifolia,* and *Panicum hemitomon)* found that as abiotic stress was increased, the importance of competition decreased (La Peyre, Grace, et al. 2001). Growth of a subtropical mangrove *(A. germinans)* was dramati-

TABLE 7.1
Biomass production (g m^{-2} yr^{-1}) of neotropical mangrove, freshwater marsh, and seagrass communities

Location	Neotropical mangrove		Freshwater marsh	Seagrass	Source
	Aboveground	Belowground	Aboveground	Aboveground	
Bahamas				602–835	Koch and Madden 2001
Bahamas				360	Dierssen, Zimmerman, et al. 2003
Belize		82–525			McKee, Cahoon, et al. 2007
Belize	280–700			942	Koltes, Tschirky, et al. 1998
Cayman Islands	942				UNESCO 1998
Dominican Republic	1,020–1,280				Sherman, Fahey, et al. 2003
Florida (Everglades)	340–2,208		255–620	91–396	Ewe, Gaiser, et al. 2006
Florida (Everglades)			419–1,744		Browder, Cottrell, et al. 1982
Florida (Everglades)			802–2,028		Davis 1989
Florida (Everglades)			945–3,620[a]		Daoust and Childers 1998
Florida (Naples)	361–1,347	18–1,146			McKee and Faulkner 2000
Florida (Rookery Bay)	444–810				Twilley, Lugo, et al. 1986
Florida (Rookery Bay)	101–263	106–842			Giraldo 2005
Honduras		311–333			Cahoon, Hensel, et al. 2003
Mexico (Boca Chico)	1,252				Day, Conner, et al. 1987
Mexico (Estero Pargo)	835				Day, Conner, et al. 1987
Mexico (Laguna de Terminos)	301–496				Day, Coronado-Molina, et al. 1996
Panama (Bocas del Toro)	34			664	Guzman, Barnes, et al. 2005
Trinidad and Tobago	1,410				UNESCO 1998

NOTE: Mangrove production estimated from litterfall (aboveground) and root ingrowth cores (belowground); marsh and seagrass aboveground production estimated by destructive harvest or both destructive and nondestructive phenometric methods.

[a] Value ranges represent different habitat types, treatments, or methods.

cally suppressed by competition when grown in mixed culture with a temperate salt marsh grass (S. alterniflora) (McKee and Rooth 2008). In seagrass beds of Florida Bay, USA, fertilization with bird guano caused a shift in species dominance from T. testudinum to H. wrightii, which persisted for eight years after nutrient addition ceased (Fourqurean, Powell, et al. 1995).

In contrast to competition, facilitation is a mechanism whereby establishment or growth of one species is benefitted by another species. Facilitation is particularly important in habitats characterized by adverse conditions, such as those found in disturbed wetlands. Few studies, however, have investigated facilitative interactions in wetlands, and most of these have focused on temperate wetlands. In southwest Florida, the presence of saltwort (Batis maritima) lowered mortality of black mangrove (A. germinans) seedlings, indicating that recolonization of disturbed mangrove areas might be improved by nurse plants (Milbrandt and Tinsley 2006). Herbaceous vegetation facilitated mangrove recruitment in a clear-cut forest in Belize by several mechanisms: trapping of dispersing propagules, structural support of seedlings, and promotion of survival or growth through amelioration of adverse conditions (temperature, aeration) (McKee, Rooth, et al. 2007). Although a number

of animal facilitation and mutualism studies have been carried out in marine environments, many of these have occurred at temperate latitudes (e.g., rocky intertidal habitats). However, a few studies have examined interactions between bivalves (mussels, clams, and oysters) and seagrasses in the Gulf of Mexico and Florida Bay (Peterson and Heck 2001; Reynolds, Berg, et al. 2007). The suspension-feeding mussel Modiolus americanus increased productivity of the seagrass T. testudinum (via nutrient enrichment, reduced epiphytic load), and the seagrass improved mussel survivorship (via reduced predation) (Peterson and Heck 2001).

Seed Dispersal and Predation

Distribution and relative abundance of Neotropical mangrove species are influenced by dispersal patterns and by losses to seed predators. Tidal sorting of mangrove propagules was first described in Panama (Rabinowitz 1978), in which differential dispersal of propagules across an elevation gradient caused a physical "sorting out" of species by tidal action, leading to vegetation zonation. Other work in the Neotropics, however, found that although propagule buoyancy and water depth influence seedling establishment, the evidence does not support tidal sorting as a primary mechanism regulating zonation patterns (Jimenez and Sauter 1991; McKee 1995a; Patterson, McKee, et al. 1997; Sousa, Kennedy, et al. 2007).

Seed predation is a process that received considerable attention by mangrove researchers because of its potential effect on seedling survival. Experiments initially conducted in Australian mangroves found that differential consumption of propagules by crabs occurred across the intertidal zone in a pattern inversely related to the dominance of mangrove species in the canopy (Smith 1987). These studies led to the "predation hypothesis," which proposed propagule predation as a determinant of forest zonation. Work carried out in Belize, Panama, and the U.S. (Louisiana), however, found that although crab and snail predation on propagules varied by species and intertidal position, the pattern for all mangrove species was not consistent with the predation hypothesis (McKee 1995a; Patterson, McKee, et al. 1997; Sousa and Mitchell 1999). Other work has shown that predispersal damage by insects also affects mangrove seedling performance on the Caribbean coast of Panama (Sousa, Kennedy, et al. 2003).

Herbivory and Detritivory

Herbivory was initially considered to play a minor role in mangrove ecosystems and it was thought that mangrove tissues were generally unpalatable to herbivores. Subsequent work, however, discovered that a variety of animals, including insects, crabs, and snails, feed on mangrove leaves and propagules in the canopy, on fallen litter, and on algae and detritus. A number of insect species feed on mangrove foliage and wood (Feller and Chamberlain 2007). Rates of herbivory in Neotropical mangrove systems are comparable to those in other tropical and temperate forests (Farnsworth and Ellison 1993). Although folivory can be low in some mangrove areas (0 to 0.4% leaf area per month), loss of yield caused by the bud moth *Ecdytolopha* sp. can be high (20% of buds killed) (Feller 2002). Early work found that mangrove islands used as bird rookeries exhibited higher rates of herbivory than islands not receiving additional nutrients (Onuf, Teal, et al. 1977). An experimental study found that while herbivory by some insects (leaf miners) increased with nutrient addition, herbivory by others (crab folivores, bud moths) did not, suggesting that responses varied by feeding strategies (Feller and Chamberlain 2007). Woodboring beetles, which girdle trees or prune branches, killed over 50% of the canopy on mangrove islands in Belize (Feller 2002) and created light gaps for seedling regeneration (Feller and McKee 1999). Premature leaf loss due to woodborer damage also influenced the quantity and quality of mangrove litter, suggesting an important role in nutrient cycling. In comparison, leaf-feeding herbivores removed less than 6% of the canopy. The mangrove tree crab *(A. pisonii)* is an omnivore that feeds on green leaves and propagules of mangrove and leaves distinctive damage in the canopy (Feller and Chamberlain 2007). Tissue chemistry of red mangrove leaves, the preferred food source of *A. pisonii,* was correlated with leaf damage in a study in south Florida, but other factors likely influenced feeding patterns (Erickson, Bell, et al. 2004). Another omnivorous crab, *G. cruentata,* feeds on fallen mangrove leaves and propagules (McKee 1995a). A large, herbivorous land crab *(U. cordatus)* cleans the forest floor of fallen leaves and propagules and carries them into its large burrows excavated in red mangrove stands. The feeding activities of crabs accelerated the degradation of mangrove leaf litter in Belizean forests (Middleton and McKee 2001). Burrowing land crabs such as *U. cordatus* and *C. guanhumi* also influence mangrove forest growth and biogeochemistry by excavating burrows, aerating soils, burying leaves and other organic matter, and building soil mounds (Middleton and McKee 2001; Lindquist, Krauss, et al. 2009). Faunal impacts on mangrove structure and function have been reviewed in detail elsewhere (Cannicci, Burrows, et al. 2008).

Disturbance

Small-scale and large-scale disturbances are important organizing forces in Neotropical mangroves. Small-scale events include loss of branches or single trees caused by windstorms, lightning strikes (Smith, Robblee, et al. 1994), frost damage (Lugo and Zucca 1977), or wood-boring beetles (Feller and McKee 1999). Large-scale events include hurricanes (Baldwin, Platt, et al. 1995; Cahoon, Hensel, et al. 2003) and occasional oil spills. Although such disturbances have been described, their influence on wetland functioning is not well studied. In marshes, the deposition of wrack (plant debris) can smother and kill living vegetation, creating bare ground. However, little information exists about the role of this process in Neotropical marshes. The formation of canopy gaps, which are common in mangrove forests, is important in forest regeneration since the gaps allow penetration of light to the forest floor, where seedlings and saplings establish. Effects of canopy gaps on seedling survival and growth and on soil chemistry have been studied in Belize and Puerto Rico (Sherman, Fahey, et al. 1998; Feller and McKee 1999; Sherman, Fahey, et al. 2000). Canopy gaps can alter temperature and salinity, which may influence seedlings directly or the crab fauna feeding on fallen litter or propagules.

Hurricane disturbance has been studied in mangrove forests throughout the Neotropics where immediate damage and/or recovery has been described (Roth 1992; Baldwin, Platt, et al. 1995). Site productivity of Nicaraguan mangroves determined posthurricane recovery and influenced the subsequent species zonation of the forest (Ross, Ruiz, et al. 2006). In Honduras, mass mortality of mangroves caused by Hurricane Mitch led to peat collapse and increased susceptibility to submergence (Cahoon, Hensel, et al. 2003).

Human Interactions and Conservation

Mangroves and other Neotropical wetlands have not been afforded the same concern and protection as have coral reefs and rainforests and consequently have been subjected to unsustainable human activities (Valiela, Bowen, et al. 2001). Humans have exploited these ecosystems for various uses for thousands of years. Ancient artifacts (pottery, charcoal, wooden structures) preserved in mangrove peat reveal that groups of Mayan coastal peoples extracted salt along the southern coast of Belize (Punta Ycacos Lagoon), which was later transported inland for sale (McKillop 2005). Evidence of Maya wetland agriculture in northern Belize also indicates an influence on the nutrient and salinity regimes of freshwater marshes and swamps in the coastal plain (Rejmankova, Pope, et al. 1995). Historically, human impacts to mangroves on the Caribbean coasts of Mexico and Central America have been

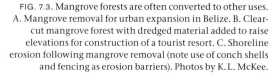
FIG. 7.3. Mangrove forests are often converted to other uses. A. Mangrove removal for urban expansion in Belize. B. Clear-cut mangrove forest with dredged material added to raise elevations for construction of a tourist resort. C. Shoreline erosion following mangrove removal (note use of conch shells and fencing as erosion barriers). Photos by K. L. McKee.

relatively minimal and confined to extraction of trees for fire-wood, fencing, and construction. Other areas, however, have suffered major impacts from conversion to shrimp farming and other activities such as extraction of salt, wood and bark, and artisanal fishing. Mangroves, seagrass beds, and coral reefs throughout the island states in Caribbean region have under-gone substantial degradation due to early pressures from agri-cultural practices and charcoal production (Lugo and Brown 1988) and later from pollution and expansion of ecotourism (Uyarra, Cote, et al. 2005). Mangrove clearing along the Carib-bean coast of Yucatán and on Belizean islands has occurred to build tourist resorts (Macintyre, Toscano, et al. 2009; McKee and Vervaeke 2009) (Fig. 7.3). Such unsustainable practices pose serious threats to coastal wetlands in the Neotropics.

Conservation and restoration of Neotropical coastal wet-lands are spotty at best, but increasing efforts to bring atten-tion to the need for action has occurred in the past fifteen years (Gottgens and Fortney 2003). Seventy-five sites containing mangroves and other wetlands in the Neotropics (excluding South America) have been designated as Wetlands of Interna-tional Importance by the Ramsar Convention (http://ramsar.wetlands.org/, accessed March 20, 2010), which emphasizes values of these ecosystems. Ecological research in this region as well as the training of students from these areas has fur-

ther focused attention on Neotropical wetlands and provided much-needed data. Despite such efforts, destruction and deg-radation of Neotropical wetlands are outpacing the acquisi-tion of information necessary to conserve them. In particular, information on the extent, distribution, and condition of man-grove and other coastal wetlands in the Neotropics is incom-plete, and what information is available becomes quickly out-dated (FAO 2007). Although some efforts have been made to quantify mangrove losses, the data for other coastal wetland types in the Neotropics is sketchy and often unpublished.

Conclusions

Unlike many of the other wetlands described in this book, we have only a rudimentary understanding of Neotropical coastal wetlands—their spatial extent, biodiversity, ecological func-tioning, and losses to natural and human causes. The infor-mation provided in this chapter shows the need for additional data, especially comparative studies that will aid in a deeper understanding of these ecosystems. Much of what is known about Neotropical coastal wetlands derives from site-specific studies, which may or may not be focused on the most repre-sentative or important sites. In other cases, the information is not published or is not readily available. Many of the detailed surveys and inventories of Neotropical coastal wetlands are decades old and require updating. However, coordinated efforts are underway to gather information in a consistent and comprehensive manner and to provide those data in an online clearinghouse. One example is the Caribbean Comparative Marine Productivity (CARICOMP) program (www.unesco.org/csi/pub/papers/kjerfve.htm, accessed March 21, 2010), which has collected data on factors regulating productivity of three habitats: mangroves, seagrasses, and coral reefs at 29 sites in 22 countries and territories throughout the Caribbean. Individual countries also have programs to inventory their wetlands, such as the geographical information system (GIS) database of Costa Rican wetlands (www.una.ac.cr/ambi/puch/ index. htm, accessed March 22, 2010) and classification systems for wetlands of Mexico (Berlanga-Robles, Ruiz-Luna, et al. 2008). These examples and others serve as a starting point to build upon as well as provide models to guide future inventories and comparative research. Such efforts, however, require funding, regional cooperation, and strong leadership.

Although some coastal wetlands are protected by law or have been designated as Wetlands of International Importance by the Ramsar Convention, most of these areas remain vulnerable to exploitation and development. To be successful, conservation efforts require documentation of the biodiversity of wetland flora and fauna and identification of those sites with threatened or endangered species. Remote sensing techniques are quantifying the areal extent of mangroves, seagrass beds, and other wetlands in the region as well as documenting recent and ongoing destruction of these ecosystems. In addition to complete inventories of Neotropical coastal wetlands, ecological research that goes beyond descriptive studies of the biota and correlations with environmental conditions is greatly needed. The diverse and extensive coastal wetlands of the Neotropics provide a wonderful palette of habitats in which many important biological and ecological questions may be addressed. Future research should focus on investigating ecological functioning and how human activities may lead to degradation and loss of ecosystem services. Although some intensive work has examined nutrient enrichment effects on oligotrophic wetlands in Florida and Belize, effects of other anthropogenic activities as well as global change factors need to be assessed. Conservation and management of wetlands in this region must account for anticipated changes in sea level, climate, and intensity or frequency of hurricanes. In particular, we need a better understanding of resilience and how it varies with biodiversity or type of wetland. Future cooperation among researchers, land managers, and policymakers will fill these information gaps and promote the preservation of the unique wetland ecosystems found in the Neotropics.

References

Baldwin AH, Platt WJ, et al. 1995. Hurricane damage and regeneration in fringe mangrove forests of southeastern Florida, USA. *J. Coast. Res.* SI21:169–83.

Berlanga-Robles CA, Ruiz-Luna A, et al. 2008. Esquema de clasificación de los humedales de México. *Investigaciones Geográficas, Boletín del Instituto de Geografía* 66:25–46.

Bouillon S, Borges AV, et al. 2008. Mangrove production and carbon sinks: a revision of global budget estimates. *Global Biogeochem. Cycles* 22:GB2013.

Browder JA, Cottrell D, et al. 1982. Biomass and primary production of microphytes and macrophytes in periphyton habitats of the southern Everglades. Report T-662. Homestead: South Florida Research Center.

Cahoon DR, Hensel P, et al. 2003. Mass tree mortality leads to mangrove peat collapse at Bay Islands, Honduras, after Hurricane Mitch. *J. Ecol.* 91:1093–105.

Campbell JA. 1998. *Amphibians and reptiles of northern Guatemala, the Yucatan, and Belize.* Norman: Univ. Oklahoma Press.

Cannicci S, Burrows D, et al. 2008. Faunal impact on vegetation structure and ecosystem function in mangrove forests: a review. *Aquat. Bot.* 89:186–200.

Cintron G, Lugo AE, et al. 1978. Mangroves of arid environments in Puerto Rico and adjacent islands. *Biotropica* 10:110–21.

Corstanje R, Reddy KR, et al. 2007. Soil microbial eco-physiological response to nutrient enrichment in a sub-tropical wetland. *Ecol. Indic.* 7:277–89.

Costa CSB, Davy AJ. 1992. Coastal saltmarsh communities of Latin America. In *Coastal plant communities of Latin America,* Seeliger U, editor. San Diego: Academic Press, pp. 179–99.

Daoust RJ, Childers DL. 1998. Quantifying aboveground biomass and estimating net aboveground primary production for wetland macrophytes using a non-destructive phenometric technique. *Aquat. Bot.* 62:115–33.

Davis SM. 1989. Sawgrass and cattail production in relation to nutrient supply in the Everglades. In *Freshwater wetlands and wildlife,* Sharitz RR, Gibbons JW, editors. Oak Ridge, TN: USDOE Off. Sci. Tech. Inf., pp. 357–78.

Davis SM. 1991. Growth, decomposition, and nutrient retention of *Cladium jamaicense* Crantz and *Typha domingensis* Pers. in the Florida Everglades. *Aquat. Bot.* 75:199–215.

Davis WP, Taylor DS, et al. 1990. Field observations of the ecology and habits of mangrove *Rivulus (Rivulus marmoratus)* in Belize and Florida. *Ichthyol. Explor. Freshw.* 1:123–34.

Davy AJ, Costa CSB. 1992. Development and organization of salt-marsh communities. In *Coastal plant communities of Latin America,* Seeliger U, editor. San Diego: Academic Press, pp. 179–99.

Day JW, Jr., Conner WH, et al. 1987. The productivity and composition of mangrove forests, Laguna de Terminos, Mexico. *Aquat. Bot.* 27:267–84.

Day JW, Coronado-Molina C, et al. 1996. A 7 year record of aboveground net primary production in a southeastern Mexican mangrove forest. *Aquat. Bot.* 55:39–60.

Dierssen HM, Zimmerman RC, et al. 2003. Ocean color remote sensing of seagrass and bathymetry in the Bahamas Banks by high-resolution airborne imagery. *Limnol. Oceanogr.* 48:444–55.

Domning DP, Yayek LC. 1986. Interspecific and intraspecific morphological variation in manatees (Sirenia: *Trichechus). Mar. Mamm. Sci.* 2:87–144.

Egler FE. 1948. The dispersal and establishment of red mangrove, *Rhizophora,* in Florida. *Caribb. For.* 9:299–310.

Ellison AM. 2004. Wetlands of Central America. *Wetl. Ecol. Manage.* 12:3–55.

Ellison AM, Farnsworth EJ. 1992. The ecology of Belizean mangrove-root fouling communities: patterns of epibiont distribution and abundance, and effects on root growth. *Hydrobiologia* 247:87–98.

Erickson AA, Bell SS, et al. 2004. Does mangrove leaf chemistry help explain crab herbivory patterns? *Biotropica* 36:333–43.

Ewe ML, Gaiser EE, et al. 2006. Spatial and temporal patterns of aboveground net primary productivity (ANPP) along two freshwater-estuarine transects in the Florida Coastal Everglades. *Hydrobiologia* 569:459–74.

FAO. 2007. *The world's mangroves: 1980–2005.* Rome: Food and Agriculture Organization of the United Nations.

Farnsworth EJ, Ellison AM. 1993. Dynamics of herbivory in Belizean mangal. *J. Trop. Ecol.* 9:435–55.

Feller IC. 1995. Effects of nutrient enrichment on growth and herbivory of dwarf red mangrove *(Rhizophora mangle). Ecol. Monogr.* 65:477–505.

Feller IC. 2002. The role of herbivory by wood-boring insects in mangrove ecosystems in Belize. *Oikos* 97:167–76.

Feller IC, Chamberlain A. 2007. Herbivore responses to nutrient enrichment and landscape heterogeneity in a mangrove ecosystem. *Oecologia* 153:607–16.

Feller IC, Mathis WN. 1997. Primary herbivory by wood-boring insects along an architectural gradient of *Rhizophora mangle. Biotropica* 29:440–51.

Feller IC, McKee KL. 1999. Small gap creation in Belizean mangrove forests by a wood-boring insect. *Biotropica* 31:607–17.

Feller IC, Whigham DF, et al. 1999. Effects of nutrient enrichment on within-stand cycling in a mangrove forest. *Ecology* 80:2193–205.

Feller IC, Whigham DF, et al. 2003. Nitrogen limitation of growth and nutrient dynamics in a disturbed mangrove forest, Indian River Lagoon, Florida. *Oecologia* 134:405–14.

Fourqurean JW, Powell GVN, et al. 1995. The effects of long-term manipulation of nutrient supply on competition between the seagrasses *Thalassia testudinum* and *Halodule wrightii* in Florida Bay. *Oikos* 72:349–58.

Garcia-Rodriguez AI, Bowen BW, et al. 1998. Phylogeography of the West Indian manatee *(Trichechusmanatus):* how many populations and how many taxa? *Mol. Ecol.* 7:1137–49.

Giraldo B. 2005. Belowground productivity of mangroves in southwest Florida. Ph.D. diss., Louisiana State Univ., Baton Rouge.

Gottgens JF, Fortney RH. 2003. Neotropical wetlands: building links among wetland scientists. *Wetl. Ecol. Manag.* 12:543–46.

Greenberg R, Maldonado JE, et al. 2006. Tidal marshes: a global perspective on the evolution and conservation of their terrestrial invertebrates. *Bioscience* 56:675–85.

Guzman HM, Barnes PAG, et al. 2005. A site description of the CARICOMP mangrove, seagrass, and coral reef sites in Bocas del Toro, Panama. *Carib. J. Sci.* 41:430–40.

Hester MW, Mendelssohn IA, et al. 2001. Species and population variation to salinity stress in *Panicum hemitomon, Spartina patens,* and *Spartina alterniflora:* morphological and physiological constraints. *Env. Exp. Bot.* 46:277–97.

Jimenez JA. 1992. Mangrove forests of the Pacific coast of Central America. In *Coastal plant communities of Latin America,* Seeliger U, editor. San Diego: Academic Press, pp. 259–67.

Jimenez JA, Sauter K. 1991. Structure and dynamics of mangrove forests along a flooding gradient. *Estuaries* 14:49–56.

Joye SB, Lee RY. 2004. Benthic microbial mats: important sources of fixed carbon and nitrogen to the Twin Cays, Belize ecosystem. *Atoll Res. Bull.* 520:1–28.

Koch MS, Madden CJ. 2001. Patterns of primary production and nutrient availability in a Bahamas lagoon with fringing mangroves. *Mar. Ecol. Prog. Ser.* 219:109–19.

Koltes KH, Tschirky JJ, et al. 1998. Carrie Bow Cay, Belize. In *Caribbean coastal marine productivity (CARICOMP): coral reef, seagrass, and mangrove site characteristics,* Kjerfve B, editor. Paris: UNESCO, pp. 79–94.

La Peyre MKG, Grace JB, et al. 2001. The importance of competition in regulating plant species abundance along a salinity gradient. *Ecology* 82:62–69.

Lee RY, Joye SB. 2006. Seasonal patterns of nitrogen fixation and denitrification in oceanic mangrove habitats. *Mar. Ecol. Prog. Ser.* 307:127–41.

Lindquist ES, Krauss KW, et al. 2009. Land crabs as key drivers in tropical coastal forest recruitment. *Biol. Rev.* 84:203–23.

Lopez-Portillo J, Ezcurra E. 1989. Zonation in mangrove and salt marsh vegetation at Laguna de Mecoacan, Mexico. *Biotropica* 21:107–14.

Lovelock CE, Feller IC, et al. 2005. Variation in mangrove forest structure and sediment characteristics in Bocas del Toro, Panama. *Carib. J. Sci.* 41:456–64.

Lugo A. 1986. Mangrove understory: an expensive luxury? *J. Trop. Ecol.* 2:287–88.

Lugo AE, Brown S. 1988. The wetlands of Caribbean islands. *Acta Cientifica* 2:48–61.

Lugo AE, Snedaker SC. 1974. The ecology of mangroves. In *Annu. Rev. Ecol. Syst.,* Johnston RF, Frank PW, Michener CD, editors. Palo Alto, CA: Annual Reviews, pp. 39–64.

Lugo AE, Zucca CP. 1977. The impact of low temperature stress on mangrove structure and growth. *Trop. Ecol.* 18:149–61.

Luther DA, Greenberg R. 2009. Mangroves: a global perspective on the evolution and conservation of their terrestrial vertebrates. *Bioscience* 59:602–12.

Macintyre IG, Toscano MA, et al. 2004. Holocene history of the mangrove islands of Twin Cays, Belize, Central America. *Atoll Res. Bull.* 510:1–16.

Macintyre IG, Toscano MA, et al. 2009. Decimating mangrove forests for commercial development in the Pelican Cays, Belize:

long-term ecological loss for short-term gain? *Smithson. Contrib. Mar. Sci.* 38:281–90.

McKee KL. 1995a. Mangrove species distribution and propagule predation in Belize: an exception to the dominance-predation hypothesis. *Biotropica* 27:334–45.

McKee KL. 1995b. Seedling recruitment patterns in a Belizean mangrove forest: effects of establishment and physico-chemical factors. *Oecologia* 101:448–60.

McKee KL. 2011. Biophysical controls on accretion and elevation change in Caribbean mangrove ecosystems. *Estuar. Coast. Shelf Sci.* 91:475–83.

McKee KL, Cahoon DR, et al. 2007. Caribbean mangroves adjust to rising sea level through biotic controls on change in soil elevation. *Glob. Ecol. Biogeogr.* 16:545–56.

McKee KL, Faulkner PL. 2000. Restoration of biogeochemical function in mangrove forest. *Restor. Ecol.* 8:247–59.

McKee KL, Feller IC, et al. 2002. Mangrove isotopic (δ^{15}N and δ^{13}C) fractionation across a nitrogen vs. phosphorous limitation gradient. *Ecology* 83:1065–75.

McKee KL, Rooth JE. 2008. Where temperate meets tropical: multifactorial effects of elevated CO_2, nitrogen enrichment, and competition on a mangrove-salt marsh community. *Glob. Change Biol.* 14:1–14.

McKee KL, Rooth JE, Feller IC. 2007. Mangrove recruitment after forest disturbance is facilitated by herbaceous species in the Caribbean. *Ecol. Appl.* 17:1678–93.

McKee KL, Vervaeke WC. 2009. Impacts of human disturbance on soil erosion and habitat stability of mangrove-dominated islands in the Pelican Cays and Twin Cays ranges, Belize. *Smithson. Contrib. Mar. Sci.* 33:415–28.

McKeon CS, Feller IC. 2004. The supratidal fauna of Twin Cays, Belize. *Atoll Res. Bull.* 526:1–22.

McKillop H. 2005. Finds in Belize document Late Classic Maya salt making and canoe transport. *Proc. Natl. Acad. Sci.* 102:5630–34.

Mendelssohn IA, McKee KL. 2000. Salt marshes and mangroves. In *North American terrestrial vegetation,* Barbour MG, Billings WD, editors. Cambridge: Cambridge Univ. Press, pp. 501–36.

Mendelssohn IA, McKee KL, et al. 1982. Sublethal stresses controlling *Spartina alterniflora* productivity. In *Wetlands: ecology and management,* Gopal B, Turner RE, et al., editors. Jaipur: National Institute of Ecology, pp. 223–42.

Merkt RE, Ellison AM. 1998. Geographic and habitat specific morphological variation of *Littoraria (Littorinopsis) anguilifera* (Lamark, 1822). *Malacologia* 40:279–95.

Middleton BA, McKee KL. 2001. Degradation of mangrove tissues and implications for peat formation in Belizean island forests. *J. Ecol.* 89:818–28.

Milbrandt EC, Tinsley MN. 2006. The role of saltwort (*Batis maritima* L.) in regeneration of degraded mangrove forests. *Hydrobiologia* 568:369–77.

Oliver JE, editor. 2005. *Encyclopedia of world climatology.* Dordrecht: Springer.

Onuf CP, Teal JM, et al. 1977. Interactions of nutrients, plant growth and herbivory in a mangrove ecosystem. *Ecology* 58:514–26.

Patterson S, McKee KL, et al. 1997. Effects of tidal inundation and predation on *Avicennia germinans* seedling establishment and survival in a sub-tropical mangal/salt marsh community. *Mangroves and Salt Marshes* 1:103–11.

Peterson BJ, Heck JKL. 2001. Positive interactions between suspension-feeding bivalves and seagrass—a facultative mutualism. *Mar. Ecol. Prog. Ser.* 213:143–55.

Pohl MD. 1990. *Ancient Maya wetland agriculture.* Boulder, CO: Westview Press.

Por FD. 1984. The ecosystem of the mangal: general considerations. In *Hydrobiology of the mangal,* Por FD, Dor I, editors. The Hague: Dr. W. Junk Publishers, pp. 1–14.

Poret N, Twilley RR, et al. 2007. Belowground decomposition of mangrove roots in Florida Coastal Everglades. *Estuaries and Coasts* 30:491–96.

Proffitt CE, Devlin DJ. 2005. Grazing by the intertidal gastropod *Melampus coffeus* greatly increases mangrove leaf litter degradation rates. *Mar. Ecol. Prog. Ser.* 296:209–18.

Rabinowitz D. 1978. Early growth of mangrove seedlings in Panama, and an hypothesis concerning the relationship of dispersal and zonation. *J. Biogeogr.* 5:113–33.

Rejmankova E, Houdkova K. 2006. Wetland plant decomposition under different nutrient conditions: what is more important, litter quality or site quality? *Biogeochemistry* 80:245–62.

Rejmankova E, Komarkova J. 2005. Response of cyanobacterial mats to nutrient and salinity changes. *Aquat. Bot.* 83:87–107.

Rejmankova E, Pope KO, et al. 1995. Freshwater wetland plant communities of northern Belize: implications for paleoecological studies of Maya wetland agriculture. *Biotropica* 27:28–36.

Reynolds LK, Berg P, et al. 2007. Lucinid clam influence on the biogeochemistry of the seagrass *Thalassia testudinum* sediments. *Estuaries and Coasts* 30:482–90.

Rivera-Arriaga E, Lara-Domínguez AL, et al. 2003. Trophodynamic ecology of two critical habitats (seagrasses and mangroves) in Terminos Lagoon, southern Gulf of Mexico. *Fish. Centre Res. Rep.* 11:245–54.

Rodriguez C, Stoner AW. 1990. The epiphyte community of mangrove roots in a tropical estuary—distribution and biomass. *Aquat. Bot.* 36:117–26.

Romero LM, Smith TJ III, et al. 2005. Changes in mass and nutrient content of wood during decomposition in a south Florida mangrove forest. *J. Ecol.* 93:618–31.

Ross MS, O'Brien JJ, et al. 1992. Ecological site classification of Florida Keys terrestrial habitats. *Biotropica* 24:488–502.

Ross MS, Ruiz PL, et al. 2006. Early post-hurricane stand development in fringe mangrove forests of contrasting productivity. *Plant Ecol.* 185:283–97.

Roth LC. 1992. Hurricanes and mangrove regeneration: effects of Hurricane Joan, October 1988, on the vegetation of Isla del Venado, Bluefields, Nicaragua. *Biotropica* 24:375–84.

Saenger P. 2002. *Mangrove ecology, silviculture and conservation.* Dordrecht: Kluwer Acad. Publ.

Seeliger U, editor. 1992. *Coastal plant communities of Latin America.* San Diego: Academic Press.Sherman RE, Fahey TJ, et al. 1998. Soil-plant interactions in a neotropical mangrove forest: iron, phosphorus and sulfur dynamics. *Oecologia* 115:553–63.

Sherman RE, Fahey TJ, et al. 2000. Small-scale disturbance and regeneration dynamics in a neotropical mangrove forest. *J. Ecol.* 88:165–78.

Sherman RE, Fahey TJ, et al. 2003. Spatial patterns of biomass and aboveground net primary productivity in a mangrove ecosystem in the Dominican Republic. *Ecosystems* 6:384–98.

Smith NF, Ruiz GM. 2004. Phenotypic plasticity in the life history of the mangrove snail, *Cerithidea scalariformis. Mar. Ecol. Prog. Ser.* 284:195–209.

Smith TJ III. 1987. Seed predation in relation to tree dominance and distribution in mangrove forests. *Ecology* 68:266–73.

Smith TJ III, Robblee MB, et al. 1994. Mangroves, hurricanes, and lightning strikes. *Bioscience* 44:1–20.

Sousa WP, Kennedy PG, et al. 2003. Propagule size and predispersal damage by insects affect establishment and early growth of mangrove seedlings. *Oecologia* 135:564–75.

Sousa WP, Kennedy PG, et al. 2007. Supply-side ecology in mangroves: do propagule dispersal and seedling establishment explain forest structure? *Ecol. Monogr.* 77:53–76.

Sousa WP, Mitchell BJ. 1999. The effect of seed predators on plant distributions: is there a general pattern in mangroves? *Oikos* 86:55–66.

Spaulding MD, Kainuma M, et al. 2010. *World atlas of mangroves.* Earthscan Ltd.

Stevens PW, Fox SL, et al. 2006. The interplay between mangroves and saltmarshes at the transition between temperate and subtropical climate in Florida. *Wetl. Ecol. Manage.* 14:435–44.

Thom BG. 1967. Mangrove ecology and deltaic geomorphology: Tabasco, Mexico. *J. Ecol.* 55:301–43.

Thom BG. 1984. Coastal landforms and geomorphic processes. In *The mangrove ecosystems: research methods,* Snedaker SC, Snedaker JG, editors. Paris: UNESCO, pp. 3–17.

Tomlinson PB. 1994. *The botany of mangroves.* Cambridge: Cambridge Univ. Press.

Twilley RR, Lugo AE, et al. 1986. Litter production and turnover in basin mangrove forests in southwest Florida. *Ecology* 67:670–83.

UNESCO. 1998. *CARICOMP—Caribbean coral reef, seagrass, and mangrove sites.* Coastal Region and Small Island Papers 3347. Paris.

Uyarra MC, Cote IM, et al. 2005. Island-specific preferences of tourists for environmental features: implications of climate change for tourism-dependent states. *Env. Conserv.* 32:11–19.

Valiela I, Bowen JL, et al. 2001. Mangrove forests: one of the world's threatened major tropical environments. *BioScience* 51:807–15.

West RC. 1977. Tidal salt-marsh and mangal formations of Middle and South America. In *Ecosystems of the World: Wet Coastal Ecosystems,* Chapman VJ, editor. New York: Elsevier, pp. 193–213.

Whelan KRT, Smith TJ, et al. 2005. Groundwater control of mangrove surface elevation: shrink and swell varies with soil depth. *Estuaries* 28:833–43.

Whelan KRT, Smith TJI, et al. 2009. Hurricane Wilma's impact on overall soil elevation and zones within the soil profile in a mangrove forest. *Wetlands* 29:16–23.

White JR, Reddy KR. 2003. Nitrification and denitrification rates of Everglades wetland soils along a phosphorus-impacted gradient. *J. Env. Qual.* 32:2436–43.

Yáñez-Arancibia A, Lara-Domínguez AL. 1999. *Ecosistemas de manglar en América tropical.* Xalapa, Veracruz: Instituto de Ecología.

CHAPTER 8

Pacific Coast Tidal Wetlands

JOHN C. CALLAWAY, AMY B. BORDE, HEIDA L. DIEFENDERFER,
V. THOMAS PARKER, JOHN M. RYBCZYK, and RONALD M. THOM

Vegetated tidal wetlands on the Pacific coast have many similarities with tidal wetland systems in other regions, including the importance of hydrology for driving their development and function. However, Pacific coast wetlands have been poorly studied in comparison with tidal wetlands from the Gulf and Atlantic coasts, and there are notable differences from these systems. Physically, Pacific coast tidal wetlands are smaller and more isolated, with a strong tidal influence and a wide range in freshwater effects, from the enormous flows of the Columbia River to intermittent annual flows in some Southern California systems. Freshwater inflows vary strongly from south to north along the coast, as do other important factors.

The similarity to tidal systems of other coasts extends to general ecological processes, with tidal wetlands providing linkages between marine and terrestrial ecosystems, as well as habitat and food-web support for a wide range of resident wetland species. At the same time, climatic differences between Pacific coast tidal systems and those of the Gulf and Atlantic coasts affect the relative importance of physical processes and their influence on wetland dynamics. Significant biological differences also exist. For example, *Spartina alterniflora* and *S. patens,* the dominant species of other North American temperate coasts, are not native to Pacific coast tidal salt marshes. In addition, marsh plains of the Pacific coast are more diverse and are dominated in more arid parts of the coast by salt-tolerant succulent species, including *Sarcocornia pacifica* (formerly *Salicornia virginica*).

Conservation and management priorities for Pacific coast tidal wetlands are relatively consistent along the coast. Similar to other regions, the restoration of tidal wetlands is a high priority for the Pacific coast, although among locales the particular focus varies. The emphasis in the Pacific Northwest (hereafter PNW; it includes Northern California, Oregon, and Washington) is on salmon habitat restoration, but emphasis shifts to other threatened and endangered species in California. High rates of wetland loss and public interest have motivated restoration in the region. Invasive species have also received significant attention, with introduced *Spartina* species a focus in multiple estuaries in all three states; other plants and invasive animals, including the green crab (*Carcinus mae-*

nas; Yamada, Dumbauld, et al. 2005), have also been the target of management efforts. More recently, climate change effects have received substantial consideration, in particular sea-level rise.

We review a range of issues, from physical factors to biological communities, ecological controls, and management dilemmas across Pacific coast wetlands, including salt marshes, brackish marshes, and tidal freshwater wetlands. This review focuses on tidal wetlands of California, Oregon, and Washington, excluding for the most part the important systems of Baja California, British Columbia, and Alaska because of limited space.

Geology, Hydrology, and Biogeochemistry

Geology

Tidal wetlands on the Pacific coast are influenced by a diverse topography, geology, and climate (Emmett, Llanso, et al. 2000). Mountains parallel the Pacific coastline of North America and constrain the size of estuaries, from the Olympic and Cascade mountains in Washington to the Oregon Coast Range to the Siskiyou Mountains, Klamath Range, and Coastal Range in California. The outer coast is generally characterized by rocky headlands composed primarily of erosion-resistant Miocene basalts (Franklin and Dyrness 1988) with pocket beaches. Coastal mountain ranges restrict not only the size of the actual estuaries, but also the surrounding watersheds. With the exception of three estuaries with relatively extensive watersheds (the San Francisco Bay–Delta, Columbia River, and Puget Sound), watersheds are relatively small and steep, resulting in many small coastal rivers and streams. The transboundary Puget Sound–Georgia Basin estuarine ecosystem, approximately 18,000 km^2 in size and including portions of the Strait of Juan de Fuca, has recently been recognized by governments in the United States and Canada under a new name, the Salish Sea. To the north, the coastline is also steep, which restricts marsh development to relatively small areas; extensive tidal marshes are found on large river deltas such as the Fraser River in lower British Columbia and the Copper River in Alaska.

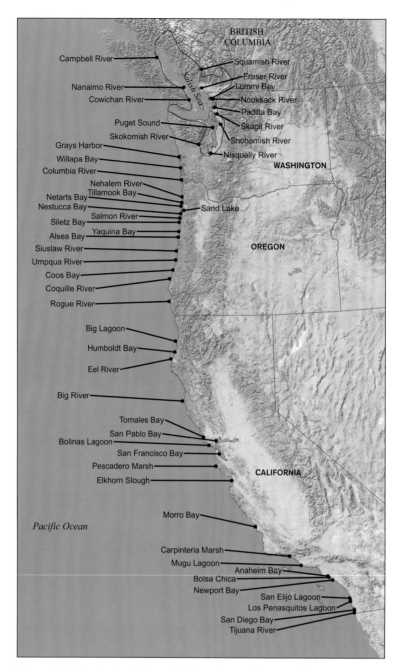

FIG. 8.1. Pacific Coast estuaries from the Tijuana Estuary, just across the Mexican border in the south, to the Salish Sea, which crosses the Canadian border in the north. Estuaries identified in the figure support coastal wetlands of least 100 ha or contain smaller but significant wetlands that are important regionally. Artist: Amy B. Borde.

In addition to the very narrow coastal plain available for the development of flat tidal wetlands, the continental shelf off the Pacific coast is relatively narrow, with deep oceanic waters extremely close to shore relative to the Gulf and Atlantic coasts of North America.

These conditions create small, isolated estuaries (Fig. 8.1); of the 24 estuaries in Washington and Oregon identified by Proctor, Garcia, et al. (1980), 8 are smaller than 2 km² and numerous unidentified estuarine areas, associated with small streams, are present. Thirteen others range in size between 2 and 50 km² (Proctor, Garcia, et al. 1980). Similar isolated conditions are also found on the California coast, with the San

Francisco Bay estuary orders of magnitude larger than other estuarine systems (Grewell, Callaway, et al. 2007); approximately half of the tidal wetland area in Washington, Oregon, and California occurs in San Francisco Bay (NOAA 1990).

The rugged, steep coastline that restricts development of the large estuarine systems typically seen on coastlines with broad coastal plains is primarily the result of the tectonically active faults found on the leading edge of the continent, such as the San Andreas fault, paralleling most of the California coast (Josselyn, Zedler, et al. 1990). Along this zone, the sea floor has folded over the margin of the North American Plate, resulting in the formation of the Coast and Transverse ranges, which are composed primarily of crushed and folded sea-floor sediments. Farther north, the Cascadia subduction zone, marking the subduction of the Juan de Fuca Plate beneath North America along the coast between Northern California and British Columbia, has influenced the formation of the coastal zone through ongoing tectonic activity and subsidence (Nelson, Kelsey, et al. 2006). Evidence for these subsidence events has been built using the examination of tidal wetlands buried by tsunamis; peat and mud couplets; tree rings from buried or flooded *Picea sitchensis* and *Thuja plicata;* and fossilized *Deschampsia cespitosa* (Atwater and Yamaguchi 1991). Most *P. sitchensis* in tidal wetlands of Washington postdate the earthquake of 1700, and following the 1964 Alaska earthquake, subsided tidal flats quickly aggraded sediment and recovered vegetation; they supported meadows and thickets within nine years, and *P. sitchensis* seedlings had established by 1980 (Benson, Atwater, et al. 2001).

While this geology forms the coastal structure, considerable climatic variation interacts with this morphological context to influence present-day tidal wetlands. The steep topography of the coast creates a wide range of microclimates within even a very small area. In addition, long-term climate change has had substantial influence on the development of coastal wetlands. Most notable is sea level, which has risen considerably since the end of the last ice age, drowning river and canyon mouths and coastal valleys. This rise in sea level has formed and affected current estuaries, fostering the development of wetland areas that are thousands of years in age at the oldest sites, with recent sediments following upward and landward movements of tidal wetlands. A rise in sea level also resulted in a landward migration of sand dunes, contributing to the formation of many of the smaller estuaries, seasonally blocking off rivers, canyons, or lagoons and producing variation in salinity and inundation among the small wetlands that form.

Slightly different approaches have been used to classify estuarine types on the Pacific coast (e.g., Emmett, Llanso, et al. 2000; Grewell, Callaway, et al. 2007). There are seven types of estuaries on the Pacific coast: *fjords* (created by glaciation and occurring only along the northern part of the coast); *drowned river valleys* (the majority of Pacific coast estuaries, formed after the last glacial period, when sea level rose and flooded river valleys); *bar-built estuaries* (dominated by long-shore sand movement and sandbar formation); *lagoons* (formed when river flows are low and systems are closed to tidal action for extended periods); *structural basins* (formed in synclines and fault valleys); *bays* (systems with extensive deepwater habitat); and *deltas* (depositional areas where high-energy rivers deposit sediments into shallow, low-energy coastal systems).

Hydrology

As with any tidal wetland system, the relative balance of freshwater inflow and tidal flows is critical in determining hydrologic processes on the Pacific coast. The entire region has a Mediterranean-type climate, with little to no rainfall in summer months and marked seasonal patterns of river inflow to estuaries that affect tidal wetland soil salinity. While differences exist in conditions on the microclimate scale, there is a predominant south-to-north gradient in terms of the importance of precipitation versus evapotranspiration. In the arid climate of Southern California, precipitation inputs are

extremely low and strongly seasonal, with virtually no rainfall from May to October. This can produce hypersaline soils in high marsh areas, while winter rains dilute soil salinities, leading to very large annual variation. Going north, precipitation becomes much more significant and summer temperatures are moderated, with average rainfall varying from approximately 50 cm/yr south of San Francisco to 100 to 200 cm/yr in most areas north of San Francisco. Southern Oregon experiences similar rates of precipitation, with > 127 cm/yr in most of this region, and > 254 cm/yr in much of northern Oregon and Washington. However, as noted, there is substantial variation in local climates, with much of the eastern Puget Sound receiving only 76 to 127 cm/yr average annual rainfall because of the rain shadow of the Olympic Mountains, which also greatly reduces rainfall in the San Juan Islands and on the northeastern Olympic Peninsula (Franklin and Dyrness 1988).

Climatic variations and watershed size directly control freshwater inputs to coastal watersheds. On the border between Washington and Oregon, the Columbia River has the largest annual discharge of any river on the Pacific coast of North America, with flows prior to regulation estimated to have reached maximums of 28,317 $m^3 s^{-1}$ (Sherwood, Jay, et al. 1990). As an extension of the estuary, the Columbia River plume is a dominant factor affecting the hydrography of PNW coastal waters (Hickey and Banas 2003). San Francisco Bay receives freshwater from the second-largest watershed in the region, the Sacramento–San Joaquin River Basin, and the Puget Sound Basin is the third largest in area (Emmett, Llanso, et al. 2000). The smallest systems of the Pacific coast are intermittent, with watersheds of only a few square kilometers. Dams and water diversions have significantly affected coastal wetlands, with decreased flows and sediment inputs in many major estuaries and increased flows in some smaller systems in Southern California because of the reliance on imported water for residential and agricultural uses (Callaway and Zedler 2009).

Together with this large-scale climatic gradient, individual small estuaries are likely to be more temporally variable than larger, buffered systems. In particular, some bar-built or drowned river valley estuaries and lagoons may close occasionally because of excessive sediment accumulation at the tidal inlet. The closure of tidal inlets leads to highly variable conditions, with extremely high salinities if closures occur in summer months in Southern California and low salinities if closures occur under periods of significant precipitation and runoff (Callaway and Zedler 2009). Winter closures are likely to be shorter-lived because of accumulated hydrologic pressure from watershed runoff.

On the ocean side, Pacific coast wetlands are affected by mixed, semidiurnal tides. Tidal ranges tend to increase from south to north, with a relatively strong tidal signal across the entire coast. Tidal ranges in much of California are typically just less than 2 m (e.g., 1.75 m in San Diego Bay, 1.62 m in Morro Bay, and 1.78 m in San Francisco Bay), although within any particular system there can be both attenuation and magnification of the tidal range depending on the local geography (especially true in larger systems such as San Francisco Bay). North of San Francisco Bay, the range is 2.06 in Humboldt Bay, 2.32 m in Coos Bay, and 2.62 m at the mouth of the Columbia River. Within Washington, the range is 2.72 m in Willapa Bay, 3.08 m in Grays Harbor, and 3.46 m at Seattle in Puget Sound. Estuaries with constricted inlets that close seasonally have reduced tidal ranges, as in many small estuaries in Southern California and elsewhere.

Tidal channels are a critical part of tidal wetland hydrology, as they deliver water from the estuary into the vegetated wetland. Channels tend to have relatively gradual slopes at lower intertidal elevations, but in the marsh plain they are often deeply incised and can be well over 2 m deep. To the north, in areas such as Katchemak Bay and Cook Inlet, Alaska salt marshes are characterized by deep (~3 m) channels caused by macrotidal amplitudes in excess of 18 m. The morphology of tidal channels in *P. sitchensis* swamps in the PNW is consistent with the forced step-pool type seen in mountain streams, with large woody debris, including log jams and beaver dams, controlling pool development (Diefenderfer and Montgomery 2009).

Biogeochemistry

Very little research has been completed on the biogeochemistry of Pacific coast tidal wetlands. A search of the Web of Science for articles on the biogeochemistry of tidal, estuarine, or brackish wetlands identified a total of 245 articles from 1984 through early 2010. Only eight of these studies were conducted in Pacific coast wetlands, all within California or Baja California in Mexico, and a number of these eight focused on subtidal habitats rather than intertidal vegetated wetlands. Given the paucity of research on Pacific coast wetland biogeochemistry, it is difficult to identify any significant trends or critical differences between Pacific coast wetlands and other, better-studied wetland ecosystems. This area presents a fundamental gap in the understanding of Pacific coast wetlands and an opportunity for future research. As indicated above, the Mediterranean climate of the Pacific coast affects wetland soil salinity, with effects of salinity on soil biogeochemistry including nutrient uptake and decomposition rates.

Plant Communities

As with other tidal wetlands, salinity influences the horizontal distribution of vegetation on the broadest scale, with a gradient of salt, brackish, and freshwater tidal wetlands as one moves upstream in the estuarine system. This gradient may be very steep in smaller systems that are intermittently or frequently closed. On the Pacific coast, tidal wetlands are predominantly composed of herbaceous or emergent vegetation, although shrub-dominated and forested tidal wetlands are found at the upstream extent and along lateral fringes of PNW estuaries. Within a particular wetland type, relatively predictable shifts in tidal wetland species and plant communities occur across elevation or inundation gradients, from submerged aquatic vegetation at the low end to wetland-upland transitional communities at the high end (Ewing 1986). MacDonald (1977) and Emmett, Llanso, et al. (2000) have described plant assemblages, diversity, and distribution of tidal wetlands along the Pacific coast, including those farther north of the region covered here. Josselyn (1983), Onuf (1987), Zedler, Nordby, et al. (1992), and Grewell, Callaway, et al. (2007) provided similar information for California and Seliskar and Gallagher (1983) for the PNW. Ibarra-Obando and Poumian-Tapia (1991) and Zedler, Callaway, et al. (1999) provided information on salt marshes in Baja California. Below, we review vegetation separately within California and the PNW along gradients of salinity (large-scale) and inundation (within wetlands); dominant species from both areas are provided in Table 8.1.

California Floristic Province

From northern Baja California to just across the Oregon border lies a distinct floristic province, the California Floristic Province (Raven and Axelrod 1978), a biodiversity hot spot. The tidal plant communities found within this floristic province are reflective of the Mediterranean climate, but they have many species in common with tidal wetlands in other regions (e.g., *S. pacifica, Distichlis spicata, Schoenoplectus americanus, Bolboschoenus maritimus, Jaumea carnosa, Triglochin maritima,* and others). What distinguishes these plant communities from other tidal wetlands is the increased dominance of species tolerant of higher levels of salinity during the growing season (Josselyn 1983; Zedler, Nordby, et al. 1992).

The principal species in subtidal and intertidal submerged aquatic plant communities is *Zostera marina* (eelgrass), found in estuaries with regular tidal action and light levels suitable to support subtidal growth. The largest populations of *Z. marina* in California are found in San Diego Bay, Morro Bay, San Francisco Bay, and Humboldt Bay. In particular, Morro Bay retains large expanses of *Z. marina* and supports significant migrating populations of black brant.

Several species characterize the lowest elevations of tidal wetlands in California. *Spartina foliosa* is often found in monocultures in saltier systems, present as a dominant up to mean high water. *Spartina foliosa* is common in the larger Southern California tidal wetlands that retain regular tidal flushing, such as Tijuana Estuary, Newport Bay, and Mugu Lagoon. It is absent from estuaries and lagoons where tidal flushing may become restricted from inlet closure (Zedler 2001), including smaller estuaries as well as larger systems, such as Morro Bay and Elkhorn Slough. Why *S. foliosa* is not found in Morro Bay and Elkhorn Slough is unclear, although this may be an indication of past seasonal closures of these systems, given the sensitivity of *S. foliosa* to seasonal disruptions of tidal flow. *Spartina foliosa* is the dominant low-marsh species in San Francisco Bay and occurs north to Bodega Bay, with no native *Spartina* species found north of Bodega Bay. In less saline areas of estuaries, *Schoenoplectus acutus* can be found in the same zone as *S. foliosa,* and *S. acutus* becomes dominant under brackish conditions (Fig. 8.2). *Bolboschoenus maritimus* and *Schoenoplectus californicus* may coexist with *S. acutus,* depending on salinity and site history, and these areas are commonly referred to as tule marshes. Other species, such as *Typha* spp., *Phragmites australis,* and *Persicaria maculata,* can also be found in this zone if the salinity is sufficiently low. In addition to freshwater emergent vegetation, some tidal freshwater wetlands in California include shrubs and trees, primarily *Salix* spp., *Cornus sericea* ssp. *occidentalis,* and *Cephalanthus occidentalis* var. *californicus.* In general, lower-elevation areas of the marsh typically have lower plant species diversity than the marsh plain, especially in salt and brackish marshes.

The large plains of salt marshes in California are dominated by *Sarcocornia pacifica,* the most common plant in California tidal wetlands (Fig. 8.3) (Zedler, Callaway, et al. 1999). Salt marsh dodder, *Cuscuta salina,* is also found throughout the marsh plain on *S. pacifica,* as well as many other species. Most of the plant diversity in the marsh plain is found along the tidal channels (Zedler, Callaway, et al. 1999; Sanderson, Ustin, et al. 2000), including *D. spicata, J. carnosa, Frankenia salina,* and *Limonium californicum;* additionally, *Grindelia stricta* var. *angustifolia* is present near channels in San Francisco Bay. In areas of tidal wetlands with slightly lower salinities, *B. maritimus* is common in Central and Northern California estuar-

TABLE 8.1

Common coastal wetland plants in California and the Pacific Northwest

Most plants are herbaceous.

Saline	Brackish	Freshwater
California		
Atriplex triangularis	*Bolboschoenus maritimus*	*Calystegia sepium*
Batis maritima	*Euthamia occidentalis*	*Carex* spp.
Cuscuta salina	*Juncus balticus*	*Cephalanthus occidentalis*[a]
Distichlis spicata	*Lepidium latifolium*[b]	*Cornus sericea*[a]
Frankenia salina	*Potentilla anserina*	*Eleocharis* spp.
Grindelia stricta	*Schoenoplectus acutus*	*Lycopus americanus*
Jaumea carnosa	*Schoenoplectus americanus*	*Persicaria maculata*
Limonium californicum	*Schoenoplectus californicus*	*Phragmites australis*
Sarcocornia pacifica	*Triglochin maritima*	*Rubus armeniacus*[b]
Spartina alterniflora and hybrids	*Typha domingensis*	*Salix lasiolepis*[a]
Spartina foliosa		*Stachys albens*
		Typha latifolia
Pacific Northwest		
Atriplex patula	*Agrostis stolonifera*	*Alnus rubra*[a]
Cakile edentula	*Bolboschoenus maritimus*	*Carex obnupta*
Cotula coronopifolia[b]	*Carex lyngbyei*	*Cornus sericea*[a]
Distichlis spicata	*Deschampsia cespitosa*	*Fraxinus latifolia*[a]
Glaux maritima	*Eleocharis* spp.	*Juncus effusus*
Grindelia integrifolia	*Juncus balticus*	*Lonicera involucrata*[a]
Jaumea carnosa	*Juncus gerardii*	*Lysichiton americanus*
Sarcocornia pacifica	*Malus fusca*[a]	*Phalaris arundinacea*[b]
Spergulatia canadensis	*Myrica californica*[a]	*Picea sitchensis*[a]
Zostera japonica[b]	*Myrica gale*[a]	*Populus balsamifera*[a]
Zostera marina	*Phragmites australis*[b]	*Prunus emarginata*[a]
	Potentilla anserina	*Rubus spectabilis*[a]
	Ruppia maritima	*Rubus ursinus*[b]
	Schoenoplectus americanus	*Sagittaria latifolia*
	Schoenoplectus tabernaemontani	*Salix* spp.[a]
	Symphotrichum subspicatum	*Spiraea douglasii*[a]
	Triglochim maritima	*Thuja plicata*[a]
	Typha angustifolia[b]	*Typha latifolia*

[a] Woody species (shrubs and trees).

[b] Nonnative species.

NOTE: Plant species are listed according to the most saline conditions that they can tolerate; many are also found in less saline conditions. Salinity categories are > 25 pp (Saline), 0.5–25 ppt (Brackish), and < 0.5 ppt (Freshwater), although some tidal wetlands may have wider seasonal variations in soil salinities. Authorities for plant species names are Hitchcock and Cronquist (1973) or Hickman (1993) except for new treatments in Flora of North America (http://fna.huh.harvard.edu/.)

ies, with *Bolboschoenus robustus* more common in these areas in the southern portion of the state. At even lower salinity, in brackish marshes in San Francisco Bay, *S. americanus* is very abundant on the marsh plain. Diversity increases in these tidal wetlands wherever estuarine freshwater can prevent hypersaline conditions in the rainless summers. Additional species found in the marsh plains in less saline conditions include *Cordylanthus maritimus, C. mollis, T. maritima, T. concinnum, Juncus lesueurii, J. balticus, Atriplex triangularis,* and *Potentilla anserina* var. *pacifica.*

The transition to upland/nonwetland conditions represents a reduction in flooding and anaerobic conditions as well as a shift in soil salinity, accompanied by an increase in plant diversity. A common species within the transitional zone in Southern California is *Arthrocnemum subterminale,* along with many of the common species found on high ground adjacent to tidal channels, such as *F. salina, L. californicum, D. spicata,* and *A. triangularis.* In Northern California, *G. stricta* var. *angustifolia* is abundant in transitional areas, along with *Juncus lesueurii, Spergularia macrotheca,* and *Polypogon monspeliensis* (nonnative). Under low salinity conditions, as in Suisun Bay, *Baccharis pilularis* can establish and become a prominent member of the higher portions of the tidal wetland.

Pacific Northwest

Dynamic conditions in PNW marshes produce species assemblages containing 15 or more species in salt marshes (Thom, Zeigler, et al. 2002) and up to 40 species in Columbia River tidal freshwater marshes (Borde pers. observation). *Zostera marina* occupies the low intertidal and shallow subtidal zone

FIG. 8.2. Tidal freshwater marsh community from Sand Mound Slough in the Sacramento–San Joaquin Delta. The dense vegetation is *Schoenoplectus acutus* (tule), with various species of *Juncus, Carex, Eleocharis,* and *Persicaria* in the understory. Photographer: V. Thomas Parker

FIG. 8.3. Salt marsh community from China Camp State Park in San Francisco Bay. Plant species include *Spartina foliosa* in the tidal channel, *Grindelia stricta* var. *angustifolia,* in flower adjacent to the channel, and *Sarcocornia pacifica* across the marsh plain. Other dominants include *Distichlis spicata, Jaumea carnosa,* and *Limonium californicum.* Photographer: V. Thomas Parker

in estuarine areas where salinities remain above about 5 ppt (Thom, Borde, et al. 2003; Rumrill and Sowers 2008). *Ruppia maritima* is common in brackish areas along much of the coastline. The nonnative *Zostera japonica* is present in the higher intertidal zones of many estuaries; however, *Z. marina* is the predominant seagrass species throughout the PNW.

Seliskar and Gallagher (1983) described seven marsh types in Oregon, which also generally apply in Washington. The marsh types (with characteristic marsh taxa in parentheses), ordered from the lowest elevation to highest elevation, are low sandy *(S. pacifica, T. maritima, J. carnosa),* low silty *(T. maritima, Eleocharis* spp.), sedge *(C. lyngbyei),* immature high *(Deschampsia cespitosa, D. spicata),* mature high *(D. cespitosa, J. balticus, A. stolonifera),* bulrush and sedge *(Schoenoplectus tabernaemontani, C. lyngbyei),* and intertidal gravel *(Eleocharis* spp.). In the extensive tidal freshwater zone of the Columbia River estuary, 25 native marsh community types (Kunze 1994; Christy and Brophy 2007) occur in a narrow elevation band of approximately 3 m (Borde pers. observation). The communities vary widely, from monocultures of *Sagittaria latifolia* to a diverse assemblage of species occurring in a variety of habitats including backwater sloughs and riverine islands. Nonnative communities (e.g., *Phalaris arundinacea*) also compose large portions of tidal wetlands in this system.

Hutchinson (1988) identified 8 plant communities associated with brackish and saline conditions in an analysis of the 17 deltas in Puget Sound; in order of frequency of occurrence, they are (1) *C. lyngbyei–T. maritima,* (2) *S. pacifica–D. spicata,* (3) *S. americanus–B. maritimus,* (4) *Juncus balticus–Potentilla anserina,* (5) *T. maritima–Glaux maritima,* (6) *B. maritimus–Spergularia canadensis,* (7) *T. maritima–S. americanus,* and (8) *D. spicata–Juncus* spp. The *S. pacifica–D. spicata* and *D. spicata–Juncus* spp. communities were associated with more saline conditions induced by variable freshwater inputs, high rates of evapotranspiration, and greater tidal range and prism.

Seliskar and Gallagher (1983) described typical lateral zonation patterns (from mudflat to upland boundary) for saline (above 25 ppt) and brackish marshes in the PNW. In the saline marshes, the lowest elevations are inhabited by the eelgrass *Z. marina,* followed by *T. maritima, J. carnosa, S. pacifica, D. spicata, Deschampsia cespitosa,* with *P. anserina* at the upland boundary (Fig. 8.4). In brackish marshes, the lowest elevations

are occupied by *C. lyngbyei,* followed by *J. balticus,* with *D. cespitosa* and *Agrostis stolonifera* at the upland boundary. Vince and Snow (1984) describe eight marsh vegetation zones between the shoreline and the upland shrub zone in Cook Inlet, Alaska. Peak aboveground standing crop ranged from 50 to 466 g dry wt m^{-2}. *Triglochin maritima* and *Potentilla egedii* occurred over the entire elevation range of the marsh that they studied.

The dominant trees of tidal forested wetlands in the PNW are *Picea sitchensis* and *Thuja plicata* on the coast and *Populus balsamifera* ssp. *trichocarpa* inland on tidal rivers. Historically, *P. sitchensis* was commonly named tideland spruce, and, like *T. plicata,* it expresses morphological adaptations to wet soils as well as tolerance of salt spray. *P. sitchensis* swamps occur on freshwater and brackish tidal waterways in the PNW, where beaver are active, and the largest occurrences remaining on the Pacific coast are on the Columbia River estuary. However, today only 6% of the historical extent of this ecosystem is in existence on the Washington shore, and 23% on the Oregon shore of the Columbia River estuary (Christy and Putera 1993). The *P. sitchensis* plant association has been variously described for areas within the PNW: (1) *P. sitchensis–Alnus rubra/Rubus spectabilis/Carex obnupta* for Puget Sound, rivers on the outer coast of Washington, and the lower Columbia River estuary (Kunze 1994); (2) *P. sitchensis/Lonicera involucrata–Malus fusca* for estuarine intertidal areas of Oregon; and (3) *P. sitchensis/Cornus sericea/Lysichiton americanus* for palustrine (tidal or nontidal freshwater) areas of Oregon (Christy and Brophy 2007).

Few tidal swamps remain in Puget Sound, though Boule (1981) reported dominance by *P. balsamifera* ssp. *trichocarpa* in association with *A. rubra, Salix* spp., and *T. plicata. Populus balsamifera* forested associations also exist in tidal freshwater areas of the Columbia River estuary and Oregon coastal rivers (Kunze 1994; Christy and Brophy 2007). The association of *A. rubra/R. spectabilis/C. obnupta–L. americanus* has been identified throughout Washington, and three *Fraxinus latifolia* associations have been identified in areas of the Columbia with relatively less tidal influence (Kunze 1994).

Salix species occur in the understory of *P. sitchensis* and *P. balsamifera* ssp. *trichocarpa* swamps and are the dominant species in six other tidal freshwater plant associations; brackish associations have also been documented on the outer coast (Kunze 1994; Christy and Brophy 2007). Prominent species

FIG. 8.4. Salt marsh community from Washington Harbor on the Strait of Juan de Fuca. Turning red in the fall is *Sarcocornia pacifica* mixed with *Distichlis spicata,* and along the upper fringing marsh is *Deschampsia cespitosa.* Photo: Ronald M. Thom.

are *Salix hookeriana, S. lucida, S. lasiandra, S. sitchensis, S. fluviatilis,* and *S. piperi.* Other shrub species can be present or codominant in these associations, and other estuarine shrub-dominated associations are also in existence.

Animal Communities

Pacific coast tidal wetlands provide habitat for a wide range of animals. For example, a review of wildlife including mammals, birds, amphibians, and reptiles by Johnson and O'Neil (2001) documented 175 species in Oregon and Washington bays and estuaries, 66 of which were closely associated with wetlands. Similar diversity can be seen in fishes and invertebrates.

Invertebrates

Invertebrate fauna are abundant in Pacific coast wetlands, although the majority of research has focused on communities in adjacent intertidal, unvegetated mudflats and subtidal areas. Oligochaetes, amphipods, and some insect larvae can reach densities in marsh soil on the order of 12,000 individuals m^{-2} (reviewed in Seliskar and Gallagher 1983). The dense roots and rhizomes in vegetated marshes restrict organisms, and abundances of invertebrates can be much higher in adjacent mudflats, where larger organisms are also found. Within marshes, some common infaunal invertebrates include oligochaetes and polychaetes. Larger epifauna within marshes include gastropods, bivalves (mussels), amphipods, isopods, and crabs (Zedler, Callaway, et al. 2001). While much of the focus of invertebrate monitoring and research has been on benthic organisms, terrestrial insects also may play an important role, especially in upper reaches of the marsh that are only intermittently flooded.

Salinity, sediment texture, and organic matter content are important factors affecting overall invertebrate community composition and abundances. Recent research that evaluated the development of invertebrate communities within restored marshes has reiterated the importance of sediment texture and organic content for invertebrate communities and high-

lighted differences between natural and restored marshes (Talley and Levin 1999). In addition, Whitcraft and Levin (2007) have shown that aboveground vegetation affects marsh invertebrate communities by ameliorating stressful environmental conditions through shading.

Invertebrates play an important role in larger food webs, with potential links to fish, mammals, and birds. Creekbanks within the marsh can have very high abundances of both epifauna and infauna, and are especially important feeding areas for fish and birds. Although much more interest and research have been focused on the importance of planktonic food webs within San Francisco Bay and some other estuaries, Howe and Simenstad (2007) used a translocation experiment in San Francisco Bay to identify the importance of marsh plant productivity moving through mussels and into the broader food web. Nonnative invertebrates, from green crabs to burrowing isopods, have had significant impacts on wetland ecosystems, affecting food webs and wetland stability (Talley, Crooks, et al. 2001; Yamada, Dumbauld, et al. 2005), with even larger numbers of nonnative invertebrates in adjacent mudflats and shallow subtidal areas (Ruiz, Carlton, et al. 1997).

Fish

Most research has investigated fish use of deepwater estuarine habitats, and the majority of research in tidal wetland ecosystems has concerned salt marshes rather than brackish and freshwater types. Nevertheless, it is known that some fish species move up into the vegetated marsh on high tides and even more use channels within tidal wetlands.

Many of the fish that use tidal wetland habitats are juveniles, seeking foraging areas or refuge from predators that live in deepwater habitats and cannot move into small channels within the marsh (Simenstad, Hood, et al. 2000). Williams and Zedler (1999) identified the importance of channel size and morphology for fish composition and numbers in Southern California. Similarly, Hood (2002) correlated channel perimeter with the abundance of salmonid fish prey in the PNW, and it is assumed that similar relationships are found in other estuaries. Tidal channels are critical for fish because they are the conduit for movement of both organisms and macro-organic matter between the marsh and deeper habitats. In this sense, channels provide both a physical link and a food-web link between marshes and adjacent ecosystems. Kwak and Zedler (1997) showed that productivity from *S. foliosa* and algae contributed to estuarine fish food webs in Tijuana Estuary, while *S. pacifica* made little contribution. Bioenergetic modeling and ecophysiological studies indicate that marsh access provides increased growth for both halibut and killifish (Madon, Williams, et al. 2001; Madon 2002). Small-scale habitat heterogeneity and pannes in upper marsh areas also affect fish distributions and abundances across the marsh (Larkin, Madon, et al. 2008).

In the San Francisco Bay region, substantial research has been carried out on Suisun Bay brackish marshes by Moyle and colleagues (e.g., Matern, Moyle, et al. 2002), where some common estuarine residents that use the marsh surface include California killifish *(Fundulus parvipinnis),* longjaw mudsuckers *(Gillichthys mirabilis),* Pacific staghorn sculpin *(Leptocottus armatus),* arrow goby *(Clevelandia ios),* bay goby *(Lepidogobius lepidus),* yellowfin goby, a nonnative *(Acanthogobius flavimanus),* and threespine stickleback *(Gasterosteus aculeatus).* These species also may use channels and adjacent subtidal habitats, as do many other estuarine and marine species, including top-smelt *(Atherinops affinis),* Pacific herring *(Clupea harengus pallasi),* northern anchovy *(Engraulis mordax),* starry flounder *(Platichthys stellatus),* and California halibut *(Paralichthys californicus;* Matern, Moyle, et al. 2002). Delta smelt *(Hypomesus transpacificus)* is a threatened species within San Francisco Bay found in both brackish and freshwater tidal wetlands, and it has received considerable attention while its population numbers have declined substantially over the last few decades (Moyle, Herbold, et al. 1992; Sommer, Armor, et al. 2007). Tidewater goby *(Eucyclogobius newberryi)* is another listed species in California, found from San Diego to Humboldt County in estuaries and lagoons that seasonally close to tidal flow (Swift, Haglund, et al. 1993).

In the PNW, much of the motivation for tidal wetland management and restoration has come from the endangered status of anadromous salmonids (see Emmett, Llanso, et al. 2000 and www.salmonrecovery.gov for listed salmon species and runs). As with other fish species, juvenile salmon use tidal wetlands primarily for foraging and refuge; they may spend anywhere from a few days to a few months in tidal marshes (Simenstad, Hood, et al. 2000; Miller and Sadro 2003). Pacific coast salmon species include pink *(Oncorhynchus gorbuscha),* chum *(O. keta),* coho *(O. kisutch),* sockeye *(O. nerka),* and Chinook *(O. tshawytscha),* as well as steelhead *(O. mykiss).* Maier and Simenstad (2009) evaluated food-web connections for chinook salmon in the Columbia River estuary and found that large-scale loss of tidal wetlands in the estuary may have reduced food availability for subyearlings.

Birds

Pacific coast wetlands lie along the Pacific Flyway and provide habitat for the shorebirds, waterfowl, waders, and other birds that rely on eelgrass beds, intertidal mudflats, and salt, brackish, and freshwater marshes during migration and overwintering. Shorebird and waterfowl abundance and diversity are low during the summer breeding season in Pacific coast wetlands, in contrast to high numbers during spring and fall migrations. Some important sites along the flyway include Morro Bay (stopover for black brant), San Francisco Bay (more than a million shorebirds during migration), Coos Bay (over 90 avian species), and Padilla Bay (over 50,000 ducks representing 26 species in winter).

Although the importance of small tidal wetlands cannot be ignored, San Francisco Bay had the largest number of shorebirds across all years and seasons in a multiyear survey of shorebirds in Pacific coast wetlands; other important migrating and overwintering habitats included Humboldt Bay, Elkhorn Slough, San Diego Bay, Mugu Lagoon, Willapa Bay, Morro Bay, Point Reyes, and Mission Bay (Page, Stenzel, et al. 1999). Western sandpipers are the most abundant shorebird on the Pacific coast flyway, followed by dunlin and dowitchers (Page, Stenzel, et al. 1999). In an exhaustive study of waterbird use in the Skagit River Delta wetlands, Slater (2004) found that shorebird abundance and diversity were highest during the lengthy fall migration, in contrast to the shorter spring migration. In the winter, shorebird density was high, but diversity was low. While specifics on exact sampling locations are not provided in many studies, shorebird use appears to be highest in adjacent mudflats rather than in vegetated wetlands. However, many shorebirds roost in vegetated marshes during higher tides when mudflats are underwater.

Waterfowl are also more abundant in adjacent deepwater habitats, although they do use channels through wetlands and some species may roost in the wetland itself or use shallow ponds for feeding or resting. Waterfowl (e.g., ducks, swans, geese) abundance and diversity were highest in the late fall and winter. Common Pacific coast species included American widgeons, northern shovelers, mallards, gadwall, and northern pintails. Black brant are closely associated with eelgrass and other submerged aquatic vegetation, and notably large numbers are found at Padilla Bay and Morro Bay. The deltas and marshes of British Columbia and Alaska harbor massive populations of shorebirds and waterfowl during migration. Lesser snow geese and Canada geese can be so abundant that their grazing significantly alters plant community structure and biomass (Zacheis, Hupp, et al. 2001).

In addition to shorebirds and waterfowl, a number of heron, egret, and rail species actively feed and nest in Pacific coast tidal wetlands. Great and snowy egrets and great blue herons commonly are seen capturing fish congregated in marsh channels. Night herons may roost in marshes, and nesting areas for herons and egrets are found in larger marshes. Two endangered subspecies of clapper rail are found in California salt marshes, the light-footed clapper rail in Southern California and the California clapper rail in San Francisco Bay. Both are marsh residents, nesting primarily in *S. foliosa* and feeding in adjacent channels (Zedler 1993). Black rails are not as well studied as clapper rail but are found in both salt and brackish marshes within San Francisco Bay, preferring dense pickleweed habitat in salt marshes (Conway and Sulzman 2007; Tsao, Takekawa, et al. 2009). Passerine species, including song sparrows, common yellowthroat, marsh wrens, and red-winged blackbirds (Stralberg, Herzog, et al. 2010), use the vegetated portion of the marsh. A large number of raptors also feed in tidal wetlands; 13 species of raptors are found in the estuaries of the PNW, the most common of which is the northern harrier. Osprey, bald eagle, and peregrine falcon are also prominent in PNW estuaries.

Mammals

Mammals within Pacific coast tidal wetlands range in size from elk to small rodents. Both the largest and smallest subspecies of North American elk use Pacific coast tidal wetlands. Roosevelt elk *(Cervus elaphus rooseveltii)* use tidal wetland habitat from Northern California to Olympic National Park in Washington and were found historically in San Francisco Bay. The tule elk *(C. e. nannodes)* is native to California and has been reestablished at reserves such as Point Reyes National Seashore and Grizzly Island Wildlife Area in Suisun Bay. The Columbian white-tailed deer *(Odocoileus virginianus leucurus),* an endangered species that has been extirpated from most of its range, has recovered in Douglas County, Oregon, but the population on the floodplain of the lower Columbia River and estuary remains listed.

The beaver *(Castor canadensis)* is abundant in freshwater tidal marshes throughout the coast and is unique in its effect on coastal landscape structure, hydrology, and habitat function through the creation of pools and modification of riparian vegetation. Beaver ponds are used for refuge and rearing by juvenile salmon, particularly coho. Its numbers were reduced substantially by hunting, but populations have recovered more recently. The California golden beaver *(C. c. subauratus)* was found throughout the lower San Joaquin and Sacramento

River systems and was once exceedingly plentiful; however, it experienced an even greater population decline, and its population status today remains uncertain.

The river otter *(Lutra canadensis)* and the much larger sea otter *(Enhydra lutris)* also use tidal wetland habitats (Mason and Macdonald 1986). The California ("southern") sea otter *(E. l. nereis)* is listed as threatened, and the Alaskan ("northern") sea otter *(E. l. kenyoni)* was successfully transplanted from Alaska to Washington State, where it previously had been extirpated. Efforts to restore Oregon populations are ongoing. Harbor seals *(Phoca vitulina)* haul out in tidal wetlands along the Pacific coast, sometimes in large numbers, and muskrats *(Ondatra zibethicus)* are found in the waterways of brackish marshes.

Robust communities of small mammals, including mice, shrews, and rabbits, occur in salt marshes, as well as larger predators including the long-tailed weasel *(Mustela frenata),* raccoon *(Procyon lotor),* striped skunk *(Mephitis mephitis),* gray fox *(Urocyon cinereoargenteus),* bobcat *(Lynx rufus),* and coyote *(Canis latrans;* MacDonald 1977). The endangered salt marsh harvest mouse *(Reithrodontomys raviventris),* endemic to the San Francisco Bay area, has received substantial attention for recovery since it was listed in 1970; a recent federal review confirmed its endangered status (USFWS 2010). Other common small mammals in Pacific coast marshes include the house mouse *(Mus musculus),* California vole *(Microtus californicus),* wandering shrew *(Sorex vagrans),* and deer mouse *(Peromyscus maniculatus).*

Key Ecological Controls

Historically, understanding of plant dynamics in Pacific coast wetlands has focused on physical processes. Within San Francisco Bay, Mahall and Park (1976a,b) identified the importance of both salinity and inundation regimes in affecting the distribution of *S. foliosa* and *S. pacifica.* In the PNW, plant productivity and community composition have been correlated with salinity, flood frequency, soil texture, and redox potential (Ewing 1983). Hutchinson (1988) found salinity to be the best predictor of plant community type in the 17 deltas of the Puget Sound. More recent work has also shown the influence of these factors on germination and establishment (Noe 2002).

Based on studies in 18 estuaries from British Columbia through Oregon, primary production in tidal wetlands ranges from 17 to 1,501 g C m^{-2} yr^{-1} (summarized in Emmett, Llanso, et al. 2000). Productivity of macroalgae and diatoms associated with the marshes and adjacent flats can range from 3 to over 1,200 g C m^{-2} yr^{-1}. Eelgrass productivity values of 84 to 1,355 g C m^{-2} yr^{-1} have been reported (summarized in Emmett, Llanso, et al. 2000). Within San Francisco Bay, Mahall and Park (1976a) measured annual productivity of 270–690 g m^{-2} yr^{-1} for *S. foliosa* and 550–960 g m^{-2} yr^{-1} for *S. pacifica,* while Atwater (Atwater, Conard 1979) measured peak annual biomass of 300–1,700 g m^{-2} for *S. foliosa* and 500–1,200 g m^{-2} for *S. pacifica.* Peak biomass for *S. californicus* in fresh and brackish marshes was approximately 2,500 g m^{-2} (Atwater, Conard, et al. 1979). Parker and Callaway (unpublished data) have found a similar trend of reduced biomass with increasing salinity; end-of-year biomass was 300–600 g m^{-2} in salt marshes and 800–2,400 g m^{-2} in brackish and freshwater marshes.

Additional research has evaluated the importance of nutrients, primarily nitrogen, in limiting productivity in Pacific coast tidal wetlands, both natural and restored. Most of the nutrient-related work has focused on salt marshes, with little related research in brackish and freshwater wetlands. Within salt marshes, nitrogen has been shown to be limiting based on a number of fertilization studies on the Pacific coast and elsewhere; Covin and Zedler (1988) found that *S. pacifica* outcompeted *S. foliosa* for nitrogen in experimental mixed plots in Tijuana Estuary. Recently, Moseman (2007) demonstrated the importance of nitrogen fixation for supplying nitrogen to salt marshes and found indications that *S. foliosa* may be more dependent on nitrogen fixation than *S. pacifica.* Substantial effort has also focused on understanding nitrogen dynamics within restored wetlands because many restored wetlands have low soil nitrogen content, particularly those that are created with dredged materials or other coarse substrates (Langis, Zalejko, et al. 1991). Boyer and Zedler (1998) tried using soil amendments and fertilization to improve soil nitrogen status and increase growth of *S. foliosa;* they found significant short-term increases in growth but little long-term effect.

Seed banks are often a critical biological dimension of tidal wetland dynamics (Parker and Leek 1985), yet systems such as Pacific coast wetlands that are dominated by perennials generally show lower reliance on seed banks (Hopkins and Parker 1984). However, the dependence of restoration actions on seed rain suggests that seed banks may have indirect ecological influences in these systems. Seed rain has been documented in some San Francisco Bay wetlands; Diggory and Parker (2011) found substantial seed rain into newly restored sites (some in excess of 150,000 m^{-2}), although tidal deposition, resuspension, and scour reduced the density of seeds in the seed bank (varying from 4,600–83,000 m^{-2}). These inputs from seed rain are similar to or greater than those found in other tidal wetlands. Rare species are usually missing from the seed rain, and seed rain and seed bank dynamics reflect species with high frequency and large reproductive output.

While earlier research focused on the importance of physical gradients of salinity, inundation, and nitrogen to sort the pool of potential species, more recent efforts have evaluated community interactions, including competition, facilitation, and the effects of parasitic plants on the broader plant community. Other studies have treated both environmental and biological factors, e.g., showing that effects of interspecific competition between *S. pacifica* and *Arthrocnemum subterminalis* in Carpenteria Marsh in Southern California are greatest in the more benign middle portion of the marsh, with greater salt stress at higher elevations and greater inundation stress at lower elevations (Pennings and Callaway 1992). In the same marsh, a mix of competitive and facilitative effects promoted increased diversity in high marsh communities, with *Monanthecloe littoralis* a competitive dominant and *A. subterminalis* facilitating annuals (Callaway and Pennings 2000). In the Skagit River delta, the presence of large woody debris facilitated the presence of the dominant estuarine shrub, *Myrica gale* (a nitrogen fixer), by providing an elevated platform from which saplings could escape flooding stress (Hood 2007). Additional research on *Cuscuta salina* and *Cordylanthus* spp. has highlighted the importance of parasitic plants for salt-marsh plant communities (Pennings and Callaway 1996; Grewell 2008).

Conservation Concerns

Restoration

Given the history of impacts to tidal wetlands along the Pacific coast, restoration has been a major focus of management activity and scientific research. Within California, approximately 90% of historical coastal wetland area has been lost (NOAA 1990), and rates are similar within San Francisco Bay, where large areas of freshwater tidal wetlands within the Sacramento–San Joaquin Delta have been converted to agriculture. Similarly, Puget Sound has lost 70 to 80% of its deltaic marshes (Collins and Sheikh 2005). Other large estuaries of the PNW coast have widely varying rates of tidal wetland loss, e.g., ~30% loss of the original 476 ha of tidal wetlands in Coos Bay, ~70% loss of the once extensive tidal wetlands in the Columbia River estuary, but only ~3% loss of the 22,555 ha of historical Willapa Bay marshes, perhaps the lowest rate of any PNW estuary (Borde, Thom, et al. 2003). Losses in Grays Harbor are undocumented, but substantial areas are cut off from tidal connection. Eelgrass changes are much more difficult to assess because of the lack of historical data and the subtidal distribution of much of the habitat. Tidal flats and eelgrass apparently have expanded in Grays Harbor but have decreased in Coos Bay and Willapa Bay (Borde, Thom, et al. 2003). In addition, throughout the Pacific coast, land conversion has resulted in substantial subsidence of potential restoration sites behind dikes, and sediment accretion may take decades to build elevations to thresholds necessary for vegetation establishment (Thom, Zeigler, et al. 2002; Diefenderfer, Coleman, et al. 2008; Callaway and Zedler 2009).

Early tidal wetland restoration projects were primarily undertaken as mitigation for permitted wetland impacts and were monitored for regulatory compliance, with significant debate about the relative effectiveness of mitigation projects (Race 1985). Two of the most common restoration strategies have been to breach levees around former tidal wetlands to restore natural tidal hydrology and salinity (e.g., Josselyn and Buchholz 1984; Josselyn, Zedler, et al. 1990; Frenkel and Morlan 1991; Thom, Zeigler, et al. 2002) or to build up low-elevation sites with dredged material (e.g., Sonoma Baylands; Marcus 2000). Tidal wetlands have also been constructed by excavating uplands (e.g., San Dieguito Wetlands, the Tidal Linkage in Tijuana Estuary, Crims Island in the Columbia River, and Gog-Le-Hi-Te in Washington State), although this method has not been as widely used.

Although only a few early sites received detailed evaluations, significant lessons have been gained from them. Zedler and colleagues followed the development of the Connector Marsh, a salt-marsh mitigation project in San Diego Bay. From this project, Langis, Zalejko, et al. (1991) identified the importance of initial soil conditions for marsh development and limitations of organic matter and nitrogen on plant growth, even after 11 years (Zedler and Callaway 1999). Research at this site also identified the challenges of restoring endangered species habitat (Zedler 1993, 1998) and the limitations of fertilization for improvement of soil conditions and plant growth (Boyer and Zedler 1998). In California, the collective evaluation of a number of projects in San Francisco Bay has resulted in changes to marsh restoration designs, with most projects adopting elevations below the target elevation of plant recruitment in order to allow for natural channel development and sediment accumulation in the top 10 cm of the marsh (Williams and Faber 2001; PWA and Faber 2004).

In the PNW, the Salmon River estuary in Oregon was restored over a 20-year time period, which enabled a space-for-time substitution to be used in postrestoration monitoring (Gray, Simenstad, et al. 2002) and improved methods of determining functional indicators of ecosystem development. In Washington, the Gog-Le-Hi-Te wetland adjacent to the Puyal-lup River in the commercial harbor of Tacoma was excavated from upland, with large-scale planting of *C. lyngbyei* (50,000 shoots), although ultimately *Typha* spp. became the dominant plant (Simenstad and Thom 1996). Fish, including target juvenile salmon species, accessed and utilized the system for refuge and feeding and grew faster than those not utilizing the system (Shreffler, Simenstad, et al. 1992). In contrast to Gog-Le-Hi-Te wetland, Elk River wetland restoration in Grays Harbor was a more typical dike breach to restore tidal hydrodynamics and an estuarine salinity regime to a 23-ha former tidal salt marsh that had subsided up to 1 m (Thom, Zeigler, et al. 2002). Vegetation at the restoration site was highly dynamic, but reference site plant composition also varied as much as 30% annually during 11 years of monitoring, confirming the critical importance of monitoring reference ecosystems.

Zedler has strongly promoted the incorporation of experimentation into wetland restoration projects, including experiments focusing on the link between diversity and ecosystem function (Zedler, Callaway, et al. 2001) and the importance of physical heterogeneity and creek formation (Wallace, Callaway, et al. 2005). In South Slough, Oregon, restoration of the Winchester Tidelands marsh was set up using an experimental design to provide information on the best elevations for marsh development (Cornu and Sadro 2002). Only a tiny proportion of restoration efforts on the Pacific coast have been designed to test hypotheses of importance to future project planning, and as a result there is great potential for more experimental projects to identify cause-effect linkages for restoration development and thus move the field forward rapidly. Such experiments should be implemented across the range of ecosystems as well as the range of potential actions (e.g., dike breaching, tide gate installation, culvert installation, excavation, and planting). In addition, most of the research to date on Pacific coast wetland restoration has focused on salt marshes. However, many future restoration opportunities exist in brackish and freshwater wetlands and in tidal floodplains of large rivers, with research particularly needed for these ecosystems.

More recently, interest has grown in larger restoration projects and regional planning. In contrast to earlier project-based mitigation efforts, much of this large-scale restoration planning and implementation has been government funded and focused on publicly owned lands. The Southern California Wetlands Recovery Project has encouraged large-scale regional restoration and emphasizes incorporating scientific knowledge into restoration prioritization, promoting citizen involvement and research. Similarly, the multidecadal restoration that is planned for 15,000 acres of salt ponds through the South San Francisco Bay Salt Pond Project has encouraged regional planning with a strong focus on adaptive management. In the lower Columbia River and estuary, a large multiagency restoration program focused on rearing habitat for juvenile salmonids has protected habitat through acquisition, undertaken complex hydrologic reconnection efforts, and conducted riparian plantings (Diefenderfer, Thom, et al. 2011). In Puget Sound, a similar large-scale program, currently in the feasibility phase, has been implemented to address ecosystem degradation of the nearshore. The plan is to implement projects that support or restore natural ecosystem processes, which in turn generate or maintain desirable nearshore ecosystem structure and function and enable the ecosystem to be naturally productive and resilient (Simenstad, Logsdon, et al. 2006). These large-scale restoration programs have necessitated the development of appropriately scaled assessment methods, such as the levels-of-evidence approach to evaluate multiproject cumulative effects that is proposed for the Columbia River estuary (Diefenderfer, Thom, et al. 2011).

In addition to the major focus on marsh restoration, eelgrass restoration has been attempted at numerous locations throughout the PNW, as well as in San Francisco and San Diego Bays, largely through transplanting former eelgrass areas. However, the success of restoration efforts has been moderate (Thom 1990). Newer projects are having more success primarily because more is known about the growth requirements of the plant, and more careful studies are being done to evaluate restoration sites (Thom, Williams, et al. 2005). State and local regulations have been developed to minimize and avoid the loss of eelgrass that occurs because of public and private development projects.

Invasive Species

Spartina species are the most common invasive plants across the Pacific coast. *Spartina foliosa* is native to California and Baja California, occurring as far north as Bodega Bay. A number of nonnative *Spartina* species have been introduced along the Pacific coast, both intentionally and accidentally. San Francisco Bay has four species of introduced *Spartina (S. alterniflora, S. densiflora, S. anglica,* and *S. patens),* as well as a very prolific hybrid between *S. alterniflora* and *S. foliosa.* Within the Bay, *S. alterniflora* and the hybrid have the largest distribution, and a substantial control effort has reduced their populations over the last five years.

Within Humboldt Bay, *S. densiflora* became established by seed and/or propagules from lumber trade with South America in the early 1900s. It was thought to be a local ecotype of *S. foliosa* for many years; however, it lacks rhizomes and grows at higher elevations than the native species (Spicher and Josselyn 1985). Given the earlier misidentification, it spread widely within Humboldt Bay and was intentionally planted in a San Francisco Bay restoration project. Control efforts have been limited given its widespread distribution and co-occurrence with pickleweed throughout Humboldt Bay, although recently interest in control has intensified.

In Oregon and Washington, there is no native congener of *Spartina. Spartina alterniflora* was introduced into Willapa Bay in 1894 as packing material for commercially grown eastern oysters (*Crassostera virginica;* Simenstad and Thom 1995); the species has spread to most estuaries in Oregon and Washington except the Columbia River estuary, where low salinity may limit establishment. *Spartina anglica* is present in northern Puget Sound, and *S. patens* is also found in parts of the PNW. The most northerly population of *S. alterniflora* is in Padilla Bay, Washington, where its net aboveground primary production (NAPP) in salt marshes has been measured at 1,520 g m^{-2}yr^{-1} (Riggs and Bulthuis 1994). While most *Spartina* spp. in the PNW do not compete with other marsh plants, they do invade mudflats that are important for invertebrates, including commercially grown oysters, and contribute to the loss of important shorebird feeding areas. For example, Patten and O'Casey (2007) found that *Spartina* meadows in Willapa Bay were rarely used by shorebirds or waterfowl, supporting only 7 small sandpipers and < 1 waterfowl per ha, whereas adjacent intertidal mudflats supported 450 small sandpipers and 11 waterfowl per ha. These impacts have prompted intensive control efforts in Washington, including herbicides, mowing, manual removal, rototilling, crushing/disking, and biological control (Hedge, Kriwoken, et al. 2003).

The combined stress of inundation and salinity in tidal wetlands probably limits the ability of other nonnative plant species to establish in tidal wetlands. Within California, other nonnative plants of concern include *Lepidium latifolium* (perennial peppergrass) and a number of salt-tolerant species that occur along the wetland-upland transition (e.g., *Polypogon monspeliensis, Parapholis incurva, Mesembryanthemum* spp., *Carpobrotus edulis,* and *Tamarix* spp.). Most of these species appear to be more abundant with reduced salinity (i.e., in brackish marshes or along local freshwater inputs to salt marshes). These species have become well established in many Southern California estuaries where increased freshwater inputs from anthropogenic sources are commonplace. In other Pacific coast estuaries with tidal freshwater zones (e.g., Columbia River estuary), numerous nonnative species of concern occur including *Lythrum salicaria, Iris pseudacorus,* and *Phalaris arundinacea,* the latter being extremely invasive and forming extensive monocultures (Sytsma, Cordell, et al. 2004).

In additional to invasive plants, invasive invertebrates are of concern in tidal wetlands, especially due to impacts on food webs and marsh stability (Ruiz, Carlton, et al. 1997; Talley, Crooks, et al. 2001; Yamada, Dumbauld, et al. 2005). Also, a number of problematic invasive fish species are found in coastal wetlands, including yellowfin gobies and sailfin mollies, as well as many other species (Williams, Desmond, et al. 1998; Matern, Moyle, et al. 2002).

Climate Change

Increases in global sea level associated with climate change will have substantial effects on the relative elevation and sustainability of Pacific coast tidal wetlands. Within estuaries where long-term accretion rates have been measured using sediment cores and isotopic data—e.g., Tijuana Estuary (Weis, Callaway, et al. 2001), San Francisco Bay (Callaway pers. observation), and the PNW (Thom 1992)—tidal wetlands are able to keep pace with current rates of sea-level rise, with accretion rates typically varying from 2 to 8 mm yr^{-1}. Other factors will also affect the relative elevation of coastal wetlands, including subsidence. Areas with high rates of ongoing subsidence are unusual on the Pacific coast, although some locations, particularly the southern extreme of San Francisco Bay, historically experienced high rates because of previous groundwater pumping. Many diked former wetlands have subsided significantly, and this creates challenges for their future restoration (Callaway and Zedler 2009). Tectonic activity on the Pacific coast is likely to cause major shifts in coastal elevations; however, these shifts are unpredictable and could result in uplift or subsidence (Nelson, Kelsey, et al. 2006).

While rates of accretion are greater than current rates of sea-level rise, they are less than predicted rates of future sea-level rise under medium to worst-case scenarios (e.g., sea-level rise of 80 to 140 cm by 2100). Current rates of accretion are not absolute predictors of the ability of wetlands to withstand future increases in sea level because accretion rates are affected by sea-level rise; however, these rates, along with predicted shifts in suspended sediment loads, provide some insight into longer-term sustainability of tidal wetlands. While suspended sediment loads to some estuaries may be decreasing as more sediment is held back in upstream dams, it is difficult to make general predictions for trends across the region. Many tidal wetlands in San Francisco Bay have expanded with inputs of upstream sediments associated with hydraulic mining over the past century; however, this expansion is likely to be unsustainable with decreased sediment inputs into San Francisco Bay. Given these shifts and current rates of sedimentation, tidal wetlands may not be sustainable if future rates of sea-level rise are greater than 10 mm/yr, as is predicted in 50–100 years under worst-case scenarios.

Changes in precipitation also will affect tidal wetlands through shifts in estuarine salinity patterns (Callaway, Parker, et al. 2007). Regional predictions of climate change–related precipitation patterns are somewhat uncertain and likely to vary with microclimates; however, there is agreement that seasonal shifts in watershed runoff are likely, as warmer temperatures lead to less snow and earlier snowmelt. Within Mediterranean regions such as the Pacific coast, this may exacerbate seasonal shifts in water and soil salinities in tidal wetlands, potentially leading to greater salinity stress during summer periods and the upstream shift of salt-tolerant species. Such salinity shifts may also lead to losses in plant species diversity and primary productivity within San Francisco Bay (Callaway, Parker, et al. 2007). Increases in anthropogenic water withdrawals associated with population growth may also affect estuarine salinities and biotic assemblages. Beyond shifts in inundation and salinity regimes, climate change will also affect CO_2 concentrations and air and water temperatures, with potential effects on species composition, productivity, growth rates, and other processes; however, most research to date on Pacific coast tidal wetlands has focused on inundation and salinity regimes, and no direct experiments have evaluated effects of CO_2 or temperature shifts on Pacific coast wetlands.

In addition to tidal wetlands, climate change will affect adjacent seagrass ecosystems. Variations in monthly mean sea level associated with major El Niño events affect interannual differences in eelgrass cover and density (Thom, Borde, et al. 2003). Although mechanisms are still under study, reduced desiccation and heat stress associated with higher sea levels during strong El Niño periods apparently result in faster growth rates and higher densities of eelgrass in the lower intertidal zone. We would expect eelgrass distribution to shift upward in elevation (where possible) under a scenario of sea-level rise because of reduced light at the lower edge of the meadow (Thom, Southard, et al. 2008). Seagrasses are often carbon limited (Mommer and Visser 2005), and eelgrass likely will respond positively to increased concentrations of CO_2.

Conclusions

California, Oregon, and Washington are characterized by diverse tidal wetlands that occur across broad salinity regimes. These wetlands share many similarities with other tidal wetlands in North America but also have unique characteristics. The Mediterranean climate and mixed, semidiurnal tides, in combination with the narrow confines of the coastal mountain ranges, shape tidal wetlands of the Pacific coast. As with physical processes, many species and genera are common to tidal wetlands in other parts of the world; however, Pacific coast salt marshes are not dominated by *Spartina* species and are more diverse than Gulf and Atlantic coast salt marshes. Losses of tidal wetlands to land conversion have been significant on the Pacific coast, and impacts from invasive species are also significant. Of particular concern is *S. alterniflora*, which has invaded mudflats in the PNW and hybridized with the native *S. foliosa* in California; introduced invertebrates have also affected wetland ecosystem functions. Interest in restoration of tidal wetlands has increased in recent years, whether for mitigation,

threatened and endangered species recovery, or other publicly funded projects. Over time, wetland restoration and planning efforts at multiple scales across the Pacific coast could impact regional estuarine ecosystem functions. Finally, climate change is expected to pose a significant concurrent challenge for tidal wetlands along the Pacific coast, particularly because shifts in both salinity and inundation regimes could have major impacts on tidal wetland distribution and sustainability.

References

Atwater BF, Conard SG, et al. 1979. History, landforms, and vegetation of the estuary's tidal marshes. In *San Francisco Bay: the urbanized estuary*, TJ Conomos, editor. San Francisco: Pacific Division, American Association for the Advancement of Science, pp. 347–85.

Atwater BF, Yamaguchi DK. 1991. Sudden, probably coseismic submergence of Holocene trees and grass in coastal Washington State. *Geology* 19:706–09.

Benson BE, Atwater BF, et al. 2001. Renewal of tidal forests in Washington State after a subduction earthquake in AD 1700. *Quat. Res.* 56:139–47.

Borde AB, Thom RM, et al. 2003. Geospatial habitat change analysis in Pacific Northwest coastal estuaries. *Estuaries* 26:1104–16.

Boule ME. 1981. Tidal wetlands of the Puget Sound region, Washington. *Wetlands* 1:47–60.

Boyer KE, Zedler JB. 1998. Effects of nitrogen additions on the vertical structure of a constructed cordgrass marsh. *Ecol. Appl.* 8:692–705.

Callaway JC, Parker VT, et al. 2007. Emerging issues for the restoration of tidal marsh ecosystems in the context of predicted climate change. *Madroño* 54:234–48.

Callaway JC, Zedler JB. 2009. Conserving the diverse marshes of the Pacific coast. In *Human impacts on salt marshes: a global perspective*, Silliman BR, Grosholz ED, Bertness MD, editors. Berkeley: Univ. Calif. Press, pp. 285–306.

Callaway RM, Pennings SC. 2000. Facilitation may buffer competitive effects: indirect and diffuse interactions among salt marsh plants. *Am. Nat.* 156:416–24.

Christy JA, Brophy LS. 2007. *Estuarine and freshwater tidal plant associations in Oregon*. Corvallis: Oregon Natural Heritage Information Center, Oregon State Univ.

Christy JA, Putera JA. 1993. *Lower Columbia River natural area inventory*. Seattle: Nature Conservancy, Washington Field Office.

Collins BD, Sheikh AJ. 2005. *Historical reconstruction, classification, and change analysis of Puget Sound tidal marshes*. Seattle: Univ. Washington, Puget Sound River History Project, Dept. Earth and Space Sciences.

Conway CJ, Sulzman C. 2007. Status and habitat use of the California black rail in the southwestern USA. *Wetlands* 27:987–98.

Cornu CE, Sadro S. 2002. Physical and functional responses to experimental marsh surface elevation manipulation in Coos Bay's South Slough. *Restor. Ecol.* 10:474–86.

Covin JD, Zedler JB. 1988. Nitrogen effects on *Spartina foliosa* and *Salicornia virginica* in the salt marsh at Tijuana estuary, California. *Wetlands* 8:51–65.

Diefenderfer HL, Coleman AM, et al. 2008. Hydraulic geometry and microtopography of tidal freshwater forested wetlands and implications for restoration, Columbia River, U.S.A. *Ecohydrol. Hydrobiol.* 8:339–61.

Diefenderfer HL, Montgomery DR. 2009. Pool spacing, channel morphology, and the restoration of tidal forested wetlands of the Columbia River, USA. *Restor. Ecol.* 17:158–68.

Diefenderfer HL, Thom RM, et al. 2011. A levels-of-evidence approach for assessing cumulative ecosystem response to estuary and river restoration programs. *Ecol. Restor.* 29:111–32.

Diggory ZE, Parker VT. In press. Seed supply and revegetation dynamics at restored tidal marshes, Napa River CA. *Restor. Ecol.* 19(101):121–30.

Emmett R, Llanso R, et al. 2000. Geographic signatures of North American West Coast estuaries. *Estuaries* 23:765–92.

Ewing K. 1983. Environmental controls in Pacific Northwest intertidal marsh plant communities. *Can. J. Bot.* 61:1105–1116.

Ewing K. 1986. Plant growth and productivity along complex gradients in a Pacific Northwest brackish intertidal marsh. *Estuaries* 9:49–62.

Franklin J, Dyrness CT. 1988. *Natural vegetation of Oregon and Washington.* Corvallis: Oregon State Univ. Press.

Frenkel RE, Morlan JC. 1991. Can we restore our salt marshes? Lessons from the Salmon River, Oregon. *Northw. Env. J.* 7:119–35.

Gray A, Simenstad CA, et al. 2002. Contrasting functional performance of juvenile salmon habitat in recovering wetlands of the Salmon River estuary, Oregon, USA. *Restor. Ecol.* 10:514–26.

Grewell BJ. 2008. Hemiparasites generate environmental heterogeneity and enhance species coexistence in salt marshes. *Ecol. Appl.* 18:1297–1306.

Grewell BJ, Callaway JC, et al. 2007. Estuarine wetlands. In *Terrestrial vegetation of California,* Barbour MG, Keeler-Wolf T, Schoenherr AA, editors. Berkeley: Univ. Calif. Press, pp. 124–54.

Hedge P, Kriwoken LK, et al. 2003. A review of *Spartina* management in Washington State, US. *J. Aquat. Plant Manag.* 41:82–90.

Hickey BM, Banas NS. 2003. Oceanography of the U.S. Pacific Northwest coastal ocean and estuaries with application to coastal ecology. *Estuaries* 26:1010–1031.

Hickman JC, editor. 1993. *The Jepson manual: higher plants of California.* Berkeley: University of California Press.

Hitchcock CL and Cronquist A. 1973. *Flora of the Pacific Northwest.* Seattle: University of Washington Press.

Hood WG. 2002. Application of landscape allometry to restoration of tidal channels. *Restor. Ecol.* 10:213–22.

Hood WG. 2007. Large woody debris influences vegetation zonation in an oligohaline tidal marsh. *Estuar. Coast.* 30:441–50.

Hopkins DR, Parker VT. 1984. A study of the seed bank of a salt marsh in northern San Francisco Bay. *Am. J. Bot.* 71:348–55.

Howe ER, Simenstad CA. 2007. Restoration trajectories and food web linkages in San Francisco Bay's estuarine marshes: a manipulative translocation experiment. *Mar. Ecol. Prog. Ser.* 351:65–76.

Hutchinson I. 1988. The biogeography of the coastal wetlands of the Puget Trough: deltaic form, environment, and marsh community structure. *J. Biogeogr.* 15:729–45.

Ibarra-Obando SE, Poumian-Tapia M. 1991. The effect of tidal exclusion on salt marsh vegetation in Baja California, México. *Wetl. Ecol. Manag.* 1:131–48.

Johnson DH, O'Neil, TA. 2001. *Wildlife-habitat relationships in Oregon and Washington.* Corvallis: Oregon State Univ. Press.

Josselyn M. 1983. *The ecology of San Francisco Bay tidal marshes: a community profile.* Washington, DC: USFWS Div. Biol. Serv.

Josselyn MN, Buchholz JW. 1984. *Marsh restoration in San Francisco Bay: a guide to design and planning.* Tiburon, CA: Paul F. Romberg Tiburon Center for Environmental Studies.

Josselyn M, Zedler J, et al. 1990. Wetland mitigation along the Pacific coast of the United States. In *Wetland creation and restoration: the status of the science,* Kusler J, Kentula M, editors. Washington, DC: Island Press, pp. 3–36.

Kunze LM. 1994. *Preliminary classification of native, low elevation, freshwater wetland vegetation in western Washington.* Olympia: Washington State DNR.

Kwak TJ, Zedler JB. 1997. Food web analysis of Southern California coastal wetlands using multiple stable isotopes. *Oecologia* 110:262–77.

Langis R, Zalejko M, et al. 1991. Nitrogen assessment in a constructed and a natural salt marsh of San Diego Bay. *Ecol. Appl.* 1:40–51.

Larkin DJ, Madon SP, et al. 2008. Topographic heterogeneity influences fish use of an experimentally restored tidal marsh. *Ecol. Appl.* 18:483–96.

MacDonald KB. 1977. Plant and animal communities of Pacific North American salt marshes. In *Wet coastal ecosystems,* Chapman VJ, editor. New York: Elsevier, pp. 167–91.

Madon SP. 2002. Ecophysiology of juvenile California halibut *Paralichthys californicus* in relation to body size, water temperature and salinity. *Mar. Ecol. Prog. Ser.* 243:235–49.

Madon SP, Williams GD, et al. 2001. The importance of marsh access to growth of the California killifish, *Fundulus parvipinnis,* evaluated through bioenergetics modeling. *Ecol. Model.* 136:149–65.

Mahall BE, Park RB. 1976a. The ecotone between *Spartina foliosa* Trin. and *Salicornia virginica* L. in salt marshes of northern San Francisco Bay: II. Soil water and salinity. *J. Ecol.* 64:793–809.

Mahall BE, Park RB. 1976b. The ecotone between *Spartina foliosa* Trin. and *Salicornia virginica* L. in salt marshes of northern San Francisco Bay: III. Soil aeration and tidal immersion. *J. Ecol.* 64:811–19.

Maier GO, Simenstad CA. 2009. The role of marsh-derived macrodetritus to the food webs of juvenile chinook salmon in a large altered estuary. *Estuar. Coast.* 32:984–98.

Marcus L. 2000. Restoring tidal wetlands at Sonoma Baylands, San Francisco Bay, California. *Ecol. Eng.* 15:373–83.

Mason CF, Macdonald SM. 1986. *Otters: ecology and conservation.* London: Cambridge Univ. Press.

Matern SA, Moyle PB, et al. 2002. Native and alien fishes in a California estuarine marsh: twenty-one years of changing assemblages. *Trans. Am. Fish. Soc.* 131:797–816.

Miller BA, Sadro S. 2003. Residence time and seasonal movements of juvenile coho salmon in the ecotone and lower estuary of Winchester Creek, South Slough, Oregon. *Trans. Am. Fish. Soc.* 132:546–59.

Mommer L, Visser EJW. 2005. Underwater photosynthesis in flooded terrestrial plants: a matter of leaf plasticity. *Ann. Bot.* 96:581–89.

Moseman SM. 2007. Opposite diel patterns of nitrogen fixation associated with salt marsh plant species *(Spartina foliosa* and *Salicornia virginica)* in Southern California. *Mar. Ecol.* 28:276–87.

Moyle PB, Herbold B, et al. 1992. Life history and status of Delta smelt in the Sacramento–San Joaquin Estuary, California. *Trans. Am. Fish. Soc.* 121:67–77.

Nelson AR, Kelsey HM, et al. 2006. Great earthquakes of variable magnitude at the Cascadia subduction zone. *Quat. Res.* 65:354–65.

NOAA. 1990. *Estuaries of the United States: vital statistics of a national resource base.* Rockville, MD: NOAA Nat. Ocean Serv.

Noe GB. 2002. Temporal variability matters: effects of constant vs. varying moisture and salinity on germination. *Ecol. Monogr.* 72:427–43.

Onuf CP. 1987. *The ecology of Mugu Lagoon, California: an estuarine profile.* Washington, DC: USFWS.

Page GW, Stenzel LE, et al. 1999. Overview of shorebird abundance and distribution in wetlands of the Pacific coast of the contiguous United States. *Condor* 101:461–71.

Parker VT, Leck MA. 1985. Relationships of seed banks to plant-distribution patterns in a fresh-water tidal wetland. *Am. J. Bot.* 72:161–74.

Patten K, O'Casey C. 2007. Use of Willapa Bay, Washington, by shorebirds and waterfowl after *Spartina* control efforts. *J. Field Ornithol.* 78:395–400.

Pennings SC, Callaway RM. 1992. Salt marsh plant zonation: the relative importance of competition and physical factors. *Ecology* 73:681–90.

Pennings SC, Callaway RM. 1996. Impact of a parasitic plant on the structure and dynamics of salt marsh vegetation. *Ecology* 77:1410–19.

PWA (Philip Williams and Associates Ltd.), Faber PM. 2004. *Design guidelines for tidal wetland restoration in San Francisco Bay.* Oakland: Bay Inst. and Calif. State Coastal Conserv. www.wrmp.org/design/.

Proctor CM, Garcia JC, et al. 1980. *An ecological characterization of the Pacific Northwest coastal region.* 5 vols. Washington, DC: USFWS Biol. Serv. Prog.

Race MS. 1985. Critique of present wetlands mitigation policies in the United States based on an analysis of past restoration projects in San Francisco Bay. *Env. Manag.* 9:71–82.

Raven PH, Axelrod DI. 1978. Origin and relationships of the California flora. *Univ. Calif. Publ. Bot.* 72:1–134.

Riggs SR, Bulthuis DA. 1994. Estimated net aerial primary productivity and monitoring of selected characteristics of *Spartina alterniflora* in Padilla Bay, Washington, April 1992–May 1993. Padilla Bay National Estuarine Research Reserve Technical Report no. 11. Mount Vernon: Washington State Department of Ecology (Publication no. 94-176).

Ruiz GM, Carlton JT, et al. 1997. Global invasions of marine and estuarine habitats by non-indigenous species: mechanisms, extent, and consequences. *Am. Zool.* 37:621–32.

Rumrill SS, Sowers DC. 2008. Concurrent assessment of eelgrass beds *(Zostera marina)* and salt marsh communities along the estuarine gradient of the South Slough, Oregon. *J. Coast. Res.* SI55:121–34.

Sanderson EW, Ustin SL, et al. 2000. The influence of tidal channels on the distribution of salt marsh plant species in Petaluma Marsh, CA, USA. *Plant Ecol.* 146:29–41.

Seliskar DM, Gallagher JL. 1983. *The ecology of tidal marshes of the Pacific Northwest coast: a community profile.* FWS/OBS-82/32. Washington, DC: USFWS Div. Biol. Serv.

Sherwood CR, Jay DA, et al. 1990. Historical changes in the Columbia River estuary. *Prog. Oceanogr.* 25:299–352.

Shreffler DK, Simenstad CA, et al. 1992. Foraging by juvenile salmon in a restored estuarine wetland. *Estuaries* 15:204–13.

Simenstad CA, Hood WG, et al. 2000. Landscape structure and scale constraints on restoring estuarine wetlands for Pacific coast juvenile fishes. In *Concepts and controversies in tidal marsh ecology,* Weinstein MP, Kreeger DA, editors. Boston, MA: Kluwer, pp. 597–630.

Simenstad C, Logsdon M, et al. 2006. *Conceptual model for assessing restoration of Puget Sound nearshore ecosystems.* Puget Sound Nearshore Partnership Report no. 2006-03. Seattle: Washington Sea Grant Program, Univ. Washington.

Simenstad CA, Thom RM. 1995. *Spartina alterniflora* (smooth cordgrass) as an invasive halophyte in Pacific Northwest estuaries. *Hortus Northwest* 6:9–12.

Simenstad CA, Thom RM. 1996. Functional equivalency trajectories of the restored Gog-Le-Hi-Te estuarine wetland. *Ecol. Appl.* 6:38–56.

Slater G. 2004. *Waterbird monitoring in estuarine habitat of Port Susan Bay and adjacent agricultural lands during fall migration.* Mount Vernon, WA: Nature Conservancy, Skagit River Office.

Sommer T, Armor C, et al. 2007. The collapse of pelagic fishes in the upper San Francisco estuary. *Fisheries* 32:270–77.

Spicher D, Josselyn M. 1985. *Spartina* (Gramineae) in Northern California: distribution and taxonomic notes. *Madroño* 32:158–67.

Stralberg D, Herzog MP, et al. 2010. Predicting avian abundance within and across tidal marshes using fine-scale vegetation and geomorphic metrics. *Wetlands* 30:475–87.

Swift CC, Haglund TR, et al. 1993. The status and distribution of the freshwater fishes of Southern California. *Bull. South. Calif. Acad. Sci.* 92:101–67.

Sytsma MD, Cordell JR, et al. 2004. *Lower Columbia River aquatic nonindigenous species survey 2001–2004: Final Technical Report.* Prepared for the United States Coast Guard and the USFWS. www.clr.pdx.edu/docs/LCRANSFinalReport.pdf.

Talley TS, Crooks JA, et al. 2001. Habitat utilization and alteration by the invasive burrowing isopod, *Sphaeroma quoyanum,* in California salt marshes. *Mar. Biol.* 138:561–73.

Talley TS, Levin LA. 1999. Macrofaunal succession and community structure in *Salicornia* marshes of Southern California. *Estuar. Coast. Shelf Sci.* 49:713–31.

Thom RM. 1990. A review of eelgrass (*Zostera marina* L.) transplanting projects in the Pacific Northwest. *Northw. Env. J.* 6:121–37.

Thom RM. 1992. Accretion rates of low intertidal salt marshes in the Pacific Northwest. *Wetlands* 12:147–56.

Thom RM, Borde AB, et al. 2003. Factors influencing spatial and annual variability in eelgrass (*Zostera marina* L.) meadows in Willapa Bay, Washington, and Coos Bay, Oregon, estuaries. *Estuaries* 26:1117–29.

Thom RM, Southard SL, et al. 2008. Light requirements for growth and survival of eelgrass (*Zostera marina* L.) in Pacific Northwest (USA) estuaries. *Estuar. Coast.* 31:969–80.

Thom RM, Williams GW, et al. 2005. Balancing the need to develop coastal areas with the desire for an ecologically functioning coastal environment: is net ecosystem improvement possible? *Restor. Ecol.* 13:193–203.

Thom RM, Zeigler R, et al. 2002. Floristic development patterns in a restored Elk River estuarine marsh, Grays Harbor, Washington. *Restor. Ecol.* 10:487–96.

Tsao DC, Takekawa JY, et al. 2009. Home range, habitat selection, and movements of California black rails at tidal marshes at San Francisco Bay, California. *Condor* 111:599–610.

USFWS. 2010. *Salt marsh harvest mouse* (Reithrodontomys raviventris) *5-year review: summary and evaluation.* Sacramento, CA: USFWS.

Vince SW, Snow AA. 1984. Plant zonation in an Alaskan salt-marsh: 1. distribution, abundance and environmental factors. *J. Ecol.* 72:651–67.

Wallace KJ, Callaway JC, et al. 2005. Evolution of tidal creek networks in a high sedimentation environment: a 5-year experiment at Tijuana estuary, California. *Estuaries* 28:795–811.

Weis DA, Callaway JC, et al. 2001. Vertical accretion rates and heavy metal chronologies in wetland sediments of the Tijuana estuary. *Estuaries* 24:840–50.

Whitcraft CR, Levin LA. 2007. Regulation of benthic algal and animal communities by salt marsh plants: impact of shading. *Ecology* 88:904–17.

Williams GD, Desmond JS, et al. 1998. Extension of 2 nonindigenous fishes, *Acanthogobius flavimanus* and *Poecilia latipinna,* into San Diego Bay marsh habitats. *Calif. Fish Game* 84:1–17.

Williams GD, Zedler JB. 1999. Fish assemblage composition in constructed and natural tidal marshes of San Diego Bay: relative influence of channel morphology and restoration history. *Estuaries* 22:702–16.

Williams PB, Faber PM. 2001. Salt marsh restoration experience in the San Francisco Bay estuary. *J. Coast. Res.* SI27:203–11.

Yamada SB, Dumbauld BR, et al. 2005. Growth and persistence of a recent invader *Carcinus maenas* in estuaries of the northeastern Pacific. *Biol. Invasions* 7:309–21.

Zacheis A, Hupp JW, et al. 2001. Effects of migratory geese on plant communities of an Alaskan salt marsh. *J. Ecol.* 89:57–71.

Zedler JB. 1993. Canopy architecture of natural and planted cordgrass marshes: selecting habitat evaluation criteria. *Ecol. Appl.* 3:123–38.

Zedler JB. 1998. Replacing endangered species habitat: the acid test of wetland ecology. In *Conservation biology for the coming age,* Fiedler PL, Kareiva PM, editors. New York: Chapman and Hall, pp. 364–79.

Zedler, JB, editor. 2001. *Handbook for restoring tidal wetlands.* Boca Raton, FL: CRC Press.

Zedler JB, Callaway JC. 1999. Tracking wetland restoration: do mitigation sites follow desired trajectories? *Restor. Ecol.* 7:69–73.

Zedler JB, Callaway JC, et al. 1999. Californian salt marsh vegetation: an improved model of spatial pattern. *Ecosystems* 2:19–35.

Zedler JB, Callaway JC, et al. 2001. Declining biodiversity: why species matter and how their functions might be restored in Californian tidal marshes. *Bioscience* 51:1005–17.

Zedler JB, Nordby CS, et al. 1992. *The ecology of Tijuana estuary, California: a National Estuarine Research Reserve.* Washington, DC: NOAA Office of Coastal Resource Management, Sanctuaries and Reserves Division.

PART II

INLAND WETLANDS

CHAPTER 9

Northern Peatlands

LINE ROCHEFORT, MARIA STRACK, MONIQUE POULIN,
JONATHAN S. PRICE, MARTHA GRAF,
ANDRÉ DESROCHERS, and CLAUDE LAVOIE

Peatlands are best defined by their capacity to accumulate organic matter, thus forming an organic soil named peat. This means that over time, the productivity of the system is greater than its rate of decomposition. Development of peatlands in the landscape is favored in cool, moist climates and in landscapes with poor drainage. Despite their peculiarities, the delineation of peatlands from other wetlands is not always straightforward. For global understanding, we are adopting the following definitions: *peat:* a sedentarily (in situ) accumulated material composed of > 30% (dry mass) of dead and partly decomposed organic matter; and *peatland:* an area with or without vegetation, with a naturally accumulated peat layer of ≥ 30 cm at the surface. Peat accumulation can reach considerable depths, up to 11–15 m, but usually will range between 2–6 m in boreal regions. The minimum depth of 30 cm is often chosen as a somewhat arbitrary threshold for peat formation, but it is useful for classification purposes, such as gathering statistics among different countries or modeling global carbon cycles (IMCG Website, RAMSAR, Wetlands International).

Two main types of northern peatlands are commonly recognized: bogs and fens. Fens are peatland systems influenced by flowthrough drainage, where enriched water coming from the surrounding watershed provides an array of mineral elements for a diverse plant community. This flowing water brings a certain degree of oxygenation to the organic substrate, which accelerates peat decomposition. Hence, fen peat deposits are usually not as thick as bog peat formed in rain-fed-only systems. The different types of vegetation in fens coincide relatively well with the degree of minerotrophy. Fen vegetation is often dominated by sedges (*Carex* and other Cyperaceae) and brown mosses (Amblystegiaceae bryophytes), some shrubs (willows, alders, or dwarf birches), and trees (larches); *Sphagnum* mosses are rare or absent when the pH is high (Amon, Thompson, et al. 2002; Bedford and Godwin 2003).

Bogs are mostly rain-fed systems, and thus poor in mineral nutrients, except when under oceanic influence. They rarely develop directly on mineral substrate (Sundberg, Hansson, et al. 2006), and most often bogs succeed in chronosequence from fen habitats (Kuhry and Turunen 2006). Indeed the accumulation of fen peat with time slowly diminishes plant access to the mineral pool of nutrients. At one point in their devel-opment, plant roots can no longer reach the mineral nutrient pool supplied by groundwater, and vegetation better adapted to poor nutrient conditions succeeds. *Sphagnum* mosses are by far the most common and abundant plant component in bogs. Cotton grass *(Eriophorum vaginatum),* ericaceous shrubs, and coniferous trees grow in association with the *Sphagnum* carpet. In North American peatlands, ericaceous shrubs in bogs are composed of a mix of *Kalmia, Ledum, Chamaedaphne, Vaccinium,* and *Gaylussacia* species. Black spruce *(Picea mariana)* is ubiquitous, but tamarack *(Larix laricina)* is also regularly found on wetter, more minerotrophic sites (Montague and Givnish 1996). Simply put, northern peatlands are mossy, spongy habitats. One walks on a soft carpet of vegetation, although it can be through dense black spruce thickets. In a nonpeatland wetland, a person will most likely get muddy feet.

Hydrology

The form and function of fens and bogs are strongly related to hydrological processes, which control the availability of water, dissolved minerals and nutrients, and ultimately the nature of the biotic environment. Fens generally occupy a relatively low position in the landscape, where they receive surface or groundwater from the surrounding mineral sediments. Where suitable climate and landscape exist, peat continues to accumulate, the water table rises, and hydraulic gradients between the fen and the upland decrease and may eventually reverse. The result is a peatland that is entirely ombrogenous (fed only by precipitation, P), and is defined as "bog" (Fig. 9.1).

The regional distribution of bogs and fens is related to landscape factors, but also to latitudinal and zonal gradients. Latitudinal effects control peat accumulation through (1) moisture availability (precipitable moisture), which is a function of atmospheric temperature; (2) the effect of temperature on productivity and decomposition rates; and (3) energy available for evapotranspiration (ET). Zonal (east/west) effects are related to the degree of continentality, i.e., moisture restrictions. Damman (1979) noted that in eastern North America there are northern and southern limits to bog occurrence, since they are reliant on ombrogenous water. Precipitation decreases

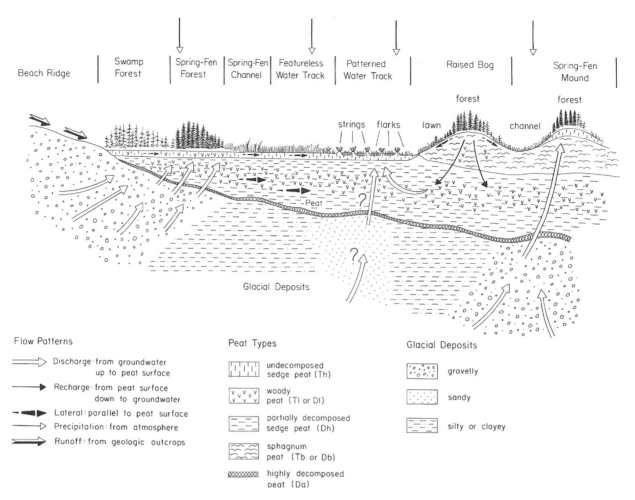

Beach Ridge | Swamp Forest | Spring-Fen Forest | Spring-Fen Channel | Featureless Water Track | Patterned Water Track | Raised Bog | Spring-Fen Mound

strings flarks lawn channel

forest forest

Peat

Glacial Deposits

Flow Patterns

⇨ Discharge: from groundwater up to peat surface

→ Recharge: from peat surface down to groundwater

◄━ Lateral: parallel to peat surface

⇾ Precipitation: from atmosphere

⇒ Runoff: from geologic outcrops

Peat Types

undecomposed sedge peat (Th)

woody peat (Tl or Dl)

partially decomposed sedge peat (Dh)

sphagnum peat (Tb or Db)

highly decomposed peat (Da)

Glacial Deposits

gravelly

sandy

silty or clayey

FIG. 9.1. Peatland types according to landform type, water chemistry, and hydrology. The sources of water and mineral ions are indicated by arrows. The alkalinity in the surface water decreases with increasing distance from the source of the groundwater or runoff draining from mineral soils. (Glaser 1992.)

northward and potential evapotranspiration (PET) increases southward; both conditions limit water supply. A similar effect occurs with decreasing precipitation and increasing PET in continental locations. Bogs cannot exist where P < ET, although they occur in the Western Boreal Plain (Vitt, Halsey, et al. 1994), where P < PET and bog ET << PET (Petrone, Silins, et al. 2007). However, since fens have an additional water source through surface and/or groundwater, they become more common than bogs where the atmospheric water deficit is more intense.

Hydrological processes within peatlands and their role in downstream aquatic systems are dominated by the structure and character of the peat soil, which ranges from living and dead but undecomposed plant material near the surface through poorly to well-decomposed materials at depth. Ingram (1978) defines the upper layer (acrotelm) as a variably saturated zone that extends to the depth of the average lowest annual water table and where biological activities are concentrated and nutrient exchange occurs (Fig. 9.2). The lower layer (catotelm) is the permanently saturated layer below which biological activity is considerably reduced, facilitating the accumulation of plant remains. The acrotelm is usually distinct in bogs, typically 35–50 cm in thickness (Belyea and Clymo 2001) and thinner (~10–20 cm) and less distinct in fens (Price and Maloney 1994) because of a higher, less variable water

table. The saturated hydraulic conductivity of the acrotelm can decrease from the surface by four or five orders of magnitude in bogs (Hoag and Price 1995; Letts, Roulet, et al. 2000) and three or four orders of magnitude in fens (Price and Maloney 1994; Ferone and Devito 2004).

Peatlands have the ability to self-regulate their hydrology, keeping water levels relatively stable. When water tables are high, such as following snowmelt or during prolonged wet periods, near-surface water flows readily through the permeable acrotelm, facilitating runoff (Quinton, Hayashi, et al. 2008). As the water table declines, the system's transmissivity decreases significantly, and runoff is inhibited. During extended dry periods, runoff from bogs may cease altogether and moderate amounts of rain may not produce any outflow (Bay 1969). Fens, whose water supply is supplemented by groundwater inflow, maintain a higher water table and consequently are less likely to dry (Ingram 1983). Patterned bogs and fens are very effective at retaining water (Price and Maloney 1994). In spring snowmelt, water flows readily around ridges (Quinton and Roulet 1998), but after snowmelt, water must seep through the peat matrix of ridges; thus runoff responses are slow and ET losses dominate (Price and Maloney 1994).

Water flow through the catotelm is minimal (Ingram 1983) because of low hydraulic conductivity; horizontal water flows are also low (Belyea and Clymo 2001). Upward flow from mineral substrates can be important water sources for fens (Devito, Waddington, et al. 1997), while mineral soils underlying bogs typically restrict seepage losses (Ingram 1983). Water content of saturated catotelm peat is frequently at or slightly greater than 0.9 cm^{-3} (Hayward and Clymo 1982), and it is a source of water for evaporation during dry periods as hydraulic gradients reverse from recharge to discharge, even in bogs (Devito, Waddington, et al. 1997; Fraser, Roulet, et al. 2001).

Water-storage changes in peatlands are typically assumed to be manifest entirely by changes in water table as pores drain or refill according to the specific yield of the acrotelm (Ingram 1983). However, dilation and contraction of peat volume (specific storage), causing surface swelling or subsidence, can be more important than pore drainage (specific yield) mechanisms in determining water-storage changes (Price and Schlotzhauer 1999). Seasonal contraction of peat volumes leading to subsidence can also reduce hydraulic conductivity by several orders of magnitude (Price 2003; Hogan, van der Kamp, et al. 2006). The effect is more prominent in fen pool and lawn communities than in more structurally rigid ridges, minimizing water table drop below the (descending) surface (Whittington and Price 2006), having implications for ecological and biogeochemical processes (Strack and Waddington 2007).

Evapotranspiration is the dominant water loss from bogs, ranging up to 4–5 mm d^{-1} (Lafleur, Hember, et al. 2005), but it decreases markedly if *Sphagnum* moss dries (Admiral, Lafleur, et al. 2006); the upward capillary flow that sustains ET (Price, Edwards, et al. 2009) becomes limited by the low hydraulic conductivity of drained moss (Price, Whittington, et al. 2008). In fens, ET can be sustained at or near PET when vascular plants are growing and the water table is within the rooting zone (Kim and Verma 1996). Price and Maloney (1994) noted that evapotranspiration from a fen surface was ~60% greater than from a bog surface. Where surface subsidence keeps the water table near the surface, evapotranspiration rates are higher and more consistent (Lafleur and Roulet 1992).

Hydrological processes in northern peatlands can be strongly affected by freezing and permafrost. Seasonal frost is persistent and permafrost is common in northern peatlands because of the thermally insulative properties of dry moss in the summer and thermally transmissive properties when wet in fall and winter (Brown and Williams 1972). Ice-cored palsas and peat plateaus form up to 2–3 m above the drainage level of some fens (Dever, Hillaire-Marcel, et al. 1984). Their raised profile isolates them from surface water inflows, and hence they are a characteristic bog landform. Water in these features has a relatively short residence time, being quickly translated into runoff (Dever, Laithier, et al. 1982; Quinton and Hayashi 2005). Their elevated position with respect to the regional water table ensures rapid water delivery to adjacent fen peatlands, which are the major regional or watershed conduits for runoff (Price 1987; Quinton and Hayashi 2005). Frost causes a perched water table, which facilitates runoff and keeps the system wetter than it would be otherwise. This can be an important mechanism to explain the occurrence of bogs in the relatively dry Western Boreal Plain (Petrone, Devito, et al. 2008). In winter, differential rates of seasonal frost penetration can alter groundwater flow paths (Price and Woo 1988). Winter drainage produces little flow from bogs, but inflow from mineral uplands can sustain flow into and from fens (Price and FitzGibbon 1987). ET rates in winter are low, but can represent 23–30% of the total annual flux (Lafleur, Hember, et al. 2005).

Biogeochemistry

As with all wetland ecosystems, the oxidation-reduction (or redox) potential is an important control on the availability of chemical elements and cycling of materials in soils. Water-logged soil conditions limit oxygen availability and result in anaerobic metabolism of organic matter, slowing decomposition and resulting in the substantial accumulation of soil carbon. As a result, northern peatlands are estimated to store between 270 and 455 × 10^{15} g of carbon (Gorham 1991; Turunen, Tomppo, et al. 2002), an amount equivalent to approximately one-third of all soil carbon stocks and 34–57% of the carbon currently held in the atmosphere (IPCC 2007). Northern peatlands are also estimated to contribute 5–10% of global CH$_4$ emissions (Mikaloff Fletcher, Tans, et al. 2004). Because of this important role in the global carbon cycle, it is not surprising that much peatland biogeochemical research has focused on carbon cycling. Variability in cation concentrations and acidity among northern peatlands has been linked to hydrogeology and availability of elements from atmospheric sources. Lately an increasing interest is being paid to nutrient cycling as atmospheric deposition of nitrogen increases (Limpens, Heijmans, et al. 2006).

Carbon Cycling

Temperate and boreal peatlands have accumulated soil carbon since the last glaciation (~10,000–14,000 years ago), and studies using soil cores give long-term accumulation rates of 19 to 25 g C m^{-2} yr^{-1} (Roulet, Lafleur, et al. 2007). Carbon accumulates in peatlands because uptake of carbon via gross ecosystem photosynthesis (GEP) exceeds losses via decomposition. Changes in stored carbon (ΔC) can be expressed as:

$$\Delta C = -(NEE + F_{CH4} + F_{NMVOC} + F_Q),$$

where NEE is the net flux of carbon as CO$_2$ from the ecosystem to the atmosphere (i.e., GEP minus autotrophic and heterotrophic respiration), F$_{CH4}$ is the flux of CH$_4$, F$_{NMVOC}$ is the flux of nonmethane volatile organic compounds, and F$_Q$ is the flux of carbon in particulate and dissolved forms carried by hydrological inputs/outputs to the ecosystem. In all cases fluxes are positive if carbon is lost from the ecosystem.

Contemporary rates of carbon exchange are known to vary widely from year to year, controlled largely by growing season temperature and water table position. Saarnio, Morero, et al. (2007) compiled values for NEE ranging from an uptake of 67 to a release of 80 g C m^{-2} yr^{-1} for bogs to an uptake of 98 to release of 101 g C m^{-2} yr^{-1} for fens. These broad ranges likely result from the fact that most studies are conducted for only one or two years and thus poorly represent average conditions at sites. Several peatlands with longer records report similarly large ranges, but average rates of carbon accumulation of ~22–24 g C m^{-2} yr^{-1} (Roulet, Lafleur, et al. 2007; Nilsson, Sagefors, et al. 2008) are similar to long-term accumulation rates determined from cores.

Methane emissions also vary both within and among peatlands. Bogs are reported to emit < 1 to 16 g CH$_4$–C m^{-2} yr^{-1} and fens < 1 to 42 g CH$_4$–C m^{-2} yr^{-1} (Saarnio, Morero, et al. 2007). Since CH$_4$ is produced under highly reduced conditions and may be oxidized to CO$_2$ above the water table, water table position is an important control on CH$_4$ emissions, with higher

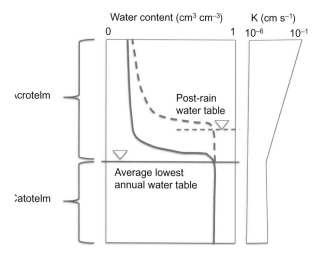

Water content (cm³ cm⁻³)

K (cm s⁻¹)

crotelm

Post-rain
water table

Average lowest
annual water table

atotelm

FIG. 9.2. Hydrological processes within peatlands and their role in downstream aquatic systems are dominated by the structure and character of the peat soil.

fluxes from wetter sites. Temperature is positively correlated to CH_4 emissions in many studies (e.g., Dise, Gorham, et al. 1993). Vegetation type (Bubier 1995) and productivity (Waddington, Roulet, et al. 1996; Tuittila, Komulainen, et al. 2000) are also related to CH_4 flux because plants provide labile substrate for CH_4 production and some species can transport CH_4 from the soil to the atmosphere. Once produced in soil, CH_4 can also accumulate as free-phase gas, or bubbles (Strack, Kellner, et al. 2005; Comas, Slater, et al. 2008; Waddington, Harrison, et al. 2009), and recent research suggests that CH_4 release via bubbling (ebullition) may account for a substantial portion of total peatland CH_4 emissions (Glaser, Chanton, et al. 2004; Comas, Slater, et al. 2008).

Carbon is also lost from peatlands via hydrologic output in both particulate and dissolved organic and inorganic forms. These outputs may account for a significant portion of peatland carbon cycles (Billett, Palmer, et al. 2004). Some suggest that hydrologic export of carbon from peatlands is increasing (Freeman, Evans, et al. 2001), leading to concerns over destabilization of these soil carbon stocks. Causes of increasing exports, particularly of dissolved organic carbon (DOC), are still uncertain, but possible mechanisms include warming temperatures (Freeman, Evans, et al. 2001), severe drought (Worrall, Burt, et al. 2004), increasing vegetation productivity (Freeman, Fenner, et al. 2004), and decreasing atmospheric deposition of sulphate (Evans, Chapman, et al. 2006).

Recent research has also shown that release of carbon to the atmosphere as nonmethane volatile organic compounds (NMVOCs) may account for up to 5% of the total carbon balance of northern peatlands (Bäckstrand, Crill, et al. 2008). Efflux of NMVOCs appears correlated to temperature, water table, and vegetation type (Bäckstrand, Crill, et al. 2008), with vascular plants likely responsible for most emissions (Tiiva, Faubert, et al. 2009).

Mineral and Nutrient Availability

Mineral concentrations in peatlands are largely controlled by the source of hydrologic inputs. Because fens receive inputs of surface and groundwater that has interacted with mineral soil, concentrations of cations and alkalinity are higher than bogs

receiving only precipitation (Table 9.1). Mineral inputs can also be atmospherically derived. Gorham and Janssens (2005) assessed peat chemistry in five bogs and observed a higher concentration of sea salt–derived minerals (Cl, S, Br) in maritime locations and more wind-blown soil–derived minerals (Al, Ce, Cr) in midcontinental sites.

Several studies have found that the hydrogeologic setting of the peatland can have an important control on mineral and nutrient concentrations and turnovers. For example, Devito and Hill (1997) observed that small headwater peatlands exhibited variable sulphate retention depending on till depth in the catchment. Shallow till depth resulted in elimination of groundwater inputs in dry summers, resulting in water table drawdown and sulphate mobilization. Similarly, Mitchell, Branfireun, et al. (2009) compared porewater chemistry at peatland sites with variable upland slope geometries. They found higher concentrations of methylmercury in porewater adjacent to concave slopes, likely due to larger hydrologic inputs supplying sulphate and DOC, important for mercury methylation.

In general, concentrations of nutrients such as nitrogen and phosphorus are relatively low in peatlands and may vary inconsistently along bog-fen gradients (Table 9.1). However, minerotrophic peatlands are often slightly more nutrient rich than ombrotrophic sites (Laine, Komulainen, et al. 2004; Keller, Bauers, et al. 2006). At many sites, primary productivity is phosphorus limited (Kellogg and Bridgham 2003). Despite low nutrient availability, peat accumulation into thick organic soils represents a long-term accumulation of nutrients (Laine, Komulainen, et al. 2004; Gorham and Janssens 2005).

Because northern peatlands are dominated by vegetation and microbial communities adapted to low nutrient conditions, ecosystem response to fertilization, particularly atmospheric nitrogen deposition, has been the focus of many recent experiments. Fertilization with N has been observed to increase the abundance of vascular vegetation at the expense of bryophytes, particularly *Sphagnum* (Limpens and Berendse 2003; Keller, Bauers, et al. 2006; Bubier, Moore, et al. 2007). This shift in vegetation can increase GEP and ecosystem respiration (Lund, Christensen, et al. 2009); however, in some cases, net uptake of CO_2 is reduced by fertilization because of the loss of mosses (Bubier, Moore, et al. 2007). A meta-analysis of N-fertilization experiments in *Sphagnum*-dominated peatlands (Limpens, Granath, et al. 2011) determined that low levels of N addition enhance *Sphagnum* production, whereas higher levels reduce production. The rate of N application that reduces moss production is lower when background N deposition is high. Higher temperatures and low phosphorus levels exacerbated detrimental effects of N application. Generally fertilization has little effect on CH_4 emissions (Keller, Bridgham, et al. 2005; Lund, Christensen, et al. 2009); however, emissions of the greenhouse gas nitrous oxide (N_2O) are increased when N is added (Lund, Christensen, et al. 2009).

Microtopography and Peatland Biogeochemistry

While it is clear that biogeochemistry varies among peatlands ecosystems, within-site variability is also important. Water tracks within a peatland complex support vegetation communities adapted to more nutrient-rich conditions because the water flow provides a constant supply of nutrients (Malmer 1986). In addition, differences in elevation of the peatland surface create zones with varying water table and vegetation

TABLE 9.1
Summary of chemical data for surface water for four peatlands in western Canada

	Bog	Poor fen	Moderately rich fen	Extremely rich fen
pH	3.96 (0.07)	5.38 (0.13)	6.14 (0.27)	6.88 (0.30)
Conductivity (µS/cm)	39.0 (11.0)	48.0 (14.0)	85.0 (16.3)	187.0 (35.0)
Ca^{2+} (mg/L)	3.00 (0.96)	5.88 (1.88)	11.09 (2.92)	23.28 (6.52)
Mg^{2+} (mg/L)	0.72 (0.35)	3.14 (1.05)	5.07 (1.37)	7.78 (1.76)
Alkalinity (µequiv./L)	< 0 (–)	198.0 (51.0)	694.0 (186.0)	1,716.0 (401.0)
NO_3-N (µg/L)	5.74 (2.10)	4.90 (1.68)	4.48 (2.55)	3.64 (1.82)
NH_4 (µg/L)	17.6 (8.40)	13.2 (8.82)	12.2 (10.5)	6.44 (5.88)
SRP (µg/L)	8.27 (6.10)	52.7 (27.9)	77.7 (101.0)	7.34 (7.03)

NOTE: Modified from Vitt, Bayley, and Jin 1995. Values are averages of 18 water samples (36 for moderately rich fen) with standard deviation in parenthesis. SRP is soluble reactive phosphorus.

communities. These features, often called microforms, may be one to several meters in extent and centimeters to meters in height. Because water table and vegetation are such important controls on carbon and nutrient cycling, microforms have been observed to have significant differences in carbon accumulation (Belyea and Clymo 2001), CH_4 fluxes (Waddington and Roulet 1996), nutrient (Eppinga, Rietkerk, et al. 2010), and methylmercury concentrations (Branfireun 2004). Microforms also respond differently to disturbances such as drought and warming (Strack and Waddington 2007; Sullivan, Arens, et al. 2008). More than simple differences between microforms, it is clear that the composition and distribution of these features within a peatland can affect whole ecosystem function (Waddington and Roulet 2000; Becker, Kutzbach, et al. 2008; Baird, Belyea, et al. 2009). Thus, in addition to local and regional hydrogeology, microtopography should be considered when studying peatland biogeochemistry.

Vegetation Gradients

Vegetation gradients exist at several spatial scales in northern peatlands. A vegetation gradient is defined as a change in abundance, composition, or growth of plant species or communities in relation to space or another physical, chemical, or biological gradient. One reason why gradients have received so much attention by scientists is their clear expression in peatland landscapes (Sjörs 1948; Bridgham, Pastor, et al. 1996; Økland, Økland, et al. 2001). Bryophytes have a different nutrient acquisition strategy than vascular plants. Given their lack of vascular structure and unistratose cellular leaf composition, bryophytes are more influenced by growing conditions at the soil-atmosphere interface than vascular plants depending more on deeper substrate layers. Consequently, changes of vascular plants and bryophytes along gradients are not always controlled in similar ways (Glaser, Janssens, et al. 1990; Vitt and Chee 1990; Bragazza and Gerdol 2002).

Sjörs (1948) identified three gradients that are important to determining patterns in peatland vegetation: (1) the microtopographical gradient between vegetation and the water table (often referred to as the hummock-hollow gradient); (2) the degree of openness from peatland margin to peatland expanse; and (3) the degree of minerotrophy (as defined by pH and cation base richness, referred to as the pH-alkalinity gradient). When discussing chemical gradients, the term *minerotrophy* strictly refers to base richness (metallic cations and pH), whereas the terms *oligotrophic, mesotrophic,* and *eutrophic* refer only to nutrient richness (mainly N and P) as used in limnology. Lately, a gradient in fertility related to the availability of the limiting nutrient elements N and P has been revealed for vascular plants (Bridgham, Pastor, et al. 1996; Wheeler and Proctor 2000). In terms of predicting the response of plant communities of northern peatlands to climate change and a wide-scale pattern of nitrogen depositions, both pH-alkalinity and nutrient gradients must be addressed and vegetation surveys must include both mosses and vascular plants (Bedford, Walbridge, et al. 1999; Limpens, Granath, et al. 2011) to adequately assess responses of peat moss–dominated peatlands.

Hummock-Hollow Gradient

The hummock-hollow gradient is the linear sequence over a few meters of microstructure. Microtopographical levels along a water table gradient are identified as hummock, lawn, carpet, and hollow/mud-bottom/pool (Fig. 9.3). This gradient is usually described by the distribution of *Sphagnum* mosses or other bryophytes (e.g., Vitt, Crum, et al. 1975; Wagner and Titus 1984; Bubier 1995), but vascular plants can also be useful (Damman and Dowhan 1981). Hummocks are raised 20–80 cm above the water surface and are characterized by dwarf shrubs and *Sphagnum fuscum* (Fig. 9.4a). Lawns are 5–20 cm above the water level and are characterized by graminoids and *Sphagnum* species such as *S. rubellum* and *S. magellanicum.* Floating carpets or hollows are between 5 cm below to 5 cm above the surface and have a sparser cover of graminoids and mosses (e.g., *S. angustifolium*). Mud-bottoms are often flooded and may lack vascular plant cover. They may support mosses or liverworts, but are often simply bare peat with a cover of algae (Karofeld and Toom 1999). Pools are water basins that are permanently filled, often with vegetation such as *Warnstorfia fluitans* (Fig. 9.4a) around the edges. In bogs (sensu lato for *Sphagnum*-dominated peatlands), hummock mosses are dominated by species

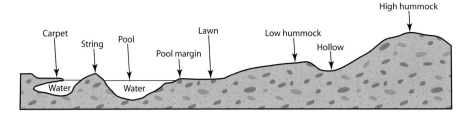

FIG. 9.3. Schematic drawing representing typical microstructures encountered in peatlands. (Drawing by Denis Bastien.)

from the Acutifolia taxonomic section of Sphagna, whereas species from the Cuspidata section frequently grow in wet hollow habitat.

Although less studied, microtopographical gradients also exist in moderate-rich and rich fens (Fig. 9.4b). Vitt (1990) described this gradient as hummock (or string), carpet, lawn, and flark (or marl pool). In fens, the microtopographical gradient is more difficult to study because the topographical height gradient is superposed with a minerotrophic gradient between hummocks and depressions. Hence, in relatively rich fens, *Sphagnum fuscum,* a typical bog species, can be found on high hummocks or well-developed strings. Note that the indicative species enumerated in Fig. 9.4 do not correspond to plant communities, but are just presented as examples of species distributed along the bog or fen microtopographical gradient. The duality of middle-range topographical gradient and minerotrophic gradient is exemplified by *Scirpus cespitosus, S. hudsonianus, Carex exilis,* and *Potentilla palustris* for vascular plants and *Loeskhypnum badium* for bryophytes (Bubier 1995; Campbell and Rochefort 2001).

Swamp Forest–Open Peatland Gradient

The swamp forest–open peatland gradient described by Sjörs (1948) is evident when one walks from upland forests through a forested peatland into a less densely forested peatland, and finally into an open peatland. Vitt and Slack (1984) describe the following moss indicator species for the shade gradient of bogs and forested fens of northern Minnesota: (1) communities within a closed tree canopy, dominated by *Sphagnum teres* and *S. warnstorfii;* (2) those with scattered, individual trees to those with an open tree cover, dominated by *S. fuscum, S. capillifolium, S. magellanicum, S. angustifolium,* and *S. fimbriatum;* and (3) those with no shade, dominated by *S. papillosum, S. rubellum, S. centrale, S. obtusum,* and *S. contortum.* But it is more the tree and shrub spatial pattern that reveals the margin-expanse gradient. When approaching the margin of a peatland, the density and size of trees of species such as *Picea mariana* and *Larix laricina* increase, forming a swampy forested zone (Bubier 1991). Shrubs such as *Viburnum nudum* ssp. *cassinoides, Ilex (Nemopanthus) mucronatus,* and *Alnus incana* ssp. *rugosa* have greater abundance in that zone (Damman and Dowhan 1981). The lagg, an ecotone quite variable in species composition at the transition between peatland and forest ecosystems but usually rich in species, exists at the margin of some peatlands (Conway 1949). Typical lagg species include *Carex riparia, C. rostrata, Osmunda cinnamomea,* and *Calamagrostis canadensis.*

Although this gradient is mostly influenced by shade (Vitt and Slack 1984; Anderson, Davis, et al. 1995), it is conditioned by hydrogeological conditions. The deeper and more variable water table at the margins (Damman and Dowhan

1981) enables trees to grow larger. The gradient also parallels minerotrophy change, as swamp forest margins are close to the mineral soil beneath, which most likely sustains the greater biomass found at peatland-forest margins. Along with the presence of more shrubs and trees, light availability is diminished, causing a change in bryophyte communities, as not all *Sphagnum* species have similar requirements in term of irradiance (Gignac 1992). Some ecologists studying temperate peatlands argue that the swamp forest–open peatland gradient may lack ecological usefulness (Wheeler and Proctor 2000); most admit that the direction of variation in vegetation remains unclear but still argue that this gradient is caused by a specific set of factors (Økland, Økland, et al. 2001). In North American peatlands, scant attention has been given to the study of the swampy forest–open peatland margin ecotone.

Ombrotrophy-Minerotrophy Gradient

A gradient of vegetation going from "poor in indicative species" to "rich in indicative species" exists among bogs, and poor, moderate, and rich fens (Sjörs 1963). This gradient is defined by the presence of indicative species, particularly minerotrophic species. Bogs have very few or no minerotrophic indicative species, whereas fens have few, several, or many indicative species according to the degree of minerotrophy. Some examples of moss species indicative of minerotrophic conditions in boreal North America are *Campylium stellatum, Scorpidium scorpioides, S. cossinii, Sphagnum warnstorfii, S. subsecundum,* and *Warnstorfia exannulata,* and vascular plant species include *Carex aquatilis, C. lasiocarpa, C. exilis, Calamagrostis canadensis,* and *Myrica gale.* Although ombrotrophic peatlands are characterized by a lack of indicative species, an abundance of *Sphagnum fuscum, S. magellanicum, S. angustifolium,* and *S. cuspidatum,* along with the vascular plants *Eriophorum spissum, Kalmia angustifolia, K. polifolia,* and *Rubus chamaemorus,* can indicate a bog environment.

Floristic multivariate analyses of peatland vegetation point to a primary division between *Sphagnum*-dominated and brown moss–dominated (Amblystegiaceae) peatlands. This plant division corresponds well to the bimodal frequency distribution of peatlands related to pH (Gorham and Janssens 1992). Experts believe that grouping peatlands into *Sphagnum*-dominated (bogs and poor fens with pH lower than 5.5–5.7) and brown moss–dominated (moderately rich and rich fens with pH greater than 5.5) habitats makes more ecological sense than using the strict concept of bog (fed only by precipitation) and DuRietz's (1949) notion of indicative species (Vitt 2000; Wheeler and Proctor 2000). With such a system, the categories of bog and poor fen in Table 9.1 would be merged to represent chemistry of *Sphagnum*-dominated peatlands.

The ombrotrophy-minerotrophy gradient is expressed at

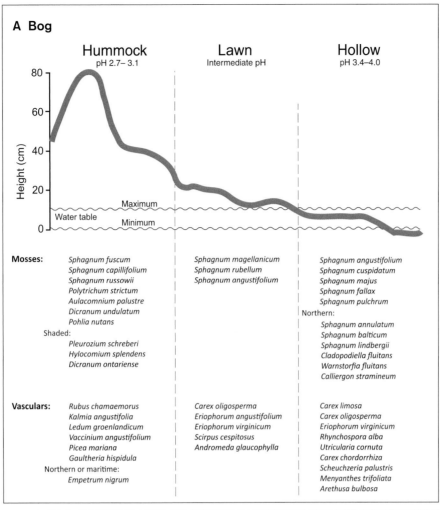

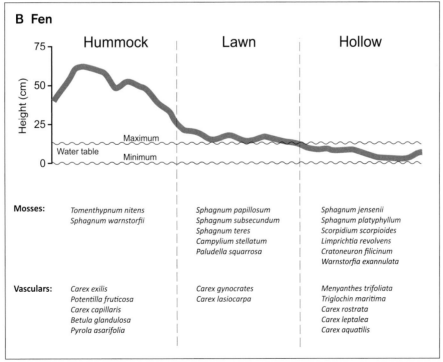

FIG. 9.4. Hummock-hollow gradient showing typical eastern North American species for each micro-habitat: A. bog species along with average pH; and B. fen species.

regional scales across different peatlands. But it can also be observed within a peatland complex, such as the extensively studied Red Lake peatlands in Minnesota (Janssens and Glaser 1986) and the Mariana Lakes region in Alberta (Nicholson and Vitt 1990). Changes in species in the ombrotrophy-minerotrophy gradient tend to follow a gradient of pH and conductivity/alkalinity/base cations (Sjörs 1950; Gorham 1953). Factors that explain the distribution of plants along this gradient are not well understood. However, two important factors are the presence of *Sphagnum* mosses (which can lower pH) and the development of the peatland (which, with time, reduces the influence of flow-through runoff). A fertility gradient, or one of nutrient supply during a given time, may also explain the distribution of plants along the ombrotrophic-minetrophic gradient. Difficulties in studying fertility gradients stem from the time and costs associated with complete nutrient budgets involving annual water balance, rate of water flow, and nutrient assimilation and decomposition rates of plants (Bridgham, Pastor, et al. 1996).

Biogeographical Gradient (Distance from the Sea)

To the original work of Sjors (1948), Malmer (1986) adds a fourth gradient: a biogeographical wetness gradient, most evident in raised bogs, that influences vegetation structure of peatlands. Broadly, three types are recognized in North America: (1) continental regions that broadly support forested (often densely) or shrubby peatlands; (2) wetter areas that harbor semiforested peatlands; and (3) the wettest areas, which have open peatlands with pools. Tree and shrub density gradually decreases in peatlands as you move farther east until you reach open peatlands with pools of the maritime region (Glaser and Janssens 1986). In Europe, Malmer (1986) ascertained that climatic conditions were most important in establishing regional differences, whereas in North America, Glaser and Janssens (1986) revealed the importance of autogenic processes and age of the peatlands to the structure of raised bogs.

Plant Adaptations in Peatlands

Sphagnum mosses are often considered eco-engineers in the sense that once established in a peatland, they induce changes in water regimes, acidity of the environment, and the sequestration of nutrients through slowly decomposing peat (van Breemen 1995). Peatland vascular plants grow in wet, partly anoxic, often nutrient-poor and acidic environments. According to Grime's (2001) plant strategies, peatland vascular plants are "stress-tolerators" due to slow growth rate and longevity and because they invest little in the production of seeds. Strategies to deal with environmental stress are more pronounced in bog species and become less pronounced in moderate-rich and rich fens. Ericaceous shrubs in particular have developed adaptations to the wet, acid-poor environment of bogs: persistent resinous leaves and involuted margins of the leaves conserve humidity, and association with ericoid mycorrhizae helps in nutrient sequestration.

Low Nutrient Availability

Several strategies allow peatland plants to live in nutrient-poor environments. Most peatland vascular plants are perennial, an efficient way to ensure large biomass above- and belowground (Rydin and Jeglum 2006). A large underground biomass is essential to procure enough nutrients in a nutrient-poor habitat. Additionally, some ericaceous shrubs *(Rhododendron, Chamaedaphne, Andromeda)* conserve nutrients by retaining their leaves over several growth seasons (Crawford 1993). In deciduous peatland species (e.g., *Rubus chamaemorus* and *Vaccinium* spp. in bogs and many grasses and sedges in fens), nutrients are transferred from leaves to the roots and rhizomes in autumn and then back to new leaves in spring (Grace 1993). Sedges additionally conserve nutrients by reproducing asexually by either aboveground stolons or belowground rhizomes. Nutrients are conserved by translocating them from the old tissue to the new plant.

Some peatland species increase nutrient intake (P, N, and K) through mycorrhizal associations between the plant roots and fungi. The plant has an increased ability to capture water, phosphorus, and other nutrients, and the fungi receive carbohydrate in return. Species that benefit from mycorrhizal associations include various peatland woody species, such as *Larix laricina, Picea mariana, Alnus incana, Betula glandulosa,* and *B. pumila,* as well as ericaceous and orchid species (Cronk and Fennessy 2001). However, sedges and cotton grass, dominant vascular species in many peatlands, generally do not have mycorrhizae (Thormann, Currah, et al. 1999).

The most spectacular example of a plant adaptation to nutrient-poor environments is carnivory in such plants as *Drosera, Utricularia,* and *Sarracenia* species. These plants increase nutrient intake by trapping and digesting invertebrates. The benefits of carnivory must balance the cost of making and maintaining the traps (Cronk and Fennessy 2001). Some carnivorous plants are facultative carnivores, relying on carnivory only in nutritionally hard times, such as a prolonged period without fire (Folkerts 1982).

Waterlogging

Anoxic conditions common in peatlands can hinder root growth and the uptake of minerals and nutrients. Some vascular peatland plants have adapted to these conditions by developing large intercellular spaces, called aerenchyma, that extend from leaves through stems and down into roots or rhizomes. This space transports oxygen to belowground parts (Crawford 1978).

Additional adaptations help peatland vegetation cope with variable water levels, such as after snowmelt or heavy precipitation. The sedge family Cyperacae forms tussocks to elevate leaves above the water. Floating mats, common where fens border lakes, allow vegetation to cope with water fluctuation by moving with the water surface (Rydin and Jeglum 2006). Some peatland plants, especially woody species, adapt their roots to cope with flooded conditions. Two common root adaptations are the development of shallow rooting and adventitious roots (roots made from tissue other than root tissue) (Crawford 1978). Due to a lack of aerenchyma and a reliance on mycorrhizae, many peatland woody species have shallow root systems. These species, such as *Picea mariana, Larix laricina,* and *Thuja occidentalis,* grow in the aerated zone, which is often just tens of centimeters deep (Rydin and Jeglum 2006).

As peatland trees grow, their weight may cause them to sink into the peat, exacerbating anoxic conditions. *Sphagnum* species also grow up around the trees and slowly raise the water level. *Salix* spp., *Alnus glutinosa, Pinus contorta, Larix laricina,* and *Picea mariana* are all peatland species that can form adventitious roots (Cronk and Fennessy 2001; Rydin and Jeglum 2006). Adventitious roots grow either directly on the trunk or can form from low branches. These new branches grow new roots and a new main shoot, leading to clonal reproduction.

Fauna

Peatlands are home to a high diversity of invertebrates; individual peatlands with well over 1,000 arthropod species are not uncommon (Blades and Marshall 1994). Together, vertebrate and invertebrate species assemblages of northern peatlands are unique. In fact, peatlands often contribute significantly to regional wildlife diversity, especially in temperate latitudes bordering the boreal biome (Calmé, Desrochers, et al. 2002; Spitzer and Danks 2006). Although most invertebrates found in peatlands occur in a variety of habitats, several species are found almost exclusively in bogs or fens (Spitzer and Danks 2006). Herbivore insects restricted to peatland plants, such as aphids and moths, dominate this group, but insect predators and parasitoids also occur as peatland specialists (Gotelli and Ellison 2002; Spitzer and Danks 2006). Peatland pools in particular harbor highly specialized invertebrate predators, including dragonflies *(Aeshna)* and water bugs *(Notonecta).*

In contrast to invertebrates, no vertebrate species is thought to occur only in peatlands, even though species of every vertebrate class will use peatlands. Bogs rarely harbor fishes in their pools due to acidic condition and isolation. Occasionally, small fish such as mudminnows *(Umbra limi)* can be found in bogs. Because of the high acidity, bogs have long been presumed hostile to amphibians, as amphibians undergo major exchanges with their environment through their skin (Pough 1976; Leuven, den Hartog, et al. 1986). However, recent investigations indicate that bogs and fens harbor abundant amphibian populations and even offer opportunities for reproduction (Mazerolle and Cormier 2003). One rare amphibian species, the four-toed salamander *(Hemidactylium scutatum),* may occur in peatlands because of its association with *Sphagnum* (Wood 1955), but its occurrence in peatlands remains to be documented (Mazerolle 2003). Few reptiles are reported in peatlands; scarcity may result from northern latitudes or a lack of detailed studies.

By far, birds are the most studied peatland vertebrates, and over 100 bird species are known to breed in North American peatlands (Desrochers and van Duinen 2006). North American peatlands are characterized by a high diversity of lesser-known songbirds. Among the most frequent birds are ubiquitous species such as white-throated sparrow *(Zonotrichia albicollis),* common yellowthroat *(Geothlypis trichas),* and hermit thrush *(Catharus guttatus),* and more specialized species such as palm warbler *(Dencroida palmarum)* and Lincoln's sparrow *(Melospiza lincolnii).* Those birds can reach high population densities on the order of 5 to 10 pairs per ha (A. Desrochers unpublished data). The species listed can be found either in bogs or fens, but fens often harbor additional species such as American bittern *(Botaurus lentiginosus),* swamp sparrow *(Melospiza georgiana),* and the ubiquitous red-winged blackbird *(Agelaius phoeniceus).*

Bogs in particular are attractive to game birds such as spruce grouse *(Falcipennis canadensis)* and sharp-tailed grouse *(Tympanuchus phasianellus).* The impressively large sandhill crane *(Grus canadensis)* is a noteworthy resident in western boreal peatlands, and appears to be expanding in eastern boreal peatlands. Other significant peatland birds are those where recent

population declines have raised concerns, including rusty blackbird *(Euphagus carolinus),* a common breeder of boreal muskeg whose numbers have plummeted since the mid-1960s (Sauer, Hines, et al. 2008); upland sandpiper *(Bartramia longicauda);* and most species of shorebirds (Morrison, Aubry, et al. 2001). The role of peatlands as staging areas for migrating shorebirds merits more investigation. Interestingly, migrating shorebirds occur not only in natural peatlands, but migrating flocks also occur regularly in barren expanses of peatlands cut over by the *Sphagnum* peat moss industry (A. Desrochers unpublished data). It is likely that the extinct Eskimo curlew *(Numenius borealis)* used northeastern peatlands regularly in the fall, in search of crowberries *(Empetrum nigrum)* as fuel for their journey south (Bent 1962).

Mammals are rarely abundant in peatlands. Like most terrestrial ecosystems, peatlands support a suite of small rodents, but none are specifically associated to this habitat. Mazerolle, Drolet, et al. (2001) found that only 2 of 15 small-mammal species encountered in eastern Canadian bogs exhibited a preference for bogs: the Arctic shrew *(Sorex arcticus)* and the southern bog lemming *(Synaptomys cooperi).* Moose *(Alces alces)* are often found in peatlands, particularly near edges between adjoining forest patches and open ericaceous habitats that provide food and cover against predators and extreme weather.

Ecological Controls

Peatland Development

Peatlands form by paludification or terrestrialization. These two processes describe the transformation of aquatic or terrestrial habitat into peatlands following changes in hydrological conditions of the substrate or climatic conditions. Specifically, paludification is the swamping of a terrestrial site and terrestrialization is the filling-in of a lake or shallow water body. These two processes do not operate necessarily in an exclusive manner, but it is generally recognized that the inception of peatlands is mostly climatically controlled, whereas their subsequent development is dominated by autogenic processes (Vitt 2006). The interplay between the influence of allogenic factors (external influences to the ecosystem such as climate, fire, large-scale human impact) and autogenic factors (internal influences such as plant succession) is well described by Payette and Rochefort (2001), Charman (2002), and Rydin and Jeglum (2006).

Peatlands are characterized by a striking heterogeneous surface topography that is expressed at several spatial scales: from a few meters (hummock-hollow microstructures) to hundreds of meters (pool macrostructure) to landscape scales (bog islands; Weltzin, Harth, et al. 2001). The main macrostructures in northern peatlands are the alternating pattern of strings and flarks or the presence of pools. Several hypotheses have been formulated about mechanisms of control (an active area of research among peatland ecologists), but none is yet universally recognized.

Macrostructures

Among allogenic processes, the influence of freeze-thaw actions, gravity through solifluxion, and permafrost creation of surface polygons shaped by the presence of ice wedges are considered important to macrostructure (Seppälä and Koutaniemi 1985; Swanson and Grigal 1988). However, in general, minimal quantitative data support allogenic development of macrostructures in boreal peatlands (Payette 2001). On the other hand, autogenic biotic processes are gaining support to explain the formation of strings and pools. From stratigraphic analyses of several peat profiles within a region, Anderson, Foster, et al. (2003) have shown that plant abundance will vary even if plant succession is under the influence of a uniform climate, suggesting that it is mostly autogenic factors controlling peat accumulation and in turn the development of macrostructures. Indeed, pools do not appear synchronously within the same climatic region or even the same site (Foster, Wright, et al. 1988; Tallis and Livett 1994; Karofeld 1998), implying a stronger influence from local variation in vegetation or hydrology (Charman 2002). Glaser and Janssens (1986) maintained that peat accumulation per se can induce changes in the hydraulic properties of peat, leading to a subsequent influence on macrostructure development. Lately, several researchers (reviewed in Kuhry and Turunen 2006) advocated that the interplay of both allogenic and autogenic factors (such as plant productivity, decomposition, peat accumulation, and *Sphagnum* acidification) is basic to the presence of macrostructrure, but that the inception and rate of change are more related to external factors, particularly the influence of climate on hydrological conditions and water table fluctuations. Some simulation models support the interplay of both internal and external factors (Belyea and Baird 2006).

Microstructures

Patterns of hummock-hollow formation and their resilience through time can be explained by various factors, such as intrinsic decomposition rates of *Sphagnum* species (Johnson and Damman 1993; Belyea 1996), water table position and climatic conditions (Rydin 1985; Belyea 1996; Karofeld 1998), interactions among plant species (Vitt, Achuff, et al. 1975; Malmer, Svensson, et al. 1994; Malmer, Albinsson, et al. 2003), nutrient regimes (Damman 1978; Luken 1985), and pH (Clymo 1963). These factors influence the development of the microtopographical gradient and the resulting thickness of the acrotelm.

Water table levels do not follow the relief of the microtopographical gradient; thus a wet-moist to drier gradient from hollows to hummocks is created. Hydrological influences on species distribution along the wetness gradient come from the fact that certain *Sphagnum* mosses have a higher resistance to desiccation conditions that develop on hummocks. This resistance results from their habit of living in tight colonies or communities where fascicle of branches are intermixed together and the structural architecture of the Acutifolia species (the most common peat mosses on hummocks), which has more branches and a denser cover of stem leaves, aiding the transmission of water upward (Hayward and Clymo 1982). This relation does not hold when isolated individual stems of hummock species are submitted to drying conditions (Sagot and Rochefort 1996). In fact, individuals can be less tolerant than hollow species, which survive cycles of drought through rapid physiological recovery in photosynthetic rates (Wagner and Titus 1984). Differences in pH and nutrient elements can also explain hummock-hollow gradients. The lower pH of hummocks, caused by the presence of efficient acid-producing species, such as *S. fuscum*, and the higher relief, impeding dilu-

tion of the acids, would exclude species less resistant to low pH (Vitt, Crum, et al. 1975). Concentrations of nutrients can be higher in depressions than on hummocks (Damman 1978). Higher concentrations of nutrients and mineral elements in the upper part of the acrotelm where the depressions are found (hollows, mud-bottoms, pools) would come in part from the buoyancy-driven water flow found in *Sphagnum* bogs (Adema, Baaijens, et al. 2006).

Finally, differences in production and decomposition between hummock and hollow habitats can also maintain microtopographical gradients. *Sphagnum* mosses decompose at a much slower rate on hummocks, even though the microhabitat is more oxygenated than the more anaerobic hollow habitat. Thus intrinsic structural properties of each *Sphagnum* species are more important in defining microtopographical gradients than the wet environment. Once established, hummock species can initiate and maintain differences in microtopography (Pouliot, Rochefort, et al. 2011).

Habitat Size

We have established that peatlands, like most ecosystems, are not homogeneous. They often harbor a high structural diversity, leading to well-defined and often predictable species distribution patterns. Large peatlands, in particular, typically offer many more habitats for wildlife than small ones, for two reasons: (1) large areas provide a greater diversity of microhabitats, and (2) many animal species are partial to large patches of habitat as opposed to small ones. As a result, species found in small peatlands are often simply subsets of species found in larger peatlands, leading to a system of nested species assemblages (Calmé and Desrochers 1999). Species associated to large peatlands include savannah sparrow (*Passerculus sandwichensis*), palm warbler, upland sandpiper (*Bartramia longicauda*), and sandhill crane. All of those species, except the warbler, appear to be attracted to large peatlands because they generally offer expanses of grassy habitats not generally found in small peatlands. The reason why palm warblers occur predominantly in large peatlands is not known, but it may be because of its tendency to congregate in loose "colonies" (Bourque and Desrochers 2006). Perhaps the most conspicuous features of large peatlands are pools. Those small bodies of open water are often the first feature to disappear as a result of land use by humans, leading to significant losses of aquatic insects, amphibians, and migrant birds, particularly ducks (*Anas crecca, A. rubripes*) and shorebirds (*Calidris melanotos, Tringa solitaria*).

For species with large home ranges or territories, peatlands may be important as part of their daily or annual movements. For example, spruce grouse and moose normally require the presence of extensive conifer or mixed forests in their home ranges, but typically venture into open bogs either to feed or, in the case of grouse, nest and raise their broods. Also, owing to their complex life cycles, amphibians may use peatlands only during certain stages, e.g., during dispersal between other types of wetlands, or as wet refuges during periods of the year when other wetlands are dry.

Fire as a Natural and Anthropogenic Disturbance

Fire is one of the few natural disturbances in North American peatlands, being especially common in the western boreal region. During drought, water table levels of bogs may rapidly drop, creating conditions propitious to surface fires, especially where inflammable ericaceous shrubs dominate. About 1,850 ha of bogs and 375 ha of fens burn each year in central Alberta, compared to 5,900 ha of uplands (Turetsky, Amiro, et al. 2004).

In western Canada, mean fire-free intervals (time between two consecutive fires) estimated from analysis of charcoal layers in peat cores are about 600 to 2,900 years (Kuhry 1994; Robinson and Moore 2000; Camill, Barry, et al. 2009). Data from bogs in eastern Québec (Canada) suggest natural fire-free intervals were 2,000 to 2,500 years prior to the 19th century. Fire-free intervals became much shorter (10 times) during the 19th and 20th centuries because until recently, farmers used fire to clear tree stumps before cultivation, and fire can easily spread from clearings to adjacent bogs on dry summer days (Lavoie and Pellerin 2007).

A 100-year postfire chronosequence of vegetation changes has been documented for *Sphagnum*-dominated bogs of central Alberta (Fig. 9.5) (Benscoter 2006; Benscoter and Vitt 2008). Because fire eliminates vascular plants, evapotranspirational water losses are diminished, which contributes to a rise in the water table (Wieder, Scott, et al. 2009). The greatest changes in the vegetation cover occur during the first 10 years, during which bare and burned peat is rapidly colonized by true mosses (mainly *Polytrichum strictum*), *Sphagnum* species, and vascular plants. True mosses are initially abundant because of their ability to colonize bare peat (Groeneveld, Massé, et al. 2007), competition from *Sphagnum* species has been removed, and they benefit from the release of nutrients from the burning of plants. Cover of true mosses rapidly declines after about 10 years, whereas abundance of *Sphagnum* species (mainly *S. fuscum*) and vascular plants continues to increase. Once *S. fuscum* dominates, plant assemblages remain relatively stable. As time progresses, canopy closure and microtopographic elevation facilitate establishment of feathermoss species (e.g., *Pleurozium schreberi*) on hummocks (Benscoter and Vitt 2008).

Fire has an impact on the carbon (C) balance of boreal bogs. Direct combustion of peat releases on average 3.2 ± 0.4 kg m^{-2} yr^{-1} of C (Turetsky and Wieder 2001; Turetsky, Wieder, et al. 2002). Immediately after fire, the bog understory (including the underlying peat) is a net source of C. About 12 to 13 years postfire, bogs switch from a source to a net C sink. This sink increases as bog trees produce roots and aboveground tissues, and reaches a maximum 75 years after fire. Then, as tree growth rates decline, C accumulation decreases (Wieder, Scott, et al. 2009).

Conservation Concerns

Few organizations specifically promote conservation of peatlands in North America. Typically programs for conserving wetlands are based on their capacity to support animal populations, and sites are evaluated and ranked according to productivity. This puts peatlands at a disadvantage since they are relatively poor or unproductive systems, especially bogs. By 2004, the North American Waterfowl Management Plan, signed by Canada and the United States in 1986, had 130,000 ha of wetlands protected, but a small proportion of this area was composed of peatlands. In 1996, less than 6% of sites protected by the international Ramsar wetland convention were peatlands (Lindsay 1996), but recent political pressure has increased this to more than 30%.

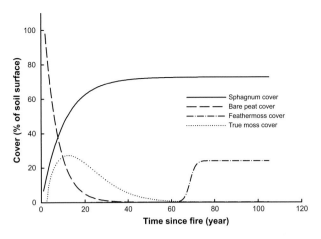

FIG. 9.5. Cover changes of main groups of moss species over time since the last fire (year zero) in bogs of north central Alberta, Canada (modified from Benscoter and Vitt 2008).

Conservation concepts specific to peatlands are emerging (Poulin, Rochefort, et al. 2004; Poulin et al. 2006), beyond only protecting large areas or huge peat volumes. Peatlands are now facing important threats that should be considered when setting conservation priorities. For instance, peatland vegetation structure and species composition are often believed to remain stable in time (centuries). This may be true for peatlands that do not face anthropogenic disturbances, but the combined effect of anthropogenic fire and of a drier-than-average climate may initiate afforestation of peatlands (Pellerin and Lavoie 2003), undermining initial conservation objectives. Anthropogenic drainage can directly affect plant communities, especially in cases where the peat is fibric (with high hydraulic conductivity) (Boelter 1972; Braekke 1983; Rothwell, Silins, et al. 1996). *Carex* species are among the first plants to decline following drainage, and may disappear within 10 years (Vasander and Laiho 1995). Following postdrainage increases in tree cover and associated shade, forest mosses may replace *Sphagnum* (Laine and Vanha-Majamaa 1992). Even natural remnants near mined areas are susceptible to afforestation by peripheral drainage (Poulin, Rochefort, et al. 1999). Afforestation is a major impact on peatland biodiversity, especially in bogs, when vascular plant and bird diversity declines after forest cover increases (Lachance, Lavoie, et al. 2005). Management plans should minimize drainage and tree invasion of peatlands.

Peat extraction for the production of horticultural compost is another threat to North American peatlands. Peat extraction severely damages peatlands, mainly due to intensive drainage, and abandoned sites are poorly recolonized spontaneously by peatland plants (Poulin, Rochefort, et al. 2005; Graf, Rochefort, et al. 2008). *Sphagnum* mosses are completely absent from residual peat surfaces, even decades after peat extraction activities have ceased (Poulin, Rochefort, et al. 2005). Fortunately, the horticultural peat industry affects only a small fraction of peatlands in North America (0.02% of Canadian peatland areas; Rubec 1996) and is limited to specific regions. Bog habitats can now be re-created in the landscape after peat extraction due to efficient restoration techniques, which are also being developed for fens (see chapter 14).

Energy production is a major threat to boreal peatlands in North America. Construction of hydroelectric dams has flooded more than 1,000,000 ha of peatlands in Québec, Manitoba, and Alberta (Rubec 1991). More recently, energy production from oil sands has expanded dramatically, and presents perhaps the greatest source of disturbance to peatlands of boreal Alberta (Forest 2001), where nearly 50% of the landscape is peatland (Vitt, Halsey, et al. 1996). One-third of the 500 km² of land impacted by open-pit mining to extract oil from sands were peatlands. If all available resources are mined, new oil extracting techniques such as in situ mining may eventually affect 138,000 km² (Schneider and Dyer 2006), an area the size of Florida and 50 times more area than that affected by actual open-pit mining activity.

One of the most influential properties of peatlands for wildlife conservation is their area. Large peatlands are not only more diverse in microhabitats and bird species but, more importantly, they support biotic assemblages rarely found in smaller, less diverse peatlands. Birds such as palm warbler (*Dendroica palmarum*) and upland sandpiper (*Bartramia longicauda*) are found only in large peatlands (Calmé and Haddad 1996; Calmé and Desrochers 2000). Smaller peatlands are often isolated, and this isolation may compound problems of small area. Distributions of palm warblers and upland sandpipers depend both on peatland area and the amount of peatland habitats available in a 10-km radius (Calmé and Desrochers 2000). As palm warbler is strictly associated to peatlands of southern Canada (Calmé and Desrochers 1999), it is a species of special concern when selecting conservation sites. Peatlands should be considered as a network, and protecting very isolated sites, especially if they are small, may be unproductive unless they support rare species.

Mapping peatland habitats using remote sensing tools may facilitate conservation network planning. Peatlands can easily be delineated in the landscape and characterized into habitat types with Landsat imagery (Poulin, Careau, et al. 2002), including habitats of special interest for conservation. For example, herbs-dominated habitats are often highly variable in terms of species composition from site to site (Poulin, Careau, et al. 2002). Although fens are not individually richer in bryophyte species than bogs, their variability from site to site leads to a higher total diversity of species when a group of fens is considered (Vitt, Bayley, et al. 1995). Variation among sites might thus complement species diversity when setting conservation priorities, because these two variables are not necessarily correlated.

Pools are a critical habitat for the conservation of peatland plant diversity. They are particularly distinct habitats in terms of species composition (Poulin, Careau, et al. 2002), and significantly increase species richness within peatlands (Fontaine, Poulin, et al. 2007). In southeastern Canada, natural bogs average 35 plant species. but this figure drops to 24 if surveys around pools are omitted (Fontaine, Poulin, et al. 2007). Thus pools deserve special attention in conservation planning. More globally, information on habitat diversity and distinctiveness is of considerable value when deciding whether all habitats deserve equal levels of protection, and determining amounts of habitat to set aside for conservation. This can be coupled with other criteria (habitat rarity, vulnerability) to set conservation targets (Pressey and Taffs 2001).

Representativeness should also include ecological diversity (Noss 1990), meaning that each type of peatland should have its own representative in a conservation network. This should maximize not only species diversity but also structural diversity, which is related to the physical organization or patterns of habitats, from the communities to the landscape scale. The Canadian wetland classification recognizes 16 forms of bogs (e.g., palsa bogs, blanket bogs, plateau bogs, polygonal peat plateau bogs, and string bogs; National Wetlands Working Group 1997). These bogs represent different shapes and surface patterning as well as different development processes, and should be considered as part of ecological diversity or biodiversity (Noss 1990). Representing each peatland type within a conservation network would favor preservation of different functions such as nutrient cycling and water regulation.

Finally, the distribution of peatlands in regard to hot spots of disturbances should be considered. For example, in North America, peatlands reach very high concentrations in the largely uninhabited Hudson Bay lowlands, whereas they are much more scattered in more densely populated areas. Conservation efforts should probably focus on populated areas, where peatlands are more susceptible to being disturbed. Remote areas in the boreal zones should not be ignored, however, since hydroelectric projects and oil sand mining now threaten peatlands there. On an international scale, North America encompasses one-third of the world's peatland (Gorham 1990), and thus we have major responsibility in regard to peatland conservation, particularly in regard to processes associated with carbon fluxes (Gorham 1991).

References

Adema EB, Baaijens GJ, et al. 2006. Field evidence for buoyancy-driven water flow in a *Sphagnum* dominated peat bog. *J. Hydrol.* 327(1–2):226–34.

Admiral SW, Lafleur PM, Roulet NT. 2006. Controls on latent heat flux and energy partitioning at a peat bog in eastern Canada. *Agri. For. Meteorol.* 140:308–21.

Amon JP, Thompson CA, et al. 2002. Temperate zone fens of the glaciated Midwestern USA. *Wetlands* 22:301–17.

Anderson DS, Davis RB, Janssens JA. 1995. Relationships of bryophytes and lichens to environmental gradients in Maine peatlands. *Vegetatio* 120:147–59.

Anderson R, Foster DR, Motzkin G. 2003. Integrating lateral expansion into models of peatland development in temperate New England. *J. Ecol.* 91:68–76.

Bäckstrand K, Crill PM, et al. 2008. Non-methane volatile organic compound flux from a subarctic mire in northern Sweden. *Tellus* 60B:226–37.

Baird AJ, Belyea LR, Morris PJ. 2009. Upscaling of peatland-atmosphere fluxes of methane: small-scale heterogeneity in process rates and pitfalls of "bucket-and-slab" models. In *Carbon cycling in northern peatlands,* Slater LD, Baird AJ, et al., editors. Geophysical Monogr. Ser. 184, Am. Geophys. Union, pp. 37–53.

Bay RR. 1969. Runoff from small peatland watersheds. *J. Hydrol.* 9:90–102.

Becker T, Kutzbach L, et al. 2008. Do we miss the hot spots?—the use of very high resolution aerial photographs to quantify carbon fluxes in peatlands. *Biogeosciences* 5:1387–93.

Bedford BL, Godwin KS. 2003. Fens of the United States: distribution, characteristics, and scientific connection versus legal isolation. *Wetlands* 23:608–29.

Bedford BL, Walbridge MR, Aldous A. 1999. Patterns in nutrient availability and plant diversity of temperate North American wetlands. *Ecology* 80:2151–69.

Belyea LR. 1996. Separating the effects of litter quality and microenvironment on decomposition rates in a patterned peatland. *Oikos* 77:529–39.

Belyea LR, Baird AJ. 2006. Beyond the "limits to peat bog growth": cross-scale feedback in peatland development. *Ecol. Monogr.* 76:299–322.

Belyea LR, Clymo RS. 2001. Feedback control of the rate of peat formation. *Proc. Royal Soc. London* B268:131521.

Benscoter BW. 2006. Post-fire bryophyte establishment in a continental bog. *J. Veg. Sci.* 17:647–52.

Benscoter BW, Vitt DH. 2008. Spatial patterns and temporal trajectories of the bog ground layer along a post-fire chronosequence. *Ecosystems* 11:1054–64.

Bent AC. 1962. *Life histories of North American shorebirds,* part II. New York: Dover.

Billett MF, Palmer SM, et al. 2004. Linking land-atmosphere-stream carbon fluxes in a lowland peatland system. *Glob. Biogeochem. Cycles* 18, GB1024, DOI: 10.1029/2003GB002058.

Blades DCA, Marshall SA. 1994. Terrestrial arthropods of Canadian peatlands: synopsis of pan trap collections at four southern Ontario peatlands. *Memoirs Ento. Soc. Can.* 169:221–84.

Boelter DH. 1972. Water table drawdown around an open ditch in organic soils. *J. Hydrol.* 15:329–40.

Bourque J, Desrochers A. 2006. Spatial aggregation of forest songbird territories and possible implications for area-sensitivity. *Avian Conserv. Ecol.* 1:3. www.ace-eco.org/vol1/iss2/art3/.

Braekke FH. 1983. Water table levels at different drainage intensities on deep peat in northern Norway. *For. Ecol. Manage.* 5:169–92.

Bragazza L, Gerdol R. 2002. Are nutrient availability and acidity-alkalinity gradients related in *Sphagnum*-dominated peatlands? *J. Veg. Sci.* 13:473–82.

Branfireun BA. 2004. Does microtopography influence subsurface pore-water chemistry? Implications for the study of methylmercury in peatlands. *Wetlands* 24:207–11.

Bridgham SD, Pastor J, et al. 1996. Multiple limiting gradients in peatlands: a call for a new paradigm. *Wetlands* 16:45–65.

Brown RJE, Williams GP. 1972. *The freezing of peatland.* Natur. Res. Counc. Can., Div. Building Res. Tech. Paper 381, NRC12881.

Bubier JL. 1991. Patterns of *Picea mariana* (black spruce) growth and raised bog development in Victory Basin, Vermont. *Bull. Torrey Botan. Club* 118:399–411.

Bubier JL. 1995. The relationship of vegetation to methane emission and hydrochemical gradient in northern peatlands. *J. Ecol.* 83:403–20.

Bubier JL, Moore TR, Bledzki LA. 2007. Effects of nutrient addition on vegetation and carbon cycling in an ombrotrophic bog. *Glob. Change Biol.* 13:1168–86.

Calmé S, Desrochers A. 1999. Nested bird and micro-habitat assemblages in a peatland archipelago. *Oecologia* 118:361–70.

Calmé S, Desrochers A. 2000. Biogeographic aspects of the distribution of bird species breeding in Québec's peatlands. *J. Biogeogr.* 27:725–32.

Calmé S, Haddad S. 1996. Peatlands: a new habitat for the upland sandpiper, *Bartramia longicauda,* in eastern Canada. *Can. Field Natur.* 110:326–30.

Calmé S, Desrochers A, Savard JPL. 2002. Regional significance of peatlands for avifaunal diversity in southern Québec. *Biol. Conserv.* 107:273–81.

Camill P, Barry A, et al. 2009. Climate-vegetation-fire interactions and their impact on long-term carbon dynamics in a boreal peatland landscape in northern Manitoba, Canada. *J. Geophy. Res.* 114, G04017, DOI: 10.1029/2009JG001071.

Campbell D, Rochefort L. 2001. La végétation: gradients. In *Écologie des tourbières du Québec-Labrador,* Payette S, Rochefort L, editors. Sainte-Foy, Québec: Presses Univ. Laval., pp. 129–40.

Charman D. 2002. *Peatlands and environmental change.* Chichester, UK: John Wiley & Sons Ltd.

Clymo RS. 1963. Ion exchange in *Sphagnum* and its relation to bog ecology. *Ann. Bot.* 27:309–24.

Comas X, Slater L, Reeve A. 2008. Seasonal geophysical monitoring of biogenic gases in a northern peatland: implications for temporal and spatial variability in free phase gas production rates. *J. Geophys. Res.* 113, G01012, DOI: 10.1029/2007JG000575.

Conway VM. 1949. The bogs of central Minnesota. *Ecol. Monogr.* 19(2):173–206.

Crawford RMM. 1978. Metabolic adaptations to anoxia. In *Plant life in anaerobic environments,* Hook DD, Crawford RMM, editors. Ann Arbor, MI: Ann Arbor Sci. Publ., pp. 119–36.

Crawford RMM. 1993. Root survival in flooded soils. In *Mires: swamp, bog, fen and moor,* Ecosystems of the world, vol. 4A, Gore AJP, ed. Amsterdam: Elsevier, pp. 257–83.

Cronk JK, Fennessy MS. 2001. *Wetland plants: biology and ecology.* Boca Raton, FL: Lewis Pub.

Damman AWH. 1978. Distribution and movement of element in ombrotrophic peat bogs. *Oikos* 30:480–95.

Damman AWH. 1979. Geographic patterns in peatland development in eastern North America. In *Proceedings of the International Symposium on Classification of Peat and Peatlands,* Kivenen E, Heikurainen L, Pakarinen, editors. Hyytiala, Finland: Internat. Peat Soc., pp. 42–57.

Damman AWH, Dowhan JJ. 1981. Vegetation and habitat conditions in Western Head Bog, a southern Nova Scotian plateau bog. *Can. J. Bot.* 59:1343–59.

Desrochers A, van Duinen GA. 2006. Peatland fauna. In *Boreal peatland ecosystems,* Wieder RK, Vitt DH, editors. Berlin: Springer-Verlag, pp. 67–100.

Dever L, Hillaire-Marcel C, Fontes JC. 1984. Composition isotopique, géochimie et genèse de la glace en lentilles (Palsen) dans les tourbières au Nouveau Québec (Canada). *J. Hydrol.* 71:107–30.

Dever L, Laithier M, Hillaire-Marcel C. 1982. Caractéristiques isotopiques (^{18}O, $^{13}CO_2$, ^{3}H) des écoulements dans une tourbière sur pergélisol au Nouveau-Québec. *Can. J. Earth Sci.* 19:1255–63.

Devito KJ, Hill AR. 1997. Sulphate dynamics in relation to groundwater-surface water interactions in headwater wetlands of the southern Canadian shield. *Hydrol. Processes* 11:485–500.

Devito KJ, Waddington JM, Branfireun BA. 1997. Flow reversals in peatlands influenced by local groundwater systems. *Hydrol. Processes* 11:103–10.

Dise NB, Gorham E, Verry ES. 1993. Environmental factors controlling methane emissions from peatlands in Northern Minnesota. *J. Geophy. Res.* 98:10583–94.

DuRietz GE. 1949. Huvudenheter och huvudgränser i svensk myr-vegetation. (Main units and main limits in Swedish mire vegetation.) *Svensk Bot. Tidskrift* 48:274–309.

Eppinga MB, Rietkerk M, et al. 2010. Resource contrast in patterned peatlands increases along a climatic gradient. *Ecology* 91:2344–55.

Evans CD, Chapman PJ, et al. 2006. Alternative explanations for rising dissolved organic carbon export from organic soils. *Glob. Change Biol.* 12:2044–53.

Ferone JM, Devito KJ. 2004. Shallow groundwater–surface water interactions in pond-peatland complexes along a boreal plains topographic gradient. *J. Hydrol.* 292:75–95.

Folkerts GW. 1982. The Gulf coast pitcher plant bogs. *Am. Sci.* 70:260–67.

Fontaine N, Poulin M, Rochefort L. 2007. Plant diversity associated with pools in natural and restored peatlands. *Mires and Peat* 2: art. 6. www.mires-and-peat.net/map02/map_02_06.htm.

Forest S. 2001. *Peatland management and conservation in boreal Alberta, Canada.* MS thesis, Univ. Alberta, Edmonton.

Foster DR, Wright HE Jr., et al. 1988. Bog development and land-form dynamics in central Sweden and south-eastern Labrador, Canada. *J. Ecol.* 76:1164–85.

CJ, Roulet NT, Lafleur PM. 2001. Groundwater flow patterns in a large peatland. *J. Hydrol.* 246:142–54.

Freeman C, Evans CD, et al. 2001. Export of organic carbon from peat soils. *Nature* 412:785.

Freeman C, Fenner N, et al. 2004. Export of dissolved organic carbon from peatlands under elevated carbon dioxide levels. *Nature* 430:195–98.

Gignac LD. 1992. Niche structure, resource partitioning, and species interactions of mire bryophytes relative to climatic and ecological gradients in western Canada. *Bryologist* 95:406–18.

Glaser PH. 1992. Vegetation and water chemistry. In *Patterned peatlands of Minnesota,* Wright HE Jr., Coffin BA, Aaseng NE, editors. Minneapolis: Univ. Minnesota Press, pp. 15–44.

Glaser PH, Janssens JA. 1986. Raised bogs of eastern North America: transitions in landforms and gross stratigraphy. *Can. J. Bot.* 64:395–415.

Glaser PH, Janssens JA, Siegel DI. 1990. The response of vegetation to chemical and hydrological gradients in the Lost River peatland, northern Minnesota. *J. Ecol.* 78:1021–48.

Glaser PH, Chanton JP, et al. 2004. Surface deformations as indicators of deep ebullition fluxes in a large northern peatland. *Glob. Biogeochem. Cycles* 18, GB1003, DOI: 10.1029/2003GB002069.

Gorham E. 1953. Chemical studies on the soils and vegetation of waterlogged habitats in the English Lake District. *J. Ecol.* 41:345–60.

Gorham E. 1990. Biotic impoverishment in northern peatlands. In *The earth in transition: patterns and processes of biotic impoverishment,* Woodwell GM, editor. Cambridge: Cambridge Univ. Press, pp. 65–98.

Gorham E. 1991. Northern peatlands: role in the carbon cycle and probable responses to climatic warming. *Ecol. Appl.* 1:182–95.

Gorham E, Janssens JA. 1992. Concepts of fen and bog re-examined in relation to bryophyte cover and the acidity of surface waters. *Acta Soc. Botan. Poloniae* 61(1):7–20.

Gorham E, Janssens JA. 2005. The distribution and accumulation of chemical elements in five peat cores from the mid-continent to the eastern coast of North America. *Wetlands* 25:259–78.

Gotelli NJ, Ellison AM. 2002. Biogeography at a regional scale: determinants of ant species density in New England bogs and forests. *Ecology* 83:1604–09.

Grace JB. 1993. The adaptive significance of clonal reproduction in angiosperms: an aquatic perspective. *Aquat. Bot.* 44:159–80.

Graf MD, Rochefort L, Poulin M. 2008. Spontaneous revegetation of cutaway peatlands of North America. *Wetlands* 28:28–39.

Grime JP. 2001. *Plant strategies, vegetation processes, and ecosystem properties,* 2nd ed. Chichester, UK: John Wiley & Sons.

Groeneveld EVG, Massé A, Rochefort L. 2007. *Polytrichum strictum* as a nurse-plant in peatland restoration. *Restor. Ecol.* 15:709–19.

Hayward PM, Clymo RS. 1982. Profiles of water content and pore size in *Sphagnum* peat and their relation to peat bog ecology. *Proc. Royal Soc. London,* Ser. B, 215:299–325.

Hoag RS, Price JS. 1995. A field-scale, natural gradient solute transport experiment in peat at a Newfoundland blanket bog. *J. Hydrol.* 172(1–4):171–84.

Hogan JM, van der Kamp G, et al. 2006. Field methods for measuring hydraulic properties of peat deposits. *Hydrol. Processes* 20:3635–49.

Ingram HAP. 1978. Soil layers in mires: function and terminology. *J. Soil Sci.* 29:224–27.

Ingram HAP. 1983. Hydrology. In *Mires: Swamp, Bog, Fen and Moor,* Gore AJP, editor. New York: Elsevier, pp. 67–158.

IPCC (Intergovernmental Panel on Climate Change). 2007. *Climate change 2007: the physical science basis: contribution of Working Group I to the Fourth Assessment Report of the Intergovernmental Panel on Climate Change,* Solomon S, Qin D, et al., editors. Cambridge, New York: Cambridge Univ. Press.

Janssens JA, Glaser PH. 1986. The bryophyte flora and major peat-forming mosses at Red Lake Peatland, Minnesota. *Can. J. Bot.* 64:427–42.

Johnson LC, Damman AW. 1993. Decay and its regulation in *Sphagnum* peatlands. *Adv. Bryol.* 5:249–96.

Karofeld E. 1998. The dynamics of the formation and development of hollows in raised bogs in Estonia. *The Holocene* 8:697–704.

Karofeld E, Toom M. 1999. Mud-bottoms in Männikjarve bog, central Estonia. *Proc. Estonian Acad. Sci. Biol./Ecol.* 48(3):216–35.

Keller J, Bauers AK, et al. 2006. Nutrient control of microbial carbon cycling along an ombrotrophic-minerotrophic peatland gradient. *J. Geophys. Res.* 111, G03006, DOI: 10.1029/2005JG000152.

Keller JK, Bridgham SD, et al. 2005. Limited effects of six years of fertilization on carbon mineralization dynamics in a Minnesota fen. *Soil Biol. Biochem.* 37:1197–1204.

Kellogg LE, Bridgham SD. 2003. Phosphorus retention and movement across an ombrotrophic-minerotrophic peatland gradient. *Biogeochemistry* 63:299–315.

Kim J, Verma SB. 1996. Surface exchange of water vapor between an open *Sphagnum* fen and the atmosphere. *Boundary-Layer Meteorol.* 79:243–64.

Kuhry P. 1994. The role of fire in the development of *Sphagnum*-dominated peatlands in western boreal Canada. *J. Ecol.* 82:899–910.

Kuhry P, Turunen J. 2006. The postglacial development of boreal and subarctic peatlands. In *Boreal peatlands ecosystems,* vol. 188, Wieder RK, Vitt DH, editors. Berlin: Springer-Verlag, pp. 25–46.

Lachance D, Lavoie C, Desrochers A. 2005. The impact of peatland afforestation on plant and bird diversity in southeastern Québec. *Écoscience* 12:161–71.

Lafleur PM, Roulet NT. 1992. A comparison of evaporation rates from two fens of the Hudson Bay lowland. *Aquat. Bot.* 44:59–69.

Lafleur PM, Hember RA, et al. 2005. Annual and seasonal variability in evapotranspiration and water table at a shrub-covered bog in southern Ontario, Canada. *Hydrol. Processes* 19:3533–50.

Laine J, Vanha-Majamaa I. 1992. Vegetation ecology along a trophic gradient on drained pine mires in southern Finland. *Ann. Bot. Fennici* 29:213–33.

Laine J, Komulainen V-M, et al. 2004. *Lakkasuo—a guide to mire ecosystem.* Publ. Dept. Forest Ecology, Univ. Helsinki 31.

Lavoie C, Pellerin S. 2007. Fires in temperate peatlands (southern Quebec): past and recent trends. *Can. J. Bot.* 85:263–72.

Letts MG, Roulet NT, et al. 2000. Parameterization of peatland hydraulic properties for the Canadian Land Surface Scheme. *Atmosphere-Ocean* 38:141–60.

Leuven RSEW, den Hartog C, et al. 1986. Effects of water acidification on the distribution pattern and the reproductive success of amphibians. *Experienta* 42:495–503.

Limpens J, Berendse F. 2003. Growth reduction of *Sphagnum magellanicum* subjected to high nitrogen deposition: the role of amino acid nitrogen concentration. *Oecologia* 135:339–45.

Limpens J, Heijmans MMPD, Berendse F. 2006. The nitrogen cycle in boreal peatlands. In *Boreal peatland ecosystems,* Wieder RK, Vitt DH, editors. New York: Springer, pp. 195–230.

Limpens J, Granath G, et al. 2011. Climatic modifiers of the response to nitrogen deposition in peat-forming *Sphagnum* mosses: a meta-analysis. *New Phytologist* (2011), doi: 10.1111/j.1469-8137.2011.03680.x.

Lindsay R. 1996. Thèmes pour l'avenir: les tourbières, un rôle clé pour la convention Ramsar. In *La conservation mondiale des tourbières: compte-rendu d'un atelier international,* Rubec CDA, editor. Union mondiale de la conservation de la nature (UICN), Service canadien de la faune, Environnement Canada, Gouvernement de la Norvège, Groupe international pour la conservation des tourbières et Société internationale de la tourbe, Ottawa, Rapport no. 96–1:7–10.

Luken JO. 1985. Zonation of *Sphagnum* mosses: interactions among shoot growth, growth form, and water balance. *Bryologist* 88:374–79.

Lund M, Christensen TR, et al. 2009. Effect of N and P fertilization on the greenhouse gas exchange in two northern peatland with contrasting N deposition rates. *Biogeosciences* 6:2135–44.

Malmer N. 1986. Vegetational gradients in relation to environmental conditions in northwestern European mires. *Can. J. Bot.* 64:375–83.

Malmer N, Svensson BM, Wallén B. 1994. Interactions between *Sphagnum* mosses and field layer vascular plants in the development of peat-forming systems. *Folia Geobot. Phytotax.* 29:483–96.

Malmer N, Albinsson C, et al. 2003. Interferences between *Sphagnum* and vascular plants: effects on plant community structure and peat formation. *Oikos* 100:469–82.

Mazerolle MJ. 2003. Detrimental effects of peat mining on amphibian abundance and species richness in bogs. *Biol. Conserv.* 113:215–23.

Mazerolle M, Cormier M. 2003. Effects of peat mining intensity on green frog *(Rana clamitans)* occurrence in bog ponds. *Wetlands* 23:709–16.

Mazerolle MJ, Drolet B, Desrochers A. 2001. Small-mammal responses to peat mining of southeastern Canadian bogs. *Can. J. Zool.* 79:296–302.

Milakoff Fletcher SE, Tans PP, et al. 2004. CH_4 sources estimated from atmospheric observations of CH_4 and its C-13/C-12 isotopic ratios: 2. Inverse modeling of CH_4 from geographical regions. *Glob. Biogeochem. Cycles* 18, GB4005, DOI: 10.1029/2004GB002224.

Mitchell CPJ, Branfireun BA, Kolka RK. 2009. Methylmercury dynamics at the upland-peatland interface: topographic and hydrogeochemical controls. *Wat. Resour. Res.* 45, W02406, DOI: 10.1029/2008WR006832.

Montague TG, Givnish TJ. 1996. Distribution of black spruce versus eastern larch along peatland gradients: relationship to relative stature, growth rate, and shade tolerance. *Can. J. Bot.* 74:1514–32.

Morrison RIG, Aubry Y, et al. 2001. Declines in North American shorebird populations. *Wader Study Group Bull.* 94:39–43.

National Wetlands Working Group. 1997. *The Canadian wetland classification system,* 2nd ed., Warner BG, Rubec CDA, editors. Waterloo, ON: Wetlands Research Centre, Univ. Waterloo.

Nicholson BD, Vitt DH. 1990. The paleoecology of a peatland complex in continental western Canada. *Can. J. Bot.* 68:121–38.

Nilsson M, Sagerfors J, et al. 2008. Contemporary carbon accumulation in a boreal oligotrophic minerogenir mire—a significant sink after accounting for all C-fluxes. *Glob. Change Biol.* 14:2317–32.

Noss R. 1990. Indicators for monitoring biodiversity: a hierarchical approach. *Conserv. Biol.* 4:355–64.

Økland RH, Økland T, Rydgren K. 2001. A Scandinavian perspective on ecological gradients in north-west European mires: reply to Wheeler and Proctor. *J. Ecol.* 89:481–86.

Payette S. 2001. Les principaux types de tourbières. In *Écologie des tourbières du Québec-Labrador,* Payette S, Rochefort L, editors. Sainte-Foy, Québec: Presses Univ. Laval. pp. 39–89.

Payette S, Rochefort L, editors. 2001. *Écologie des tourbières du Québec-Labrador.* Sainte-Foy, Québec: Presses Univ. Laval.

Pellerin S, Lavoie C. 2003. Reconstructing the recent dynamics of mires using a multitechnique approach. *J. Ecol.* 91:1008–21.

Petrone RM, Devito K, et al. 2008. Importance of seasonal frost to peat water storage: western boreal plains, Canada. Groundwater–Surface Water Interactions: Process Understanding, Conceptualization and Modelling. In *Proceedings of Symposium HS1002 at IUGG 2007,* Perugia, July 2007. IAHS Publ. 321:61–66.

Petrone RM, Silins U, Devito KJ. 2007. Dynamics of evapotranspiration from a riparian pond complex in the western boreal forest, Alberta, Canada. *Hydrol. Processes* 21:1391–1401.

Pough FH. 1976. Acid precipitation and embryonic mortality of spotted salamanders, *Ambystoma maculatum. Science* 192(4234):68–70.

Poulin M., Bélisle M., Cabeza M. 2005. Within-site habitat configuration in reserve design: a case study with a peatland bird. *Biol. Conserv.* 128:55–66.

Poulin M, Careau D, et al. 2002. From satellite imagery to peatland vegetation diversity: how reliable are habitat maps? *Conserv. Ecol.* 6(2):16. www.consecol.org/vol6/iss2/art16.

Poulin M, Rochefort L, Desrochers A. 1999. Conservation of bog plant species assemblages: assessing the role of natural remnants in mined sites. *Appl. Veg. Sci.* 2:169–80.

Poulin M, Rochefort L, et al. 2004. Threats and protection for peatlands in eastern Canada. *Géocarrefour* 79:331–344.

Poulin M, Rochefort L, et al. 2005. Spontaneous revegetation of mined peatlands in eastern Canada. *Can. J. Bot.* 83:539–57.

Pouliot R, Rochefort L, Karofeld E. 2011. Initiation of microtopography in re-vegetated cutover peatlands: evolution of plant species composition. *Appl. Veg. Sci.,* Doi: 10.1111/j.1654-109X.2011.01164.x.

Pressey RL, Taffs KH. 2001. Scheduling conservation action in production landscapes: priority areas in western New South Wales defined by irreplaceability and vulnerability to vegetation loss. *Biol. Conserv.* 100:355–76.

Price JS. 1987. The influence of wetland and mineral terrain types on snowmelt runoff in the subarctic. *Can. Water Resour. J.* 12:43–52.

Price JS. 2003. Role and character of seasonal peat soil deformation on the hydrology of undisturbed and cutover peatlands. *Water Resour. Res.* 39(9):1241, DOI: 10.1029/2002WR001302.

Price JS, FitzGibbon JE. 1987. Groundwater storage—streamflow relations during winter in a subarctic wetland, Saskatchewan. *Can. J. Earth Sci.* 24:2047–81.

Price JS, Maloney DA. 1994. Hydrology of a patterned bog-fen complex in southeastern Labrador, Canada. *Nordic Hydrol.* 25:313–30.

Price JS, Schlotzhauer SM. 1999. Importance of shrinkage and compression in determining water storage changes in peat: the case of a mined peatland. *Hydrol. Processes* 13:2591–601.

Price JS, Woo MK. 1988. Studies of a subarctic coastal marsh. I. Hydrology. *J. Hydrol.* 103:275–92.

Price JS, Whittington PN, et al. 2008. Determining unsaturated hydraulic conductivity in living and undecomposed *Sphagnum* moss hummocks. *Soil Sci. Soc. Am. J.* 72:487–91.

Price JS, Edwards TWD, et al. 2009. Physical and isotopic characterization of evaporation from *Sphagnum* moss. *J. Hydrol.* 369:175–82.

Quinton WL, Hayashi M. 2005. The flow and storage of water in the wetland-dominated central Mackenzie River basin: recent advances and future directions. In *Prediction in ungauged basins: approaches for Canada's cold regions,* Spence C, Pomeroy JW, Pietroniro A, editors. Can. Water Resour. Assoc., pp. 45–66.

Quinton WL, Roulet NT. 1998. Spring and summer runoff hydrology of a subarctic patterned wetland. *Arct. Alp. Res.* 30:285–94.

Quinton WL, Hayashi M, Carey SK. 2008. Peat hydraulic conductivity in cold regions and its relation to pore size and geometry. *Hydrol. Processes* 22:2829–37.

Robinson SD, Moore TR. 2000. The influence of permafrost and fire upon carbon accumulation in high boreal peatlands, Northwest Territories, Canada. *Arct. Antarct. Alpe. Res.* 32:155–66.

Rothwell RL, Silins U, Hillman GR. 1996. The effects of drainage on substrate water content at several forested Alberta peatlands. *Can. J. For. Res.* 26:53–62.

Roulet NT, Lafleur PM, et al. 2007. Contemporary carbon balance and Holocene carbon accumulation in a northern peatland. *Glob. Change Biol.* 13:397–411.

Rubec CDA. 1991. Peat resources use in Canada: a national conservation issue. In *Peat and peatlands: the resource and its utilization. Proceedings of the International Peat Symposium, Duluth, Minnesota, 19–23 August 1991,* Grubich DN, Malterer TJ, editors.

Rubec C. 1996. The status of peatland resources in Canada. In *Global peat resources,* Lappalainen E, editor. Jyskä, Finland: Internat. Peat Soc., pp. 243–52.

Rydin H. 1985. Effect of water level on desiccation of *Sphagnum* in relation to surrounding Sphagna. *Oikos* 45:374–79.

Rydin H, Jeglum J. 2006. *The biology of peatlands.* Oxford: Oxford Univ. Press.

Saarnio S, Morero M, et al. 2007. Annual CO_2 and CH_4 fluxes of pristine boreal mires as a background for the lifecycle analyses of peat energy. *Boreal Env. Res.* 12:101–13.

Sagot C, Rochefort L. 1996. Tolérance des sphaignes à la dessiccation. *Cryptogamie, Bryol.-Lichénol.* 17:171–83.

Sauer JR, Hines JE, Fallon J. 2008. *The North American Breeding Bird Survey: results and analysis, 1966–2007* (version 5.15.2008). Laurel, MD: USGS Patuxent Wildl. Res. Center.

Schneider R, Dyer S. 2006. *Death by a thousand cuts: impact of in situ oil sands development on Alberta's boreal forest.* Pembina Institute. www.pembina.org; www.cpaws-sask.org/common/pdfs/Death_by_thousand_cuts.pdf.

Seppälä M, Koutaniemi L. 1985. Formation of a string and pool topography as expressed by morphology, stratigraphy and current processes on a peatland in Kuusamo, Finland. *Boreas* 14:287–309.

Sjörs H. 1948. Myrvegetation i Bergslagen. (Mire vegetation in Bergslagen, Sweden.) *Acta Phytogeogr. Suecica* 21:1–299.

Sjörs H. 1950. On the relation between vegetation and electrolytes in north Swedish mire waters. *Oikos* 2:241–57.

Sjörs H. 1963. Bogs and fen on Attawapiskat River, northern Ontario. *Bull. Nat. Mus. Can.* 186:45–133.

Spitzer K, Danks HV. 2006. Insect biodiversity of boreal peat bogs. *Annu. Rev. Ent.* 51:137–61.

Strack M, Waddington JM. 2007. Response of peatland carbon dioxide and methane fluxes to a water table drawdown experiment. *Glob. Biogeochem. Cycles* 21, GB1007, DOI: 10.1029/2006GB002715.

Strack M, Kellner E, Waddington JM. 2005. Dynamics of biogenic gas bubbles in peat and their effects on peatland biogeochemistry. *Glob. Biogeochem. Cycles* 19, GB1003, DOI: 10.1029/2004GB002330.

Sullivan PF, Arens SJT, et al. 2008. Temperature and microtopography interact to control carbon cycling in a high arctic fen. *Ecosystems* 11:61–76.

Sundberg S, Hansson J, Rydin H. 2006. Colonization of *Sphagnum* on land uplift islands in the Baltic Sea: time, area, distance and life history. *J. Biogeogr.* 33:1479–91.

Swanson DK, Grigal DF. 1988. A simulation model of mire patterning. *Oikos* 53:309–14.

Tallis JH, Livett EA. 1994. Pool-and-hummock patterning in a southern Pennine blanket mire. I. Stratigraphic profiles for the last 2800 years. *J. Ecol.* 82:775–88.

Thormann MN, Currah RS, Bayley SE. 1999. The mycorrhizal status of the dominant vegetation along a peatland gradient in southern boreal Alberta, Canada. *Wetlands* 19:438–50.

Tiiva P, Faubert P, et al. 2009. Contribution of vegetation and water table on isoprene emission from boreal peatland microcosms. *Atmos. Env.* 43:5469–75.

Tuittila E-S, Komulainen V-M, et al. 2000. Methane dynamics of a restored cut-away peatland. *Glob. Change Biol.* 6:569–81.

Turetsky MR, Wieder RK. 2001. A direct approach to quantifying organic matter lost as a result of peatland wildfire. *Can. J. For. Res.* 31:363–66.

Turetsky MR, Amiro BD, et al. 2004. Historical burn area in western Canadian peatlands and its relationship to fire weather indices. *Glob. Biogeochem. Cycles* 18, GB4014, DOI: 10.1029/2004GB002222.

Turetsky MR, Wieder RK, et al. 2002. Current disturbance and the diminishing peatland carbon sink. *Geophy. Res. Letters* 29, 1526, DOI: 10.1029/2001GL014000.

Turunen J, Tomppo E, et al. 2002. Estimating carbon accumulation rates of undrained mires in Finland—application to boreal and subarctic regions. *Holocene* 12:69–80.

van Breemen N. 1995. How *Sphagnum* bogs down other plants. *Trends Ecol. Evol.* 10:270–75.

Vasander JH, Laiho R. 1995. Long-term effects of water level drawdown on the vegetation of drained pine mires in southern Finland. *J. Appl. Ecol.* 32:785–802.

Vitt DH. 1990. Growth and production dynamics of boreal mosses over climatic, chemical and topographic gradients. *Bot. J. Linnean Soc.* 104:35–59.

Vitt DH. 2000. Peatlands: ecosystems dominated by bryophytes. In *Bryophyte biology,* Shaw AJ, Goffinet B, editors. Cambridge: Cambridge Univ. Press, pp. 312–43.

Vitt DH. 2006. Functional characteristics and indicators of boreal peatlands. In *Boreal peatland systems,* Wieder RK, Vitt DH, editors. Berlin: Springer-Verlag, pp. 9–24.

Vitt DH, Chee W-L. 1990. The relationship of vegetation to surface water chemistry and peat chemisty in fens of Alberta, Canada. *Vegetatio* 89:87–106.

Vitt DH, Slack NG. 1984. Niche diversification of *Sphagnum* relative to environmental factors in northern Minnesota peatlands. *Can. J. Bot.* 62:1409–30.

Vitt DH, Achuff P, Andrus RE. 1975. The vegetation and chemical properties of patterned fens in the Swan Kills, north central Alberta. *Can. J. Bot.* 53:2776–95.

Vitt DH, Bayley SE, Jin T-L. 1995. Seasonal variation in water chemistry over a bog-rich fen gradient in continental western Canada. *Can. J. Fish. Aquat. Sci.* 52:587–606.

Vitt DH, Crum HA, Snider JA. 1975. The vertical zonation of *Sphagnum* species in hummock-hollow complexes in northern Michigan. *Michigan Bot.* 14:190–200.

Vitt DH, Halsey LA, Zoltai SC. 1994. The bog landforms of continental Canada in relation to climate and permafrost patterns. *Arct. Alp. Res.* 26:1–13.

Vitt DH, Halsey LA, et al. 1996. *Peatland inventory of Alberta.* Alberta Peat Task Force, National Center of Excellence in Sustainable Forest Management, Univ. Alberta, Edmonton.

Waddington JM, Roulet NT. 1996. Atmosphere-wetland carbon exchanges: scale dependency on CO_2 and CH_4 exchange on the developmental topography of a peatland. *Glob. Biogeochem. Cycles* 10:233–45.

Waddington JM, Roulet NT. 2000. Carbon balance of a boreal patterned peatland. *Glob. Change Biol.* 6:87–97.

Waddington JM, Harrison K, et al. 2009. Effect of atmospheric pressure and temperature on entrapped gas content in peat. *Hydrol. Processes* 23:2970–80.

Waddington JM, Roulet NT, Swanson RV. 1996. Water table control of CH_4 emission enhancement by vascular plants in boreal peatlands. *J. Geophy. Res.* 101:22775–85.

Wagner DJ, Titus JE. 1984. Comparative desiccation tolerance of two *Sphagnum* mosses. *Oecologia* 62:182–87.

Weltzin JF, Harth C, et al. 2001. Production and microtopography of bog bryophytes: response to warming and water-table manipulations. *Oecologia* 128:557–65.

Wheeler BD, Proctor MCF. 2000. Ecological gradients, subdivisions and terminology of north-west European mires. *J. Ecol.* 88:187–203.

Whittington PN, Price JS. 2006. The effects of water table drawdown (as a surrogate for climate change) on the hydrology of a patterned fen peatland near Quebec City, Quebec. *Hydrol. Processes* 20:3589–600.

Wieder RK, Scott KD, et al. 2009. Postfire carbon balance in boreal bogs of Alberta, Canada. *Glob. Change Biol.* 15:63–81.

Wood JT. 1955. The nesting of the four-toed salamander, *Hemidactylium scutatum* (Schlegel), in Virginia. *Am. Midl. Natur.* 53:381–89.

Worrall F, Burt T, Adamson J. 2004. Can climate change explain increases in DOC flux from upland peat catchments? *Sci. Total Env.* 326:95–112.

CHAPTER 10

Northeastern Seasonal Woodland Pools

ARAM J. K. CALHOUN, MEGAN K. GAHL, and ROBERT F. BALDWIN

Seasonal woodland pools (also known as vernal pools or ephemeral isolated wetlands) have been called the "jewels in the crown" of northeastern landscapes (Hunter 2008). Woodland pools, often less than 0.5 ha in size, may function as keystone ecosystems by enhancing local and regional biodiversity, serving as aquatic stepping stones for dispersers across taxa, and by exporting substantial amounts of secondary production (in the form of amphibian biomass to adjacent ecosystems) (Gibbons, Winne, et al. 2006). Seasonal woodland pools are regulated in our region primarily as specialized amphibian breeding habitat, as they provide optimal breeding conditions for wood frogs *(Lithobates sylvaticus)* and ambystomatid salamanders *(Ambystoma* spp.), which are adapted to development in fishless waters. However, their ecological role far exceeds the pool boundary. Pools are open systems, much like salt marshes, where nutrients and energy are exchanged between the adjacent forested matrix and other wetland systems. Furthermore, the amphibians that typically breed in these pools spend the majority of their lives in terrestrial habitat, often migrating to and from pools at the scale of hundreds of meters (with dispersal distances being measured in kilometers) (Berven and Grudzien 1990; Smith and Green 2005).

Conservation of seasonal woodland pool ecosystems requires management of both terrestrial and wetland ecosystems. This complexity poses conservation challenges to resource managers and biologists alike. To better understand these challenges, a firm grasp of the complexity of pool systems is required. Accordingly, the goals of this chapter are to (1) present key concepts pertaining to the environment within the pool (hydrology, biogeochemistry, dominant flora and fauna, and key ecological processes); (2) explore linkages among pools and the terrestrial realm; and (3) to identify key challenges and solutions to maintaining seasonal woodland pool functions in developing landscapes.

Geology, Hydrology, and Geochemistry

Geologic Setting

In glaciated northeastern North America, seasonal woodland pools generally have temporary to semipermanent water

regimes occurring in shallow depressions (ranging from as little as 100 m^2 to 0.8 ha). Pools typically fill with snowmelt or precipitation during the spring or fall and may dry during the summer or in drought years. The spatial configuration of pools in northeastern landscapes varies regionally as influenced by topography, surficial geology, and climate. Reported pool densities in the northeastern U.S. range from 0.2 to 5 pools per km^2 (Calhoun, Walls, et al. 2003; Skidds and Golet 2005), but this may vary geographically. Most seasonal woodland pools are associated with morainal and lacustrine glacial deposits (Palik, Buech, et al. 2003; Rheinhardt and Hollands 2008).

Seasonal woodland pools occur in five major geomorphic settings, depending on topographic position and surficial geology (Rheinhardt and Hollands 2008): (1) depression, (2) slope, (3) flats, (4) riverine, and (5) anthropogenic (Table 10.1). Each geomorphic setting also has subclasses based on surficial geology (bedrock, till, drift) and water source (precipitation, groundwater, overbank flow). Pools associated with till tend to rely on precipitation for water. Pools underlain with stratified drift have moderate to high permeability and may have some groundwater exchange (Rheinhardt and Hollands 2008). In slope settings, groundwater input is typically through seeps and springs. In riverine floodplain settings, most pools fill with surficial water through overbank flow, but often intercept groundwater (Rheinhardt and Hollands 2008).

Hydrology

WATER SOURCES AND DURATION OF FLOODING

Because seasonal woodland pools are not permanently connected to open water bodies such as lakes or rivers, their primary water source is either precipitation (especially for perched pools on tills or clay deposits) or through groundwater exchange (particularly for pools with organic soils or outwash materials), although pools associated with riverine floodplains can fill with surface water through overbank flow. In the Northeast, pools primarily fill from snowmelt and from spring and fall rains, and dry during the mid- to late summer. Subsidies from regional groundwater inputs or hydrologic connec-

Major geomorphic settings in which seasonal woodland pools occur

Geomorphic setting	Pool description
Depression	Concave landforms surrounded by higher elevation; low-energy sedimentary environments
Slope	Perched on an incline; downslope, unidirectional flows dominate hydrodynamics
Flats	Located in low-relief landscapes; usually underlain by low-permeability glacio-lacustrine deposits
Riverine	Pools in headwater streams may occur in steplike series with other pools; seasonal connection between pools; formed by tree tip-ups, abandoned beaver dams, debris dams, or years of frost heaving
	Pools associated with floodplains are usually filled or created by overbank flooding in scour, abandoned, or high-flow channels
Anthropogenic	Excavated or impounded by human activity, such as abandoned borrow pits, quarries, drainage ditches, skidder ruts, or detention basins

tions with permanent water bodies are typically ephemeral (Leibowitz and Brooks 2008). Inputs from local groundwater sources are largely unknown, primarily because so few studies have developed water budgets for these small systems. Overall, groundwater inputs are considered minor and drawn from shallow, adjacent sources (Brooks 2009).

Local-scale climate patterns of precipitation and temperature have significant effects on the hydrology of these small systems because the hydrology of pools is largely a function of precipitation and evapotranspiration. This can cause considerable annual variation in hydroperiod (Boone, Johnson, et al. 2006; Brooks 2009). Regardless, because pool hydrology also reflects geomorphic settings, which do not vary annually, pools can be generally categorized into five broad inundation regimes depending on when they dry (short-cycle, long-cycle, semipermanent) and when they refill (spring or fall; Fig. 10.1a) (Colburn 2004).

EFFECTS OF HYDROLOGY ON POOL COMMUNITIES

Seasonal shifts in pool hydrology are the driving mechanism in structuring pool communities, both biotic and abiotic components. Different inundation regimes show marked effects on the geochemical environment, rate of litter breakdown (Inkley, Wissinger, et al. 2008), composition and richness of invertebrate (Brooks 2000; Batzer, Palik, et al. 2004; Colburn, Weeks, et al. 2008) and plant (Palik, Streblow, et al. 2007) communities, and composition and breeding success of pool-breeding amphibians (Brodman, Ogger, et al. 2003; Baldwin, Calhoun, et al. 2006a). For example, longer-hydroperiod pools may develop deep organic substrates and will support amphibians such as *Ambystoma* salamanders and spring peepers *(Pseudacris crucifer)*, which require longer development times than other pool-breeding species. In contrast, shorter-hydroperiod pools typically have leaf litter substrates and may support only wood frogs *(Lithobates sylvaticus)*, which can develop relatively quickly (although they may not develop quickly enough in some years). In addition, these systems often contain highly specialized biota (with the exception of plants) because of the

adaptations and plasticity necessary for survival in such an ephemeral and variable environment (Snodgrass, Komoroski, et al. 2000; Babbitt, Baber, et al. 2003).

In general, duration of inundation can influence the diversity of a resident community and the dominant community-structuring mechanism. Longer-hydroperiod pools typically have higher richness and diversity of invertebrates (Schneider 1999; Batzer, Palik, et al. 2004), plants (Palik, Streblow, et al. 2007), and amphibians (Sadinski and Dunson 1992; Rowe and Dunson 1993; Snodgrass, Komoroski, et al. 2000) (Fig. 10.1b). These longer-duration pools are increasingly structured by biotic interactions, primarily competition and predation, because of their increasing diversity (Fig. 10.1b). In contrast, short-duration pools are structured primarily by abiotic factors and associated adaptations to pool hydroperiod, with only a few species typically interacting with conspecifics. The longest-duration pools are likely structured by predation, as increasing numbers of predaceous invertebrates that are habitat generalists colonize pools (Schneider 1999).

Geochemistry

Northeastern seasonal woodland pools tend to be oligotrophic and acidic because the greatest proportion of their water comes from precipitation. Exceptions to this are pools located in disturbed watersheds, which may have more water from surface runoff and, therefore, have higher pH and greater algal biomass than those in more pristine locations (Colburn 2004; Carrino-Kyker and Swanson 2007). In addition, dissolved oxygen is generally low because pools are small, which subjects them to influences on oxygen such as high atmospheric diffusion, algal photosynthesis, variable temperatures, soil respiration, and litter decomposition. However, pools exhibit high variation in physical and chemical attributes even within a local area. This variability has been attributed to diurnal fluctuations, shallow water depths, temporary hydroperiod, biological processes, and variability in water sources, as well as small areas (Bonner, Diehl, et al. 1997; Colburn 2004; Carrino-Kyker and Swanson 2007).

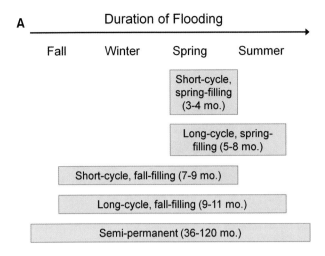

A
Duration of Flooding

Fall   Winter   Spring   Summer

Short-cycle, spring-filling (3-4 mo.)

Long-cycle, spring-filling (5-8 mo.)

Short-cycle, fall-filling (7-9 mo.)

Long-cycle, fall-filling (9-11 mo.)

Semi-permanent (36-120 mo.)

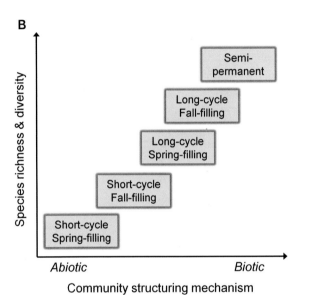

B

Species richness & diversity

Semi-permanent

Long-cycle Fall-filling

Long-cycle Spring-filling

Short-cycle Fall-filling

Short-cycle Spring-filling

Abiotic   *Biotic*

Community structuring mechanism

FIG. 10.1. A. General seasonal woodland pool inundation regimes. (Following Colburn 2004.) B. Relationship of pool hydroperiod to dominant community-structuring mechanisms and species richness and diversity.

DIURNAL AND SEASONAL VARIATION

Diurnal fluctuations in pools are often stronger than those in larger wetland or pond systems because of their small size and shallow depth, which results in a strong response to local climatic patterns. Dissolved oxygen, carbon dioxide, and water temperature exhibit the largest diurnal fluctuations. Substantial diurnal fluctuations of dissolved oxygen are caused by (1) light availability throughout the water column that initiates photosynthesis; and (2) community respiration overnight, which can drive dissolved oxygen levels to anoxia in some pools. Carbon dioxide also exhibits strong diurnal fluctuations, caused by community respiration and temperature, with higher carbon dioxide levels overnight in most pools. Acidity can also fluctuate diurnally, but northeastern seasonal woodland pools tend to be well buffered by naturally occurring organic acids, and, therefore, many pools exhibit little pH fluctuation.

Seasonal fluctuations in geochemistry in seasonal woodland pools are largely driven by snowmelt, pool evaporation, and pool refill. In pools with high amphibian biomass, geochemical changes can also result from the mass migration of metamorphs from the aquatic system, which can significantly increase algal production (Seale 1980; MK Gahl unpublished data). Snowmelt and spring rains drive the early spring water chemistry of pools and often result in a strong acid pulse event combined with low conductivity (Fig. 10.2). Water depth is usually at its highest, and therefore most solutes are relatively dilute (Gahl and Calhoun 2010). As pools evaporate in midsummer, water temperature increases and most other solutes become more concentrated (Fig. 10.2) (Gahl and Calhoun 2010). In contrast, dissolved oxygen typically decreases over the summer as seasonal pool fauna colonize, grow larger, and increase activity (Bonner, Diehl, et al. 1997; Carrino-Kyker and Swanson 2007). Pool drying changes the sediment environment from reducing to oxidizing. When pools refill from a dry basin, episodic hydrological flowpaths reactivate and mobilize accumulated reactants such as methyl-mercury and aluminum into the aquatic system (Wetzel 2001; McClain, Boyer, et al. 2003).

EFFECTS OF GEOCHEMISTRY ON POOL COMMUNITIES

Most research to date on geochemistry in seasonal woodland pools has focused on using water chemistry to predict species assemblages (Rowe and Dunson 1993; Hecnar and M'Closkey 1996; Brodman, Ogger, et al. 2003) or on toxicity to amphibians (Freda and Dunson 1986; Rowe, Sadinski, et al. 1992). Dissolved organic carbon, metals, and pH are the most important factors for both toxicological effects and for shaping community structure (Horne and Dunson 1995). Algal communities are largely determined by these three components, but invertebrate communities do not seem to be as sensitive to pool geochemistry (Horne and Dunson 1995; Batzer, Palik, et al. 2004). Low pH and short hydroperiods may be important in shaping amphibian communities in pools, but this is not consistent across all studies, primarily because low pH does not typically limit breeding success of wood frogs or spotted salamanders (*Ambystoma maculatum*), two key pool-breeding amphibians (Sadinski and Dunson 1992; Rowe and Dunson 1993).

Vegetation

There are few, if any, known obligate seasonal woodland pool plant species (e.g., featherfoil, *Hottonia inflata*), with most pools being dominated by cosmopolitan species (for an extensive list of plants associated with pools in northeastern North America, see Cutko and Rawinski 2008). Vegetation composition may not be a defining biotic feature of pools (Batzer, Palik, et al. 2004), but structural diversity provided by plants is important for ovipositing amphibians and emerging invertebrates, as substrate for algae and biofilms consumed by herbivores, and as cover for larval amphibians (deMaynadier and Houlahan 2008).

In general, pools are difficult to classify by vegetation type alone, as floristic patterns generally reflect local pool physical conditions (e.g., substrate, depth, hydroperiod, chemistry, size, canopy cover, local seed sources) and biogeophysical region (Cutko 1997; Cutko and Rawinski 2008). Palik, Streblow, et al.

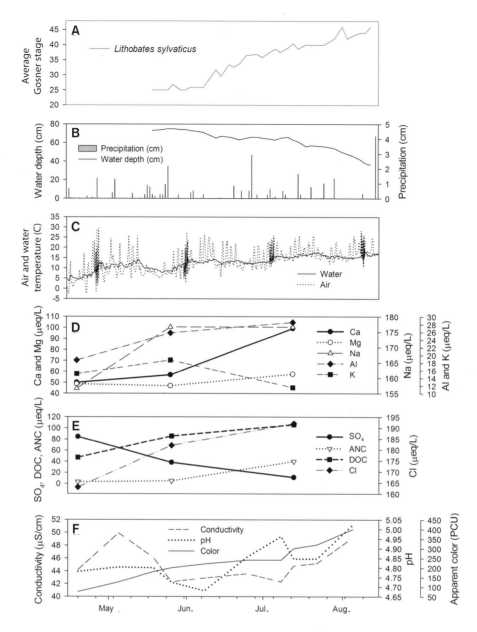

FIG. 10.2. Seasonal changes in water chemistry from a seasonal woodland pool in Acadia National Park, Maine (2004), and the relationship to amphibian development and local climate patterns. A. Average Gosner stage of wood frog larvae. B. Water depth and precipitation. C. Water and air temperature. D. Cation concentration. E. Anion and dissolved organic carbon concentrations and acid-neutralizing capacity. F. Conductivity, pH, and apparent color (platinum-cobalt units). (Modified from Gahl and Calhoun 2010.)

(2007) studied 64 seasonal pools in Minnesota and quantified the range of variation in plant communities. They found that pool-scale physical parameters were generally highly variable among pools and collectively explained a larger portion of the differences in plant functional groups as compared to glacial landform and land vegetation class. Attempts to classify seasonal woodland pools are limited overall, but those that exist classify pools by plant structure and/or composition (e.g., forested wetland, shrub swamp, coniferous swamp pools, water willow pools, aquatic vegetation; Colburn 2004) or landscape setting as a proxy (e.g., floodplain pool, wetland complex, or upland isolated; Calhoun and deMaynadier 2008). Although few plants serve as ecosystem indicators, seasonal woodland pool plant communities contribute to regional biodiversity

and may harbor rare or listed plants. In northeastern North America, for example, 20 at-risk species are closely associated with "isolated" wetlands, including seasonal woodland pools (Comer, Goodin, et al. 2005).

Fauna

Invertebrates

Invertebrates may well be the backbone of seasonal pool ecosystems. Hundreds of invertebrate species are associated with seasonal woodland pools, as compared to fewer than 20 amphibian specialists (Colburn, Weeks, et al. 2008). Forty-six taxa (orders and families) were tallied in a study of 66 pools in relatively pristine, mature forests in Minnesota, with 18 being widespread (Batzer, Palik, et al. 2004). Woodland pool invertebrates are distinguished by the key roles they play in energy and nutrient cycling and food-web interactions (Strayer 2006; Colburn, Weeks, et al. 2008).

Colburn (2004) and Colburn, Weeks, et al. (2008) recognized three major roles of pool invertebrates: as consumers, as prey for other animals (Stout and Stout 1992; Rowe, Sadinski, et al. 1994; Colburn 2004), and as controls on animal community structure through competition and predation. For example, caddisflies and leeches are important predators of amphibian eggs, and their presence may affect egg development rates (Rowe, Sadinski, et al. 1994), while odonate nymphs and diving beetle adults and larvae can be important predators of amphibian larvae. Invertebrate scrapers compete with amphibian tadpoles for algae, while predatory invertebrates compete with larval salamanders for prey. For an overview of key invertebrate taxa and functional groups in the region, see Colburn, Weeks, et al. (2008), Batzer, Rader, et al. (1999), and Batzer, Palik, et al. (2004).

Invertebrate taxon richness and evenness may change with pool hydroperiod (Tarr, Baber, et al. 2005), pool substrate and chemistry (Rowe, Sadinski, et al. 1994), canopy cover, temperature, and food availability (Colburn 2004; Batzer, Palik, et al. 2004). However, Batzer, Palik, et al. (2004) studied the relationship between macroinvertebrate communities and environmental variables in 66 seasonal woodland pools in Minnesota and concluded that most macroinvertebrates in pools are habitat generalists (but see Tarr, Baber, et al. 2005).

Colburn, Weeks, et al. (2008) noted two key adaptations employed by pool invertebrates for living in temporary waters: (1) early colonization to ensure time for larval development; and (2) behaviors to avoid, resist, or tolerate pool drying (see also Wiggins, Mackay, et al. 1980; Williams 1997). Winged insects may colonize pools as soon as the ice is out (Colburn, Weeks, et al. 2008) or use pools seasonally as breeding or feeding sites (e.g., some mosquitoes, water boatmen, backswimmers, and some predaceous diving beetles). Permanent residents, or less mobile species, may remain dormant as juveniles and adults in pool sediments until the pool is inundated (e.g., fingernail clams), while others produce desiccant-resistant eggs (e.g., fairy shrimp) or dormant cysts (e.g., flatworms, oligochaetes).

Amphibians

Salamanders (*Ambystoma* spp.) and wood frogs are the signature pool-breeding amphibian species in northeastern forested landscapes. However, seasonal woodland pools may host a broader assemblage of facultative species that use pools for breeding, foraging, resting, or aestivating. Of the 48 species of amphibians that occur in the Northeast, more than half (27) regularly use seasonal pools (Colburn 2004). We focus on wood frogs and marbled (*Ambystoma opacum*), spotted (*A. maculatum*), blue-spotted [complex] (*A. laterale* complex), and Jefferson (*A. jeffersonianum*) salamanders, the species most tightly associated with seasonal woodland pools in the region (Skelly, Halverson, et al. 2005). Although life history traits vary among pool-breeding species, and even within the same species, as a function of geography (see Semlitsch, Todd, et al. 2009), all share complex life cycles and adaptations to breeding in temporary waters.

BREEDING AND LARVAL DEVELOPMENT

Seasonal woodland pools present both opportunities and challenges to breeding amphibians. Pools often thaw well before lakes and rivers, providing early breeding opportunities for amphibians and a source of detrital-based nutrients and invertebrate prey for developing larvae (Smith, Rettig, et al. 1999; Maret, Snyder, et al. 2006). Yet pools are characterized by extremes in hydrology, temperature, solute concentrations, and oxygen. Eggs are at risk of freezing if water levels and temperatures drop, and larvae may fail to complete development if pools dry too early (Babbitt, Baber, et al. 2003). However, pool-breeding amphibians are well adapted to these pressures and employ some of the same life history strategies used by invertebrates. For example, wood frogs and salamanders migrate to breeding pools before the ice is out to maximize larval development periods. Strategies for avoiding or tolerating drying conditions are also evident. Marbled salamanders deposit eggs in the fall on the dry pool edge, enabling eggs to hatch immediately upon pond filling so that larvae can overwinter in the pools, conferring an advantage over later-breeding ambystomatids the following spring (Petranka 1998; Jenkins, McGarigal, et al. 2006). Adult ambystomatids and wood frogs exhibit high fidelity to their natal pools (Hopey and Petranka 1994; Vasconcelos and Calhoun 2004), a behavior that limits breeding attempts in pools with extremely short hydroperiods.

Amphibian eggs and larvae are often heavily depredated by invertebrates and other amphibians (Baldwin and Calhoun 2002; Sours and Petranka 2007), reptiles, birds, and mammals (Mitchell, Paton, et al. 2008). Predator avoidance or minimization behaviors increase breeding success. For example, pool-breeding species may detect the presence of fish or other predators in pools and reject those pools as breeding sites (Resetarits and Wilbur 1989; Kats and Sih 1992). Strategies for ensuring egg success vary among species. Blue-spotted salamanders often deposit eggs singly on pool bottoms, making them less visible to potential predators. Wood frogs employ a predator-swamping strategy by laying rafts of egg masses (often among hundreds of other masses), conferring protection to eggs deposited in the center (Hunter, Calhoun, et al. 1999).

Larvae may adapt behavior or morphology to local pond conditions (Relyea 2002). For example, salamander and wood frog larvae may increase the rate of development to metamorphosis in the face of rapid pool drying or rising temperatures (Berven 1990). Conversely, they may slow development in the case of food limitation (Newman 1992; Denver, Mirhadi, et al. 1998). Differences in larval feeding strategies (temporal and spatial) also decrease competition and predation pressures (Werner 1986; Relyea 2002).

JUVENILE AND ADULT AMPHIBIANS: LINKING TERRESTRIAL AND AQUATIC ECOSYSTEMS

Land-use practices within kilometers of amphibian breeding pools influence the health and diversity of amphibian populations (Guerry and Hunter 2002; Smith and Green 2005; Bauer, Paton, et al. 2010). The poolscape, or landscape defined by amphibian breeding pools and the matrices that support both migration (intrapopulational movements to and from breeding pools) and dispersal movements (interpopulational unidirectional movements from breeding pools to new breeding sites; Semlitsch 2008), should be considered relevant to conservation of functions associated with seasonal woodland pools.

Only recently has research on terrestrial habitat requirements of amphibians come to the forefront as a key issue in the conservation of pool-breeding species (Gamble, McGarigal, et al. 2006). Recent experiments (reviewed by Semlitsch and Skelly 2008) and theoretical studies (see Biek, Funk, et al. 2002; Vonesh and De la Cruz 2002) suggest that juvenile (pre-breeding-age) and adult survival in the terrestrial realm may underpin population trends. In a 21-year study of a wood frog population in Michigan, Berven (2009) identified juvenile and adult population size as the single most important factor explaining year-to-year variation in juvenile and adult birth and death rates. Ultimately, the quality of terrestrial habitat is key to species persistence (see review by Cushman 2006 and online appendix 10.1 for details). For seasonal woodland pool breeders specifically, the average migration distance is reported to be 123 m (Semlitsch and Skelly 2008), with maximum distances recorded as > 300 m in one migration event for a wood frog (Baldwin, Calhoun, et al. 2006b). Juveniles, the key dispersers to new breeding sites, may travel up to tens of kilometers from natal pools (Smith and Green 2005). This dispersal enhances genetic diversity and results in recolonization of pools where local populations have been extirpated (Semlitsch and Bodie 2003; Trenham and Shaffer 2005).

Facultative Vertebrate Species

The role of seasonal woodland pools as "keystone ecosystems" (see Hunter 2008) might be elucidated by more research on linkages between pools and other vertebrates. Mitchell, Paton, et al. (2008) reviewed the limited body of literature on pool use by other animals. Seasonal woodland pools serve as stepping stones for wetland-dependent species moving through uplands to permanent water bodies, including moose *(Alces alces)* (Mitchell, Paton, et al. 2008), nonbreeding amphibians (Paton and Crouch 2000; Gahl, Calhoun, et al. 2009), snakes (Ernst and Ernst 2003; Baldwin, Calhoun, et al. 2006b), and turtles (Kenney and Burne 2000; Joyal, McCollough, et al. 2001; Ernst and Ernst 2003), including a number of threatened and endangered species (Mitchell, Paton, et al. 2008).

Because pools thaw earlier in the growing season than large water bodies, they also provide food resources for an array of non-wetland-dependent species that are food limited in late winter, emerging from hibernation, or early spring migrants. Mitchell, Paton, et al. (2008) report use of seasonal woodland pools by 64% of the region's freshwater turtles, 51% of snakes, and 81% of the migrating or breeding avifauna. Eighty-six species of mammals have been reported foraging in seasonal woodland pools (Brooks and Doyle 2001). These movements link aquatic and terrestrial systems, as animals serve as vectors for transferring plants' seeds, invertebrate eggs, and cysts among pools (Colburn 2004).

Key Ecological Processes

Plant-Animal Interactions

The strongest plant-animal interactions in seasonal woodland pools are based on vegetation structure rather than species-specific interactions, although some rare and endangered species are associated with specific vegetation. For example, four-toed salamanders *(Hemidactylium scutatum)* and ringed-boghaunter dragonflies *(Williamsonia lintneri)* are typically found in *Sphagnum*-dominated pools (deMaynadier and Carlson 1998; Cutko and Rawinski 2008). Vegetation structure is an important microhabitat component for both amphibians and invertebrates as egg attachment sites and larval refugia. Key amphibians in seasonal woodland pools often partition egg attachment sites: *Ambystoma maculatum* tend to lay eggs on the previous year's perennial vegetation, low in the water column, while *A. laterale* complexes and wood frogs attach their eggs to downed woody debris or shrubs (Hunter, Calhoun, et al. 1999).

Food-Web Interactions

Seasonal woodland pools are generally considered heterotrophic, detrital-based systems fueled by allochthonous inputs of terrestrial leaf litter, woody debris, and dissolved organic matter as a primary energy source and base of the food chain (Fig. 10.3) (Rubbo and Kiesecker 2004; Palik, Batzer, et al. 2006). Terrestrial inputs of organic carbon increase secondary production in pools, likely because there is more surface area and nutrients for periphyton production. Periphyton, the algal, bacterial, and fungal films that form on substrates, provides forage for a suite of invertebrates, such as snails and other scrapers, and omnivorous tadpoles such as wood frogs.

The proportion of allochthonous to autochthonous inputs varies from pool to pool, is often associated with canopy closure, and can drive the composition of the aquatic faunal community. Closed-canopy pools show lower primary productivity and higher allochthonous inputs (Skelly, Friedenburg, et al. 2002; Schiesari 2006). In contrast, open-canopy pools receive more light, and thus have more herbaceous vegetation and autochthonous carbon through primary production than closed-canopy pools (Colburn 2004; Schiesari 2006). Open-canopy pools typically have more herbivorous fauna, particularly scrapers, that can take advantage of biofilms.

Predation is also a powerful top-down mechanism structuring seasonal woodland pools (Fig. 10.3). Besides direct mortality, predation can alter distribution patterns of amphibian larvae in space or by size (Urban 2007) and can alter species composition (Morin 1983). For example, marbled salamander larvae hatch after fall reflooding and overwinter in the pools. Thus, the following spring, marbled salamander larvae are much larger than those ambystomatid larvae developing from eggs deposited in spring. Marbled salamander larvae can heavily depredate the smaller amphibians' larvae (Urban 2007). Gape-limited predators such as marbled salamanders and eastern newts *(Notophthalmus viridescens viridescens)* can affect the size distribution of their prey by allowing larger individuals to survive. This change in size distribution can lead to differing community dynamics and generate divergent selection on early growth and body size in the prey species (Urban 2007, 2008). Omnivorous wood frogs hatch quickly and can depredate spring-laid ambystomatid or American toad embryos (Petranka, Hopey, et al. 1994; Petranka, Rushlow, et al. 1998; Baldwin and Calhoun 2002). This predation can affect the distribution and density of amphibian larvae in a pool, and therefore change the effects of predation by ambystomatids and other amphibians on wood frog larvae later in the season.

Herbivory as a top-down control in seasonal woodland pools can be driven by the amphibian species present. Tadpoles that consume periphyton can dramatically affect nutrient flows. For example, after metamorphosis of wood frog tadpoles, we

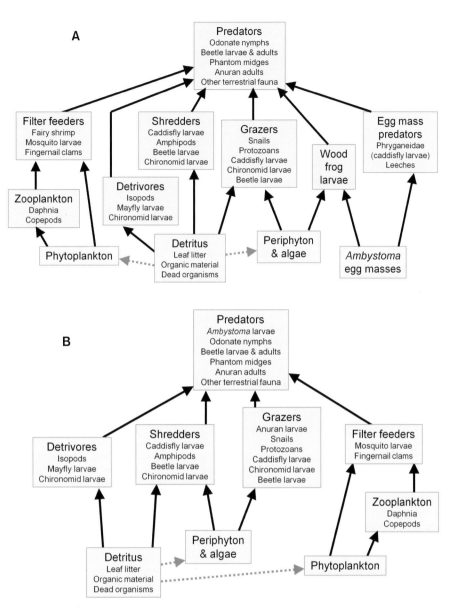

FIG. 10.3. Example of food webs in seasonal woodland pools in (A) early season (spring) and (B) midseason (early/midsummer). Black arrows represent transfer of energy from food sources to consumers. Gray dashed arrows represent transfer of nutrients from source to consumer. Abundant or important species are identified in each category, but species lists are not complete. Artist: M. K. Gahl.

have observed pools turning green from filamentous algae and periphyton, presumably from a lack of tadpole herbivory.

Amphibian breeding phenology in seasonal pools can strongly influence predator-prey interactions. For example, because wood frogs hatch quickly and are omnivorous, they can depredate spring-laid ambystomatid or American toad embryos (Petranka, Hopey, et al. 1994; Petranka, Rushlow, et al. 1998; Baldwin and Calhoun 2002).

Seasonal woodland pool communities are complex, and species composition and abundance may not be predictable. The aquatic community in seasonal woodland pools changes throughout the seasonal hydrologic cycle as key species colonize or emerge from a pool (Fig. 10.3). Community composition can also vary annually because it reflects the responses of resident species to changes in hydrology, water quality, preda-

tors, competitors, differences in colonization by migrants from one year to the next, and stochastic events. For example, in exceptionally wet years, green frogs, which have an extended larval period, may breed in seasonal woodland pools. All of these changes can influence food-web dynamics.

Transfer of Energy between Pools and Uplands

The seasonal pool food web reaches beyond the borders of the pools as biomass is distributed to the surrounding terrestrial ecosystems when invertebrates and amphibians leave the pool and organic material is deposited into the pool from the surrounding terrestrial system (Fig. 10.4). The contribution of amphibian biomass to terrestrial carbon reserves in

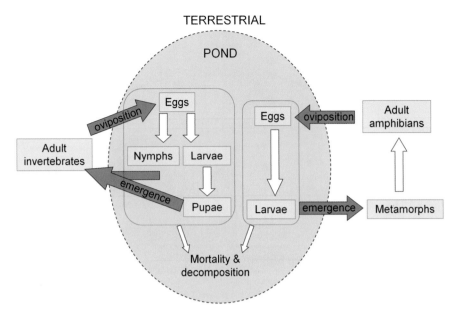

FIG. 10.4. Biotic connections between seasonal woodland pools and the terrestrial environment. Darker arrows represent energy flow across aquatic-terrestrial system boundaries. Artist: M. K. Gahl.

both southeastern (Gibbons, Winne, et al. 2006) and potentially northeastern seasonal wetland ecosystems (Windmiller 1996) may be more significant than currently documented (Unrine, Hopkins, et al. 2007). Energy and nutrients are transferred to the upland through the pulse of metamorphs from breeding pools each summer and early fall (Regester, Lips, et al. 2005; Regester, Whiles, et al. 2008), which provides important food resources for terrestrial predators such as snakes and birds (Mitchell, Paton, et al. 2008). Seasonal pools are also dependent upon the surrounding forest for nutrient inputs from both biotic and abiotic sources. When adult amphibians return to the breeding pools in spring, nutrients from the forests are returned to the pool through egg mass deposition and larval and adult mortality (Regester, Lips, et al. 2005; Regester and Whiles 2006) (Fig. 10.4). Upland leaf litter and organic material transported to pools form the base of the food web and can define the composition of the pool community (Palik, Batzer, et al. 2006; Batzer and Palik 2007; Rubbo, Belden, et al. 2008).

Conservation Concerns

Seasonal woodland pools are regionally among the most threatened wetland resource by virtue of their small size, surficial isolation from more strictly regulated rivers, streams, and lakes, and their occurrence on predominantly private property (Dahl 2006; Calhoun and deMaynadier 2008). Pools and their associated wildlife may be temporally ephemeral in more than one way if conservation issues are not directly addressed. Federal and state protections for pools in the Northeast are ineffective and are frequently challenged by legislators or special-interest groups (Preisser, Kefer, et al. 2000; Mahaney and Klemens 2008). Many pools are not regulated, and losses through filling or use as pollution detention basins may be substantial (Stedman and Dahl 2008).

State regulations in the Northeast are limited to the pool depression and a minimal "buffer" area around the pool ranging from 15 to 76 m (50 to 250 feet; Mahaney and Klemens

2008). These buffers were modeled after buffer widths used for maintaining water quality, or were chosen to match buffers used for shoreland zoning or existing resource protection values with which the public is familiar. While existing regulations may raise the profile of seasonal woodland pools for landowners, consultants, and resource managers, current regulations are not adequate for ensuring the maintenance of seasonal woodland pool functions.

We make a distinction in this discussion between conserving seasonal woodland pools (discrete depressional wetlands) and conserving the poolscape necessary to maintain seasonal woodland pool functions. Because a key function of pools in our region is as breeding habitat for a specialized suite of amphibians adapted to life in temporary waters, we focus our attention on improving terrestrial linkages among pools, other wetlands, and the terrestrial matrix that connects them. We believe that by addressing terrestrial habitat requirements of pool-breeding amphibians, we will conserve the bundle of pool functions (i.e., nutrient cycling and export, hydrologic discharge and recharge, biodiversity, facultative wildlife habitat) provided by seasonal woodland pools in northeastern forests.

How do managers conserve small, often ephemeral, wetlands that are difficult to remotely identify and fall largely on private property? We identify specific challenges and suggest some solutions for conserving poolscapes.

Defining Seasonal Woodland Pools

There is no standard definition of seasonal woodland pools among either the scientific community or policymakers. Some pools are defined strictly by biological criteria (e.g., presence of indicator amphibian species or fairy shrimp), while others are defined by hydroperiod and geomorphic setting (Calhoun and deMaynadier 2008). They are variously known as vernal pools, ephemeral wetlands, seasonally ponded isolated wetlands, or seasonal ponds. This lack of standardization at the federal and state levels can be confusing to the public and to resource managers. There must be clear identification criteria and terminology, whether at the state, regional, or local levels, in order for management to be transparent and effective.

Creating a Pool Digital Database for Land-Use Planning

The first step in effectively managing pool resources is preidentification through mapping and inventory. State-level mapping of seasonal woodland pools is rare, and even when it is done, mapping efforts only suggest potential pools (Burne and Lathrop 2008). Existing maps of wetlands are rarely sufficient, including the National Wetland Inventory (NWI) maps produced by the U.S. Fish and Wildlife Service. NWI maps are developed from aerial photography flown at scales too coarse to detect most seasonal woodland pools. For example, in a regional study of seasonal woodland pools in mid-coast Maine (unpublished), less than 50% of the 1,800 potential pools documented were captured on NWI maps. Mapping at a finer scale than NWI (1":1000' or 1":400'), using color infrared photography (CIR), and viewing in stereo improve detection rates but are still problematic. Errors of omission with 1":1000' panchromatic photography often exceed 30% (Calhoun, Walls, et al. 2003). Small pool size and mixed or evergreen canopy cover can also confound pool identification (Burne and Lathrop 2008).

More recent attempts to identify pools with other methods have had mixed results. Efforts using surficial geology and topography to preidentify pool-rich landscapes suggest this could be a promising tool in some regions but may not be reliable in others (Grant 2005; Skidds and Golet 2005). Pool identification through LIDAR (light detection and ranging) may hold promise for the future as a preidentification tool, but for the present, remote sensing for seasonal woodland pools is an inexact science requiring extensive field verification (Van Meter, Bailey, et al. 2008).

Conserving Terrestrial Habitat

The existing regulatory buffers fall short of the core amphibian terrestrial habitat suggested by many scientists (Semlitsch and Bodie 2003; Calhoun, Miller, et al. 2005; Harper, Rittenhouse, et al. 2008). Adjacent forests provide the shade and organic matter necessary to maintain water quality and to provide organic input to fuel pool food webs (deMaynadier and Houlahan 2008). Fragmentation of amphibian terrestrial habitat and migratory and dispersal corridors by agriculture (Guerry and Hunter 2002; Babbitt, Baber, et al. 2009), roads (Fahrig, Pedlar, et al. 1995; Lehtinen, Galatowitsch, et al. 1999), and development (Homan, Windmiller, et al. 2004; Cushman 2006) can cause declines or extirpation of local populations. Wood frogs are particularly sensitive to urbanization and disappear from degraded landscapes even if pools are present (Korfel, Mitsch, et al. 2009). Without protections for terrestrial habitat associated with pools, regulators and resource managers may be left with an array of intact pool depressions that lack the target species (Gibbs and Reed 2008).

Terrestrial habitat requirements of pool-breeding species vary regionally (Semlitsch, Todd, et al. 2009), thus making a "one size fits all" regulatory approach ineffective. Relatively little research in urbanizing landscapes has been done to assess viability thresholds for pool-breeding amphibians

with respect to both pool loss and loss of terrestrial habitat (but see Homan, Windmiller, et al. 2007). Issues of connectivity among pools and terrestrial habitat are further complicated by disagreement over which levels of connectivity are appropriate: too much allows for flow of invasive species, disease, or predators and potential outbreeding depression, while too little may genetically isolate populations of pool-breeding fauna (Petranka and Holbrook 2006; Gibbs and Reed 2008). These issues underscore the importance of designing management strategies sensitive to local conditions.

Wetland Mitigation

It may seem counterintuitive to list wetland mitigation as a threat to seasonal woodland pools. The U.S. Clean Water Act states that impacts to wetlands should be first avoided, then minimized, and finally compensated. However, "avoidance" is often dismissed (Calhoun and Windmiller 2008). With the increase in wetland losses to exurban development, mitigation for woodland pool losses is more common and often results in creation of permanent ponds in open settings (Windmiller and Calhoun 2008). This practice results in a net loss of natural wetland functions, but it is documented in trends analyses as national *increases* in wetland area (Stedman and Dahl 2008).

The issues of pool creation and success are far more complex than the engineering itself. Consultants regularly attempting pool creation in the Northeast are quick to maintain that creation of pools, and re-creating seasonal hydroperiods in particular, is tricky and often results in failure. Replication of the seasonal hydrology that drives pools' unique ecosystem functions and emulating the natural spatial distribution of pools in the landscape are key challenges to successful creation (see Petranka and Holbrook 2004). Studies comparing created pool functions with natural pools have shown that created pools have significantly longer hydroperiods than natural pools (Gamble and Mitsch 2009), do not mimic the chemistry of natural pools (Korfel, Mitsch, et al. 2009), and often do not support viable populations of wood frogs, a target species for pool creation projects (Vasconcelos and Calhoun 2006; Gamble and Mitsch 2009). Longer-hydroperiod pools may create biological traps for the target species because predator populations—both invertebrates and vertebrates (such as green frogs and bullfrogs)—may increase to levels that are detrimental to target pool species.

Climate Change

Wetland community composition and structure is driven by hydrology, which is determined by hydrogeomorphic setting (see Rheinhardt and Hollands 2008) and climate. Climate projections in the Northeast include temperature increases; changes in precipitation patterns, with more rain in the winters and drier summers; increased intensity of storms (leading to flashier hydroperiods); and decreases in fall water surpluses from reduced snowpack (Brooks 2009). The potential for drier, warmer summers suggests that shorter-hydroperiod pools may be lost, increasing interpool distances and potentially leading to isolation of amphibian populations (Gibbs and Reed 2008) and other species dependent on pools for foraging or resting (Gibbs 1998). The loss of shorter-hydroperiod pools may lead to less variability in hydroperiods at the landscape scale and a resultant loss of pool faunal diversity. Furthermore, decreased snowpack could lead to drier pools in the fall, potentially detrimental to fall breeders such as the marbled salamander, which may be locally adapted to fall and winter precipitation patterns for nest site selection (Croshaw and Scott 2006).

Climate change may also affect the terrestrial habitat of pool-breeding amphibians. Decreased snowpack and winter insulation may lead to extended freezing and mortality of wood frogs hibernating in shallow depressions in the leaf litter (Baldwin, Calhoun, et al. 2006b). Drier, hotter summers may change summer refugia and food availability. For example, accelerated decomposition of leaf litter (and hence material for moist refugia) may make conditions more conducive to invasive species (plants/earthworms) that could change forest floor microclimate and arthropod composition (Maerz, Nuzzo, et al. 2009).

Distribution ranges for pool-breeding amphibians, as well as for potential competitors and predators, may similarly change. If conservation biologists focus strictly on the ecological needs of pool-breeders (static pool depression and adjacent forest) and discount the need for accommodation of microevolutionary processes (i.e., responses to selection pressures from competition, predation, or new gene pools), loss of genetic diversity may result in the loss of variation important for future selection pressures (Rice and Emery 2003).

Solutions

A review of major challenges associated with conservation of pool-breeding amphibian populations brings to mind the mantra commonly invoked in the 1970s: "Think globally, act locally." These challenges can be met only by supplementing current regulatory approaches with a mechanism for conservation planning at the local scale that addresses a regional poolscape instead of focusing on pool-by-pool regulation in response to development pressures. Seasonal woodland pools perform a variety of ecosystem functions that require consideration of the matrix and connectivity to other wetland resources. This can be achieved most effectively through local efforts. Conserving seasonal woodland pools, or any natural resource on private lands, always poses socioeconomic as well as ecological challenges. Here we provide some general guidelines for meeting these key challenges to conservation.

Local Stewardship of Seasonal Woodland Pools

To develop effective conservation strategies that embrace some of the principles listed above, managers must engage a diverse team of problem-solvers through collaborations between social and biophysical experts and local stakeholders. Public attitudes toward conserving resources on private land are tightly wed to political and economic concerns. Interdisciplinary problem-solving that addresses both social and ecological concerns, coupled with local stakeholder engagement, will yield more creative approaches to conservation planning and to local stewardship initiatives (see Hart and Calhoun 2010; Jansujwicz and Calhoun 2010).

DEFINE SEASONAL WOODLAND POOLS

Defining seasonal woodland pools, criteria for assessment, and providing the public with the overarching goal of regulation are critical steps in effective natural resources management. Public education is essential for compliance. Federal regulators generally define seasonal woodland pools in either their State Programmatic Permits or General Permits. State officials may elect to refine those definitions depending on state goals. Maine developed its state definition, which served as a model for local governments, through a working group of diverse stakeholders. The key task was to define seasonal woodland pools and to provide justification for proposed regulatory solutions. Extensive public educational outreach about seasonal woodland pools and the proposed regulations accompanied these efforts (Jansujwicz and Calhoun 2010).

CREATE A SEASONAL WOODLAND POOL DATABASE

Researchers in Maine are currently using an interdisciplinary approach to addressing practical woodland pool conservation solutions in 12 municipalities. In these towns, trained citizen scientists are mapping and assessing amphibian use of seasonal woodland pools to provide a digital pool database for community natural resource planning and landowner education (see www.umaine.edu/vernalpools; Oscarson and Calhoun 2007; Morgan and Calhoun 2010). In addition, municipalities and biologists are working with social scientists and economists to identify citizen concerns and to investigate the cost of pool conservation (and conservation of other natural resources) on private land. With this information, stakeholders and experts will explore existing economic incentives (e.g., conservation easements, open space benefits, tax incentives, mitigation options) for property owners and work on creating novel approaches that address both poolscape conservation issues and economic sustainability of communities.

GIS TECHNOLOGY AND NATURAL RESOURCES PLANNING

GIS technology and modeling are powerful tools for informing conservation decisions (Margules and Pressey 2000; Baldwin and deMaynadier 2009). While there are many approaches and software packages (including corridor, reserve selection, and population viability analysis packages) currently available to assist wetland conservation planners, seasonal woodland pools present a unique spatial problem with the need to conserve wildlife populations that require both aquatic and terrestrial habitats. Two approaches that were designed specifically for identifying critical habitat for amphibians dependent on seasonal woodland pools are presented in a case study available in online appendix 10.1 for this chapter.

DEVELOP ORDINANCES OR CONSERVATION ZONING

Local ordinances and development of pool conservation zones (areas of pool clusters, significant productivity, and proximity to terrestrial habitat) are two approaches that can fine-tune management strategies that take into account pool-breeding and terrestrial habitat needs. For example, for zones slated for commercial or high-use development, protection for individual pools could be relaxed and mitigation dollars could be redirected to high-priority areas, including pool clusters, pools with intact adjacent habitat, and those that are biologically exemplary. Seasonal woodland pool (and other natural resource) conservation zones would be analogous to the Special Area Management Plans (SAMPS) developed by the U.S. Army Corps of Engineers (USACE) or Advanced Identification wetland projects (ADID) implemented by USACE and the Environmental Protection Agency that enable all stakeholders to take a comprehensive look at the past and future of a geographic area and decide what resources should receive the most protection. This approach may be attractive to U.S. states with a strong "home rule" foundation (Jansujwicz and Calhoun 2010).

Wetland Mitigation

Avoid and minimize impacts to seasonal woodland pools. Although wetland restoration and creation may have a role for supporting some amphibian populations in severely altered landscapes (Brand and Snodgrass 2010; Simon, Snodgrass, et al. 2009), this approach may not be appropriate in other contexts or for all pool breeders. Particularly at risk are those species sensitive to predators associated with more permanent waters and those that are dependent on adjacent terrestrial habitat (e.g., wood frog and ambystomatid salamanders; Boone, Semlitsch, et al. 2008). Over time, low juvenile recruitment associated with suboptimal pool conditions may lead to extirpation of local populations (Marsh and Trenham 2001).

EMULATE POOL CHARACTERISTICS TYPICAL OF THE FOCUS AREA

Given that scientists have not been able to answer the questions "How many pools are enough?" and "How much terrestrial habitat is necessary for each species of concern?" managers should start by emulating natural pool hydrogeomorphic settings, hydroperiods, and densities and distribution in a suitable upland matrix. For functional evolutionary units of organisms, conservation efforts will need to encompass groups of pool-based amphibian populations at spatial scales that support dispersal (Gibbs and Reed 2008). Some of this information may be available through Geographic Information Systems (GIS) analyses.

Information on native vegetation patterns may be useful for pool conservation efforts beyond maintaining local and regional biodiversity. In some cases, plants may be used as surrogates for hydroperiod (Mitchell 2005) and may provide guidance in conserving a variety of pool types (hydrogeomorphic or wetland classes) in any given landscape. Restoration or other mitigation efforts should encourage the establishment of native vegetation associated with pools in similar hydrogeomorphic settings in the region and avoid the introduction of exotic or invasive species that may choke pools (e.g., *Typha* spp. or other aggressive colonizers; Vasconcelos and Calhoun 2006).

Climate Change

Clearly, the effects of climate change on seasonal woodland pools (and other wetlands) and their associated biota are uncertain. Maintaining connectivity among pools and other wetlands, conserving the range of pool hydrogeomorphic settings, and minimizing other environmental stressors (e.g., pollution, introduction of invasive species) on wildlife may help to conserve pool functions. Maintaining a range of seasonal pool hydroperiods and recognizing natural agents of amphibian breeding habitat creation may provide the buffer needed in the face of uncertain rainfall patterns. For example, recent research on beavers' relationship with amphibians has suggested that beavers may play a substantial role in maintaining pool-breeding amphibian populations in the Northeast by providing alternative breeding habitat in landscapes with low pool density (Cunningham, Calhoun, et al. 2006; Stevens, Paszkowski, et al. 2007; Karraker and Gibbs 2009; Popescu and Gibbs 2009). Other natural disturbance regimes that create "natural" pools should be conserved when possible, including floodplain scouring and development of oxbows, tree blowdowns in forested wetlands, and fire, which reverses succession (Semlitsch and Skelly 2008).

Conclusion

Seasonal woodland pools are unique aquatic habitats in northeastern North America, providing breeding habitat for a specialized array of invertebrates and amphibians adapted to life in temporary waters. They also serve as foraging and resting refugia for both wetland-dependent and facultative species, a number of which are regionally threatened or endangered. Although pools typically have been regulated as isolated ecosystems, their interdependence on adjacent terrestrial ecoystems through exchange of nutrients and energy resources is increasingly recognized by conservation practitioners and resource managers. Research advances in documenting the terrestrial habitat needs of pool-breeding amphibians, the importance of pool density and spatial distribution in supporting wetland-dependent fauna, and the sensitivity of within-pool dynamics to biophysical context and local forest conditions have provided the foundation for proactive management of seasonal woodland pool ecosystem processes. This is particularly important in the face of changing environmental conditions and land-use practices. Advances in technology using GIS with natural resources databases empower local entities to plan for maintaining functioning pool resources that ultimately will complement other conservation goals.

References

Babbitt KJ, Baber MJ, Tarr TL. 2003. Patterns of larval amphibian distribution along a wetland hydroperiod gradient. *Can. J. Zool.* 81:1539–52.

Babbitt KJ, Baber MJ, et al. 2009. Influence of agricultural upland habitat type on larval anuran assemblages in seasonally inundated wetlands. *Wetlands* 29:294–301.

Baldwin RF, Calhoun AJK. 2002. *Ambystoma laterale* (blue-spotted salamander) and *Ambystoma maculatum* (spotted salamander) predation. *Herp. Rev.* 33:44–45.

Baldwin RF, deMaynadier PG. 2009. Assessing threats to pool-breeding amphibian habitat in an urbanizing landscape. *Biol. Conserv.* 142:1628–38.

Baldwin RF, Calhoun AJK, deMaynadier PG. 2006a. The significance of hydroperiod and stand maturity for pool-breeding amphibians in forested landscapes. *Can. J. Zool.* 84:1604–15.

Baldwin RF, Calhoun AJK, deMaynadier PG. 2006b. Conservation planning for amphibian species with complex habitat requirements: a case study using movements and habitat selection of the wood frog (*Rana sylvatica*). *J. Herp.* 40:443–54.

Batzer DP, Palik BJ. 2007. Variable response by aquatic invertebrates to experimental manipulations of leaf litter input into seasonal woodland ponds. *Fund. Appl. Limnol.* 168:155–62.

Batzer DP, Palik BJ, Buech R. 2004. Relationships between environmental characteristics and macroinvertebrate communities in seasonal woodland ponds of Minnesota. *J. N. Am. Benthol. Soc.* 23:50–68.

Batzer DP, Rader RB, Wissinger SA, editors. 1999. *Invertebrates in freshwater wetlands of North America: ecology and management.* New York: John Wiley and Sons.

Bauer DM, Paton PWC, Swallow SK. 2010. Are wetland regulations cost effective for species protection? A case study of amphibian metapopulations. *Ecol. Appl.* 20:798–815.

Berven KA. 1990. Factors affecting population fluctuations in larval and adult stages of the wood frog *(Rana sylvatica). Ecology* 71:1599–1608.

Berven KA. 2009. Density dependence in the terrestrial stage of wood frogs: evidence from a 21-year population study. *Copeia* 2009:328–38.

Berven KA, Grudzien TA. 1990. Dispersal in the wood frog *(Rana sylvatica):* implications for genetic population structure. *Evolution* 44:2047–56.

Biek R, Funk WC, Maxell BA, Mills LS. 2002. What is missing in amphibian decline research: insights from ecological sensitivity analysis. *Conserv. Biol.* 16:728–34.

Bonner LA, Diehl WJ, Altig R. 1997. Physical, chemical, and biological dynamics of five temporary dystrophic forest pools in central Mississippi. *Hydrobiologia* 353:77–89.

Boone MD, Semlitsch RD, Mosby C. 2008. Suitability of golf course ponds for amphibian metamorphosis when bullfrogs are removed. *Conserv. Biol.* 22:172–79.

Boone RB, Johnson CM, Johnson LB. 2006. Simulating vernal pool hydrology in central Minnesota, USA. *Wetlands* 26:581–92.

Brand AB, Snodgrass J. 2010. Value of artificial habitats for amphibian reproduction in altered landscapes. *Conserv. Biol.* 10:295–301.

Brodman R, Ogger J, et al. 2003. Multivariate analyses of the influences of water chemistry and habitat parameters on the abundances of pond-breeding amphibians. *J. Freshw. Ecol.* 18:425–35.

Brooks RT. 2000. Annual and seasonal variation and the effects of hydroperiod on benthic macroinvertebrates of seasonal forest ("vernal") ponds in central Massachusetts, USA. *Wetlands* 20:707–15.

Brooks RT. 2009. Potential impacts of global climate change on the hydrology and ecology of ephemeral freshwater systems of the forests of the northeastern United States. *Clim. Change* 95:469–83.

Brooks RT, Doyle KL. 2001. Shrew species richness and abundance in relation to vernal pool habitat in southern New England. *Northeast. Nat.* 8:137–48.

Burne MR, Lathrop RG. 2008. Remote and field identification of vernal pools. In *Science and conservation of vernal pools in northeastern North America,* Calhoun AJK, deMaynadier PG, editors. Boca Raton, FL: CRC Press, pp. 55–68.

Calhoun AJK, Walls T, et al. 2003. Developing conservation strategies for vernal pools: a Maine case study. *Wetlands* 23:70–81.

Calhoun AJK, deMaynadier PG, editors. 2008. *Science and conservation of vernal pools in northeastern North America.* Boca Raton, FL: CRC Press.

Calhoun AJK, Miller N, Klemens MW. 2005. Conservation strategies for pool-breeding amphibians in human-dominated landscapes. *Wetl. Ecol. Manage.* 13:291–304.

Carrino-Kyker SR, Swanson AK. 2007. Seasonal physiochemical characteristics of thirty northern Ohio temporary pools along gradients of GIS-delineated human land-use. *Wetlands* 27:749–60.

Colburn EA. 2004. *Vernal pools: natural history and conservation.* Blacksburg, VA: McDonald and Woodward.

Colburn EA, Weeks SC, Reed SK. 2008. Diversity and ecology of vernal pool invertebrates. In *Science and conservation of vernal pools in northeastern North America,* Calhoun AJK, deMaynadier PG, editors. Boca Raton, FL: CRC Press, pp. 105–26.

Comer P, Goodin K, et al. 2005. *Biodiversity values of geographically isolated wetlands in the United States.* Arlington, VA: NatureServe.

Croshaw DA, Scott DE. 2006. Marbled salamanders *(Ambystoma opacum)* choose low elevation nest sites when cover availability is controlled. *Amphibia-Reptilia* 27:359–64.

Cunningham J, Calhoun AJK, Glanz WE. 2006. Patterns of beaver colonization and wetland change in Acadia National Park: implications for pond-breeding amphibian species distribution. *Northeast. Nat.* 13:583–96.

Cushman SA. 2006. Effects of habitat loss and fragmentation on amphibians: a review and prospectus. *Biol. Conserv.* 128:231–40.

Cutko A. 1997. *A botanical and natural community assessment of selected vernal pools in Maine.* Augusta: Maine Natural Areas Program.

Cutko A, Rawinski TJ. 2008. Flora of northeastern vernal pools. In *Science and conservation of vernal pools in northeastern North America,* Calhoun AJK, deMaynadier PG, editors. Boca Raton, FL: CRC Press, pp. 71–104.

Dahl TF. 2006. *Status and trends of wetlands in the conterminous United States 1998 to 2004.* Washington, DC: USFWS.

deMaynadier PG, Carlson B. 1998. A survey and evaluation of habitat potential for *Williamsonia lintneri* in southern Maine. Bangor: Report to Maine Dept. Inland Fish. Wildl.

deMaynadier PG, Houlahan JE. 2008. Conserving vernal pool amphibians in managed forests. In *Science and conservation of vernal pools in northeastern North America,* Calhoun AJK, deMaynadier PG, editors. Boca Raton, FL: CRC Press, pp. 127–48.

Denver, RJ, Mirhadi N, Phillips M. 1998. Adaptive plasticity in amphibian metamorphosis: response of *Scaphiopus hammondii* tadpoles to habitat desiccation. *Ecology* 79:1859–72.

Ernst CH, Ernst EM. 2003. *Snakes of the United States and Canada.* Washington, DC: Smithsonian Institute Press.

Fahrig L, Pedlar JH, et al. 1995. Effect of road traffic on amphibian density. *Biol. Conserv.* 73:177–82.

Freda J, Dunson WA. 1986. Effects of low pH and other chemical variables on the local distribution of amphibians. *Copeia* 2:454–66.

Gahl MK, Calhoun AJK. 2010. The role of multiple stressors in ranavirus-caused amphibian mortalities in Acadia National Park wetlands. *Can. J. Zool.* 88:108–21.

Gahl MK, Calhoun AJK, Graves R. 2009. Facultative use of seasonal pools by American bullfrogs *(Rana catesbeiana). Wetlands* 29:697–703.

Gamble DL, Mitsch WJ. 2009. Hydroperiods of created and natural vernal pools in central Ohio: a comparison of depth and duration of inundation. *Wetl. Ecol. Manage.* 17:385–95.

Gamble LR, McGarigal K, et al. 2006. Limitations of regulated "buffer zones" for the conservation of marbled salamanders. *Wetlands* 26:298–306.

Gibbons JW, Winne CT, et al. 2006. Remarkable amphibian biomass and abundance in an isolated wetland: implications for wetland conservation. *Conserv. Biol.* 20:1457–65.

Gibbs, JP. 1998. Amphibian movements in response to forest edges, roads, and streambeds in southern New England. *J. Wildl. Manage.* 62: 584–89.

Gibbs JP, Reed JM. 2008. Population and genetic linkages of vernal pool associated amphibians. In *Science and conservation of vernal pools in northeastern North America,* Calhoun AJK, deMaynadier PG, editors. Boca Raton, FL: CRC Press, pp. 149–68.

Grant EHC. 2005. Correlates of vernal pool occurrence in the Massachusetts, USA, landscape. *Wetlands* 25:480–87.

Guerry AD, Hunter ML Jr. 2002. Amphibian distributions in a landscape of forests and agriculture: an examination of landscape composition. *Conserv. Biol.* 16:745–54.

Harper EB, Rittenhouse TAG, Semlitsch RD. 2008. Demographic consequences of terrestrial habitat loss for pool-breeding amphibians: predicting extinction risks associated with inadequate size of buffer zones. *Conserv. Biol.* 22:1205–15.

Hart D, Calhoun AJK. 2010. Rethinking the role of ecological research in the sustainable management of freshwater ecosystems. *Freshw. Biol.* 55:258–69.

Hecnar SJ, M'Closkey RT. 1996. Amphibian species richness and distribution in relation to pond water chemistry in south-western Ontario, Canada. *Freshw. Biol.* 36:7–15.

Homan RN, Windmiller BS, Reed JM. 2004. Critical thresholds associated with habitat loss for two vernal pool-breeding amphibians. *Ecol. Appl.* 14:1547–53.

Homan RN, Windmiller BS, Reed JM. 2007. Comparative life histories of two sympatric *Ambystoma* species at a breeding pond in Massachusetts. *J. Herp.* 41:401–09.

Hopey ME, Petranka JW. 1994. Restriction of wood frogs to fish-free habitats: how important is adult choice? *Copeia* 1994:1023–25.

Horne MT, Dunson WA. 1995. The interactive effects of low pH, toxic metals, and DOC on a simulated temporary pond community. *Env. Pollu.* 89:155–61.

Hunter ML Jr. 2008. Valuing and conserving vernal pools as small-scale ecosystems. In *Science and conservation of vernal pools in northeastern North America,* Calhoun AJK, deMaynadier PG, editors. Boca Raton, FL: CRC Press, pp. 1–10.

Hunter ML Jr, Calhoun AJK, McCollough M. 1999. *Maine amphibians and reptiles.* Orono: Univ. Maine Press.

Inkley MD, Wissinger SA, Baros BL. 2008. Effects of drying regime on microbial colonization and shredder preference in seasonal woodland wetlands. *Freshw. Biol.* 53:435–45.

Jansujwicz JS, Calhoun AJK. 2010. Protecting natural resources on private lands: the role of collaboration in land-use planning. In *Landscape-scale conservation planning,* Trombulak SC, Baldwin RF, editors. New York: Springer-Verlag, pp. 205–33.

Jenkins CL, McGarigal K, Timm BC. 2006. Orientation of movements and habitat selection in a spatially structured population of marbled salamanders *(Ambystoma opacum). J. Herp.* 40:240–48.

Joyal LA, McCollough M, Hunter ML Jr. 2001. Landscape ecology approaches to wetland species conservation: a case study of two turtle species in Maine. *Conserv. Biol.* 15:1755–62.

Karraker NE, Gibbs JP. 2009. Amphibian production in forested landscapes in relation to wetland hydroperiod: a case study of vernal pools and beaver ponds. *Biol. Conserv.* 142:2293–3002.

Kats LB, Sih A. 1992. Oviposition site selection and avoidance of fish by streamside salamanders *(Amybystoma barbouri). Copeia* 1992:468–73.

Kenney LP, Burne MR. 2000. *A field guide to the animals of vernal pools.* Westborough: Mass. Div. Fish. Wildl. Natural Heritage and Endangered Species Program.

Korfel CA, Mitsch WJ, et al. 2009. Hydrology, physiochemistry, and amphibians in natural and created vernal pool wetlands. *Restor. Ecol.* 2:1–12.

Lehtinen RM, Galatowitsch SM, Tester JR II. 1999. Consequences of habitat loss and fragmentation for wetland amphibian assemblages. *Wetlands* 19:1–12.

Leibowitz SG, Brooks RT. 2008. Hydrology and landscape connectivity of vernal pools. In *Science and conservation of vernal pools in northeastern North America,* Calhoun AJK, deMaynadier PG, editors. Boca Raton, FL: CRC Press, pp. 31–54.

Maerz JC, Nuzzo VA, Blossey B. 2009. Declines in woodland salamander abundance associated with non-native earthworm and plant invasions. *Conserv. Biol.* 23:975–81.

Mahaney WS, Klemens MW. 2008. Vernal pool conservation policy: the federal, state, and local context. In *Science and conservation of vernal pools in northeastern North America,* Calhoun AJK, deMaynadier PG, editors. Boca Raton, FL: CRC Press, pp. 193–212.

Maret TJ, Snyder JD, Collins JP. 2006. Altered drying regime controls distribution of endangered salamanders and introduced predators. *Biol. Conserv.* 127:129–38.

Margules CR, Pressey RL. 2000. Systematic conservation planning. *Nature* 405:243–53.

Marsh DM, Trenham PC. 2001. Metapopulation dynamics and amphibian conservation. *Conserv. Biol.* 15:40–49.

McClain ME, Boyer EW, et al. 2003. Biogeochemical hot spots and hot moments at the interface of terrestrial and aquatic systems. *Ecosystems* 6:301–12.

Mitchell J. 2005. *Using plants as indicators of hydroperiod class and amphibian habitat suitability in Rhode Island seasonal ponds.* Master's thesis, Univ. of Rhode Island.

Mitchell JC, Paton PWC, Raithel CJ. 2008. The importance of vernal pools to reptiles, birds and mammals. In *Science and conservation of vernal pools in northeastern North America,* Calhoun AJK, deMaynadier PG, editors. Boca Raton, FL: CRC Press, pp. 169–92.

Morgan DE, Calhoun AJK. 2010. *Maine municipal guide to mapping and conserving vernal pools.* Falmouth: Maine Audubon Society.

Morin PJ. 1983. Predation, competition, and the composition of larval anuran guilds. *Ecol. Mongr.* 53:119–38.

Newman RA. 1992. Adaptive plasticity in amphibian metamorphosis. *BioScience* 42:671–78.

Oscarson D, Calhoun AJK 2007. Developing vernal pool conservation plans at the local level using citizen scientists. *Wetlands* 27:80–95.

Palik B, Batzer DP, Kern C. 2006. Upland forest linkages to seasonal wetlands: litter flux, processing, and food quality. *Ecosystems* 9:142–51.

Palik BJ, Buech R, Egeland L. 2003. Using an ecological land hierarchy to predict seasonal-wetland abundance in upland forests. *Ecol. Appl.* 13:1153–63.

Palik B, Streblow D, Egeland L, Buech R. 2007. Landscape variation of seasonal pool plant communities in forests of northern Minnesota, USA. *Wetlands* 27:12–23.

Paton PWC, Crouch WB III. 2002. Using the phenology of pond-breeding amphibians to develop conservation strategies. *Conserv. Biol.* 16:194–204.

Petranka JW. 1998. *Salamanders of the U.S. and Canada.* Washington, DC: Smithsonian Institution Press.

Petranka JW, Holbrook CT. 2006. Wetland restoration for amphibians: should local sites be designed to support metapopulations or patchy populations? *Restor. Ecol.* 14:404–11.

Petranka JW, Rushlow AW, Hopey ME. 1998. Predation by tadpoles of *Rana sylvatica* on embryos of *Ambystoma maculatum:* implications of ecological role reversals by *Rana* (predator) and *Ambystoma* (prey). *Herpetologica* 54:1–13.

Petranka JW, Hopey ME, et al. 1994. Breeding habitat segregation of wood frogs and American toads: the role of interspecific tadpole predation and adult choice. *Copeia* 3:691–97.

Popescu VD, Gibbs JP. 2009. Interactions between climate, beaver activity, and pond occupancy by the cold-adapted mink frog in New York State, USA. *Biol. Conserv.* 142:2059–68.

Preisser EL, Kefer JY, et al. 2000. Vernal pool conservation in Connecticut: assessment and recommendations. *Env. Manage.* 26:503–13.

Regester KJ, Whiles MR. 2006. Decomposition rates of salamander *(Ambystoma maculatum)* life stages and associated energy and nutrient fluxes in ponds and adjacent forest in southern Illinois. *Copeia* 2006:640–49.

Regester KJ, Lips KR, Whiles MR. 2005. Energy flow and subsidies associated with the complex life cycle of ambystomatid salamanders in ponds and adjacent forest in southern Illinois. *Oecologia* 147:303–14.

Regester KJ, Whiles MR, Lips KR. 2008. Variation in the trophic basis of production and energy flow associated with emergence of larval salamander assemblages from forest ponds. *Freshw. Biol.* 53:1754–67.

Relyea RA. 2002. Local population differences in phenotypic plasticity: predator-induced changes in wood frog tadpoles. *Ecol. Monogr.* 72:77–93.

Resetarits WJ Jr, Wilbur HM. 1989. Choice of oviposition site by *Hyla chrysoscelis:* role of predators and competitors. *Ecology* 70:220–28.

Rheinhardt RD, Hollands GG. 2008. Classification of vernal pools: geomorphic setting and distribution. In *Science and conservation of vernal pools in northeastern North America,* Calhoun AJK, deMaynadier PG, editors. Boca Raton, FL: CRC Press, pp. 11–30.

Rice KJ, Emery NC. 2003. Managing microevolution: restoration in the face of global change. *Frontiers Ecol. Env.* 1:469–78.

Rowe CL, Dunson WA. 1993. Relationships among abiotic parameters and breeding effort by three amphibians in temporary wetlands of central Pennsylvania. *Wetlands* 13:237–46.

Rowe CL, Sadinski WJ, Dunson WA. 1992. Effects of acute and chronic acidification on three larval amphibians that breed in temporary ponds. *Arch. Env. Contam. Toxic.* 23:339–50.

Rowe CL, Sadinski WJ, Dunson WA. 1994. Predation on larval and embryonic amphibians by acid-tolerant caddisfly larvae *(Ptilostomis postica). J. Herp.* 28:357–64.

Rubbo MJ, Kiesecker JM. 2004. Leaf litter composition and community structure: translating regional species changes into local dynamics. *Ecology* 85:2519–25.

Rubbo MJ, Belden LK, Kiesecker JM. 2008. Differential responses of aquatic consumers to variations in leaf litter inputs. *Hydrobiologia* 605:37–44.

Sadinski WJ, Dunson WA. 1992. A multilevel study of effects of low pH on amphibians of temporary ponds. *J. Herp.* 26:413–22.

Schiesari L. 2006. Pond canopy cover: a resource gradient for anuran larvae. *Freshw. Biol.* 51:412–23.

Schneider DW. 1999. Snowmelt ponds in Wisconsin: influence of hydroperiod on invertebrate community structure. In *Invertebrates in freshwater wetlands of North America: ecology and management,* Batzer DP, Rader RB, Wissinger SA, editors. New York: Wiley. pp. 299–318.

Seale DB. 1980. Influence of amphibian larvae on primary production, nutrient flux, and competition in a pond ecosystem. *Ecology* 61:1531–50.

Semlitsch RD. 2008. Differentiating migration and dispersal processes for pond-breeding amphibians. *J. Wildl. Manage.* 72:260–67.

Semlitsch RD, Bodie JR. 2003. Biological criteria for buffer zones around wetlands and riparian habitats for amphibians and reptiles. *Conserv. Biol.* 17:1219–28.

Semlitsch RD, Skelly DK. 2008. Ecology and conservation of pool-breeding amphibians. In *Science and conservation of vernal pools in northeastern North America,* Calhoun AJK, deMaynadier PG, editors. Boca Raton, FL: CRC Press, pp. 127–48.

Semlitsch RD, Todd BD, et al. 2009. Effects of timber harvest on amphibian populations: understanding mechanisms from forest experiments. *Bioscience* 59:853–62.

Simon JA, Snodgrass JW, et al. 2009. Spatial correlates of amphibian use of constructed wetlands in an urban landscape. *Landscape Ecol.* 24:361–73.

Skelly DK, Freidenburg LK, Kiesecker JM. 2002. Forest canopy and the performance of larval amphibians. *Ecology* 83:983–92.

Skelly DK, Halverson MA, et al. 2005. Canopy closure and amphibian diversity in forested wetlands. *Wetl. Ecol. Manage.* 13:261–68.

Skidds DE, Golet FC. 2005. Estimating hydroperiod suitability for breeding amphibians in southern Rhode Island seasonal forest ponds. *Wetl. Ecol. Manage.* 13:349–66.

Smith GR, Rettig JE, et al. 1999. The effects of fish on assemblages of amphibians in ponds: a field experiment. *Freshw. Biol.* 41:829–37.

Smith MA, Green DM. 2005. Dispersal and the metapopulation paradigm in amphibian ecology and conservation: are all amphibian populations metapopulations? *Ecography* 28:110–28.

Snodgrass JW, Komoroski MJ, et al. 2000. Relationships among isolated wetland size, hydroperiod, and amphibian species richness: implications for wetland regulations. *Conserv. Biol.* 14:414–19.

Sours GN, Petranka JW. 2007. Intraguild predation and competition mediate stage-structured interactions between wood frog *(Rana sylvatica)* and upland chorus frog *(Pseudacris feriarum)* larvae. *Copeia* 1:131–39.

Stedman S, Dahl TE. 2008. *Status and trends of wetlands in the coastal watersheds of the eastern United States, 1998 to 2004.* National Oceanic and Atmospheric Administration, National Marine Fisheries Service, and U.S. Department of the Interior, Fish and Wildlife Service.

Stevens CE, Paszkowski CA, Foote AL. 2007. Beaver *(Castor canadensis)* as a surrogate species for conserving anuran amphibians on boreal streams in Alberta, Canada. *Biol. Conserv.* 134:1–13.

Stout BM III, Stout KK. 1992. Predation by the caddisfly *Banksiola dossuaria* on egg masses of the spotted salamander *Ambystoma maculatum. American Midland Naturalist* 127:368–72.

Strayer DL. 2006. Challenges for freshwater invertebrate conservation. *Journal of the North American Benthological Society* 25:271–87.

Tarr TL, Baber MJ, Babbitt KJ. 2005. Macroinvertebrate community structure across a wetland hydroperiod gradient in southern New Hampshire, USA. *Wetl. Ecol. Manage.* 13:321–34.

Trenham PC, Shaffer HB. 2005. Amphibian upland habitat use and its consequences for population viability. *Ecol. Appl.* 15:1158–68.

Unrine JM, Hopkins WA, et al. 2007. Bioaccumulation of trace elements in omnivorous amphibian larvae: implications for amphibian health and contaminant transport. *Env. Pollu.* 149:182–92.

Urban MC. 2007. Predator size and phenology shape prey survival in temporary ponds. *Oecologia* 154:571–80.

Urban MC. 2008. Salamander evolution across a latitudinal cline in gape-limited predation risk. *Oikos* 117:1037–49.

Van Meter R, Bailey LL, Grant EHC. 2008. Methods for estimating the amount of vernal pool habitat in the northeastern United States. *Wetlands* 28:585–93.

Vasconcelos D, Calhoun AJK. 2004. Movement patterns of adult and juvenile wood frogs *(Rana sylvatica)* and spotted salamanders *(Ambystoma maculatum)* in three restored vernal pools. *J. Herp.* 38:551–61.

Vasconcelos D, Calhoun AJK. 2006. Monitoring created seasonal pools for functional success: a six-year case study of amphibian responses, Sears Island, Maine, USA. *Wetlands* 26:992–1003.

Vonesh JR, De la Cruz O. 2002. Complex life cycles and density dependence: assessing the contribution of egg mortality to amphibian declines. *Oecologia* 133:325–33.

Werner EE. 1986. Amphibian metamorphosis: growth rate, predation risk, and the optimal size at transformation. *Am. Nat.* 128:319–41.

Wetzel RG. 2001. *Limnology: lake and river ecosystems.* San Diego: Academic Press.

Wiggins GB, Mackay RJ, Smith IM. 1980. Evolutionary and ecological strategies of animals in annual temporary pools. *Archiv für Hydrobiologie* (Supplement) 38:97–206.

Williams DD. 1997. Temporary ponds and their invertebrate communities. *Aquatic Conservation—Marine and Freshwater Ecosystems* 7:105–17.

Windmiller BS. 1996. The pond, the forest and the city: spotted salamander ecology and conservation in a human-dominated landscape. Ph.D. diss., Tufts Univ., Boston.

Windmiller B, Calhoun AJK. 2008. Conserving vernal pool wildlife in urbanizing landscapes. In *Science and conservation of vernal pools in northeastern North America,* Calhoun AJK, deMaynadier PG, editors. Boca Raton, FL: CRC Press, pp. 233–52.

CHAPTER 11

Northern Red Maple and Black Ash Swamps

JOAN EHRENFELD

In the northeastern portions of the United States, the most abundant types of wetlands are deciduous hardwood swamps. While these swamps can have a variety of tree species in their canopies, the most abundant species is red maple *(Acer rubrum)*. These wetlands are found over the entire range of possible hydrogeomorphic settings; they can occupy areas ranging from small (< 1 ha) patches to large regional wetland systems; they are found on both mineral and organic soils and on both acidic and alkaline soils; they can support communities of high diversity, very low diversity, and anything in between; and red maple can range from a minor component of the canopy to the dominant, if not sole, member of the canopy. In short, they represent a wide range of wetland diversity, and play an important role in northeastern landscapes. However, despite their ubiquity, they have attracted relatively little research effort and are thus relatively poorly documented, unlike other northern forested wetlands (Trettin, Jurgensen, et al. 1997) or southern forested wetlands (Messina and Conner 1998). The ecology of red maple swamps in much but not all of their range was reviewed in a classic publication by Golet, Calhoun, et al. (1993), and this community profile still serves as the basis for much knowledge about these wetlands.

Black ash swamps are also relatively poorly known. Although the distribution of the species *(Fraxinus nigra)* extends from western Newfoundland (Canada) across southern Manitoba to eastern North Dakota, and south through Indiana and Ohio to the Appalachian Mountains in Virginia, it is often a minor component of mixed hardwood swamps and several types of conifer swamps. Like red maple, it is tolerant of a wide range of hydrological and soil conditions, and similarly has attracted little research attention.

This chapter will summarize what is known about these wetland types, and suggest topics that would reward more detailed research. It is difficult to set geographical bounds for the wetlands considered here. Northern red maple swamps grade into and are one form of bottomland hardwood swamps. Maple swamps also grade into many other types of deciduous and mixed coniferous-deciduous wetlands throughout their geographic range. Black ash swamps may be considered coextensive with the range of this species, but, like red maple, the species may be found at low abundance in a variety of wetland types. Thus, this chapter will arbitrarily limit its scope to the structure and function of hardwood swamps dominated by either species and found within the New England, mid-Atlantic, and northern midwestern U.S. states and the eastern provinces of Canada.

Biology of the Species

Red Maple

Acer rubrum is one of the most widespread tree species in North America, occurring from central Quebec and Ontario south to the Gulf coast, and from the eastern seaboard west to Missouri, Oklahoma, and eastern Texas (Fig. 11.1a). The species occurs in both uplands and wetlands; in both habitats it can be found on an extremely wide range of geological terrains, soil types, and hydrological settings. Its widespread distribution reflects its broad physiological tolerances as a "super-generalist" (Abrams 1998). It flowers early in spring, and may be an important pollen source for early-flying bees, which are seen visiting the flowers (Anderson and Neson 2006). Numerous seeds are produced, with larger crops observed biennially, and they germinate immediately, under a wide variety of light, temperature, and moisture conditions. Seedling growth requires moderate to high light. The species also reproduces through prolific sprouting. Mature trees are relatively small (18–27 m tall, 46–76 cm diameter breast height [DBH]), and they live a maximum of 150 years. Although it is classed as a "pioneer" species that occupies disturbed or open sites well, it is also moderately shade tolerant, and persists within mature communities. It is widely used by wildlife, both for browse and for the seeds. Its sap can be used for syrup, and although its wood is softer than that of other maple species and its growth form is frequently poor, it can be used as saw timber for many purposes as well as pulpwood (Neson 2006). It is prized by Native Americans as a source of splints for basket-making (Benedict and Frelich 2008).

Red maple has three recognized varieties that occur in wetlands (www.itis.gov). The most common variant is *Acer*

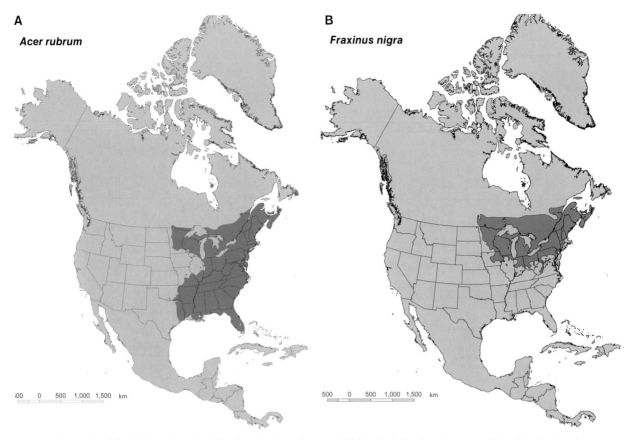

A

Acer rubrum

B

Fraxinus nigra

FIG. 11.1. Geographical distributions (green) of (A) red maple, *Acer rubrum,* and (B) black ash, *Fraxinus nigra,* trees. These distributions do not necessarily coincide with the distributions of wetlands that are dominated by these species. (Burns and Honkala 1990, courtesy of USDA Forest Service.)

rubrum var. *rubrum,* the variety ranging from dry uplands to wetlands. It is classified as a "facultative" wetland species throughout its range (https://rsgis.crrel.usace.army.mil/apex/f?p=703:1:2217343648658295). *Acer rubrum* var. *drummondii* is mostly found in the Midwest through the South, extending only as far north as southern New Jersey to southern Illinois. It has three-lobed leaves with dense whitish pubescence on their lower surfaces, is primarily if not exclusively found in wetlands, and is classified as facultative-wet to obligate. A third variety, *Acer rubrum* var. *trilobum,* is found throughout the range of the main variety, has three-lobed leaves with some pubescence on the undersurfaces, and is also primarily found in wetlands (classified as facultative-wet to obligate). Because none of the literature reviewed for this chapter distinguished the variety under study, the species will be simply referred to as *A. rubrum* or red maple.

Flooding tolerance in *A. rubrum* may reflect ecotypic differentiation from adjacent upland populations, insofar as seedlings from wetlands show a wide range of physiological adaptations to flood conditions. These include reduced photosynthetic rates under flooded conditions, a growth rate that reduces but continues under floods, and characteristic changes in electron transport rates, maximum carboxylation rates, dark respiration, and quantum use efficiency of flood-adapted species, which distinguish them from plants from upland environments (Anella and Whitlow 2000; Bauerle, Whitlow, et al. 2003). Under wetland conditions, *A. rubrum* seedlings show greater decreases in growth, especially in roots, under continuously flooded conditions than under intermittently flooded conditions (Day 1987). However, under the latter conditions,

morphological adaptations, such as hypertrophied lenticels on the stem near the water line, abundant adventitious roots, and increased leaf senescence, are observed (Day 1987; Kellison, Young, et al. 1998). Although the species occurs over a wide range of hydrological conditions, from intermittently saturated or flooded to permanently saturated or flooded, it is unknown if different suites of adaptations to anoxia and/or flooding are used by individuals in different conditions. It is also not known if there are differences in adaptive physiology or morphology between the three recognized varieties. In one of the few studies of leaf nutrient content, Day (1985) found that nutrient contents tended to be lower than in co-occurring species in Virginia swamps, but that there was significant variation among sites, within the species, and across seasons, making it difficult to describe a "typical" nutrient content. Nutrient contents were comparable to values observed in a range of other forested communities (not necessarily wetlands). Day noted that there was not a close correspondence between leaf nutrient content and soil nutrient content.

Black Ash

Black ash is found almost exclusively in wetlands, as is evidenced by its other common names ("swamp ash" or "water ash"). It is restricted to the Northeast and northern Midwest south of the boreal forest biome (Fig. 11.1b). It grows to be a relatively small tree (12–18 m, maximum 21 m tall, 20–25 cm DBH), with a narrow crown (Burns and Honkala 1990; Anderson and Neson 2006). Although it is generally described as

TABLE 11.1
Areal extent (ha) of palustrine nontidal and tidal
forested wetlands in the Northeast

State	Palustrine nontidal forested	Palustrine tidal forested	Palustrine forest as % of state wetland total
Connecticut	43,082	20	26.6
Delaware	57,041	2,235	55.6
District of Columbia	42	32	44.3
Maine	481,257	2,487	54.9
Maryland	130,744	16,178	51.4
Massachusetts	118,000	732	54.7
New Hampshire	56,652	210.5	48.0
New Jersey	201,247	7,640	55.1
New York	360,101	1,040	56.7
Pennsylvania	88,616	89	50.6
Rhode Island	19,664	38	68.8
Vermont	47,693	—	44.7
Virginia	305,612	22,768	55.2

SOURCE: Tiner 2010.

short-lived (130-year lifespan), trees up to 240 years old have been found in northern Quebec (Tardif and Bergeron 1999). It produces abundant seed crops relatively infrequently (about 33% of the time), the seeds require stratification for germination, and regenerating stems are intolerant of shade. The seeds are eaten by a variety of birds and mammals. Reproduction also occurs through stump sprouting. Saplings and trees grow slowly, and are readily overtopped by co-occurring species. Black ash is one of the first species to drop its deciduous leaves in the autumn, a phenological characteristic that allows reliable identification of black ash stands using multitemporal remote sensing imagery taken during summer and early autumn (Wolter, Mladenoff, et al. 1995). Like red maple, it is found in a variety of hydrogeomorphic settings, and on both organic and wet mineral soils. It is usually found in species mixtures rather than monodominant stands, although the latter do occur. The species has been widely used by Native Americans throughout its northern range as a source of splints for basket-weaving, for lacrosse sticks, and for several medicinal uses (Anderson and Neson 2006; Benedict and Frelich 2008).

Black ash is classified as Facultative-Wet FAC-WET) and FAC-WET+ throughout its range. It occasionally is found in uplands, and can reproduce rapidly through sprouting after disturbances (Arévalo, DeCoster, et al. 2000). Aside from the observation by Tardif, Dery, et al. (1994) that saplings can produce hypertrophied lenticels, there does not appear to have been any detailed studies of its physiology or adaptations to wetland conditions.

Geomorphic Settings

Both red maple and black ash swamps are found over the entire range of geological and geomorphic settings in the region of interest. As summarized by Golet, Calhoun, et al. (1993) for the glaciated Northeast, this includes many different physiographic provinces, representing elevations from sea level to 1,200 m and bedrock types including granites, schists, slates, shales, limestones, sandstones, conglomerates, recent and Cenozoic unconsolidated sediments, with and without glacial surficial layers (tills, moraines, outwash, glacial lake clays, and other deposits). Over the larger range considered here, these wetlands are found in an even wider variety of physiographic provinces (12 provinces, from the New England Province to the Central Lowlands of the Midwest [http://tapestry.usgs.gov/physiogr/physio.html], and 8 ecoregions, as mapped by Bailey [1995]). Because there is no well-defined western boundary for the distribution of red maple–dominated wetlands, the western physiographic provinces may be less well represented.

Red maple swamps are found across the range of hydrogeomorphic settings for wetlands (depressions, slopes [seeps], riverine, lacustrine, organic and mineral flats). However, red maple–dominated wetlands are less common in alluvial or riverine settings. Black ash, while also found in a range of hydrogeomorphic settings, is most commonly associated with floodplains. These associations are discussed below more extensively in the context of plant community composition and structure.

As noted above, and as discussed in more detail below, red maple and black ash occur as both dominants and subordinate species in a wide range of different community types across their species ranges, and different sources of community classification yield different definitions of what constitutes a red maple or black ash swamp. In addition, national- and state-level analyses of wetland distribution only report "forested wetland" or other broad classes of wetland, which may be largely but not entirely represented by the wetlands of interest here. Thus, it is at present not possible to accurately estimate the abundance of these community types. How-

TABLE 11.2

Representative data on red maple stand structure

Parameter	Range of values	Data source
Stand height (m)	7.9–17.7	31 stands in RI, MA, NJ
Tree density (stems/ha)	225–3,067	33 stands in RI, NY, NJ
Basal area (m²/ha)	11.6–39.0	41 stands in RI, NY, NY, NJ
Shrub cover (%)	3–99	30 stands in RI, CT
Shrub density (stems/ha)	470–86,440	27 stands in RI, NY, NH, NJ
Herb cover (%)	0–88	30 stands in RI, CT

NOTE: From Golet, Calhoun, et al. (1993). Different studies used different criteria for counting stems as "trees" or "shrubs."

ever, a recent survey of major wetland types in the northeastern region (defined as the states from Maine to Virginia along the East Coast, west only to Pennsylvania and West Virginia) (Tiner 2010) gives some idea of the areal extent and relative importance, if it is assumed that the majority of palustrine forested wetlands in this area are dominated by red maple. In most of these states with extensive coastal marshes, palustrine forested wetlands account for over 50% of all wetlands, with most occurring in nontidal locations (Table 11.1). Abundance of black ash swamps is, at present, not known.

Plant Communities

A comprehensive overview of plant community composition for either red maple or black ash wetlands is difficult to present, largely because the literature is so sparse. Golet, Calhoun, et al. (1993) provided comprehensive descriptions of both species composition and vegetation structure for red maple swamps in different portions of the glaciated Northeast, summarizing the existing literature as of the early 1990s, including many unpublished theses. This publication remains the best source for a detailed consideration of red maple swamps in this portion of the community's range. State-based vegetation surveys each give descriptions of red maple and black ash swamps (for example, Breden 1989; Fike 1999; Metzler and Barrett 2006), with lists of typical species, but these descriptions do not have equivalent amounts of information. No profile of black ash communities has been done, and the literature on these wetlands is sparse.

The most comprehensive and nationally applicable description of both red maple–dominated and black ash–dominated communities available at this time is the community classification developed by NatureServe, a nonprofit organization that brings together natural heritage program information and state-based biological inventories. They have produced a comprehensive classification of terrestrial ecosystems of the United States (Comer, Faber-Langendoen, et al. 2003), which is available online at www.natureserve.org/index.jsp. This classification is based on the American component of the International Vegetation Classification (U.S. National Vegetation Classification). It uses a combination of environmental factors (geology, topography, soils, geographic extent and location, climate, elevation), important dynamic processes (hydrologic regime, fire regime), and plant community composition (both

species composition and vegetation structure) to define ecological units. The most specific level of the hierarchical system is the "association"; associations are grouped into "alliances," which are then grouped into "ecological systems." Associations and alliances are based primarily on floristic criteria, but include in their descriptions and definitions the environmental and dynamic criteria mentioned above (Comer, Faber-Langendoen, et al. 2003). The development of this classification system permits a comprehensive overview of both the floristics and environmental determinants of all communities in which a particular species is a dominant species. Although the descriptions of each alliance and association provide some floristic information, the level of detail of this information varies greatly among the associations, and none present quantitative data on either overall species richness or on the abundance of particular species. Therefore, this information has not been further analyzed, as the extent to which descriptions of different communities are comparable is not clear. The reader is referred to the NatureServe website listed above for available floristic information for each alliance or association.

Red Maple Communities

Red maple communities range from those with dense woody understories to those with few shrubs but dense and often diverse herb strata (Fig. 11.2). This range of community structure is well described by the data presented in Golet, Calhoun, et al. (1993) (Table 11.2) and confirmed by subsequent studies (Ehrenfeld 2005; Rheinhardt 2007; Peterson-Smith, Wardrop, et al. 2009). Red maple is most commonly the canopy dominant, but tends to be mixed with other species in floodplains (Aronson, Hatfield, et al. 2004; Baker and Wiley 2004). Canopy composition ranges from monodominant stands (Society of American Foresters cover type no. 108) to stands in which it is a codominant or associated species.

Online appendix 11.1 lists alliances in which red maple is a dominant or codominant species. The large number of alliances (24) and larger number of associations (85) vividly illustrate the extremely wide ecological amplitude of the species, both geographically and ecologically. Fig. 11.3 illustrates the abundance of associations within each state and Canadian province. Clearly, New England, the mid-Atlantic region, and Quebec host the greatest diversity of red maple–dominated communities. However, the southern and north-midwestern

FIG. 11.2. Characteristic appearance of red maple swamps with (A) herbaceous understories and (B) woody understories.

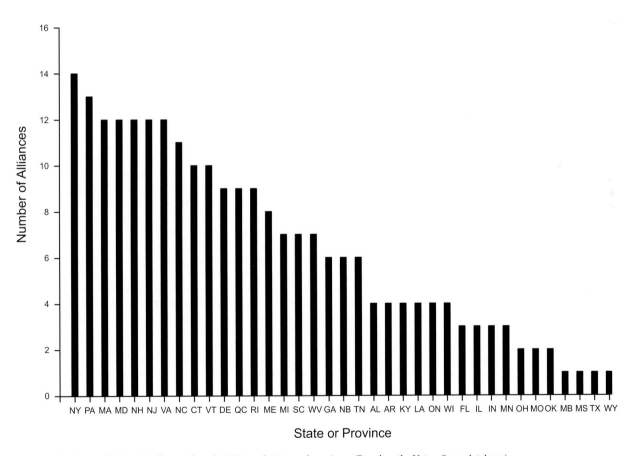

FIG. 11.3. Numbers of red maple alliances found within each state and province. (Based on the NatureServe database.)

states included in many of the descriptions illustrate how red maple swamps grade into southern bottomland hardwoods and northern peatland communities.

Red maple forms associations with other deciduous trees and evergreen coniferous species. The latter communities include associations with conifers that have northern *(Picea rubens, Tsuga canadensis, Pinus strobus),* midwestern *(Thuja occidentalis),* eastern *(Chamaecyparis thyoides, Pinus rigida),* and southern distributions *(Pinus taeda).* Some alliances are widespread, occurring across the East Coast from New England to the Gulf and including numerous associations. Others have more restricted distributions (for example, the *Pinus taeda–Chamaecyparis thyoides–Acer rubrum–Nyssa biflora* saturated forest alliance, found only in North Carolina and Virginia). More than half of the alliances (14) are characterized by saturated, rather than flooded, conditions; the others are divided between seasonally and temporarily flooded conditions. One alliance *(Fraxinus pennsylvanica–Acer rubrum–Ulmus americana* tidal forest alliance), found primarily on the mid-Atlantic Coastal Plain, is characterized by tidal flooding.

In the hydrologic descriptions of each alliance, riverine and alluvial hydrologies are notably absent. Only those communities associated with headwaters, small rivers, or bottoms or lower terraces within floodplain systems are described as being subject to surface-water flooding. Thus, while red maple is a frequent component of many riparian communities throughout its range, as described in, e.g., Messina and Conner (1998), it is rarely a dominant species when surface-water flooding is the dominant source of water. Indeed, groundwater sources, either as high water tables that maintain soil saturation, as headwaters regions (Morley and Calhoun 2009), or as discharge at seeps or within portions of floodplains with mixtures of water sources, appear to be the primary hydrological conditions, although exceptions occur in isolated instances (Rheinhardt 2007). Peterson-Smith, Wardrop, et al. (2009) examined the relationship of community composition to hydrogeomorphic setting in sites from the Adirondacks to Virginia, and found that community types were more strongly related to hydrogeomorphology within each region than across the entire latitudinal gradient, suggesting that hydrology is only one of many factors determining community composition.

Soil properties, both physical and chemical, are also quite variable among the alliances (insofar as this information is provided). Alliances are found on both mineral and organic soils, and the latter include both deep peats and mucky, highly decomposed organic matter. The majority of soils data indicate that these communities are more frequently associated with acidic conditions than with calcareous conditions.

Species composition of red maple swamps is as varied as environmental properties and geographic locations. Golet, Calhoun, et al. (1993) described the flora of swamps in the glaciated Northeast as "rich," containing at least 50 species of trees, 90 species of shrubs and vines, and over 300 species of herbaceous plants. Ehrenfeld (2005) described a set of red maple–dominated swamps from a small urban region of New Jersey that contained 300 species of vascular plants. Paratley and Fahey (1986) examined a 40-ha wetland in New York and reported 272 species from that one site. In contrast, Rheinhardt (2007) found only 106 species in a sample of 16 red maple swamps in southeastern Massachusetts. This overall diversity clearly reflects the diversity of hydrogeomorphic settings and soils that characterize these communities. Nevertheless, all of these studies found that the number of species per site ranged between 20–30 to at most 100–120 vascular species, with high

dominance of a few select species (Paratley and Fahey 1986; Golet, Calhoun, et al. 1993; Ehrenfeld 2005). Higher richness is associated with less acidic soils, less coniferous cover, and more microtopographic relief (hummock-hollow microtopography). Higher species richness has also been associated with moderate amounts of flooding on low-gradient rivers, in contrast to depression wetlands (Rheinhardt 2007).

Red maple swamps also vary greatly in the relative abundance of shrubs and herbs, ranging from sites with dense shrub strata and few herbaceous species to sites with few shrubs and dense (and diverse) herbaceous communities (Fig. 11.2). In New Jersey sites, most shrub species are classified as facultative species, and thus are found over a wide range of site types (Ehrenfeld 2005). Herbaceous species, in particular the graminoid species, constitute most of the obligate wetland species, and account for much of the difference in overall diversity among wetlands. Dense shrub layers have been associated with high water tables and prolonged wetness (Golet, Calhoun, et al. 1993) based on several studies in Rhode Island, New York, and New Jersey, but this observation has not been more extensively tested and verified. In addition, Ehrenfeld (2005) found in the sample of New Jersey swamps that tree, shrub, and herb strata were structured by different sets of environmental variables.

In the urban red maple swamps of New Jersey, the presence of exotic plant species was also found to vary greatly, with some urban sites not heavily invaded, contrary to expectation (Ehrenfeld 2008; Cutway and Ehrenfeld 2009). Exotic invasion was associated with adjacent land use, with higher rates of invasion in wetlands adjacent to residential areas than those near industrial-commercial areas, and with increasing soil nutrient content and sandy textures. In a review of urban wetlands in general (many of which were red maple swamps), Ehrenfeld and Stander (2011) found that patterns of exotic species invasions were complex, with many different factors in addition to urban land use affecting the degree of invasion.

Black Ash Communities

Unlike red maple communities, there are relatively few black ash–dominated communities; these are summarized in Table 11.3. Although the species is found on a wide range of soil types and over a wide range of pH values, many of the described wetlands in which it is a dominant species occur on calcareous substrates and/or are associated with base-rich groundwater or circumneutral to alkaline pH values. Two of these limestone-associated communities are globally rare, with one type *(Fraxinus nigra–Abies balsamea / Rhamnus alnifolia* forest) known from only seven sites in West Virginia. Most of the black ash communities are also described as being rich in herbaceous species, particularly graminoids.

Black ash forms variable associations with other hardwoods (primarily *A. rubrum,* but also *Tilia cordata, Ulmus americana,* and *Fraxinus pennsylvanica)* and with several coniferous species, including *T. canadensis, A. balsamea,* and especially *Thuja occidentalis,* a common associate in the upper Midwest. In the upper Midwest (Michigan and Wisconsin), it is primarily found as part of a black ash–elm–red maple community type on somewhat poorly drained soils, and as almost pure black ash stands on poorly drained organic soils (Erdman, Crow, et al. 1987; MacFarlane and Meyer 2005). A community classification from northern Quebec (Tardif and Bergeron 1992) identified several types of community, but it is not clear how these community types correspond to those delimited by Nature-Serve (Table 11.3). The NatureServe data suggest that some communities have geographically restricted distributions. For example, the *Acer rubrum–Fraxinus americana–Fraxinus nigra–Betula alleghaniensis / Veratrum viride–Carex bromoides* forest is found only on metabasalt substrates in the northern Blue Ridge. Conversely, the *Fraxinus nigra–Acer rubrum* saturated forest alliance is found across 24 states and Canadian provinces. However, most states have only one or two association types present.

A series of studies conducted at Lake Duparquet in northwest Quebec have illuminated some aspects of the ecology of black ash communities, at least in the boreal forest biome. Wetlands along the shore of the lake contain combinations of *F. nigra, Picea mariana, T. occidentalis,* and several less abundant species. Sites with a high abundance (often pure) stands of black ash are located on low surfaces (50 cm to < 2 m elevation above the lake), and include both floodplains receiving inundation from the lake and flats constructed of lake-derived deposits, with glaciolacustrine clayey soils (Denneler, Bergeron, et al. 1999; Tardif and Bergeron 1999; Denneler, Asselin, et al. 2008). Differences in community composition of black ash–dominated sites reflect small differences in elevation and drainage, which determine flooding frequency and intensity (Tardif and Bergeron 1992). Black ash seedlings recruit well in the range of 50–200 cm above the lake level, and recruitment at higher or lower elevations is poor. These riparian stands have uneven age-structured populations that fit a negative exponential model well (Denneler, Asselin, et al. 2008). At higher elevations, sensitivity to fire, drought, and shading from other species limits recruitment. As a riparian species, it is tolerant of high levels of disturbance not only from flooding, but also from ice pushed up during spring melt. Old-growth stands can develop with trees exceeding 200 years in age. Detailed studies of population dynamics in stands with different flooding regimes on this lake showed that the ability of the species to sprout from the stumps allows stands to survive and spread with high amounts of flooding damage (Tardif and Bergeron 1999). The sprouting ability renders these stands resistant to long-term fluctuations in flood frequency, as low-elevation stands recover through sprouting while less flooded populations rely on sexual reproduction. However, sexual reproduction in turn depends on moisture conditions, including both winter and summer precipitation levels, with different controls operating in different stands (Tardif, Dery, et al. 1994). Precipitation also affects radial growth, as does temperature, and again, stands in different geomorphic positions respond to different combinations of precipitation and temperature, particularly the conditions in the previous year (Tardif and Bergeron 1993, 1997). Radial growth varies on 3.5- and 7.5-year periodicities (Tardif, Dutilleul, et al. 1998), which may also reflect periodicities in flooding and flood stress. While this exemplary series of studies illuminates many aspects of black ash stands, it is not known whether the ecological relationships demonstrated for these populations at the northern limit of both the species' and the community type's ranges are applicable to populations elsewhere. Moreover, the dynamics and ecological controls demonstrated for the boreal sites have unknown relevance for the range of associations reported by NatureServe (Table 11.3) on different types of hydrogeomorphic positions and soils. Finally, it should be noted that black ash is among the last species to leaf out in the spring and among the first to shed leaves in the fall (C. Johnston pers. communication). How it competes successfully with other trees with such a short growing season remains an open and intriguing research question.

Biogeochemistry

As with other aspects of red maple swamps, there is a dearth of studies specifically addressing biogeochemical functions. There is even less information on this topic for black ash swamps. Golet, Calhoun, et al. (1993) lamented the lack of data on northern red maple swamps, and relied on studies from Virginia's Great Dismal Swamp (Day 1979, 1982; Gomez and Day 1982; Megonigal and Day 1988) and northern peatlands to broadly examine basic nutrient cycling processes. While there has been extensive study of biogeochemical processes in wetlands throughout the regions covered by these wetland types, many, if not most, do not clearly indicate whether red maple is present, and if so, whether it is the dominant canopy species. This is especially the case because most biogeochemical attention has been focused on riparian wetlands because of their great importance in regulating surface water quality and hydrology, but, as discussed above, red maple dominance is less common in these geomorphic settings than in depression, slope, and mineral and organic flat settings.

A recent series of studies of red maple swamps in New York and Rhode Island by Groffman and colleagues have explored nitrogen cycling, and especially denitrification potential, in riparian red maple swamps. In a comparison of New York red maple swamps of moderate pH (~ 6) with other kinds of wetlands, Groffman, Hanson, et al. (1996) found that the maple swamps had low levels of extractable ammonium but variable levels of extractable nitrate, soil carbon, and nitrogen (N), conductivity, potential net N mineralization and nitrification rates among three replicate sites. The authors related these differences to site hydrology: a site with higher water tables had, not surprisingly, higher organic matter content in the soil, and higher microbial biomass and microbially mediated processes than the drier sites. Similar variability among replicate sites was observed in a sample of three red maple swamps of low pH (~ 3–4) in Rhode Island (Simmons, Gold, et al. 1992; Duncan and Groffman 1994). These sites showed high abilities to remove nitrate through microbial denitrification, particularly when upland residential land use supplied high levels of nitrate in groundwater (Nelson, Gold, et al. 1995). Denitrification rates were higher in the red maple swamps on poorly and very poorly drained soils than in the transitional and upland (not red maple–dominated), better-drained soils. Hydrology and soil organic matter exert strong controls over the size and characteristics of the soil microbial community, such that surface soils have higher denitrification activities than do deeper soils, although plant uptake of nitrate from deep roots may also have an effect (Groffman, Gold, et al. 1992).

Nelson, Gold, et al. (1995) noted that nitrate removal capacity had high spatial and temporal variability. Part of the spatial patchiness in denitrification potential, particularly in subsoil materials, is due to variability in the location and size of patches of organic matter associated with decaying tree roots; patches of dead roots promote denitrification of groundwater nitrate because they are a source of carbon for microbial populations (Gold, Jacinthe, et al. 1998; Rotkin-Ellman, Addy, et al. 2004). Despite the ability of red maple swamps on poorly and very poorly drained soils to remove significant amounts of nitrate in both surface and subsurface soils, large inputs of N from adjacent developed land can result in nitrogen enrich-

TABLE 11.3
Black ash associations, as reported in the NatureServe database

Association name	Hydrology and soils
Acer rubrum–Fraxinus americana–Fraxinus nigra–Betula alleghaniensis / Veratrum viride–Carex bromoides forest	Groundwater-saturated headwater streams; large spring seeps; groundwater discharge zones along slope bottoms; soils with high Ca, Mg
Acer rubrum–Fraxinus nigra–(Tsuga canadensis) / Tiarella cordifolia forest	Organic (peat or muck) soils; minerotrophic (circumneutral pH)
Fraxinus nigra–Abies balsamea / Rhamnus alnifolia forest	Seepage-fed, frost-pocket wetlands on limestone; high-elevation (> 900 m) temporarily to semipermanently flooded flat headwaters and basins. Muck or organic-rich silt loams over clay; high base saturation; pH ~ 5–6
Fraxinus nigra–Acer rubrum–(Larix laricina) / Rhamnus alnifolia forest	Calcareous groundwater seepage sites along streams or headwaters; organic soils; Ca-rich groundwater
Fraxinus nigra–Acer rubrum / Rhamnus alnifolia / Carex leptalea saturated forest	Unglaciated seepage zones and depressions, often on calcareous bedrock. Muck soils, but no peat deposits
Fraxinus nigra–mixed hardwoods–conifers / *Cornus sericea / Carex* spp. forest	Perched water tables or other impeded drainage sites; also near shores. Seasonally flooded to saturated. Well-decomposed woody peat or fine-textured mineral soils
Populus balsamifera–Fraxinus nigra / Matteuccia struthiopteris forest	Floodplains on moderate-energy boreal rivers; spring flooding, silty alluvial soils
Quercus palustris–(Fraxinus nigra) / Lindera benzoin / Carex bromoides forest	Floodplain forests on low-gradient reach, sloughs and oxbows; silty clay loam soils; seasonal and periodic flooding from bank overflow
Thuja occidentalis–Fraxinus nigra forest	Well-decomposed peat or mineral saturated soils, minerotrophic

ment of both soils and vegetation, and produce symptoms of nitrogen saturation (Hanson, Groffman, et al. 1994).

The carbon that fuels denitrification in these wetlands is generally assumed to be derived from recent photosynthate (fresh litter, dissolved organic carbon from this litter, labile forms of soil organic matter), but a recent analysis of red maple sites on both alluvial and glaciofluvial soils in Rhode Island showed that ancient carbon (> 500 years old) in buried horizons at 3–4 m depth may also be used. Gurwick, Groffman, et al. (2008) examined soil profiles in 14 riparian red maple swamps in Rhode Island and found both alluvial and glaciolacustrine sites could have buried organic or organic matter-rich A horizons. They further found that the organic matter from these buried horizons, aged at 16,270–17,050 years before present, was available for microbial metabolism, and supported microbial biomass proportional to the amount of carbon min-

eralization (Gurwick, McCorkle, et al. 2008). The ancient carbon may reflect buried flow channel deposits, which appear to be common in glaciated landscapes. These studies support other work suggesting that buried horizons are a major control on overall denitrification rates in wetlands, at least within these glaciated regions. The role of buried carbon in maple swamps in glaciated landscapes deserves further investigation.

These studies all emphasize the role of soil type (in particular, soil texture and organic matter quantity, quality, and distribution through the profile) and hydrology as fundamental controls on nitrogen cycling in red maple swamps, fully in line with conclusions of many other studies of nitrogen cycling in wetlands (Reddy and DeLaune 2008). To what extent red maple swamps may have unique properties cannot be evaluated from the available information. While it is known that different plant species can have dramatic effects on soil microbial com-

Distribution	Plant community characteristics	Alliance
Northern Blue Ridge on metabasalt (base-rich bedrock); small patch sizes; VA, MD; also DE, NJ. VA occurrence is southernmost location	Mixed overstory; *F. nigra* more common in understory; canopy partially open due to blowdowns; very wet microsites. Diverse, dense shrub layer. High herb cover; high microtopographic relief	*Fraxinus nigra–Acer rubrum* saturated forest alliance; global status G3
Central New England and MI; groundwater-discharge zones in basins, stream headwaters; MA, NH, VT, MI	*A. rubrum* as canopy codominant; *Tsuga canadensis* and/or *Pinus strobus* may be present. Herb layer with dense layer of ferns and nonvascular plants	*Fraxinus nigra–Acer rubrum* saturated forest alliance
Allegheny Mountains, WV; small patches	Stunted, open canopy of *F. nigra, Abies balsamea, Tsuga canadensis*. High herb diversity and microtopographic relief; several rare calciphiles; graminoids dominate	*Fraxinus nigra–Acer rubrum* saturated forest alliance; global status G1; known from 7 patches in WV
Northeast U.S.: CT, MA, NH, NJ, NY, PA, RI, VT. Canada: QC	*A. rubrum, Larix laricina* canopy associates. Dense shrub and vine strata	*Fraxinus nigra–Acer rubrum* saturated forest alliance
Narrow zones to large swamps; northern Piedmont, Allegheny Plateau, Central Appalachians. MD, NY, PA, WV	*A. rubrum, F. nigra* codominants. Patchy shrub stratum; diverse, sedge-dominated herb stratum	*Fraxinus nigra–Acer rubrum* saturated forest alliance
Northern Midwest to boreal zone. U.S.: IL, IN, MI, MN, ND, WI, WY. Canada: MB, ON, QC	Variable canopy cover (open to closed), diverse mix of hardwoods and conifers; *F. nigra* at least 50% of canopy cover. Diverse shrub and herb strata	*Fraxinus nigra–Acer rubrum* saturated forest alliance
U.S.: ME, NH (?), VT Canada: NB, QC	Canopy cover partly open (~ 80%). Patchy shrub stratum and dense herb stratum	*Populus tremuloides* temporarily flooded forest alliance
Restricted to one river (Meadow River) in WV	*F. nigra* mixed with *Q. palustris* (dominant) and other hardwoods. Diverse sedge herb stratum	*Quercus palustris–(Quercus bicolor)* seasonally flooded forest alliance
Sub-boreal Great Lakes region U.S.: MI, MN, WI Canada: ON	Canopy variable, often fairly open; strong microtopographic relief	*Thuja occidentalis–Acer rubrum* saturated forest alliance

munities and the microbially mediated processes that create biogeochemical cycles (Ehrenfeld, Ravit, et al. 2005), the evidence from wetlands for such plant species–mediated effects on wetland biogeochemistry is not yet strong. Indeed, studies in salt marshes (Ravit, Ehrenfeld, et al. 2003) have suggested that hydrology may override plant-specific effects on microbial communities. Whether these results apply to less wet sites (seasonally or temporarily saturated wetlands, as are many types of red maple swamp) remains to be determined. However, it is quite clear that alterations in hydrology, particularly the effects of urban disturbances that reduce the extent of wetland hydrology through ditches, dams, and diversions, can greatly alter biogeochemical processes. For example, Stander and Ehrenfeld (2009a,b) found that such urban disturbances resulted in net nitrate production, and a striking decrease in denitrification rates, in a population of red maple swamps in New Jersey.

Animal Communities

As with all other aspects of red maple wetlands, there has been little research beyond the summary of animal communities presented in Golet, Calhoun, et al. (1993). For black ash swamps, there is even less information available. According to Golet et al.'s review of wildlife reports for northeastern red maple swamps, numerous species of vertebrates use these wetlands. This includes numerous wetland-dependent as well as nondependent species. They list 24 species of amphibians, 18 species of reptiles, 120 species of birds, and 50 species of mammals. Of these, 103 were listed as species of "special concern" (species that are considered rare, threatened, or endangered in at least one state as reviewed by Golet et al.). Examples of such species include bog turtles *(Glyptemys muhlenbergii),* eastern mountain lions *(Puma concolor couguar),* and New England cottontail *(Sylvilagus transitionalis)*. Not surprisingly, vegetation structure (number of strata, stem and foliage densities within strata, canopy tree height, leaf area height distribution) influences all types of vertebrates. Hydrology is an equally important factor (acting in part through its effect on vegetation).

Beyond lists of species, it is not possible to deduce general relationships between faunal communities and either botanical communities or environmental factors, due to the lack of data.

Two recent studies of bird communities in nonriparian red maple swamps, one in Michigan (Riffell, Burton, et al. 2006) and one in Rhode Island (Golet, Wang, et al. 2001), illustrate the challenges of seeking general patterns about animal communities. Golet, Wang, et al. (2001) quantified bird communities in a sample of wetlands set within a largely forested landscape (Rhode Island). They found that swamp size was the primary determinant of bird richness, and plant community and landscape structure were secondary factors affecting different species and subgroups of birds. Riffell, Burton, et al. (2006) used similar metrics to quantify bird communities in depression wetlands set within small forested patches, which were located within a largely agricultural landscape. They found, in contrast to Golet's study, that swamp size was not important, but that overall forest patch size was the most important determinant of bird species richness. As Riffell et al. point out, the difference in results probably reflects the overall landscape structure: Rhode Island is extensively forested, whereas Michigan is primarily agricultural, and so forest patch size assumes an importance it lacks in a forested region. The contrast in these results underlines the fact that because many, if not most, animals use both wetland and upland habitats, animal communities are strongly influenced by landscape setting, as well as by the characteristics of particular sites and regional species pools. Without studies of animal use of red maple and black ash swamps that are dedicated to understanding the characteristics of these wetlands that structure animal communities, understanding of this topic will not advance.

Conservation Concerns and Research Needs

Both red maple and black ash swamps face the range of conservation challenges that affect virtually all natural communities: destruction for development, fragmentation, exotic species invasion, loss of rare species, nutrient and toxic pollution. But the protection and management of red maple and black ash swamps face an equally large challenge from the lack of dedicated research attention and the striking lack of detailed information about almost all aspects of the ecology of these ecosystems. Clearly, part of the problem comes from the fact that both species, especially red maple, are found over large geographic ranges, and are components of many types of wetlands across these geographic ranges. In addition, there are no clear criteria for distinguishing the point at which a wetland in which these species contribute to canopy structure becomes a "red maple swamp" or "black ash swamp." While riparian and floodplain wetlands, with or without red maple or black ash, have attracted extensive research attention because of their obvious importance to many ecosystem services, wetlands in other hydrogeomorphic locations are not prominently associated with ecosystem services and thus have received much less research attention.

Two major strands of needed research can be identified that are grounded in fundamental questions of ecology. First, the

most well-defined communities of both species have mono-dominant, or near-monodominant, canopies, and thus a single species is providing most of the biomass of these stands. Given the strong emphasis in the recent research literature on the value and importance of biodiversity (Hooper, Chapin, et al. 2005; Gamfeldt and Hillebrand 2008; Duffy 2009; Reiss, Bridle, et al. 2009), the ecosystem functions and potential ecosystem services provided by these ecosystems call out for basic research. Does ecosystem functioning vary with the diversity of a herb layer that provides a tiny fraction of the biomass but is often, as described above, highly diverse in these swamps? That is, does understory diversity mitigate effects of the low diversity of the biomass dominants? Do swamp forests with low-diversity tree assemblages function differently from swamp forests of similar hydrology but with higher-diversity tree assemblages? How do variations in function associated with the diversity of the canopy affect ecosystem services (e.g., nitrogen sequestration or removal, flood storage, carbon sequestration)? Undoubtedly, many other questions could be posed. Answers to these questions would not only greatly improve our understanding of wetlands dominated by these species or containing these species as important components of the canopy, but would also inform ecological theory. And, insofar as ecosystem function determines the services that society manages, better knowledge would help inform management—and valuation—of these wetlands.

A second important line of research concerns the structure and function of these communities along the large gradients of geography, environmental conditions, and community composition that this chapter has documented. How is community composition related to hydrogeomorphic and soil conditions? Are there identifiable environmental conditions under which either species is always or never dominant? Do canopy and understory structures reflect similar environmental factors? Ehrenfeld (2005, 2008), for example, found that species in different strata may respond in opposite fashion to the same environmental factor. Indeed, to what extent are particular understory structures dependent on canopy structures? Because most plant species of concern (rare or endangered) are understory species, answers to such questions would inform their management and conservation.

Research in both of these areas is particularly important in order to inform and guide the numerous mitigation projects that are attempting to restore deciduous forested wetlands. As described above, such wetlands account for over half of the wetland area in the Northeast, and probably similar fractions in the Midwest. They are therefore frequently the target of development permits and consequent mitigation efforts. As has been well documented (NRC 2001), forested wetlands are frequently replaced by other types of wetlands during restoration, and the loss of forested wetlands to upland land uses continues to be a significant problem (Dahl 2005). Developing appropriate guidelines for forested wetland restoration depends on having accurate data on species composition, hydrology, and soils, information that is largely lacking for the great variety of red maple and black ash communities. Indeed, knowledge of the success and status of forested wetland restoration in the Northeast and Midwest is largely unknown. A comprehensive assessment of restoration success, failures, and challenges for these community types would be a valuable contribution to both the knowledge of these ecosystems and the mitigation industry that uses this knowledge.

Finally, an emerging and significant challenge for black ash swamps is the spread of the emerald ash borer *Agrilus pla-*

nipennis (Coleoptera: Buprestidae) (Poland and McCullough 2006). This beetle, introduced into Michigan in 2002, is now established in much of the midwestern range of *F. nigra* and is expanding rapidly eastward through the rest of its range (MacFarlane and Meyer 2005). The beetle feeds and oviposits on black ash as extensively as it does on white and green ash (Pureswaran and Poland 2009). Spread of the insect involves both local diffusive dispersal and human-mediated dispersal through the movement of nursery or forestry stock, especially firewood (Muirhead, Leung, et al. 2006). The beetle is currently (2010) found extensively in southern Michigan and adjacent Indiana and northern Ohio, but is also reported from counties scattered across Illinois, Maryland, Pennsylvania, and New York (www.emeraldashborer.info/files/MultiState_EABpos.pdf). Most of the research on the beetle and its effects on ash has been devoted to the economically important white and green ash; much less is known of its effects on black ash. With the anticipated spread of this pest throughout the range of the species, major impacts on its ecosystems must unfortunately be expected.

Acknowledgments

I thank Drs. Frank P. Day Jr. and Carol Johnston for helpful comments on an earlier version of this paper. Support was provided by grants from the NSF (DEB-0948896), the U.S. EPA (EPA RD83377701-01), and the U.S. Dept of Agriculture (grant number 2009-35900-06016).

References

Abrams MD. 1998. The red maple paradox. *BioScience* 48:355–64.

Anderson MK, Neson G. 2006. *Black ash plant guide.* Washington, DC: USDA Natural Resources Conservation Service.

Anella LB, Whitlow TH. 2000. Photosynthetic response to flooding of *Acer rubrum* seedlings from wet and dry sites. *Am. Midl. Nat.* 143:330–41.

Arévalo JR, DeCoster JK, et al. 2000. Changes in two Minnesota forests during 14 years following catastrophic windthrow. *J. Veg. Sci.* 11:833–40.

Aronson MFJ, Hatfield CA, Hartman JM. 2004. Plant community patterns of low-gradient forested floodplains in a New Jersey urban landscape. *J. Torrey Bot. Soc.* 131:232–42.

Bailey RG. 1995. *Description of the ecoregions of the United States,* 2nd ed. Misc. Pub. no. 1391. Washington, DC: USDA Forest Service.

Baker ME, Wiley MJ. 2004. Characterization of woody species distribution in riparian forests of lower Michigan, USA, using map-based models. *Wetlands* 24:550–61.

Bauerle WL, Whitlow TH, et al. 2003. Ecophysiology of *Acer rubrum* seedlings from contrasting hydrologic habitats: growth, gas exchange, tissue water relations, abscisic acid and carbon isotope discrimination. *Tree Physiol.* 23:841–50.

Benedict MA, Frelich LE. 2008. Site factors affecting black ash ring growth in northern Minnesota. *For. Ecol. Manage.* 255:3489–93.

Breden T. 1989. A preliminary natural community classification for New Jersey. In *New Jersey's rare and endangered plants and animals.* Mahwah: School of Theoretical and Applied Science, Ramapo College of New Jersey, pp. 157–91.

Burns RM, Honkala BH. 1990. Silvics of North America. 1. Conifers; 2. Hardwoods. Agricultural Handbook 654. Washington, DC: USDA Forest Service.

Comer PD, Faber-Langendoen D, et al. 2003. *Ecological systems of the United States: a working classification of U.S. terrestrial systems.* Arlington, VA: NatureServe.

Cutway HB, Ehrenfeld JG. 2009. Exotic plant invasions in forested wetlands: effects of adjacent urban land use type. *Urban Ecosystems* 12:371–90.

Dahl T. 2005. *Status and trends of wetlands in the conterminous United States 1998–2004.* Fish and Wildlife Service 112. Washington, DC: USDI.

Day FP. 1979. Litter accumulation in four plant communities in the Dismal Swamp, Virginia. *Am. Midl. Nat.* 102:281–89.

Day FP. 1982. Litter decomposition rates in the seasonally flooded Great Dismal Swamp. *Ecology* 63:670–78.

Day FP. 1985. Influence of species, season, and soil on foliar macronutrients in the Great Dismal Swamp. *Bull. Torrey Bot. Club* 112:146–57.

Day FP. 1987. Effects of flooding and nutrient enrichment on biomass allocation in *Acer rubrum* seedlings. *Am. J. Bot.* 74:1541–54.

Denneler B, Asselin H, et al. 2008. Decreased fire frequency and increased water levels affect riparian forest dynamics in southwestern boreal Quebec, Canada. *Can. J. For. Res.—Rev. Can. Rech. For.* 38:1083–94.

Denneler B, Bergeron Y, Begin Y. 1999. An attempt to explain the distribution of the tree species composing the riparian forests of Lake Duparquet, southern boreal region of Quebec, Canada. *Can. J. Bot.y—Rev. Can. Bot.* 77:1744–55.

Duffy JE. 2009. Why biodiversity is important to the functioning of real-world ecosystems. *Frontiers Ecol. Env.* 7:437–44.

Duncan CP, Groffman PM. 1994. Comparing microbial parameters in natural and constructed wetlands *J. Env. Qual.* 23:298–305.

Ehrenfeld JG. 2005. Vegetation of forested wetlands of urban and suburban landscapes in New Jersey. *J. Torrey Bot. Soc.* 132:262–79.

Ehrenfeld J. 2008. Exotic invasive species in urban wetlands: environmental correlates and implications for wetland management. *J. Appl. Ecol.* 45:1160–69.

Ehrenfeld JG, Ravit B, Elgersma K. 2005. Feedback in the plant-soil system. *Annu. Rev. Env. Resour.* 30:75–115.

Ehrenfeld JG, Stander E. 2010. Habitat functions in urban riparian zones. In *Urban ecosystem ecology,* Aitkenhead-Peterson J, Volder A, editors. Madison, WI: ACA-CSSA-SSSA. pp. 103–118.

Erdman G, Crow TR, et al. 1987. *Managing black ash in the Lake States.* USDA Forest Service N. Central For. Exp. Sta. Gen. Tech. Rep. NC-115.

Fike J. 1999. *Terrestrial and palustrine communities of Pennsylvania.* Harrisburg: Pennsylvania Dept. Conserv. Nat. Resour. and Nature Conservancy.

Gamfeldt L, Hillebrand H. 2008. Biodiversity effects on aquatic ecosystem functioning—maturation of a new paradigm. *Internat. Rev. Hydrobiol.* 93:550–64.

Gold AJ, Jacinthe PA, et al. 1998. Patchiness in groundwater nitrate removal in a riparian forest. *J. Env. Qual.* 27:146–55.

Golet FC, Calhoun JK, et al. 1993. Ecology of red maple swamps in the glaciated Northeast: a community profile. Washington, DC: USFWS, Biological Report 12.

Golet FC, Wang Y, et al. 2001. Relationship between habitat and landscape features and the avian community of red maple swamps in southern Rhode Island. *Wilson Bull.* 113:217–27.

Gomez MM, Day FP. 1982. Litter nutrient content and production in the Great Dismal Swamp. *Am. J. Bot.* 69:1314–21.

Groffman PM, Gold AJ, Simmons RC. 1992. Nitrate dynamics in riparian forests: microbial studies. *J. Env. Qual.* 21:666–71.

Groffman PM, Hanson GC, et al. 1996. Variation in microbial biomass and activity in four different wetland types. *Soil Sci. Soc. Am. J.* 60:622–29.

Gurwick NP, Groffman PM, et al. 2008. Microbially available carbon in buried riparian soils in a glaciated landscape. *Soil Biol. Biochem.* 40:85–96.

Gurwick NP, McCorkle DM, et al. 2008. Mineralization of ancient carbon in the subsurface of riparian forests. *J. Geophys. Res. Biogeosci.* 113: Art. G02021.

Hanson GC, Groffman PM, Gold AJ. 1994. Symptoms of nitrogen saturation in a riparian wetland. *Ecol. Appl.* 4:750–56.

Hooper DU, Chapin FS, et al. 2005. Effects of biodiversity on ecosystem functioning: a consensus of current knowledge. *Ecol. Monogr.* 75:3–35.

Kellison RC, Young MJ, et al. 1998. Major alluvial floodplains. In *Southern forested wetlands,* Messina MG, Conner WH, editors. Boca Raton, FL: CRC Press, pp. 291–323.

MacFarlane DW, Meyer SP. 2005. Characteristics and distribution of potential ash tree hosts for emerald ash borer. *For. Ecol. Manage.* 213:15–24.

Megonigal JP, Day FP. 1988. Organic matter dynamics in four seasonally flooded forest communities of the Dismal Swamp. *Am. J. Bot.* 75:1334–43.

Messina MG, Conner WH, editors. 1998. *Southern forested wetlands ecology and management.* Boca Raton, FL: CRC Press.

Metzler K, Barrett JP. 2006. *The vegetation of Connecticut: a preliminary classification.* Hartford: State Geol. and Nat. Hist. Surv. CT, Dept. Env. Protection.

Morley TR, Calhoun AJK. 2009. Vegetation characteristics of forested hillside seeps in eastern Maine, USA. *J. Torrey Bot. Soc.* 136:520–31.

Muirhead JR, Leung B, et al. 2006. Modelling local and long-distance dispersal of invasive emerald ash borer *Agrilus planipennis* (Coleoptera) in North America. *Diversity and Distributions* 12:71–79.

Nelson WM, Gold AJ, Groffman PM. 1995. Spatial and temporal variation in groundwater nitrate removal in a riparian forest. *J. Env. Qual.* 24:691–99.

Neson G. 2006. *Red maple plant guide.* Washington, DC: USDA Nat. Resour. Conserv. Serv.

NRC. 2001. *Compensating for wetland losses under the Clean Water Act.* Washington, DC: National Acad. Press.

Paratley RD, Fahey TJ. 1986. Vegetation-environment relations in a conifer swamp in central New York. *Bull. Torrey Bot. Club* 113:357–71.

Peterson-Smith J, Wardrop DH, et al. 2009. Hydrogeomorphology, environment, and vegetation associations across a latitudinal gradient in highland wetlands of the northeastern USA. *Plant Ecol.* 203:155–72.

Poland TM, McCullough DG. 2006. Emerald ash borer: invasion of the urban forest and the threat to North America's ash resource. *J. For.* 104:118–24.

Pureswaran DS, Poland TM. 2009. Host selection and feeding preference of *Agrilus planipennis* (Coleoptera: Buprestidae) on ash (*Fraxinus* spp.). *Env. Ent.* 38:757–65.

Ravit B, Ehrenfeld JG, Haggblom M. 2003. A comparison of sediment microbial communities associated with *Phragmites australis* and *Spartina alterniflora* in brackish wetlands of New Jersey. *Estuaries* 26(2B):465–74.

Reddy KR, DeLaune RD. 2008. *Biogeochemistry of wetlands science and application.* Boca Raton, FL: CRC Press.

Reiss J, Bridle JR, et al. 2009. Emerging horizons in biodiversity and ecosystem functioning research. *Trends Ecol. Evol.* 24:505–14.

Rheinhardt RD. 2007. Hydrogeomorphic and compositional variation among red maple *(Acer rubrum)* wetlands in southeastern Massachusetts. *NE Nat.* 14:589–604.

Riffell S, Burton T, Murphy M. 2006. Birds in depressional forested wetlands: area and habitat requirements and model uncertainty. *Wetlands* 26:107–18.

Rotkin-Ellman M, Addy K, et al. 2004. Tree species, root decomposition and subsurface denitrification potential in riparian wetlands. *Plant & Soil* 263:335–44.

Simmons RC, Gold AJ, Groffman PM. 1992. Nitrate dynamics in riparian forests: groundwater studies. *J. Env. Qual.* 21:659–65.

Stander E, Ehrenfeld J. 2009a. Rapid assessment of urban wetlands: do hydrogeomorphic classification and reference criteria work? *Env. Manage.* 43:725–42.

Stander EK, Ehrenfeld JG. 2009b. Rapid assessment of urban wetlands: functional assessment model development and evaluation. *Wetlands* 29:261–76.

Tardif J, Bergeron Y. 1992. Ecological analysis of black ash stands *(Fraxinus nigra)* on the shore of Lake Duparquet (northwestern Quebec). *Can. J. Bot.* 70:2294–2302.

Tardif J, Bergeron Y. 1993. Radial growth of *Fraxinus nigra* in a Canadian boreal floodplain in response to climatic and hydrological fluctuations. *J. Veg. Sci.* 4:751–58.

Tardif J, Bergeron Y. 1997. Comparative dendroclimatological analysis of two black ash and two white cedar populations from contrasting sites in the Lake Duparquet region, northwestern Quebec. *Can. J. For. Res.—Rev. Can. Rech. For.* 27:108–16.

Tardif J, Bergeron Y. 1999. Population dynamics of *Fraxinus nigra* in response to flood-level variations, in northwestern Quebec. *Ecol. Monogr.* 69:107–25.

Tardif J, Dery S, Bergeron Y. 1994. Sexual regeneration of black ash (*Fraxinus nigra* Marsh.) in a boreal floodplain. *Am. Midl. Nat.* 132:124–35.

Tardif J, Dutilleul P, Bergeron Y. 1998. Variations in periodicities of the ring width of black ash (*Fraxinus nigra* Marsh.) in relation to flooding and ecological site factors at Lake Duparquet in northwestern Quebec. *Biol. Rhythm Res.* 29:1–29.

Tiner RW. 2010. *Wetlands of the Northeast: results of the National Wetlands Inventory.* Hadley, MA: USFWS, Northeast Region.

Trettin CC, Jurgensen MF, et al., editors. 1997. *Northern forested wetlands: ecology and management.* Boca Raton, FL: Lewis Publishers, CRC Press.

Wolter PT, Mladenoff, DJ, et al. 1995. Improved forest classification in the northern Lake State using multi-temporal Landsat imagery. *Photogram. Engin. Remote Sensing* 61:1129–43.

CHAPTER 12

Beaver Wetlands

CAROL A. JOHNSTON

The beaver is nature's original wetland creation and restoration expert. Stimulated by the sound of running water, the beaver builds dams that create new ponds and wetlands or raise water levels in existing wetlands and water bodies (Johnston 1994). The beaver is the epitome of an ecological engineer (Müller-Schwarze and Sun 2003; Rosell, Bozser, et al. 2005; Wright and Jones 2006) and is a keystone species (Power, Tilman, et al. 1996) that disproportionately affects its environment relative to its abundance.

The North American beaver, *Castor canadensis,* occurs in aquatic habitats in Alaska and Canada south of the Arctic Circle, most of the continental United States (absent from parts of southwestern USA and most of Florida), and extending into northern Mexico (Jenkins and Busher 1979). *Castor canadensis* has been introduced to South America and Eurasia, including northwestern Russia, Poland, Germany, Finland (Hyvönen and Nummi 2008), and Austria (Wilson and Reeder 2005). The Eurasian beaver, *Castor fiber,* occupies aquatic habitats throughout northern Eurasia (Curry-Lindahl 1967; Wilson and Reeder 2005), and at least 13 countries have carried out reintroduction programs to restore the range of *C. fiber* in Europe (MacDonald, Tattersall, et al. 1995).

This chapter describes wetlands created and altered by beaver dams. Although the majority of the literature cited describes *C. canadensis* activity, the effects of *C. fiber* dams on wetlands are also included in this chapter (Curry-Lindahl 1967; Wilsson 1971; Gurnell 1998; Collen and Gibson 2001; Rosell, Bozser, et al. 2005). Beaver ponds are the archetypal beaver wetland (Fig. 12.1a), whereas beaver meadows (Fig. 12.1b) are former beaver ponds that have drained and revegetated (Johnston, Pinay, et al. 1995; Pastor, Downing, et al. 1996; Wright, Flecker, et al. 2003; Simonavičiūtė and Ulevičius 2007). Beaver dams frequently raise the water level in existing wetlands, which are also discussed here.

Geology, Hydrology, and Biogeochemistry

Geology

Beaver occur in a variety of geologic settings within their extensive range, including mountain streams (Margolis, Castro, et al. 2001; Westbrook, Cooper, et al. 2006), river deltas and floodplains (Gill 1972; Dieter and McCabe 1989; Demmer and Beschta 2008; Diefenderfer and Montgomery 2009), southeastern U.S. blackwater streams (Snodgrass and Meffe 1998; Jakes, Snodgrass, et al. 2007), karst terrain (Cowell 1984), and peatlands (Harkonen 1999). The beaver's extensive range and continued expansion into new territory make it difficult to generalize about suitable beaver habitat from one region to another (Barnes and Mallik 1997).

Beaver have been called geomorphic agents due to the long-term accumulation of sediments in valley bottoms impounded by their dams (Rudemann and Schoonmaker 1938; Ives 1942; Butler and Malanson 1994; Gurnell 1998). However, the interpretation of these landforms is complicated by the fact that beaver dams are often built in glaciated terrain, where U-shaped valleys may have been caused by glacial and postglacial geomorphologic processes rather than beaver activity (Retzer, Swope, et al. 1956). Beaver dams have influenced the establishment and expansion of peatlands (Kaye 1962; Johnston 2000) and the formation of palsa mounds in peatlands (Lewkowicz and Coultish 2004). The establishment and abandonment of beaver ponds increases stream channel complexity through the formation of new meanders, pools, and riffles (Demmer and Beschta 2008).

Beaver dams are generally thought to reduce channel incision and streambank erosion by slowing water velocity (Maret, Parker, et al. 1987), and the capacity of beaver ponds to reduce erosion is so well accepted that restoration of beaver populations is a recommended management technique for stream restoration, particularly in the semiarid western U.S. (FISRWG 2001). Eroded sediments settle out when they reach the placid waters of beaver ponds (Naiman, Melillo, et al. 1986; Devito and Dillon 1993; Butler and Malanson 1995; Meentemeyer and Butler 1999; Pollock, Beechie, et al. 2007). Published sedimentation rates vary from 0.4 cm yr^{-1} in a headwater beaver pond in central Ontario (Devito and Dillon 1993) to 27.9 cm yr^{-1} in a pond in the Rocky Mountains of Montana (Butler and Malanson 1995). Soil scientists have cautioned, however, that some of these studies may have erroneously interpreted materials deposited by glacial and fluvial action as beaver pond sediments, thereby inflating accretion rates (Retzer, Swope, et al. 1956; Johnston 2000). Beaver pond sediments span the range

FIG. 12.1. Typical beaver wetlands. A. Beaver pond on Pancake-Hall Creek in the Adirondack Mountains of New York. B. Beaver meadow in Voyageurs National Park, northern Minnesota.

FIG. 12.2. Rushing water from the collapse of an upstream beaver dam after a heavy summer rainfall eroded fine sediments in this streambed at Voyageurs National Park, leaving behind gravel, cobbles, and boulders.

of textures from clay to sands and gravels (Johnston 2000; Bigler, Butler, et al. 2001).

Catastrophic failure of beaver dams can cause erosion (Fig. 12.2), a process that is less well documented in the literature (Butler 1989). A stream in Alberta was drastically altered when a June 1994 flood wave resulting from a breached beaver dam eroded and redeposited large amounts of debris and sediment (Hillman, Feng, et al. 2004). Outburst floods from beaver dam failure have been responsible for 13 deaths and numerous injuries in the U.S. and Canada, including significant impacts on railway lines (Butler and Malanson 2005). The 2001 breach of the beaver dam at the outlet of Shoepack Lake in VNP released 2.16×10^6 kL of water (Frohnauer, Pierce, et al. 2007).

Hydrology

Beaver are semiaquatic mammals that use water for mobility and protection from predators, but characteristics of beaver-inhabited water bodies are highly variable. Beaver can live along the margins of lakes and rivers that are too large to dam, dwelling in lodges or burrows excavated into the banks (Wilsson 1971; Gill 1972; Dieter and McCabe 1989; Smith and Peterson 1991; Wheatley 1997; Collen and Gibson 2001; Raffel, Smith, et al. 2009). Within a 100-km² area in Minnesota surveyed between 1979 and 1981, 58% of the 221 active beaver colonies occupied lakes, 36% occupied bogs, and 6% occupied rivers (Rebertus 1986).

Beaver often dam the outlets of lakes, increasing lake surface area and depth, and flooding lakeside wetlands (Reddoch and Reddoch 2005; Bertolo and Magnan 2006; Bertolo, Magnan, et al. 2008). Approximately half of 1,085 "drainage lakes" sampled in the Adirondack Mountains of New York had beaver dams at their outlets (Kretser, Gallagher, et al. 1989). In Voyageurs National Park (NP) in northern Minnesota, the 2001 collapse of an outlet beaver dam reduced the surface area of Shoepack Lake by 47% (Frohnauer, Pierce, et al. 2007), draining adjacent wetlands. The prevalence and ecological influence of lake-outlet beaver dams are relatively unknown.

Beaver commonly dam ditches and culverts (Fig. 12.3), often causing substantial economic damage (Boyles and Savitzky 2008). In New York, beaver roadside occupancy was predicted by stream gradient, the percentage of roadside area devoid of woody vegetation, the interaction between these two variables, and stream width (Curtis and Jensen 2004); oversized culverts were the best deterrent to beaver plugging activity (Jensen, Curtis, et al. 2001).

Beaver have been observed to impound a variety of wetland types, including bogs (Rebertus 1986; Mitchell and Niering 1993; Ray, Ray, et al. 2004), fens (Reddoch and Reddoch 2005), deciduous swamps (Naiman, Johnston, et al. 1988), and tidal forested wetlands (Diefenderfer and Montgomery 2009). In Massachusetts, beaver colony density was greatest on poorly drained soils (Howard and Larson 1985), presumably because poor soil drainage allowed beaver ponds to better retain water. At Voyageurs NP, 59% of lands impounded by beaver were wet-

FIG. 12.3. A semicircular beaver dam surrounds the road culvert (at arrow) along Rainbow Shores Road, Oswego County, New York, making use of the roadbed to flood a much larger area.

FIG. 12.4. A beaver dam across Oak Creek near Mahto, South Dakota, on July 20, 2006. Note that green vegetation is restricted to the riparian corridor adjacent to the creek.

lands *prior* to impoundment (Johnston 1994), and impounded peatlands had more stable hydrology than did impoundments on upland or wetland mineral soils (Pastor, Bonde, et al. 1993).

Stream gradient is one of the most important factors determining beaver dam site suitability (Retzer, Swope, et al. 1956; Howard and Larson 1985; Beier and Barrett 1987). The U.S. Fish and Wildlife Service habitat suitability index (HSI) for beaver optimizes suitability at stream gradients of 6% or less, with stream gradients > 15% considered unsuitable for beaver (Allen 1983). Steeper slopes increase the force of the stream, increasing the likelihood that high flows will burst beaver dams. In blackwater streams of the South Carolina Coastal Plain, beaver were most likely to impound streams of < 1.2% slope draining moderate-sized watersheds (1,000 to 5,000 ha) that were crossed by roads (Jakes, Snodgrass, et al. 2007). Pond areas are generally smaller in steeper terrain and may not provide sufficient protection and foraging access for the beaver colony (Johnston and Naiman 1987; Gurnell 1998).

Water force and fluctuation also influence beaver dam establishment. The beaver HSI model defines optimum sites as those with a permanent source of surface water with little or no fluctuation (Allen 1983). During a period of beaver recolonization at Voyageurs NP, beaver dams were first established at areas that created the largest ponds with the greatest potential for expansion, but subsequent ponds were successively smaller as the most suitable sites were occupied (Johnston and Naiman 1990a). Beaver generally dam streams of first to fifth order because larger-order streams have too much flow (Naiman, Melillo, et al. 1986; Johnston and Naiman 1990b; Jakes, Snodgrass, et al. 2007; Stevens, Paszkowski, et al. 2007). Rapidly varying winter flows associated with hydropower generation in Sweden were detrimental to beaver colonization (Curry-Lindahl 1967).

Too little stream flow can be detrimental to beaver habitat. The number of beaver dams on a previously ephemeral creek in Wyoming was tripled after its flow was augmented by a transbasin diversion to convey water to the city of Cheyenne (Wolff, Wesche, et al. 1989). In regions where stream flow is inherently variable, however, beaver may still adapt to extreme water-level fluctuations. Beaver colonized a creek in western South Dakota with daily discharge rates ranging during 1997 from 0.3 to 193 $m^3 s^{-1}$ (Striped Face-Collins and Johnston 2007). The beaver dams were built between the high creekbanks, creating a series of stair-stepped pools within the creekbed that

retained water while the rest of the creek dried out during summer drought, seasonally converting a river into a series of wetlands (Fig. 12.4).

In addition to creating surface water bodies, beaver dams raise water tables in adjacent riparian zones (Westbrook, Cooper, et al. 2006; Hill and Duval 2009). A study of a 1.5-km reach of the fourth-order Colorado River in Rocky Mountain National Park showed that the main effects of beaver on hydrologic processes occurred downstream from the dam rather than being confined to the near-pond area (Westbrook, Cooper, et al. 2006). The beaver dams caused river water to move around them as surface runoff and groundwater seepage during both high- and low-flow periods, and attenuated the expected water table decline in the drier summer months over roughly one-quarter of the 58-ha study area, suggesting that beaver can create and maintain hydrologic regimes suitable for the formation and persistence of wetlands (Westbrook, Cooper, et al. 2006).

The construction of beaver ponds alters hydrology at the watershed level. Comparing the water balance in subarctic drainage basins with and without beaver dams at their outlets showed that the dammed basin lost more water to evaporation, had suppressed peak and low flows, and had increased water basin storage (Woo and Waddington 1990). A beaver pond can significantly affect the downstream delivery of event water through evaporation and mixing but provides minimal retention during large runoff events such as snowmelt (Burns and McDonnell 1998).

Beaver meadows, like many wetlands, have complicated internal water flowpaths due to their subtle topography. The modeling of diffuse water flow to and within a Voyageurs NP beaver meadow using a conventional elevation-based flow routing model generated many artifacts in the predicted flow pattern, whereas a more sophisticated aspect-based stream tube flow routing model predicted a more realistic flow pattern (Brown, Johnston, et al. 2003).

Biogeochemistry

The creation of beaver ponds induces a number of biogeochemical changes, many of which are affected by the enhanced microbial activity in beaver ponds (Songsteralpin and Klotz 1995). The impoundments created by beaver deplete oxygen, particularly during winter when ice cover and cold temperatures limit subaqueous photosynthesis (Smith, Driscoll, et al. 1991; Devito and Dillon 1993; Hill and Duval 2009). The anaerobic conditions promote denitrification in beaver ponds and meadows (Naiman, Pinay, et al. 1994), and several studies have documented that beaver wetlands are sinks for nitrate (NO_3^-) (Devito, Dillon, et al. 1989; Cirmo and Driscoll 1993; Devito and Dillon 1993; Correll, Jordan, et al. 2000; Margolis, Castro, et al. 2001; McHale, Cirmo, et al. 2004; Hill and Duval 2009). Beaver ponds enrich stream-water concentrations of reduced metals (Fe^{2+} and Mn^{2+}) and retain sulfate (SO_4^{2-}) (Driscoll, Wyskowski, et al. 1987; Smith, Driscoll, et al. 1991; Cirmo and Driscoll 1993, 1996; Johnston, Pinay, et al. 1995; Margolis, Castro, et al. 2001), consistent with redox reactions expected under anaerobic conditions.

Methane is produced at extremely low redox potentials, and beaver ponds have been shown to be hot spots of methane flux by eddy covariance (Roulet, Crill, et al. 1997) and flux chamber measurements (summarized by Scott, Kelly, et al. 1999), with flux rates much greater than from other northern wetlands (Roulet, Ash, et al. 1992). Daily methane fluxes as high as 300 mg CH_4 m^{-2} have been measured from beaver ponds (Yavitt, Lang, et al. 1990; Bubier, Moore, et al. 1993), and even higher rates (440 ± 350 mg CH_4 m^{-2} d^{-1}) have been measured from floating peat mats, which are commonly associated with beaver impoundments (Scott, Kelly, et al. 1999). A major reason for the source strength of beaver ponds is bubble flux (ebullition), whereby methane produced at depth in organic-rich sediments rises quickly through the water column to the overlying air (Dove, Roulet, et al. 1999); in saturated soils that are not covered by water, methanotrophs in the aerated soil surface consume methane before it can reach the atmosphere (Bridgham, Johnston, et al. 1995). Beaver ponds are a minor component of most landscapes, so these high rates of methane flux are normally negligible in terms of landscape methane emissions. However, in places like Voyageurs NP, where beaver ponds are prevalent, landscape-scale methane flux can triple as a result of beaver pond construction (Bridgham, Johnston, et al. 1995).

An undesirable biogeochemical change associated with beaver ponds is the generation of methylmercury (CH_3Hg^+), a toxic trace metal that has been linked to human illness and environmental damage. Net mercury methylation in an Adirondack beaver pond (Fig. 12.1a) occurred at rates comparable to values reported in the literature for other wetlands (Driscoll, Holsapple, et al. 1998). Stream concentrations of CH_3Hg^+ were greatest during low-flow summer conditions, and the annual flux of CH_3Hg^+ was greater than literature values of atmospheric deposition, suggesting that the watershed was a net source of CH_3Hg^+.

In addition to the aforementioned effects of beaver ponds on NO_3^-, beaver ponds alter other aspects of the N cycle. Pore-water ammonium (NH_4^+) concentrations were significantly greater in beaver pond sediments than in beaver meadows, forest soils, or stream sediments (Naiman, Pinay, et al. 1994; Hill and Duval 2009). Beaver ponds were a net annual source of streamwater NH_4^+ in Precambrian shield beaver ponds (Devito, Dillon, et al. 1989; Cirmo and Driscoll 1993), but NH_4^+ export was only seasonal in other beaver ponds (Devito and Dillon 1993; Correll, Jordan, et al. 2000; Margolis, Castro, et al. 2001). Summer NH_4^+ concentrations in a Maryland Coastal Plain stream were negatively correlated with stream flow, a relationship that was amplified by the subsequent construction of a beaver pond; during periods of low flow the pond may have been more hypoxic and produced more NH_4^+ (Correll, Jordan, et al. 2000). Beaver ponds seasonally retain total organic N (Correll, Jordan, et al. 2000), but on an annual basis, Precambrian shield beaver ponds exported more total organic N than they received from stream inflows (Devito, Dillon, et al. 1989). Overall, beaver wetlands have been found to reduce annual discharge of total N by 0 to 18% (Devito, Dillon, et al. 1989; Devito and Dillon 1993; Correll, Jordan, et al. 2000).

Beaver ponds raise the pH and acid-neutralizing capacity (ANC) of streamwater, which is beneficial in regions subject to acid precipitation (Driscoll, Wyskowski, et al. 1987; Smith, Driscoll, et al. 1991; Cirmo and Driscoll 1993; Margolis, Castro, et al. 2001). In an Adirondack beaver pond (Fig. 12.1a), losses of ANC resulting from Al^{n+} retention, basic cation retention, and organic anion release (RCOO-) were more than offset by gains in ANC from SO_4^{2-} and NO_3^- retention and Fe^{2+} and NH_4^+ release, resulting in a net increase of ANC (Driscoll, Wyskowski, et al. 1987; Smith, Driscoll, et al. 1991; Cirmo and Driscoll 1993). A liming ($CaCO_3$) treatment of a beaver pond catchment (Cirmo and Driscoll 1996) resulted in an immediate increase in ANC associated with Ca^{2+} release, and caused the pond to release silicate, even though beaver ponds are normally a sink for dissolved silicate (Cirmo and Driscoll 1993; Correll, Jordan, et al. 2000). The geologic origin of beaver meadow soils also influences cation concentrations: porewater Ca^{2+}, Mg^{2+}, and K^+ concentrations were much greater in Voyageurs NP beaver meadows with glacio-lacustrine soils than in those with glacio-fluvial soils (Johnston, Pinay, et al. 1995).

Beaver ponds reduced downstream fluxes of total suspended solids and total P, probably due to sedimentation of suspended particulates along with their constituent phosphorus (Maret, Parker, et al. 1987; Correll, Jordan, et al. 2000). The Maryland Coastal Plain beaver pond studied by Correll, Jordan, et al. (2000) retained 35 kg total P ha^{-1} yr^{-1}, which was 21% of total inputs. On the Precambrian shield, Devito, Dillon, et al. (1989) found that one of their beaver ponds retained 0.1 kg total P ha^{-1} yr^{-1} while the other exported 0.3 kg total P ha^{-1} yr^{-1}. A study of five beaver ponds in New York also showed that some retained and some released soluble reactive P (Klotz 1998). Winter is a critical time for beaver pond P dynamics because prolonged ice cover increases P concentrations that are flushed out during peak snowmelt (Devito and Dillon 1993; Klotz 1998).

Plant Communities

Beaver dam construction in forested regions causes a fairly predictable sequence of vegetation changes: (1) flooded forest, (2) tree death and toppling, (3) pond containing submergent, floating-leaved, and emergent wetland plants, (4) drained pond with exposed sediments, and (5) drained pond revegetated to grasses and sedges (Johnston 1994; Sturtevant 1998; Pastur, Lencinas, et al. 2006; Wright 2009). Beaver meadows also succeed to shrubs in some regions (Remillard, Gruendling, et al. 1987), but this transition was uncommon at Voyageurs NP (Erickson 1994). Beaver often reflood areas that they have previously abandoned (Fig. 12.5a–b), converting beaver meadows back into beaver ponds (Pastor, Bonde, et al. 1993).

Tussock-forming graminoids such as tussock sedge (*Carex stricta*), woolgrass (*Scirpus cyperinus*), and common rush (*Juncus effusus*) are commonly associated with beaver meadows (Fig. 12.1b), and their tussocks may facilitate the growth of other

FIG. 12.5. Beaver pond on Nelson Creek, upper peninsula of Michigan. A. Abandoned pond reverting to a beaver meadow in September 2002. B. Beaver had reflooded the area as of August 2005.

plant species (Parker, Caudill, et al. 2007; Ervin 2009). Tussocks can persist under slightly fluctuating water levels but are killed by rapid inundation (Johnston and Naiman 1987; Johnston 2000). Of the 37 identifiable plant species that germinated from soil seed banks collected at 14 beaver ponds in Quebec, the 5 most abundant species were *J. effusus, Leersia oryzoides, S. cyperinus, J. brevicaudatus,* and *Ludwigia palustris* (Le Page and Keddy 1998). Other graminoid species commonly associated with North American beaver meadows include beaked sedge *(Carex rostrata)* and bluejoint grass *(Calamagrostis canadensis)* (Remillard, Gruendling, et al. 1987; Pastor, Downing, et al. 1996; Wright, Flecker, et al. 2003). Reed canary grass *(Phalaris arundinacea)* is also common as a native species in European beaver meadows (Simonavičiūtė and Ulevičius 2007) and as an invasive species in U.S. beaver meadows (Perkins and Wilson 2005).

Beaver meadows have been found to increase herbaceous plant diversity. In east-central Alberta, the diversity of emergent plants was greatest in wetlands having the greatest ungulate and beaver activity (Hood and Bayley 2009). By increasing habitat heterogeneity, beaver increased the number of species of herbaceous plants of riparian zones in the Adirondack region of New York by over 33% (Wright, Jones, et al. 2002), and beaver meadow plant diversity increased with increasing meadow age and water-level fluctuation (Wright, Flecker, et al. 2003). However, such a large increase in diversity was possible only because there were no other open wetlands in the landscape where obligate wetland plant species were found; in other landscapes, the impact of beaver may be reduced.

When beaver flood existing wetlands, the sequence of vegetation changes incorporates plant species from the antecedent wetland (Mitchell and Niering 1993). Flooded peatlands can form floating mats of sedges and/or *Sphagnum* moss and ericaceous shrubs that rise and fall with the water level (Rebertus 1986; Johnston and Naiman 1987, 1990b). Trees in the peatland are killed, but the cover of low ericaceous shrubs, especially *Chamaedaphne calyculata* and *Kalmia angustifolia,* increases (Mitchell and Niering 1993).

Species richness of submerged and floating macrophytes increased with pond age in Minnesota beaver ponds (Ray, Rebertus, et al. 2001). Species composition also changed with pond age, succeeding from free-floating plants (e.g., *Lemna, Spirodela, Wolffia, Utricularia*) in ponds aged 1–10 years to floating-leaved plants (e.g., *Brasenia, Nymphaea, Nuphar*) or a rich assemblage of *Potamogeton* species in ponds older than 40 years.

Animal Communities

Mammals and Birds

The beaver itself is the prime benefactor of the ponds and wetlands it creates. The proportion of land area impounded as shallow marsh at Voyageurs NP was a reliable predictor ($R^2 =$ 0.93) of beaver colony density (Broschart et al. 1989). Beaver ponds and dens also provide important habitat for river otters, *Lontra canadensis* (Newman and Griffin 1994; LeBlanc, Gallant, et al. 2007; Gallant, Vasseur, et al. 2009), and a partial commensalism appears to exist between the two species, with otters benefitting from creation and maintenance of fish habitats by beaver (Reid, Herrero, et al. 1988). Beaver ponds can be drained, however, when otters dig passages through beaver dams for under-ice access between ponds (Reid, Herrero, et al. 1988). Beaver ponds also increase the available habitat for muskrats, *Ondatra zibethicus,* which have been observed to use active beaver lodges (McKinstry, Kahru, et al. 1997).

The number of small mammals trapped in beaver meadows of northern Minnesota was significantly less than the number trapped in an adjacent forest or the edge between them. Two species, red-backed vole *(Clethrionomys gapperi)* and deer mouse *(Peromyscus maniculatus),* dominated the forest and edge habitats, whereas the meadow vole *(Microtus pennsylvanicus)* was the primary species in beaver meadows. Voles play a complex role in beaver meadow recolonization by conifers, which depend on ectomycorrhizae for germination. The red-backed vole disperses spores of mycorrhizal fungi in its feces (Pastor, Dewey, et al. 1996) but is often limited in distribution to forested habitat with abundant woody debris and may be excluded from graminoid habitats by interactions with the meadow vole, which eats primarily conifer seeds and insects (Terwilliger and Pastor 1999). The lack of ectomycorrhizal fungi in soils of beaver meadows due to the absence of red-backed voles may limit the rate of conifer invasion.

Both beaver and ungulates utilize woody forage, and the interaction effects of the two herbivores may be different than their independent effects. In the Rocky Mountains of Colorado, beaver benefit willow *(Salix* spp.) by creating bare, moist soil for seed germination, by increasing late-season moisture regimes for seedling survival, and by increasing willow sprouting through their herbivory (Baker, Ducharme, et al. 2005). The willows provide important browse for elk, but heavy browsing by elk and beaver strongly suppresses shrub biomass (Baker, Ducharme, et al. 2005). In east-central Alberta, there were no significant effects exclusively related to beaver activities on the overall composition and structure of woody riparian plant communities, but areas with no beaver and lower ungulate densities had a positive growth response in preferred shrub species (e.g., *Salix* spp., *Prunus* spp.), which demonstrated the combined influence of these herbivores on riparian communities (Hood and Bayley 2009). Moose frequent areas around beaver ponds in boreal forests because of their abundant trembling aspen *(Populus tremuloides)* and shrub forage, but heavy browsing by moose on small aspen prevents them from attaining the larger diameters preferred by beaver (Johnston, Pastor, et al. 1993).

Beaver ponds create new habitat for waterfowl and other birds (Renouf 1972; Ringelman 1991; Merendino, McCullough, et al. 1995; Brown, Hubert, et al. 1996; McCall, Hodgman, et al. 1996; Nummi and Poysa 1997; McKinstry, Caffrey, et al. 2001; Cooke and Zack 2008). Some researchers have found that active beaver ponds have greater bird species richness than abandoned beaver ponds (Grover and Baldassarre 1995), whereas others have found the opposite (Aznar and Desrochers 2008). Avian omnivores and insectivores benefit from the increased invertebrate production that occurs in beaver ponds (Longcore, McCauley, et al. 2006). Standing dead trees in beaver ponds are important roosting habitat for birds (Grover and Baldassarre 1995) and bats (Menzel, Carter, et al. 2001). Other habitat characteristics of beaver wetlands that benefit birds include ponded water and cover of emergent and deciduous shrub vegetation (Brown, Hubert, et al. 1996; Cooke and Zack 2008).

Fish and Aquatic Invertebrates

The lentic environment created by beaver ponds differs from the lotic conditions of free-flowing streams, which alters the species composition of fish and aquatic invertebrates (Duffy and LaBar 1994; Collen and Gibson 2001; Margolis, Raesly, et al. 2001; Anderson and Rosemond 2007). Collen and Gibson's 2001 review summarized the positive and negative effects of beaver dams on habitat for aquatic fauna. Negative effects include impeded upstream migration, siltation and inundation of spawning beds, alteration of fish species composition and interactions, and creation of habitat advantageous to predators (Collen and Gibson 2001; Bertolo and Magnan 2006; Mitchell and Cunjak 2007). Positive effects include expansion of aquatic habitat, habitat creation for larger fish with attendant angling opportunities, augmented woody debris cover that benefits some fish and invertebrate species, stabilization of stream flows, sediment trapping in streams with high particulate loads, retention of organic matter that provides food for invertebrates, establishment of refugia for fish to escape adverse conditions during winter or summer, faster fish growth rates, and changes in water chemistry (acidity, nutrients, Al) that can benefit fish (Collen and Gibson 2001; Rolauffs, Hering, et al. 2001; Pollock, Pess, et al. 2004; Ray, Ray, et al. 2004; Sigourney, Letcher, et al. 2006; Frohnauer, Pierce, et al. 2007; White and Rahel 2008). Where beaver are invasive, such as *C. canadensis* in Tierra del Fuego, they can greatly

impact native fish species present in streams (Moorman, Eggleston, et al. 2009).

Some effects of beaver ponds, such as warming of water temperatures, are detrimental to some fish yet beneficial to others. For example, where water temperatures rise above their optimum preferenda, salmonids may be replaced by species such as cyprinids, catostomids, percids, or centrarchids (Hale 1966; Collen and Gibson 2001). Warming of water temperatures by beaver dams has been found by some studies (Cirmo and Driscoll 1993; Margolis, Raesly, et al. 2001), but not others (McRae and Edwards 1994; Sigourney, Letcher, et al. 2006).

Amphibians and Reptiles

Numerous studies in the northern U.S. and Canada have found beaver ponds to increase the abundance and diversity of amphibians, particularly anurans. In Maine, sites with high amphibian species richness were best predicted by connectivity of wetlands in the landscape through stream corridors and wetland modification by beaver, although wood frog *(Rana sylvatica)* breeding habitat was best predicted by temporary hydroperiod, lack of fish, and *absence* of current beaver activity (Cunningham, Calhoun, et al. 2007). Anuran call surveys in Alberta indicated that beaver create breeding habitat for wood frogs, boreal chorus frogs *(Pseudacris maculata),* and western toads *(Bufo boreas);* no calling males of any species were recorded on unobstructed boreal streams (Stevens, Paszkowski, et al. 2007). Older beaver ponds supported more breeding wood frogs than younger ponds (Stevens, Paszkowski, et al. 2006). Mink frog *(R. septentrionalis)* occurrence was strongly and positively influenced by the presence of beaver (Popescu and Gibbs 2009). Beaver wetlands produced annually 1.2–23 times the number of wood frogs as did temporary vernal pools in the Adirondack Mountains of New York (Karraker and Gibbs 2009).

In contrast, researchers in the South Carolina Piedmont found that the richness, diversity, and evenness of amphibians were comparable (Russell, Moorman, et al. 1999) or significantly greater (Metts, Lanham, et al. 2001) at unimpounded streams than at beaver ponds. Turtles, lizards, and anurans were significantly more abundant at beaver ponds than along unimpounded streams, whereas salamanders were significantly more abundant at unimpounded streams than at beaver ponds (Metts, Lanham, et al. 2001). However, the richness and total abundance of reptiles (turtles, lizards, and snakes) were significantly greater at old beaver ponds when compared to new beaver ponds and unimpounded streams (Russell, Moorman, et al. 1999; Metts, Lanham, et al. 2001).

The structure provided by beaver lodges constructed by lake-dwelling beaver also promotes amphibians and other fauna. The richness and abundance of 10 benthic macroinvertebrate taxa, six species of small fishes, and two species of amphibians were significantly greater near beaver lodges versus littoral zones of lakes in northwestern Ontario (France 1997).

Key Ecological Controls

Beaver Population Changes

Beaver dam construction is the key ecological process that maintains beaver wetlands, so changes in beaver population influence the existence of beaver wetlands. Overzealous trap-

TABLE 12.1
Beaver impoundments as a proportion of landscape area

Location	Year	Beaver ponds as % of landscape	All beaver wetlands as % of landscape	Source
Minnesota, USA	1988	6.20	12.40	Naiman, Pinay, et al. 1994[a]
Georgia, USA	1992	0.17	0.48	Snodgrass 1997[b]
Virginia, USA	1994	0.76	—	Syphard and Garcia 2001[a]
Alberta, Canada	1996	3.23	—	Hood and Bayley 2008[c]
Finland	1998	0.14	—	Hyvönen and Nummi 2008
Tierra del Fuego, Argentina	—	—	2–15	Anderson, Pastur, et al. 2009

[a] Area of permanent lakes excluded from the landscape area.
[b] Open water and flooded hardwoods included as beaver ponds.
[c] Increase in open water area from 1948 to 1996 divided by 194-km^2 area of Elk Island National Park.

ping during the 17th through 19th centuries caused the beaver's demise throughout much of the world, but increasing conservation concerns and a decline in the demand for beaver pelts led to a remarkable recovery in beaver populations during the 20th century (Naiman, Johnston, et al. 1988). Now that the expansion of beaver into its pre-Columbian habitats has restored many beaver wetlands, the prevalence of the beaver's influence as an ecosystem engineer is becoming evident (Litvaitis 2003). Although it is uncertain whether current beaver population levels rival those that occurred prior to the 17th century, it is clear that populations of *C. canadensis* and *C. fiber* are increasing worldwide. Beaver population growth is likely to continue, given low prices for beaver pelts and the endangered status of the beaver's primary natural predator, the wolf, throughout most of the United States.

Disease has temporarily reduced beaver numbers in recent history. Tularemia *(Francisella tularensis)* is the major beaver epizootic and caused major beaver die-offs in the early 1950s (Stenlund 1953; Banfield 1954; Lawrence, Fay, et al. 1956). Beaver shed live *F. tularensis* and *Giardia* spp. into streamwater, which can cause human disease (Parker, Steginhaus, et al. 1951; Monzingo and Hibler 1987). Scientists have no explanation for the beaver tularemia outbreak of the 1950s, but a future recurrence could impact beaver populations.

Landscape Alteration

Beaver dams and ponds are relatively easy to identify using aerial photos, so the extent and rate of beaver landscape alteration can be documented using a series of historical aerial photos and a geographic information system (Remillard, Gruendling, et al. 1987; Johnston and Naiman 1990b; Snodgrass 1997; Syphard and Garcia 2001; Cunningham, Calhoun, et al. 2006; Hood and Bayley 2008). In certain landscapes, beaver have altered as much as 15% of land area through construction of beaver ponds and meadows, but other landscapes are less susceptible to beaver flooding (Table 12.1). Between 1940 and 1961, beaver at Voyageurs NP created new wetlands at the rate of 0.42% y^{-1} (i.e., each 10,000-ha area of land would have 42 new ha of beaver ponds each year) (Johnston 1994). By comparison, human development of land within 1 km of the Great Lakes shoreline between 1992 and 2001 was 0.48% y^{-1} (Wolter,

Johnston, et al. 2006), an indication that beaver are capable of altering landscapes at rates comparable to humans.

Conservation Concerns

The habitat created by beaver wetlands has been shown to indirectly maintain populations of an endangered insect, the St. Francis' satyr butterfly *(Neonympha mitchellii francisci)*. Beaver-created wetland habitats supported plant species not found elsewhere in riparian zones and increased plant species diversity across the landscape by creating a novel combination of patch types conducive to the butterfly populations (Bartel et al. 2010).

The recovery of beaver has been so successful throughout North America that they are now considered a pest in many areas (Payne and Peterson 1986). Plugging of culverts (Fig. 12.2) and flooding by beaver damages roads and railroads (Jensen, Curtis, et al. 2001; Curtis and Jensen 2004), can kill valuable timber (Bhat, Huffaker, et al. 1993; Harkonen 1999), and can kill desirable wetland plant species (Mitchell and Niering 1993; Reddoch and Reddoch 2005).

Beaver herbivory has been reported to indirectly enhance riparian zone invasion by the exotic woody plants Russian olive *(Elaeagnus angustifolia)* and tamarisk *(Tamarix* spp.) in the western U.S. (Lesica and Miles 2004). Fear that beaver would adversely alter the habitat for endangered songbirds led to the beaver's removal from a biological reserve in California (Longcore, Rich, et al. 2007).

Beaver have been particularly destructive in South America, where they are an invasive exotic species. The availability of suitable feeding and lodging sites coupled with the lack of natural predators or competitors favored rapid beaver population growth and range expansion in Tierra del Fuego, where beaver have altered streams, forests, and riparian zones (Anderson, Pastur, et al. 2009; Moorman, Eggleston, et al. 2009). Beaver meadows created by beaver on Cape Horn had nearly twice the herbaceous species richness and abundance when compared to forested sites, but much of this richness was due to invasion by exotic plants (Anderson, Griffith, et al. 2006). Beaver herbivory in the Cape Horn study significantly reduced forest canopy up to 30 m away from streams, essentially eliminating *Nothofagus* forests and their seedling bank.

Conclusions

Beaver were creating and modifying wetlands long before humans influenced wetlands. Beaver existed throughout the Pleistocene, and giant beaver the size of bears existed as recently as the deglaciation of the North American continent (Erickson 1962; Robinson, Beaudoin, et al. 2007; Rybczynski 2008). As more and more wetlands are affected by beaver, it is important to keep in mind that beaver were a very important part of the landscape for millennia and are only now regaining their rightful role as wetland stewards.

References

Allen AA. 1983. *Habitat suitability index models: beaver.* FWS/OBS-82/10.30. Washington, DC: US Dept. Int., Div. Biol. Serv.

Anderson CB, Rosemond AD. 2007. Ecosystem engineering by invasive exotic beavers reduces in-stream diversity and enhances ecosystem function in Cape Horn, Chile. *Oecologia* 154:141–53.

Anderson CB, Griffith CR, et al. 2006. The effects of invasive North American beavers on riparian plant communities in Cape Horn, Chile—do exotic beavers engineer differently in sub-Antarctic ecosystems? *Biol. Conserv.* 128:467–74.

Anderson CB, Pastur GM, et al. 2009. Do introduced North American beavers *Castor canadensis* engineer differently in southern South America? An overview with implications for restoration. *Mammal Rev.* 39:33–52.

Aznar JC, Desrochers A. 2008. Building for the future: abandoned beaver ponds promote bird diversity. *Ecoscience* 15:250–57.

Baker BW, Ducharme HC, et al. 2005. Interaction of beaver and elk herbivory reduces standing crop of willow. *Ecol. Appl.* 15:110–18.

Banfield AWF. 1954. Tularemia in beavers and muskrats, Waterton Lakes National Park, Alberta, 1952–53. *Can. J. Zool.—Rev. Can. Zool.* 32:139–43.

Barnes DM, Mallik AU. 1997. Habitat factors influencing beaver dam establishment in a northern Ontario watershed. *J. Wildl. Manage.* 61:1371–77.

Bartel RA, Haddad NM, Wright JP. 2010. Ecosystem engineers maintain a rare species of butterfly and increase plant diversity. *Oikos* 119:883–890.

Beier P, Barrett RH. 1987. Beaver habitat use and impact in the Truckee River basin, California. *J. Wildl. Manag.* 51:794–99.

Bertolo A, Magnan P. 2006. Spatial and environmental correlates of fish community structure in Canadian Shield lakes. *Can. J. Fish. Aquat. Sci.* 63:2780–92.

Bertolo A, Magnan P, Plante M. 2008. Linking the occurrence of brook trout with isolation and extinction in small Boreal Shield lakes. *Freshw. Biol.* 53:304–21.

Bhat MG, Huffaker RG, Lenhart SM. 1993. Controlling forest damage by dispersive beaver populations—centralized optimal management strategy. *Ecol. Appl.* 3:518–30.

Bigler W, Butler DR, Dixon RW. 2001. Beaver-pond sequence morphology and sedimentation in northwestern Montana. *Phys. Geogr.* 22:531–40.

Boyles SL, Savitzky BA. 2008. An analysis of the efficacy and comparative costs of using flow devices to resolve conflicts with North American beavers along roadways in the Coastal Plain of Virginia. In *Proc. 23rd Vertebrate Pest Conf.* Davis: Univ. Calif., pp. 47–52.

Bridgham SD, Johnston CA, Pastor J, Updegraff K. 1995. Potential feedbacks of northern wetlands on climate change. *Bioscience* 45:262–74.

Broschart MR, Johnston CA, Naiman RJ. 1989. Prediction of beaver colony density using impounded habitat variables. *Journal of Wildlife Management* 53:929-934.

Brown D, Hubert W, Anderson S. 1996. Beaver ponds create wetland habitat for birds in mountains of southeastern Wyoming. *Wetlands* 16:127–33.

Brown TN, Johnston CA, Cahow KR. 2003. Lateral flow routing into a wetland: field and model perspectives. *Geomorphology* 53:11–23.

Bubier JL, Moore TR, Roulet NT. 1993. Methane emissions from wetlands in the midboreal region of northern Ontario, Canada. *Ecology* 74:2240–54.

Burns DA, McDonnell JJ. 1998. Effects of a beaver pond on runoff processes: comparison of two headwater catchments. *J. Hydrol.* 205:248–64.

Butler DR. 1989. The failure of beaver dams and resulting outburst flooding: a geomorphic hazard of the southeastern Piedmont. *Geogr. Bull.* 31:29–38.

Butler DR, Malanson GP. 1994. Beaver landforms. *Can. Geogr.* 38:76–79.

Butler DR, Malanson GP. 1995. Sedimentation rates and patterns in beaver ponds in a mountain environment. *Geomorphology* 13:255–69.

Butler DR, Malanson GP. 2005. The geomorphic influences of beaver dams and failures of beaver dams. *Geomorphology* 71:48–60.

Cirmo CP, Driscoll CT. 1993. Beaver pond biogeochemistry—acid neutralizing capacity generation in a headwater wetland. *Wetlands* 13:277–92.

Cirmo CP, Driscoll CT. 1996. The impacts of a watershed $CaCO_3$ treatment on stream and wetland biogeochemistry in the Adirondack Mountains. *Biogeochemistry* 32:265–97.

Collen P, Gibson RJ. 2001. The general ecology of beavers (*Castor* spp.), as related to their influence on stream ecosystems and riparian habitats, and the subsequent effects on fish—a review. *Rev. Fish Biol. Fish.* 10:439–61.

Cooke HA, Zack S. 2008. Influence of beaver dam density on riparian areas and riparian birds in shrubsteppe of Wyoming. *West. N. Am. Natur.* 68:365–73.

Correll DL, Jordan TE, Weller DE. 2000. Beaver pond biogeochemical effects in the Maryland Coastal Plain. *Biogeochemistry* 49:217–39.

Cowell DW. 1984. The Canadian beaver, *Castor canadensis*, as a geomorphic agent in karst terrain. *Can. Field-Natur.* 98:227–30.

Cunningham JM, Calhoun AJK, Glanz WE. 2006. Patterns of beaver colonization and wetland change in Acadia National Park. *Northeast. Natur.* 13:583–96.

Cunningham JM, Calhoun AJK, Glanz WE. 2007. Pond-breeding amphibian species richness and habitat selection in a beaver-modified landscape. *J. Wildl. Manage.* 71:2517–26.

Curry-Lindahl K. 1967. The beaver *Castor fiber* Linnaeus, 1758 in Sweden—extermination and reappearance. *Acta Theriol.* 12:1–15.

Curtis PD, Jensen PG. 2004. Habitat features affecting beaver occupancy along roadsides in New York State. *J. Wildl. Manage.* 68:278–87.

Demmer R, Beschta RL. 2008. Recent history (1988–2004) of beaver dams along Bridge Creek in central Oregon. *Northw. Sci.* 82:309–18.

Devito KJ, Dillon PJ. 1993. Importance of runoff and winter anoxia to the P and N dynamics of a beaver pond. *Can. J. Fish. Aquat. Sci.* 50:2222–34.

Devito KJ, Dillon PJ, Lazerte BD. 1989. Phosphorus and nitrogen retention in five Precambrian shield wetlands. *Biogeochemistry* 8:185–204.

Diefenderfer HL, Montgomery DR. 2009. Pool spacing, channel morphology, and the restoration of tidal forested wetlands of the Columbia River, USA. *Restor. Ecol.* 17:158–68.

Dieter CD, McCabe TR. 1989. Factors influencing beaver lodge-site selection on a prairie river. *Am. Midl. Natur.* 122:408–11.

Dove A, Roulet NT, et al. 1999. Methane dynamics of a northern boreal beaver pond. *Ecoscience* 6:577–86.

Driscoll C, Holsapple J, et al. 1998. The chemistry and transport of mercury in a small wetland in the Adirondack region of New York, USA. *Biogeochemistry* 40:137–46.

Driscoll C, Wyskowski B, et al. 1987. Processes regulating temporal and longitudinal variations in the chemistry of a low-order woodland stream in the Adirondack region of New York. *Biogeochemistry* 3:225–41.

Duffy WG, LaBar DL. 1994. Aquatic invertebrate production in southeastern USA wetlands during winter and spring. *Wetlands* 14:88–97.

Erickson BR. 1962. A description of *Castoroides ohioensis* from Minnesota. *Minn. Acad. Sci. Proc.* 30:7–13.

Erickson HE. 1994. Nitrogen and phosphorus availability, ecosystem processes and plant community dynamics in boreal wetland meadows. Ph.D. diss., Univ. Washington, Seattle.

Ervin GN. 2009. An experimental study on the facilitative effects of tussock structure among wetland plants. *Wetlands* 27:620–30.

FISRWG. 2001. Restoration design. In *Stream corridor restoration: principles, processes, and practices.* Fed. Interagency Stream Restor. Working Group (15 federal agencies of the U.S. government).

France RL. 1997. The importance of beaver lodges in structuring littoral communities in boreal headwater lakes. *Can. J. Zool.—Rev. Can. Zool.* 75:1009–13.

Frohnauer NK, Pierce CL, Kallemeyn LW. 2007. Population dynamics and angler exploitation of the unique muskellunge population in Shoepack Lake, Voyageurs National Park, Minnesota. *N. Am. J. Fish. Manage.* 27:63–76.

Gallant D, Vasseur L, et al. 2009. Habitat selection by river otters *(Lontra canadensis)* under contrasting land-use regimes. *Can. J. Zool.—Rev. Can. Zool.* 87:422–32.

Gill D. 1972. The evolution of a discrete beaver habitat in the Mackenzie River Delta, Northwest Territories. *Can. Field-Natur.* 86:233–39.

Grover AM, Baldassarre GA. 1995. Bird species richness within beaver ponds in south-central New York. *Wetlands* 15:108–18.

Gurnell AM. 1998. The hydrogeomorphological effects of beaver dam-building activity. *Progr. Phys. Geogr.y* 22:167–89.

Hale JG. 1966. Influence of beaver on some trout streams along the Minnesota north shore of Lake Superior. *Minn. Fish. Invest.* 4:5–29.

Harkonen S. 1999. Forest damage caused by the Canadian beaver *(Castor canadensis)* in South Savo, Finland. *Silva Fenn.* 33:247–59.

Hill AR, Duval TP. 2009. Beaver dams along an agricultural stream in southern Ontario, Canada: their impact on riparian zone hydrology and nitrogen chemistry. *Hydrol. Proc.* 23:1324–36.

Hillman GR, Feng JC, et al. 2004. Effects of catchment characteristics and disturbances on storage and export of dissolved organic carbon in a boreal headwater stream. *Can. J. Fish. Aquat. Sci.* 61:1447–60.

Hood GA, Bayley SE. 2008. Beaver *(Castor canadensis)* mitigate the effects of climate on the area of open water in boreal wetlands in western Canada. *Biol. Conserv.* 141:556–67.

Hood GA, Bayley SE. 2009. A comparison of riparian plant community response to herbivory by beavers *(Castor canadensis)* and ungulates in Canada's boreal mixed-wood forest. *For. Ecol. Manage.* 258:1979–89.

Howard RJ, Larson JS. 1985. A stream habitat classification system for beaver. *J. Wildl. Manage.* 49:19–25.

Hyvönen T, Nummi P. 2008. Habitat dynamics of beaver *Castor canadensis* at two spatial scales. *Wildl. Biol.* 14:302–08.

Ives RL. 1942. The beaver-meadow complex. *J. Geomorph.* 5:191–203.

Jakes AF, Snodgrass JW, Burger J. 2007. *Castor canadensis* (beaver) impoundment associated with geomorphology of southeastern streams. *Southeast. Natur.* 6:271–82.

Jenkins SH, Busher PE. 1979. *Castor canadensis. Mammal. Species* 120:1–8.

Jensen PG, Curtis PD, et al. 2001. Habitat and structural factors influencing beaver interference with highway culverts. *Wildl. Soc. Bull.* 29:654–64.

Johnston CA. 1994. Ecological engineering of wetlands by beavers. In *Global wetlands: old world and new,* Mitsch WJ, editor. Amsterdam: Elsevier Sci., pp. 379–84.

Johnston CA. 2000. Wetland soil and landscape alteration by beavers. In *Wetland soils: their genesis, morphology, hydrology, landscapes, and classification,* Richardson JL, Vepraskas MJ, editors. Boca Raton, FL: CRC Press, pp. 391–408.

Johnston CA, Naiman RJ. 1987. Boundary dynamics at the aquatic-terrestrial interface: the influence of beaver and geomorphology. *Landsc. Ecol.* 1:47–57.

Johnston CA, Naiman RJ. 1990a. Aquatic patch creation in relation to beaver population trends. *Ecology* 71:1617–21.

Johnston CA, Naiman RJ. 1990b. The use of a geographic information system to analyze long-term landscape alteration by beaver. *Landsc. Ecol.* 4:5–19.

Johnston CA, Pastor J, Naiman RJ. 1993. Effects of beaver and moose on boreal forest landscapes. In *Landscape ecology and geographical information systems,* Cousins SH, Haines-Young R, Green D, editors. London: Taylor & Francis, pp. 236–54.

Johnston CA, Pinay G, et al. 1995. Influence of soil properties on the biogeochemistry of a beaver meadow hydrosequence. *Soil Sci. Soc. Am. J.* 59:1789–99.

Karraker NE, Gibbs JP. 2009. Amphibian production in forested landscapes in relation to wetland hydroperiod: a case study of vernal pools and beaver ponds. *Biol. Conserv.* 142:2293–02.

Kaye CA. 1962. Early postglacial beavers in southeastern New England. *Science* 138:906–07.

Klotz RL. 1998. Influence of beaver ponds on the phosphorus concentration of stream water. *Can. J. Fish. Aquat. Sci.* 55:1228–35.

Kretser W, Gallagher J, Nicolette J. 1989. *Adirondack lakes study 1984–1987: an evaluation of fish communities and water chemistry.* Ray Brook, NY: Adirondack Lakes Surv. Corp.

Lawrence WH, Fay LD, Graham SA. 1956. A report on the beaver die-off in Michigan. *J. Wildl. Manage.* 20:184–87.

LeBlanc FA, Gallant D, et al. 2007. Unequal summer use of beaver ponds by river otters: influence of beaver activity, pond size, and vegetation cover. *Can. J. Zool.—Rev. Can. Zool.* 85:774–82.

Le Page C, Keddy PA. 1998. Reserves of buried seeds in beaver ponds. *Wetlands* 18:242–48.

Lesica P, Miles S. 2004. Beavers indirectly enhance the growth of Russian olive and tamarisk along eastern Montana rivers. *West. N. Am. Natur.* 64:93–100.

Lewkowicz AG, Coultish TL. 2004. Beaver damming and palsa dynamics in a subarctic mountainous environment, Wolf Creek, Yukon Territory, Canada. *Arct. Antarct. Alpine Res.* 36:208–18.

Litvaitis JA. 2003. Are pre-Columbian conditions relevant baselines for managed forests in the northeastern United States? *For. Ecol. Manage.* 185:113–26.

Longcore JR, McAuley DG, et al. 2006. Macroinvertebrate abundance, water chemistry, and wetland characteristics affect use of wetlands by avian species in Maine. *Hydrobiologia* 567:143–67.

Longcore T, Rich C, Muller-Schwarze D. 2007. Management by assertion: beavers and songbirds at Lake Skinner (Riverside County, California). *Env. Manage.* 39:460–71.

MacDonald DW, Tattersall FH, et al. 1995. Reintroducing the European beaver to Britain: nostalgic meddling or restoring biodiversity? *Mammal Rev.* 25:161–200.

Maret TJ, Parker M, Fannin TE. 1987. The effect of beaver ponds on the nonpoint source water quality of a stream in southwestern Wyoming. *Water Res.* 21:263–68.

Margolis BE, Castro MS, Raesly RL. 2001. The impact of beaver impoundments on the water chemistry of two Appalachian streams. *Can. J. Fish. Aquat. Sci.* 58:2271–83.

Margolis BE, Raesly RL, Shumway DL. 2001. The effects of beaver-created wetlands on the benthic macroinvertebrate assemblages of two Appalachian streams. *Wetlands* 21:554–63.

McCall TC, Hodgman TP, et al. 1996. Beaver populations and their relation to wetland habitat and breeding waterfowl in Maine. *Wetlands* 16:163–72.

McHale MR, Cirmo CP, et al. 2004. Wetland nitrogen dynamics in an Adirondack forested watershed. *Hydrol. Processes* 18:1853–70.

McKinstry MC, Caffrey P, Anderson SH. 2001. The importance of beaver to wetland habitats and waterfowl in Wyoming. *J. Am. Water Resour. Assoc.* 37:1571–77.

McKinstry MC, Kahru RR, Anderson SH. 1997. Use of active beaver, *Castor canadensis,* lodges by muskrats, *Ondatra zibethicus,* in Wyoming. *Can. Field-Natur.* 111:310–11.

McRae G, Edwards CJ. 1994. Thermal-characteristics of Wisconsin headwater streams occupied by beaver—implications for brook trout habitat. *Trans. Am. Fish. Soc.* 123:641–56.

Meentemeyer RK, Butler DR. 1999. Hydrogeomorphic effects of beaver dams in Glacier National Park, Montana. *Phys. Geogr.* 20:436–46.

Menzel MA, Carter TC, et al. 2001. Tree-roost characteristics of subadult and female adult evening bats *(Nycticeius humeralis)* in the upper Coastal Plain of South Carolina. *Am. Midl. Natur.* 145:112–19.

Merendino MT, McCullough GB, North NR. 1995. Wetland availability and use by breeding waterfowl in southern Ontario. *J. Wildl. Manage.* 59:527–32.

Metts BS, Lanham JD, Russell KR. 2001. Evaluation of herpetofaunal communities on upland streams and beaver-impounded streams in the upper Piedmont of South Carolina. *Am. Midl. Natur.* 145:54–65.

Mitchell CC, Niering WA. 1993. Vegetation change in a topogenic bog following beaver flooding. *Bull. Torrey Bot. Club* 120:136–47.

Mitchell SC, Cunjak RA. 2007. Stream flow, salmon and beaver dams: roles in the structuring of stream fish communities within an anadromous salmon dominated stream. *J. Anim. Ecol.* 76:1062–74.

Monzingo DLJ, Hibler CP. 1987. Prevalence of *Giardia* sp. in a beaver colony and the resulting environmental contamination. *J. Wildl. Diseases* 23:576–85.

Moorman MC, Eggleston DB, et al. 2009. Implications of beaver *Castor canadensis* and trout introductions on native fish in the Cape Horn Biosphere Reserve, Chile. *Trans. Am. Fish. Soc.* 138:306–13.

Müller-Schwarze D, Sun L. 2003. *The beaver: natural history of a wetlands engineer.* Ithaca, NY: Cornell Univ. Press.

Naiman RJ, Johnston CA, Kelley JC. 1988. Alteration of North American streams by beaver. *Bioscience* 38:753–62.

Naiman RJ, Melillo JM, and Hobbie JE. 1986. Ecosystem alteration of boreal forest streams by beaver *(Castor canadensis). Ecology* 67:1254–1269.

Naiman RJ, Pinay G, et al. 1994. Beaver influences on the long-term biogeochemical characteristics of boreal forest drainage networks. *Ecology* 75:905–21.

Newman DG, Griffin CR. 1994. Wetland use by river otters in Massachusetts. *J. Wildl. Manage.* 58:18–23.

Nummi P, Poysa H. 1997. Population and community level responses in *Anas*-species to patch disturbance caused by an ecosystem engineer, the beaver. *Ecography* 20:580–84.

Parker JD, Caudill CC, Hay ME. 2007. Beaver herbivory on aquatic plants. *Oecologia* 151:616–25.

Parker R, Steginhaus E, et al. 1951. Contamination of natural waters and mud with *Pasteurella tularensis* and tularemia in beavers and muskrats in the northwestern United States. *Nat. Inst. Health Bull.* 193:1–61.

Pastor J, Bonde J, et al. 1993. Markovian analysis of the spatially dependent dynamics of beaver ponds. In *Predicting spatial effects in ecological systems,* Gardner RH, editor. Providence, RI: Am. Mathematical Soc., pp. 5–27.

Pastor J, Dewey B, Christian DP. 1996. Carbon and nutrient mineralization and fungal spore composition of fecal pellets from voles in Minnesota. *Ecography* 19:52–61.

Pastor J, Downing A, Erickson HE. 1996. Species-area curves and diversity-productivity relationships in beaver meadows of Voyageurs National Park, Minnesota, USA. *Oikos* 77:399–406.

Pastur GM, Lencinas MV, et al. 2006. Understorey succession in *Nothofagus* forests in Tierra del Fuego (Argentina) affected by *Castor canadensis. Appl. Veg. Sci.* 9:143–54.

Payne NF, Peterson RP. 1986. Trends in complaints of beaver damage in Wisconsin. *Wildl. Soc. Bull.* 14:303–07.

Perkins TE, Wilson MV. 2005. The impacts of *Phalaris arundinacea* (reed canarygrass) invasion on wetland plant richness in the Oregon Coast Range, USA, depend on beavers. *Biol. Conserv.* 124:291–95.

Pollock MM, Beechie TJ, Jordan CE. 2007. Geomorphic changes upstream of beaver dams in Bridge Creek, an incised stream channel in the interior Columbia River basin, eastern Oregon. *Earth Surf. Processes Landf.* 32:1174–85.

Pollock MM, Pess GR, Beechie TJ. 2004. The importance of beaver ponds to coho salmon production in the Stillaguamish River basin, Washington, USA. *N. Am. J. Fish. Manage.* 24:749–60.

Popescu VD, Gibbs JP. 2009. Interactions between climate, beaver activity, and pond occupancy by the cold-adapted mink frog in New York State, USA. *Biol. Conserv.* 142:2059–68.

Power ME, Tilman D, et al. 1996. Challenges in the quest for keystones. *Bioscience* 46:609–20.

Raffel TR, Smith N, et al. 2009. Central place foraging by beavers *(Castor canadensis)* in a complex lake habitat. *Am. Midl. Natur.* 162:62–73.

Ray HL, Ray AM, Rebertus AJ. 2004. Rapid establishment of fish in isolated peatland beaver ponds. *Wetlands* 24:399–405.

Ray AM, Rebertus AJ, Ray HL. 2001. Macrophyte succession in Minnesota beaver ponds. *Can. J. Bot.—Rev. Can. Bot.* 79:487–99.

Rebertus AJ. 1986. Bogs as beaver habitat in north-central Minnesota. *Am. Midl. Natur.* 116:240–45.

Reddoch JM, Reddoch AH. 2005. Consequences of beaver, *Castor canadensis,* flooding on a small shore fen in southwestern Quebec. *Can. Field-Natur.* 119:385–94.

Reid DG, Herrero SM, Code TE. 1988. River otters as agents of water loss from beaver ponds. *J. Mammal.* 69:100–07.

Remillard MM, Gruendling GK, Bogucki DJ. 1987. Disturbance by beaver *(Castor canadensis* Kuhl) and increased landscape heterogeneity. In *Landscape heterogeneity and disturbance,* Turner MG, editor. New York: Springer-Verlag, pp. 103–22.

Renouf RN. 1972. Waterfowl utilization of beaver ponds in New Brunswick. *J. Wildl. Manage.* 36:740–44.

Retzer JL, Swope HM, et al. 1956. *Suitability of physical factors for beaver management in the Rocky Mountains of Colorado.* Tech. Bull. no. 2. Denver: CO Dept. Game, Fish & Parks.

Ringelman JK. 1991. *Managing beaver to benefit waterfowl.* Washington, DC: USFWS.

Robinson S, Beaudoin AB, et al. 2007. Plant macrofossils associated with an early Holocene beaver dam in interior Alaska. *Arctic* 60:430–38.

Rolauffs P, Hering D, Lohse S. 2001. Composition, invertebrate community and productivity of a beaver dam in comparison to other stream habitat types. *Hydrobiologia* 459:201–12.

Rosell F, Bozser O, et al. 2005. Ecological impact of beavers *Castor fiber* and *Castor canadensis* and their ability to modify ecosystems. *Mammal Rev.* 35:248–76.

Roulet NT, Ash R, Moore TR. 1992. Low boreal wetlands as a source of atmospheric methane. *J. Geophys. Res.* 97(D4):3739–49.

Roulet NT, Crill PM, et al. 1997. CO_2 and CH_4 flux between a boreal beaver pond and the atmosphere. *J. Geophys. Res.* 102:29313–19.

Rudemann R, Schoonmaker WJ. 1938. Beaver dams as geologic agents. *Science* 88:523–25.

Russell KR, Moorman CE, et al. 1999. Amphibian and reptile communities associated with beaver *(Castor canadensis)* ponds and unimpounded streams in the Piedmont of South Carolina. *J. Freshw. Ecol.* 14:149–58.

Rybczynski N. 2008. Woodcutting behavior in beavers (Castoridae, Rodentia): estimating ecological performance in a modern and a fossil taxon. *Paleobiology* 34:389–402.

Scott KJ, Kelly CA, Rudd JWM. 1999. The importance of floating peat to methane fluxes from flooded peatlands. *Biogeochemistry* 47:187–202.

Sigourney DB, Letcher BH, Cunjak RA. 2006. Influence of beaver activity on summer growth and condition of age-2 Atlantic salmon parr. *Trans. Am. Fish. So.* 135:1068–75.

Simonavičiūtė L, Ulevičius A. 2007. Structure of phytocenoses in beaver meadows in Lithuania. *Ekologija* 53:34–44.

Smith DW, Peterson RO. 1991. Behavior of beaver in lakes with varying water levels in northern Minnesota. *Env. Manag.* 15:395–401.

Smith ME, Driscoll CT, et al. 1991. Modification of stream ecosystem structure and function by beaver *(Castor canadensis)* in the Adirondack Mountains, New York. *Can. J. Zool.—Rev. Can. Zool.* 69:55–61.

Snodgrass JW. 1997. Temporal and spatial dynamics of beaver-created patches as influenced by management practices in a southeastern North American landscape. *J. Appl. Ecol.* 34:1043–56.

Snodgrass JW, Meffe GK. 1998. Influence of beavers on stream fish assemblages: effects of pond age and watershed position. *Ecology* 79:928–42.

Songsteralpin MS, Klotz RL. 1995. A comparison of electron-transport system activity in stream and beaver pond sediments. *Can. J. Fish. Aquat. Sci.* 52:1318–26.

Stenlund MH. 1953. Report of Minnesota beaver die-off, 1951–1952. *J. Wildl. Manage.* 17:376–77.

Stevens CE, Paszkowski CA, Foote AL. 2007. Beaver *(Castor canadensis)* as a surrogate species for conserving anuran amphibians on boreal streams in Alberta, Canada. *Biol. Conserv.* 134:1–13.

Stevens CE, Paszkowski CA, Scrimgeour GJ. 2006. Older is better: beaver ponds on boreal streams as breeding habitat for the wood frog. *J. Wildl. Manage.* 70:1360–71.

Striped Face-Collins M, Johnston CA. 2007. Rangeland drought mitigation by beaver *(Castor canadensis)* impounded water. *Proc. So. Dakota Acad. Sci.* 86:228.

Sturtevant BR. 1998. A model of wetland vegetation dynamics in simulated beaver impoundments. *Ecol. Model.* 112:195–225.

Syphard AD, Garcia MW. 2001. Human- and beaver-induced wetland changes in the Chickahominy River watershed from 1953 to 1994. *Wetlands* 21:342–53.

Terwilliger J, Pastor J. 1999. Small mammals, ectomycorrhizae, and conifer succession in beaver meadows. *Oikos* 85:83–94.

Westbrook CJ, Cooper DJ, Baker BW. 2006. Beaver dams and overbank floods influence groundwater–surface water interactions of a Rocky Mountain riparian area. *Water Resourc. Res.* 42:W06404.

Wheatley M. 1997. Beaver, *Castor canadensis,* home range size and patterns of use in the taiga of southeastern Manitoba. 3. Habitat variation. *Can. Field-Natur.* 111:217–22.

White SM, Rahel FJ. 2008. Complementation of habitats for Bonneville cutthroat trout in watersheds influenced by beavers, livestock, and drought. *Trans. Am. Fish. Soc.* 137:881–94.

Wilson DE, Reeder DM. 2005. *Mammal species of the world: a taxonomic and geographic reference,* 3rd ed. Baltimore: Johns Hopkins Univ. Press.

Wilsson L. 1971. Observations and experiments on the ethology of the European beaver (*Castor fiber* L.). *Viltrevy* 8:115–266.

Wolff SW, Wesche TA, Hubert WA. 1989. Stream channel and habitat changes due to flow augmentation. *Regul. Riv.: Res. & Manage.* 4:225–33.

Wolter PT, Johnston CA, Niemi GJ. 2006. Land use land cover change in the U.S. Great Lakes Basin 1992 to 2001. *J. Great Lakes Res.* 32:607–28.

Woo MK, Waddington JM. 1990. Effects of beaver dams on subarctic wetland hydrology. *Arctic* 43:223–30.

Wright JP. 2009. Linking populations to landscapes: richness scenarios resulting from changes in the dynamics of an ecosystem engineer. *Ecology* 90:3418–29.

Wright JP, Jones CG. 2006. The concept of organisms as ecosystem engineers ten years on: progress, limitations, and challenges. *Bioscience* 56:203–09.

Wright JP, Flecker AS, Jones CG. 2003. Local vs. landscape controls on plant species richness in beaver meadows. *Ecology* 84:3162–73.

Wright JP, Jones CG, Flecker AS. 2002. An ecosystem engineer, the beaver, increases species richness at the landscape scale. *Oecologia* 132:96–101.

Yavitt JB, Lang GE, Sexstone AJ. 1990. Methane fluxes in wetland and forest soils, beaver ponds, and low-order streams of a temperate forest ecosystem. *J. Geophys. Res.* 95:22463–74.

CHAPTER 13

Great Lakes Coastal Marshes

DOUGLAS A. WILCOX

Great Lakes Geology and Hydrology

The Great Lakes system consists of Lakes Superior, Huron, Michigan, Erie, and Ontario, as well as their connecting channels and the St. Lawrence River, which connects the lakes to the Atlantic Ocean (Fig. 13.1). The Great Lakes Basin includes the Canadian province of Ontario and the U.S. states of Minnesota, Wisconsin, Illinois, Indiana, Michigan, Ohio, Pennsylvania, and New York. The basin covers about 765,000 km², including the upper St. Lawrence River (Neff and Nicholas 2005).

The surficial geology of the Great Lakes Basin is highly variable. Lake Superior and northern Lake Huron are surrounded by metamorphic and igneous rocks of Precambrian age, with little or no overburden. The remainder of the basin is underlain by sedimentary rocks of Cambrian through Cretaceous ages (Wilcox, Thompson, et al. 2007) and covered by unconsolidated glacial deposits. Water chemistry of the lakes reflects the underlying geology; Lake Superior is less mineralized (specific conductance 95–100 uS/cm; pH 7.4–8.0; alkalinity 40–50 mg/L as $CaCO_3$) compared to the other lakes, which are more calcareous, with limestone and dolomite bedrock (specific conductance 200–300 uS/cm; pH 7.8–8.5; alkalinity 80–110 mg/L as $CaCO_3$) (Keough, Thompson, et al. 1999; Mechenich, Kraft, et al. 2006; www.ilec.or.jp/database/index/idx-lakes.html).

Lake Superior is at the upstream end of the Great Lakes and discharges to Lake Huron via the St. Marys River (Fig. 13.1). Lakes Huron and Michigan are one lake hydrologically because the connection between lakes at the Straits of Mackinac is very wide. Lake Huron discharges to Lake Erie by way of the St. Clair River, Lake St. Clair, and the Detroit River; Lake Erie connects to Lake Ontario largely via the Niagara River.

Mean annual precipitation ranges from 0.7 m north of Lake Superior to 1.3 m east of Lake Ontario. Snowbelt areas downwind from open waters of the lakes receive lake-effect snow that can average 3.5 m and exceed 8.9 m annually (Wilcox, Thompson, et al. 2007). Evaporation from the lake surface, especially when cooler dry air passes over warmer open water in fall and early winter, results in atmospheric outflows composing as much as one-third of the water balance in lakes Superior and Michigan-Huron (Wilcox, Thompson, et al. 2007).

Great Lakes water levels vary considerably on timescales from hours to millennia and are influenced by both natural processes and human activities. Storm surges, seiches, and barometric pressure changes can create localized changes in water levels that last hours to days. Wind-driven seiches with amplitudes of 10 to 30 cm are common across most Great Lakes and larger embayments within the lakes, but seiches with amplitudes of over 3 m have been recorded in Lake Erie. Seasonal and annual data systematically recorded by the U.S. and Canadian governments since 1860 show cycles of low winter levels and high summer levels that vary in magnitude by lake (Fig. 13.2). Based on the monthly average water levels, the magnitudes of unregulated seasonal fluctuations are relatively small, averaging about 0.4 m on lakes Superior and Michigan-Huron, about 0.5 m on Lake Erie, and about 0.6 m on Lake Ontario (Wilcox, Thompson, et al. 2007).

Longer-term (multiyear, decadal, and longer) fluctuations are recognizable in the historical lake-level record and show some similarities among lakes (Fig. 13.2). Pronounced low lake levels occurred in the mid-1920s, mid-1930s, mid-1960s, and starting again in 1999. Periods of higher lake levels generally occurred in the late 1800s, the late 1920s, the mid-1950s, and from the early 1970s to mid-1980s. However, Lake Superior water levels have been regulated since about 1914, and levels of Lake Ontario have been regulated since about 1960. Therefore, lake-level patterns on those lakes since regulation began do not reflect all of the natural variability that would have occurred. Other human activities affecting lake levels include diversions into or out of the basin, consumption of water, and dredging of outlet channels.

Water-level changes have also been recorded in the late Holocene geologic record as sequences of beach ridges of similar origin but different age (chronosequences) that formed during repeated occurrences of high lake levels, with intervening low levels. Baedke and Thompson (2000) used the elevations of foreshore deposits in these ridges coupled with radiocarbon dates from the wetlands between the ridges to develop a 4,700-year lake-level record for lakes Michigan-Huron (Fig. 13.3). The record shows a quasi-periodic behavior, with short-term fluctuations with a range of 0.5 to 0.6 m that occur about every 32 ± 6 years superimposed on longer-term fluctuations with a

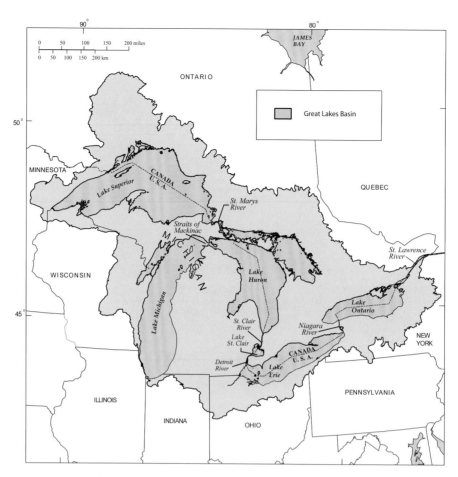

FIG. 13.1. Map of the Great Lakes showing the extent of the drainage basin. Base from ESRI, 2001; U.S. Army Corps of Engineers, 1998; and Environment Canada, 1995; digital data sets at various scales. (From Neff and Nicholas 2005.)

range of 0.8 to 0.9 m that occur about every 160 ± 40 years. Over millennia, three high phases occurred from 2,300 to 3,300, 1,100 to 2,000, and 0 to 800 years ago.

A preliminary paleo-record of Lake Superior water levels was also created, using dating of sand grains by a technique called optically stimulated luminescence to determine the age of the ridges (Argyilan, Forman, et al. 2005). It shows patterns similar to those of lakes Michigan-Huron until about 1,200 years ago because lakes Superior, Michigan, and Huron had been joined as one lake prior to that time (Johnston, Baedke, et al. 2004; Johnston, Thompson, et al. 2007). It appears that Lake Superior has taken on its own lake-level pattern following its split from the other lakes.

The hydrographs recording long-term patterns of lake-level change also reflect long-term patterns of vertical ground movement in response to glacial isostatic adjustment (GIA), in which the earth's crust is warping in response to the melting of the last glacial ice sheets that crossed the area. The glacial ice was thickest north of the Great Lakes Basin, so these areas of the earth's crust were depressed the most. Today, areas depressed the most are rising the fastest (Baedke and Thompson 2000; Mainville and Craymer 2005). GIA influences long-term lake levels by warping each lake's basin and changing the elevation of the lake's coastline in relationship to its outlet. Segments of coastline rebounding more rapidly than the lake's outlet experience a long-term lake-level fall, whereas coastlines rebounding more slowly than the outlet experience

a long-term lake-level rise (Wilcox, Thompson, et al. 2007). In areas under a long-term rise, lake waters advance into river and stream valleys along the shoreline, creating drowned river mouths that are a major setting for wetland development.

Great Lakes coastal wetlands can be separated into three specific hydrogeomorphic systems—lacustrine, riverine, and barrier-protected—based on geomorphic position, dominant hydrologic source, and current hydrologic connectivity to the lake (Keough, Thompson, et al. 1999; Environment Canada 2002; Albert, Wilcox, et al. 2005). In addition to the three general hydrogeomorphic systems, this classification includes further breakdown into geomorphic type and geomorphic modifiers that reflect specific site conditions.

Lacustrine (lake-influenced) systems (Fig. 13.4a) are controlled directly by waters of the Great Lakes and are strongly affected by lake-level fluctuations, nearshore currents, seiches, and ice scour. Geomorphic formations such as embayments and sand spits along the shoreline provide varying degrees of protection from coastal processes. Open lacustrine wetlands are exposed to the full force of winds and waves, and they accumulate little organic sediment. Protected lacustrine wetlands have more organic sediments and typically have more extensive vegetation development (Environment Canada 2002; Albert, Wilcox, et al. 2005).

Riverine (river-influenced) system wetlands (Fig. 13.4b) occur in rivers and streams that flow into or between the Great Lakes. The water quality, flow rate, and sediment input are con-

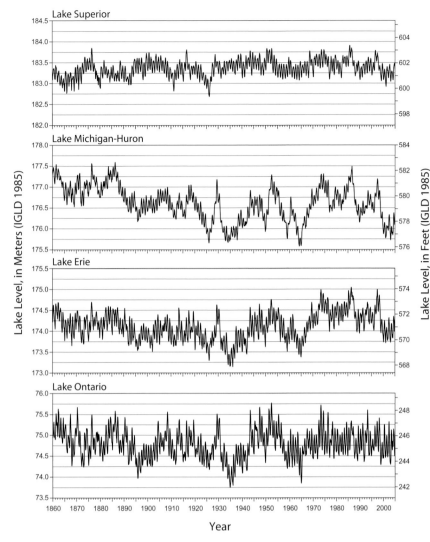

FIG. 13.2. Hydrograph showing historical lake levels for the Great Lakes, 1860–2005.

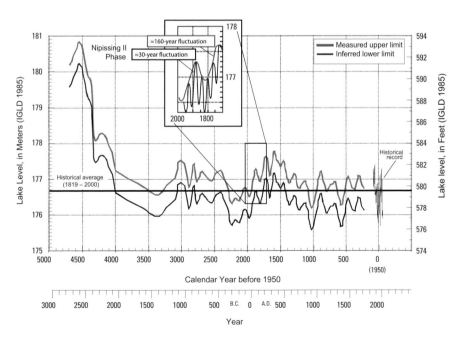

FIG. 13.3. Hydrograph of the late Holocene lake level and historical lake level for Lake Michigan-Huron. The upper line is interpreted from beach-ridge studies, whereas the lower line is an inferred lower limit using the range of the historical record as a guide. (From Baedke and Thompson 2000 as presented by Wilcox, Thompson, et al. 2007.)

FIG. 13.4. Oblique aerial photographs of Lake Ontario wetlands of differing geomorphic type. A. Braddock Bay, open embayment; *lacustrine.* B. Stony Creek, drowned river mouth; *riverine.* C. South Colwell Pond, barrier-beach lagoon; *barrier-protected.*

trolled in large part by their individual drainage basins. However, water levels and fluvial processes in these wetlands are also determined by the Great Lakes because lake waters flood back into the lower portions of the drainage system (drowned river mouth wetlands). Protection from wave attack is provided in the river channels by bars and channel morphology. Riverine wetlands also include those wetlands found along large connecting channels, such as the St. Marys and St. Clair Rivers. In addition, delta wetlands formed from alluvial materials that extend into the lake or connecting channel are also included as riverine; they may be extensive and typically have well-developed organic soils (Environment Canada 2002; Albert, Wilcox, et al. 2005).

Barrier-protected system wetlands (Fig. 13.4c) may have originated from either coastal or fluvial processes. However, due to nearshore processes, the wetlands have become separated from the Great Lakes by a barrier beach or series of beach ridges. Barrier-beach lagoon wetlands are protected from wave attack but may be periodically or continuously connected directly to the lake by a channel or inlet crossing the barrier. When connected to the lake, water levels in these wetlands are determined by lake levels, while during isolation from the lake, groundwater and surface drainage from the basin of the individual wetland provide the dominant source of water input. Inlets to protected wetlands may be permanent or temporary due to nearshore processes that can close off inlets from the lake. Swale complexes are wetlands that occur between recurved fingers of sand spits or relict beach ridges. Oftentimes, only the first few swales are directly connected to the lake, but groundwater discharges related to lake levels often supply water to swales farther from the lake (Environment Canada 2002; Albert, Wilcox, et al. 2005).

Plant Communities

Wetland plant communities in the Great Lakes vary according to factors that include underlying geology and resultant water chemistry, lake-level variability, geomorphic type, human disturbance, and location within the geographic range of the basin. Differences can be seen even among wetlands of the same geomorphic type from northern Lake Superior to the more southerly lakes. A lake-by-lake tour of selected wetlands illustrates this point, with descriptions reflecting plant communities commonly found when lake levels are not at extreme high or low levels.

Bark Bay is a lake-connected, barrier-beach lagoon wetland with two small inflowing streams on the Bayfield Peninsula in western Lake Superior (Fig. 13.5a). Behind the protective barrier beach is a large, shallow lagoon containing pondweeds (*Potamogeton* spp.), common watermilfoil (*Myriophyllum sibiricum*), stonewort (*Chara* spp.), and other submersed plants. The perimeter of the lagoon has a narrow band of emergent marsh containing broad-leaf cattail (*Typha latifolia*), lake sedge (*Carex lacustris*), bur-reed (*Sparganium* spp.), rushes (*Juncus* spp.), three-way sedge (*Dulichium arundinaceum*), and increasing amounts of common reed (*Phragmites australis*). Large areas also consist of floating fen mat—peatland where slow decomposition of plants allows development of deep organic soils. Rhizomes of wool-fruited sedge (*Carex lasiocarpa*) intertwine to form the mat, which supports other sedge species, as well as mat-forming leatherleaf (*Chamaedaphne calyculata*) and peatland plants such as sphagnum moss (*Sphagnum* spp.), sundew (*Drosera* spp.), small cranberry (*Vaccinium oxycoccos*), and pitcherplant (*Sarracenia purpurea*). The shrub sweet gale (*Myrica gale*) is also common on the floating mats (Epstein, Judziewicz, et al. 1997; Wilcox, Meeker, et al. 2002).

The Kakagon River flows into Chequamegon Bay, on western Lake Superior near Ashland, Wisconsin (Fig. 13.5b). Seiches with amplitudes of 30 cm occur regularly and cause reverses in river flow direction as much as 2 km upstream in this drowned river mouth wetland. A dominant wetland plant is northern wild rice (*Zizania palustris*), a tall annual grass with large nutrient requirements that benefits from the nutrient-rich sediment deposited in response to flow reversals (Meeker 1996). Other dominant plants include pondweeds, waterweed (*Elodea canadensis*), coontail (*Ceratophyllum demersum*), bullhead pond lily *(Nuphar variegata)*, white water lily *(Nymphaea odorata)*, and pickerelweed *(Pontederia cordata)* in the aquatic zone and Canada bluejoint grass *(Calamagrostis canadensis)* and wool-fruited sedge in the peatlands (Meeker 1993).

A narrow fringe of wet meadow and emergent marsh follows long stretches of the St. Marys River (Fig. 13.5c), with beds of submersed vegetation, including stonewort, naiads *(Najas* spp.), quillworts *(Isoetes* spp.), and pondweeds, along the outside border. The emergent zone in these connecting channel riverine wetlands contains bulrushes *(Schoenoplectus* spp.) and spike-rushes *(Eleocharis* spp). The wet meadow at slightly higher elevation contains Canada bluejoint grass, tussock sedge *(Carex stricta)*, wool-fruited sedge, lake sedge, broad-leaf cattail, and water knotweed *(Polygonum amphibium)* (Albert 2003; D. Albert pers. comm.).

Duck Bay is a protected lacustrine wetland in an embayment on Marquette Island, in the Les Cheneaux Islands of northern Lake Huron (Fig. 13.5d). Protection from wave action allows development of broad bands of emergent plants and wet meadows, with beds of submersed vegetation extending to depths of about 2 m. Submersed plants include pondweeds, naiads, waterweed, watermilfoil, and wild celery *(Vallisneria americana);* floating white water lily and spatterdock *(Nuphar advena)* are also common. The emergent community contains wave-tolerant hardstem bulrush *(Schoenoplectus acutus)* and spike-rushes along the outer edge and bulrushes, horsetails *(Equisetum* spp.), arrowhead *(Sagittaria latifolia)*, pickerelweed, and bur-reed closer to shore. Wet meadows are dominated by Canada bluejoint grass and sedges, with scattered marsh fern *(Thelypteris palustris)*, marsh bellflower *(Campanula aparinoides)*, marsh pea *(Lathyrus palustris)*, marsh cinquefoil *(Potentilla palustris)*, and other forbs. At slightly higher elevations, a narrow band of shrubs includes speckled alder *(Alnus incana)*, sweet gale, and willows *(Salix* spp.) among grasses and sedges, giving way to northern white cedar *(Thuja occidentalis)* swamp above the highest lake level (Albert 2003).

Limestone bedrock underlying open embayments, such as El Cajon Bay, along the shores of northern Lake Huron (Fig. 13.5e), supports development of highly minerotrophic fens with thin organic soils and marl flats. Standing water may contain lawns of stonewort and sparse stands of hardstem bulrush, but slightly higher elevations support plants such walking sedge *(Eleocharis rostellata)*, Indian paintbrush *(Castilleja coccinea)*, Kalm's lobelia *(Lobelia kalmii)*, grass-of-Parnassus *(Parnassia glauca)*, and insectivorous butterwort *(Pinguicula vulgaris)*, pitcherplant, and sundews. Characteristic shrubs are sweet gale and shrubby cinquefoil *(Potentilla fruticosa);* common trees are northern white cedar and tamarack *(Larix laricina)* (Albert 2003).

Saginaw Bay, on Lake Huron, is an open lacustrine wetland (Fig. 13.5f). Seiches with an amplitude of 10–20 cm are routine, and they can be greater following storm events. The very gradual slope of the wetland basin thus allows seiches to flood and dewater large areas of wetland, affecting seed germination and the extent of submersed vegetation (Wilcox and Nichols 2008). The southern portion of Saginaw Bay is characterized by a 200- to 300-m-wide band of emergent marsh along much of its perimeter. Lakeward from the marsh and interspersed within it are submersed plants such as stonewort, naiads, common watermilfoil, water star-grass *(Heteranthera dubia)*, and wild celery. The emergents are dominated by three-square bulrush *(Schoenoplectus pungens)* and softstem bulrush *(S. tabernaemontani)*, with invading cattails and, more recently, common reed (Wilcox and Nichols 2008).

FIG. 13.5. Map of the Great Lakes showing locations of wetlands for which plant and animal communities are described. a. Bark Bay, Lake Superior. b. Kakagon River, Lake Superior. c. St. Marys River. d. Duck Bay, Lake Huron. e. El Cajon Bay, Lake Huron. f. Saginaw Bay, Lake Huron. g. Arcadia Lake, Lake Michigan. h. Dickinson Island, St. Clair River. i. Metzger Marsh, Lake Erie. j. South Colwell Pond, Lake Ontario. k. Kents Creek, Lake Ontario.

Arcadia Lake contains a drowned river mouth wetland in which three tributary creeks coalesce and enter a small lake formed in the now-flooded river valley before exiting to Lake Michigan along its eastern shore (Fig. 13.5g). Much of the wetland is dominated by a sedge/grass meadow plant community composed of Canada bluejoint grass and tussock sedge, with jewelweed *(Asclepias incarnata)*, marsh bellflower, and invading reed canarygrass *(Phalaris arundinacea)* also prominent. A short emergent community occurs along the water's edge that contains arrowhead, softstem bulrush, bur-reed, rice cutgrass *(Leersia oryzoides)*, spike-rushes, and several sedges. The aquatic zone contains bullhead pond lily, pondweeds, waterweed, and other submersed aquatic plants. Unsuccessful attempts to ditch and drain the wetland allowed some of the emergent wetland to be invaded by narrow-leaf cattail *(Typha angustifolia)*.

Dickinson Island is a riverine delta wetland that is part of the St. Clair River delta, which formed where the river flows into Lake St. Clair (Fig. 13.5h). Topographic relief varies across the island, with beaches, beach ridges, natural levees, and shallow swales and pools (Jaworski, Raphael, et al. 1979). Dominant plants include buttonbush *(Cephalanthus occidentalis)*, Canada rush *(Juncus canadensis)*, rice cutgrass, Canadian St. John's wort *(Triadenum fraseri)*, bur-reed, pickerelweed, common arrowhead, stonewort, white water lily, pondweeds, and sedges. Common reed is a more recent invader (Albert 2003; unpublished data).

Metzger Marsh formed as a barrier-beach lagoon wetland in western Lake Erie (Fig. 13.5i), but the protective barrier was lost to erosion during a high lake-level period in the 1970s (Kowalski and Wilcox 1999; Wilcox and Whillans 1999). A dike was constructed in the 1990s to mimic the protective function of a barrier beach, with inclusion of a water-control structure to maintain hydrologic connection to the lake. Large areas of submersed vegetation are dominated by coontail, waterweed, Eurasian watermilfoil *(Myriophyllum spicatum)*, and naiads. Emergent vegetation has changed periodically since the 1990s and is now dominated by areas of cattail, arrowhead, softstem bulrush, and invasive common reed, flowering rush *(Butomus umbellatus)*, and reed canarygrass. American lotus *(Nelumbo lutea)*, which begins as a floating-leaf plant but matures as an emergent, is also very prevalent (Kowalski and Wilcox 2002).

South Colwell Pond is a barrier-beach lagoon wetland on

the eastern shore of Lake Ontario (Fig. 13.5j). The native plant community of much of the wetland was meadow marsh dominated by Canada bluejoint grass, with jewelweed, sensitive fern *(Onoclea sensibilis)*, spinulose woodfern *(Dryopteris carthusiana)*, and shrubs such as red-osier dogwood *(Cornus sericea)*. Following regulation of Lake Ontario water levels when the St. Lawrence Seaway began operation in 1960, the narrow emergent marsh along the edge of the lagoon expanded, with domination by hybrid *(Typha × glauca)* and narrow-leaf cattail, but also containing bur-reed, arrowhead, and European frogbit *(Hydrocharis morsus-ranae)*. The adjacent aquatic zone contains emergent northern wild rice and pickerelweed, submersed vegetation such as coontail, bladderwort *(Utricularia* spp.), nodding waternymph *(Najas flexilis)*, and stonewort, and floating white water lily, bullhead pond lily, and duckweeds *(Lemna* spp.). The meadow marsh at higher elevations has been invaded by hybrid cattail, along with reed canarygrass and multiflora rose *(Rosa multiflora)* (Wilcox, Ingram, et al. 2005; Wilcox, Kowalski, et al. 2008).

Kents Creek is a drowned river mouth wetland in northeastern Lake Ontario near the outlet into the St. Lawrence River (Fig. 13.5k). The native sedge/grass–dominated meadow marsh contains Canada bluejoint grass, tussock sedge, forbs such as jewelweed, and shrubs such as red-osier dogwood. Following regulation of Lake Ontario water levels, the emergent marsh along the creek's edge expanded both landward and toward the water. Narrow-leaf cattail now dominates the lower-elevation emergent zone, with European frogbit floating among the stems. The adjacent aquatic zone contains submersed vegetation such as pondweeds, coontail, wild celery, and stonewort, as well as floating white water lilies. The meadow marsh at higher elevations has been invaded by hybrid cattail, along with reed canarygrass (Wilcox, Ingram, et al. 2005; Wilcox, Kowalski, et al. 2008).

Animal Communities

Great Lakes wetlands also provide valuable habitat for fish and wildlife (Wilcox 1995; Environment Canada 2002). Many invertebrates are closely associated with macrophyte beds; waterfowl, aquatic mammals, and small fish are attracted to these areas because they provide food and shelter. When water levels change, habitats and biotic interactions change as well. Flooding of emergent plant communities allows access for spawning fish, reduces mink *(Mustela vison)* predation on muskrats *(Ondatra zibethicus)*, and increases the interspersion of vegetated and open-water areas preferred by waterfowl. Flooded, detrital plant materials are also colonized by invertebrates that are consumed by waterfowl. Low water levels can jeopardize fish spawning and reduce waterfowl nesting areas; yet they provide the opportunity for regeneration of the plant communities that are the foundation of the habitat.

Fish

Fish use Great Lakes wetlands for spawning, rearing, and adult feeding habitat. Some species, such as northern pike *(Esox lucius)*, deposit their eggs in early spring in flooded grasses, thus taking advantage of warmer shallow-water temperatures and the higher dissolved oxygen concentrations required for egg respiration. Other species, such as largemouth bass *(Micropterus salmoides)*, spawn in late spring or early sum-

mer. The male remains with the eggs while fanning them to increase oxygen availability and guarding both eggs and juveniles from predators. Many young-of-year fish remain in wetlands, taking advantage of the protective cover of the vegetation and feeding on plentiful invertebrates. Some adult fish use wetlands seasonally but abandon them when warm water and decomposing vegetation reduce dissolved oxygen levels. Others, such as bowfin *(Amia calva)*, are more tolerant and remain in the wetlands throughout the summer (Environment Canada 2002).

Fish common to Bark Bay in Lake Superior (Fig. 13.5a) include rock bass *(Ambloplites rupestris)*, black bullhead *(Ameiurus melas)*, northern pike, and spottail shiner *(Notropis hudsonius)*, as well as mottled sculpin *(Cottus bairdi)* and central mudminnow *(Umbra limi)* (Wilcox, Meeker, et al. 2002; unpublished data). The emergent bulrush marshes of Saginaw Bay (Fig. 13.5f) support many alewife *(Alosa pseudoharengus)* (young-of-year), pumpkinseed *(Lepomis gibbosus)*, white bass *(Morone chrysops)*, yellow perch *(Perca flavescens)*, blacknose shiner *(Notropis heterolepis)*, and largemouth bass, as well as longnose gar *(Lepisosteus osseus)*, spottail shiner, and other species (Wilcox, Meeker, et al. 2002; unpublished data). Prominent fish in the Arcadia Lake drowned river mouth wetland (Fig. 13.5g) are largemouth bass, pumpkinseed, rockbass, brown bullhead, yellow bullhead *(Ameiurus natalis)*, yellow perch, and common carp *(Cyprinus carpio)* (Wilcox, Meeker, et al. 2002; unpublished data). Abundant fish species in Metzger Marsh of western Lake Erie (Fig. 13.5i) include gizzard shad *(Dorosoma cepedianum)*, bluegill *(Lepomis macrochirus)*, pumpkinseed, largemouth bass, common carp, and white bass; other prominent species are spottail shiner, emerald shiner *(Notropis atherinoides)*, goldfish *(Carassius auratus)*, and white perch *(Morone americana)* (Wells, McClain, et al. 2000; Johnson, Braig, et al. 2004). Kents Creek and adjacent Mud Bay in Lake Ontario (Fig. 13.5k) support golden shiner *(Notemigonus crysoleucas)*, yellow perch, pumpkinseed, largemouth bass, black crappie *(Pomoxis nigromaculatus)*, and banded killifish *(Fundulus diaphanous)*, as well as spotfin shiner *(Cyprinella spiloptera)*, rockbass, brown bullhead *(Ameiurus nebulosus)*, round goby *(Neogobius melanostomus)*, and northern pike (J. Farrell pers. comm.). Other fish species found in Great Lakes wetlands include shortnose gar *(Lepisosteus platostomus)*, muskellunge *(Esox masquinongy)*, walleye *(Sander vitreus)*, smallmouth bass *(Micropterus dolomieu)*, logperch *(Percina caprodes)*, trout-perch *(Percopsis omiscomaycus)*, johnny darter *(Etheostoma nigrum)*, ninespine stickleback *(Pungitius pungitius)*, fivespine stickleback *(Culaea inconstans)*, threespine stickleback *(Gasterosteus aculeatus)*, channel catfish *(Ictalurus punctatus)*, tadpole madtom *(Noturus gyrinus)*, brindled madtom *(N. miurus)*, white sucker *(Catostomus commersonii)*, shorthead redhorse *(Moxostoma macrolepidotum)*, quillback *(Carpiodes cyprinus)*, fathead minnow *(Pimephales promelas)*, bluntnose minnow *(P. notatus)*, common shiner *(Luxilus cornutus)*, and rainbow smelt *(Osmerus mordax)* (Goodyear, Edsall, et al. 1982; Jude and Pappas 1992; Wilcox 1995; Uzarski, Burton, et al. 2005; Seilheimer and Chow-Fraser 2007).

Other Animals

Invertebrates in Great Lakes wetlands range from microinvertebrates commonly termed zooplankton to macroinvertebrates such as insects, clams, and crayfish. Wetland invertebrates provide an important food source for fish and wildlife, both in aquatic habitats and, if emerging from larval life stages, on land or in the air. The large numbers of invertebrate taxa and difficulty in identifying many of them often result in broad taxonomic classifications. Published lists of taxa are available in Burton and Uzarski (2009).

Amphibians depend on the mix of land and water provided by wetlands, feeding on insects that emerge en masse from aquatic larval forms to flying adults. The amphibians, in turn, provide important food for wading birds and fish. Wetlands also provide habitat and food for many reptiles, and these turtles and snakes are important predators in the wetland ecosystem (Environment Canada 2002). Published lists of taxa are found in Maynard and Wilcox (1997), Hecnar (2004), Price, Howe, et al. (2007), and Burton and Uzarski (2009).

Just as Great Lakes wetlands vary in vegetation, invertebrate assemblages, and physical conditions, so too do these habitats vary in bird community composition. During spring and fall migration, coastal wetlands provide critical habitat for literally millions of birds as they forage along shorelines, marshes, and swamps (Diehl, Larkin, et al. 2003; www.jstor.org/stable/4090180). During winter, on the other hand, Great Lakes coastal wetlands can be nearly devoid of birds, especially at northern latitudes. More than 150 bird species are known to use Great Lakes coastal wetlands during the breeding season, the majority breeding or feeding extensively within wetland habitats (Howe, Regal, et al. 2007). Published lists of taxa are available in Maynard and Wilcox (1997), Hanowski, Danz, et al. (2007), Howe, Regal, et al. (2007), and Miller, Niemi, et al. (2007).

Muskrat and beaver (Castor canadensis) are keystone mammals in Great Lakes wetlands. Muskrats cut emergent wetland plants (especially cattails) for food and to build lodges, thus opening the canopy and enhancing habitat for many bird species. The lodges also serve as nesting habitat for some bird species. Beaver act on a grander scale by cutting woody vegetation for food and to build lodges and dams. The dams may alter water levels in some drowned river mouth wetlands. Many other mammals reside in Great Lakes wetlands or include them within their larger habitat. Published lists of taxa are available in Maynard and Wilcox (1997) and Burton and Uzarski (2009).

Key Ecological Processes

Coastal wetlands of the Great Lakes are, by nature, stress-controlled systems. An understanding of human-induced stresses to these wetlands requires an initial understanding of natural stresses.

Water-Level Change

The major stressor and key ecological process affecting Great Lakes wetlands is water-level change, which is caused by a combination of seasonal and longer-term weather conditions and climate changes. Water-level fluctuations are the primary driver affecting wetland vegetation, as even small changes in lake level can shift large areas from flooded to exposed conditions and vice versa. Individual plant species and communities of species have affinities and physiological adaptations for certain water-depth ranges and durations, and their life forms may show adaptations for different water-depth environments. Changes in water level add a dynamic aspect to the species-depth relationship and result in shifting mosaics

of wetland vegetation types. In general, high water levels kill trees, shrubs, and other emergent vegetation, and low water levels following these highs result in seed germination and growth of a multitude of species (Keddy and Reznicek 1986; Maynard and Wilcox 1997) (Fig. 13.6). Some species are particularly well suited to recolonizing exposed areas during low water phases, and several emergents may coexist there because of their diverse responses to natural disturbance.

In the first year following a reduction in water levels, the distribution of new seedlings is due to the distribution of seeds in the sediments. In ensuing years, the distribution of mature plants is due to seedling survival dictated by competitive interactions and changes in abiotic conditions (Welling, Pederson, et al. 1988; Seabloom, van der Valk, et al. 1998; Seabloom, Maloney, et al. 2001; Keddy 2000). If one species is favored in early colonization, its density may be great enough that it can maintain dominance of an area. In most cases, early-colonizing species or communities are later lost through competitive displacement, but the opportunity to go through a life cycle allowed them to replenish the seed bank in the sediments (van der Valk and Davis 1978; Keddy and Reznicek 1982). Occasional low water levels are also needed to restrict growth of plants that require very wet conditions.

The magnitude of water-level fluctuations is of obvious importance to wetland vegetation because it directly results in different water-depth environments (Environment Canada 2002). The different plant communities that develop in a Great Lakes wetland shift from one location to another in response to changes in water depth. Flooding/dewatering history largely determines the species composition of a particular site at a given point in time, with resultant zonation patterns sometimes becoming obvious (Environment Canada 2002; Wilcox and Nichols 2008) (Fig. 13.7).

In general, elevations that have not been flooded for many years are dominated by shrubs, grasses, and old-field plants. If flooding has been more recent, small shrubs may be present, as well as grasses, sedges, and forbs (Keddy and Reznicek 1986). Elevations that are flooded periodically, each 10 to 20 years, and dewatered for successive years between floods have the greatest diversity of wetland vegetation. These plant communities contain the most wetland taxa and the highest diversity of plant structural types. Dominants include grasses, sedges, forbs, rushes, short emergent plants, and submersed aquatic vegetation. At elevations that are rarely or never dewatered, submersed and floating plants are dominant, with emergent plants also occurring at some sites (Keddy and Reznicek 1986; Maynard and Wilcox 1997; Environment Canada 2002).

The frequency, timing, and duration of water-level fluctuations are important for several reasons. Effects of seiches are poorly understood, although they can affect zonation of plant communities by keeping soils wet and limiting germination from the seed bank. Seasonal differences in the timing of water-level declines are important, especially in the Great Lakes, where peak water levels occur in the summer and lows occur in the winter (the reverse of the changes in most inland wetlands). An early summer peak and the subsequent beginning of water-level decline allow more plants to grow from the seed bank than a later peak. Water-level declines in winter can result in ice-induced sediment erosion. Consistent annual fluctuations during the growing season favor the species that are most competitive under those conditions, while variable summer water levels produce changing environmental conditions and result in variability in the vegetation (Wilcox, Thompson, et al. 2007).

Year 1. High water levels

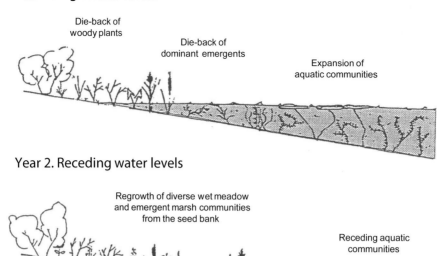

Die-back of
woody plants

Die-back of
dominant emergents

Expansion of
aquatic communities

Year 2. Receding water levels

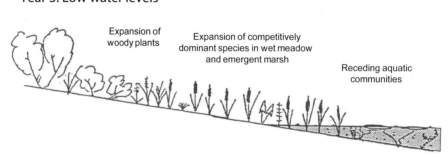

Regrowth of diverse wet meadow
and emergent marsh communities
from the seed bank

Receding aquatic
communities

Year 3. Low water levels

Expansion of
woody plants

Expansion of competitively
dominant species in wet meadow
and emergent marsh

Receding aquatic
communities

FIG. 13.6. Simplified diagram of the effects of water-level fluctuations on Great Lakes coastal wetland plant communities. (From Maynard and Wilcox 1997.)

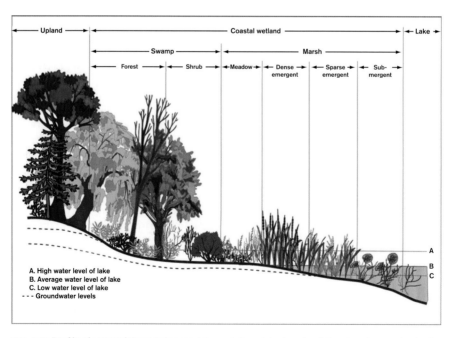

FIG. 13.7. Profile of a typical Great Lakes coastal marsh from lake to upland showing changes in plant communities related to lake-level history. (From Environment Canada 2002.)

Successional processes often occur in plant communities. However, the hydrologic variability of the Great Lakes does not allow succession to proceed for long in most geomorphic settings. The ridge and swale terrains in many large embayments of the Great Lakes contain sequences of wetlands of similar origin but different ages that can be several thousand years old, with older wetlands always farther from the lake. These settings suggest an opportunity for successional processes. Analyses of plant communities across a sequence of wetlands at the south end of Lake Michigan showed an apparent successional pattern from submersed to floating to emergent plants as water depth decreased with wetland age. However, paleoecological analyses showed that the observed vegetation changes were driven largely by disturbances associated with increased human settlement in the area. Climate-induced hydrologic changes were also shown to have greater effects on plant-community change than autogenic, or self-driven, processes (Wilcox and Simonin 1987; Jackson, Futyma, et al. 1988; Wilcox 2004).

Sediment Supply and Transfer

Another key ecological process affecting Great Lakes coastal wetlands is the constant change in the location and movement of sediments. These sediments can form barrier beaches and sand spits that protect wetlands; their erosion can expose wetlands to wave attack. If deposited onto existing wetlands, they can bury wetland plant communities. Coastal processes are greatly affected by lake-level changes, both through net erosion and net deposition of sediments at specific wetland sites and through changes in sediment transport mechanisms. Waves from storms that occur during periods of high lake levels can erode materials not accessible at low stages and increase the load of sediment transported in the littoral drift. At low lake levels, sediments are exposed to transport by wind. These processes also serve to determine and perhaps change the exposure of a wetland to the forces of the open lake (Maynard and Wilcox 1997).

Ice and Storms

Great Lakes wetlands are also affected by ice and storms, both of which are affected by lake-level changes. Ice formed before water levels decline in winter can come to rest on bare sediments and freeze them, thus affecting the survival and dominance of plants at those sites (Renman 1989; Wilcox and Meeker 1991). Frozen sediments can be dislodged and float away with the ice pack in spring (Geis 1985). Large ice packs washing onto the shore during storms can also gouge away sediments. Large waves associated with storms not only erode sediments, but also can physically destroy vegetation in exposed wetlands (Maynard and Wilcox 1997).

Biological Stressors

Natural stressors of Great Lakes wetlands include certain native plants and animals. Invasive emergent plants such as cattails can stress wetlands by forming monotypic stands that greatly reduce wetland diversity. However, the most invasive species are hybrid and narrow-leaf cattail, which may or may not be native. Muskrats can substantially alter wetland habitat

by cutting emergent vegetation, such as cattails and bulrushes, for food and shelter. The unvegetated pools around lodges, formed by cutting activity, create open areas within the wetland. When muskrat populations are high, extensive areas of emergent vegetation may be cut. Beavers also use wetlands of the Great Lakes in some locations and have similar habitat-altering effects. Diseases of both plants and animals are natural phenomena that also stress wetland communities (Maynard and Wilcox 1997).

Conservation Concerns

Large areas of Great Lakes wetlands have been converted to other uses, most notably in the lake plains of western Lake Erie and Saginaw Bay, where ditches and dikes were constructed to drain wetlands for agricultural and urban use. Other alterations include filling, excavating, clearing vegetation, and introduction of nutrients and toxic chemicals. Despite stricter regulations, wetlands continue to be lost, degraded, and altered by human activities. Some alterations are temporary; others may be permanent.

Water-Level Regulation

High water levels create problems for lakeshore property owners and industries with structures built in the flood hazard zone. Low water levels create problems for the shipping, hydropower, and recreational boating industries (Gauthier and Donahue 1999). Regulation of water levels on lakes Superior and Ontario at their outlets seeks to reduce the occurrence of both high and low lake levels. Regulation of water levels creates problems for wetlands; it is a human-induced stressor. It reduces the diversity of wetland plant communities and alters habitat values for wetland fauna.

Water levels on Lake Superior have been regulated for much of the 20th century. The range of fluctuations and the cyclic nature of high and low lake levels have not been altered substantially (Wilcox and Meeker 1995; Wilcox, Thompson, et al. 2007), although periods of low lake levels seem to have been eliminated (Fig. 13.2). Over 275 plant taxa were recorded in a sampling of 18 wetlands along the U.S. shoreline, and 78% of them were obligate or facultative wetland species (Wilcox, Meeker, et al. 1992). Most upland plant species were found at elevations that had not been flooded for four or more years. These invading upland plants composed about one-third of the total number of taxa at those elevations, and many of them were found only at a certain elevation with a specific water-level history. Vegetation mapping from aerial photographs showed the most prevalent vegetation types in the Lake Superior wetlands to be those dominated by submersed aquatic vegetation that had not been affected by low lake levels or shrubs that had not been affected by extremely high lake levels. Both vegetation types were present in all sites and averaged about 25% of the cover. Vegetation types dominated by cattails (or other taxa plus cattails) occurred in about half the sites but averaged only about 6% of the cover. Across all sites, 27 different vegetation types were mapped.

Water levels on Lake Ontario have been regulated since the St. Lawrence Seaway began operation. Prior to regulation, the range of fluctuations during the 20th century was about 2 m. Following initiation of regulation, the range was reduced slightly during the period between 1960 and 1976, but low water-supply conditions in the mid-1960s and high supplies in the mid-1970s maintained much of the range. Regulation reduced the range to about 1.3 m in the years following 1973 (Wilcox, Thompson, et al. 2007) (Fig. 13.2). The lack of alternating flooded and dewatered conditions at the upper and lower edges of the wetlands, especially the lack of low lake levels, resulted in establishment of extensive stands of cattail at the expense of other plant community types, especially the sedge/grass community (Wilcox, Kowalski, et al. 2008). In a preliminary study of the effects of regulation on Lake Ontario wetlands (Wilcox, Meeker, et al. 1992), more than 250 taxa were recorded in sampling of 17 wetlands along the U.S. shoreline; however, only 58% were obligate or facultative wetland plants. Most of the upland species were found at elevations that had not been flooded for 15 to 38 years, and they composed over half of the total number of taxa at those elevations. Of the 54 taxa found only at the elevation not flooded for 38 years, 45 were upland plants, again demonstrating the role of water-level history as a critical plant habitat characteristic in the coastal zone of the Great Lakes.

An extensive follow-up study of Lake Ontario water-level regulation at 32 U.S. and Canadian wetlands tied plant community type to lake-level history and lake-level regulation (Wilcox, Ingram, et al. 2005; Wilcox, Kowalski, et al. 2008; Wilcox and Xie 2007, 2008). Portions of wetlands at elevations that had not been flooded for 5 or more years were dominated by sedges and grasses, with shrubs invading. Elevations that had not been dewatered for 4–38 years were dominated by cattails. The intervening elevations that were intermittently flooded and dewatered over a 5-year span contained a combination of sedges, grasses, cattails, and other emergent species. Plant communities that had not been dewatered in the growing season for many years were dominated by floating and submersed species.

Photointerpretation studies used photographs from the 16 sites in the U.S. (4 each from drowned river mouth, barrier beach, open embayment, and protected embayment wetlands) and spanned a period from the 1950s to 2001 at roughly decadal intervals (Wilcox, Kowalski, et al. 2008). Sedge/grass meadow was the most prominent vegetation type in most wetlands in the late 1950s, when water levels had declined following high lake levels in the early 1950s (Fig. 13.2). Sedge/grass meadow marsh increased at some sites in the mid-1960s in response to low lake levels and decreased at all sites in the late 1970s following a period of high lake levels. Cattail increased at nearly all sites, except wave-exposed open embayments, in the 1970s. Sedge/grass meadow continued to decrease and cattail to increase at most sites during sustained higher lake levels through the 1980s, 1990s, and into 2001 (Fig. 13.2). Site-by-site analyses showed that most vegetation changes could be correlated with lake-level changes and with life-history strategies and physiological tolerances to water depth of prominent taxa. Much of the cattail invasion, largely by hybrid cattail, was landward into meadow marsh. Lesser expansion toward open water included both narrow-leaf and hybrid cattail. The results suggested that canopy-dominating, moisture-requiring cattail was able to invade meadow marsh at higher elevations because sustained higher lake levels following regulation allowed it to survive and overtake sedges and grasses that can tolerate periods of drier soil conditions.

In addition to having adverse effects on wetland plant communities, reduction of water-level fluctuations can affect wetland animal communities. High water levels (i.e., levels above the historical long-term mean) increase fish access to spawning and nursery habitat in emergent vegetation, and flooded detrital plant materials are also colonized by invertebrates that are fed upon by fish and waterfowl. Structural complexity of vegetation resulting from water-level fluctuations creates more diverse habitat for a variety of waterbirds. Although low water levels can jeopardize fish spawning and reduce waterfowl nesting areas, they provide the opportunity for regeneration of the plant communities that are the foundation of the habitat.

Shoreline Modification

A common response to the threat of flooding and erosion along the shoreline of the Great Lakes is to construct revetments or breakwalls along the shore, which can affect wetlands. By reducing erosion, these structures also reduce the supply of sediments that naturally nourishes the shoreline and replaces eroded sediments. Barrier-beach wetlands may thus lose the protection of a barrier beach. Hard shoreline structures also shift wave energy farther downshore and may locally accelerate erosion of beaches and wetlands elsewhere. When revetments are constructed along the gently sloping shore of a wetland, a "backstopping" effect can result. Wave energy can scour sediments from in front of the revetment, leaving an abrupt boundary between upland and deep water and no migrating, sloping shoreline with the required water depths for various wetland plant communities (Maynard and Wilcox 1997). In response to low lake levels, common actions that modify the shoreline include dredging of marinas and recreational boating access channels (Uzarski, Burton, et al. 2009).

Dike Construction

Although diking of wetlands is considered a solution to management problems when protection from water-level change and wave action is required, dikes also create problems for wetlands along the Great Lakes shoreline (Wilcox and Whillans 1999). Isolation from lake waters and the surrounding landscape results in elimination or reduction of many of the values of wetlands, including flood conveyance, sediment control, and improvement of water quality. Habitat for waterfowl and certain other animals may be improved by diking, but shorebirds and many less common plants and animals lose the habitat provided by a continually changing boundary between land and water. In addition, fish and invertebrates not capable of overland travel do not have access to diked marshes and lose valuable habitat. Fish larvae pumped into diked wetlands during filling operations cannot leave and are thus lost to the lake population. Trapped common carp remain in diked wetlands through adulthood and cause management problems by uprooting vegetation and increasing turbidity (Maynard and Wilcox 1997).

Road Construction

Coastal wetlands of the Great Lakes occupy the shoreline, which also serves as a transportation corridor connecting coastal cities and providing access for owners of private land along the coast. Roadways following the shoreline and crossing wetlands serve as stressors on wetlands (Maynard and Wilcox

1997). A substantial percentage of the drowned river mouth wetlands on all the lakes are crossed by roadways, which alter natural hydrology. The often broad, multichanneled river is constricted to pass under a narrow bridge placed along a roadbed causeway, partially damming the river and wetland. Floodwaters slowed by the causeway dam and narrowed outlet deposit excessive sediments in the wetlands and raise the elevation of the substrate. This allows invasion of plant species that would otherwise not tolerate the hydrologic regime of the wetland. Water-level changes due to seiches are also dampened by the reduced connection with the lake. Barrier beaches are commonly used for roadbeds, with similar hydrologic impacts to wetlands behind them and added alteration of the coastal processes that create and maintain them. In addition, roadways can contaminate wetlands with by-products of combustion and with road salt in winter.

Other Physical Alterations

Large-scale physical alteration and destruction have been the greatest sources of wetland loss in the Great Lakes. While the conversion of wetlands to agricultural, urban, and industrial uses has decreased, it has not ended. Filling of nearshore lake waters for urban development continues at a decreased rate. Dredging and channelizing for boat harbors continue in many river mouths, representing a loss of significant wetland habitat (Limno-Tech 1993). Development of shoreline for recreation and residential uses continues seemingly unchecked, and likely affects adjacent wetlands. Dams constructed on tributary rivers trap sediment that may be necessary to maintain wetlands at the river mouth. Conversely, deforestation for agriculture and timber production has increased sediment loading in other streams and rivers flowing into wetlands, adding pollutants, reducing photosynthesis, reducing dissolved oxygen concentrations, and affecting the survival rates of invertebrate and fish eggs. Increased turbidity caused by sediments in suspension may also seriously interfere with the food-finding activities of many valuable predator fish. Water temperatures can increase as a result of removal of shade from streamside vegetation. The narrow temperature requirements of many fish are relatively well documented. Increased temperature fluctuations have restricted the habitat of fish species (Dodge and Kavetsky 1995; Maynard and Wilcox 1997).

Water Quality

Pollutants, turbidity, and increased water temperatures, along with increased nutrient concentrations, can decrease wetland water quality. Wetlands may be stressed by enrichment of nutrients from agricultural runoff (Trebitz, Brazner, et al. 2007) and also from residential runoff and sewage discharges. Wetland and aquatic plants can obtain nutrients from both sediments and the water column; the predominant source of nutrient uptake is generally species specific. Therefore, the trophic status of the water in a wetland has obvious importance in determining productivity and species composition (Wisheu, Keddy, et al. 1990). Plant communities in nutrient-enriched wetlands may differ from those in other areas. The growth of some plant species is enhanced by nutrient enrichment; other plants, adapted to low-nutrient environments, can be displaced by species better adapted to greater nutrient concentrations. In addition, nutrient enrichment may cause excessive algal blooms that can reduce light available to macrophytes for photosynthesis. Excessive growth of macrophytes or algae can also result in depletion of dissolved oxygen when these plants die and decay; this is especially critical in shallow basins with little mixing, such as barrier-beach wetlands (Maynard and Wilcox 1997). Oxygen depletion can also be caused by discharge of organic wastes into wetlands.

Toxic chemicals can also stress wetland biological systems, especially animal communities. Through the processes of biomagnification and bioaccumulation, the impact of toxic chemicals has been greatest on animal species at the top of the food web, such as predatory birds, fish, and mammals (Wren 1991; Hoffman, Smith, et al. 1993). The highest concentrations of these chemicals have been observed in top predators in nutrient-poor systems with reduced overall productivity and few prey species. Because these systems are simple, the potential for biomagnifaction is greater. Animal health and reproduction can also be affected by contaminants. Contaminated sediments may be toxic to fish eggs. Thinning of eggshells and deformities are well documented among fish-eating birds of the Great Lakes (Hoffman, Smith, et al. 1993). Although levels of banned DDT, PCBs, and their metabolites will likely continue to decline, the effect of the continuing discharge of other persistent toxic chemicals on the quality of the chemical regime of habitats is not well understood.

Long-term effects of toxic chemicals on plants and herbivores are also not well understood. Herbicides (e.g., Atrazine) from cropland may be interfering with aquatic plant growth. Herbicides are present in the wetlands and bays of Lake Erie at levels high enough to alter planktonic species composition and inhibit photosynthesis of algal and rooted plant communities (Dodge and Kavetsky 1995). Increased salinity caused by road salt runoff can alter algal and macrophyte communities of wetlands, as well as animal communities.

Other water-quality alterations that can stress wetlands are temperature and turbidity (Trebitz, Brazner, et al. 2007). Temperature differs most between protected wetlands (e.g., behind barrier beaches) and those with greater mixing of lake water. Water temperature may affect the length of the growing season and thus productivity. In some cases, such as shallow barrier-beach wetlands with dark sediments, extremely high water temperatures may inhibit plant growth, exceed the tolerance limit of invertebrates and fish, and result in oxygen depletion. In wetlands with a strong discharge of groundwater, low water temperatures may limit productivity and species tolerance. High turbidity reduces the availability of light to submersed plants and can limit growth. It can also limit feeding activity by sight-feeding fish such as northern pike. Turbidity can be affected by the source of water, the type of sediment, exposure to wave attack that suspends sediments by mixing, and biological action, such as feeding activity by common carp.

Nonindigenous Species

The most serious biological stressors affecting wetlands of the Great Lakes are species not native to the area and aggressive species of uncertain origin that compete with native biota. Methods of introduction include intentional release, deposition of ship ballast, escape from cultivated or cultured populations, and migration along travel routes such as railroads, highways, and canals (which may also overcome natural physical barriers to aquatic travel). In many cases, introductions may not be successful in a healthy ecosystem. However, given the means and extent of wetland alteration in the Great Lakes, habitats and food webs have been sufficiently disturbed to allow many introduced species to thrive (Maynard and Wilcox 1997).

As many as 180 nonindigenous aquatic organisms have been documented in the Great Lakes (Mills, Leach, et al. 1993; Ricciardi 2001, 2006); many of them do not occur in wetlands or do not cause identifiable problems, but several do cause or have the potential to cause considerable problems. Examples of such plants include submersed aquatics such as Eurasian watermilfoil, curlyleaf pondweed *(Potamogeton crispus),* slender naiad *(Najas minor),* and common waterweed; floating European frogbit; and emergents such as purple loosestrife *(Lythrum salicaria),* reed canarygrass, flowering rush, and common reed (Trebitz and Taylor 2007). Although biological controls may be reducing purple loosestrife locally, common reed has been highly invasive in recent years and is difficult and costly to control.

Animal invaders that may affect Great Lakes wetlands include zebra and quagga mussels (*Dreissena* spp.), rusty crayfish *(Orconectes rusticus),* and common carp. The latter fish species has been shown to affect wetlands by reducing the diversity and biomass of macrophytes (King and Hunt 1967; Crivelli 1983). Changes in macrophyte communities may also contribute to reduced abundance of emergent insects in wetlands where common carp are abundant (McLaughlin and Harris 1990). Although common carp have been found to dominate larval fish samples from some Great Lakes marshes (Chubb and Liston 1986; Johnson 1989; Petering and Johnson 1991) and are often very abundant as adults, they cause the greatest problems in diked marshes, where they remain in residence year-round and are in greater abundance than in lake-connected wetlands (Johnson 1989). Common carp begin to enter wetlands as early in the year as February; their numbers are greatly reduced by the end of summer, and nearly all carp have returned to the lake by autumn. Common carp may cause problems in degraded coastal wetlands, but they seem to have little effect on healthy marshes. Management becomes a major concern when wetlands are diked, common carp larvae enter through screens or via pumping operations, and adult fish have no means of returning to the lake.

Climate Change

Great Lakes water levels typically increase during cool climatic periods and decrease during warm periods (Baedke and Thompson 2000) (Fig. 13.3). The expected linear response of plant communities in the short term is a reduction in emergent species in years when water levels are high and a resurgence of emergents from the seed bank when water levels are lower and expose underlying sediments (Keddy and Reznicek 1986). Over longer time periods, ranging from decades to centuries to millennia, the expected linear response is also deeper open water with few emergent species during cool, wet climate phases and shallow marsh with shoreline and mudflat species during warm, dry phases (Singer, Jackson, et al. 1996). Prolonged warm, dry phases with greater primary production by emergent species may accelerate basin infilling in protected areas not subject to wave attack (Wilcox, Shedlock, et al. 1986; Wilcox and Simonin 1987). Successional processes may accompany shallowing of the basins, leading to further vegetation changes that include the invasion of shrubs and trees, although the return of high water can reset the successional stage (van der Valk 1981; Jackson, Futyma, et al. 1988; Wilcox 2004).

Work in chronosequences of wetlands occurring in ridge and swale terrains of lakes Michigan and Superior, however, suggests that groundwater may mediate effects of climate and successional processes on plant communities in some wetlands. During warm climate phases, plant communities with sufficient groundwater supplies may be resistant to climate-related water-level reductions that drive vegetation change. Over prolonged periods with no climate-driven flooding to reset the successional stage, plant communities may develop with greater fidelity to groundwater influences than to assumed successional processes (Burkett, Wilcox, et al. 2005).

Conclusions

The large expanse of the Great Lakes Basin encompasses a broad geographic range with concomitant variability in underlying geology. Together, these factors result in considerable differences among wetlands across the basin. However, the lakes share many similarities in hydrology that affect wetlands, with peak annual water levels in summer and lows in winter. Prior to regulation of lakes Superior and Ontario, all lakes experienced wide fluctuations in water levels at decadal to millennial intervals in response to climatic changes. Coastal processes are also important to wetlands across all the Great Lakes; wetlands occur in similar geomorphic settings that provide varying degrees of protection from wave energy.

Wetland plant communities have many similarities among lakes, but differing geology and resultant differences in water chemistry sometimes cause stark differences in wetland type. Climatic differences related to latitude add to plant community variability. Animal communities respond both to habitat variability associated with vegetation and to physical habitat characteristics related to geology, water chemistry, and latitude-driven temperature ranges. As with plants, however, many features of animal communities are similar across lakes.

Although Great Lakes wetlands can be affected at the local level by numerous natural stressors, their broader ecological processes are driven by water-level change. Human disturbance can affect Great Lakes wetlands at the local level; however, alteration of natural water-level fluctuations through regulation affects all wetlands on a regulated lake. The relation between ecological processes and lake-level variability often overrides other processes affecting Great Lakes wetlands.

Periodic high lake levels kill invading trees, shrubs, and large, canopy-dominating emergent plants. Succeeding low lake levels expose the sediment and stimulate germination of a variety of species from the seed bank, thus increasing diversity. The open canopy provides the opportunity for these plants to grow, reproduce, and replenish the seed bank. Trees, shrubs, and canopy-dominating emergent plants also recolonize the wetland, but the next cycle of high lake levels begins the process again. Habitat diversity for many animal species is also maintained by this process. As demonstrated in Figure 13.8, lake-level variability provides periodic wetland restoration.

When water levels are regulated and the range and periodicity of fluctuations are altered, wetlands lose diversity. Invasion of Lake Ontario wetlands by cattail is a classic example (see Figure 13.9), but similar problems have been noted in regulated lakes elsewhere. The case for natural lake-level variability and wetlands must be made in relation to other interests. Although hydropower industries tend to seek full water-storage capacity

A. Drowned river-mouth wetland in Pigeon River near Port Sheldon, Michigan; photo taken in spring 1999 after Lake Michigan water levels had dropped more than 0.5 m from the previous year. Note the lack of emergent vegetation along the shore.

B. Same wetland in late summer 2000; photo shows mostly annual emergent plants along the shore that grew from the seed bank.

C. Same wetland in 2001; photo shows perennial emergent plants displacing annuals along the shore.

D. Same wetland in 2003; photo shows a shift in vegetation to a different perennial plant community.

FIGURE 13.8. Some species are particularly well suited to recolonizing exposed areas during low-water phases, and several emergents may coexist there because of their diverse responses to natural disturbance.

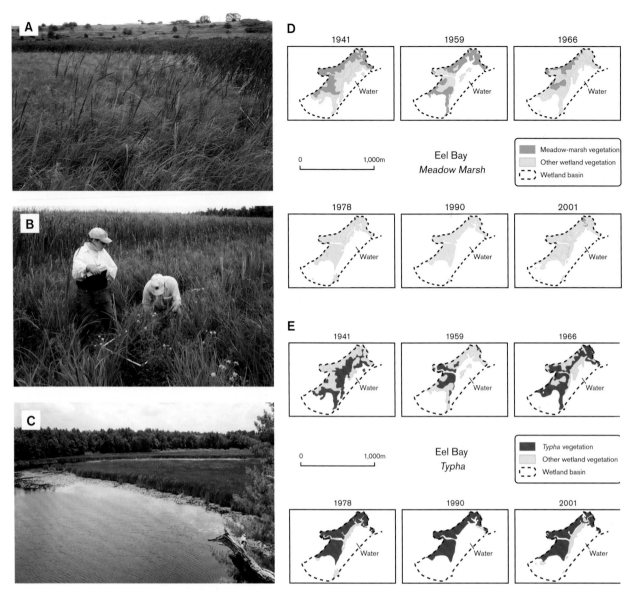

FIG. 13.9. The different plant communities that develop in a Great Lakes wetland shift from one location to another in response to changes in water depth. Illustrations redrawn by Chris Hall.

A. Meadow-marsh vegetation in a Lake Ontario wetland with invading cattails.

B. Scientists sampling vegetation in the narrow band of remaining meadow marsh in a Lake Ontario wetland.

C. Cattail domination of a Lake Ontario wetland extending from near shore to deeper water, with abrupt transition of floating and submersed plant communities.

D. Vegetation maps from Eel Bay near Alexandria Bay, New York, derived from analyses of aerial photographs taken before regulation of Lake Ontario water levels (1960) and continuing through 2001. The loss of meadow-marsh vegetation following regulation is highlighted.

E. Vegetation maps from Eel Bay highlighting the increase in cattail (Typha)-dominated plant communities following regulation of lake levels.

to maximize potential electricity generation, they would benefit in years with low water supplies by allowing more water to pass through the turbines instead of holding it back to create unnaturally high lake levels. The resultant lower lake levels would mimic natural conditions. Shoreline property owners tend to prefer average lake levels in all years in an effort to reduce erosion during high-water years. However, all storms then hit the shoreline at the same elevation, and erosion is accelerated. Periodic low lake levels would expose sand that could rebuild protective beaches and dunes through aeolian processes, but some shoreline property owners oppose low lake

levels because they allow regeneration of wetland plants from the seed bank (Uzarski, Burton, et al. 2009).

Recreational boaters and marinas tend to prefer higher lake levels to avoid damage to boats from underwater structures, as well as high levels that extend longer into autumn to increase the length of the boating season. Those who use their boats for fishing, as well as the marinas and lakeshore communities that rely on the recreational fishing industry, could receive benefits from wetland habitat enhanced by periodic low lake levels—the foundation for the food web supporting target fish species. Environmental advocates (for wetlands in particular) seek regulation plans that allow both periodic high and low lake levels at the proper frequency to drive ecological processes. The best answer for all interests is rather straightforward: a regulation plan promoting lake levels that mimic natural amplitudes and frequencies as closely as possible while protecting all interests from damages incurred by extremely high or low lake levels.

In common with wetlands found in other geographic settings, conservation of wetlands of the Great Lakes requires protection from a variety of human disturbances at the local and landscape levels. Indeed, physical, chemical, and biological alterations have already degraded nearly all Great Lakes wetlands to varying degrees. However, the high-energy coastal setting of Great Lakes wetlands sets them apart from most inland wetlands. Conservation of Great Lakes wetlands requires maintenance of natural lake-level variability coupled with maintenance of natural shoreline processes that determine the geomorphic settings where wetlands can persist.

References

Albert DA. 2003. *Between land and lake: Michigan's Great Lakes coastal wetlands.* East Lansing: Michigan State Univ. Extension Bull. E-2902.

Albert DA, Wilcox DA, et al. 2005. Hydrogeomorphic classification for Great Lakes coastal wetlands. *J. Great Lakes Res.* 31 (Suppl. 1):129–46.

Argyilan EP, Forman SL, et al. 2005. Optically stimulated luminescence dating of late Holocene raised strandplain sequences adjacent to southern Lake Superior, Upper Peninsula, Michigan, USA. *Quaternary Res.* 63:122–35.

Baedke SJ, Thompson TA. 2000. A 4,700-year record of lake level and isostacy for Lake Michigan. *J. Great Lakes Res.* 26:416–26.

Burkett VR, Wilcox DA, et al. 2005. Nonlinear dynamics in ecosystem response to climatic change: case studies and management implications. *Ecol. Complexity* 2:357–94.

Burton TM, Uzarski DG. 2009. Biodiversity in protected coastal wetlands along the west coast of Lake Huron. *Aquat. Ecosys. Health Manage.* 12:63–76.

Chubb SL, Liston CR. 1986. Density and distribution of larval fishes in Pentwater Marsh, a coastal wetland on Lake Michigan. *J. Great Lakes Res.* 12:332–43.

Crivelli AJ. 1983. The destruction of aquatic vegetation by carp. *Hydrobiologia* 106:37–41.

Diehl RH, Larkin RP, Black JE. 2003. Radar observations of bird migration over the Great Lakes. *Auk* 120:278–90.

Dodge D, Kavetsky R. 1995. Aquatic habitat and wetlands of the Great Lakes. State of the Lakes Ecosys. Conf. Background Pap. EPA 905-R-95-014. Toronto: Env. Canada, Chicago: USEPA.

Environment Canada. 2002. *Where land meets water: understanding wetlands of the Great Lakes,* Wilcox DA, Patterson N, et al., contributors. Toronto: Env. Canada.

Epstein EJ, Judziewicz EJ, Smith WA. 1997. *Wisconsin's Lake Superior coastal wetlands evaluation.* WI Nat. Heritage Inventory Prog. WI PUBL ER-803 2002. Madison: WI DNR.

Gauthier R, Donahue MJ, editors. 1999. *Living with the lakes: understanding and adapting to Great Lakes water level changes.* Ann Arbor, MI: Great Lakes Commission.

Geis JW. 1985. Environmental influences on the distribution and composition of wetlands in the Great Lakes Basin. In *Coastal wetlands,* Prince HH, D'Itri FM, editors. Chelsea, MI: Lewis Publ., pp. 15–31.

Goodyear CD, Edsall TA, et al. 1982. *Atlas of the spawning and nursery areas of Great Lakes fishes,* vols. 1–5. FWS/OBS-82/52. Washington, DC: USFWS.

Hanowski JM, Danz NP, et al. 2007. Considerations for monitoring breeding birds in Great Lakes coastal wetlands. *J. Great Lakes Res.* 33 (Sp. Issue 3):245–52.

Hecnar SJ. 2004. Great Lakes wetlands as amphibian habitats: a review. *Aquat. Ecosys. Health Manage.* 7:289–303.

Hoffman DJ, Smith GJ, Rattner BA. 1993. Biomarkers of contaminant exposure in common terns and black-crowned night herons in the Great Lakes. *Env. Toxicol. Chem.* 12:1095–103.

Howe RW, Regal RR, et al. 2007. An index of ecological condition based on bird assemblages in Great Lakes coastal wetlands. *J. Great Lakes Res.* 33 (Sp. Issue 3):93–105.

Jackson ST, Futyma RP, Wilcox DA. 1988. A paleoecological test of a classical hydrosere in the Lake Michigan dunes. *Ecology* 69:928–36.

Jaworski E, Raphael CN, et al. 1979. *Impact of Great Lakes water level fluctuations on coastal wetlands.* Ypsilanti: Eastern Michigan Univ.

Johnson DL. 1989. Lake Erie wetlands: fisheries considerations. In *Lake Erie estuarine systems: issues, resources, and management,* Krieger KA, editor. Washington, DC: NOAA Sem. Ser. 14, pp. 257–74.

Johnson DL, Braig EC IV, Lynch WL Jr. 2004. *The fish assemblage of Metzger Marsh after restoration.* Columbus: Ohio State Univ. Press.

Johnston JW, Baedke SJ, et al. 2004. Late Holocene lake-level variation in southeastern Lake Superior: Tahquamenon Bay, Michigan. *J. Great Lakes Res.* 30 (Sup. 1):1–19.

Johnston JW, Thompson TA, et al. 2007. Comparison of geomorphic and sedimentologic evidence for the separation of Lake Superior from Lake Michigan and Huron. *J. Paleolimn.* 37:349–64.

Jude DJ, Pappas J. 1992. Fish utilization of Great Lakes coastal marshes. *J. Great Lakes Res.* 18:651–72.

Keddy PA. 2000. *Wetland ecology: principles and conservation.* Cambridge: Cambridge Univ. Press.

Keddy PA, Reznicek AA. 1982. The role of seed banks in the persistence of Ontario's coastal plain flora. *Am. J. Bot.* 69:13–22.

Keddy PA, Reznicek AA. 1986. Great Lakes vegetation dynamics: the role of fluctuating water levels and buried seeds. *J. Great Lakes Res.* 12:25–36.

Keough JR, Thompson TA, et al. 1999. Hydrogeomorphic factors and ecosystem responses in coastal wetlands of the Great Lakes. *Wetlands* 19:821–34.

King DR, Hunt GS. 1967. Effect of carp on vegetation in a Lake Erie marsh. *J. Wildl. Manage.* 31:181–88.

Kowalski KP, Wilcox DA. 1999. Use of historical and geospatial data to guide the restoration of a Lake Erie coastal marsh. *Wetlands* 19:858–68.

Kowalski KP, Wilcox DA. 2002. *Alternative management strategies for diked marshes: summary results from 1994–2001 studies of Metzger Marsh plant communities.* Ann Arbor, MI: USGS.

Limno-Tech. 1993. *Great Lakes environmental assessment.* Ann Arbor, MI: National Council of the Paper Industry for Air and Stream Improvement.

Mainville A, Craymer MR. 2005. Present-day tilting of the Great Lakes region based on water-level gauges. *Geol. Soc. Am. Bull.* 117:1070–80.

Maynard L, Wilcox DA. 1997. *Coastal wetlands of the Great Lakes.* State of the Lakes Ecosys. Conf. Background Paper EPA 905-R-97-015b. Burlington, ON: Env. Canada; Chicago: USEPA.

McLaughlin DB, Harris HJ. 1990. Aquatic insect emergence in two Great Lakes marshes. *Wetl. Ecol. Manage.* 1:111–21.

Mechenich C, Kraft GJ, et al. 2006. Assessment of coastal water resources and watershed conditions at Pictured Rocks National Lakeshore. Ashland, WI: NPS Tech. Rep. NPS/NRWRD/NRTR-2006/361.

Meeker JE. 1993. The ecology of wild rice (*Zizania palustris* var. *palustris*) in the Kakagon sloughs, a riverine wetland on Lake Superior. Ph.D. diss., Univ. Wisc., Madison.

Meeker JE. 1996. Wild-rice and sedimentation processes in a Lake Superior coastal wetland. *Wetlands* 16:219–31.

Miller C, Niemi GJ, et al. 2007. Breeding bird communities across and upland disturbance gradient in the western Lake Superior region. *J. Great Lakes Res.* 33 (Sp. Issue 3):305–18.

Mills EL, Leach JH, et al. 1993. Exotic species in the Great Lakes: a history of biotic crises and anthropogenic introductions. *J. Great Lakes Res.* 19:1–54.

Neff BP, Nicholas JR. 2005. *Uncertainty in the Great Lakes water balance.* USGS Sci. Investigations Rep. 2004-1500.

Petering RW, Johnson DL. 1991. Distribution of fish larvae among artificial vegetation in a diked Lake Erie wetland. *Wetlands* 11:123–38.

Price SJ, Howe RW, et al. 2007. Are anurans of Great Lakes coastal wetlands reliable indicators of ecological condition? *J. Great Lakes Res.* 33 (Sp. Issue 3):211–23.

Renman G. 1989. Distribution of littoral macrophytes in a north Swedish riverside lagoon in relation to bottom freezing. *Aquat. Bot.* 33:243–56.

Ricciardi A. 2001. Facilitative interactions among aquatic invaders: is an "invasional meltdown" occurring in the Great Lakes? *Can. J. Fish. Aquat. Sci.* 58:2513–25.

Ricciardi A. 2006. Patterns of invasion in the Laurentian Great Lakes in relation to changes in vector activity. *Diver. Distrib.* 12:425–33.

Seabloom EW, Maloney KA, van der Valk AG. 2001. Constraints on the establishment of plants along a fluctuating water-depth gradient. *Ecology* 82:2216–32.

Seabloom EW, van der Valk AG, Maloney KA. 1998. The role of water depth and soil temperature in determining initial composition of prairie wetland coenoclines. *Plant Ecol.* 138:203–16.

Seilheimer TS, Chow-Fraser P. 2007. Application of the wetland fish index to northern Great Lakes marshes with emphasis on Georgian Bay coastal wetlands. *J. Great Lakes Res.* 33 (Sp. Issue 3):154–71.

Singer DK, Jackson ST, et al. 1996. Differentiating climatic and successional influences on long-term development of a marsh. *Ecology* 77:1765–78.

Trebitz AS, Brazner JC, et al. 2007. Water quality in Great Lakes coastal wetlands: basin-wide patterns and responses to an anthropogenic disturbance gradient. *J. Great Lakes Res.* 33 (Sp. Issue 3):67–85.

Trebitz AS, Taylor DL. 2007. Exotic and invasive aquatic plants in Great Lakes coastal wetlands: distribution and relation to watershed land use and plant richness and cover. *J. Great Lakes Res.* 33:705–21.

Uzarski DG, Burton TM, et al. 2005. Fish habitat use within and across wetland classes in coastal wetlands of the five Great Lakes: development of a fish-based index of biotic integrity. *J. Great Lakes Res.* 31 (Sup. 1):171–87.

Uzarski DG, Burton TM, et al. 2009. The ecological impacts of fragmentation and vegetation removal in Lake Huron's coastal wetlands. *Aquat. Ecosys. Health Manage.* 12:45–62.

van der Valk AG. 1981. Succession in wetlands: a Gleasonian approach. *Ecology* 62:688–96.

van der Valk AG, Davis CB. 1978. The role of seed banks in the vegetation dynamics of prairie glacial marshes. *Ecology* 59:322–35.

Welling CH, Pederson RL, van der Valk AG. 1988. Recruitment from the seed bank and the development of zonation of emergent vegetation during a drawdown in a prairie wetland. *J. Ecol.* 76:483–96.

Wells SE, McClain JR, Hill TD. 2000. *Fish passage between Lake Erie and Metzger Marsh: monitoring of an experimental fish passage structure.* Alpena, MI: USFWS.

Wilcox DA. 1995. The role of wetlands as nearshore habitat in Lake Huron. In *The Lake Huron ecosystem: ecology, fisheries and management*, Munawar M, Edsall T, Leach J, editors. Amsterdam: Ecovision World Monogr. Ser., S.P.B. Acad. Publ., pp. 223–45.

Wilcox DA. 2004. Implications of hydrologic variability on the succession of plants in Great Lakes wetlands. *Aquat. Ecosys. Health Manage.* 7:223–32.

Wilcox DA, Ingram JW, et al. 2005. *Evaluation of water-level regulation influences on Lake Ontario and Upper St. Lawrence River coastal wetland plant communities.* Washington, DC: Internat. Joint Comm.

Wilcox DA, Kowalski KP, et al. 2008. Cattail invasion of sedge/grass meadows and regulation of Lake Ontario water levels: photointerpretation analysis of sixteen wetlands over five decades. *J. Great Lakes Res.* 34:301–23.

Wilcox DA, Meeker JE. 1991. Disturbance effects on aquatic vegetation in regulated and non-regulated lakes in northern Minnesota. *Can. J. Bot.* 69:1542–51.

Wilcox DA, Meeker JE. 1995. Wetlands in regulated Great Lakes. In *Our living resources: a report to the nation on the distribution, abundance, and health of U.S. plants, animals, and ecosystems*, LaRoe ET, Farris GS, et al., editors. Washington, DC: USDOI, Nat. Biol. Serv., pp. 247–49.

Wilcox DA, Meeker JE, Elias J. 1992. *Impacts of water-level regulation on wetlands of the Great Lakes.* Phase 2 Rep. Working Comm. 2, Water-Levels Ref. Study. Washington, DC: Internat. Joint Comm.

Wilcox DA, Meeker JE, et al. 2002. Hydrologic variability and the application of index of biotic integrity metrics to wetlands: a Great Lakes evaluation. *Wetlands* 22:588–615.

Wilcox DA, Nichols SJ. 2008. The effect of water-level fluctuations on plant zonation in a Saginaw Bay, Lake Huron wetland. *Wetlands* 28:487–501.

Wilcox DA, Shedlock RJ, Hendrickson WH. 1986. Hydrology, water chemistry, and ecological relations in the raised mound of Cowles Bog. *J. Ecol.* 74:1103–17.

Wilcox DA, Simonin HA. 1987. A chronosequence of aquatic macrophyte communities in dune ponds. *Aquat. Bot.* 28:227–42.

Wilcox DA, Thompson TA, et al. 2007. *Lake-level variability and water availability in the Great Lakes.* USGS Circular 1311.

Wilcox DA, Whillans TH. 1999. Techniques for restoration of disturbed coastal wetlands of the Great Lakes. *Wetlands* 19:835–57.

Wilcox DA, Xie Y. 2007. Predicting wetland plant responses to proposed water-level-regulation plans for Lake Ontario: GIS-based modeling. *J. Great Lakes Res.* 33:751–73.

Wilcox DA, Xie Y. 2008. Predicted effects of proposed new regulation plans on sedge/grass meadows of Lake Ontario. *J. Great Lakes Res.* 34:745–54.

Wisheu IC, Keddy PA, et al. 1990. Effects of eutrophication on wetland vegetation. In *Proceedings of an international symposium: wetlands of the Great Lakes: protection and restoration policies: status of the science*, Niagara Falls, New York, May 16–18, 1990, Kusler J, Smardon R, editors. Niagara Falls, NY: Assoc. State Wetl. Managers, pp. 112–21.

Wren CD. 1991. Cause-effect linkages between chemicals and populations of mink *(Mustela vison)* and otter *(Lutra canadensis)* in the Great Lakes Basin. *J. Toxic. Env. Health* 33:549–86.

CHAPTER 14

Pocosins

Evergreen Shrub Bogs of the Southeast

CURTIS J. RICHARDSON

Pocosins comprise the largest extent of true bogs in the southeastern U.S. (Richardson 1981a,b, 1983). They once covered over one million ha in North Carolina alone, but the area has been greatly diminished by agricultural development and forestry conversions to loblolly pine *(Pinus taeda)* plantations (Richardson 1981a,b, 1983, 2003). The word *pocosin* is an ancient Algonquin Indian word meaning "swamp-on-a-hill" (Tooker 1899). It has over 20 different spellings and is often seen on old maps and records as *poquosin, poquoson, percoason, pekoson, pocoson, pocason*, etc. One of the earliest reported usages of the term *pocosin* to indicate low, marshy ground or swamp is by the eighteenth-century explorer John Lawson (1709): "The swamp I now spokd of, is not a miry Bog, but you go down to it thro' a steep Bank, at the Foot of which begins this Valley. . . . The Land in this Percoarson, or Valley, being extraordinary rich, and the Runs of Water well stor'd with Fowl." Tooker (1899) reviewed numerous documents, provided several names that he considered dialectical corruptions of the word *pocosin,* and stated, "The application of the term, therefore, in its linguistic sense, was to indicate or to describe localities where water 'backed up' as in spring freshets, or in rainy seasons, which, by reason of such happenings, become necessarily more or less marshy or boggy." He reports the name of a river in North Carolina that was called the Poquosen and points out that the term *pocoson* was frequently used by George Washington in 1763, for example, "Black mould taken out of the pocoson on the creek side . . . " (Richardson 1981a). In fact, George Washington was among the first landowners to attempt large-scale drainage of pocosins in the Dismal Swamp of coastal Virginia, giving him another, less glamorous title: "the father of wetland drainage in the U.S."

The geologist W. C. Kerr (1875) defined pocosins as "flatwoods with no natural drainage ways, different from swamps in that they are not alluvial, occurring on divides between rivers and sounds and frequently elevated above streams of which they were the source." Harper (1907) characterized a pocosin as an "extensive, flat damp, sandy or peaty area usually remote from large streams, supporting a scattered growth of pine (mostly *Pinus serotina*) and a very dense growth of shrubs, mostly evergreen, giving the whole a decided heathlike aspect." The most holistic definitions of pocosins were pro-

posed by Wells (1928), Woodwell (1958), and Kologiski (1977). They described pocosins as being primarily restricted to the southeastern coastal plain, occurring in broad, shallow basins, in drainage basin heads, and on broad, flat uplands. These areas have long hydroperiods, temporary surface water, periodic burning, and soils of sandy humus, muck, or peat. These definitions suggest that pocosins are not adjacent or connected to flowing water bodies or rivers but imply that pocosins are the source of water on the coastal landscape. Thus, understanding their role in coastal hydrology is critical to managing the region's water supply and estuarine interactions.

Pocosins are classified as palustrine wetland ecosystems since they are nontidal wetlands and trees, shrubs, persistent emergents, emergent mosses, or lichens cover 30% or more of the area (Cowardin, Carter, et al. 1979) (Fig. 14.1). The Indians used the term *pocosin* to describe a variety of bog and swamp ecosystems; thus, the term was not used by them to delineate a single class of wetlands. A broad definition of pocosins *(sensu lato)* would include all shrub and forested bogs, as well as Atlantic white cedar stands and some pine stands on flooded soils on the Coastal Plain. A stricter definition *(sensu stricto)* of pocosins would include only the classic shrub-scrub (short pocosin) and pond-pine-dominated tall pocosin. Thus, the term *pocosin* (Richardson, Evans, et al. 1981) can be used to cover a number of subclasses of wetlands found on the Coastal Plain of the southeastern U.S. Specifically, the dominant subclasses from the 1954 report by the United States Fish and Wildlife Service (USFWS) that were all included under the term *bog* (called "pocosin" by Richardson, Evans, et al. 1981) were pond pine *(Pinus serotina)* and scrub-shrub along with Atlantic white cedar *(Chamaecyparis thyoides),* savanna, and pond pine stands on hydric soils. In the current USFWS wetland classification system (Cowardin, Carter, et al. 1979), pocosins are classified as palustrine systems: class: scrub-shrub (vegetation less than 6 m high, also referred to as short pocosin; see Fig. 14.2) or forested (vegetation more than 6 m high, also referred to as tall pocosin; see Fig. 14.3a); subclass: broad-leaved evergreen; water regime: saturated, semipermanently flooded, intermittently flooded, or seasonally flooded; water chemistry: fresh-acid; soil: organic (Medisaprist) (Cowardin, Carter, et al. 1979). Common synonyms for *pocosin*

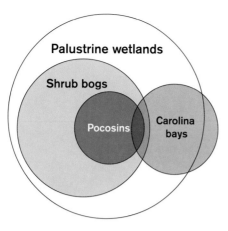

FIG. 14.1. A Venn diagram displaying that all pocosins are classified as palustrine wetlands and are shrub bogs. Carolina bays and pocosins do show some overlap in terms of similar plant species and would be classified as shrub bogs and palustrine systems, but many Carolina bays with open water would be classified as lacustrine systems according to Cowardin, Carter, et al. (1979).

FIG. 14.2. Short pocosin, 2009, at the Pocosins Lakes Wildlife Refuge in coastal North Carolina. Note the short stature of the vegetation (1–2 m), including the pond pine *(Pinus serotina)* in the background. Here the vegetation is dominated by *Lyonia Lucida* (fetter bush) and *Ilex* sp. Peat depths are in excess of 3 m. (Photo by C. J. Richardson.)

FIG. 14.3. A. Tall pocosin, 2009, at the Pocosins Lakes Refuge. Note the density and height of the vegetation (> 6 m). The vegetation is dominated by *Pinus serotina* (pond pine) and *Gordonia laisianthus* (loblolly bay), and the trees are > 6 m in height. The peat depths are < 1 m. (Photo by C. J. Richardson.) B. Aerial view of young bay forest (gum swamp) in Pocosins Lakes Wildlife Refuge. Key species here are red maple *(Acer rubrum),* loblolly bay *(Gordonia laisianthus),* magnolia bay *(Magnolia virginiana),* gum *(Nyssa sylvatica),* and Atlantic white cedar *(Chamaecyparis thyoides).* (Photo by C. J. Richardson.) See also Table 14.3a–b.

include bay, bayland, bayhead, xeric shrub bog, and evergreen shrub bog (Kologiski 1977). Bay forests or gum swamps, as they are often called, are often found adjacent to pocosins, generally on shallower peat soils and in the downstream flow of water from the higher pocosin sites (Fig. 14.3b). Only Carolina bays on the lower Coastal Plain have similar pocosin vegetation (Fig. 14.1). However, differences in size and geologic origin exist between large pocosin tracts and elliptical Carolina bays (Richardson and Gibbons 1993). Carolina bays are ovate-shaped, shallow depressions found primarily on the Coastal Plain of North and South Carolina and Georgia (Sharitz and Gibbons 1984; Ross 1987; see Kirkman et al., this volume). For a more extensive analysis of pocosins versus Carolina bays, the reader is referred to Richardson (1981a), Sharitz and Gresham (1998), Savage (1982), Ross (1987), and Richardson and Gibbons (1993).

The purpose of this chapter is to: (1) provide a brief overview of the origin and geographic distribution of pocosins, as well as provide an update on what is known about the ecological, hydrologic, and biogeochemical status of these poorly studied wetlands; (2) give an overview of the dominant plant and animal communities; (3) assess the key ecological controls; and (4) present current conservation concerns.

Geographic Distribution, Geology, Hydrology, and Biogeochemistry

Distribution

Surveys have shown that pocosins occurred on the southeastern Coastal Plain from Virginia to north Florida and once cov-

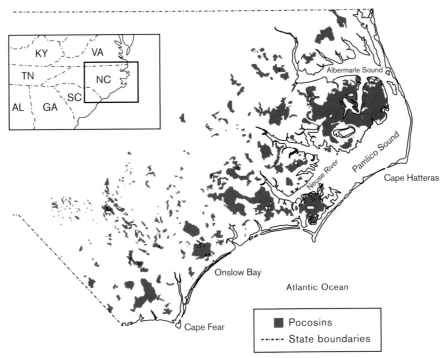

FIG. 14.4. Distribution of pocosin bogs (and Carolina bays, mainly isolated wetlands found inland in the southern part of the state) in North Carolina in the 1950s. Total area was estimated to be 908,000 ha by Wilson (1962). The figure was compiled by Richardson (1981a). The vast majority of the wetlands are found in the large expanses of pocosins. Carolina bays make up the majority of the wetland type in the smaller wetlands found in the southern inland coastal counties of North Carolina. Redrawn by Chris Hall.

ered more than 1.5 million ha in the Southeast (Richardson 1981a, 1983). Pocosin vegetation has been found as far west as coastal Alabama and as far south as northern Florida (Monk 1968). The exact distribution of pocosins along the Coastal Plain has not been mapped for most states, but their major location as of 1950 in North Carolina is shown in Fig. 14.4. This pocosin and Carolina bay map was based on a report by Wilson (1962), which in turn utilized USFWS aerial surveys taken from 1939 to 1949 (USFWS 1954). As noted earlier, a broad definition of pocosins resulted in the inclusion of all shrub and forested bogs, as well as Atlantic white cedar stands and some loblolly pine stands on flooded soils. The exact breakdown by bog subclasses in the 1954 report was as follows: pond pine: 413,797 ha; scrub-shrub: 332,452 ha; savanna: 24,700 ha; and loblolly pine: 391,000 ha. Seventy percent of the nation's pocosins are found in North Carolina, and they comprise more than 50% of North Carolina freshwater wetlands (Richardson et al. 1981a, 1983, 2003).

Geology

Pocosin tracts often cover hundreds of square kilometers and are found on flat, clay-based soils, in shallow basins on divides between ancient rivers and sounds on the South Atlantic Coastal Plain. Impeded runoff of freshwater (i.e., blocked drainage due to sediment build-up, rising sea levels, and peat formation) coupled with the milder climate since the Wisconsin Ice Age (about 18,000 years ago) resulted in a shift from boreal forest species to present-day southern wetland forests and evergreen shrub bog communities (Whitehead 1972, 1981). Based on ^{14}C dating from the Dismal Swamp, the deposition of most organic clays and overlaying peat within

this region began between 10,340 ± 130 and 8,135 ± 160 years before the present (Daniel 1981). However, radiocarbon dates from much of the peat forest present today in the Dismal Swamp indicate ages of less than 3,500 years. This information, when coupled with the changes in pollen profiles (Whitehead 1972, 1981), the presence of charcoal at various depths (Dolman and Buol 1967), and the evidence of decreased rainfall (McComas, Kempton, et al. 1972; Whitehead 1981), indicates fluctuations in peat oxidation and carbon accumulation rates, the occurrence of extensive fires in pocosin peatlands, and a dynamic peat development history. For example, a recent study estimated carbon emissions for a large peatland fire in North Carolina using remote sensing to reconstruct burn severity and topographic lidar to constrain peat burn depths (Poulter, Christensen, et al. 2006). This study estimated that total carbon emissions for a 40,000-ha 1985 fire ranged from 1 to 3.8 Tg, with spatially heterogeneous patterns of carbon fluxes (0.2 to 11 kg C m^{-2}) responding to variation in vegetation type, peat burn depth, soil substrate (mineral or organic), and fire severity. A more recent fire in the Pocosins Lakes Wildlife Refuge in 2008 burned 16,500 ha of drained peatlands, releasing an estimated 22 million metric tons of carbon to the atmosphere (USFWS 2008, unpublished data). Estimates of peat accretion rates for a pocosin peatland in the Croatan National Forest, North Carolina, via the ^{210}Pb technique showed approximately 2.6 mm per year (Craft and Richardson 1998). This annual rate of accretion is 1 mm higher than has been reported for the Everglades (Craft and Richardson 1998) and for many peatland systems in Europe, and is closer to tropical peatland rates (Moore and Bellamy 1974; Page, Wust, et al. 2004). However, this high accretion rate has never been independently checked.

Pocosin vegetation is found on mineral soils, sandy humus,

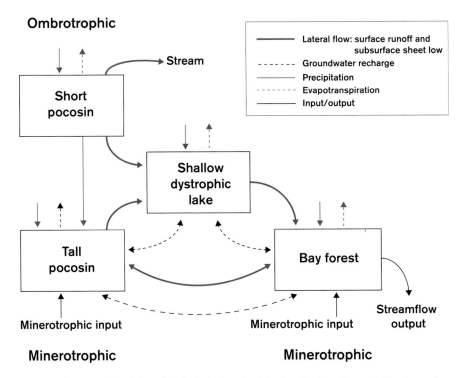

FIG. 14.5. A cross-sectional view of the hydrologic and nutrient gradients on the coastal landscape for the large pocosin complexes found in the Southeast.

and organic mucks and peats (histosols, terric or typic Medis-parist) (Barnes 1981; Gilliam and Skaggs 1981; Bridgham and Richardson 2003). These soils are saturated or shallowly flooded primarily during the cool seasons. On these raised organic soils, precipitation is virtually the only external source of plant nutrients, the peat is thick enough to keep the underlying mineral soil out of contact with plant roots, and there is no external drainage of water into these bogs because they are the topographic high on the landscape. These peatlands are referred to as oligotrophic (i.e., having water poor in nutrients). Peat depths of greater than 3 m are found in the most extensive remaining pocosins, which are in the Alligator River National Wildlife Refuge in northeastern North Carolina. It has been estimated that over 529 million metric tons of peat (298 million tons of carbon) exist in North Carolina peatlands and that pocosins comprise 82% of the peat (Otte 1981).

Hydrology

As mentioned earlier, pocosins are the topographic high on the regional landscape, and as such they are the source of water for downstream areas. A graphic view of their hydrologic gradient on the landscape is shown in Fig. 14.5. The short pocosin is the largest area of the wetland complex, has the deepest peat, is fed primarily by rainfall (ombrotrophic), and is thus nutrient poor. It is the source of water for the region, as runoff drains slowly from short pocosins to shallow dystrophic lakes or the surrounding tall pocosins. The water that flows laterally into shallow lakes or into small streams then flows to the bay forest communities at the downstream end of pocosin systems. These bay forest sites are more nutrient rich (minerotrophic) since they are in contact with mineral soils and have nutrient inputs from the pocosin runoff. Shallow groundwater transfers

also are thought to take place among the components of the pocosin complex, but no extensive studies have been done to quantify this. However, it is clear that pocosins are the main source of freshwater on the coastal landscape where they cover large areas. The amount and timing of the runoff from these wetlands are critical to downstream flows and estuarine water quality (Richardson 1983).

In natural pocosins, > 90% of water output is through evapotranspiration (ET) if the rainfall is during the summer and fall, but output shifts to runoff if precipitation occurs in winter and spring (Daniel 1981). The water storage capacity of pocosins is thus limited in the winter and early spring months, when low evapotranspiration and high rainfall have caused the soil to become saturated. High evapotranspiration during the summer can lower the water table 60 to 90 cm below the land surface, giving the wetlands extensive stormwater storage capacity (Gilliam and Skaggs 1981; Bridgham and Richardson 2003). Studies of annual differences in rainfall and ET over several decades show that runoff from pocosins can vary considerably during periods of drought or extreme rainfall. Following several years of high rainfall and reduced soil storage capacity, runoff reached nearly 75 cm/yr in wet years, while runoff dropped to nearly 10 cm/yr following low rainfall periods and higher ET (Gilliam and Skaggs 1981).

The hydrologic model DRAINMOD (Skaggs 1978; Gregory, Skaggs, et al. 1984; Amatya 1993) was utilized to simulate evapotranspiration and runoff for a typical pocosin in North Carolina or Virginia for a 20-year period, using climate data from Richardson and McCarthy (1994). The average annual rainfall for the coastal region was 123 cm, but monthly and yearly distributions varied considerably. On average, the wettest months are July and August (Fig. 14.6). Evaporation exceeds rainfall mainly in the summer months. Runoff is highest during the winter months and lowest during the summer

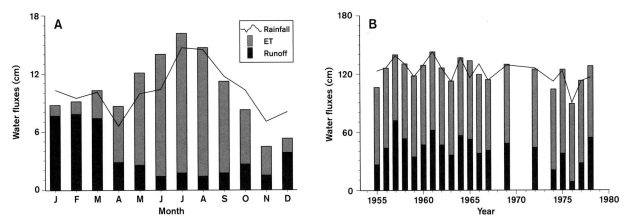

FIG. 14.6. A. Seasonal rainfall, evapotranspiration (ET), and runoff from natural pocosin sites in northeastern North Carolina and southeastern Virginia. Values represent monthly means from a 20-year simulation utilizing the Skaggs (1978) model DRAINMOD (modified from Richardson and Gibbons 1993). B. A 20-year simulation of mean annual rainfall, ET, and runoff for mature natural pocosin sites in northeastern North Carolina (from Richardson and McCarthy 1994). Missing years in the simulation are due to a lack of weather data for those years. The model utilized is from Skaggs (1978).

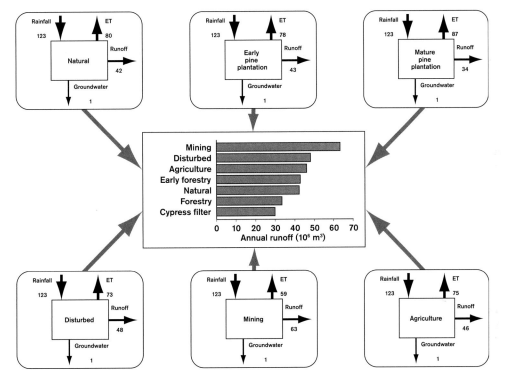

FIG. 14.7. Hydrologic inputs and outputs for pocosins by land-use type in cm/yr. The bar graph indicates annual runoff (m³ × 10⁶ yr) from a 404-ha block of peat-based pocosins under different land-use types as simulated for a 20-year period using the model DRAINMOD (from Richardson and McCarthy 1994).

months. Average yearly rainfall compared to ET in most years shows that 65% (80 cm) of the annual precipitation input of 123 cm leaves pocosins as ET. Groundwater losses are less than 1% of rainfall (Heath 1975).

To test the actual effect of various development activities that occur in pocosins, a hydrologic study and modeling simulation were completed on a series of pocosin lands that were converted to agriculture, forestry, and peat mining (Richardson and McCarthy 1994). The hydrologic outputs by land-use type were compared to natural pocosin runoff, and the results were dramatic (Fig. 14.7). The peat mining activity resulted in 63 cm/yr runoff compared to 42 cm/yr for natural pocosins. The disturbed (i.e., land-clearing) pocosin lands released

the next highest amount of water, at 48 cm/yr. Agriculture increased runoff by 9% over its natural level, but, surprisingly, mature pine reduced it by 19%, due to increased ET (Richardson and McCarthy 1994). In summary, undrained pocosins function as significant water storage systems on the coastal landscape and primarily release water as ET or slowly diffuse freshwater runoff across a broad surface to the adjacent estuarine ecosystems. This runoff clearly establishes their role as a source of water and connects them to downstream waters or coastal waters (Richardson and McCarthy 1994). Thus, their regulation (slow release across a broad surface area) of freshwater may be their most important contribution to regional ecosystem stability, especially for adjacent estuarine habitats.

Biogeochemistry

Very few studies have been done on the biogeochemistry of pocosins. The most complete work was done by Bridgham and Richardson (1992, 1993, 2003), who looked at nutrient gradients, gas flux losses of CO_2 and CH_4, and the role of nutrient additions in decomposition and mineralization along a N and P nutrient availability gradient. Exchange of hydrogen ions for cations resulted in a low soil pH of < 4.0 (Table 14.1). Soil N:P ratio, total P and N, peat depth, and bulk density also differ among pocosin sites. Total soil P and PO_4-P contents and N:P ratios show a P-availability gradient, with larger soil P pools in the gum swamp, smaller soil P pools in the short pocosin, and soil P pools in the tall pocosin that were similar or slightly larger than in the short pocosin (Table 14.1). Total soil N and NO_3-N contents were also greater in the gum swamp than in the other communities, although NH_4-N contents did not differ. The lower organic matter concentration and higher Mg, Ca, and K contents in the gum swamp than in the short pocosin and tall pocosin reflect the minerotrophic (i.e., influenced by groundwater and overland flow) status of the gum swamp, as noted earlier. Despite the clear minerotrophic status of the gum swamp based upon most soil chemical variables and its landscape position, it had a low pH, similar to the pocosin sites. In contrast to most northern peatlands, degree of minerotrophy and pH may be unrelated in peatlands along the North Carolina Coastal Plain because of the underlying sandy mineral substrata with low cation exchange capacity (Bridgham and Richardson 1993). Drained pocosin sites retained soil chemistry characteristics that were quite similar to the short pocosin in all aspects other than somewhat higher Ca content. Thus, natural sites reflect a gradient of N, P, and cation availability under low soil pH conditions.

A number of studies, including greenhouse bioassays (Woodwell 1958; Wilbur and Christensen 1983) and fertilization of natural ecosystems (Simms 1985) and managed ecosystems (Maki 1974; Ralston and Richter 1980; Bridgham and Richardson 2003), have suggested that phosphorus is the proximal limiting nutrient in pocosins. Recent studies have indicated that pocosin soils have average N:P ratios of > 35, which further suggests P limitation (Richardson unpublished data). Despite the extremely low nutrient availability in the pocosins and low soil pH, cross-community comparison and amendment experiments in the short pocosin demonstrated that exogenous nutrient availability, endogenous nutrient concentrations in litter, and low soil pH do not inhibit decomposition in these sites (Bridgham and Richardson 2003).

Soil gas release is important in nutrient and carbon cycling, particularly in peatlands due to their potentially large atmospheric emissions of several greenhouse gases, especially following drainage (Mitsch and Gosselink 2007). A test of the effects of anaerobic and aerobic conditions on the release and storage of greenhouse gases in short pocosins, tall pocosins, and gum swamps (bay forests) revealed that short pocosin had the lowest soil CO_2 production rates under both aerobic and anaerobic conditions in laboratory experiments, while rates in tall pocosin were similar to or somewhat less than in the gum swamp (Bridgham and Richardson 1992). Methanogenesis rates were extremely low and suggested that CH_4 production is not a significant pathway of carbon flow in these peatlands. Amendment experiments revealed that the poor substrate quality of the highly decomposed, humified peat limits both CO_2 and CH_4 production rates, even though the peat is 95%

organic matter (Table 14.1). Low soil nutrient concentrations and low pH do not directly limit soil respiration in these peatlands, although there is a positive feedback of nutrients with organic matter inputs and litter quality, causing greater soil respiration in nutrient-rich sites, as found in pocosins converted to agriculture.

In situ CO_2 emissions differ between the communities, with the highest rates in the gum swamp and lowest rates in the pocosins (Bridgham and Richardson 1992). Their studies showed that emissions are highly seasonal, with soil temperature explaining the majority of the temporal variability. Maximum potential CH_4 emission estimates, derived from both laboratory temperature relationships and in situ soil temperature data, indicated that pocosins make an insignificant contribution to global atmospheric CH_4 flux. This was further supported by a recent study by Morse (2010) in restored and natural pocosins, where she found very low levels of CH_4 release to the atmosphere in comparison to CO_2 and N_2O. Her study did find dramatic differences in seasonal fluxes of CO_2 flux to the atmosphere, further supporting the earlier findings of Bridgham and Richardson (1992). Research in nearby peatland tidal freshwater forests also revealed low CH_4 emissions due to soil oxidation (Megonigal and Schlesinger 2002).

Other research by Bridgham and Richardson (2003) clearly showed that the most important factor controlling peat decomposition rates in pocosins was the water table, with greater rates of decay in drained sites. High initial soluble phenolic concentrations and a low holocellulose quotient (percentage holocellulose/percentage lignocellulose) in litter also inhibited decay rates. In contrast, immobilization-mineralization dynamics of N and P were largely driven by a source-sink relationship, with greatest immobilization found with high exogenous nutrient availability and low initial endogenous nutrient concentrations. The continued existence of pocosin peats in the warm southeastern climates may to a large extent depend on the low substrate quality of their soil organic matter, which maintains low decomposition rates under both aerobic and anaerobic conditions.

A summary of the hydrologic and biogeochemical differences between short and tall pocosins and bay forest demonstrates a similar low groundwater loss pattern, but there are major differences in other such variables, due in large part to their different locations on regional landscape and their hydrogeology, which is influenced by the depth to the sandy or mineral substrate below (Table 14.2). Important differences also occur in their nutrient concentrations, annual nutrient return in litterfall, nutrient use efficiency, and belowground-aboveground C allocation dynamics (Bridgham, Richardson, et al. 1991; Bridgham, Pastor, et al. 1995; Walbridge 1991; Bridgham and Richardson 2003). For example, P in litterfall was 32, 174, and 626 mg m^{-2} yr^{-1} in short pocosin, tall pocosin, and gum swamp respectively, indicating differences in both biomass and P content in litter (Bridgham 1991).

It has been proposed (Clymo 1983; Shotyk 1988) that a Ca:Mg of near 1 is an indication of the minerotrophic/ombrotrophic boundary in peatlands. The gum swamp has a ratio above 1, while the pocosin sites are less than 1 (Table 14.2). Around 75% of the Mg was exchangeable in pocosin sites but only 34% in the gum swamps, indicating a lower percentage of base cation exchange in the gum swamps. This suggests that the classic bog-fen gradient of increasing pH and exchangeable Ca and decreasing OM typically found in northern peatlands does not exist in the pocosin peatlands of North Carolina. By

TABLE 14.1

Total nutrient and carbon concentrations, root-free bulk density (BD), and organic matter content (OM)
at three depth intervals for short pocosin (SP), tall pocosin (TP), and bay forest (BF)
Significant differences (P < 0.05) between sites within a depth interval are shown by different small letters,
while significant differences between depths within a site are shown by different numbers.

Site	Depth (cm)	BD (g/cm³)	OM (%)	pH	C (mg/cm³)	N (mg/cm³)	P (mg/cm³)	Mg (mg/cm³)	Ca (mg/cm³)	N:P
SP	0–5	0.027 (0.001)[b3]	95.3 (0.3)[a1]	3.8*	16.5 (0.6)[b3]	0.393 (0.009)[b3]	9.63 (0.10)[b3]	32.5 (1.1)[a3]	22.6 (6.6)[a2]	46.9 (1.8)[a†]
	5–10	0.049 (0.008)[b2]	95.0 (0.9)[a1]		29.2 (4.6)[ab2]	0.793 (0.133)[b2]	16.2 (2.7)[b2]	52.9 (8.3)[a3]	19.0 (2.0)[a1]	
	10–20	0.115 (0.009)[b1]	95.5 (1.3)[a1]		69.7 (5.1)[b1]	1.74 (0.14)[b1]	36.1 (1.7)[b2]	117.0 (8.0)[b2]	25.2 (1.8)[b2]	
TP	0–5	0.028 (0.002)[b3]	93.2 (3.1)[a1]	3.7*	15.4 (1.5)[b3]	0.345 (0.034)[b2]	12.5 (1.1)[b2]	32.8 (3.9)[a2]	50.2 (10.1)[a1]	31.8 (3.2)[b†]
	5–10	0.042 (0.002)[b3]	89.7 (5.0)[a1]		21.1 (1.3)[b3]	0.520 (0.061)[b2]	17.2 (1.6)[b2]	42.1 (5.0)[a2]	26.0 (8.0)[a1]	
	10–20	0.132 (0.008)[b2]	79.1 (11.0)[ab1]		56.0 (6.8)[b2]	1.57 (0.27)[b1]	48.0 (4.1)[b1]	94.2 (17.6)[b1]	27.2 (12.2)[ab1]	
BF	0–5	0.047 (0.007)[a3]	81.2 (6.2)[b1]	3.9*	23.3 (2.4)[a3]	0.923 (0.117)[a2]	71.2 (15.7)[a2]	28.3 (6.1)[a3]	43.9 (18.0)[a1]	10.1 (1.2)[c†]
	5–10	0.095 (0.025)[a3]	70.3 (8.0)[b1]		38.9 (5.5)[a3]	(0.26)[a2]	151.0 (41.0)[a2]	62.8 (20.6)[a3]	35.5 (7.4)[a1]	
	10–20	0.265 (0.042)[a2]	57.4 (9.1)[b1]		89.7 (5.8)[a2]	3.35 (0.05)[a1]	347.0 (41.0)[a1]	190.0 (35.0)[a2]	69.7 (10.8)[a1]	

* pH values are for 0–10 cm only.
† N:P at 0–30 cm only.
SOURCE: Modified from Bridgham and Richardson 1993.

TABLE 14.2
A summary of the hydrologic and biogeochemical differences between
three peatland communities on the North Carolina Coastal Plain

Variable	Short pocosin	Tall pocosin	Gum swamp
HYDROLOGY			
Trophic status	Ombrotrophic	Weakly minerotrophic?	Minerotrophic
Water table	Perched	Not perched?	Not perched
Seasonal water table change	Smallest	Large	Largest
Surface soil moisture	Highest	Lowest	Intermediate
Soil oxidation zone	Smallest	Large in growing season	Large in growing season
Groundwater loss	Low	Low	Low
Evapotranspiration	Smallest	Intermediate	Largest
BIOGEOCHEMISTRY			
Peat depth	1 to 5 m	≤ 1.5 m	≤ 1 m
Soil	Medisaprist	Medisaprist	Medisaprist
Bulk density	Lowest	Low	Highest
% organic matter (0–30 cm)	95–97	76–93	50–81
Soil pH	< 4	< 4	< 4
Total nutrient concentrations	Lowest P and K; low N, Mg, Ca	Low N, P, Mg, Ca, K	Highest N, P, Mg, Ca, K
N:P ratio	Highest	Intermediate	Lowest
Extractable nutrient concentrations	Low N and P, high Mg and Ca	Low N and P; high Mg and Ca	Highest N, P, Mg, Ca, K
% humic matter	Low	Low	High
CEC	High	High	High
% base saturation	Low	Low	Lowest
Ca:Mg ratio	< 1	< 1	> 1
% exchangeable nutrients	Low N and P; high Mg and Ca	Low N and P; high Mg and Ca	Low N; higher P; high Ca; lowest Mg
P mineralization	Low	Low	High
Anion exchange resin-P[a]	Lowest	Low	Highest
Nutrient return in litterfall[b]	Lowest	Intermediate	Highest
Nutrient use efficiency[b]	High N; highest P	High N; intermediate P	Lowest N and P
Below-/aboveground C allocation[b]	High	Low	Low

[a] From Walbridge 1991.
[b] From Bridgham 1991.
SOURCE: Bridgham and Richardson 1993.

contrast, the pocosin–gum swamp gradient was better separated by N and P status since both the pocosin and gum swamp sites had < 4 pH (Bridgham and Richardson 1993).

Importantly, community studies have related environmental soils variables to plant community assemblages (Christensen, Wilbur, et al. 1988). Christensen found that short pocosin stands had greater peat depth, lower exchangeable Mg, K, and CEC, and lower bulk density, as well as extractable P, Ca:Mg ratios, and pH. He also noted the importance of fire in controlling community age and structure. Later it was

reported that peatland plant communities were also related to N:P ratios, extractable PO_4^{-3} and NO_3^-, and total N and P, as well as OM, pH, and water table depth (Bridgham, Richardson, et al. 1991).

Plant Communities

The pocosin communities of today are only a remnant of the vegetation of presettlement times (Lilly 1981; Christensen,

Wilbur, et al. 1988). Most of the once-extensive stands of Atlantic white cedar, cypress, pine, gum, etc. were harvested during the past 200 years (Frost 1995). However, a unique mosaic of wetland ecosystems still exists across the Coastal Plain landscape. Distinct ecosystems, varying in vegetational composition (Table 14.3a–b) and soil nutrient status (Table 14.1), occur along a topographic gradient, even though local relief is generally 2 m or less. Topographic highs are occupied by nutrient-deficient short pocosins, ombrotrophic shrub bogs that occur over relatively deep peat accumulations (> 1 m) (Fig. 14.2). Tall pocosins, and sometimes shallow dystrophic lakes, border short pocosins (Fig. 14.5). Tall pocosins occur over shallower peat deposits (approximately 50 to 100 cm), have higher soil nutrient content, and exhibit greater vegetation height and aboveground biomass than short pocosins (Wendel, Storey, et al. 1962; Christensen, Burchell, et al. 1981) (Fig. 14.2). Relatively nutrient-rich gum swamps/bay forests occur along the southern margins of the lakes and along outflow stream drainages (Fig. 14.5). Peat depths in gum swamps/bay forest stands can range from approximately 50 cm to > 150 cm of organic matter depending on the age of the stand, and soil mineral content is somewhat greater than in pocosins (Table 14.2). A comparison of short and tall pocosin community vegetation as well as bay forests in North Carolina is shown in Table 14.3a–b. Of note is the fact that many of the shrub species are similar. Pocosins and bay forests also share a number of species, such as *Persea borbonia, Gordonia lasianthus, Cyrilla racemiflora,* and *Pinus serotina,* although the numbers and basal area vary greatly. The number of tree stems per hectare and the number of short stems are very much reduced in tall pocosins as compared to short pocosins. Herb cover is lowest in tall pocosins (Snyder 1980). In north Florida, Monk (1968) found a 50% similarity in tree species between the flatwoods savanna and bayheads (pocosins). Jones (1981), in a comparison study in South Carolina, also found a greater number of tree species, shrub species, and total number of woody species, as well as greater basal area, in bay forests versus pocosins. Species evenness is highest in the low pocosin type and decreases steadily as productivity increases (Woodwell 1956; Christensen 1979).

Plants that are dependent in part on pocosin-type habitat or adjacent coastal savanna are the threatened Venus flytrap *(Dionaea muscipula),* dwarf fothergilla *(Fothergilla gardenii),* sweet pitcher plant *(Sarracenia rubra),* and the endangered white beakrush *(Rynchospora alba)* (Cooper, Robinson, et al. 1977). Other endangered plants, such as white wicky *(Kalmia cuneata),* arrowleaf shieldwort *(Peltandra sagittae-folia),* spring-flowering goldenrod *(Solidago verna),* and rough-leaf loosestrife *(Lysimachia asperulaefolia),* are also found in these habitats. If extensive natural fires remove the peat substrate and the bay or pocosin reverts to a marsh, or if the ecosystem type is developed by man, these species will face extinction.

Animal Communities

Very little is known about the fauna of pocosin ecosystems. Pocosins serve as habitat for the specialized swallowtail *(Papilio palamedes)* and the Hessel's hairstreak butterfly *(Mitoura hesseli)* and are important to the federally endangered pine barrens tree frog *(Hyla andersoni)* (Wilbur 1981). The state (North Carolina) endangered eastern diamondback rattlesnake *(Crotalus adamanteus)* and American alligator *(Alligator mississippi-*

ensis) are also found here. Pocosins are refuges for native big game species such as black bear *(Ursus americanus)* and white-tailed deer *(Odocoileus virginianus),* and smaller mammals such as the bobcat *(Lynx refus),* marsh rabbit *(Sylvilagus floridanus),* and gray squirrel *(Sciurus carolinensis)* (Monschein 1981). The largest population of black bear on the East Coast now exists in the pocosin refuges. The federally endangered red-cockaded woodpecker *(Picoides borealis)* inhabits mature pond pines in pocosins. Importantly, the red wolf *(Canis rufus),* one of two species of wolves in the U.S., was extinct in the wild, but a successful reintroduction into the Pocosin Lakes National Wildlife Refuge has established a small population. For a more detailed analysis of the animals found in pocosins, see Sharitz and Gibbons (1984) and Richardson and Gibbons (1993).

Ecological Controls

Pocosin vegetation and, in turn, animal communities are controlled primarily by nutrient-poor regional precipitation patterns since they are the topographic high on the Coastal Plain and are mainly fed by rainfall. The excessive amount of annual precipitation over evapotranspiration over the past 4,000–5,000 years has resulted in massive amounts of peat accumulation, further resulting in the isolation of these ecosystems from the nutrients and minerals of the ancient marine sandy terraces found beneath (Richardson 1981a,b). Thus, pocosin cation chemistry is controlled by low pH and low Ca due to the siliceous parent material directly beneath and the extremely low concentrations of phosphorus. A test of nutrient use efficiency, which defines changes in production due to nutrient availability, showed that tall pocosin had the greatest P uptake and appeared to be close to the optimum nutrient availability for uptake and use of nutrients, while even greater nutrient deficiency in short pocosin caused a reduction in nutrient efficiency (Bridgham, Pastor, et al. 1995). They also reported that N and P values for short pocosin are much lower than those found in tropical systems and suggested that collectively these data support the hypothesis that nutrient efficiency must decrease at low, suboptimal concentrations of limiting nutrients.

The role of disturbance events as a long-term controlling factor has not been well understood, and a check of peat profiles reveals that these systems are subject to intense fires, droughts, and hurricanes, as evidenced by thick charcoal layers and species changes. Entire mature stands of flattened Atlantic white cedar and cypress are found often buried at depths > 3 m (Daniel 1981; Richardson pers. observation). These findings and historical studies by Wells (1928) have led to several theories about how pocosins are formed and maintained in their current state. The two basic theories of pocosin succession are in sharp contrast with each other. Wells (1928) proposed that the frequency and intensity of fire controls successional development. According to this theory, the pioneer stage is short pocosin, which succeeds to the bay forest climax within a few hundred years if disturbance is prevented. The second theory of pocosin succession (Otte 1981) assumes that nutrient levels are the controlling factor. The limiting soil nutrient is primarily phosphorus (Richardson 1983; Walbridge 1991; Bridgham and Richardson 2003). According to this hypothesis, the successional sequence is marsh to swamp forest to bay forest to tall pocosin to short pocosin. Pollen analysis supports Otte's proposed sequence in the communities. This succession has taken

TABLE 14.3A
A comparison of short pocosin and tall pocosin vegetation in Croatan National Forest, North Carolina

Species name	Short pocosin					Tall pocosin				
	Frequency[a] 25 plots	Number of tree stems[b]	Basal area[c]	Herb covers[d]	Number of shrub stems[b]	Frequency[a] 25 plots	Number of tree stems[b]	Basal area[c]	Herb covers[d]	Number of shrub stems[b]
Andropogon sp.	1			0.05		1				
Aronia arbutifolia	19			1.08	200	6			0.36	1,625
Carex walteriana	6			0.47		5			0.41	
Chamadaphne calyculata	1			0.10						
Cladonia	3			0.20						
Cyrilla racemiflora	22			2.33	5,400	19			2.63	6,500
Gaylussacia frondosa	14			2.17		4			0.51	
Gordonia lasianthus	13			0.48	1,100	9	13	0.041	0.46	875
Ilex coriaceae									0.10	
Ilex glabra	23			2.01	900	16			1.45	
Kalmia Carolina	17			1.11		5			0.75	500
Lyonia lucida	25			2.84	6,666	20			3.56	1,000
Persea borbonia	23			1.48	100	16			1.04	625
Pinus serotina	22	395	3.89	0.25	900	15	156	2.929	0.05	
Rhododendron atlanticum	1			0.10	2,500	1			0.01	250
Sarracenia flava	2			0.20		2			0.04	
Sarracenia purpurea						1			0.01	
Smilax laurifolia	23			1.79	300	18			1.68	
Sphagnum bartlettianum	1			0.15						
Sphagnum spp.	4			0.22		12			1.08	
Vaccinium corymbosum	6			0.56		2			0.16	
Vaccinium crassifolium	5			0.22						
Woodardia virginica	22			0.90	200	16			1.41	
Xyris caroliniana	1			0.15						
Zenobia pulverulenta	22			2.31	500	18			2.13	
Acer rubrum						3	13	0.044	0.01	125
Arundinaria gigantea										
Chamaecyparis throides						7	75	2.078	0.58	625
Peltandra virginica						2			0.05	
Total		395	3.89	21.17	18,766		169	5.092	18.48	12,125

[a] Frequency is the number of quadrats in which the species appeared, regardless of stratum.
[b] Tree and shrub stem numbers are calculated on a hectare basis.
[c] Basal area is m²/ha.
[d] Herb cover is the average of 1–5 Daubenmire (1968) cover scale.
NOTE: Data recalculated from Christensen (1988). Taxonomy follows Radford, Ahles, and Ritchie (1968).

TABLE 14.3B
Bay/gum forest vegetation in Croatan National Forest
(Compare with the short and tall pocosins in Table 14.3a)

Species name	Frequency 15 plots	Bay/gum forest			
		Number of tree stems	Basal area	Herb cover	Number of shrub stems
Acer rubrum	9	133	15.07	0.68	
Arundinaria gigantea	2			0.28	4,833
Cyrilla racemiflora	5	108	0.32	0.38	3,333
Eryngium prostatum	1			0.03	
Gelsemium sempervirens	1			0.03	
Gordonia lasianthus	4	233	0.98	0.18	666
Ilex coriacea	2			0.40	2,000
Ilex glabra	1			0.03	
Ilex opaca	5	25	0.11	0.01	166
Liquidambar styraciflua	9	175	18.88	0.03	
Lyonia lucida	10			1.43	1,666
Magnolia virginiana	3	75	0.37		
Nyssa sylvatica	7	33	7.13	0.20	
Panicum sp.	1			0.08	
Persea borbonia	15	308	4.74	2.00	3,500
Pinus serotina	5	166	5.10		
Rhus radicans	2			0.05	
Smilax laurifolia	10			0.26	
Sphagnum spp.	1			0.10	
Tillandsia usneoides	1			0.03	
Vaccinium corymbosum	4			1.30	1,500
Vitis rotundifolia	1			0.10	
Woodardia virginica	1			0.05	
Total		1,256	52.70	7.58	17,664

NOTE: Data recalculated from Christensen (1988). Taxonomy follows Radford, Ahles, and Ritchie (1968).

place over the past 5,000 years as paludification (peat expansion over the landscape) has resulted in an extensive peat-covered landscape in part of the southeastern coast and an associated gradual rise in the water table. The importance of fire versus nutrients or hydroperiod in controlling pocosin succession is, however, not clear. These factors are so interrelated that it is impossible to separate out one as the primary control, according to Otte (1981).

One interpretation of how these factors control the patterns of wetland communities on the Coastal Plain is Kologiski's model (1977) of the relationship among vegetation types, hydroperiod, soil type, and fire for the Green Swamp area of North Carolina (Fig. 14.8). He noted that hydroperiod was probably the most important variable since it controls the establishment and growth of plants and, to some extent, the severity of fire. Pocosins occur in areas with deeper peat, longer hydroperiods (6 to 12 months), and fires occurring on a 20- to 50-year cycle (Christensen, Wilbur, et al. 1988). Pine savannas (shrub understory) occur on mineral soils with short hydroperiods and very low fire frequency. Frequent fires (3 to 10 years) on mineral soils and short hydroperiod result in a pine savanna with a grass understory (Fig. 14.8). Marsh bogs

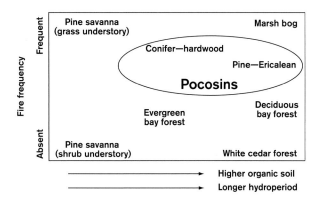

FIG. 14.8. A soil type, hydroperiod, and fire frequency–control model depicting the relationship among wetland vegetation types in pocosin, pine forest, and bay and cedar forests on the Southeastern Coastal Plain (based on Kologiski 1977). Pocosins-type wetlands exist within a regime of higher fire frequency and longer hydroperiod. White cedar communities, by contrast, are found only on sites with fire but with deep peat and longer hydroperiods. Importantly, Atlantic white cedar (*Chamaecyparis thyoides*) germinates best on land with mineral soil or after a fire (Korstian 1928; Frost 1995).

are theorized to be the result of severe fires that result in deeply burned-out peat areas, and have a combination of marsh and bog species. The bay forest, divided into evergreen and deciduous types by Kologiski (1977), is found on organic soils with moderate to long hydroperiods and a highly variable fire pattern of often > 50 years (Christensen, Wilbur, et al. 1988).

Conservation Concerns

Pocosins have come under threat many times during the past three centuries. The first drainage of the peatlands started in the late 1700s, the time of George Washington, but really expanded during the slavery era of the mid-1800s as lands were converted to cotton plantations and farms (Lilly 1981). The second wave of drainage occurred during the early 1900s, when logging of giant cypress (*Taxodium distichum*) and Atlantic white cedar (*Chamaecyparis thyoides*) trees became the main industry on the Coastal Plain. The next impact accompanied the idea that peat soils would be great for farming: by the 1980s, nearly 66% of the 908,000 ha of pocosins in North Carolina were drained or in farmland or were being prepared for pine plantations (Richardson 1981a,b, 1983). It was also at this time that pocosins were considered a great source of fuel as "peat for energy." There was a large effort by several corporations to develop peat harvesting plans over hundreds of thousands of acres for fuel for power plants. Fortunately, cooler heads prevailed after it was realized that environmental damage to the wetlands and adjacent estuaries could be massive and that the entire supply of peat for energy (reserves equal to 12 quadrillion British thermal units [BTUs] of energy) would meet less than a decade's energy requirements for North Carolina (Harwood and McMullan 1981).

A parallel wave of preservation activity started in the mid-1980s and continues to the present, aimed at preserving as much of the remaining pocosin as possible. The creation of the Alligator River National Wildlife Refuge (61,408 ha) in 1984 and the Pocosin Lakes National Wildlife Refuge (44,482 ha) in 1990, in addition to the creation of the Great Dismal Swamp National Wildlife Refuge in 1973 in coastal Virginia (44,844 ha), has resulted in the preservation of over 150,000 ha of

pocosin-type wetlands under former threat of agriculture and forestry conversions.

A new threat to these wetlands occurred with a recent change in wetland laws. The change by the U.S. Supreme Court in the federal statutory authority over isolated wetlands (SWANCC 2001; *Rapanos v. U.S.* 2006) put additional pressures on individual states to strengthen their rules regarding wetland protection (Richardson 2003). The Supreme Court ruled "For isolated wetlands that do not have a surface water connection to other waters of the United States, the Corps can exert Section 404 jurisdiction only if it can document that an interstate commerce connection exists for that specific wetland or water." Immediately pocosins were perceived to be without wetland protection under Section 404 of the Clean Water Act of 1972. In addition, the Supreme Court Rapanos ruling in 2006 clarified that the term "waters of the United States" "includes only those relatively permanent, standing or continuously flowing bodies of water 'forming geographic features' that are described in ordinary parlance as "streams, . . . oceans, rivers, and lakes." All waters with a "significant nexus" to "navigable waters" are covered under the CWA; however, the words "significant nexus" remains open to judicial interpretation and considerable controversy. Practically speaking, a significant nexus is difficult to establish for relatively small, isolated wetlands; accordingly, the U.S. Army Corps of Engineers (USACE, Wilmington office, personal communication) is generally not able to exert Section 404 jurisdiction in these cases. However, for larger isolated wetlands and waters, interstate commerce is usually easier to identify and document, providing the USACE with the necessary documentation to allow regulation of discharges into those wetlands and waters. However, as stated earlier, pocosins do not have an abundance of streams or rivers within their systems, thus lack navigable waters.

Therefore, it is important to determine pocosins' degree of hydrologic connection to, or isolation on the landscape from, other waters of the U.S. As mentioned in the hydrology section, pocosins are the headwaters for large areas of the Coastal Plain and are a source of sheet flow for the region. They often have shallow groundwater connections and are part of a wetland–lake–stream–coastal estuary system, and thus they are not isolated on the landscape (Daniel 1981; Richardson 2003). Importantly, most pocosins have some ditching, which further connects them with other waters of the U.S., including coastal waters. Finally, the USACE district offices in Wilmington and Washington, DC, have stated that pocosins are not being treated as isolated due to both their hydrologic connection and importance to estuarine systems. Hence, they are currently under Section 404 jurisdiction. However, the 2006 Supreme Court ruling and redefinition of the Clean Water Act's jurisdiction over isolated wetlands may remove federal oversight on large numbers of the nation's wetlands, including pocosins or Carolina bays not immediately adjacent to estuaries. Importantly, what few streams emanate from pocosins are not navigable waters, and this may further weaken the future interpretation of their hydrologic connection at the federal level. Decisions will be made on a case-by-case basis in each Corps region.

Many states in the Southeast, such as Georgia, have no state wetland laws or regulations. Nor have they addressed the isolated wetland issue, but, in a 2010 South Carolina Supreme Court ruling, isolated coastal wetlands received protection. However, pocosins in some states will be under increased development pressure if they are deemed isolated. Fortunately, two recent rulings in North Carolina have provided significant protection to wetlands, including isolated wetlands such as Carolina bays. In March 2003 the North Carolina Supreme Court ruled that the state's Environmental Management Commission has the authority to make rules to protect wetlands and that wetlands are waters of the state (John Dorney, NC Division of Water Quality, pers. communication). Second, and most important for the isolated wetlands, the North Carolina Division of Water Quality promulgated a new rule (15A NCAC O2H.1301), which became part of the NC Administrative Code on April 1, 2003, regarding discharges to isolated wetland and isolated waters. The rule was specifically put in place to offset the lack of federal regulation of water that is isolated and not regulated under Section 404 of the Clean Water Act. While there are some exemptions from this rule, it does provide the state with a clear set of rules from which to regulate dredge or fill material in isolated wetlands.

In summary, pocosins are often found adjacent to estuaries and have surface hydrological connections that are linked to the regional water quality and salinity gradients found in estuarine areas along the southeastern coast. This hydrologic connection, combined with the vast, continuous expanses of pocosin on the landscape, suggests that they are connected to regulated tributary waters of the United States. In addition, a survey of USACE personnel in North Carolina indicates that most pocosins are considered hydrologically connected to regional water supplies since they are the source of water flow on the landscape where they dominate, although small, isolated remnants of formerly larger pocosins may be now hydrologically isolated and not under full protection.

Conclusions

Pocosins are unique to the southeastern Coastal Plain, and short and tall pocosins are quite distinct hydrologically and biogeochemically from adjacent bay swamps. They are fed mainly by rainfall and are phosphorus-limited wetlands. They are hydrologically connected to the waters of the Coastal Plain communities mainly by broad-scale surface flow connections to adjacent estuaries. Short and tall pocosins with large land areas are currently not being treated as isolated wetlands by the district USACE in North Carolina, but smaller, isolated pockets of remaining pocosin wetlands are under intense development pressure. This pressure will continue as lands become scarcer with increased urbanization, highway construction, and agricultural development. Care must be taken to recognize their ecological importance, since their presence is essential to the survival of the native flora and fauna of the coastal landscape and the productivity of adjacent estuaries. They contain rare and endangered species of both plants and animals. They are currently the main refuge for the black bear in the Southeast, and they are home to the only remaining native population of red wolves in the United States.

References

Amatya DM. 1993. Hydrologic modeling of drained forested lands. Ph.D. diss., North Carolina State Univ., Raleigh.

Barnes S. 1981. Agricultural adaptability of wet soils of the North Carolina coastal plain. In *Pocosin wetlands: an integrated analysis of coastal plain freshwater bogs in North Carolina,* Richardson CJ, editor. Stroudsburg, PA: Hutchinson Ross, Inc., pp. 225–37.

Bridgham SD, Richardson CJ. 1992. Mechanisms controlling soil respiration (CO_2 and CH_4) in southern peatlands. *Soil Biol. Biochem.* 24:1089–99.

Bridgham SD, Richardson CJ. 1993. Hydrology and nutrient gradients in North Carolina peatlands. *Wetlands* 13:207–18.

Bridgham SD, Richardson CJ. 2003. Endogenous versus exogenous nutrient control over decomposition and mineralization in North Carolina peatlands. *Biogeochemistry* 65:151–78.

Bridgham SD, Pastor J, et al. 1995. Nutrient-use efficiency: a litter-fall index, a model, and a test along a nutrient-availability gradient in North Carolina peatlands. *Am. Natur.* 145:1–21.

Bridgham SD, Richardson CJ, et al. 1991. Cellulose decay in natural and disturbed peatlands in North Carolina. *J. Env. Qual.* 20:695–701.

Christensen NL. 1979. Shrublands of the southeastern United States. In *Heathlands and related shrublands of the world,* Specht RL, editor. Amsterdam: Elsevier, 9A (Descriptive Studies):441–49.

Christensen NL. 1988. Vegetation of the southeastern Coastal Plain. In *North American terrestrial vegetation,* Barbour MG, Billings WD, editors. New York: Cambridge Univ. Press, pp. 317–63.

Christensen NL, Burchell R, et al. 1981. The structure and development of pocosin vegetation. In *Pocosin wetlands: an integrated analysis of coastal plain freshwater bogs in North Carolina,* Richardson CJ, editor. Stroudsburg, PA: Hutchinson Ross, Inc., pp. 43–61.

Christensen NL, Wilbur RB, McLean JS. 1988. *Soil-vegetation correlations in the pocosins of Croatan National Forest, North Carolina.* Biol. Report 88. Washington, DC: USFWS.

Clymo RS. 1983. Peat. In *Mires: Swamp, Bog, Fen and Moor, Ecosystems of the World 4A,* Gore AJP, editor. Elsevier, Amsterdam: Elsevier, pp. 159–224.

Cooper JE, Robinson SS, Funderburg JB. 1977. *Endangered and threatened plants and animals of North Carolina.* Raleigh: North Carolina Museum of Natural History.

Cowardin LM, Carter V, et al. 1979. *Classification of wetlands and deepwater habitats of the United States.* FWS/OBS-79/31. Washington, DC: USFWS.

Craft CB, Richardson CJ. 1998. Recent (^{137}Cs) and long-term (^{210}Pb, ^{14}C) organic soil accretion and nutrient accumulation in the Everglades. *Soil Sci. Soc. Am. J.* 62:834–43.

Daniel CC III. 1981. Hydrology, geology and soils of pocosins: a comparison of natural and altered systems. In *Pocosin wetlands: an integrated analysis of coastal plain freshwater bogs in North Carolina,* Richardson CJ, editor. Stroudsburg, PA: Hutchinson Ross, Inc., pp. 69–108.

Daubenmire BF. 1968. *Plant communities: a textbook of plant autecology,* 2nd ed. New York: John Wiley & Sons.

Dolman JD, Buol SW. 1967. A study of organic soils (histosols) in the tidewater region of North Carolina. Tech. Bull. no. 181. Raleigh: North Carolina Agricultural Exper. Sta.

Frost C. 1995. Atlantic white cedar forests. PhD diss., Univ. North Carolina, Chapel Hill.

Gilliam JW, Skaggs RW. 1981. Drainage and agricultural development: effects on drainage waters. In *Pocosin wetlands: an integrated analysis of coastal plain freshwater bogs in North Carolina,* Richardson CJ, editor. Stroudsburg, PA: Hutchinson Ross, Inc., pp. 109–24.

Gregory JD, Skaggs RW, et al. 1984. *Hydrologic and water quality impacts of peat mining in North Carolina.* Report no. 214. Raleigh: Univ. NC Water Resour. Research Inst.

Harper RM. 1907. A midsummer journey through the coastal plain of the Carolinas and Virginia. *Bull. Torrey Bot. Club* 34:351–77.

Harwood H, McMullan P, Jr. 1981. Peat energy for North Carolina: An economic analysis. In *Pocosin wetlands: an integrated analysis of coastal plain freshwater bogs in North Carolina,* Richardson CJ, editor. Stroudsburg, PA: Hutchinson Ross, Inc., pp. 255–269.

Heath RC. 1975. *Hydrology of the Albemarle-Pamlico region of North Carolina: a preliminary report on the impact of agricultural development.* USGS Water Resources Investigation 75-9. Raleigh, NC: USGS.

Jones RH. 1981. A classification of lowland forests in the northern coastal plain of South Carolina. Master's thesis, Clemson Univ., Clemson, SC.

Kerr WC. 1875. *Geological survey of North Carolina,* vol. 1: *Physical geography, resume, economical geology.* Raleigh, NC: Josiah Turner.

Kologiski RL. 1977. *The phytosociology of the Green Swamp, North Carolina.* Tech. Bull. no. 250. Raleigh: North Carolina Agricultural Exper. Sta.

Korstian CF. 1928. Soil temperature and forest cover. *Ecology* 9:102–3.

Lawson J. 1709. *A new voyage to Carolina: containing the exact description and natural history of that country; together with the present state thereof; and a journal of a thousand miles travel'd thro' several nations of Indians; giving a particular account of their customs, manners, etc.* London: [n.p.].

Lilly JP. 1981. A history of swamp land development in North Carolina. In *Pocosin wetlands: an integrated analysis of coastal plain freshwater bogs in North Carolina,* Richardson CJ, editor. Stroudsburg, PA: Hutchinson Ross, Inc., pp. 20–39.

Maki TE. 1974. Factors affecting forest production on organic soils. In *Histosols: their characteristics, classification and use.* SSSA Special Publication no. 6, Stelly M, Dinauer RC, editors. Madison, WI: Soil Sci. Soc. Am., pp. 119–36.

McComas MR, Kempton JP, Hinckley KC. 1972. *Geology, soils and hydrology of Volo Bog and vicinity, Lake County, Illinois.* Illinois Geological Environmental Geology Notes no. 57. Champaign: Illinois State Geol. Surv.

Megonigal JP, Schlesinger WH. 2002. Methane production and oxidation in a tidal freshwater swamp. *Glob. Biogeochem. Cycles* 16(4), 1088, doi:10.1029/2001GB001594.

Mitsch MJ, Gosselink JG. 2007. *Wetlands,* 4th ed. New York: John Wiley & Sons.

Monk CD. 1968. Successional and environmental relationships of the forest vegetation of north central Florida. *Am. Midl. Natur.* 74:441–57.

Monschein T. 1981. Values of pocosins to game and fish species in North Carolina. In *Pocosin wetlands: an integrated analysis of coastal plain freshwater bogs in North Carolina,* Richardson CJ, editor. Stroudsburg, PA: Hutchinson Ross, Inc., pp. 155–70.

Moore PD, Bellamy DJ. 1974. *Peatlands.* New York: Springer-Verlag.

Morse JL. 2010. Farm fields to wetlands: biogeochemical consequences of re-flooding in coastal plain agricultural land. PhD diss., Duke Univ., Durham, NC.

Otte LJ. 1981. *Origin, development, and maintenance of the pocosin wetlands of North Carolina: report to the North Carolina Natural Heritage Program.* Raleigh: NC Dept. Resour. Commun. Devel.

Page SE, Wust RAJ, et al. 2004. A record of Late Pleistocene and Holocene carbon accumulation and climate change from an equatorial peat bog (Kalimantan, Indonesia): implications for past, present and future carbon dynamics. *J. Quaternary Sci.* 19:625–35.

Poulter B, Christensen NL Jr, Halpin PN. 2006. Carbon emissions from a temperate peat fire and its relevance to interannual variability of trace atmospheric greenhouse gases. *J. Geophys. Res.* 111, D06301, doi:10.1029/2005JD006455.

Radford AE, Ahles HE, Ritchie BC. 1968. *Manual of the vascular flora of the Carolinas.* Chapel Hill: Univ. North Carolina Press.

Ralston CW, Richter DD. 1980. Identification of lower coastal plain sites of low fertility. *S. J. Appl. For.* 4:84–88.

(Rapanos v. U.S. 2006). *Rapanos v. United States.* 547 US 715 (2006).

Richardson CJ, editor. 1981a. *Pocosin wetlands: an integrated analysis of coastal plain freshwater bogs in North Carolina.* Stroudsburg, PA: Hutchinson Ross, Inc.

Richardson CJ. 1981b. Pocosins: ecosystem processes and the influence of man on system response. In *Pocosin wetlands: an integrated analysis of coastal plain freshwater bogs in North Carolina,* Richardson CJ, editor. Stroudsburg, PA: Hutchinson Ross, Inc., pp. 135–51.

Richardson CJ. 1983. Pocosins: vanishing wastelands or valuable wetlands? *Bioscience* 33:626–33.

Richardson CJ. 2003. Pocosins: Isolated or integrated wetlands on the landscape? *Wetlands* 23:563–576.

Richardson CJ, Gibbons LW. 1993. Pocosins, Carolina bays and mountain bogs. In *Biotic communities of the Southeast,* vol. 2: *Lowland terrestrial communities,* Martin WH, Boyce SG, Echternacht AC, editors. New York: John Wiley & Sons, pp. 257–310.

Richardson CJ, McCarthy EJ. 1994. Effect of land development and forest management on hydrologic response in southeastern coastal wetlands: a review. *Wetlands* 14:56–71.

Richardson CJ, Evans R, Carr D. 1981. Pocosins: an ecosystem in transition. In *Pocosin wetlands: an integrated analysis of coastal plain freshwater bogs in North Carolina,* Richardson CJ, editor. Stroudsburg, PA: Hutchinson Ross, Inc., pp. 3–19.

Ross TE. 1987. A comprehensive bibliography of the Carolina bays literature. *J. Elisha Mitchell Soc.* 103:28–42.

Savage H Jr. 1982. *The mysterious Carolina bays.* Columbia: Univ. South Carolina Press.

Sharitz RR, Gibbons JW. 1984. The ecology of evergreen shrub bogs (pocosins) and Carolina bays: a community profile. FWS/OBS-82/04. Slidell, LA: USFWS Biol. Serv. Program.

Sharitz RR, Gresham CA. 1998. Pocosins and Carolina bays. In *Southern forested wetlands: ecology and management,* Messina MG, Conner WH, editors. Boca Raton, FL: Lewis Publ., pp. 343–77.

Shotyk W. 1988. Review of the inorganic geochemistry of peats and peatland waters. *Earth Sci. Rev.* 25:95–176.

Simms EL. 1985. Growth response to clipping and nutrient addition in *Lyonia lucida* and *Zenobia pulverulenta. Am. Midl. Natur.* 114:44–50.

Skaggs RW. 1978. *A water management model for shallow water table soils.* Report no. 134. Raleigh: Univ. NC Water Resour. Res. Inst.

Snyder JR. 1980. Analysis of coastal plain vegetation, Croatan National Forest, North Carolina. *Veroffentlichongen des Geobotanischen Institutes der Eidgenoessiche Technische Hochschule Stiftung Rubel* 69:40–113.

SWANCC 2001. Solid Waste Agency of Northern Cook County v. US Army Corps of Engineers. 531 US 159 (2001).

Tooker WW. 1899. The adapted Algonquin term "Poquosin." *Am. Anthropol.* 1:162–70.

USFWS. 1954. *The wetlands of North Carolina in relation to their wildlife value.* Office of River Basin Studies Report. Raleigh, NC: USDI.

Walbridge M. 1991. Phosphorus availability in acid organic soils of the lower North Carolina coastal plain. *Ecology* 73:2083–100.

Wells BW. 1928. Plant communities of the coastal plain of North Carolina and their successional relations. *Ecology* 9:230–42.

Wendel GW, Storey TG, Byram GM. 1962. *Forest fuels on organic and associated soils in the coastal plain of North Carolina.* Paper 144. Asheville, NC: USDA For. Serv. SE Exper. Sta.

Whitehead DR. 1972. Developmental and environmental history of the Dismal Swamp. *Ecol. Monogr.* 42:301–15.

Whitehead DR. 1981. Late-Pleistocene vegetational changes in northeastern North Carolina. *Ecol. Monogr.* 51:451–71.

Wilbur HM. 1981. Pocosin fauna. In *Pocosin wetlands: an integrated analysis of coastal plain freshwater bogs in North Carolina,* Richardson CJ, editor. Stroudsburg, PA: Hutchinson Ross, Inc., pp. 62–68.

Wilbur RB, Christensen NL. 1983. Effects of fire on nutrient availability in a North Carolina coastal plain pocosin. *Am. Midl. Natur.* 110:54–61.

Wilson KA. 1962. *North Carolina wetlands: their distribution and management.* Federal Aid in Wildlife Restoration Project W-6-R. Raleigh: NC Wildl. Resour. Commission.

Woodwell GM. 1956. Phytosociology of coastal plain wetlands of the Carolinas. Master's thesis, Duke Univ., Durham, NC.

Woodwell GM. 1958. Factors controlling growth of pond pine seedlings in organic soils of the Carolinas. *Ecol. Monogr.* 28:219–36.

CHAPTER 15

Southeastern Depressional Wetlands

L. KATHERINE KIRKMAN, LORA L. SMITH, and STEPHEN W. GOLLADAY

Isolated depressional wetlands are common landscape features throughout the Coastal Plain of the southeastern U.S. Broadly defined, they are wetlands that are surrounded by uplands and lack surface water inputs and outputs (Tiner 2003). They occur in topographic depressions ranging from less than 1 ha to several square kilometers, and their hydrology is dominated by precipitation inputs and evapotranspiration losses. Variations among these wetlands are reflected in many regional colloquial names, such as Carolina bays, grady ponds, limesink ponds, cypress domes, oak domes, citronelle ponds, gum ponds, seasonal ponds, and flat-bottom ponds.

In the Southeast (and similarly in other regions), depressional wetlands have many of the structural and functional attributes associated with other types of wetlands; however, their ecological role has been greatly undervalued, particularly in regard to the important habitats they provide (National Research Council 1995). Ironically, the absence of a clear surface-water connection contributes to the uniqueness of these wetland habitats; yet this defining feature has also played a role in society's failure to recognize and protect the ecological services associated with them.

Often these wetlands support unique suites of species, including several rare species of conservation concern. Relative to their collective area in the region, isolated depressional wetlands contribute disproportionately to the maintenance of biodiversity (both fauna and flora) (Whigham 1999), particularly when they are embedded within minimally disturbed uplands or buffer zones (Kirkman, Goebel, et al. 2000). Despite this fact, depressional wetlands do not receive the federal protection afforded to other wetland types. Even less awareness exists of the upland-wetland connectivity of ecosystem functions and delivery of ecosystem services. The reason for this may be that these values are less obvious than in other types of wetlands and are not easily measured because the wetlands are integral parts of the landscape (Ewel 1990a; Whigham 1999). For some depressional wetlands in the Southeast, little is known about their hydrologic connectivity to surface flows through subsurface or short-duration surface waters or to groundwater, or even their potential role in regulation of nutrient assimilation processes in agriculturally impacted landscapes (Ewel 1990a; Whigham and Jordan 2003).

In this chapter we characterize the physiognomic variation of depressional wetlands in the region. We emphasize the importance of seasonally fluctuating water levels and frequent fire as drivers of the structural and functional diversity of depressional wetlands, as well as the primary factors controlling the notable similarities in appearance and constituent species that occur across the region. Finally, we identify conservation concerns and information needs that are critical to the development of strategic management and protection plans of these vulnerable southeastern wetlands.

Geology, Hydrology, and Biogeochemistry

Distribution and Geomorphology

The origins of depressions vary across the region depending on topographic position and underlying geology. In karst regions of southwestern Georgia, southern Alabama, and northern Florida, irregular depressions called limesinks appear to result from solution processes in the underlying limestone bedrock. As mildly acidic rainwater infiltrates soils, it dissolves the calcium carbonate and creates underground voids. The overlying land surface eventually subsides, and an accumulation of sand and clay results in impermeable soil horizons that lead to the ponding of water and a semi-perched water table (Hendricks and Goodwin 1952; Lide, Meentemeyer, et al. 1995).

In southeastern North Carolina and throughout the Coastal Plain of South Carolina, depressional wetlands that have a distinctive elliptical shape and northwest-southeast orientation are called Carolina bays and are particularly abundant. Based on their position on sandy, relatively undissected surfaces, the geomorphologic origin of these depressions is attributed to unidirectional wind on water in surface depressions (Soller and Mills 1991). Although numerous wetland depressions exhibit the elliptical shape ascribed to Carolina bays, others within the same range are less well defined geomorphically (Lide 1997). Irregularly ovoid depressions that lack consistent orientation occur throughout the southeastern Atlantic and Gulf Coastal Plain westward to Alabama; these may have originated from dissolution of underlying weathered clay or iron-oxide cementing materials that resulted in volume loss and soil settling (Folkerts 1997).

Soils

Isolated depressional wetlands are situated within Coastal Plain uplands on deep, well-drained sand and loamy sand soils to poorly drained upland soils. Characteristically, these wetlands have relatively impervious clay or sandy clay layers beneath the basin that restricts surface-water and groundwater interactions. The permeability and infiltration rate of these sediments depend on the soil texture and depth. Commonly, in the interior of the depression this aquitard is composed of alternating clay and sand layers several meters deep and is thinner toward the upland margin (Lide, Meentemeyer, et al. 1995). Although the clayey hardpan may remain saturated throughout the period of inundation (Lide, Meentemeyer, et al. 1995), unsaturated layers of clay and sand beneath saturated zones also commonly occur (West, Shaw, et al. 1998).

Surficial soils above the clayey layers are extremely variable among wetlands and may range from sandy substrates to organic layers several meters deep (Bliley and Pettry 1979; Stolt and Rabenhorst 1987; Newman and Schalles 1990). A distinction is often made between "peat-based" wetlands and "clay-based" wetlands, reflecting the accumulation of organic materials (Sharitz 2003). In a regional transect from the upper Coastal Plain to the Atlantic Coast, Newman and Schalles (1990) reported a trend of greater peat depth toward the lower Coastal Plain, particularly in more poorly drained upland soils. The degree of organic soil or peat accumulation depends on hydroperiod, nutrient levels, and fire. Peat buildup occurs when primary production exceeds decomposition of the peat substrates (Clymo, Turnen, et al. 1998). Litter decomposition is particularly slow if pH and dissolved oxygen (DO) are low (Ewel 1990b). In wetlands that frequently dry down, organic soils typically do not accumulate, because plant litter rapidly decomposes when substrates are exposed to oxygen (e.g., Battle and Golladay 2007). Also, in wetlands that frequently dry, fire often plays an important role in reducing organic matter accumulation (Schalles and Shure 1989; Ewel 1990b; Sharitz and Gresham 1998; Craft and Casey 2000).

Geomorphic controls of wetland processes and community development include the topographic setting and the associated soils of the uplands surrounding the depressions. Evidence that depressional wetlands located in interridge depressions of sandy uplands or in former floodplain terraces tend to have finer-textured soils and longer hydroperiods suggest that topo-edaphic conditions drive variations in hydrologic regime and potential fire frequency (Kirkman, Goebel, et al. 2000; De Steven and Toner 2004). Similarly, cypress swamps or shrubbogs located in the flatwoods of the lower Coastal Plain are surrounded by seasonally wet Spodosols that affect upland-wetland hydrologic interactions (Richardson 2003; Sun, Callahan, et al. 2006).

Hydrology

The hydrologic regime of depressional wetlands is strongly driven by precipitation, evapotranspiration, basin morphometry, and topographic position. Thus, timing and duration of inundation vary widely among wetlands, even when in close geographical proximity. Water levels in the wetlands fluctuate seasonally and among years, largely depending on precipitation. Hydroperiod ranges from semipermanent inundation with dry down occurring only during prolonged periods of drought to wetlands that dry nearly every year (Dierberg and Brezonik 1984a; Mitsch 1984; Schalles and Shure 1989; Lide, Meentemeyer, et al. 1995; Kirkman, Goebel, et al. 2000; De Steven and Toner 2004). Seasonal patterns of inundation occur, with filling in winter and spring when precipitation exceeds evaporative water loss. With increasing temperatures and vegetation growth responses, gradual dry down occurs in summer with increased evapotranspiration. Inundation may occur rapidly in response to large rainfall events (Sharitz 2003); however, there may be considerable lag time between change in prevailing weather and change in water level, depending on antecedent wetland water levels (Lide, Meentemeyer, et al. 1995).

While hydrologic connectivity of depressional wetlands to groundwater is often assumed to be minimal because of the relatively impervious basin materials, several studies have demonstrated hydrologic coupling during certain conditions that depend on water table depth, subsurface topography, and the permeability of clay layers beneath the wetland. For example, in some depressional wetlands of southwestern Georgia, Hendricks (1954) found that in wet conditions when groundwater was high, lateral seepage into the wetland occurred. Alternatively, when groundwater level was below the ponded-water level, a hydraulic gradient developed and the rate of seepage out of the pond was influenced, provided that the substrate permitted hydraulic connectivity. Hendricks (1954) also demonstrated a water table mounding effect beneath the basin of some wetlands when groundwater levels were lower than the basin of the wetland, but in such conditions, the groundwater level had no control on the rate of seepage. Similar interpretations were drawn from a water budget study in an isolated depressional wetland in South Carolina (Lide, Meentemeyer, et al. 1995). Pyzoha, Callahan, et al. (2008) developed a conceptual model describing hydrology of depressional wetlands, suggesting that during years of above-normal rainfall, surficial groundwater moves laterally into the wetland from the catchment basin associated with the depression. When precipitation and inundation conditions change, such as at the initial onset of drought or at the end of a drought, this gradient is reversed. Shallow groundwater transfers between depressional wetlands and extensive shrub-bog flats are presumed to take place, although quantification of the degree of hydrologic connectivity is lacking (Richardson 2003).

In the upper Coastal Plain, ephemeral surface-water connections between depressional wetlands and streams during extreme storm events are also possible (Heimberg 1984). As depressions fill, they act as corridors for surface-water movement. For example, in 1994 and 1998, southwestern Georgia experienced greater than 100-year floods due to tropical storms, and some depressional wetlands became briefly linked to other depressions as well as a nearby fifth-order creek (Michener, Blood, et al. 1998; Battle and Golladay 2002). In such events, the surface flow of water likely serves as a mechanism for nutrient pulses into wetlands, as well as for propagule dispersal between wetlands.

Biogeochemistry and Nutrient Cycling

Water chemistry in depressional wetlands is influenced by many factors, including hydroperiod, vegetation, position within the landscape, surrounding land use, fire, and relative contribution of shallow groundwater versus precipitation. Although they exhibit heterogeneity in water chemistry, most southeastern depressional wetlands derive nutrients primarily from precipitation, and are usually acidic and nutrient poor. Across a regional transect of depressional wetlands in North Carolina and South Carolina, Newman and Schalles (1990) reported a median pH value of 4.6. Similar acidic conditions occur in depressional wetlands in Florida (Dierberg and Brezonik 1984a), whereas somewhat higher average pH has been reported in wetlands of southwestern Georgia (Battle and Golladay 2001).

Among wetlands of differing vegetation types, Battle and Golladay (2001) reported similar water chemistry characteristics at the initial period of inundation, presumably reflecting precipitation. However, over the course of the hydroperiod, closed-canopy wetlands differed significantly from cypress savannas or grass-sedge marshes, particularly in maintaining higher levels of PO_4-P, benthic organic matter, and organic C. As water levels receded, NH_4-N and organic C levels increased in the swamps and the water became darkly stained. Differences in water chemistry among wetlands are probably attributable to larger amounts of litterfall and wood inputs into the forested sites relative to those wetlands that are dominated by herbaceous vegetation. Similar seasonal patterns in ammonia have been reported in cypress ponds in Florida when the diluting effect of rainfall was not present (Mitsch 1984).

Surrounding land use is a potential factor influencing water quality of depressional wetlands. Because they are topographically low, these wetlands appear to be sinks for sediment and nutrients (Craft and Casey 2000; Whigham and Jordon 2003). Relative to minimally altered sites, elevated N, P, and suspended sediments have been observed in wetland waters located within intensive agricultural areas in Florida (Reiss 2006) and in southwestern Georgia (Battle and Golladay 2007; Atkinson, Golladay 2011). The degree of nutrient retention or transport to surface streams or groundwater is not well documented and appears to depend on the specific hydrologic characteristics of the depressional wetland (Whigham and Jordan 2003), as well as intensive storm events (Battle and Golladay 1999). Some studies of Florida cypress swamps receiving wastewater indicated no significant hydrologic or nutrient connections of the depressional wetland with downstream systems. In this case, nearly all of the introduced organic matter and nutrients was retained through soil processes (Deghi, Ewel, et al. 1980; Dierberg and Brezonik 1984b). However, in a similar study in which intermittent surface flows occurred from a cypress pond to a downstream wetland, export of wastewater nutrients to the downstream wetland were observed (Nessel and Bayley 1984).

Regardless of vegetation type, net primary productivity in depressional wetlands is generally thought to be P-limited (Ewel 1990b; Koerselman and Mueleman 1996). In addition to low input of nutrients, acidic conditions in depressional wetlands make nutrients unavailable for plant uptake, partly because of slow decomposition rates of dead organic material, and also because P becomes bound with iron and aluminum. Craft and Chiang (2002) found that plant available N (nitrate), organic N, and total N were greater in wetlands than in longleaf pine–wiregrass uplands and that C:N increased from wetland to upland soils. Even though total P was greater in wetland than in upland soils, most of it was in recalcitrant organic forms. They concluded that periodic inundation results in retention of organic N and P in soil, with greater retention of N than of P. This process results in a shift from N limitation of plant growth in uplands toward P limitation or N and P co-limitation in wetlands.

Some comparisons of productivity in Florida wetlands suggest that relative to swamps receiving flowing water from streams or rivers, depressional cypress swamps that were supplied primarily by rainfall had lower net primary productivity (Brown 1981). However, generalizations regarding the influence of nutrient inputs versus inundation period on decomposition rates in various wetlands are difficult to make, particularly because these roles may change with prolonged drought or prolonged inundation, as well as type of plant material (Brinson, Lugo, et al. 1981; Battle and Golladay 2007). Water level fluctuations may diminish nutrient limitation by encouraging decomposition and nutrient mineralization processes (Brinson, Lugo, et al. 1981). For example, in depressional wetlands with highly fluctuating water levels in Georgia and South Carolina, Watt and Golladay (1999) and Busbee, Conner, et al. (2003) reported litterfall values that were similar to those of alluvial river systems.

The degree to which fire influences overall nutrient balances within a wetland is not well understood. In general, fire consumes much aboveground biomass and litter, increasing the rate of nutrient turnover. However, the type of vegetation, soils, timing of rainfall, intensity of fire, and hydrologic regime also influence nutrient turnover and availability. Wilbur and Christensen (1983) found that following burning in shrub-bog wetlands, a considerable enrichment of nutrients occurred, including Mg, K, PO_4-P, NH_3-N, and NO_3-N. It was unclear as to whether the increase in nitrate in burned peat was a consequence of ash addition, reduced plant uptake, or changes in rates of nitrification and denitrification. Nutrient volatilization associated with fires that consume vegetation in herbaceous wetlands with mineral soils probably results in losses of N and C due to combustion, but little loss of P, similar to that reported in adjacent upland longleaf pine–wiregrass forests (Boring, Hendricks, et al. 2004). Nutrient subsidies associated with fire may also be attributable to the transport of ash into the wetlands, primarily when coupled with rainfall (Battle and Golladay 2003).

Changes in soil nutrient concentrations have been examined relative to land uses surrounding depressional wetlands. A consistent pattern of increased total P concentration in soils of wetlands impacted by agricultural runoff relative to reference sites has been reported, although seasonal fluxes have not been thoroughly examined (Paris 2005; Reiss 2006). Craft and Casey (2000) attributed declines in rates of soil P accumulation over the last 100 years to decreased anthropogenic disturbances in a group of depressional wetlands located within landscapes currently managed for conservation of longleaf pine forests. Although they reach tentative conclusions, these studies suggest that P accumulation in wetland soils may be a sensitive metric that could be developed into a useful indicator of depressional wetland condition.

Vegetation

Vegetation of isolated depressional wetlands varies widely because of the spatial and temporal variation in hydrologic regimes, topographic settings, and the influence of fire. The hydrologic regime directly influences vegetation composition by filtering out species based on their tolerance of inundated or dry conditions. Hydroperiod also regulates fire frequency and intensity when prescribed fire management is occurring on

FIG. 15.1. Vegetation types in depressional wetlands. A. Grass-sedge marsh. B. Cypress savanna. C. Cypress-gum swamp. D. Shrub bog. (A–C: Photos from J. W. Jones Ecological Research Center archives; D: Photo from Hugh and Carol Nourse.)

the landscape. During dry periods, both upland and wetland sites will burn provided that fire fuels are available, but they are not susceptible to fire when inundated. Thus, during dry conditions, fire removes species intolerant of fire. Regional fire suppression and landscape fragmentation have significantly altered the influence of fire in plant community succession in many to most depressional wetlands. Differences in plant community development associated with topographic position and geomorphology are likely linked through the influence of these physical differences on hydrologic regime (Kirkman, Goebel, et al. 2000; De Steven and Toner 2004; Stroh, De Steven, et al. 2008).

Plants inhabiting depressional wetlands must cope with anaerobic conditions when soils are saturated or inundated, partial submergence of leaves during inundation, periods of dry soil or even drought conditions, and, potentially, fire. In addition to seed dormancy characteristics, other life-history traits that contribute to success in wetland environments include seed dispersal by animals or water, nutritional value to waterfowl, first-year reproductive maturity of perennials, and flood-induced petiole elongation (Kirkman and Sharitz 1993).

Plant Communities

Numerous distinct plant assemblages have been described for Coastal Plain depressional wetlands (Sharitz and Gresham 1998; Sharitz 2003). Structurally, this diverse vegetation can

be grouped into three major categories: open-canopied herbaceous-dominated communities, closed-canopy swamps, and shrub-bogs (Fig. 15.1a–d).

OPEN-CANOPIED HERBACEOUS-DOMINATED COMMUNITIES

Grass-sedge marshes and cypress savannas occur primarily in wetlands having sandy surficial soils over clay that frequently experience dry-down conditions. The vegetation is composed of a species-rich herbaceous flora. Dominant species are often distributed in distinct zonal patterns in response to water depth, fire, or even historical anthropogenic disturbances (Tyndall, McCarthy, et al. 1990; Sharitz and Gresham 1998). Floating species dominate in the deepest part of the depression or across entire wetlands with semipermanent hydroperiods. Emergent grasses and sedges often occur in more intermediate water conditions, and woody shrubs may be present along the wetland edge. Droughts, or periods of greater than average precipitation, may result in shifts in species zones (Stroh, De Steven, et al. 2008). Collins and Battaglia (2001) concluded that zonation is less distinct in wetlands with greater fluctuations in hydroperiod and less gradient in slope.

Several interacting factors contribute to directional or cyclical patterns of change in vegetation over time in grass-sedge marshes. Based on chronosequences of aerial photographs, many depressional marshes appear to be temporally stable if

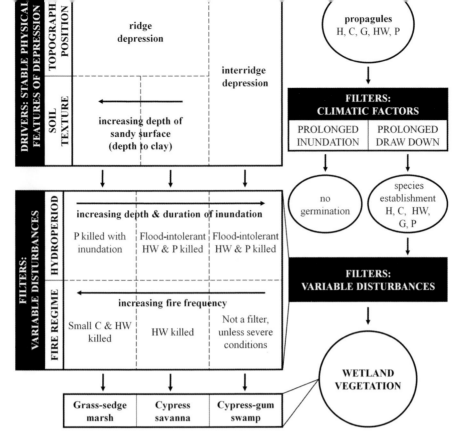

FIG. 15.2. Conceptual model of ecosystem development in depressional wetlands. Drivers (stable physical features of depression that control hydrologic and fire-disturbance regimes) and filters (climatic and disturbance factors that control the establishment of species) are identified in black boxes. Bold arrows from these boxes indicate the resulting environmental conditions or vegetation from each influencing factor. Abbreviations of vegetation: H (herbs), C (cypress), G (gum), HW (other hardwoods), P (pine). Resulting depressional wetland vegetation is indicated in lowest boxes. (From Kirkman, Goebel, et al. 2000.)

they have escaped direct hydrologic alterations (Kirkman, Lide, et al. 1996; Stroh, De Steven, et al. 2008). Dominance by herbaceous vegetation may be maintained for many decades without encroachment of hardwoods or pond cypress *(Taxodium ascendens).* Because fire and inundation both inhibit establishment of woody species, the absence of one factor may be offset by the presence of the other, and, consequently, change in the plant community can be very slow. In depressions with prolonged or semipermanent inundation, hydrology alone may exclude woody establishment. Alternatively, extended dry periods in the absence of fire can result in rapid shrub and tree encroachment in which the size of the wetland, the land-use history, or the landform may be factors (Kirkman, Goebel, et al. 2000; Stroh, De Steven, et al. 2008) (Fig. 15.2).

In depressional marshes with irregularly fluctuating water levels, a persistent seed bank is usually present and guilds of species adapted to germination under different hydrologic conditions have been identified (Kirkman and Sharitz 1994; Poiani and Dixon 1995; Collins and Battaglia 2001; Mulhouse, Burbage, et al. 2005). Some species are adapted to drought and germinate in exposed soil conditions, others are stimulated to germinate only when inundated, and some are generalists and can germinate in both flooded and dry soil conditions (Hook 1984). The species richness of persistent seed banks in grass-

sedge depressional wetlands is among the highest of freshwater wetlands in North America (Kirkman and Sharitz 1994).

Cypress savannas are similar to marshes floristically, but have an open to sparse canopy (25–50% cover) of pond cypress. For cypress to become established, the wetland must be dry long enough for seeds to germinate (Demaree 1932) and seedlings must attain a height that will not be submerged with inundation, as well as attaining a size that can withstand fire. Once established, mature pond cypress trees are relatively fire tolerant and extremely flood tolerant (Ewel 1995, 1998). Even-aged stands of cypress may reflect past timber harvest or may be the result of episodic recruitment events. With prolonged dry down and absence of fire, cypress savannas can become invaded by hardwoods, particularly oaks *(Quercus* spp.) and swamp black gum *(Nyssa biflora)* (Ewel 1998).

Vegetation of some shallow depressional wetlands, particularly those at the dry end of the hydrologic gradient, succeed from herbaceous-dominated marshes to mesic hardwood communities with prolonged fire exclusion (DeSteven and Toner 2004). Martin and Kirkman (2009) describe such depressional wetlands in southwestern Georgia as islands of evergreen and semievergreen hardwoods, particularly flood-tolerant live oaks *(Q. virginiana),* water oaks *(Q. nigra),* and laurel oaks *(Q. laurifolia)* within a matrix of fire-maintained longleaf pine

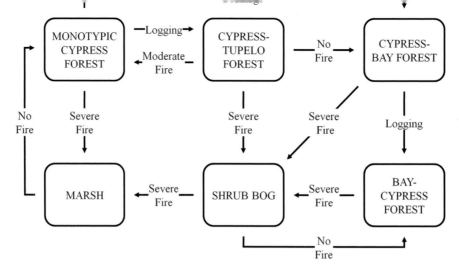

FIG. 15.3. Generalized model for succession in medium-depth basins in north-central Florida. (From Casey and Ewel 2006.)

uplands. The largest and oldest trees usually occur in the deepest part of the depression, where these fire-intolerant species can become established. Based on aerial photography and the presence of a persistent seed bank of obligate wetland herbaceous species, the presence of mesophytic oaks suggests that during dry periods they become established and are then protected from fire when the wetlands are ponded or have saturated soils. The accumulation of fire-resistant oak leaves and low light conditions result in little or no shrub layer or herbaceous ground cover. The layer of oak leaves also holds moisture and, consequently, the leaf litter becomes increasingly less prone to carry fire. Thus, over time, as fire is prevented from being carried beneath the oaks, additional oaks become established and the oak-dominated patch encroaches outward toward the upland. As a consequence, these wetlands remain in a persistent alternate state as a hardwood-dominated community because fire exclusion is perpetuated (Martin and Kirkman 2009).

CLOSED-CANOPY SWAMPS

Cypress-gum swamps tend to develop in depressions with longer hydroperiods than those of cypress savannas or grass-sedge marshes and may even be semipermanently inundated. These depression swamps occur throughout the Coastal Plain and are generally located in interridge landscape positions or floodplain terraces in the upper Coastal Plain (Kirkman, Goebel, et al. 2000; De Steven and Toner 2004) or are surrounded by pine flatwoods in the lower Coastal Plain and peninsular Florida (Ewel 1998; Casey and Ewel 2006). Surface soils are usually highly acidic organic mucks and peats. Because of the longer hydroperiod, fires are typically less frequent in these wetlands than in cypress savannas or grass-sedge marshes.

The canopy composition of cypress-gum swamps ranges from monospecific stands of either pond cypress or swamp black gum to a mixture of both species. The dominance of one species over the other may reflect chance historical establishment conditions and fire events, or even timber harvest patterns in which cypress was selectively removed. Mixtures of slash pine *(Pinus elliottii)* or loblolly pine *(P. taeda)* and red maple *(Acer rubrum)* are also frequently present, as well as numerous shrub species. Characteristic assemblages vary across the region (Newman and Schalles 1990; Folkerts 1997; Edwards and Weakly 2001; Sharitz 2003; De Steven and Toner 2004). In some cypress wetlands, the trees form a domelike profile, with taller, older, and more fire-protected trees in the center and shorter, younger trees on the edges. These are often called cypress domes or gum domes (Ewel 1998). A cypress dome with an open center is sometimes referred to as a cypress doughnut. The closed canopy and frequent inundation of these wetlands result in sparse, herbaceous ground cover.

Because pond cypress is more fire tolerant than swamp black gum, more frequently burned sites may be maintained as monospecific stands of cypress (Ewel and Mitsch 1978). Protection from fire, in addition to commercial harvesting of cypress, increases the dominance of hardwoods (Ewel 1990b; Casey and Ewel 2006). De Steven and Toner (2004) examined environmental factors influencing vegetation in depressional wetlands in South Carolina and suggested that hardwoods that colonize following prolonged drought or altered hydrologic conditions depend in part on the forest composition of the adjacent uplands and proximity to other wetlands. Additionally, Kirkman, Lide, et al. (1996) observed that vegetation of smaller wetlands in South Carolina with a history of cultivation has a high probability of developing into mixed stands of flood-tolerant hardwoods after several decades of abandonment from agriculture. Casey and Ewel (2006) examined successional relationships among depressional wetlands in north-central Florida based on depth of basin and accumulation of organic materials. They reported wider fluctuations in hydroperiod in shallow-basin swamps, and noted that under certain combinations of fire and hydroperiod, slash pine becomes established. They reasoned that fire results in mineral soil for seed germination, but successful establishment requires a subsequent prolonged period with the absence of fire and inundation. In medium-basin swamps, they proposed successional pathways linking cypress or cypress-gum swamps to shrub-bogs through a combination of logging, severe fire, and drainage (Fig. 15.3).

Shrub-bog vegetation develops in depressional wetlands with peat or sandy peat soils, with long hydroperiods of 6–12 months and fire return intervals of 20–50 years (Christensen 1988; Casey and Ewel 2006). This vegetation type most commonly occurs in the lower Coastal Plain (Sharitz and Gresham 1998; Richardson 2003; Laliberte, Luken, et al. 2007) or in Florida (Richardson and Gibbons 1993). The vegetation is characterized by dense stands of shrubs such as loblolly bay *(Gordonia lasianthus),* red bay *(Persea palustris),* sweet bay *(Magnolia virginiana),* and other shrub species. Pond pine *(Pinus serotina)* or pond cypress are occasionally scattered as canopy emergents (Christensen, Burchell, et al. 1981; Sharitz and Gresham 1998). Overall species richness in shrub-bogs is much lower than that of other types of depressional wetland vegetation (Laliberte, Luken, et al. 2007). Otte (1981) suggested that the shrub-bog vegetation develops with increased peat accumulation and in response to nutrient limitation. However, fire, hydroperiod, and nutrients are intricately linked (Christensen 1988). One interpretation of the occurrence of a mix of marsh and shrub-bog vegetation is a result of severe fires that burn out deep layers of peat in shrub-bogs (Richardson 2003; Casey and Ewel 2006).

Animal Communities

Southeastern depressional wetlands support a remarkably diverse fauna, particularly among aquatic invertebrates (Mahoney, Mort, et al. 1990; Golladay, Entrekin, et al. 1999; Battle and Golladay 2001) and amphibians (Moler and Franz 1987; Dodd 1992; Liner, Smith, et al. 2008). Some animals use depressional wetlands opportunistically, whereas others have specialized life-history characteristics that allow them to persist in temporary aquatic systems (Wiggins, Mackay, et al. 1980; Semlitsch and Ryan 1999). The distinctive fluctuating hydroperiods of depressions limit the presence of predatory fish and many invertebrates and amphibians are adapted to the fishless conditions in these wetlands (Semlitsch 2000).

Invertebrates

Depressional wetlands support diverse communities of invertebrates. Arthropods, in particular, tend to be very diverse and abundant. Major groups of arthropods include aquatic insects and crustaceans of subclasses Branchiopoda, Copepoda, Ostracoda, and Malacostraca (Taylor, Leeper, et al. 1999). Generally, copepods, cladocerans, and ostracods are very small taxa (< 500 μm at maturity) and considered microinvertebrates, while the larger groups are considered macroinvertebrates (> 500 μm at maturity) (Taylor, Leeper, et al. 1999). Other invertebrate groups observed in depressional wetlands include annelids, nematodes, rotifers, mollusks, bryozoans, sponges, hydrozoans, tardigrades, turbellarians, and water mites (Taylor, Leeper, et al. 1999).

Invertebrate assemblages of depressional wetlands vary with season, hydroperiod, and wetland vegetation type (Golladay, Taylor, et al. 1997; Battle and Golladay 2001). Invertebrate abundance is greatest early in the hydroperiod, reflecting the rapid response of taxa capable of surviving the dry period in these habitats. Early in the hydroperiod, predator abundance tends to be low (Schneider and Frost 1996; Moorhead, Hall, et

al. 1998), and physical conditions, such as moderate temperature and abundant DO, are optimal for invertebrate growth (Wiggins, Mackay, et al. 1980; Sklar 1985). After prolonged flooding or dry down, many early-hydroperiod taxa exhibit physiological or behavioral adaptations (migration or production of a resistant life-history stage) (Sklar 1985; Dietz-Brantley, Taylor, et al. 2002) to avoid stressful conditions.

The most taxonomically diverse groups of invertebrates in depressional wetlands are Diptera, Coleoptera, Hemiptera, and Odonata (Battle and Golladay 2001; Entrekin, Golladay, et al. 2001); these are primarily migrants that colonize wetlands and oviposit in response to seasonal flooding. Some invertebrate taxa, especially the relatively abundant crustaceans, live in seasonally flooded depressional wetlands but are seldom found in nearby permanently flooded aquatic habitats (Wiggins, Mackay, et al. 1980). This is often attributed to the absence or low numbers of predaceous fish.

As with plant communities, marshes have greater diversity and density of aquatic invertebrates than other depressional wetland vegetation types (Battle and Golladay 2001). This may be due to a combination of habitat complexity and trophic diversity. Emergent plants provide both food and habitat for invertebrates, particularly taxa capable of clinging to plants. While few aquatic invertebrates eat living aquatic vascular plants (Newman 1991), decomposing macrophytes, periphyton, and planktonic microorganisms provide high-quality food resources for these organisms (Golladay unpublished data). Closed-canopy depressional wetlands have abundant detrital food resources from the forest canopy, and species assemblages are dominated by detritivorous crustaceans early in the hydroperiod. However, invertebrate abundance and diversity declines later in the hydroperiod, possibly due to low DO concentrations (Golladay, Entrekin, et al. 1999; Battle and Golladay 2001).

Amphibians

Most amphibians that use depressional wetlands spend much of their life in adjacent uplands and migrate to wetlands to breed. These species are able to persist in upland habitats during the nonbreeding season by adopting a largely fossorial lifestyle. However, to support an aquatic larval stage, they must lay their eggs in water or in a moist environment that will ultimately be inundated. The length of the larval stage ranges from a few weeks in some frog species to 6–8 months for a few frogs and most salamanders. A few fully aquatic amphibians, the dwarf salamander *(Pseudobranchus striatus),* two-toed amphiuma *(Amphiuma means),* and siren *(Siren* spp.), persist in depressional wetlands during dry downs by aestivating in moist substrate or burrows of other animals. Some amphibians breed early in the hydroperiod, presumably to minimize competition and predation, whereas others breed later in the hydroperiod and have other survival strategies. Species such as the pinewoods treefrog *(Hyla femoralis)* breed only in wetlands that have dried in the previous year and are thus unlikely to have populations of predatory fish (Pechmann, Scott, et al. 1989). Amphibians that breed in depressional wetlands have exceptionally high fecundity and are believed to be long-lived, traits that enable them to produce large numbers of offspring when conditions are appropriate (Gibbons, Winne, et al. 2006). A single female eastern spadefoot toad *(Scaphiopus holbrookii),* for example, can lay > 2,000 eggs at one time and can breed multiple times in one year (Wright 1932). This spe-

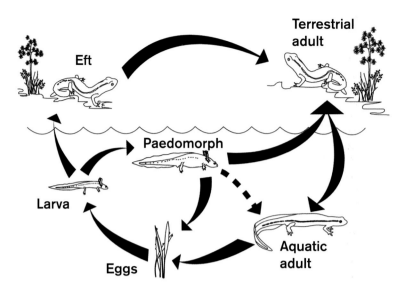

FIG. 15.4. Life history of the striped newt *(Notophthalmus perstriatus)*. Adult striped newts migrate to depressional wetlands to breed. Eggs are laid in the wetlands and hatch into aquatic larvae. As wetlands dry in late spring or summer, larvae transform into terrestrial juveniles called efts. Efts mature in the uplands, after which they return to wetlands to breed, repeating the cycle. In very wet years, if wetlands hold water through the following fall and winter (dashed arrow), larvae may remain in the wetland, retain their aquatic morphology (gills and tail fin), and become sexually mature. The sexually mature larval forms are called paedomorphs. (From Johnson 2001.)

cies also has a short larval period (2–3 weeks), which allows the larvae to take advantage of highly ephemeral water bodies that support fewer predators.

One of the most dramatic examples of adaptations to the unpredictable breeding environment of depressional wetlands is that of the striped newt *(Notophthalmus perstriatus),* which, in addition to being long-lived and highly fecund, is also paedomorphic (Dodd 1993). Paedomorphism is a phenomenon in which an organism with a multistage life cycle becomes reproductively mature while retaining some larval characteristics (Fig. 15.4) (Johnson 2002). Eggs hatch into fully aquatic larvae with external gills for respiration and tail fins for aquatic locomotion. As the wetland dries down in late spring or summer, the larvae transform (i.e., external gills are absorbed and lungs develop to breathe air) into terrestrial juveniles called efts that live a fossorial existence in the uplands until they reach sexual maturity, and eventually migrate overland back to wetlands to breed. However, in years when a wetland holds water through the summer, striped newts may remain in the wetland, retain their external gills while their reproductive organs develop, and then breed the following fall and winter. This complex life history allows the species to mature quickly and breed immediately in extremely wet years, thus avoiding the risk of the additional migration.

Landscape connectivity among and between depressional wetlands, terrestrial habitats, and permanent aquatic systems (e.g., streams and rivers) is critical to maintaining the diverse amphibian fauna of depressional wetlands. For example, some amphibians that breed in depressional wetlands migrate considerable distances through uplands to nonbreeding habitat (Gibbons 2003; Semlitsch 2003). Therefore, they need navigable corridors between the two habitats. Although some amphibians exhibit fidelity to their natal wetland, many species also need corridors between wetlands to maintain viable metapopulations (Marsh and Trenham 2001). Altered habi-

tats such as agricultural fields, roads, or other forms of human development can act as barriers to amphibian movements because of the increased risk of desiccation or predation (Rittenhouse 2002; Rothermel 2004). Many amphibians are particularly susceptible to mortality on roadways because they migrate en masse to breeding wetlands on rainy nights (Smith, Smith, et al. 2005).

Other Herpetofauna

Depressional wetlands are also important habitat for semiaquatic turtles and American alligators *(Alligator mississippiensis).* Chicken turtles *(Deirochelys reticularia)* and eastern mud turtles *(Kinosternon subrubrum)* inhabit wetlands in spring, summer, and early fall and overwinter belowground in adjacent uplands (Buhlmann and Gibbons 2001; Steen et al. 2007). Therefore, the ecotone surrounding wetlands is important to these taxa. Navigable corridors between wetlands are also important to aquatic turtles, which frequently move from depressional wetlands to more permanent water bodies during drought (Buhlmann and Gibbons 2001). Adult male alligators typically inhabit permanent water bodies with large prey, including fish, and utilize open water for courtship. However, smaller adult female alligators may inhabit depressional wetlands or migrate from permanent water bodies to depressional wetlands to nest. Dense emergent vegetation in depressional wetlands offers suitable substrate for constructing nest mounds, and the abundant cover, invertebrate prey base, and low numbers of predators are ideal for juvenile alligator survival (Subalusky, Fitzgerald, et al. 2009). Juvenile alligators leave depressional wetlands as they approach maturity to seek more permanent water bodies that support fish and other large prey (Subalusky, Fitzgerald, et al. 2009). As alligators migrate between habitats, they also use depressional wetlands as tempo-

FIG. 15.5. American alligator *(Alligator mississippiensis)* in a burrow within a depressional wetland. The photo was taken during a regional drought, and at least six yellow-bellied sliders *(Trachemys scripta)* are visible within the burrow. (Photo by Beth and Dirk Stevenson.)

rary stopping points; thus a complex of wetlands within a larger landscape appears to be important to alligator populations.

The American alligator also plays an important functional role in southeastern wetlands by creating wallows and dens that offer refugia for aquatic fauna such as amphiuma, siren, and turtles to persist in depressional wetlands during droughts (Kushlan 1974; Mazzotti and Brandt 1994) (Fig. 15.5). Alligators further modify the wetland environment when females construct nest mounds from dead and decaying vegetation. In Florida, alligator nest mounds in marshes are used as nest sites by red-bellied *(Pseudemys nelsoni),* Florida softshell *(Apalone ferox),* and eastern mud turtles (Deitz and Jackson 1979). Nest mounds also are colonized by plants intolerant of inundation.

Key Ecosystem Services

One of the most important ecosystem services ascribed to southeastern depressional wetlands is providing unique habitats for aquatic and semiaquatic wetland flora and fauna, including numerous endemic, threatened, or endangered species (Sutter and Kral 1994; Kirkman, Drew, et al. 1998; Edwards and Weakly 2001; Dodd and Smith 2003; Sharitz 2003; Smith, Steen, et al. 2006). The relative contribution of these wetlands to regional diversity is disproportionate to their total area (Semlitsch and Bodie 1998). High floristic richness is attributable in part to the variable hydrologic conditions both within and among wetlands, but also to variable fire regimes and the fire-maintained upland-wetland ecotonal habitats (e.g., longleaf pine ecosystem) (Kirkman and Mitchell 2006; Kaeser and Kirkman 2009). Furthermore, at a landscape level, the collective habitats of large and small depressions, wet and dry years, and long and short hydroperiods provide an exceptionally diverse and dynamic assemblage of environmental conditions (Sharitz 2003; Whigham and Jordan 2003).

In a survey of rare plants in six states, Edwards and Weakly (2001) found nearly 200 species of concern associated with depressional wetlands, 69 of which were in a threatened status. Most of these were perennial species and occurred in grass-sedge marsh and cypress savanna habitats. At least two federally endangered species are associated primarily with ecotonal zones between depressional wetlands and pine-dominated

uplands, including American chaffseed *(Schwalbea americana)* (Norden and Kirkman 2004) and pondberry *(Lindera melissifolia)* (Aleric and Kirkman 2005).

Amphibians dependent on depressional wetlands as their primary breeding habitat are among the most threatened vertebrates in the Southeast. The Mississippi gopher frog *(Rana sevosa),* for example, is federally listed as endangered (USFWS 2008), with only one known breeding site for the species remaining. The federally listed (as threatened) frosted flatwoods salamander *(Ambystoma bishopi),* which was recently recognized as unique from the reticulated flatwoods salamander *(A. cingulatum),* is known from only a handful of sites in southwestern Georgia and the Florida panhandle. No successful breeding has been reported for this species since the late 1990s. The reticulated salamander also is listed as a threatened species, with fewer than 20 known populations in Florida and southeastern Georgia.

Other ecosystem services of depressional wetlands include water storage, nutrient assimilation, and carbon sequestration; however, quantification of most of these in economic terms or environmental consequences is generally lacking, particularly in the southeastern U.S. Depressional wetlands function similarly to other wetlands by providing water storage during periods of heavy rainfall. These wetlands have the potential to improve water quality by assimilating nonpoint-source nutrients released within their basins, particularly in agricultural or urban settings (Dierberg and Brezonik 1984b; Leibowitz 2003; Whigham and Jordan 2003). Although not well documented, depressional wetlands may have important roles in carbon sequestration (Craft and Casey 2000) and the maintenance of human health through food webs that limit zoonotic disease vectors (Kirkman, Whitehead, et al. 2010). Furthermore, nutrient transfer associated with large migrations of amphibians likely represents an important linkage between depressional wetlands and adjacent uplands (Gibbons, Winne, et al. 2006). For example, Smith LL (unpublished data) recorded more than 276,000 juvenile spadefoot toads emigrating from a 0.25-ha wetland in a single breeding event. Although individual toads weighed only about 0.5 g, the total biomass of juveniles exiting the wetland was 560 kg/ha. Although the role of depressional wetlands in the maintenance of regional biodiversity is recognized as an ecosystem service, it is the collective landscape in which these wetlands occur that offers the greatest manifestation of this ecosystem service.

Conservation Concerns

Our current national wetland policy fails to recognize and adequately protect depressional wetlands. Without greater recognition of the values and services they provide, the future of these unique wetlands is precarious. Throughout much of the Southeast, depressional wetlands have been altered or destroyed by a wide variety of human activities, including ditching, drainage, agriculture, silviculture, and urbanization (Brinson and Malvárez 2002). Fire suppression within and around many depressional wetlands has promoted successional trajectories toward hardwood domination. In many wetlands, hydrologic modifications have either extended wetland hydroperiods, allowing establishment of fish populations, or have drained the wetlands entirely. Urban development, agriculture, and silvicultural activities have fragmented the larger landscape, presenting challenges to the restoration of these wetlands and regional biodiversity. In addition, potential climate change in the southeastern U.S. may affect the amount and timing of annual precipitation, which, in turn, will modify depressional wetland hydroperiods (Brinson and Malvárez 2002; Stroh, De Steven, et al. 2008). Ultimately, these changes affect wetland vegetation structure, functional processes, and habitat suitability for fauna.

Owing to a 2001 Supreme Court decision *(Solid Waste Agency of Northern Cook County [SWANCC] v. U.S. Army Corps of Engineers)*, current U.S. policy fails to adequately recognize and protect the values and services of depressional wetlands because they are deemed "isolated" from other surface waters. Knowledge of the condition of depressional wetlands relative to their support of biotic communities across the Southeast is generally lacking, and methods to assess ecological functions of degraded wetlands are currently limited. Refinement of techniques for creating wetlands or enhancing wetlands through best management practices is necessary to promote policies for delivery of some of the biophysical processes and ecological functions of depressional wetlands.

Indices of biotic integrity have been developed for depressional wetlands in Florida (Florida Wetland Condition Indices [FWCIs]; Lane, Brown, et al. 2002; Cohen, Carstenn, et al. 2004; Reiss 2006), which could serve as models for other southeastern states. The FWCIs include both abiotic and biotic metrics, such as water quality parameters, soils, diatoms, macroinvertebrates, and macrophytes. Initial evaluation of the FWCIs revealed that agricultural and urban wetlands had lower biotic integrity relative to reference wetlands (Reiss 2006); however, even in highly urbanized environments, wetlands offered water storage and potential ecological services related to nutrient assimilation. An amphibian index of biotic integrity has been developed for wetlands in Ohio (Micacchion 2002); given the high numbers of amphibian specialists in southeastern depressional wetlands, use of amphibians as indicator taxa warrants investigation.

Practical approaches to process-based restoration of depressional wetlands, as well as financial incentives for restoration, are needed. Monitoring and adaptive management can help guide restoration of depressional wetlands. In some cases, wetland seed banks may provide a passive means of revegetation (De Steven, Sharitz, et al. 2006). However, despite the apparent resilience of wetland seed banks, more drastic intervention may be necessary to achieve restoration goals if a threshold to change is surpassed (Martin and Kirkman 2009). Stochastic events such as drought can alter the trajectory of wetland restoration and result in the need for adjustments to management and restoration strategies to achieve desired future conditions (De Steven and Sharitz 2007; Martin and Kirkman 2009). At the national level, the USDA Farm Bill, Wetland Reserve Program (WRP), offers financial incentives to private landowners to restore previously altered wetlands on agricultural lands; however, in parts of the Southeast, the program may be underutilized (De Steven and Lowrance in press). Furthermore, detailed guidelines for restoration in this program are lacking.

The current challenge in the Southeast is the development of best management practices for depressional wetlands in agricultural and urban landscapes that can promote components of ecosystem functions. Revegetation of these wetlands with native wetland plants can increase nutrient assimilation and their use by native wildlife. Establishing buffers around the wetlands would further enhance their suitability as wildlife habitat. In many cases, restoration of natural drainage patterns through removal of ditches can provide water quality benefits (Bruland, Hanchey, et al. 2003). Understanding fundamental biogeochemical and hydrologic processes is essential for successfully enhancing and restoring ecological integrity. Correspondingly, a process-based perspective that can promote recognition of the value of inherent services provided by depressional wetlands in the Southeast is central to implementation of policies and management practices that will protect them.

References

Aleric KM, Kirkman LK. 2005. Growth and photosynthetic responses of the federally endangered shrub, *Lindera melissifolia* (Lauraceae), to varied light environments. *Am. J. Bot.* 92:682–89.

Battle JM, Golladay SW. 1999. Water quality and aquatic macroinvertebrates in 3 types of reference limesink wetlands in southwest Georgia. In *Proceedings of the 1999 GA Water Resour. Conf.,* Hatcher KJ, editor. Athens, GA: Institute of Ecology, pp. 439–42.

Battle JM, Golladay SW. 2001. Water quality and macroinvertebrate assemblages in three types of seasonally inundated limesink wetlands in southwest Georgia. *J. Freshw. Ecol.* 16:189–207.

Battle JM, Golladay SW. 2002. Aquatic invertebrates in hardwood depressions of southwest Georgia. *Southeast. Nat.* 1:149–58.

Battle JM, Golladay SW. 2003. Prescribed fire's impact on water quality of depressional wetlands in southwestern Georgia. *Am. Midl. Natur.* 150:15–25.

Battle JM, Golladay SW. 2007. How hydrology, habitat type, and litter quality affect leaf breakdown in wetlands on the Gulf Coastal Plain of Georgia. *Wetlands* 27:251–60.

Bliley DJ, Pettry DE. 1979. Carolina bays on the eastern shore of Virginia. *Soil Sci. Soc. Am. J.* 43:558–64.

Boring LR, Hendricks JJ, et al. 2004. Season of burn and nutrient losses in a longleaf pine ecosystem. *Int. J. Wildland Fires* 13:443–53.

Brinson MM, Malvárez AI. 2002. Temperate freshwater wetlands: types, status, and threats. *Env. Conserv.* 29:115–33.

Brinson MM, Lugo AE, Brown S. 1981. Primary productivity, decomposition and consumer activity in freshwater wetlands. *Ann. Rev. Ecol. Sys.* 12:123–61.

Brown SL. 1981. Comparison of the structure, primary production and transpiration of cypress ecosystems in Florida. *Ecol. Monogr.* 51:403–27.

Bruland GL, Hanchey MF, Richardson CJ. 2003. Effects of agriculture and wetland restoration on hydrology, soils and water quality of a Carolina bay complex. *Wetl. Ecol. Manag.* 11:141–56.

Buhlman KA, Gibbons, JW. 2001. Terrestrial habitat use by aquatic turtles from a seasonally fluctuating wetland: implications for wetland conservation boundaries. *Chelonian Conserv. and Biol* 41:115–127.

Busbee WS, Conner WH, et al. 2003. Composition and aboveground productivity of three seasonally flooded depressional forested wetlands in coastal South Carolina. *Southeast. Nat.* 2:335–46.

Casey WP, Ewel KC. 2006. Patterns of succession in forested depressional wetlands in North Florida, USA. *Wetlands* 26:147–60.

Christensen NL. 1988. Vegetation of the southeastern Coastal Plain. In *North American terrestrial vegetation,* Barbour MG, Billings WD, editors. New York: Cambridge Univ. Press, pp. 317–64.

Christensen NL, Burchell RB, et al. 1981. The structure and development of pocosin vegetation. In *Pocosin wetlands,* Richardson CJ, editor. Stroudsburg, PA: Hutchinson Ross, pp. 43–61.

Clymo RS, Turnen J, Tolonen K. 1998. Carbon accumulation in peatland. *Oikos* 81:368–88.

Cohen MJ, Carstenn S, Lane CR. 2004. Floristic quality indices for biotic assessment of depressional marsh condition in Florida. *Ecol. Appl.* 14:784–94.

Collins BS, Battaglia LL. 2001. Hydrology effects on propagule bank expression and vegetation in six Carolina bays. *Commun. Ecol.* 2:23–33.

Craft CB, Casey CP. 2000. Sediment and nutrient accumulation in floodplain and depressional freshwater wetlands of Georgia, USA. *Wetlands* 20:323–32.

Craft CB, Chiang C. 2002. Forms and amounts of soil nitrogen and phosphorus across a longleaf pine–depressional wetland landscape. *Soil Sci. Soc. Am. J.* 66:1713–21.

Deghi GS, Ewel KC, Mitsch WJ. 1980. Effects of sewage effluent application on litter fall and decomposition in cypress swamps. *Jour. Appl. Ecol.* 17:397–408.

Deitz DC, Jackson DR. 1979. Use of American alligator nests by nesting turtles. *J. Herpetol.* 13:510–12.

Demaree D. 1932. Submerging experiments with *Taxodium. Ecology* 13:258–62.

De Steven D, Lowrance R. 2011. Agricultural conservation practices and wetland ecosystem services in a wetland-rich landscape: the Piedmont–Coastal Plain region. *Ecol. Appl.* 21:S3–S17.

De Steven D, Sharitz RR. 2007. Transplanting native dominant plants to facilitate community development in restored Coastal Plain wetlands. *Wetlands* 27:972–78.

De Steven D, Toner MM. 2004. Vegetation of upper Coastal Plain depression wetlands: environmental templates and wetland dynamics within a landscape framework. *Wetlands* 24:34–42.

De Steven D, Sharitz RR, Singer JH, Barton CD. 2006. Testing a passive revegetation approach for restoring Coastal Plain depression wetlands. *Restor. Ecol.* 14:452–60.

Dierberg FE, Brezonik PL. 1984a. Water chemistry of a Florida cypress dome. In *Cypress swamps,* Ewel KC, Odum HT, editors. Gainesville: Univ. Presses of Florida, pp. 34–50.

Dierberg FE, Brezonik PL. 1984b. The effect of wastewater on the surface water and groundwater quality of cypress domes. In *Cypress swamps,* Ewel KC, Odum HT, editors. Gainesville: Univ. Presses of Florida, pp. 164–70.

Dietz-Brantley SE, Taylor BE, Batzer DP, DeBiase AE. 2002. Invertebrates that aestivate in dry basins of Carolina bay wetlands. *Wetlands* 22:767–75.

Dodd CK Jr. 1992. Biological diversity of a temporary pond herpetofauna in north Florida sandhills. *Biodiv. Conserv.* 1:125–42.

Dodd CK Jr. 1993. Cost of living in an unpredictable environment: the ecology of striped newts (*Notophthalmus perstriatus*) during a prolonged drought. *Copeia* 1993:605–14.

Dodd CK Jr, Smith LL. 2003. Habitat destruction and alteration: historical trends and future prospects for amphibians. In *Amphibian conservation,* Semlitsch RD, editor. Washington, DC: Smithsonian Institution, pp. 94–112.

Edwards AE, Weakly AS. 2001. Population biology and management of rare plants in depression wetlands of the southeastern Coastal Plain, USA. *Nat. Areas J.* 21:12–35.

Entrekin SA, Golladay SW, Batzer DP. 2001. The influence of plant community on chironomid secondary production in two wetland types: cypress-gum swamps and grass-sedge marshes. *Archiv. Hydrobiol.* 152:369–94.

Ewel KC. 1990a. Multiple demands on wetlands. *BioScience* 40:660–66.

Ewel KC. 1990b. Swamps. In *Ecosystems of Florida,* Myers RL, Ewel JJ, editors. Gainesville, FL: Univ. Presses of Florida, pp. 281–323.

Ewel KC. 1995. Fire in cypress swamps in the southeastern United States. In *Fire in wetlands: a management perspective.* Proc. Tall Timbers Fire Ecology Conf. no. 19, Cerulean S, Engstrom TR, editors. Tallahassee, FL: Tall Timbers Res. Sta., pp. 111–16.

Ewel KC. 1998. Pondcypress swamps. In *Southern forested wetlands: ecology and management,* Messina M, Conner W, editors. Boca Raton, FL: Lewis Publ., pp. 405–20.

Ewel KC, Mitsch WJ. 1978. The effects of fire on species composition in cypress dome ecosystems. *Fl. Sci.* 4:25–31.

Folkerts GW. 1997. Citronelle ponds: little-known wetlands of the central Gulf Coastal Plain, USA. *Nat. Areas J.* 17:6–16.

Gibbons JW. 2003. Terrestrial habitat: a vital component for herpetofauna of isolated wetlands. *Wetlands* 23:630–35.

Gibbons JW, Winne CT, et al. 2006. Remarkable amphibian biomass and abundance in an isolated wetland: implications for wetland conservation. *Conserv. Biol.* 20:1457–65.

Golladay SW, Taylor BW, Palik BJ. 1997. Invertebrate communities of forested limesink wetlands in southwest Georgia, USA: habitat use and influence of extended inundation. *Wetlands* 17:383–93.

Golladay SW, Entrekin S, Taylor BW. 1999. Forested limesink wetlands of southwest Georgia: invertebrate habitat and hydrological variation. In *Invertebrates in freshwater wetlands of North America: ecology and management,* Batzer DP, Rader RB, Wissinger SA, editors. New York: John Wiley & Sons, Inc., pp. 197–216.

Heimberg K. 1984. Hydrology of north-central Florida cypress domes. In *Cypress swamps,* Ewel KC, Odum HT, editors. Gainesville: Univ. Presses of Florida, pp. 72–82.

Hendricks EL. 1954. Some notes on the relation of ground-water levels to pond levels in limestone sinks of southwestern Georgia. *Trans. Amer. Geophys. Union* 35:796–804.

Hendricks EL, Goodwin MH. 1952. Water-level fluctuations in limestone sinks in southwestern Georgia. U.S. Geol. Survey Water-Supply Paper 1110-E.

Hook DD. 1984. Adaptations to flooding with fresh water. In *Flooding and plant growth,* Kozlowski TT, editor. New York: Academic Press, pp. 265–94.

Johnson SA. 2001. Life history, ecology, and conservation genetics of the striped newt (*Notophthalmus perstriatus*). Unpublished Ph.D. diss., Univ. of Florida, Gainesville.

Johnson SA. 2002. Life history of the striped newt at a north-central Florida breeding pond. *Southeast. Nat.* 1:381–402.

Kaeser MJ, Kirkman LK. 2009. Estimating total plant species richness in seasonally inundated depressional wetlands in the longleaf pine ecosystem. *Wetlands* 20:373–85.

Kirkman LK, Mitchell RJ. 2006. Conservation management of *Pinus palustris* ecosystems from a landscape perspective. *Appl. Veg. Sci.* 9:67–74.

Kirkman LK, Sharitz R. 1993. Growth in controlled water regimes of three grasses common in freshwater wetlands of the southeastern USA. *Aquat. Bot.* 44:345–59.

Kirkman LK, Sharitz RR. 1994. Vegetation disturbance and maintenance of diversity in intermittently flooded Carolina bays in South Carolina. *Ecol. Appl.* 4:177–88.

Kirkman LK, Goebel PC, et al. 2000. Depressional wetland vegetation types: a question of plant community development. *Wetlands* 20:373–85.

Kirkman LK, Lide R, et al. 1996. Vegetation changes and land-use legacies of depression wetlands of the western Coastal Plain of South Carolina: 1951–92. *Wetlands* 16:564–76.

Kirkman LK, Whitehead EA, et al. 2011. A research framework for identifying potential linkages between isolated wetlands and disease ecology. *Ecol. Res.* 26:875–883.

Kirkman LK, Drew MB, West LT, Blood ER. 1998. Ecotone characterization between upland longleaf pine/wiregrass stands and seasonally-ponded isolated wetlands. *Wetlands* 18:346–64.

Koerselman W, Mueleman AFM. 1996. The vegetation N:P ratio: a new tool to detect the nature of nutrient limitation. *J. Appl. Ecol.* 33:1441–50.

Kushlan JA. 1974. Observations on the role of the American alligator (*Alligator mississippiensis*) in the southern Florida wetlands. *Copeia* 1974:993–96.

Laliberte L, Luken JO, et al. 2007. The ecological boundaries of six Carolina bays: community composition and ecotone distribution. *Wetlands* 27:873–83.

Lane CR, Brown MT, et al. 2002. *The development of the wetland condition index for Florida.* Final report to the Florida Department of Environmental Protection. Howard T. Odum Center for Wetlands, Univ. of Florida, Gainesville.

Leibowitz SG. 2003. Isolated wetlands and their functions: an ecological perspective. *Wetlands* 23:517–31.

Lide R. 1997. When is a depression wetland a Carolina bay? *Southeast. Geogr.* 38:90–98.

Lide RF, Meentemeyer VG, et al. 1995. Hydrology of a Carolina bay located on the upper Coastal Plain of western South Carolina. *Wetlands* 15:47–57.Liner AE, Smith LL, et al. 2008. Amphibian distributions within three types of isolated wetlands in southwest Georgia. *Am. Midl. Natur.* 160:69–81.

Liner AE, Smith LL, Castleberry SB, Golladay SW, Gibbons JW 2008. Amphibian distributions within three types of isolated wetlands in southwest Georgia. *Amer. Midl. Nat.* 160:69–81.

Mahoney DL, Mort MA, Taylor BE. 1990. Species richness of calanoid copepods, cladocerans and other Branchiopods in Carolina Bay temporary ponds. *Am. Midl. Natur.* 123:244–58.

Marsh DM, Trenham PC. 2001. Metapopulation dynamics and amphibian conservation. *Conserv. Biol.* 15:40–49.

Martin KL, Kirkman LK. 2009. Management of ecological thresholds to re-establish disturbance-maintained herbaceous wetlands of the south-eastern USA. *Ecol. Appl.* 46:906–14.

Mazzotti FJ, Brandt LA. 1994. Ecology of the American alligator in a seasonally fluctuating environment. In *Everglades: the ecosystem and its restoration,* Ogden JC, Davis SM, editors. Delray Beach, FL: St. Lucie Press, pp. 485–505.

Micacchion M. 2002. Amphibian index of biotic integrity (AmphIBI) for wetlands. Final report. Columbus, OH: U.S. EPA.

Michener WK, Blood ER, et al. 1998. Tropical storm flooding of a Coastal Plain landscape: extensive floodplains ameliorated potential adverse effects on water quality, fishes, and molluskan communities. *BioScience* 48:696–705.

Mitsch WJ. 1984. Seasonal patterns of a cypress dome in Florida. In *Cypress swamps,* Ewel KC, Odum HT, editors. Gainesville: Univ. Presses of Florida, pp. 25–33.

Moler P, Franz R. 1987. Wildlife values of small isolated wetlands in the southeastern Coastal Plain. In *Third southeast. nongame endanger. wildl. symp,* Odom RR, Riddleberger KA, Ozier JC, editors. Athens: GA Department of Natural Resources, Game and Fish Division, pp. 234–41.

Moorhead DL, Hall DL, Willig MR. 1998. Succession of macroinvertebrates in playas of the southern High Plains, USA. *J. N. Am. Benthol. Soc.* 17:430–43.

Mulhouse JM, Burbage LE, Sharitz RR. 2005. Seed bank-vegetation relationships in herbaceous Carolina bays: responses to climatic variability. *Wetlands* 25:738–47.

National Research Council. 1995. *Wetlands: characteristics and boundaries.* Washington, DC: National Academy Press.

Nessel JK, Bayley SE. 1984. Distribution and dynamics of organic matter and phosphorus in a sewage-enriched cypress swamp. In *Cypress swamps,* Ewel KC, Odum HT, editors. Gainesville: Univ. Presses of Florida, pp. 262–78.

Newman MC, Schalles JR. 1990. The water chemistry of Carolina bays: a regional study. *Archiv. Hydrobiol.* 118:147–68.

Newman RM. 1991. Herbivory and detritivory on freshwater macrophytes by invertebrates: a review. *J. N. Am. Benthol. Soc.* 10:89–114.

Norden AH, Kirkman LK. 2004. Persistence and prolonged winter dormancy of *Schwalbea americana* L. (Scrophulariaceae) following experimental management techniques. *Nat. Areas J.* 24:129–34.

Otte LJ. 1981. Origin, development and maintenance of pocosin wetlands of North Carolina. Unpublished report to the North Carolina Natural Heritage Program. Raleigh, NC: North Carolina Dept. Natural Resour. Commun. Devel.

Paris JM. 2005. Southeastern wetland biogeochemical survey: determination and establishment of numeric nutrient criteria. M.S. thesis, Univ. of Florida, Gainesville.

Pechmann JHK, Scott DE, Gibbons JW, Semlitsch RD. 1989. Influence of wetland hydroperiod on diversity and abundance of metamorphosing juvenile amphibians. *Wetl. Ecol. Manag.* 1:3–11.

Poiani K, Dixon P. 1995. Seed banks of Carolina bays—potential contributions from surrounding landscape vegetation. *Am. Midl. Nat.* 134:140–54.

Pyzoha JE, Callahan JJ, et al. 2008. A conceptual hydrologic model for a forested Carolina bay depressional wetland on the Coastal Plain of South Carolina, USA. *Hydrol. Process.* 22:1689–98.

Reiss KC. 2006. Florida wetland condition index for depressional forested wetlands. *Ecol. Indic.* 6:337–52.

Richardson CJ. 2003. Pocosins: hydrologically isolated or integrated wetlands on the landscape? *Wetlands* 23:563–76.

Richardson C, Gibbons JW. 1993. Pocosins, Carolina bays and mountain bogs. In *Biodiversity of the southeastern United States,* Martin WH, Boyce SG, Echternacht AC, editors. New York: Wiley & Sons, pp. 257–310.

Rittenhouse TAG. 2002. Spotted salamander migration at a pond located on a forest-grassland edge. M.A. thesis, Univ. Missouri–Columbia.

Rothermel BB. 2004. Migratory success of juveniles: a potential constraint on connectivity for pond-breeding amphibians. *Ecol. Appl.* 14:1535–46.

Schalles JR, Shure DJ. 1989. Hydrology, community structure, and productivity patterns of a dystrophic Carolina bay wetland. *Ecol. Monogr.* 59:65–85.

Schneider DW, Frost TM. 1996. Habitat duration and community structure in temporary ponds. *J. N. Am. Benthol. Soc.* 15:64–86.

Semlitsch RD. 2000. Principles for management of aquatic-breeding amphibians. *J. Wildl. Manag.* 64:615–31.

Semlitsch RD. 2003. Conservation of pond breeding amphibians. In *Amphibian conservation,* Semlitsch RD, editor. Washington, DC: Smithsonian Institution, pp. 8–23.

Semlitsch RD, Bodie JR. 1998. Are small, isolated wetlands expendable? *Conserv. Biol.* 12:1129–33.

Semlitsch RD, Ryan TJ. 1999. Migration, amphibians. In *Encyclopedia of reproduction,* Neill EK, Neill JD, editors. San Diego, CA: Academic Press, Inc., pp. 221–27.

Sharitz RR. 2003. Carolina bay wetlands: unique habitats of the southeastern U.S. *Wetlands* 23:550–62.

Sharitz RR, Gresham CA. 1998. Pocosins and carolina bays. In *Southern forested wetlands ecology and management,* Messina MG, Conner WH, editors. Boca Raton, FL: Lewis Publ., pp. 343–77.

Sklar FH. 1985. Seasonality and community structure of the backswamp invertebrates in a Louisiana cypress-tupelo wetland. *Wetlands* 5:69–86.

Smith LL, Smith KG, et al. 2005. Roads and Florida's herpetofauna: a review and mitigation case study. In *Amphibians and reptiles: status and conservation in Florida,* Meshaka WE Jr, Babbitt KJ, editors. Malabar, FL: Krieger Publ Co., pp. 32–40.

Smith LL, Steen DA, et al. 2006. The vertebrate fauna of Ichauway, Baker County, GA. *Southeast. Nat.* 5:599–620.

Soller DR, Mills HH. 1991. Surficial geology and geomorphology. In *The geology of the Carolinas,* Horton W Jr, Zullo VA, editors. Knoxville: Univ. Tennessee Press, pp. 290–308.

Solid Waste Agency of Northern Cook County [SWANCC] v. U.S. Army Corps of Engineers, 531 U.S. 159 (2001)

Steen DA, Sterrett SC, et al. 2007. Terrestrial movements and microhabitat selection of overwintering subadult eastern mud turtles *(Kinosternon subrubrum)* in southwest Georgia. *J Herpetol.* 41:115–127.

Stolt MH, Rabenhorst MC. 1987. Carolina bays on the eastern shore of Maryland. II. Distribution and origin. *Soil Sci. Soc. Am. J.* 51:399–405.

Stroh CL, De Steven D, Guntenspergen GR. 2008. Effect of climate fluctuation on long-term vegetation dynamics in Carolina bay wetlands. *Wetlands* 28:17–27.

Subalusky AL, Fitzgerald LA, Smith LL. 2009. Ontogenetic niche shifts in the American alligator establish functional connectivity between aquatic systems. *Biol. Conserv.* 142:1507–14.

Sun G, Callahan TJ, et al. 2006. Modeling the climatic and subsurface stratigraphy controls on the hydrology of a Carolina bay wetland in South Carolina, USA. *Wetlands* 26:567–80.

Sutter RD, Kral R. 1994. The ecology, status, and conservation of two non-alluvial wetland communities in the south Atlantic and eastern Gulf Coastal Plain, USA. *Biol. Conserv.* 68:235–43.

Taylor BE, Leeper DA, et al. 1999. Carolina bays: ecology of aquatic invertebrates and perspectives on conservation. In *Invertebrates in freshwater wetlands of North America: ecology and management,* Batzer DP, Rader RB, Wissinger SA, editors. New York: John Wiley & Sons, Inc., pp. 167–96.

Tiner RW. 2003. Geographically isolated wetlands of the United States. *Wetlands* 23:494–516.

Tyndall RW, McCarthy KA, et al. 1990. Vegetation of six Carolina bays in Maryland. *Castanea* 55:1–21.

USFWS (US Fish and Wildlife Service). 2008. Endangered and threatened wildlife and plants. 50 CFR 17.11 and 17.12. Washington DC.

Watt KM, Golladay SW. 1999. Organic matter dynamics in seasonally inundated, forested wetlands of the Gulf Coastal Plain. *Wetlands* 19:139–48.

West LT, Shaw JN, Blood ER, Kirkman LK. 1998. Correlation of water tables to redoximorphic features in the Dougherty Plain, southwest Georgia. In *Quantifying soil hydromorphology,* SSSA

Special Publication no. 54, Rabenhorst MC, Bell JC, McDaniel PA, editors. Madison, WI: Soil Sci. Soc. Am., pp. 247–58.

Whigham DF. 1999. Ecological issues related to wetland preservation, restoration, creation and assessment. *Sci. Total Env.* 240:31–40.

Whigham DF, Jordan TE. 2003. Isolated wetlands and water quality. *Wetlands* 23:541–49.

Wiggins GB, Mackay RJ, Smith IM. 1980. Evolutionary and eco- logical strategies of animals in annual temporary pools. *Archiv. Hydrobiol. Suppl.* 58:97–206.

Wilbur RB, Christensen NL. 1983. Effects of fire on nutrient availability in a North Carolina Coastal Plain pocosin. *Am. Midl. Natur.* 110:54–61.

Wright AH. 1932. *Life-histories of the frogs of the Okefinokee Swamp, Georgia.* New York: Macmillan Co.

CHAPTER 16

Southeastern Swamp Complexes

DAROLD P. BATZER, FRANK DAY, and STEPHEN W. GOLLADAY

The southeastern U.S. is extremely rich in wetlands, and other chapters in this book are devoted to coastal systems, river floodplains, pocosins, and depressional wetlands of the region, and the Florida Everglades. In terms of large southeastern wetlands, the Everglades immediately comes to mind, but several other expansive wetland complexes exist across the area. Among the largest of these complexes are the Great Dismal Swamp of Virginia and North Carolina, the Okefenokee Swamp of Georgia and Florida, and the perhaps lesser-known Chickasawhatchee Swamp in southwest Georgia. Each of these three wetlands is geologically and ecologically unique, and each could merit its own chapter. By virtue of being largely forested, and hence having the moniker "swamp," these three wetlands are grouped together for this publication. Perhaps a better reason to group these habitats is that they characterize the mystical flavor of southeastern wetlands, with darkly stained tannic waters, buttressed cypress trees, fascinating bird and reptilian life, and exotic-sounding names.

The Great Dismal Swamp

The Great Dismal Swamp is the largest intact remnant of a habitat that once covered more than one million ha in southeastern Virginia and northeastern North Carolina (USFWS 2006). The remaining protected area currently includes about 45,000 ha in the two states (online appendix 16.A). Dismal Swamp has been impacted by over 200 years of anthropogenic disturbance from fires, logging, and construction of over 100 km of drainage ditches with parallel roads (Fig. 16.1a) (Levy 1991). Human history in the area is long and storied. Native Americans were very active in the swamp. Early European explorers made note of the swamp but rarely ventured into it. George Washington and other land speculators organized the Dismal Swamp Land Company, which started draining and logging the swamp. Dense vegetation provided an Underground Railroad refuge for escaped slaves prior to the Civil War (Stewart 1979).

The Dismal Swamp is well known for the unique blending of northern and southern flora and fauna, and thus an intense interest in its protection has developed. In 1974, the Virginia portion of the swamp was established as a US Fish and Wildlife Service (USFWS) National Wildlife Refuge (NWR), which was the first time an NWR unit was created for the primary purpose of protecting an ecosystem (Culp 2000). Dismal Swamp State Park in North Carolina and other state-owned local units were also established. The Nature Conservancy received the original land gift and still retains some oversight rights.

Geology

The Dismal Swamp is a relatively young feature. This extensive forested wetland developed along drainage lows during the most recent late-glacial period (Whitehead 1972). Postglacial rise of sea level resulted in wetland development and accumulation of fine-grained organic sediments. The western boundary is defined by the Suffolk Scarp (a sharply delineated Pleistocene shoreline), the eastern boundary by the Fentress Rise (a north-south linear high consisting of interglacial marine and barrier sediments), and the northern boundary by topographic lows extending almost to the James River and Chesapeake Bay (online appendix 16.A). The swamp gently slopes toward the southeast, originally reaching the Albemarle Sound in North Carolina.

Pleistocene deposits are underlain by a complex series of marine, barrier, and lagoonal deposits, with as many as five transgressions (Whitehead 1972). The oldest and deepest formation is the Yorktown (impermeable clay), overlain by the Norfolk Formation (sands), then London Bridge and Sandbridge (which confine the Norfolk aquifer), and the cap consists of peat deposits and mineral soils (USFWS 2006). Peat, as much as 4 m deep but highly variable throughout the swamp, lies over the clays and sandy clays of the Sandbridge Formation.

Hydrology

Severe historic manipulations of hydrology have amplified the spatial and temporal variability of water levels in the Dismal Swamp. Water levels fluctuate widely, both seasonally and annually (Fig. 16.2). The Dismal Swamp can be exceptionally

FIG. 16.1. Great Dismal Swamp. Washington ditch adjacent to (A) maple-gum forest; (B) cypress tree in Lake Drummond; (C) regenerating Atlantic white cedar following logging; and (D) black bear. (A: Photo by Frank Day; B–D: photos by U.S. Fish and Wildlife Service, Great Dismal Swamp National Wildlife Refuge.)

dry, with water levels below a meter depth in the soil, or wet, with saturated soils or surface flooding (most commonly during the winter). Surface flooding is a poor indicator of the influence of hydrology on ecosystem processes in the habitat. Duration of soil saturation is the better indicator, and it does not correlate well with surface flooding duration (Day, West, et al. 1988).

Interrelationships between surface water and groundwater are basic to understanding Dismal Swamp hydrology (Lichtler and Walker 1979). The primary source of water in the swamp is seepage of groundwater; surface inflow is minimal during summer, but is three to four times greater in winter. Groundwater inflow is mostly from the west through the Norfolk aquifer and surficial sand overlying the Sandbridge confining layer. Aquifer flow has been modified by human withdrawals. Rain on or near the swamp may stand on the soil surface before soaking into peat and underlying formations. Surface water moves laterally toward areas of discharge, such as canals and ditches.

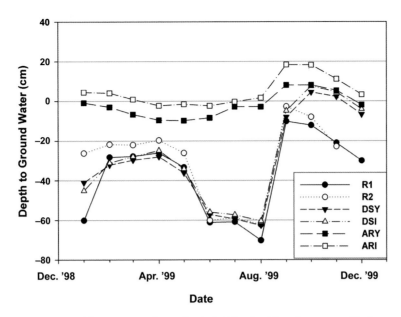

FIG. 16.2. Monthly mean groundwater depths in Atlantic white cedar communities in the Dismal Swamp (DSY: young; DSI: intermediate age); Alligator River National Wildlife Refuge, North Carolina, sites (ARY: young; ARI: intermediate age); and two cedar restoration sites (R1 and R2) for 1999. Means obtained from daily water depths averaged from two readings (morning and evening) from a continuous-recording well installed at the center of each study site. The 0 on the y-axis represents the soil surface. (Adapted from DeBerry, Belcher, et al. 2003; published in Crawford, Day, et al. 2007.)

TABLE 16.1

Selected features of four long-term research sites in the Dismal Swamp
(Day 1982; Megonigal and Day 1988; J. Rule and T. Matthews unpublished data)

Feature	Cedar	Maple-gum	Cypress	Mixed hardwoods
Months flooded	4	6	6	0
Maximum flooding depth (cm)	20	17	21	No surface flooding
Soil pH (range)	3.3–4.4	4.3–5.6	4.5–5.5	3.2–4.9
Soil organic matter (%)	85	14	4	2
CEC (meq/11 g)	54	39	10	21
Exchangeable P (mg/g)	1.68	1.10	1.36	2.27

NOTE: Modified from Day and Megonigal 2000.

Parts of the Dismal Swamp remain wet even during droughts because of upward seepage of groundwater.

Carter, Gammon, et al. (1994) examined ecotones and natural wetland boundaries along transects in the Dismal Swamp. The water table was within the root zone (0–30 cm) 25–100% of the growing season in the wetland, < 25–100% in the ecotone, and < 25–50% in the upland. Wetland boundaries based on vegetation, hydrology, or soils varied among different transects, indicating great spatial variability and varied controlling factors.

Biogeochemistry

Mineral and organic properties and organic matter turnover rates are quite variable spatially in Dismal Swamp soils as a result

of hydrologic variability among sites (Table 16.1). Soil organic matter is variable among flooded sites, ranging from 85% in an Atlantic white cedar *(Chamaecyparis thyoides)* site to 4% in a bald cypress *(Taxodium distichum)* site. An unflooded site had the lowest organic matter content (2%). Greatest accumulations in wet sites are due primarily to higher aboveground net primary productivity (NPP) (Megonigal and Day 1988; Day and Megonigal 1993). Decomposition rates vary primarily as a result of litter quality rather than hydrology (Day 1982). Biomass allocation patterns (above versus belowground) vary in response to a flooding gradient, and these patterns in turn determine the array of litter types that affect decomposition rates and thus nutrient availability (Day and Megonigal 1993). Based on research in the Dismal Swamp, Harriss, Sebacher, et al. (1982) published the first report that swamp soils can serve as a methane sink or source, depending on soil moisture and anoxia.

TABLE 16.2
Dominant plant species in four major plant community types of the Great Dismal Swamp

	Species	Basal area (m²/ha)	Density (stems/ha)	Biomass (kg/ha)
Atlantic white cedar	*Chamaecyparis thyoides*	31	460	103,169
	Nyssa biflora	14	640	67,613
	Acer rubrum	9	480	42,999
	Other	1	420	6,667
	Total	55	2,000	220,448
Bald cypress	*Taxodium distichum*	28	290	173,097
	A. rubrum	10	270	61,988
	N. biflora	9	190	49,973
	Other	13	810	60,207
	Total	60	1,560	345,265
Maple-gum	*Nyssa aquatica*	18	570	91,449
	A. rubrum	13	760	64,315
	N. biflora	6	210	32,432
	Other	2	540	7,543
	Total	39	2,080	195,739
Mixed hardwoods	*Quercus laurifolia*	10	60	63,880
	Quercus alba	5	30	33,323
	Liquidambar styraciflua	5	120	25,471
	Other	13	1,230	71,892
	Total	33	1,440	194,566

NOTE: Data are for trees with stems > 2.54 cm dbh; biomass is for aboveground vegetation. Modified from Dabel and Day 1977.

Plant Communities

Most plant communities in Dismal Swamp (Table 16.2) are dense, shrub-dominated second- or third-growth forests. Bald cypress was historically the dominant tree but was intensively logged along with Atlantic white cedar. The cypress-gum forest type is now represented by only a few remnants and some individual cypress trees around the shore of Lake Drummond (Fig. 16.1b). Little remains of the once extensive and ecologically unique Atlantic white cedar forest. Red maple *(Acer rubrum)* dominates many Dismal Swamp communities today (Levy 1991).

Four major community types in the Dismal Swamp have been extensively studied (Dabel and Day 1977; Day and Megonigal 1993, 2000) (Table 16.2). Hardwood-dominated communities represent about 64% of the swamp's vegetation, followed by 6% Atlantic white cedar and 2% bald cypress (Dabel and Day 1977). The remaining area is composed of pine forest and mixed tree species.

During the 1900s, Atlantic white cedar declined by over 90% in Virginia and North Carolina due to ditching, logging, and fire suppression, and it was replaced primarily by red maple and other hardwoods. Low water tables likely contributed substantially to cedar's decline (Shacochis, DeBerry, et al. 2000). Hydrology is exceptionally important in cedar establishment

and maintenance (Atkinson, DeBerry, et al. 2003; DeBerry, Belcher, et al. 2003). Cedar appears to require a relatively specific set of hydrologic conditions for maintenance: saturated soils for a substantial portion of the year, but with periods dry enough to allow low-temperature surface fires (Harrison, DeBerry, et al. 2003). Reestablishment can occur under the right circumstances, natural or manipulated (Fig. 16.1c). Hurricane Isabel (2003) had a great impact on Dismal Swamp community structure that will be apparent for many years (USFWS 2006). The storm caused extensive blowdown of several thousand hectares of Atlantic white cedar and bald cypress.

Threatened or endangered plant species include Virginia least trillium *(Trillium pusillum* var. *virginianum),* silky camellia *(Stewartia malacodendron),* sheep laurel *(Kalmia angustifolia),* and purple bladderwort *(Utricularia purpurea).* Problem invasive plants include common reed *(Phragmites australis)* and privet *(Ligustrum* spp.) (USFWS 2006).

Animal Communities

The Dismal Swamp is probably the most important refugium in the eastern U.S. for mammals dependent on coastal freshwater swamps (Webster 2000). Elevated richness in Dismal

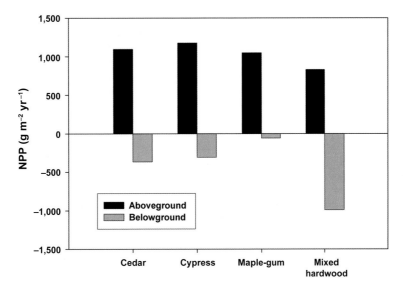

FIG. 16.3. Net primary production (NPP) in g m⁻² yr⁻¹ in four Dismal Swamp communities. Belowground production is only for fine roots in the top 40 cm of soil. (From Megonigal and Day 1988; Powell and Day 1991.)

Swamp is attributed to maple-gum, bald cypress, and Atlantic white cedar forests and interior upland islands providing habitat for animals with boreal, temperate, and subtropical affinities. Rose (2000) and the Dismal Swamp's Comprehensive Conservation Plan (USFWS 2006) provide comprehensive lists of species for most animal groups.

The most important animal in the Dismal Swamp is probably the black bear *(Ursus americanus)* (Webster 2000) (Fig. 16.1d), and the swamp supports the most northerly black bear population in the Atlantic Coastal Plain (Hellgren and Vaughn 2000). Bear density in the 1980s was 0.5–0.7 bears/km². Based on a year-round radio tracking study, females preferred pocosins and mesic areas and males preferred cypress-gum and red maple/pine areas (Hellgren, Vaughn, et al. 1991). Winter-active bears frequented pocosin-type habitats of evergreen shrubs and inundated cypress-gum swamps; the unusually high frequency of winter activity has been attributed to mild winter temperatures, lack of persistent snow, and diverse food sources.

After black bear, Swainson's warbler *(Limnothlypis swainsonii)* has received the most attention among animal residents. Extensive clearing of bottomland forests in the southeastern United States restricted the warbler to seasonally inundated buffer zones bordering swamps. In the Dismal Swamp, hydrology is the driving force influencing warbler distribution, and the bird is found more often on the drier end of the hydrologic gradient in swamp undergrowth thickets, greenbriar *(Smilax* spp.) tangles, and deep shade (Graves 2001). Swainson's warbler avoids flooding due to its ground-foraging behavior.

Southern bog lemming *(Synaptomys cooperi helaletes)* was thought to be extinct due to human-induced habitat changes, including lowered water tables and fire prevention (which reduced the number of openings in the canopy). The species, however, was rediscovered in the Dismal Swamp in 1980 (Rose 1981).

The most important game species is white-tail deer *(Odocoileus virginianus)*. Beavers *(Castor canadensis)* were once depleted in the area but have recently returned in significant numbers (USFWS 2006). Federally listed rare species include red-cockaded woodpecker *(Picoides borealis)* and red wolf *(Canis rufus)* (not currently present). State listed species include cane-

brake rattlesnake *(Croatalus horridus atricaudatus)* and the Dismal Swamp southeastern shrew *(Sorex longirostris fisheri)*. Invasives of most concern are coyote *(Canis latraus)* and nutria *(Myocastor coypus)*.

Ecological Controls

Hydrology is clearly the primary driving force in the Dismal Swamp, and historical alterations to the natural hydrology are the principal reasons for dramatic changes in ecosystem structure and function. Plant organic matter pools have been quantified on four sites representing different community types in the Dismal Swamp (Megonigal and Day 1988; Powell and Day 1991) (Fig. 16.3). Aboveground annual net primary production was greatest on the flooded sites, but belowground net primary production was higher on the least-flooded site. Even though the least-flooded site had greater potential inputs to soil organic matter via root production, accumulations of soil organic matter continued to be greatest on the more extensively saturated sites, as slow decomposition rates permitted accumulation (Day 1982; Tupacz and Day 1990). An important implication is that manipulations and alterations of hydrology can have large impacts on biomass allocation, organic matter accumulation, and basic ecosystem integrity in forested wetlands (Day and Megonigal 2000).

Fire is an important driver, in concert with hydrology, in the establishment and maintenance of Atlantic white cedar. Periodic fire removes competing understory species, reduces the organic layer, and promotes seed germination. A delicate balance exists between hydrology and fire for cedar establishment. Water levels must be low enough to permit fire, but if it gets too dry, fire will burn into the peat and destroy the seed bank.

Conservation Concerns

Forest management includes fire management to maintain Atlantic white cedar without conflicting with the need to suppress wildfire because of drier hydrology, and water management to limit hardwoods but allow bald cypress seedlings to establish. Both prescribed fire and fire suppression are practiced. Hydrologic management is challenging because some irreparable damage has occurred (e.g., removal of the confining clay layer by ditch construction), but some drainage control has been achieved with water control structures. The USFWS maintains over 30 water control structures to slow drainage (Culp 2000).

A major management goal is to restore and expand Atlantic white cedar and cypress communities (Culp 2000). Hydrologic restoration is key to cypress reestablishment. Without the appropriate hydrology, bald cypress is outcompeted by hardwoods. The restoration of Atlantic white cedar is more complex, and studies have been conducted to establish the requirements for successful reestablishment. A study of natural and mitigation planted sites found that hydrology was exceptionally important to cedar establishment and growth (Atkinson, DeBerry, et al. 2003). It is unlikely that the full complement of cedar ecosystem functions, such as peat accumulation, will develop in former agricultural fields unless appropriate hydrologic regimes are reestablished (Brown and Atkinson 2003). High planting density and elevated groundwater tables may be necessary to ensure successful cedar restoration (DeBerry, Belcher, et al. 2003). Sufficient root production coupled with low root decomposition rates should result in peat accumulation (Rodgers, Day, et al. 2004; Crawford, Day, et al. 2007).

Wildlife management goals are to maintain a black bear population that is viable and within the carrying capacity of the refuge (USFWS 2006) and to regulate the white-tail deer population with a managed hunting program (Culp 2000). The greatest threat to the black bear population is continued expansion of human development into bear habitat, causing habitat loss and fragmentation and an increase in bear-human encounters (Lane 2000). Most bear mortality is due to legal and illegal harvest, vehicle collisions, and intraspecific predation. Conservation easements and other incentive programs are needed to preserve habitat. Conservation can succeed by maintaining large, contiguous forest tracts and connecting corridors, restricting human access, and enhancing key habitats (pocosins, mesic islands, gum-cypress swamps) (Hellgren and Vaughn 2000). Maintenance and enhancement of preferred habitats would benefit bears by providing a variety of foods throughout the year (Hellgren, Vaughn, et al. 1991).

Swainson's warbler is also a species identified for management and protection. It has been recommended that the water table be maintained at subsurface levels during the summer months in areas managed for this species (Graves 2001). Patterns of genetic variation suggest local and regional conservation programs may be necessary to maintain warbler genetic diversity (Winker and Graves 2008).

Exploited for Centuries: Can the Great Dismal Swamp Be Great Again?

The Dismal Swamp has been severely altered in many ways, especially hydrologically, over the past couple of centuries. Some of the most severe impacts are irreversible; thus, it is highly unlikely the Dismal Swamp will ever appear or function as it did before the arrival of Europeans. The altered hydrology cannot be completely restored, and the water regime is the principal determinant of swamp structure and function. Can the swamp be restored to a more functional state than currently exists? Time will tell, but the present management efforts appear to offer a path toward successful recovery to a more natural state.

Okefenokee Swamp

At almost 200,000 ha, the Okefenokee Swamp in southeastern Georgia and northeastern Florida (online appendix 16.B) is among the largest freshwater wetlands in North America. The name is of Native American origin, meaning "land of trembling earth," presumably due to the peat deposits and floating islands. The area is managed by the USFWS as a National Wildlife Refuge, much of it designated as wilderness. Although it was historically impacted by extensive logging (Izlar 1984), human access to the Okefenokee is now limited to recreational uses along rivers, canals, and canoe trails.

Geology, Hydrology, and Biogeochemistry

GEOLOGY AND HYDROLOGY

In terms of geo-hydrology, the Okefenokee could be viewed as an enormous depressional wetland. It was created in the Pleistocene behind "Trail Ridge," a long sand rim of marine origin along the eastern side. Water budgets indicate inputs are dominated by direct precipitation (70–90%), with some inflow from small tributary creeks and off uplands (Rykiel 1984; Brook and Hyatt 1985). Surficial discharge of groundwater into the Okefenokee from the deep (Floridan) aquifer is minimal. Water outputs, again as in a depression wetland, are dominated by evapotranspiration (~85%). Remaining water losses are from stream flow out the Suwannee and St. Mary's rivers to the south, with seepage into groundwater being negligible (< 3%). Relative hydrologic inputs and outputs vary greatly with patterns of precipitation (Brook and Hyatt 1985).

Water budgets also vary across the Okefenokee (Loftin, Rasberry, et al. 2000). The eastern half is influenced primarily by inputs of direct precipitation and outputs via evapotranspiration; Trail Ridge limits flows off uplands. The western half of the Okefenokee is strongly influenced by inflows from tributary streams and uplands to the west and outflows via the Suwannee River. Western areas take on characteristics of floodplain wetlands, with water level fluctuations being pronounced.

The hydrology of the Okefenokee is minimally affected by humans. Early efforts to drain it failed (Izlar 1984). Networks of canals (Suwannee and Kingfisher canals) and managed canoe trails exist in some areas, but they do not drain wetland. In 1960 a long earthen dam, the Suwannee River Sill, was constructed where the Suwannee River exits, designed to keep water levels higher and reduce threats of wildfire. However, the Sill's influence was spatially limited (Loftin, Kitchens, et al. 2001), and its gates are now kept open to maintain natural hydrology and allow fish migration.

BIOGEOCHEMISTRY

Being primarily precipitation based, the Okefenokee shares some chemical characteristics with ombrotrophic bogs. Water and sediment pH is acidic (3.5–4.0) (Blood 1980). Mineral concentrations (Ca, Mg, Na, K, Cl) are low, even lower than in many bogs (Rykiel 1984). Dissolved nutrient concentrations (N, P) are also low (Schlesinger 1978a). However, because the overall system is largely closed, nutrients are intensively recycled by biota (Hopkinson 1992). Many nutrients are lost to peat deposition (Schlesinger 1978a). For plants, N limitation is most

FIG. 16.4. A. Marsh and tree island habitat in Chesser Prairie, Okefenokee Swamp. B. Florida sandhill cranes. (A: Photo by M. Galatowitsch, University of Georgia; B: photo by S. Gentry, USFWS.)

important during drought, while P limitation is greatest during high water (Gerritsen and Greening 1989).

Levels of dissolved carbon (C), however, are quite high (46–58 mg C l⁻¹) (Bano, Moran, et al. 1997) due to organic acids from plant decomposition. Humic compounds give the water a characteristic tea-colored appearance. As in ombrotrophic bogs, extensive deposits of peat (1.0–4.5 m thick), derived mostly from remnant water lily or cypress debris, have developed across the Okefenokee (Cohen, Andrejko, et al. 1984), providing a significant sink for C.

Epiphytic bacterial production in the Okefenokee is typical for aquatic systems (Moran and Hodson 1992). However, high levels of dissolved C contribute to particularly high bacterial production in the water (Murray and Hodson 1985; Moran and Hodson 1992). When dissolved humic substances are exposed to intense sunlight, they break down into more labile components, serving as a nutrient source for bacteria (Bano, Moran, et al. 1998).

Plant Communities

Major wetland plant communities of the Okefenokee include (1) forested swamp, (2) scrub-shrub thickets, (3) emergent (grasses, sedges) marsh, and (4) water lily *(Nymphaea, Nuphar)* beds (McCaffrey and Hamilton 1984) (Fig. 16.4a). Marshes and beds of water lily are locally called prairies. Plant species exhibit a diversity of seed-bank responses to water level variation. Some species germinate in newly exposed dry soil (rushes, sedges), others germinate only underwater (water lily), and others germinate across a diversity of conditions (Gerritsen and Greening 1989). Distinct floras exist in long-inundation areas (floating and submersed plants) versus short-inundation areas (emergent and woody plants, *Sphagnum* moss) (Greening and Gerritsen 1987).

Although most attention focuses on forested or prairie habitats, scrub-shrub is most expansive (McCaffrey and Hamilton 1984). Even in forests, scrub-shrub understory is pervasive (Schlesinger 1978b). The shrubs, consisting of both deciduous and evergreen species, are very productive (>100 g m⁻² yr⁻¹) (Schlesinger 1978b). Specific leaf mass, rather than leaf longevity, explains most of the variation in photosynthetic rates and nutrient-use efficiency among shrubs (DeLucia and Schlesinger 1995).

Bald cypress and pond cypress *(Taxodium ascendens)* are the dominant overstory trees in wetland forests, and compose much of the aboveground plant biomass (Schlesinger 1978a). Most biomass is in boles (96%), with little in foliage (0.8%). Stem densities can be high (> 1,500 stems ha⁻¹), but net primary production of cypress compared to other trees is relatively low (692 g m⁻² yr⁻¹).

Small tree islands are common across the Okefenokee (Fig. 16.4a), and are believed to arise when peat masses (called batteries) break loose from the substrate, providing habitat for nonaquatic plants. This process of "terrestrialization" is more rapid than peat accumulation. Duever and Riopelle (1983) and Glasser (1985) suggested that disturbance from fire and relative light and flood tolerances of plants affect the sequence of plant succession on islands. Species requiring full sunlight and tolerant of root flooding dominate early seral stages; shade-tolerant and more xeric species dominate late stages. Tree ring analyses indicate islands can persist for > 500 years (Duever and Riopelle 1983).

Animal Communities

Kratzer and Batzer (2007) identified 103 aquatic macroinvertebrate taxa across the Okefenokee. This fauna is more similar to that of local depressional wetlands (Carolina bays) than that of other large complexes (Everglades), more evidence of a functional similarity to depressional wetlands. Chironomid midge larvae by themselves composed 66% of abundance. Mollusks are rare, probably because acid waters lack calcium for shell formation. Although plants exist in patchy mosaics, the aquatic macroinvertebrate fauna is more homogenous, comprised of habitat generalists (Kratzer and Batzer 2007; Beganyi and Batzer 2011). Most taxa lack seasonality, although microcrustaceans decline in winter from cool temperatures, and in summer from fish predation (Schoenberg 1988).

Unlike many blackwater systems, fish productivity in the Okefenokee Swamp is high (Freeman and Freeman 1985). Most productivity is from diminutive species with rapid turnover rates, such as killifish *(Fundulus* spp.), pygmy sunfish *(Elassoma* spp.), and mosquitofish *(Gambusia* spp.). These small fishes feed primarily on midge larvae and microcrustaceans (Freeman and Freeman 1985; Oliver 1991). Larger fishes (sunfishes, *Lepomis* spp.; pickerels, *Esox* spp.; bowfin, *Amia calva*) primarily occur in the deeper river channels, lakes, and canals. A small population of largemouth bass *(Micropterus salmoides)* persists in the Double Lakes area. While fish typically exclude most predatory invertebrates (Wellborn, Skelly, et al. 1996), they readily coexist in the Okefenokee, probably because both groups are of similar size. Interestingly, B. Freeman (unpublished data) observed large dragonfly nymphs frequently eating small fish.

A diversity of wetland and forest birds use the Okefenokee (Meyers and Odum 1991). Several birds of conservation concern occur, including red-cockaded woodpeckers and various neotropical migrants. The most noteworthy bird is the Florida sandhill crane (*Grus canadensis pratensis;* Fig. 16.4b), a nonmigratory subspecies with a local population of around 400 birds (Bennett 1989). Migratory cranes *(G. c. tabida)* also winter in the area (Bennett and Bennett 1989). Cranes favor prairie habitats in the eastern portion of the Okefenokee, with Grand Prairie being especially important. Because of low dissolved nutrients, enrichment of bird guano from colonial bird rookeries is important to the functioning of aquatic ecosystems (Oliver and Legovic 1988; Oliver and Schoenberg 1989).

The Okefenokee supports a large population of alligators (*Alligator mississippiensis;* around 1,000 individuals), and the population is now relatively stable (R. H. Hunt unpublished data). Hunt and Ogden (1991) found that bear predation is a major mortality factor for eggs. When densities are concentrated during droughts, cannibalism of large individuals on small ones is common. Studies of alligators and other reptiles from the Okefenokee are remarkably limited, and this is a major research need.

The Okefenokee supports one of the largest remaining populations of Florida black bears *(U. americanus floridanus)* in the U.S. (~70 individuals; Dobey, Masters, et al. 2005). Hunting is a major mortality factor, and current harvest rates are at the maximum for a sustainable population. The viable bear population in the Okefenokee was a factor in the USFWS deciding against listing the subspecies as threatened (Dobey, Masters, et al. 2005). Based on habitat quality considerations, the Okefenokee may be a desirable location for reintroducing endangered Florida panther *(Puma concolor)* (Thatcher, van Manen, et al. 2006).

Key Ecological Controls

Fire, integrated with drought, is probably the most important factor controlling the structure of Okefenokee plant communities (Schlesinger 1978a; Glasser 1985). Fires occur sporadically, with especially large fires occurring every few decades (Cypert, 1961; Yin 1993). In 1954–55 and 2007, fires burned > 75% of the Okefenokee. Prairies are believed to be maintained by fire, and would otherwise convert to woody vegetation. Some of the deeper "lakes" scattered across the Okefenokee may have developed in hotspots that burned deep into the peat layer. As mentioned, plant succession is, in part, fire regulated. However, a wildfire in 2007 did not markedly affect composition of aquatic invertebrate communities (Beganyi and Batzer 2011).

Conservation Concerns

The Okefenokee is less imperiled than many wetland complexes because hydrologic regimes remain largely unaltered, the surrounding uplands are minimally developed, and virtually the entire habitat is controlled by the USFWS as a refuge and wilderness area. Most conservation concerns focus on factors that operate at regional or global scales.

Climate change is of special concern because Okefeno-

kee wetlands are controlled hydrologically by precipitation and evapotranspiration, and ecologically by fire. Changes in temperature and/or rainfall could alter water depths and flood duration, and in turn biota, especially if conditions dry. With drying, wildfire could become more frequent and more intense, further altering community structure.

Heavy metals are also a concern. Frequent anoxic, high-temperature conditions in sediments are conducive to mercury methylation, the form most toxic and most likely to bioaccumulate. Mercury levels in macroinvertebrates are unusually high (George and Batzer 2008), but levels in alligators are typical for the Southeast (Jagoe, Arnold-Hill, et al. 1998). Human consumption advisories exist for several fish. After the 2007 wildfire, however, mercury levels in macroinvertebrates did not increase (Beganyi and Batzer 2011). Patterns of both mercury and lead across the Okefenokee are consistent with aerial deposition (Jackson, Winger, et al. 2004; George and Batzer 2008).

The human population around the Okefenokee is growing rapidly, and upland development near the wetlands may pose a threat. Trail Ridge, on the Okefenokee's east side, has valuable deposits of titanium oxide; plans were made to mine the resource but later abandoned over concerns of potential negative impacts to the Okefenokee.

Chickasawhatchee Swamp

Chickasawhatchee Swamp is a large wetland complex in southwest Georgia (Dougherty, Baker, and Calhoun counties) (online appendix 16.C). Approximately 7,967 ha of this swamp system comprises the Chickasawhatchee Wildlife Management Area (WMA; GA WRD 2008). In the 19th century into the early 20th century, upland areas of the Chickasawhatchee were converted into small subsistence farms and plantations, mostly of cotton and pecans (GA WRD 2008). In the mid 20th century, the area was owned by the Grand Cypress Lumber Company and used mostly for livestock and timber production, with much of the remaining old-growth cypress logged (GA WRD 2008). In 1958, St. Joe Timber Company purchased approximately 12,950 ha of the Chickasawhatchee Swamp and associated uplands. It converted much of the remnant upland and bottomland forests and remaining agricultural fields and pastureland to pine plantations.

In 1965, portions of Chickasawhatchee were leased into the Georgia WMA system. In 2000, the Nature Conservancy (TNC), Georgia Conservancy, Doris Duke Foundation, Woodruff Foundation, State of Georgia, and others purchased 5,750 ha of the St. Joe holdings, and ownership was transferred to Georgia. In December 2001, TNC and the USFWS purchased the 2,217-ha Kiokee Creek Tract from private landowners, and the WMA now comprises 7,967 ha (GA WRD 2008).

Geology and Hydrology

The swamp is located in the Dougherty Plain of the Coastal Plain physiographic province. Topography is relatively flat, with gentle slopes interspersed with wetlands along creek drainages. Elevations range from 52 to 76 m above sea level, with the highest elevations occurring on the northwestern portion of the WMA (GA WRD 2008). Depressions formed by the subsidence of the underlying Ocala Limestone form the low-lying wetlands associated with the Chickasawhatchee (Golladay and Battle 2002). These lowlands provide a direct connection between the Chickasawhatchee Swamp and the Upper Floridan aquifer, making the Chickasawhatchee hydrologically distinct from most deepwater swamps. With this connection, rapid exchange of water takes place as aquifer recharge and as natural discharge to area streams through numerous springs and seeps (Clayton and Hicks 2003).

Three major creeks, the Chickasawhatchee, Spring, and Kiokee, converge in Chickasawhatchee Swamp to form Chickasawhatchee Creek (Clayton and Hicks 2003). After leaving the swamp, Chickasawhatchee Creek flows into Ichawaynochaway Creek, a major tributary of the lower Flint River. During much of the year, the Upper Floridan aquifer discharges water into Spring Creek and contributes substantially to downstream flows even under drought conditions (Golladay and Battle 2002).

Chemically, water discharging from the swamp varies with regional hydrologic conditions (Golladay and Battle 2002). Generally, suspended sediment, DOC, and NH_4-N have highest concentrations during "wet" or "flooded" conditions, reflecting connection between surface flows and floodplain soils. During low or baseflow conditions, water quality reflects aquifer chemistry, having high inorganic carbon concentration from dissolved carbonates and low DOC concentration.

Plant Communities

Chickasawhatchee WMA's current plant communities were largely shaped by the interaction of historical land use, soil conditions, hydrology, and other management activities (e.g., fire history). Land cover of the Chickasawhatchee includes eight types: upland pine plantation (3,072 ha), mixed pine hardwood (271 ha), upland hardwood (117 ha), herbaceous wetlands (101 ha), bottomland hardwood (2,447 ha), gum-cypress swamp (1,868 ha), open land (80 ha), and roads (98 ha) (GA WRD 2008; online appendix 16.C). Upland pine plantation consists of planted pines. Mixed pine hardwood comprises natural stands, cutover hardwood stands with significant pine regeneration, and planted pine stands with a significant hardwood component. Upland hardwood stands are dominated by hardwood species associated with more xeric sites. Herbaceous wetlands include all areas consisting of depressional, seasonally flooded, nonforested wetlands. Forested wetlands are differentiated into bottomland hardwood and gum-cypress swamp communities. Open land is wildlife openings, powerline areas, and miscellaneous nonforested or wetland areas. Roads consist of all access roads and trails located in or adjacent to the swamp (GA WRD 2008).

HERBACEOUS WETLANDS

These are seasonally inundated depressional wetlands dominated by herbaceous groundcover with few trees or shrubs present, representing about 1.3% of the total area. Hydrology of these wetlands shows considerable annual variation depending upon regional weather patterns, and these sites exhibit high biological diversity (Kirkman, Golladay, et al. 1999). A majority are small, averaging 2.8 ha in size, and only four herbaceous wetlands exceed 8.1 ha (GA WRD 2008). Tree species include cypress *(Taxodium* spp.), blackgum *(Nyssa sylvatica),* persimmon *(Diospyros virginiana),* and various oaks. Buttonbush *(Cephalanthus occidentalis)* is the dominant shrub while herbaceous species include rushes *(Juncus* spp.), sedges *(Carex* spp.), and grasses (GA WRD 2008).

FIG. 16.5. The Chickasawhatchee Swamp near 13 bridges during early-spring (March 2003) inundation. This is looking upstream at the main channel of Chickasawhatchee Creek as it appears in much of the swamp. The surrounding forest is dominated by second-growth swamp tupelo and bald cypress. Photo by Stephen Golladay.

BOTTOMLAND HARDWOODS

Bottomland hardwood forests compose 30.5% of the area. Forest composition generally consists of second- and possibly third-growth hardwood stands (GA WRD 2008). Several distinct subcategories of bottomland hardwood exist, including oak-gum-dominated wetlands, bottomland forests, floodplain forests, and regenerating hardwoods.

Oak-gum wetlands are dominated by swamp tupelo *(Nyssa biflora)* and often include a mixture of several oaks, sweetgum, persimmon, red maple, hickory *(Carya* spp.), and scattered pines. Understory includes grape *(Vitus* spp.), greenbrier, and palmetto *(Sabal* sp.) (GA WRD 2008). Oak-gum stands occur at higher elevation than gum-cypress swamp forest.

Floodplain forests occur on drier soils within the floodplain and are dominated by hardwoods such as laurel oak *(Quercus laurifolia),* overcup oak *(Q. lyrata),* swamp chestnut oak *(Q. michauxii),* and water hickory *(Carya aquatica),* with some willow oak *(Q. phellos),* sweetgum, sugarberry *(Celtis laevigata),* sweetbay *(Magnolia virginiana),* hawthorn *(Crataegus* sp.), red maple, and tulip poplar *(Liriodendron tulipifera).* Understory vegetation varies considerably but typically includes palmetto and wild iris *(Iris virginica)* (GA DNR 2008).

Bottomland forests occur on low-lying flatlands that border streams with distinct banks. This forest type is dominated by water oak *(Quercus nigra),* live oak *(Q. virginiana),* red maple, sweetgum, loblolly pine *(Pinus taeda),* spruce pine *(P. glabra),* southern magnolia *(Magnolia grandiflora),* blackgum, and beech *(Fagus grandifolia).* These forests are typically inundated only during floods.

GUM-CYPRESS SWAMP

Composing 22.9% of the Chickasawhatchee Swamp, this forest is dominated by buttressed hydrophytic trees such as swamp tupelo and bald cypress (Fig. 16.5). Found along creek bottoms, it can be flooded for much of the year, with aerobic water on sites located along stream channels or anaerobic water where no distinct stream channel exists. Secondary overstory trees include overcup oak, sweetgum, tulip poplar, persimmon, hickory, red

TABLE 16.3

Rare and listed species of Chickasawhatchee Swamp

"Present" indicates that the species are currently present in the swamp. "Suitable habitat" indicates species that have been historically present and/or reported from nearby areas with similar habitat.

	Common name	Scientific name	Federal status[a]	State status[a]
MAMMALS				
Present	None			
Suitable habitat	Rafinesque's big-eared bat	*Corynorhinus rafinesquii*	—	R
	Gray myotis	*Myotis grisescens*	E	E
BIRDS				
Present	Bachman's sparrow	*Aimophilia aestivalis*	—	R
	Bald eagle	*Haliaeetus leucocephalus*	—	T
	Wood stork	*Mycteria americana*	E	E
Suitable habitat	Red-cockaded woodpecker	*Picoides borealis*	E	E
REPTILES AND AMPHIBIANS				
Present	Spotted turtle	*Clemmys guttata*	—	R
	Gopher tortoise	*Gopherus polyphemus*	T	T
	Alligator snapping turtle	*Macroclemys temminckii*	—	T
Suitable habitat	Flatwoods salamander	*Ambystoma cingulatum*	T	T
	Eastern indigo snake	*Drymarchon corias couperi*	T	T
	Barbour's map turtle	*Graptemys barbouri*	—	T
	Striped newt	*Notophthalmus perstriatus*	—	T
	Gopher frog	*Rana capito*	—	T
FISHES				
Present	None			
Suitable habitat	Alabama shad	*Alosa alabamae*	—	T
	Spotted bullhead	*Ameiurus serracanthus*	—	T
	Blue-stripe shiner	*Cyprinella caerulea*	T	R
	Goldstrip darter	*Etheostoma parvipinne*	—	R
INVERTEBRATES				
Present	Shiny-rayed pocketbook	*Hamotia subangulata*	E	E
	Oval pigtoe	*Pleurobema pyriforme*	E	E
	Gulf moccasinshell			
Suitable habitat	Delicate spike	*Elliptio arctata*	—	E

maple, spruce pine, southern magnolia, sweetbay, beech, American elm *(Ulmus americana),* sugarberry, and swamp dogwood *(Cornus foemina).* Common understory species include buttonbush, Virginia willow *(Itea virginica),* white titi *(Cyrilla racemiflora),* and wax myrtle *(Morella cerifera)* (GA DNR 2008).

Fauna of Interest

Chickasawhatchee Swamp provides habitat to a variety of nongame species, including several species that are state or fed- erally listed as rare, threatened, or endangered (RTE). Management priorities for the swamp and adjacent areas include control of undesirable hardwoods in pine stands adjacent to gopher tortoise *(Gopherus polyphemus)* habitat and incorporation of growing-season burns into prescribed burning schedules to promote native understory vegetation. Restoration of contiguous blocks of longleaf pine and enhancement or restoration of native groundcover will help to provide sufficient habitat to support viable populations of RTE or special-concern species that depend upon pine savannas or early successional habitat (GA WRD 2008).

TABLE 16.3 *(continued)*

	Common name	Scientific name	Federal status[a]	State status[a]
PLANTS				
Present	Variable-leaf plantain	*Arnoglossum diversifolium*	—	T
	Swamp buckthorn	*Sideroxylon thornei*	—	R
Suitable habitat	Hirst witch grass	*Dichanthelium hirstii*	C	—
	Harper's fimbristylis	*Fimbristylis perpusilla*	—	E
	Harper's yellow-eyed grass	*Xyris scabrifolia*	—	E
	Corkwood	*Leitneria floridana*	—	T
	Pondberry	*Lindera melissifolia*	E	E
	Curtiss loosestrife	*Lythrum curtissii*	—	T
	Canby's dropwort	*Oxypolis canbyi*	E	E
	White pitcherplant	*Sarracenia leucophylla*	—	E
	American chaffseed	*Schwalbea americana*	E	E
	Relic trillium	*Trillium reliquum*	E	E

[a] R = rare, T = threatened, E = endangered, C = candidate for listing, — = not listed.

Other critical habitats for nongame species, particularly birds, include bottomland forest and high-quality freshwater wetlands. These habitats provide important foraging and breeding habitat for many wading birds, including snowy egret *(Egretta thula),* little blue heron *(E. caerulea),* and white ibis *(Eudocimus albus)* (GA WRD 2008). A large rookery, known as Bird Roost Pond, is located in the southern portion of the swamp. Large numbers of wading birds, including numerous species of egrets and herons, have been documented using this area. Solitary sandpipers *(Tringa solitaria)* and spotted sandpipers *(Actitus macularia)* likely use the extensive freshwater wetlands found here. Depending on water levels, the site could provide important fall stopover habitat for stilt sandpipers *(Micropalama himantopus).*

The forested wetlands also are critical stopover areas for many species of Neotropical migratory birds, such as cerulean *(Dendroica cerulea)* and worm-eating warblers *(Helmitheros vermivorus).* Substantial populations of forest interior songbirds—Swainson's warblers, hooded warblers *(Wilsonia citrina),* Kentucky warblers *(Oporornis formosus),* yellow-billed cuckoo *(Coccyzus americanus),* northern parula *(Parula americana)*—have been observed in the swamp and surrounding forest during the breeding season (GA WRD 2008). Swallow-tailed kites *(Elanoides forficatus)* have not been documented as breeding in the swamp, but suitable nesting habitat is available.

torical records, and their presence in nearby areas (Table 16.3). Protection of freshwater wetlands and the insurance of water quality are essential in providing foraging habitats for wood storks and bald eagles, and breeding and wintering habitats for the listed freshwater mussels, blue-stripe shiner, and Barbour's map turtle. Frequently burned, mature pine uplands with little or no soil disturbance and seasonally flooded depressional wetlands are ideal for flatwoods salamander, striped newt, and gopher frog (GA WRD 2008). The site supports a significant breeding density of Bachman's sparrow, well in excess of 25 breeding pairs. Large areas of freshwater wetlands provide foraging habitat for the listed bat species. Freshwater mussel communities of the Flint River basin are among the richest in the region, and the Chickasawhatchee Swamp offers high mussel conservation potential because of the long-term protection of the land adjacent to important streams (Golladay, Gagnon, et al. 2004). Chickasawhatchee Creek has been proposed as a site for intensive hydrologic study and possible reintroduction of endangered mussel species (Golladay and Muenz 2006). Historically, eastern indigo snakes were found in the area, but none have been observed recently (GA WRD 2008).

Two state-listed plant species occur in the swamp (swamp buckthorn and variable-leaf plantain). Suitable habitat is present that could support an additional 10 state- and/or federally listed plant species (GA WRD 2008).

Conservation Concerns

LISTED SPECIES

Federally or state-listed animal species found in the Chickasawhatchee Swamp (see Table 16.3 for all species names) include the wood stork, bald eagle, Bachman's sparrow, and three native freshwater mussels species (Bivalvia, Unionidae) (GA WRD 2008; Golladay and Muenz 2006) (Table 16.3). A number of listed and candidate animal species could be present or were present historically based on habitat suitability, his-

INVASIVE EXOTIC SPECIES

Known invasive plant species found in Chickasawhatchee Swamp include Chinese privet *(Ligustrum sinense),* chinaberry *(Melia azedarach),* Japanese honeysuckle *(Lonicera japonica),* bamboo *(Phyllostachys* sp.), kudzu *(Pueraria montana),* bicolor lespedeza *(Lespedeza bicolor),* and Japanese climbing fern *(Lygodium japonicum)* (GA WRD 2008). Among these, Chinese privet and chinaberry are the most common. These species are associated with disturbed areas in bottomland hardwoods (Chinese privet) and upland pines, old logging decks, and roadways (chinaberry). Japanese climbing fern can be found along roadways in bottomland hardwoods, while bicolor lespedeza is confined to areas where it was planted along the main powerline rights-of-way. Imported fire ants (Solenopsis invicta) and feral hogs (Sus scrofa) are the most significant invasive animal species found (GA WRD 2008).

References

Atkinson RB, DeBerry JW, et al. 2003. Water tables in Atlantic white cedar swamps: implications for restoration. In *Atlantic white cedar restoration ecology and management: proceedings of a symposium,* Atkinson RB, Belcher RT, et al., editors. May 31–Jun. 2, 2000. Newport News, VA: Christopher Newport Univ., pp. 137–50.

Bano N, Moran MA, Hodson RE. 1997. Bacterial utilization of dissolved humic substances from a freshwater swamp. *Aquat. Microb. Ecol.* 12:233–38.

Bano N, Moran MA, Hodson RE. 1998. Photochemical formation of labile organic matter from two components of dissolved organic carbon in a freshwater wetland. *Aquat. Microb. Ecol.* 16:95–102.

Beganyi SR, Batzer DP. 2011. Wildfire induced changes in aquatic invertebrate communities and mercury bioaccumulation in the Okefenokee Swamp. *Hydrobiologia.* 669:237–247.

Bennett AJ. 1989. Population size and distribution of Florida sandhill cranes in the Okefenokee Swamp, Georgia. *J. Field Ornith.* 60:60–67.

Bennett AJ, Bennett LA. 1989. Wintering population of greater sandhill cranes in the Okefenokee Swamp, Georgia. *Wilson Bull.* 101:87–93.

Blood ER. 1980. Surface water hydrology and biogeochemistry of the Okefenokee Swamp watershed. Ph.D. diss., Univ. Georgia, Athens.

Brook GA, Hyatt RA. 1985. A hydrological budget for the Okefenokee Swamp watershed, 1981–82. *Phys. Geogr.* 6:127–41.

Brown DA, Atkinson RB. 2003. Influence of environmental gradients on Atlantic white cedar wetlands in southeastern Virginia. In *Atlantic white cedar restoration ecology and management: proceedings of a symposium,* Atkinson RB, Belcher RT, et al., editors. May 31–Jun. 2, 2000. Newport News, VA: Christopher Newport Univ., pp. 151–63.

Carter V, Gammon PT, Garrett MK. 1994. Ecotone dynamics and boundary determination in the Great Dismal Swamp. *Ecol. Appl.* 4:189–203.

Clayton B, Hicks DW. 2003. Water monitoring network in the Chickasawhatchee Swamp, southwest Georgia. In *Proc. 2003 Georgia Water Resour. Conf.,* Hatcher KJ, editor. Athens: Inst. Ecol., Univ. Ga., pp. 864–66.

Cohen AD, Andrejko MJ, et al. 1984. Peat deposits of the Okefenokee Swamp. In *The Okefenokee Swamp: its natural history, geology, and geochemistry,* Cohen AD, Casagrande DJ, et al., editors. Los Alamos, NM: Wetland Surveys, pp. 493–553.

Crawford ER, Day FP, Atkinson RB. 2007. The influence of environment and substrate quality on root decomposition in naturally regenerating and restored Atlantic white cedar wetlands. *Wetlands* 27:1–11.

Culp LA. 2000. Refuges and ecosystem protection. In *The natural history of the Great Dismal Swamp,* Rose R, editor. Madison, WI: Omni Press, pp. 261–66.

Cypert E. 1961. The effects of fires in the Okefenokee Swamp in 1954 and 1955. *Am. Midl. Nat.* 66:485–503.

Dabel CV, Day FP. 1977. Structural comparisons of four plant communities in the Great Dismal Swamp, Virginia. *Bull. Torrey Botan. Club* 104:352–60.

Day FP. 1982. Litter decomposition rates in the seasonally flooded Great Dismal Swamp. *Ecology* 63:670–78.

Day FP, Megonigal JP. 1993. The relationship between a variable hydroperiod, production allocation, and belowground organic turnover in forested wetlands. *Wetlands* 13:115–21.

Day FP, Megonigal JP. 2000. Plant organic matter dynamics in the Dismal Swamp. In *The natural history of the Great Dismal Swamp,* Rose R, editor. Madison, WI: Omni Press, pp. 51–58.

Day FP, West SK, Tupacz EG. 1988. The influence of groundwater dynamics in a periodically flooded ecosystem, the Great Dismal Swamp. *Wetlands* 8:1–13.

DeBerry JW, Belcher RT, et al. 2003. Comparison of aboveground structure of four Atlantic white cedar swamps. In *Atlantic white cedar restoration ecology and management: proceedings of a symposium,* Atkinson RB, Belcher RT, et al., editors. May 31–Jun. 2, 2000. Newport News, VA: Christopher Newport Univ., pp. 67–80.

DeLucia EH, Schlesinger WH. 1995. Photosynthetic rates and nutrient-use efficiency among evergreen and deciduous shrubs in Okefenokee Swamp. *Int. J. Plant Sci.* 156:19–28.

Dobey S, Masters DV, et al. 2005. Ecology of Florida black bears in the Okefenokee-Osceola ecosystem. *Wildl. Monogr.* 158:1–41.

Duever MJ, Riopelle LA. 1983. Successional sequences and rate on tree islands in the Okefenokee Swamp. *Am. Midl Nat.* 110:186–93.

Freeman BJ, Freeman MC. 1985. Production of fishes in a subtropical blackwater ecosystem: the Okefenokee Swamp. *Limnol. Oceanogr.* 30:686–92.

GA WRD (Georgia Wildlife Resources Division). 2008. *Fifty (50) Year Habitat Management Plan for Chickasawhatchee Wildlife Management Area.* Albany: GA WRD.

George BM, Batzer DP. 2008. Spatial and temporal variations of mercury levels in Okefenokee invertebrates: southeast Georgia. *Env. Pollu.* 152:484–90.

Gerritsen J, Greening HS. 1989. Marsh seed banks of the Okefenokee Swamp: effects of hydrologic regime and nutrients. *Ecology* 70:750–63.

Glasser JE. 1985. Successional trends on tree islands in the Okefenokee Swamp as determined by interspecific association analysis. *Am. Midl. Natur.* 113:287–93.

Golladay SW, Battle JM. 2002. Effects of flooding and drought on water quality in Gulf Coastal Plain streams in Georgia. *J. Env. Qual.* 31:1266–72.

Golladay SW, Muenz TK. 2006. *Survey and relocation study of unionids in Chickasawhatchee Creek and Elmodel Wildlife Management Areas, southwest Georgia.* Report GA DNR Nat. Heritage Prog., Social Circle.

Golladay SW, Gagnon P, et al. 2004. Response of freshwater mussel assemblages (Bivalvia: Unionidae) to a record drought in the Gulf Coastal Plain of southwestern Georgia. *J. N. Am. Benthol. Soc.* 23:494–506.

Graves GR. 2001. Factors governing the distribution of Swainson's warbler along a hydrologic gradient in Great Dismal Swamp. *Auk* 118:650–64.

Greening HS, Gerritsen J. 1987. Changes in macrophyte community structure following drought in the Okefenokee Swamp, Georgia, U.S.A. *Aquat. Bot.* 28:113–28.

Harrison JM, DeBerry JW, et al. 2003. Effects of water table on survival and growth of Atlantic white cedar in two young planted sites. In *Atlantic white cedar restoration ecology and management: proceedings of a symposium,* Atkinson RB, Belcher RT, et al., editors. May 31–Jun. 2, 2000. Newport News, VA: Christopher Newport Univ., pp. 181–96.

Harriss RC, Sebacher DI, Day FP. 1982. Methane flux in the Great Dismal Swamp. *Nature* 297:673–74.

Hellgren EC, Vaughn MR. 2000. Ecology, conservation, and management of black bears in the Great Dismal Swamp. In *The natural history of the Great Dismal Swamp,* Rose R, editor. Madison, WI: Omni Press, pp. 199–208.

Hellgren EC, Vaughn MR, Stauffer DF. 1991. Macrohabitat use by black bears in a southeastern wetland. *J. Wildl. Manage.* 55:442–48.

Hopkinson CS. 1992. A comparison of ecosystem dynamics in freshwater wetlands. *Estuaries* 15:549–62.

Hunt RH, Ogden JJ. 1991. Selected aspects of the nesting ecology of American alligators in the Okefenokee Swamp. *J. Herpetol.* 25:448–53.

Izlar RL. 1984. A history of Okefenokee logging operations. In *The Okefenokee Swamp: its natural history, geology, and geochemistry,* Cohen AD, Casagrande DJ, et al., editors. Los Alamos, NM: Wetland Surveys, pp. 5–17.

Jackson BP, Winger PV, Lasier PJ. 2004. Atmospheric lead deposition to Okefenokee Swamp, Georgia, USA. *Env. Pollu.* 130:445–51.

Jagoe CH, Arnold-Hill B, et al. 1998. Mercury in alligators (*Alliga-*

tor mississippiensis) in the southeastern United States. *Sci. Total Env.* 213:255–62.

Kirkman LK, Golladay SW, et al. 1999. Biodiversity in southeastern seasonally ponded, isolated wetlands: management and policy perspectives for research and conservation. *J. N. Am. Benthol. Soc.* 18:553–62.

Kratzer EB, Batzer DP. 2007. Spatial and temporal variation in aquatic macroinvertebrates in the Okefenokee Swamp, Georgia, USA. *Wetlands* 27:127–40.

Lane M. 2000. Conservation of black bear habitat on private land in the Great Dismal Swamp ecosystem. In *The natural history of the Great Dismal Swamp,* Rose R, editor. Madison, WI: Omni Press, pp. 209–26.

Levy GF. 1991. The vegetation of the Great Dismal Swamp: a review and overview. *Va. J. Sci.* 42:411–17.

Lichtler WF, Walker PN. 1979. Hydrology of the Dismal Swamp, Virginia–North Carolina. In *The Great Dismal Swamp,* Kirk PW, editor. Charlottesville: Univ. Va. Press, pp. 140–66.

Loftin CS, Kitchens WM, Ansay N. 2001. Development and application of a spatial hydrology model of Okefenokee Swamp, Georgia. *J. Am. Water Resour. Assoc.* 37:935–56.

Loftin CS, Rasberry W, Kitchens WM. 2000. Development of a grid-cell topographic surface for Okefenokee Swamp, Georgia. *Wetlands* 20:487–99.

McCaffrey CA, Hamilton DB. 1984. Vegetation mapping of the Okefenokee ecosystem. In *The Okefenokee Swamp: its natural history, geology, and geochemistry,* Cohen AD, Casagrande DJ, et al., editors. Los Alamos, NM: Wetland Surveys, pp. 201–11.

Megonigal JP, Day FP. 1988. Organic matter dynamics in four seasonally flooded forest communities of the Dismal Swamp. *Am. J. Bot.* 75:1334–43.

Meyers JM, Odum EP. 1991. Breeding bird populations of the Okefenokee Swamp in Georgia: baseline for assessing future avifaunal changes. *J. Field Ornithol.* 62:53–68.

Moran MA, Hodson RE. 1992. Contributions of three subsystems of a freshwater marsh to total bacterial secondary productivity. *Microb. Ecol.* 24:161–70.

Murray RE, Hodson RE. 1985. Annual cycle of bacterial secondary production in five aquatic habitats of the Okefenokee Swamp ecosystem. *Appl. Env. Microb.* 49:650–55.

Oliver JD. 1991. Consumption rates, evacuation rates, and diets of pygmy killifish, *Leptolucania-ommata,* and mosquitofish, *Gambusia-affinis* (Osteichthyes, Atheriniformes) in the Okefenokee Swamp. *Brimleyana* 17:89–103.

Oliver JD, Legovic T. 1988. Okefenokee marshland before, during and after nutrient enrichment by a bird rookery. *Ecol. Model.* 43:195–223.

Oliver JD, Schoenberg SA. 1989. Residual influence of macronutrient enrichment on the aquatic food web of an Okefenokee Swamp abandoned bird rookery. *Oikos* 55:175–82.

Powell SK, Day FP. 1991. Root production in four communities in the Great Dismal Swamp. *Am. J. Bot.* 78:288–97.

Rodgers HL, Day FP, Atkinson R. 2004. Root dynamics in restored and naturally regenerated Atlantic white cedar wetlands. *Restor. Ecol.* 16:401–11.

Rose R. 2000. *The natural history of the Great Dismal Swamp.* Madison, WI: Omni Press.

Rose RK. 1981. *Synaptomys* not extinct in the Dismal Swamp. *J. Mammal.* 62:844–45.

Rykiel EJ Jr. 1984. General hydrology and mineral budgets for Okefenokee Swamp. In *The Okefenokee Swamp: its natural history, geology, and geochemistry,* Cohen AD, Casagrande DJ, et al., editors. Los Alamos, NM: Wetland Surveys, pp. 212–28.

Schlesinger WM. 1978a. Community structure, dynamics and nutrient cycling in the Okefenokee cypress swamp-forest. *Ecol. Monogr.* 48:43–65.

Schlesinger WM. 1978b. On the relative dominance of shrubs in Okefenokee Swamp. *Am. Natur.* 112:949–54.

Schoenberg SA. 1988. Microcrustacean community structure and biomass in marsh and lake habitats of the Okefenokee Swamp: seasonal dynamics and responses to resource manipulations. *Holarct. Ecol.* 11:8–18.

Shacochis KM, DeBerry JW, et al. 2000. The effects of hydrology on *Chamaecyparis thyoides* growth in wetland restoration efforts. *Va. J. Sci.* 51:114.

Stewart PC. 1979. Man and the swamp: the historical dimension. In *The Great Dismal Swamp,* Kirk PW, editor. Charlottesville: Univ. Va. Press, pp. 57–73.

Thatcher CA, van Manen FT, Clark JD. 2006. Identifying suitable sites for Florida panther reintroduction. *J. Wildl. Manage.* 70:752–63.

Tupacz EG, Day FP. 1990. Decomposition of roots in a seasonally flooded swamp ecosystem. *Aquat. Bot.* 37:199–214.

USFWS (US Fish and Wildlife Service). 2006. *Great Dismal Swamp Nat. Wildl. Refuge and Nansemond Nat. Wildl. Refuge final comprehensive conserv. plan.* www.fws.gov/northeast/greatdismalswamp/CCP%20final%20announcement8-17-06.htm.

Webster WD. 2000. Coastal freshwater swamps as mammal refugia: the role of the Great Dismal Swamp. In *The natural history of the Great Dismal Swamp,* Rose R, editor. Madison, WI: Omni Press, pp. 227–34.

Wellborn GA, Skelly DK, Werner EE. 1996. Mechanisms creating community structure across a freshwater habitat gradient. *Annu. Rev. Ecol. System.* 27:337–64.

Whitehead DR. 1972. Developmental and environmental history of the Dismal Swamp. *Ecol. Monogr.* 42:301–15.

Winker K, Graves GR. 2008. Genetic structure of breeding and wintering populations of Swainson's warbler. *Wilson J. Ornithol.* 120:433–45.

Yin ZY. 1993. Fire regime of the Okefenokee Swamp and its relation to hydrological and climatic conditions. *Int. J. Wildl. Fire* 3:229–40.

CHAPTER 17

The Florida Everglades

EVELYN E. GAISER, JOEL C. TREXLER, and PAUL R. WETZEL

The gently sloping margins of landmasses in the Caribbean Sea harbor expansive wetlands of great distinction. Inundated by the sea for several millennia, these shallow, warm coastal waters sustained a rich, abundant sea life that flourished and died to eventually form a vast, flat carbonate platform. Today, freshwater meanders over, under, and through this very porous limestone, making its way toward the sea through a mosaic of wet prairies, sloughs, forested swamps, and hammocks. Subtle variation in topography causes them to be highly vulnerable to changes in freshwater supply and the rise and fall of the sea. Further, the subtropical seasonality and mosaic of carbonates encourage distinctive biological communities and ecological functions. Although their distribution is poorly documented, these karstic freshwater wetlands occur on the margins of landmasses throughout the Caribbean Sea (Kueny and Day 1998), but are well represented by the "River of Grass" (Douglas 1947), the Florida Everglades.

Portrayed as a watery Eden by early explorers (in Blake 1980), the freshwater marshlands of the Everglades once covered more than 15,000 km^2 of South Florida in an elongated basin spanning 175 km, representing by far the largest karstic wetland in the world (Fig. 17.1a). Humans have been an important part of the Everglades landscape for centuries (Ogden 2011) but their impact on the landscape accelerated in the early 1900s, when the quest for rich soils for farming, swamp timber, and the subtropical, coastal lifestyle met with the manufacture of machinery to efficiently drain, harvest, build, and develop (Hollander 2008). South Florida's landscape was gradually converted from one where the types and distribution of ecological communities and people were controlled largely by geology and climate to one controlled by engineering (Fig. 17.1b). Today, freshwater is removed from the surface and aquifer to drain the land and control flooding and then redistributed for agricultural and urban uses; most of the rest is sent directly to the sea through canals, with only a small residual, often of compromised quality, left for the remaining wilderness, which requires clean water to persist (Sklar, McVoy, et al. 2001). The extent to which the Everglades has been damaged by unmitigated development was recognized by the federal government in the 1980s and resulted in a multibillion-dollar restoration effort, authorized in 2000, to rehabilitate water flow, timing, and quality in the Everglades (Comprehen-

sive Everglades Restoration Plan [CERP]) (RECOVER 2010) (Fig. 17.2). However, for many reasons, the restorative process has been painstakingly slow, and all the more frustrating as past mistakes in the Everglades are replayed in the underappreciated sister wetlands of the subtropics, where development has only just begun in earnest (Nature Conservancy 2007).

The purpose of this chapter is to focus on the most distinctive features of subtropical, karstic wetlands that have been revealed through scientific investigations in the Florida Everglades, rather than reviewing the voluminous scholarly material written about the Everglades (see Myers and Ewel 1990; Davis and Ogden 1994; McCally 1999; Porter and Porter 2002; Lodge 2010). By examining the unusual features of the Everglades in the context of other North American wetlands, we can more broadly conceptualize how wetlands are organized. Together with sea-level rise and climate change, the imposition of human activities on this landscape is creating unique troubles for these fragile coastal ecosystems. By understanding how karstic wetland ecosystem structure and function are regulated in the context of large restoration efforts, we may be able to better inform management practices to reduce or prevent these detrimental effects in the Everglades and other, comparable wetlands.

Geology, Hydrology, and Biogeochemistry

Climate Drivers of Hydrogeology

Everything in the Everglades, from the gently sloping, porous bedrock to the muds of Florida Bay and the small microbes in periphyton mats to the fringing mangrove forests, is ultimately molded by a single sculptor—water. The push and pull of fresh and saltwater, driven by tides and climate variability and, more recently, human intervention, control the form and function of the physical, chemical, and biological template on the broad, flat trough that cradles Everglades wetlands. At the millennial and centurial scales, the rise and fall of sea level created the sediments that form and sculpt the gently sloping floor of the modern Everglades. At decadal to subannual scales, the extreme variability in rainfall controls interannual and seasonal patterns of plant and animal production. Humans

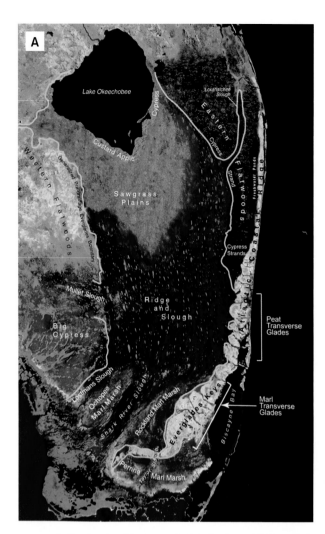
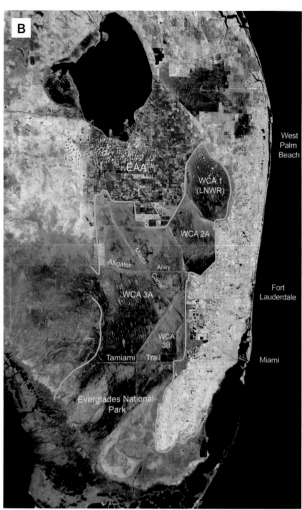

FIG. 17.1. A. Simulated satellite image of original (prior to 1882) Everglades. B. The modern landscape showing the Loxahatchee National Wildlife Refuge (LNWR), water conservation areas (WCAs), the Everglades Agricultural Area (EAA), and Everglades National Park. (Reprinted with permission from the National Academies Press: C. McVoy, 1999, in Central and Southern Florida Project Comprehensive Review Study, Final Integrated Feasibility Report and Programmatic Environmental Impact Statement. [U.S. Army Corps of Engineers and South Florida Water Management District].)

played a role in South Florida even before Everglades wetlands existed, influencing fire regimes, water flow patterns, and wildlife populations and today have dramatically altered the way that water moves through the ecosystem. (McVoy et al 2011)

CHANGES OVER MILLENNIA

The oldest rocks in the northwestern parts of South Florida contain layers of fossil shells, sands, and rock that indicate transgressions of the sea during the Pliocene (2.5–5 million years before present [ybp]) (Gleason and Stone 1994), as well as the terminus of the influence of littoral drift providing clastic sediments to South Florida. Fluctuations in sea level continued during the glacial and interglacial sequences of the Pleistocene (12,000–2.5 million ybp), causing South Florida to be intermittently occupied by freshwater and marine communities (Wanless, Parkinson, et al. 1994). A sandy-shelly formation to the northeast and oolitic limestone covering the majority of the southern Everglades were formed when sea level was 8 m above current levels and the basin harbored productive lagoons. Largely dry during the most recent Wisconsin Glaciation (10,000–100,000 ybp), the basin last flooded in the mid-

Holocene, between 4,000–6,500 ybp. This flooding was due to a combination of rapidly rising seas (ca. 12 cm/100 years) and greater wetness associated with a northward movement of the intertropical convergence zone (ITCZ) and increased periodicity of the El Niño Southern Oscillation (ENSO) (Donders, Wagner, et al. 2005; Bernhardt and Willard 2009). This latest transgression was highly significant; it allowed for the widespread flooding of depressions and establishment of the contemporary distribution and expanse of wetlands throughout the southeastern United States (Gaiser, Taylor, et al. 2001). Expansion of aquatic resources enabled the Mayan and North American Paleo-Indian cultures to spread across the southeastern United States and Caribbean Basin (McCally 1999). The Everglades is therefore very young geologically and has supported human populations throughout its history.

CHANGES OVER RECENT CENTURIES

Since the mid-Holocene flooding, the Everglades has been subjected to dry and wet phases, indicated by alternating layers of organic and autogenic inorganic soils and fossils (Gleason and Stone 1994). Highly organic soils (peats) produced by plants

Pre-Drainage Flow   Current Flow   Restored Flow

FIG. 17.2. A. Water flows in the predrainage ecosystem, the current system, and the theoretical future restored system. B. Areal photograph of the Tamiami Trail and Canal, which separates Water Conservation Area 3 (left, north) from Shark River Slough (right, south), showing early clearing for the construction of a 1-mile bridge (at right; photo taken June 14, 2011) that will allow more water flow into Everglades National Park. (A. Photo courtesy of the South Florida Water Management District; B. Photo by Evelyn Gaiser.)

and algae accumulate in the deepest parts of the Everglades trough, where they reduce groundwater seepage and decompose slowly. This peat, building slowly at a rate of ~5 mm y^{-1} (Saunders et al. 2006), is often intercalated with light-colored calcitic soils called marl. Marl forms more slowly (~1 mm y^{-1}; Gaiser, Zafiris et al. 2006), in shallow water where frequent drying promotes organic matter oxidation and mineral precipitation. There was a persistent dry phase between 2,000–3,000 ybp, possibly caused by a southward migration of the ITCZ and a decelerating rate of sea-level rise (Winkler, Sanford, et al. 2001; Donders, Wagner, et al. 2005). Although it is clear that there were intense hydrologic fluctuations in the mid-Holocene Everglades, their causes are unknown. This is a puzzle worthy of attention, as understanding the temporal patterns and drivers of hydrologic shifts can provide important guidance for hydrologic restoration.

INTERANNUAL CLIMATE VARIABILITY

In South Florida, as in much of the subtropics, interannual variation in rainfall (86–224 cm) is often as great as the long-term (1895–2009) mean annual rainfall (130 cm; Fig. 17.3a). There is also very large spatial variability in precipitation on small scales, so that no two series of rainfall data from weather stations in South Florida look identical (Duever, Meeder, et al. 1994) (Fig. 17.3b). A substantial component of this variability is driven by large-scale oceanic climate cycles and associated major precipitation events caused by tropical weather systems (including hurricanes) (Enfield, Mestas-Nunez, et al. 2001) (Fig. 17.3a). The most important appear to be the Atlantic Multidecadal Oscillation, which causes rainfall and runoff in South Florida to fluctuate on a 30- to 40-year cycle (Miralles-Wilhelm, Trimble, et al. 2005), and the ENSO, operating on a shorter, 7- to 10-year cycle that controls the magnitude of the difference between wet- and dry-season rainfall and runoff (Childers, Boyer, et al. 2006). The discrimination of climate cycles from directional climate controls on changes observed in South Florida wetlands is critical to proper restoration planning and will require continued commitment to long-term data collection and dynamic ecosystem modeling.

SEASONALITY

The most predictable changes in water availability in South Florida result from the subtropical seasonal climate, characterized by a pronounced bimodal pulse of precipitation between the months of May and October, when more than 75% of the annual precipitation is received (Fig. 17.3b). During the wet season and in preparation for storms, managers increase water releases from water conservation areas (Fig. 17.1b), resulting in a slow (0–0.8 cm s^{-1}) flow of water through much of the ecosystem (Harvey, Schaffranek, et al. 2009). The climate of the

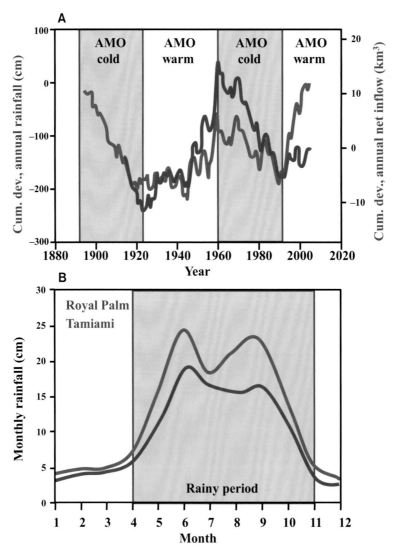

FIG. 17.3. A. Long-term interannual trends in Florida rainfall in the upper Everglades watershed and inflows to Lake Okeechobee (cum. dev. = cumulative deviation from average), showing relationship to the phases of the Atlantic Multidecadal Oscillation (AMO). B. Intraannual trends from two weather stations in the northern (Tamiami) and southern (Royal Palm) locations in Everglades National Park (mean of 1948–2009), showing spatial differences in rainfall and demarcating the distinct wet and dry seasons. (A. Redrawn from J. Obeysekera, South Florida Water Management District. B. Courtesy of the Florida Coastal Everglades Long-Term Ecological Research program, fcelter.fiu.edu.)

wet season is also characterized by an abundance of isolated afternoon thunderstorms that move about the landscape in a shifting patchwork. Lightning strikes are frequent during these storms, and resultant fires are important agents of ecosystem disturbance (Beckage, Platt, et al. 2003). These storms can be persistent and severe when driven by tropical weather systems that generate tropical storms and hurricanes, and create a patchwork of change in the landscape (Zhang, Simard, et al. 2008). Tropical-storm and hurricane winds defoliate and topple trees (Smith, Anderson, et al. 2009) and can deliver salt and marl sediment into the marsh interior, which affects productivity (Castañeda-Moya, Twilley, et al. 2010). These storms reconfigure the landscape, and their legacy creates a new template on which longer-term changes, such as sea-level rise and directional climate change, are imposed (Wanless, Parkinson, et al. 1994). Further, wetland losses and reductions of sheet

flow resulting from compartmentalization may have reduced the resiliency of the South Florida landscape to severe storm and drought events.

As autumn meets winter and the tropical-storm season comes to a close, rainfall tapers from 15–20 cm to ~5 cm per month (Fig. 17.3b). Impacts of the dry season on the marsh vary from year to year, depending on the extent of below-average rainfall as well as regulation that further reduces water flow to the marsh from peripheral canals. Large expanses of the ecosystem go dry, leaving desiccated, cracked soils and standing water that is confined to solution holes and remnant sloughs. Plants senesce and aquatic animals retreat to these deeper, ponded areas (Fig. 17.4a–f).

Inundation is typically continuous in the central drainage of Shark and Taylor River Sloughs and in some of the water conservation areas, where water is artificially confined by canals.

Peripheral areas of the marsh, including the marl prairie and rocky glades, are dry for extended periods (perhaps 9–12 months), and the water table may drop well below the surface of the marsh. Some of the plant and animal species occupying these areas are adapted to frequent drying, while others are stressed by the long-term reduction in water flow to this formerly much wetter area. Much native ridge and slough habitat has been converted to marl prairie, and former marl prairie to farmland and housing (Davis, Gaiser, et al. 2005). Residual, often small, populations of prairie species have been driven to the interior, and many of these species are threatened or endangered, and therefore protected by federal laws. Overdrainage of wet prairies has also increased the frequency and severity of peat fires, further threatening these fragile communities (Craighead 1971).

The Distinctive Biogeochemistry of the Everglades

Geology, freshwater source and availability, land use, and biota control the concentrations and fluxes of chemicals in Everglades water. From an ecosystem standpoint, the most important chemical constituents in the Everglades are calcium carbonate ($CaCO_3$) and phosphorus (P). Groundwater flow through the karst bedrock delivers water of high pH and calcium concentrations (Harvey and McCormick 2009), except in northern areas of the Everglades, where silica sands overlay the limestone bedrock. P supply is very limited, the primary natural source (> 90%) being atmospheric deposition. Much of this P chemically adsorbs to $CaCO_3$ or is taken up into organic form by microbial (periphyton) assemblages. As a result, areas of the Everglades protected from anthropogenic enrichment are P depleted (< 10 μg L^{-1}), and productivity is largely controlled by P availability (Noe, Childers, et al. 2002).

Because the P supply is so depleted, resident bacterial and algal populations are adapted for rapid uptake, long-term storage, and efficient recycling of available nutrients (Scinto and Reddy 2003). Periphyton mats and microbially active detritus cause water column concentrations to converge to 5–7 μg L^{-1} (Thomas, Gaiser, et al. 2006), which is close to the background water TP concentration commonly found in the pristine southern Everglades marsh (<10 μg L^{-1}, Flora and Rosendahl 1982; 5–7 μg L^{-1}, McCormick and O'Dell 1996). Thus, the majority of P is stored in the soil, periphyton and microbial communities, and dead and living plant material rather than the water column (Reddy, Wang, et al. 1998). Soil oxidation, either by microbial decomposition (especially high when water levels are lowered) or fire, can increase available P. As a result, P availability cycles seasonally, with oxidative P released during the dry season, fueling productivity when flooding commences in the wet season (Childers, Boyer, et al. 2006).

In areas of the Everglades underlain by clastic sediment (rather than limestone) or where thick peats retard the interaction between limestone bedrock and the water column, P-sorption is reduced. Marshes of the northern Everglades, including the Loxahatchee River drainage and the Arthur R. Marshall Loxahatchee National Wildlife Refuge (the refuge, now comprising Water Conservation Area-1 [WCA-1]), have mineral-depleted soils (which can be as deep as 6 m) and have soft-water chemistry resembling tributaries to Lake Okeechobee. For this reason, the lake itself likely had a predrainage TP range greater than the central Everglades (~20 to 30 μg L^{-1}; Brezonik and Pollman 1999). Phosphorus draining from the lake was probably attenuated by the former pond apple forest and vast "sawgrass plain," both in the location of the present Everglades Agricultural Area, so that levels downstream in the ecosystem (now the water conservation areas and Everglades National Park) were at 10 μg L^{-1} or less (Davis 1994). At the coastal end of the Everglades drainage, ion concentrations are enhanced by tides and directional landward brackish-water discharge (Price, Swart, et al. 2006) that is becoming more noticeable as sea-level rise is unmitigated by natural freshwater flow to the sea.

Hydrological and Biochemical Patterns Imposed by Water Management

Agricultural and urban development has decreased the spatial extent of the Everglades by more than 50%, as well as the landscape connectivity. In places where natural patterns of water flow from the north were severed, such as in much of the refuge, WCA-2A, and northeast Shark River Slough, hydroperiods have shortened and droughts have a more widespread influence than in the past (Davis, Gaiser, et al. 2005). Other places are experiencing drying reversals, such as where controlled discharges from the canals bounding Everglades National Park release unseasonable pulses of water into Shark and Taylor River Sloughs during the normal dry season (Sklar, Chimney, et al. 2005). Recognition of the extent to which engineering has disconnected natural climate variability from the hydrologically dependent processes in the Everglades is driving the multibillion-dollar restoration effort (CERP). The goal of CERP is to balance the needs of the environment with the complex management of water and unbridled human development of southern Florida. The hydrological restoration goals in CERP were created under the assumption that water-quality problems would be solved before hydropattern restoration proceeds (Sklar, Chimney, et al. 2005). In the following sections, we provide details on the composition, structure, and ecology of native plant and animal communities and address the ways in which they have been impacted by hydrologic and biogeochemical shifts in the landscape. By returning to these concepts in the "Conservation Concerns" section, we hope to provide a backdrop for the sense of urgency in restoring the Everglades.

Plant Communities

The plant communities of the Everglades are dynamic and constantly changing as a result of environmental drivers, internal feedback loops, and external disturbances. The interplay of these processes with the life-history characteristics of a distinctive group of plants has created a fascinating ecosystem. The Everglades is located in a transition zone between tropical and temperate vascular floras. Tropical species migrated to the peninsula from the Antilles, Mexico, and Central and South America (61% of the flora), while other members of the flora are common to continental North America (Long 1984). A third contributor is the approximately 160 endemic species (9% of the flora) that have persisted since Miocene times. Finally, people have introduced about 250 exotic species (~16% of the flora) (Long 1984). Overall, about 850 vascular plant species are found in the Everglades that sort into about 20 community associations (Gunderson 1994).

The composition, structure, and landscape location of vascular-plant communities in the Everglades are controlled by three

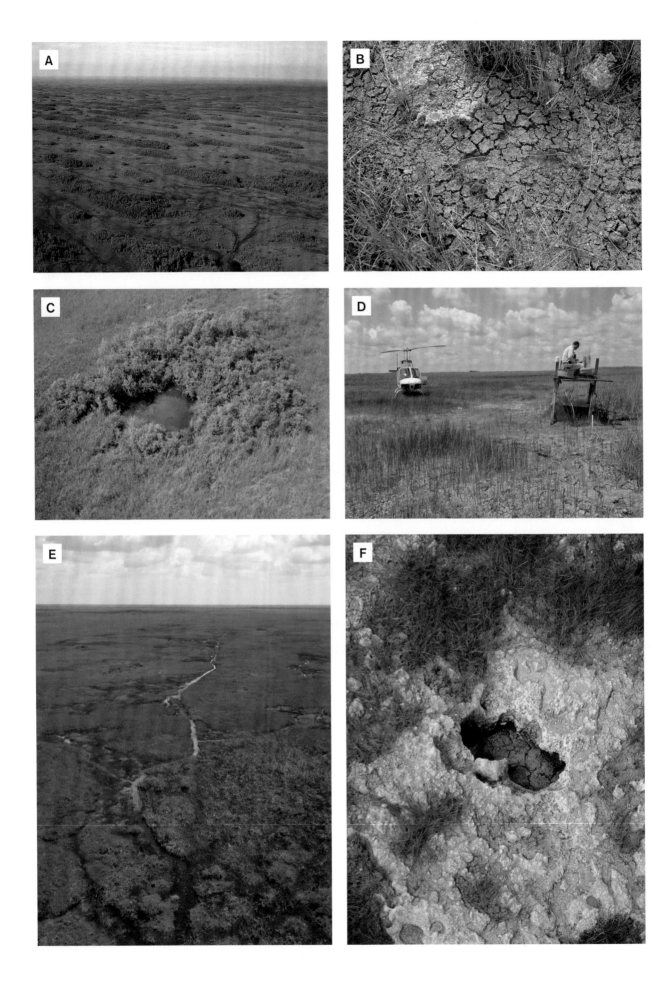

primary environmental drivers: hydrology, nutrient levels, and fire/droughts. Other environmental factors, such as salinity (Ross, Meeder, et al. 2000; Childers, Boyer, et al. 2006), hurricanes (Smith, Anderson, et al. 2009), and freezing temperatures (Duever, Meeder, et al. 1994), are important in shaping plant communities, but these factors are more localized or occur less frequently than the primary drivers. The effects of the primary environmental drivers are best understood for the marshes, wet prairies, and sloughs, and these plant communities are the focus of the discussion of how environmental drivers interact to shape the plant communities on the Everglades landscape.

Hydrologic Drivers of Plant Communities

As with all wetland ecosystems, hydrology has a major effect on Everglades plant communities. Most simply, plant communities may be classified by their hydroperiods (defined here as the average number of days per year that the water level is at or above the soil surface), although flow rates and water depth also affect composition. Hydroperiods range from the driest conditions, 0 to 45 days yr^{-1} for tropical hardwood hammocks, to deepwater sloughs that can be inundated all year (Fig. 17.5a–i).

Changing hydrology will cause shifts from one plant community to another, creating a blurring of community boundaries and a variety of community subtypes. Marsh community succession occurs rapidly, with measurable changes occurring within one year of hydrologic change (Childers, Boyer, et al. 2006) and complete plant community transformation occurring within four years or less (Armentano, Sah, et al. 2006; Zweig and Kitchens 2008). For example, sawgrass (Cladium jamaicense) is generally a superior competitor in short-hydroperiod wetlands (Steward and Ornes 1975), being able to persist under very low P concentrations (Richardson, Ferrell, et al. 1999) and resist both drought and fire (Urban, Davis, et al. 1993). However, if sawgrass communities experience water depths greater than 61 cm for over two years during the wet season, these communities begin to fragment (Zweig and Kitchens 2009) and can be replaced by spikerush-dominated (Eleocharis spp.) assemblages (Childers, Boyer, et al. 2006). On the other hand, if sloughs experience water levels below the soil surface for three consecutive dry seasons or more, sawgrass will encroach from the ridges (Zweig and Kitchens 2009). A number of studies have suggested that hydrologic extremes, i.e., wet and dry season maximums and minimums, may exert a greater effect on both herbaceous and woody plant communities than seasonal means (Wetzel 2002; Miao, Zou, et al. 2009). Although hydrology is an important environmental driver of plant community composition and succession, its interactions with nutrient levels and fire must also be considered, especially in parts of the Everglades modified by humans.

Effects of Fire on Plant Communities

The distinct annual winter dry periods in South Florida create conditions that support wildfires, which, in addition to incendiary (vandalism-started) and prescribed fires, create an ecologically important disturbance. In Everglades National Park, where consistent wildfire records are available, most wildfires occur during the dry-wet season transition in April and May, when water levels are lowest (Gunderson and Snyder 1994). Everglades fires appear to occur at three periodicities: 1, 3.4–5, and ~12.3-year cycles (Beckage, Platt, et al. 2003). Years with large areas burned (20,000–80,000 ha) occur every ~12 years, often during the La Niña phase of the ENSO, which brings a decrease in dry-season rainfall and lower water levels. Years with medium-sized burned areas (2,000–20,000 ha) occur every 3.4 to 5.0 years, while the effect of the annual dry-wet cycle is reflected in the one-year fire regime in which 0–2,000 ha may burn.

Everglades fires are of two intensities: either severe peat-burning fires (muck fires) or modest surface fires, depending on water level and fuel load in the ecosystem. Severe muck fires can reduce the soil surface 10–20 cm and destroy hammocks and tree islands (Newman, Schuette, et al. 1998). Such a loss of peat will take 20–40 years to restore at an average accretion rate of 5 mm per year (Saunders et al. 2006). Once an herbaceous plant community has burned, it takes about three years to restore the plant biomass back to prefire levels (Steward and Ornes 1975; Schmalzer, Hinkle, et al. 1991), although cattail (Typha latifolia) marshes recover more quickly (~18 months; Tian, Xu, et al. 2010).

Lowering of the peat surface after a muck fire alters plant communities and initiates a new succession pathway. Wet prairies succeed to plant communities with longer hydroperiods following fires (Newman, Schuette, et al. 1998), and muck fires burn woody plant roots, changing tree island patches to herbaceous plant communities (Zaffke 1983). Fires that burn the surface vegetation and not the peat soil generally will not cause one plant community to succeed to another.

Patterns on the Landscape: The Tree Island, Ridge, and Slough Continuum

Plant communities in the central and southern Everglades are arranged in a distinctive spatial pattern, with thousands of teardrop-shaped tree islands interspersed with regularly spaced, narrow sawgrass ridges and alternating deepwater water lily sloughs. This landscape-scale patterning generally runs north to south, following the predrainage water flow (Fig. 17.4a). However, reduced water storage on the landscape and compartmentalization in the northern and central managed Everglades have altered these landscape patterns, resulting in a topographic flattening of the marsh soil surface and a corresponding reduction in elevation between ridges and sloughs (Sklar, McVoy, et al. 2002; Larsen, Harvey, et al. 2007).

Patterning in the landscape began ~5,000 ybp, although two more recent dry periods—~1,000 ybp (the Medieval Warm Period) and ~400 ybp—saw an expansion of sawgrass ridges and the formation of many tree islands (Willard, Bernhardt, et al. 2006). Although the origin of patterning is poorly understood, Larsen, Harvey, et al. (2007) postulate that flood pulses deposit sediment that is eventually colonized by sawgrass dur-

FIG. 17.4. (opposite) Photos of the Everglades, contrasting wet and dry habitats. A. Aerial image showing linear patterning of ridges, sloughs, and tree islands arising from directional sheetflow of water. B. A 1-m^2 patch of marsh in the dry season, showing desiccated, cracked periphyton. C. Water sampling station during the dry season. D–F. Dry-season refuges for aquatic animals, including alligator holes (D), deeper pools and sloughs (E), narrow tidal channels (E), and a ~1-m^2 solution hole in the rocky glades (F). (A: Photo by D. Kilbane; B–F: photos by E. Gaiser.)

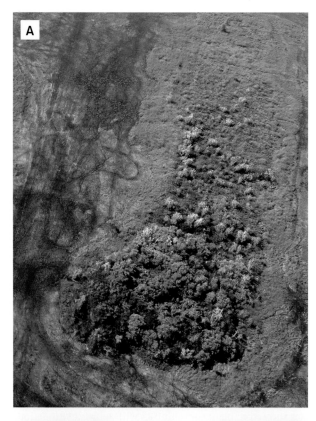

A. Tree island, bayhead

Description: Large low-stature swamps, bayhead forest, and tree islands. *Annona glabra, Magnolia virginiana, Persea palustris.*

Hydroperiod: 60–150d (Schomer and Drew [1982, 120–150d]; Gunderson and Loftus [1993, 60–180d]; Drew and Schomer [1984, 100–150d]; Ross, Mitchell-Bruker, et al. [2006, 157d]; Wetzel, Pinion, et al. [2008, 80d].)

B. Bayhead swamp

Description: Shrub wetlands. *Salix* spp., *Cephalanthus occidentalis,* and sometimes high proportions of *Typha* spp. or *Cladium jamaicense.*

Hydroperiod: 110–320d (Wetzel [2002, 110–365d]; Schomer and Drew [1982, 150–300d]; McPherson [1973, 110–365d]; Kolipinski and Higer [1969, 244d].)

C. Cypress and mixed swamp forest

Description: Swamp forests: *Gordonia lasianthus, Magnolia virginiana, Persea palustris* (bays), *Nyssa* spp. (gum), *Taxodium* spp.; cypress forests: *Taxodium distichum, T. ascendens.*

Hydroperiod: 120–290d; 200–340d (Ewel [1990, 180–270d]; Schomer and Drew [1982, 120–210d]; Duever, Carlson, et al. [1978, 155–290d]; Wharton, Odum, et al. [1977, 200–240d]; Sun, Riekert, et al. [1995, 212–340d].)

FIG. 17.5. Major plant communities in the freshwater Everglades, with dominant species and annual hydroperiod ranges. The hydroperiod range assigned to a plant community either encompasses the ranges reported in the literature or is averaged from the data available. (A: Photo by D. Kilbane; B–C: photos by J. Richards; D–E: photos by F. Tobias; F: photos by C. Zweig)

D

D. Wet prairie

Description: Muhly grass prairie. *Muhlenbergia capillaries, Cladium jamaicense, Schoenus nigricans, Schizachyrium rhizomatum.*

Hydroperiod: 60–120d (Kushlan [1990, < 180d]; Porter [1967, 60–210d]; Loope [1980, 60–120d]; Duever, Carlson, et al. [1978, 111–155d]; Brown, Flohrschutz, et al. [1984, 120d]; Gunderson and Loope [1982, 70d]; Duever, Meeder, et al. [1984, 70d].)

E

E. Marsh (sawgrass)

Description: Tall, dense or short, sparse. *Cladium jamaicense, Panicum virginica, Pontedria cordata, Eleocharis elongata.*

Hydroperiod: 130–330d (Kushlan [1990, 180–270d]; Schomer and Drew [1982, 150–300d]; David [1996, 117–310d]; Lowe [1986, 168–303d]; McPherson [1973, 175–365d]; Hagenbuck et al. [1974, 73–180d]; Ross, Mitchell-Bruker, et al. [2006, 339d, sparse; 323d, tall].)

F

F. Marsh (spikerush)

Description: Wet prairie. *Eleocharis cellulosa, E. elongata, Hymenocallis palmeri, Panicum hemitomon, Utricularia spp., Sagittaria lancifolia.*

Hydroperiod: 150–300d (Kushlan [1990, 180–270d]; Schomer and Drew [1982, 150–300d]; David [1996, 193–310d]; Loope [1980, > 270d]; Hagenbuck et al. [1974, 73–180d]; Ross, Meeder, et al. [2000, 266–333d], Ross, Mitchell-Bruker, et al. [2006, 344d].)

ing periods of drought or low flow. This increase in sawgrass further slows water flow, increasing sedimentation, and favors greater accumulation of plant material on the ridges compared to sloughs even when wetter conditions return. If an elevated patch of sediment or ridge becomes dry enough to support woody plant invasion, prototype tree islands may form (Wetzel, van der Valk, et al. 2005). The presence of trees allows the focused concentration of nutrients from bird and animal

guano or dust deposition onto the proto-island, causing litter and peat to accumulate at a higher rate than on the surrounding ridges or sloughs. Thus, our understanding of the ridge and slough landscape patterning is that the formation and maintenance of the ridge and slough landscape represents a balance between peat accumulation controlled by water levels and sediment redistribution controlled by water velocity and direction (Brandt et al. 2000).

Animal Communities

Freshwater animal communities of the Everglades are characterized by abundant macroinvertebrates and small fishes less than 4 cm in length. Amphibians and reptiles are also important members of the aquatic community; American alligators *(Alligator mississippiensis)* in particular have received much attention, both because of conservation concerns and their key role as ecosystem engineers (Mazzotti and Brandt 1994). Frogs and salamanders, particularly the siren *(Siren lacertina),* are not well studied in the Everglades but are clearly important predators and food for alligators and humans. There is a poorly documented but thriving pig frog *(Rana grylio)* harvest in parts of the Everglades (Ugarte, Rice, et al. 2007). Several threatened or endangered animal species inhabit the region, notably the American alligator, wood stork *(Mycteria americana),* snail lite *(Rostrhamus sociabilis),* Cape Sable seaside sparrow *(Ammodramus maritimus mirabilis),* and Florida panther *(Felis concolor coryi).*

Everglades animal communities are often characterized as diverse, but in fact most groups are relatively species poor. For example, reptiles and amphibians (Means and Simberloff 1987) and freshwater fish (Trexler 1995) have fewer species than would be expected for comparably sized habitats elsewhere, probably because the unusual biogeochemical conditions exclude some species found farther north, but also because of the isolated location at the tip of a peninsula and the relatively short period of time since the area was most recently under sea level. The native members of groups such as freshwater fish and amphibians that do not commonly cross saltwater are all temperate in origin. More mobile freshwater animals, including many aquatic insects with flying stages, include taxa with links to the West Indies and broader Caribbean Basin (Rader 1999). Of course, in recent years a great diversity of species has been added to the Everglades from around the world through human-assisted migration.

Animal communities of southern Florida and the Everglades have been comprehensively and systematically described in other places (Loftus and Kushlan 1987; Gunderson and Loftus 1993; Davis and Ogden 1994; Lodge 2010), so we will focus on one aspect of animals in Everglades ecology: the aquatic food web. While this focus leaves many important stories untold here, the aquatic food web, including small fishes and crustaceans, supports charismatic species such as wading birds and alligators that are of great conservation concern because of their depleted numbers compared to historical records (Frederick, Gawlik, et al. 2009). The decline of these taxa is tied to diminished food availability in the places and times that sustained their historical abundance (Bancroft, Strong, et al. 1994). Thus, recovery of their numbers and spatial distribution will require restoring hydropatterns to recapture historical spatial and temporal patterns of secondary productivity.

Hydrological Drivers of Freshwater Animal Communities

Seasonal changes of water level have a profound impact on aquatic animals inhabiting the Everglades. Aquatic animals can be divided into two life-history patterns: those that can survive drying by tolerating it or those that must move to aquatic refuges to escape it. Toleraters include species that burrow (e.g., Everglades crayfish, *Procambarus alleni*) (Dorn and Trexler 2007; Dorn and Volin 2009), diapause (copepods and cladocerans) (Bruno, Loftus, et al. 2001) or aestivate (e.g., apple snails, *Pomacea paludosa*) (Darby, Bennetts, et al. 2008), or emerge to a flying life stage (e.g., midges, dragonflies). Refuging species must be mobile and able to locate deep habitats because a failure in choice leads to stranding and death. All freshwater fish of the Everglades must have this attribute to some degree. However, one species, the marsh killifish *(Fundulus confluentus),* has been shown to lay diapausing eggs in Florida marshes outside the Everglades (Harrington 1959), and it is possible that a second species, flagfish *(Jordanella floridae),* may be able to accomplish this feat.

Several types of aquatic refuges are used by different members of the Everglades fish communities, including alligator ponds, solution holes, creeks (Fig. 17.4d–f), and, more recently, canals. Alligator ponds are found throughout the Everglades, although they are less frequent in short-hydroperiod wetlands than in long-hydroperiod ones (Palmer and Mazzotti 2004). In the wet season, alligator ponds are sparsely populated by fish (Trexler, Loftus, et al. 2002), but in the dry season, they can have high concentrations of yellow bullhead catfish *(Ameiurus natalis),* warmouth *(Lepomis gulosus),* and Florida gar *(Lepisosteus playrhincus)* (Nelson and Loftus 1996). Some small fishes enter alligator ponds in the dry season, but clearly at great risk of predation. In a similar way, solution holes in short-hydroperiod marshes of the southern Everglades and Rocky Glades were once thought to be potentially important dry-season refuges for communities in this region (Loftus, Johnson, et al. 1992), although now it appears that water tables drop low enough to dry out the vast majority of solution holes and can be the favored home of predatory nonnative species (Kobza, Trexler, et al. 2004).

Creeks draining the southern Everglades into the mangrove-dominated oligohaline zone are also densely populated by freshwater fishes, especially Florida gar, eastern mosquitofish *(Gambusia* spp.), largemouth bass *(Micropterus salmoides),* and snook *(Centropomus undecimalis),* in the dry season each year (Rehage and Loftus 2007). It is believed that these same fish move long distances when marshes reflood early in the wet season. Canals now cross the Everglades and provide a large volume of dry-season refuges that have diminished the use of natural dry-season refuges in their proximity by alligators (Mazzoti and Brandt 1994; Palmer and Mazzotti 2004) and fish (J. Parkos unpublished data). The open waters of canals are also ready conduits for dispersal and modify population structure.

When marshes in the Everglades dry, the fish community is dispersed and experiences high mortality, and recolonization takes place over a number of years following reflooding (Trexler, Loftus, et al. 2001; Trexler, Loftus, et al. 2005). Three life histories have been identified for fish recovery following drought: eastern mosquitofish recolonize in a matter of weeks; bluefin killifish and least killifish *(Heterandria formosa)* reappear in a period of three to six months; and flagfish and marsh killifish also recolonize rapidly but become less abundant as time passes (Fig. 17.6) (DeAngelis, Trexler, et al. 2005). Macroinvertebrates display a similar array of life-history responses to drying, also tied to their dispersal abilities, yielding predictable temporal patterns of recovery. For example, the spatial dynamics of crayfish and grass shrimp appear to be tied to their abilities to recolonize by walking or swimming into reflooded sites. Everglades crayfish, which appear to be excellent dispersers, colonize rapidly following a drought, are most dense in short-hydroperiod wetlands, and diminish to zero after two years of continuous inundation (Hendrix and Loftus

2000; Dorn and Trexler 2007). Slough crayfish *(Procambarus fallax)* dominate long-hydroperiod marshes and recolonize slowly following a drought. Riverine grass shrimp *(Palaemonetes paludosus)* reach their highest density in marshes that have been inundated for at least two years, and can reach very high densities when forced into pools by regional drying. Macroinvertebrates with aquatic larval stages that recolonize by egg deposition of flying adults, such as naiads of dragonflies, also display species-specific patterns of density associated with the time since a site has most recently been flooded (Urgelles 2009). Gastropods must survive a drying event in situ and are more abundant in longer- than in shorter-hydroperiod marshes because of demographic impacts of desiccation; the most common Everglades snails, Seminole ramshorn *(Planorbella duryi)* and apple snail *(Pomacea paludosa),* can survive extended periods of dry conditions, but juvenile stages in particular incur increased mortality in such events (Darby, Bennetts, et al. 2008; Ruehl 2010). As years pass following a drying event, its impact and that of recolonization abilities is obscured by other biological interactions. For example, both of these common snails, and some small fish, are less abundant in very long-hydroperiod sites (white water lily–dominated sloughs) than in long-hydroperiod wet prairies because their aquatic predators also recolonize and increase in abundance over time post-drought (Trexler, Loftus, et al. 2005; Karunaratne, Darby, et al. 2006; Ruehl 2010).

Hydroperiod and time passed since the most recent drought also affect food-web structure in Everglades marshes. Detritivory is an important route of energy flow in the Everglades (Williams and Trexler 2006). Trophic position indicated by nitrogen isotopes of eastern mosquitofish, and to a less extent riverine grass shrimp, increases with increasing time since marsh drying. These data and others (Sargeant, Gaiser, et al. 2010) are consistent with the diet of these abundant consumers shifting to higher trophic-level prey, leading to more of these animals in long- versus short-hydroperiod sites.

Local Control of Freshwater Animal Communities

Though local control of fish and macroinvertebrate density is often strongly correlated with the frequency and duration of drying, predators also play an important role in Everglades communities. Excluding large predators often leads to more small fish, crayfish, and shrimp, which in turn reduce new periphyton growth, suggesting a trophic cascade (Dorn, Trexler, et al. 2006). Interestingly, these studies have never documented an effect of grazers directly on the local periphyton, suggesting that periphyton is physically and/or chemically defended from strong grazing impacts (Chick, Geddes, et al. 2008); nutrient regeneration may also be important in this system (Geddes and Trexler 2003). In fact, intact Everglades periphyton mats were not consumed by grass shrimp unless the mat structure was disrupted (Geddes and Trexler 2003).

Trexler, Loftus, et al. (2005) proposed that the relative importance of hydrological disturbance and predation replace each other as the time since a drought event increases (online appendix 1). Hydrological impacts become increasingly less important in controlling community structure after approximately three years, while the role of large fishes as predators becomes more apparent. However, the Trexler, Loftus, et al. (2005) conceptual model does not include effects of nutrient enrichment, which impacts Everglades aquatic community structure, discussed below.

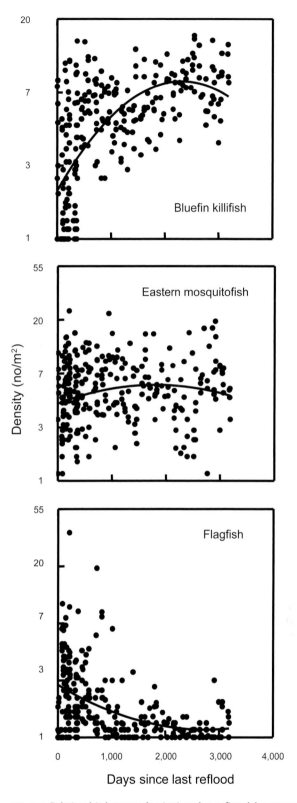

FIG. 17.6. Relationship between density (number m⁻²) and days passed since study site reflooded for three species of fish. Data were collected from Shark River Slough, Everglades National Park. (Redrawn from DeAngelis, Trexler, et al. 2005.)

Key Ecological Processes

The ecology of the Everglades is controlled by interactions between the climatological and biogeochemical template and the changing abundances of plants, animals, and detrital material in the ecosystem. Examples of these interactions are threaded throughout this chapter, but below we provide examples of ecological processes that are distinctive in the Everglades, including the regulatory role played by abundant, calcareous microbial mats, the resultant food-web paradox, and the biogeochemical patterning caused by tree islands that dot the Everglades.

Periphyton as an Ecosystem Engineer

One of the most conspicuously unusual features of Everglades freshwater wetlands is the copious microbial mats that blanket the surface of the water, sediments, and plants (Fig. 17.7). These communities are composed of microalgae, cyanobacteria, fungi, bacteria, small animals, and associated detritus, and are colloquially termed "periphyton." In the shallow waters of the limestone-based Everglades, the biomass of periphyton can be one to two orders of magnitude greater than in other freshwater marshes, lake littoral zones, ponds, and shallow marine habitats (online appendix 2). Average reported ash-free dry (organic) biomass values from surveys throughout the Everglades range from 200–500 g m^{-2} (Gaiser 2009), and are similar only to values from other karstic marshes in the Caribbean and tropical Central America (80 g m^{-2}, 370 g m^{-2}; La Hée 2010). In these quantities, periphyton plays a regulatory role in the environment: it stabilizes and accretes soils, controls the concentration of gases and ions in the water, and is the base of a complex food web.

The great biomass of periphyton in karstic marshes is unexpected, given the extreme stresses of periodic drying and unpredictable flooding, exposure to high temperatures and occasional fires, and unusual water chemistry, with high concentrations of carbonates and very low concentrations of dissolved nutrients. Karstic wetland periphyton communities appear to be uniquely adapted to this combination of stressful environmental conditions. The cyanobacterially dominated mats contain species that protect themselves from desiccation by forming resistant resting stages or exuding mucilaginous coatings that resist drying and recover within days of reflooding (Thomas, Gaiser, et al. 2006). The mucilage allows the mat to function as a sponge, trapping moisture and promoting seed germination, enhancing survival of macrophyte seedlings in the following wet period (Gaiser et al. 2011). High temperatures and even occasional fires do not appear to deter growth; instead, these processes mobilize nutrients, allowing mats to reform from inocula surviving in the abundant dissolution pools that dot the landscape (Gaiser, pers. observation).

The dominant cyanobacterial species in desiccation-prone karstic environments include filamentous blue-green algae, *Schizothrix calcicola* and *Scytonema hofmannii* (McCormick and O'Dell 1996). Within this matrix of filaments resides a distinct diatom and green algal assemblage that appears to be endemic to karstic wetlands of the subtropics and tropics (La Hée 2010), as well as a rich and metabolically diverse heterotrophic bacterial community (Fig. 17.7). Together this community functions in a manner similar to marine stromatolites; the algae efficiently utilize bicarbonate in photosynthesis, depleting the supply of inorganic carbon, causing calcium carbonate

FIG. 17.7. Exposed periphyton mat at ground level in Taylor Slough. (Photo by F. Tobias.)

crystals to deposit (Fig. 17.7). Thick, laminated layers of marl soil accumulate at a rate of ~1 mm yr^{-1} (Gaiser, Zafiris, et al. 2006), especially in the short-hydroperiod Everglades, where organic accumulations seasonally oxidize (Gleason and Spackman 1974). In long-hydroperiod sites with thick peat soils, particularly in the southern portion of the refuge, the lower pH promotes a flora dominated by desmid algae and acidophilic diatoms, similar to that of ponds and wetlands of the southeastern United States (McCormick 2010).

High productivity rates and the calcium carbonate matrix cause calcitic periphyton mats and associated marl soils to regulate water total phosphorus concentrations to ~5–7 µg L^{-1} (McCormick and O'Dell 1996; Thomas, Gaiser, et al. 2006). When water column concentrations are naturally or artificially increased, periphyton very quickly removes all available P from the water column, rendering water concentrations of a very poor metric of P load or availability (Gaiser, Scinto, et al. 2004). Instead, shifts in algal P concentration, productivity, and species composition provide reliable metrics of P load and enrichment history (see "Conservation Concerns," below).

Paradox of Production

The structure of production across trophic levels in the Everglades presents three paradoxes, one at each major level of the food web (primary producers, primary consumers, and top predators) (Fig. 17.8). The first is how high levels of periphyton primary production, described above, can be sustained under P-depleted conditions. A satisfactory explanation for this paradox is still forthcoming, although this issue has received considerable attention in recent years. It is well known that calcitic periphyton mats have a considerable capacity to store P, by adsorption onto calcium carbonate and within the extracellular polymeric substances (EPS) that can make up 90% of their biomass (Bellinger et al. 2010). Bacteria living within this EPS matrix exhibit high levels of enzyme activity, particularly alkaline phosphatase, indicating rapid mobilization and cycling of nutrients. In addition, algal cells can increase their chlorophyll *a* content and subsequent photosynthetic efficiency under P-starved conditions (Gaiser, Richards, et al. 2006). It is likely that the answer lies in the nutrient recycling

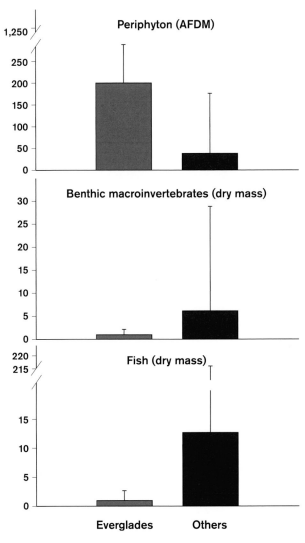

FIG. 17.8. Biomass (g m⁻²) of periphyton ash-free dry mass (AFDM), benthic macroinvertebrates (dry mass), and fish (dry mass) from the Everglades and other wetlands reported in the literature. (Data from Turner, Trexler, et al. 1999).

efficiency afforded by very tight algal-bacterial coupling, but methodologies are only recently developing to address this in detail.

The second paradox is the very low standing crop of primary consumers despite very high periphyton primary productivity (Fig. 17.8). This paradox is explained partly by the stress imposed on aquatic animals by seasonal drying, but likely more significant is the composition of the periphyton matrix. The dominant filamentous algae and calcium carbonate crystals are highly inedible and, to some degree, toxic to small invertebrate and fish grazers (Geddes and Trexler 2003; Chick, Geddes, et al. 2008). Thus, energy appears to reach the food web primarily through less efficient detrital pathways (Williams and Trexler 2006), thereby supporting lower densities and biomass of primary consumers.

Finally, the third paradox is how an ecosystem with a relatively low standing crop of small fishes and macroinvertebrates can sustain large populations of top predators. Standing crops of small fishes and macroinvertebrates are surprisingly low for an ecosystem known for its high production of top carnivores, the wading birds (Turner, Trexler, et al. 1999). This paradox is

explained by the interaction of landscape and seasonal hydrology that serves to concentrate prey over large areas timed to the nesting season. High productivity of wading birds is sustained by the annual process of prey concentration. The Everglades landscape and seasonal hydrological cycle concentrates prey during the early spring nesting season to provide the critical foraging opportunities to support, at times, the massive nesting effort of these birds.

Tree Islands as Biogeochemical Hot Spots

The Everglades landscape is dotted with islands of trees organized into nonrandom spatial patterns: round clumps of trees surrounded by water lily sloughs, teardrop-shaped islands oriented in the direction of surface water flow, long strands parallel to sawgrass or marsh ridges, and a labyrinth of trees with gaps occupied by herbaceous communities. Tree islands number in the thousands and range in size from 0.01 to 70 ha and cover 3 to 14% of the Everglades (Patterson and Finck 1999).

Tree islands rise in elevation 18 to 160 cm higher than the surrounding sloughs (Wetzel, Sklar, et al. 2011), a topographic difference that is large enough to support a wide variety of plant and animal species that otherwise could not survive in the Everglades (Meshaka, Snow, et al. 2002). Tree island elevation generally decreases from the upstream head to the downstream tail, creating distinctive vegetation zones influenced by the corresponding hydrologic gradient (Fig. 17.9a–b). For teardrop-shaped islands, the upstream, or head, of the island has the highest elevation and generally supports the largest trees, in both trunk diameter and height. Plant communities immediately downstream of the head, known as the near tail, are shorter and contain low-stature trees, shrubs, and a dense herbaceous understory, including shrubs, ferns, and forbs. Farther downstream of the near tail are very dense herbaceous communities, dominated by sawgrass and sporadic shrubs, known as the tail. Eventually, in the far tail region, the tree island vegetation becomes similar to the surrounding marsh communities (Mason and van der Valk 2002). This distribution is largely controlled by hydroperiod, which is controlled by the elevation gradient (Zaffke 1983).

These forested patches are now recognized to be a driving force for localized P accumulation in the landscape, making every tree island a biogeochemical hot spot in the ecosystem (Wetzel, van der Valk, et al. 2005; Ross, Mitchell-Bruker, et al. 2006; Wetzel, Sklar, et al. 2011) (Fig. 17.9c). Soil TP concentration on tree island heads has been found to be 3 to 170 times greater than in the surrounding marsh (Wetzel, Sklar, et al. 2011). Wetzel, van der Valk, et al. (2005) proposed that the focused redistribution of P on tree islands causes them to accumulate biomass at a greater rate than the surrounding sloughs. As the tree island grows, more nutrients are redistributed to the island, creating a positive feedback mechanism that increases the size of tree islands (Fig. 17.9c). Several different mechanisms have been proposed that contribute to this positive feedback, including wading bird roosting and nesting (Frederick and Powell 1994), forest trapping of dry fallout (Weathers, Cadenasso, et al. 2001), and evapotranspirative pumping of nutrients from groundwater (Wetzel, van der Valk, et al. 2005). Through mechanisms that are still not clear, tree islands are biogeochemical hot spots for P, and they appear to be the result of material fluxes of a limiting resource operating at multiple spatial and temporal scales. Thus, positive and negative feedbacks between biomass and resources create a spatially orga-

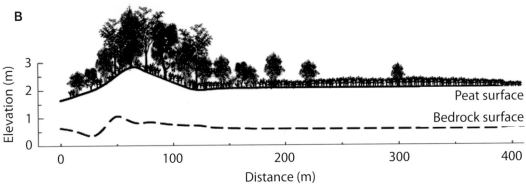

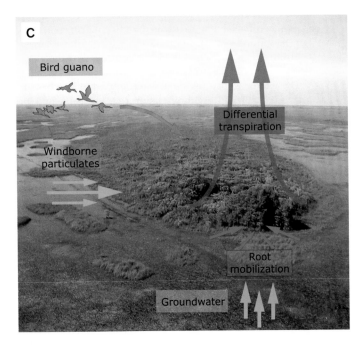

FIG. 17.9. A. Tree island. B. Longitudinal section of a tree island from the central Everglades (peat and bedrock elevations from D. Mason, unpublished data), with the locations shown of the head, near tail, far tail, and surrounding marsh. Elevation exaggerated 20x. C. Conceptual model of proposed mechanisms of phosphorus redistribution onto tree islands resulting from the presence of tree patches on the landscape. See text for explanations of the various mechanisms. (Photo: D. Kilbane.)

nized landscape with strong hydrologic and nutrient gradients that contribute to the overall biocomplexity of the Everglades landscape.

Conservation Concerns

The Everglades is an ecosystem in peril because of unsustainable patterns of water extraction and land development that conflict with beneficial wetland functions. Hydrological modifications have not only displaced species and their ecological functions, but have altered processes controlling the patterning of the landscape that was a distinctive feature of the ecosystem. Water-quality problems are equally severe, resulting from decades of unregulated inflows of nutrient-enriched waters and culminating in abrupt and widespread alterations of ecosystem function in a naturally nutrient-limited landscape. Large-scale restoration efforts are underway to mitigate these impacts, though political conflicts and tradeoffs among competing conservation and development goals continue to stall their progress. Additional threats posed by climate change only increase the urgency of implementation. Each restoration success story and approval for a long-awaited project provides glimmers of hope for eventually rehabilitating the Everglades.

Conservation Issues Related to Hydrology

Hydrology is the major environmental driver shaping the plant communities in the Everglades and therefore a critical factor in the restoration of the ecosystem. However, hydrology is not a single factor but a force of interacting components, all of which are necessary for restoration, including the length of time that water is above the soil surface, the height of the water, and the rate of water flow. Take away or alter beyond historical bounds any one of these components of hydrology and the result will be a change in Everglades plant and animal communities.

Hydrologic alteration is exactly what happened in the Everglades with the construction of an extensive canal and levee system. Hydroperiods have been extended in some areas and shortened in others, while flow is reduced or stopped and water levels are static—all disrupting the annual wet- and dry-season cycles. The result has been community-level shifts from grasses to spikerush in wet prairies or monotypic cattail stands (Zweig and Kitchens 2008). Many communities and their associated ecological functions were diminished or lost outright, such as the *Rhynchospora* flats plant community described by Loveless (1959), the pond apple forest and the large sawgrass plain south of Lake Okeechobee, and the eastern pinelands.

Given that humans have modified the Everglades enough to create an assemblage of species and environmental conditions that has not existed on the Everglades landscape, it can be argued that the modern Everglades is a novel ecosystem (Zweig and Kitchens 2010). Recognizing that either parts or all of the Everglades have been transformed into an entirely new ecosystem complicates the goals of restoration and defining success criteria. Restoration goals were already complicated by unrelenting societal demands for land, water supply, and flood control, as well as the practical aspect of having only a partial understanding of how the historic Everglades, a dynamic ecosystem in itself, looked and functioned. Furthermore, in addition to being in conflict with societal values, restoration goals are often in conflict with other conservation goals. For exam-

ple, preserving habitat for the endangered Cape Sable seaside sparrow can limit options for hydrologic restoration in certain areas. Sparrows need marl prairies dominated by *Muhlenbergia* sp. grasses with at least 45 days of dry conditions to successfully nest (Pimm, Lockwood, et al. 2002). Development and drainage have eliminated much of this habitat and pushed the remaining sparrow populations into marginal habitat that floods more frequently. Concern for the sparrow's survival limits hydrologic restoration in areas that were historically wetter than the bird's preferred habitat (Rizzardi 1999).

How should Everglades plant communities be conserved and restored? Even without human disruption of the hydrology and nutrient cycles and the creation of novel plant species, plant communities can change rapidly on the landscape. Managers and scientists must consider the larger perspective and perhaps establish restoration goals focused on restoring basic abiotic processes, such as hydrology, nutrient cycles, and soil accretion, that will in turn support biotic (biodiversity and biomass) and trophic (predation, competition, reproduction) processes (Zweig and Kitchens 2008). Focusing on basic abiotic processes will also simplify restoration goals and make it easier to understand novel communities and gauge the effect of restoration actions.

Conservation Issues Related to Landscape Pattern

MAINTAINING RIDGES AND SLOUGHS

Water flow is vital to the creation and maintenance of the Everglades slough–ridge–tree island topography. Satellite images of the Everglades clearly show the effect of water sweeping across the landscape in a southerly arc, orientating sloughs, ridges, and tree islands, as well as sculpting islands into teardrop shapes. Restoring a pulsed water flow in the Everglades will be necessary to conserve areas with well-defined landscape patterning and to restore degraded areas.

The velocity of historic flows in the Everglades is not known, but modern flows in sloughs are generally less than 2 cm s^{-1} (Harvey, Schaffranek, et al. 2009). Water flow depends on slope but also on vegetation density in the water column and the presence of periphyton; consequently, water was found to flow 29 to 50% faster in sloughs than on ridges (Ho, Engel, et al. 2009). Higher water-flow velocities (up to ~5 cm s^{-1}) do occur on the leading edges of waves created by pulsed flows during intense rainfall events, large water releases from hydraulic structures, and changes in barometric pressure during hurricanes (Harvey, Schaffranek, et al. 2009). The surface water slopes of the current Everglades ecosystem are lower than the slopes that occurred historically because of landscape drainage and dissection. Drainage has caused peat to subside, while levees create ponding in the WCAs. Larsen, Harvey, et al. (2009) determined that water surface slopes in the current system are an order of magnitude less than the slopes required to move sediment from the slough to the ridge. They suggested that to redistribute sediment from the slough to the ridge, the surface water slope can be increased with pulsed releases of water from impounded areas. However, creating conditions that will move sediment from the sloughs to the ridges will require removing not only barriers to flow, such as levees and roadways, but also emergent vegetation that has grown into sloughs over decades of reduced pulsed water delivery. Storm events may facilitate this process, but the details of this important ecological process remain largely unknown.

MAINTAINING TREE ISLANDS

Human engineering of the South Florida landscape has reduced or eliminated the number and aerial extent of tree islands throughout the Everglades (Patterson and Finck 1999; Sklar, Chimney, et al. 2005). Only the faint outlines of tree islands, known as ghost islands, remain in WCA-2A due to hydrologic and water quality shifts. In WCA-3A, fires, resulting from increased drainage, have destroyed tree islands to the north, whereas impounding of water has flooded remaining islands in the south (Loveless 1959). Elsewhere, many have been partially or completely overtaken by the exotic climbing vine *Lygodium microphyllum* (Volin, Lott, et al. 2004). These alterations resulted in a 54% decline in the number of hardwood communities greater than 1 ha and a 67% decline in the total area of trees (Patterson and Finck 1999).

Recently developed models of patterned landscapes have identified trees and shrubs as the concentration mechanism of scarce resources that explains the characteristic vegetation patterns of these ecosystems (Lejeune, Tlidi, et al. 2004). The loss of trees, the concentrating mechanism, will cause the system to shift from the patterned state to a homogenous vegetation state with reduced biocomplexity. The human-induced hydrologic changes and added P in the marshes of the northern Everglades have reduced tree island area and created large, homogenous cattail stands (Sklar, Chimney, et al. 2005). The loss of the nutrient-concentrating mechanism of trees in the Everglades also means that the marshes will naturally receive a higher nutrient load, which may affect the oligotrophy of the entire system (Wetzel, van der Valk, et al. 2009).

What actions must be taken to preserve tree islands and create a fully restored Everglades? First, the hydrology of the remaining Everglades must allow the survival of woody species, which will likely require the reestablishment of hydroperiods similar to historic conditions. Second, tree island loss in some parts of the Everglades has been so complete that planting trees on the heads of ghost tree islands will be required once the hydroperiod and nutrient levels are restored. Finally, understanding the importance of material fluxes beyond the visible boundaries of an individual tree island is critical to the restoration of the tree islands and, by extension, the Everglades itself.

Conservation Issues Related to Water Quality

PHOSPHORUS

Enrichment by P draining to canals, then marshes, from surrounding fertilized agriculture and urban landscapes poses one of the greatest water-quality threats to the ecology of the Everglades (Noe, Childers, et al. 2001). Currently, about 69% of the P inputs into the WCAs and 12% of the P inputs into Everglades National Park are anthropogenic in origin and enter through overland flow or are pumped into their respective areas (Davis 1994). One of the most conspicuous signals of this chronic enrichment is the monospecific stands of cattail, readily visible from satellite imagery, that have developed downstream of canal control structures (McCormick, Newman, et al. 2009). The realization that P-driven ecosystem shifts were quickly migrating to the interior of Everglades marshes prompted a 1988 lawsuit by the federal government and led to the 1994 Everglades Forever Act, which called for research to determine a protective, numeric P criterion that would prevent imbalance in natural populations of aquatic flora or fauna. A major component of this research was field dosing studies in Everglades wetlands that have been protected from excessive P enrichment (Childers, Jones, et al. 2001; Richardson 2008). These studies showed that even slightly elevated concentrations of P, if delivered continuously, cause a sequence of predictable responses over time, beginning with microbial communities and cascading to eventually shift the ecosystem to a new, cattail-dominated regime (Gaiser, Trexler, et al. 2005; Hagerthey, Newman, et al. 2008) (Fig. 17.10). All levels of sustained P enrichment ultimately result in long-term ecosystem shifts over time, such that the history of P loading (P concentration × discharge), rather than existing P concentration alone, best explains observed patterns of change (Gaiser, Trexler, et al. 2005).

The cascade of responses to P enrichment is now well documented, and useful in adaptive management, as initial responses can provide warning signals before the ecosystem has reached an unmanageable endpoint. The first, easily observable change in the southern Everglades marsh ecosystem in response to P loading is the disintegration of the calcareous, cyanobacterially dominated mat and its replacement by a mucilaginous, green-algal-dominated community (McCormick and O'Dell 1996; Gaiser, Trexler, et al. 2005) (Fig. 17.10). While the absolute biomass of periphyton mats paradoxically declines with enrichment, the green algal community has a higher nutrient content (Gaiser, Trexler, et al. 2005) (Fig. 17.10). This shift leads to greater palatability of the consumer food base, so standing stocks of many aquatic animals increase (McCormick, Shuford, et al. 2004). However, once the enrichment reaches a point where phytoplankton replaces periphyton, aquatic animal density declines, probably due to a loss of food and cover (Liston, Newman, et al. 2008). Prolonged enrichment also causes oxygen depletion that may decrease aquatic animal abundance, leading to a unimodal pattern of consumer biomass and P enrichment (King and Richardson 2007). It is only after sustained above-ambient P delivery that soil, plant, and water column P concentrations begin to reflect P inputs, but by this point individualistic and community responses to increased availability of this extremely limiting nutrient have already led to large-scale ecosystem shifts (Hagerthey, Newman, et al. 2008) (Fig. 17.10).

OTHER IONS

In addition to impacting P loading rates, water delivery alterations also lead to changes in ion chemistry (Price, Swart, et al. 2006; McCormick 2010). Canal excavation increases water $CaCO_3$ concentrations and increases connectivity to groundwater supplies of other ions, including magnesium, sodium, potassium, chloride, and sulfate (Hagerthey et al. 2011). Ecological consequences of mineral loading include increased development of calcite-precipitating blue-green algal mats, particularly noticeable in areas adjacent to canals, where water management alterations increased pH and ion concentrations in downstream marshes. For example, the lower pH flora of the refuge is gradually shifting to one dominated by calcite-precipitating mats that had never been noted in this part of the system (Gaiser et al. 2011). Paleoecological data suggest that similar changes occurred in WCA-2A following the dredging of peripheral canals (Slate and Stevenson 2000).

Natural marsh with periphyton   **Replacement by green algae**   **Open-water, low D.O. phase**   **Invasion by cattail**

FIG. 17.10. Hypothesis guiding phosphorus enrichment research at the experimental dosing facility in Everglades National Park (see Childers, Jones, et al. 2001), showing that continuous exposure to elevated phosphorus causes shifts at dose-dependent rates that ultimately converge toward a persistent disturbed end state. These effects are not static but cascade through the ecosystem, with microbial communities responding first, followed by soils and rooted-plant communities and finally by aquatic consumers that depend on microbes and plants for food and refuge. Photos of a 1-m^2 quadrant show the successive collapse of the calcareous mat matrix, replacement by a green algae–dominated community, followed by an open-water but low-dissolved oxygen (DO) clear phase that was colonized by tall, monospecific stands of cattail. This sequence occurred at all P dose levels (5, 15, and 30 μg L^{-1}) but at rates dependent on P load. (Redrawn from Gaiser, Trexler, et al. 2005.)

WATER QUALITY RESTORATION AND ASSESSMENT

The lawsuit enacted by the federal government over water-quality deterioration in the Everglades is still active, and represents the longest-running, and probably the most expensive, environmental litigation in U.S. history. The lawsuit not only called for research to determine the P threshold for Everglades wetlands, as described above, but also required the agricultural community to implement Best Management Practices and required the state to build > 40,000 acres of constructed wetlands (Stormwater Treatment Areas, or STAs) in the Everglades Agricultural Area (EAA) to clean up nutrients before they are discharged into the Everglades Protection Area (the three WCAs and the park). More than $1.5 billion has been directed toward these goals, mostly by the state of Florida. However, STAs are insufficient in area and inefficient at P removal relative to the loading rates of P into the ecosystem (Knight, Gu, et al. 2003), and it is likely that recent court actions may require another $1.5 billion to mitigate these effects. In 2008, the state of Florida announced a plan, hailed as the largest land conservation deal ever and a hopeful step toward storing and cleaning water on a scale never before contemplated, to purchase 73,000 ha of land from the United States Sugar Corporation. However, by 2010 this project had been downscaled to an 11,000-ha purchase, a baby step in a process necessitating greater urgency and large-scale commitment.

In order to document changes resulting from modifications

in land-use management and water flow, large-scale assessment efforts have been undertaken to evaluate a full suite of chemical, physical, and biological parameters relevant to restoration assessment (Scheidt and Kalla 2007; Doren, Trexler, et al. 2009; RECOVER 2010). These are coupled with long-term ecological studies, including the Long-Term Ecological Research program (established in the Everglades in 2001 by the National Science Foundation) and others operated by Everglades National Park, the South Florida Water Management District, and others, undertaken in order to understand the causes and consequences of these shifts at all levels of ecological organization and apply them in adaptive ecosystem management.

Invasive Species

Human modifications to the Everglades have created plant communities that never existed there. The vast cattail-dominated communities described earlier are an example of a new plant community in the Everglades consisting of species already present in the system (Sklar, Chimney, et al. 2005). New plant communities have also arisen because of the introduction of exotics, such as *Melaleuca quinquenervia* and *Schinus terebinthifolius* (Brazilian pepper), that create dense, nearly impenetrable forests or shrub thickets (Doren, Richards, et al. 2009). These species modify their local environment to create environmental conditions that further increase their spread. Dense stands of *Melaleuca* prevent competition from other plants by shading and allelopathy (Doren, Richards, et al. 2009). *Melaleuca* and other invasive natives, such as cattail, produce dense litter that create new soil types and raise soil elevations, reducing hydroperiod faster than native peat producers (Sklar, Chimney, et al. 2005; Doren, Richards, et al. 2009). Other exotic plants, such as *Lygodium microphyllum,* a climbing fern from Asia that smothers understory and canopy trees, have been found to alter fire regimes by providing a pathway for fire to reach tree island canopies, resulting in their death (Doren, Richards, et al. 2009). Thus, these exotic species are not only creating new plant communities, but are also capable of modifying the overall ecosystem. Furthermore, it is likely that these species will never be completely eradicated from the Everglades ecosystem.

The aquatic ecosystems of South Florida have been subjected to numerous additions of animal species, notably (but not limited to) fishes. The invasion of fishes is facilitated by the presence of canals that serve as conduits for their spread across the ecosystem. However, several species have been tracked spreading through Everglades marshes, and at least one species appears to have expanded across the breadth of the system in a period as short as three years (pike killifish, *Belanesox belizanus*). A second species, the jewelfish *(Hemichromis leternauxi),* spread across the ecosystem in less than five years and has reached high density in many sites (J. Kline pers. comm.). The nonnative species invading the Everglades represent a diversity of life histories and foraging styles, and several have highly developed and specialized behaviors and anatomy to tolerate conditions of low oxygen (Schofield, Loftus, et al. 2007).

Documenting the regional impacts of these invading species on native taxa and ecological processes has been challenging because of the large and complex nature of this ecosystem, though local impacts on native fishes have been shown. At present, these impacts are primarily in edge habitats of the freshwater Everglades. For example, Mayan cichlids *(Cichlasoma urophthalmus)* are at times over 50% of the biomass and numbers of fishes in some areas of the mangrove zone in southeastern Everglades National Park (Trexler, Loftus, et al. 2001). The implications of this new community dynamic for higher trophic levels have yet to be explored. Nonnative fishes are also abundant in solution holes in the short-hydroperiod regions of Everglades National Park called the Rocky Glades (Kobza, Trexler, et al. 2004). However, at present, the density and biomass of nonnative fishes remain low in the core areas of Everglades marshes, although it is unclear what management actions can be taken to keep these areas from being flooded by nonnative taxa whose cumulative effects, if not individually large, may be overwhelming.

Climate Change

The dynamic South Florida landscape is confronted by one certainty: climate change. Climate change comes in the form of directional, continuous shifts and abrupt, episodic ones, which shape the interactions between humans and the services provided by the ecosystem (online appendix 3). The National Research Council (2008) summarized the following expectations for South Florida by 2100: (1) temperatures will increase by 3–5°C; (2) rainfall will decrease by 10%; (3) tropical storms will be less frequent but have greater intensity; and (4) sea level will continue to rise at an accelerating rate. These changes will increase the stress on freshwater resources in the ecosystem, particularly increasing reliance on stored water to alleviate sustained periods of drought. The ecosystem must be able to withstand extremes, including large storms, known to reconfigure the coastal landscape. Sea-level rise will continue to cause saltwater encroachment where soil accretion rates are lower than the rate of rise (Lodge 2010). Peat accretion rates are highly variable, ranging from 1–10 mm yr^{-1} in mangrove forests and deeper sloughs, at times and in places keeping pace with the rate of rise (Chen and Twilley 1999). However, peat accretion requires constant inundation and anaerobic soils, which will be threatened by increased droughts. The marl prairies and the mangrove zone of Taylor Slough that is highly unproductive are in great jeopardy, accreting at rates less than 2 mm yr^{-1} (Gaiser, Zafiris, et al. 2006; Smith, Anderson, et al. 2009). The ability of mangrove swamps to sustain the landscape in the face of rising seas is largely dependent on successful restoration of water flows that reach the estuaries, and do so in volumes that compensate for losses due to projected increases in evaporation and reductions in rainfall. And all of these changes will transpire in a human-dominated landscape that continues to make increasing demands on water and land resources, so recognizing the feedbacks between these systems has become of utmost importance.

Conclusion

The Everglades is a wetland of great distinction due to its unusual geologic history and the interrelatedness of hydrology, biochemistry, and tropical and temperate species pools. By examining how these unusual species, communities, and landscapes respond to the climate dynamics from millennial to seasonal scales, we can better plan, and adapt to, changes imposed by projects geared to rehabilitate the wetland in the face of climate change. By revealing how biochemical cycles are controlled by geology, hydrology, and biotic interactions, we can better inform managers about the tradeoffs between delivering more water to the system and concerns that the delivered water is clean. In addition, we can use success stories, such as restoration efforts in the Kissimmee River (Toth 2010), where the "kinks" were put back into a once channelized river, resulting in the revitalization of the upper Everglades, as inklings that the very large-scale restoration needed for the Everglades is indeed possible. Finally, it is important to remember that the Everglades was, is, and will continue to be a human-occupied landscape, and that it is through appreciation of the services it provides that restoration will be possible (Zweig and Kitchens 2010). Many new fields of cultural ecology are rapidly developing to help bridge the gap between decision-making and the quality of the environment that sustains us.

Acknowledgments

Thanks to Nick Aumen, Jeff Kline, William Loftus, Laura Brandt, and an anonymous reviewer for providing expertise, helpful comments, and references to improve this chapter. The preparation of this chapter was generously supported by cooperative agreements with Everglades National Park, South Florida Water Management District, and Everglades Foundation and Florida International University, and by the Florida Coastal Everglades Long-Term Ecological Research Program (U.S. National Science Foundation cooperative agreement #DEB-9910514).

References

Armentano TV, Sah JP, et al. 2006. Rapid responses of vegetation to hydrological changes in Taylor Slough, Everglades National Park, Florida, USA. *Hydrobiologia* 569:293–309.

Bancroft GT, Strong AM, et al. 1994. Relationships among wading bird foraging patterns, colony locations, and hydrology in the Everglades. In *Everglades: the ecosystem and its restoration,* Davis SM, Ogden JC, editors. Delray Beach, FL: St. Lucie Press, pp. 615–57.

Beckage B, Platt WJ, et al. 2003. Influence of the El Niño Southern Oscillation on fire regimes in the Florida Everglades. *Ecology* 84:3124–30.

Bellinger BJ, Gretz MR, et al. 2010. Composition of extracellular polymeric substances from periphyton assemblages in the Florida Everglades. *J. Phycol.* 46: 484–496.

Bernhardt CE, Willard DA. 2009. Response of the Everglades ridge and slough landscape to climate variability and 20th-century water management. *Ecol. Appl.* 19:1723–38.

Blake NM. 1980. *Land into water—water into land: a history of water management in Florida.* Tallahassee: Univ. Presses of Florida.

Brandt LA, Portier KM, Kitchens WM. 2000. Patterns of change in tree islands in Arthur R. Marshall Loxahatchee National Wildlife Refuge from 1950 to 1991. *Wetlands* 20:1–14.

Brezonik PL, Pollman CD. 1999. Phosphorus chemistry and cycling in Florida lakes: global issues and local perspectives. In *Phosphorus biogeochemistry in subtropical ecosystems,* Reddy KR, O'Connor GA, Schelske CL, editors. Boca Raton, FL: Lewis Publ. pp. 69–110.

Brown SL, Flohrschutz EW, Odum HT. 1984. Structure, productivity, and phosphorus cycling of the scrub cypress ecosystem. In *Cypress swamps,* Ewel KC, Odum HT, editors. Gainesville: Univ. Florida Press, pp. 304–17.

Bruno MC, Loftus WF, et al. 2001. Diapause in copepods (Crustacea) from ephemeral habitats with different hydroperiods in Everglades National Park (Florida, USA). *Hydrobiologia* 453:295–308.

Castañeda-Moya E, Twilley RR, et al. 2010. Sediment and nutrient deposition associated with hurricane Wilma in mangroves of the Florida Coastal Everglades. *Estuar. Coasts* 33:45–58.

Chen R, Twilley RR. 1999. A simulation model of organic matter and nutrient accumulation in mangrove wetland soils. *Biogeochemistry* 44:93–118.

Chick JH, Geddes P, Trexler JC. 2008. Periphyton mat structure mediates trophic interactions in a subtropical wetland. *Wetlands* 28:378–89.

Childers DL, Boyer JN, et al. 2006. Relating precipitation and water management to nutrient concentration patterns in the oligotrophic "upside down" estuaries of the Florida Everglades. *Limnol. Oceanogr.* 51:602–16.

Childers DL, Jones RD, et al. 2002. Quantifying the effects of low level phosphorus enrichment on unimpacted Everglades wetlands with in situ flumes and phosphorus dosing. In *The Everglades, Florida Bay, and coral reefs of the Florida Keys: an ecosystem sourcebook,* Porter J, Porter K, editors. Boca Raton, FL: CRC Press, pp. 127–52.

Craighead FC. 1971. *The natural environments and their succession: trees of South Florida.* Coral Gables, FL: Univ. Miami Press.

Darby PC, Bennetts RE, Percival HF. 2008. Dry down impacts on apple snail *(Pomacea paludosa)* demography: implications for wetland water management. *Wetlands* 28:204–14.

David PG. 1996. Changes in plant communities relative to hydrologic conditions in the Florida Everglades. *Wetlands* 16:15–23.

Davis SM. 1994. Phosphorus inputs and vegetation sensitivity in the Everglades. In *Everglades: the ecosystem and its restoration,* Davis SM, Ogden JC, editors. Delray Beach, FL: St. Lucie Press, pp. 357–78.

Davis SM, Ogden JC, editors. 1994. *Everglades: the ecosystem and its restoration.* Delray Beach, FL: St. Lucie Press.

Davis SM, Gaiser EE, et al. 2005. Southern marl prairies conceptual ecological model. *Wetlands* 25:821–31.

DeAngelis DL, Trexler JC, Loftus WF. 2005. Life history trade-offs and community dynamics of small fishes in a seasonally pulsed wetland. *Can. J. Fish. Aq. Sci.* 62:781–90.

Donders TH, Wagner F, et al. 2005. Mid- to late-Holocene El Niño–Southern Oscillation dynamics reflected in the subtropical terrestrial realm. *Proc. Nat. Acad. Sci.* 102:10904–08.

Doren RF, Richards JH, Volin JC. 2009. A conceptual ecological model to facilitate understanding the role of invasive species in large-scale ecosystem restoration. *Ecol. Indic.* 9S:150–60.

Doren RF, Trexler JC, et al. 2009. Ecological indicators for system-wide assessment of the Greater Everglades Ecosystem Restoration Program. *Ecol. Indic.* 9S:2–16.

Dorn NJ, Trexler JC. 2007. Crayfish assemblage shifts in a large drought-prone wetland: the roles of hydrology and competition. *Freshw. Biol.* 52:2399–2411.

Dorn NJ, Volin JC. 2009. Resistance of crayfish *(Procambarus* spp.) populations to wetland drying depends on species and substrate. *J. N. Am. Benthol. Soc.* 28:766–77.

Dorn NJ, Trexler JC, Gaiser EE. 2006. Exploring the role of large predators in marsh food webs: evidence for a behaviorally-mediated trophic cascade. *Hydrobiologia* 569:375–386.

Douglas MS. 1947. *The Everglades: river of grass.* New York: Rinehart and Company.

Drew RD, Schomer NS. 1984. An ecological characterization of the Caloosahatchee River/Big Cypress watershed. FWS/OBS-82/58.2. Washington, DC: USFWS.

Duever MJ, Carlson JE, et al. 1978. Ecosystem analyses at Corkscrew Swamp. In *Cypress wetlands for water management, recycling and conservation,* Odum HT, Ewel KC, editors. Fourth Annual Report to National Science Foundation and Rockefeller Foundation. University of Florida, Center for Wetlands, Gainesville, FL, USA. pp. 534–570.

Duever MJ, Meeder JF, Duever LC. 1984. Ecosystems of the Big Cypress Swamp. In *Cypress wetlands for water management, recycling and conservation,* Odum HT, Ewel KC, editors. Gainesville: Univ. Florida Press, pp. 294–302.

Duever MJ, Meeder JF, et al. 1994. The climate of South Florida and its role in shaping the Everglades ecosystem. In *Everglades: the ecosystem and its restoration,* Davis SM, Ogden JC, editors. Delray Beach, FL: St. Lucie Press, pp. 225–48.

Enfield DB, Mestas-Nunez AM, Trimble PJ. 2001. The Atlantic multidecadal oscillation and its relation to rainfall and river flows in the continental U.S. *Geophys. Res. Lett.* 28:2077–80.

Ewel KC. 1990. Swamps. In *Ecosystems of Florida,* Myers RL, Ewel JJ, editors. Orlando: Univ. Central Florida Press, pp. 281–323.

Flora MD, Rosendahl PC. 1982. An analysis of surface water nutrient concentrations in the Shark River Slough, 1972–1980. Report T-653. Homestead: South Florida Research Center.

Frederick P, Gawlik DE, et al. 2009. The white ibis and wood stork as indicators for restoration of the Everglades ecosystem. *Ecol. Indic.* 9S:83–95.

Frederick PC, Powell GVN. 1994. Nutrient transport by wading birds in the Everglades. In *Everglades: the ecosystem and its restoration,* Davis SM, Ogden JC, editors. Delray Beach, FL: St. Lucie Press, pp. 571–84.

Gaiser E. 2009. Periphyton as an indicator of restoration in the Everglades. *Ecol. Indic.* 9S:37–45.

Gaiser EE, Taylor BE, Brooks MJ. 2001. Establishment of wetlands on the southeastern Atlantic Coastal Plain: paleolimnological evidence of a mid-Holocene hydrologic threshold from a South Carolina pond. *J. Paleolimnol.* 26:373–91.

Gaiser EE, Richards JH, et al. 2006. Periphyton responses to eutrophication in the Florida Everglades: cross-system patterns of structural and compositional change. *Limnol. Oceanogr.* 51:617–30.

Gaiser EE, Scinto LJ, et al. 2004. Phosphorus in periphyton mats provides the best metric for detecting low-level P enrichment in an oligotrophic wetland. *Water Res.* 38:507–16.

Gaiser EE, Trexler JC, et al. 2005. Cascading ecological effects of low-level phosphorus enrichment in the Florida Everglades. *J. Env. Qual.* 34:717–23.

Gaiser EE, Zafiris A, et al. 2006. Tracking rates of ecotone migration due to salt-water encroachment using fossil mollusks in coastal South Florida. *Hydrobiologia* 569:237–57.

Gaiser E, McCormick P, Hagerthey S. 2011. Landscape patterns of periphyton in the Florida Everglades. *Critical Reviews in Environmental Science and Technology.* 41(S1): 92–120.

Geddes P, Trexler JC. 2003. Uncoupling of omnivore-mediated

positive and negative effects on periphyton mats. *Oecologia* 136:585–95.

Gleason PJ, Spackman W. 1974. Calcareous periphyton and water chemistry in the Everglades. Environments of South Florida Present and Past, *Miami Geol. Soc. Memoir 2,* Miami, FL.

Gleason PJ, Stone P. 1994. Age, origin, and landscape evolution of the Everglades peatland. In *Everglades: the ecosystem and its restoration,* Davis SM, Ogden JC, editors. Delray Beach, FL: St. Lucie Press, pp. 157–166.

Gunderson LH. 1994. Vegetation of the Everglades: determinants of community composition. In *Everglades: the ecosystem and its restoration,* Davis SM, Ogden JC, editors. Delray Beach, FL: St. Lucie Press, pp. 323–40.

Gunderson LH, Loftus WF. 1993. The Everglades. In *Biodiversity of the southeastern United States,* Martin WH, Boyce SG, Echternacht AC, editors. New York: John Wiley, pp. 199–256.

Gunderson LH, Loope LL. 1982. An inventory of the plant communities within the Deep Strand Lake Area, Big Cypress National Preserve. SFRC Tech. Rep. T-666, Homestead, FL.

Gunderson LH, Snyder JR. 1994. Fire patterns in the southern Everglades. In *Everglades: the ecosystem and its restoration,* Davis SM, Ogden JC, editors. Delray Beach, FL: St. Lucie Press, pp. 291–305.

Hagenbuck WW, et al. 1974. A preliminary investigation of the effects of water levels on vegetative communities of Loxahatchee National Wildlife Refuge, Florida. DOI PB-231 611.

Hagerthey SE, Newman S, et al. 2008. Multiple regime shifts in a subtropical peatland: community-specific thresholds to eutrophication. *Ecol. Monogr.* 78:547–65.

Hagerthey S, Bellinger B, et al. 2011. Everglades periphyton: A biogeochemical perspective. *Critical Reviews in Environmental Science and Technology.* 41(S1): 309–343.

Harrington RW. 1959. Delayed hatching in stranded eggs of marsh killifish, *Fundulus confluentus. Ecology* 40:430–37.

Harvey JW, McCormick PV. 2009. Groundwater's significance to changing hydrology, water chemistry, and biological communities of a floodplain ecosystem, Everglades, South Florida, USA. *Hydrogeol. J.* 17:185–201.

Harvey JW, Schaffranek RW, et al. 2009. Hydroecological factors governing surface water flow on a low-gradient floodplain. *Wat. Resour. Res.* 45:W03421, doi:10.1029/2008WR007129.

Hendrix AN, Loftus WF. 2000. Distribution and relative abundance of the crayfishes *Procambarus alleni* (Faxon) and *P. fallax* (Hagen) in southern Florida. *Wetlands* 20:194–99.

Ho DT, Engel VC, et al. 2009. Tracer studies of sheet flow in the Florida Everglades. *Geophys. Res. Lett.* 36:L09401, doi:10.1029/2009GL037355.

Hollander GM. 2008. *Raising cane in the 'Glades: the global sugar trade and the transformation of Florida.* Chicago: Univ. Chicago Press.

Karunaratne LB, Darby PC, Bennetts RE. 2006. The effects of wetland habitat structure on Florida apple snail density. *Wetlands* 26:1143–50.

King RS, Richardson CJ. 2007. Subsidy-stress response of macroinvertebrate community biomass to a phosphorus gradient in an oligotrophic wetland ecosystem. *J. N. Am. Benthol. Soc.* 26:491–508.

Knight RL, Gu B, et al. 2003. Long-term phosphorus removal in Florida aquatic systems dominated by submerged aquatic vegetation. *Ecol. Eng.* 20:45–63.

Kobza RM, Trexler JC, et al. 2004. Community structure of fishes inhabiting aquatic refuges in a threatened karstic wetland and its implication for ecosystem management. *Biol. Conserv.* 116:153–65.

Kolipinski MC, Higer AL. 1969. *Some aspects of the effects of the quantity and quality of water on biological communities in Everglades National Park.* Tallahassee, FL: USGS.

Kueny JA, Day MJ. 1998. An assessment of protected karst landscapes in the Caribbean. *Carib. Geogr.* 9:87–101.

Kushlan JA. 1990. Freshwater marshes. In *Ecosystems of Florida,* Myers RL, Ewel JJ, editors. Orlando: Univ. Central Florida Press, pp. 324–63.

La Hée J. 2010. The influence of phosphorus on periphyton mats from the Everglades and three tropical karstic wetlands. Ph.D. diss., Florida International Univ., Miami.

Larsen LG, Harvey JW, Crimaldi JP. 2007. A delicate balance: ecohydrological feedbacks governing landscape morphology in a lotic peatland. *Ecol. Monogr.* 77:591–614.

Larsen LG, Harvey JW, Crimaldi JP. 2009. Predicting bed shear stress and its role in sediment dynamics and restoration potential of the Everglades and other vegetated flow systems. *Ecol. Eng.* 35:1773–85.

Lejeune O, Tlidi M, Lefever R. 2004. Vegetation spots and stripes: dissipative structures in arid landscapes. *Intern. J. Quantum Chem.* 98:261–71.

Liston SE, Newman S, Trexler JC. 2008. Macroinvertebrate community response to eutrophication in an oligotrophic wetland: an in situ mesocosm experiment. *Wetlands* 28:686–94.

Lodge TE. 2010. *The Everglades handbook: understanding the ecosystem,* 3rd ed. Boca Raton, FL: CRC Press.

Loftus WF, Kushlan JA. 1987. Freshwater fishes of southern Florida. *Bull. Fla. State Mus. Biol. Sci.* 31:147–344.

Loftus WF, Johnson RA, Anderson GH. 1992. Ecological impacts of the reduction of groundwater levels in short-hydroperiod marshes of the Everglades. In *Proc. 1st Intern. Conf. Ground Water Ecol.,* Stanford JA, Simons JJ, editors. Am. Wat Resour. Assoc., Middleburg, VA, pp. 199–208.

Long RW. 1984. Origin of the vascular flora of southern Florida. In *Environments of south Florida present and past II,* Gleason PJ, editor. Coral Gables, FL: Miami Geol. Soc., pp. 118–26.

Loope LL. 1980. Phenology of flowering and fruiting in plant communities of Everglades National Park and Biscayne National Monument, Florida. SFRC T-586, Everglades Nat. Park, Homestead, FL.

Loveless, CM. 1959. A study of the vegetation of the Florida Everglades. *Ecology* 40:1–9.

Lowe EF. 1986. The relationship between hydrology and vegetational pattern within the floodplain marsh of a subtropical, Florida lake. *Fla. Sci.* 1986:213–33.

Mason D, van der Valk AG. 2002. Vegetation, peat elevation, and peat depth on two tree islands in Water Conservation Area 3-A. In *Tree islands of the Everglades,* Sklar FH, van der Valk AG, editors. Dordrecht: Kluwer, pp. 337–56.

Mazzotti FJ, Brandt LA. 1994. Ecology of the American alligator in a seasonally fluctuating environment. In *Everglades: the ecosystem and its restoration,* Davis SM, Ogden JC, editors. Delray Beach, FL: St. Lucie Press, pp. 485–505.

McCally D. 1999. *The Everglades: an environmental history.* Tallahassee: Univ. Presses of Florida.

McCormick, PV (2010). Soil and periphyton indicators of anthropogenic water-quality changes in a rainfall-driven wetland. *Wetlands Ecology and Management* (31 July 2010): 1-16-16. doi: 10.1007/s11273-010-9196-9.

McCormick PV, O'Dell MB. 1996. Quantifying periphyton responses to phosphorus in the Florida Everglades: a synoptic-experimental approach. *J. N. Am. Benthol. Soc.* 15:450–68.

McCormick PV, Newman S, Vilcheck LW. 2009. Landscape responses to wetland eutrophication: loss of slough habitat in the Florida Everglades, USA. *Hydrobiologia* 621:105–14.

McCormick PV, Shuford RBE, Rawlik PS. 2004. Changes in macroinvertebrate community structure and function along a phosphorus gradient in the Florida Everglades. *Hydrobiologia* 529:113–32.

McPherson BF. 1973. Vegetation in relation to water depth in Conservation Area 3, Florida. Tallahassee, FL: USGS Open File Report no. 73025.

McVoy CW, Said WP, et al. 2011. *Landscapes and hydrology of the pre-drainage Everglades.* Gainesville: Univ. Press of Florida.

Means DB, Simberloff D. 1987. The peninsula effect: habitat-correlated species decline in Florida's herpetofauna. *J. Biogeogr.* 14:551–68.

Meshaka WE, Snow R, et al. 2002. Occurrence of wildlife on tree islands in the southern Everglades. In *Tree islands of the Everglades,* Sklar FH, van der Valk AG, editors. Dordrecht: Kluwer. pp. 391–427.

Miao S, Zou CB, Breshears DD. 2009. Vegetation responses to extreme hydrological events: sequence matters. *Am. Nat.* 173:113–18.

Miralles-Wilhelm F, Trimble PJ, et al. 2005. Climate-based estimation of hydrologic inflow into Lake Okeechobee, Florida. *J. Wat. Resour. Plan. Manag.* 131:394–401.

Myers RL, Ewel JJ. 1990. *Ecosystems of Florida.* Orlando: Univ. Central Florida Press.

National Research Council. 2008. *Progress toward restoring the Everglades: the second biennial review—2008.* Washington, DC: National Academies Press.

Nature Conservancy. 2007. *Parks in peril.* Mexico Partners, Arlington, VA.

Nelson CM, Loftus WF. 1996. Effects of high-water conditions on fish communities in Everglades alligator ponds. In *Proc. 1996 conference: ecological assessment of the 1994–1995 high water conditions in the southern Everglades,* Armentano TV, editor. Miami: Florida Internat. Univ., pp. 89–101.

Newman S, Schuette J, et al. 1998. Factors influencing cattail abundance in the northern Everglades. *Aquat. Bot.* 60:265–80.

Noe GB, Childers DL, Jones RD. 2001. Phosphorus biogeochemistry and the impact of phosphorus enrichment: why is the Everglades so unique? *Ecosystems* 4:603–24.

Ogden, L. 2011. *Swamplife: People, Gators, and Mangroves Entangled in the Everglades.* Minneapolis, MN: University of Minnesota Press. 224 pp.

Palmer ML, Mazzotti FJ. 2004. Structure of Everglades alligator holes. *Wetlands* 24:115–22.

Patterson K, Finck R. 1999. Tree islands of the WCA3 aerial photointerpretation and trend analysis project summary report. SFWMD Report, St. Petersburg, FL.

Pimm SL, Lockwood JL, et al. 2002. Sparrow in the grass: a report on the first ten years of research on the Cape Sable seaside sparrow *(Ammodramus maritimus mirabilis).* Report to the National Park Service, Everglades National Park, FL.

Porter CL. 1967. Composition and productivity of a subtropical prairie. *Ecology* 48:937–42.

Porter J, Porter K. 2002. *The Everglades, Florida Bay and coral reefs of the Florida Keys: an ecosystem sourcebook.* Boca Raton, FL: CRC Press.

Price RM, Swart PK, Fourqurean JW. 2006. Coastal groundwater discharge—an additional source of phosphorus for the oligotrophic wetlands of the Everglades. *Hydrobiologia* 569:23–36.

Rader RB. 1999. The Florida Everglades: natural variability, invertebrate diversity, and foodweb stability. In *Invertebrates in freshwater wetlands of North America,* Batzer DP, Rader RB, Wissinger SA, editors. New York: John Wiley, pp. 25–54.

RECOVER. 2010. *2009 comprehensive Everglades restoration plan system status report.* SFWMD, West Palm Beach, FL.

Reddy KR, Wang Y, et al. 1998. Forms of soil phosphorus in selected hydrologic units of the Florida Everglades. *Soil Sci. Soc. Am. J.* 62:1134–47.

Rehage JS, Loftus WF. 2007. Seasonal fish community variation in headwater mangrove creeks in the southwestern Everglades: an examination of their role as dry-down refuges. *Bull. Mar. Sci.* 80:625–45.

Richardson CJ. 2008. *The Everglades experiments: lessons for ecosystem restoration.* New York: Springer.

Richardson CJ, Ferrell GM, Vaithiyanathan P. 1999. Nutrient effects on stand structure, resorption efficiency, and secondary compounds in Everglades sawgrass. *Ecology* 80:2182–92.

Rizzardi KW. 1999. Everglades in jeopardy: a drama of water management and endangered species. *Florida State Univ. Law Rev.* 27:349–95.

Ross MS, Meeder JF, et al. 2000. The southeast saline Everglades revisited: 50 years of coastal vegetation change. *J. Veg. Sci.* 11:101–12.

Ross MS, Mitchell-Bruker S, et al. 2006. Interaction of hydrology and nutrient limitation in the ridge and slough landscape of the southern Everglades. *Hydrobiologia* 569:37–59.

Ruehl CB. 2010. Quantifying the interactive effects of predators, resources, and disturbance on multiple traits of a freshwater snail from the Everglades. Ph.D. diss., Florida International Univ., Miami.

Sargeant B, Gaiser EE, Trexler JC. 2010. Biotic and abiotic determinants of community trophic diversity in an Everglades food web. *Mar. Freshw. Ecol.* 61:11–22.

Saunders CJ, Gao M, et al. 2006. Using soil profiles of seeds and molecular markers as proxies for sawgrass and wet prairie slough vegetation in Shark Slough, Everglades National Park. *Hydrobiologia* 569:475–92.

Scheidt DJ, Kalla PI. 2007. Everglades ecosystem assessment: water management and quality, eutrophication, mercury contamination, soils and habitat: monitoring for adaptive management: a R-EMAP status report. USEPA Region 4, Athens, GA. 904-R-07-001.

Schmalzer PA, Hinkle CR, Mailander JL. 1991. Changes in community composition and biomass in *Juncus roemerianus* Scheele and *Spartina bakeri* Merr. marshes one year after a fire. *Wetlands* 11:67–86.

Schofield PJ, Loftus WF, Brown ME. 2007. Hypoxia tolerance of two centrarchid sunfishes and an introduced cichlid in karstic Everglades wetlands of southern Florida, U.S.A. *J. Fish Biol.* 71:87–99.

Schomer NS, Drew RD. 1982. An ecological characterization of the lower Everglades, Florida Bay and the Florida Keys. USFWS, Washington, DC. FWS/OBS-82/58.1.

Scinto LJ, Reddy KR. 2003. Biotic and abiotic uptake of phosphorus by periphyton in a subtropical freshwater wetland. *Aquat. Bot.* 77:203–22.

Sklar F, Chimney MJ, et al. 2005. The ecological-societal underpinnings of Everglades restoration. *Frontiers Ecol. Env.* 3:161–69.

Sklar F, McVoy C, et al. 2002. The effects of altered hydrology on the ecology of the Everglades. In *The Everglades, Florida Bay, and coral reefs of the Florida Keys: an ecosystem sourcebook,* Porter J, Porter K, editors. Boca Raton, FL: CRC Press, pp. 39–82.

Slate JE, Stevenson RJ. 2000. Recent and abrupt environmental change in the Florida Everglades indicated from siliceous microfossils. *Wetlands* 20:346–56.

Smith TJ, Anderson GH, et al. 2009. Cumulative impacts of hurricanes on Florida mangrove ecosystems: sediment deposition, storm surges and vegetation. *Wetlands* 29:24–34.

Steward KK, Ornes WH. 1975. The autecology of sawgrass in the Florida everglades. *Ecology* 56:162–71.

Sun G, Riekert H, Korhnak LV. 1995. Shallow groundwater table dynamics of cypress wetland/pine upland systems in Florida flatwoods. *Soil Crop Sci. Soc. Fla.* 54:66.

Thomas SE, Gaiser EE, et al. 2006. Quantifying the responses of calcareous periphyton crusts to rehydration: a microcosm study (Florida Everglades). *Aquat. Bot.* 84:317–23.

Tian H, Xu X, et al. 2010. Modeling ecosystem responses to prescribed fires in a phosphorus-enriched Everglades wetland: I. Phosphorus dynamics and cattail recovery. *Ecol. Model.* doi:10.1016/j.ecolmodel.2009.12.025.

Toth LA. 2010. Restoration response of relict broadleaf marshes to increased water depths. *Wetlands* 30:263–74.

Trexler JC. 1995. Restoration of the Kissimmee River: a conceptual model of past and present fish communities and its consequences for evaluating restoration success. *Restor. Ecol.* 3:195–210.

Trexler JC, Loftus WF, et al. 2001. Empirical assessment of fish introductions in a subtropical wetland: an evaluation of contrasting views. *Biol. Invasions* 2:265–77.

Trexler JC, Loftus WF, et al. 2002. Ecological scale and its implications for freshwater fishes in the Florida Everglades. In *The Everglades, Florida Bay and coral reefs of the Florida Keys: an ecosystem sourcebook,* Porter J, Porter K, editors. Boca Raton, FL: CRC Press, pp. 153–81.

Trexler JC, Loftus WF, Perry S. 2005. Disturbance frequency and community structure in a twenty-five-year intervention study. *Oecologia* 145:140–52.

Turner AM, Trexler JC, et al. 1999. Targeting ecosystem features for conservation: standing crops in the Florida Everglades. *Conserv. Biol.* 13:898–911.

Ugarte CA, Rice KG, Donnelly MA. 2007. Comparison of diet, reproductive biology, and growth of the pig frog *(Rana grylio)* from harvested and protected areas of the Florida Everglades. *Copeia* 2007:436–48.

Urban NH, Davis SM, Aumen NG. 1993. Fluctuations in sawgrass and cattail densities in Everglades Water Conservation Area 2A under varying nutrient, hydrologic and fire regimes. *Aquat. Bot.* 46:203–23.

Urgelles R. 2009. Dragonfly assemblage structure in relation to hydroperiod and vegetation gradients in freshwater wetlands of the Florida Everglades. MS thesis, Florida International Univ., Miami.

Volin JC, Lott MS, et al. 2004. Predicting rapid invasion of the

Florida Everglades by Old World climbing fern *(Lygodium microphyllum). Divers. Distrib.* 10:439–46.

Wanless HR, Parkinson RW, Tedesco LP. 1994. Sea level control on stability of Everglades wetlands. In *Everglades: the ecosystem and its restoration,* Davis SM, Ogden JC, editors. Delray Beach, FL: St. Lucie Press, pp. 199–222.

Weathers KC, Cadenasso ML, Pickett STA. 2001. Forest edges as nutrient and pollutant concentrators: potential synergisms between fragmentation, forest canopies, and the atmosphere. *Conserv. Biol.* 15:1506–14.

Wetzel PR. 2002. Analysis of tree island vegetation communities. In *Tree islands of the Everglades,* Sklar FH, van der Valk AG, editors. Dordrecht: Kluwer, pp. 357–89.

Wetzel PR, Pinion T, et al. 2008. Landscape analysis to tree island head vegetation in Water Conservation Area 3, Florida Everglades. *Wetlands* 28:276–89.

Wetzel PR, Sklar FH, et al. 2011. Biogeochemical processes on tree islands in the Greater Everglades: initiating a new paradigm. *Crit. Rev. Environ. Sci. Technol.* 41(S1):670–701.

Wetzel PR, van der Valk AG, et al. 2005. Maintaining tree islands in the Florida Everglades: nutrient redistribution is the key. *Frontiers Ecol. Env.* 3:370–76.

Wetzel PR, van der Valk AG, et al. 2009. Heterogeneity of phosphorus distribution in a patterned landscape, the Florida Everglades. *Plant Ecol.* 200:83–90.

Wharton CH, Odum HT, et al. 1977. Forested wetlands of Florida—their management and use. Tallahassee, FL: Div. State Plan.

Willard DA, Bernhardt CE, et al. 2006. Response of Everglades tree islands to environmental change. *Ecol. Monogr.* 76:565–83.

Williams AJ, Trexler JC. 2006. A preliminary analysis of the correlation of food-web characteristics with hydrology and nutrient gradients in the southern Everglades. *Hydrobiologia* 569:493–504.

Winkler MG, Sanford PR, Kaplan SW. 2001. Hydrology, vegetation, and climate change in the southern Everglades during the Holocene. *Bull. Am. Paleontol.* 361:57–98.

Zaffke M. 1983. Plant communities of water conservation area 3A; base-line documentation prior to the operation of S-339 and S-340. SFWMD Report, West Palm Beach, FL.

Zhang K, Simard M, et al. 2008. Airborne laser scanning quantification of disturbances from hurricanes and lightning strikes to mangrove forests in Everglades National Park, USA. *Sensors* 8:2262–92.

Zweig CL, Kitchens WM. 2008. Effects of landscape gradients on wetland vegetation communities: information for large-scale restoration. *Wetlands* 28:1086–96.

Zweig CL, Kitchens WM. 2009. Multistate succession wetlands: a novel use of state and transition models. *Ecology* 90:1900–09.

Zweig CL, Kitchens WM. 2010. The semiglades: the collision of restoration, social values, and the ecosystem concept. *Restor. Ecol.* 18:138–42.

CHAPTER 18

Floodplain Wetlands of the Southeastern Coastal Plain

SAMMY L. KING, LORETTA L. BATTAGLIA, CLIFF R. HUPP,
RICHARD F. KEIM, and B. GRAEME LOCKABY

Floodplains achieve their greatest extent in North America on the Coastal Plain Physiographic Province (Fig. 18.1) (Hunt 1967), predominantly in the southeastern U.S. These ecosystems are integrally linked to the rivers that have led to their formation and have supported human uses simultaneously with other biological functions for about 10,000 years (King, Shepard, et al. 2005). Conservation and management of these systems necessitate an integrated understanding of geomorphology, hydrology, ecology, and other biotic and abiotic processes (King, Sharitz, et al. 2009). The objective of this chapter is to provide a basic overview of nontidal, lowland southeastern floodplain ecosystems.

Geomorphology, Hydrology, Soils, and Biochemistry

Geomorphology

Variation in climate and tectonics has led to a complex modern landscape in the southeastern Coastal Plain. For instance, many rivers on the Coastal Plain are underfit: that is, the present channel does not carry sufficient discharge or sediment to have created the broad alluvial floodplain within which the river now flows. This underfit condition may have resulted from a present-day reduction in rainfall compared to a pluvial period 18,000 to 10,000 years ago when rainfall and floodplain development may have been 18 times greater. (Dury 1977). Stream captures (i.e., when one stream intersects another and the flow of the intersected stream begins to flow down the channel of the first stream) have contributed to the underfit nature of some fluvial systems (e.g., the Cache River, Arkansas; Bennett and Saucier 1988).

Floodplains that occur along most meandering alluvial streams are broad, flat to gently sloping alluvial surfaces that are inundated every one to three years by out-of-bank flooding (Osterkamp and Hupp 1984). Floodplains, like most fluvial landforms, are dynamic features where meandering channel dynamics cause constant erosion in some places and aggradation elsewhere. Meanders typically extend and erode accreted sediments until they are cut off from the main channel, leaving an oxbow lake and a new channel (Fig. 18.2).

Within river valleys of the Southeast, there may be multiple terraces, also known as bottoms. The first bottom is the one currently occupied by the river and its floodplain. It is often topographically diverse with ridge-and-swale topography, features reminiscent of former point bars and channel locations. Adjacent terraces (e.g., second and third bottoms) that flank the active floodplain are essentially abandoned floodplains. Although originally created by fluvial processes, the processes of erosion and deposition, coupled with channel migration, have left them hydrologically disconnected from the river.

Spatial and temporal variation in both vertical and lateral sediment deposition creates the fluvial features that typify floodplains (Fig. 18.2). Slight differences in elevation associated with floodplain geomorphic features and large woody debris create a complex pattern of microsite velocity regimes during flooding that ultimately affect intrasite sedimentation regimes. Coarse sediments require greater water velocities for transport; thus, as floodwaters overtop the bank and encounter the hydraulically rough floodplain, water velocities slow and coarse sediments are deposited, forming natural levees along the floodplain margin (Hupp, Demas, et al. 2008). Fine sediments require lower water velocities for transport and require a longer period of interaction on the floodplain for deposition to occur. Vertical deposition is greatest in low areas with long hydroperiods and connectivity to sediment-laden flow (Hupp, Walbridge, et al. 2005).

Natural levee building and crevasse splay deposits may occur from both vertical and lateral depositional events (Fig. 18.2). Levees tend to be most pronounced along relatively straight reaches between meanders and are often the highest ground on the floodplain. Breaches in natural levees can create crevasse splays that may insert coarse material deep into the otherwise fine-grained floodplain (Fig. 18.2). Lateral deposition of relatively coarse sediment occurs within the channel and produces features such as point bars. Features formed by lateral deposition may become isolated when channels are cut off, thus forming relict features such as ridge-and-swale topography.

Fluvial geomorphic systems, by nature, tend to maintain a dynamic equilibrium among ambient sediment load, water discharge, and channel geometry (Osterkamp and Hedman 1977). Stream reaches are deemed to be "in equilibrium" when

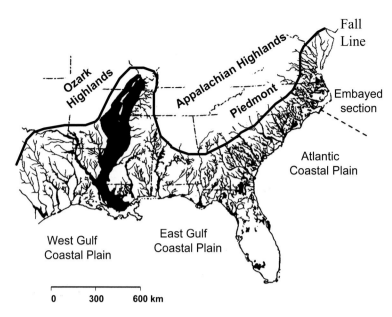

FIG. 18.1. The Coastal Plain of the southeastern United States. Potential extent of bottomland hardwood forest (BLH; forested riparian wetlands) is shown along major streams. Note that the extent of BLH forests nearly matches the inland extent of the Coastal Plain delineated by the Fall Line.

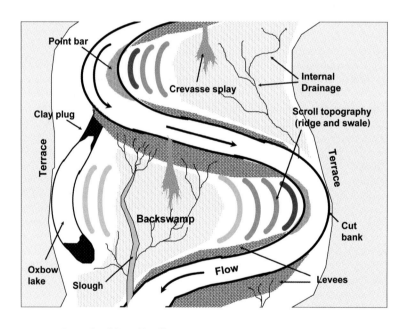

FIG. 18.2. Generalized fluvial landforms on a Coastal Plain bottomland. Point bars, cut banks, and to a large degree scroll topography are developed by lateral fluvial processes, whereas backswamps, sloughs, oxbows, and internal drainage are maintained by vertical fluvial processes.

the stream and its hydrogeomorphic form and process are sufficiently (but not overly) competent to entrain (i.e., initiate movement), transport, and store the sediment provided by the catchment (Hack 1960); this equilibrium, by definition, is not static but dynamic. Streams that are not in dynamic equilibrium typically have been subjected to dramatic, usually rapid, regime shifts; this may happen naturally (e.g., earthquakes) or through human alteration. Sediment grain size, stream gradient, and channel pattern (meandering, cascading, and straight) may adjust along the conceptual gradient to maintain near-equilibrium conditions (Hupp 2000). Streams that

have been affected by substantial human alteration usually exhibit an unstable regime shift away from equilibrium conditions (Fig. 18.3).

In the Coastal Plain, widespread stream channelization has resulted in severe channel erosion because of the increased gradient (Simon and Hupp 1987) (e.g., channel incision, from a meandering regime to a straight regime). This instability normally initiates a complex but predictable sequence of process responses (Schumm and Parker 1973) back toward the original equilibrated state. Typical responses are channel widening and filling following channel incision (Simon and Hupp 1992)

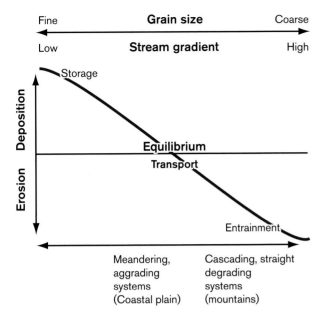

FIG. 18.3. Conceptual gradient of erosion and deposition in relation to channel gradient, sediment grain size, channel pattern, and general physiography. The equilibrium area represents conditions where there is no significant net deposition or erosion. Most stream systems in equilibrium lie on either side of the equilibrium area. (Hupp, Pierce et al. 2009).

in response to severe floodplain aggradation (Pierce and King 2007). These erosional adjustments typically form knickpoints (a point or area of increased erosion downstream that migrates into equilibrated areas) that migrate upstream. Another, nearly ubiquitous disturbance on Coastal Plain floodplains is the impact of legacy sedimentation following European settlement (Jackson, Martin, et al. 2005).

Hydrology

The regional climate of the southeastern U.S. is typified by precipitation that is relatively evenly distributed throughout the year but decreased evapotranspiration during winter (Muller and Grymes 1998). The result is annual river hydrographs dominated by high discharge in the winter and spring and decreasing discharge during summer. Exceptions are in southern Florida, where summer precipitation is normally sufficient to exceed evapotranspiration (Kelly and Gore 2008). Interannual variability in rainfall and discharge is greatest in coastal watersheds where summer precipitation may vary by up to 40%, depending on climatic cycles such as the Atlantic Multidecadal Oscillation (Enfield, Mestas-Nuñez, et al. 2001). Multiyear droughts and wet periods are typical throughout the region, but interannual variability in stream flow is greatest in southern Florida (Patrick 1995).

The hydrology of many wetlands in Coastal Plain floodplains is dominated by river flows. Floodplain geomorphology affects surface connectivity between rivers and the floodplain, so that the frequency, duration, and sources of floodwaters vary spatially and temporally. Small geomorphic features control surface connectivity between rivers and floodplains. Natural levees that form adjacent to channels restrict surface flow connections below bank-full stage, but crevasses in natural levees and minor channels and swales within the floodplain allow for localized hydrologic connectivity (Hupp 2000).

Because many southeastern streams are underfit, overbank flooding events are typically of long duration and low flow velocity, and floodplains are typified by frequent inundation of large areas. The duration of overbank flood events is generally inversely proportional to watershed size, both because large watersheds integrate more climatic variability and because storage of floodwaters on floodplains attenuates flood peaks downstream (Walton, Davis, et al. 1996).

The underfit floodplain morphology of most floodplains can result in local dominance of water sources other than streamflow (Williams 1998), especially when the main river is not above flood stage. There is substantial mixing of river water with local rainfall and runoff from small tributaries, which are not always synchronous with river flow (Mertes 1997). Kroes and Brinson (2004) concluded that groundwater influence is required for the formation of wetlands on floodplains, regardless of the duration of overbank flows. Rainwater ponding dominates some floodplain wetlands, especially where natural or artificial barriers to flow impound water or isolate topographic low points from surface flows.

Within the floodplain, topographical features typical of river meandering, such as sloughs, relict ridges, and scrollbar topography, control flowpaths and retention of floodwaters and rainwater (Steiger, Tabacchi, et al. 2005; Jones, Poole, et al. 2008). Ponding of rainwater and groundwater can occur prior to overbank flooding and may be important biologically for organisms that require fishless ponds for reproduction (see "Herpetofauna," below). Geomorphic controls on hydrologic processes can be highly variable in time as a result of progressive geomorphic changes such as river incision, meandering, and sediment deposition; ephemeral, biologically derived flow impedances such as beaver dams; and anthropogenic geomorphic alterations such as roads, levees, dredging, and water control structures. Thus, stage-discharge relationships vary through time and surface flooding may persist locally long after overbank flooding has ceased.

Subsurface hydrological processes in floodplain wetlands of the region have not been extensively studied. Groundwater in floodplain microtopography is highly variable locally and has spatial patterns that vary seasonally (Fig. 18.4). Many floodplains have sufficient microtopographical relief that the water table is deep enough during large portions of the year to stop hydric soils from forming (Dewey, Schoenholtz, et al. 2006); these floodplains can be considered complexes of mesic and hydric sites. Transient groundwater conditions resulting from rain events can form groundwater ridges within topographic ridges (Newman 2010); the longevity of these ridges and their relevance for ecological processes remain poorly understood.

Soils

Given the dynamic nature of soil formation processes that may occur across a floodplain, a high degree of microsite soil variability is reasonable compared to that of more stable surfaces. In floodplains, the occurrence of deposition and scouring may be simultaneous in either a spatial or temporal context. Furthermore, within each of the broad geomorphic features common to floodplains (Fig. 18.2), convex and concave microrelief are associated with seemingly minor elevational changes of a few centimeters. This results in a great deal of variation in soil aeration, texture, chemistry, and microbiology that is often not apparent in soil classification reports.

Floodplains have long been perceived to be highly fertile

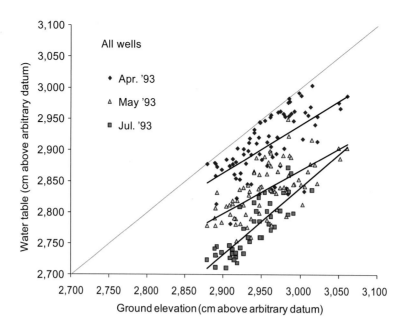

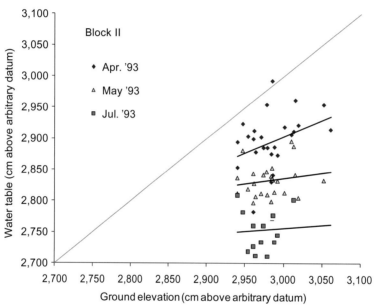

FIG. 18.4. Water table measurements in shallow wells in the floodplain of the Neches River, Texas. Each dot is a spot measurement of water table elevation in a well. The "All Wells" data include three blocks, which together covered ~ 5 linear km of floodplain. The "Block II" data is from wells in a single 8-ha area. (Data from Wang 1996.)

locations as a result of nutrient sink activity normally associated with depositional landscape positions, and this perception is generally correct (Brinson 1990). Soil biological and chemical characteristics may be quite different, however, between concave and convex microrelief sites (Stoeckel and Miller-Goodman 2001).

Fluvial processes govern soil morphogenesis in southeastern floodplains; thus it is not surprising that soil orders such as entisols and inceptisols (i.e., young soils in a morphological sense with minimal horizonation compared to older soils that weathered in place on uplands and exhibit more pronounced horizonation) are most common. In addition, histosols (i.e., wet soils with high organic matter content due to slow rates of decomposition) are often found in backswamp areas as well as other poorly drained microsites.

Floodplain soils of the Atlantic Coastal Plain (ACP) are more diverse morphologically than those of the Gulf Coastal Plain (GCP) (Anderson and Lockaby 2007). Soils along lower floodplains of the GCP are primarily entisols and inceptisols, while similar reaches in the ACP exhibit ultisols, alfisols, and mollisols (e.g., soils that are more developed morphologically compared to those previously mentioned) in addition to entisols and inceptisols (Anderson and Lockaby 2007). Because Piedmont and Coastal Plain material sources are low in base saturation, soils derived from both tend to be acidic (pH 3.5–5.5). Exceptions occur where calcareous material lies near the surface along some Coastal Plain streams such as the Coosawhatchie River in South Carolina. In the GCP, there is less distinction between material sources internal and external to the Coastal Plain than in the ACP (Stanturf and Schoenholtz 1998).

Many soils in the Lower Mississippi Alluvial Valley (LMAV) have high base saturation and are near neutral or slightly alkaline in pH. This is particularly true for soils formed on young levees, whereas base cations may have been leached to a greater extent on older soils (Stanturf and Schoenholtz 1998). Meander belt soils on point bars and natural levees are generally classified as entisols, inceptisols, and alfisols and are moderately well drained (Aslan and Autin 1998). The high fertility levels associated with many LMAV soils are unique among other floodplains in the Southeast. The common occurrence of vertisols (soils with high shrink-swell potential) is a second factor that distinguishes the LMAV soils from those on more acidic floodplains in the remainder of the Southeast.

Biogeochemistry

One of the foremost societal values placed upon riverine wetlands of the southeastern U.S. is water filtration or material trapping. Floodplains may function as sinks, sources, or transformation zones for nutrients (Brinson 1993). When loadings of nutrients are low, the net balance of nutrients may be maintained, albeit in different forms (Brinson 1993). An example is that of the Apalachicola River, where inorganic nitrogen loads were transformed to organic upon contact with the floodplain (Elder 1985). Floodplains may act as sinks in cases where inputs are high, such as under high sediment loads generated by catchment disturbances. Examples of the latter scenario include the Mobile-Tensas Delta in Alabama and the Cache River floodplain in Arkansas. If nutrient assimilation capacities related to soil and vegetation have been maximized, high inputs may pass through the system with little change. Floodplains disturbed by hurricanes, fires, or development may act as sources of sediment and nutrients. However, where forest vegetation recovers quickly (e.g., natural regeneration following harvests), the potential for sink activity may be enhanced (Aust, Schoenholtz, et al. 1997). In oligotrophic (i.e., low-nutrient) systems, expected stimulation of soil N or P mineralization following harvests may not result in increased export (source activity), particularly if the vegetation and microbes are strongly nutrient deficient (Lockaby, Thornton, et al. 1994). In these situations, any increase in soil mineral N or P may become quickly assimilated in vegetation or microbial sinks.

As is the case with all wetland processes, hydrology drives biogeochemistry in terms of the timing and nature of litterfall, release and/or immobilization of nutrients by forest litter, nitrogen mineralization, and vegetation uptake (Lockaby and Walbridge 1998). The hydrologic influence on biogeochemistry may drive significant variation among floodplain vegetation communities and among floodplains, and spatial variation in microsite types can play a considerable role in defining intrasystem cycling at the community level (Lockaby and Walbridge 1998). Decomposition rates may be maximized on microsites with intermediate wetness where flooded and nonflooded cycles predominate. Such cycles stimulate microbial activity as well as promote physical fragmentation of litter (e.g., Lockaby, Wheat, et al. 1996). Despite variation in processes across microsites, there is mixed evidence of whether they result in significant differences in litter quality among microsites within the same floodplain (Burke, Lockaby, et al. 1999; Schilling and Lockaby 2005).

Southeastern floodplains are primarily occupied by hardwoods, which require more nutrients than most evergreen species, and, consequently, even though soil fertility levels are much higher than on upland sites, nutrient deficiencies may still restrict net primary productivity (NPP; Lockaby, Conner, et al. 2008). In one study (Dunn, Farrish, et al. 1999), an application of N and P resulted in a 70% increase in diameter increment for naturally regenerated hardwoods in a minor stream bottom in north Louisiana on a soil that is generally considered to be quite productive (i.e., Guyton series, typic glossaqualf). There is also evidence that on more acidic floodplains such as those of the Satilla and Altamaha Rivers in Georgia, differences among floodplains in terms of base cation availability may partially explain differences in aboveground NPP (Schilling and Lockaby 2006). While soil fertility is generally higher on floodplains than on upland sites, the soil-vegetation systems of most floodplains operate under conditions of varying degrees of nutrient deficiency.

High productivity, coupled with anaerobic conditions that limit decomposition, gives bottomland forests the potential to function as large belowground sinks for carbon (Giese, Aust, et al. 2003). As with shoot production, root production and sequestration of carbon in the soil can be quite high in these systems. However, belowground productivity is not always strongly correlated with aboveground NPP (Megonigal and Day 1992) and is often more sensitive to differences in flooding (Day and Megonigal 1993). The balance between production and decomposition, determined primarily by hydrology but also influenced by species composition, is critical for determining rate of carbon sequestration and degree of protection in the soil (Burke and Chambers 2003).

Plant Communities

Floodplains of the southeastern U.S. were historically dominated by bottomland hardwood forests. However, oxbow lakes, sloughs, baldcypress/tupelo swamps, and other wetlands, as well as cane thickets, were embedded within this forested matrix (Fig. 18.2) (Wharton, Kitchens, et al. 1982). Floodplain plant species are highly adapted to and dependent upon periodic flooding, or what has been termed the flood pulse (Junk, Bailey, et al. 1989; see following). The timing, periodicity, duration, and extent of flooding influence nutrient cycling (Lockaby and Walbridge 1998), seed dispersal (Schneider and Sharitz 1988), regeneration (Streng, Glitzenstein, et al. 1989), tree growth (Keeland and Sharitz 1995), and productivity (Conner and Day 1976).

Natural floodplains are defined by a shifting habitat mosaic dependent upon the flooding regime (Bornette, Tabacchi, et al. 2008). Floodplain plant species differentially establish across this habitat template, exhibiting species-specific preferences (Sharitz and Mitsch 1993) and setting into motion successional patterns in community composition that are closely tied to fluvial processes (Meitzen 2009).

Natural levees are generally the best-drained, highest points in the floodplain and therefore least susceptible to flooding and persistence of low oxygen conditions. Accordingly, species that are moderately intolerant to intolerant of flooding are relegated to this part of the floodplain (Table 18.1) (Battaglia, Collins, et al. 2004a). Point bars, which are also characterized by coarse soil particles, develop as the channel migrates and sediments are deposited along the convex bends of the river. Early successional species are the first to colonize, and as other vegetation becomes established over time, point bars become stabilized. Several shade-intolerant species that also require

TABLE 18.1

List of select species present in the major hydrogeomophological zones of bottomland hardwood forest communities

Vertical strata/ topographic position	Backswamps/sloughs (lowest)	Low floodplain flats	High floodplain flats	Newly formed levees	Old levee ridges (Highest)
Tree (overstory and subcanopy)	*Taxodium distichum* *Nyssa aquatica* *Fraxinus profunda*	*Quercus lyrata* *Quercus nigra* *Carya aquatica* *Acer rubrum*	*Quercus pagoda* *Celtis laevigata* *Celtis occidentalis* *Fraxinus pennsylvanica* *Acer rubrum* *Liquidambar styraciflua*	*Populus deltoides* *Salix nigra* *Betula nigra* *Platanus occidentalis* *Acer negundo* *Acer saccharinum*	*Fagus grandifolia* *Ilex opaca* *Celtis occidentalis* *Celtis laevis* *Ulmus americana* *Acer negundo*
Shrub	*Itea virginica* *Morella cerifera* *Cephalanthus occidentalis*	*Ilex decidua* *Cephalanthus occidentalis*	*Lindera benzoin* *Asimina triloba* *Crataegus marshallii*	*Forestiera acuminata* *Planera aquatica*	*Asimina triloba*
Vines	n/a	*Campsis radicans*	*Vitis rotundifolia* *Toxicodendron radicans* *Campsis radicans* *Parthenocissus quinquefolia* *Ampelopsis arborea*	*Ampelopsis arborea* *Toxicodendron radicans*	*Vitis rotundifolia* *Toxicodendron radicans* *Campsis radicans* *Parthenocissus quinquefolia*
Understory	*Carex* spp. *Polygonum* spp.	*Saururus cernuus*	*Viola* spp. *Leersia virginica*	*Arundinaria gigantea* *Carex* spp.	*Arundinaria gigantea*
Floating	*Azolla caroliniana* *Lemna minor* *Wolffia* spp. *Wolfiella* spp. *Eichhornia crassipes*[a] *Salvinia molesta*[a]	n/a	n/a	n/a	n/a
Submerged	*Ceratophyllum demersum* *Myriophyllum aquaticum*	n/a	n/a	n/a	n/a

[a] Indicates nonnative species.

mineral substrate to establish depend upon provision of this habitat for successful regeneration (Robertson and Augspurger 1999).

Fluvial processes also create habitat that is frequently flooded. Oxbow lakes can support diverse aquatic and wetland plant populations based on lake morphometry, flow rates, light penetration, depth and turbidity of the water column, and sediment characteristics (Wharton, Kitchens, et al. 1982). As point bars develop and the river migrates laterally, sloughs become disconnected from the river's flow, fill with water, and quickly become stagnant. Expansive, low-lying backswamps are commonly found between the river's natural levee and valley wall. Deepwater swamp communities composed of the most flood-tolerant tree species, as well as floating leaf aquatics and submergent plants, often occur in all three of these habitats (Conner and Buford 1998) (Table 18.1). Although established trees may be tolerant of flooding and pervasive anaerobic conditions, successful regeneration is dependent upon periodic drawdown events to meet seed germination and seedling establishment requirements (Sharitz, Schneider, et al. 1990). Given that these sites are often flooded, vegetation cover and diversity in the understory are usually limited. Some herbaceous species may colonize floating logs and stumps (Dennis and Batson 1974). Although they may be long-lived, deepwater swamps and oxbow lakes are not permanent features on the floodplain, as they fill in with sediment over time. Channel incision can also lead to vegetation changes of floodplain wetlands and forests as they are increasingly isolated from the river (Bornette, Amoros, et al. 1996), leading to reduced water-level fluctuations and eventual decline in macrophyte and aquatic diversity, as well as reduced tree growth and altered forest composition (Van Geest, Wolters, et al. 2005).

Biodiversity in floodplain forests is related, in part, to the rapid species turnover that accompanies slight elevation changes (Sharitz and Mitsch 1993). Thus, first and second bottoms generally have high diversity and are often compositionally similar, although the abundances of species may differ (Kellison, Young, et al. 1998). Many of the moderately flood- and shade-tolerant species occur here, including most of the bottomland oaks and hickories (Wharton, Kitchens, et al. 1982).

Aboveground NPP is generally high in bottomland forest-swamp ecosystems, but varies widely depending upon hydroperiod, flow (and related dissolved oxygen), and species composition (Sharitz and Pennings 2006). In general, sites that are frequently and deeply flooded where waters become stagnant and anaerobic conditions are prevalent, have lower aboveground NPP (Conner and Day 1976) than those where water levels fluctuate and anoxia is limited.

Animal Communities

Fish

Floodplain fish communities of the southeastern U.S. are species rich (Hoover and Kilgore 1998). Fish assemblages vary longitudinally within a watershed (Schmutz, Kauffmann, et al. 2000), latitudinally among the river channel and floodplain habitats, and within habitats of the river channel and its floodplain (Winemiller, Tarim, et al. 2000). Within broad habitat types (e.g., river channels, oxbow lakes), there are important differences that drive the composition of fish communities.

For example, bed type, water velocity, coarse woody debris loads, and water temperature influence the composition of fish communities within the channel (Jackson 2005). In oxbow lakes, the frequency and duration of connection to the river, water depth, nutrient status, substrate type, vegetation communities, and dissolved oxygen concentrations can influence species composition (Sabo, Kelso, et al. 1991).

With slight modifications due to water temperature (Tockner, Malard, et al. 2000), floodplain fish move from the river onto the floodplain during flood pulses (Junk, Bailey, et al. 1989) to take advantage of food resources for growth and reproduction (Hoover and Kilgore 1998). Reproduction in floodplain fish collectively can occur throughout the year, although reproductive requirements vary by species and depend on temperature, day length, and length of floodplain inundation (Hoover and Kilgore 1998).

Land use within a watershed can have important implications to community structure, growth, and/or reproduction of floodplain fish. Agricultural areas can be sources of sediments, nutrients, and chemicals that can degrade habitat structure, physiochemical characteristics of the water, alter food webs, and directly affect fish health (Weijters, Janse, et al. 2009). Forested watersheds tend to support more complete fish fauna than urbanized or agriculturally dominated watersheds and/or support different fish assemblages (Schweizer and Matlack 2005). Furthermore, land legacy effects on aquatic systems can linger for decades (Jackson, Martin, et al. 2005).

Herpetofauna

Over 175 species of reptiles and amphibians inhabit southeastern floodplain ecosystems (Jones and Taylor 2005). No single wetland or forest type can provide habitat for all species. Many species of reptiles and amphibians require aquatic/wetland and terrestrial (or nonaquatic) habitats in relatively close proximity (Semlitsch 2005). Semiaquatic turtles use a diversity of wetland and nonwetland habitats throughout the floodplain (Bodie and Semlitsch 2000a). Several species of anurans and salamanders breed in wetlands or permanent waters before retreating to terrestrial areas for the remainder of their life cycle (Petranka 1998; Semlitsch 2005). Many herptofaunal species use upland areas adjacent to floodplains for hibernacula or refugia from flooding; some species traverse several kilometers to reach overwintering sites (Ernst and Ernst 2003; Sexton, Drda, et al. 2007).

Flooding can have a substantial effect on community structure, reproductive success, food habits, and mortality of herptofauna, so a matrix of wetlands with diverse hydroperiods and vegetation structure supports the greatest amphibian diversity (Lichtenberg, King, et al. 2006). Most amphibians and many other herpetofauna have relatively small home ranges; thus the availability of upland habitats in close proximity to floodplains can affect herptofaunal communities. Nests of riverine turtles can be destroyed by flooding (Horne, Brauman, et al. 2003), and some species often nest during a point in the season when stream levels are historically dropping (Tucker, Janzen, et al. 1997). Drying of wetlands during winter combined with low temperatures can kill estivating turtles (Bodie and Semlitsch 2000b). Many species of amphibians are more common on higher elevation sites in floodplains, including ephemeral wetlands on terraces and high ridges because they require fishless ponds for successful reproduction (Lamb, Gaul, et al. 1998).

Birds

Floodplain ecosystems support a diverse avifauna, including songbirds, waterfowl, wading birds, and secretive marshbirds. Floodplain forests are used throughout the year by songbirds, and some species are closely associated with geomorphic or biological features (Pashley and Barrow 1993). During migration, floodplain forests that are in large forest blocks and close to the Gulf coast receive extensive use (Buler, Moore, et al. 2007). During the breeding season, over 70 species of birds nest in bottomland hardwood forests (Pashley and Barrow 1993). Segregation across plant community types and among microhabitats is common among breeding and wintering songbirds in these ecosystems (Pashley and Barrow 1993). At the community scale, many breeding songbirds can be broadly divided along a wetness gradient (Sallabanks, Walters, et al. 2000).

Structural and compositional features are also important. The Swainson's warbler *(Limnothlypis swainsonii)* nests in dense thickets at higher elevations and is commonly associated with cane (Benson, Anich, et al. 2009). Bowen, Moorman, et al. (2007) observed more birds, including forest-edge species, forest-interior species, field-edge species, and several individual species, in artificially created canopy gap and gap-edge habitats than in the surrounding mature forest. Some species shift habitat use during seasons, particularly during nesting.

Landscape structure affects occupancy, but more importantly can also affect nest success (Robinson, Thompson, et al. 1995). Many floodplain forest ecosystems are remnant patches embedded within an agricultural or urban matrix. Within small patches, several factors including increased predation, parasitism by brown-headed cowbirds *(Molothrus ater)* (Robinson, Thompson, et al. 1995), and competition can limit occupancy and nest success (Twedt and Wilson 2007).

Flooding can affect breeding success and distribution of floodplain avifauna, including songbirds. Nests of the eastern wild turkey *(Meleagris gallopavo)*, a ground nester, can be destroyed by flooding (Cobb and Doerr 1997). In contrast, nest predation of cavity-nesting wood ducks *(Aix sponsa)* and prothonotary warblers *(Protonotaria citrea)* can be reduced by flooding (Nielsen and Gates 2007; Cooper, Wood, et al. 2009). However, late-spring/early-summer flooding can submerge and destroy prothonotary warbler nests (Cooper, Wood, et al. 2009).

There are at least eight species of waterfowl that use forested wetlands during the winter: hooded merganser *(Lophodytes cucullatus)*, gadwall *(Anas strepera)*, Canada goose *(Branta canadensis)*, northern pintail *(Anas acuta)*, green-winged teal *(Anas carolinensis)*, ring-necked duck *(Aythya collaris)*, mallard *(Anas platyrhyncos)*, and wood duck (Fredrickson and Heitmeyer 1988). Numerous other waterbird and shorebird species are common during winter and migration within managed moist-soil units and flooded agricultural fields (Twedt, Nelms, et al. 1998; Twedt and Nelms 1999). The specific food items consumed vary among species, sex, and life-cycle events (e.g., molt, prebreeding, migration) (Fredrickson and Heitmeyer 1988).

Mammals

Over 35 species of mammals use southeastern floodplains, including 14 rodent species, 3 shrew species, and 11 bat species (Heitmeyer, Cooper, et al. 2005). Some species, such as the North American beaver *(Castor canadensis)* and muskrat *(Ondatra zibethicus)*, are adapted to aquatic environments, but most species lack aquatic adaptations.

Beaver are one of the most visible animals in floodplain environments because of large flooded areas behind their dams. Beaver ponds create important wetland diversity on the floodplain that benefits a wide range of fish and wildlife species (Snodgrass and Meffe 1999; Folk and Hepp 2003). Backswamps, sloughs, and other areas that are easily impounded are the most common locations for beaver dams and are the most frequent locations of timber mortality (Townsend and Butler 1996). Many of the remaining bottomland forests in the LMAV are backswamps or ridge-swale complexes that are easily dammed by beavers.

Mammals respond to both local and landscape habitat characteristics (Scharine, Nielsen, et al. 2009). Frequently flooded areas and/or areas with dense overstory canopy that support little ground cover are of less value to many small mammal species (Scharine, Nielsen, et al. 2009). Forest structure and composition are important habitat considerations for several mammals. Several species of bats, including the Rafinesque's big-eared bat *(Plecotus rafinesquii)* and southeastern myotis *(Myotis austroriparius)*, are cavity roosters and use large (> 115 cm diameter-at-breast height), hollow trees as roost cavities (Gooding and Langford 2004). American black bears *(Ursus americanus)* also use cavities inside large bald cypress and oak trees as dens; these dens are important due to the danger of ground dens flooding (Hightower, Wagner, et al. 2002). Raccoons *(Procyon lotor)*, striped skunks *(Mephitis mephitis)*, and other mesopredators (i.e., medium-sized predators) have expanded rapidly in the last several decades due to habitat fragmentation and the loss or reduction of top predators (Prugh, Stoner, et al. 2009). These species are important predators of nests for many avian species, and inflated populations are an important conservation concern (Ritchie and Johnson 2009).

Flooding can have substantial effects on mammal communities depending on a number of flood parameters, including the rate at which the water rises, maximum water depth, and flood duration (e.g., Anderson, Wilson, et al. 2000). Prolonged flooding generally reduces densities of small mammals (Chamberlain and Leopold 2003), although productivity during nonflood periods can be higher than adjacent uplands (Batzli 1977).

Key Ecological Controls

Flood Pulse

The flood pulse concept (Junk, Bailey, et al. 1989) was developed to explain the major role of a pulsing river discharge on the biota in river-floodplain ecosystems, particularly those in low-gradient rivers in large alluvial valleys that have frequent, predictable, long-duration flood pulses. During flood events, nutrients and water are transported from the river to the floodplain, generally stimulating productivity of floodplain biota. Floodwaters also provide riverine organisms, particularly fishes, access to the nutrient-rich floodplain environment. The main functions of the river channel for plants and animals are as a migration route and a dispersal system to access resources and as a low-water refuge (Junk, Bailey, et al. 1989).

Although the flood-pulse concept, with key modifications

(e.g., Tockner, Malard, et al. 2000), accurately describes river-floodplain processes for many river systems, including many rivers in the Southeast, it is not applicable to all rivers regionally or globally. Headwater and/or low-order rivers generally lack a predictable, long-duration flood pulse, and the flood pulse concept does not apply. Furthermore, even in unmodified, low-gradient rivers in large alluvial valleys, it does not fully describe the role of flooding in structuring and maintaining biological diversity (Opperman, Luster, et al. 2010). The flood-pulse concept was developed to explain biological processes in river-floodplain systems, but it failed to explicitly recognize the interrelationships of flooding, fluvial geomorphic processes, biological diversity, and other ecosystem processes. Geomorphic diversity is the template for spatial heterogeneity in biological resources because it affects numerous processes and properties, including soil nutrients and drainage capacity and elevation. High-magnitude, low-frequency floods are important for bank erosion and sediment transport onto the floodplain, thus creating topographic heterogeneity on the floodplain (Florsheim, Mount, et al. 2006; Opperman, Luster, et al. 2010). The frequency and magnitude of flood events are critical for reworking floodplain surfaces and the development of oxbow lakes and other floodplain wetlands (Whiting 2002). Alterations in the flood pulse can also disrupt nutrient cycling processes in the floodplain (Schramm, Cox, et al. 2009). Thus, the disconnection of floodplains or the alteration of flow regimes can have direct and indirect impacts on biological diversity and other ecosystem functions.

Disturbance

Clearly, fluvial processes affect the rate, trajectory, and temporal interval of plant community succession, but other types of allogenic and autogenic disturbances can also drive compositional changes (Battaglia, Sharitz, et al. 1999). Hydroperiod and light are the principal factors that influence population dynamics and regeneration in wetland forests (Mann, Harcombe, et al. 2008). Therefore, events that alter flooding and light availability have a major influence on community composition and dynamics (Putz and Sharitz 1991). Tolerance to flooding and shade can be used to predict regeneration and compositional changes during forest succession (Battaglia, Collins, et al. 2004a), but they are at best coarse predictors, due to small-scale environmental variation and the randomness associated with propagule dispersal.

Disturbances can set back succession and favor establishment of shade-intolerant plant species, or, in some cases, accelerate succession by disproportionately removing these species, thereby favoring shade-tolerant species already established in the seedling and sapling layers (Zhao, Allen, et al. 2006). Windstorms and treefall disturbances produce microtopographic variation in bottomland forests and open the canopy, thereby modifying the amount and pattern of light availability (Zhao, Allen, et al. 2006). Microtopographic variation (e.g., pit and mound topography associated with uprooted trees) creates a patchwork of flooding conditions and is a key factor that influences regeneration, seedling recruitment patterns, and composition (Collins and Battaglia 2002). Similarly, interannual variability in flow combined with species-specific temporal windows of germination can substantially influence regeneration patterns (Streng, Glitzenstein, et al. 1989). Successful regeneration of shade-intolerant and moderately shade-toler-

ant species relies on canopy openings for seedling establishment (Battaglia, Collins, et al. 2004b). Some species exhibit tradeoffs between flood and shade tolerance whereby they occupy a less stressful part of one gradient than predicted, which may allow them to avoid the combined effects of both stresses (Battaglia and Sharitz 2005). Microtopographic variation can also interact with regimes of canopy gap formation, and some areas of the floodplain such as ridges may be more susceptible to frequent canopy opening (Almquist, Jack, et al. 2002).

Although fire is not common in floodplain environments, natural and anthropogenically driven conditions may occur periodically that promote fire disturbance (Nelson, Ruffner, et al. 2008), and the legacies of these disturbances can be very important for establishment and maintenance of certain vegetation types. Historically, canebrakes were common in floodplain ecosystems, and they provided important habitat for many wildlife species (Cirtain, Franklin, et al. 2004). These habitats are thought to be maintained by fire and/or wind disturbance (Gagnon, Platt, et al. 2007; Gagnon 2009). Along with other losses of bottomland habitat, canebrakes have been almost entirely eliminated (Brantley and Platt 2001).

Animal responses to disturbance are varied and depend upon the species of interest and the type, intensity, frequency, and/or spatial scale of disturbance. Canopy disturbance from windfall gaps not only stimulates production of herbaceous plants, vines, and trees, but the increased vegetative structure affects invertebrate and avian populations (Gorham, King, et al. 2002; Bowen, Moorman, et al. 2007). Prolonged flooding can reduce herbaceous understories and reduce cover and food for a variety of wildlife species, and, as noted above, high-elevation areas are needed by some species for refugia from floods. Extreme floods, however, are also necessary for geomorphic processes that create topographic and vegetative heterogeneity, which are important for maintaining biological diversity in floodplain forests (Opperman, Luster, et al. 2010).

LMAV versus Coastal Plain

The bottomland hardwood ecosystem is quite similar ecologically throughout its range. However, there are some subtle differences in vegetation between the LMAV and Coastal Plain provinces that are partially related to the differences in floodplain characteristics, such as size, hydroperiod, and soils, described above and elsewhere (Hupp 2000; King, Sharitz, et al. 2009). In addition to these abiotic factors, there are also biogeographic differences between the provinces. Although there are several dominant tree species that occur throughout the bottomland hardwood ecosystem, producing widespread overlap in species composition between the provinces, there is some separation due to some species that are more restricted in their distribution (Fig. 18.5). For example, several species that are more common in Coastal Plain floodplains than the LMAV are *Nyssa ogeche, N. biflora,* and *Ilex verticillata* (USDA Plants Database). In contrast, *Carya illinoensis, Quercus nuttallii,* and *Ulmus crassifolia* are common in LMAV floodplains but not in the Coastal Plain (Kellison, Young, et al. 1998).

There is also some variation in river and floodplain animal communities across the region as well. Variation in fish communities is not limited to differences between LMAV and Coastal Plain, but rather often differs among watersheds due to differences in geological change (Swift, Gilbert, et al.

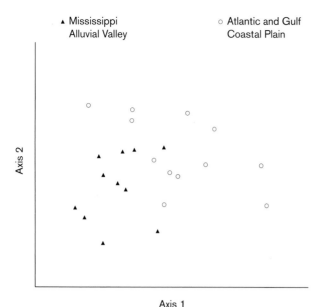

△ Mississippi
Alluvial Valley

○ Atlantic and Gulf
Coastal Plain

Axis 2

Axis 1

FIG. 18.5. Non-metric multidimensional scaling ordination of bottomland forests of the southeast. Sources of data from Atlantic and Gulf Coastal Plain forests include: Jones 1981, Marks and Harcombe 1981, Dabel and Day 1977, and White 1983. Sources of data from the Mississippi Alluvial Valley include: Robertson, Weaver et al. 1978, Denslow and Battaglia 2002, Thieret 1971, and Devall 1990.

1986). Distributions of many amphibian species, however, are affected by the Mississippi River drainage, as their range is truncated at the Mississippi River (Dundee and Rossman 1989). More mobile groups, such as birds and mammals, may be less affected but can be still influenced by the barrier posed by the Mississippi River. The plains pocket gopher *(Geomys bursarius)*, for example, occurs west of the Mississippi River in Louisiana, but presumably suitable habitat east of the Mississippi River is unoccupied because of the formidable barrier posed by the Mississippi and Atchafalaya Rivers (Lowery 1974).

Conservation Concerns

Geomorphic and Hydrologic Alterations

Channelization and the construction of levees and dams for flood protection for agriculture and human settlements have led to widespread alteration of geomorphic and hydrologic processes of southeastern floodplain ecosystems. Channelization has led to incision and lowered water tables for many rivers of the region, which can effectively convert adjacent floodplains from dominance by stream flow to dominance by rainfall (Richardson, Rating, et al. 2006). Furthermore, excessive sedimentation and rapid runoff associated with channelization sometimes result in increased localized flooding of downstream areas (Shankman 1996). Channel modifications for navigation have affected water levels even on the Mississippi River, where geomorphic adjustments to meander cutoffs have continued for at least 50 years (Biedenharn and Watson 1998). Levees preclude overbank flooding for most of the floodplain and often increase flood depths and durations for the immediate riparian zone. Dams have widespread and long-

term geomorphic and hydrologic impacts on river and floodplain ecosystems (Petts and Gurnell 2005), including accelerated bank erosion, channel incision immediately below the dam, reduced peak flows, higher low flows, and accelerated deposition in certain habitats (Hupp, Schenk, et al. 2009). The extent and type of impact varies among rivers for several reasons, including geology of the river basin, size of the dam, and how it is managed. Finally, groundwater pumping for agriculture has locally reduced stream flow and lowered floodplain water tables (e.g., Golladay, Hicks, et al. 2007) and can affect floodplain ecosystems because of groundwater linkages to river flows and tree growth.

Water quantity in rivers is a critical issue and will continue to be so into the forseeable future. No general quantitative relationships exists among flow parameters and ecological response, although it is clear that flow alteration is associated with ecological change and the risk of ecological change increases with the degree of flow alteration (Poff and Zimmerman 2010). Improved techniques are needed to determine the effects of altered flow patterns on floodplain and riverine plant and animal communities, and, possibly more importantly, to prescribe flows that sustain human populations and the biological communities associated with floodplain ecosystems (Poff, Richter, et al. 2010).

Timber Management

Timber management is an important economic activity in southeastern floodplain forests. The overall effects of timber harvesting on floodplain systems vary, but in general, the effects are positive or at least neutral for most ecological functions (Lockaby, Stanturf, et al. 1997). Watersheds dominated by forest management often have higher water quality than watersheds with other land uses, such as agriculture and urban areas (Schoonover and Lockaby 2006). Short-term increases in sediment and nutrient export can occur, although rapid revegetation following timber harvest stabilizes sites in two to three years. Once revegetation has occurred, harvested sites are effective at filtering sediment and other nonpoint-source pollutants from sheet flow. In addition, current forest management techniques have little impact on floodplain hydrology and, consequently, key functions are maintained (Sun, McNutly, et al. 2001).

Historical practices of timber exploitation by high-grading (i.e., taking the highest-quality trees and leaving the rest) have had significant impacts on structure and composition of floodplain forests (King, Shepard, et al. 2005). Appropriate timber management, however, can be used to improve the structure and composition of floodplain forests, thereby increasing the economic and wildlife value of future forests (LMVJV 2007).

Responses by wildlife are varied and depend upon many factors, including the species of interest, the type and frequency of harvest, and the overall landscape structure. Forest management is a critical component of songbird, black bear, and other wildlife conservation programs because when used appropriately it can enhance forest structure and species composition (LMVJV 2007). This is particularly important when considering that altered hydrologic regimes, reduced river meandering, and past high-grading and timber exploitation have affected current forest structure. Furthermore, because regeneration processes are strongly affected by hydrologic processes (Streng, Glitzenstein, et al. 1989), alterations in flooding patterns are influencing future forest composition and structure. Thus, the natural dynamics in these systems are heavily modified and forest management can assist in creating and maintaining diverse plant and animal communities.

Reforestation of Agricultural Lands

The area of forested wetlands directly lost to agriculture has declined in the last decade (Dahl 2006). In recent years, over 275,000 ha have been reforested in the Mississippi Alluvial Valley, with the majority enrolled in the Wetland Reserve Program (King, Twedt, et al. 2006). Improving timber quality and forest structure of these reforestation sites is a major challenge (Wilson, Ribbeck, et al. 2007). Developing markets for carbon and nutrient sequestration may increase the attractiveness of restoration of floodplain forests, including connectivity to river systems (Lal, Delgado, et al. 2009).

Few reforested sites have full functional capacity because nearly all have only local hydrologic restoration (i.e., water control structures), are in the lowest topographic positions, and lack connectivity to rivers. Removal of levees, or moving them farther back from the river, has been suggested as a viable alternative (Mitsch and Day 2006; Opperman, Galloway, et al. 2009), yet this strategy is unattractive on many floodplains because of conflicting land uses.

Invasive Species

Invasive species pose a major threat to the biodiversity and ecosystem functioning of floodplain wetlands of the southeastern U.S. because of their high productivity and predilection for frequent disturbance. Further, the movement of water through riparian systems such as these puts them at risk for invasion by hydrochoric (i.e., water-dispersed seeds) exotics (Thomas, Gibson, et al. 2005). Chinese tallow *(Triadica sebifera),* Chinese privet *(Ligustrum sinense),* and Japanese climbing fern *(Lygodium japonicum)* are some common plant invaders. Chinese tallow has a broad flood tolerance and is dispersed by birds and water. It can invade areas of high native species diversity and forest management and roads enhance its invasion (Wall and Darwin 1999; Jianbang, Miller, et al. 2009). For invasives in general, sites that have experienced anthropogenic disturbances are especially at risk, which can compromise success of restoration projects (McLane 2009).

Feral pigs *(Sus scrofa)* and nutria are common animal invaders that can create substantial management challenges. Stomach content analyses of feral pigs in the United States indicate that they eat a wide variety of animals, including various birds, small mammals, fawns, terrapins, and herpetofauna (Oliver and Brisbin 1993; Jolley, Ditchkoff, et al. 2010). Feral pigs also disrupt forest plant communities and can negatively affect invertebrate and microbial communities of streams (Kaller, Kelso, et al. 2006; Siemann, Carrillo, et al. 2009).

Existing control measures for invasive plant and animal species are costly to implement and vary in their long-term success; the development of improved control measures and understanding overall system impacts of invasive species are major research needs.

References

Almquist BE, Jack SB, Messina MG. 2002. Variation of the treefall gap regime in a bottomland hardwood forest: relationships with microtopography. *For. Ecol. Manage.* 157:155–63.

Anderson CJ, Lockaby BG. 2007. Soils and biogeochemistry of tidal freshwater forested wetlands. In *Ecology of tidal freshwater forested wetlands of the southeastern United States,* WH Conner, TW Doyle, KW Krauss, editors. The Netherlands: Springer, pp. 65–88.

Anderson DC, Wilson KR, et al. 2000. Movement patterns of riparian small mammals during predictable floodplain inundation. *J. Mammal.* 81:1087–99.

Aslan A, Autin WJ. 1998. Holocene floodplain soil formation in the southern lower Mississippi Valley: implications for interpreting alluvial paleosols. *Geol. Soc. Am. Bull.* 110:433–49.

Aust WM, Schoenholtz SH, et al. 1997. Recovery status of a tupelo-cypress wetland seven years after disturbance: silvicultural implications. *For. Ecol. Manage.* 90:161–70.

Battaglia LL, Sharitz RR. 2005. Effects of natural disturbance on bottomland hardwood regeneration. In *Ecology and management of bottomland hardwood systems: the state of our understanding,* Fredrickson LH, King SL, Kaminski RM, editors. Puxico, MO: Univ. Missouri–Columbia, Gaylord Memorial Laboratory Special Publ. no. 10, pp. 121–36.

Battaglia LL, Collins BS, Sharitz RR. 2004a. Do published tolerance and dispersal factors predict species distributions in bottomland hardwood forests? *For. Ecol. Manage.* 198:15–30.

Battaglia LL, Collins BS, Weisenhorn PB. 2004b. *Quercus michauxii* regeneration in and around aging canopy gaps. *Can. J. For. Res.* 34:1359–64.

Battaglia LL, Sharitz RR, Minchin PR. 1999. Patterns of seedling and overstory composition along a gradient of hurricane disturbance in an old-growth bottomland hardwood community. *Can. J. For. Res.* 29:144–56.

Batzli GO. 1977. Population dynamics of the white-footed mouse in floodplain and upland forests. *Am. Midl. Nat.* 97:18–32.

Bennett WJ Jr, Saucier RT. 1988. *Cultural resources survey: West Woodruff Water Association proposed route, Woodruff County, Arkansas.* Nashville, AR: Archeol. Assess. Rep. no. 84.

Benson TJ, Anich NM, et al. 2009. Swainson's warbler nest-site selection in eastern Arkansas. *Condor* 111:694–705.

Biedenharn DS, Watson CC. 1998. Stage adjustments in the lower Mississippi River, USA. *Regul. Riv.: Res. Manage.* 13:517–36.

Bodie JR, Semlitsch RD. 2000a. Spatial and temporal use of floodplain habitats by lentic and lotic species of turtles. *Oecologia* 122:138–46.

Bodie JR, Semlitsch RD. 2000b. Size-specific mortality and natural selection in freshwater turtles. *Copeia* 2000:732–39.

Bornette G, Amoros C, Rostan JC. 1996. River incision and vegetation dynamics in cut-off channels. *Aquat. Sci.* 58:31–51.

Bornette G, Tabacchi E, et al. 2008. A model of plant strategies in fluvial hydrosystems. *Freshw. Biol.* 53:1692–05.

Bowen LT, Moorman CE, Kilgo JC. 2007. Seasonal bird use of canopy gaps in a bottomland forest. *Wilson J. Ornith.* 119:77–88.

Brantley CG, Platt SG. 2001. Canebrake conservation in the southeastern United States. *Wildl. Soc. Bull.* 29:1175–81.

Brinson MM. 1990. Riverine forests. In *Ecosystems of the world,* 15: *Forested wetlands,* Lugo AE, Brinson M, Brown S, editors. New York: Elsevier, pp. 87–41.

Brinson MM. 1993. Changes in functioning of wetlands along an environmental gradient. *Wetlands* 13:65–74.

Buler JJ, Moore FR, Woltmann S. 2007. A multi-scale examination of stopover habitat use by birds. *Ecology* 88:1789–1802.

Burke MK, Chambers JL. 2003. Root dynamics in bottomland hardwood forests of the southeastern United States Coastal Plain. *Plant and Soil* 250:141–53.

Burke MK, Lockaby BG, Conner WH. 1999. Aboveground primary productivity and nutrient circulation across a flooding gradient in a South Carolina Coastal Plain forest. *Can. J. For. Res.* 29:1402–18.

Chamberlain MJ, Leopold BD. 2003. Effects of a flood on relative abundance and diversity of small mammals in a regenerating bottomland hardwood forest. *SW Natur.* 48:306–09.

Cirtain MC, Franklin SB, Pezeshki R. 2004. Effects of nitrogen and moisture regimes on *Arundinaria gigantea* (Walt.) Muhl. seedling growth. *Natur. Areas J.* 24:251–57.

Cobb DT, Doerr PD. 1997. Eastern wild turkey reproduction in an area subjected to flooding. *J. Wildl. Manage.* 61:313–17.

Collins BS, Battaglia LL. 2002. Microenvironmental heterogeneity and *Quercus michauxii* regeneration in experimental selection gaps. *For. Ecol. Manage.* 155:279–90.

Conner WH, Buford MA. 1998. Southern deepwater swamps. In *Southern forested wetlands: ecology and management,* Messina MG, Conner WH, editors. Boca Raton, FL: Lewis Publ., pp. 263–89.

Conner WH, Day JW Jr. 1976. Productivity and composition of a baldcypress–water tupelo site and a bottomland hardwood site in a Louisiana swamp. *Am. J. Bot.* 63:1354–64.

Cooper RJ, Wood LA, et al. 2009. Effects of timber harvest and other factors on a floodplain forest indicator species, the prothonotary warbler. *Wetlands* 29:574–85.

Dabel CV, Day FP. 1977. Structural comparisons of four plant communities in Great Dismal Swamp, Virginia. *Bull. Torrey Bot. Club* 104:352–60.

Dahl TE. 2006. *Status and trends of wetlands in the conterminous United States, 1998 to 2004.* Washington, DC: USDI, Fish Wildl. Serv., Fisheries and Habitat Conservation.

Day FP, Megonigal JP. 1993. The relationship between variable hydroperiod, production allocation, and belowground organic turnover in forested wetlands. *Wetlands* 13:115–21.

Dennis W, Batson W. 1974. The floating log and stump communities in the Santee Swamp of South Carolina. *Castanea* 39:166–70.

Denslow JS, Battaglia LL. 2002. Stand composition and structure across a changing hydrologic gradient: Jean Lafitte National Park, Louisiana, USA. *Wetlands* 22:738–52.

Devall MS. 1990. Cat Island Swamp—window to a fading Louisiana ecology. *For. Ecol. Manage.* 33–34:303–14.

Dewey JC, Schoenholtz SH, et al. 2006. Issues related to wetland delineation of a Texas, USA bottomland hardwood forest. *Wetlands* 26:410–29.

Dunn MA, Farrish KW, Adams JC. 1999. Fertilization response in a natural bottomland hardwood stand in north-central Louisiana. *For. Ecol. Manage.* 114:261–64.

Dundee HA, Rossman DA. 1989. *The amphibians and reptiles of Louisiana.* Baton Rouge: Louisiana State Univ. Press.

Dury G. 1977. Underfit streams: retrospect, perspect and prospect. In *River channel changes,* Gregory KJ, editor. New York: Wiley, pp. 281–93.

Elder JF. 1985. Nitrogen and phosphorus speciation and flux in a large Florida river—wetland system. *Water Resour. Res. Bull.* 21:724–32.

Enfield DB, Mestas-Nuñez AM, Trimble PJ. 2001. The Atlantic multidecadal oscillation and its relation to rainfall and river flows in the continental U.S. *Geophy. Res. Letters* 28:2077–80.

Ernst CH, Ernst EM. 2003. *Snakes of the United States and Canada.* Washington, DC: Smithsonian Books.

Florsheim JL, Mount JF, Constantine CR. 2006. A geomorphic monitoring and adaptive assessment framework to assess the effect of lowland floodplain river restoration on channel-floodplain sediment continuity. *River Res. Applic.* 22:353–75.

Folk TH, Hepp GR. 2003. Effects of habitat use and movement patterns on incubation behavior of female wood ducks *(Aix sponsa)* in southeast Alabama. *Auk* 120:1159–67.

Fredrickson LH, Heitmeyer ME. 1988. Waterfowl use of forested wetlands of the southern United States: an overview. In *Waterfowl in winter,* MW Weller, editor. Minneapolis: Univ. Minnesota Press, pp. 307–23.

Gagnon PR. 2009. Fire in floodplain forests in the southeastern USA: insights from disturbance ecology of native bamboo. *Wetlands* 29:520–26.

Gagnon PR, Platt WJ, Moser EB. 2007. Response of a native bamboo [*Arundinaria gigantea* (Walt.) Muhl.] in a wind-disturbed forest. *For. Ecol. Manage.* 241:288–94.

Giese LAB, Aust WM, et al. 2003. Biomass and carbon pools of disturbed riparian forests. *For. Ecol. Manage.* 180:493–508.

Golladay SW, Hicks DW, Muenz TK. 2007. Stream flow changes associated with water use and climatic variation in the lower Flint River Basin, southwest Georgia. In *Proceedings of the 2007 Georgia Water Conference,* Rasmussen TC, Carroll GD, Georgakakos AP, editors. Athens: School Ecol., Univ. Georgia, pp. 479–82.

Gooding G, Langford JR. 2004. Characteristics of tree roosts of Rafinesque's big-eared bat and southeastern bat in northeastern Louisiana. *SW Natur.* 49:61–67.

Gorham LE, King SL, Keeland BD, Mopper S. 2002. Effects of canopy gaps and flooding on homopterans in a bottomland hardwood forest. *Wetlands* 22:541–49.

Hack JT. 1960. Interpretation of erosional topography in humid temperate regions. *Am. J. Sci.* 258:80–97.

Heitmeyer ME, Cooper RJ, et al. 2005. Ecological relationships of warmblooded vertebrates in bottomland hardwood ecosystems. In *Ecology and management of bottomland hardwood systems: the state of our understanding,* Fredrickson LH, King SL, Kaminski RM, editors. Puxico: Univ. Missouri–Columbia, Gaylord Mem. Lab. Special Publ. no. 10, pp. 281–306.

Hightower DA, Wagner RO, Pace RM III. 2002. Denning ecology of female American black bears in south central Louisiana. *Ursus* 13:11–17.

Hoover JJ, Kilgore KJ. 1998. Fish communities. In *Southern forested wetlands: ecology and management,* Messina MG, Conner WH, editors. Boca Raton, FL: Lewis Publ., pp. 237–60.

Horne BD, Brauman RJ, et al. 2003. Reproductive and nesting ecology of the yellow-blotched map turtle, *Graptemys flavimaculata:* implications for conservation and management. *Copeia* 2003:729–38.

Hunt CB. 1967. *Physiography of the United States.* San Francisco: WH Freeman.

Hupp CR. 2000. Hydrology, geomorphology, and vegetation of Coastal Plain rivers in the southeastern United States. *Hydrol. Processes* 14:2991–3010.

Hupp CR, Walbridge MR, Lockaby BG. 2005. Fluvial geomorphic processes and landforms, water quality, and nutrients in bottomland hardwood forests of southeastern USA. In *Ecology and management of bottomland hardwood systems: the state of our understanding,* Fredrickson LH, King SL, Kaminski RM, editors. Puxico: Univ. Missouri–Columbia, Gaylord Mem. Lab. Special Publ. no. 10, pp. 37–55.

Hupp CR, Demas CR, et al. 2008. Recent sedimentation patterns within the central Atchafalya Basin, Louisiana. *Wetlands* 28:125–40.

Hupp, CR, Pierce AR, et al. 2009. Floodplain geomorphic processes and environmental impacts of human alteration along Coastal Plain rivers, USA. *Wetlands* 29:413–429.

Hupp CR, Schenk ER, et al. 2009. Bank erosion along the dam-regulated lower Roanoke River, North Carolina. In *Management and restoration of fluvial systems with broad historical changes and human impacts,* Geological Society of America Special Paper 451, James LA, Rathburn SL, Whitecar GR, editors. Geological Society of America, pp. 97–108.

Jackson CR, Martin JK, et al. 2005. A southeastern Piedmont watershed sediment budget: evidence for a multi-millenial agricultural legacy. *J. Soil Water Conserv.* 60:298–310.

Jackson DC. 2005. Fisheries dynamics in temperate floodplain rivers. In *Ecology and management of bottomland hardwood systems: the state of our understanding,* Fredrickson LH, King SL, Kaminski RM, editors. Puxico: Univ. Missouri–Columbia, Gaylord Mem. Lab. Special Publ. no. 10, pp. 202–12.

Jianbang, G, Miller JH, et al. 2009. Invasion of tallow tree into southern US forests: influencing factors and implications for mitigation. *Can. J. For. Res.* 39:1346–56.

Jolley DB, Ditchkoff SS, et al. 2010. Estimate of herpetofauna depredation by a population of wild pigs. *J. Mammal.* 91:519–24.

Jones JC, Taylor JD II. 2005. Herpetofauna communities in temperate river floodplain ecosystems of the southeastern United States. In *Ecology and management of bottomland hardwood systems: the state of our understanding,* Fredrickson LH, King SL, Kaminski RM, editors. Puxico: Univ. Missouri–Columbia, Gaylord Mem. Lab. Special Publ. no. 10, pp. 235–37.

Jones KL, GC Poole et al. 2008. Surface hydrology of low-relief landscapes: assessing surface water flow impedance using LIDAR-derived digital elevation models. *Remote Sens. Env.* 112:4148–58.

Jones RH. 1981. *A classification of lowland forests in the northern Coastal Plain of South Carolina.* MS thesis, Clemson Univ.

Junk WJ, Bailey PB, Sparks RE. 1989. The flood-pulse concept in river floodplain systems. *Can. Special Publ. Fish. Aquat. Sci.* 106:110–27.

Kaller MD, Kelso WE. 2006. Swine activity alters invertebrate and microbial communities in a Coastal Plain watershed. *Am. Midl. Nat.* 156:163–77.

Keeland BD, Sharitz RR. 1995. Season growth patterns of *Nyssa sylvatica* var *biflora, Nyssa aquatica,* and *Taxodium distichum* as affected by hydrologic regime. *Can. J. For. Res.* 25:1084–96.

Kellison RC, Young MJ, et al. 1998. Major alluvial floodplains. In *Southern forested wetlands: ecology and management,* Messina MG, Conner WH, editors. Boca Raton, FL: Lewis Publ., pp. 291–323.

Kelly MH, Gore JA. 2008. Florida river flow patterns and the Atlantic multidecadal oscillation. *Riv. Res. Appl.* 24:598–616.

King SL, Twedt DJ, Wilson RR. 2006. The role of the Wetland Reserve Program in conservation efforts in the Mississippi Alluvial Valley. *Wildl. Soc. Bull.* 34:914–20.

King SL, Sharitz RR, et al. 2009. The ecology, restoration, and management of southeastern floodplain ecosystems: a synthesis. *Wetlands* 29:624–34.

King SL, Shepard JP, et al. 2005. Bottomland hardwood forests: past, present, and future. In *Ecology and management of bottomland hardwood systems: the state of our understanding,* Fredrickson LH, King SL, Kaminski RM, editors. Puxico: Univ. Missouri–Columbia, Gaylord Mem. Lab. Special Publ. no. 10, pp. 1–17.

Kroes DE, Brinson MM. 2004. Occurrence of riverine wetlands on floodplains along a climatic gradient. *Wetlands* 24:167–77.

Lal H, Delgado JA, et al. 2009. Market-based approaches and tools for improving water and air quality. *Env. Sci. Policy* 12:1028–39.

Lamb T, Gaul RW Jr, et al. 1998. A herptofaunal inventory of the lower Roanoke River floodplain. *J. Elisha Mitchell Soc.* 114:43–55.

Lichtenberg JS, King SL, et al. 2006. Habitat associations of chorusing anurans in the lower Mississippi River Alluvial Valley. *Wetlands* 26:736–44.

Lockaby BG, Thornton FC, et al. 1994. Ecological responses of an oligotrophic floodplain forest to harvesting. *J. Env. Qual.* 23:901–06.

Lockaby BG, Wheat RS, Clawson RG. 1996. Influence of hydroperiod on conversion of litter to SOM in a floodplain forest. *Soil Sci. Soc. Am. J.* 60:1989–93.

Lockaby BG, Walbridge MR. 1998. Biogeochemistry. In *Southern forested wetlands: ecology and management,* Messina MG, Conner WH, editors. Boca Ratonm FL: Lewis Publ., pp. 149–72.

Lockaby BG, Conner WH, Mitchell J. 2008. Floodplains. In *Encyclopedia of ecology,* vol. 2: *Ecosystems,* Jorgensen SE, Fath BD, editors. Oxford: Elsevier, pp. 1616–26.

Lockaby BG, Stanturf JS, Messina M. 1997. Harvesting impacts on functions of forested floodplains: a review of existing reports. *For. Ecol. Manage.* 90:93–100.

Lower Mississippi Valley Joint Venture Forest Resource Conservation Working Group (LMVJV). 2007. Restoration, management, and monitoring of forest resources in the Mississippi Alluvial Valley: Recommendations for enhancing wildlife habitat. Wilson R, Ribbeck K, King SL, Twedt D, eds.

Lowery, GH Jr. 1974. *The mammals of Louisiana and adjacent waters.* Baton Rouge: Louisiana State Univ. Press.

Mann LE, Harcombe PA, et al. 2008. The trade-off between flood- and shade-tolerance: a mortality episode in *Carpinus caroliniana* in a floodplain forest, Texas. *J. Veg. Sci.* 19:739–46.

Marks PL, Harcombe PA. 1981. Forest vegetation of the Big Thicket, southeast Texas. *Ecol. Monogr.* 51:287–305.

McLane CR. 2009. *Evaluating exotic species assemblages across a chronosequence of restored floodplain forests.* MS thesis, Southern Illinois Univ., Carbondale.

Megonigal JP, Day FP. 1992. Effects of flooding on root and shoot production of bald cypress in large experimental enclosures. *Ecology* 73:1182–93.

Meitzen KM. 2009. Lateral channel migration effects on riparian forest structure and composition, Congaree River, South Carolina, USA. *Wetlands* 29:465–75.

Mertes LAK. 1997. Documentation and significance of the perirheic zone on inundation in floodplains. *Water Resour. Res.* 33:1749–62.

Mitsch WJ, Day JW Jr. 2006. Restoration of wetlands in the Mississippi-Ohio-Missouri (MOM) River Basin: experience and needed research. *Ecol. Engin.* 26:55–69.

Muller RA, Grymes JM III. 1998. Regional climates. In *Southern forested wetlands: ecology and management,* Messina MG, Conner WH, editors. Boca Raton, FL: Lewis Publ., pp. 87–101.

Nelson JL, Ruffner CM, et al. 2008. Drainage and agriculture impacts on fire frequency in southern Illinois forested bottomland. *Can. J. For. Res.* 38:2932–41.

Newman AE. 2010. *Water and solute transport in the shallow subsurface of a riverine wetland natural levee.* MS thesis, Louisiana State Univ., Baton Rouge.

Nielsen CLR, Gates RJ. 2007. Reduced nest predation of cavity-nesting wood ducks during flooding in a bottomland hardwood forest. *Condor* 109:210–15.

Oliver WLR, Brisbin IL. 1993. Introduced and feral pigs: problems, policy and priorities. In *Pigs, peccaries and hippos: status survey and action plan,* Oliver WLR, editor. Electronic file. Gland, Switzerland: IUCN, pp. 269–86.

Opperman JJ, Galloway GE, et al. 2009. Sustainable floodplains through large-scale reconnection to rivers. *Science* 326:1487–88.

Opperman JJ, Luster, R, et al. 2010. Ecologically functional floodplains: connectivity, flow regime, and scale. *J. Am. Water Resour. Assoc.* 46:211–26.

Osterkamp WR, Hedman ER. 1977. Variation of width and discharge for natural high-gradient stream channels. *Water Resour. Res.* 13:256–58.

Osterkamp WR, Hupp CR. 1984. Geomorphic and vegetative characteristics along three northern Virginia streams. *Bull. Geol. Soc. Am.* 95:501–13.

Pashley DN, Barrow WC. 1993. Effects of land use practices on neotropical migratory birds in bottomland hardwood forests. In *Status and management of neotropical migratory birds,* Finch DM, Stangel PW, editors. Washington, DC: USFS Gen. Tech. Rep. RM-229, pp. 315–20.

Patrick R. 1995. *Rivers of the United States,* vol. 2: *Chemical and physical characteristics.* New York: Wiley.

Petranka JW. 1998. *Salamanders of the United States and Canada.* Washington, DC: Smithsonian Inst. Press.

Petts GE, Gurnell AM. 2005. Dams and geomorphology: research progress and future directions. *Geomorphology* 71:27–47.

Pierce AR, King SL. 2007. The influence of valley plugs in channelized streams on floodplain sedimentation dynamics over the last century. *Wetlands* 27:631–43.

Poff NL, Zimmerman JKH. 2010. Ecological responses to altered flow regimes: a literature review to inform the science and management of environmental flows. *Freshw. Biol.* 55:194–205.

Poff NL, Richter BD, et al. 2010. The ecological limits of hydrological alteration (ELOHA): a new framework for developing regional environmental flow standards. *Freshw. Biol.* 55:147–70.

Prugh LR, Stoner CJ, et al. 2009. The rise of the mesopredator. *Bioscience* 59:779–90.

Putz FE, Sharitz RR. 1991. Hurricane damage to old-growth forest in Congaree Swamp National Monument, South Carolina, U.S.A. *Can. J. For. Res.* 21:1765–70.

Richardson CJ, Rating R, et al. 2006. Restoration of hydrologic and biogeochemical functions in bottomland hardwoods. In *Hydrology and management of forested watersheds: proceedings of the international conference,* Amayta D, editor. New Bern, NC: Am. Soc. Agri. Biol. Engin., pp. 150–57.

Ritchie EG, Johnson CN. 2009. Predator interactions, mesopredator release, and biodiversity conservation. *Ecol. Letters* 12:982–98.

Robertson JM, Augspurger CK. 1999. Geomorphic processes and spatial patterns of primary forest succession on the Bogue Chitto River, USA. *J. Ecol.* 87:1052–63.

Robertson PA, Weaver GT, Cavanaugh JA. 1978. Vegetation and tree species patterns near the northern terminus of the southern floodplain forest. *Ecol. Monogr.* 48:249–67.

Robinson SK, Thompson FR III, et al. 1995. Regional forest fragmentation and the nesting success of migratory birds. *Science* 267:1987–90.

Sabo MJ, Kelso WE, et al. 1991. Physiochemical factors affecting larval fish densities in Mississippi River floodplain ponds, Louisiana (U.S.A.). *Regul. Riv.: Res. Manage.* 6:109–16.

Sallabanks R, Walters JR, Collazo JA. 2000. Breeding bird abundance in bottomland hardwood forests: habitat, edge, and patch size effects. *Condor* 102:748–58.

Scharine PD, Nielsen CK, et al. 2009. Swamp rabbits in floodplain ecosystems: influence of landscape- and stand-level habitat on relative abundance. *Wetlands* 29:615–23.

Schilling E, Lockaby BG. 2005. Microsite influences on productivity and nutrient circulation within two southeastern floodplain forests. *Soil Sci. Soc. Am. J.* 69:1185–95.

Schilling EB, Lockaby BG. 2006. Relationships between productivity and nutrient circulation within two contrasting floodplain forests. *Wetlands* 26:181–92.

Schmutz S, Kaufmann M, et al. 2000. A multi-level concept for fish-based, river-type-specific assessment of ecological integrity. *Hydrobiologia* 422/423:279–89.

Schoonover JS, Lockaby BG. 2006. Land cover impacts on stream nutrients and fecal coliform in the lower Piedmont of west Georgia. *J. Hydrol.* 331:371–82.

Schramm HL, Cox MS et al. 2009. Nutrient dynamics in the lower Mississippi River floodplain: comparing present and historic hydrologic conditions. *Wetlands* 29:476–87.

Schumm SA, Parker RS. 1973. Implications of complex response of drainage systems for Quaternary alluvial stratigraphy. *Nature* 243:99–100.

Schweizer PE, Matlack GR. 2005. Annual variation in fish assemblages of watersheds with stable and changing land use. *Am. Midl. Natur.* 153:293–308.

Semlitsch RD. 2005. Management of amphibians in floodplain wetlands: importance of local population and landscape processes. In *Ecology and management of bottomland hardwood systems: the state of our understanding,* Fredrickson LH, King SL, Kaminski RM, editors. Puxico, MO: Univ. Missouri–Columbia, Gaylord Memorial Laboratory Special Publ. no. 10, pp. 259–71.

Sexton OJ, Drda WJ, et al. 2007. The effects of flooding upon the snake fauna of an isolated refuge. *Natur. Areas J.* 27:133–44.

Shankman D. 1996. Stream channelization and changing vegetation patterns in the U.S. Coastal Plain. *Geogr. Rev.* 86:216–32.

Sharitz RR, Mitsch WJ. 1993. Southern floodplain forests. In *Biodiversity of the southeastern United States: lowland terrestrial communities,* Martin WH, Boyce SG, Esternacht AC, editors. New York: John Wiley & Sons, Inc., pp. 311–72.

Sharitz RR, Pennings SC. 2006. Development of wetland plant communities. In *Ecology of freshwater and estuarine wetlands,* Batzer DP, Sharitz RR, editors. Berkeley: Univ. Calif. Press, pp. 177–241.

Sharitz RR, Schneider RL, Lee LC. 1990. Composition and regeneration of a disturbed river floodplain forest in South Carolina. In *Ecological processes and cumulative impacts: illustrated by bottomland hardwood ecosystems,* Gosselink JG, Lee LC, Muir TA, editors. Chelsea, MI: Lewis Publ., pp. 195–218.

Siemann E, Carrillo JA, et al. 2009. Experimental test of the impacts of feral hogs on forest dynamics and processes in the southeastern U.S. *For. Ecol. Manage.* 258:546–53.

Simon A, Hupp CR. 1987. Geomorphic and vegetative recovery processes along modified Tennessee streams: an interdisciplinary approach to disturbed fluvial systems. *Proc. For. Hydrol. Watershed Manage. Symp. Publ.* 167:251–61.

Simon A, Hupp CR. 1992. Geomorphic and vegetative recovery processes along modified stream channels of West Tennessee. USGS Open-File Report, vol. 91–502.

Snodgrass JW, Meffe GK. 1999. Habitat use and temporal dynamics of blackwater stream fishes in and adjacent to beaver ponds. *Copeia* 1999:628–39.

Stanturf JA, Schoenholtz SH. 1998. Soils and landforms. In *Southern forested wetlands: ecology and management,* Messina MG, Conner WH, editors. Boca Raton, FL: Lewis Publ., pp. 123–47.

Steiger J, Tabacchi E, et al. 2005. Hydrogeomorphic processes affecting riparian habitat within alluvial channel-floodplain river systems: a review for the temperate zone. *Riv. Res. Appl.* 21:719–37.

Stoeckel DM, Miller-Goodman MS. 2001. Seasonal nutrient dynamics of forested floodplain soil influenced by microtopography and depth. *Soil Sci. Soc. Am. J.* 65:922–31.

Streng DR, Glitzenstein JS, Harcombe PA. 1989. Woody seedling dynamics in an east Texas floodplain forest. *Ecol. Monogr.* 59:177–204.

Sun G, McNutly SG, et al. 2001. Effects of timber management on the hydrology of wetland forests in southern United States. *For. Ecol. Manage.* 143:227–36.

Swift CC, Gilbert CR, et al. 1986. Zoogeography of the freshwater fishes of the southeastern United States: Savannah River to Lake Pontchartrain. In *The zoogeography of North American freshwater fishes,* Hocutt CH, Wiley EO, editors. New York: John Wiley and Sons, pp. 213–65.

Thieret JW. 1971. Quadrat study of a bottomland forest in St. Martin Parish, Louisiana. *Castanea* 36:174–81.

Thomas JR, Gibson DJ, Middleton BA. 2005. Water dispersal of vegetative bulbils of the invasive exotic *Dioscorea oppositifolia* in southern Illinois. *J. Torrey Bot. Soc.* 132:187–96.

Tockner K, Malard F, Ward JV. 2000. An extension of the flood-pulse concept. *Hydrol. Processes* 14:2861–83.

Townsend PA, Butler DR. 1996. Patterns of landscape use by beaver on the lower Roanoke River floodplain, North Carolina. *Phys. Geogr.* 17:253–69.

Tucker JK, Janzen FJ, Paukstis GL. 1997. Responses of embryos of the red-eared turtle (*Trachemys scripta elegans*) to experimental exposure to water-saturated substrates. *Chelonian Conserv. Biol.* 2:345–51.

Twedt DJ, Nelms CO. 1999. Waterfowl density on agricultural fields managed to retain water in winter. *Wildl. Soc. Bull.* 27:924–30.

Twedt DJ, Wilson RR. 2007. Management of bottomland forests for birds. In *Proc. Louisiana Natur. Resour. Symp.,* Shupe TF, editor. Baton Rouge LA: LSU AgCenter, pp. 49–64.

Twedt DJ, Nelms CO, et al. 1998. Shorebird use of managed wetlands in the Mississippi Alluvial Valley. *Am. Midl. Natur.* 140:140–52.

USDA Plants Database. http://plants.usda.gov/ (accession date August 24, 2010).

Van Geest GJ, Wolters H, et al. 2005. Water-level fluctuations affect macrophyte richness in floodplain lakes. *Hydrobiologia* 539:239–48.

Wall DP, Darwin SP. 1999. Vegetation and elevational gradients within a bottomland hardwood forest of southeastern Louisiana. *Am. Midl. Nat.* 142:17–30.

Walton R, Davis JE, et al. 1996. Hydrology of the black swamp wetlands on the Cache River, Arkansas. *Wetlands* 16:279–87.

Wang Z. 1996. *Effects of harvesting intensity on water quality, nitrogen mineralization and litter decomposition in a bottomland hardwood floodplain forest in southeastern Texas.* Ph.D. diss., Mississippi State Univ.

Weijters MJ, Janse JH, et al. 2009. Quantifying the effect of catchment land use and water nutrient concentrations on freshwater river and stream biodiversity. *Aquat. Conserv.: Marine Freshw. Ecosys.* 19:104–12.

Wharton CH, Kitchens WM, et al. 1982. *The ecology of bottomland hardwood swamps of the southeast: a community profile.* Washington, DC: USDI FWS, FWS/OBS-81/37.

White DA. 1983. Plant communities of the Lower Pearl River Basin, Louisiana. *Am. Midl. Nat.* 110:381–96.

Whiting PJ. 2002. Streamflow necessary for environmental maintenance. *Annu. Rev. Earth Planet Sci.* 30:181–206.

Williams TM. 1998. Hydrology. In *Southern forested wetlands: ecology and management,* Messina MG, Conner WH, editors. Boca Raton, FL: CRC Press, pp. 103–22.

Wilson R, Ribbeck K, et al. eds. 2007. *Restoration, management, and monitoring of forest resources in the Mississippi Alluvial Valley: recommendations for enhancing wildlife habitat.* Vicksburg, MS: Lower Mississippi Valley Joint Venture.

Winemiller KO, Tarim S, et al. 2000. Fish assemblage structure in relation to environmental variation among Brazos River oxbow lakes. *Trans. Am. Fish. Soc.* 129:451–68.

Zhao DH, Allen B, Sharitz RR. 2006. Twelve year response of old-growth southeastern bottomland hardwood forests to disturbance from Hurricane Hugo. *Can. J. For. Res.* 36:3136–47.

CHAPTER 19

Tropical Freshwater Swamps and Marshes

PATRICIA MORENO-CASASOLA,
DULCE INFANTE MATA, and HUGO LÓPEZ ROSAS

Tropical wetlands have been important to human societies on all continents for millennia. The Egyptian dynasties flourished on the floodplain of the Nile. Sumerians based their economic and social development on the resources and environmental services of the Euphrates and Tigris Rivers and associated wetlands, as did the Harappas along the Indus River and the Khmer kingdom along the Mekong River. In South America, the Los Ajos people relied on wetlands around Lake Merin, where they were the first to plant corn, pumpkin, beans, and tubers. On the coast of the central Gulf of Mexico, the Olmecs, from whom descended the Mesoamerican civilizations, including the Maya, developed a civilization along the floodplains of the Papaloapan, San Juan, Coatzacoalcos, and Grijalva-Usumacinta Rivers (Veracruz and Tabasco, Fig. 19.1). Regrettably, wetlands in all of these tropical regions have largely disappeared or have been transformed by draining, channel construction, pollution, plant and animal species invasions, nutrient enrichment, and other human impacts. However, substantial wetland resources remain in tropical North America, and this chapter reviews the ecology and conservation of freshwater wetlands of Mexico and Central America.

Geomorphology, Hydrology, and Soils

There are no comprehensive data on the total extent of wetlands in Mexico and Central America. Olmsted (1993) developed a distributional map of the major Mexican wetlands, estimating 33,185 km², including mangroves, salt marshes, salt flats, low inundated forests, freshwater marshes, savannas, prairies, and palm thickets. INEGI (2010) also developed a wetland map of Mexico (1:250,000 scale), based on aerial and satellite images from 1979–91 to assess the extent and distribution of freshwater wetlands at that time (Fig. 19.1). This effort indicated that wetlands occupied 128,124 km² (or 6.5%) of the country's area. Ellison (2004) estimated the area covered by freshwater wetlands in Central America at 17,500 km² (Aselmann and Crutzen 1989).

Tropical Mexico and Central America are split longitudinally by high mountain ranges bordered by coastal lowlands on both the Atlantic and Pacific sides. In Mexico, the Sierra Madre Oriental and Sierra Madre Occidental extend north to south, where they merge into more southerly mountain ranges that extend east to west. In Central America, 75% of the area is composed of mountain ranges, and the largest wetlands are found in the lowlands along the east and west coasts. The mountain ranges and coastal plains provide corridors for the exchange of biota between temperate and tropical latitudes (Stehli and Webb 1985), but function as a barrier between the Atlantic (Gulf of Mexico, Caribbean Sea) and Pacific sides.

The climate of tropical Mexico and Central America is mostly warm and humid, with a summer rainy season. Along the central Gulf coast of Mexico, annual rainfall ranges from 1,200 to 3,000 mm, being somewhat lower (600–800 mm) in the northern Yucatán Peninsula (Moreno-Casasola, Espejel, et al. 1998). The Caribbean region of Nicaragua is extremely wet, receiving between 2,500 and 6,500 mm of rain annually. The Pacific coast is typically drier than the Atlantic coast. Hurricanes (from June to November) and *nortes* (winter cold fronts) induce much of the regional rainfall. Rainfall that drains from the highlands to the lowlands floods many of the coastal freshwater marshes, even late into the dry season.

The combination of copious rains and the proximity of mountain ranges provide the setting for extensive wetland formation. Most tropical wetlands in North America and elsewhere exhibit considerable water-level fluctuations between dry and rainy seasons (Junk 2002), and function as floodplains where flood pulses control their ecology (Junk, Bayley, et al. 1989). Swamps and marshes can be found both along river floodplains and in isolated basins. Permanent water wetlands are less prevalent, and when present, are often parts of larger, seasonally flooded wetland complexes.

Figure 19.2a shows the hydroperiod of two swamps in Veracruz, one of them an isolated depression in La Mancha, north of the Port of Veracruz, and the other in the floodplain of the Tecolutla River in the Ciénága del Fuerte Reserve. Both hydroperiods have similarities but also important differences. The wetland on the river floodplain has strong pulses associated with river overflows, but remains flooded for short periods of time. The depression wetland is fed by groundwater (Yetter 2004) and remains flooded for longer periods of time, depending on the amount of water flowing down to the coastal plain.

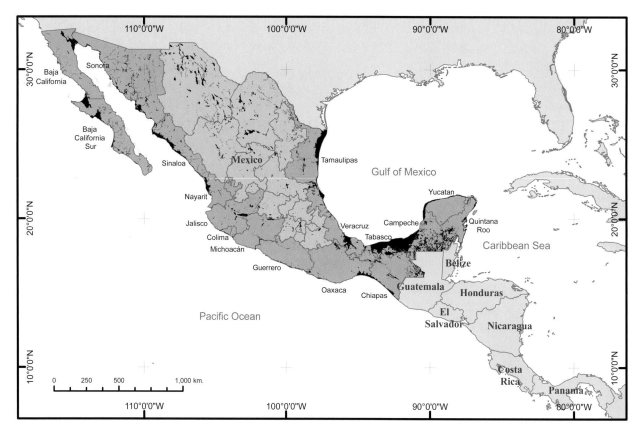

FIG. 19.1. Mexico and Central America, showing the geographical names used in the text. For Mexico, wetland distribution is shown in black shading, with lighter shading indicating the central plateau (INEGI 2010).

Figure 19.2b shows hydroperiods for an additional five wetlands along the River Papaloapan floodplain, south of Veracruz. All these wetlands flood during the rainy season and dry by April or May. The *Pachira aquatica–Annona glabra* swamp remains dry for the longest period (February–June). In contrast, the *Typha domingensis–Eleocharis cellulosa* marsh remains flooded for the longest period, and water depths of 60–70 cm occur during peak flooding. In the *Avicennia germinans–Laguncularia racemosa* mangrove and the *Spartina spartinae* marsh, water tables can drop to more than 1 m below the soil level.

Yetter (2004) studied water budgets of two herbaceous freshwater wetlands in a dune system in Veracruz, dominated by *T. domingensis* and *Sagittaria lancifolia,* and found that groundwater discharge comprised 76% of inputs, with remaining inputs coming from precipitation (19%) and surface flow (5%). Precipitation and surfacewater inputs occur almost exclusively in the June–October rainy season, and groundwater was the only source of water during the dry season (November–May). Groundwater recharge accounted for 68% of water loss from the wetland, and evapotranspiration contributed the remaining 32%. Losses to groundwater were highest at the end of the dry season, coinciding with rising temperatures and a regional drop in the water table. Stable isotope (^{18}O and ^2H) and tritium data indicated that groundwater from local and regional flow systems was discharging into the wetlands.

Swamps, marshes, and mangroves can be found on both organic and mineral soils. A study of 13 marshes in Veracruz found that they occurred on two types of soils: gleysols (mineral soils) and histosols (organic soils). Marshes along the fluvial system of the Papaloapan were mostly on histosols

(Moreno-Casasola, Cejudo-Espinosa, et al. 2010). Analysis of eight swamps in Veracruz found that these wetlands occurred mostly on histosols, but also on fluvisols and gleysols.

Lakes occur both in the highlands and plateaus and the lowlands (García Calderón and de la Lanza 1995; Ellison 2004), and many of these lakes have emergent, floating, and submerged wetland vegetation along their margins. In Mexico, many lakes occur along the Eje Neovolcánico Transversal, where tectonic activity has created geomorphological features where water accumulates, including volcanic calderas. Similar lakes have developed along the Cordillera Central in Central America. Freshwater lakes, varying in size from 1 to 150 ha, often occur in the extensive coastal dune systems of the central Gulf coast of Mexico (Peralta Peláez 2007). In Mexico, there are more than 4,000 reservoirs created by dams, many of which harbor wetland vegetation.

Plant Communities

There are numerous floristic studies of freshwater wetlands in tropical Mexico and Central America. However, this literature is widely scattered and not easily accessed, and materials often do not address the structure of the vegetation, the ecological processes, or the plant-animal interactions in any detail. Mexico's scientists classify vegetation using species composition and physiognomy (general appearance of the vegetation, such as height, amount of leaf fall during the dry season, and species richness). Miranda and Hernández-X (1963) recognized mangroves, broad-leaved marshes, *Typha* marshes, and reed marshes. Rzedowski (1978) recognized aquatic and subaquatic

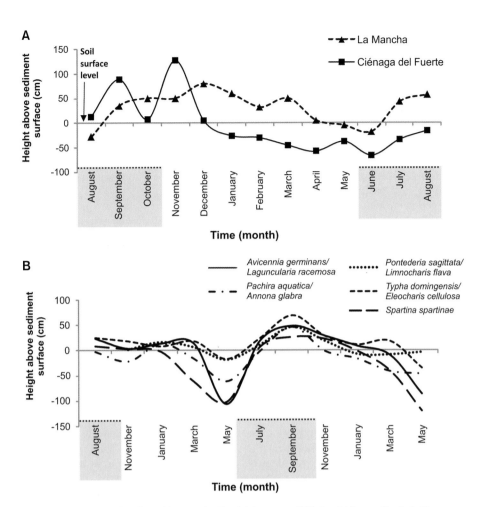

FIG. 19.2. A. Hydrographs of a *Pachira aquatica* floodplain swamp (Ciénága del Fuerte, Tecolutla River floodplain) and an *Annona glabra* dune depression swamp (La Mancha, north of the Port of Veracruz). In both sites, flooding takes place during the rainy season (June to October). Ciénága del Fuerte shows pulses associated with river overflow, remaining flooded for a shorter period of time. The hydroperiod in La Mancha wetlands is fed by groundwater and remains flooded for longer periods. (D. Infante Mata, 2011.) B. Hydrographs from five freshwater wetlands on the floodplain of the Papaloapan River, Veracruz, with flooding during the rainy season. The *Pachira aquatica–Annona glabra* swamp remains dry for the longest period (February–June), while the *Typha domingensis–Eleocharis cellulosa* marsh remains flooded for almost 10 months. Shaded areas indicate rainy season. (P. Moreno-Casasola, unpublished data.)

vegetation, which includes mangroves, broad- and narrow-leaved marshes, reed marshes, floating communities, and tropical forest. Scientists in Central America use the Holdridge Life Zone system (Holdridge 1967) to categorize habitats, but that system does not include wetlands as a distinct vegetation type (see Ellison 2004). Common and family names of all plant species listed in the below community decriptions can be found in online appendix 19.1.

Tropical Swamps

Several types of swamps (forested wetlands) are distributed throughout the coastal plains of Mexico (Lot-Helgueras and Novelo 1990) and Central America (Ellison 2004). Ewel (2010) recently brought attention to freshwater forested wetlands, often found just upslope from mangrove forests in both high- and low-rainfall zones, and highlighted how important both wetland types are to each other from the hydrological perspective and to local economies. The importance of mangroves is

well recognized, but goods and services provided by freshwater wetlands are not nearly as well documented.

In Mexico, swamps are mainly distributed in lowlands along the Gulf coast and the Yucatán Peninsula (Atlantic coast), where the coastal plain is wide and receives drainage water from the Mexican plateau, and in the coastal plain of Chiapas, in the southwest. Swamp area is diminishing quickly, but extensive remnants can still be found, especially in the southeast. In Mexico, some swamps are dominated by only a few species, while others are quite diverse. In Central America, swamps tend to have fairly low plant species diversity (Ellison 2004; Ibáñez 2006) in comparison to tropical swamps elsewhere.

Along the Mexican Gulf coast in Veracruz, three types of swamps can be found, characterized by their dominant plants (Fig. 19.3a–c): *Annona glabra* swamps, *Pachira aquatica* swamps, and *Ficus* spp. swamps. Orozco-Segovia and Lot-Helgueras (1976) described *Annona glabra–Chrysobalanus icaco* and *Calophyllum brasiliense–Calyptranthes* spp. swamps in the southern part of Veracruz and Tabasco. All these commonly occur along river borders, lagoon fringes, and floodplains lacking marine influence. They can occur in almost monotypic stands, or can support relatively high species richness. Tree species associated with *Annona* swamps include *Diospyros digyna, Ficus insipida,* and *P. aquatica* (Moreno-Casasola, López-Rosas, et al. 2009). Species associated with *Pachira* swamps include *D. digyna, Inga vera, Zygia latifolia, Hasseltia floribunda, Hippocratea celastroides,* and *Ficus insipida* trees, and *Roystonea dunlapiana* and *Attalea liebmanii* palms. Species associated with *Ficus* swamps include *Ficus pertusa, F. insipida* subsp. *insipida,* and *F. maxima,* and other trees such as *Stemmadenia obovata, Bursera simaruba, Tabebuia rosea, D. digyna,* and *Brosimum alicastrum.* The latter two trees are also common elements of evergreen rainforests. Figure 19.4 shows some physico-chemical environmental parameters of interstitial water and groundwater taken from piezometers for the first three types of swamps. Conductivity, total dissolved solids, and salinity from *Pachira* swamps tend to differ from *Annona* or *Ficus* swamps, with values from piezometer water showing the greatest differences. *Pachira* swamps often border mangroves, in areas where freshwater predominates, and can tolerate more salt than the other two types of swamp.

In southern Tabasco and northern Chiapas, a *Bravaisia integerrima* association is common, occurring as intermediate-sized evergreen wetland forest. This association covers flat terrain with shallow, calcareous, highly organic soils. *Bravaisia integerrima* often forms pure stands, but in areas with less flooding, associated species include *Andira inermis, Calophyllum brasiliense, Ceiba pentandra, D. digyna, Ficus panamensis, Lonchocarpus cruentus,* and *Tabebuia rosea. Pterocarpus officinalis* is a very common wetland species in Central America, and appears as an accompanying species in this association (Miranda and Hernández-X 1963; Gómez-Pompa 1965; Rzedowski 1978; Lot-Helgueras and Novelo 1990). In wetlands along Lake Nicaragua, pure stands of *B. integerrima, A. glabra, Anacardium excelsum, Clusia rosea,* or *Erythina glauca* can be found (Taylor 1959 cited in Ellison 2004).

The Mexican Pacific has a narrow coastal plain and only small patches of tropical swamps can be found, often associated with lakes or coastal lagoons. *Pachira* swamps also cover extensive regions in Chiapas, especially in the Encrucijada Reserve. They are frequently mapped with mangroves, but are predominantly freshwater communities. Swamps of *Hippomane mancinella* form small, species-poor patches, sometimes grading into mangroves, and occur along the Pacific coast of Mexico in Jalisco, Guerrero, Oaxaca, and Chiapas. This species has been also recorded in the Caribbean and Florida Keys, but not the Gulf of Mexico.

The calcareous plains of the coastal Yucatán Peninsula harbor a unique type of swamp called *petenes,* which contain tree islands of mixed tropical forest or mangroves in a matrix of flooded grasslands or dwarf mangroves. They are widespread in the Yucatán Peninsula and have similar counterparts in the Everglades in Florida and some Caribbean islands. They are located near the sea, so their coastal fringes are influenced by marine water. Their size is variable (1–30 ha), as is their topography, degree of inundation, and species composition. Durán (1987), Olmsted and Durán (1988), and Zamora (2003) have described two fundamental types of *petenes.* One is characterized by the almost pure stands of the red mangrove, *Rhizophora mangle* (> 90% cover), often with white mangrove (*Laguncularia racemosa).* Tree height varies between 15 and 30 m. Farther away from the area dominated by tall red mangrove, *L. racemosa* disappears, *R. mangle* is substituted by *Avicennia ger-*

minans, and tree heights are only 2 m. The general physiognomy is a tall patch of mangroves surrounded by an extensive plain with low or even dwarf mangroves. The second type of *peten* is more speciose, with trees such as *R. mangle, L. racemosa, Tabebuia rosea, Manilkara zapota, Ficus* spp., *Dendrosicus latifolius, Swietenia macrophylla, Cedrela* sp., and *Sabal* sp., shrubs such *Malvaviscus arboreus* and *Bravaisia tubiflora,* and the giant fern *Acrostichum* spp. Trees are 20–25 m tall, soils are deep and highly organic, and flooding (10–20 cm) occurs only during the rainy season. An abrupt vegetative change occurs between these tall patches and the surrounding herbaceous emergent vegetation.

Haematoxylon campechianum swamps were once common throughout Campeche (Yucatán Peninsula) and northern Belize (Ellison 2004), but were cut extensively through the 19th century. These swamps flood during the rainy season. Soils are shallow, derived from calcareous materials, and have a high percentage of organic matter (Lot-Helgueras and Novelo 1990). Other associated trees include *Bucida buceras, Cameraria latifolia, Coccoloba reflexiflora, Crescentia cujete, Curatella americana, Eugenia lundellii, Hampea trilobata, Hyperbaena winzerlingii,* and *Metopium brownei.* Schultz (2005) describes a *H. campechianum* seasonally inundated forest with variously aged stands of forest inundated for 4–6 months each year. Patchy thickets of trees and shrubs on rock outcrops are interspersed with open areas of sedges. The epiphyte flora is rich and includes many species of Orchidaceae, Bromeliaceae, and Cactaceae.

Also in Yucatán, *Metopium brownei* swamps are dominated by species with wide tolerance to flooding and salinity. They grow in the ecotone of mangroves or form part of drier tropical forests, sometimes in association with *Manilkara zapota.* The trees *M. brownei* and *M. zapota* can also occur with *Bucida buceras* or *H. campechianum* (Rzedowski 1978; Lot-Helgueras and Novelo 1990; Zamora 2003).

In Belize, swamp forests floristically resemble those in the Yucatán Peninsula, and *M. brownei* is associated with various tree species (Wright, Romey, et al. 1959 cited in Ellison 2004). Low broad-leaved swamps include *Spondias mombin* trees, which can be found with *Sabal mauritiiformis* palms and *P. aquatica* trees. Another association is formed by *P. aquatica, Chrysobalanus icaco,* and *Pterocarpus officinalis.* In a 1.6-ha riparian forest patch in the Neotropical savanna of Belize, 292 plant species were identified (Meave and Kellman 1994). Riparian forests here are characterized by low biomass and high stem densities; most species are typical rainforest taxa, suggesting that this flora is not specialized for riparian environments.

Across Central America, in the absence of palms, there is a preponderance of leguminous trees. Forests dominated by *Pterocarpus officinalis* are found ranging from river margins and floodplains to rain-fed upland swamps. The wide range of habitats this tree occupies has been attributed to both a broad spectrum of morphological and physiological ecotypes, and taxonomic confusion. When the understory develops it is dominated by the swamp lily, *Crinum erubescens* (Ellison 2004). In Nicaragua, semiseasonal permanent freshwater swamp with *Erythrina glauca* and *P. aquatica* is reported and brackish swamp with *A. glabra.* In Costa Rica, Hartshorn (1983) described a *Pentaclethra macroloba* swamp, with *P. officinalis* and *P. aquatica* as other canopy species and several palms in the understory. *Prioria copaifera* forms isolated patches on the Osa Peninsula (Costa Rica), and in Nicaragua and Panama it occurs only on the Pacific coast (Ibáñez 2006). Along the Gulf of Chiriquí, mainly to the south, this species is codominant with another legume, *Peltogyne purpurea,* reaching a height of

FIG. 19.3. Swamp trees: A. *Annona glabra* (pond apple); B. *Pachira aquatica* (Guiana chestnut or money tree); and C. *Ficus insipida* subsp. *insipida* (fig). Palm wetland species: D. *Roystonea dunlapiana* (yagua palm); E. *Sabal mexicana* (Mexican palmetto, apachite); and F. *Attalea liebmannii* (coyol real palm). Marsh species: G. *Thalia geniculata* (alligator flag); and H. *Cyperus giganteus* (giant flatsedge). (Photographs by Gerardo Sánchez Vigil.)

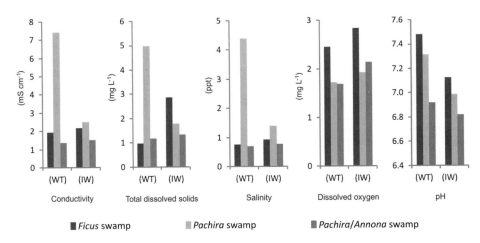

FIG. 19.4. Physico-chemical environmental characteristics for three types of swamps in water taken from groundwater (WT) and interstitial water (IW). *Pachira* swamps tolerate higher salinity values (groundwater) than do the other two freshwater forested wetlands. This tree is sometimes found accompanying mangrove species.

40–50 m. Wetland forests dominated by *Campnosperma panamense* occur in Nicaragua, Costa Rica, and Panama (Ellison 2004). In the Pacific lowlands of Panama, Ibañez (2006) has recorded monotypic formations of the legume *Mora oleifera* as well as 10-m-high swamps dominated by *A. glabra*, sometimes associated with the palm *Elaeis oleifera*, as well as mixed swamps of *Prioria copaifera*, *M. oleifera*, and *P. officinalis*, others with *M. oleifera* and *P. aquatica*, and still others with *P. officinalis* and the mangrove *Pelliciera rhizophorae*.

In coastal regions of Mexico and Central America, both *P. aquatica* and *P. officinalis* can grade into mangroves (Holdridge and Budowski 1956; Vázquez-Yanes 1971; Lot-Helgueras 2004) or *M. oleifera* swamps (Hartshorn 1988; Ibañez 2006). The latter form ecotones between the mangroves and tropical forests and are flooded almost daily from tidal influences, although they are flooded less often than mangroves (Ibañez 2006). Table 19.1 presents some environmental data related to hydrology of three swamps: a freshwater forested wetland dominated by *P. aquatica* in La Mancha (Veracruz); a *P. aquatica–R. mangle* community; and a mangrove community dominated solely by *R. mangle*. A broad spectrum of physiological ecotypes and a broad ecological tolerance probably can explain presence of dominants in freshwater forested swamps as well as accompanying species in mangroves (Ellison 2004).

Palm Swamps

Forested wetlands dominated by palms occur throughout the tropics. In southeastern Mexico they form dense swamps or parts of savannas. Different palm associations grow in long-inundated floodplains, seasonally flooded areas, and uplands. *Acoelorraphe wrightii* characterizes a flood-tolerant palm association. They grow in fringes around other wetlands (swamps, marshes, or inland edges of mangroves) or in the interior of flooded savannas. Soils are highly organic and may be saline. Water depths may reach 1.5 m. Plants also tolerate dry soils and even periodic burning. Associated woody species include *A. glabra*, *Bactris balanoidea*, *Dalbergia glabra*, and *H. campechianum* (Miranda 1958; Lot-Helgueras and Novelo 1990).

In southeast Mexico, *Roystonea dunlapiana* (Fig. 19.3d) and *R. regia* form palm associations, with the latter species having a restricted distribution (Miranda and Hernández-X 1963; Rzedowski 1978). *Sabal morrisiana* associations occur in saturated soils, and trees can reach 25 m tall (Miranda 1958).

In Chiapas, *Sabal mexicana* (Fig. 19.3e) tolerates temporary flooding (Miranda 1952). It also forms part of the floodplain around Veracruz and is associated with grasslands used for cattle ranching, often occurring in abandoned pasture. In the Yucatán Peninsula, dwarf *Bactris balanoidea* and *B. trichophylla* form shallow, fringing, forested wetlands below 200 m elevation. Other flood-tolerant palms of Mexico include *Sabal mauritiiformis*, *S. yapa*, and *Attalea liebmannii* (Fig. 19.3f) (Miranda 1958; Miranda and Hernández-X 1963; Gómez-Pompa 1965, 1973; Rzedowski 1978).

Palm swamps are particularly prevalent from Nicaragua to Panama. *Raphia taedigera* palm swamps cover 600 km² (including 1.2% of Costa Rica) and occur as both river and rain-fed wetlands. The understory is also dominated by palms (*Asterogyne martiana* and *Calyptrogyne ghiesbreghtiana* subsp. *glauca*), but overall the habitats have low diversity (Myers 1990). To a lesser extent, *Manicaria saccifera* palm swamps are also found along the Atlantic lowlands of Costa Rica. In these swamps, two other palms, *Astrocaryum alatum* and *Euterpe oleracea*, can co-dominate.

One can conclude that the tropical region of North America is very diverse in swamp composition. It is a long stretch of land, at times very narrow, with strong maritime influences, frequently subjected to heavy rains induced by hurricanes. This geographical space harbors a great variety of tree species combinations along the coastal plains, although palm swamps are more diverse in Central America. They are found in depressions inland and along floodplains that merge into mangrove forests.

Shrub Wetlands

Wetlands are often dominated by shrubs (< 4 m height, generally branched from the base), although most shrubs also grow as understory or ecotonal species in the forested wetlands already described. Human or natural disturbances of trees, such as logging, cattle grazing, or fire, can leave shrubs as the main residual plant community or promote conditions that favor shrubs. The most common shrub wetland is dominated

TABLE 19.1
Data on water salinity, redox potential, and inundation in forested wetlands of
the coastal plain of Veracruz in the Gulf of Mexico

	Pachira aquatica swamps	*Pachira–Rhizophora mangle*	Mangroves
Inundation limit (m)	–0.90 to 1.0	–0.50 to 0.30	0.82 edge; 0.56 basin
Inundation time (months)	4 to 10	8 to 10	8 to 9
Redox potential (mV)	–63 to 490	–220 to 209	–164 to 116
Water salinity (ppt)			
Superficial	0.21 to 0.4	0.3 to 18.7	10.0 to 45.0
Interstitial	0.22 to 1.2	1.0 to 8.4	1.8 to 28
Groundwater	0.15 to 2.8	5.0 to 19	17.7

NOTE: Data for *Pachira aquatica* swamps of Ciénaga del Fuerte, La Mancha, Laguna La Apompal, and El Salado from Yetter (2004) and Infante Mata, Moreno-Casasola, et al. (2011). Data for *Pachira–Rhizophora mangle* swamps of Laguna Chica, La Mancha lagoon, from P. Moreno-Casasola (unpublished data). Data for mangroves of La Mancha from Flores-Verdugo, Moreno-Casasola, et al. (2007) and Utrera-López and Moreno-Casasola (2008).

by *Mimosa pigra,* which is common in flooded pastures and other human-modified wetlands (Ocaña and Lot-Helgueras 1996). Establishment is facilitated by grazing disturbances on floodplains (Zedler and Rea 1998).

Dalbergia brownei forms dense communities in flooded zones behind mangroves, particularly where the mangroves have been converted to pasture. This community may be transitional between freshwater marshes and mangroves. It can invade freshwater wetlands or tree gaps in swamps. In Ciénaga del Fuerte (Veracruz), many *P. aquatica* trees toppled during hurricanes Dean (2007) and Lorenzo (2009), and *D. brownei* rapidly invaded. Its branches can climb tree trunks and retard succession. In La Mancha (Veracruz), this shrub became problematic in a newly restored freshwater wetland (López Rosas, López-Barrera, et al. 2010).

Marshes

Most freshwater marshes in Mexico and Central America, both temporarily and permanently flooded, occur on coastal plains. However, some occur on plateaus and in depressions more than 2000 m above sea level. For example, cattail marshes (*Typha domingensis* and *T. latifolia*) occur in the Mexico City vicinity (Novelo and Gallegos 1988) and around lakes in Michoacán and Jalisco. In Xochimilco, near Mexico City, cattails form extensive floating mats.

Narrow-leaved marshes are dominated by *Typha* spp., *Scirpus* spp., and/or *Cyperus* spp. (Rzedowski 1978). Wetlands dominated by *Phragmites australis* or *Cladium jamaicense* are generally restricted to coastal areas and are frequently monocultures (Rzedowski 1972), although *Arundo donax,* an introduced species, is sometimes associated. Moreno-Casasola, López-Rosas, et al. (2009) describe in detail a *Cyperus articulatus* and *Eleocharis mutata* marsh in the lowlands of Veracruz.

Typha domingensis marshes are most extensive. They occur in isolated depressions or along river borders and floodplains. Species-poor communities develop, dominated by one or two species, although we have recorded as many as 14 species in a *T. domingensis* marsh in southern Veracruz (Moreno-Casasola, Cejudo-Espinosa, et al. 2010). Research is still needed to establish if *T. domingensis* can potentially become an invasive species and outgrow and replace broad-leaved tropical marshes when the water level is altered or quality is enriched with nutrients.

The coastal plain of northern Belize consists of relatively undisturbed freshwater marshes that are strongly phosphorus (P)-limited and characterized by monodominant stands or mixtures of emergent macrophytes. Increases in soil P augment *T. domingensis* abundance, while *Eleocharis* spp. and *C. jamaicense* are negatively affected (Johnson and Rejmánková 2005). Rejmánková, Pope, et al. (1995) found that *Eleocharis cellulosa* dominated marshes with high conductivity caused by gypsum and calcium carbonate.

Broad-leaved marshes are found mostly in the Atlantic lowlands, primarily in alluvial floodplains and depressions from Veracruz to Chiapas and Campeche. Some of the most extensive broad-leaved marshes are found in Centla Reserve, in Tabasco (Novelo and Ramos 2005). Dominant species are *Pontederia sagittata, Thalia geniculata* (Fig. 19.3g), which also forms isolated patches in Pacific lowlands, *Sagittaria lancifolia, Calathea lutea,* and *Heliconia latispatha.* The reed *Cyperus giganteus* (Fig. 19.3h) can also be present. These species can form monospecific patches or mix with other species, forming rich communities. Richness of broad-leaved species is greatest in more southerly latitudes and on extensive floodplains, such as the Papaloapan River floodplain, where floating mats develop (Moreno-Casasola, Cejudo-Espinosa, et al. 2010). López-Rosas, Moreno-Casasola, et al. (2005) reported 29 species in a La Mancha broad-leaved marsh (and compared species diversity, hydrology, and soils between narrow- and broad-leaved habitats).

Dune lakes have both narrow- and broad-leaved marshes (Peralta Peláez and Moreno-Casasola 2009). Plant communities include 46 families (27 strictly aquatic) and 82 species, with *Sagittaria lancifolia, P. sagittata,* and *Ceratophyllum demersum* often being dominants. Richness per lake fluctuates between 5 and 33 species. Classification identified one assemblage dominated by aquatic species and a second with flood-tolerant grass species (e.g., *Cynodon dactylon, Echinochloa pyramidalis*) that had invaded from surrounding uplands. Groups were associated with pH and the number of dry months. In dune lakes surrounded by cattle ranches or sugar cane plantations, water had high levels of nutrients (ammonium concentrations > 1 mgL⁻¹), which promoted grass invasion.

Along the plateau of the states of Michoacán, Mexico, Jalisco, and Guanajuato, several herbaceous wetland complexes exist. Marsh species distributions from Mexican lakes have been described in Lago Pátzcuaro (Lot and Novelo 1988) and Lago Chapala. Species lists for several lakes in Central America are published in Ellison (2004). Around both Mexican and Central American lakes, many of the same marsh plant species occur. Novelo and Gallegos (1988) describe an interesting situation in Xochimilco (Mexico City), where raised agricultural terraces *(chinampas)* were built in wetlands by the Aztecs. Today these terraces are still being used for flower and vegetable production, and aquatic vegetation grows in flooded channels. In Lago Cuitzeo (Michoacán), the second-largest lake in Mexico, the lakeshore wetland vegetation is dominated by *T. domingensis, Scirpus validus, Schoenoplectus americanus, S. californicus, P. australis,* and *Eleocharis* spp. (Rojas and Novelo 1995). Along the southeast shore, there are considerable expanses dominated by the sedges *S. americanus, Eleocharis rostellata, Cyperus digitatus, C. niger,* and *C. laevigatus,* associated with the herbs *Sagittaria latifolia, Arenaria bourgaei, Polygonum hydropiperoides,* and *Echinochloa crus-pavonis,* among many others. Submerged aquatic plants have also been found in this lake, including *Potamogeton pectinatus, Zannichellia palustris, Najas guadalupensis,* and *C. demersum.* In the Lerma region (state of México), there are several shallow lakes associated with the Lerma River. Ramos (2000) recorded over 200 aquatic and subaquatic plant species. Lake levels have been drastically reduced and habitats are degraded, but they still harbor numerous wetland species. In general these higher-altitude wetland complexes are richer in species than wetlands along the coastal plains (with the exception of the Centla marshes in Tabasco). They support combinations of aquatic and wetland habitat, with diverse growth forms and numerous aquatic herbaceous species. Coastal plains may support more types of wetlands—swamps, palms, savannas, broad- and narrow-leaved marshes—but highland wetlands have greater plant richness.

Volcanic crater lakes are a unique habitat found both in Mexico and Central America. Crater lakes in Puebla and Veracruz (Ramírez-García and Novelo 1984) typically range from 40–60 m depths (although one is only 2.5 m deep), have high salinities (e.g., Alchichica 10.5%; Atexcac 11.3%; Aljojuca, Tecuitlapa, Quechulac, La Preciosa 0.2–0.9%), and pH ranges from 6.9 to 8.2. In the more saline lakes, *Ruppia maritima, P. australis,* and *Potamogeton pectinatus* are widespread. In freshwater lakes, *Eleocharis montevidensis, Cyperus laevigatus, Juncus andicola,* and *Hydrocotyle verticillata* dominate. However, all volcanic lakes tend to be species poor.

Some volcanic lakes can have extremely low levels of pH, ranging down to 2 in Lake Alegria, El Salvador, where only *Eleocharis sellowiana* exists, or extremely high levels, up to 10 in Lake Nejapa, Nicaragua, where only phytoplankton persist (Armitage 1971; Armitage and Fassett 1971 cited in Ellison 2004). Several species *Nymphaea odorata* var. *gigantea, Proserpinaca palustris* var. *crebra, Potamogeton pusillus, Brasenia schreberi)* reach their southern range limit in Central American lakes.

Floating Communities

Floating vegetation includes numerous species with diverse growth forms. True free-floating species include *Salvinia* spp., *Lemna* spp., *Eichhornia* spp., and *Pistia stratiotes,* among others. However, rooted species also occur, including the genera *Nymphaea, Nymphoides, Brasenia, Callitriche, Hydrochloa, Ludwigia, Neptunia,* and *Potamogeton,* as well as submerged species, including the genera *Cabomba, Ceratophyllum, Myriophyllum, Nitella, Ruppia,* and *Vallisneria* (Rzedowski 1972; Lot-Helgueras, Novelo, et al. 1999).

Rojas and Novelo (1995) described floating and submerged communities in Lake Cuitzeo. *Lemna aequinoctialis, L. gibba, Spirodela polyrhiza, Wolffiella lingulata, Pistia stratiotes,* and *Eichhornia crassipes* formed monodominant floating patches, sometimes with *Heteranthera reniformis* or *Azolla mexicana* as associates. Common rooted or submerged species included *Zannichellia palustris, P. pectinatus, C. demersum, Nymphaea gracilis, Nymphoides fallax,* and *Marsilea mollis.* The varied nature of environmental conditions in this lake (extensive shallows and springs, variable depths, different kinds of sediments and rocks) probably contributed to the high species richness of plants (40 families, 92 species). In Central America, free-floating plants in lacustrine wetlands are dominated by *Azolla* spp., *Salvinia* spp., *Lemna* spp., and *Eichhornia* spp. (Ellison 2004). Free-floating plants (especially *E. crassipes* and *P. stratiotes)* can cause problems when they cover water bodies completely. For example in Lake Yuriria, Michoacán (Ramos and Novelo 1993), floating species relegated other wetland plant species (*T. domingensis,* and *Taxodium mucronatum* and *Salix chilensis* trees) to small areas along lake edges.

Animal Communities

While comprehensive descriptions of plant communities in tropical wetlands of Mexico and Central America are rare, descriptions of animal communities are in even shorter supply. We highlight those studies available, and generate faunal lists of some taxa using general habitat knowledge for individual species.

Peralta Peláez, Deloya, et al. (2007) sampled freshwater marshes and floating communities in dune lakes and recorded 62 insect families. Coleoptera (beetles) was the order with the highest number of families, followed by Diptera (flies) (Fig. 19.5a), in which the family Chironomidae (midges) was most abundant, representing 40% of the total collected. Trophic structure was dominated by detritivorous groups (57% were scrapers, collectors, or shredders), followed by predators (38%) and herbivores (5%), which suggests that dune lakes have copious amounts of organic detritus.

Amphibians in La Mancha wetlands, Veracruz, were sampled by Valdez Lares (2010). That data, together with a list assembled by González-Romero and Lara-López (2006), reports 16 total species. The frog *Leptodactylus melanonotus* was the dominant species (Fig. 19.5b). The broadfoot climbing salamander, *Bolitoglossa platydactyla,* was associated with leaves of *Sagittaria lancifolia.*

Reptiles are frequent inhabitants of wetlands. *Crocodylus moreleti* (Morelet's crocodile) lives in mangroves, freshwater marshes, and swamps in the Gulf of Mexico, while *C. acutus* (American crocodile) has a more extensive distribution, both on the Pacific and Caribbean coasts. Caymans *(Caiman crocodylus)* are less common. Other reptiles often associated with freshwater wetlands include striped basilisks *(Basiliscus vittatus),* green iguanas *(Iguana iguana),* rainbow lizards *(Aspidocelis deppei),* rose-bellied spiny lizards *(Sceloporus variabilis),* and various snakes.

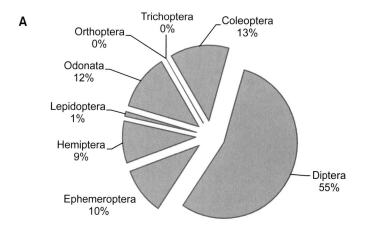

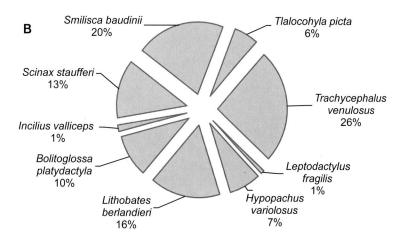

FIG. 19.5. A. Percentage of individuals in the various orders of insects sampled in fresh-water marshes in dune lakes (Diptera 12,399, Coleoptera 3,055, Odonata 2,794, Ephemeroptera 2,306, Hemiptera 1,968, Lepidoptera 137, Orthoptera 21, Trichoptera 11). (Data from Peralta-Peláez, Deloya, et al. 2007.) B. Amphibian composition recorded during a study of communities in two freshwater marshes in La Mancha. The frog *Leptodactylus melanonotus* is not included in the chart because of its dominance (79% of total). (Data from Valdez Lares 2010.)

Crocodylus moreleti has not been well studied, and many aspects of its life history are unknown. It occurs in the Atlantic and Caribbean lowlands of Mexico, Guatemala, and Belize and is considered an endangered species. However, in a recent revision of IUCN Red List categories, based largely on survey data from Mexico, the extinction risk of this species was considered low, but continued survival is contingent on current conservation efforts (Platt and Thorbjarnarson 2000). As a result of commercial skin hunting, populations were greatly diminished, but since hunting and trade controls were enacted, populations have recovered. Spotlight surveys from 1992 to 1997 in northern Belize reported 754 crocodiles over 482 km surveyed. Encounter rates were highest in nonalluvial and alluvial lagoons, and low in rivers, creeks, and mangroves. Nesting occurs in the wet season (mid-June through mid-July), and eggs hatch in mid-August through September, with islands used heavily as nesting sites. Nest losses were primarily due to flooding and raccoon *(Procyon lotor)* predation, and low water levels facilitate predator access to nests (Platt, Rainwater, et al. 2008).

Numerous species of freshwater turtles live in marshes, swamps, and flooded pastures. Common species include Cen-tral American snapping turtle *(Chelydra rossignoni),* Tabasco mud turtle *(Kinosternon acutum),* white-lipped mud turtle *(K. leucostomum),* narrow-bridged musk turtle *(Claudius angustatus),* Mesoamerican slider turtle *(Trachemys venusta),* and Mexican giant musk turtle *(Staurotypus triporcatus).* Turtles can be an important food source for local people, resulting in local population reductions (although some species are now protected in Mexico and Costa Rica) (G. Aguirre pers. comm.). Platt and Rainwater (2011) reported significant turtle predation by the otters.

Migrating and resident birds frequently use freshwater wetlands along the coasts of Mexico (Baldassarre, Brazda, et al. 1989; Kramer and Migoya 1989) and Central America (Frederick, Correa, et al. 1997). Tarabini (2006) recorded 59 species of aquatic and wading birds, belonging to 16 families, in three water bodies in La Mancha (Veracruz): a freshwater dune lake (16 species), a volcanic lake surrounded by marshes (40 species), and an estuary with mangroves (44 species). Herons and bitterns (Ardeidae) were most diverse, with 12 species, with 8 species of duck, sandpiper, and snipe (Anatidae, Scolopacidae), 5 gulls (Laridae), 4 plovers (Charadriidae), and 4 grebes (Podicipedidae), among others. Resident birds preferred the wetlands of the freshwater dune lake and volcanic lake. The lagoonal estuary supported similar numbers of resident and migratory bird families. Ducks and grebes preferred the volcanic lake; plovers, gulls and snipes preferred the estuary; and herons and bitterns preferred the freshwater dune lake. The more common species in the freshwater swamps and dune lake were migratory *Ardea alba* (great egret), *Egretta thula* (snowy egret), *E. caerulea* (little blue heron), *E. tricolor* (tricoloured heron), *Bubulcus ibis* (cattle egret), *Nycticorax nycticorax* (black-crowned night heron), *Nyctanassa violacea* (yellow-crowned night heron), and *Cochlearius cochlearius* (boat-billed heron). Only small populations of *Jacana spinosa* (northern jacana) and *Aramides cajanea* (grey-necked wood rail) were year-round residents and reproduced there. Frederick, Correa, et al. (1997) surveyed Atlantic coastal wetlands of Nicaragua and Honduras and found that great egrets were widespread, representing 53% (Nicaragua) and 46% (Honduras) of waterbird sightings. Wood storks *(Mycteria americana)* and *Egretta* herons were the next two most abundant groups. Breeding colonies of wood storks, roseate spoonbills *(Platalea ajaja),* great egrets, and previously unrecorded populations of jabiru storks *(Jabiru mycteria)* occurred in both areas.

Several mammal species are wetland inhabitants, but many are rare or have declining populations. The neotropical river otter *(Lontra longicaudis)* and the West Indian manatee *(Trichechus manatus)* reside permanently in wetlands and associated aquatic/marine habitats. But most mammals live along flooded wetland borders, catching insects, fish, reptiles, and amphibians for food (e.g. the greater grison *Galictis vittata,* the greater bulldog bat *Noctilio leporinus*). The Central American tapir *(Tapirus bairdii)* grazes and wallows in freshwater wetlands, and the marsupial water opossum *(Chironectes minimus)* lives and forages aquatically for prey along riverbanks.

Key Ecological Processes

Regrettably minimal empirical information exists, beyond the species descriptions already reviewed, to explain which key ecological processes control tropical wetlands. La Mancha in Veracruz and Palo Verde in Costa Rica are two of the areas where there is active ongoing research on freshwater wetlands. We present some case studies that address the roles of plant competition and herbivory.

Competition

Impacts of a nonindigenous invasive grass, *Echinochloa pyramidalis,* on the ecology of narrow-leaved marshes have been addressed in a series of experiments in La Mancha. *E. pyramidalis,* or antelope grass, is a very productive, perennial, rhizomatous, stoloniferous C4 grass, native to the floodplains of tropical Africa, where it grows in dense, pure stands (Howard-Williams and Walker 1974; John, Lévêque, et al. 1993; López-Rosas 2007). This grass is drought tolerant, able to withstand a wide range in water depths and duration of flooding, and tolerates intensive grazing. It was introduced into tropical wetlands of North America as a fodder plant, and is now invading the marshes of Mexico and Central America, displacing native vegetation.

In a tropical freshwater marsh, López Rosas et al. (2006) performed a series of experiments to assess the responses of invasive *E. pyramidalis* versus native plant species. They found cover and biomass of *E. pyramidalis* could be reduced by disking the soil, although the practice did not eliminate the invader. López Rosas and Moreno-Casasola (unpublished data). Each treatment was replicated once in each of 7 blocks, following a randomized block design (N = 42). As in earlier studies, treatments that included disking of the soil successfully prevented reestablishment of *E. pyramidalis* and increased the diversity and cover of native species (Fig. 19.6). Treatments using shade cloth efficiently controlled *E. pyramidalis,* but did not increase overall plant diversity.

López Rosas and Moreno-Casasola (in press) conducted yet another field experiment to determine if changes in topography affected the competitive capacity of nonindigenous *E. pyramidalis* versus native *S. lancifolia* and *T. domingensis.* The experiment was conducted using 0.7 × 0.7 m plots, with treatments replicated five times, using a factorial design. Three hydroperiod levels were used: (1) normal soil moisture; (2) dry conditions, where soil levels were elevated 30 cm; and (3) wet conditions, where soil levels were excavated by 40 cm. Two species combinations were used: (1) *E. pyramidalis* (E) versus *S. lancifolia* (S); and (2) *E. pyramidalis* (E) versus *T. domingensis* (T). Initial densities of each species were developed in the following combinations: (a) 0E vs. 4S or T, (b) 1E vs. 3S or T, (c) 2E vs. 2S or T; (d) 3E vs. 1S or T; and (e) 4E vs. 0S or T. Biomass of *E. pyramidalis* did not vary among hydrology levels or combinations of species (two-way ANCOVA; $F_{1,33}$ = 1.33; P = 0.25). When *E. pyramidalis* grew together with *S. lancifolia,* its biomass was 725.1 ± 56.3 g per quadrat, and when it grew with *T. domingensis* its biomass was 781.6 ± 69.5 g per quadrat. Biomass of *E. pyramidalis* was consistently greater than the native species in the drier marsh plots (normal and dry) (Fig. 19.7), which would coincide with natural marsh of higher elevation. The biomass difference between *E. pyramidalis* and the two native marsh species was least in the wettest hydroperiods (Fig. 19.7), indicating that native species may not be significantly affected by competition with *E. pyramidalis* at lower topographical levels.

Herbivory

Infante Mata (2004) assessed the impacts of herbivory by Lepidoptera larvae on seedling growth responses of two swamp tree species, *Annona glabra* and *Pachira aquatica,* in situ in a tropical swamp along the border of a dune lake. Seedling survival and growth were analyzed in the presence/absence of herbivory and under two levels of soil saturation. Seedlings of *A. glabra* and *P. aquatica* show unique responses. *Annona glabra* was heavily attacked by herbivores, and its growth rate was severely limited (0.017 ± 0.003 g d⁻¹) compared with that of plants that were isolated from herbivores (0.032 ± 0.004 g d⁻¹). Leaf area and total dry weight of *A. glabra* seedlings declined in response to herbivory (Fig. 19.8). *Pachira aquatica* seedlings also had lower leaf area in response to herbivory (Fig. 19.8), but dry weight was not affected (Fig. 19.8). The herbivory treatment revealed that the seedlings of *A. glabra* were highly susceptible, while those of *P. aquatica* experienced minimal damage from herbivores. This suggests that more *P. aquatica* than *A. glabra* seedlings would survive in the presence of the herbivorous caterpillars.

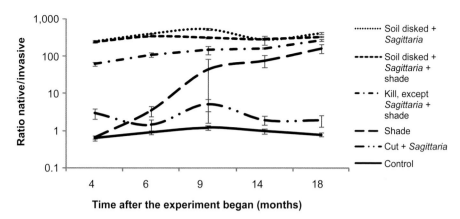

FIG. 19.6. Ratio between the cover of native species/cover of *E. pyramidalis* obtained through experimentation using six treatments. (1) Control: ambient conditions, with an extensive cover of invasive *E. pyramidalis;* (2) cut + *Sagittaria:* all vegetation was clipped to soil level, and then five individuals of *S. lancifolia* were transplanted into the plots; (3) shade: all vegetation was covered with shade cloth, yielding 50% light reduction; (4) kill, except *Sagittaria* + shade: all plants in the plot were eliminated with herbicide, except individuals of *S. lancifolia,* which were protected, and then the plot was covered with shade cloth; (5) soil disked + *Sagittaria* + shade: all vegetation was clipped, the soil was disked by hand to a depth of 37 cm, five individuals of *S. lancifolia* were transplanted, and finally the plot was covered with shade cloth; and (6) soil disked + *Sagittaria:* all vegetation was clipped, the soil was disked by hand to a depth of 37 cm, and five individuals of *S. lancifolia* were transplanted. Density and percent cover by species in each quadrant was measured 5 times over 18 months. The mean for data of 7 quadrants is presented by treatment and by sampling date. The ratio values are expressed on a logarithmic scale. (López Rosas and Moreno-Casasola unpublished data.)

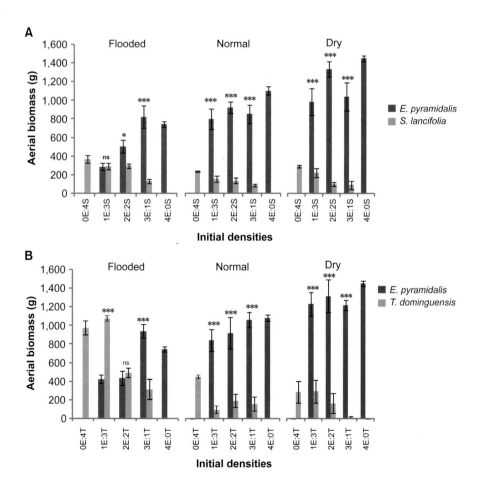

FIG. 19.7. Aboveground biomass of *E. pyramidalis* versus *S. lancifolia* (A) and *T. domingensis* (B) for different hydroperiod treatments and among different initial densities (mean ± 1 SE). Significant differences among pairs of species are indicated (paired t, ns = not significant, * *P* < 0.05, ** *P* < 0.01, *** *P* < 0.001).

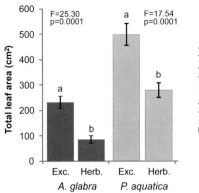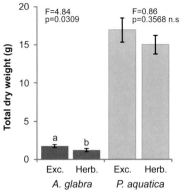

FIG. 19.8. Seedling response of *Annona glabra* and *Pachira aquatica* when exposed to hervibory in the swamp of La Mancha, Veracruz. Different letters indicate significant differences between treatments (N = 80). The first graph shows the leaf area of *A. glabra* and *P. aquatica* seedlings under excluded conditions (Exc.) and subjected to herbivory (Herb.). The second graph shows the values obtained for total dry weight of both *A. glabra* and *P. aquatica* seedlings under these two conditions (Infante Mata 2004).

Conservation Concerns

Tropical wetlands, in general, are highly threatened ecosystems (Junk 2002). Moreno-Casasola (2008) provides a synthesis of the main problems affecting wetlands in Mexico. Two of the most important threats are the expansion of cattle ranching and wetland drainage for urban/tourist development. In Mexico, mangroves have legal protection, and draining or cutting them is forbidden (although some efforts are being made to weaken protections). Inland freshwater wetlands have much weaker legal protection, mainly because of a lack of definition of the different types of wetlands and the species that indicate their presence. For the Tempisque Basin of northwest Costa Rica, Daniels and Cumming (2008) related the locations of wetlands with the rate of change in wetland area and found that landscape settings with highest probabilities of wetland conversion were readily accessible and occurred in regions lacking legal protections.

Impacts of Cattle Ranching

Cattle ranching is a major economic activity in the tropics, both dry and humid. Cebu cattle were introduced in the 1950s to replace the small longhorn cows first introduced by the colonial Spanish (Skerritt 1993; Guevara and Lira-Noriega 2004). Historically cattle could be left unattended to graze on native trees, shrubs, and herbs. However, cebu cattle need open pasture, which led to increased cutting of forests and the introduction of nonindigenous forage grasses (Parsons 1972). Swamp forests have been extensively clear-cut for cattle ranching, and broad-leaved marshes are burned annually (and sometimes drained) to encourage resprouting of cattle forage. In the tropical lowlands, a common practice is to graze cattle on uplands during the summer wet season when wetlands are flooded, and then move them to wetlands during the winter-spring dry season.

Cattle ranching can alter wetlands in many ways. Cattle trampling compacts soil, which changes wetland capacity for water percolation and can lead to decreased plant diversity (Travieso-Bello, Moreno-Casasola, et al. 2005). Seeds that survive being consumed by cattle can germinate in cattle dung, providing a ready way for nonindigenous species to be introduced into wetlands. To increase fodder productivity, some cattle ranchers drain wetlands and introduce African grass species, including *Cynodon plectostachyus* (Parsons 1972) and *E. pyramidalis* (Lopez-Rosas, Moreno-Casasola, et al. 2006), among others. These grasses displace native vegetation either through direct planting or through invasive expansion. Moreno-Casasola, López-Rosas, et al. (2009), working in La Mancha along the Gulf of Mexico, found that most of the area wetlands had been transformed into inundated pastures.

Escutia-Lara, Lara-Cabrera, et al. (2009) analyzed fire effects in a tropical marsh in Michoacán. Fire had different effects depending on the plant species. *Schoenoplectus americanus* was not affected, but cover of *T. domingensis* was altered across the wetland gradient, with a consequent loss of the normal zonation pattern of these species. Fire reduced plant species richness from 34 species during 2005 to 26 in 2007. *Carex comosa* increased its cover by 133%.

Cattle grazing can benefit some aspects of marsh ecology. Palo Verde wildlife refuge in Costa Rica (OTS Field station) is dominated by a seasonally flooded marsh on the floodplain of the Tempisque River. It is an important feeding and breeding area for waterfowl. Historically, cattle commonly grazed in the marsh, but they were removed in 1979, when the refuge was established. Removal led to expanded *T. domingensis* cattail cover (from 5 to 95%) and the disappearance of open water, which led to a decline in waterfowl (McCoy and Rodriguez 1994). Mechanical removal of cattail led to an initial recovery of open water, but those areas were subsequently colonized by dense stands of *Paspalidium* spp. *Typha* was also managed by crushing and then removing it, using a tractor with metal paddle wheels (Osland 2009). When applied at the beginning of the dry season, this practice resulted in a large reduction in aboveground biomass, ramet density, and ramet height. This was coupled with an increase in open water, and a 98-fold and 5-fold increase in avian density and richness, respectively. After the decrease in *Typha* cover, Trama (2005) found that 12 bird species nested in the restored wetland, 30% among the *Typha* plants, 30% in trees, and the other 40% in floating and emergent vegetation or on crushed *Typha* stems.

Invasive Species

Above we described the invasive ability of the African grass *E. pyramidalis*. Nonindigenous invasive plants in general have negative effects on the structure and function of ecosystems, including wetlands. Nonindigenous plant introductions can alter food webs (MacDonald and Frame 1988; O'Connor, Covich, et al. 2000), increase erosion and sedimentation rates of streams (Lacey, Marlow, et al. 1989), alter hydrologic cycle (Loope and Sánchez 1988; Vitousek 1990; López-Rosas 2007), change nutrient cycles (Ramakrishnan and Vitousek 1989; Vitousek 1990), or cause other disturbances (Brandt and Rickard 1994). Invasive grasses possess features that make them better competitors than plants from other families, such as increased litter production, dense root systems, highly efficient acquisition of water and soil nutrients, large sexual and vegetative reproductive capacities, and some degree of tolerance to drought (D'Antonio and Vitousek 1992; Chapman 1996; López-Rosas, Moreno-Casasola, et al. 2006; López-Rosas 2007). Perennial C4 species from Africa are particularly successful invaders in tropical and subtropical regions of North America because their adaptations give them a strong competitive advantage over native plants (D'Antonio and Vitousek 1992), especially tolerance to grazing, fire, and low soil nutrient availability (Parsons 1972; D'Antonio and Vitousek 1992; Williams and Baruch 2000). Some of the changes induced by nonindigenous *Brachiaria mutica* in wetlands are aggressive colonization and displacement of native plants, facilitation of invasion by other nonindigenous grasses, and formation of large floating mats in ponds and other wetlands (Parsons 1972; Humphries, Groves, et al. 1992; Low 1997). *Hyparrhenia rufa* has been reported to impede the regeneration of trees at riverine forest edges (Nepstad, Uhln, et al. 1991; Rodríguez 2001), and *E. pyramidalis* displaces native wetland plants and has a high production of roots that increases soil levels, "drying up the marsh" (López-Rosas 2007).

Some native wetland species have invasive qualities. Hall, Zedler, et al. (2008) experimentally harvested stands of *T. domingensis* in central Mexico. After one year, relative to control plots, harvested treatments had increased species richness at the plot and the wetland scales, and changed plant community compositions.

Human Encroachment and Urban Growth

Many cultures and human settlements have developed close to wetlands, and there is no exception in the tropics. However, now urbanization is occurring rapidly. Towns and cities have spread over fertile lands and wetlands, and environmental legislation has not been able to appreciably slow this trend. Two conditions particularly favor urban sprawl into wetlands. The first is a lack of continuity in urban plans by governments, and the second is the transformation of inundated pasturelands and wetlands into housing units. Pasturelands are often owned by ranchers with the money and political power to obtain permits to change land use (Guevara and Moreno-Casasola 2008). Also, wetlands usually have a lower market price than uplands, and thus are readily bought around rapidly growing cities that need housing facilities. Urban plans are often changed, with little concern for wetlands.

The poorer sectors of society are often forced to settle in the least hospitable environments, wetlands among them. Floods

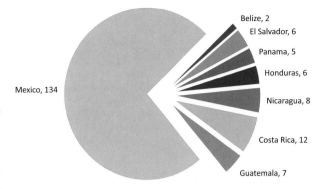

FIG. 19.9. Ramsar sites in Mexico and the Central American countries. The total area of Ramsar reserves in Central America is 2,076,917 ha and in Mexico 8,911,049 ha.

can become disasters with numerous human deaths because people have settled on river floodplains or drained swamps and marshes. In very rainy years or during hurricanes, these areas flood and can retain water for days or weeks, and soils can liquefy and mudslides can develop. Hurricane Karl (2010) caused extensive flooding in coastal cities of Veracruz, largely in urban development on wetlands.

Conservation Efforts and Policies

A wetland conservation effort is currently taking place in Mexico and Central America in which protected areas and Ramsar sites are being established. The most important type of protected area in the region is the Biosphere Reserve, a category recognized internationally by UNESCO. These sites combine conservation of biological and cultural diversity with sustainable development (Guevara and Laborde 2008), and include many wetlands. There are currently 44 Biosphere Reserves in Mexico, of which Centla (Tabasco), Tuxtlas (Veracruz), Los Petenes and Calakmul (Campeche), Sierra Gorda (Querétaro), and La Encrucijada (Chiapas) are prominent (www.conanp.gob.mx/que_hacemos/reservas_biosfera.php).

The establishment of Ramsar sites is another important way that wetlands are being conserved in Mexico and Central America. Ramsar designation does not change land ownership but requires a participatory management plan to insure sustainable use of the wetlands. There are 114 Ramsar sites in Mexico and 41 in Central America (Fig. 19.9). Because Central America is one-fourth the size of Mexico, proportionally the number of Ramsar reserves in Central America is somewhat higher than for Mexico. Despite the fact that international mechanisms such as the Ramsar Convention have no power to impose specific management or conservation measures, they provide "moral authority" and guidelines for local governments (Junk 2002).

Slowly governments and society are coming to understand the importance of wetlands and the need for their conservation. But legislation remains weak. There is a vital need for environmental education of society and decisionmakers, including government authorities at federal, state, and local levels. Many wetlands are lost because permits for changing land use are being provided at the local level. Transformation of wetlands into inundated pastures does not require a special permit. Transforming an inundated pasture into a housing facility needs a permit, but weak enforcement of legislation can easily overcome this requirement.

In many places, wetland functions are appreciated by one sector, but not by another. In Mexico and Central America, both international and national NGOs should play an increasing role in the future to promote protection of wetlands, promote regulations that protect wetlands and ensure they are applied, create cogent watershed management plans, and integrate diverse perspectives on urban development.

Sustainable use of wetlands is valued by many local people of Mexico and Central America. In Costa Rica, projects on ecotourism and local art and crafts focus on wetland areas (Grupo de Mujeres de Santa Fe, Asociación de Desarrollo Integral de Ostional), and restoration activities have been conducted (Carbonell, Nathai-Gyan, et al. 2001). In Nicaragua, Grupo de Trabajo en Humedales de Nicaragua monitors waterbirds. In Mexico, several local associations of fishermen, peasants, or women work in environmentally friendly projects and actively participate in ecotourism (e.g., Red de Humedales de la Costa de Chiapas, Asociación de Silvicultores Marisma y Selva de Nayarit, Red de Humedales de la Costa de Oaxaca, Cooperativa La Mujer Costeña, Mujeres Experimentando, Ejido San Crisanto, Fundación San Crisanto AC., La Mancha en Movimiento). Universities and research institutions also work with local people and NGOs on conservation and restoration strategies in Costa Rica (FUNGAP; www.fungap.org/) and Mexico (Costa Sustentable—Instituto of Ecología AC; www1.inecol.edu.mx/costasustentable/; Moreno-Casasola and Salinas 2005).

Conclusion

Tropical North America is a region rich in wetland types and wetland plant and animal species. The geographical position of the wetlands, many of them along the coastal floodplains, where there is intensive agricultural activity, tourism and port development, city growth, and water and oil/gas extraction, has taken a toll on these habitats. A lack of watershed management is increasing sediment and nutrient loads. Governments, politicians, and the general public lack awareness about the importance of the environmental and societal services and benefits that wetlands provide. The region clearly needs more research and environmental education to change the perception of wetland roles in providing goods and services.

Acknowledgments

We are grateful to Roberto Monroy for help with the maps and figures, Gerardo Sánchez Vigil for the photographs, and Evelyn Gaiser for helpful comments.

References

Armitage KB. 1971. A highly alkaline lake in Nicaragua. *Hydrobiologia* 38:437–39.

Armitage KB, Fassett NC. 1971. Aquatic plants of El Salvador. *Arch. Hydrobiol.* 69:234–55. *Wetl. Ecol. Manage.* 12:3–55. (Cited in Ellison 2004.)

Aselmann I, Crutzen PJ. 1989. Global distribution of natural freshwater wetlands and rice paddies, their net primary productivity, seasonality and possible methane emissions. *J. Atmos. Chem.* 8:307–58.

Baldassarre GA, Brazda AR, Woodyard ER. 1989. The east coast of Mexico. In *Habitat management for migrating and wintering waterfowl in North America,* Smith LM, Pederson RG, Kaminski RM, editors. Lubbock: Texas Tech Univ. Press, pp. 407–25.

Brandt CA, Rickard WH. 1994. Alien taxa in the North American shrub-steppe four decades after cessation of livestock grazing and cultivation agriculture. *Biol. Conserv.* 68:95–105.

Carbonell M, Nathai-Gyan N, Finlayson CM. 2001. *Science and local communities: strengthening partnerships for effective wetland management.* Memphis, TN: Ducks Unlimited, Inc., USA.

Chapman GP. 1996. *The biology of grasses.* Wallingford, UK: CAB International.

Daniels AE, Cumming GS. 2008. Conversion or conservation? Understanding wetland change in northwest Costa Rica. *Ecol. Appl.* 18:49–63.

D'Antonio CM, Vitousek PM. 1992. Biological invasions by exotic grasses, the grass/fire cycle, and global change. *Annu. Rev. Ecol. System.* 23:63–87.

Durán R. 1987. Descripción y análisis de la estructura y composición de la vegetación de los petenes del noroeste de Campeche. *Biotica* 12:181–92.

Ellison A. 2004. Wetlands of Central America. *Wetl. Ecol. Manage.* 12:3–55.

Escutia-Lara Y, Lara-Cabrera S, Lindig-Cisneros RA. 2009. Efecto del fuego y dinámica de las hidrófitas emergentes en el humedal de la Mintzita, Michoacán, México. *Rev. Mex. Biodiv.* 80(3):771–78.

Ewel KC. 2010. Appreciating tropical coastal wetlands from a landscape perspective. *Front. Ecol. Env.* 8:20–26.

Flores-Verdugo F, Moreno-Casasola P, et al. 2007. La topografía y el hidroperiodo: dos factores que condicionan la restauración de los humedales costeros. *Bol. Soc. Bot. Méx.* 80(Suplemento):33–47.

Frederick PC, Correa JS, et al. 1997. The importance of the Caribbean coastal wetlands of Nicaragua and Honduras to Central American populations of waterbirds and jabiru storks (*Jabiru mycteria*). *J. Field Ornithol.* 68:287–95.

García Calderón JL, de la Lanza G. 1995. La cuenca de México. In *Lagos y presas de México,* de la Lanza G, García Calderón JL, editors. México: Editorial Centro de Ecología y Desarrollo, pp. 27–50.

Gómez-Pompa A. 1965. La vegetación de México. *Bol. Soc. Bot. Méx.* 29:76–120.

Gómez-Pompa, A. 1973. Ecology of the vegetation of Veracruz. In *Vegetation and vegetational history of northern Latin America,* Graham A, editor. Amsterdam: Elsevier, pp. 73–148.

González-Romero A, Lara-López MS. 2006. Los anfibios, los reptiles y los mamíferos. In *Entornos Veracruzanos: la costa de La Mancha,* Moreno-Casasola P, editor. Xalapa, México: Instituto de Ecología AC, pp. 407–22.

Guevara S, Laborde J. 2008. The landscape approach: designing new reserves for protection of biological and cultural diversity in Latin America. *Env. Ethics* 30:251–62.

Guevara SS, Lira-Noriega A. 2004. De los pastos de la selva a la selva de los pastos: la introducción de la ganadería en México. *Pastos* 34(2):109–50.

Guevara SS, Moreno-Casasola P. 2008. El dilema de los recursos naturales: la ganadería en el trópico de México. *Guararaguao* 12(29):9–23.

Hall S, Zedler JBC, Lindig-Cisneros R. 2008. Does harvesting sustain diversity in central Mexican wetlands? *Wetlands* 28:776–92.

Hartshorn GS. 1983. Plants. Introduction. In *Costa Rican natural history,* Janzen DH, editor. Univ. Chicago Press, pp. 118–57.

Hartshorn GS. 1988. Tropical and subtropical vegetation of Meso-America. In *North American terrestrial vegetation,* Barbour MG, Billings WD, editors. Cambridge: Cambridge Univ. Press, pp. 365–90.

Holdridge LR. 1967. *Life zone ecology.* San José, Costa Rica: Tropical Science Center.

Holdridge LR, Budowski G. 1956. Report of an ecological survey of the Republic of Panama. *Caribbean Forester* 17(3–4):92–110.

Howard-Williams C, Walker BH. 1974. The vegetation of a tropical African lake: classification and ordination of the vegetation of Lake Chilwa (Malawi). *J. Ecol.* 62:831–54.

Humphries SE, Groves RH, Mitchell DS. 1992. Plant invasions of Australian ecosystems: a status review and management directions. In *Plant invasions: the incidence of environmental weeds in*

Australia, Longmore R, editor. Canberra: Kowari 2, Australian Nat. Parks Wildl. Serv., pp. 1–27.

Ibañez A. 2006. Golfo de Chiriquí. In *Ecosistemas y conservación de la zona insular y costera.* Panama: Nature Conservancy, 98.

INEGI (Inst. Na. Estad., Geogr. Inform.). 2010. www.inegi.org. mx/geo/contenidos/recnat/humedales/Metodologia.aspx.

Infante Mata D. 2004. Germinación y establecimiento de *Annona glabra* (Annonaceae) y *Pachira aquatica* (Bombacaceae) en humedales, La Mancha, Actopan, Ver. MS thesis, Instituto de Ecología AC, Xalapa, México.

Infante Mata D, Moreno-Casasola P, et al. 2011. Floristic composition and soil characteristics of tropical freshwater forested wetlands of Veracruz on the coastal plain of the Gulf of Mexico. *Forest Ecol. Manag.* 262:1514–1531.

John EM, Lévêque C, Newton LE. 1993. Western Africa. In *Wetlands of the world.* I: *Inventory, ecology and management,* Whigham DF, Dykyjová D, Hejný S, editors. Dordrecht: Kluwer Academic, pp. 47–78.

Johnson S, Rejmánková E. 2005. Impacts of land use on nutrient distribution and vegetation composition of freshwater wetlands in northern Belize. *Wetlands* 25:89–100.

Junk WJ. 2002. Long term environmental trends and the future of tropical wetlands. *Env. Conserv.* 29:414–35.

Junk WJ, Bayley PB, Sparks RE. 1989. The flood pulse concept in river floodplain systems. In *Proceedings of the International Large River Symposium, Can. Spec. Publ. Fish. Aquat. Sci.* 106:110–27, Doge DP, editor.

Kramer GW, Migoya R. 1989. The Pacific coast of Mexico. In *Habitat managment for migrating and wintering waterfowl in North America,* Smith LM, Pederson RG, Kaminski RM, editors. Lubbock: Texas Tech Univ. Press, pp. 507–28.

Lacey JR, Marlow CB, Lane JR. 1989. Influence of spotted knapweed *(Centaurea maculosa)* on surface runoff and sediment yield. *Weed Technol.* 3:627–31.

Loope LL, Sánchez PG. 1988. Biological invasions of arid land nature reserve. *Biol. Conserv.* 44:95–118.

López-Rosas H. 2007. Respuesta de un humedal transformado por la invasión de la gramínea exótica *Echinochloa pyramidalis* Hitchc. & A. Chase a los disturbios inducidos (cambios en el hidroperíodo, apertura de espacios y modificación de la intensidad lumínica). Ph.D. diss., Instituto de Ecología AC, Xalapa, México.

López-Rosas H, Moreno-Casasola P, Mendelssohn I. 2005. Effects of an African grass invasion on vegetation, soil and interstitial water characteristics in a tropical freshwater marsh in La Mancha, Veracruz (Mexico). *J. Plant Interaction* 1:187–95.

López-Rosas H, Moreno-Casasola P, Mendelssohn I. 2006. Effects of experimental disturbances on a tropical freshwater marsh invaded by the African grass *Echinochloa pyramidalis. Wetlands* 26:593–604.

López-Rosas H, López-Barrera F, et al. 2010. Indicators of recovery in a tropical freshwater marsh invaded by an African grass. *Ecol. Restor.* 28:324–32.

López-Rosas H, Moreno-Casasola P. In Press. Invader versus natives: Effects of hydroperiod on competition between hydrophytes in a tropical freshwater marsh. *Basic and Applied Ecology* (http://dx.doi.org/10.1016/j.baae.2011.10.004).

Lot A, Novelo A. 1988. Vegetación y flora acuática del Lago de Pátzcuaro, Michoacán. *SW Natur.* 33:167–75.

Lot-Helgueras A. 2004. Flora and vegetation of freshwater wetlands in the coastal zone of the Gulf of Mexico. In *Environmental analysis of the Gulf of Mexico,* Caso M, Pisanty I, Ezcurra E, editors. SEMARNAT—Inst. Nacional Ecol., Inst. Ecol. AC, Harte Res. Inst. Gulf of Mexico Studies, Texas A&M Univ., pp. 314–39.

Lot-Helgueras A, Novelo A. 1990. Forested wetlands of Mexico. In *Ecosystems of the world: forested wetlands of the world,* Lugo AE, Brinson MM, Brown S, editors. Amsterdam: Elsevier, pp. 287–98.

Lot-Helgueras A, Novelo AR, et al. 1999. *Catálogo de angiospermas acuáticas de México: hidrófitas estrictas emergentes, sumergidas y flotantes.* México, DF: Cuadernos Inst. Biol. 33. Univ. Nacional Autónoma de México.

Low T. 1997. Tropical pasture plants as weeds. *Trop. Grasslands* 31:337–43.

MacDonald IAW, Frame GW. 1988. The invasion of introduced species into nature reserves in tropical savannas and dry woodlands. *Biol. Conserv.* 44:67–93.

McCoy MBC, Rodríguez J. 1994. Cattail *(Typha domingensis)* eradication methods in the restoration of a tropical, seasonal, freshwater marsh. In *Global wetlands old world and new,* Mitsch WJ, editor. Amsterdam: Elsevier, pp. 469–82.

Meave J, Kellman M. 1994. Maintenance of rain forest diversity in riparian forests of tropical savannas: implications for species conservation during Pleistocene drought. *J. Biogeogr.* 21:121–35.

Miranda F. 1952. *La vegetación de Chiapas.* Tuxtla Gutiérrez: Ediciones del Gobierno del Estado.

Miranda F. 1958. Estudios acerca de la vegetación. In *Los recursos naturales del sureste y su aprovechamiento,* vol. 2, Beltrán E, editor. México, DF: Edic. Inst. Mex. Rec. Nat. Renov., pp. 215–71.

Miranda F, Hernández XE. 1963. Los tipos de vegetación de México y su clasificación. *Bol. Soc. Bot. Méx.* 28:29–178.

Moreno-Casasola P. 2008. Los humedales en México: tendencias y oportunidades. *Cuadernos de Biodiversidad* 28 (Univ. de Alicante, España):10–18.

Moreno-Casasola P, Salinas S. 2005. Scientists and rural stakeholders develop enterprises designed to restore Gulf wetlands (Mexico). *Ecol. Rest.* 23:120–21.

Moreno-Casasola P, Cejudo-Espinosa E, et al. 2010. Composición florística, diversidad y ecología de humedales herbáceos emergentes en la planicie costera central de Veracruz, México. *Bol. Soc. Bot. Méx.* 87:29–50.

Moreno-Casasola P, Espejel I, et al. 1998. Flora de los ambientes arenosos y rocosos de las costas de México. In *Biodiversidad en Iberoamérica,* vol. 2, Halffter G, editor. CYTED—Instituto de Ecología AC, Xalapa, Ver. pp. 177–258.

Moreno-Casasola P, López-Rosas H, et al. 2009. Environmental and anthropogenic factors associated with coastal wetland differentiation in La Mancha, Veracruz, Mexico. *Plant Ecol.* 200:37–52.

Myers RL. 1990. Palm swamps. In *Forested wetlands,* Lugo AE, Brinson M, Brown S, editors. New York: Elsevier, pp. 267–86.

Nepstad DC, Uhln C, Serrao EAE. 1991. Recuperation of a degraded Amazonian landscape: forest recovery and agricultural restoration. *Ambio* 20:248–55.

Novelo R, Ramos L. 2005. Vegetación acuática. In *Biodiversidad del estado de Tabasco.* Bueno J, Álvarez F, Santiago S, editors. Inst. Biol., UNAM-CONABIO, Mexico, pp. 111–44.

Novelo RA, Gallegos M. 1988. Estudio de la flora y la vegetación acuática relacionada con el sistema de Chinampas en el sureste del Valle de México. *Biótica* 13(1,2):121–39.

Ocaña D, Lot Helgueras A. 1996. Estudio de la vegetación acuática vascular del sistema fluvio-lagunar-deltaico del Río Palizada, en Campeche, México. *Anal. Inst. Biol., UNAM. Ser. Botánica* 67:303–27.

O'Connor PJ, Covich AP, et al. 2000. Non-indigenous bamboo along headwater streams of the Luquillo Mountains, Puerto Rico: leaf fall, aquatic leaf decay, and patterns of invasion. *J. Trop. Ecol.* 16:499–516.

Olmsted I. 1993. Wetlands of Mexico. In *Wetlands of the world.* I: *Inventory, ecology and management,* Whigham DF, Dykyjová D, Hejný S, editors. Handbook of Vegetation Science. Dordrecht: Kluwer, pp. 637–77.

Olmsted I, Duran R. 1988. Aspectos ecológicos de los petenes de Florida, Campeche y Quintana Roo. In *Memorias del Simposio Internacional sobre la Ecología y Conservación del Delta de los ríos Usumacinta y Grijalva, Tabasco,* 2–7 Feb. 1987, 517–36. INIREB-Tabasco.

Orozco-Segovia A, Lot-Helgueras A. 1976. La vegetación de las zonas inundables del sureste de Veracruz. *Biotica* 1:1–44.

Osland MJ. 2009. *Managing invasive plants during wetland restoration: the role of disturbance, plant strategies, and environmental filters.* Ph.D. diss., env. sci., Duke Univ.

Parsons JJ. 1972. Spread of African pasture grasses to the American tropics. *J. Range Manage.* 25:12–17.

Peralta-Peláez LA. 2007. *Diseño de un índice de integridad biótica para los lagos interdunarios de la región costera central del estado de Veracruz, México.* Ph.D. diss., Instituto de Ecología AC, Xalapa, México.

Peralta-Peláez LA, DeloyaC, Moreno-Casasola P. 2007. Insectos acuáticos asociados a las lagunas interdunarias de la región central del Estado de Veracruz, México. *Neotrop. Ent.* 36:342–55.

Peralta-Peláez L, Moreno-Casasola P. 2009. Composición florística y diversidad de la vegetación de humedales en los lagos interdunarios de Veracruz. *Bol. Soc. Bot. Méx.* 85:89–99.

Platt SG, Thorbjarnarson JB. 2000. Population status and conservation of Morelet's crocodile, *Crocodylus moreletii,* in northern Belize. *Biol. Conserv.* 96:21–29.

Platt SG, Rainwater TR. 2011. Predation by neotropical otters *(Lontra longicaudis)* on turtles in Belize. *IUCN Otter Spec. Group Bull.* 28:4–10.

Platt SG, Rainwater TR, et al. 2008. Reproductive dynamics of a tropical freshwater crocodilian: Morelet's crocodile in northern Belize. *J. Zool.* 275:177–89.

Ramakrishnan PS, Vitousek PM. 1989. Ecosystem-level processes and the consequences of biological invasions. In *Biological invasions: a global perspective,* Drake JA, editor. Chichester, UK: Wiley, pp. 281–300.

Ramírez-García P, Novelo AR. 1984. La vegetación acuática vascular de seis lagos-cráter del estado de Puebla, México. *Bot. Soc. Bot. Méx.* 46:75–88.

Ramos LJ, Novelo A. 1993. Vegetación y flora acuáticas de la laguna de Yuriria, Guanajuato, México. *Acta Bot. Mex.* 25:61–79.

Ramos VLJ. 2000. *Estudio de la flora de la vegetación acuáticas vasculares de la cuenca alta del Río Lerma, en el Estado de México.* MS thesis, ecol. envi. sci., Univ. Nacional Autónoma de México, México, DF.

Rejmánková E, Pope K, et al. 1995. Freshwater wetland plant communities of northern Belize: implications for paleoecological studies of Maya wetland agriculture. *Biotropica* 27:28–36.

Rodríguez JP. 2001. Exotic species introductions as a challenge for the conservation of South American biodiversity. *Interciencia* 26:479–84.

Rojas J, Novelo A. 1995. Flora y vegetación acuáticas del Lago de Cuitzeo, Michoacán, México. *Acta Bot. Mex.* 31:1–17.

Rzedowski J. 1972. Contribuciones a la fitogeografía florística e histórica de México. II. Afinidades geográficas de la flora fanerogámica de diferentes regiones de la República Mexicana. *Anal. Esc. Nac. Cienc. Biol. Méx.* 19:45–48.

Rzedowski J. 1978. *Vegetación de México.* México, DF: Limusa.

Schultz GP. 2005. Vascular flora of the El Eden Ecological Reserve, Quintana Roo, Mexico. *J. Torrey Bot. Soc.* 132:311–22.

Skerritt D. 1993. *Rancheros sobre tierra fértil.* Xalapa: Univ. Veracruzana.

Stehli FG, Webb SD. 1985. A kaleidoscope of plates, faunal and floral dispersals, and sea level changes. In *The great American biotic interchange,* Stehli FG, Webb SD, editors. New York: Plenum Press, pp. 3–16.

Tarabini S. 2006. Aves acuáticas y vadeadoras. In *Entornos Veracruzanos: la costa de La Mancha,* Moreno-Casasola P, editor. Xalapa, México: Inst. Ecol. AC, pp. 363–80.

Taylor BW. 1959. *Estudios ecológicos para el aprovechamiento de la tierra en Nicaragua* (Ecological land use survey in Nicaragua). *Wetl. Ecol. Manage.* 12:3–55. (Cited in Ellison 2004.)

Trama FA. 2005. *Manejo activo y restauración del humedal palo verde: cambios en las coberturas de vegetación y respuesta de las aves acuáticas.* MS thesis, Univ. Nac. Inst. Internac. Conserv. Manejo de Vida Silvestre. Univ. Nac., Heredia, Costa Rica.

Travieso-Bello AC, Moreno-Casasola P, Campos A. 2005. Efecto de diferentes manejos pecuarios sobre el suelo y la vegetación en humedales transformados a pastizales. *Interciencia* 30:12–18.

Utrera-López ME, Moreno-Casasola P. 2008. Mangrove litter dynamics in La Mancha Lagoon, Veracruz, Mexico. *Wetl. Ecol. Manage.* 16:11–22.

Valdez Lares R. 2010. El ensamble de anfibios de un humedal en proceso de restauración (La Mancha, Veracruz, México): diversidad y su relación con el ambiente. MS thesis, Instituto Ecología AC, Xalapa, Veracruz, México.

Vázquez-Yánez C. 1971. La vegetación de la Laguna de Mandinga, Veracruz. *Anal. Inst. Biol. UNAM. 42. Ser. Botánica* 1:49–94.

Vitousek PM. 1990. Biological invasions and ecosystem properties: toward an integration of population biology and ecosystem studies. *Oikos* 57:7–13.

Williams DG, Baruch Z. 2000. African grass invasion in the Americas: ecosystem consequences and the role of ecophysiology. *Biol. Invasions* 2:123–40.

Wright ACS, Romey DH, et al. 1959. *Land in British Honduras: report of the British Honduras Land Survey Team. Wetl. Ecol. Manage.* 12:3–55. (Cited in Ellison 2004.)

Yetter J. 2004. *Hydrology and geochemistry of freshwater wetlands on the Gulf coast of Veracruz, Mexico.* MS thesis, Univ. Waterloo, Canada.

Zamora PC. 2003. Contribución al estudio florístico y descripción de la vegetación del municipio de Tenabo, Campeche, México. *Polibotánica* 15:1–40.

Zedler JB, Rea N. 1998. Introduction to the ecology and management of wetland plant invasions. *Wetl. Ecol. Manage.* 5:161–63.

CHAPTER 20

Northern Great Plains Wetlands

SUSAN GALATOWITSCH

Most individual prairie potholes are small wetlands that appear to be simple, closed ecosystems. To understand both the ecological processes and conservation issues of prairie potholes, one needs to look beyond an individual marsh, and even beyond the clusters of wetlands within a locale, and consider the vast landscape of the northern Great Plains that once was a mosaic of wetlands and prairie. This region occupies 750,000 km² in the center of North America, bounded by the Rocky Mountains to the west, the Canadian Shield to the east and north, and the limits of the Wisconsin glaciation to the south (Fig. 20.1).

The rich glacial till soils and oscillating wet and dry periods typical of the midcontinent create conditions that support exceptional biological productivity. Historically, about half of the continent's waterfowl population likely bred in the region, along with a tremendous variety of other waterbirds (Smith, Stoudt, et al. 1964). These supported extensive agricultural production, once excess water was drained. Artificial drainage of wetlands and conversion of the landscape to agriculture in the past century transformed all but the most arid parts of the region.

Not surprisingly, conservationists registered concerns about dwindling waterfowl populations resulting from development of agriculture, cities, and roads and looked for ways to stem or even reverse the declines. For over 50 years, ecological research on prairie marshes and lakes, particularly long-term, multidisciplinary studies at Cottonwood Lakes, North Dakota; Delta Marsh, Manitoba; St. Denis, Saskatchewan; and Orchid Meadows, South Dakota, has advanced our understanding of these wetlands and provided a foundation for conservation and restoration. Our knowledge of these systems has improved conservation, management, and restoration in the region, but stemming or reversing wetland habitat losses continues to be an elusive goal. And key knowledge gaps remain that, if filled, could contribute to addressing future challenges.

Geology, Hydrology, and Biochemistry

Glaciation and Landform Patterns

The northern Great Plains is one of the youngest landscapes on earth, with landforms developing after the Wisconsin as glaciers retreated from the region, as recently as 10,000 years ago (Patterson 1997). A layer of glacial drift, ranging from 30–180 m thick, blankets sedimentary rocks from the Mesozoic and Cenozoic ages (Winter 1989). This mantle of drift is thinnest across ground moraines, with greater accumulations along end and stagnation moraines. These end and dead-ice moraines, some extending for hundreds of kilometers, rise up from the flat plains, forming bands of relatively rugged terrain. The local relief within an end moraine is typically 15–45 m, compared to a few meters across ground moraine (Winter 1989). The lower relief terrain of ground moraines formed when till was deposited as glaciers moved or melted and collapsed. Dead-ice moraines formed when glaciers stopped advancing; sediments exposed during the initial melting insulated the ice below, causing ice to melt slowly but irregularly. The slumping and sliding of the semisolid debris over thousands of years created a complex terrain of depressions and hills, common in places like the Prairie Coteau, Missouri Coteau, and Turtle Mountains.

Across most of the northern Great Plains, the glacial till is unusually fine textured because it originated from sandstone, siltstone, and marine shale bedrock. These fine-textured glacial deposits impede water infiltration, prolonging ponding within depressions of the hummocky morainal terrain and even across flat expanses of lake and till plains. Most of the palustrine wetlands, or prairie potholes, occur in the depressions of end and ground moraines. Although a variety of wetlands occur across the range of landforms in the northern Great Plains, these palustrine wetlands are such a prominent feature that this landscape is commonly called the Prairie Pothole Region (PPR).

Retreat of the continental ice sheet was accompanied by outwash deposits, the formation of glacial lakes, and even ice streams with surging glaciers. Each created locally distinctive landforms within the PPR. Heavy loads of materials embedded in ice flowed in the meltwater onto newly exposed land, into glacial rivers, and even on top of still unmelted ice. Large lakes and depressions are common across many of the resulting outwash plains. Glacial rivers carried meltwater, often with heavy bed loads of sediments, to the edge of the retreating ice sheets, which acted as dams. As the ice retreated, the glacial lakes that formed on the margin changed in extent and configuration, depending on their position relative to inflow and outflow riv-

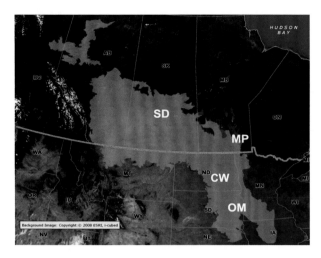

FIG. 20.1. Long-term northern prairie wetland research sites: SD (Saint Dennis), MP (Marsh Ecology Research Program), CW (Cottonwood Lakes), OM (Orchid Meadows). MP is situated on the south shore of Lake Manitoba, the other three in prairie pothole complexes. Image courtesy of Ducks Unlimited.

evapotranspiration deficits trend from 60 cm in southwestern Saskatchewan and eastern Montana to only 10 cm in Iowa (Winter 1989). Annual variability in precipitation and temperature results in wet and dry cycles of varying duration and extent. During severe droughts, most wetlands may remain dry for multiple years. When precipitation is extremely high, some typically isolated wetlands overflow, connecting to other depressions.

Hydrology

Wetland hydrology that depends on exchange of water with the atmosphere is a legacy of the region's recent glacial past. Few prairie potholes have stream inlets, and so contributing surface-water catchments tend to be small, and the glacial tills that underlie them are fine textured, with very low permeability, limiting groundwater inputs. Glacial tills in the region are less permeable than tills characteristic of other regions of the U.S. and Canada (Winter 1989). For the majority of wetlands in the PPR, the source of most of the water is snowmelt runoff, windblown snow, and summer precipitation that falls directly on the wetland (van der Kamp and Hayashi 2009). Melting snow runs off the frozen, impermeable soils early in spring; late spring and summer rains across the surrounding uplands infiltrate the dry soils, only contributing to overland flows during intense rainfall events (Hayashi, van der Kamp, et al. 1998a). Evapotranspiration is the primary way water is lost from these wetlands.

Along beach ridges of the former Glacial Lake Agassiz, as well as some moraines and river valleys, groundwater recharge areas are situated on topographic high locations of sands and gravels confined by layers of less permeable till (Almendinger and Leete 1998a). These coarse glacial deposits of high permeability transmit large amounts of water to discharge areas, which can occur at slope breaks or along the seepage faces of relatively uniform slopes (Thompson, Bettis, et al. 1992). In wetlands that form in these localized areas, called fens, groundwater discharge is the primary water supply and surface runoff is the primary way water is lost.

Although glacial till below 4–5 m in depth typically has very low hydraulic conductivity (< 0.1 m/yr), macropores created by fractures, decayed root channels, and animal burrows facilitate water movement (1,000 m/yr) near the surface with prairie wetlands. This pattern of decreasing conductivity with depth has been observed in native grasslands across the PPR. Water in prairie wetlands is pulled laterally through the high-conductivity zone by transpiration toward the periphery of the depressions (van der Kamp and Hayashi 2009) (Fig. 20.2). Fluxes between depressional wetlands and deeper groundwater are now thought to be minimal, although classic models of prairie wetland hydrology suggested connections between regional groundwater flows and wetlands (Lissey 1971). In fact, hydraulic conductivity is so low that unfractured tills still contain pre-Holocene water (Remenda, van der Kamp, et al. 1996; Hendry and Wassenaar 1999).

In locales with high evapotranspirational deficits, the rate of water loss via infiltration to offset transpiration is strongly affected by the shoreline/area ratio, reflecting the relatively greater influence of riparian vegetation. Millar (1971) observed that a small wetland, with a greater shoreline/area ratio than a larger wetland, consistently had a much higher rate of summer water-level recession. Further studies of this smaller wetland by Hayashi, van der Kamp, et al. (1998a) estimated that infiltra-

ers. At their greatest extent, some were over 200 m deep, with a flooded area of more than 200,000 km². Wind and water currents redistributed much of the incoming sediment, with the finer sediments forming vast, flat lakebeds, bordered by ridges of coarser deposits (called beach ridges). One of the largest of these lakes, Glacial Lake Agassiz, drained as outlets emerged, leaving only remnants, the present-day Lake Winnipeg and Lake Manitoba. Massive ice streams draining through Lake Winnipeg drove lobes of ice southward into present-day Iowa and South Dakota. These ice sheets, known as the James and Des Moines Lobes, partially stagnated, becoming riddled with cavities and tunnels. As the ice melted, the tunnels formed networks of drainageways connecting depressions.

In total, 5 to 8 million glacially formed wetlands occur across the PPR of the United States and Canada (van der Valk 1989). The contemporary distribution of wetlands across most of the region reflects the glacial history of the landscape. Areas of lower relief, such as ground moraine, are typified by smaller, more ephemerally ponded wetlands, compared to areas of dead-ice and terminal moraines. Larger wetlands that often hold water throughout most summers are most common there. The highest densities of wetlands, sometimes greater than 40/km², are also found in dead-ice and terminal moraines (Kantrud, Krapu, et al. 1989).

Climatic Variation

Complex interactions among three air masses (i.e., Continental Polar, Maritime Tropical, Maritime Polar) over the center of the North American continent create some of the most extreme and dynamic climates on earth (Bryson and Hare 1974; Millett, Johnson, et al. 2009). Winter temperatures can drop below –40°C, while summer temperatures can exceed 40°C. Evapotranspiration from wetlands and water exceeds precipitation across the region, drying shallow wetlands in all but the wettest years. Precipitation ranges from approximately 300 mm/yr in the west to 900 mm/yr in the east. The temperature gradient is orthogonal to precipitation, with the mean annual temperatures as low as 1°C in the north to nearly 10°C in the south (Millett, Johnson, et al. 2009). Consequently,

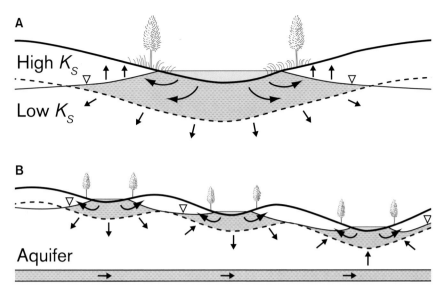

FIG. 20.2. A. Groundwater flow under a recharge wetland. B. Groundwater flow under wetlands in recharge, flow-through, and discharge settings. (From van der Kamp and Hayashi 2009.) Redrawn by David R. Dudley.

tion was responsible for 75–80% of this water loss. Infiltrating water moved laterally to be taken up by riparian vegetation. The downward flux into the low conductivity till was only 2 mm/yr, on average, across the wetland basin. The diurnal patterns of lateral groundwater fluxes observed by several investigators point to plant transpiration as the key process driving infiltration losses (e.g., Rosenberry and Winter 1997). Groundwater fluxes are greatest at midday and lowest at night. Under wetter conditions, shallow groundwater more frequently flows toward the center of wetlands. If the water table is shallow and higher than the water level of most wetlands, there is likely significant groundwater flow among wetlands (Johnson, Boettcher, et al. 2004). In the relatively humid, southern PPR, this additional water supply likely contributes to longer ponding duration.

Prairie wetlands are hydrologically variable, reflecting local differences in landform and land use, as well as hydrology. Shallow wetlands may be ponded for only a few weeks after snowmelt each year. On terminal moraines, these so-called ephemeral or temporary wetlands may be small, but across ground moraines and lake plains, vast areas of ephemeral sheetwater wetlands were once common prior to agricultural drainage. Wetlands that in most years retain standing water until midsummer are considered seasonal wetlands; those that may not completely recede until late summer, if at all, are semipermanent wetlands (Stewart and Kantrud 1971) (Fig. 20.3). Fens are saturated throughout the year and do not collect water (Amon, Thompson, et al. 2002), although some may have small pools created by groundwater discharge.

The hydrological classification of prairie wetlands as temporary, seasonal, or seminpermanent is based on typical duration of ponding. However, the annual change in water levels varies among different kinds of wetlands. Within a locale, the annual water-level recession is often less for semipermanent wetlands than for seasonal or temporary wetlands. For example, Johnson, Boettcher, et al. (2004) observed the annual range of water level in South Dakota semipermanent wetlands to be < 20 cm and in seasonal wetlands to be approximately 50 cm. Water table depths followed the same pattern. This difference may

be linked to inputs or outputs; temporary and seasonal wetlands tend to have small watersheds and so are more sensitive to droughts. They are also small in size, and so have relatively high infiltration and evaporative losses.

The region's strong climatic variability, with multiyear wet and dry periods, also results in pronounced interannual differences in wetland water levels. Based on information from Cottonwood Lakes, North Dakota, and St. Denis, Saskatchewan, differences are more pronounced in semipermanent than seasonal or temporary wetlands (van der Valk 2005). In contrast, Johnson, Boettcher, et al. (2004) observed semipermanent wetlands to be more hydrologically stable than temporary ones through a wet-dry cycle.

Biogeochemistry

The fresh bedrock ground and transported across the region by glaciers was rich in carbonates and pyrites (Van der Kamp and Hayashi 2009). Weathering and dissolution of this glacial till produce the carbonate and sulfate salts typical of the waters in prairie wetlands (e.g., Arndt and Richardson 1993). As a result of weathering of carbonates, as well as photosynthetic uptake of dissolved carbon dioxide, prairie potholes are alkaline (i.e., pH > 7.4) (Hem 1970). Specific conductance, the concentration of dissolved solid in water, varies in prairie wetlands from approximately 50 to 200,000 µS/cm (LaBaugh 1989).

Coinciding with the climate gradient, there is a trend from bicarbonate to sulfate waters from east to west (Gorham, Dean, et al. 1983). Wetlands with sulfates as the most abundant anion are common in the Dakotas and Canadian prairies but not in Minnesota and Iowa (LaBaugh 1989). High-sulfate waters derive from weathering of high-sulfur tills, such as those incorporating a large fraction of Pierre Shale materials (Richardson, Arndt, et al. 1994). The lowest sulfate concentrations are found in landscapes not formed from marine shale deposits, such as sandy outwash plains and glacial lakebeds. Of the four common cations, calcium, magnesium, sodium and potassium, increased specific conductance is associated

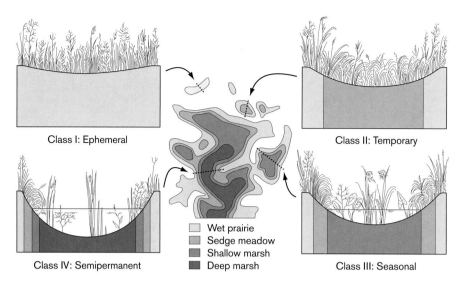

FIG. 20.3. Wetland vegetation zones corresponding to the typical duration of ponding each year. (From Galatowitsch and van der Valk 1994.) Redrawn by David R. Dudley.

with a shift from calcium to magnesium and sodium. Sodium-chloride and sodium-sulfate wetlands are common in North Dakota but not eastward.

The water chemistry of an individual prairie pothole wetland is affected by spatial and temporal variability, as well as regional trends in climate and geology. Water chemistry can be highly variable among wetlands within a relatively small area (i.e., often less than a few square kilometers) corresponding to surface water and groundwater sources contributing to each basin. Wetlands with the lowest specific conductance typically occur in topographically high locations where the net outward flow of groundwater (i.e., recharge) transports salts out of the depression (Hayashi, van der Kamp, et al. 1998a). Wetlands with the highest specific conductance are often lower in the landscape where groundwater discharge contributes salts (LaBaugh 1989). Even though groundwater discharge is a minor part of the overall water balance, its salt concentration can be high (Van der Kamp and Hayashi 2009). Strong upward hydraulic gradients associated with regional groundwater discharge prevent dissolved salts from leaching, containing them within the wetland basin and further concentrating them through evapotranspiration.

Specific conductance within prairie wetlands increases, often dramatically, throughout the year as the concentrating effects of evaporation outstrip the dilution from precipitation and runoff. Specific conductance increases up to sixfold through the summer; ice formation further concentrates the solutes within prairie wetlands (LaBaugh 1989). Changes in specific conductance also reflect annual variation in rainfall, increasing through dry periods. LaBaugh, Winter, et al. (1996) observed that wet-dry cycles caused a shift in major ion chemistry in North Dakota semipermanent wetlands. One wetland with a long-term record of bicarbonate dominance changed to a sulfate-type water during the 1988–92 drought; the reverse shift occurred in a sulfate wetland following the deluges of 1993.

In all but extremely wet years, prairie wetlands are closed depressions that trap sediments and associated minerals transported in surface water runoff. Calcite and gypsum salts that are transported into the wetland either through surface or groundwater flow toward the periphery via capillary rise and evapotranspiration, sometimes resulting in a ring of soils with relatively high calcite and/or gypsum concentration (e.g., Arndt and Richardson 1989, 1993; Steinwand and Richardson 1989; Hayashi, van der Kamp, et al. 1998b; Berthold, Bentley, et al. 2004).

In addition to being less rich in mineral salts, wetland centers often have thicker organic and inorganic sediments and are finer textured (Richardson, Arndt, et al. 1994). In general, organic matter accumulates when the rate of plant tissue production exceeds oxidation losses (e.g., decomposition, fire) and removal (e.g., herbivory) (van der Valk 1989). Frequent drawdowns throughout temporary and seasonal wetlands and along the periphery of semipermanent and permanent wetlands aerate soils, favoring oxidation of organic matter. Soils in the center of semipermanent wetlands have surface accumulations of organic matter mixed with sediments over 1 m thick, whereas thicknesses at the periphery are typically half that (Richardson, Arndt, et al. 1994). In sulfate-rich prairie wetlands, oxidation of organic matter also occurs when soils are saturated and anaerobic, due to sulfate reduction (Korner 1992). Consequently, organic matter accumulations decline westward in the region, as a function of both precipitation deficits and the composition of glacial tills.

Plant Communities

Vegetation Dynamics and Hydrology

The combined effects of water-level fluctuations that occur on two time scales—annual recession and multiyear oscillations—result in very different environmental conditions for plant growth along topographic gradients within prairie pothole wetlands. One of the most striking features of prairie wetlands are the concentric bands of vegetation (called zones) that correspond to differences in annual flooding duration. The wetland periphery, normally inundated for a few weeks during the growing season, is typically dominated by a mixture of grasses, fine sedges, and forbs. In some locales, though, the wetland periphery is a ring of woody vegetation (primarily *Salix* and *Populus*). Where inundation typically extends into

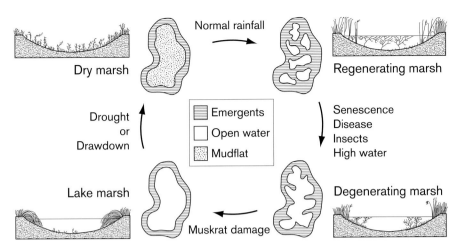

FIG. 20.4. Vegetation changes through wet and dry cycles. (From Galatowitsch and van der Valk 1994.) Redrawn by David R. Dudley.

midsummer and early fall, coarse sedges and other midheight hydrophytes form the patchy vegetation of what is known as the shallow emergent marsh. Interannual variability, multi-year wet and dry phases, shifts the relative abundance of species in these shallow zones but does not trigger replacement of one assemblage of species with another (van der Valk 2005).

In contrast, wet-dry cycles trigger vegetation succession in deeper zones (Fig. 20.4). Strongly clonal macrophyte species, such as *Typha* and *Scirpus,* tolerate prolonged flooding with minimal periods of drawdown but cannot regenerate from seed under these conditions. So, they become established only on the mudflats exposed during prolonged drought. Emergent macrophytes spread as wetlands reflood. High water levels during wet phases eradicate emergent vegetation over a few years. Only submersed and floating aquatic plants remain until the next drawdown, which again releases the emergent seedbank, as well as supporting a flush of terrestrial annuals (van der Valk and Davis 1978). Seed-bank stores of emergent marshes are much greater than for wet meadows, i.e., 3,000–25,000 versus 1,000–2,000 seeds/m^2, as expected given the importance of episodic seed regeneration to sustain emergent vegetation (Galatowitsch and Biederman 1998).

Van der Valk (2005) hypothesized that cyclic succession is a feature of deep but not shallow emergent marsh vegetation because the range of oscillatory water-level fluctuations is much greater in semipermanent wetlands than in seasonal wetlands, which lack the deeper zone. Oscillatory fluctuations greater than 150 cm appear to trigger successional vegetation dynamics, whereas a small range of water-level changes (i.e., 50 cm or less) does not. Long-term experimental studies of water-level effects on emergent macrophytes at Delta Marsh (i.e., MERP, the Marsh Ecology Research Program) demonstrated that high water level is the primary reason emergent macrophytes are eliminated during wet periods (van der Valk 2005). Two or more years of water 1 m or more above the mean level cause macrophyte stands to be eliminated.

Differences in annual fluctuations between semipermanent and seasonal fluctuation could also contribute to these contrasting dynamics. Although semipermanent wetlands have greater interannual water level variability than seasonal wetlands, their annual fluctuations are typically less (Johnson, Boettcher, et al. 2004). In addition, wet meadow and shallow emergent marsh vegetation must respond to soil flooding and drying cycles at a much higher frequency (annually rather

than every 5–10 years). Whether wet meadow and shallow marsh vegetation respond to annual and interannual water variability differently if they occupy the deepest zone of small wetlands versus rings of large wetlands is unknown.

Plant Distributions in Relation to Hydrology and Water Chemistry

The vegetation composition of prairie wetlands is influenced by water permanence, water chemistry, and land-use history (Kantrud, Krapu, et al. 1989; Aronson and Galatowitsch 2008). Wetlands with a greater period of inundation often support higher species diversity than those flooded less persistently because they provide suitable environmental conditions for a greater array of functional groups. Submersed and floating-leaved functional groups are missing or depauperate in temporary and seasonal wetlands, for example. Within emergent zones, more species are present during the dry phase because flooding hinders the recruitment of moist soil annuals and short-lived perennials (Galinato and van der Valk 1986; Welling, Pederson, et al. 1988a,b).

The dissolved salt concentration (specific conductivity) also serves as an important environmental determinant of species composition. The hydrophytic species of the region vary greatly in their maximum tolerance to dissolved salts, ranging from 2 to 76.4 μS, although there is little variability in their minimum range, with few greater than 0.5 μS (Kantrud, Krapu, et al. 1989). So, as a regionwide trend, wetlands with higher specific conductivity have lower wetland plant species richness. However, because solute concentration can fluctuate widely, especially in small, seasonal wetlands, plant community composition may shift between species more and less tolerant to high salinity. Spring flooding in seasonal marshes dilutes soil salinity during peak plant production, and so may regulate the abundance of relatively salt-intolerant species, such as whitetop *(Scolochloa festucacea),* in shallow, seasonal marshes (Neil 1993). At the most saline end of the gradient, prairie wetlands sometimes contain only a single angiosperm *(Ruppia maritima)* (Kantrud, Krapu, et al. 1989), in contrast to freshwater wetlands, which frequently have 50–100 species. Although fens comprise a very small portion of wetlands in the region, they support a high number of uncommon and rare species that require the distinctive hydrology and water chemistry created by calcareous groundwater discharge (e.g., Amon, Thompson, et al. 2002).

Vegetation and Nutrient Cycling

Sediments contain more than 75% of the carbon (C), nitrogen (N), and phosphorus (P) pools in prairie wetlands, even when nonsediment pools are at their maxima (Murkin, van der Valk, et al. 2000a). Macrophyte uptake is responsible for most of the fluxes to and from the sediment, so patterns in their production regulate resources available for other biota in prairie wetlands, including algae, invertebrates, and vertebrates. A 10-year large-scale field experiment at Delta Marsh (Manitoba) elucidated nutrient flux patterns during in wet-dry cycles of emergent marshes (Murkin, van der Valk, et al. 2000a). As emergent vegetation regenerates and spreads during the dry marsh phase, nutrients are taken up from sediments, and cycle relatively rapidly as nutrients are incorporated into plant tissues, with some released to other pools (e.g., algae, invertebrates, vertebrates), which eventually decompose and return to sediment pools. With the elimination of emergent vegetation during the continuous inundation of the wet state, nutrients become "locked" in sediment pools. Release of these nutrients occurs with the reestablishment of emergent vegetation during the next dry stage.

Murkin, van der Valk, et al. (2000a) observed a pulse of productivity upon reflooding following a dry phase, as has been widely reported. They found that this pulse is triggered by rapid leaching of nutrients from litter that stimulates algal growth, which in turn supports increases in invertebrate populations. Increased decomposition and associated release of nutrients because of sediment aeration had been assumed to drive this productivity pulse (e.g., Kadlec 1962), but was not observed to be important at Delta Marsh.

Similar to many other kinds of wetlands, uptake by emergent plants is greater than inorganic N and P available in sediment porewater. Organic nutrient pools from the sediment must replenish porewater pools to sustain plant productivity (Murkin, van der Valk, et al. 2000a). The rates of N and P release from litter decomposition do not offset peak plant uptake in the spring, so some sediment mineralization occurs. Nitrogen supplies may also be augmented by N fixation. However, seasonal patterns in porewater nutrient levels suggest a mismatch between plant uptake and likely contributions from microbial mineralization, given suboptimal temperatures for microbial processes in spring. Verma, Robarts, et al. (2003) suggested that fungi may be important in the prairie wetland nutrient cycling; fungi that degrade labile portions of bound nutrients are productive in the spring, followed later in the season by those capable of digesting more refractive plant tissues. So, although plants play a major role in the flux of nutrients to aboveground pools, a better understanding of litter decomposition and microbial processes in the water column is needed to determine what controls nutrient cycles in prairie wetlands (Murkin, van der Valk, et al. 2000a).

Vegetation Effects on Environmental Conditions

In addition to unlocking sediment nutrients, emergent vegetation alters other physical and chemical attributes of sediments and waters within prairie wetlands (Rose and Crumpton 1996). Water temperature and dissolved oxygen vary less diurnally and are lower in emergent vegetation stands than in open water within prairie wetlands. In a dense stand of emergent vegetation, much of the ambient light is intercepted by the vascular plant canopy, reducing the photosynthetic production of oxygen by algae and temperature in the water column. Emergent stands also have much higher rates of oxygen demand in response to respiration of organisms associated with decomposing litter (Rose and Crumpton 1996), which is often an order of magnitude greater than in open-water areas (Davis and van der Valk 1978). Compared to the effects of submersed macrophytes (e.g., Carpenter and Lodge 1986), emergent vegetation depresses oxygen levels more peristently and to a greater extent. By limiting oxygen supplies, emergent vegetation may increase the importance of nutrient fluxes through anaerobic pathways, such as denitrification, sulfate reduction, and methanogenesis.

Animal Communities

Invertebrates

The aquatic invertebrate fauna of prairie potholes possess a wide range of life-history strategies for coping with anoxia, desiccation, salinity, and prolonged flooding, as well for capitalizing on diverse food sources including hydrophytic plants, algae, microbes, and fish (Euliss, Wrubelski, et al. 1999). Prairie wetlands have long periods of anoxia; in the winter, the sediment-water interface is usually anoxic, and during the summer, oxygen is depleted within stands of emergent vegetation. Freshwater invertebrates include mollusks, leeches, and amphipods that are replaced by salt-tolerant species such as brine shrimp and shore flies in wetlands with higher salinity (Murkin and Ross 2000). Differences in the composition of invertebrate communities occupying a prairie wetland are, however, mostly responses to the hydrologic conditions there, and the resulting vegetation. For prairie wetlands that typically go dry each year, ephemeral, temporary, and seasonal wetlands, the duration of inundation determines how extensive the invertebrate community is (Murkin and Ross 2000). Some invertebrate species cannot complete their life cycles with only a few weeks of ponding and so must rely on other wetlands to sustain populations. Consequently, many invertebrates in ephemeral and temporary wetlands are vagile. Diversity increases with longer periods of flooding; more species can reproduce and increased algal production and hydrophytic plant diversity provide suitable conditions for more species. In addition, an increased prey base attracts mobile invertebrate predators that leave as wetlands dry.

Multiyear wet-dry cycles in semipermanent wetlands cause major shifts in faunal communities (Murkin and Ross 2000). If drawdowns last more than a couple of years, species that depend on flooded conditions (e.g., amphipods and some chironomids) dwindle. After reflooding, they recolonize via active or passive dispersal (e.g., attached to birds). Initially, the invertebrate community of a recently reflooded wetland includes many taxa of temporary wetlands (Neckles, Murkin, et al. 1990). New algal growth and flooded remnant plant litter provide a food supply as water returns. With persistently flooded conditions, invertebrates intolerant of dessication replace those, such as ostracods and mosquitoes, which are tolerant. As emergent vegetation regenerates and spreads, invertebrate diversity and abundance increase. Patches of submersed and emergent hydrophytes are presumed to support the greatest array of species (Murkin and

Ross 2000). Invertebrates in prairie wetlands rely on living and dead emergent hydrophytes, beds of submersed aquatic plants, and floating algal masses (i.e., metaphytic algae) for habitat structure; the greatest abundances are associated with fine-leaved submersed aquatics. With prolonged flooding and the decline of emergent vegetation, a lack of habitat structure supports fewer invertebrate species.

Invertebrates are the principal link between primary producers and higher-order consumers, such as waterfowl, in prairie wetlands. They are relatively unimportant for breaking down litter but consume significant quantities of algae and microbes that coat plant litter. So, prairie wetlands have less of a detrital-based trophic structure than has often been assumed (Murkin 1989; Murkin and Ross 2000). A diverse array of microorganisms, including bacteria and fungi, colonize plant litter and accumulate nutrients from the surrounding water column to support their growth. Invertebrate consumption of litter increases after microbial colonization, likely because these detrivores rely on nutrients associated with microbes. Invertebrate herbivory on algae in prairie wetlands is another significant trophic pathway. Although the standing crop of algae at any point in time is not great, rapid turnover of algal biomass results in high annual production (Murkin and Ross 2000). A wide range of species, including many midges and snails, feed on epiphytic algae that encrust the surfaces of submersed aquatic leaves, emergent stems, and the sediment surface. Other groups, such as cladocerans, copepods, and midges, are filter feeders of planktonic algae. Hanson and Butler (1994) reported daily cladoceran filtration rates in prairie wetlands that exceeded 100% of its water volume.

Predators are a significant part of both the abundance and diversity of prairie wetland invertebrate communities. At some times of the year, the abundance of predators is as high as that of prey species, an indication of their important role in the trophic structure of prairie potholes (Murkin and Ross 2000). Although most feed on other invertebrates, larger species (giant water bugs, dragonflies) prey on small fish and tadpoles.

Invertebrates are a primary food source for many vertebrates in prairie wetlands, including waterfowl, song birds, mammals, and amphibians (Murkin and Batt 1987). For waterfowl, invertebrate protein is essential to meet higher physiological demands of breeding adults, for eggshell development, and to support rapid juvenile growth. Not surprisingly, where waterfowl forage reflects the availability of invertebrates determines, to a great extent, where waterfowl forage. Temporary and seasonal wetlands thaw earlier than deeper, more permanent wetlands, and so have a spring emergence of invertebrates that coincides with the breeding season of early-nesting species such as mallards and pintails. By the time later-nesting species breed, these shallow wetlands have dried, and they must rely on semipermanent and permanent wetlands.

Fish, Amphibians, and Reptiles

Because the juveniles of native amphibians (except salamanders and mudpuppies) grow rapidly and reach adulthood in a short period of time, temporary and seasonally flooded wetlands can support breeding populations, except during drought years. Eighteen amphibian species occur in prairie potholes in the United States (Balas 2008), with the greatest diversity occurring in the southeast, where salinity is low, droughts less frequent, and the climate warmer. Of these, there are 16 anurans and 2 salamanders. The eastern tiger salaman-

der (*Ambystoma tigrinum*), the American toad (*Bufo americana*), and the northern leopard frog (*Rana pipiens*) are particularly widespread. The leopard frog was so abundant about a century ago that it was harvested commercially for bait and food (Lannoo, Lang, et al. 1994). One species, the American bullfrog (*R. catesbeiana*), was introduced into the region during fish stocking, and unlike most native amphibians, it breeds in permanent wetlands. The reptile fauna is less species rich and includes 3 turtles and 3 snakes. Western painted turtles (*Chrysemys picta*) and snapping turtles (*Chelydra serpentina*) are mobile and widespread, and snapping turtles can be important predators. Western plains garter snakes (*Thamnophis radix*) and eastern garter snakes (*T. sirtalis*) are not aquatic, and use wet meadows and deeper zones only during drawdowns to search for prey.

A lack of permanent water, low dissolved oxygen, and high salinities make prairie wetlands unsuitable for most fish species (Peterka 1989; Benoy 2008). Two species are tolerant of these conditions, however, the fathead minnow (*Pimephales promelas*) and brook stickleback (*Culaea inconstans*). Both are common in semipermanent and permanent wetlands throughout the region. Lawler, Sunde, et al. (1974) reported 10–20% of prairie potholes in southern Manitoba support fish populations. During drawdowns, fathead minnow and stickleback populations are lost; they recolonize via overland dispersal, although how this occurs has not been reported. Some prairie wetlands are stocked with fathead minnows for commercial bait and walleye (*Sander vitreus*) fry to eventually move to recreational lakes, but some of these fish persist.

In many other aquatic systems, fish are the primary consumers of zooplankton; some have conjectured that in prairie wetlands, tiger salamander may be their functional equivalent. Benoy (2008) tested this hypothesis in 45 Manitoba prairie wetlands. He found that as tiger salamander abundance increased, so did algal standing crop; macroinvertebrate abundance, however, declined. This suggests salamanders may exert some level of trophic control over the community structure of fishless prairie wetlands. Dabbling ducks forage less frequently in prairie wetlands with high tiger salamander densities, presumably because they reduce invertebrate food resources (Benoy 2005). Zimmer, Hanson, et al. (2000) observed a similar pattern for waterfowl in prairie wetlands with fathead minnows; fish were important determinants of invertebrate abundance (and indirectly algal productivity).

Mammals

Currently, 19 species of mammals use of prairie pothole wetlands, including 3 that depend on flooded wetlands to complete their life cycles: beaver (*Castor canadensis*), muskrat (*Ondatra zibethicus*), and mink (*Mustela vison*). Of these, beaver rely primarily on riverine wetlands rather than prairie wetlands. Certain voles, shrews, and mice live primarily along wetland perimeters. The immense herds of bison (*Bison bison*) that once roamed the Great Plains likely had profound effects on the prairie wetlands, although these were never documented (Kantrud, Krapu, et al. 1989).

Muskrats have a conspicuous impact on vegetation. They prefer cattails (*Typha*) and bulrush (*Scirpus*) for lodge building and food, although they consume other emergent macrophytes as well as submersed aquatics, algae, and even animal matter (Fritzell 1989). Spring populations are typically 1–2 muskrats/ha, swelling to as many as 50/ha by autumn (Clark

FIG. 20.5. Muskrat herbivory. Courtesy of Michele Rundquist-Franz.

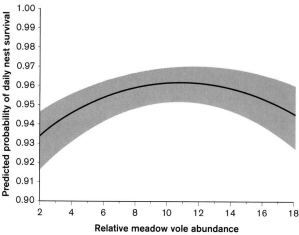

FIG. 20.6. The effects of meadow vole abundance on waterfowl nest success, modeled from data collected on six prairie wetlands in Canada (95% confidence interval is shaded). (Modified from Brooks, Pasitschniak-Arts, et al. 2008.)

2000). Within their home ranges, extending about 15 m from lodges, muskrat herbivory diminishes the emergent canopy, and thus influences trophic structure and biogeochemical processes (Fig. 20.5) (Murkin, van der Valk, et al. 2000b). At high densities, herbivory by muskrats has often been assumed to exceed regrowth of emergent vegetation, causing "eat-outs," shifting semipermanent marshes to the degeneration stage (e.g., Errington, Siglin, et al. 1963; Weller and Spatcher 1965; Fritzell 1989). However, in MERP wetlands, Clark (2000) estimated that < 10% of the standing crop of emergents was removed by muskrats at population densities of 20–30/ha. In addition, MERP experiments were able to distinguish the relative importance of flooding and herbivory on vegetation decline. Although muskrat herbivory hastened decline of emergent vegetation, flooding was the primary cause. Muskrat populations oscillate in the PPR (Errington 1954), in part as a result of wet-dry cycles. During drawdown, muskrat overwinter survival is very low because soils freeze, access to food is limited, and predation increases (Murkin, van der Valk, et al. 2000b). But intrinsic factors (social structure, disease, physiology) also likely influence muskrat population cycles.

Predation pressure by mammals in prairie wetlands is greatest in peripheral zones because all but the mink are primarily terrestrial (Kantrud, Krapu, et al. 1989). Weasels prey primarily on voles, but most predatory mammals consume a wide variety of prey, including small mammals, birds and their eggs, and insects. Most waterfowl species nest in uplands and so are preyed on by coyotes (Canis latrans) and red fox (Vulpes vulpes); striped skunks (Mephitis mephitis) and raccoons (Procyon lotor) readily consume waterfowl eggs. Nest predation depresses waterfowl reproductive success and so has received considerable research attention (e.g., Sargeant, Greenwood, et al. 1993). In Iowa, for example, Fleskes and Klaas (1991) reported an 11% nest success for waterfowl; predators (primarily mammalian) caused 89% of the nest failures. Nest predation rates are higher in territories of red fox than of coyotes, but red fox avoids denning in coyote territories, creating significant spatial and temporal variability in waterfowl nest success (Sovada, Sargeant, et al. 1995; Pieron and Rohwer 2010).

The abundance of alternative prey species, especially meadow voles, can affect predation rates on waterfowl by mammalian predators (Brook, Pasitschniak-Arts, et al. 2008).

Vole population cycles are very pronounced, with populations ranging from 2.5/ha to 617/ha, up to 75% of the small mammals in prairie wetlands (Jones et al. 1983). Voles are a primary food source for most of the common mammal predators, as well as several raptors (Brook, Pasitschniak-Arts, et al. 2008). Waterfowl are buffered from predation until vole populations reach a high enough density to trigger changes in both predator numbers and their foraging behavior (Fig. 20.6).

Birds

Over 50 bird species rely on prairie wetlands for some aspect of breeding (Kantrud, Krapu, et al. 1989; Galatowitsch and van der Valk 1994) or migration (Batt, Anderson, et al. 1989). Fifteen species of ducks and geese commonly breed in prairie wetlands (Table 20.1). Once common breeders, the trumpeter swan (Cygnus buccinator) and whooping cranes (Grus americana) were extirpated from the region nearly a century ago; many others, like the common sandhill crane (G. canadensis) and marbled godwit (Limosa fedoa), are now rare (Kantrud, Krapu, et al. 1989).

Most waterfowl are omnivores and shift the proportion of plant and animal matter they consume depending on life-history demands and resource availability (Murkin and Caldwell 2000). Only a few waterbirds, notably geese and swans, are strictly herbivorous. Predators are a major component of the avian fauna of prairie wetlands. Shorebirds and passerines primarily consume invertebrates; herons, pelicans, and grebes are piscivorous, but also take amphibians and large invertebrates.

Habitat conditions are temporally and spatially variable in a prairie pothole landscape. The shallowest wetlands are the first to be ice-free and so provide early-season food resources to the earliest migrants, such as mallards, Canada geese, and northern pintails. The periphery of seasonal and semipermanent wetlands also thaw early, but deeper centers retain water longer in most years, and so offer greater variety and abundance of food, especially invertebrates, and cover. Permanent wetlands are generally too deep to provide food and cover for dabbling ducks, but support submersed aquatics, which are used by diving ducks, such as canvasbacks and redhead. In addition, many waterfowl species use permanent wetlands during migration

TABLE 20.1
Avian conservation priority species for the PPR:
Waterfowl and wetland nongame birds with small or declining populations.

	Common name	Scientific name
WATERFOWL	Canada goose	*Branta canadensis*
	Wood duck	*Aix sponsa*
	Green-winged teal	*Anas crecca*
	Mallard	*A. platyrhynchos*
	Northern pintail	*A. acuta*
	Blue-winged teal	*A. discors*
	Northern shoveler	*A. clypeata*
	Gadwall	*A. strepera*
	American wigeon	*A. americana*
	Canvasback	*Aythya valisineria*
	Redhead	*A. americana*
	Ring-necked duck	*A. collaris*
	Lesser scaup	*A. affinis*
	Hooded merganser	*Lophodytes cucullatus*
	Ruddy duck	*Oxyura jamaicensis*
WETLAND NONGAME BIRDS WITH SMALL OR DECLINING POPULATIONS	Pied-billed grebe	*Podilymbus podiceps*
	American bittern	*Botaurus lentignosus*
	Northern harrier	*Circus cyaneus*
	Ferruginous hawk	*Buteo regalis*
	Yellow rail	*Coturnicops noveboracensis*
	Virginia rail	*Rallus limicola*
	Sora rail	*Porzana carolina*
	Piping plover	*Charadrius melodus*
	Willet	*Catoptrophorus semipalmatus*
	Long-billed curlew	*Numenius americanus*
	Marbled godwit	*Limosa fedoa*
	Wilson's phalarope	*Phalaropus tricolor*
	Franklin's gull	*Larus pipixcan*
	Least tern	*Sternula antillarum*
	Black tern	*Childonias niger*
	Short-eared owl	*Asio flammeus*
	Sedge wren	*Cistothorus platensis*
	Sprague's pipit	*Anthus spragueii*
	Loggerhead shrike	*Lanius ludovicianus*
	Clay colored sparrow	*Spizella pallida*
	Lark bunting	*Calamospiza melanocorys*
	Baird's sparrow	*Ammodramus bairdii*
	Grasshopper sparrow	*A. savannarum*
	LeConte's sparrow	*A. leconteii*
	Nelson's sharp-tailed sparrow	*A. nelsoni*
	McCown's longspur	*Calcarius mccownii*
	Bobolink	*Dolichonyx oryzivorus*

SOURCE: Pashley and Warhurst 1999.

and some species rely on them for molting. Because vegetation and invertebrate communities of semipermanent wetlands exhibit high interannual variability in response to wet-dry cycles, birds that rely on prairie wetlands must be adapted to highly variable and unpredictable conditions (Murkin and Caldwell 2000). Nearly all of the common breeding waterbirds accomplish this by opportunistically shifting their habitat use from one kind of wetland to another, rather than specializing on one kind of habitat (Swanson and Duebbert 1989). For example, early migrants forage in ephemeral wetlands but typically often choose permanent wetlands for cover. Some piscivorous birds, such as herons, capitalize on stranded fish in receding pools of semipermanent wetlands early in a drawdown, but move to permanent wetlands if drought conditions persist. So, complexes of various types of wetlands—ranging from ephemeral to permanent—are widely considered essential for sustaining the greatest diversity and abundance of birds in the region.

Although inundated wetlands are focal foraging habitats for many waterbirds, their cover requirements are variable and species specific, with some, such as pintails, utilizing upland habitats even several kilometers from open water. A major determinant of avian habitat use in prairie wetlands is the cover needed to meet the range of breeding season requirements, including courtship, mating, nesting, and brood-rearing. These requirements are species specific, with colonial birds seeking large blocks of cover to support many individuals, whereas solitary, territorial species (e.g., sora rail, *Porzana carolina*) seek out dense cover to minimize inter- and intraspecific interactions (Murkin and Caldwell, 2000). Red-winged blackbirds *(Agelaius phoeniceus)* avoid territories of marsh wrens because they are nest predators, and are outcompeted for optimal territorial space in emergent wetlands by the more aggressive yellow-winged blackbirds *(Xanthocephalus xanthocephalus).*

Changes in food and cover resources can affect the size of local breeding populations. An interspersed pattern of emergent and submersed vegetation typically supports the highest use and production of dabbling ducks, as well as red-winged blackbirds (Weller and Spatcher 1965; Kaminski and Prince 1981; Murkin 1989). Ducks rely on invertebrates to meet the protein and calcium needs of reproduction; the habitat heterogeneity provided by the interspersion of emergent and submersed vegetation supports a rich invertebrate community for optimal waterfowl foraging. This vegetation pattern, called hemi-marsh, occurs in the wet-dry cycle of semipermanent wetlands during the transition from regenerating to degenerating stages. Wildlife managers often manipulate the water levels and vegetation (e.g., by cutting), and even excavate, with varying results, to create more interspersed habitat. Other measures used to increase local waterfowl populations include predator control, artificial nest structures, and planting upland cover (Nudds 1983; Williams, Koneff, et al. 1999).

At a regional scale, waterfowl populations change in response to climatic cycles, with wet years offering the greatest number of breeding ponds and highest resource availability (Johnson and Grier 1988; Bethke and Nudds 1995; Drever 2006). During droughts, some species, such as mallards and canvasbacks, are displaced to less favorable breeding areas north of the PPR (Johnson and Grier 1988). Because droughts typically reduce populations of resident mammalian predators, average waterfowl nest success may increase immediately following years of low precipitation (Krapu, Klett, et al. 1983; Beauchamp, Koford, et al. 1996; Beauchamp, Nudds, et al. 1996).

Land-Use Changes and Ecological Responses

Agricultural Transformation

European settlement began in the PPR in the mid- to late 1800s, but the maze of wetlands hindered agricultural production, as well as transportation. In some areas, early settlers reported needing mudboats to move between towns that became isolated each spring as wetlands filled with snowmelt and runoff (Galatowitsch and van der Valk 1994). Wetland drainage began in earnest around 1900, progressing from open ditch systems to subsurface tiles (i.e., subsurface perforated pipes) (Fig. 20.7). Drainage systems lowered the water table enough to reliably grow row crops, such as corn. Agricultural conversion of both wetlands and the surrounding prairie accelerated in the early 1900s, leading to significant habitat losses. For example, Iowa has lost 99% of its native prairie and 89% of its wetlands (Bishop, Joens, et al. 1998; Smith 1998). In North Dakota and South Dakota, wetland losses have been estimated at 35% and 49%, respectively (Dahl 1990). In the U.S., the Clean Water Act (1972) and the "Swampbuster" provision of the 1985 Food Security Act created disincentives for wetland conversion, which reduced loss rates. Losses continue, though, because small, isolated wetlands have been variably protected.

With relatively high annual precipitation and temperatures, the eastern PPR is best suited for high-yield crop production and so has experienced the greatest degree of habitat fragmentation. Although the Des Moines Lobe landscape had a high density of wetlands prior to European settlement, there are currently about 3–4 wetlands/km², compared to > 15 wetlands/km² to the west (Millett, Johnson, et al. 2009). Historically, the less frequently ponded kinds of wetlands were much more abundant than semipermanent wetlands (Galatowitsch and van der Valk 1996b; Miller, Crumpton, et al. 2009). However, shallow wetlands were easier to drain and more reliable for agriculture, so are virtually absent from intensively farmed areas. Even those that were not drained are frequently cultivated (Richardson, Arndt, et al. 1994).

Landscape-scale habitat fragmentation and loss resulting from the region's agricultural conversion have dramatically diminished populations of many wetland animal and plant species. The loss of temporary and seasonal wetlands has been especially damaging for species that primarily relied on those habitats. Native amphibians rely on breeding success in temporary and seasonal wetlands to sustain populations because fish and bullfrog predation is high in more permanently inundated wetlands (Lannoo 1994). Increased isolation of wetlands likely limits postdrought recolonization of invertebrates from more refugial wetlands that have longer periods of inundation (Bataille and Baldassarre 1993). In response to habitat loss and fragmentation, waterfowl populations have precipitously declined in recent decades and an additional 28 bird species are also declining or have small populations that warrant special conservation attention (Table 20.1) (Pashley and Warhurst 1999). To a great extent, this reflects the loss of upland tallgrass prairie, which has reduced critical breeding habitat for many prairie wetland birds and increased mammalian predation (Sargeant, Greenwood, et al. 1993; Greenwood, Sargeant, et al. 1995; Naugle, Johnson, et al. 2001; Sovada, Anthony, et al. 2001; Pieron and Rohwer 2010). Not only have populations and distributions of some mammalian predators, such as red fox, raccoons, and striped skunks, increased during the agricultural transformation of the region, but their foraging efficiency has also increased. Small, isolated tracts of grasslands

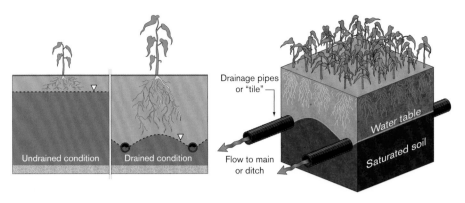

FIG. 20.7. Subsurface drainage tiles used to drain prairie wetlands in agricultural landscapes. (From Blann, Anderson, et al. 2009.) Redrawn by David R. Dudley.

are searched more thoroughly and frequently than larger tracts (Sovada, Zicus, et al. 2000; Phillips, Clark, et al. 2003).

Prairie Wetlands in Agricultural Landscapes

The remaining wetlands in the PPR are often surrounded by cropland, isolated from other wetlands. They may be grazed by domestic livestock or, in dry years, cultivated. Stressors to remnant prairie wetlands are numerous: increased runoff, sediments, nutrients, contaminants, and introduced species. Runoff from tilled drainage basins is much greater than from grassland basins where macropores allow more infiltration. Conversion of tilled lands to grasslands can therefore substantially decrease the inundation of prairie wetlands (van der Kamp, Stolte, et al. 1999; van der Kamp, Hayashi, et al. 2003). Detenbeck et al. (2002) observed that small, occasionally cultivated wetlands (i.e., not drained) have greater seasonal drawdown than comparable, untilled wetlands, most likely due to higher infiltration losses. Cultivated drainage basins deliver about twice as much sediment to wetlands as do prairie basins (Adomaitis, Kantrud, et al. 1967; Martin and Hartman 1987). If the wet meadow perimeter remains, the sediment load may largely be trapped there, rather than reach the emergent zone (Detenbeck et al. 2002). Where tillage has removed perennial wetland vegetation, sediment additions reach deeper portions of wetlands and open-water conditions are more likely to result in resuspension and high turbidity (Dieter 1991).

Significant amounts of fertilizers and pesticides applied to cultivated lands are lost via surface runoff and groundwater transport (Fig. 20.8) (Neely and Baker 1989). In row crop systems of corn and soybeans, approximately 10–50% of N, 5% of P, and less than 2% of pesticides move overland and into ditch systems or infiltrate into tile drains. In addition to fertilizer, N mineralization, the conversion of organic N to ammonium, is greater in cultivated soils than in native prairie (Keeney and DeLuca 1993). Ditch and tile drainage systems are designed to rapidly move water through landscapes with minimal, natural conveyance; wetlands that receive ditch or tile effluent can be exposed to unusually high loads of N and P. The greatest fraction of P and organic N moves with sediment, whereas ammonium moves primarily in surface runoff and nitrates in subsurface (i.e., tile flow) (Neely and Baker 1989). Nitrogen additions have been observed to stimulate the production of emergent species (Neil 1990) and wet meadow species (Green and Galatowitsch 2002), although there is insufficient information to

estimate the effects of increased N loads on primary production (Crumpton and Goldsborough 1989).

Both N and P concentrations in the water column of prairie wetlands are often more influenced by changes in water level and vegetation structure than agricultural additions. Phosphate concentrations decline when dissolved oxygen increases, causing the precipitation of phosphate; these conditions occur when wetlands are inundated and sparsely vegetated (Detenbeck 2002). Denitrification, the conversion of nitrate to nitrogen gas, increases with nitrate additions, as long as conditions are suitable (i.e., anaerobic, adequate C). More than 80% of nitrate additions can be lost through denitrification in prairie pothole wetlands (Crumpton and Goldsborough 1998). A major effect of agricultural nitrate additions to prairie wetlands may be to substantially increase anaerobic and total C metabolism, but the effects to various microbial pathways in these systems have not yet been reported.

Prairie wetlands are exposed to herbicides and pesticides applied by ground or aerial methods to maximize yields in agricultural fields (Donald, Syrgiannis, et al. 1999; Cessna and Elliott 2004; Waite, Cessna, et al. 2004). Agricultural chemicals can enter prairie potholes through application drift, wet and dry atmospheric deposition, surface runoff, and deposition of wind/water-eroded soil (Waite, Grover, et al. 1995). In Saskatchewan, the proportion of wetlands with detectable levels of pesticides was reported by Donald, Syrgiannis, et al. (1999) to be greater where precipitation was higher. Pesticide levels exceeded Canadian aquatic protection guidelines in 60% of wetlands where rainfall 15 days prior to application was > 90 mm. Herbicides, 2,4-D, MCPA, and triallate were frequently detected above aquatic protection thresholds, as was the pesticide lindane. In a survey of 189 Iowa prairie potholes, agricultural chemicals were detected from all but 2 (Iowa DNR 2008). Atrazine, acetochlor, alachlor, and flumetsulam (and degradates of each) were most widespread. On average, 7 herbicides and pesticides were detected in each prairie wetland in Iowa; in Saskatchewan an average of 2–3 were detected, depending on precipitation.

Although poorly studied, pesticides likely have a significant affect on aquatic food webs. Epiphytic insects are especially sensitive to herbicides (Murkin and Ross 2000), which impact both the vascular plant and metaphyton habitat structure they rely on, as well as algal food supplies. Algae are often more sensitive to herbicides than vascular plants (Fletcher 1990); 7 of 21 herbicides used in the PPR are toxic to algae at concentrations expected in wetlands (Sheehan, Baril, et al. 1987). The

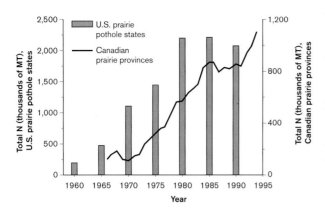

FIG. 20.8. Fertilizer nitrogen use in the Canadian prairie provinces (Alberta, Manitoba, Saskatchewan) and U.S. prairie pothole states (Iowa, Minnesota, North Dakota, South Dakota). (Crumpton and Goldsborough 1998.) MT = measurement ton.

impacts of multiple agricultural contaminants are poorly documented; Forsyth, Martin, et al. (1997) showed that a combination of herbicides piclorum and 2,4-D had synergistic effects on two submersed macrophytes in prairie potholes.

The direct effects of agricultural development on wetlands in the region are not dichotomous, i.e., drained and farmed versus intact. Wetland land use covers a spectrum, varying in frequency and practices, reflecting the costs of land improvement balanced against likelihood of financial gains. While some wetlands are drained and annually cultivated, many others are grazed by livestock or cultivated only in dry years because drainage is cost-prohibitive. Still others are partially drained; semipermanent wetlands can be difficult to adequately drain for crop production and so may end up with a hydrologic regime similar to a temporary wetland and used for pasture. To improve forage yields, many wet pastures in the eastern part of the region were planted with agronomic cultivars of the circumboreal perennial grass, *Phalaris arundinacea,* belatedly recognized as an invasive species. In other cases, if wetlands could not be drained, their periphery was cultivated, eliminating the wet-meadow vegetation. So, nearly all remnant wetlands in the eastern part of the region usually have some combination of partial drainage, high nutrient and sediment additions, and invasive *Phalaris* cover. Compared to the very few high-quality prairie wetlands that remain within prairie preserves, these agriculture-impacted wetlands are depauperate, with particularly poor representation of wet-meadow plant species (Galatowitsch, Whited, et al. 2000).

Westward, where pastured wetlands are not typically planted with improved forage species, changes to wetland vegetation depend on grazing intensity. The dominant species in grazed wetlands differ from those that are not grazed, likely due to higher herbivory of palatable species (Kantrud 1986). Low to moderate levels of grazing can increase plant diversity, perhaps because a more open canopy allows species to establish that are unable to do so with closed canopies and a dense litter layer.

High fish densities in semipermanent wetlands are common when they are connected via tiles or ditches to permanent water bodies such as lakes and rivers. Carp populations, for example, easily move into prairie wetlands through agricultural tile drains, and thrive there because of their tolerance to low dissolved oxygen. As in other aquatic systems, they generate high sediment turbidity, which limits plant and inverte-

brate productivity. Poorly regulated baitfish stocking reduces aquatic invertebrate abundance of these wetlands (Hanson and Riggs 1995). Fish stocking likely inadvertently introduced bullfrogs into the region, and has been linked to declines of other amphibians (Lannoo, Lang, et al. 1994). Seasonal wetlands are sometimes impounded or excavated, so at least some portion is permanently flooded for gamefish or livestock use. Euliss and Mushet (2004) reported that deepening prairie potholes allowed tiger salamanders to develop resident populations, and predation pressure from salamanders reduced populations of native frogs.

Prairie Wetland Restoration

Prior to the mid-1980s, opportunities to reverse losses of wetlands and prairies in the region had been limited to a few isolated restorations. Declining waterfowl populations in the early 1980s led to a joint agreement between the U.S. and Canada, the North American Waterfowl Management Plan, to promote innovative habitat management strategies and less destructive agricultural land-use practices (Environment Canada, Canadian Wildlife Service and United States Department of Interior, Fish and Wildlife Service 1986). In 1985, the United States' Food Security Act created a mechanism to pursue regional-scale wetland restoration in North America. One provision of the act, the Conservation Reserve Program (CRP), was primarily intended to reduce soil erosion and reduce surplus grain production but resulted in the restoration of thousands of wetlands in the region because water was considered to be an appropriate soil cover for enrolled, set-aside farmland. Under the CRP, farmers received financial incentives for planting and maintaining unused perennial cover on highly erodible land for 10 years. Reynolds, Shaffer, et al. (2001) estimated that over 2 million ducks a year were produced annually from 1992–97 as a result of the CRP, based on annual US Fish and Wildlife Surveys. CRP wetlands that were surrounded by planted perennial cover attracted more breeding duck pairs than similar wetlands in crop fields (Reynolds 2005). Phillips, Clark, et al. (2003) reported higher nest success in large tracts of planted perennial grassland, which they surmised had lower predatory foraging efficiency. Some wetlands restored under the CRP were re-enrolled under the Wetland Reserve Program (WRP), a permanent land retirement program established in 1990.

Wetlands restored under programs such as the CRP and WRP are reflooded by interrupting agricultural drainage systems (i.e., breaking tile drains or plugging ditches); enrolled uplands are planted with one to few perennial grasses (not necessarily native) to stabilize soils. The prevailing assumption was that upon reflooding, recolonization of plants and animals would be efficient, and restored wetlands similar to intact, remnant wetlands (e.g., Galatowitsch and van der Valk 1996a). Breeding waterfowl, submersed and emergent aquatic plants, and insects with aerial dispersal capabilities recolonized within the first few years of reflooding (e.g., van Rees-Siewert and Dinsmore 1996), but other organismal groups did not.

The colonization of less mobile and passively dispersed invertebrates, amphibians, wet-meadow plants, and nonwaterfowl birds has lagged (Delphey and Dinsmore 1993; Galatowitsch and van der Valk 1996a; Lehtinen and Galatowitsch 2001). Gleason, Euliss, et al. (2004) found that the redevelopment of invertebrate egg banks in restored wetlands was slower in parts of the PPR that had experienced greater agricultural wetland loss. Because prolonged drainage and cultivation is known to diminish invertebrate egg banks (Euliss and Mushet 1999), they concluded that recolonization was limited by a lack of propagule sources in the landscape. Likewise, the accumulation of amphibian species is adversely affected by increasing distance to source wetlands, although some species, such as *Rana pipiens* and *Pseudacris triseriata,* colonize rapidly (Lehtinen and Galatowitsch 2001). Mulhouse and Galatowitsch (2003) showed that even after a decade, fewer plant species had accumulated in wetlands that were more isolated from natural wetland propagule sources, but were also negatively related to flooding frequency and size. These vegetation differences continued to persist after 19 years (Aronson and Galatowitsch 2008), despite use by waterfowl, which can disperse viable seeds of some species that seldom colonize (e.g., *Carex* spp.; Mueller and van der Valk 2002). Lags in recolonization have resulted in dominance by a few invasive plant species, with especially depauperate wet meadows. Restored wetlands that lack wet-meadow vegetation are not used by some sparrows, wrens, and warblers (Delphey and Dinsmore 1993). Total bird species richness in restored prairie potholes was found by van Rees-Siewert and Dinsmore (1996) to be more influenced by vegetation characteristics than wetland area, whereas the reverse was true for waterfowl.

Conclusions

Wetland drainage and agricultural conversion of upland prairies mean that we are increasingly reliant on less habitat and lower-quality habitat to sustain the region's biodiversity. In some cases, wetland managers actively manipulate conditions in remnant wetlands, attempting to maximize benefits to specific species, usually waterfowl, as a way of compensating for these regional losses. However, many species with declining populations, especially nongame birds and amphibians, do not benefit from the habitat management for duck productivity (e.g., Koper and Schmiegelow 2006). The importance of wetland complexes and of the surrounding grasslands to wetland functions was apparent to the earliest scientists and conservationists in the region and has been reaffirmed by researchers who have delved into the details of many different organismal groups and environmental processes. Environmental policy, e.g., Swampbuster, has provided protection for some wetlands, but grasslands remain especially vulnerable to agricultural conversion. The CRP demonstrated that landscape-scale restoration in the PPR is possible, but the program was temporary and so many of these gained wetlands and grasslands were converted back to agriculture when enrollments ended. In recent years, interest in biofuels has greatly accelerated these grassland losses.

Given that the PPR is one of the most intensively used agricultural areas on earth, it is surprising how little is known of the effects of herbicides and pesticides on the region's biota. In particular, the potential for adverse impacts of herbicides on food webs and for synergistic effects of agricultural chemicals (including their surfactants) on wetland biota warrants significant research attention.

Over the past century, the PPR's strong east-west precipitation gradient steepened (Millett, Johnson, et al. 2009). Scientists predict it will become warmer but not necessarily wetter in the coming decades due to increased concentrations of greenhouse gases (Johnson, Werner, et al. 2010). A warmer climate seems likely to result in earlier snowpack melting,

diminished inputs from snowmelt and rainfall, reduced wetland water depths and volumes, shorter hydroperiods, and faster drawdowns. Wetlands across much of the region, especially those that are currently semipermanent, may become too dry to support waterfowl production. The region's climate refuge is the eastern part of the region, where little wetland and prairie habitat remains. Policy mechanisms to protect groundwater resources regionwide and to spur permanent landscape-scale restoration in the eastern part of the region are urgently needed to salvage what we can of the prairie pothole landscape.

References

Adomaitis V, Kantrud H, Shoesmith J. 1967. Some chemical characteristics of aeolian deposits of snow-soil on prairie wetlands. *N. Dak. Acad. Sc.* 21:65–69.

Almendinger J, Leete J. 1998. Regional and local hydrogeology of calcareous fens in the Minnesota River Basin, USA. *Wetlands* 18:184–202.

Amon J, Thompson C, et al. 2002. Temperate zone fens of the glaciated midwestern USA. *Wetlands* 22:301–17.

Arndt J, Richardson J. 1989. Geochemical development of hydric soil salinity in a North Dakota prairie-pothole wetland system. *Soil Sci. Soc. Am. J.* 53:848–55.

Arndt J, Richardson J. 1993. Temporal variations in the salinity of shallow groundwaters collected from the periphery of some North Dakota USA wetlands. *J. Hydrol.* 141:75–105.

Aronson M, Galatowitsch S. 2008. Long-term vegetation development of restored prairie wetlands. *Wetlands* 28:883–95.

Balas C. 2008. The effects of conservation programs on amphibians of the PPR's Glaciated Plain. MS thesis, Humboldt State University, Arcata, CA.

Bataille K, Baldassarre G. 1993. Distribution and abundance of aquatic macroinvertebrates following drought in three prairie pothole wetlands. *Wetlands* 13:260–69.

Batt B, Anderson M, et al. 1989. The use of prairie potholes by North American ducks. In *Northern prairie wetlands,* van der Valk A, editor. Ames: Iowa State Univ. Press, pp. 204–27.

Beauchamp W, Koford R, et al. 1996. Long term declines in nest success of prairie ducks. *J. Wildl. Manage.* 60:247–57.

Beauchamp W, Nudds T, Clark R. 1996. Duck nest success declines with and without predator management. *J. Wildl. Manage.* 60:258–64.

Benoy G. 2005. Variation in tiger salamander density within prairie potholes affects aquatic bird foraging behavior. *Can. J. Zool.* 83:926–34.

Benoy G. 2008. Tiger salamanders in prairie potholes: a "fish in amphibian's garments"? *Wetlands* 28:464–72.

Berthold S, Bentley L, Hayashi M. 2004. Integrated hydrogeological and geophysical study of depression-focused groundwater recharge in the Canadian prairies. *Water Resour. Res.* 40:1–14.

Bethke R, Nudds T. 1995. Effects of climate change and land use on duck abundance in Canadian prairie-parklands. *Ecol. Appl.* 5:588–600.

Bishop R, Joens J, Zohrer J. 1998. Iowa's wetlands, present and future with a focus on prairie potholes. *J. Iowa Acad. Sci.* 105:89–93.

Blann K, Anderson J, et al. 2009. Effects of agricultural drainage on aquatic ecosystems. *Crit. Rev. Env. Sci. Tech.* 39:909–1001.

Brook RW, Pasitschniak-Arts M, et al. 2008. Influence of rodent abundance on nesting success of prairie waterfowl. *Can. J. Zool.* 86:497–506.

Bryson R, Hare F. 1974. *Climates of North America,* Vol. 11. In *World survey of climatology,* Landsberg H, editor. New York: Elsevier, pp. 1–47.

Carpenter S, Lodge D. 1986. Effects of submersed macrophytes on ecosystem processes. *Aquat. Bot.* 26:341–70.

Cessna A, Elliott J. 2004. Seasonal variation in herbicide concentrations in prairie farm dugouts. *J. Env. Qual.* 33:302–315.

Clark W. 2000. Ecology of muskrats in prairie wetlands. In *Prairie wetland ecology: the contribution of the Marsh Ecology Research Pro-*

gram, Murkin H, van der Valk A, Clark W, editors. Ames: Iowa State Univ. Press, pp. 287–313.

Crumpton W, Goldsborough L. 1998. Nitrogen transformation and fate in prairie wetlands. *Great Plains Res.* 8:57–72.

Dahl T. 1990. Wetlands: losses in the United States, 1780's to 1980's. Washington, DC: USFWS Report to Congress.

Davis C, van der Valk A. 1978. The decomposition of standing and fallen litter of *Typha glauca* and *Scirpus fluviatilis*. *Can. J. Bot.* 56:662–75.

Delphey P, Dinsmore J. 1993. Breeding bird communities of recently restored and natural prairie potholes. *Wetlands* 13:200–06.

Detenbeck N, Elonen C, et al. 2002. Effects of agricultural activities and best management practices on water quality of seasonal prairie pothole wetlands. *Wetl. Ecol. Manage.* 10:335–54.

Dieter CD. 1991. Water turbidity in tilled and untilled prairie wetlands. *J. Freshw. Ecol.* 6:185–89.

Donald D, Syrgiannis J, et al. 1999. Agricultural pesticides threaten the ecological integrity of northern prairie wetlands. *Sci. Total Env.* 231:173–81.

Drever M. 2006. Spatial synchrony of prairie ducks: roles of wetland abundance, distance, and agricultural cover. *Oecologia* 147:1432–39.

Environment Canada, Canadian Wildlife Service and United States Department of Interior, Fish and Wildlife Service. 1986. North American Waterfowl Management Plan.

Errington P. 1954. On the hazards of overemphasizing numerical fluctuations in studies of "cyclic" phenomena in muskrat populations. *J. Wildl. Manage.* 18:66–90.

Errington P, Siglin R, Clark R. 1963. The decline of a muskrat population. *J. Wildl. Manage.* 27:1–8.

Euliss N, Mushet D. 2004. Impacts of water development on aquatic macroinvertebrates, amphibians, and plants in wetlands of a semi-arid landscape. *Aquat. Ecosys. Health Manage.* 7:73–84.

Euliss N, Wrubelski D, Mushet D. 1999. Wetlands of the PPR: invertebrate species composition, ecology and management. In *Invertebrates in freshwater wetlands of North America: ecology and management,* Batzer D, Rader R, Wissinger S, editors. New York: John Wiley and Sons, pp. 471–514.

Euliss NH Jr, Mushet DM. 1999. Influence of agriculture on aquatic invertebrate communities of temporary wetlands in the PPR of North Dakota, USA. *Wetlands* 19:578–83.

Fleskes J, Klaas E. 1991. Dabbling duck recruitment in relation to habitat and predators at Union Slough National Wildlife Refuge, Iowa. USFWS, Fish. Wildl. Tech. Rep. 32.

Fletcher JS. 1990. Use of algae versus vascular plants to test for chemical toxicity. In *Plants for toxicity assessment,* Wang W, Gorsuch JW, Lower WR, editors. Philadelphia: Am. Soc. Testing and Materials, pp. 33–39.

Forsyth D, Martin P, Shaw G. 1997. Effects of herbicides on two submersed aquatic macrophytes, *Potamogeton pectinatus* L. and *Myriophyllum sibiricum* Komarov. in a prairie wetland. *Env. Pollu.* 90:259–68.

Fritzell E. 1989. Mammals in prairie wetlands. In *Northern prairie wetlands,* van der Valk A, editor. Ames: Iowa State Univ. Press, pp. 268–301.

Galatowitsch S, Biderman L. 1998. Vegetation and seedbank composition of temporarily flooded *Carex* meadows and implications for restoration. *Internat. J. Ecol. Env. Sci.* 24:253–70.

Galatowitsch S, van der Valk A. 1994. *Restoring prairie wetlands: an ecological approach.* Ames: Iowa State Univ. Press.

Galatowitsch S, van der Valk A. 1996a. The vegetation of restored and natural prairie wetlands. *Ecol. Appl.* 6:102–12.

Galatowitsch SM, van der Valk AG. 1996b. Characteristics of newly restored prairie potholes. *Wetlands* 16:75–83.

Galatowitsch S, Whited D, et al. 2000. The vegetation of wet meadows in relation to their land use. *Env. Monitoring Assess.* 60:121–44.

Galinato M, van der Valk A. 1986. Seed germination traits of annuals and emergents recruited during drawdowns in the Delta Marsh, Manitoba, Canada. *Aquat. Bot.* 26:89–102.

Gleason R, Euliss N, et al. 2004. Invertebrate egg banks of restored, natural, and drained wetlands in the PPR of the United States. *Wetlands* 24:562–72.

Gorham E, Dean W, Sanger J. 1983. The chemical composition of lakes in the north central United States. *Limnol. Oceanogr.* 28:287–301.

Green E, Galatowitsch S. 2002. Effect of *Phalaris arundinacea* and nitrate-N addition on the establishment of wetland plant communities. *J. Appl. Ecol.* 39:134–44.

Greenwood R, Sargeant A, et al. 1995. Factors associated with duck nest success in the PPR of Canada. *Wildl. Monogr.* no. 128.

Hanson M, Butler M. 1994. Responses of plankton, turbidity, and macrophytes to biomanipulation in a shallow prairie lake. *Can. J. Fish. Aquat. Sci.* 51:1180–88.

Hanson M, Riggs M. 1995. Potential effects of fish predation on wetland invertebrates: a comparison of wetlands with and without fathead minnows. *Wetlands* 15:167–75.

Hayashi M, van der Kamp G, Rudolph D. 1998a. Water and solute transfer between a prairie wetland and adjacent uplands. 1. Water balance. *J. Hydrol.* 207:42–55.

Hayashi M, van der Kamp G, Rudolph D. 1998b. Water and solute transfer between a prairie wetland and adjacent uplands. 2. Chloride cycle. *J. Hydrol.* 207:56–67.

Hem J. 1970. *Study and interpretation of the chemical characteristics of natural waters,* 2nd ed. Washington, DC: USGS Water Supply Paper 1473.

Hendry M, Wassenaar L. 1999. Implications of the distribution of #D in pore waters for groundwater flow and the timing of geologic events in a thick aquitard system. *Water Resour. Res.* 35:1751–60.

Iowa DNR. 2008. Results of wetland monitoring 2005–2007. Water Fact Sheet 2008-3. Iowa City: IA DNR, Geol. Surv.

Johnson D, Grier J. 1988. Determinants of breeding distributions of ducks. *Wildl. Monogr.* no. 100.

Johnson W, Boettcher S, et al. 2004. Influence of weather extremes on the water levels of glaciated prairie wetlands. *Wetlands* 24:385–98.

Johnson W, Werner B, et al. 2010. Prairie wetland complexes as landscape functional units in a changing climate. *BioScience* 60:128–40.

Kadlec J. 1962. Effect of a drawdown on the ecology of a waterfowl impoundment. *Ecology* 43:267–81.

Kaminski R, Prince H. 1981. Dabbling duck activity and foraging response to aquatic macroinvertebrates. *Auk* 98:115–26.

Kantrud H. 1986. *Effects of vegetation manipulation on breeding waterfowl in prairie wetlands—a literature review.* USFWS Tech. Rep. 3.

Kantrud H, Krapu G, Swanson G. 1989. *Prairie basin wetlands of the Dakotas: a community profile.* USFWS Biol. Rep. 85(7.28). Washington, DC: USDI.

Keeney D, DeLuca T. 1993. Des Moines River nitrate in relation to watershed agricultural practices: 1945 versus 1980s. *J. Env. Qual.* 22:267–72.

Koper N, Schmiegelow F. 2006. Effects of habitat management for ducks on target and nontarget species. *J. Wildl. Manage.* 70:823–34.

Korner S. 1992. Bidirectional sulfate diffusion in saline-lake sediments: evidence from Devil's Lake, northeast North Dakota. *Geology* 20:314–22.

Krapu G, Klett A, Jorde D. 1983. The effect of variable spring water conditions of mallard reproduction. *Auk* 100:689–98.

LaBaugh J. 1989. Chemical characteristics of water in northern prairie wetlands. In *Northern prairie wetlands,* van der Valk A, editor. Ames: Iowa State Univ. Press, pp. 57–90.

LaBaugh J, Winter T, et al. 1996. Changes in atmospheric circulation patterns affect midcontinental wetlands sensitive to climate. *Limnol. Oceanogr.* 41:864–70.

Lannoo M, Lang K, et al. 1994. An altered amphibian assemblage: Dickinson County, Iowa, 70 years after Frank Blanchard's survey. *Am. Midl. Natur.* 131:311–19.

Lawler G, Sunde L, Whitaker J. 1974. Trout production in prairie ponds. *J. Fish. Res. Board Can.* 31:929–36.

Lehtinen R, Galatowitsch S. 2001. Colonization of restored wetland by amphibians in Minnesota. *Am. Midl. Natur.* 145:388–96.

Lissey A. 1971. Depression-focused transient groundwater flow patterns in Manitoba. *Sp. Pap. Geol. Assoc. Can.* 9:333–41.

Martin D, Hartman W. 1987. The effect of cultivation on sediment composition and deposition in prairie pothole wetlands. *Water Air Soil Pollu.* 34:45–53.

Millar J. 1971. Shoreline-area ratio as a factor in the rate of water loss from small sloughs. *J. Hydrol.* 14:259–84.

Miller B, Crumpton W, van der Valk A. 2009. Spatial distribution of historical wetland classes on the Des Moines Lobe, Iowa. *Wetlands* 29:1146–52.

Millett B, Johnson W, Guntenspergen G. 2009. Climate trends of the North American PPR 1906–2000. *Climatic Change* 93:243–67.

Mueller M, van der Valk A. 2002. The potential role of ducks in wetland seed dispersal. *Wetlands* 22:170–78.

Mulhouse J, Galatowitsch S. 2003. Revegetation of prairie pothole wetlands in the mid-continental US: twelve years post-flooding. *Plant Ecol.* 169:143–59.

Murkin H. 1989. The basis for food chains in prairie wetlands. In *Northern prairie wetlands,* van der Valk A, editor. Ames: Iowa State Univ. Press, pp. 316–39.

Murkin H, Batt B. 1987. Interactions of vertebrates and invertebrates in peatlands and marshes. In *Aquatic insects of peatlands and marshes,* Rosenberg D, Danks H, editors. Mem. Ent. Soc. Can. 140, pp. 15–30.

Murkin H, Caldwell P. 2000. Avian use of prairie wetlands. In *Prairie wetland ecology: the contribution of the Marsh Ecology Research Program,* Murkin H, van der Valk A, Clark W, editors. Ames: Iowa State Univ. Press, pp. 249–86.

Murkin H, Ross L. 2000. Invertebrates in prairie wetlands. In *Prairie wetland ecology: the contribution of the Marsh Ecology Research Program,* Murkin H, van der Valk A, Clark W, editors. Ames: Iowa State Univ. Press, pp. 201–48.

Murkin H, van der Valk A, Kadlec J. 2000a. Nutrient budgets and the wet-dry cycle of prairie wetlands. In *Prairie wetland ecology: the contribution of the Marsh Ecology Research Program,* Murkin H, van der Valk A, Clark W, editors. Ames: Iowa State Univ. Press, pp. 99–124.

Murkin H, van der Valk A, et al. 2000b. Marsh Ecology Research Program: management implications for prairie wetlands. In *Prairie wetland ecology: the contribution of the Marsh Ecology Research Program,* Murkin H, van der Valk A, Clark W, editors. Ames: Iowa State Univ. Press, pp. 317–44.

Naugle DE, Johnson R, et al. 2001. A landscape approach to conserving wetland bird habitat in the PPR of eastern South Dakota. *Wetlands* 21:1–17.

Neckles H, Murkin H, Cooper J. 1990. Influences of seasonal flooding on macroinvertebrate abundance in wetland habitats. *Freshw. Biol.* 23:311–22.

Neely R, Baker J. 1989. Nitrogen and phosphorus dynamics and the fate of agricultural runoff. In *Northern prairie wetlands,* van der Valk A, editor. Ames: Iowa State Univ. Press, pp. 92–131.

Neil C. 1990. Effects of nutrients and water levels on emergent macrophyte biomass in a prairie marsh. *Can. J. Bot.* 68:1007–14.

Neil C. 1993. Growth and resource allocation of whitetop *(Scolochloa festucacea)* along a water depth gradient. *Aquat. Bot.* 46:235–46.

Nudds T. 1983. Niche dynamics and organization of duck guilds in variable environments. *Ecology* 64:319–30.

Pashley D, Warhurst R. 1999. Conservation planning in the PPR of the United States: integration between an existing waterfowl plan and emerging non-game bird model. In *Partners in Flight (PIF) Conservation Plan: building consensus for action,* Bonney R, Pashley D, et al., editors. Proc. PIF Internat. Workshop, Cornell Lab Ornithol. http://birds.cornell.edu.

Patterson CJ. 1997. Southern Laurentide ice lobes were created by ice streams: Des Moines Lobe in Minnesota, USA. *Sediment. Geol.* 111:249–61.

Peterka J. 1989. Fishes in northern prairie wetlands. In *Northern prairie wetlands,* van der Valk A, editor. Ames: Iowa State Univ. Press, pp. 302–15.

Phillips M, Clark W, et al. 2003. Predator selection of prairie landscape features and its relation to duck nest success. *J. Wildl. Manage.* 67:104–14.

Pieron M, Rohwer F. 2010. Effects of large-scale predator reduction on nest success of upland nesting ducks. *J. Wildl. Manage.* 74:124–32.

Remenda VH, van der Kamp G, Cherry J. 1996. Use of vertical profiles of δ^{18}O to constrain estimates of hydraulic conductivity in a thick, unfractured aquitard. *Water Resour. Res.* 32:2979–87.

Reynolds R, Shaffer T, et al. 2001. Impact of the Conservation Reserve Program on duck recruitment in the U.S. PPR. *J. Wildl. Manage.* 65:765–80.

Reynolds RE. 2005. The Conservation Reserve Program and duck production in the U.S. PPR. In *Fish and wildlife benefits of farm bill conservation programs: 2000–2005 update,* Haufler J, editor. Tech. Rev. #05-2, 33-40. Bethesda, MD: Wildlife Society.

Richardson J, Arndt J, Freeland F. 1994. Wetland soils of the prairie potholes. *Adv. Agron.* 52:121–71.

Rose C, Crumpton W. 1996. Effects of emergent macrophytes on dissolved oxygen dynamics in a prairie pothole wetland. *Wetlands* 16:495–502.

Rosenberry D, Winter T. 1997. Dynamics of water-table fluctuations in an upland between two prairie-pothole wetlands in North Dakota. *J. Hydrol.* 191:266–89.

Sargeant A, Greenwood R, et al. 1993. *Distribution an abundance of predators that affect duck production: PPR.* USFWS Resour. Publ. no. 194.

Sheehan PJ, Baril A, et al. 1987. *The impact of pesticides on the ecology of prairie nesting ducks.* Tech. Rep. Ser. no. 19. Can. Wildl. Serv., Ottawa: Environment Canada.

Smith A, Stoudt J, Gollop J. 1964. Prairie potholes and marshes. In *Waterfowl tomorrow,* Linduska J, editor. Washington, DC: USFWS, pp. 39–50.

Smith D. 1998. Iowa prairie: original extent and loss, preservation and recovery attempts. *J. Iowa Acad. Sci.* 105:94–108.

Sovada M, Sargeant A, Grier J. 1995. Differential effects of coyotes and red foxes on duck nest success. *J. Wildl. Manage.* 59:1–9.

Sovada M, Zicus M, et al. 2000. Relationship of habitat patch size to predator community and survival of duck nests. *J. Wildl. Manage.* 64:820–31.

Sovada MA, Anthony RM, Batt BDJ. 2001. Predation on waterfowl in arctic tundra and prairie breeding areas: a review. *Wildl. Soc.y Bull.* 29:6–15.

Steinwand A, Richardson J. 1989. Gypsum occurrence in soils on the margin of semipermanent prairie pothole wetlands. *Soil Sci. Soc. Am. J.* 53:836–42.

Stewart RE, Kantrud HA. 1971. Classification of natural ponds and lakes in the glaciated prairie region. Res. Publ. 92. Bureau Sport Fish. Wildl.

Swanson G, Duebbert H. 1989. Wetland habitats of waterfowl in the PPR. In *Northern prairie wetlands,* van der Valk A, editor. Ames: Iowa State Univ. Press, pp. 228–67.

Thompson C, Bettis E, Baker R. 1992. Geology of Iowa fens. *J. Iowa Acad. Sci.* 99:53–59.

van der Kamp G, Hayashi M. 2009. Groundwater-wetland ecosystem interaction in the semiarid glaciated plains of North America. *Hydrogeol. J.* 17:203–14.

van der Kamp G, Hayashi M, Gallen D. 2003. Comparing the hydrology of grassed and cultivated catchments in the semiarid Canadian prairies. *Hydrol. Processes* 17:559–75.

van der Kamp G, Stolte W, Clark R. 1999. Drying out of small prairie wetlands after conversion of their catchments from cultivation to permanent brome grass. *Hydrol. Sci. J.* 44:387–97.

van der Valk A. 1989. *Northern prairie wetlands.* Ames: Iowa State Univ. Press.

van der Valk A. 2005. Water-level fluctuations in North America prairie wetlands. *Hydrobiologia* 539:171–88.

van der Valk A, Davis C. 1978. The role of seed banks in the vegetation dynamics of prairie glacial marshes. *Ecology* 59:322–35.

Van Rees-Siewert K, Dinsmore J. 1996. Influences of wetland age on bird use of restored wetlands in Iowa. *Wetlands* 16:577–82.

Van Rees-Siewert KL. 1993. *The influence of wetland age on bird and aquatic macroinvertebrate use of restored Iowa wetlands.* MS thesis, Iowa State Univ., Ames.

Verma B, Robarts R, Headley J. 2003. Seasonal changes in fungal production and biomass on standing dead *Scirpus lacustris* litter in a northern prairie wetland. *Appl. Env. Microbiol.* 69:1043–50.

Waite D, Cessna A, et al. 2004. Environmental concentrations of agricultural herbicides in Saskatchewan, Canada: bromoxynil, dicamba, diclofop, MCPA, and trifluralin. *J. Env. Qual.* 33:1616–28.

Waite D, Grover R, et al. 1995. Atmospheric deposition of pesticides in a small southern Saskatchewan watershed. *Env. Toxicol. Chem.* 14:1171–75.

Welling C, Pederson R, van der Valk A. 1988a. Recruitment from the seed bank and the development of zonation of emergent vegetation during a drawdown in a prairie wetland. *J. Ecol.* 76:483–96.

Welling C, Pederson R, van der Valk A. 1988b. Temporal patterns in recruitment from the seed bank during drawdowns in a prairie wetland. *J. Appl. Ecol.* 25:999–1007.

Williams B, Koneff M, Smith D. 1999. Evaluation of waterfowl conservation under the North American Waterfowl Management Plan. *J. Wildl. Manage.* 63:371–440.

Winter T. 1989. Hydrologic studies of wetlands in the northern prairie. In *Northern prairie wetlands,* van der Valk A, editor. Ames: Iowa State Univ. Press, pp. 16–54.

Zimmer K, Hanson M, Butler M. 2000. Factors influencing invertebrate communities in prairie wetlands: a multivariate approach. *Can. J. Fish. Aquat. Sci.* 57:76–85.

CHAPTER 21

High Plains Playas

LOREN M. SMITH, DAVID A. HAUKOS, and SCOTT T. MCMURRY

Playas have been loosely described as closed-basin wetlands occurring in arid to semiarid regions throughout the world (Neal 1975; Bolen, Smith, et. al. 1989; Rosen 1994), but such a definition has resulted in the inclusion of a variety of wetland types with differing hydrogeomorphic settings (e.g., Stone 1956; Droste 1959; Neal 1965). Regardless, playas are believed to occur in their highest densities as inland freshwater wetlands of the nonglaciated High Plains region of the western Great Plains in the United States (Bolen, Smith, et al. 1989) (Fig. 21.1). Here, they are more precisely defined as shallow depressional recharge wetlands, with each wetland occurring in its own catchment or watershed (Smith 2003:6). Playas of the High Plains are not directly connected to a permanent water source and naturally lose water only through aquifer recharge, evaporation, and transpiration, and primarily receive water from catchment runoff and direct precipitation.

The High Plains is a large region of the western Great Plains with limited topographical relief (Gurdak and Roe 2009). This limited relief promotes playa establishment and development as well as contributing to their primarily circular surface appearance on the elevationally and hydrologically isolated Southern High Plains of Texas and New Mexico and their more oblong appearance in more northern reaches. The historical number of playas occurring in the High Plains is unknown but certainly exceeded 30,000 and may have been as great as 60,000 (e.g., Guthery, Bryant, et al. 1981; Playa Lakes Joint Venture, www.pljv.org/cms/playa-county-maps; see discussion in the "Conservation Concerns" section).

There is also the dilemma of accurately documenting the extent of "loss" of playas from the landscape. Because playas are typically shallow (usually < 1 m) and occur at the bottom of a watershed, they often fill with soil eroded from surrounding cultivated uplands (Luo, Smith, et al. 1997) and are no longer readily identifiable as wetlands. This confounds estimation of playa numbers that occurred prior to cultivation history as well as the number potentially available to restore. A more insidious problem has arisen as a result of USDA reclassification of depressional soils in the southern High Plains, including fragmentation of the dominant hydric soil series previously used to identify playa locations into several nonhydric and hydric series (Johnson, Haukos, et al. 2010). Obviously,

hydric soil reclassified as nonhydric will reduce the number and area of potential playas. We will further address this issue later in the chapter.

The High Plains is one of the most intensively cultivated regions in North America (Samson and Knopf 1994) and, as alluded to above, playas, imbedded in that landscape, have been profoundly impacted by farming activities. To understand playa ecology, physical and hydrological modifications, and restoration potential in this region, one must have an understanding of agricultural practices over time relative to playas in the High Plains. However, histories of agricultural production vary regionally according to time since European settlement, precipitation, and availability of groundwater. The Rainwater Basin region of south-central Nebraska has been farmed since the 1860s, 40 to 80 years prior than areas to the west and south. Moreover, the Rainwater Basin receives more precipitation than other areas of the High Plains, and playas were viewed as hindering farming activities (Smith 2003). This led to widespread drainage efforts (Gersib, Cornely, et al. 1990). The High Plains west of the Rainwater Basin (western High Plains; Fig. 21.1) was not generally farmed prior to the early 1900s, primarily due to unreliable surface water and lower precipitation that did not support widespread farming until a dependable source of groundwater (i.e., High Plains or Ogallala Aquifer) was discovered and technology supporting its withdrawal could be developed. This led to a more recent cultivation history in the western High Plains; widespread farming did not occur until the 1930s and 1940s. Therefore, livestock grazing was more common following elimination of bison *(Bison bison)* and prior to cultivation in the western High Plains.

Playas are the critical ecosystem in the High Plains, providing functions that support the persistence of a majority of flora and fauna as well as contributing services in support of the overall well-being of humans residing in the region (Smith, Haukos, et al. 2011). Services include groundwater recharge, floodwater storage, biomass production, biodiversity provisioning, and contaminant filtration (Smith, Haukos, et al. 2011). Because the High Plains region containing playas is approximately 1,600 km from north to south, there is also considerable variation in the relative contribution of ecosystem services they might provide (Smith, Haukos, et al. 2011). For

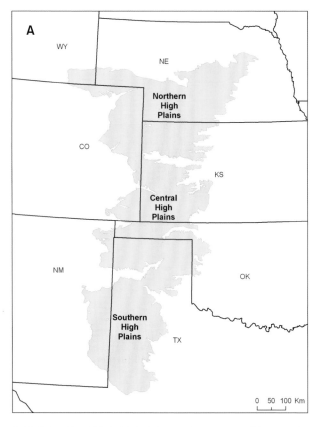

FIG. 21.1. The High Plains region of the United States contains playas in a mosaic of native grassland and cropland. (Figure courtesy of Megan McLachlan; photo by Ross Tsai.)

example, the importance of habitat provisioning for migratory birds is much different in southern playas than northern playas simply because of the different physiological requirements of migratory birds during the annual cycle. Moreover, the importance of one group of playas may be greater than another group because of habitat destruction or uniqueness of a given group. For example, approximately 90% of the estimated original 4,000 playas in the Rainwater Basin region have been destroyed, leaving the remaining 400 extremely important for a variety of services, including spring migration habitat for waterfowl (Schildman and Hurt 1984). Although an individual playa is hydrologically isolated from adjacent playas, it is the cumulative number of and ecological variation among playas in a specific area that makes them important, biotically and

abiotically. Playas as a whole form a system that, for example, allows biotic populations to persist as metapopulations. From an abiotic perspective, it is the number of playas that allows substantial aquifer recharge to occur versus the relatively small amount that infiltrates through a single basin. Therefore, loss or degradation of an individual playa, seemingly inconsequential given the large number of playas, actually reduces the ecological function of neighboring playas as well as the wetland system as a whole.

Most of our knowledge of playas, their ecosystem characteristics, and the services they provide exist for the Southern High Plains (especially Texas) and the Rainwater Basin region of Nebraska. Scientific investigation of playas in other areas, such as western Kansas, western Nebraska, and eastern Colorado, are now just beginning. Regardless, the number of ecosystem studies on playas is much fewer than those on most other major wetland types in North America, which has retarded conservation efforts throughout the region (Smith 2003).

Geology and Hydrology

A variety of processes have been proposed as responsible for the initiation of playa formation (playa origin) and their subsequent development in the High Plains. These include large mammal wallows, meteorites, wind deflation, and subsidence of underlying soil materials (e.g., carbonates) (Evans and Meade 1945; Evans 1961; Reeves 1966). A likely conclusion is that no single factor was responsible for initiation of playa formation throughout the High Plains (Smith 2003). Currently, the two most accepted theories of playa formation, following the initiation of a depression, are dissolution of the underlying calcium carbonate, or caliche, typical of the Southern High Plains (Osterkamp and Wood 1987), and wind deflation (principally on the Central and Northern High Plains) (Sabin and Holliday 1995; Reeves and Reeves 1996).

Dissolution of calcium carbonate and subsequent subsidence resulting in the formation of a playa stem from the hypothesis that accumulation of water into small depressions, resulting from any number of factors, as listed above, concentrates organic material, which is carried into the soil, wherein it oxidizes and forms a weak carbonic acid. Carbonic acid then dissolves the underlying calcium carbonate, which is transported down through the soil column, causing formation of a more pronounced depression that with subsequent inundation and organic matter input continually grows outward in a circular fashion (Osterkamp and Wood 1987). This theory on playa formation is supported by the fact that most playas are near-circular in appearance in the Southern High Plains and are relatively shallow (depth limited in part by the thickness of the calcium carbonate layer), and calcium carbonate is found only along the playa edge and not under the basin. However, exceptions have been documented in which calcium carbonate still exists under playa basins, which may be related to playa age (Reeves and Reeves 1996).

Wind deflation is another primary theory of playa formation. Although the circular shape of most playas would seem counter to their development by wind, which is predominantly out of the southwest in summer and northwest in winter, the effects of wind on playas cannot be wholly discounted. About 5% of all playas in the Southern High Plains have pronounced lunettes (small dunes of windblown lacustrine sediment) on their east and south sides, demonstrating the effects of wind on land deflation. Many more (50%) in the Rainwater

Basin have lunettes (Starks 1984). Wind also plays a role in the maintenance of playa depressions because it removes erosional sediments (Luo, Smith, et al. 1997). For example, when deep water inhibits plant communities and the playa subsequently dries during the nongrowing season, sediments are blown from the basin floor into the surrounding uplands.

Playa wetlands experience variable wet-dry fluctuations; however, their hydrological budget is quite simple. Playas receive water only from direct precipitation and runoff following precipitation events and in some cases irrigation runoff from adjacent crop fields. Each playa is hydrologically isolated from all others, with no lateral subterranean movement of water among playas. Water is lost from playas by infiltration and evapotranspiration. Infiltration can be substantial, especially during the early stages of inundation in playas that have been dry long enough to form deep cracks in the hydric soil or during periods of intense precipitation. Indeed, it is generally accepted that playas are the primary, if not only, point of recharge to the Ogallala Aquifer underlying the Southern High Plains (Gustavson, Holliday, et al. 1995). The substantial infiltration is evidenced by the freshwater conditions present in playas (61–1,177 μmhos; Hall, Sites, et al. 1999). If conditions were more saline in playas, it would be indicative of evaporative losses rather than recharge events (waters are only slightly alkaline on average; Hall, Sites, et al. 1999).

The major hydrological input is watershed runoff. As noted above, the original native prairie watersheds have been dramatically altered by agricultural impacts. Today, most playas in the High Plains are embedded in cropland-dominated landscapes (Fig. 21.1), which, over time, has resulted in significant accumulation of sediment in playas with cultivated watersheds (Luo, Smith, et al. 1997). Moreover, this results in very turbid conditions in playas embedded in cropland compared to grassland playas (Hall, Sites, et al. 1999). Most playas surrounded by cropland have lost greater than 100% of their hydric soil defined volume (sediment completely covering all hydric soil). Numerous examples demonstrate the negative effects of sediment accumulation on playa hydrology, including shorter hydroperiods and increased rate of water loss (Tsai, Venne, et al. 2007). Deep sediments rapidly absorb water, reducing the amount of available standing water. In addition, sedimentation makes a playa shallower, and water is dispersed over a larger area that increases evaporative loss. The runoff from agricultural lands also results in most playas being considered eutrophic (see nitrogen and phosphorus values in Hall, Sites, et al. 1999). Although conditions are eutrophic, there is often little variation in dissolved oxygen levels from surface to bottom water depths due to substantial mixing as a result of persistent winds (Hall, Sites, et al. 1999).

Conservation Reserve Program (CRP) land represents another land-use alteration having major impacts on playa watersheds in the High Plains. The CRP was implemented in 1985 in part to temporarily remove highly erodible farmed land from cultivation and reduce production of some commodity crops to increase prices (Young and Osborn 1990). Landowners enrolled in the CRP program were required to plant perennial grasses, but it seldom restored the native prairie. During initial enrollments in most states (except Kansas), landowners were allowed to plant exotic grasses (Berthelsen, Smith, et al. 1990). Exotic grasses (weeping love grass [*Eragrostis curvula*], old world bluestem [*Bothriochloa ischaemum*]) typical of most CRP lands in the southern Great Plains produce heavy, rank stands of vegetation in contrast to the native species. Playas with watersheds dominated by vegetation planted in the CRP experience reduced precipitation runoff (Gilley, Patton, et al. 1996). However, enrollment of playa watersheds in the CRP has been successful at slowing soil erosion and additional accumulation of sediments in playas, but probably at the expense of reduced inundation frequency and shortened hydroperiods. Although recent studies show aquifer levels as less impacted under CRP watersheds relative to cropland, the finding is perhaps more a result of reduction in aquifer exploitation for irrigation than increased recharge from playas with CRP watersheds (K. Mulligan, Center for Geospatial Technology, Texas Tech University, unpublished data).

Plant Communities

Our knowledge of playa plant communities is primarily restricted to vascular plants; little is known about algal communities (see Smith 2003 for a brief summary of algae). Vascular plants contribute to numerous services, including aquifer recharge (Osterkamp and Wood 1987; Wood and Osterkamp 1987; Zartman 1987), water quality (L. Johnson, Texas Tech University, unpublished data), stormwater catchment and storage (Nelson, Logan, et al. 1983; Tsai, Venne, et al. 2007), biomass production (Haukos and Smith 1993a; Anderson and Smith 1998), and wildlife habitat (Haukos and Smith 1994a). Due to extensive conversion of the native prairie to agriculture, urban, and industrial uses, playas serve as refugia for propagules of species from the former surrounding native prairie, and plant assemblages existing in playas represent predominant remaining native plant communities of the western High Plains (Haukos and Smith 1997, 2004; Cariveau and Pavlacky 2008, 2009).

Composition of plant species in playas changes much more frequently compared to other wetland systems (Haukos and Smith 2004). Indeed, on average, > 60% of extant species change over the growing season because of their life-history patterns and varying environmental conditions (Haukos and Smith 1993a; Smith and Haukos 2002). As such, the dominant longevity of species occurring in functional playas range from annual to short-lived perennial, which contrasts with many other interior North American freshwater wetlands, which are often dominated by longer-lived perennials (e.g., *Typha* spp., *Potamogeton* spp., and *Schoenoplectus* spp.) (van der Valk and Davis 1978; Leck 1989). In addition, perennial woody vegetation (e.g., *Salix* spp., *Ulmus pumila*) rarely occurs within unaltered playas (Haukos and Smith 1997, 2004).

There are 346 plant species reported in southern Great Plains playas (Haukos and Smith 1997). With the recent addition of subsequent surveys in the Central and Northern High Plains of Colorado and Nebraska (Cariveau and Pavlacky 2008, 2009) and using Great Plains Flora Association (1991) and the USDA PLANTS database (plants.usda.gov) as taxonomic authorities, we determined that 450 different species have been documented in playas of 6 states in the High Plains. Of these 43.5% were classified as annual and 56.5% as biannual or perennial; 16.5% were considered exotic, naturalized, or introduced. Interestingly, of the 450 species, only 2, *Oenothera canescens* and *Verbena bracteata,* are consistently reported (Reed 1930; Rowell 1971, 1981; Curtis and Beierman 1980; Hoagland 1991; Kindscher and Lauver 1993; Cushing, Mazaika, et al. 1993; Kindscher 1994; Johnston 1995; Haukos and Smith 1997, 2004; Smith and Haukos 2002; Cariveau and Pavlacky 2008, 2009). Only 17 species occurred in each of the 6 states.

Although there are no species endemic to western playas, 247 species (55%) are currently reported as unique to a single state (Texas, 94; Oklahoma, 1; New Mexico, 12; Kansas, 25; Colorado, 111; Nebraska, 4).

Plant species are typically assigned a Wetland Indicator Status (WIS) for use during determination of jurisdictional standing (USFWS 1988b; US National Wetlands Inventory 1996). The WIS categories are assigned based on Regional Indicators, with plants of High Plains playas categorized across three regions. Assigned WIS categories often vary throughout the High Plains for individual species. For our purposes, we assigned the WIS of Region 6 (South Plains, including Oklahoma and Texas) to documented species and the WIS of the region of the state in which any species not listed in Region 6 occurred (Region 5 = Colorado, Nebraska, and Kansas; Region 7 = Arizona and New Mexico). For playas in the western High Plains, 52 (11.6%) species were classified as Obligate Wetland plants (OBL) and 43 (9.5%) as Facultative Wetland plants (FACW). Categories of Facultative (FAC) and Facultative Upland (FACU) were assigned to 120 (26.6%) species. Further, 206 (46%) species did not have an assigned indicator code, 22 (4.9%) were classified as no indicator status, and 6 (1.3%) were labeled as upland (UPL).

In the Rainwater Basin playas of central Nebraska, Weaver and Bruner (1954) and Erickson and Leslie (1987) recorded 26 and 64 species, respectively. In a more extensive survey, Gilbert (1989) found 212 plant species in the Rainwater Basin, with > 80% of these also occurring in the southern Great Plains. Gilbert (1989) reported that > 10% of species were considered exotic. *Phalaris arundinacea* and *Schoenoplectus fluviatilis* are considered the most invasive (USFWS 2007; Davis, Bidwell, et al. 2009).

Playas increase the biodiversity of the native prairie (Gilbert 1989; Hoagland and Collins 1997; Smith and Haukos 2002; Cariveau and Pavlacky 2009). Considering the number of plant species occurring in playas and despite the variable climate of the western High Plains, species richness is remarkably predictable (Haukos and Smith 2004). On average, one can expect 13 species in the extant assemblage at any point during the growing season of a functional playa, and 19 species are likely to occur throughout the growing season (Haukos and Smith 2004). This pattern exists because few available niches exist in playas (Smith and Haukos 2002). The circular shape, short sloping edge, consistent soil type, and flat bottoms of playas limit variation across multiple potential gradients that influence richness of plant communities.

As a result of ordination and cluster analyses, 12 species assemblages (i.e., species most likely to occur together in a playa) exist in the western High Plains when all playas are combined in all land-use types (e.g., grassland and cropland; Haukos and Smith 2004). However, separating playas by watershed condition resulted in the identification of 14 groups in playas with cropland watersheds and 16 groups in playas in native grassland (Haukos and Smith 2004). Across the landscape of the southern Great Plains, the growing season gradient had more influence on the species composition of extant vegetation in playas than the rainfall gradient (Haukos and Smith 2004).

Composition of seed banks in playas is directly related to extant vegetation. Occurrence of any species in the extant assemblage, given appropriate environmental conditions, is limited only by occurrence in the seed bank, playa location, and potentially dispersal ability within the High Plains (Haukos and Smith 1993a, 1994b, 2004). Species persisting in

seed banks of playas do not germinate all available seeds during favorable environmental conditions, but rather some viable seed remains as a hedge against the unpredictable environment (Haukos and Smith 2001). These life-history strategies associated with seed banks allow each playa to respond rapidly and appropriately to environmental changes. Any impacts to seed banks in playas (e.g., burial or removal of the hydric soil) have significant impacts on ecological functions of playas as well as potential local extirpation of species.

Plant assemblages in playas are dependent upon natural water-level fluctuation to persist and maximize biological productivity (Haukos and Smith 1993a, 1994b, 2001). Because playas are dominated by annuals and short-lived perennials within a dynamic environment, under most conditions it is unlikely that competition is a major factor in the development of an extant plant community (Haukos and Smith 1994b). Playas with moist-soil conditions (saturated soil with little standing water) develop communities dominated by mudflat annuals capable of producing large quantities of seed and associated cover of high value for wildlife (Haukos and Smith 1993b). Dry playas are characterized by plant species more commonly found in the surrounding uplands, including species of the native prairie (Haukos and Smith 2004). In the southern Great Plains, diversity is greatest in playas with moist soil conditions, followed by those with dry conditions, and then flooded playas (Haukos and Smith 2004). Playa area positively influences the number of obligate wetland species because larger playas tend to remain flooded longer (Smith and Haukos 2002).

Unlike many other wetland systems that contain some sort of ecological gradient (e.g., elevation, salinity, soil structure, nutrients), which causes variation in species composition (Johnson, Sharik, et al. 1987; Welling, Pederson, et al. 1988), individual playas have a limited elevational gradient (Haukos and Smith 1994b). Therefore, other than a few species usually limited to the playa edge (e.g., *Oenothera canescens, Lippia nodiflora, Malvella leprosa*), there is little zonation of plant assemblages in western High Plains playas (Haukos and Smith 1994b). The Rainwater Basin playas have a more defined depth gradient, which resulted in the identification of four vegetation zones (Gilbert 1989).

Watershed disturbance negatively impacts plant communities in western High Plains playas. Smith and Haukos (2002) found that playas with cultivated watersheds had more exotic species and more annuals for both richness and percent cover than playas in native grassland. In Colorado, Cariveau and Pavlacky (2008) reported that playas with grassland watersheds had more perennial grass cover, less cover by annuals, and greater species richness than playas with cultivated watersheds. Seed banks of playas with cultivated watersheds are dominated by annuals, which is likely a response to the shortened hydroperiod for these wetlands due to increased sediment accumulation (Haukos and Smith 1993a).

Animal Communities

Many animal species in the High Plains are completely dependent on wet playas for at least part of their life cycle. Dry playas also provide critical resources for resident and migratory animals. The very nature of playas, fluctuating through unpredictable wet and dry phases, enhances their ability to provide resources to a diversity of animal life. Invertebrates contribute the most to animal diversity in playas, yet overall remain the least studied group of animals. Of the currently published work, most has focused on invertebrates in wet playas. However, the invertebrate fauna in wet playas likely differs significantly from dry playas and those recently inundated (Smith 2003). Our knowledge of invertebrates during the dry phase is less documented. Undoubtedly, many invertebrate species inhabiting playas are yet to be discovered, as evidenced by the recent description of a new species of arachnid in playas (Cokendolpher, Torrence, et al. 2007).

Invertebrates

Nonetheless, the studies that have been performed demonstrate a diverse invertebrate community inhabiting playas (Sublette and Sublette 1967; Davis 1996; Anderson 1997; Hall, Sites, et al. 1999). To date, greater than 170 taxa of invertebrates have been documented in playas. However, few studies have identified invertebrates beyond the family level, and therefore 170 taxa is an extremely conservative estimate. As a group, aquatic insects, some brachiopods, and ostracods are probably the most studied and well documented in playas. However, many of the other invertebrate groups have received far less study, and information on their diversity and natural history in playas is less well known.

Amphibians and Reptiles

Amphibians and birds are the most numerous vertebrates associated with playas. Fourteen species of amphibians, representing six families, may be found using wet playas as breeding and rearing habitat (Smith 2003). The most commonly encountered species include several species of anurans (Great Plains toad [*Bufo cognatus*], New Mexico spadefoot toad [*Spea multiplicata*], Plains spadefoot toad [*S. bomifrons*], and spotted chorus frog [*Pseudacris clarkii*]) and the tiger salamander *(Ambystoma tigrinum)*. The other species encountered less frequently include members of the families Bufonidae, Hylidae, Microhylidae, Pelobatidae, and Ranidae (Anderson, Haukos, et al. 1999).

The life history strategies employed by High Plains amphibians are well suited for life in variable hydroperiods of playas. Spadefoots (*Spea* spp.) in particular are well adapted to successfully breed in potentially short hydroperiods. These species can emerge from underground, assemble at playas immediately after inundation, and breed, and the eggs hatch within a 48-hour period (Degenhardt, Painter, et al. 1996). Spadefoot larvae have the ability to reach metamorphosis within as little as two weeks. Other species such as plains leopard frog *(Rana blairi)* have longer hydroperiod requirements for reproduction, which limits their ability for successful reproduction to playas that hold water for relatively extended periods of time (Fig. 21.2b). Salamanders are reliant on longer hydroperiods, and typically are found in their greatest numbers in those rare playas that hold water from one breeding season to the next (Ghioca and Smith 2008).

Although the amphibian community in playas is represented by only a few species, the potential production of new individuals is substantial. Next to invertebrates, the numbers of amphibians produced each year far exceeds any other animal associated with playas. Literally tens of thousands of anurans can emerge from a single playa over the course of one or two months in summer (Gray and Smith 2005). Most of these new individuals likely die before the following spring,

FIG. 21.2. Long-billed curlews (A), a species of concern in the High Plains that is associated with native grassland playas, and plains leopard frog (B), a species that requires long hydroperiods to complete metamorphosis in the High Plains, are just two of a multitude of species dependent on playas to fulfill their life cycle. (Photos by Ross Tsai.)

however, suffering losses to desiccation, predation, overwinter freezing, and starvation (Torrence 2007).

Because amphibian presence and reproductive success in a playa is tightly linked to hydrology (which is affected by land use), many recent studies have examined amphibians in playas embedded in cropland versus native grassland watersheds. Results of these studies have consistently shown land-use-related effects on resident amphibians at the individual, population, and community levels. For example, larval and adult spadefoots, Great Plains toad, and tiger salamander were typically smaller in cropland than grassland playas, which have longer hydroperiods (Gray and Smith 2005). In addition, studies of land-use-related effects on development showed altered immune system development and reduced fatty acid composition of resident spadefoots, particularly at the larval stage of development (McMurry, Smith, et al. 2009; Ghioca-Robrecht, Anderson, et al. 2010). These land-use-related effects also manifest themselves as altered phenotypic expression in the morphology of resident species known for their developmental plasticity, such as tiger salamander (Ghioca and Smith 2008) and spadefoots (Ghioca-Robrecht, Smith, et al. 2009). For example, Ghioca and Smith (2008) found typical, intermediate, and cannibal morphs of tiger salamanders in Southern High Plains playas. They identified cannibal morphs by their broader head, enlarged vomerine ridges, and elongated teeth, and intermediate morphs as those externally resembling typical salamanders but with elongated teeth. Longer hydroperiods, as typical for native grassland playas, were positively associated with the presence of cannibal morph tiger salamanders, which in turn negatively influenced the presence of intermediate morphs in favor of typical morphs (Ghioca and Smith 2008). When cannibal morphs were absent, however, intermediate and typical morphs were equally represented. New Mexico spadefoot and especially Plains spadefoot toads can express two distinct morphotypes; carnivores and omnivores. In playas, the presence of the carnivore type is strongly related to the presence of tiger salamander, which predominate in grassland playas with longer hydroperiods (Ghioca-Robrecht, Smith, et al. 2009). Thus, land use in uplands can completely alter trophic structure of wetlands. Although expression of the carnivore type has been positively correlated to the density of fairy shrimp (order Anostraca), Ghioca-Robrecht, Smith, et al. (2009) found no correlation between the presence of carnivores and shrimp in playas.

Other modifications typically associated with playas include the presence of pits and trenches in playas for holding irrigation and/or drinking water for livestock. The presence of pits in many cropland playas has altered the resident amphibian community to some degree by providing a relatively stable water supply in most years, even when the playa itself has dried (Guthery and Bryant 1982). Pits that hold water year-round can provide the resources needed for supporting salamanders, bullfrogs (Rana catesbeiana), and fish. Fish in particular are not part of the natural fauna of playas because of their frequent drying.

Reptiles occur in playas, yet their ecology therein has not been studied to any significant degree. Yellow mud turtles (Kinosternon flavescens), the only native aquatic reptile in the western Plains, are regularly encountered in wet playas and along playa edges, and several species of snakes and lizards have been observed using dry playas and playa edges, yet their ecology as related to playas has not been studied (Smith 2003). Other turtle species occur in the Rainwater Basin but have not been surveyed.

Birds

Dozens of species of waterfowl, shorebirds, passerines, and others use playas as stopover sites during migration, nesting sites, and feeding sites (Haukos and Smith 1994a). Whether inundated or dry, playas are used by birds year-round as dictated by species-specific habitat requirements and season (e.g., migration, breeding) (Smith 2003). Different accounts note a little over 100 nonwaterfowl avian species found in playas in the Southern High Plains, nearly 60 to 80% of which were migrants (Simpson and Bolen 1981; Fischer, Schibler, et al. 1982). Indeed, migrants significantly increase the number of species associated with playas, as observed by Flowers (1996), who found 168 species of birds (mostly during migration) associated with playas in Meade County, Kansas.

Shorebirds frequent playas throughout the High Plains during migration, as they provide resting and feeding sites critical for replenishing depleted energy stores. In the Southern High Plains, Davis and Smith (1998a) found 30 species of migrating shorebirds using playas, and in Kansas, 26 species were observed (Flowers 1996). Playas with mudflats are preferred (Davis and Smith 1998a), and shorebirds using these wetlands

spend most of their time feeding, typically consuming invertebrates and to a lesser extent seeds of wetland plants (Davis and Smith 1998b). Heavy reliance on invertebrates and the sheer numbers of shorebirds that use playas during migration as feeding sites (estimated in the millions; Davis and Smith 1998a) result in significant opportunities for competition for food (Davis and Smith 2001). However, differential use of habitats among foraging guilds and asynchronous migration times likely minimize competition for food (Helmers 1991; Skagen and Knopf 1994; Davis and Smith 1998a).

Far fewer shorebird species nest around playas than use them during migration. Yet playas and associated uplands are important nesting habitat for many shorebird species, including American avocets (Recurvirostra americana), killdeer (Charadrius vociferus), black-necked stilts (Himantopus mexicanus), and some snowy plovers (C. alexandrinus). Generally, these birds nest along playa edges with sparse vegetation, avoiding playas with dense vegetation. Thus, playas surrounded with CRP plantings may be less suitable as nesting sites for many shorebirds, depending on the structure of the plants. Estimates of 258,000 avocet and 30,000 killdeer nests were proposed as possible for playas in the Southern High Plains if hydrologic conditions were suitable (Conway 2001). Native grassland around playas, although limited, serves as nesting habitat for two species of concern, the long-billed curlew (Numenius americanus; Fig. 21.2a) and mountain plover (C. montanus) (Smith 2003).

The number of waterfowl using playas during migration and as wintering and nesting sites can be staggering. Indeed, millions of waterfowl, representing 25 species, are known to use playas during spring and winter (USFWS 1988a; Gersib, Cornely, et al. 1990; Smith 2003). Dabbling ducks, lesser snow geese (Chen caerulescens), cackling geese (Branta hutchinsii), and Canada geese (B. canadensis) are the most common. Estimates for playas in the Rainwater Basin suggest that 90% of the midcontinental population of white-fronted geese (Anser albifrons) use these wetlands (Benning 1987). Estimates for ducks were lower but still impressive, at 50% and 30% of the midcontinent population of mallards (Anas platyrhynchos) and northern pintails (A. acuta), respectively, using these playas in spring (USFWS and Nebraska GPC 1986). Similar estimates for other playa regions in the Great Plains do not exist.

The Southern High Plains represents a major wintering area for waterfowl in the Central Flyway, and it is estimated that 500,000 to 2.8 million ducks and 100,000 to 750,000 snow, Canada, and cackling geese winter in the region (Simpson and Bolen 1981; USFWS 1988a). Although these estimates are approximate due to reasons such as inconsistent sampling areas and techniques (Strickland, Harju, et al. 1994), Southern High Plains playas can be the most important wintering habitat in the Central Flyway for many species of waterfowl, particularly mallards and pintails (Bellrose 1980; Bergan and Smith 1993; Moon and Haukos 2006, 2008). Playas typically provide shallow water habitat favored by dabbling ducks, and consequently dabbling ducks such as mallard, northern pintail, American wigeon (Anas americana), and green-winged teal (A. crecca) are most common (Simpson and Bolen 1981). Diving ducks are less common in playas, although they can be locally abundant given suitable habitat (Smith 2003).

In addition, many duck species use playas and associated uplands as nesting and brood-rearing habitat. The most common species to nest in or near playas in the western High Plains are mallard, blue-winged teal (Anas discors), and cinnamon teal (A. cyanoptera), although others such as redhead (Aythya americana), ruddy duck (Oxyura jamaicensis), and northern pintail will nest as well (Traweek 1978; Rhodes 1978, 1979; Smith and Haukos 1995; Flowers 1996; Seyffert 2001; Ray, Sullivan, et al. 2003). The nesting season can range from April through August, making it difficult to estimate annual production. In addition, successful production of ducklings varies by year as local environmental conditions fluctuate (e.g., wet versus dry years). However, production has been estimated at 250,000 in wet years in playas throughout the traditionally defined five-state playa region (USFWS 1988a).

Waterfowl, especially ducks, derive substantial nutritional benefits from invertebrate and seed production afforded by playas. Indeed, diets composed of relatively greater amounts of invertebrates and seeds of annual wetland plants are considered to be of greater nutritional value than grains typical of agricultural fields (Haukos and Smith 1995). The importance of playas as a source of high-quality and abundant food is further supported by studies demonstrating increased body condition and survival of ducks (e.g., pintails) and postponed use of agricultural fields as feeding sites during years with greater numbers of wet playas (Smith and Sheeley 1993a,b). Observations for mallard and pintail hens during winter note body condition and survival rates were lowest in dry years (Bergan and Smith 1993; Moon and Haukos 2006, 2009). Although playas provide both seeds and invertebrates as food sources for ducks, results of studies show that invertebrates are the preferred food for some species (e.g., green-winged teal; Anderson, Smith, et al. 2000).

Mammals

More than 50 mammal species may associate with playas, yet to date, their ecology has not been studied to any significant degree. Dry playas with vegetative cover likely support the most mammals, with eastern cottontails *(Sylvilagus floridanus)* and various species of rodents most abundant (Scribner 1982; Smith 2003). Other species, including coyotes *(Canis latrans),* feral hogs *(Sus scrofa),* white-tailed and mule deer *(Odocoileus virginianus, O. hemionus),* raccoons *(Procyon lotor),* and others, utilize dry playas and in some cases wet playas as feeding areas and security cover. Generally, though, mammal ecology in playas has not been extensively studied (Smith 2003).

Ecosystem Drivers

Geomorphic setting and climate are the primary drivers influencing wetland ecosystem structure and function (Euliss, Smith, et al. 2008), including playas. Although precipitation can occur any time in the High Plains, when it does occur it is often intense, being associated with thunderstorms in late spring, then occurring sporadically through summer and reaching another high point in early autumn, albeit less frequently than spring events. Because of the intense nature of most precipitation events and the depressional wetland setting, precipitation runoff is the most important hydrologic input affecting playa water budgets. Average annual precipitation ranges from 38 cm in the southwest to 63 cm in the north-central portion of the region, while potential evaporation is 284 cm and 165 cm, respectively, for those same geographical extremes. These climatic factors, therefore, can lead to shorter hydroperiods for playas in the southern areas versus those in the north.

Playa hydroperiods can range from a few days to greater than a year, but rarely last longer than a few months following a precipitation event without additional precipitation (Tsai, Venne, et al. 2007). Regional climatic conditions cause great variability in playa hydroperiod, which in any given year can range from dry to inundated conditions for an entire year (Smith, Euliss, et al. 2008). In a recent analysis of frequency of playas inundated during midwinter (the driest time of year: January) in Texas and thus available for use by wintering waterfowl, it was found that over a 9-year period none of the sampled playas were inundated every January, and that factors contributing to likelihood of a playa being flooded during January include a negative relationship to the proportion of cropland in the watershed (i.e., reduced hydroperiods for playas with cropland watersheds) and positive relationships with average annual rainfall and playa size (W. Johnson, Texas Parks and Wildlife Department, unpublished data).

Hydroperiod is the major driver influencing all biota and other abiotic services such as recharge. For example, soil moisture influences fissure formation in the hydric vertisol (soils with a high content of expansive clay known as montmorillonite) clay soils and therefore subsequent infiltration (Wood, Rainwater, et al. 1997). Moreover, biota that inhabit playas must be adapted to variable hydroperiods. Common features of playa biota include rapid development times allowing species to complete life-history requirements before a playa dries, extended dormancy or aestivation abilities, and advanced mobility/migratory capabilities (invertebrates, vertebrates, and plants; e.g., Haukos and Smith 1994b; Anderson and Smith 2004; Ghioca and Smith 2008).

The overall trophic structure and relative abundance of different organisms change dramatically over the playa hydroperiod. Immediately following inundation, invertebrates are best characterized by low diversity but high abundance as species hatch from dormant egg banks (Moorehead, Hall, et al. 1998; Anderson and Smith 2004). Amphibians, particularly Plains and New Mexican spadefoots, immediately congregate and breed upon playa inundation, producing larvae within as little as 72 hours. With time, more species colonize the wet playa and abundances of different species increases (Skelly 1997; Moorehead, Hall, et al. 1998). However, extended hydroperiods allow for increased predation and competition among residents, which along with the completion of life cycles for certain species, results in a drop in community diversity (Neckles, Murkin, et al. 1990). This series of events obviously greatly influences the biotic relationships within a playa. Effects on hydroperiod and the distribution of functional playas in the landscape, whether from anthropogenic or natural causes, influence the presence of species and their relationships in playas.

The fluctuating hydroperiod also drives all processes such as nutrient cycling and decomposition and therefore energy flow. As with most wetlands, playas are detrital-system-based, but decomposition in playas is relatively rapid during periods of fluctuating water levels and greater availability of oxygen (Anderson and Smith 2002). Indeed, organic carbon in playa soils from southern regions is usually less than 1.5% (Allen, Harris, et al. 1972; Luo 1994). Haukos and Smith (1996) found that levels of soil nutrients in playas varied depending on soil moisture, with nitrogen and phosphorus potentially limiting during wet and dry years, respectively. Although playas are detrital-based, we know little about the fungal and bacterial communities regulating that process (Anderson and Smith 2002).

In addition to precipitation and evapotranspiration, playa

FIG. 21.3. Sediment removal as a restoration practice occurring in the Rainwater Basin. (Photo by Randy Stutheit, courtesy of the Nebraska Game and Parks Commission.)

depth and watershed land use and size (regulating runoff amounts) are primary influences on hydroperiod (Tsai, Venne, et al. 2007). Cultivated watersheds allow more water to run off and enter the wetland, and that water carries sediments and other potential pollutants (Smith, Haukos, et al. 2011). Sediment accumulation in playas negatively affects the flood storage service provided by playas and results in increased flooding of croplands, roads, utilities, and other nonwetland areas. Although effects of sediment on aquifer recharge are unknown, the potential exists for polluted water in playas to contaminate underlying aquifers (Wells, Huddleston, et al. 1970; Felty, Moeller, et al. 1972; Zartman, Ramsey, et al. 1996). As noted above, tall, dense stands of nonnative grasses typical of much of the CRP plantings effectively reduce soil erosion and sedimentation, but they also cause the wetland to increasingly become more xeric because they restrict water from entering the playa (Smith, Haukos, et al. 2011). Although native grassland (primarily shortgrass prairie in the western plains and mixed to tall grass prairie in central Nebraska) does not have as much runoff as cropland, native grassland playas typically have longer hydroperiods because there has been much less sediment deposition into these playas.

Wetland modifications that maintain water over longer periods of time also influence the hydroperiod driver that affects delivery of natural services. Playas deepened for urban floodwater storage or wastewater/sewage storage are obviously providing a municipal service, but natural ecological function is completely altered, causing changes in biological communities and permitting existence of exotic species such as fish (Smith 2003). Moreover, natural ecosystem processes such as decomposition are altered.

Conservation Concerns and Threats

The value of High Plains playas has been recognized nationally and internationally, and these valuable wetlands occur within the Playa Lakes and Rainwater Basin Joint Ventures under the North American Waterfowl Management Plan, which targets

wetland conservation within those respective regions. Playas have been included in other landscape-level conservation plans, such as with Ducks Unlimited and the Nature Conservancy. Unfortunately, conservation of playas in the western High Plains has been deficient relative to stated goals. Furthermore, the Playa Lakes Joint Venture has expanded its priorities from playa conservation to other habitats and species in the region. In contrast, the Rainwater Basin Joint Venture has maintained its playa focus and is achieving relatively greater conservation accomplishments in Nebraska (www.rwbjv.org/; Smith 2003). The Rainwater Basin playas are priorities for state (Nebraska GPC) and federal (USFWS, USDA NRCS) governmental agencies and several nongovernmental agencies (Nature Conservancy, Pheasants Forever, Ducks Unlimited). They use a variety of conservation approaches to achieve wetland protection goals, including federal and state purchases of individual wetlands, active pursuit of conservation easements, intensive restoration of lost and degraded wetlands (Fig. 21.3), and implementation of management practices (e.g., water-level management, spring flooding, prescribed fire, managed livestock grazing).

One of the most difficult obstacles to playa conservation in the western High Plains is the lack of understanding of these ecosystems by society and governmental agencies. Greater than 99% of western Great Plains playas are privately owned, and thus most management-orientated research and conservation must be acceptable to private landowners and compatible with local agricultural activities. Yet a survey of landowners in the western High Plains (Playa Lakes Joint Venture 2006) found that only half of landowners had heard the term *playa* and did not know that playas recharge the Ogallala Aquifer. As with landowners throughout the Great Plains, High Plains landowners considered wetland conservation a low priority and would require financial incentives to consider wetland protection, and were concerned with potential imposed state and federal regulations due to playas on their land. Landowners who considered playas a positive influence identified attracting wildlife as the highest-priority benefit. When landowners understand the beneficial functions of playas, efforts

TABLE 21.1
Estimated number of playa wetlands in the High Plains
from a variety of data sources

State	Number of playas	Total area (ha)	Mean playa size (ha)
Nebraska			
Western playas[a]	15,812	8,893	0.56
Rainwater basins[b]	1,811	32,313	17.84
Colorado[c]	8,347	22,537	2.70
Kansas[d]	22,045	32,929	1.49
Kansas[e]	9,900	37,000	4.22
Southern Great Plains[f]			
Kansas	2,806	11,963	4.26
Colorado	198	675	3.14
Oklahoma	585	3,876	6.62
New Mexico	2,462	9,731	3.95
Texas	19,339	140,150	7.25
Total for southern Great Plains	25,390	166,395	6.55
Texas[g]	20,577	155,974	7.58

[a] Cariveau and Pavlacky 2009 (NWI, SSURGO, LANDSAT, NAIP imagery, field observations, PLJV Landcover; 12 counties).

[b] A. Bishop, Rainwater Basin Joint Venture, personal communication (aerial surveys, historic soil surveys, SSURGO, NWI).

[c] Cariveau and Pavlacky 2008 (SSURGO, LANDSAT, National Hydrography Dataset; 27 counties).

[d] Bowen, Johnson, et al. 2010 (Aerial Photo, Digital Raster Graphics, SSURGO; 46 counties).

[e] Johnson and Campbell 2004 (SSURGO; 40 counties).

[f] Guthery, Bryant, et al. 1981 (hydric soils on historical soil surveys; 39 counties in Texas, 4 counties in New Mexico, 3 counties in Oklahoma, 7 counties in Kansas, and 1 county in Colorado).

[g] Fish, Atkinson, et al. 1998 (hydric soils on historical soil surveys; 65 counties in Texas).

to conserve playas should be enhanced (Haukos 1995), thus highlighting the need for education.

There is a vital need to identify playas that provide critical connections and ecological links among playas for conservation planning. Unfortunately, inconsistent definitions of playas, variation in spatial sampling, multiple data sources, and variable field validation efforts have led to variation and debate on the number, location, and area of playas in the western Great Plains (Table 21.1). This lack of a consistent estimate of the number of existing and functional playas results from different criteria used to define playa locations in different parts of the High Plains and the unknown rate of historical playa loss. Some studies have used the presence of hydric soils from historical United States Department of Agriculture (USDA) soil surveys (i.e., 1950–60s) to define a playa location (e.g., Guthery, Bryant, et al. 1981; Fish, Atkinson, et al. 1998), whereas others have used topographic relief data whereby any depression was counted as a playa (e.g., Sabin and Holliday 1995) and others used a combination of soil surveys, topographic maps, and aerial imagery (Cariveau and Pavlacky 2008, 2009). Each of these methods has limitations. Obviously, confirmed presence of a hydric soil leads to a known location of a playa. However,

the locations of all hydric soils have not been mapped in the High Plains. For example, if the extent of a particular hydric soil was less than 1–2 ha, the USDA soils mapping teams may have chosen to include that hydric soil area within the dominant upland series, especially in drier, western portions of the High Plains. Because playas are typically small, disregarding the occurrence of potentially hydric soil < 2 ha in area will lead to a conservative estimate of the number of playas. This has become apparent when mapping studies using other sources have resulted in a large increase in the number of playas < 1 ha (e.g., Cariveau and Pavlacky 2008, 2009; Bowen, Johnson, et al. 2010). At the other extreme are locations based solely on topographic data indicating a depression without additional supporting wetland criteria. Not all depressions are playas, and sole use of this criterion leads to liberal estimates of playa numbers. Unfortunately, few of the data sets for mapping playa locations have been ground-truthed. Although it appears that the northern states (Nebraska, Colorado, and Kansas) contain more individual playas than the southern states (Oklahoma, New Mexico, Texas), this is confounded by the previously mentioned lack of consistency in the determination of playa location across the High Plains. We propose that identification of a playa must include (1) an isolated depression capable of collecting and storing precipitation runoff via internal drainage; and (2) presence of a hydric soil buried or on the surface.

Ecological function and service loss is related to ecosystem degradation, primarily through anthropogenic impacts to playas and their watersheds. Because of the density of playas in the western High Plains, especially the Southern High Plains, it is difficult for any anthropogenic activity not to potentially impact one or more playas. Unfortunately, it is likely that a vast percentage of any estimated number of playas contains lost and degraded playas, so that the true level of cumulative ecological functions (e.g., total aquifer recharge, available volume for stormwater storage, amount of natural habitat for wildlife) is typically overestimated. Physical loss and degradation of playas primarily occur via deliberate and unintentional filling of the hydric-soil volume of playas, excavation of hydric soil to concentrate collected water, and continued cultivation of hydric soils. Draining of playas has been most extensive in the Rainwater Basin, whereas most playa impacts in the Southern High Plains have been due to sedimentation (Luo, Smith, et al. 1997). Moreover, accumulation of as little as 5 mm of sediment can nearly eliminate seedling and invertebrate emergence in wetlands (Gleason, Euliss, et al. 2003). These factors reduce hydroperiod and increase loss of available sources of plants and invertebrates, negatively influencing the ability of the ecosystem to respond to changing environmental conditions. Additional anthropogenic activities potentially impacting ecological function of playas include (1) modification of playa structure through construction of road and stormwater storage pits (typically in urban settings where playas are incorporated into stormwater drainage systems); (2) contamination of playas by feedlot, dairy, and urban runoff; (3) direct application of pesticides and fertilizers; (4) storage of industrial waste; (5) development of alternative energy (wind, solar, biofuels); (6) unsustainable grazing; (7) inconsistent application and availability of USDA conservation programs and practices among states (e.g., establishment of irrigation systems versus conservation of playas); (8) associated powerlines; and (9) oil and gas production. The individual and cumulative impacts of these activities have not been quantified but are increasing throughout the High Plains

Watershed management is critical for playa management because all activities in a playa's watershed will affect the playa (Smith, Euliss, et al. 2008). Practices to minimize impacts of cultivated watersheds include contour plowing and field listing, reduction of tillage events (including no-till practices), precision application of nutrients and pesticides (including avoidance of wetland areas), establishment of vegetated waterways, and creation of maintained vegetated buffer areas around playas (Haukos 1994, 1995; Skagen, Melcher, et al. 2008). Vegetated waterways and buffer areas should be composed of native species and extend a suggested upland buffer a minimum of 40 m from the playa edge (L. Johnson, Texas Tech University, unpublished data).

Federal protection under Section 404 of the Clean Water Act for playas and other isolated wetlands was removed by a January 2001 Supreme Court decision (Haukos and Smith 2003). Combined with the lack of state-level regulations for all playa states, loss of potential protection under the Clean Water Act has resulted in little legal protection for playas (Haukos and Smith 2003). Although still potentially subject to the USDA "Swampbuster" provision enacted by the 1985 Food Security Act, extended natural dry periods allow for frequent cultivation and other activities without incurring violation. Further-more, jurisdictional status is necessary to establish eligibility for many wetland conservation programs (e.g., North American Wetlands Conservation Act grants). At this time, it is impossible to determine the number of playas lost due to the Supreme Court decision or lack of any other federal or state laws, regulations, or policies, but we surmise the number of lost individual playas due to lack of regulatory protection is considerable.

The most subtle example of loss of jurisdictional status is the current effort by USDA to reclassify playa soils in the Southern High Plains, whereby reclassification of a former hydric soil into a nonhydric series removes potential remaining regulatory or incentive options for conservation of playas as well as eliminates the former playa location from soil survey maps. Preliminary assessment of this effort indicates the potential removal of hydric soil status from > 50% of previously defined playa wetlands in the Southern High Plains of Texas (Johnson, Haukos, et al. 2010). The ability to monitor playa loss and changes in connectivity of the landscape is reduced by the removal of hydric soil locations because it creates inaccuracies in the location of playas. Currently, the USDA Soil Survey Geographic database (SSURGO) contains both the historical soil survey for counties yet to be reclassified and some counties for which soils have been reclassified, which can cause confusion relative to playa conservation. Consequently, continued reclassification and the subsequent use of these soil surveys will impede conservation.

The most economically and ecologically sound management of playas impacted by agriculture is to protect the integrity of the wetland from sedimentation and contamination. Playa restoration should start with restoration of the watershed for native prairie. Then sediment removal and pit filling can be accomplished (Fig. 21.3). Following restoration of natural hydrology with proper vegetation response, additional management would be minimal. Managers should also consider revival of the historic role of fire (5–10 year fire frequency [Wright and Bailey 1982]) and herbivory through prescribed burning and proper grazing management of the associated watershed.

As noted above, more conservation dollars have been spent on Rainwater Basin playas than those of western High Plains. Furthermore, to dramatically reduce playa loss across the High Plains, landowners, communities, and conservation organizations in the western High Plains must be allowed access to conservation dollars and initiatives (e.g., Wetland Reserve Program, wetland easements, formation of Wetland Management Districts) similar to those available in the Rainwater Basin and other portions of the U.S. Even without sufficient conservation funding, some rural communities have gotten involved in playa education and conservation efforts through organization of rural development groups (e.g., Ogallala Commons, www.ogallalacommons.org/), but considerably more resources are needed to conserve the playa system of the High Plains.

Haukos and Smith (2003) outlined several steps that must be taken to ensure conservation of playas, including (1) increased promotion and implementation of existing federal and state conservation programs specifically for playas; (2) proposed state regulations and incentives specifically for playas; (3) recognition of agricultural impacts on wetland jurisdictional determination; (4) creation of Federal Playa Wetland Management Districts in the western High Plains to preserve intact, functioning playas as is done in the Rainwater Basin; and (5) increased public education on the value of playas. In addition, inclusion of isolated tracts containing playas in the National

Wildlife Refuge system of the USFWS would conserve playas, assist in the education of the importance of playas, provide public access for individuals to discover and understand playa ecology, help stabilize rural economies, and permit recreational activities that are rarely available in the region.

Possibilities for landowner conservation funding of playas include USDA programs (Wetland Reserve Program, Conservation Practice 23A of the Conservation Reserve Program [establishment of wetland buffer areas]), federal and state private land assistance program (e.g., USFWS Partners for Fish and Wildlife, State Wildlife Grants), nongovernmental organizations (e.g., the Nature Conservancy, Rocky Mountain Bird Observatory, Ducks Unlimited), and assistance from the Playa Lakes and Rainwater Basin Joint Ventures under the North American Waterfowl Management Plan. Seldom are these promoted within the western High Plains.

Conclusions

Without playa wetlands, the benefits of playa services to humans in the High Plains, such as aquifer recharge, flood storage, biodiversity provisioning, and recreation, are essentially gone. The number of playas necessary to fully provide the ecosystem functions necessary to support these services of the western Great Plains is unknown, but loss and degradation of playas to date have resulted in the marked decline in the delivery of ecosystem services necessary for the long-term persistence of plant and animal communities. Unless meaningful conservation occurs within the next two decades, it is unlikely that 10% of the existing playas will remain functional based on current sedimentation trends alone. Conservation over most of the region to date has failed.

References

Allen BL, Harris BL, et al. 1972. *The mineralogy and chemistry of High Plains playa lake soils and sediments.* WRC-72-4. Lubbock: Texas Tech Univ.

Anderson AM, Haukos DA, Anderson JT. 1999. Habitat use by anurans emerging and breeding in playa wetlands. *Wildl. Soc. Bull.* 27:750–69.

Anderson JT. 1997. *Invertebrate communities in vegetated playa wetlands.* Ph.D. diss., Texas Tech Univ., Lubbock.

Anderson JT, Smith LM. 1998. Protein and energy production in playas: implications for migratory bird management. *Wetlands* 18:437–46.

Anderson JT, Smith LM. 1999. Carrying capacity and diel use of managed playa wetlands by nonbreeding waterbirds. *Wildl. Soc. Bull.* 27:281–91.

Anderson JT, Smith LM. 2000. Invertebrate response to moist-soil management of playa wetlands. *Ecol. Appl.* 10:550–58.

Anderson JT, Smith LM. 2002. The effect of flooding regimes on decomposition of *Polygonum pensylvanicum* in playa wetlands (southern Great Plains, USA). *Aquat. Bot.* 29:1–12.

Anderson JT, Smith LM. 2004. Persistence and colonization strategies of playa wetland invertebrates. *Hydrobiologia* 513:77–86.

Anderson JT, Smith LM, Haukos DA. 2000. Food selection and feather molt by non-breeding American green-winged teal in Texas playas. *J. Wildl. Manag.* 64:220–30.

Bellrose FC Jr. 1980. *Ducks, geese and swans of North America.* Washington, DC: Wildlife Management Inst.

Benning DS. 1987. *Coordinated mid-continent white-fronted goose survey.* Denver: USFWS.

Bergan JF, Smith LM. 1993. Survival rates of female mallards wintering in the Playa Lakes Region. *J. Wildl. Manag.* 57:570–77.

Berthelsen PS, Smith LM, George RR. 1990. Ring-necked pheasant nesting ecology and production on CRP lands in the Texas Southern High Plains. *Trans. N. Am. Wildl. Nat. Resour. Conf.* 55:46–56.

Bolen EG, Smith LM, Schramm HL Jr. 1989. Playa lakes: prairie wetlands of the Southern High Plains. *BioScience* 39:615–23.

Bowen MW, Johnson WC, et al. 2010. A GIS-based approach to identify and map playa wetlands on the High Plains, Kansas, USA. *Wetlands* 30:675–84.

Cariveau AB, Pavlacky D. 2008. *Assessment and conservation of playas in eastern Colorado: final report to the Colorado Division of Wildlife, Playa Lakes Joint Venture, United States Environmental Protection Agency, and United States Fish and Wildlife Service.* Brighton, CO: Rocky Mountain Bird Observatory.

Cariveau AB, Pavlacky D. 2009. *Biological inventory and evaluation of conservation strategies in Southwest playa wetlands: final report to the Nebraska Game and Parks Commission and the Playa Lakes Joint Venture.* Brighton, CO: Rocky Mountain Bird Observatory.

Cokendolpher JC, Torrence SM, et al. 2007. New Linyphiidae spiders associated with playas in the Southern High Plains (Llano Estacado) of Texas (Arachnida: Araneae). *Zootaxa* 1529:49–60.

Conway WC. 2001. *Breeding ecology of shorebirds in the Playa Lakes Region of Texas.* Ph.D. diss., Texas Tech Univ., Lubbock.

Curtis D, Beierman H. 1980. *Playa lakes characterization study.* Fort Worth, TX: USFWS.

Cushing CE, Mazaika RR, Phillips RC. 1993. *Ecological investigations at the Pantex plant.* USDOE Contract DE-AC06-76RLO 1830. Amarillo, TX: Battelle, Pacific Northwest Laboratory.

Davis CA. 1996. *Ecology of spring and fall migrant shorebirds in the Playa Lakes region of Texas.* Ph.D. diss., Texas Tech Univ., Lubbock.

Davis CA, Smith LM. 1998a. Ecology and management of migrant shorebirds in the Playa Lakes Region of Texas. *Wildl. Monogr.* 140.

Davis CA, Smith LM. 1998b. Behavior of migrant shorebirds in playas of the Southern High Plains, Texas. *Condor* 100:266–76.

Davis CA, Smith LM. 2001. Foraging strategies and niche dynamics of coexisting shorebirds at stopover sites in the southern Great Plains. *Auk* 118:484–95.

Davis CA, Bidwell JR, Hickman KR. 2009. Effects of hydrological regimes on competitive interactions of *Schoenoplectus fluviatilis* and two co-occurring wetland plants. *Aquat. Bot.* 91:267–72.

Degenhardt WG, Painter CW, Price AH. 1996. *Amphibians and reptiles of New Mexico.* Albuquerque: Univ. New Mexico Press.

Droste J. 1959. Clay minerals in the playas of the Mojave Desert, California. *Science* 130:100.

Erickson NE, Leslie DM Jr. 1987. *Soil-vegetation correlations in the Sandhills and Rainwater Basin wetlands of Nebraska.* Biological Report 87(11). Washington, DC: USFWS.

Euliss NH Jr, Smith LM, et al. 2008. Linking ecological processes with wetland management goals: charting a course for a sustainable future. *Wetlands* 28:553–62.

Evans GL. 1961. *Investigations at the Odessa meteor craters.* Cratering Symposium, US Atomic Energy Commission Report 6434. Washington, DC.

Evans GL, Meade GE. 1945. Quaternary of the Texas High Plains. *University of Texas Publications* 4401:485–507.

Felty JR, Moeller RL, et al. 1972. Potential pollution of the Ogallala by recharging playa lake water. In *Playa lake symposium,* CC Reeves Jr., editor. Lubbock: International Center for Arid and Semi-Arid Land Studies, Texas Tech Univ., pp. 31–35.

Fischer DH, Schibler MD, et al. 1982. Checklists of birds from the playa lakes of the southern Texas panhandle. *Bull. Texas Ornithol. Soc.* 15:2–7.

Fish EB, Atkinson EL, et al. 1998. *Playa lakes digital database for the Texas portion of the Playa Lakes Joint Venture Region.* Tech. Publ. no. T-9-813. Lubbock: Texas Tech Univ.

Flowers TL. 1996. Classification and occurrences of the birds of the playa lakes of Meade County, Kansas. *Bull. (Kansas Ornithol. Soc.)* 47(2):21–28.

Gersib RA, Cornely J, et al. 1990. *Concept plan for waterfowl habitat protection: Rainwater Basin area of Nebraska category 25 of the North American Waterfowl Management Plan.* Denver, CO: USFWS.

Ghioca DM, Smith LM. 2008. Population structure of *Ambystoma tigrinum mavortium* in playa wetlands: landuse influence and variations in polymorphism. *Copeia* 2008:286–93.

Ghioca-Robrecht DM, Smith LM, Densmore LD. 2009. Ecological

correlates of trophic polyphenism in spadefoot tadpoles inhabiting playas. *Can. J. Zool.* 87:229–38.

Ghioca-Robrecht DM, Anderson TA, et al. 2010. Lipid mass and fatty acid composition of *Spea* spp. in playa wetlands as influenced by land use. *Wetlands* 30:220–30.

Gilbert MC. 1989. *Ordination and mapping of wetland communities in Nebraska's Rainwater Basin region.* CEMRO Environmental Report 89-1. Omaha NE: USACE.

Gilley JE, Patton BD, et al. 1996. Grazing and haying effects on runoff and erosion from a former Conservation Reserve Program site. *Appl. Eng. Agricul.* 12:681–84.

Gleason RA, Euliss NH Jr, et al. 2003. Effects of sediment load on emergence of aquatic invertebrates and plants from wetland soil egg and seed banks. *Wetlands* 23:26–34.

Gray MJ, Smith LM. 2005. Influence of land use on postmetamorphic body size of playa lake amphibians. *J. Wildl. Manage.* 69:515–24.

Great Plains Flora Association. 1991. *Flora of the Great Plains.* Lawrence: Univ. Press of Kansas.

Gurdak JJ, Roe CD. 2009. *Recharge rates and chemistry beneath playas of the High Plains aquifer—a literature review and synthesis.* USGS Circular 1333. Washington, DC.

Gustavson TC, Holliday VT, Hovorka SD. 1995. *Origin and development of playa basins, sources of recharge to the Ogallala Aquifer, Southern High Plains, Texas and New Mexico.* Bureau of Econ. Geol. Report of Investigations 229. Austin: Univ. Texas.

Guthery FS, Bryant FC. 1982. Status of playas in the southern Great Plains. *Wildl. Soc. Bull.* 10:309–17.

Guthery FS, Bryant FC, et al. 1981. *Playa assessment study.* Amarillo, TX: US Water and Power Resources Service.

Hall DL, Sites RW, et al. 1999. Playas of the Southern High Plains: the macroinvertebrate fauna. In *Invertebrates in freshwater wetlands of North America: ecology and management,* Batzer DP, Rader RB, Wissinger SA, editors. New York: Wiley, pp. 635–65.

Haukos DA. 1991. *Vegetation manipulation strategies for playa wetlands.* Ph.D. diss., Texas Tech Univ., Lubbock.

Haukos DA. 1994. Management of playas for wildlife enhancement. In *Proceedings of playa basin symposium,* Urban LV, Wyatt AW, editors. Water Resources Center, Lubbock: Texas Tech University, pp. 267–76.

Haukos DA. 1995. Management of playa wetlands impacted by agriculture. In *Proceedings of the symposium on issues and technology in the management of impacted wildlife,* Foster SO, Pas S, et al., editors. Glenwood Springs, CO: Thorne Ecological Inst., pp. 110–13.

Haukos DA, Smith LM. 1993a. Seed-bank structure and predictive ability of field vegetation in playa lakes. *Wetlands* 13:32–40.

Haukos DA, Smith LM. 1993b. Moist-soil management of playa lakes for migrating and wintering ducks. *Wildl. Soc. Bull.* 21:288–98.

Haukos DA, Smith LM. 1994a. The importance of playa wetlands to biodiversity of the Southern High Plains. *Landsc. Urban Plan.* 28:83–98.

Haukos DA, Smith LM. 1994b. Composition of seed banks along an elevational gradient in playa wetlands. *Wetlands* 14:301–07.

Haukos DA, Smith LM. 1995. Chemical constituents of seeds from moist-soil plants in playa wetlands. *Wildl. Soc. Bull.* 23:514–19.

Haukos DA, Smith LM. 1996. Effects of moist-soil management on playa wetland soils. *Wetlands* 16:143–49.

Haukos DA, Smith LM. 1997. *The common flora of playa lakes.* Lubbock: Texas Tech Univ. Press.

Haukos DA, Smith LM. 2001. Temporal emergence patterns from seed banks of playa lakes. *Wetlands* 21:274–80.

Haukos DA, Smith LM. 2003. Past and future impacts of wetland regulations on playas. *Wetlands* 23:577–89.

Haukos DA, Smith LM. 2004. *Plant communities of playa wetlands.* Special publication of the Museum of Texas Tech University 47.

Helmers DL. 1991. *Habitat use by migrant shorebirds and invertebrate availability in a managed wetland complex.* Master's thesis, Univ. of Missouri, Columbia.

Hoagland B. 1991. *Final report, Colorado playa lake study.* Denver, CO: Nature Conservancy.

Hoagland BW, Collins SL. 1997. Heterogeneity in shortgrass prairie vegetation: the role of playa lakes. *J. Veg. Sci.* 8:277–86.

Johnson L, Haukos DA, et al. 2010. *Current status and function of playa wetlands and evaluation of buffer effectiveness: implications for future conservation efforts.* Dallas, TX: USEPA.

Johnson WC, Campbell JS. 2004. *Playa lakes: database of playa distribution in western Kansas.* Kansas Geol. Survey, Lawrence: Univ. Kansas.

Johnson WC, Sharik TL, et al. 1987. Nature and cause of zonation discreetness around glacial prairie marshes. *Can. J. Bot.* 65:1622–32.

Johnston MC. 1995. *Floristic survey of the Pantex plant site, Carson County, Texas.* Amarillo, TX: USDOE.

Kindscher K. 1994. *Vegetation of western Kansas playa lakes—1994.* Salina, KS: USDA.

Kindscher K, Lauver C. 1993. *Preliminary vegetation analysis of western Kansas playa lakes.* Salina, KS: USDA.

Leck, MA. 1989. Wetland seed banks. In *The ecology of soil seed banks,* Leck MA, Parker VT, Simpson RL, editors. San Diego: Academic Press, pp. 283–305.

Luo HR. 1994. *The effects of land use on sediment deposition in playas.* MS thesis, Texas Tech Univ., Lubbock.

Luo HR, Smith LM, et al. 1997. Effects of sedimentation on playa wetland volume. *Ecol. Appl.* 7:247–52.

Luo HR, Smith LM, et al. 1999. Sources of recently deposited sediments in playa wetlands. *Wetlands* 19:176–81.

McMurry ST, Smith LM, et al. 2009. Influence of land use on body size and splenic cellularity in wetland breeding *Spea* spp. *J. Herp.* 43:421–30.

Moon JA, Haukos DA. 2006. Survival of female northern pintails wintering in the Playa Lakes Region of northwestern Texas. *J. Wildl. Manage.* 70:777–83.

Moon JA, Haukos DA. 2008. Habitat use by northern pintails wintering in the Playa Lakes Region. *Proceed. Southeast. Assoc. Fish Wildl. Agencies* 62:82–87.

Moon JA, Haukos DA. 2009. Factors affecting body condition of wintering northern pintails. *Waterbirds* 32:87–95.

Moorehead DL, Hall DL, Willig MR. 1998. Succession of macroinvertebrates in playas of the Southern High Plains, USA. *J. N. Am. Benthol. Soc.* 17:430–42.

Neal JT, editor. 1965. *Geology, mineralogy, and hydrology of U.S. playas.* Environmental Research Papers no. 96. Fort Belvoir, VA: US Air Force.

Neal JT. 1975. *Playas and dried lakes: occurrence and development.* Benchmark Papers in Geology, no. 20. New York: Halsted Press.

Neckles HA, Murkin HR, Cooper JA. 1990. Influence of seasonal flooding on macroinvertebrate abundance in wetland habitats. *Freshw. Biol.* 23:311–22.

Nelson RW, Logan WJ, Weller EC. 1983. *Playa wetlands and wildlife on the southern Great Plains: a characterization of habitat.* FWS/OBS 83/28. Washington, DC: USFWS.

Osterkamp WR, Wood WW. 1987. Playa-lake basins on the Southern High Plains of Texas and New Mexico. Part I: Hydrologic, geomorphic, and geologic evidence for their development. *Geol. Soc. Am. Bull.* 99:215–23.

Playa Lakes Joint Venture. 2006. *High Plains landowner survey 2006: farmers, ranchers, and conservation.* Lafayette, CO: Playa Lakes Joint Venture.

Ray JD, Sullivan BD, Miller HW. 2003. Breeding ducks and their habitats in the High Plains of Texas. *Southwest. Nat.* 48:341–48.

Reed EL. 1930. Vegetation of the playa lakes in the Staked Plains of western Texas. *Ecology* 11:597–600.

Reeves CC Jr. 1966. Pluvial lake basins of West Texas. *J. Geol.* 74:269–91.

Reeves CC Jr, Reeves JA. 1996. *The Ogallala Aquifer (of the Southern High Plains).* Lubbock, TX: Estacado Books.

Rhodes MJ. 1978. *Habitat preferences of breeding waterfowl on the Texas High Plains.* MS thesis, Texas Tech Univ., Lubbock.

Rhodes MJ. 1979. Redheads breeding in the Texas Panhandle. *Southwest. Nat.* 24:691–92.

Rosen MR. 1994. The importance of groundwater in playas: a review of playa classifications and the sedimentology and hydrology of playas. In *Paleoclimate and basin evaluation of playa system,* MR Rosen, editor. Geol. Soc. Am. Special Paper 289, pp. 1–18.

Rowell CM Jr. 1971. Vascular plants of the playa lakes of the Texas Panhandle and South Plains. *Southwest. Nat.* 15:407–17.

Rowell CM Jr. 1981. The flora of playas. In *Playa lakes symposium,*

Barclay JS, White WV, editors. FWS/OBS-81/07. Fort Worth, TX: USFWS, pp. 21–29.

Sabin TJ, Holliday VT. 1995. Playas and lunettes on the Southern High Plains: morphometric and spatial relationships. *Ann. Assoc. Am. Geogr.* 85:286–305.

Samson FB, Knopf FL. 1994. Prairie conservation in North America. *BioScience* 44:418–21.

Schildman G, Hurt J. 1984. *Update of Rainwater Basin wetland survey: survey of habitat work-plan K-83.* Pittman-Robertson Project W-15-8-40. Lincoln: Nebraska GPC.

Scribner KT. 1982. *Population ecology and genetics of the eastern cottontail rabbit on West Texas playa basins.* MS thesis, Texas Tech Univ., Lubbock,

Seyffert KD. 2001. *Birds of the Texas Panhandle: their status, distribution, and history.* College Station: Texas A&M Press.

Simpson CD, Bolen EG. 1981. *Wildlife assessment of playa lakes.* Amarillo, TX: US Bureau of Reclamation.

Skagen SK, Knopf FL. 1994. Migrating shorebirds and habitat dynamics at a prairie wetland complex. *Wilson Bull.* 106:91–105.

Skagen SK, Melcher CP, Haukos DA. 2008. Reducing sedimentation of depressional wetlands in agricultural landscapes. *Wetlands* 28:594–604.

Skelly DK. 1997. Tadpole communities. *Am. Sci.* 85:36–45.

Smith LM. 2003. *Playas of the Great Plains.* Austin: Univ. of Texas Press.

Smith LM, Haukos DA. 1995. *Demonstrating and testing moist-soil management plans for waterfowl and nongame birds in the Playa Lakes Region.* Final Report. Albuquerque, NM: USFWS.

Smith LM, Haukos DA. 2002. Floral diversity in relation to playa wetland area, watershed, and disturbance. *Conserv. Biol.* 16:964–74.

Smith LM, Sheeley DG. 1993a. Factors affecting condition of northern pintails wintering in the Southern High Plains. *J. Wildl. Manage.* 57:62–71.

Smith LM, Sheeley DG. 1993b. Molt patterns of wintering northern pintails in the Southern High Plains. *J. Wildl. Manage.* 57:229–38.

Smith LM, Euliss NH Jr, et al. 2008. Application of a geomorphic and temporal perspective to wetland management in North America. *Wetlands* 28:563–77.

Smith LM, Haukos DA, et al. 2011. Ecosystem services provided by playa wetlands in the High Plains: potential influences of USDA conservation programs. *Ecol. Appl.* 2011. 21:582–592.

Starks PJ. 1984. *Analysis of Rainbasin depressions of Clay County, Nebraska.* MS thesis, Univ. Nebraska, Lincoln.

Stone RO. 1956. *A geologic investigation of playa lakes.* Ph.D. diss., Univ. of Southern California, Los Angeles.

Strickland MD, Harju HJ, et al. 1994. Harvest management. In *Research and management techniques for wildlife and habitats,* 5th ed., Bookhout TA, editor. Bethesda, MD: Wildlife Society, pp. 445–73.

Sublette JE, Sublette MS. 1967. The limnology of playa lakes on the Llano Estacado, New Mexico and Texas. *Southwest. Nat.* 12:369–406.

Torrence SM. 2007. Landuse and hydroperiod influences on amphibian community structure and the role of larval amphibians in the playa food web. Ph.D. diss., Texas Tech Univ., Lubbock.

Traweek MS Jr. 1978. *Waterfowl production survey.* Austin: Texas PWD.

Tsai J-S, Venne LS, et al. 2007. Influences of landuse and wetland characteristics on water loss rates and hydroperiods of playas in the Southern High Plains, U.S.A. *Wetlands* 27:683–92.

USFWS. 1988a. *Playa Lakes Region waterfowl habitat concept plan, Category 24 of the North American Waterfowl Management Plan.* Albuquerque, NM.

USFWS. 1988b. *National list of vascular plant species that occur in wetlands.* Biological Report 88 (26.9). Washington, DC.

USFWS. 2007. *Comprehensive Conservation Plan: Rainwater Basin Wetland Management District.* Lakewood, CO.

USFWS and Nebraska GPC. 1986. *Rainwater Basin of Nebraska migratory bird habitat acquisition plan.* Denver, CO.

US National Wetlands Inventory. 1996. *National list of plant species that occur in wetlands.* St. Petersburg, FL.

van der Valk AG, Davis CB. 1978. Primary production of prairie glacial marshes. In *Freshwater wetlands: ecological processes and management potential,* Good RE, Whigham DF, Simpson RL, editors. New York: Academic Press, pp. 21–37.

Weaver JE, Bruner WE. 1954. Nature and place of transition from true prairie to mixed prairie. *Ecology* 35:117–26.

Welling CH, Pederson RL, van der Valk AG. 1988. Recruitment from the seed bank and the development of zonation of emergent vegetation during a drawdown in a prairie wetland. *J. Ecol.* 76:483–96.

Wells DM, Huddleston EW, Rekers RG. 1970. *Potential pollution of the Ogallala by recharging playa lake water: pesticides.* Water Resources Center, Lubbock: Texas Tech Univ.

Wood WW, Osterkamp WR. 1987. Playa-lake basins on the Southern High Plains of Texas and New Mexico. Part II. A hydrologic and mass-balance arguments for their development. *Geol. Soc. Am. Bull.* 99:224–30.

Wood WW, Rainwater KA, Thompson DB. 1997. Quantifying macropore recharge: examples from a semi-arid area. *Ground Water* 35:1097–106.

Wright HA, Bailey AW. 1982. *Fire ecology: United States and Canada.* New York: John Wiley.

Young CE, Osborn CT. 1990. Costs and benefits of the conservation reserve program. *J. Soil Water Conserv.* 45:370–73.

Zartman RE. 1987. Playa lakes recharge aquifers. *Crops Soils* 39:20.

Zartman RE, Ramsey RH, et al. 1996. Outerbasin, annulus, and playa basin infiltration studies. *Texas J. Agricul. Nat. Resourc.* 9:23–32.

CHAPTER 22

Western Mountain Wetlands

DAVID J. COOPER, RODNEY A. CHIMNER, and DAVID M. MERRITT

Mountains, produced by plate tectonics and volcanism, are one of the most striking features on earth. They provide relief and dramatic visual effect, and exert control over continental and regional-scale climate patterns and geomorphic processes. Mountains, more than any other landform, create and separate major biomes, and are a significant factor driving biotic evolution. Orographic lifting produces both the wettest and driest regions on earth (in rain shadows on leeward sides) (Walter 1973). Climate effects of mountains may be felt hundreds or thousands of kilometers away, making many areas wetter or drier, warmer or colder than they might be if the mountains were absent, and controlling regional vegetation patterns (Price 1981).

On regional and local scales, mountains influence total annual precipitation (as well as its seasonal distribution), air temperature, and growing season length. Any distant view of a mountain range is highlighted by changes in landform and vegetation from its base to top (Price 1981; Billings 1973), produced by the distribution of biota along the complex environmental gradients of temperature, potential evapotranspiration (ET), water availability, erosion and sediment deposition, and land-use history. In the far north and especially in the western U.S., mountains rise as islands above large expanses of conifer forest, arid and semiarid shrublands, grasslands, and desert.

Mountains receive the highest total annual precipitation in any region. For example, the windward side of Mt. Olympus in Washington State is the wettest place in the western U.S. Mountains in the Great Basin rise as high as 2,000 m above desert floors, forming sky islands that receive and trap almost three times the moisture of surrounding valleys (Chambers and Miller 2004), and in parts of the Rocky Mountains, highland areas may receive 10 times more precipitation than surrounding basins and lowlands. The combination of high precipitation and cool climate allows high mountain regions to support glaciers, lakes, and abundant wetlands and streams. Mountain streams flow from the highlands to the surrounding valleys, basins, or ocean, providing not only habitat for native organisms, but also water for agriculture and municipal and industrial uses. Mountains are often referred to as "water towers" (Messerli et al. 2004) because they accumulate snow during winter, may support glaciers, and receive higher

rainfall amounts than most lowland areas. Runoff water from snowmelt, glaciers, and high-precipitation areas is essential for human civilization in the surrounding lowlands.

Western North and South America are characterized by the Cordillera that stretches from the Arctic to Tierra del Fuego. The mountain systems are largely oriented north-south, perpendicular to the flow of the northern temperate zone westerly winds, which blocks the flow of moist air from the Pacific Ocean into the continent's interior. Due to orographic lift, the wettest areas on the North American continent occur on west-facing slopes of the Coast Range, Cascades, and Sierra Nevada in Alaska, British Columbia, Washington, Oregon, and California, with some areas receiving > 250 cm of precipitation annually. The climate blocking produces widespread aridity in areas to the east or north of the mountains, for example, in interior Alaska, the Okanogan Valley in British Columbia, and the Great Basin and Mojave deserts. Aridity extends east to middle-elevation slopes of the Rocky Mountains. Regional aridity also occurs in northern and central Mexico and the southern portions of the western U.S. due to subtropical high pressure (Walter 1968), but high-elevation areas receive greater amounts of precipitation.

Mountains break up the south to north (tropics to Arctic) climate progression not only by regional climate forcing, but also by producing vertical altitudinal belts. A characteristic of all mountains is that mean annual temperature decreases with altitude. The temperature drop when rising 300 m in elevation is approximately the same as the mean annual decrease in temperature recorded over a distance of 100 km from south to north. This produces a dramatic compression of vegetation zones, compared with latitudinal changes in vegetation. In North America the vegetation patterns produced along an elevation gradient reflect the latitudinal vegetation zones so much that Merriam (1890) named these vegetation zones after continental biomes (e.g., Arctic, Hudsonian, Canadian, Upper Sonoran). However, altitudinal belts are not merely small-scale repetitions of latitudinal gradients (Walter 1985). Although temperatures are cooler, growing season shorter, and precipitation greater at high altitudes, the day length and position of the sun are similar to all zones. Further, the rugged terrain (e.g., canyons, valleys, peaks, glacial landforms) in mountains

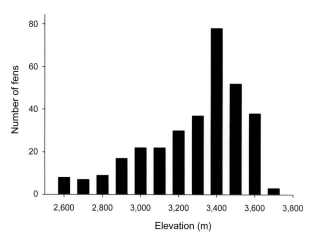

FIG. 22.1. Number of fens in 100-m elevation zones in the San Juan Mountains, Colorado. (Chimner et al. 2010.)

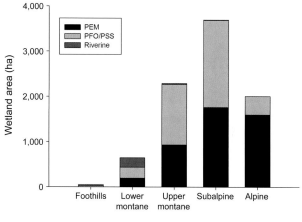

FIG. 22.2. Area (ha) of palustrine emergent (PEM), palustrine forested and shrub (PFO/PSS), and riverine wetlands in five elevation zones in Sequoia National Park, Sierra Nevada, California. Foothills = 300–900 m; lower montane = 900–2,100 m; upper montane = 2,100–2,700 m; subalpine = 2,700–3,200 m; alpine = 3200–>4,000 m elevation. (Data from National Wetlands Inventory.)

can amplify the effects of aspect on seasonal temperature fluctuations, duration of snowpack, and timing of snowmelt, influencing biota in various ways. Deep mountain canyons may be biogeographically important through serving as refugia for species adapted to a formerly wetter and cooler climate.

A number of landforms that are common in mountains promote wetland formation. For example, valley glaciers and local ice caps produced terminal moraines that blocked valley drainage, forming lakes, some of which filled with sediment and created large level areas where wetlands formed. Lateral moraines and other glacial deposits, alluvial fans, and large colluvial and eolian deposits may function as aquifers that store and supply water to wetlands. Mountains may also create intermountain basins and valleys that receive runoff from highlands and support extensive wetland complexes.

Why Mountains Support Abundant and Distinctive Wetlands

High annual precipitation, cool temperatures, and high humidity in mountains create greater water availability, particularly striking where mountains rise from arid and semiarid lowlands. The extent and density of wetlands increase with elevation due to increasing water availability and a greater abundance of landforms suitable for wetland formation. For example, the density of peatlands increases nearly linearly with elevation in the San Juan Mountains of southern Colorado, but then drops off at the highest elevation due to the lack of suitable landforms (Fig. 22.1) (Chimner et al. 2010). In the Sierra Nevada, precipitation increases from lowest to middle elevation on the western slope, but does not increase further with increasing elevation. Thus, the greatest abundance of water and wetlands occurs at middle elevations (Fig. 22.2). However, intermountain basins and valleys may also support large wetland complexes due to their level topography and surrounding mountains that provide runoff.

Mountains support a wide range of wetlands over very short distances because hydrologic characteristics needed to support a wetland, or wetland type, may change at a spatial scale

of tens of meters. In addition, local and landscape-scale landforms, bedrock outcrops, and till and alluvial deposits are spatially discrete and may create or influence the hydrologic and topographic template for wetland formation. Water flowing over and through bedrock, unconsolidated deposits, and soil results in the liberation of ions and nutrients, creating a range of geochemical environments. Groundwater and substrate biogeochemistry can influence the biotic composition and ecological processes occurring in a wetland, again often varying over small spatial scales (Cooper et al. 2010). Finally, steep elevation, aspect, and landscape position–controlled climate gradients may cause dramatic differences in wetland biotic composition over short distances. Two meadows with similar hydrologic regimes, one in the foothills and one in the subalpine zone, may support completely different species of plants and animals.

Geographic Scope of This Chapter

In this chapter we address all mountain landscapes west of the Rocky Mountain Front in the lower 48 United States and Canada, and south of the North Slope in Alaska. We define a mountain as any feature high enough to support life zones different from the surrounding basal plain or valley. Major mountain ranges include the Brooks Range, Alaska Range, Wrangell Mountains, St. Elias Range, Coast Range, Cascade Range, Sierra Nevada, Rocky Mountains, and Sierra Madre (Fig. 22.3).

We review three major wetland types: (1) herbaceous nonpeat-accumulating wetlands, including marshes, wet meadows, and salt flats; (2) peatlands (fens and bogs); and (3) riparian areas along streams and floodplain meadows and marshes.

Intermountain Basin Marshes, Wet Meadows, and Salt Flats

Geology and Hydrology

Marshes, wet meadows, and salt flats are wetlands with mineral soils. Marshes seasonally or periodically have deep

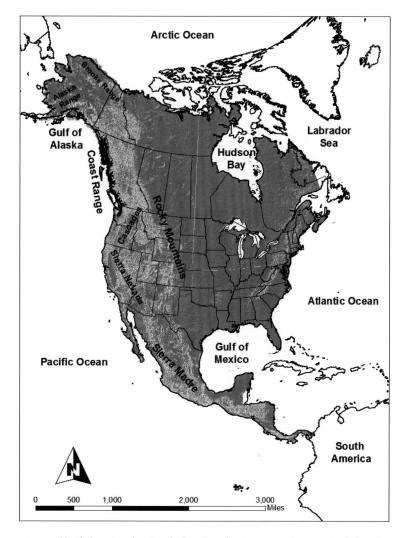

FIG. 22.3. North America, showing the location of major mountain ranges including the Brooks Range, Alaska Range, Coast Range, Cascade Range, Sierra Nevada, Rocky Mountains, and Sierra Madre.

standing water that limits their flora to submerged aquatic and relatively tall emergent herbaceous plant species. During drought periods marshes may be dry. Wet meadows are groundwater-supported sloping wetlands that are seasonally saturated. Salt flats occupy basins that periodically fill with surface water or have shallow groundwater tables and salt accumulation at the soil surface due to surface water evaporating in basins or groundwater rising by capillarity and depositing salts. The high salt concentration constrains the biota that can occur to halophytes and animals tolerant of high salinity.

These three wetland types are common throughout the western U.S. and portions of western Canada and Alaska in intermountain basins and valleys and where low precipitation or summer aridity limits peat development. Many of the largest wetland complexes in the region have formed where spring snowmelt–fed streams fill mountain front marsh basins, wet meadows, and groundwater flow systems that support wetlands far from the mountain front (Cooper et al. 2006). Some intermountain basins in the Rocky Mountains (for example, the northern part of Colorado's San Luis Valley and the Great Basin) are hydrologically closed, with inflowing sur-

face and groundwater, and outflow only by evaporation and transpiration. Other valleys have through-flowing streams. While inflows are freshwater, after thousands of years of evaporation, many closed basins have accumulated high salt concentrations.

Water is supplied to salt flats and marshes from perennial or intermittent streams that flow from high mountain watersheds during the spring or rainstorms that fill basins with surface water (Sanderson et al. 2008a), stream-recharged groundwater that discharges into and through basins (Wurster et al. 2003), or water diverted from streams and used for irrigation (Peck and Lovvorn 2001). The water table depth in wet meadows ranges from slightly above the ground surface to > 1.0 m below the ground surface (Sanderson and Cooper 2008; Cooper et al. 2006), while in marshes surface water may be > 0.5 m deep or the water table may be > 2 m below the ground surface (Sanderson and Cooper 2008). These wetlands have high annual ET rates, ranging from 0.75 to nearly 1.00 m/yr, and may figure prominently in regional water budgets. Groundwater-fed wet meadows have greater interannual hydrologic stability than surface water–fed sites, which may be dry for multiyear periods (Sanderson et al. 2008b). Salt flats typically have a water

FIG. 22.4. A. Salt flats, San Luis Valley, Colorado, dominated by *Sporobolus airoides* and *Triglochin maritimum*. B. Heart Lake marshes, Wyoming, dominated by *Carex utriculata* and *C. atherodes*. C. Marsh basins within glacial till on Yellowstone National Park's northern range; emergent vegetation is *Schoenoplectus acutus*. D. Meadow at foot of Great Basin range, Nevada, dominated by *Carex nebraskensis* and *Juncus balticus* (dark-colored plant). E. South Park meadows, Colorado, influenced by irrigation and hay cutting. F. Log meadow, Sequoia National Park, Sierra Nevada, California, dominated by *Scirpus microcarpus*. (A–C, E–F: David J. Cooper; D: D.M. Merritt.)

table within 1 m of the soil surface, or seasonally ponded shallow water.

Ecology

SALT FLAT AND MARSH GRADIENTS IN INTERMOUNTAIN BASINS

The chemical content of water and soil controls the biotic composition of montane wetlands, and soil salt content may vary by an order of magnitude along gradients as short as several meters. Wetland basins filled with snowmelt water are flushed of accumulated salts and remain relatively fresh (electrical conductivity [EC] = < 2.0 dS/m) and support plants with widespread distribution in the temperate zone, including spike rush (*Eleocharis palustris*), softstem bulrush (*Schoenoplectus lacustris*), threesquare bulrush (*S. pungens*), and submerged aquatic plants that are favored by waterfowl (e.g., *Potamogeton pectinatus* and *Zanichellia palustris*) (Sanderson et al. 2008b). In lacustrine basins near Laramie, Wyoming, *Chara* spp. dominated saline ponds, while *P. pectinatus* dominated ponds with lower salinities (Hart and Lovvorn 2000). These two different community types supported distinctive aquatic assemblages, with amphipods and gastropods (snails) in the *Chara* community, and planktonic crustaceans, chironomids, and insect predators in the *Potamogeton* community.

The margins of ponds and basins that were periodically flooded with shallow groundwater supported slightly brackish (soil EC = 2.4 dS/m) meadow communities dominated by rush (*Juncus arcticus*) and meadow foxtail (*Hordeum brachyantherum*) (Sanderson et al. 2008b). At higher landscape positions where the water table never reaches the soil surface, but where the capillary fringe does reach the surface, high salt concentrations occur. Soil pH may exceed 9.5 and soil EC ranges from 5.3 to 20.9 dS/m. These sites support halophytes such as inland saltgrass (*Distichlis spicata*), alkali cordgrass (*Spartina gracilis*), alkali sacaton (*Sporobolus airoides*), and greasewood (*Sarcobatus vermiculatus*), which can tolerate anoxic and saline soils (Fig. 22.4a).

MONTANE MARSHES

Marshes occur on pond and lake margins (Fig. 22.4b), beaver ponds, kettle ponds, and other basins created by glacial activity (Fig. 22.4c). These are highly dynamic ecosystems, with water-level depth and duration controlled by regional climate that controls snowfall and snowmelt runoff. For example, Pope Marsh, adjacent to Lake Tahoe in the California Sierra Nevada, experienced a drought in the early 1990s (Rejmankova et al. 1999). Communities dominated by *Carex utriculata* and *Juncus balticus* changed little in vegetation composition or biomass production from the dry to the wet period. However, the deeper-water area, which was dominated by *Scirpus acutus* and *Nuphar polysepalum,* experienced a significant reduction in biomass produced by these two species, and *Hippuris vulgaris* and upland ruderals invaded the pond basin during the drought. However, the *Scirpus-* and *Nuphar*-dominated communities both recovered their floristic composition and biomass when average hydrologic conditions occurred again.

East of Missoula, Montana, in the Blackfoot Valley, marshes occur in basins formed in compacted, fine-grained glacial till. The basins are supported primarily by surface snowmelt runoff, with little connection to groundwater (Cook and Hauer 2007). Vegetation patterns were tied to local-scale surface water and soil water recharge and discharge patterns, with *Potentilla anserina, Deschampsia cespitosa, J. balticus, Agrostis scabra,* and *E. palustris* being the most common species. Marshes on Yellowstone National Park's northern range also occur in a till-covered landscape. However, they are fed by surface snowmelt runoff and groundwater discharge from till and adjacent volcanic rocks (Schook and Cooper unpublished data). Springs create surface-water inflows on the upgradient side of many marshes, which support wet meadow vegetation dominated by spike rush (*Eleocharis quinqueflora*) and wooly sedge (*Carex lanuginosa),* while the basin margins supports tall marsh species such as *Schoenoplectus acutus* and *C. atherodes* (Fig. 22.4c). Interdunal marshes at Great Sand Dunes National Park in Colorado are supported almost entirely by groundwater flow (Wurster et al. 2003). The groundwater flow system was recharged by a snowmelt-fed stream.

These case studies illustrate that hydrologic processes supporting mountain valley and intermountain basin marshes vary due to the underlying substrate composition, its hydraulic conductivity, topographic gradients, and potential water sources. It should not be assumed that one model of marsh hydrologic and ecological processes should apply in all situations, or that the vegetation composition and its dynamics, vegetation zonation, geochemical gradients, and soil forming processes would apply throughout this extensive and topographically complex region.

MONTANE WET MEADOWS

Wet meadows are groundwater-driven wetlands with largely mineral soils and occur in all elevation zones from mountain foothills to the alpine. Many of the plant species that dominate montane wet meadows have broad geographic ranges and occur throughout the western U.S., for example *Carex nebraskensis, Deschampsia cespitosa, Juncus balticus,* and *Poa pratensis* (Fig. 22.4d). Wet meadows support at least one herbaceous plant–dominated community, and plants use surface water and/or shallow groundwater (generally at depths of less than 1 m). Woody vegetation (e.g., trees, particularly conifers, and shrubs in the genera *Salix*) may be locally abundant but not dominant over the entire meadow complex.

As they are groundwater-driven ecosystems, seasonal variability in water table depth strongly influences the floristic composition of wet-meadow plant communities (Table 22.1). Water table variation has been related to vegetation composition in the northern (Allen-Diaz 1991) and southern Sierra Nevada of California (Ratliff 1985), Cascade Range (Dwire et al. 2004), Great Basin (Castelli et al. 2000; Chambers and Miller 2004), and Rocky Mountains (Cooper 1990). These studies form a reasonable basis for understanding meadow hydroecology. Allen-Diaz (1991) characterized five plant communities that were correlated with water table depth patterns during the growing season: *D. cespitosa–Carex nebraskensis* (water table – 6 to –94 cm below the ground surface), *P. pratensis–Potentilla gracilis* (–26 to –62 cm), *P. pratensis–Carex* spp. (–19 to –50 cm), *Carex angustata–P. pratensis* (–32 to –51), and *Carex angustata* (– 3 to –36). In the Cascade Range of Oregon, Dwire et al. (2004) characterized wet, moist, and dry communities. Total biomass production was positively correlated with mean summer

TABLE 22.1

Plant species dominants of wet meadows, and water table depth ranges in western U.S. mountain ranges

Region	Community dominant	Water table depth range	Source
N. Sierra Nevada	*Carex nebraskensis*	0–30 cm	Allen-Diaz 1991
S. Sierra Nevada	*C. nebraskensis* *Calamagrostis breweri*	0–30 cm	Ratliff 1985
Rocky Mountains	*Deschampsia cespitosa*	0–30 cm	Cooper 1990
Cascade Range	*Carex utriculata, C. aquatilis* (wet) *D. cespitosa* (moist) *P. pratensis* (dry)	17–30 cm	Dwire, Kauffman, et al. 2004
Great Basin	*C. nebraskensis* *P. pratensis*	0–34 cm 0–149 cm	Castelli, Chambers, and Tausch 2000

water table depth and negatively correlated with mean redox potential, and belowground biomass accounted for 68–81% of annual production.

Wet meadows are key habitat for small mammals. Meadow vole and montane vole were the most abundant small mammals in meadows near Gray's Lake, Idaho, and deer mouse, vagrant shrew, and ermine also occurred (Austin and Pyle 2004); however, population sizes varied annually.

Conservation Concerns

Impacts to intermountain basin marshes have occurred from groundwater pumping and surface-water diversions (Elmore et al. 2003; Cooper et al. 2006), as well as basin-wide logging and urbanization (Kim et al. 2001). Montane marshes provide many important services, including pollution removal, flood mitigation, recreation, and habitats and resources for plants and animals (Kim et al. 2001).

Many meadows are used for hay production and grazing (Fig. 22.4e). Intensive livestock use of meadows has occurred in the American West since the mid-1800s (Ratliff 1985) because meadows provide the main forage base in most mountain regions. Regions with little summer rain, such as the California Sierra Nevada, have little suitable forage in uplands under conifer forests, or shrublands; therefore almost all livestock grazing has been in meadows (Fig. 22.4f). The vegetation composition of some meadows is reported to have changed since the 19th century due to livestock use (Dull 1999), including the reduction in nonvascular plants and *Salix,* and an increase in *Artemisia* and species of Rosaceae. The composition of the predisturbance vegetation, the changes that occurred, and its postgrazing recovery are unknown (DeBenedetti and Parsons 1979).

Mountain Peatlands

Geology and Hydrology

Peatlands form organic soil or "peat" because the rate of plant production exceeds the rate of organic matter decomposition. Most peatlands (> 90%) occur in low-relief boreal regions, but peatlands are also common in many mountain ranges (Chadde

et al. 1998; Warner and Asada 2006; Cooper and Wolf 2006; Lemly 2007; Patterson and Cooper 2007; Chimner et al. 2010). For example, approximately 2,000 peatlands occur in the San Juan Mountains of southern Colorado (Chimner et al. 2010), and over 13,000 km² of peatlands occur in the mountains of Canada (Warner and Asada 2006). Peatlands have been identified in the Rocky Mountains from New Mexico to northern Canada and the Brooks Range of Alaska (Cooper 1986), the Sierra Nevada of California, and the Coast Range and Cascades of Oregon, Washington, British Columbia, and coastal Alaska. There are no records of peatlands occurring in the mountains of Mexico, though this area is poorly studied.

In western North America, fens are supported primarily by groundwater and bogs by precipitation (Warner and Asada 2006). Bogs occur in coastal British Columbia and southern Alaska in a hypermaritime climate receiving ample rain and high humidity throughout the year (Asada et al. 2003) (Fig. 22.5a). Fens are also common in maritime climates and co-occur with bogs in peatland complexes. The Rocky Mountains, Cascade Range, and Sierra Nevada support only fens due to the dry summer climate (Cooper and Andrus 1994; Cooper and Wolf 2006). In Alaska, fens occur over continuous or discontinuous permafrost (Fig. 22.5b).

The elevation range supporting peatlands varies with latitude and total annual precipitation. In western North America, peatlands occur primarily at high elevations in southern latitudes of the Rocky Mountains and Sierra Nevada (Fig. 22.1), and at lower elevations in northern latitudes and at sea level in the Coast Ranges of Washington, British Columbia, and Alaska (Asada et al. 2003). Peatlands in southwestern Colorado occur primarily in the subalpine zone from 2,290–3,800 m (mean 3,200 m; Chimner et al. 2010). In northwestern Wyoming, peatlands occur between 1,880–2,710 m (mean 2,264 m; Lemly and Cooper 2007). In the Sierra Nevada, they occur at an average elevation of 3,100 m in the southern, drier Sierra Nevada and 1,700 m in the northern, wetter Sierra Nevada (Cooper and Wolf 2006). In Idaho and Montana, valley peatlands occur from 641–1,666 m (mean 840 m; Bursik and Henderson 1995), while mountain slope peatlands occur from 944–2,400 m (mean 1,560 m; Chadde et al. 1998).

Mountain peatlands are typically small due to valley confinement, steep slopes, and small catchment sizes (Patterson and Cooper 2007). In high-elevation regions of Colorado, California, and Wyoming, peatlands average ~2 ha in size, with the

FIG. 22.5. Peatlands in the mountains of western North America. A. Blanket bog dominated by *Sphagnum* spp. near Wrangell, Alaska. Tree is *Pinus contorta* ssp. *contorta*. B. *Eriophorum vaginatum*–dominated fen in Alaska Range. C. Floating mat dominated by *Carex limosa* in Yellowstone National Park, Wyoming. D. Big Meadows fen dominated by *Carex aquatilis* in Colorado. E. Extreme-rich High Creek fen dominated by *Kobresia simplisiuscula* in Colorado. F. Mt. Emmons iron fen dominated by *C. aquatilis* and *Sphagnum fimbriatum* in Colorado.

largest peatlands generally being < 100 ha (Cooper and Wolf 2006; Lemly 2007; Chimner et al. 2010), although a few fens in Idaho and Montana are > 500 ha (Lichthardt 2004). Watersheds supporting fens in one southern Colorado mountain region average 23 ha (Cooper unpublished data). Peatlands are much larger in maritime mountains, exceeding 6,000 ha in Alaska and other coast ranges (Riggs 1925).

Mountain peatlands occur in several different landforms. Basin peatlands form through infilling of small lakes or ponds by mineral sediment and peat. They may have open water with floating mats, or the pond may have completely filled with peat (Fig. 22.5c). In hypermaritime regions, basin peatlands can develop into bogs, but in most regions they remain fens.

Sloping fens are more common than basin fens. For example, in southwestern Colorado nearly 75% of fens are sloping (Chimner et al. 2010). Fens occur on steep (up to 30%) mountainsides (midslope) where perennial groundwater discharges (Cooper and Wolf 2006; Chimner et al. 2010), or in more gentle toe-slopes or valley bottom positions, where groundwater discharges from glacial till, alluvial fans, or colluvium (Fig. 22.5d). Some fens have formed where regional groundwater discharges (Fig. 22.5e) (Cooper 1996). Surficial patterns of strings and flarks, terraces, and pools occur in many sloping fens, but they are less well developed at southern latitudes. In maritime regions, blanket bogs are common on slopes (Warner and Asada 2006).

Water table levels and dynamics vary among mountain peatland types. Long-term measurements in Colorado indicate that sloping fens have water table levels near the soil surface during most summers, but these drop 10–20 cm below the soil surface during droughts (Figs. 22.6–22.7). Basin fens have ponded water in early summer, and water tables may drop to 50 cm below the ground surface in late summer; basin fens may remain ponded in wet summers (Fig. 22.5c). Vegetation type varies by water table level, being deeper in communities dominated by *Calamagrostis canadensis* and shallower in those dominated by *E. quinqueflora* and *Carex aquatilis* (Chimner and Cooper 2003).

Because most mountain peatlands are sloping and groundwater supported, watershed geology strongly influences the chemical content of their source water (Vitt and Chee 1990; Cooper and Andrus 1994; Chimner et al. 2010). Geochemical categories of mountain peatlands range from bogs and iron fens to extreme-rich fens. Intermediate fens are common in watersheds with granite and other intrusive igneous rocks dominating their watersheds that liberate few ions. Rich and extreme-rich fens are common in watersheds with calcareous rocks (limestone, dolomite) (Fig. 22.5f), and iron fens and acidic geothermal fens occur where outcrops of iron pyrite or sulfur from volcanic vents oxidize to form sulfuric acid, creating naturally acid groundwater (Fig. 22.5e) (Cooper and Andrus 1994; Cooper et al. 2002; McClellan et al. 2003; Lemly 2007; Chimner et al. 2010).

Ecology

Mountain peatlands can be floristically diverse. Chimner et al. (2010) identified 188 vascular and 63 bryophyte species in San Juan Mountain fens, Colorado; Lemly (2007) identified 256 vascular and 58 bryophyte species in Yellowstone National Park fens; Cooper and Wolf (2006) identified 170 vascular spe-

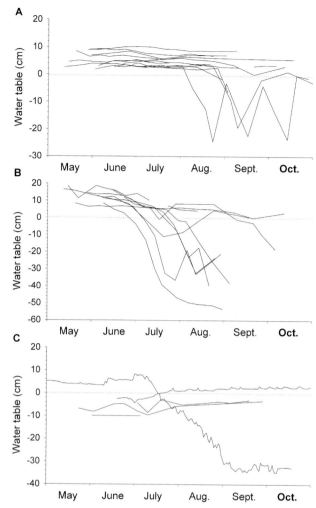

FIG. 22.6. Groundwater levels in three Colorado fens. A. 1987–98 for Big Meadows, in Rocky Mountain National Park, A sloping, *Carex aquatilis*-dominated fen. B. 1987–98 for Green Mountain trail fen in Rocky Mountain National Park, a basin, *Carex utriculata*-dominated fen. C. 2005–09 for Chattanooga iron fen in the San Juan Mountains, Colorado.

cies in 100 Sierra Nevada fens; Bursik and Henderson (1995) identified 291 vascular and 20 bryophyte species in mountain valley peatlands in Idaho; and Riswold and Fonda (2001) found 130 vascular and 9 bryophyte species in Olympic Mountain fens. This species richness is higher than in boreal peatlands (80–100 taxa; Warner and Asada 2006).

Mountain peatlands in hypermaritime climate regions support a carpet of *Sphagnum* spp. similar to low-relief boreal peatlands (Riggs 1925, 1937; Risvold and Fonda 2001; Asada et al. 2003). *Sphagnum* species are much less important in southern mountain fens. In the U.S. Rocky Mountains, 21 *Sphagnum* species are reported (Andrus unpublished report), with *S. central, S. magellanicum, S. subsecundum,* and *S. teres* being most abundant in Idaho and Montana (Chadde et al. 1998), and *S. russowii, S. fimbriatum* and *S. angustifolium* in Colorado (mostly in iron fens; Cooper et al. 1999; Chimner et al. 2010). Extreme biogeographic disjunctions occur in peatlands. For example, the boreal and subarctic peat moss *S. balticum* occurs in a few isolated populations in southern Colorado iron fens disjunct by more than 1,000 km (Cooper et al. 2002).

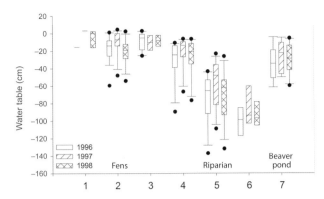

FIG. 22.7. Range of mean water levels for three years for seven wetland communities in the Colorado River Valley in Rocky Mountain National Park, Colorado. Communities 1–3 are fens, 4–5 are riparian, 6 is a wet meadow, and 7 is a beaver pond within a riparian area.

Mountain peatlands in continental climate regions are dominated by herbaceous plants, particularly species of *Carex* and brown mosses in the family Amblysegiaceae (Chadde et al. 1998; Cooper and Wolf 2007; Lemly 2007; Chimner et al. 2010) (Fig. 22.5c–d). These are rich and transitional rich fens (Cooper and Andrus 1994). Up to 50 species of Cyperaceae occur in the Rocky Mountain fen flora south of the Canadian border, and *Carex aquatilis,* which has a circumpolar distribution, is the most abundant plant in mountain fens throughout western North America, and is also present in hypermaritime region fens. Bryophyte cover and diversity is dominated by brown mosses, with 49 species in Idaho and Montana, 46 species in Wyoming, and 57 species in Colorado, including *Aulacomnium palustre, Tomenthypnum nitens, Warnstorfia fluitans, Drepanocladus aduncus, Ptychostomum pseudotriquetrum,* and *Climacium dendroides* (Chadde et al. 1998; Lemly 2007; Chimner et al. 2010).

Extreme-rich fens occur where limestone and dolomite dominate watersheds (Fig. 22.5f) in Colorado (Cooper 1996), Montana (Lesica 1986), and California (Cooper and Wolf 2006). These fens can be dominated by *Kobresia simpliciuscula* and *K. myosuroides* (Cooper 1996; Cooper and Sanderson 1997), mosses such as *Scorpidium scorpioides,* and typical halophytes such as *Triglochin maritimum* and *Glaux maritimum.* Water pH of extreme-rich fens can exceed 8.0, containing high concentrations of HCO_3, SO_4, Ca, and even Na.

Hypermaritime fens and blanket bogs in Alaska and British Columbia are *Sphagnum*-dominated but may contain high densities of conifers, including *Pinus contorta* and *Thuja heterophylla.* The dominant vascular plants include *Carex pauciflora, Scirpus caespitosus,* and several species of Ericaceae, including *Oxycocus microcarpus, Vaccinium vitis-idaea, Rubus chamaermorus,* and *Andromeda polifolia* (Fig. 22.5a).

Peat Formation

Mountain peat bodies average 70 cm thick in the Sierra Nevada (Cooper and Wolf 2007) and 125 cm in Colorado (Chimner et al. 2010). However, peat bodies > 4 m thick have been reported in the Rocky Mountains, and > 7 m thick in the Andes (Chimner et al. 2010; Cooper et al. 2010). Peat thickness tends to decrease at higher elevations and on steeper slopes.

Few mountain peatlands have been analyzed to determine the initial timing of peat formation. [14]C analysis of 29 Colorado fens suggests that peat began to accumulate soon after mountain glaciers melted, with basal ages of 8,000–12,000 ybp (Chimner 2000). Similarly ancient peat occurs in Wyoming, Montana, Idaho, and Alaska (Mehringer et al. 1977; Zicheng et al. 2009).

Most mountain peatlands occur in confined valleys among high mountains, where mineral sediment is transported from slopes by snowmelt water, eolian processes, and mass movements producing higher mineral and lower C content than low-relief boreal peatlands (Chimner and Karberg 2008). The mean C content of 419 Colorado fens was 30% (~60% organic matter) (Chimner et al. 2010), and C content varied along the Von Post decomposition scale (VP 1–2 = 36%, VP 3–4 = 31%, VP 5–10 = 27% C). The highest C content occurs in minimally decomposed *Sphagnum* peat, and the lowest in highly decomposed *Carex* peat. While mountain peat generally has lower C content than boreal peat, it is typically denser. Therefore, long-term C accumulation rates may be similar in mountain and boreal peatlands (Chimner et al. 2002).

Conservation Concerns

A range of disturbances can impact mountain peatlands. One of the most common is from roads (Chimner et al. 2010), which intercept water flow, bisect habitats, and introduce mineral sediments. Many roads have limited impacts to peatlands, but some cause severe impacts, especially where poor culvert placement creates channels and erosion, or ditches along the road intercept groundwater. Beside the physical factors of altering water flow and mineral sediment deposition, roads permit vehicle access that can directly impact peatlands. Off-roading through peatlands can create tire tracks that act as ditches and drains, and can lead to gully formation. Peatlands can also be impacted by other development (golf courses, parking structures, condos, ski areas, houses), usually from filling of portions of peatlands or building structures that alter groundwater flow to or from peatlands.

Mining impacts are common in some areas. Tailing piles can physically cover peat, or disrupt surface- and groundwater flow and alter chemical and mineral sediment influx to peatlands. Severe impacts develop when the peat itself has been mined, either for horticultural uses or to remove bog iron, and little or no vegetation remains (Cooper and MacDonald 2000; Chimner et al. 2010). Many mined peatlands have remained bare for decades and require active restoration (Cooper and MacDonald 2000; Chimner et al. 2010).

Drainage ditches, water diversions, and groundwater extraction are common disturbances encountered in mountain peatlands (Cooper et al. 1998; Patterson and Cooper 2007). These disturbances cause severe impacts because they lower the water table, allowing peat to oxidize and the peat surface to subside (Chimner and Cooper 2003). Dewatering can lead to changes in vegetation composition, facilitate invasion of pocket gophers (Patterson and Cooper 2007), and make peatlands more susceptible to fire. Reservoirs can flood peatlands in some areas.

Cattle grazing can impact peatlands by trampling peat and vegetation (Cooper and Wolf 2006) or creating trails that function as ditches (similar to vehicle tracks). Grazing impacts are particularly intense in the California Sierra Nevada and South American Andes (Cooper and Wolf 2006; Cooper et al. 2006;

Chimner et al. 2007). Trampling can also occur from native animals such as elk or deer (Chimner et al. 2010).

Riparian Floodplains

Geology and Hydrology

Networks of streams and rivers dissect the landscape and, through erosion and deposition processes, hydrologic variability, and disturbance regimes, maintain distinctive and dynamic landforms and vegetation. In mountainous landscapes (e.g., Rocky Mountains, Cascade Range, and the Coast Range), streams and their associated riparian landforms and biota are influenced by complex interactions between physical and biological characteristics, including valley constraint, streamside landforms, channel bedform, and habitat features, which in turn are shaped by watershed geology, climate, sediment supply, large woody debris, and steep mountain landscapes (Rot et al. 2000). Streams and rivers occupy the lowest portions of mountain landscapes, primarily valley bottoms. The biotic communities of streamsides and floodplains are among the most diverse in the western U.S., and the unique species that occur in these areas can enhance regional species richness by more than 50% (Sabo et al. 2005).

The form and character of mountain channels are typically constrained by bedrock and glacial history, which control valley form, as well as alluvial and colluvial landforms. Mass movement of sediment from hillslopes in steep, wet, constrained reaches and from tributary streams controls valley width and gradient at the reach scale. Valley constraint, which is influenced by mass wasting processes and stream incision into bedrock, significantly influences riparian habitat. Along steep bedrock-confined valleys, channels are typically straight and exhibit cascade and step-pool forms, while in lower-elevation, less steep valleys, channels have plane-bed and pool-riffle forms (Montgomery and Buffington 1997). At yet lower elevations, in wider valley bottoms and intermountain parks, alluvial channels may exhibit straight, meandering, island braided, and braided forms, with high rates of lateral channel migration and floodplain turnover relative to higher-elevation streams (Beechie et al. 2006). The relative increase in stream size and floodplain interactions as water descends from the mountains, combined with changes in abiotic factors and dominant geomorphic processes along a river's course, produce a gradient or continuum of riparian biota and ecosystem types from mountaintops to lowlands.

River channels are important conduits for transporting water, mineral sediment, organic matter, propagules, and organisms. River networks also serve as biotic corridors through landscapes, connecting otherwise disconnected landscape elements and laterally connecting rivers to adjacent landscapes. Air (and streamwater) temperature and evapotranspiration generally increase, as do stream order, channel size, discharge, sediment supply, and floodplain development, as streams descend from high mountains to lowlands. Along this continuum, precipitation and stream gradient decrease and valley form and dominant geomorphic influences ("process domain" *sensu* Montgomery 1999) change in predictable ways (Friedman et al. 2006). For example, along higher-elevation and steeper reaches, streams are typically highly connected to adjacent hillslopes through confinement, mass wasting, and colluvial sediment inputs (Benda et al. 2005). Such constrictions can control the longitudinal profile of chan-

nels, creating steps that punctuate lower-gradient reaches and inhibit lateral movement and floodplain formation. Stream channel form, flow regime, and sediment delivery to channels create the resource (e.g., water and nutrients) and disturbance template (e.g., energy gradients and scour and burial) upon which plant communities establish and develop.

In high mountain regions, streams originate from glacial meltwater and snow, which may contribute more than 70% of total annual streamflow in northern Rocky Mountain streams (Hauer et al. 1997). Summer snowmelt forms innumerable small rills in steep alpine and subalpine basins, eventually coalescing into larger and larger streams, filling high-elevation lakes, recharging aquifers, and forming channels as water converges and flows through valley bottoms. As first-order stream channels coalesce to form larger channels, colluvium and eroded material from sideslopes is transported, redistributed, and sorted by flooding (Wohl 2000; Benda et al. 2005). Flood-associated channel migration results in the formation and abandonment of fluvial features across valley bottoms and the sorting and layering of alluvium. Valley bottoms subjected to floodplain formation and abandonment may exhibit a mosaic of depressions, oxbow lakes, scour holes, and ridge and swale topography, as well as deposits of sorted material and splays, and chutes contributing to heterogeneity in edaphic and hydrologic conditions across mountain valley bottoms. It is upon this physical template, formed by the interactions between valley and channel processes, that fluvial marshes, wet meadows, fens, and shrub-dominated carrs and riparian forests form.

Differences in dominant life-history traits of riparian species and the composition, physiognomy, and reproductive characteristics of plant communities reflect dominant abiotic processes as they change throughout a drainage network (Samuelson and Rood 2004). In contrast to vegetation in nonriverine marshes, peatlands, and wet meadows, riparian vegetation is influenced by periodic fluvial disturbance as well as seasonally fluctuating flows that create spatial and seasonal gradients of water availability and anoxia. Primary productivity, nutrient processing, and interactions and exchanges between channels and adjacent landscapes vary along the longitudinal continuum of mountain river channels from alpine areas to lowlands and are reflected in the distinct characteristics of vegetation along this riparian continuum.

Ecology

ALPINE AND SUBALPINE RIPARIAN ZONES

In the alpine and upper subalpine zone, bedrock is typically shallow and streams originate from glacial meltwater, overland runoff from precipitation or snowmelt, shallow subsurface flow in the unsaturated zone, and groundwater discharge (Fig. 22.8a). Groundwater discharge usually is the least variable source of water in alpine and subalpine zones (Winter 2007). Kryal, krenal, and rhithral streams have been distinguished in mountainous landscapes based upon their principal water source (Hauer et al. 2007). Kryal streams have year-round snowmelt from glaciers or snowbanks; krenal streams are spring fed with water discharging from glacial till, talus, alluvium, and other aquifers, and may support wetland meadows and fens; rhithral streams are driven by seasonal snowmelt and are typically intermittent. Alpine streams are typically steep-gradient falls or cascades in steeper settings (e.g.,

FIG. 22.8. A. Subalpine brook, Mt. Hood, Oregon. B. Low-stature willow *(Salix planifolia)*–dominated riparian zone, Wind River, Wyoming.
C. Conifer-dominated riparian zone, Colorado. D. Colorado River riparian zone, Colorado. Willows dominate the floodplain. Current beaver
ponds occur, and former beaver ponds are meadowlike features. E. *Salix geyeriana*– and *S. monticola*–dominated community, Blue River,
Colorado. F. *Populus angustifolia* forest, San Miguel River, Colorado.

moraines, cliffs, and chasms), but may form low-gradient sinuous channels in wider valley bottoms.

Many alpine streams have seasonally intense disturbance
regimes from snowmelt-driven floods, which annually disturb
fluvial surfaces and erode plants and their propagules from
channel margins. Riparian vegetation composition and physiognomy are determined to a large degree by fluvial landforms
and associated edaphic, hydrologic, geochemical, and hydraulic attributes associated with them (e.g., substrate texture,
hydraulic conductivity and groundwater flow, nutrient processing, water availability, proximity to channel, shear stress,
and others) (Harris 1987).

Vegetative growth is a dominant trait relative to sexual
reproduction in alpine areas. Spring communities dominated
by herbaceous perennial plants, including *Primula parryi, Mer-
tensia ciliata, Cardamine cordifolia, Caltha leptosepala,* and *Dode-
catheon pulchellum* in the southern Rocky Mountains (Komarkova 1979), *Mimulus lewisii* farther north, and many other
obligate brook species, dominate these riparian zones. Alpine
riparian streambanks, as well as fens and wet meadows, may
be dominated by *Carex scopulorum* or *C. nigricans* in the Rocky
Mountains (Komarkova 1979). Willows, including *Salix barrat-
tiiana* on alpine fluvial soils in Banff National Park, Alberta,
Canada (Knapik et al. 1973), *S. planifolia* and *S. wolfii* in the

southern Rocky Mountains (Cooper 1990) (Fig. 22.8b), and *S. orestra* in the Sierra Nevada may provide the majority of the cover and biomass in alpine and upper subalpine areas.

In the high subalpine zone, snowmelt basins have deep winter snow and numerous small streams, and narrow *Salix*-dominated riparian zones occur, many of which are bordered directly by upland conifer forests (Fig. 22.8c). Valley morphology strongly influences stream gradient, valley width, alluvium thickness, the influence of valley sideslopes and colluvial processes, and the character of the hydrologic regime and vegetation. Narrow stream channels, avalanche chutes, or steep, sloping wetlands are often lined in the subalpine or montane zones by *Alnus incana* and species of *Salix* and/or *Betula fontinalis* and *Swida (Cornus) stolonifera* at lower elevations. *Alnus* and *Salix* stems are flexible and sprout after breakage, and their seeds readily germinate in freshly disturbed, moist, and unshaded sites. The association of *Alnus* with nitrogen-fixing bacteria significantly influences nutrient dynamics and plant community development in riparian and stream ecosystems, contributing as much as 50–200 kg N ha^{-1} yr^{-1} to soils and groundwater in pure stands (Walker and Chapin 1986; Binkley et al. 1994; Compton et al. 2003).

Within the riparian zone, successional processes and stand age influence the size of stems and the volume of wood delivered to the channel. Woody material in the channel influences channel dynamics, particularly on smaller streams and along moderately constrained to unconstrained valleys (Rot et al. 2000). Large woody debris influences flow resistance through providing boundary roughness, may increase local boundary erosion through deflecting flow against banks, may produce a stepped longitudinal profile where trunks or debris jams span the channel, and may serve as storage sites for organic and mineral sediment (reviewed in Wohl 2000). In mountain channels, woody debris has a diminishing influence on channel form as a function of stream order, the influence being greater in lower-order streams with smaller channels, lower discharge (for mobilization of debris), narrower valleys, steeper sideslopes, and higher rates of mass wasting (Wohl 2000). High-mountain riparian zones in the Rocky Mountains, Cascades, and Coastal Mountains, as well as in the Great Basin, may have no or very narrow floodplains, be dominated by conifer trees, and have greater species diversity compared to hillslope vegetation. In contrast, lower-elevation, unconstrained riparian zones along higher-order streams are highly dynamic, and may have well-developed and extensive floodplains with deciduous species well adapted to flood-related disturbance (Gregory et al. 1991).

MONTANE FLUVIAL MARSHES, WET MEADOWS, AND SHRUBLANDS

Vegetation along topographically heterogeneous valley bottoms along midelevation, low-gradient reaches of mountain streams often exhibits a variety of growth forms. Patches of willow may be interspersed with grass, rush- and sedge-dominated wet and mesic meadow, patches of shrubs and isolated trees, and moss-dominated areas as well as open water and bare ground. Fluvial depressions and stream channels may receive groundwater from side slopes for part or most of the year and experience seasonal peaks associated with snowmelt runoff delivered via streams.

Potential distributions of species are governed by depth to water table, soil moisture, texture and chemistry, degree of connectivity to stream channels, and intensity of fluvial disturbance, which are conditioned by fluvial landform (Chambers et al. 2004; Bayley and Guimond 2008). Chance dispersal coupled with suitable conditions may determine which species colonize open sites. The paring of tolerances of colonizing species to inundation and burial may dictate long-term community composition on these sites. Competition for resources (e.g., light, space, water, and nutrients) also plays an important role in the distribution of various growth forms in high-elevation riparian areas (Kotowski et al. 2006). Species with tolerances of extremes (fluvial disturbance versus xeric conditions farther from stream channels) may dominate entirely different positions on the landscape, with generalists or particularly good competitors occupying intermediate, and presumably more optimal, positions. Affinities of certain vegetation to specific fluvial features may be striking in alluvial valleys. For example, in the Cascade Range, riparian plant community composition was differentiated into classes based on associated landforms: floodplain dominated by *Alnus rubra,* low terrace, high terrace, as well as areas dominated by hillslope processes (Villarin et al. 2009). Along montane streams in the Great Basin, Chambers et al. (2004) reported *Carex nebraskenis, Deschampsia cespitosa,* and *Juncus balticus*–dominated meadow vegetation nearest stream channels (0.38 m above the channel); *Salix*-dominated mesic meadow (at elevations of 0.49 to 0.73 m) occurring with *Populus tremuloides, P. angustifolia,* and *P. balsamifera;* drier meadow dominated by *Poa pratensis* and *Elymus trachycaulus;* and forbs meadows at higher elevations (0.87 m). The outward extent of riparian areas in these Great Basin streams were composed of *Betula occidentalis* (1.04 m above the channel), *Prunus viginiana–Rosa woodsii* (1.8 m), and *Artemisia tridentata* furthest from the channel (1.85 m above the channel).

In high-elevation floodplain wetlands in Alberta, Canada, differences in plant community composition in riparian meadows was best explained by soil attributes (electrical conductivity and sediment organic content), hydrology (water depth), and microtopography (the number of hummocks) (Bayley and Guimond 2008). At the wetter and less hummocky end of the gradient, monocots such as *Carex aquatilis, C. utriculata,* and *Eleocharis palustris* as well as mosses in the genus *Drepanocladus* and fern allies (such as *Equisetum fluviatile*) tended to dominate, whereas species of *Salix* and other shrubs tended to occur in drier areas, with deeper, more stable water tables and sites with hummocks and varied topography (Bayley and Guimond 2008). Dwire et al. (2006) found that riparian wet meadows with shallow water tables were dominated by one or a couple of *Carex* species, whereas drier sites were more species rich and dominated by grasses and forbs.

Willows (*Salix* spp.) dominate midelevation, low-gradient stream reaches throughout western North America. Willows establish on three main fluvial landforms: abandoned beaver ponds, abandoned channels, and point bars (Cooper et al. 2006) (Fig. 22.8d–e). Most montane willows reproduce by seeds, which are dispersed in early summer, just after the spring flood, and germinate on bare wet mineral sediment (Gage and Cooper 2004; Woods and Cooper 2005); however, a few species (i.e., *Salix wolfii*) are clonal, and most willow can reproduce from stem fragments and roots, including those clipped by beaver. Vegetative reproduction is a dominant trait in many high-elevation riparian willow communities (dominated by *S. planifolia* and other species) compared to lower-elevation riparian areas (although *S. exigua* is a common clonal dominant in some regions). Though *Salix* and other disturbance-adapted species tend to colonize sites freshly disturbed by fluvial processes, soil disturbances caused by burrowing mammals can also serve as sites for colonization.

Beavers *(Castor canadensis)* and *Salix* have a mutualistic relationship because beavers rely on willow for food and building material, and *Salix* benefit from the elevated water tables and habitat beavers create for establishment and growth. Stream channels that are less than 5–10 m wide and of relatively low gradient provide habitat for beaver, though beaver may be active on large rivers as well. Beaver eat willow, alder, and other woody plants as well as using them to build dams and dens. Where valleys and stream channels are wider, beaver dams strongly influence the hydrologic regime, sediment dynamics, and vegetation of floodplains (Fig. 22.8d). For example, a beaver dam on the Colorado River influenced floodplain saturation exceeding that of a 10-year return interval flood on the same river (Westbrook et al. 2006). In addition, the patterns of flooding, soil saturation, flow diversion, mineral sediment deposition, and nutrient dynamics caused by beaver dams control the landscape-scale patterns of vegetation on some floodplains (Westbrook et al. 2010).

The role of beavers along small, midelevation streams is so striking that where heavy browsing reduces willow to a short-growth form and willow plants are no longer suitable for beaver dams (Baker et al. 2005), entire valleys may dry considerably, producing extreme water stress and reduced willow growth rates (Wolf et al. 2007; Bilyeu et al. 2008). Heavy browsing by native or domestic ungulates can also severely restrict willow flowering and seed production because catkins are produced on the stems from the previous year (Gage and Cooper 2005).

Many species of montane willows can vegetatively resprout and persist as clones for decades to centuries along valley margins, supported primarily by shallow groundwater. Along channel margins, riparian woodlands often form patches that are interspersed with forest and wet meadow. Along narrow streams, coniferous forest may dominate the riparian vegetation, precluding sun-loving species such as Salix and Alnus, but supporting broadleaf herbaceous communities. Floodplain development is typically limited in narrow, high-elevation valley bottoms, and floodplain turnover is lower than along wider alluvial segments (Beechie et al. 2006), leading to narrower and less diverse and dynamic riparian vegetation in these areas.

MONTANE RIPARIAN FORESTS

Midelevation floodplains along large rivers in the Rocky Mountains and the east slope of the Sierra Nevada support riparian forests dominated by narrowleaf cottonwood *(Populus angustifolia),* which forms the majority of the biomass and creates the stand structure (Fig. 22.8f). In some areas, blue spruce *(Picea pungens)* codominates. Narrowleaf cottonwood, in contrast to plains or Fremont cottonwood *(Populus deltoides),* reproduces primarily by asexual means. Clonal recruitment accounted for 60–86% of the trees along small streams in the Wasatch Range near Logan, Utah (Roberts 1999). Stands of clones were up to 200–300 m in diameter, and some clones occurred on both sides of a stream channel due to braiding or channel avulsion that occurred after the clone with formed. Recruitment was reported to occur every 25–30 years on midchannel islands and sinuous sites that were little entrenched. Narrowleaf cottonwood seedling establishment was reported to occur an aver-

age of every 3.4 years during the past 100–150 years along the Animas River in southwestern Colorado, but stand-originating floods that produced significant erosion and recruitment occurred only every 10–15 years (Baker 1990). These recruitment events were driven by wet winters and persistent summer monsoon storms that created large floods, channel erosion, and sediment deposition, and wet summers that supported seedling establishment. Flows, exceeding 125% of bankfull flow, cause bank erosion and channel migration in the meandering Yampa River, near Hayden, Colorado (Richter and Richter 2000). Bar extension and the creation of newly disturbed sites facilitated recruitment of new cottonwood cohorts, primarily by asexual means (Richter and Richter 2000). The dominant reproductive strategy in two *Populus* species was shown to shift from primarily clonal growth in montane reaches to sexual reproduction along lower-elevation, more fluvially active reaches along two Rocky Mountain streams in Alberta, Canada (Samuelson and Rood 2004).

Most large river floodplains are composed of coarse sediments that allow the complex movement of water in three dimensions (downstream in the channel, and laterally and vertically as subsurface flow through the alluvium, i.e., hyporheic flow). These complex flow patterns, which are influenced by valley width, control the water table depth and nutrient availability (through N transformation) and control the establishment and growth of cottonwoods *(P. trichocarpa)* (Harner and Stanford 2003). Along the Middle Fork of the Flathead River, Montana, the patchy mosaic of stand age and productivity relate to areas of groundwater upwelling at valley constrictions and downwelling along reaches in wider valley bottoms (Harner and Stanford 2003). The horizontal (and vertical) distribution of various fluvial features of different elevations, soil characteristics, flood frequency, and age create a concentration of habitats across floodplains. Shifts in cottonwood understory plant species composition were shown to be more related to floodplain stratigraphy and soil texture and its influence on water availability than to hydroperiod along the Snake River in eastern Idaho (Merigliano 2005). Soil moisture and depth to water table have universally been determined to be key factors determining plant species composition (Chambers et al. 2004), species richness (Dwire et al. 2006), and dominant life form (Darrouzet-Nardi et al. 2006) along mountain river channels.

A distinct feature of most mountain stream channels is vegetation zonation—distinct bands of vegetation paralleling the stream—along channel margins. Cross-valley or transverse patterns of plant zonation are a common feature of wetland and riparian vegetation (Toner and Keddy 1997; Nilsson et al. 1999). Zonation may be conspicuous because of differences in plant physiognomy (e.g., plant height, canopy color, etc.) across different vegetation zones. In some cases, zonation is caused by the affinities and tolerances of individual species to abiotic factors as they change laterally as a function of distance away and elevation above stream channels. Soil texture, exposure to disturbance (shear stress), depth to water table, soil moisture, flow duration and anoxia, and vulnerability to ice or woody debris scour vary along the elevation gradient extending laterally from stream channels to uplands. Degree of connectivity to stream channels is also an important mediator of water chemistry and fluvial disturbance, and thus plant community composition (Bayley and Guimond 2008).

Zonation may reflect the tolerance of individual species to inundation, disturbance, and drought, or may reflect the competitive abilities of species. Zonation may also reflect a temporal or successional trend associated with river meandering, resulting in distinct even-aged stands of vegetation corresponding to rates of meandering (Nanson and Beach 1977; Scott et al. 1996). Specific sets of traits (e.g., vegetative growth, furrowed bark, adaptation to anoxia, taproots, or flexible stems) within transverse vegetation zones recur along stream channel margins throughout the West (Merritt et al. 2010). Life forms of vegetation transitioning from herbaceous, flood-tolerant species to woody species (subshrubs and shrubs) to trees as a function of distance from the channel have been documented along mountain rivers worldwide (Nilsson 1991; Toner and Keddy 1997; Friedman et al. 2006; Merritt and Wohl 2006). The steep abiotic gradients that drive such zonation form a concentrated patchwork of various habitat attributes (including disturbance frequency and magnitude) and contribute to the high number of species in riparian habitats, a trend that occurs from alpine streams to lowland riparian areas when compared to adjacent uplands.

Conservation Concerns

Flow alteration due to dams, diversions, channelization, and other water management activities is a fundamental cause of channel and vegetation change along rivers and floodplains throughout western North America. Dam construction in mountain valleys is common throughout the Rocky Mountains. Even more common are within and out-of-basin water diversions, which number in the tens of thousands in the mountains of western North America. Dams and diversions can result in reduced peak flows, reduced suspended sediment and bedload, increased or decreased base flow, shifts in flow variability, and altered timing of various hydrographic attributes. Altered streamflow regimes and sediment dynamics in streams can interrupt recruitment and other life stages of plants as well as cause changes in channel form and natural disturbance regimes. Disturbance-adapted species are particularly vulnerable to the changes in flow regime and fluvial processes imposed by dams (Merritt et al. 2010). Dams and diversions are designed to cause changes to flow regimes, but they have other unintended effects, such as to alter groundwater levels and moisture distributions across floodplains, to hinder the movement of organisms, and to interrupt sediment transport, which may influence meandering rates and alter channel form, all of which can compromise the functioning of riparian zones.

Dewatering, groundwater pumping, and channel incision can result in declines in groundwater levels, often resulting in encroachment of woody vegetation into areas formerly dominated by herbaceous vegetation (Chambers et al. 2004). Encroachment of *Artemisia* into formerly herbaceous-dominated riparian vegetation following groundwater decline is common in western riparian systems, including those in the Rocky Mountains and Great Basin. Vegetation change toward terrestrial vegetation (terrestrialization) is a common phenomenon in riparian areas as a response to dewatering or altered flow regimes.

Roads, urban development, agriculture, mining, and other human activities in valley bottoms also influence rivers and riparian areas directly. Logging in riparian areas, biomass removal through livestock grazing and fire, and recreational activities can also have measurable effects through directly altering vegetation and channel properties. Soil compaction and disturbance in riparian areas can result in erosion and bank failure, and alter rates of infiltration and rates of runoff and channel form. Browsing and grazing by domestic or native ungulates can also reduce vegetative cover and limit or restrict riparian vegetation recruitment (e.g., *Populus* and *Salix*) (Beschta 2003). Trapping of riverine mammals such as beaver, muskrat *(Ondatra zibethicus)* and otter *(Lontra canadensis)* may also have cascading effects on rivers. Naiman et al. (1998) estimate that 80% of riparian areas have been lost over the past 200 years in North America, in part because of beaver trapping and associated loss of beaver-maintained riparian marsh and wet meadows.

In addition to the direct effects of water development and human activities in river channels, humans can influence rivers through activities that alter sediment and water delivery from uplands throughout their watershed. These effects may range from increased rates of runoff due to altering vegetation to changes in hillslope processes and mass wasting. Improved management of lands throughout watersheds, road improvements, the establishment of riparian buffers, environmental flow management, the construction of fish ladders, and dam removal are among the many tools that can be used to reduce or reverse the effects of human activities on riverine ecosystems in the mountain landscapes of western North America.

References

Allen-Diaz BH. 1991. Water table and plant species relationships in Sierra Nevada meadows. *Am. Midl. Nat.* 126:30–43.

Asada T, Warner BG. 2005. Surface peat mass and carbon balance in a hyper-maritime peatland. *Soil Sci. Soc. Am. J.* 69:549–62.

Asada T, Warner BG, Pojar J. 2003. Environmental factors responsible for shaping an open peatland—forest complex on the hyper-maritime north coast of British Columbia. *Can. J. For. Res.* 33:2380–94.

Austin JE, Pyle WH. 2004. Small mammals in montane wet meadow habitat at Grays Lake, Idaho. *Northw. Sci.* 78:225–33.

Baker BW, Ducharme HC, et al. 2005. Interaction of beaver and elk herbivory reduces standing crop of willow. *Ecol. Appl.* 15:110–18.

Baker WL. 1990. Climatic and hydrologic effects on the regeneration of *Populus angustifolia* James along the Animas River, Colorado. *J. Biogeogr.* 17:59–73.

Bayley SE, Guimond JK. 2008. Effects of river connectivity on marsh vegetation community structure and species richness in montane floodplain wetlands in Jasper National Park, Alberta, Canada. *EcoScience* 15:377–88.

Beechie TJ, Liermann M, et al. 2006. Channel pattern and river-floodplain dynamics in forested mountain river systems. *Geomorphology* 78:124–41.

Benda LE, Hassan MA, et al. 2005. Geomorphology of steepland headwaters: the transition from hillslopes to channels. *J. Am. Water Resour. Assoc.* 41:835–51.

Beschta RL. 2003. Cottonwoods, elk, and wolves in the Lamar Valley of Yellowstone National Park. *Ecol. Appl.* 13:1295–09.

Binkley D, Cromack K, Baker D Jr. 1994. Nitrogen fixation by red alder: biology, rates, and controls. In *The biology and management of red alder*, Hibbs DE, DeBell DS, Tarrant RF, editors. Corvallis: Oregon State Univ. Press, pp. 57–72.

Bursik RJ, Henderson DM. 1995. Valley peatland flora of Idaho. *Madroño* 42:366–95.

Castelli RM, Chambers JC, Tausch RJ. 2000. Soil-plant relations along a soil-water gradient in a Great Basin riparian meadow. *Wetlands* 20:251–66.

Chadde SW, Shelly JS, et al. 1998. *Peatlands on national forests of the northern Rocky Mountains: ecology and conservation*. Ogden, UT: USFS Rocky Mountain Res. Sta.

Chambers JC, Miller JR, editors. 2004. *Great Basin riparian ecosystems*. Washington, DC: Island Press.

Chambers JC, Tausch RJ, et al. 2004. Effects of geomorphic processes and hydrologic regimes on riparian vegetation. In *Great*

Basin riparian ecosystems, Chambers JC, Miller JR, editors. Washington, DC: Island Press, pp. 124–161.

Chimner RA. 2000. *Carbon dynamics of southern Rocky Mountain fens.* Ph.D. diss., Colorado State Univ., Fort Collins.

Chimner RA, Cooper DJ. 2003. Carbon dynamics of pristine and hydrologically modified fens in the southern Rocky Mountains. *Can. J. Bot.* 81:477–91.

Chimner RA, Karberg J. 2008. Long-term carbon accumulation in two tropical mountain peatlands, Andes Mountains, Ecuador. *Mires and Peat* 3:Art. 4.

Chimner RA, Lemly J, Cooper DJ. 2010. Mountain fen distribution, types and restoration priorities, San Juan Mountains, Colorado, USA. *Wetlands* DOI: 10.1007/s13157-010-0039-5.

Chimner RA, Cooper DJ, Parton WJ. 2002. Modeling carbon accumulation in Rocky Mountain fens. *Wetlands* 22:100–10.

Chimner RA, Brione E, et al. 2007. Exploring the hydro-ecological conditions of high elevation wetlands in the Andes Mountains. Final report, National Geograph. Soc. Washington, DC.

Compton JE, Church MR, et al. 2003. Nitrogen export from forested watersheds in the Oregon Coast Range: the role of N-2-fixing red alder. *Ecosystems* 6:773–85.

Cook BJ, Hauer FR. 2007. Hydrologic connectivity on water chemistry, soils, and vegetation structure and function in an intermontane depressional wetland landscape. *Wetlands* 27:719–38.

Cooper DJ. 1990. The ecology of wetlands in Big Meadows, Rocky Mountain National Park, Colorado: the correlation of vegetation, soils and hydrology. *US Department of the Interior, Fish and Wildlife Service, Biological Report* 90(15).

Cooper DJ. 1996. Water and soil chemistry, floristics, and phytosociology of the extreme rich High Creek fen, in South Park, Colorado, U.S.A. *Can. J. Bot.* 74:1801–11.

Cooper DJ, Andrus RE. 1994. Patterns of vegetation and water chemistry in peatlands of the west-central Wind River Range, Wyoming, U.S.A. *Can. J. Bot.* 72:1586–97.

Cooper DJ, MacDonald LH. 2000. Restoring the vegetation of mined peatlands in the southern Rocky Mountains of Colorado, U.S.A. *Restor. Ecol.* 8:103–11.

Cooper DJ, Sanderson JS. 1997. A montane *Kobresia myosuroides* fen community type in the southern Rocky Mountains of Colorado, U.S.A. *Arct. Alp. Res.* 29:300–03.

Cooper DJ, Wolf E. 2006. *Fens of the California Sierra Nevada: landforms, geochemistry, vegetation, and influences of livestock grazing.* Report, U.S. Forest Service. Vallejo, CA.

Cooper DJ, Andrus RE, Arp CD. 2002. *Sphagnum balticum* in a southern Rocky Mountain iron fen. *Madroño* 49:186–88.

Cooper DJ, MacDonald LH, Kennedy S. 1998. Hydrologic restoration of a fen in Rocky Mt. National Park, Colorado. *Wetlands* 18:335–45.

Cooper DJ, Dickens J, et al. 2006. Hydrologic, geomorphic and climate controls on willow establishment in a montane ecosystem. *Hydrol. Processes* 20:1845–64.

Cooper DJ, Sanderson JS, et al. 2006. Effects of long-term water table drawdown on evapotranspiration and vegetation in an arid region phreatophyte community. *J. Hydrol.* 325:21–34.

Cooper DJ, Wolf EC, et al. 2010. Wetlands of the Minas Congas region, Cajamarca, Peru. *Arct. Antarct. Alp. Res.* 42:19–33.

Darrouzet-Nardi A, D'Antonio CM, Dawson TE. 2006. Depth of water acquisition by invading shrubs and resident herbs in a Sierra Nevada meadow. *Plant and Soil* 285:31–43.

DeBenedetti SH, Parsons DJ. 1979. Mountain meadow management and research in Sequoia and Kings Canyon National Parks: a review and update. In *Proceedings First Conference on Scientific Research in the National Parks,* Linn R, editor. USDI NPS Trans. Proc. 5, 2:1305–11.

Dull RA. 1999. Palynological evidence for 19th century grazing-induced vegetation change in the southern Sierra Nevada, California, USA. *J. Biogeogr.* 26:899–912.

Dwire KA, Kauffman JB, Baham JE. 2006. Plant species distribution in relation to water-table depth and soil redox potential in montane riparian meadows. *Wetlands* 26:131–46.

Dwire KA, Kauffman JB, et al. 2004. Plant biomass and species composition along an environmental gradient in montane riparian meadows. *Oecologia* 139:309–17.

Elmore AJ, Mustard JF, Manning SJ. 2003. Regional patterns of plant community response to changes in water: Owens Valley, California. *Ecol. Appl.* 13:443–60.

Friedman JM, Auble GT, et al. 2006. Transverse and longitudinal variation in woody riparian vegetation along a montane river. *West. N. Am. Natur.* 66:78–91.

Gage EA, Cooper DJ. 2005. Patterns and processes of *Salix* seed dispersal in a browsed environment. *Can. J. Bot.* 83:678–87.

Gage EA, Cooper DJ. 2004. Constraints on willow seedling establishment in a Rocky Mountain montane riparian floodplain. *Wetlands* 24:908–11.

Gregory S, Swanson FJ, et al. 1991. An ecosystem perspective of riparian zones. *BioScience* 41:540–51.

Harner MH, Stanford JA. 2003. Differences in cottonwood growth between a losing and a gaining reach of an alluvial floodplain. *Ecology* 84:1453–58.

Hart EA, Lovvorn JR. 2000. Vegetation dynamics and primary production in saline, lacustrine wetlands of a Rocky Mountain basin. *Aquat. Bot.* 66:21–39.

Hauer FR, Stanford JA, Lorang MS. 2007. Patterns and processes in northern Rocky Mountain headwaters: ecological linkages in the headwaters of the crown of the continent. *J. Am. Water Resourc. Assoc.* 43:104–17.

Hauer FR, Baron JS, et al. 1997. Assessment of climate change and freshwater ecosystems of the Rocky Mountains, USA and Canada. *Hydrol. Processes* 11:903–24.

Kim JG, Rejmánková E, Spanglet H. 2001. Implications of a sediment-chemistry study on subalpine marsh conservation in the Lake Tahoe basin, USA. *Wetlands* 21:379–94.

Komarkova V. 1979. *Alpine vegetation of the Indian Peaks Area.* Vaduz, Germany: J. Cramer. FL-9490.

Kotowski W, Van Diggelen R, Kleinke J. 1998. Behaviour of wetland plant species along a moisture gradient in two geographically distant areas. *Acta Bot. Neerlandica* 47:337–49.

Lemly JM and Cooper DJ. 2011. Multiscale factors control community and species distributions in mountain peatlands. *Botany* 89:689–713.

Lesica P. 1986. Vegetation and flora of Pine Butte fen, Teton County, Montana. *Great Basin Natur.* 46:22–32.

Lichthardt J. 2004. *Conservation strategy for Idaho Panhandle peatlands.* Rep. Idaho Panhandle Nat. For.

Maltby E, Proctor MCF. 1996. Peatlands: their nature and role in the biosphere. In *Global Peat Resources,* Lappalainen E, editor. Internat. Peat Soc. Geol. Surv. Finland, pp. 11–19.

McClellan MH, Brock T, Baichtal JF. 2003. Calcareous fens in Southeast Alaska. *Res. Note PNW-RN-536.* Portland, OR: USDA, For. Serv., Pac. NW Res. Sta.

Mehringer PJ Jr, Arno SF, Peterson KL. 1977. Postglacial history of Lost Trail Pass Bog, Bitterroot Mountains, Montana. *Arct. Alp. Res.* 9:345–68.

Merigliano MF. 2005. Cottonwood understory zonation and its relation to floodplain stratigraphy. *Wetlands* 25:356–74.

Merriam CH. 1890. Results of a biological survey of the San Francisco Mountain region and the desert of the Little Colorado, Arizona. *N. Am. Fauna* 3:1–113.

Merritt DM, Wohl EE. 2006. Plant dispersal along rivers fragmented by dams. *Riv. Res. Appl.* 22:1–26.

Merritt DM, Scott ML, et al. 2010. Theory, methods and tools for determining environmental flows for riparian vegetation: riparian vegetation-flow response guilds. *Freshw. Biol.* 55:206–25.

Messerli B, Viviroli D, Weingartner R. 2004. Mountains of the world: vulnerable water towers for the 21st century. *Ambio* 13:29–34.

Montgomery DM. 1999. Process domains and the river continuum. *J. Am. Water Resourc. Assoc.* 35:397–410.

Montgomery DR, Buffington JM. 1997. Channel-reach morphology in mountain drainage basins. *Geol. Soc. Am. Bull.* 109:596–611.

Naiman RJ, Johnston CA, Kelley JC. 1988. Alteration of North American streams by beaver. *Bioscience* 38:753–62.

Nanson GC, Beach HF. 1977. Forest succession and sedimentation on a meandering-river floodplain, northeast British Columbia, Canada. *J. Biogeogr.* 4:229–51.

Nilsson C. 1999. Rivers and streams. In *Swedish plant geography,* Rydin H, Snoeijs P, Diekmann M, editors. Uppsala: Opulus Press, pp. 135–48.

Patterson L, Cooper DJ. 2007. The use of hydrologic and ecological indicators for the restoration of drainage ditches and water diversions in a mountain fen, Cascade Range, California. *Wetlands* 27:290–304.

Peck DE, Lovvorn JR. 2001. The importance of flood irrigation in water supply to wetlands in the Laramie Basin, Wyoming, USA. *Wetlands* 21:370–78.

Ratliff RD. 1985. *Meadows in the Sierra Nevada of California: state of knowledge.* USDA For. Serv., Pac. SW For. Range Exp. Sta. Berkeley.

Rejmankova E, Rejmanek M, et al. 1999. Resistance and resilience of subalpine wetlands with respect to prolonged drought. *Folia Geobot.* 34:175–88.

Richter B, Richter H. 2000. Prescribing flood regimes to sustain riparian ecosystems along meandering rivers. *Conserv. Biol.* 14:1467–78.

Riggs GB. 1925. Some *Sphagnum* bogs of the north Pacific coast of America. *Ecology* 6:260–78.

Risvold AM, Fonda RW. 2001. Community composition and floristic relationships in montane wetlands in the north Cascades, Washington. *Northw. Sci.* 75:157–67.

Roberts MD. 1999. *Hydrogeomorphic factors influencing clonal recruitment of cottonwoods in mountain valleys.* MS thesis, Utah State Univ., Logan.

Rot BW, Naiman RJ, Bilby RE. 2000. Stream channel configuration, landform, and riparian forest structure in the Cascade Mountains, Washington. *Can. J. Fish. Aquat. Sci.* 57:699–707.

Sabo JL, Sponseller R, et al. 2005. Riparian zones increase regional species richness by harboring different, not more, species. *Ecology* 86:56–62.

Samuelson GM, Rood SB. 2004. Differing influences of natural and artificial disturbances on riparian cottonwoods from prairie to mountain ecoregions in Alberta, Canada. *J. Biogeogr.* 31:435–50.

Sanderson JS, Cooper DJ. 2008. Ground water evapotranspiration from wetlands of an arid intermountain basin. *J. Hydrol.* 351:344–59.

Sanderson JS, Kotliar NB, et al. 2008a. The simulated natural hydrologic regime of an intermountain playa conservation site. *Wetlands* 23:363–77.

Sanderson JS, Kotliar NB, Steingraeber DA. 2008b. Opposing environmental gradients govern vegetation zonation in an intermountain playa. *Wetlands* 28:1060–70.

Scott ML, Friedman JM, Auble GT. 1996. Fluvial process and the establishment of bottomland trees. *Geomorphology* 14:327–39.

Toner M, Keddy P. 1997. River hydrology and riparian wetlands: a predictive model for ecological assembly. *Ecol. Appl.* 7:236–46.

Vitt DH, Chee WL. 1990. The relationships of vegetation to surface water chemistry and peat chemistry in fens of Alberta, Canada. *Vegetatio* 89:87–106.

Viviroli D, Weingartner R, Messerli B. 2003. Assessing the hydrological significance of the world's mountains. *Mountain Res. Develop.* 23:32–40.

Walker LR, Chapin F. 1986. Physiological controls over seedling growth in primary succession on an Alaskan floodplain. *Ecology* 67:1508–23.

Walter H. 1973. *Vegetation of the Earth in relation to climate and the eco-physiological conditions,* 2nd ed. New York: Springer-Verlag.

Walter H. 1985. *Vegetation of the Earth and the ecological systems of the geo-biosphere,* 3rd revised ed. New York: Springer-Verlag.

Warner BG, Asada T. 2006. Biological diversity of peatlands in Canada. *Aquat. Sci.* 68:240–53.

Westbrook C, Cooper DJ, Baker B. 2006. Beaver dams and floods in controlling hydrologic processes of a mountain valley. *Water Resour. Res.* 42:W06404, doi:10.1029/2005WR004560.

Westbrook C, Cooper DJ, Baker B. 2010. Beaver assisted river valley formation. *Riv. Res. Appl.* doi:10.1002/rra.13.59.

Winter TC. 2007. The role of ground water in generating streamflow in headwater areas and in maintaining base flow. *J. Am. Water Resour. Assoc.* 43:15–25.

Wohl E. 2000. *Mountain rivers.* Washington, DC: Am. Geophys. Union.

Wolf EC, Cooper DJ, Hobbs NT. 2007. Beaver, streamflow and elk influence willow establishment and floodplain stability on Yellowstone's northern range. *Ecol. Appl.* 17:1572–87.

Woods SW, Cooper DJ. 2005. Hydrologic factors affecting willow seedling establishment along a subalpine stream, Colorado, USA. *Arct. Antarct. Alp. Res.* 37:636–43.

Wurster FC, Cooper DJ, Sanford WE. 2003. Stream/aquifer interactions at Great Sand Dunes National Monument, Colorado: influences on interdunal wetland disappearance. *J. Hydrol.* 271:77–100.

Zicheng Y, Beilman DW, Jones MC. 2009. Sensitivity of northern peatland carbon dynamics to Holocene climate change. In *Carbon cycling in northern peatlands,* Baird AJ, Belyea LR, et al., editors. Geophys. Monogr. Series, vol. 184.

CHAPTER 23

Desert Spring Wetlands of the Great Basin

MARY JANE KELEHER and DON SADA

Forests are absent, except for a few limited areas on the higher
mountains. One may ride hundreds of miles through the valleys
without finding a tree to shelter him from the intense heat of
summer sun.

ISRAEL C. RUSSELL, 1895

O the luxury of good sweet water to a thoroughly thirsty traveler!
O little do we value the daily common bounties of Providence! For
the past few days a draught of pure cold water has been prized at
its true value . . . only the real absence of comforts that causes us
to estimate them at their full value.

CAPTAIN J. H. SIMPSON, 1859

To the traveler the Great Basin is as described by Israel Russell and water has the premium noted by J. H. Simpson. The region is dry and is covered by expansive sagebrush valleys intervened by high mountains. While these observations are valid, they are misguided because its intrigue lies in subtleties that belie generalizations. Israel Russell was fascinated by the region's aridity and rugged topography and became intrigued by the subtle evidence of ancient lakes and past wetter climates shown by shoreline terraces tracing the base of many Great Basin mountain ranges (Russell 1889). The Great Basin was the last area explored in the U.S. and remains one of the least studied. This area is remote and sparsely populated, with most of its metropolitan areas located along its eastern, western, and southern boundaries. Aridity is a defining factor for life in the Great Basin. Its terrestrial and aquatic systems are adapted to high temperatures, high solute concentrations in soils and water, and, of course, the paucity of water.

The Great Basin

Geographical Setting

The Great Basin encompasses most of the Basin and Range Province of western North America. Boundaries of the Great Basin differ according to hydrologists, botanists, and aquatic biogeographers, but in this chapter we define its boundaries by the current hydrographic connection to adjacent watersheds (Fig. 23.1). As its name implies, its watersheds are contained within enorheic (enclosed) basins that drain internally

and do not flow to oceans. It encompasses almost one-fifth of the United States, including most of Nevada, western Utah, and fringes of California, Idaho, and Oregon. The Great Basin is bounded on the north and south by the Columbia and Colorado Plateaus, the east by the Wasatch Range, and the west by the Sierra Nevada mountains. Within its boundaries is one of the driest regions in the U.S.: the Mojave Desert. Its diverse topography consists of more than 170 north-south-oriented mountain ranges that are separated by intervening valleys (McLane 1987). The geographer Clarence Dutton likened its physiography to "a line of caterpillars marching southward toward Mexico." Many of its mountains exceed 4,000 m elevation, while valley elevations range from 83 m below sea level in Death Valley to near 1,600 m in most of the northern valleys. Most precipitation comes during the winter primarily as mountain snow. Annual precipitation varies from 350 cm in the mountains to less than 2 cm in Death Valley. Summer temperatures exceed 45°C in most of the southern Great Basin and can be less than –50°C in mountains during winter. The minimum winter temperature is often less than –30°C in higher elevation valleys, but it is rarely less than 4°C in lower valleys.

Great Basin Wetlands

Scientists and the public identify typical wetlands as expansive marshes, swamps, and bogs where wildlife is abundant and vegetation relies on the presence of water through much of the year. These impressions typify wetlands in more mesic

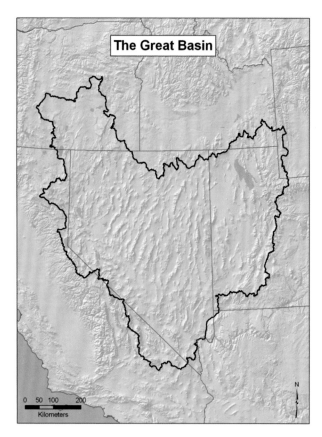

FIG. 23.1. The Great Basin. Boundary is based on the current hydrographic connection to adjacent watersheds.

our discussion focuses on characteristics of these wetland types rather than the large marshlands that also occur in the Great Basin.

Geology and Hydrology

Geology

Desert springs are small-scale unique aquatic systems that occur where groundwater reaches the surface. As such, they provide an interface between hypogean (subterranean) and epigean (surface-water) habitats (Smith et al. 2003). As mentioned, the general topography of the Great Basin Desert is a product of geological forces that created flat valleys or basins separated by many north-south-trending mountain ranges (Christiansen 1951; Wilberg and Stolp 1985; Grayson 1993). Thousands of geographically isolated desert springs ranging in elevation from 83 m below sea level (bsl) (e.g., Badwater, Death Valley, California) to 1,475 m above sea level (asl) (e.g., Gandy Salt Marsh, Snake Valley, Utah) are scattered along the base of these mountains and throughout the valley floors. Even though they vary widely in size, persistence, morphology, water quality, and habitat complexity, many have persisted for thousands of years (Waring 1920; Deacon and Minckley 1974; Deacon et al. 1980). Basic physicochemical and biological characteristics are poorly known for most desert springs. A number of the larger spring complexes have been studied (Deacon et al. 1980; Sada and Nachlinger 1996, 1998; Hoegrefe and Fridell 2000; Sada 2000; Biowest Inc. 2007; Keleher and Rader 2007; Three Parameters Plus, Inc. 2010); however, most of the smaller spring systems have not.

Great Basin desert spring ecosystems range in size from small individual springs (1.0 m^2; Fig. 23.2a) to large spring-fed wetland complexes (Fig. 23.2b), though most tend to be less than 1 ha in size. Many of the desert spring ecosystems consist solely of a spring source and the eucrenal zone. Most spring-fed complexes include three distinct habitat types: a spring source (including the eucrenal zone); a hypocrenal springbrook; and shallow (< 1 m depth), often extensive terminal marshes. The larger wetland complexes typically have multiple spring sources, some of which are connected by springbrooks that typically flow into marshes. The largest spring-fed complex is located within the Fish Springs Wildlife Refuge in Utah and is approximately 40 km^2. Springbrooks exhibit varying widths, ranging from less than 30 cm to > 3 m in width. Marsh habitats are the most variable in size ranging from only a few meters square to nearly 40 km^2.

Hydrology

Desert spring ecosystems of the Great Basin occur where groundwater from large underground aquifers discharge to the land surface through fractures or faults in underlying rock strata or through porous materials (Prudic et al. 1995; Smith et al. 2000; Anderson et al. 2005; Todd and Mays 2005). These ecosystems are dependent on recharge from mountain precipitation (Fig. 23.3), and physicochemical characteristics of each spring are a function of landscape association (e.g., valley floor playa or alluvium, bajada, etc.), geology, residence time of water in the aquifer, and depth of circulation. In general, desert springs with high concentrations of dissolved chemi-

that small wetlands had little value. During their taxonomic and biogeographic work, they also documented decreasing fish abundance and distribution caused by habitat alteration and provided a foundation for modern-day fish conservation. Though fish conservation programs have prevented extinctions and extirpations of many species (Sada and Vinyard 2002), they have focused primarily on larger systems that include only a small portion of Great Basin wetlands.

Today, thousands of desert springs occur across all Great Basin landforms. Most are geographically isolated, comparatively small, and perceived to be less important than large marshes and swamps. These comparisons are inappropriate because the value of wetlands must be considered in the context of regional climate, topography, and biodiversity. Although Great Basin desert springs tend to be small, they are biodiversity hot spots, provide the only water over vast areas, and many support a number of narrowly endemic plant species and crenobiontic (spring- and springbrook-dwelling) vertebrates and invertebrates (Myers and Resh 1999).

Several Great Basin desert spring ecosystems are within state and federal wildlife refuge systems (e.g., Fish Springs National Wildlife Refuge [NWR] in Utah, Pahranagat, Ruby Lake NWRs in Nevada). Most of these refuges consist of a large terminal marsh that is supported by springs with a distinctive crenofauna and are isolated from other aquatic systems. These refuges are some of the largest waterfowl habitats in the region and others, such as Ash Meadows NWR, were designated to conserve species listed as endangered by the US Fish and Wildlife Service (Sada 1990). Since most of the Great Basin wetlands consist of small, mostly undescribed isolated desert springs,

FIG. 23.2. Individual spring source with eucrenal zone. A. A cold spring in Gandy Salt Marsh, Snake Valley, Utah, and spring-fed complex. B. Saratoga Springs, Death Valley, California.

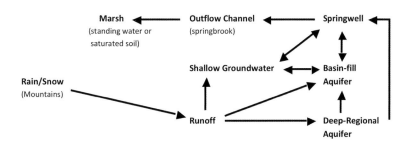

FIG. 23.3. Conceptual model of the complex hydrology of valley floor spring ecosystems of the Great Basin. (Modified from Patten, Rouse, et al. 2008.)

cal constituents are supported by larger, regional or carbonate aquifers with longer residence time (decades to millennia), deep circulation, and warm (> 20°C) temperatures (Quade et al. 1998; Smith et al. 2000; Patten et al. 2008; Hershey et al. 2009).

Because desert springs depend primarily on groundwater and very little on surface runoff (Fig. 23.3), these systems would represent a unique wetland type currently missing from diagrams presented by Brinson (1993) and Sharitz and Pennings (2006) depicting the relative contribution and importance of water sources to wetlands. In Fig. 23.4, we modify a diagram to demonstrate the hydrologic relationships of spring-fed wetlands. Many deep regional aquifers are large and composed of ancient water (Thomas et al. 1996). Because much of the water infiltrated hundreds to thousands of years ago, before modern agriculture and industrialization, water from carbonate aquifers tends to be unpolluted (Quade et al. 1998), but the quality of groundwater from shallow, unconsolidated material can be and has been affected by watershed alterations and contaminants (Barbash et al. 2001).

Depending on the source of water (e.g., aquifer or shallow groundwater) and bank slope, water depths of the spring source range considerably, from shallow (~0.25 m) to < 8.0 m in depth. Springbrooks and marshes have shallower water depths, ranging from only a few centimeters to nearly a meter. Groundwater inflow into some springs is constant and subject to little annual variation, particularly regional aquifer springs (Todd and Mays 2005), but can be variable in many systems and influenced by short-term precipitation patterns. Depending on the rate of spring discharge, water depths in spring-

brooks and marshes are usually greatest in spring and decrease in the summer and fall as evaporation rates increase and precipitation decreases.

In most wetland systems, hydrodynamics is one of the most important local factors that affect community composition. However, since desert spring ecosystems are relatively stable in terms of flooding and channel-forming processes, this abiotic factor has a lesser effect on community composition then do morphology, discharge, and chemical properties. Chemical properties (temperature, dissolved oxygen), however, can be and are driven to a great extent by the groundwater source, which is influenced by geology, climate, and topography (Sada 2008).

Water Temperature and Chemistry

Desert springs feature one of the most important contrasts known to effect community composition: constant versus variable environmental conditions (Southwood 1977). Persistent springs are one of the most constant aquatic habitats on Earth, whereas marshes can be one of the most variable (Mitsch and Gosselink 2007). Chemical conditions of marshes (e.g., oxygen, pH, nutrient levels) fluctuate on a daily basis as photosynthesis and total community respiration respond to changes in solar irradiation (Wetzel 2001). Since chemical properties of shallow, stagnant marshes fluctuate from day to night, like so many wetlands, our discussion is limited to the chemical attributes of persistent spring sources, the primary source of water for high-quality desert-spring wetlands. As

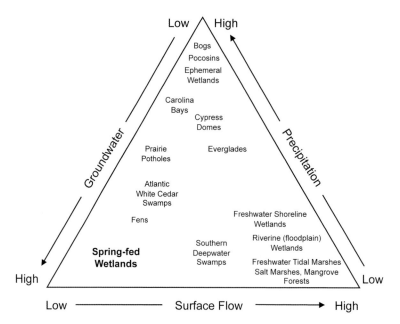

FIG. 23.4. A diagram depicts the relative contribution and importance of water sources to different wetlands. Inserting spring-fed wetlands (such those in the Great Basin) clearly completes this diagram with an example with high groundwater but low surface water contribution. (From Sharitz and Pennings 2006; reprinted with permission.)

these springs are fairly constant systems and subject to little annual variation, they tend to exhibit only slight fluctuations in daily, seasonal, and interannual variability of water chemistry (Deacon and Minckley 1974; Todd and Mays 2005). Since these desert springs are groundwater-fed, the specific groundwater source has a significant influence on the chemical attributes, particularly temperature, salinity (based on electrical conductivity given as μS/cm), dissolved chemical constituents, and dissolved oxygen (DO).

Water temperature in Great Basin desert springs ranges from cold (near 10°C) to hot (> 35°C) where magmatic proximity supports geothermal springs that are often > 50°C (e.g., 71°C Chimney Hot Springs, Railroad Valley). The coolest springs (e.g., 10°C Miller Spring, Snake Valley) are generally supported by small aquifers with short resident time and relatively few dissolved chemical constituents (Prudic et al. 1995; Thomas et al. 1996; Quade et al. 1998; Smith et al. 2000; Anderson et al. 2005; Patten et al. 2008; Hershey et al. 2010). Using water temperature, desert springs can be divided into cold springs (near or below the mean annual air temperature (< 20°C), warm or thermal springs (~ 20–30°C) and hot springs (> 30°C). Most desert spring ecosystems in the Great Basin are supported by contributions from at least two aquifers; however, each system tends to be dominated by one. For example, nearly every spring in Snake Valley is cold (mean 14.6°C), whereas nearly every spring in Fish Springs Valley is thermal (mean 25.2°C), and springs in Railroad Valley are all hot (mean 38.9°C). Snake Valley springs are supported by local aquifers with short residence times between snowmelt entering the aquifer and water discharging from a spring. Hot springs in Railroad Valley are supported by geothermal sources, and Fish Springs Valley springs are primarily supported by a regional aquifer.

Conductivity also varies widely within the Great Basin desert spring ecosystems, ranging from 100 μS/cm in bajada springs to 10,000 μS/cm in Death Valley (Thomas et al. 1996). In fact, all springs within the Fish Springs Wildlife Refuge have conductivities that exceed 3,000 μS/cm with a mean of 3,200 μS/cm. Most desert springs in the Great Basin, however, range between 300 and 700 μS/cm. Like temperature and conductivity, DO varies and is influenced primarily by the groundwater source. In systems with low DO, the water source is usually from deep aquifers, whereas springs with high levels of DO tend to be supplied by the more shallow groundwater sources. For example, in Tule Valley (Utah), many of the desert springs have DO levels near or below 2 mg/l, which probably indicates supply by groundwater from a deeper aquifer (Biowest Inc. 2007). It has been noted; however, that DO increases as the water moves away from the spring source (Biowest Inc. 2007) providing greater spring habitat heterogeneity. pH is perhaps the least variable chemical attribute, with most desert springs having a fairly constant pH near 7.7, though some range as high as 10 (Percy Spring, Fish Springs NWR). The extreme variability in chemical attributes among desert springs, coupled with the isolation that results in their unique biodiversity, plays a significant role in determining the biological communities present in desert spring ecosystems of the Great Basin.

Plant and Animal Communities

In arid regions such as the Great Basin, desert spring ecosystems often are "island" ecosystems surrounded by xerophyte-dominated (e.g., *Distichlis spicata*, *Artemisia tridentata*) deserts and are often the sole source of water for a large number of plant and wildlife species. As such, spring systems provide the majority of reliable water and food resources in the region, making them "biodiversity hot spots" that are critical to the persistence of plants, algae, macroinvertebrates, amphibians, fish, mammals, and birds, many of which are unique and endemic aquatic organisms. Though there are no birds endemic to the spring-fed wetlands of the Great Basin, these springs are of primary importance to numerous species of waterbirds, particularly ducks (Ryser 1985; Engilis and Reid 1996). For example, the Lahontan Valley provides habitat for the widest diversity and largest populations of migratory and wetland-dependent waterbirds in Nevada (Jehl 1994; Page and Gill 1994; USFWS 1994).

Plants and Algae

Vegetation communities associated with Great Basin wetlands differ in response to elevation, soil type, and water source. Additionally, alteration of these wetlands in support of livestock has greatly influenced these communities by introducing invasive species and excessive trampling. Because of these impacts, few resemble historic, prelivestock conditions and it is difficult to identify reference conditions. Great Basin wetlands are broadly associated with two soil types, with valley bottom wetlands consisting of mesic aridisols and entisols, many of which are alkaline to saline clays. At these wetlands, seasonal drying of spring borders and marsh habitats often expose fine-grained mudflats and/or surficial salt encrustations. Wetlands that occur at higher elevations (> 1,000 m) and are slightly above valley floors or on bajadas are associated with larger-grain alluvium soils that are less saline and alkaline. Vegetation associated with valley floor wetlands tends to be salt-tolerant and halophytic associations (USDI 1994), such as *Distichlis spicata*, *Schoenoplectus americanus–Eleocharis palustris*, *E. palustris–D. spicata*, and *E. palustris–Juncus balticus*.

Zonation of spring-fed wetlands typically exhibits four distinct zones: an upland border zone, a narrow rush border/bank cover zone, a shallow-water zone, and an open-water zone that is often deep (up to 2 m). Vegetation associated with the higher elevation wetlands includes a dense willow (*Salix* sp.) riparian border that may be bound laterally by *D. spicata* or even upland vegetation (usually *Artemisia* sp.). Wetlands below 1,000 m elevation may support ash (*Fraxinus* sp.) and mesquite (*Prosopis* sp.) forests that are underlain with *D. spicata*. *Distichlis spicata* occurs primarily around upland borders and is the most prominent herbaceous vegetation found at Great Basin wetlands that are associated with saline and alkaline soils (Marquis et al. 1984; Tiku 2006). However, at higher elevations species of *Salix* may be more prominent.

Adjacent to the saltbrush uplands, the bank and shallow wetted borders of most springs and springbrook habitats tend to be dominated by lower-growing emergent vegetation such as rushes (e.g., *Juncus balticus*), spikerushes (e.g., *Eleocharis palustris*), and sedges (e.g., *Carex nebrascensis*). These rush border communities occur in strips of only a few centimeters to a meter in width. However, the specific association often depends on disturbances (e.g., grazing pressure) and the stage of succession (Shupe 1986, Bolen 1964). For example, *C. nebrascensis* has a low tolerance to pressures from grazing or trampling disturbances and can easily be replaced by *J. balticus* (Pratt et al. 2002). Early successional *E. palustris* also tends to thrive in springs that have been disturbed. Other plants often associated within this zone include species of *Muhlenbergia* (e.g., *M. richardsonis*) and *Agrostis* and the invasive foxtail barley (*Hordeum jubatum*). Few native shrubs and trees occur along the outer borders of desert springs and if present typically will be *Allendolfea occidentalis*, *Populus angustifolia*, *P. fremontii*, or *Ribes aureum*. The lack of shrubs and trees, however, may be an artifact of past human land-use practices that have altered this community type. If trees are found along the borders they tend to be the invasive *Elaeagnus angustifolia* or *Tamarix ramosissima* (Deacon et al. 1980).

Similar to the typical marsh habitat, desert springs with large shallow-water borders may also be dominated by a zone of taller bulrush species such as *Schoenoplectus americanus*, one of the most common clonal species that occurs in the Great Basin. In these systems, *S. americanus* tends to be monodominant in deeper-water areas but will codominate with species of *Eleocharis*, *Carex*, and *Distichlis* (Bolin 1964) as water levels decrease and salinity increases away from the spring source (Shupe 1986). Other species commonly found in this zone include *S. maritiumus*, *Triglochin maritime*, and species of *Salicornia* as well as invasive species such as *Phragmites australis* or *Typha latifolia*. Species of *Triglochin* and *Salicornia* and *S. maritiumus* are typically found in the more hypersaline spring ecosystems, however.

Open deep-water zones in desert springs are dominated by a variety of floating and submersed vegetative species including muskgrass (*Chara vulgaris*), several species of the watercress group (*Nasturtuim* spp., *Rorripa* spp.), *Potamogeton* spp., and the spiny naiad (*Najas marina*). Charophytes and species of *Potamogeton* are particularly important in many springs for regulating water quality by binding nutrients as well as stabilizing soils and providing organic materials. In addition to species of *Chara*, horsehair algae (*Chlorophyceae* sp.) and Cyanophyta species are the most common algal groups that occur in Great Basin springs. It has been suggested that several species of Cyanophyta may be able to fix atmospheric nitrogen, a process that may be uniquely fundamental to the entire trophic structure of many of the Great Basin desert springs (Deacon et al. 1980).

A few studies have been conducted to further describe algal communities in Great Basin wetlands. For example, Keleher and Rader (2008a) examined patterns of metaphyton community composition from 150 sites in spring wetlands of the Bonneville Basin, and others have studied epiphytic diatoms from other spring systems (Grimes et al. 1980; Kaczmarska and Rushforth 1984). Based on these studies and other reports, green algae (Chlorophyta) appear to be the most common microalgal group that occurs in Great Basin spring ecosystems and quite possibly is the primary energy base of these communities. Various species of *Spirogyra* and *Cladophora* in particular appear to be common Chlorophyta taxa. Of the other algal orders, *Merismopedia elegans* (Cyanophyta), *Vaucheria geminate* (Xantophyta), and species of *Synedra* (Bacillariophyta) also appear commonly in springs of the Great Basin.

Macrophyte and algal communities of desert spring ecosystems are vital food sources, particularly high in protein content, for a variety of wildlife, including muskrat, mule deer, geese, and ducks, as well as domestic livestock (Shupe 1986). In addition to food, emergent and submersed vegetation provides significant cover value to birds, fish, amphibians, and aquatic invertebrates.

Animal Communities

Since the Great Basin's fragmented hydrologic history has left most spring systems isolated from each other, springs, regardless of their size, support diverse aquatic animal communities, and many are inhabited by obligate endemic spring-dwelling crenobiontic species of vertebrates and invertebrates (LaRivers 1949, 1962; Hershler 1998, 1999; Schmude 1999). Trophic bases of food webs for these wetlands depend on both macrophytes and algae; however, some may depend more on one than the other. For example, cooler, more freshwater systems depend primarily on floating and submersed macrophytes or *Chara*,

TABLE 23.1
Select native endemic fish species that occur in desert springs of the Great Basin

Endemic taxa	Habitat	Location[a]	Status	Trophic level/1° food
Crenichthys baileyi, White River springfish	Warm to hot springs	Ash Meadows, NV	Endangered	Opportunistic omnivore—mostly filamentous algae and caddisfly larvae
C. nevadae, Railroad Valley springfish	Warm to hot springs	Railroad Valley, NV	Threatened	Opportunistic omnivore—mostly gastropods and filamentous algae
Cyprinodon diabolis, Devils Hole pupfish	Warm to hot springs	Death Valley, CA	Endangered	Mostly herbivore—diatoms
C. nevadensis, Amargosa pupfish	Warm to hot springs	Ash Meadows, NV	Endangered	Mostly herbivore—algae, some invertebrates
C. radiosus, Owens pupfish	Warm springs	Owens Valley, CA	Endangered	Mostly carnivore—variety of invertebrates
C. salinus milleri, Cottonball marsh pupfish	Warm to hot springs	Death Valley, CA	NS	Omnivore/algae and invertebrates
C. salinus salinus, Salt Creek pupfish	Warm to hot springs	Death Valley, CA	Special Concern	Opportunistic omnivore—mostly filamentous algae, amphipods, ostracods, and snails
Empetrichthys latos, Pahrump poolfish	Warm springs	Pahrump Valley, NV	Endangered	Opportunistic omnivore—mostly amphipods, ostracods, and snails
E. acros, desert dace	Warm to hot springs	Soldier Meadows, NV	Threatened	Omnivore—mostly periphyton, filamentous algae, and some invertebrates
Gila alvordensis, Alvord chub	Cold to warm springs	Alvord Basin, OR/NV	Special Concern	Opportunistic carnivore—mostly midge, cladocerans, copepods, ostracods, and mollusks
G. robusta jordani, Pahranagat roundtail chub	Warm outflows	Ash Springs, NV	Endangered	Herbivore—mostly algae
Iotichthys phlegethontis, least chub	Cold springs	Snake Valley, UT	Special Concern	Opportunistic omnivore—mostly amphipods, gastropods, insects, and ostracods
Relictus solitarius, relict dace	Warm springs	Ruby Valley Springs, NV	Threatened	Opportunistic omnivore—mostly amphipods, gastropods, insects, and ostracods
Lepidomeda albivallis, White River spinedace	Cold springs	White River, NV	Endangered	Opportunistic omnivore

[a] Denotes general location of occurrence: CA = California; NV = Nevada, OR = Oregon; UT = Utah.
NOTE: Information primarily summarized from Sigler and Sigler (1987) and NatureServe.org.

whereas thermal springs tend to depend more on algae growth as the food web base (Deacon et al. 1980). Subsequently, overall animal productivity in desert springs is quite variable. Some may exhibit very low animal diversity, whereas some may be somewhat more diverse, particularly in terms of the macro-invertebrates. Overall, within-spring diversity (Alpha diversity) tends to be low, whereas among spring diversity within the Great Basin (Beta diversity) tends to be high, probably due to the high degree of endemism and dispersal limitations attributed to the difficulties of moving through a dry terrestrial landscape (Keleher 2007). Tables 23.1 and 23.2 list some of the unique fish and amphibian species that occur in the Great Basin; Sada and Vinyard (2002) present a more complete list of distinct aquatic species and subspecies of amphibians, fish, mollusks, aquatic insects, and fairy shrimp.

Native fishes that occur in desert springs of the Great Basin are primarily composed of Cypriniformes (Cyprinidae) and Atheriniformes (Cyprinodontidae). Overall richness of fish in individual desert springs range from fishless to four species, with an estimated average of 1.5 species. Overall 74 native fishes occur in the spring-fed wetlands of Great Basin, with all being endemic species and subspecies. The most common fish is the ubiquitous *Rhinichthys osculus* (speckled dace), though studies indicate that this species may have several endemic subspecies (Sada et al. 1995; Sada and Vinyard 2002)

Similar to vegetative communities, fish communities, though low in site-specific diversity, are uniquely adapted to the specific chemical attributes of the springs in which they occur (Sada and Vinyard 2002). For example, Sumner and Sargent (1940) were able to demonstrate that *Crenichthys baileyi*

TABLE 23.2

Native amphibians that occur in desert springs of the Great Basin

Species	Habitat	Location	Status
Bufo nelsoni, Amargosa toad	Desert springs and streams	Oasis Valley, NV	FC
B. exsul, black toad	Desert springs	Deep Springs Valley, NV	—
B. boreas, western toad	Variety of wetland habitats	Spotted throughout Great Basin	—
B. punctatus, red-spotted toad	Desert streams and oases	Throughout Great Basin	—
B. woodhousii, Woodhouse's toad	Variety of wetland habitats	Widespread in Utah, southeast NV	—
Rana luteiventris, Columbia spotted frog	Springs and riparian marshes	Throughout ID, NV, OR, UT portions of Great Basin	FC
R. pipiens, northern leopard frog	Springs and riparian marshes	Snake Valley, UT, Spring Valley, NV, and extreme western NV	FC
R. onca, relict leopard frog	Springs	Virgin River drainage	FC
Pseudacris regilla, Pacific tree frog	Variety of wetland habitats	Throughout the Great Basin	—

NOTE: FC = Federal Candidate for listing under the Endangered Species Act of 1973, as amended.

(White River springfish) from a warm spring could survive in a cool spring, but the converse was not true. Some fish only inhabit thermal springs (e.g,. *Cyprinodon nevadensis,* Amargosa pupfish; *Crenichthys nevadae,* Railroad Valley springfish; *C. baileyi,* White River springfish; Table 23.1), whereas others tend to inhabit a wider range of spring temperatures (*Eremichthys acros,* desert dace; *Gila alvordensis,* Alvord chub; *Gila robusta jordani,* Pahranagat roundtail chub, *Iotichthys phlegethontis,* least chub; *Lepidomeda albivallis,* White River spinedace; Table 23.1). Still other fish are uniquely adapted to highly saline springs, such as *Cyrinodon salinus salinus* (Salt Creek pupfish; Fig. 23.5a) and *Cyrinodon salinus milleri* (Cottonball Marsh pupfish), both occurring in desert springs on the floor of Death Valley.

Fish species that evolved as solitary occupants of any given habitat are usually feeding generalists because they have not needed to specialize to compete for limited resources (Deacon and Minckley 1974). True to this pattern, many of the endemic fish species of Great Basin desert springs are indiscriminate and opportunistic feeders (Table 23.1), ingesting a wide variety of foods (Williams 1986). Overall, the majority of native fish species that occur in the Great Basin springs are omnivores, eating primarily algae during summer and fall and switching to invertebrates during the winter and spring when algal production is low (LaRivers 1962; Naiman 1975; Soltz and Naiman 1978). The most common invertebrates eaten tend to be amphipods, gastropods, and ostracods, with filamentous algae being the preferred algal group overall. A few fish are more specialized, such as *Cyprinodon diabolis* (Devils Hole pupfish), whose diet is composed primarily of diatoms (Deacon and Deacon 1978). In general, small fish need to consume a large percentage of their body weight in food every day to meet metabolic demands, which vary directly with water temperature of the occupied habitat (Bond 1979). Since springs in the Great Basin demonstrate a wide variety of temperatures, particularly the hot springs, some fish exhibit unique respiratory adaptations. For example, studies have shown that subspecies of *C. baileyi* that inhabit hot springs have a respiratory rate four or more times greater than subspecies that inhabit cool-water springs (Bond 1979).

Amphibian diversity in the Great Basin is low and even more so in desert spring ecosystems. There are 9 anurans (5 bufonids, 3 ranids, 1 hylid) that occupy spring habitats in the Great Basin (Table 23.2). Other species may frequent springs in some systems but are not dependent upon them, including *Bufo cognatus* (Great Plains toad) and *Spea intermontana* (Great Basin spadefoot). *Rana luteiventris* (Columbia spotted frog; Fig. 23.5b), *B. exsul* (black toad), and *B. nelsoni* (Amargosa toad) are all highly aquatic and dependent on springs throughout the year (Schuierer and Anderson 1990; Perkins and Lentsch 1998; Stebbins 2003), whereas most species use springs primarily for breeding (Altig et al. 1987; Murphy et al. 2003). Within the springs themselves, frogs and toads prefer areas with abundant sedges, grasses, and floating macrophytes such as watercress (Altig et al. 1987; Murphy et al. 2003). Algae are the primary food source for most amphibian larvae, though some species may prey on aquatic macroinvertebrates when algae production is low. Adults, however, are primarily predators utilizing a wide variety of terrestrial and aquatic macroinvertebrates as prey.

Several studies have shown that aquatic invertebrates and their communities are also quite diverse and unique in the Great Basin (Hovingh 1986; Hershler 1998; Vinson 2002; Keleher 2007; Biowest Inc. 2007; Keleher and Rader 2008b). In 38 isolated wetlands in northern Utah, Vinson (2002) documented 20 orders, 56 families, and 88 genera of insects (Coleoptera, Diptera, Ephemeroptera, Hemiptera, Odonata, Plecoptera, Trichoptera), crustaceans, and mollusks, with insect diversity being highest. Vinson noted that with each new location sampled, he collected new taxa, and further noted little indication that the relationship was going to taper off. Similarly, Keleher (2007) found that the overall β-diversity in the Bonneville Basin was high because approximately half of the 288 taxa collected were found to occur in 6 or fewer sites across area; half of the taxa had very restricted distributions, with 20% collected from only single sites. Evidence from the distribution and genetics of individual species also supports this assertion. Hovingh (1993) found that Snake Valley and Tule Valley contained unique species of leeches absent from

FIG. 23.5. Representative species: A. Salt Creek pupfish *(Cyprinodon salinus milleri)* from Death Valley, California. B. Columbia spotted frog *(Rana luteiventris)* from Snake Valley, Utah (Photo by Richard Fridell).

the other valleys of the Bonneville Basin and suggested that the intervening mountains isolated these species before Lake Bonneville drained and that leeches have been unable to disperse between valleys since that time. Furthermore, Hershler (1998) described 58 previously undescribed species of hydrobiid snails, 22 of which are endemic to single locations, supporting the notion of long isolation coupled with slow dispersal leading to local speciation and extinction, and thus high endemism within valleys of the Great Basin.

Of 288 taxa of aquatic invertebrates collected, Keleher (2007) and Keleher and Rader (2008b) identified 16 orders from 280 sites in the Bonneville Basin, of which 69% consisted of Diptera, Coleoptera, or Hemiptera. Other common taxa included amphipods, ostracods, and hydrobiids. The average richness for all sites sampled in the Bonneville Basin was 20 taxa, with the most diverse site being a spring in Goshen Valley, Utah (46 taxa), and the least diverse site being a spring in Snake Valley with only 3 taxa. Biowest Inc. (2007) conducted surveys of 92 sites throughout 11 valleys of east-central Nevada and west-central Utah from 2003 to 2005 and identified 254 taxa of aquatic invertebrates, the most common being amphipods, ostracods, hydrobiids, dipterans, and ephemeropterans. Hershler (1998) and Frest (1996) found that the most common springsnail in the Great Basin is *Pyrgulopsis kolobensis* (Toquerville springsnail), which has been collected from the Virgin River Basin, southwestern Utah, the Bonneville Basin (Utah, Idaho, and Nevada), and eastern Great Basin portions of Nevada. Though these studies have contributed significantly to understanding the aquatic invertebrate diversity in

the Great Basin, more research is needed to clearly document the unique aquatic invertebrate communities that occur in the Great Basin, especially in light of the ever-increasing threats facing desert spring ecosystems (Sada and Vinyard 2002).

Endemism

Distinct species and subspecies of aquatic taxa occur throughout the Great Basin, which is a function of the uniqueness and isolation of desert spring ecosystems. Endemic taxa of amphibians, fish, and macroinvertebrates occupy a wide diversity of habitats, including rivers, lakes, and streams as well as spring-fed wetlands. Most endemic aquatic species occur in springs (153 taxa), followed by lotic (18 taxa) and lentic (10 taxa) habitats (Sada and Vinyard 2002). Some species require primarily lentic habitats but use lotic areas for spawning (e.g., *Catastomus warnerensis,* Warner sucker; *Chasmistes liorus,* June sucker). Others continuously occupy both lentic and lotic habitats (e.g., *Richardsonius egregious,* Lahontan redside). Most of endemic species, however, depend on specific habitat types such as thermal springs (*C. diabolis,* Devils Hole pupfish; *E. acros,* desert dace; *Pyrgulopsis militaris,* northern Soldier Meadow pyrg) or cold springs (*I. phlegethontis,* least chub; *L. albivallis,* White River spinedace).

Endemism in spring systems has inspired a number of biogeographic studies (Echelle and Dowling 1992; Hershler and Sada 2002; Liu and Hershler 2007) or physiological studies examining adaptations of desert fishes to life in harsh environments (Feldmeth et al. 1974; Hillyard 1981). Several studies have focused on individual springs and the natural history of fishes and springsnails (La Bounty and Deacon 1972; Deacon and Deacon 1978; Vinyard 1996) or gastropod assemblages (Sada 2008). Few studies have examined the ecology of desert springs in context of their diversity across the landscape (Keleher 2007). Myers et al. (2001) and Keleher and Rader (2008a,b) examined invertebrate and metaphyton algae dispersal among springs, and Sada et al. (2005), Fleischman et al. (2006), and Keleher and Rader (2008b) considered the influence of land use on spring-fed benthic and riparian communities.

The importance of small spring-fed wetlands to benthic macroinvertebrates with limited distribution was first revealed by Hershler and Sada (1987) and Hershler (1989) with description of springsnails (Gastropoda: Hydrobiidae) in several systems. More than 150 springsnail species are now known from the Great Basin, many of them endemic and occupying either single springs, spring provinces, or single basins (Hershler 1998, 1999; Hershler and Sada 2002; Hershler et al. 2007). Other taxonomic studies have also documented the presence of endemic aquatic insects and crustaceans in Great Basin spring-fed systems (LaRivers 1948, 1949, 1953; Shepard 1992; Schmude 1999), and approximately 200 endemic aquatic vertebrate taxa (including fish, amphibians) are presently known from the Great Basin (Sada and Vinyard 2002).

Recent studies have suggested that free-living microbial species, including algae, have a global distribution because of their vast numbers and small size, which facilitate dispersal (Finlay 2002; Fenchel and Finlay 2004; Londry et al. 2005). Freshwater algae have commonly been thought to possess exceptional dispersal capabilities (Kristiansen 1996; McCormick 1996) because many taxa have a cosmopolitan distribution (Round 1981; Finley and Clarke 1999). However, the importance of dispersal limitations in constraining the composition of algal communities has rarely been investigated

(Round 1981; Stevenson and Peterson 1991; Foissner 2006). A recent review (Foissner 2006) suggests that many microorganisms may have restricted geographic distributions and that some appear to be endemic. Endemic algal species occur in wetlands of Antarctica (Sabbe et al. 2003) and in lakes and springs of Australia (Tyler 1996). Foissner (2006) suggested that about 30% of microorganisms might be morphological and/or genetic endemics. Keleher and Rader (2008a) found that 67% of metaphyton taxa in desert springs of the Bonneville Basin appear to have restricted distributions. Based on Foissner's (2006) estimation, half of these taxa may be endemic to individual springs or wetlands.

Unlike the high degree of endemism seen in the aquatic fauna and potentially in algal groups, desert springs of the Great Basin do not support a large number of unique higher plants. Some of the more noted unique and sensitive species include *Calochortus striatus* (alkali mariposa lily), which is found in moist alkaline meadows and around springs in the creosote bush zones of Clark and Nye counties, Nevada; and *Castilleja salsuginosa* (Monte Neva paintbrush), which is found in damp, open, and alkaline to saline clay soils of hummocks and drainages on travertine hot-spring mounds in Eureka and White Pine counties, Nevada. *Spiranthes diluvialis* (Ute ladies' tresses), listed as federally threatened, is another perennial herb found in somewhat alkaline or calcareous springs in many sporadic locations throughout the Great Basin. Ash Meadows has perhaps the highest number of endemic plants, including *Astragalus phoenix* (Ash Meadows milkvetch), *Centaurium namophilum* (spring-living centaury), *Grindelia fraxinopratensis* (Ash Meadows gumplant), and *Ivesia kingii* var. *eremica* (Ash Meadows mousetails), all of which are federally listed as threatened.

Taxonomic studies over the past 140 years have increased recognition of distinct plants and animals in Great Basin wetlands. Although many taxa have been described, many populations within a species may warrant recognition as either unique endemic species or endemic subspecies (Hubbs et al. 1974; Deacon and Williams 1984; Sada et al. 1995). Unfortunately, many endemic aquatic organisms of the Great Basin are particularly susceptible to disturbance and have undergone declines in distribution or abundance since the late 1800s; at least 16 Great Basin taxa have now gone extinct (Deacon et al. 2007; Sada and Vinyard 2002).

Conservation Concerns

Human Encroachment

Like many arid and semiarid regions around the world, the Great Basin is experiencing major social, economical, and ecological changes that are having widespread detrimental effects on the composition, structure, and function of its native ecosystems (Chambers and Wisdom 2009). In fact, the Great Basin is currently considered one of the most endangered ecoregions in the United States (Center for Science, Economics and Environment 2002). Similar to most ecosystems worldwide, the primary threats facing this region include the growth of human populations, past and present land use, climate change, and a rapid expansion of invasive species. In addition, the Great Basin is also experiencing alteration of fire regimes and water resources. A detailed summary of threats and issues facing Great Basin ecosystems can be found at the Great Basin Research and Management Partnership Web page (http://greatbasin.wr.usgs.gov/gbrmp/).

The human population of the Great Basin is growing at one of the highest rates in the U.S. (US Census Bureau 2010), with most individuals living in urban areas located at the base of watersheds such as Salt Lake City, Utah, and Reno, Nevada. Growth in these cities, coupled with limited supplies of water and anticipated exportation of water to other areas, has resulted in aquatic ecosystems becoming more and more stressed (Fitzhugh and Richter 2004; Deacon et al. 2007). For example, explosive growth in Las Vegas has stimulated a significant demand for new water supplies, particularly groundwater supplies. As demonstrated in areas such as Ash Meadows and Pahrump Valley, Nevada, and Owens Valley, California, excessive groundwater withdrawal and surface-water diversions can alter wetland habitats, groundwater flow, and recharge patterns, all of which result in loss of connectivity between groundwater and surface-water habitats.

As a result of human encroachment, desert springs of the Great Basin are now some of the most threatened wetlands in the U.S. Many springs have been eliminated (capped and filled), while the vast majority of others have been seriously degraded by water depletions, livestock use, agricultural inputs, and the introduction of nonnative species (Shepard 1993). Though small and isolated, they harbor a large proportion of the region's biodiversity (Myers and Resh 1999). As such, they are beginning to receive a significant conservation attention (Deacon and Minckley 1991; Engilis and Reid 1996; Sada and Vineyard 2002; Deacon et al. 2007; Keleher 2007; Chambers and Wisdom 2009).

Nonnative Species

Many of the larger spring systems in the Great Basin support nonnative animals (including sport and aquarium fishes, amphibians, crustaceans, and mollusks) and a diversity of nonnative invasive plants. The establishment of thermally tolerant invasive species into warm and thermal spring systems of the Great Basin represents the single greatest threat to a number of aquatic species of conservation concern through competition and predation (NDOW 2006). Unfortunately, the introduction of nonnative species has subsequently altered the functional characteristics, trophic dynamics, and energy flow in these aquatic systems (Sada 2008). Furthermore, the establishment of emergent vegetation (e.g., *Phragmites, Typha*) and trees (e.g., *Eleagnus, Tamarix*), coupled with excessive grazing by nonnative ungulates and diversion of surface flow, has severely modified and altered habitats, resulting in a sparse or monotypic riparian vegetation at most springs (Fleischner 1994; Sada 2008).

Nonnative fish species in the Great Basin have been introduced from elsewhere in North America and from Europe, Asia, Africa, and South America (Deacon and Williams, 1984; Sigler and Sigler 1987). Many of introduced species (e.g., *Gambusia affinis,* mosquitofish) are now widespread, and most Great Basin fish assemblages are dominated by nonnative taxa (Sada and Vinyard 2002; Ayala et al. 2007). Deacon and Williams (1984) and Sigler and Sigler (1987) identified 50 nonnative fish taxa in the region, which exceeds the total number of native Great Basin fishes (43 species). Predators such as *Salmo gairdneri* (rainbow trout) and *Micropterus* spp. (bass) and competitors such as *G. affinis, Carassois auratis* (goldfish), and a variety of tropical fish present particular problems for native fish of Great Basin springs.

The widespread and invasive *Lithobates catesbieana* (bullfrog) not only presents competitive impacts to all native aquatic species, but is also an avid predator on both adult and larvae of native amphibians, fish, and macroinvertebrates in the Great Basin. Adults consume birds, rodents, other frogs, snakes, turtles, lizards, and bats as well as the many invertebrates that are the usual food of native frogs (McKercher and Gregoire 2010). Stomach content studies going back to 1913 suggest the bullfrog preys on "any animal it can overpower and stuff down its throat" (Cardini 1974). Larvae can have a significant impact upon benthic algae, and thus perturb aquatic community structure (McKercher and Gregoire 2010).

The introduction of *Melanoides tuberculata* (Malaysian trumpet snail) into the Great Basin has raised some significant concern. Hovingh (1998) noted changes in the molluscan species of Fish Springs NWR from 1986 to 1997, and correlated this change with the introduction of *M. tuberculata*. Recent efforts by Rader et al. (2003) highlight the widespread and invasive nature of *M. tuberculata* and have found that the snail has become one of the most abundant species in the entire Fish Springs complex. They found that *Melanoides* dominance occurs rapidly, within a span of 5 to 8 years after introduction, and that average densities of the invasive species range from 4,895 to 7,340 organisms/m^2 (Rader et al. 2003).

Threatened Species and Management

Federally listed threatened and endangered aquatic species can be found throughout the Great Basin, as well as a host of federally listed species of concern and state-listed rare and sensitive species, primarily fish, amphibians, and springsnails, many of which have been highlighted in previous sections. Some of the most notable species are the *Gila robusta jordani* (Pahranagat roundtail chub) and *C. diabolis* (Devils Hole pupfish). The *G. robusta jordani* is perhaps the most endangered native fish in North America, as its population has been estimated to be less than 50 individuals (Sigler and Sigler 1987); *C. diabolis* depends precariously on a single limestone cavern whose opening at the surface is no more than 2 m by 6 m in size.

Mollusks are among the most endangered of animal groups in North America and this new awareness has recently focused conservation management attention on Great Basin taxa (Biowest Inc. 2007). Little is known concerning threats and population trends for most Great Basin mollusk species. For example, eight species in Snake Valley, Utah, alone fall within the "at risk" category and are in need of further surveys and genetic studies to determine if they are endemic to a single location. Currently, *Pyrgulopsis notidicola*, the elongate mud meadows springsnail, is the only Great Basin candidate for federal listing (NVNHP 2010); however, recent surveys have documented more than 55 additional springsnail species within the Great Basin (Hershler 1998, 1999). Currently 82 springsnail species are listed on the State of Nevada's Rare (At-Risk) species list (NVNHP 2010) or the State of Utah's Rare Species List (UDWR 2010).

Concerns exist that current management and protection are not sufficient to sustain the ecological integrity of these springs or long-term water production. Field studies have documented degraded habitat conditions, declines in sensitive plant and animal populations, and species extinctions (Sigler and Workman 1975; Workman et al. 1979; Toone 1991; Cuel-

lar 1994; Ross et al. 1994; Hershler 1998; Oliver and Bosworth 1999; Hogrefe and Fridell 2000; Sada 2001; Fridell et al. 2004, Wheeler et al. 2004, Mills et al. 2004, Sada 2005; Biowest Inc. 2007; Keleher and Rader 2008). However many actions are being undertaken to protect and restore these unique wetlands and the fauna and flora that depend upon them. Conservation agreements have been developed for many species (UDWR 2005a, 2006), habitat protection and restoration efforts are being implemented (e.g., USFWS 1987, 1993, 1994), and larger, state-wide Comprehensive Wildlife Conservation Plans (UDWR 2005b; IDFG 2006; NDOW 2006; ODFW 2006; CDFG 2007) have been developed. The small size of most of the desert springs and the controllable threats causing degradation of these habitats and their communities suggests that stopping the continued declines and losses does not require substantial funding or even a large commitment of natural resources. Conserving these habitats simply requires collaborative partnerships among research and management organizations and innovative programs that allow reasonable human use while protecting these aquatic systems from further degradation.

Conclusion

Desert springs around the world are centers of biological diversity embedded in a dry terrestrial landscape (Curtis et al. 1998, Fensham 2003), but often are overlooked. Spring ecosystems on all major continents are now the focus of intense conservation because they are threatened by a variety of anthropogenic stressors. Our ability to preserve these ecosystems depends in part, on our understanding of their unique biological properties. As they are critical habitat for many endemic aquatic taxa, the degradation and loss of these springs has resulted in several species receiving sensitive designations. Efforts to protect desert spring wetlands of the arid west lack the information needed to determine their health and integrity. Chambers and Wisdom (2009) provided a comprehensive discussion on priority research and management issues of the Great Basin. Research coupled with effective monitoring strategies and large-scale assessments is desperately needed to understand and track ongoing changes on all fronts (biological and anthropocentric) of these systems. Collaboration among all involved parties (stakeholders, managers, researchers) has greatly improved in recent years, but as with most conservation issues, limited water and limited funding greatly reduces conservation action options.

References

Altig R, Dodd K Jr. 1987. The status of the the Amarogosa toad *(Bufo nelsoni)* in the Amargosa River drainage of Nevada. *Southw. Nat.* 32:276–78.

Anderson K, Nelson S, et al. 2006. Interbasin flow revisited: the contribution of local recharge to high-discharge springs, Death Valley, CA. *J. Hydrol.* 323:276–302.

Ayala J, Rader RB, et al. 2007. Ground-truthing the impact of invasive species: spatio-temporal overlap between native least chub and introduced western mosquitofish. *Biol. Invasions* 9:857–69.

Barbash JE, Thelin GP, et al. 2001. Major herbicides in ground water: results from the National Water-Quality Assessment.

Batzer DP, Rader RB, Wissinger SA. 2001. *Invertebrates in freshwater wetlands of North America: ecology and management.* New York: Wiley.

Biowest Inc. 2007. *Ecological evaluation of selected aquatic ecosystems in the Biological Resources Study Area for the Southern Nevada*

Water Authority's proposed Clark, Lincoln, and White Pine Counties Groundwater Development Project. Final Rep: vol. 1: PR 987-1.

Bolen EG. 1964. Plant ecology of spring-fed salt marshes in western Utah. Ecol. Monogr. 34:143–66.

Bond CE. 1979. The biology of fishes. New York: Holt, Reinhart, Winston, CBS College Publ.

Brinson MM. 1993. A hydrogeomorphic classification for wetlands. Wetlands Res. Progr. Tech. Report WRP-DE-4. USACE.

Brues CT. 1932. Further studies on the fauna of North American hot springs. Proc. Am. Acad. Arts Sci. 67:185–303.

CDFG (Calif. Dept. Fish Game). 2007. California wildlife: conservation challenges. California's Wildlife Action Plan. UC Davis Wildlife Health Center CDFG.

Cardini F. 1974. Specializations of the feeding response of the bullfrog, Rana catesbeiana, for the capture of prey submerged in water. MS thesis, Univ. Massachusetts, Amherst.

Center for Science, Economics and Environment. 2002. The state of the nation's ecosystems: measuring lands, waters and living resources of the United States. Cambridge: Cambridge Univ. Press.

Chambers JC, Wisdom MJ. 2009. Priority research and management issues for the imperiled Great Basin of the western United States. Restor. Ecol. 17:707–14.

Christiansen FW. 1951. Geology of the Canyon, House and Confusion ranges, Millard County, Utah. Guidebook Geol. Utah 6:68–80.

Cuellar O. 1994. Ecological observations on Rana pretiosa in western Utah. Alytes (Paris) 12:109–21.

Curtis B, Roberts KS, et al. 1998. Species richness and conservation of Nambian freshwater macro-invertebrates, fish and amphibians. Biodiv. Conserv. 7:447–66.

Deacon JE, Minckley WL. 1974. Desert fishes. In Desert biology, vol. 2, GW Brown Jr., editor. New York: Academic Press, pp. 385–488.

Deacon JE, Deacon M. 1978. Research on endangered fishes in the National Parks, with special emphasis on the Devil's Hole pupfish. First Annu. Symp. Research National Parks, USNPS.

Deacon JE, Hardy TB, et al. 1980. Environmental analysis of four aquatic systems in east-central Nevada, June–July 1980. Interim summary report, HDR Sci. (Contr. no. HDR/RPA15).

Deacon JE, Williams JE. 1984. Annotated list of the fishes of Nevada. Proc. Biol. Soc. Wash. 97:103–18.

Deacon JE, Minckley WL. 1991. Western fishes and the real world: the enigma of "endangered species" revisited. In Battle against extinction: native fish management in the American West, Minckley WL, Deacon JE, editors. 405–13. Tucson: Univ. Arizona Press.

Deacon JE, Williams AE, et al. 2007. Fueling population growth in Las Vegas: how large-scale groundwater withdrawal could burn regional biodiversity. BioScience 57:688–98.

Echelle AA, Dowling TE. 1992. Mitochondrial DNA variation and evolution of the Death Valley pupfishes (Cyprinodon, Cyprinodontidae). Evolution 46:193–206.

Engilis A Jr, Reid FA. 1996. Challenges in wetland restoration of the western Great Basin. Internat. Wader Studies 9:71–79.

Feldmeth CR, Stone EA, Brown JH. 1974. An increased scope for thermal tolerance upon acclimating pupfish (Cyprinodon) to cycling temperatures. J. Compar. Physiol. 89:39–44.

Fenchel T, Finlay BJ. 2004. The ubiquity of small species: patterns of local and global diversity. BioScience 54:777–84.

Fensham RJ. 2003. Spring wetlands of the Great Artesian Basin, Queensland, Australia. Wetl. Ecol. Manage. 11:343–63.

Finlay BJ. 2002. Global dispersal of free-living microbial eukaryote species. Science 296:1061–63.

Finlay B, Clarke KJ. 1999. Ubiquitous dispersal of microbial species. Nature 400:828.

Fitzhugh TW, Richter BD. 2004. Quenching urban thirst: growing cities and their impacts on freshwater ecosystems. BioScience 54:741–54.

Fleischner TL. 1994. Ecological cost of livestock grazing in western North America. Conserv. Biol. 8:629–44.

Fleishman E, Murphy DD, Sada SW. 2006. Effects of environmental heterogeneity and disturbance on the native and nonnative flora of desert springs. Biol. Invasions 8:1091–1101.

Foissner W. 2006. Biogeography and dispersal of micro-organisms: a review emphasizing protists. Acta Protozool. 45:111–36.

Frémont JC. 1845. Report of the exploring expeditions to the Rock Mountains in the year 1842, and to Oregon and Northern California in the years 1843–1844. By Order of The Senate of the United States. Washington, DC: Gales and Seaton Printers.

Fridell RA, Schroeder KL, et al. 1999. Least chub (Iotichthys phlegethontis) monitoring summary, Snake Valley, 1999. Utah Div. Wildl. Resour., Salt Lake City. Publ. no. 99-37.

Fridell R, Nonne DV, Wheeler KK. 2004. Columbia spotted frog (Rana luteiventris) population monitoring summary: Gandy, Bishop Springs, Tule Valley, 2004. Utah Div. Wildl. Resour., Salt Lake City. Publ. no. 04-32.

Frest T. 1996. Mollusk collection report to USFWS at Fish Springs National Wildlife Refuge. Fish Springs National Wildlife Refuge, Dugway, UT.

Gilbert CH. 1893. Report on the fishes of the Death Valley Expedition, collection in southern California and Nevada in 1891, with descriptions of new species. No. Am. Fauna 7:229–34.

Goldsborough LG, Robinson GGC Patterns in wetlands. In Algal ecology: freshwater benthic eco-systems, Stevenson RJ, Bothwell MK, Lowe RL, editors. San Diego: Academic Press, pp. 77–117.

Grayson D. 1993. The desert's past: a natural prehistory of the Great Basin. Washington, DC: Smithsonian Inst. Press.

Grimes JA, St Clair LL, Rushforth SR. 1980. A comparison of epiphytic diatom assemblages on living and dead stems of the common grass Phragmites australis. Great Basin Nat. 40:223–28.

Hall ER. 1995. Mammals of Nevada, rev. ed. Reno: Univ. Nevada Press.

Hershey RL, Mizell SA, Earman S. 2009. Chemical and physical characteristics of springs discharging from regional flow systems of the carbonate-rock province of the Great Basin, western United States. Hydrogeol. J. DOI 10.1007/s10040-009-0571-7.

Hershler R. 1989. Springsnails (Gastropoda: Hydrobiidae) of Owens and Amargosa River (exclusive of Ash Meadows) drainages, Death Valley system, California-Nevada. Proc. Biol. Soc. Wash. 102:176–248.

Hershler R. 1998. A systematic review of the Hydrobiid Snails (Gastropoda: Rissooidea) of the Great Basin, Western United States. Part I. Genus Pyrgulopsis. Veliger 41:1–132.

Hershler R. 1999. A systematic review of the hydrobiid snails (Gastropoda: Rissooidea) of the Great Basin, western United States. Part II. Genera Colligyrus, Eremopyrgus, Fluminicola, Prinstinicola, and Tryonia. Veliger 42:306–37.

Hershler R, Sada DW. 1987. Springsnails (Gastropoda: Hydrobiidae) of Ash Meadows, Amargosa basin, California-Nevada. Proc. Biol. Soc. Wash. 100:776–843.

Hershler R, Sada DW. 2002. Biogeography of Great Basin aquatic snails of the genus Pyrgulopsis. In Great Basin aquatic systems history, Hershler R, Madison DB, Currey RD, editors. Smithsonian Contrib. Earth Sci., 33. Washington, DC: Smithsonian Inst. Press, pp. 255–76.

Hershler R, Liu H-S, Sada DW. 2007. Origin and diversification of the Soldier Meadow springsnails (Hydrobiidae: Pyrgulopsis), a species flock in the northwestern Great Basin. J. of Mollus. Studies 73:167–83.

Hillyard SD. 1981. The evolution of thermal tolerance in desert fishes. In Fishes in North American deserts, Naiman RJ, Soltz DL, editors. New York: Wiley, pp. 385–410.

Hovingh P. 1986. Biogeographic aspects of leeches, molluscs, and amphibians in the Intermountain region. Great Basin Nat. 46:736–44.

Hovingh P. 1993. Aquatic habitats, life history observations, and zoogeographic considerations of the spotted frog (Rana pretiosa) in Tule Valley, Utah. Great Tule Valley, Utah. Great Basin Nat. 53:168–79.

Hovingh P. 1998. Melanoides turberculata study report to Fish Springs National Wildlife Refuge. Fish Springs Nat. Wildl. Refuge, Dugway, UT.

Hubbs CL, Miller RR, Hubbs LC. 1974. Hydrographic history and relict fishes of the north-central Great Basin. Mem. Calif. Acad. Sci., vol. VII.

IDFG (Idaho Department of Fish and Game). 2006. Idaho Comprehensive Wildlife Conservation Strategy. Idaho Conservation Data Center, IDFG, Boise.

Jehl Jr., JR. 1994. Changes in saline and alkaline lake avifauna in western North American in the past 150 years. Studies Avian Biol. 15:258–72.

Kaczmarska I, Rushforth SR. 1984. Diatom associations in Blue Lake Warm Spring, Utah. USA. *Bibliogr. Diatomol.* 2:1–123.

Keleher MJ. 2007. *Bioassessment and the partitioning of community composition and diversity across spatial scales in wetlands of the Bonneville Basin.* Ph.D. diss., Brigham Young Univ., Provo, UT.

Keleher MJ, Rader RB. 2008a. Dispersal limitations and history explain community composition of metaphyton in desert springs of the Bonneville Basin, Utah: a multiscale analysis. *Limn. Oceanogr.* 53:1604–13.

Keleher MJ, Rader RB. 2008b. Bioassessment of artesian springs in the Bonneville Basin, Utah, USA. *Wetlands* 28:1048–59.

Kristiansen J. 1996. Dispersal of freshwater algae—a review. *Hydrobiologia* 336:151–57.

La Bounty JF, Deacon JE. 1972. *Cyprinodon milleri,* a new species of pupfish from Death Valley, California. *Copeia* 1972(4):769–80.

La Rivers I. 1948. A new species of *Ambrysus* from Death Valley, with notes on the genus in the United States (Hemiptera: Naucoridae). *Bull. So. Calif. Acad. Sci.* 47:103–10.

La Rivers I. 1949. A new species of *Microcylleopus* from Nevada (Coleoptera: Dryopidae). *Ent. News* 60:205–09.

La Rivers I. 1953. New Gelastocorid and Naucorid records and miscellaneous notes, with a description of a new species, *Ambrysus amargosus* (Hemiptera: Naucoridae). *Wasmann J. Biol.* 11:83–96.

La Rivers, I. 1962. *Fishes and fisheries of Nevada.* Carson City: NV State Fish Game Comm.

Liu H-P, Hershler R. 2007. A test of the vicariance hypothesis of western North American freshwater biogeography. *J. Biogeogr.* doi: 10.1111/j.1365-2699.2006.01611.x.

Londry KL, Badiou PH, Grasby SE. 2005. Identification of a marine green alga *Percursaria percursa* from hypersaline springs in the middle of the North American continent. *Can. Field-Nat.* 119:82–87.

Marquis LY, Comes RD, Yang C. 1984. Relative tolerance of desert saltgrass *(Distichlis stricta)* and reed canarygrass *(Phalaris arundinacea)* to boron. *Weed Sci.* 32:534–38.

McCormick PV. 1996. Resource competition and species coexistence in freshwater benthic algal assemblages. In *Algal ecology: freshwater benthic ecosystems,* Stevenson RJ, Bothwell MK, Lowe RL, editors. San Diego: Academic Press, pp. 229–49.

McKercher L, Gregoire DR. 2010. *Lithobates* [= *Rana*] *catesbeianus.* USGS Nonindigenous Aquatic Species Database, Gainesville, FL.

McLane AR. 1987. The mountain ranges of Nevada. *Camp Nevada Monograph* 4. Reno, NV.

Merriam CH. 1893. The Death Valley Expedition: a biological survey of parts of California, Nevada, Arizona, and Utah. Part II. *No. Am. Fauna* 7:1–394.

Miller RR. 1961. Man and the changing fish fauna of the American Southwest. *Pap. Mich. Acad. Sci. Arts Lett.* 46:365–404.

Miller RR, Hubbs C, Miller FH. 1991. Ichthyological exploration of the American West: the Hubbs-Miller era, 1915–1950. In *Battle against extinction: native fish management in the American West,* Minckley ML, Deacon JE, editors. Tucson: Univ. Arizona Press, pp. 19–42.

Mills MD, Rader RB, Belk MC. 2005. Complex interactions between native and invasive fish: the simultaneous effects of multiple negative interactions. *Oecologia* 141:713–21.

Minckley WL, Deacon JE. 1968. Southwestern fishes and the "enigma" of endangered species management. *Science* 159:1424–32.

Minckley WL, Douglas ME. 1991. Discovery and extinction of western fishes: a blink of the eye in geologic time. In *Battle against extinction: native fish management in the American West,* Minckley ML, Deacon JE, editors. Tuscon: Univ. Arizona Press, pp. 7–18.

Mitsch WJ, Gosselink JG. 2007. *Wetlands,* 4th ed. New York: Wiley.

Murphy JF, Simandle ET, Becker DE. 2003. Population status and conservation of the black toad, *Bufo exsul. Southw. Nat.* 48:54–60.

Myers MJ, Resh VH. 1999. Spring-formed wetlands of the arid west: islands of aquatic invertebrate biodiversity. In *Invertebrates in freshwater wetlands of North America: ecology and management,* Batzer DP, Rader RB, Wissinger SA, editors. New York: Wiley, pp. 811–28.

Myers JM, Sperling FAH, Resh VH. 2001. Dispersal of two species of Trichoptera from desert springs: conservation implications for isolated vs. connected populations. *J. Insect Conserv.* 5:207–15.

Naiman RJ. 1975. Food habits of the Amargosa pupfish in a thermal stream. *Trans. Am. Fish. Soc.* 104:536–38.

NDOW (Nevada Department of Wildlife). 2006. *Nevada Wildlife Action Plan.* Reno NV.

NDOW. 2006. *Nevada Wetlands Priority Conservation Plan.* NV DNR, NV Heritage Progr., Carson City.

ODFW (Oregon Department of Fish and Wildlife). 2006. *The Oregon Conservation Strategy.*

Oliver GV, Bosworth WR III. 1999. Rare, imperiled, and recently extinct or extirpated mollusks of Utah: a literature review. Publ. no. 99-29. UT Div. Wildlife Resources, Salt Lake City.

Page WP, Gill RE Jr. 1994. Shorebirds in western North America: late 1800's to late 1900's. *Studies Avian Biol.* 15:147–60.

Patten DT, Rouse L, Stromberg JC. 2008. Isolated spring wetlands in the Great Basin and Mojave Deserts, USA: potential response of vegetation to groundwater withdrawal. *Env. Manage.* 41:398–413.

Perkins J, Lentsch LD. 1998. Conservation agreement and strategy for spotted frog *(Rana pretiosa).* UT Div. Wildl. Resour., Salt Lake City.

Pratt M, Browns J, et al. 2002. Range plants of Utah. Utah State Univ. Coop. Ext. http://extension.usu.edu/rangeplants/. Accessed September 2010.

Prudic DE, Harrill JR, Burbey TJ 1995. Conceptual evaluation of regions ground-water flow in the carbonate-rock province of the Great Basin, Nevada, Utah and adjacent states. USGS Professional Pap. 1409-D. Reston, VA.

Quade J, Forester RM, et al. 1998. Black mats, spring-fed streams, and late-glacial-age recharge in the southern Great Basin. *Quaternary Res.* 49:129–48.

Rader RB, Belk MC, Keleher MJ. 2003. The introduction of an invasive snail *(Melanoides tuberculata)* to spring ecosystems of the Bonneville Basin, Utah. *J. Freshw. Ecol.* 18:647–57.

Ross DA, Stanger MC, et al. 1994. *Distribution, habitat use and relative abundance indices of spotted frogs in the West Desert, Utah, 1993.* Utah Div. Wildl. Resour. Publ. no. 93-15.

Round FE. 1981. *The ecology of algae.* Cambridge: Cambridge Univ. Press.

Russell IC. 1895. Present and extinct lakes of Nevada. *Natl. Geogr. Monogr.* 1:101–32.

Russell IC. 1889. Quaternary history of the Mono Valley, California. Eighth Annual Report United States Geological Survey to the Secretary of Interior 1886–'87, Part I:267–394.

Ryser Jr., FA. 1985. *Birds of the Great Basin: a natural history.* Reno: Univ. Nevada Press.

Sabbe K, Verleyen E, et al. 2003. Benthic diatom flora of freshwater and saline lakes in the Larsemann Hills and Rauer Islands, East Antarctica. *Antarctic Sci.* 15:227–48.

Sada DW. 1990. A recovery plan for the endangered and threatened species of Ash Meadows, Nevada. USFWS, Portland OR.

Sada DW. 2000. Geologically persistent springs in southern Nevada and southeastern California as indicated by aquatic assemblages. Unpubl. rep., USEPA, Las Vegas, NV.

Sada DW. 2001. Demography and habitat use of the Badwater snail *(Assiminea infima),* with observations on its conservation status, Death Valley National Park, California, U.S.A. *Hydrobiologia* 466:255–65.

Sada DW. 2005. Personal communication with Mike Golden of BIO-WEST, Inc. regarding springsnail species found throughout the BRSA. December 9, 2005.

Sada DW. 2008. Synecology of a springsnail (Caenogastropoda: Hydrobiidae) assemblage in a western U.S. thermal spring province. *Veliger* 50:59–71.

Sada DW, Nachlinger JL. 1996. Spring Mountains ecosystems: vulnerability of spring-fed aquatic and riparian systems to biodiversity loss. Unpubl. rep., USBLM, Las Vegas, NV.

Sada DW, Nachlinger JL. 1998. Spring Mountains ecosystem: vulnerability of spring-fed aquatic and riparian systems to biodiversity loss. Part II. Springs surveyed in 1997. Unpubl. rep., USBLM, Las Vegas, NV.

Sada DW, Britten HB, Brussard PB. 1995. Desert aquatic ecosystems and the genetic and morphological diversity of Death Valley System speckled dace. In *Evolution and the aquatic ecosystem, defining unique units in population conservation,* Nielsen J, editor. Am. Fish. Soc. Symp. 17, pp. 350–59.

Sada DW, Vinyard GL. 2002. Anthropogenic changes in historical biogeography of Great Basin aquatic biota. In *Great Basin aquatic systems history,* Hershler R, Madsen DB, Currey D, editors. Smithsonian Contrib. Earth Sci. no. 33, pp. 277–95.

Sada DW, Fleishman E, Murphy DD. 2005. Associations among spring-dependent aquatic assemblages and environmental and land use gradients in a Mojave Desert mountain range. *Diver. Distrib.* 11:91–99.

Schmude KL. 1999. Riffle beetles in the genus *Stenelmis* (Coleoptera: Elmidae) from warm springs in southern Nevada: new species, new status, and a key. *Ent. News* 110(1):1–12.

Schuierer FW, Anderson SC. 1990. Population status of *Bufo exsul* Myers. *Herp. Rev.* 21:57.

Sharitz RR, Pennings SC. 2006. Development of wetland plant communities. In *Ecology of freshwater and estuarine wetlands,* Batzer DP, Sharitz RR, editors. Berkeley: Univ. Calif. Press, pp. 177–241.

Shepard WD. 1993. Desert springs—both rare and endangered. *Aquat. Conserv. Mar. Freshw. Ecosys.* 3:351–59.

Shupe JB, Brotherson JD, Rushforth SR. 1986. Patterns of vegetation surrounding springs in Goshen Bay, Utah County, Utah. U.S.A. *Hydrobiologia* 139:97–107.

Sigler WF, Workman GW. 1975. Studies on the least chub (*Iotichthys phlegethontis*—Cope) in geothermal activities area of Snake and Tule Valleys, UT. UT Div. Wildl. Resour., Salt Lake City.

Sigler WF, Sigler JW. 1987. *Fishes of the Great Basin: a natural history.* Reno: Univ. Nev. Press.

Simpson JH. 1859. Report of explorations about the Great Basin of the territory of Utah for a direct wagon-route from Camp Floyd to Genoa in Carson Valley in 1859. Republished by Nabu Press, January 2010.

Smith GI, Friedman I, et al. 2000. Stable isotope compositions of waters in the Great Basin, United States. Comparison of groundwater with modern precipitation. *J. Geophy. Res.* 107:4403.

Soltz DL, Naiman RJ. 1975. The natural history of native fishes in the Death Valley system. *Science Series* 30. Natur. Hist. Mus. Los Angeles County, Los Angeles.

Southwood T. 1977. Habitat, the templet for ecological strategies? *J. Anim. Ecol.* 46:337–65.

Stearns REC. 1893. Report on the land and fresh-water shells collected in California and Nevada by the Death Valley Expedition, including a few additional species obtained by Dr. C. Hart Merriam and assistants in parts of the southwestern United States. *N. Am. Fauna* 7:26–283.

Stebbins RC. 2003. *Western reptiles and amphibians.* New York: Houghton Mifflin Co.

Stevenson RJ, Peterson CG. 1991. Emigration and immigration can be important determinants of benthic diatom assemblages in streams. *Freshw. Biol.* 26:279–94.

Sumner FB, Sargent MC. 1940. Some observations on the physiology of warm spring fishes. *Ecology* 21:45–54.

Thomas JM, Welch AH, Dettinger MD. 1996. Geochemistry and isotope hydrology of representative aquifers in the Great Basin region of Nevada, Utah, and adjacent states. USGS Professional Pap. 1409-C.

Tiku BL. 2006. Effect of salinity on the photosynthesis of the halophyte *Salicornia rubra* and *Distichlis stricta. Physiol. Plantarum* 37:23–28.

Todd, DK, Mays LW. 2005. *Groundwater hydrology,* 3rd ed. New York: Wiley.

Toone RA. 1991. General inventory for western spotted frogs (*Rana pretiosa*) in the House Range Resource Area, Utah. UT Natural Heritage Progr.

Three Parameters Plus, Inc. 2010. *Baseline physical habitat conditions of wetlands in Snake Valley, Utah.* Final Rep. Vol. 1. UT DNR, Endangered Species Mitigation Fund, Salt Lake City.

Tyler PA. 1996. Endemism in freshwater algae. *Hydrobiologia* 336:127–35.

US Census Bureau. 2007. Census 2000, Summary File 3 (SF 3). (Online.)

USDI (US Dept. Interior). 1994. *Standardized national vegetation classification system.* Washington DC: USDI, NBS, NPS, TNC, Env. Systems Res. Inst.

USFWS (US Fish Wildl. Serv.). 1986. *Pahranagat roundtail chub recovery plan.* Portland, OR: USFWS.

USFWS. 1987. *Borax Lake chub recovery plan.* Portland, OR: USFWS.

USFWS. 1993. *Big Spring spinedace,* Lepidomeda mollispinis pratensis, *recovery plan.* Portland, OR: USFWS.

USFWS. 1994. *White River spinedace,* Lepidomeda albivallis, *recovery plan.* Portland, OR: USFWS.

UDWR (Utah Division of Wildlife Resources). 2005a. *Conservation agreement and strategy for least chub* (Iotichthys phlegethontis) *in the state of Utah.* Publication no. 05-24.

UDWR. 2005b. *Utah comprehensive wildlife conservation plan.* Utah Comprehensive Wildlife Conservation Strategy (CWCS).

UDWR. 2006. *Conservation agreement and strategy for Columbia spotted frog* (Rana luteiventris) *in the state of Utah.* Publication no. 06-01.

UDWR. 2010. Utah sensitive species list. Salt Lake City: Utah Div. Wildl. Resour.

Vinson M. 2002. Preliminary assessment of wetland invertebrate assemblages in northern Utah. Final Report for State of Utah Contract no. 010681.

Vinyard GL. 1996. Distribution of a thermal endemic minnow, the desert dace (*Eremichthys acros),* and observations of impacts of water diversion on its population. *Great Basin Nat.* 56:360–68.

Waring GA. 1920. Ground water in Pahrump, Mesquite, and Ivanpah Valleys, Nevada and California. Water-Supply Paper 450-C.

Wetzel RG. 2001. *Limnology: lake and river ecosystems,* 3rd ed. New York: Academic Press.

Wheeler KK, Fridell RA, Bryant JA. 2004. Least chub (*Iotichthys phlegethontis*) monitoring summary: Snake Valley, 2004. UT Div. Wildl. Resour., Salt Lake City.

Wilberg DE, Stolp BJ. 1985. Physical characteristics and chemical quality of selected springs in parts of Juab, Millard, Tooele, and Utah counties, Utah. USGS Water-Resource Invest. Rep. 85-4324.

Williams CD. 1986. *Life history of the Railroad Valley springfish, Crenichthys nevadae Hubbs (Cyprinodontidae), of east-central Nevada.* MS thesis, California State Univ., Sacramento.

Williams JE, Bowman DB, et al. 1985. Endangered aquatic ecosystems of North American deserts with a list of vanishing fishes of the region. *Arizona-Nevada Acad. Sci.* 20:1–62.

Workman GW, Workman WG, et al. 1979. Studies 37 on the least chub in geothermal active areas of western Utah. Contract no YA-512-CT7-21, USDI Bur. Land Manage., Utah State Office.

CHAPTER 24

Riparian Floodplain Wetlands of the Arid and Semiarid Southwest

JULIET C. STROMBERG,
DOUGLAS C. ANDERSEN, and MICHAEL L. SCOTT

The riparian forests that line alluvial, perennial rivers of the arid and semiarid American Southwest present a striking visual contrast to the bordering desert shrublands and grasslands (Fig. 24.1). In this chapter, we discuss rivers within two physiographic provinces—the Basin and Range physiographic province of the southwestern USA and northern Mexico, and the Colorado Plateau (Fig. 24.2). In these arid and semiarid settings, perennial rivers originate in the mountains, whether continuous ranges or isolated peaks. We focus on the lower segments of the rivers, after they descend from the montane zone into the comparatively warm, dry basins below. The upper catchment areas (often snow-covered in winter) are pivotal in supplying these desert streams with summer base flow as well as contributing, along with lower parts of the catchment, to seasonal flood pulses (Baillie et al. 2007). Streams whose primary water source is derived from a different region or climate zone are referred to as exotic, allogenic, or interregional rivers.

The predominant biotic communities along rivers in our study region are tropical and subtropical riparian wetlands and warm temperate riparian wetlands (Brown 1994). Depending on location, the floodplain forests are vegetated by one of three closely related cottonwoods: Fremont cottonwood *(Populus fremontii* ssp. *fremontii),* Mexican cottonwood *(P. fremontii* ssp. *mesetae),* and Rio Grande cottonwood *(P. deltoides* ssp. *wislizeni),* and/or Goodding's willow *(Salix gooddingii).* These tall pioneer species are renowned for supporting diverse bird life. They often occur with later-successional forests of mesquite *(Prosopis velutina, P. glandulosa).* Also present in the desert riparian landscape mosaic are shrublands, grasslands, marshlands, and sparsely vegetated patches of mineral soil.

Ecological studies of southwestern desert rivers began decades ago but intensified in the 1990s following management shifts toward preservation of riparian ecosystems (Fig. 24.3). Drawing on this research, our chapter focuses on the importance of stream flows and geomorphic processes to desert riparian biotic communities and concludes with efforts to restore and sustain riparian ecosystems and the services they provide. Identifying and sustaining flows to meet environmental needs is at the heart of many of these efforts. Scarcity of freshwater resources is an issue of concern worldwide, and preeminent within the arid and semiarid Southwest.

Hydrology

The coupled interaction of surface and groundwater controls riparian ecosystem structure and functioning along rivers in dry regions of the Southwest. Most drainages in desert basins have *ephemeral* flow, wherein flow is present for only short periods (in response to surface runoff), with the water table always remaining below the channel (Fig. 24.4). Also present are *intermittent* streams, which cease flowing for weeks to months during dry seasons and where floodplains often have highly fluctuating water tables. Perennial streams flow year-round (except during severe drought), with dry-season flows sustained by groundwater inflow. Over the length of southwestern rivers, downstream flow is typically lost to evapotranspiration and infiltration into deep basin fills, but flow may increase in areas where bedrock rises close to the surface or where tributaries provide water inputs (Graf 1988). Such rivers that have a mix of perennial and nonperennial segments are classified as *interrupted perennial.*

Mountains and alluvial basins are dominant features throughout western North America. All four major North American deserts—Great Basin, Mojave, Sonoran, and Chihuahuan—lie within the Basin and Range physiographic province, a tectonically active region characterized by isolated, north-south-trending mountain ranges that serve as moisture-gathering "islands." The two primary ways in which mountains supply water to streams and their aquifers in the alluvial valleys are through snowmelt or rain runoff to tributary streams and "mountain block" recharge of basin aquifers. Determining rates and patterns of water flow from mountains to streams is an active area of research (Magruder et al. 2009).

Geographic and seasonal variation in storm tracks contributes to distinctive climates and thus distinctive stream flow patterns in individual deserts (Fig. 24.5). The warm-season southwestern monsoon, with a geographic center in northwest Mexico, produces convective thunderstorms that diminish in intensity northward and westward. Thus, hydrographs of Chihuahuan Desert rivers have predictable flooding during late summer. The Mojave Desert receives minimal summer rain, as does the central Great Basin. Winter rains and snow are supplied by Pacific frontal storms, producing a bimodal flood

FIG. 24.1. Gila River at Cliff, New Mexico. This section of the river is in the upper portion of the Gila catchment (above 1,200 m in elevation) and more than 700 river km from the Gila's confluence with the Colorado River. (Photo credit: Michael Collier.)

pattern, most apparent in the Sonoran Desert. Localized low-pressure storms from March to May supply additional moisture to the Great Basin.

Precipitation and stream flow in the region have large temporal variability, reflecting in part the interacting effects of annual (El Niño Southern Oscillation) and multidecadal (Pacific Decadal Oscillation) shifts in sea surface temperatures and atmospheric circulation patterns. Drought and intense floods are recurring features (Ely et al. 1993; Woodhouse 2004). In some areas, multiyear droughts of sufficient intensity to cause famine among farmers and ranchers have occurred repeatedly in recent centuries (Endfield and Tejedo 2006).

Geomorphology and Soils

Catchments in semiarid regions have some of the highest rates of sediment production in North America (Langbein and Schumm 1958). Soil surfaces can be hydrophobic (promoting overland runoff rather than infiltration) and vegetation is sparse, leaving hillslopes unprotected from the erosive forces of intense rainfall, especially where biological soil crusts have been destroyed (Belnap 1995). The combination of large floods and abundant sediment input creates a dynamic riparian system, with high rates of aggradation and degradation of alluvial surfaces.

Given their position in the stream network, most alluvial

desert rivers are sand-bedded, with coarser material—gravel, cobbles, and boulders—sometimes prominent at the mouths of steep tributaries. Soils of the fluvial landforms are young and poorly developed, often lacking distinct horizons. Soil development is slowest in the active channel, where alluvial sediments are reworked most years, and fastest on portions of the floodplain where both soil moisture and aeration are high, geomorphic disturbance is minimal, and organic matter is added through ecological processes. Mature soils on floodplains range from sandy loams to clay loams and have complex horizontal and vertical heterogeneity. Histosols, hydric soils that develop under anoxic conditions with high organic matter content, are limited. Among the areas that develop histosols are spring-fed marshes, some of which regionally are called *ciénegas* (Green et al. 2009).

Channel form can vary, but the compound channel wherein a low-flow meandering channel is nested within a larger braided channel (Fig. 24.1) is a common type in many desert rivers (Graf 1988). Floodplains can be several miles wide for lower reaches of larger rivers. Interestingly, many dryland rivers have their current high-flow channel incised into ancient alluvial plains (also called fluvial terraces) created in Holocene or late Pleistocene periods when the region was cooler and wetter and discharge was larger (Waters 2008; Bacon et al. 2010).

Riparian Plant Communities

Factors Influencing Riparian Plant Communities

Perennial desert rivers sustain several hundreds of plant species, encompassing a wide variety of functional types. The modern riparian plant assemblages of the region arose from three continental-scale geofloras (Arcto-, Madro- and Neotropical-Tertiary) in response to tectonic processes and to increasing aridity beginning in the Cretaceous (Axelrod 1958). *Populus* and *Salix* were in existence as early as 60 million years ago (Tuskan et al. 2006), and were the genetic forebears of heat-tolerant taxa such as Fremont cottonwood and Goodding's willow.

Among the factors allowing for a high degree of species coexistence in desert riparian zones are temporal variation in flood patterns and the presence of complex spatial gradients of inundation frequency, depth to water table, and soil texture and moisture from the channel to the uplands. Disturbance-adapted wetland taxa (a.k.a. core riparian species; McLaughlin 2004) establish on channel bars and low topographic positions on floodplains, while more drought-tolerant and less flood-tolerant individuals occur on higher surfaces. A large fraction of the plants present are facultative riparian species, i.e., those that also grow in upland areas of the catchment. This group can appreciably add to diversity levels. For example, along perennial rivers in Sonora, Mexico, plant diversity increased from north to south, reflecting retention of upland species of tropical origin that established in the riparian zone (Scott et al. 2009).

WATER SOURCES

The shallow water table that lies beneath the floodplains and terraces of perennial to intermittent desert rivers is a key water

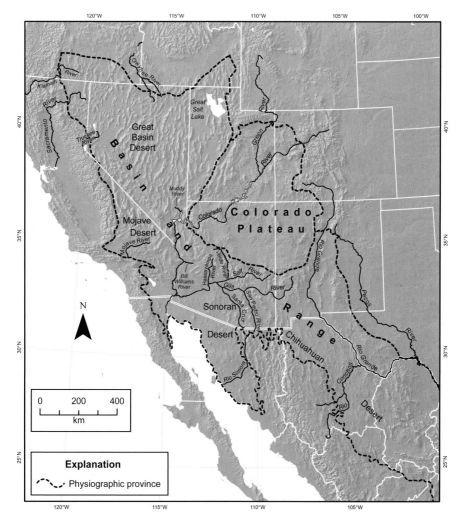

FIG. 24.2. Boundaries of the Colorado Plateau and Basin and Range physiographic provinces, and of the Great Basin, Mojave, Sonoran, and Chihuahuan deserts. Also indicated are major rivers and other rivers mentioned in the text. (Map credit: Tammy Fancher.)

source for many plants. In these alluvial rivers with coarse substrates (e.g., sand, gravel), the water table fluctuates in tandem with stream stage. Both depth to water table and degree of water-level fluctuation influence plant response. Cottonwood and willow trees are obligate phreatophytes—species that in arid regions are dependent on groundwater for long-term survival (Meinzer 1927; Busch et al. 1992). Mesquite, introduced tamarisk (*Tamarix* ssp.), and the bunchgrass big sacaton *(Sporobolus wrightii)* are examples of facultative phreatophytes. Such species can survive without continuous access to groundwater, although their stature and productivity are enhanced by its availability. Many facultative phreatophytes have deep taproots and sinker roots (often to depths of 5 to 15 m) as well as wide-spreading lateral roots. This allows plants to switch water sources from groundwater to flood or rainwater, when available. Some deep-rooted trees, including mesquite, influence growth of shorter-rooted plants through hydraulic redistribution of water within the soil profile (Hultine et al. 2004).

Given interspecific differences in rooting depth and drought tolerance, riparian plants are distributed along gradients of depth to groundwater (Stromberg et al. 1996; Naumburg et al. 2005). Where declines in water inflow cause the water table to drop to about 3 m below the floodplain surface,

the cottonwoods and willows are replaced by deeper-rooted or shrubbier species such as tamarisk or burrobrush *(Ambrosia monogyra)* (Scott et al. 1999; Horton et al. 2001; Stromberg et al. 2007). The herbaceous communities along the channel also change with water availability, with species richness declining and composition shifting from obligate wetland to facultative upland species as a stream becomes intermittent.

FLOOD DISTURBANCE

Fluvial landforms of desert streams present a challenging suite of physical conditions to plant growth (Johnson 2010). In addition to fluctuations in water availability and soil fertility, plants are subjected to frequent mechanical disturbance and erosion and deposition of sediment. Many stoloniferous or rhizomatous grasses such as knotgrass *(Paspalum distichum)* and Bermudagrass *(Cynodon dactylon)* persist on frequently flooded surfaces because their buried stems can quickly produce adventitious roots to exploit water, nutrients, and oxygen in freshly deposited sediment. Cottonwoods and willows are well adapted to fluvial disturbance owing to life-history traits including vegetative reproduction, highly flexible stems, and

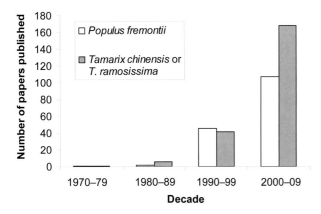

FIG. 24.3. The number of journal articles in the ISI Web of Knowledge database with the respective terms *Populus fremontii* and *Tamarix chinensis* or *Tamarix ramosissima* in the title, abstract, or keywords has increased in recent decades (database accessed June 15, 2009).

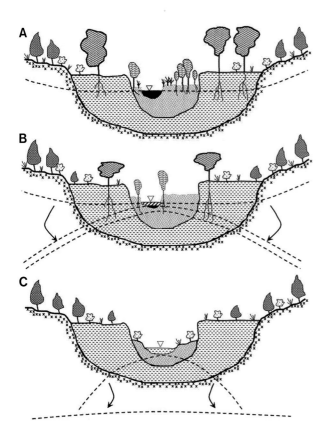

FIG. 24.4. Depiction of riparian vegetation in an alluvial valley, relative to the stream channel, surface water, alluvial water table (dashed line), and upland vegetation for (A) a perennial stream in a gaining reach where a stable water table maintains base flow (solid fill); (B) an intermittent stream where a seasonally high water table supports surface flow for a portion of the year, after which the water table drops below the channel and surface flow ceases (lowest dashed line); and (C) an ephemeral stream where groundwater is disconnected from the channel except during brief storm-related flow events when surface flow (horizontal dash fill) is rapidly lost to the alluvium. (Modified from Goodwin, Archer, et al. 1997.)

tolerance of burial, as well as abundant production of small wind- and water-dispersed seeds. Evolutionarily, these traits also may confer high levels of genetic diversity (Karrenberg et al. 2002).

Many attributes of floods, including intensity and timing, are important forces structuring riparian plant communities (Merritt et al. 2010). Intense floods, through scour, abrasion, erosion, and sedimentation, cause mortality of plants while also creating bare patches available for colonization by propagules. This results in ongoing change in species composition and forest age structure. Shade-intolerant seedlings of cottonwood and willow, for example, germinate and grow on moist, bare sediments following floods of appropriate timing and rate of flow recession (Scott et al. 1997; Mahoney and Rood 1998; Shafroth et al. 1998). The spatial patterns of pioneer trees in the riparian zone reflect the recent flood history as conditioned by geomorphic setting (Johnson 1994; Auble and Scott 1998). It is not uncommon to find arcuate bands of similar-aged cottonwood cohorts on the inside bends of meandering channels (Bradley and Smith 1984) and linear bands of multi-aged trees on the former beds of braided channels (Friedman and Lee 2002).

In addition to creating short-term anoxic stress and physical disturbance, floods also supply a limiting resource—water—to plants on floodplains and channel bars and banks. Soil moisture and aquifer recharge provided by large floods produce pulses of growth, recruitment, and productivity of woody plants as well as of the many herbaceous species that occur along desert rivers. Many of these opportunists arise from persistent soil seed banks, with the buried seed reserves allowing plants to survive the long dry periods that may occur between regenerative flood cycles (Stromberg et al. 2008).

Flood transport of seeds (or hydrochory) helps maintain species diversity in riparian zones. Large floods distribute seed broadly, uniting into a metacommunity the various plant communities that form along lateral hydrogradients. This provides ecosystem resiliency by increasing the probability that plants of a particular habitat affinity have seed available to germinate after large floods reconfigure the channel and reshuffle microsites.

EXOTIC SPECIES

High rates of fluvial geomorphic and hydrological disturbance plus high edge-to-area ratios at both the landscape and patch scales create opportunities for influx of new plant species. Human use of riparian areas as travel corridors and for agricultural and urban purposes provides a ready source of seeds. Thus, exotic species commonly constitute 15 to 30% of desert riparian floras (McLaughlin 2004). Exotic species often increase overall richness, but in some cases a significantly altered disturbance regime may simultaneously cause a non-native to become a dominant species and reduce richness.

The two most abundant woody exotics in the riparian west are tamarisk and Russian olive (*Elaeagnus angustifolia*) (Friedman et al. 2005). Tamarisk shares several life-history traits with cottonwood and willow, which explains its success in flood-disturbed riparian zones, but is more tolerant of drought and salinity. Although abundant in a variety of riverine settings (Birken and Cooper 2006), tamarisk generally is favored over cottonwood by flow regulation, river drying, and land uses including livestock grazing (Everitt 1998; Stromberg et al.

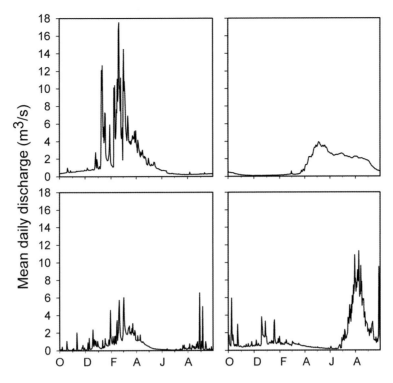

FIG. 24.5. Stream hydrographs differ greatly between rivers in the Mojave (top left), Great Basin (top right), Sonoran (bottom left), and Chihuahuan (bottom right) deserts. Respective rivers and gauges are the Mojave (USGS 10261500), Owyhee (USGS 13174500), Hassayampa (USGS 9515500), and San Pedro (USGS 9471000). All figures show the mean of daily mean values for the water year. The letters along the x axis indicate months. (Figure by Julian Scott.)

2009; Merritt and Poff 2010; Mortenson and Weisberg 2010). Russian olive is a shade-tolerant species abundant along regulated and unregulated rivers alike (Katz and Shafroth 2003; Mortenson and Weisberg 2010).

FIRE

Fire has indirect and direct effects on riparian ecosystems (Pettit and Naiman 2007; Rood et al. 2007). Upland fires increase hillslope runoff and erosion following intense rains, and the increased sedimentation and flooding create disturbance in downstream riparian systems. Fires within the lowland riparian zones exert direct effects on plants. Riparian trees differ in their ability to survive fire, and in their capacity to resprout after top-kill. Shrubby species such as tamarisk resprout the most prodigiously. Thus, one common outcome of fire in the Southwest, particularly on dammed or diverted rivers, is increased relative abundance of tamarisk. Where tamarisk grows in the shady understory of mature cottonwood, however, it has few storage reserves available for postfire resprouting, with the net result being greater postfire population decline for tamarisk (Stromberg and Rychener 2010).

SALINITY

Some rivers in the Southwest traverse geologic marine deposits of high salt content and others receive irrigation return flows high in salts; thus surface and alluvial groundwater may

become saline (Williams 1987). High rates of evaporation can concentrate these salts in upper soil layers, and this can be exacerbated by extrusion of salts and dehiscence of salty leaves by halophytes. Common halophytes along saline reaches of rivers such as the lower Gila and lower Colorado include the shrubs Mojave seepweed *(Suaeda moquinii)*, fourwing saltbush *(Atriplex canescens)*, quailbush *(A. lentifomis)*, arrowweed *(Pluchea sericea)*, and tamarisk (Marks 1950).

Plant-Environment Interactions

Riparian vegetation influences many hydrologic and geomorphic processes. With respect to the hydrologic cycle, riparian plants exert their main effect through evapotranspiration (ET) (Scott et al. 2008). Phreatophytes have high rates of transpiration, sufficient to produce a daily signal in the stream stage, and this has lead to many ill-fated attempts to "salvage" water through "phreatophyte control" (Graf 1992). Present measurement techniques, however, reveal lower rates of floodplainwide ET than were reported in earlier decades. Recent studies also reveal less interspecies variability in ET among riparian trees and large shrubs than once suspected, with cottonwood, willow, and tamarisk having generally similar rates of ET (Glenn and Nagler 2005; Shafroth et al. 2005).

Riparian plants modulate the effects of flood flows on channel and bank form through various processes. Their stems reduce flow velocity and their roots (particularly of grasses) increase soil cohesion and soil strength (Simon and Collison 2002). The stabilization of channel banks by vegetation can lead to conversion of a braided channel form to a single-thread channel (Tal and Paola 2007). Such issues are of management relevance on desert streams where efforts are underway to remove tamarisk from stream margins (see "Recovering Endangered Species").

Riparian Animals

Riparian areas of the North American deserts support a large array of animals that take advantage of the seasonally lush herbaceous growth, tall-statured woody vegetation, proximity to scarce surface water, and other resources. The strips of forest, patches of nonwoody vegetation, and marshes created by flow-related geomorphic processes provide internal edges and increase habitat complexity. Animals, in turn, must be able to tolerate or avoid the periodic disturbance and physical danger associated with floods.

Factors Influencing Riparian Animal Abundance and Richness

WATER AVAILABILITY

Availability of water, either directly or indirectly, is clearly a major contributor to the rich diversity found in assemblages of desert riparian animals. Some species are riparian-obligates, tied to the presence of free water, the riparian microclimate, a riparian-obligate plant (or prey) species, or some combination thereof. Presence of surface water increases richness of birds by providing drinking water, as does depth to the water table by controlling the composition and structural diversity of riparian vegetation (Brand et al. 2008). Several species or subspecies of small mammals are restricted to riparian or similarly moist areas, in that they lack the water-conserving adaptations of rodents living in xeric habitats (Andersen and Nelson 1999).

The western viceroy *(Limenitis archippus obsoleta),* whose larvae feed on willow species, is one of several riparian-obligate butterflies (Nelson 2003). As adults, butterflies forage broadly for nectar, but the quality of riparian plant species as nectar resources varies widely depending on soil moisture. Ground arthropods are influenced by permanence of surface flow, with different assemblages found at intermittent versus perennial sites. Some taxa, such as the damp-loving field cricket *(Gyryllus alogus),* avoid the seasonal drought that occurs at intermittent streams by feeding on "greenfall" of Fremont cottonwood leaves (Sabo et al. 2008).

FLOODS

Flood pulses are paramount in influencing riparian animal communities. Seasonal flood pulses that raise groundwater and create temporary floodplain pools allow amphibians to increase in abundance (Bateman et al. 2008). Further, floods can maintain water quality within the tolerance range for amphibians such as lowland leopard frogs *(Rana yavapaiensis)* that require a freshwater environment for reproduction (Ruibal 1959). For herbivorous insects, summer floods create a pulse of productivity by stimulating growth of plants. On the other hand, flash floods can cause high mortality of animals unable to escape (Andersen and Cooper 2000). For some species, such as Ord's kangaroo rats *(Dipodomys ordii),* the mortal-

ity caused by flooding may cause riparian habitats to function as a population sink (Miller et al. 2003).

LANDSCAPE COMPLEXITY

As the structural complexity of vegetation increases, so does avian species richness. This pattern applies broadly across regions, and is pronounced in arid and semiarid riparian forests (Scott et al. 2003; van Riper et al. 2008). Cottonwood-willow forests, with their tall and multilayered canopies, typically support the highest richness and abundance of breeding birds, followed by mesquite forests (often called bosques) (Hunter et al. 1987; Brand et al. 2008). Tamarisk, with its short canopy, tends to support fewer breeding birds. Riparian grasslands and marshlands each support a distinctive avian community. Collectively, breeding bird richness is highest where many structural and floristic types coexist in the riparian mosaic.

Other taxa similarly increase in richness with structural and floristic complexity of the landscape. For example, many butterflies are abundant in grassy meadows and marshes, while others are associated with dense forests (Hannon et al. 2009). Short stretches of floristically rich riparian zones can support upward of 100 species of butterflies. Bats select habitat based on roosting site preferences and foraging traits such as insect abundance and canopy gaps; thus bat richness is high where a mosaic of vegetation structure types exists (Williams et al. 2006).

Migratory Species

Hundreds of migrant birds, bats, and butterflies seasonally use desert riparian areas as travel corridors, as stopover sites to refuel or drink, or as places to breed or to overwinter. One of the many neotropical migrant birds that rely on desert riparian corridors is the endangered southwestern willow flycatcher *(Empidonax traillii extimus;* see "Recovering Endangered Species"). Another is the western yellow-billed cuckoo *(Coccyzus americanus occidentalis),* a candidate for listing as federally threatened or endangered in the U.S. Cuckoos winter in South America and return to southwestern cottonwood forests to breed. They are one of the few birds to nest in midsummer, when air temperatures are highest. This unusual timing allows the breeding birds to feed on summer insects, including the root-feeding cicadas that emerge each year from the riparian forest floor (Andersen 1994; Smith et al. 2006).

Endemic and Rare Species

A few riparian species (or subspecies) in the North American deserts are endemic to particular rivers or river basins. (All species of concern are listed in online appendix 1.) Many have become geographically isolated along a large river as desert conditions formed or intensified beginning in the Cenozoic era. Large river corridors also served to isolate desert populations from one another, with the result that species or subspecies pairs now occur on opposite banks of the lower Colorado River, the Rio Conchos, and other desert rivers. For example, along the lower Colorado, mammalian species pairs include antelope ground squirrels *(Ammospermophilus harrisii* and *A. leucurus),* pocket mice *(Perognathus intermedius* and both *P. formosus* and *P. spinatus),* and subspecies pairs of a pocket gopher *(Thomomys bottae)* (Grinnell 1914).

Interactions among Zones

The influence of a riparian zone can extend deeply into the uplands (Soykan and Sabo 2009). Large, mobile desert mammals, such as desert bighorn sheep *(Ovis canadensis mexicana)*, collared peccary (javelina, *Pecari tajacu)*, or Sonoran pronghorn antelope *(Antilocapra americana sonoriensis)*, often visit riparian areas to obtain water or forage. Similarly, the wide-ranging large predators in these desert regions, such as coyote *(Canis latrans)*, mountain lion *(Puma concolor)*, and jaguar *(Panthera onca)*, opportunistically use riparian areas to hunt and drink. Desert habitat generalists such as Mojave rattlesnakes *(Crotalus scutulatus)* range into riparian habitat when dispersing or searching for food.

Plant-Animal Interactions

Despite the well-documented negative effects from excessive numbers of livestock (see "Agro-Ecosystems," below), common wisdom holds that physical factors structure desert riparian plant communities. Increasingly, however, researchers are addressing the roles of animals, including "ecosystem engineers" such as beaver *(Castor canadensis)*. Beaver can have large local effects on hydrology and geomorphology in smaller streams such as the Bill Williams River through their dam-building activities (Andersen and Shafroth 2010). Other animals affecting riparian hydrology include pocket gophers *(Thomomys* spp.), whose tunnels serve as underground water distribution systems during floods, and desert cicadas, whose emergence tunnels facilitate infiltration (Andersen 1994).

Beavers aside, the role of native herbivores in dynamics of riparian plant populations has received little attention. Grasshoppers are important herbivores found in floodplains throughout all four deserts, with some taxa rarely found away from water (Rehn and Grant 1957). Cottonwood leaf beetles *(Chrysomela scripta)* can defoliate trees during their population irruptions (Andersen and Nelson 2002). Ungulates such as the desert mule deer *(Odocoileus hemionus)* can influence survivorship of young cottonwoods, but they generally do not form large herds; thus, population- and landscape-level effects are negligible except where habitat is limited due to factors such as flow regulation (Andersen 2005). Bison *(Bison bison)* were once present in Chihuahuan and Sonoran deserts, but their effects on riparian vegetation are not well known.

Many riparian animals serve as pollinators and seed dispersers. Although cottonwoods and other pioneer trees are wind-pollinated and wind- and water-dispersed, plants associated with less flood-prone surfaces often are animal-pollinated and their seeds are animal-dispersed. Riparian pollinators include bees, butterflies, and numerous other insects as well as several species of hummingbirds. Frugivorous birds such as phainopeplas *(Phainopeplanitens)*and omnivorous mammals such as coyotes feed on fleshy-fruited riparian plants, providing a mechanism for movement of plant seeds and genes.

Ecosystem Processes

After water, the environmental factor most limiting riparian productivity is probably nitrogen (N). In the coarse, dry sediments of the floodplain, N can be sparse, but is seasonally supplemented by upland runoff and flood-associated depositional processes (Adair et al. 2004; Brooks et al. 2007; Harms and

Grimm 2008). The N delivered in floodwaters and subsurface flows is rapidly taken up by young floodplain trees close to the channel (Schade et al. 2002).

Nitrogen also is supplied to desert floodplain soils by biological fixation. Along streams in the Chihuahuan, Sonoran, and Mojave deserts, N-fixing bacteria in roots of mesquite increase soil N (Schade and Hobbie 2005). In cold-desert floodplains of the Great Basin and Colorado Plateau, actinorhizal associations of *Shepherdia* sp. and Russian olive do the same (Harner et al. 2009). These N-fixing woody plants are most prevalent on high floodplains and terraces, and may be particularly important for maintaining productivity in older forest stands.

Mycorrhizae are important in maintaining plant vigor in desert river floodplains. The two predominant mycorrhizal associations in our study region are ectomycorrhizae (EM) and arbuscular mycorrhizae (AM) (Stutz et al. 2009). Several new species of AM fungi have been reported from riparian areas in the Southwest, and undoubtedly more remain to be described. Goodding's willow and cottonwoods are unusual in forming a tripartate relationship, hosting both AM and EM fungi. *Tamarix* apparently is nonmycorrhizal in the desert Southwest, contrasting with patterns in Eurasia (Yang et al. 2008).

Cycling of nutrients and carbon within the floodplain depends on a variety of organisms and processes. Scavengers consume moist, high-quality animal material. Arthropods can be important detritivores (Tibbets and Molles 2005), and leaching and photochemical processes also contribute to breakdown of riparian plant litter. Breakdown of woody debris may be accelerated by xylophagous beetles, whose larvae bore through (and consume) dead wood (Kukor and Martin 1986; MacKay et al. 1987). Mineralization ultimately results from microbial (including fungal) activity, which requires a moist environment. Decomposition of surface litter can be very slow (years to decades) on dry surfaces (Andersen and Nelson 2006).

Conservation Concerns

Stream Flow Alteration

The flow regime of every major desert river in North America has been altered by man, with that alteration in some cases initiated hundreds or even thousands of years ago. Human impacts on hydrology accelerated during the 20th century through construction of large flood control, water storage, and power-generating dams. Prehistoric diversion canals were rebuilt and expanded, and new water supply and delivery systems constructed, including interbasin water transfer systems such as the Central Arizona Project. Thousands of wells were drilled into stream aquifers to sustain irrigated agriculture and mining operations, and even today they are being drilled into regional (basin) aquifers to support urban growth and associated needs such as power production.

The combined freshwater extraction for agriculture, municipal use, and industries led to dramatic changes in riparian ecosystem conditions. Surface-water diversion and groundwater pumping locally reduced base flows, lowered water tables, and increased the spatial extent of intermittent and ephemeral (vs. perennial) stream reaches. Cottonwood, willow, and mesquite trees died from water extraction on rivers such as the Santa Cruz (Webb and Leake 2006), causing declines in riparian bird species. Flood control and water storage dams, by altering flood patterns and sediment inflows, reduced recruitment rates of floodplain cottonwood and willow trees (Rood et al.

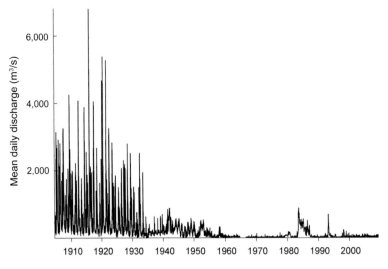

FIG. 24.6. Discharge for the Colorado River near its mouth (data from USGS gauge "Colorado River at Yuma, Arizona" or equivalent for post-1966 period). Construction of the first large flood-control dam in the catchment (Hoover Dam, near Las Vegas, Nevada) was completed in 1935.

2010). By reducing scour and other fluvial disturbance, dams decreased heterogeneity and species diversity, but increased woody debris in some cases (Shafroth et al. 2002). Accumulations of dead wood and litter increase intensity of riparian fire (Ellis 2001).

Recovering Endangered Species

Precise values for the acreages of riparian wetlands in the American Southwest that have been converted to human use or otherwise substantially altered by actions such as dam building and stream diversion remain unknown. It is clear that habitat loss and alteration have resulted in the endangerment and extirpation of many species (online appendix 1) and driven shifts in species compositions. One well-documented case of riparian ecosystem loss and alteration is the lower Colorado River, where flows are now diminished to the point that in drought years no water reaches the Gulf of California (Glenn et al. 2007) (Fig. 24.6). Increased salinity and a greatly altered flow regime have shifted plant species toward more drought- and salt-tolerant taxa such as tamarisk. Largely owing to hydrogeomorphic changes and extensive land conversion to agriculture, 45 of the ecoregion's species are listed as endangered, threatened, or sensitive (U.S. Bureau of Reclamation 1996, in Glenn et al. 2001).

The flagship endangered species (technically, subspecies) of desert riparian areas is the southwestern willow flycatcher, a small, riparian-obligate, neotropical migrant songbird. The birds nest in dense, young stands of willows and tamarisks growing near perennial water. Collectively, water extraction, river damming, land conversion, and grazing (which can attract cowbirds, *Molothrus* spp., a nest parasite) have reduced flycatcher abundance.

One component of the flycatcher recovery plan calls for improving riparian habitat conditions on rivers that sustain the few remaining large populations of the birds, thereby increasing regional metapopulation stability. Thus, within Arizona, ranchland has been acquired on the lower San Pedro River and ranch-related pumping from the alluvial aquifer stopped, with the expectation that perennial flow will occupy a greater portion of the river, leading to more riparian-obligate plants and then more flycatchers. On some parts of the river, the hydrologic response has been rapid (Katz et al. 2009). On others, change has yet to be realized, perhaps because long-term groundwater pumping reduced aquifer permeability—an irreversible impediment to restoration—or perhaps because recharging depleted aquifers is a slow process.

Another "tool" being used for flycatcher habitat restoration is beaver. Once common throughout the region, beavers were widely trapped out over a century ago for their pelts. They also declined as riverine marshlands were drained (in some cases to eliminate malaria) and as rivers entrenched. Today, beaver have repopulated or are being reintroduced to rivers from which they were extirpated. For example, reintroduction of beaver to catchments on the Zuni Reservation (Arizona/New Mexico border) has expanded riparian and wetland cover and has contributed to a doubling of flycatcher nesting territories (Albert and Trimble 2000).

Another factor listed by the US Fish and Wildlife Service as a cause of endangerment of the flycatcher is tamarisk. Recent evidence, however, suggests that tamarisk provides habitat of positive value at sites no longer hydrologically suitable for willow and also provides fuel for stopover migrants (Sogge et al. 2008; Cerasale and Guglielmo 2010) (Fig. 24.7a–b). This has raised controversy among those who value endangered species and those who vilify exotic species. "Your weed is our habitat" (seen on a poster at a scientific meeting) captures the sentiment of this controversy. Tamarisk removal efforts continue, however, exemplified most recently by the introduction of a herbivorous beetle as a biological control agent (Hudgeons et al. 2007).

Restoring Foundation Species

Many people wish to shift river and riparian ecosystems toward a more desired condition. The factors that motivate restoration efforts range from legal mandates to recover an endangered species to a desire to bring back "what was." For example, the Mojave Indian Nation, whose ancestors farmed the lower Colorado River floodplain, is active in planting riparian woodlands on the Colorado River Indian Reservation, including the mes-

FIG. 24.7. Arizona Game and Fish personnel using mirrors (A) to observe a nest of the southwestern willow flycatcher (B), here shown in a *Tamarix* stand. (Photos by Arizona Game and Fish Department [left] and Jim Burns [right].)

quite bosques that play an important role in their traditional ceremonies.

Many restoration efforts have targeted cottonwoods and willows. Past failures involving restoration plantings testify to the extensive changes that have occurred in riparian landscapes, and indicate that the past is not necessarily an effective guide to present potential. Of note, many of the cottonwoods and willows planted on fallowed farm fields along the lower Gila and lower Colorado rivers died because site conditions on these partially dewatered and highly regulated rivers were no longer favorable. Plants with deeper roots and greater salt tolerance, such as mesquite and saltbush, had greater success (Cohn 2001).

Other efforts to restore riparian zones have involved release of appropriately timed flood pulses. For the Bill Williams River, stakeholders have collaborated to combine development of riparian habitat (involving flood releases from an upstream dam) with other goals such as sustaining reservoir recreation. The Truckee River is another case wherein scientists and agency personnel have worked together to implement dam releases as a restoration tool (Rood et al. 2005). The original impetus was to create spawning habitat for an endangered fish, but the flood also stimulated cottonwood recruitment, thus demonstrating that restoration of a single form of flood pulse can meet multiple species' needs.

On desert rivers with complex natural flow patterns, multiple floods of different sizes and in different seasons may be needed to create the temporal and spatial diversity of habitats and regeneration niches that typified these ecosystems pre-dam. Many desert rivers present viable options for restoration via release of flood flows and/or base flows (Boudell and Stromberg 2008), and await stakeholder groups to plan and implement actions. Often, however, rehabilitation (improved habitat condition) rather than restoration is undertaken, as it is less water-demanding and politically easier to accomplish. Of note, the major ecosystem management efforts underway along the lower Colorado River do not include flood restoration.

Revising Water Laws

Maintaining water flows to riparian wetlands can require maintaining hydrological linkages at large spatial scales. Research in Nevada, for example, revealed connections between regional aquifers and discharge at distant desert springs in the Mojave and Great Basin deserts (Patten et al. 2008). Thus, conserving endemic wetland plants at spring-fed sites in areas such as southern Nevada's Ash Meadows National Wildlife Refuge may require that urbanizing parts of Nevada seek water from sources other than rural aquifers. Laws governing water use, however, provide little protection for riparian habitat. For example, although surface and groundwater sometimes are managed conjunctively in some states, in others they are treated as legally distinct entities.

With respect to surface water laws, individual states in the dry, western U.S. began adopting laws in the mid-1800s separating the right to use stream water from ownership of riparian land. The "prior appropriation doctrine" evolved as a simple priority rule that gave a right to a volume of water to the individual who first diverted that volume and put it to "beneficial" use *outside the channel*. In recent decades, many states have adopted rules allowing surface water rights for beneficial *instream* uses such as sustaining fish and wildlife or recreation. However, many rivers have become "overappropriated" in that the volume of water to which rights have been extended exceeds the volume of stream flow, and many instream water right holders do not have seniority.

Restoring Urban Riparian Amenities

Urban populations in southwestern deserts are expanding rapidly. Urbanized rivers in these areas share many attributes: their floodplains often are narrowed, with the river disconnected from its historic floodplain by levees or channelization, and their flows of water and sediment are altered by upstream dams. Desert riparian streams provide water (and crops) essential to people, but they also are valued for their aesthetic and recreational value, as reflected in local economic benefits derived from bird watching and in people's willingness to pay higher prices for homes located near flowing streams (Bark et al. 2009). The streams and the biota they sustain also can provide flood amelioration, water storage, pollution control, pollination services, carbon sequestration, climate regulation, and biodiversity maintenance, depending on how they are managed.

One urban reach that is the focus of restoration efforts is the Salt River in the Phoenix metropolitan area, where more than 4 million people now live and work. Prior to extensive channelization and diversion, people would picnic along the river under shady cottonwoods and catch now-extirpated "big river" fish such as Colorado pikeminnow (*Ptychocheilus lucius*). Today, the stream water is distributed in canals throughout the metropolitan area, where it sustains urban forests that counteract the urban heat island and furnish habitat for some riparian biota (Rosenberg et al. 1987). The fragmentation and hydrogeomorphic alteration of the waterway, however, have profoundly altered the riparian communities along the river. In response, multimillion-dollar restoration projects have been initiated by cities and the federal government (authorized by the Water Resources Development Act of 1996). In such urban settings, though, ecosystem restoration in the strict sense is impossible because it is not feasible to reinstate the physical forces and processes that historically sustained the biota. On the Salt River in Phoenix, project efforts thus have emphasized reengineering of the local water infrastructure and surface topography, together with planting and weeding, effectively creating an aesthetically pleasing urban park that also sustains riparian wildlife.

One water source that is increasing in the urbanizing Southwest is municipal effluent. In some areas, effluent is intentionally discharged to support wetlands and the services they provide, notably water-quality purification. In Las Vegas, Nevada, for example, treated wastewater is released into Las Vegas Wash. The marshlands and riparian shrublands that are sustained by the flows, in conjunction with the wash sediments, purify the water during its journey to Lake Mead. There are some environmental concerns about the quality of municipal effluent, but many treatment plants are being upgraded. For those who enjoy recreating in riparian zones, this is a double-edged sword: As water quality improves, increasing volumes of effluent are directly reused for municipal purposes ("toilet to tap") rather than being discharged to streambeds to sustain riparian wetlands.

Agro-Ecosystems

In dryland regions, the lands most suitable for farming are along the river courses. Thus, considerable acreage of southwestern riparian land has been converted to irrigated crops (Doolittle 2006; Andersen et al. 2007). Conversion rates are highest for the lower reaches of the main drainages such as the lower Rio Grande and lower Colorado. The wide valleys of these reaches offered expansive flood-free terraces for profitable crop production and, once floods were controlled, the modern floodplain as well. In such reaches, it is not uncommon for the majority of the bottomland to be in agriculture.

Although industrialized agriculture—with a primary focus on maximizing productivity—is common, small-scale organic

FIG. 24.8. Riparian trees and shrubs serve as fence rows and channel buffers, reflecting traditional agricultural practices on the floodplain of the Río Sonora near Aconchi, Sonora, Mexico. (Photo by Michael Scott.)

agriculture is a growing practice. Multifunctional landscapes exist in which crop production is integrated with other ecosystem services. For example, small farms along the Santa Cruz and San Pedro rivers in Arizona sustain hedgerows of flowering shrubs along the agricultural fields, thereby attracting insects, including dozens of bee species that can pollinate agricultural crops (Hannon and Sisk 2009). In parts of Mexico, cottonwood and willow pole plantings have long been used as living fencerows on cultivated floodplains to reduce erosion, and the plantings also provide habitat for wildlife (Scott et al. 2009) (Fig. 24.8). Patches of woodland in southwestern agricultural landscapes likely maintain high avian abundance, as they do elsewhere in the West (Perkins et al. 1993; Tewksbury et al. 1998).

A major land use in the arid and semiarid American West was (and remains) livestock grazing. Unregulated grazing in the 1800s and early 1900s caused significant and long-lasting changes in the riparian landscape. For example, reductions in fire frequency from overgrazing contributed to the current predominance of woody riparian vegetation (vs. grassland and marshland) along many desert rivers (Hendrickson and Minckley 1984). Further, overgrazing shifted upland vegetation in some areas from desert grassland to desert scrub. This shift was accompanied by severe soil erosion and loss of topsoil, with persistent effects on water infiltration and runoff processes. Still being debated is the role of overgrazing (in concert with climate fluctuation) in contributing to the early 19th-century entrenchment of many desert rivers. This entrenchment or arroyo-cutting desiccated marshlands and shifted vegetation towards deeply rooted facultative phreatophytes (Hastings 1959), and, for some streams, set in motion a century-long process of cottonwood expansion in the inset channel.

Stocking rates on public lands in the USA declined considerably after passage of federal grazing laws in the 1930s. Particularly during times of drought and heat, however, thirsty cattle will congregate, if allowed, in and near streambeds, and their concentrated grazing and trampling can alter riparian soil properties, geomorphic processes, and plant communities. Selective foraging promotes plants that are chemically or structurally well defended (e.g., mesquite and tamarisk) and rhizomatous grasses tolerant of repeated herbivory. Bare

FIG. 24.9. A. Many riparian preserves have been established along the San Pedro River, shown here upstream of Benson, Arizona. B. On many other desert rivers, such as the Rio Grande (shown here at its confluence with the Rio Conchos in southwestern Texas), irrigated agriculture is a primary land use. (Photos by Michael Collier.)

ground expands and vegetation structure simplifies (Scott et al. 2003). If these changes substantially alter hydrologic processes such as water infiltration and bank storage, dry-season stream flow rates decline.

In the 1970s, surveys estimated that 83% of the riparian area under management of the federal Bureau of Land Management (BLM) in the western U.S. was in unsatisfactory condition (Almand and Krohn 1979). About one-third of the drylands in the USA's Southwest and Intermountain West were severely desertified, conditions that affect water and sediment delivery to streams (Dregne 1983). In response, the BLM and USDA Forest Service attempted to restore streams on public lands by restricting the timing of grazing or the stocking rate allowed by grazing permit holders. Some federal riparian preserves were established from which livestock are excluded (Fig. 24.9a), and many other preserves were established by conservation organizations. There remains a need, however, for more long-term monitoring, as well as for experimental study, to clarify the effects of cattle, as well as feral burros *(Equus asinus)*, on desert riparian ecosystems (Sarr 2002; Abella 2008).

Climate Change

Efforts to restore and sustain riparian ecosystems in the North American deserts are taking place literally in a climate of uncertainty. However, Seager et al. (2007) predict that the Southwest is becoming more arid. Warmer temperatures increase evaporation rates, thus reducing surface runoff and recharge. The ensuing reductions in base flows and water tables, if sufficiently large, will shift vegetation from obligate to facultative phreatophytes, reduce primary productivity, and simplify vegetation structure. Further, with climate-related shifts in the ratio of snowfall to rainfall, human demands on water resources of the major river basins are likely to intensify (Christensen et al. 2004). Some climate models predict increases in winter rains, which could offset warming-related declines in base flows, but precipitation predictions are particularly uncertain (Dixon et al. 2009). Further reducing uncertainty are the many feedbacks that will occur between physical and biotic components of the ecosystem as climate changes.

Conclusion

In the arid and semiarid American Southwest, periodically flooded perennial river floodplains harbor cottonwood-willow forests and other riparian vegetation types, and provide habitat for a wide array of animals. In this harsh environment, people too have concentrated their livelihoods along the rivers: virtually all North American desert rivers have been hydrologically modified and many acres of riparian bottomland have been converted to irrigated croplands. Biotic communities have been "reshuffled" and conflicts have arisen over management efforts to remove exotic species (e.g., tamarisk) that now provide nesting habitat for endangered species (e.g., southwestern willow flycatcher). Restoration of riparian vegetation to its original spatial extent is impossible, but some efforts are underway to reinstate the key processes—including flood pulses and low flows—that sustain riparian wetlands. Such efforts will become more challenging as climate change dries headwaters and shifts flow regimes, and as human populations expand. Sustaining riparian environments is but one of many issues that will be considered as governmental agencies face the daunting task of determining how to deal with water scarcity. Revitalizing streams with emerging water sources, notably municipal effluent, and integrating crop production with riparian communities to create multifunctional landscapes may be key for creating sustainable systems. Catchment-scale perspectives will help ensure that the important and sometimes long-lasting effects from fire, grazing, and other activities outside the riparian zone will be considered in riparian restoration and management plans. Information exchange among agencies, scientists, and the public are paramount for sustaining riparian ecosystems. For rivers like the Colorado, Rio Grande, Rio Conchos, and San Pedro, international collaboration also is a necessity.

References

Abella SR. 2008. A systematic review of wild burro grazing effects on Mojave Desert vegetation, USA. *Env. Manage.* 41:809–19.
Adair EC, Binkley D, Andersen DC. 2004. Patterns of nitrogen accumulation and cycling in riparian floodplain ecosystems along the Green and Yampa rivers. *Oecologia* 139:108–16.

Albert S, Trimble T. 2000. Beavers are partners in riparian restoration on the Zuni Indian reservation. *Ecol. Restor.* 18:87–92.

Almand J, Krohn W. 1979. The position of the Bureau of Land Management on the protection and management of riparian ecosystems. US Forest Serv. GTR-WO-12:359–361.

Andersen DC. 1994. Are cicadas *(Diceroprocta apache)* both a "keystone" and a "critical-link" species in lower Colorado River riparian communities? *Southwest. Nat.* 39:26–33.

Andersen DC. 2005. Characterizing flow regimes for floodplain forest conservation: an assessment of factors affecting sapling growth and survivorship on three cold desert rivers. *Can. J. For. Res.* 35:2886–99.

Andersen DC, Cooper DJ. 2000. Plant-herbivore-hydroperiod interactions: effects of native mammals on floodplain tree recruitment. *Ecol. Appl.* 10:1384–99.

Andersen DC, Nelson SM. 1999. Rodent use of anthropogenic and "natural" desert riparian habitat, lower Colorado River, Arizona. *Regul. Rivers: Res. & Manage.* 15:377–93.

Andersen DC, Nelson SM. 2002. Effects of cottonwood leaf beetle *Chrysomela scripta* (Coleoptera: Chrysomelidae) on survival and growth of Fremont cottonwood *(Populus fremontii)* in northwest Colorado. *Am. Midl. Nat.* 147:189–203.

Andersen DC, Nelson SM. 2006. Flood pattern and weather determine *Populus* leaf litter breakdown and nitrogen dynamics on a cold desert floodplain. *J. Arid Env.* 64:626–50.

Andersen DC, Shafroth PB. 2010. Beaver dams, hydrological thresholds, and controlled floods as a management tool in a desert riverine ecosystem, Bill Williams River, Arizona. *Ecohydrology* 3:325–38.

Andersen DC, Cooper DJ, Northcott K. 2007. Dams, floodplain land use, and riparian forest conservation in the semiarid upper Colorado River basin, USA. *Env. Manage.* 40:453–75.

Auble GT, Scott ML. 1998. Fluvial disturbance patches and cottonwood recruitment along the upper Missouri River, Montana. *Wetlands* 18:546–56.

Axelrod DI. 1958. Evolution of the Madro-Tertiary geoflora. *Bot. Rev.* 24:434–62.

Bacon SN, McDonald EV, et al. 2010. Timing and distribution of alluvial fan sedimentation in response to strengthening of late Holocene ENSO variability in the Sonoran Desert, southwestern Arizona, USA. *Quat. Res.* 73:425–38.

Baillie MN, Hogan, JF, et al. 2007. Quantifying water sources to a semiarid riparian ecosystem, San Pedro River, Arizona. *J. Geophys. Res.-Biogeo.* 112 (G3): Art. no. G03S02.

Bark RH, Osgood DE, et al. 2009. Habitat preservation and restoration: do homebuyers have preferences for quality habitat? *Ecol. Econ.* 68:1465–75.

Bateman HL, Harner MJ, Chung-MacCoubrey A. 2008. Abundance and reproduction of toads *(Bufo)* along a regulated river in the southwestern United States: importance of flooding in riparian ecosystems. *J. Arid Env.* 72:1613–19.

Belnap J. 1995. Surface disturbances: their role in accelerating desertification. *Env. Monit. Assess.* 37:39–57.

Birken AS, Cooper DJ. 2006. Processes of *Tamarix* invasion and floodplain development along the lower Green River, Utah. *Ecol. Appl.* 16:1103–20.

Boudell JA, Stromberg JC. 2008. Propagule banks: potential contribution to restoration of an impounded and dewatered riparian ecosystem. *Wetlands* 28:656–65.

Bradley CE, Smith DG. 1986. Plains cottonwood recruitment and survival on a prairie meandering river flood plain, Milk River, southern Alberta and northern Montana. *Can. J. Bot.* 64:1433–42.

Brand LA, White GC, Noon BR. 2008. Factors influencing species richness and community composition of breeding birds in a desert riparian corridor. *Condor* 110:199–210.

Brooks PD, Haas PA, Huth AK. 2007. Seasonal variability in the concentration and flux of organic matter and inorganic nitrogen in a semiarid catchment, San Pedro River, Arizona. *J. Geophys. Res.* 112, Art. no. G03S04.

Brown D, ed. 1994. *Biotic communities: southwestern United States and northwestern Mexico.* Salt Lake City: Univ. Utah Press.

Busch DE, Ingraham NL, Smith SD. 1992. Water uptake in riparian phreatophytes of the southwestern U.S.: a stable isotope study. *Ecol. Appl.* 2:450–59.

Cerasale DJ, Guglielmo CG. 2010. An integrative assessment of the effects of tamarisk on stopover ecology of a long-distance migrant along the San Pedro River, Arizona. *Auk* 127:636–46.

Christensen NS, Wood AW, et al. 2004. The effects of climate change on the hydrology and water resources of the Colorado River basin. *Clim. Change* 62:337–63.

Cohn JP. 2001. Resurrecting the dammed: a look at Colorado River restoration. *BioSci.* 51:998–1003.

Dixon MD, Stromberg JC, et al. 2009. Potential effects of climate change on the upper San Pedro riparian ecosystem. In *Ecology and conservation of the San Pedro River,* Stromberg JC, Tellman B, editors. Tucson: Univ. Arizona Press, pp. 57–72.

Doolittle WE. 2006. Agricultural manipulation of floodplains in the southern Basin and Range province. *Catena* 65:179–99.

Dregne HE. 1983. *Desertification of arid lands.* Chur, Switzerland: Harwood Press.

Ellis LM. 2001. Short-term response of woody plants to fire in a Rio Grande riparian forest, central New Mexico, USA. *Biol. Conserv.* 97:159–70.

Ely LL, Enzel Y, et al. 1993. A 5000-year record of extreme floods and climate-change in the southwestern United States. *Science* 262:410–12.

Endfield GH, Tejedo IF. 2006. Decades of drought, years of hunger: archival investigations of multiple year droughts in late colonial Chihuahua. *Clim. Change* 75:391–419.

Everitt BL. 1998. Chronology of the spread of saltcedar in the central Rio Grande. *Wetlands* 18:658–68.

Friedman JM, Auble GT, et al. 2005. Dominance of non-native riparian trees in western USA. *Biol. Invas.* 7:747–51.

Friedman JM, Lee VJ. 2002. Extreme floods, channel change, and riparian forests along ephemeral streams. *Ecol. Monogr.* 72:409–25.

Glenn EP, Flessa KW, et al. 2007. Just add water and the Colorado River still reaches the sea. *Env. Manage.* 40:1–6.

Glenn EP, Nagler PL. 2005. Comparative ecophysiology of *Tamarix ramosissima* and native trees in western US riparian zones. *J. Arid Env.* 61:419–46.

Glenn EP, Zamora-Arroyo F, et al. 2001. Ecology and conservation biology of the Colorado River delta, Mexico. *J. Arid Env.* 49:5–15.

Goodwin CN, Archer CP, Kershner JL. 1997. Riparian restoration in the western United States: overview and perspective. *Restor. Ecol.* 5:4–14.

Graf WL. 1988. *Fluvial processes in dryland rivers.* Berlin: Springer-Verlag.

Graf WL. 1992. Science, public-policy, and western American rivers. *T. I. Brit. Geogr.* 17:5–19.

Green DM, Stromberg JC, Tiller RL. 2009. Riparian soils. In *Ecology and conservation of the San Pedro River,* Stromberg JC, Tellman B, editors. Tucson: Univ. Arizona Press, pp. 268–84.

Grinnell J. 1914. An account of the mammals and birds of the Lower Colorado Valley. *U. Calif. Pub. Zool.* 12:51–294.

Hannon LE, Ries L, Williams KS. 2009. Terrestrial arthropods along the San Pedro: three case studies. In *Ecology and conservation of the San Pedro River,* Stromberg JC, Tellman B, editors. Tucson: Univ. Arizona Press, pp. 127–52.

Hannon LE, Sisk TD. 2009. Hedgerows in an agri-natural landscape: potential habitat value for native bees. *Biol. Conserv.* 142:2140–54.

Harms TK, Grimm NB. 2008. Hot spots and hot moments of carbon and nitrogen dynamics in a semiarid riparian zone. *J. Geophys. Res.* 113, G01020, doi:10.1029/2007JG000588.

Harner MJ, Crenshaw CL, et al. 2009. Decomposition of leaf litter from a native tree and an actinorhizal invasive across riparian habitats. *Ecol. Appl.* 19:1135–46.

Hastings JR. 1959. Vegetation change and arroyo cutting in southeastern Arizona. *J. Arizona-Nevada Acad. Sci.* 1:60–67.

Hendrickson DA, Minckley WL. 1984. Ciénegas—vanishing climax communities of the American Southwest. *Desert Plants* 6:130–75.

Horton JL, Kolb TE, Hart SC. 2001. Responses of riparian trees to interannual variation in groundwater depth in a semi-arid river basin. *Plant Cell Env.* 24:293–304.

Hudgeons JL, Knutson AE, et al. 2007. Establishment and biological success of *Diorhabda elongata elongata* on invasive *Tamarix* in Texas. *Southwest. Entomol.* 32:157–68.

Hultine KR, Scott RL, et al. 2004. Hydraulic redistribution by a dominant, warm-desert phreatophyte: seasonal patterns and response to precipitation pulses. *Funct. Ecol.* 18:530–38.

Hunter WC, Ohmart RD, Anderson BW. 1987. Status of breeding riparian-obligate birds in southwestern riverine systems. *Western Birds* 18:10–18.

Johnson WC. 2000. Tree recruitment and survival in rivers: influence of hydrological processes. *Hydrol. Process.* 14:3051–74.

Johnson WC. 1994. Woodland expansion in the Platte River, Nebraska: patterns and causes. *Ecol. Monogr.* 64:45–84.

Karrenberg S, Edwards PJ, Kollmann J. 2002. The life history of Salicaceae living in the active zone of floodplains. *Freshw. Biol.* 47:733–48.

Katz GL, Shafroth PB. 2003. Biology, ecology and management of *Elaeagnus angustifolia* L. (Russian olive) in western North America. *Wetlands* 23:763–77.

Katz GL, Stromberg JC, Denslow MW. 2009. Streamside herbaceous vegetation response to hydrologic restoration on the San Pedro River, Arizona. *Ecohydrology* 2:213–25.

Krueper D, Bart J, Rich TD. 2003. Response of vegetation and breeding birds to the removal of cattle on the San Pedro River, Arizona (USA). *Conserv. Biol.* 17:607–15.

Kukor JJ, Martin MM. 1986. Cellulose digestion in *Monochamus marmorator* Kby (Coleoptera, Cerambycidae)—role of acquired fungal enzymes. *J. Chem. Ecol.* 12:1057–70.

Langbein WB, Schumm SA. 1958. Yield of sediment in relation to mean annual precipitation. *T. Am. Geophys. Un.* 39:1076–84.

MacKay WP, Zak JC, Hovore FT. 1987. Cerambycid beetles (Coleoptera: Cerambycidae) of the northern Chihuahuan Desert (south central New Mexico). *Coleopt. Bull.* 41:361–69.

Magruder IA, Woessner WW, Running SW. 2009. Ecohydrologic processs modelling of mountain block groundwater recharge. *Ground Water* 47:774–85.

Mahoney JM, Rood SB. 1998. Streamflow requirements for cottonwood seedling recruitment—an integrative model. *Wetlands* 18:634–45.

Marks JB. 1950. Vegetation and soil relations in the lower Colorado desert. *Ecology* 31:176–93.

McLaughlin SP. 2004. Riparian flora. In *Riparian areas of the southwestern United States: hydrology, ecology and management,* Baker MB Jr., Ffolliott PF, et al., editors. Boca Raton, FL: Lewis Publishers, pp. 127–67.

Meinzer OE. 1927. *Plants as indicators of ground water.* Washington, DC: United States Department of the Interior, US Geological Survey Water-Supply Paper 577.

Merritt DM, Poff NL. 2010. Shifting dominance of riparian *Populus* and *Tamarix* along gradients of flow alteration in western North American rivers. *Ecol. Appl.* 20:135–52.

Merritt DM, Scott ML, et al. 2010. Theory, methods and tools for determining environmental flows for riparian vegetation: riparian vegetation-flow response guilds. *Freshwater Biol.* 55:206–25.

Miller MS, Wilson KR, Andersen DC. 2003. Ord's kangaroo rats living in floodplain habitats: factors contributing to habitat attraction. *Southwest. Nat.* 48:411–18.

Mortenson SG, Weisberg PJ. 2010. Does river regulation increase the dominance of invasive woody species in riparian landscapes? *Global Biol. Biogeogr.* 19:562–74.

Naumburg E, Mata-Gonzalez R, et al. 2005. Phreatophytic vegetation and groundwater fluctuations: a review of current research and application of ecosystem response modeling with an emphasis on Great Basin vegetation. *Env. Manage.* 35:726–40.

Nelson SM. 2003. The western viceroy butterfly (Nymphalidae: *Limenitis archippus obsoleta*): an indicator for riparian restoration in the arid southwestern United States? *Ecol. Indic.* 3:203–11.

Patten DT, Rouse L, Stromberg JC. 2008. Isolated spring wetlands in the Great Basin and Mojave deserts, U.S.A.: potential response of vegetation to groundwater withdrawal. *Env. Manage.* 41:398–413.

Perkins AW, Johnson BJ, Blankenship EE. 1993. Response of riparian avifauna to percentage and pattern of woody cover in an agricultural landscape. *Wildl. Soc. B.* 31:642–60.

Pettit NE, Naiman RJ. 2007. Fire in the riparian zone: characteristics and ecological consequences. *Ecosystems* 10:673–87.

Rehn JAG, Grant HJ Jr. 1957. The genus *Paratettix* as found in North America (Orthoptera: Acridoidea: Tetrigidae). *P. Acad. Nat. Sci. Phila.* 109:247–319.

Rood SB, Braatne JH, Goater LA. 2010. Responses of obligate versus facultative riparian shrubs following river damming. *River Res. Appl.* 26:102–17.

Rood SB, Goater LA, et al. 2007. Floods, fire, and ice: disturbance ecology of riparian cottonwoods. *Can. J. Bot.* 85:1019–32.

Rood SB, Samuelson GM, et al. 2005. Managing river flows to restore floodplain forests. *Front. Ecol. Env.* 3:193–201.

Rosenberg KV, Terrill SB, Rosenberg GH. 1987. Value of suburban habitats to desert riparian birds. *Wilson Bull.* 99:642–54.

Ruibal R. 1959. The ecology of a brackish water population of *Rana pipiens. Copeia* 1959:315–22.

Sabo JL, McCluney KE, et al. 2008. Greenfall links groundwater to aboveground food webs in desert river floodplains. *Ecol. Monogr.* 78:615–31.

Sarr DA. 2002. Riparian livestock exclosure research in the western United States: a critique and some recommendations. *Env. Manage.* 30:516–26.

Schade JD, Marti E, et al. 2002. Sources of nitrogen to the riparian zone of a desert stream: implications for riparian vegetation and nitrogen retention. *Ecosystems* 5:68–79.

Schade JD, Hobbie SE. 2005. Spatial and temporal variation in islands of fertility in the Sonoran Desert. *Biogeochemistry* 73:541–53.

Scott RL, Cable WL, et al. 2008. Multiyear riparian evapotranspiration and groundwater use for a semiarid watershed. *J. Arid Env.* 72:1232–46.

Scott ML, Nagler PL, et al. 2009. Assessing the extent and diversity of riparian ecosystems in Sonora, Mexico. *Biodivers. Conserv.* 18:247–69.

Scott ML, Auble GT, Friedman JM. 1997. Flood dependency of cottonwood establishment along the Missouri River, Montana, USA. *Ecol. Appl.* 7:677–90.

Scott ML, Shafroth PB, Auble GT. 1999. Responses of riparian cottonwoods to alluvial water table declines. *Env. Manage.* 23:347–58.

Scott ML, Skagen SK, Merigliano MF. 2003. Relating geomorphic change and grazing to avian communities in riparian forests. *Conserv. Biol.* 17:284–96.

Seager R, Ting M, et al. 2007. Model projections of a more arid climate in southwestern North America. *Science* 316:1181–84.

Shafroth PB, Auble GT, et al. 1998. Establishment of woody riparian vegetation in relation to annual patterns of streamflow, Bill Williams River, Arizona. *Wetlands* 18:577–90.

Shafroth PB, Cleverly JR, et al. 2005. Control of *Tamarix* spp. in the western U.S.: implications for water salvage, wildlife use, and riparian restoration. *Env. Manage.* 35:231–46.

Shafroth PB, Stromberg JC, Patten DT. 2002. Riparian vegetation response to altered disturbance and stress regimes. *Ecol. Appl.* 12:107–23.

Simon A, Collison AJC. 2002. Quantifying the mechanical and hydrologic effects of riparian vegetation on streambank stability. *Earth Surf. Processes* 27:527–46.

Smith DM, Kelly JF, Finch DM. 2006. Cicada emergence in southwestern riparian forest: influences of wildfire and vegetation composition. *Ecol. Appl.* 16:1608–18.

Sogge M, Sferra S, Paxton E. 2008. Saltcedar as habitat for birds: implications to riparian restoration in the southwestern United States. *Restor. Ecol.* 16:146–54.

Soykan CU, Sabo JL. 2009. Spatiotemporal food web dynamics along a desert riparian-upland transition. *Ecography* 32:354–68.

Stromberg JC, Rychener TJ. 2010. Effects of fire on riparian forests along a free-flowing dryland river. *Wetlands* 30:75–86.

Stromberg JC, Boudell JA, Hazelton AF. 2008. Differences in seed mass between hydric and xeric plants influence seed bank dynamics in a dryland riparian ecosystem. *Funct. Ecol.* 22:205–12.

Stromberg JC, Tiller R, Richter B. 1996. Effects of groundwater decline on riparian vegetation of semiarid regions: the San Pedro River, Arizona, USA. *Ecol. Appl.* 6:113–31.

Stromberg JC, Beauchamp VB, et al. 2007. Importance of low-flow and high-flow characteristics to restoration of riparian vegetation along rivers in arid southwestern United States. *Freshw. Biol.* 52:651–79.

Stromberg JC, Chew MK, et al. 2009. Changing perceptions of change: the role of scientists in *Tamarix* and river management. *Restor. Ecol.* 17:177–86.

Stutz JC, Beauchamp VB, et al. 2009. Mycorrhizal ecology. In *Ecology and conservation of the San Pedro River,* Stromberg JC, Tellman B, editors. Tucson: Univ. Arizona Press, pp. 73–88.

Tal M, Paola C. 2007. Dynamic single-thread channels maintained by the interaction of flow and vegetation. *Geology* 35:347–50.

Tewksbury JJ, Hejl SJ, Martin TE. 1998. Breeding productivity does not decline with increasing fragmentation in a western landscape. *Ecology* 79:2890–903.

Tibbets TM, Molles MC. 2005. C : N : P stoichiometry of dominant riparian trees and arthropods along the Middle Rio Grande. *Freshw. Biol.* 50:1882–94.

Tuskan GA, DiFazio S, et al. 2006. The genome of black cottonwood, *Populus trichocarpa* (Torr. & Gray). *Science* 313:1596–604.

van Riper III, C, Paxton KL, et al. 2008. Rethinking avian response to tamarisk on the Lower Colorado River: a threshold hypothesis. *Restor. Ecol.* 16:155–67.

Waters MR. 2008. Alluvial chronologies and archaeology of the Gila River drainage basin, Arizona. *Geomorphology* 101:332–41.

Webb RH, Leake SA. 2006. Ground-water surface-water interactions and long-term change in riverine riparian vegetation in the southwestern United States. *J. Hydrol.* 320:302–23.

Williams JA, O'Farrell MJ, Riddle BR. 2006. Habitat use by bats in a riparian corridor of the Mojave Desert in southern Nevada. *J. Mamm.* 87:1145–53.

Williams WD. 1987. Salinization of rivers and streams: an important environmental hazard. *Ambio* 16:180–85.

Woodhouse CA. 2004. A paleo perspective on hydroclimatic variability in the western United States. *Aquat. Sci.* 66:346–56.

Yang YH, Chen YN, Li WH. 2008. Arbuscular mycorrhizal fungi infection in desert riparian forest and its environmental implications: a case study in the lower reach of Tarim River. *Prog. Nat. Sci.* 18:983–91.

CHAPTER 25

Wetlands of the Central Valley of California and Klamath Basin

JOSEPH P. FLESKES

The Central Valley of California (CVCA) and Upper Klamath Basin (KLBA) in southern Oregon and northeastern California contain some of the most important wetland habitats in North America (see area maps in Fig. 25.1). Wetlands in these regions are habitat for a large variety of fauna and flora and provide other important ecosystem functions, such as sediment and nutrient reduction, floodwater storage, and groundwater recharge (Novitzki et al. 1996). Wetlands in these regions are especially critical for migratory birds, with KLBA providing spring and fall migration staging habitats for many of the 10–12 million waterfowl and hundreds of thousands of other migratory waterbirds that winter in or pass through the CVCA annually (Fig. 25.2a–f; Gilmer et al. 1982, 2004; Warnock et al. 1998; Fleskes and Yee 2007). Waterfowl and other waterbirds also breed in both regions in large numbers (Baldassarre and Bolen 1994), which was a major reason that Lower Klamath National Wildlife Refuge (NWR) was established by President Theodore Roosevelt in 1908 as the first waterfowl refuge in the United States. The wetlands in these regions are of international importance, as evidenced by their designation as Ramsar Convention of International Importance sites, Western Hemisphere Shorebird Reserve Network sites, Audubon Important Birds Areas, and North American Waterfowl Management Plan Priority Conservation areas (North American Waterfowl Management Plan Committee 1986). The KLBA and surrounding region is recognized as a global center of biodiversity and is one of the seven North American International Union for Conservation of Nature Areas of Global Botanical Significance. The KLBA and surrounding region is also proposed as a World Heritage Site and United Nations Educational, Scientific and Cultural Organization Biosphere Reserve (Vance-Borland et al. 1995). The CVCA and KLBA have both become the focus of large-scale, multipartner, public-private conservation efforts (e.g., Central Valley Joint Venture [CVJV], Intermountain West Joint Venture) that have been the main forces for wetland habitat conservation in these regions since 1988. Despite these efforts, the large and diverse plant and wetland-dependent wildlife communities in both regions face immense challenges. While KLBA is sparsely populated, CVCA is inhabited by one of the most rapidly increasing human populations in the United States (American Farmland Trust 1995).

Irrigated agriculture dominates the landscape in both regions, and along with urban areas, put high demands on land and water resources (Hathaway and Welch 2002). The unfortunate outcome is that many plants and animals in these regions are in peril (e.g., 44 plant and 47 animal species in CVCA are threatened or endangered; www.library.ca.gov/crb/97/09/index.html#Heading37).

Hydrogeology

Central Valley

Totaling about 52,000 km², CVCA spans 640 km from Red Bluff in the north to the Tehachapi Mountains in the south, and is 48–112 km wide between the foothills of the Sierra Nevada and the Pacific Coastal Ranges (Gilmer et al. 1982). CVCA is composed of three regions: the Sacramento Valley in the north, the San Joaquin Valley in the south, and the Sacramento–San Joaquin River Delta (hereafter the Delta) in between (Fig. 25.1). The Sacramento Valley drains into the south-flowing Sacramento River. The San Joaquin River runs north and drains the northern third of San Joaquin Valley, including, in exceptionally wet years, the Tulare Lake Bed. However, in most years, Tulare Lake serves as the terminus sink for the Kings, Kern, and Tule Rivers. The Sacramento and San Joaquin Rivers meet in the Delta, with the conjoined waters flowing through Suisun Marsh into San Francisco Bay and out to the Pacific Ocean.

The CVCA is a structural trough filled with Jurassic- to Holocene-aged sediments to a depth of nearly 10 km. Groundwater–surface water interaction is primarily through gaining and losing sections of streambeds, with water percolating into the ground as streams flow into CVCA. Water discharges through evapotranspiration of marsh vegetation, and historically directly into the Tulare Lake; aquifer pumping is now another major source of groundwater outflow (Mullen and Nady 1985; Williamson et al. 1989). Soils are diverse, with many in San Joaquin Valley poorly drained and high in salts, alkalinity, and trace elements, which make management of water quality difficult (Heitmeyer et al. 1989; http://soils.usda

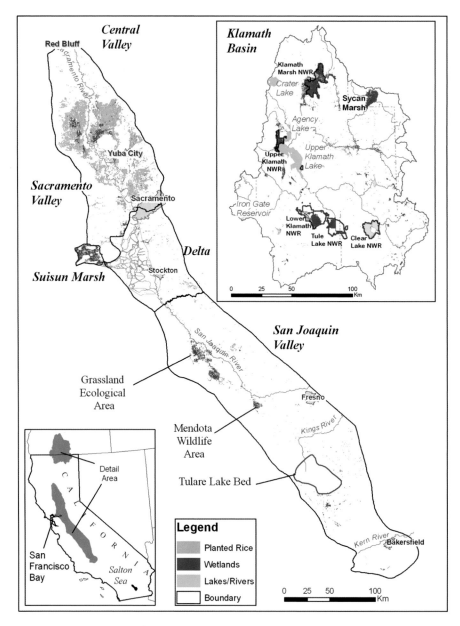

FIG. 25.1. The Central Valley of California and the Klamath Basin of northeastern California and southern Oregon.

.gov/survey/online_surveys/). Climate is Mediterranean, with dry, warm summers and wet, mild winters; > 97% of the precipitation falls October–May (www.wrcc.dri.edu). Evapotranspiration greatly exceeds summer precipitation, especially in the San Joaquin Valley (Faunt 2009), where wetland evapotranspiration is as high as 1.5 cm per day (Heitmeyer et al. 1989) and summer rain rare (e.g., Bakersfield: June–Aug. avg. precipitation = 0.004 cm per day).

Prior to the construction of dams, rivers meandered and flooded widely over the valley most winters. However, hydrology has been greatly altered since European settlement to facilitate agriculture, mining, flood protection, and urbanization. About 70% of the wetland area was modified from 1850 to the 1920s by local drainage, levee, and water diversion (Harding 1960; McGowan 1961), followed by large-scale federal and state projects (Shelton 1987; Frayer et al. 1989). Today, a system of more than 100 dams and numerous reservoirs and canals

move water, with pumps in the Delta directing a portion of the flow to Southern California via the 1,151-km-long California Aqueduct.

Wetland loss has been extensive. The estimated 1.6–2 million ha of wetlands in CVCA pre-European settlement were reduced to 1.5 million ha in 1906; 485,600 ha in 1922; 220,415 ha in 1960; 172,000 ha in 1977 (United States Fish and Wildlife Service [USFWS] 1978); and 53,930 ha in 2003 (USFWS and U.S. Bureau of Reclamation 2003), which represents a 97% loss. However, loss estimates vary, ranging from a 91% loss by 1990 (Dahl 1990) to a 96% loss by 2006, based on 83,000 ha of managed wetlands in 2006 (CVJV 2006). The magnitude of loss and types of wetland habitats remaining differ by region. Historically, about 40% of CVCA wetlands occurred in San Joaquin Valley, with 60% in the Sacramento Valley, Delta, and Suisun Marsh (USFWS 1978). The southern San Joaquin Valley had the largest block of wetlands, but most were lost by the 1920s

FIG. 25.2. Wetlands in the Central Valley (A, B, C) tend to be smaller, more intensively managed, and situated in more urbanized landscapes than those in the Klamath Basin (D,E,F), but both areas support large populations of waterfowl and other wildlife. A. Wetland on Yolo Bypass State Wildlife Area, with Sacramento in the background. (Dave Feliz, CA DFG.) B. Aerial view of seasonal wetland on Sacramento NWR showing areas of mowed vegetation and constructed islands. (Anonymous, USFWS.) C. Northern pintail and other waterfowl concentrated on a Sacramento NWR wetland. (Robert McLandress, CA Waterfowl Assoc.) D. View of a large wetland complex in Klamath Basin. (Dan Skalos, USGS.) E. Large wetland unit on Lower Klamath NWR. (Dan Skalos, USGS.) F. Greater white-fronted geese flushing from a Klamath Basin wetland. (Colin Tierney, USGS.)

with conversion of Tulare Lake (once the largest freshwater lake west of the Mississippi River) and associated wetlands to agricultural lands (Kirk 1994). Wetland loss in Sacramento Valley and the Delta was also severe, but many wetlands in Sacramento Valley were converted to rice and in the Delta to grain fields that retain higher value for waterbirds than the cotton, orchards, and nongrain croplands that dominate the San Joa-

quin Valley landscape (Fleskes et al. 2005). Today, wetlands and flooded rice provide nearly contiguous waterbird habitat in Sacramento Valley, whereas in San Joaquin Valley, large expanses of agriculture of relatively low waterbird value separate wetland habitats into three distinct blocks (i.e., Grassland Ecological Area, Mendota Wildlife Area, and Tulare Lake Bed and vicinity).

Klamath Basin

The 20,720-km² KLBA lies in a broad, relatively flat basin within a Pleistocene lakebed (Gannett et al. 2007). The KLBA extends along the east slope of the Cascade Range and includes the Klamath River drainage upstream of Iron Gate Reservoir (Fig. 25.1). Geology reflects repeated volcanic activity, erosion, and sedimentary rock deposition. KLBA spans parts of the Cascade Range, and is underlain mostly by late Tertiary and Quaternary volcanic deposits that are generally permeable, with a substantial groundwater system recharged from Cascade Range precipitation. Valleys are 792–1,524 m above sea level, with a high natural water table (Fretwell et al. 1996) and a diverse set of highly organic muck soils of drained lakebeds and sand-to-loam mineral upland soils (Jahnke 1994). However, drainage and subsequent intensive grazing have compacted wetland soils and promoted erosion (USFWS 2009b). The climate is semiarid, characterized by relatively dry, moderate summers and wet, cold winters. Most (e.g., 70% in Klamath Falls, Oregon) of the annual 38–64 cm of precipitation falls during November–April (www.ocs.orst.edu/). Maximum temperatures average 33°C during summer, and winter minimums average –7.2°C; a killing frost can occur during any month.

About 85–90% of KLBA's original wetlands have been lost, with only about 60,000 ha remaining (Akins 1970; Bottorff 1989). In 1905, the U.S. Bureau of Reclamation initiated the Klamath Reclamation Project: three large storage reservoirs, hundreds of diversion structures, > 2,260 km of canals, and a 2.4-km tunnel now deliver water throughout KLBA (Hathaway and Welch 2002).

Current Wetland Hydrology

Hydrology of most wetlands in CVCA and KLBA is extensively modified and intensively managed, primarily to provide food and refuge for the millions of migratory waterfowl that use regional habitats (CVJV 2006). Natural overflow flooding from snowmelt and rain has mostly been replaced by managed flooding via controlled diversions, timed reservoir releases, and pumped water delivery from ditches, rivers, sloughs, and wells. Regional wetlands can be generally classified by hydropattern as semipermanent-permanent (hereafter "semi-perm"), seasonal, or temporary (mostly vernal pools and alkali sinks). In many cases, the lowest parts of wetland basins are semi-perms and the shallower portions are seasonal. Managed wetlands are mostly seasonal and semi-perms. Differences in geomorphology, climate, water availability, and timing of use by waterfowl have resulted in a greater portion of KLBA wetlands managed as semi-perms than in CVCA. For instance, semi-perms comprise 59% of the managed wetlands on Lower Klamath and Tule Lake NWRs (Dugger et al. 2008) versus 13% in CVCA (CVJV 2006).

Hydropattern differs by wetland type. In wetlands managed as semi-perms, water is usually maintained year-round in at least part of the basin to provide habitat for breeding and molting waterfowl as well as other wetland-dependent birds (i.e., waterbirds) and other fauna. However, if emergent vegetation overtakes the basin (which commonly occurs in shallow basins after a few years), and if water levels can be manipulated, wetlands are drained and emergent vegetation disked or burned to restore the desired "hemi-marsh" interspersion of open water and vegetation. Hydrology of most seasonal wetlands, which

comprise about 87% of the managed wetlands in CVCA and 41% of the managed wetlands on Lower Klamath and Tule Lake NWRs, is designed to maximize production of waterbird food resources (primarily seeds but also aquatic invertebrates), and on most private and many public lands, provide opportunity for waterfowl sport harvest. Exact timing of flooding differs somewhat among regions and years to match timing of waterfowl use and hunting seasons. Waterfowl from northern breeding grounds begin to arrive in KLBA and CVCA in early August, with most migrants departed by late April. Waterfowl hunting season usually begins in early (KLBA) to mid-October (CVCA) and ends in mid- (KLBA) to late January (CVCA). Thus, most seasonal wetlands are unflooded, but irrigated periodically during summer to promote seed production, and are flooded starting in mid-August to late October, with water maintained through at least January. Due to higher water costs, many southern San Joaquin Valley wetlands are not summer-irrigated and fall flooding is delayed to reduce evapotranspiration and to coincide with the later opening date of the local hunting season. Due to logistical constraints, wetland drawdowns on private lands often begin when hunting season ends, even though drawdowns would be more effective in simultaneously promoting plant growth and providing invertebrate resources for birds if timed to occur with peak migrations (Heitmeyer et al. 1989; Fredrickson 1991). Soil temperature has considerable influence on moist-soil plant community composition and seed production (Fredrickson 1991), and drawdown timing varies regionally and by target species. For instance, in the San Joaquin Valley, wetlands managed for swamp timothy (*Crypsis schoenoides*) are drawn down in mid-April to early May, whereas those managed for alkali bulrush (*Scirpus paludosus*) are drawn down in March (Smith et al. 1994). A small percentage (e.g., 7% in Grassland EA; Chouinard 2000) of seasonal wetlands in CVCA are managed in reverse cycle (i.e., flooded March–August and left dry September–February) to supplement semi-perms as waterbird breeding and brood habitat. The annual vegetation that grows in reverse-cycle wetlands decomposes rapidly when flooded and provides optimal conditions for invertebrate production. Unlike the intensively managed hydropattern of most seasonal and semi-perm wetlands in KLBA and CVCA, hydrology of most temporary wetlands, including the 5–25% of the original vernal pools that still exist (Holland 1978) and most alkali sink wetlands, primarily reflects local precipitation events. Thus, most temporary wetlands are flooded for a shorter duration than seasonal and semi-perm wetlands.

Biogeochemistry and Microbial Processes

Biogeochemical processes regulate the exchange of materials between the abiotic and biotic components of the environment. Microbes alter the chemistry and productivity of wetland environments by performing complex transformations of organic and inorganic molecules. These processes occur in both the soil and water column of wetlands. Biogeochemical processes include settling of suspended matter, adsorption and desorption of chemical elements from particles, transformations between contaminants in surface water and sediments, and uptake, transformation, and release of nutrients and other chemical elements in plants, algae, microbes, and other fauna. Microbes are important for nutrient cycling and soil carbon turnover and sequestration (Frenzel et al. 2000) and impact the speciation, mobility, bioavailability, and toxicity of toxic elements. Anaerobic microbial processes are especially important, affecting nutrient transport, water quality, and greenhouse gas fluxes (Whitmire and Hamilton 2005). Several processes are especially important to the ecology and conservation of wetlands and wetland fauna in KLBA and CVCA.

NUTRIENT RETENTION AND RELEASE

A variety of interacting factors determine whether wetlands serve as sinks or sources for nutrients. Soils play an important role in wetland water quality and productivity because they serve as sinks, sources, and transformers of nutrients. Thus, differences in soil types as well as source waters and evapotranspiration rates result in variation of water chemistry among regional wetlands. In addition, while wetlands often are net sinks for nutrients, such as phosphorus (P) and nitrogen (N), and even a small area of wetland can greatly improve local water quality (Whitmire and Hamilton 2005), if sediments are disturbed by tillage or other means and then reflooded, the nutrients are often released into the water column. For instance, wetlands restored from agricultural lands adjacent to Upper Klamath Lake released P to surface waters when first flooded (Aldous et al. 2007). At Lower Klamath NWR, water quality impacts of wetlands include higher conductivity and water temperatures but lower turbidity. Outflow P and N concentrations are higher than inflow concentrations, but loads are lower, with 19–51% of the mass of P and 55–77% of the mass of N entering wetlands on Lower Klamath NWR retained; seasonal wetlands retain less P than permanent wetlands. The overall effect of Klamath NWR wetlands is to decrease net N and P loads but increase the ratio of bioavailable P to N in outflows (Mayer 2005).

AGRICULTURAL CHEMICAL SEQUESTRATION

Wetlands also serve as sinks for agricultural chemicals. With numerous urban areas and about 2.8 million ha of irrigated agricultural lands in CVCA (Budd et al. 2009) and 200,000 ha in KLBA (Gannett et al. 2007), a wide variety of agricultural and urban chemicals, including an increasingly potent class of pyrethroid insecticides (Weston et al. 2004), find their way into regional wetlands. Constructed wetlands in the San Joaquin Valley have been shown to be effective at reducing the levels of pyrethroid and organophosphate insecticides (as well as bioavailable P) in agricultural drainwaters, primarily through sedimentation of particles (Budd et al. 2009; Maynard et al. 2009).

MERCURY METHYLATION

Methylation is a product of complex processes that move and transform mercury from its elemental form to its more bioavailable form, methylmercury (Conaway et al. 2008). Sulfate-reducing bacteria are the primary methylators in anoxic estuarine sediment (Compeau and Bartha 1985), although iron-reducing bacteria may also have a role (Kerin et al. 2006). Formation of methylmercury, particularly monomethylmercury, is of environmental concern because it is bioaccumulated and biomagnified to toxic concentrations in higher-trophic-level organisms, including birds and mammals (Conaway et al. 2008). Historical mercury mines in the Pacific Coastal Range and the historical use of mercury for gold amalgamation during gold-mining operations in the Sierra Nevada Mountains introduced large quantities of mercury into CVCA (Domagalski 1998; Alpers et al. 2005). Atmospheric deposition, mostly from coal-fired power plants, is the source of the inorganic divalent form of mercury, which, although occurring in much smaller quantities than mine-derived mercury in CVCA, is more readily converted to methylmercury. Once in surface water, mercury can be converted to another form or attach to particles that settle onto sediments, where it can diffuse into the water column or be resuspended, buried by other sediments, or methylated. Methylmercury can enter the food chain or be released back to the atmosphere by volatilization. Bird feather data (Schwarzbach 2009) indicate that concentrations of mercury in San Francisco Bay have declined over the last 120 years, but Conaway et al. (2007) found no decreasing trends in fish or bivalves. Interestingly, selenium can provide protection from toxic effects of methylmercury in mammals (Yang et al. 2008) and adult birds but worsen them in bird embryos and hatchlings (Hoffman and Heinz 1998).

BIOACCUMULATION AND TRANSFORMATION OF SELENIUM

The toxic effects of selenium in CVCA wetlands made national headlines in the mid-1980s, when waterbird deformities were linked to high levels of selenium in agricultural drainwaters stored in constructed wetlands in Kesterson NWR (Ohlendorf et al. 1986) in the Grassland Ecological Area (Fig. 25.1). Soils in western San Joaquin Valley are rich in selenium, which leaches into the shallow groundwater of the region, a process accelerated by agricultural irrigation. When selenium-rich drainwaters are stored in ponds or wetlands, evaporation can greatly concentrate the element to dangerously high levels. Although removal and burying of contaminated soils was the method used at Kesterson NWR, microbial volatilization of selenium to detoxify soils is also being considered (Wu 2003). These include metal-reducing bacteria such as *Geobacter sulfurreducens*, *Shewanella oneidensis*, and *Veillonella atypica*, which use different mechanisms to transform bioavailable sodium selenite to less toxic, nonmobile elemental selenium and then to selenide in anaerobic environments (Pearce et al. 2009).

OXIDATION OF PEAT SOILS

In parts of KLBA (Lindenberg and Wood 2009) and in the Delta, microbial oxidation of organic carbon in peat soils is a major factor in the subsidence of drained wetlands (Deverel and Rojstaczer 1996). Exposed wetland soils are subject to aerobic microbial activity, which accelerates organic matter decomposition, mobilizes peat soil nutrients, and increases the subsidence rate. This is accelerated by tillage, especially at high temperatures, which increases air and oxygenated water penetration into the soils. Subsidence occurs as porewater is replaced by air, which more easily compresses than water. Subsidence can be rapid under continual farming (e.g., 6 m in 150 years in the Delta [Miller et al. 2008]), greatly increasing the potential for levee failure and flooding. Restoring marshes to rebuild organic matter shows promise as a way of reversing or slowing subsidence (Miller et al. 2008).

GREENHOUSE GASES

Wetlands can be both important sinks and sources for greenhouse gases. Because of their low turnover rate of organics, wetlands can be an important sink for C and N. However, because of their water-saturated anaerobic soils, wetlands can be an important source of methane (Intergovernmental Panel on Climate Change 2007), which is a much more potent greenhouse gas than carbon dioxide and responsible for about a quarter of all global warming (Mosier 1998). The amount of methane emitted from a wetland is largely determined by the nature of its vegetation and soil microbes that interfere with the production and consumption of methane (Laanbroek 2010). When sulfate is highly available, as in many brackish and tidal wetlands, production of methane is inhibited. However, most CVCA and KLBA wetlands are freshwater, with low sulfates, and are likely not to sequester enough carbon to offset methane release. One exception is the Delta, where, although now mostly freshwater, wetlands were once tidal. Thus, sulfates are common, and restoration on peat islands there to reverse subsidence (Miller et al. 2008) may also reduce greenhouse gases (http://miller-mccune.com/science_environment/ Protect-a-Levee-Protect-the-World-844).

Plant Communities

Community Composition

Wetland plant communities in CVCA and KLBA vary by wetland type, water salinity, soils, and regional climate (Mason 1957). They are greatly impacted by management. Plants in deep semi-perms commonly include milfoil *(Myriophyllum)* and other submergents, floating plants such as water lilies *(Nuphar luteum)* and duckweed *(Lemna),* rooted aquatics such as watercress *(Rorippa nasturtium-aquaticum),* and emergents such as bulrushes *(Scirpus)* and cattails *(Typha)* (Fiedler 1996). Seasonal wetlands usually include more sedges *(Carex),* spikerushes *(Eleocharis),* rushes *(Juncus),* smartweeds *(Polygonum),* horsetails *(Equisetum),* and grasses. Other common plant species include dock *(Rumex)* and various willows *(Salix).*

Most seasonal and semi-perm wetlands in CVCA and KLBA are managed primarily to provide food and refuge for wintering waterfowl. Managers use flooding schedules and periodic disking or burning to encourage plant species that provide abundant seeds and habitat for aquatic invertebrates preferred as food for ducks and to avoid dense stands of less desirable plants such as cocklebur *(Xanthium strumarium),* Baltic rush *(Juncus balticus),* saltgrass *(Distichlis spicata),* and bermudagrass *(Cynodon dactylon)* (Smith et al. 1994). In most CVCA wetlands, managers target growth of swamp timothy, watergrass *(Echinochloa crusgalli),* and smartweed *(Polygonum),* or a mix of these and other wetland (e.g., alkali bulrush, *Juncus, Paspalum distichum)* or moist-soil plants. In KLBA, these include red goosefoot *(Chenopodium rubrum),* witchgrass *(Panicum capillare),* and beggartick *(Bidens)* (Fregien 1998). The plant community of managed wetlands in Suisun Marsh (a naturally brackish marsh) is quite different from elsewhere in CVCA and KLBA (Baldassarre

and Bolen 1994). Pickleweed *(Salicornia virginica)* and saltgrass cover the greatest area of Suisun wetlands. However, management has reduced these and encouraged duck food species such as fathen *(Atriplex patula),* brass button *(Cotula coronopifolia),* and alkali bulrush (Rollins 1991), although sea purslane *(Sesuvium verrucosum)* and watergrass seeds were preferred by ducks feeding there in a recent study (Burns 2003). The natural plant communities of vernal pools and alkali sinks differ from those of managed wetlands.

Vernal pools hold water long enough to inhibit upland plants but not long enough to permit typical marsh plants. Vernal pools contain a wide variety of locally unique and endemic plants (e.g., Solano grass, *Tuctoria mucronata;* Holland and Jain 1977) that changes as pools flood and then desiccate after winter rains (Silveira 2000). Exotic species richness and cover are greater in altered than in natural pools (Gerhardt and Collinge 2003). Alkali sinks are shallow basins with prolonged inundations and sparse vegetation due to calcium-derived salts. Typical plants include iodine bush *(Allenrrolfea occidentails),* bush seepweed *(Suaeda moquinii),* saltgrass, saltbush *(Atriplex),* and arrowgrass *(Triglochin).*

Animals

There are 490 vertebrate species that regularly inhabit CVCA (279 bird, 88 mammal, 40 reptile, 18 amphibian, 65 fish; Bunn et al. 2007) and 420 that have been recorded from KLBA (274 bird, 78 mammal, 32 reptile and amphibian, 36 fish; www.fws. gov/klamathbasinrefuges/1KBNWRchecklist.pdf). Specific taxa are important to regional wetlands because of their direct impact on wetland ecology or because they are a focus of management because they are hunted or of conservation concern (i.e., state or federal endangered, threatened, sensitive, or vulnerable species).

Birds

CVCA and KLBA are both internationally renowned for their great abundance and diversity of birds, including North America's largest wintering population of bald eagles *(Haliaeetus leucocephalus)* in KLBA. As part of the Pacific Flyway, CVCA and KLBA regions share many of the same migratory bird species. Although many birds use dry wetland basins and associated habitats, wetland-dependent species (i.e., waterbirds) in KLBA and CVCA can be grouped based on taxonomy and ecology into eight groups (see below). KLBA wetlands are frozen throughout winter, and their primary importance to waterbirds is as breeding and migration habitat. CVCA wetlands rarely freeze, and so they provide wintering habitat for most Pacific Flyway waterbirds in addition to migration and breeding habitat.

WATERFOWL

Most ducks and geese, but not swans, are hunted in KLBA and CVCA during fall and winter. Substantial numbers of waterfowl, mostly dabbling ducks, breed in CVCA and KLBA. California breeding populations during 1990–2008 averaged 605,000 ducks, composed mostly of mallards *(Anas platyrhynchos,* 64%), gadwall *(A. strepera,* 14%), cinnamon teal *(A.*

cyanoptera, 7%), and northern shoveler *(A. clypeata,* 6%), but also 12 other species (USFWS 2009a). About 1,200 pairs of western Canada geese *(Branta canadensis moffitti)* nest in California (Pacific Flyway 2000), primarily in KLBA and Sierra foothills, but also in CVCA.

Although breeding populations are substantial, abundance and species diversity are much greater during winter in CVCA and during spring and fall migration in KLBA, with 20 duck and 5 goose species common. Gilmer et al. (1982) estimated about 10–12 million waterfowl annually winter in or pass through CVCA. Recent (1998–2001) peak abundance averaged 4.8 million in California during early January (> 90% in CVCA) and 1.1 million during fall and 670,000 during spring migration in KLBA (Gilmer et al. 2004). Up to 65% of the northern pintails *(A. acuta)* in North America winter in CVCA, and despite continental declines, they are still the most common species (Fleskes and Yee 2007). During the January 2009 "midwinter" survey, about 3.6 million ducks (33% northern pintail, 20% northern shoveler, 14% green-winged teal [*A. crecca*], 11% American wigeon [*A. americana*], 6% mallard, and 16% other species), 1.3 million geese (61% snow [*Chen caerulescens*] or Ross' goose [*C. rossii*], 30% greater white-fronted goose [*Anser albifrons*], 9% Canada [*Branta canadensis*] or cackling [*B. hutchinsii*] goose), and 98,000 tundra swans *(Cygnus columbianus)* were counted in California (89% of the ducks and > 97% of geese and swans were in CVCA) (USFWS 2009c).

The types of wetlands used by waterfowl vary among species and season. Only diving ducks (mostly ruddy duck [*Oxyura jamaicensis*], canvasbacks [*Aythya valisineria*], redheads [*A. Americana*]), wood ducks *(Aix sponsa),* and some Canada geese and mallards commonly nest over water in emergent vegetation, on muskrat *(Ondatra zibethica)* huts, or (for wood ducks) in trees or nest boxes. Thus, for most breeding waterfowl, wetlands are used primarily for pair isolation, feeding, and brood habitat. Semi-perms also provide critical molting habitat for postbreeding ducks; these habitats are more abundant in KLBA, and many mallards and other waterfowl breeding in CVCA travel to KLBA marshes to undergo feather molt (Yarris et al. 1994). During winter, wetlands are important for roosting, feeding, and courtship. During hunting season, waterfowl concentrate during the day on areas where hunting is not allowed and fly out (ducks primarily at dusk, geese in the morning and evening) to other wetlands and rice (Sacramento Valley) and other crop fields to feed (Fleskes et al. 2003, 2005).

SHOREBIRDS

CVCA supports more shorebirds during winter and spring than any other inland site in western North America and, in fall, is the second most important inland site after Great Salt Lake, Utah (Hickey et al. 2003). About 33 shorebird species migrate through KLBA and CVCA or winter in CVCA, with total abundance in CVCA during the early 1990s averaging 134,000 in August, 211,000 in November, 303,000 in January, and 335,000 in April (Shuford et al. 1998). Most species primarily use open habitats such as seasonal wetlands, mudflats, and agricultural fields. Although shorebirds were widely hunted until the early 1900s, only Wilson's snipe *(Gallinago delicate)* is currently considered a game species. Seven species nest in CVCA and KLBA, with black-necked stilt *(Himantopus mexicanus),* American avocet *(Recurvirostra americana),* and kill-deer *(Charadrius vociferus)* most common (Hickey et al. 2003; Shuford 2009).

COOTS AND SECRETIVE MARSH BIRDS

The American coot *(Fulica americana)* is an abundant breeder and migrant in KLBA and CVCA and year-round resident in CVCA (> 550,000 counted in January 2009; USFWS 2009c). Coots are highly visible and use a wide variety of wetland types, whereas other species in this group are more secretive and mostly use dense emergents. The common moorhen *(Gallinula chloropus)* is a common resident in CVCA but is very rare in KLBA (Greij 1994). Sora *(Porzana carolina)* and Virginia rails *(Rallus limicola)* are less common but regular breeders in KLBA and year-round residents in CVCA marshes. Although rails are hunted in many states, only coots and moorhens are currently legal game species in California and Oregon. The yellow rail *(Coturnicops noboboracensis)* is a rare local breeder in KLBA (previously in CVCA) and a rare winter visitor in Suisun Marsh (Stern et al. 1993; California Department of Fish and Game [CDFG] 2008). The California subspecies of black rail *(Laterallus jamaicensis coturniculus)* is found mostly in tidal marshes of San Francisco Bay but also occur in small numbers in some CVCA and Sierra foothill marshes (Estep et al. 2009). American *(Botaurus lentiginosus)* and least bitterns *(Ixobrychus exilis)* are regular breeders in KLBA and year-round residents in CVCA marshes.

COLONIAL-NESTING WADERS

Waders are common in CVCA and KLBA, nesting in colonies in dense emergent wetland vegetation or trees and feeding in flood-irrigated pastures, hayfields, and wetlands. Shuford et al. (2004) estimated 339 pairs of great egrets *(Casmerodius albus),* 3,162 pairs of white-faced ibis *(Plegadis chihi),* and 98 pairs of great blue herons *(Ardea herodias)* nesting in KLBA in 2003. During the same May–August surveys, they also recorded up to 392 black-crowned night herons *(Nycticorax nycticorax),* 88 snowy egrets *(Egretta thula),* and 2 green herons *(Butorides striatus).* These species are all also common in CVCA, and their populations increased during 1966–89; white-faced ibis, a species of special concern (CDFG 2008), increased faster than others (Fleury and Sherry 1995). Cattle egrets *(Bubulcus ibis)* have been a common resident and local breeder in CVCA since the 1960s, but are rare in KLBA (Garrett and Dunn 1981).

COLONIAL-NESTING SEABIRDS

American white pelicans *(Pelecanus erythrorhynchos),* double-crested cormorants *(Phalacrocorax auritus),* gulls, and terns typically nest in colonies, mostly on islands in large wetlands isolated from disturbance and mammalian predators. An exception is the black tern *(Chlidonias niger),* which nests in floating-anchored substrates or on mounds in marshes (CDFG 2009). Large wetlands with isolated islands are more prevalent in KLBA, and KLBA is a more important breeding area than CVCA (Shuford et al. 2004; CDFG 2009). Both regions host breeding populations of Caspian *(Sterna caspia),* Forster's *(S. forsteri),* and black terns; ring-billed *(Larus delawarensis)* and some Franklin's gulls *(L. pipixcan)* also breed in KLBA.

GREBES

KLBA and CVCA are important to several species of grebes. KLBA is of regional or continental importance to breeding populations of eared *(Podiceps nigricollis)*, western *(Aechmophorus occidentalis)*, and Clark's *(A. clarkia)* grebes (Shuford et al. 2004); eared and western grebes also nest irregularly in small numbers on a few wetlands in CVCA (CDFG 2009). Pied-billed grebes *(Podilymbus podiceps)* are common nesters in both regions and year-round residents in many CVCA wetlands. A few horned *(Podiceps auritus)* and red-necked grebes *(P. grisegena)* are present during breeding season and may nest in KLBA.

SANDHILL CRANES

Two populations of sandhill cranes *(Grus canadensis)* migrate through KLBA and winter almost exclusively in CVCA; both have special conservation status (Littlefield and Ivey 2000; CDFG 2008). The CVCA population of the greater sandhill crane *(G. c. tabida)* is state-threatened (CDFG 2008) and breeds in KLBA; about 8,500 winter in CVCA. The Pacific Flyway population of the lesser sandhill crane *(G. c. canadensis)* is a species of state concern and breeds in southern Alaska; about 25,000 winter in CVCA. Nesting in KLBA typically occurs in open-grazed meadow-wetland habitat, and wintering cranes forage mostly in crop, alfalfa, or fallow fields but use open wetlands as night-roost habitat (CDFG 2009).

OTHER WETLAND-DEPENDENT BIRDS

Other birds that rely heavily on flooded wetlands in KLBA and CVCA include blackbirds, marsh wrens *(Cistothorus palustris)*, belted kingfishers *(Ceryle alcyon)*, and northern harriers *(Circus cyaneus)*. Tricolored blackbirds *(Agelaius tricolor)* are largely endemic and resident to California and are of state and federal concern (CDFG 2008). Most nest in large (thousands of birds) colonies in CVCA marshes; a few colonies are in KLBA (Beedy and Hamilton 1999). Populations declined > 90% during 1930–2000 to about 260,000 in 2005 (CDFG 2008). Yellow-headed blackbirds *(Xanthocephalus xanthocephalus)* are also of state concern and occur primarily as a summer breeder and migrant, with some wintering in CVCA (CDFG 2008). They nest in small colonies in emergents over deep water. The red-winged blackbird *(Agelaius phoeniceus)* is an abundant resident, but the rare Kern red-winged blackbird *(A. p. aciculatus)* is a subspecies of concern that breeds only east of, and winters in, San Joaquin Valley (CDFG 2008).

Mammals

Several mammals are important to the ecology of KLBA and CVCA wetlands. Muskrats feed upon emergent vegetation, creating open-water habitat; their houses are also used by nesting waterbirds. Beavers *(Castor canadensis)* create ponds in streams but are often a nuisance to managers when they dam water control structures and destroy tree plantings. River otters *(Lutra canadensis)*, mink *(Mustela vison)*, and raccoons *(Procyon lotor)* are important predators of waterbirds and their eggs and other wetland wildlife. Several bat species of conservation concern occur in CVCA and KLBA; because these bats forage over

water on insects and require drinking water, wetland management plays an important role in their ecology. The San Joaquin antelope squirrel *(Ammospermophilus nelson)*, two species of kangaroo rats *(Dipodomys ingens, D. nitratoides)* that occur in San Joaquin Valley alkali sinks, and the salt marsh harvest mouse *(Reithrodontomys raviventris halicoetes)* in Suisun Marsh are of conservation concern (Bias 1995; CDFG 2009).

Amphibians and Reptiles

The California red-legged frog *(Rana aurora draytonii)* has almost completely disappeared from CVCA (Jennings 1995) and, along with the California tiger salamander *(Ambystoma californiense)* and western spadefoot toad *(Spea [Scapbioupus] hammondii)*, which remain largely in rain-pool habitats in San Joaquin Valley (Jennings and Hayes 1994), is of conservation concern. Native western toads *(Bufo boreas)* and Sierran tree-frog *(Pseudacris sierra)* are common in both CVCA and KLBA. In KLBA, the Oregon spotted frog *(R. pretiosa)*, which remain only in isolated populations, the Southern long-toed salamander *(A. macrodactylum sigillatum)*, and Great Basin spadefoot *(S. intermonana)* are also present (www.uoregon.edu/~titus/herp/rangemaps.html). The introduced American bullfrog *(R. catesbiana)* is a very common invader in both regions. Native aquatic reptiles that are the focus of wetland managers are the threatened giant garter snake *(Thamnophis gigas)* in CVCA and Pacific pond turtle *(Actinemys marmorata)* in both CVCA and KLBA. Nonnative red-eared sliders *(Trachemys scripta)* and soft-shelled turtles *(Apalone)* (www.californiaherps.com) may negatively impact native species in some CVCA wetlands.

Fish

CVCA and KLBA wetlands are important fish habitat, with cyprinids (minnows and shiners), centrarchids (sunfish, crappie, and bass), and ictalurids (catfish, bullheads) most common (Moyle 2002). The introduced common carp *(Cyprinus carpio)* is a problem in many semi-perms, uprooting plants and reducing water clarity and invertebrate populations (Smith et al. 1994). The maze of canals that connect many marshes to rivers entrap migrating anadromous fish, including Chinook salmon *(Oncorhynchus tshawytscha)*, steelhead trout *(O. mykiss irideus)*, lampreys *(Lampetra)*, sturgeons *(Acipenser)*, and striped bass *(Morone saxatilis,* introduced in CVCA in 1879). Two endangered species, the Lost River *(Deltistes luxatus)* and shortnose *(Chasmistes brevirostris)* suckers, are present in wetlands in Upper Klamath and Tule Lake NWRs (Hicks et al. 1999).

Insects and Other Invertebrates

The community of aquatic and semiaquatic invertebrates in CVCA and KLBA wetlands varies by hydropattern, plant community species and biomass, water chemistry, soil, and wetland age (Eldridge 1990). In seasonal wetlands, Chironomidae, Cladocera, and Copepoda were consistently most numerically dominant in both KLBA and CVCA; Hemiptera (primarily Corixidae) was also dominant in Sacramento Valley. Ostracoda, Oligochaeta, and Hemiptera were also dominant in restored seasonals in KLBA (Fregien 1998). Invertebrates are important to regional wetlands mainly because they are a focus of management due to their importance as waterfowl food or because they are rare and of conservation concern. Diptera, especially Chironomidae, are very important foods for waterfowl, whereas highly mobile species, such as water boatmen (Corixidae), are generally consumed less than available (Batzer et al. 1993). Species of conservation concern are mostly vernal pool species and include the delta green ground beetle *(Elaphrus viridis),* summer tadpole shrimp *(Triops longicaudatus),* and several species of fairy shrimp *(Linderiella occidentalis, Lepidurus packardi, Branchinecta).*

Key Ecological Controls

Management Objective

With the hydrology of KLBA and CVCA greatly altered and most wetlands under intensive management, the management objective of a particular wetland largely controls its ecology. Thus, two groups of species focused upon by managers, hunted waterfowl and species of conservation concern, are key ecological controls for CVCA and KLBA wetlands.

HUNTED WATERFOWL

Most CVCA and KLBA wetlands are managed primarily to provide food and refuge for wintering, migrating, and breeding waterfowl. These include wetlands on most NWRs and State Wildlife Areas that were purchased and are managed, at least in part, with hunting-based funds, and the > 60% of California's wetlands that are privately owned and managed due to hunter support (Baldassarre and Bolen 1994; CVJV 2006). Hydropatterns, timing of fall flood-up, vegetation, and other wetland characteristics are managed primarily to provide habitat, maximize production of food resources, and facilitate sport harvest of these species.

SPECIES OF CONSERVATION CONCERN

Some wetlands, mostly vernal pools but also others, are protected and managed primarily to support threatened, endangered, or other species of conservation concern. In addition, management practices on all wetlands are restricted in that they must not harm these species. Also, management of many NWR wetlands, even though focused on waterfowl, is often tailored toward improving habitat for species of concern. One key species is the threatened and CVCA-endemic giant garter snake. The giant garter snake has summer-flooded habitat needs that are not fulfilled by seasonal wetlands left unflooded during summer to grow food plants for wintering waterfowl (www.californiaherps.com/snakes/pages/t.gigas.html). Thus, inclusion of some semi-perms in wetland restoration projects is encouraged to avoid negative impacts on the giant garter snake, especially if conversion of rice fields (an important snake habitat) is involved (USFWS 2006). Endangered fish, such as the spring run of Chinook salmon, and in KLBA, the Lost River, shortnose, and Klamath largescale suckers *(Catostomus snyderi),* are key species that compete for water and restrict timing and quality of wetland outflows. In addition, some wetlands in the Yolo Bypass part of the upper Delta region may be managed specifically to provide important rearing habitats for endangered fish (www.yolobypass.net/docs/FINAL_PF_Bypass_Conservation_Measure.pdf). Other rare, endemic,

or sensitive species include the native amphibian species that have declined (Fisher and Shaffer 1996) in CVCA due to habitat destruction, windborne pesticides (Davidson et al. 2002), introduced species, and other factors (www.californiaherps.com). Also important are the many locally rare endemic vernal pool plants and invertebrates, and palmate-bracted bird's beak *(Cordylanthus palmatus),* an endangered San Joaquin Valley alkali sink plant (Coats et al. 1993).

Water Availability

In addition to management objectives, the timing, amount, and quality of water supplies available are key factors controlling the types, quality, and amount of wetlands in CVCA and KLBA. Evapotranspiration rates are greater and precipitation lower in CVCA (especially the San Joaquin Valley) than in KLBA. Thus, water required for wetlands in CVCA (seasonals: 4.1–8.5 acre-ft/acre; semi-perms: 7.4–14.3 acre-ft/acre) is much greater than in KLBA (seasonals: 1.8–3.5 acre-ft/acre; semi-perms: 3.1 acre-ft/acre) (Mayer and Thomasson 2004; USFWS 2000). Multiyear drought reduces water availability that restricts summer irrigations, reduces seed production, and delays fall flooding.

The discovery of embryotoxic effects of selenium on waterbird reproduction at Kesterson NWR (Ohlendorf et al. 1986) caused managers to eliminate or modify their use of agricultural drainwaters to manage wetlands, especially in San Joaquin Valley (Paveglio and Kilbride 2007). During the 1960s and 1970s, many wetlands were laser-leveled, especially in San Joaquin Valley, to reduce wetland water needs. However, the Central Valley Improvement Act of 1992 (Davis 1992) enhanced CVCA refuge water supplies and, along with recognition of the value of habitat diversity, has led to reconstruction of wetland basin contours and increased plant diversity (www.dfg.ca.gov/lands/wetland/public.html).

Conservation Concerns and Challenges

The majority of the concerns and challenges that wetlands and wetland-dependent species face in CVCA and KLBA can be traced to the rapid rate of human population growth and the resulting increased pressures on the landscape. The challenges are especially great in CVCA, where the human population is expected to triple by 2040, a much higher rate than in nearly all other regions (American Farmland Trust 1995). The impact of this population growth on wetland conservation can be manifested in several ways.

Urbanization and Agricultural Conversion

Habitat loss and fragmentation due to urbanization and increased need for agricultural production are the most important factors affecting wetland-dependent species in CVCA and KLBA (CDFG 2005). Expansion of urban areas and road and power networks can lead to wetland loss and fragmentation. Recent examples include the District 10 Bypass in the Sacramento Valley (Griffiths et al. 2000), the proposed City of Los Banos expansion (Weissman and Strong 2001), the High Speed Rail route (Grassland Staff 2007) dissecting the Grassland Ecological Area, and routing of proposed power lines through CVCA wetlands (Ducks Unlimited 2009). The quality of urbanized wetlands is often lower due to altered hydropattern and biogeochemistry, runoff of contaminants and fertilizers, increased mosquito abatement, increased human disturbance, and increased predation by homeowner cats. Although wetlands are protected, development pressure in CVCA is high, and any reduction in official protection status is a concern (Kay 2001).

Inadequate Water Supplies

Water is limited and is key to wetland maintenance in CVCA and KLBA (Mayer and Thomasson 2004). Increased competition from urban and agricultural users, along with in-stream demands for maintaining endangered salmon and other fish species (e.g., suckers in KLBA, delta smelt [*Hypomesus transpacifcus*] in CVCA [CDFG 2005]) will continue to reduce availability and increase costs of water for wetland management. Pumping groundwater is an expensive alternative to surface-water diversions, and some aquifers in southern San Joaquin Valley are already depleted and contain elevated arsenic levels (Welch et al. 2006; Faunt et al. 2009). Add in projected impacts of climate change and an aging water delivery infrastructure, and KLBA and CVCA are among the most likely regions in the United States to experience major water supply conflicts (Dziegielewski and Kiefer 2007). Water shortages can negatively impact wetland-dependent wildlife even if adequate water is maintained for wetlands. Water transfers from water-"rich" regions of CVCA (i.e., the Sacramento Valley rice-growing region) to water-"poor" regions (e.g., Southern California, San Joaquin Valley) are viewed as a useful method of dealing with critical regional shortages (U.S. Department of Interior 2009). However, one potential outcome of water transfers is idling of irrigated crops such as rice, which provide many of the same functions as wetlands (Elphick 2000). The mix of wetlands and flooded rice fields in the Sacramento Valley provides superior waterbird habitat compared with wetlands within a non-rice landscape (Fleskes et al. 2007). Thus, water transfers that reduce acreage or postharvest flooding of rice may be detrimental to waterbirds even if water supplies for wetlands are maintained.

Poor-Quality Wetland Water Supply

Poor-quality water can have detrimental impacts on wetland fauna and result in suboptimal wetland management. With water in short supply in CVCA and KLBA, most water used for wetland management has passed through agricultural lands or has been comingled with urban and agricultural runoff. CVCA waters are laden with up to 40,000 tons of contaminants annually (Bunn et al. 2007), including chemical fertilizers, herbicides, and pesticides, and from San Joaquin Valley soils, trace elements such as selenium that can concentrate to dangerous levels in wetland organisms (Ohlendorf et al. 1986). In addition, the estrogenic activity of some agricultural chemicals is a potential concern for both wildlife and humans (Johnson et al. 1998). Use of agricultural drainwaters can also lead to discharge restrictions that inhibit wetland management. For example, concerns about the quality of waters entering the San Joaquin River from wetlands in the Grassland Ecological Area may require that spring drawdowns be delayed by a month so that the highly saline water enters the river when reservoir releases are adequate to dilute the salts (Quinn and

Hanna 2003). This modified hydrology may cause retention of salts, reducing wetland plant productivity and waterbird food availability (Ortega 2009). Waters used for management of KLBA wetlands were found to have high temperatures, elevated pH, low dissolved oxygen, and un-ionized ammonia at levels known to kill fish and cause malformation of developing frog embryos (see Boyer and Grue 1995).

Reduced Support for Wetland Conservation and Management

Concerns over the perceived role that wetlands can play in human disease and contamination of water supplies, and impacts of a perceived oversupply of wetlands on waterfowl hunting success may erode public support for continued wetland conservation and restoration programs in CVCA and KLBA. This could result in fewer resources (monetary and water) available for wetland conservation and management.

HUMAN DISEASE

Wetlands, especially those in CVCA, are interspersed among large centers of human population. Concerns over the possible role of wetlands in harboring vectors of West Nile virus, equine encephalitis, avian flu, and other human diseases may erode public support for continued wetland conservation and restoration programs. As society is confronted with new and emerging mosquito-borne diseases, the need to simultaneously protect human health and wetland functions will only increase (Society of Wetland Scientists 2009). Costs assessed for mosquito abatement may inhibit habitat managers from flooding wetlands when potential liability exists, thus reducing wetland productivity and seasonal availability. In addition, laser leveling to precisely control water levels has been recommended for restored wetlands (Knight et al. 2003), but, at the same time, this reduces habitat diversity. Some commonly used organophosphate (e.g., malathion, naled) and synthetic pyrethroid (e.g., permethrin, resmethrin, sumithrin) adulticides kill not only mosquitoes but also other invertebrates (www.epa.gov/opppmsd1/PR_Notices/pr2005-1.pdf). Widespread introduction of mosquitofish (*Gambusia affinis*) into wetlands can have detrimental impacts on native fauna and may not be any more effective than native species (Pyke 2008). Solutions will depend upon improved communication between the mosquito abatement and wetland management communities (Dale and Knight 2008) to develop protocols that provide adequate wildlife habitat while avoiding creation of habitat for mosquito species that most threaten human health.

METHYLMERCURY

Concerns over the role of wetlands in conversion of environmental mercury to the more dangerous methylmercury form may impede wetland restoration in CVCA. For example, a high proportion of the methylmercury entering the Delta comes from upstream areas (Marvin-Dipasquale et al. 2007), and local governments may restrict that new wetland restoration not contribute further (www.delta.ca.gov/meetings/pdf/2008/112008_item_24_Y.pdf). The production of methylmercury in individual wetlands depends upon an array of factors, including labile organic matter production, timing and inundation of flooding, and wetland location within a drainage basin. For instance, Delta marshes had higher monomethylmercury/total mercury ratios than open water (Heim et al. 2007), and Ackerman et al. (2010) found that total mercury concentrations were higher in some insects in permanent wetlands than in temporary wetlands or rice fields. However, mercury concentrations in fish were higher in rice fields than in permanent wetlands (Ackerman and Eagles-Smith 2010). This issue will require careful placement and design of wetland restoration projects.

WATERFOWL HUNTER DISSATISFACTION

Over 60% of wetlands in California are privately owned and managed, and since hunters provide much of the political and financial support for wetland conservation in the region, the future of wetland conservation depends heavily on the continued support of the hunting community (Baldassarre and Bolen 1994; CVJV 2006). Wetland restoration and increased postharvest flooding of rice fields (Fleskes et al. 2005b) have improved body condition (Fleskes et al. 2009), reduced daily flight distances, and changed local movement patterns and regional distribution of some hunted species of waterfowl (Fleskes et al. 2005). Thus, hunters in some traditional hunting areas have reported seeing fewer waterfowl and have experienced reduced harvest rates (http://madduck.org). Over time, this could erode hunter support for continued wetland conservation.

Bioenergetics modeling (CVJV 2006) indicates that food resources in CVCA are currently adequate to support current and goal populations of wintering waterfowl. However, food supplies are currently abundant in large part because rice and other crop seeds are plentiful. Modeling indicates that if changes in agricultural policy, cropping patterns, water transfers, or increased harvester efficiency significantly reduce availability of these crop seeds, current wetlands alone could not support desired waterbird populations (CVJV 2006). Thus, to ensure adequate waterbird habitat and food supplies in the future, managers must maintain support for continued wetland conservation from waterfowl hunters, even though doing so may reduce present-day harvest success. Effective communication between conservation program managers and the hunting community will be required to arrive at innovative solutions.

Invasive Species

Invasives are not new to California, likely arriving as early as 1542 with the first European explorers (Williams et al. 2005), but the problem has escalated along with the speed and reach of global trade. Invasive plants are especially problematic in wetlands because they outcompete and hybridize with native plants, reduce habitat value for native wildlife, provide habitat for exotic wildlife and mosquitoes, alter ecosystem functions and hydrology, and reduce efficiency of water delivery by slowing flow, clogging structures, and increasing evapotranspiration (Bossard et al. 2000). Especially or potentially problematic invasive plants in regional wetlands (www.cal-ipc.org/ip/management/plant_profiles/index.php) include (1) perennial pepperweed (Lepidium latifolium), an aggressive invader that forms dense rooted stands and has increased greatly since 1995; (2) water-primrose (Ludwigia hexapetala, L. peploides), which

forms dense mats on and below the water surface and has expanded greatly in CVCA during the 2000s; (3) purple loosestrife (Lythrum salicaria), a perennial wetland herb that forms monotypic stands; (4) water hyacinth (Eichhornia crassipes), widespread throughout CVCA, with heavy infestations in the Delta that require repeated treatment; (5) Eurasian watermilfoil (Myriophyllum spicatum), a submergent that creates dense mats found in several CVCA counties; (6) azolla (Azolla), a 1.5–2 cm floating fern that forms dense mats (www.ars.usda.gov/SP2UserFiles/Program/304/ActionPlan2008–2013/3c.pdf), first reported in CVCA in 2008; (7) saltcedar (Tamarix), which forms dense thickets in wetland and riparian areas in CVCA that may lower water tables; and (8) bioengineered plants, which provide numerous advantages but also risks (Whitman 2000), and are considered a special class of invasives by some. Although their environmental impact is uncertain, waterfowl and other wetland-dependent wildlife would likely be negatively impacted if cross-contamination by bioengineered rice reduces the overseas market for CVCA rice, and rice acreage declines (Environment California Research and Policy Center 2004).

Other invasive organisms also impact wetlands and wetland-dependent wildlife. Several of the more problematic species in CVCA and KLBA include (1) feral and free-ranging cats (Felis catus), which are important predators on birds and small mammals where wetlands are near urban areas (www.dfg.ca.gov/wildlife/nongame/nuis_exo/dom_cat/index.html); (2) red fox (Vulpes vulpes), which in CVCA were, until recently, all thought to be nonnative (Lewis et al. 1999) and managed as such (www.dfg.ca.gov/wildlife/nongame/nuis_exo/red_fox/index.html). However, recent genetic analysis indicates red fox in Sacramento Valley are distinct and should be considered native (Moore et al. 2009). Change in red fox status and management could increase predation of wetland birds and their nests, including several of conservation concern (Lewis et al. 1999). Also problematic are (3) bullfrogs, a predator of young endangered giant garter snakes (Wylie et al. 2003) and an obvious threat to native amphibians (but see Hayes and Jennings 1986); (4) chytrid fungus, a fungal pathogen (Batrachochytrium dendrobatidis) that has been recently associated with deaths of a wide array of amphibians (Daszak et al. 2003); and (5) exotic crustaceans and mollusks (e.g., Chinese mitten crab [Eriocheir sinensis; CDFG 2003], New Zealand mudsnail [Potamopyrgus antipodarum], quagga mussel [Dreissena bugensis], and zebra mussel [D. polymorpha]), capable of impacting water delivery or wetland environments.

Global Climate Change

Climate change models predict substantial changes in temperature and precipitation in CVCA and KLBA watersheds (Cayan et al. 2008), which have potential to exacerbate all of the above issues. These include worsening water shortages and quality by altering timing and amounts of rainwater and snowmelt flooding and increasing evapotranspiration rates that could lead to less water available for wetland management; changing the environment in favor of exotic diseases and invasives; changing ecology of wetlands and wetland-dependent wildlife (Bauer et al. 2008); and altering when and where resources are available and needed for migratory birds. For example, warmer springs may dry CVCA habitats quicker, forcing waterbirds to KLBA earlier, where they may find reduced availability of temporary wetland habitats. Extreme winter storms and sea-level rise will increase the likelihood of levee collapse in the Delta and conversion of Delta and Suisun Marsh wetlands from fresh to saltwater. Conservation programs and reservoir operations will need to adjust to avoid misdirecting priorities and optimally manage flood risk and water supplies (Brekke et al. 2009).

Conclusions

Wetlands and wetland-dependent wildlife in both KLBA and CVCA face immense challenges due to intense agriculture, increasing urbanization, increasingly limited water resources, and an altered landscape. Despite great losses, both regions are still rich in diversity and immense abundance of natural resources that are the focus of broadly supported conservation efforts. The importance of these wetland ecosystems to the economy and health of humans and natural fauna requires that managers overcome uncertainties of possible climate change impacts and other challenges and work to ensure wetland ecosystems in the regions continue to flourish.

References

Ackerman JT, Miles AK, Eagles-Smith CA. 2010. Invertebrate mercury bioaccumulation in permanent, seasonal, and flooded rice wetlands within California's Central Valley. *Sci. Total Env.* 408:666–71.

Akins GJ. 1970. *The effects of land use and land management on the wetlands of the Upper Klamath Basin.* MS thesis, Western Washington State College, Ellensburg.

Aldous AR, Craft CB, et al. 2007. Soil phosphorus release from a restoration wetland, Upper Klamath Lake, Oregon. *Wetlands* 27:1025–35.

Alpers CN, Hunerlach MP, et al. 2005. *Mercury contamination from historical gold mining in California.* USGS Fact Sheet 2005-3014.

American Farmland Trust. 1995. *Alternatives for future urban growth in California's Central Valley: the bottom line for agriculture and taxpayers.* Washington, DC, and Davis, CA: American Farmland Trust.

Baldassarre GA, Bolen EG. 1994. *Waterfowl ecology and management.* New York: Wiley.

Batzer DP, McGee M, Resh VH, Smith RR. 1993. Characteristics of invertebrates consumed by mallards and prey response to flooding schedules. *Wetlands* 13:41–49.

Bauer S, Dinther MV, et al. 2008. The consequences of climate-driven stop-over sites changes on migration schedules and fitness of Arctic geese. *J. Anim. Ecol.* 77:654–60.

Beedy EC, Hamilton WJ III. 1999. Tricolored blackbird *(Agelaius tricolor).* In *The birds of North America,* no. 423, A Poole, F Gill, editors. Philadelphia: Am. Ornithol. Union, Acad. Nat. Sci.

Bias MA. 1995. Wildlife resources of the Central Valley, California: important wetland-associated mammals. In *Valley habitats: a technical guidance series for private land managers in California's Central Valley,* no. 10. Sacramento: Ducks Unlimited.

Bossard CC, Randall JM, Hoshovsky MC, editors. 2000. *Invasive plants of California's wildlands.* Berkeley: Univ. Calif. Press.

Bottorff J. 1989. *Concept plan for waterfowl habitat protection, Klamath Basin.* Portland, OR: USFWS.

Boyer R, Grue CE. 1995. The need for water quality criteria for frogs. *Env. Health Perspect.* 103:352–57.

Brekke LD, Maurer EP, et al. 2009. Assessing reservoir operations risk under climate change. *Water Resour. Res.* 45. W04411, doi:10.1029/2008WR006941.

Budd R, O'Geen A, et al. 2009. Efficacy of constructed wetlands in pesticide removal from tailwaters in the Central Valley, California. *Env. Sci. Tech.* 43:2925–30.

Bunn D, Mummert A, et al. 2007. *California wildlife: conservation challenges (California's Wildlife Action Plan).* Sacramento: Calif. DFG.

Burns EG. 2003. An analysis of food habits of green-winged teal,

northern pintails, and mallards wintering in the Suisun Marsh to develop guidelines for food plant management. MS thesis, Univ. Calif., Davis.

California Department of Fish and Game. 2003. *Atlas of the biodiversity of California.* Sacramento: California DFG. www.dfg.ca.gov/biogeodata/atlas.

California Department of Fish and Game. 2005. *The status of rare, threatened, and endangered plants and animals of California 2000–2004.* Sacramento: California DFG. http://www.dfg.ca.gov/wildlife/nongame/t_e_spp/docs/2004/t_esummary.pdf.

California Department of Fish and Game. 2008. *Bird species of special concern.* Sacramento: California DFG. www.dfg.ca.gov/wildlife/nongame/ssc/birds.html.

California Department of Fish and Game. 2009. *Life history accounts and range maps—California wildlife habitat relationships system.* Sacramento: California DFG. www.dfg.ca.gov/biogeodata/cwhr/cawildlife.aspx.

Cayan DR, Maurer EP, et al. 2008. Climate change scenarios for the California region. *Clim. Chang. Suppl.* 1:S21–S42.

Central Valley Joint Venture. 2006. *Central Valley Joint Venture Implementation Plan—conserving bird habitat.* Sacramento: USFWS.

Chouinard MP Jr. 2000. *Survival and habitat use of mallard broods in the San Joaquin Valley, California.* MS thesis, Humboldt State Univ., Arcata, CA.

Coats R, Showers MA, Pavlik B. 1993. Management plan for an alkali sink and its endangered plant *Cordylanthus palmatus. Env. Manage.* 17:115–27.

Compeau GC, Bartha R. 1985. Sulfate-reducing bacteria: principal methylators of mercury in anoxic estuarine sediment. *Appl. Env. Microbiol.* 50:498–502.

Conaway CH, Black FJ, et al. 2008. Mercury in the San Francisco Estuary. *Rev. Env. Contam. Toxicol.* 194:29–54.

Conaway CH, Ross JRM, et al. 2007. Decadal mercury trends in San Francisco Estuary sediments. *Env. Res.* 105:53–66.

Dahl TE. 1990. *Wetland losses in the United States 1780's to 1980's.* Washington, DC: USFWS.

Dale PER, Knight JM. 2008. Wetlands and mosquitoes: a review. *Wetl. Ecol. Manage.* 16:255–76.

Daszak P, Cunningham AA, Hyatt AD. 2003. Infectious disease and amphibian population declines. *Divers. Distrib.* 9:141–50.

Davidson C, Shaffer HB, Jennings MR. 2002. Spatial tests of the pesticide drift, habitat destruction, UV-B, and climate change hypotheses for California amphibian declines. *Conserv. Biol.* 16:1588–1601.

Davis PA. 1992. Omnibus western water law. *Congressional Quarterly* 21 (November):3687–90.

Deverel SJ, Rojstaczer SA. 1996. Subsidence of agricultural lands in the Sacramento–San Joaquin Delta, California: role of aqueous and gaseous carbon fluxes. *Water Resour. Res.* 32:2359–67.

Domagalski J. 1998. Occurrence and transport of total mercury and methyl mercury in the Sacramento River Basin, California. *J. Geogchem. Explor.* 64:277–91.

Ducks Unlimited. 2009. *Central Valley wetlands, hunting areas threatened by power lines.* Sacramento: Ducks Unlimited.

Dugger BD, Petrie MJ, Mauser D. 2008. *A bioenergetic approach to conservation planning for waterfowl at Lower Klamath and Tule Lake National Wildlife Refuge.* Tulelake, CA: USFWS.

Dziegielewski B, Kiefer JC. 2007. U.S. water demand, supply and allocation: trends and outlook. Alexandria, VA: USACE Inst. Water Resour. Rep. 2007-R-3.

Eldridge J. 1990. Aquatic invertebrates important for waterfowl production: waterfowl management handbook. *Fish and Wildl. Leafl.* 13.3.3:1–7.

Elphick CS. 2000. Functional equivalency between rice fields and seminatural wetland habitats. *Conserv. Biol.* 14:181–91.

Environment California Research and Policy Center. 2004. *Voters in seven California counties consider banning genetically engineered agriculture: a white paper.* http://cdn.publicinterestnetwork.org/assets/Nzk7e2xdZVhQnxr3pHrE8w/Voters_in_7_California_Counties.pdf.

Estep J, Beedy T, et al. 2009. *California black rail.* Yolo Natural Heritage Program, Draft Species Accounts. www.yoloconservationplan.org/yolo_pdfs/speciesaccounts/birds/Cal-black-rail.pdf.

Faunt CC. 2009. *Groundwater availability of the Central Valley aquifer, California.* USGS Prof. Pap. 1766.

Faunt CC, Hanson RT, et al. 2009. California's Central Valley groundwater study: a powerful new tool to assess water resources in California's Central Valley. *Fact Sheet* 2009-3057. Washington, DC: USGS.

Fiedler PL. 1996. *Common wetland plants of central California.* Sacramento: USACE.

Fisher RN, Shaffer HB. 1996. The decline of amphibians in California's Great Central Valley. *Conserv. Biol.* 10:1387–97.

Fleskes JP, Yee JL. 2007. Waterfowl distribution and abundance during spring migration in southern Oregon and northeastern California. *West. N. Am. Nat.* 67:409–28.

Fleskes JP, Jarvis RL, Gilmer DS. 2003. Selection of flooded agricultural fields and other landscapes by female northern pintails wintering in Tulare Basin, California. *Wildl. Soc. Bull.* 31:793–803.

Fleskes JP, Miller MR, et al. 2009. Increased winter habitat improves body condition of ducks in the Central Valley of California. *Wildlife Soc. 16th Annu. Conf.* Monterey, CA (Abstract).

Fleskes JP, Perry WM, et al. 2005b. Change in area of winter-flooded and dry rice in the northern Central Valley of California determined by satellite imagery. *Calif. Fish Game* 91:207–15.

Fleskes JP, Yee JL, et al. 2005. *Waterfowl distribution, movements and habitat use relative to recent habitat changes in the Central Valley of California: a cooperative project to investigate impacts of Central Valley Habitat Joint Venture and changing agricultural practices on the ecology of wintering waterfowl. Final Report.* Dixon, CA: USGS, West. Ecol. Res. Center, Dixon Field Sta.

Fleskes JP, Yee JL, et al. 2007. Pintail and mallard survival in California relative to habitat, abundance, and hunting. *J. Wildl. Manage.* 71:2238–48.

Fleury BE, Sherry TW. 1995. Long-term population trends of colonial wading birds in the southern United States: the impact of crayfish aquaculture on Louisiana populations. *Auk* 112:613–32.

Frayer WE, Peters DD, Pywell HR. 1989. *Wetlands of the California Central Valley: status and trends 1939 to mid-1980s.* Portland, OR: USFWS.

Fredrickson LH. 1991. *Strategies for water level manipulation in moist-soil systems: waterfowl management handbook. Fish and Wildl. Leafl.* 13.4.6.

Fregien SL. 1998. *Characterization of moist-soil plant and macroinvertebrate communities within seasonal wetlands created by flooding agricultural fields on the Tule Lake National Wildlife Refuge.* MS thesis, Univ. Washington, Seattle.

Frenzel P, Arth I, et al. 2000. Linking nitrogen and carbon cycles: methane oxidation and nitrification in the rhizophere of wetland plants. *Internat. Peat Congr., Soc. Wetl. Sci./INTECOL.* Session 110. Global Climate Change. Quebec, Canada (Abstract).

Fretwell JD, Williams JS, Redman PJ. 1996. National water summary on wetland resources. *Water-Supply Paper* 2425. Washington, DC: USGS.

Gannett MW, Lite KE Jr, et al. 2007. Ground-water hydrology of the Upper Klamath Basin, Oregon and California. *USGS Sci. Investig. Rep.* 2007-5050.

Garrett K, Dunn J. 1981. *Birds of Southern California.* Los Angeles: Audubon Soc.

Gerhardt F, Collinge SK. 2003. Exotic plant invasions of vernal pools in the Central Valley of California, USA. *J. Biogeogr.* 30:1043–52.

Gilmer DS, Miller MR, et al. 1982. California's Central Valley wintering waterfowl: concerns and challenges. *Trans. N. Am. Wildl. Nat. Resour. Conf.* 47:441–52.

Gilmer DS, Yee JL, et al. 2004. Waterfowl migration on Klamath Basin National Wildlife Refuges 1953–2001. *Biol. Sci. Rep.* USGS/BRD/BSR-2003-0004, USGS.

Grassland staff. 2007. High-speed rail alternative route threatens Grassland wetlands. *Grassl. Today* 17:6.

Greij ED. 1994. Common moorhen. *Migratory shore and upland game bird management in North America,* TC Tacha, CE Braun, editors. Washington, DC: Internat. Assoc. Fish Wildl. Agencies, pp. 145–57.

Griffiths T, Gaines B, Smith D. 2000. District 10 wetlands at risk from highway project. *Calif. Waterfowl* April/May:9–11.

Harding ST. 1960. *Water in California.* Palo Alto, CA: N-P Publications.

Hathaway R, Welch T. 2002. Background. *Water allocation in the Klamath Reclamation Project, 2001: an assessment of natural resource, economic, social, and institutional issues with a focus on Upper Klamath Basin,* Braunworth B, Hathaway R, Carlson H, editors. Corvallis: Oregon State Univ.; Davis and Berkeley: Univ. California, pp. 31–43.

Hayes MP, Jennings MR. 1986. Decline of Ranid frog species in western North America: are bullfrogs *(Rana catesbeiana)* responsible? *J. Herpetol.* 20:490–509.

Heim WA, Coale KH, et al. 2007. Spatial and habitat-based variations in total and methyl mercury concentrations in surficial sediments in the San Francisco Bay-Delta. *Env. Sci. Tech.* 41:3501–07.

Heinz GH, Hoffman DJ. 1998. Methylmercury chloride and selenomethionine interactions on health and reproduction in mallards. *Env. Toxicol. Chem.* 17:139–45.

Heitmeyer ME, Connelly DP, Pederson RL. 1989. The Central, Imperial, and Coachella Valleys of California. In *Habitat management for migrating and wintering waterfowl in North America,* Smith LM, Pedersen RL, Kaminski RM, editors. Lubbock: Texas Tech Press, pp. 475–505.

Hickey C, Shuford WD, et al. 2003. *Version 1.1. The Southern Pacific Shorebird Conservation Plan: a strategy for supporting California's Central Valley and coastal shorebird populations.* Stinson Beach, CA: PRBO Conserv. Sci.

Hicks LA, Mauser DM, et al. 1999. *Ecology of shortnose and Lost River suckers in Tule Lake National Wildlife Refuge, California, progress report, April–November 1999.* Tulelake, CA: USFWS Klamath Basin Nat. Wildl. Refuge.

Hoffman DJ, Heinz GH. 1998. Effects of mercury and selenium on glutathione metabolism and oxidative stress in mallard ducks. *Env. Toxicol. Chem.* 17:161–66.

Holland RF. 1978. Geographic and edaphic distribution of vernal pools in the Great Central Valley, California. *CA Native Plant Soc. Spec. Publ.* no. 4. Sacramento: CA Native Plant Soc.

Holland RF, Jain SK. 1977. Vernal pools. In *Terrestrial vegetation of California,* Barbour MG, Major J, editors. New York: Wiley-Intersci., pp. 258–90.

Intergovernmental Panel on Climate Change. 2007. Climate change 2007. Synthesis report. *Contribution of Working Groups I, II, and III to the Fourth Assessment Report of the Intergovernmental Panel on Climate Change.* New York: Cambridge Univ. Press.

Jahnke JJ. 1994. Soil survey of Butte Valley–Tule Lake Area, California: parts of Siskiyou and Modoc Counties. USDA Soil Conserv. Serv.

Jennings M. 1995. Native ranid frogs in California. In *Our living resources: a report to the nation on the distribution, abundance, and health of U.S. plants, animals, and ecosystems,* LaRoe ET, Farris GS, et al., editors. Washington, DC: USDI, Nat. Biol. Serv., pp. 131–34.

Jennings MR, Hayes MP. 1994. *Amphibian and reptile species of special concern in California.* Rancho Cordova: California DFG, Inland Fish. Div.

Johnson ML, Salveson A, et al. 1998. Environmental estrogens in agricultural drain water from the Central Valley of California. *Bull. Env. Contam. Toxicol.* 60:609–14.

Kay J. 2001. Justices' ruling could affect scores of California wetlands. *San Francisco Chronicle.* January 11, 2001. Page A6.

Kerin EJ, Gilmour CC, et al. 2006. Mercury methylation by dissimilatory iron-reducing bacteria. *Appl. Env. Microbiol.* 72:7919–21.

Kirk A. 1994. Vanished lake, vanished landscape. In *Life on the edge,* Thelander CG, editor. Santa Cruz, CA: Biosystems Books, pp. 171–79.

Knight RL, Walton WE, et al. 2003. Strategies for effective mosquito control in constructed treatment wetlands. *Ecol. Eng.* 21:211–32.

Laanbroek HJ. 2010. Methane emission from natural wetlands: interplay between emergent macrophytes and soil microbial processes. a mini-review. *Ann. Bot.* 105:141–53.

Lewis JC, Sallee KL, Golightly RT Jr. 1999. Introduction and range expansion of nonnative red foxes *(Vulpes vulpes)* in California. *Am. Midl. Nat.* 142:372–81.

Lindenberg MK, Wood TM. 2009. *Water quality of a drained wetland, Caledonia Marsh on Upper Klamath Lake, Oregon, after flooding in 2006.* USGS Sci. Investig. Rep. 2009-5025.

Littlefield CD, Ivey GL. 2000. *Conservation assessment for greater sandhill cranes wintering on the Consumnes River Floodplain and Delta Regions of California.* Galt, CA: Nature Conservancy.

Marvin-Dipasquale MC, Windham-Myers L, et al. 2007. Mercury cycling in agricultural and non-agricultural wetlands of the Yolo Bypass Wildlife Area, California: sediment biogeochemistry. *Am. Geophys. Union, Fall Meeting 2007* (Abstract #B14B-03).

Mason HL. 1957. *A flora of the marshes of California.* Berkeley, Los Angeles: Univ. Calif. Press.

Mayer T. 2005. Water-quality impacts of wetland management on Lower Klamath National Wildlife Refuge. *Wetlands* 25:697–712.

Mayer TD, Thomasson R. 2004. Fall water requirements for seasonal diked wetlands at Lower Klamath National Wildlife Refuge. *Wetlands* 24:92–103.

Maynard JJ, O'Geen AT, Dahlgren RA. 2009. Bioavailability and fate of phosphorus in constructed wetlands receiving agricultural runoff in the San Joaquin Valley, California. *J. Env. Qual.* 38:360–72.

McGowan JA. 1961. *History of the Sacramento Valley,* vol. 2. New York: Lewis Historical Publ. Co.

Miller RL, Fram MS, et al. 2008. Subsidence reversal in a re-established wetland in the Sacramento–San Joaquin Delta, California, USA. *San Francisco Estuar. Watershed Sci.* 6:1–20.

Moore M, Brown S, et al. 2009. Use of genetic tools to assess impacts of encroaching non-native red foxes on the native Sacramento Valley red fox. *Wildl. Soc. 16th Annu. Conf.,* Monterey, CA (Abstract).

Mosier AR. 1998. Soil processes and global change. *Biol. Fertil. Soils* 27:221–29.

Moyle PB. 2002. *Inland fishes of California,* rev. and expanded ed. Berkeley: Univ. Calif. Press.

Mullen JR, Nady P. 1985. *Water budgets for major streams in the Central Valley, California, 1961–77.* USGS Open-File Report 85-401.

North American Waterfowl Management Plan Committee. 1986. *North American Waterfowl Management Plan 1986: strategy for cooperation.* Can. Wildl. Serv., USFWS.

Novitzki RP, Smith RD, Fretwell JD. 1996. Restoration, creation, and recovery of wetlands: wetland functions, values, and assessment. In *National Water Summary of Wetland Resources, USGS Water Supply Paper 2425,* Fretwell JD, Williams JS, Redman PJ, editors.

Ohlendor, HM, Hoffman DJ, et al. 1986. Embryonic mortality and abnormalities of aquatic birds: apparent impacts of selenium from irrigation drainwater. *Sci. Total Env.* 52:49–63.

Ortega R. 2009. Wetland response to adaptive salinity drainage management. MS thesis, Univ. California, Davis.

Pacific Flyway. 2000. *Pacific Flyway management plan for the Pacific population of western Canada geese.* Portland, OR: Pacific Flyway Study Committee, USFWS.

Paveglio FL, Kilbride KM. 2007. Selenium in aquatic birds from central California. *J. Wildl. Manage.* 71:2550–55.

Pearce CI, Pattrick RAD, et al. 2009. Investigating different mechanisms for biogenic selenite transformations: *Geobacter sulfurreducens, Shewanella oneidensis* and *Veillonella atypical. Env. Tech.* 30:1313–26.

Pyke GH. 2008. Plague minnow or mosquito fish? A review of the biology and impacts of introduced *Gambusia* species. *Annu. Rev. Ecol. Evol. Syst.* 39:171–91.

Quinn NWT, Hanna WM. 2003. *Env. Model. Softw.* 18:503–11.

Rollins GL. 1991. A guide to waterfowl habitat management in Suisun Marsh. Sacramento: California DFG.

Schwarzbach SE. 2009. Mercury contamination of San Francisco Bay marshes—a 120 year perspective using museum specimens and structural equation modeling. *Wildl. Soc. 16th Annu. Conf.* Monterey, CA (Abstract).

Shelton ML. 1987. Irrigation induced change in vegetation and evapotranspiration in the Central Valley of California. *Landsc. Ecol.* 1:95–105.

Shuford D. 2009. Klamath Basin CA/OR. In *U.S. shorebird conservation plan: Intermountain West regional shorebird plan, version 1.0,* Oring LW, Neel L, Oring KE, editors. pp. 39–41.

Shuford WD, Page GW, Kjelmyr JE. 1998. Patterns and dynamics of shorebird use of California's Central Valley. *Condor* 100:227–44.

Shuford WD, Thomson DL, et al. 2004. *Abundance, distribution, and phenology of nongame waterbirds in the Klamath Basin of Oregon and California in 2003: final report.* Tulelake, CA: USFWS, Klamath Basin Nat. Wildl. Refuge.

Silveira JG. 2000. Alkali vernal pools at Sacramento National Wildlife Refuge. *Fremontia* 27(4) and 28(1):10–18.

Smith WD, Rollins GL, Shinn R. 1994. *A guide to wetland habitat management in the Central Valley.* Sacramento: CA DFG, CA Waterfowl Assoc.

Society of Wetland Scientists. 2009. *Current practices in wetland management for mosquito control.* www.sws.org/wetland_concerns/docs/SWS-MosquitoWhitePaperFinal.pdf.

Stern MA, Morawski JF, Rosenberg GA. 1993. Rediscovery and status of a disjunct population of breeding yellow rails in southern Oregon. *Condor* 95:1024–27.

United States Department of Interior. 2009. *Reality check: California's water crisis.* Office of Communications. www.doi.gov/documents/CA_Water_Reality_Check.pdf.

United States Fish and Wildlife Service. 1978. *Concept plan for waterfowl wintering habitat preservation, Central Valley, California.* Portland, OR: USFWS.

United States Fish and Wildlife Service. 2000. *Central Valley wetlands water supply investigations: CVPIA 3406(d)(6)(A,B): a report to Congress: final report.* Portland, OR: USFWS.

United States Fish and Wildlife Service. 2006. *Giant garter snake* (Thamnophis gigas), *5-year review: summary and evaluation.* Sacramento: USFWS.

United States Fish and Wildlife Service. 2009a. *2009 Pacific Flyway data book.* Portland, OR: USFWS.

United States Fish and Wildlife Service. 2009b. *Klamath Marsh National Wildlife Refuge: draft comprehensive conservation plan and environmental assessment.* Tulelake, CA: USFWS.

United States Fish and Wildlife Service. 2009c. *Winter waterfowl survey, Pacific Flyway, January 5–9, 2009.* Sacramento: USFWS.

United States Fish and Wildlife Service and United States Bureau of Reclamation. 2003. *Central Valley Project Improvement Act, Section 3406 (b)(1) "Other" Habitat Restoration Program Project Plan.*

Vance-Borland K, Noss R, et al. 1995. A biodiversity conservation plan for the Klamath/Siskiyou region. *Wild Earth* 5(4):52–59.

Warnock N, Haig SM, Oring LW. 1998. Monitoring species richness and abundance of shorebirds in the western Great Basin. *Condor* 100:589–600.

Weissman KG, Strong D. 2001. *Land use and economics study: Grassland Ecological Area, Merced County, California.* Los Banos, CA: Grassland Water District.

Welch AH, Oremland RS, et al. 2006. Arsenic in ground water: a review of current knowledge and relation to the CALFED Solution Area with recommendations for needed research. *San Francisco Estuar. Watershed Sci.* 4:1–32.

Weston DP, You J, Lydy MJ. 2004. Distribution and toxicity of sediment-associated pesticides in agriculture-dominated water bodies of California's Central Valley. *Env. Sci. Tech.* 38:2752–59.

Whitman DB. 2000. Genetically modified foods: harmful or helpful? *CSA Discovery Guides* April 2000:1–13. www.csa.com/discoveryguides/gmfood/review.pdf.

Whitmire SL, Hamilton SK. 2005. Rapid removal of nitrate and sulfate in freshwater sediments. *J. Env. Qual.* 34:2062–71.

Williams JW, Seabloom EW, et al. 2005. Anthropogenic impacts upon plant species richness and net primary productivity in California. *Ecol. Letters* 8:127–37.

Williamson AK, Prudic DE, Swain LA. 1989. Ground-water flow in the Central Valley, California. *USGS Prof. Pap.* 1401-D.

Wu L. 2003. Review of 15 years of research on ecotoxicology and remediation of land contaminated by agricultural sediment rich in selenium. *Ecotoxicol. Env. Safety* 57:257–69.

Wylie GD, Casazza ML, Carpenter M. 2003. Diet of bullfrogs in relation to predation on giant garter snakes at Colusa National Wildlife Refuge. *Calif. Fish Game* 89:139–45.

Yang D-Y, Chen Y-W, et al. 2008. Selenium and mercury in organisms: interactions and mechanisms. *Env. Rev.* 16:71–92.

Yarris GS, McLandress MR, Perkins AEH. 1994. Molt migration of postbreeding female mallards from Suisun Marsh, California. *Condor* 96:36–45.

CHAPTER 26

Freshwater Arctic Tundra Wetlands

LAURA GOUGH

The Arctic conjures up visions of sea ice and polar bears, Northern Lights in winter, midnight sun in summer, swarms of mosquitoes, herds of caribou, and fossil fuel exploration. The Arctic is a huge expanse of wilderness that lies frozen most of the year, but during the brief summer, biologically rich wetlands support an array of microbial, plant, and animal species adapted to weather extremes and multiple environmental stresses. Understanding ecosystem processes in these wetlands contributes to region-specific knowledge and helps illuminate patterns of global element cycling because tundra soils contain huge carbon reserves.

Tundra is an open habitat where trees do not normally occur because of limitations imposed by cold temperatures, short growing seasons, frequently waterlogged soils, and permafrost (permanently frozen ground). For this chapter, I define the Arctic tundra as the area north of treeline. Precipitation is low, similar to deserts, but evapotranspiration rates are even lower because of low temperatures and energy inputs. Peat-accumulating soils and permafrost prevent soil drainage, creating expansive wetland conditions following snowmelt each spring.

Arctic ecologists typically divide tundra into communities based on soil moisture and reserve the term *wetland* for wet meadow mires and marshes that remain flooded or completely saturated for the entire growing season. Here I include moist and wet tundra since both support hydrophytic vegetation, typically have organic wetland soils, and remain saturated for substantial periods during the growing season. Tundra wetlands generally fall in the palustrine-emergent-flooded and palustrine-emergent-saturated categories (USFWS 1994).

The Circumarctic Vegetation Map (CAVM) provides estimates for extent of different Arctic tundra communities and can be used to develop estimates of wetland area (Fig. 26.1, Table 26.1). According to the CAVM, the area covered by wetlands is ~37% of Canada's Arctic region and ~82% of Alaska's, with more of this area "moist" than "wet" (Fig. 26.1, Table 26.1). The CAVM does not include riparian habitats because they are too narrow to dominate the polygons used to calculate identities. In the High Arctic (e.g., Canadian Archipelago), wetlands are present but patchy and often too small to be mapped. The North American Arctic contains wetland (~44%) in similar proportion to the entire Arctic (~37%; Table 26.1).

I describe the characteristics of inland freshwater wetlands in Arctic North America focusing on results from a few locations in Canada (Ellesmere Island, Daring Lake, Inuvik) and Alaska (Toolik Lake, Atqasuk). Studies in freshwater coastal marshes at Barrow, Alaska, are also included because intensive research during the International Biosphere Program (Brown et al. 1980) can be applied to many Arctic wet meadows. For a description of coastally influenced Arctic and subarctic wetlands, see Martini et al. (2009).

Climate, Geology, Hydrology, and Biogeochemistry

Climate and Geology

Climatic constraints in the Arctic are severe. The region has very little daylight through the long winter, with a short one-to four-month growing season, depending on latitude, during which there is light 24 hours a day. Precipitation and evapotranspiration are low. Temperatures remain cold year-round, generally averaging less than 10°C even during July. Snowmelt occurs near the peak of available solar radiation, so photosynthesis must be carried out as solar radiation is beginning to decline (Fig. 26.2). High interannual variability in climate results in varying dates of snowmelt and ice-out, and snow and ice storms can occur at any time during the growing season, killing plants and restricting food availability for consumers.

Much of the North American Arctic has been influenced by glaciers (Bliss and Matveyeva 1992), but during the most recent glacial maximum, significant areas of Alaska as well as the Yukon region of Canada were not glaciated. Because of this history, at a regional scale, vegetation throughout the North American Arctic is believed to have been relatively stable for as long as 10,000 years (Oswald et al. in preparation). Landscape age (time since deglaciation) and loess inputs from rivers affect soil pH and wetland community development (Hamilton 2003). Plant community type is also affected by topography (Ostendorf and Reynolds 1998) because depressions, slope, and aspect all affect hydrology.

The presence of permafrost dominates Arctic ecosystem

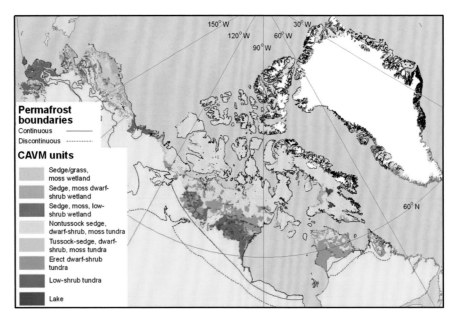

FIG. 26.1. Wetland communities of Arctic North America. White indicates ice and glacier cover, gray is areas of the Arctic that are not wetland, and beige is non-Arctic land. (Adapted from the CAVM [Walker, Raynolds, et al. 2005] by M. Raynolds, Alaska Geobotany Center, University of Alaska, Fairbanks.)

TABLE 26.I

Estimated area (km²) of wetlands of North America from the Circumarctic Vegetation Map focused on moist and wet tundra

Mapping unit	Plant community	Canada		U.S.		North America total		Arctic total	
		Area	%	Area	%	Area	%	Area	%
G3	Nontussock sedge, dwarf shrub, moss	32,754	12	3,922	8	36,676	11	60,314	8
G4	Tussock sedge, dwarf shrub, moss	3,074	1	13,866	27	16,960	5	35,616	4.7
S1	Erect dwarf-shrub tundra	37,206	14	5,194	10	42,400	13	73,034	9.7
S2	Low-shrub tundra	15,900	6	6,148	12	22,048	7	64,978	8.6
W1	Sedge/grass, moss	5,300	2	742	1.4	6,042	2	10,706	1.4
W2	Sedge, moss, dwarf shrub	2,862	1	4,770	9	7,632	2	14,416	1.9
W3	Sedge, moss, low shrub	2,014	1	7,632	15	9,646	3	16,854	2.2
Other	Dry tundra, barrens, glaciers, lakes	171,720	63	9,010	18	180,836	56	477,742	63
Total		270,618	100	51,410	100	322,240	100	753,660	100

NOTE: See text and Walker, Raynolds, et al. (2005) for more details regarding the plants and soils associated with each mapping unit.

G (graminoid) and S (shrub) tundra are considered moist, while W (wetland) tundra represents wet meadows. Riparian communities were too small to be included in the coarse scale of the analysis.

processes. Permafrost affects soil temperature, moisture, and depth as well as depth to water table and groundwater flow. Permafrost depth depends on climate, soil type, insulating vegetation, and topography. Where permafrost is continuous (Fig. 26.1), the active layer (surface soil that thaws each summer and is biologically active) generally reaches at most 1 m (Kane et al. 1992), restricting groundwater movement to the upper soil horizon. Even where permafrost is discontinuous, hydraulic conductivity of peat is low, and water moves very slowly.

Arctic soils are classified as gelisols because they formed over permafrost, with wetland soils additionally being classified as histosols or inceptisols. Arctic wetlands are generally peatlands because of slow decomposition rates and hydrology, but in the High Arctic, patchy wetlands occur over mineral soils (W1 in Fig. 26.1) (Woo and Young 2006). Cryoturbation occurs somewhat randomly across the landscape, generating local-scale heterogeneity in soil conditions (Munroe and Bockheim 2001). When soils freeze and thaw differentially, patterned ground (frost boils, sorted circles, and polygons) forms. Frost boils, areas of bare mineral soil, are correlated with soil

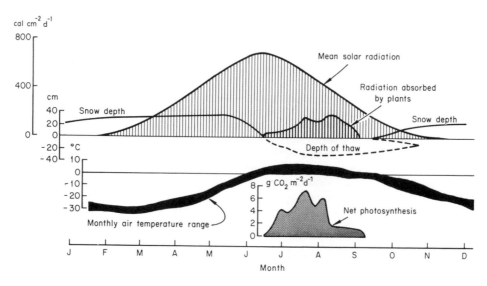

FIG. 26.2. Annual pattern of environmental variables and net photosynthesis at Barrow, Alaska. (From Chapin and Shaver 1985; reprinted with kind permission of Springer Science+Business Media B.V. and the authors.)

texture, hydrology, and topography, among other variables, in moist and wet tundra (Michaelson et al. 2008).

Hydrology

Arctic tundra hydrology is strongly affected by climate and permafrost (Rydén 1981; Kane et al. 1992; Rouse et al. 1997). Total precipitation is typically < 300 mm annually, with more falling as rain than as snow (Rouse et al. 1997). Peak runoff usually occurs during snowmelt (late May or early June), and spring flooding at ice-out of major rivers may dominate wetland hydrographs. During floods, soils become saturated, and depending on geomorphology, may remain that way for the rest of the growing season until freezing again in early fall.

In the Low Arctic, huge expanses of wetland dominate the landscape (Fig. 26.1). In contrast, in the High Arctic, wetlands are patchy and determined mostly by hydrogeomorphology (Fig. 26.3) (Woo and Young 2003), often restricted to snowbanks, groundwater-fed depressions, riverine areas, and lake outflows (Woo and Young 2006). In High Arctic watersheds, snowfall is so low that early-growing-season precipitation contributes as much runoff as snowmelt to wetlands (Dugan et al. 2009).

Dominant hydrological inputs to Arctic wetlands are usually lateral, although ombrogeneous wetlands exist (Jonasson and Shaver 1999). Water moves easily toward the surface of soils because of large soil pores (Quinton et al. 2000), but is restricted from percolating downward by permafrost. Snowfall is relatively light, and topography and wind exposure determine where snow accumulates, influencing spring water presence, especially in the High Arctic (Woo and Young 2003).

More pronounced water movement occurs in "water tracks," channels of subsurface precipitation flow (Kane et al. 1992). Near Toolik Lake, water tracks had deeper thaw, greater productivity of tussock-forming sedge *(Eriophorum vaginatum),* and faster nutrient cycling rates than adjacent areas, highlighting the positive influence of water flow on plant growth (Chapin et al. 1988). In areas where geothermal springs keep

the ground thawed, balsam poplar *(Populus balsamifera)* trees can grow (Bockheim et al. 2003).

Biogeochemistry

Biogeochemistry of Arctic wetland soils is strongly influenced by cold and waterlogged conditions. Plant-available inorganic nutrients are limited because inputs are low, and most are tied up in soil organic matter and microbial biomass (Robinson and Wookey 1997; Jonasson and Shaver 1999). Nutrient recycling rates are also low because cold, anoxic conditions limit microbial activity. Arctic soils contain massive amounts of carbon (C) (Ping et al. 2008), much of which remains frozen in permafrost.

Seasonally, nutrient availability changes dramatically in Arctic wetland soils, primarily because of temperature effects on microbes (ACIA 2004). Soil nutrients are released from microbes in winter and again in the spring around the time of snowmelt. In a calcareous fen near Churchill, Manitoba, peak nutrient availability occurred early in the freeze-thaw phase, and as soils thawed, microbial biomass declined (Edwards et al. 2006). During the growing season, plants actively compete with microbes for soil nutrients, reducing availability.

Patterns of element cycling also vary spatially across Arctic landscapes. Hydrology, slope, and aspect all affect which element is most limiting. Moist acidic and nonacidic tundra can differ in C and nitrogen (N) cycling (Walker et al. 1998; Hobbie et al. 2005). Giblin et al. (1991) found that all communities along a short toposequence in northern Alaska were limited by N and phosphorus (P), but in different ways; P was more limiting in wet sedge meadow (also see Shaver et al. 1998), while N was more limiting in moist tussock and riverside willow habitats. Most P was supplied by recycling rather than weathering. Among these plant communities, standing stocks of N, P, and C as well as plant productivity and biomass differed significantly, with the greatest values found in riverside willow (also see Shaver and Chapin 1991).

Of course, elements do not cycle in isolation. The Simple Arctic Model (Fig. 26.4) proposed by Shaver, Billings, et al. (1992) provides a conceptual basis for understanding how

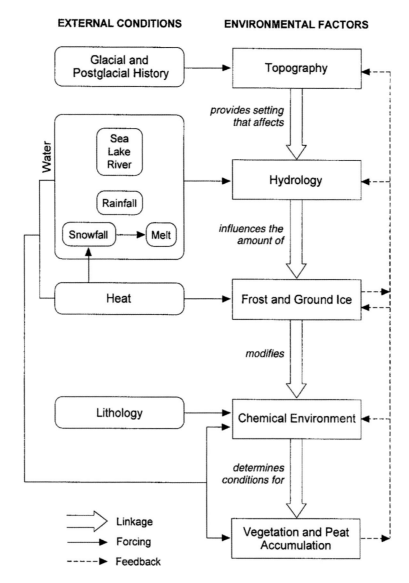

FIG. 26.3. Overview of the environmental factors governing the occurrence of patchy wetlands in the High Arctic. (From Woo and Young 2003.)

C and N cycling are intertwined in tundra wetlands. Essentially, the C:N ratios of the vegetation and soil determine element movement. N must be available for uptake by plants in order for them to accumulate biomass via net primary productivity (NPP). Atmospheric nutrient inputs are low in the Arctic, so most N for plants must come from decomposition and associated N mineralization during which soil organic matter is respired to release carbon dioxide (CO_2). This model highlights how predicting effects of climate change on Arctic wetlands requires consideration of multiple elements and environmental variables. Because vegetation C:N ratios are affected by plant species and growth form, shifts in plant composition induced by cryoturbation, increased temperatures, or biotic factors (e.g., herbivory) may affect both C and N cycling.

Arctic wetland plants show various adaptations to low nutrients (Chapin 1989), several of which affect local N cycling. Some moist tundra plant species use organic N to avoid competition for limited inorganic N (McKane et al. 2002). Mycorrhizae may play an important role in providing N to certain moist tundra species as well (Hobbie and Hobbie 2006). Pres-

ence of N-fixing lichens can affect N availability, especially in the High Arctic, while vascular plants with associated N-fixing root endosymbionts may contribute to N availability in the Low Arctic.

Experiments in wet meadows (Shaver et al. 1998; Boelman et al. 2003) and moist tundra (Shaver et al. 2001; Gough and Hobbie 2003; Hobbie et al. 2005) at Toolik Lake have increased nutrients, increased temperature, and decreased light for many years. Results highlight the importance of shifts in plant growth form that have subsequent effects on element cycling. Warming experiments across wetland and terrestrial communities as part of the International Tundra Experiment (ITEX) also suggest that changes in plant community structure and growth alter biogeochemical cycles (Walker et al. 2006).

Plant Communities

Hydrology, topography, and permafrost interact to control soil moisture and determine plant communities. Along with vas-

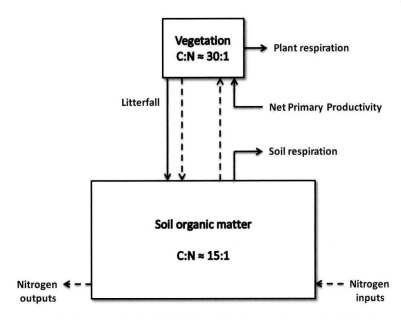

FIG. 26.4. The Simple Arctic Model (SAM), describing how the ratio of carbon (C) to nitrogen (N) controls movement of both elements through tundra ecosystems. Solid arrows represent C, while dashed arrows represent N. (Adapted from Shaver, Billings, et al. 1992.)

cular plants, mosses, liverworts, lichens, and cyanobacteria are important components of many tundra wetland communities. The Arctic flora is small relative to the expansive area covered, and species richness of cryptogams and lichens tends to exceed that of vascular plants (ACIA 2004). However, vascular species richness per unit area is often similar to temperate wetlands. Across relatively short distances, distinctly different plant communities can develop if topography and hydrology vary (Giblin et al. 1991). Epstein et al. (2004) found that transitions between plant community types were controlled by climate, parent material, topography, disturbance, permafrost, hydrology, and snow cover.

Arctic vascular plants use the C_3 photosynthetic pathway, are perennial (with one exception), reproduce mostly through clonal growth, and tend to be mycorrhizal. They must be adapted to cold, wind, short growing seasons, saturated soils, and low soil nutrients. Many plants experience anoxia when the ground freezes, and in wet tundra they must also cope with soil anoxia during the growing season. Given these constraints, NPP in the Arctic is low, with most biomass developing belowground (Table 26.2) (Billings et al. 1978).

Despite the predominance of clonal growth, Arctic plants often produce viable seeds. Germination is limited by environmental constraints (Oberbauer and Dawson 1992; Baskin and Baskin 2001) and, in the Low Arctic, by competition for space from mosses and other plants (Gartner et al. 1986; Gough 2006). Seed dispersal ensured survival of many Arctic species when past glaciation forced migration, and dispersal capabilities may remain high (Alsos et al. 2007).

Height of Arctic plants, and thus presence of trees, is restricted by permafrost, which precludes deep roots, and by abrasion by wind in the winter, causing plants growing on exposed areas to be stunted. Tree seeds are not establishing on the North Slope of Alaska because of the barrier created by the Brooks Range (Rupp et al. 2001). Some evidence of northward movement has been found, however, in northwestern Alaska (Suarez et al. 1999) and in the Canadian Arctic in response to fire (Landhausser and Wein 1993).

The patterned ground of Arctic landscapes has dramatic effects on plant communities at small spatial scales. High-centered tundra polygons are typically surrounded by wet-meadow plants but support species better adapted for drained soil. As polygons age, soil sinking creates ponds that support wetland vegetation (Woo and Young 2006). Similarly, palsas (raised islands of peat also caused by cryoturbation) support moist tundra species because soils are better drained than surrounding habitat. Palsas go through a series of successional stages, beginning as *Carex* wet meadow, then transitioning to fen and then bog vegetation (Bhiry and Robert 2006).

Wet Meadows

Throughout the North American Arctic, wet meadows predominate on saturated soils flooded throughout the growing season (a.k.a. graminoid-moss tundra; Bliss 2000). Wet-meadow soils thaw more slowly than moist tundra, and typically retain standing water through much of the growing season, creating anoxia and low plant diversity.

Plants in wet meadows include pond and lake margin species, such as *Menyanthes trifoliata, Arctophila fulva,* and *Potentilla palustris*. In shallower areas, *Carex* and *Eriophorum* sedges are common, as well as *Sphagnum* and other mosses. This community is analogous to W2 and W3 in the CAVM (Fig. 26.1, Table 26.1). In western and northern Alaska, wet-meadow communities are extensive (Fig. 26.1) and have been studied intensively near Barrow (Brown et al. 1980). Results there suggest that lemmings are important herbivores, and their predators play a role in controlling plant-herbivore dynamics (Batzli et al. 1980).

In the High Arctic, wet meadows have unique species composition, occur on mineral soils, and are more restricted in area (W1 in Fig. 26.1). Less than 2% of the unglaciated land area supports these oases that remain wet throughout the growing season. Wet meadows are usually more productive than the surrounding, drier communities (Henry 1998), and are dom-

TABLE 26.2
Net primary productivity (NPP) and root:shoot ratios for
North American Arctic wetlands

| Plant community | CAVM mapping unit | NPP (g/m²/yr) | | Root:shoot |
		Vascular	Cryptogams	Phytomass
Low Arctic				
Tall shrub	S2	250–400	5–25	1:2
Low shrub	S1	125–175	25–50	1:2
Cottongrass-herb	G4	150–200	25–100	3:1
Wet sedge-moss	W2/W3	150–200	5–25	20:1
High Arctic				
Wet sedge-moss	W1	100–175	10–40	20:1

NOTE: Adapted from Bliss 2000.

inated by graminoid species including sedges, grasses, and rushes, and occasionally *Salix arctica* and *Polygonum viviparum*. Community structure is controlled by grazing intensity, availability of N, and soil moisture (Henry 1998).

Moist Tundra

Moist tundra is the most expansive Arctic wetland (Table 26.1), occurring in areas better drained than wet meadows. Peat and active layer thickness vary over both small and large scales. Communities are dominated by a mixture of sedges *(Eriophorum, Carex),* dwarf shrubs (Ericaceae heaths, *Betula, Salix*), and mosses. On acidic soils, *Sphagnum* mosses proliferate. Moist tundra commonly has patterned ground, with hummocks and tussocks creating drier soil conditions, and surrounding, lower wet areas remaining saturated all summer (Quinton et al. 2000). On acidic soils, *Sphagnum* mosses dominate intertussock or interhummock spaces, insulating soil surfaces, reducing rates of thaw, and retaining meltwater, thus creating saturated soil conditions.

CAVM classification distinguishes different types of moist tundra. Moist graminoid tundra is divided into moist acidic tundra (MAT; G4), composed of tussock sedge (cottongrass, *E. vaginatum),* dwarf shrubs, and mosses; and moist nonacidic tundra (MNT; G3), composed of nontussock *Carex* sedges, dwarf shrubs, forbs, and non-*Sphagnum* mosses. MAT has been well studied in the vicinity of Toolik Lake and other North Slope areas, and is extensive in the Yukon Territory and the Mackenzie River Delta. MNT occurs where loess inputs from rivers keep soil pH high as well as in recently deglaciated areas (Hamilton 2003); *Sphagnum* mosses are rare in MNT and thus cannot drive down pH. MNT communities support the highest plant species richness in the region (Gough et al. 2000; Kade et al. 2005).

The CAVM divides moist shrub tundra (a.k.a. low shrub tundra; Bliss 2000) into erect dwarf-shrub tundra (S1) (common in Alaska and northwestern Canada; a.k.a. mesic dwarf shrub tundra; Nobrega and Grogan 2008) and low-shrub tundra (S2) (often supporting larger alder and willow) (Fig. 26.1, Table 26.1). These communities share species with G3 and G4, including Ericaceae *(Vaccinium, Ledum, Empetrum),* graminoids, and larger shrubs *(Betula, Salix).* Moist shrub tundra generally differs from moist graminoid tundra in that soil depths are shallow (3–10 cm), C and N soil pools are smaller, C:N is lower, and winter soil temperatures are higher.

Riparian willow sites (a.k.a. tall shrub; Bliss 2000) are generally subsumed within other CAVM categories because they exist only in narrow bands. In general, tall shrubs in the Arctic are restricted to riparian areas and watertracks. Gould and Walker (1999) described plant communities at 17 sites along the Hood River, Northwest Territories, and found disturbance, topography, and soil pH affected community occurrence (Fig. 26.5). Riparian sites often support unique species of forbs because flowing water provides nutrients and aeration to the soil, facilitating growth of species not as well adapted to moist or wet-meadow conditions.

Animal Communities

Harsh abiotic factors also limit animal populations in the Arctic. Dark, cold winter conditions require particular adaptations for growth, survival, and reproduction. During the short growing season, numerous animals can take advantage of milder conditions by migrating to the tundra or becoming active in summer. Because plant productivity is low, consumers are less numerous and diverse than at temperate latitudes. Trophic dynamics are often complex because animals must be opportunistic, and many employ omnivory.

Invertebrates

Danks (2004) reported that the North American Arctic supports more than 2,200 species of arthropods. To tolerate winter conditions and exploit the short, cold, and unpredictable growing seasons, invertebrates exhibit various physiological, structural, and ecological adaptations (Danks 2004). Primitive groups such as springtails are better represented than more evolutionarily advanced groups such as beetles (ACIA 2004). Most animal pollination of Arctic plants is by flies, followed

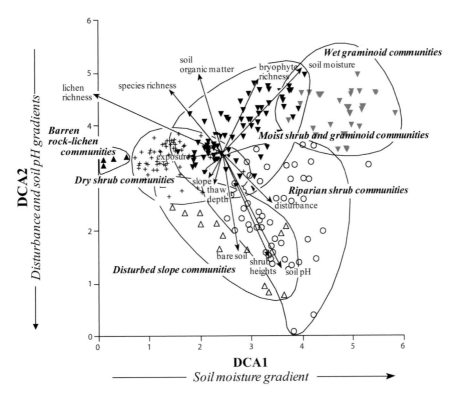

FIG. 26.5. Major physiognomic-ecological vegetation categories from 17 sites along the Hood River, NWT. Six vegetation groups separated along gradients of soil moisture, elevation, topographic position, disturbance, and soil pH. (Figure provided by W. A. Gould; adapted from Gould and Walker 1999.)

by bumblebees and butterflies. Arctic soils harbor numerous invertebrate species (see Fig. 26.6).

Larvae of many Arctic insects are aquatic, with many exploiting wetlands. Arctic mosquitoes develop enormous populations because wetlands provide ample larval habitat in summer. Invertebrates serve as crucial food sources for birds: aquatic larvae for waterfowl and flying adults for passerines. Oestrid flies and mosquitoes harass caribou and other mammals to such an extent that some caribou calves die because they do not eat. Caribou migrate in part to avoid insect harassment (White and Trudell 1980).

Vertebrates

Amphibians and reptiles cannot survive the cold of the Arctic. Birds and mammals, however, are relatively diverse, with a few species overwintering but most being migratory.

BIRDS

Arctic freshwater wetlands serve as crucial stopover habitat and breeding grounds for migratory birds and year-round habitat for other species. Fewer than a dozen bird species, including Arctic redpoll *(Carduelis hornemanni),* ptarmigan *(Lagopus* spp.), raven *(Corvus corax),* gyrfalcon *(Nyctea scandiaca),* and snowy owl *(Bubo scandiacus),* winter in the Arctic, but more than 180 species breed there (Pitelka 1974). In summer, large populations of waterbirds breed, nest, and forage on the tundra, where wetland plants and invertebrates provide nutritious

sources of energy. Charismatic wetland species include tundra swans *(Cygnus columbianus)* that consume submerged vegetation along lake and pond margins and in river deltas, and sandhill cranes *(Grus canadensis)* that nest in marshy tundra. Most birds nest in areas with cover, which in a treeless landscape is usually associated with shrub habitat or emergent vegetation of wet meadows. Because of strong interannual variability in climate, Arctic birds may not breed every year.

Jaegers *(Stercorarius* spp.), golden eagles *(Aquila chrysaetos),* gyrfalcons, rough-legged hawks *(Buteo lagopus),* short-eared owls *(Asio flammeus),* and snowy owls are important predatory birds that frequent Arctic wetlands. Predation, in general, causes significant loss of eggs and young birds each year. Passerine birds are preyed on by Arctic foxes *(Alopex lagopus),* ermines *(Mustela ermine),* jaegers, and gulls. Nesting success of snow geese *(Chen caerulescens)* in Nunavut, Bylot Island, relies on multiple factors, including access to a source of water for females incubating eggs (Lecomte et al. 2009). Foxes have difficulty preying on eggs and young in wetlands, while predatory birds do not. Many predators rely on lemmings for food, and since lemming populations are cyclical, their abundance may increase or decrease predation pressure on birds (Lecomte et al. 2008). In the Yukon-Kuskokwim Delta, Sovada et al. (2001) also found that fox predation affected nesting success of geese, swans, and northern pintails.

MAMMALS

Caribou *(Rangifer tarandus)* and musk ox *(Ovibos moschatus)* are important mammalian residents of the Arctic. Arc-

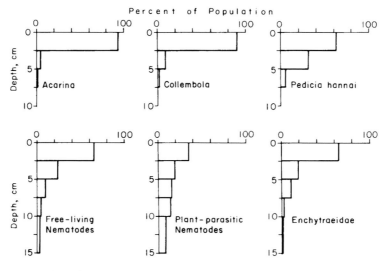

FIG. 26.6. Annual mean depth distribution of representative groups of soil invertebrates sampled in wet coastal meadow at Barrow, Alaska. (From MacLean 1980).

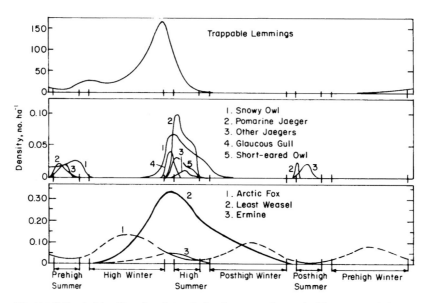

FIG. 26.7. Estimated densities of predators during the course of a standard lemming cycle for the coastal tundra at Barrow. Periods of snowmelt and freeze-up are indicated between summer and winter. (From Batzli, White, et al. 1980.)

tic mammals tolerate the cold climate with thick coats of fur, rounder bodies, shorter extremities, and efficient fat storage (ACIA 2004). Herbivores include small (voles, lemmings, ground squirrels) and large (caribou, musk ox, moose) species. Mammalian herbivores consume a small percentage of available plant productivity, while a large percentage of herbivore biomass is consumed by predators, suggesting that top-down dynamics are important (Krebs et al. 2003).

Microtine rodents (voles, lemmings) have been especially well studied, with considerable focus on their role as herbivores in wet and moist tundra. Microtine rodent diversity decreases with increasing latitude. They remain active through the winter, living beneath the snow; thus they must store food, create dens, and harbor resources each summer. In wet meadows in northern Alaska, brown lemmings (*Lemmus sibiricus*) prefer low, marshy ground, while collared lemmings (*Dicrostonyx*

groenlandicus) avoid wetlands. Brown lemmings consume sedges, while collared lemmings consume willow (Batzli et al. 1980), suggesting niche partitioning. Tundra voles (*Microtus oeconomus*) are most active where lemmings are not common (Batzli and Jung 1980). Important controls on rodent populations are food availability in summer and deep snow for nests in winter.

Lemmings are the subject of many misconceptions. Population swings of brown lemmings in wet-meadow vegetation at Barrow, Alaska, were initially explained by variation in food availability, with populations building and then crashing after overconsumption of food resources (MacLean et al. 1974). Others speculated that predation caused steep declines (Batzli et al. 1980) (Fig. 26.7). Recent studies document synchronous population cycles across regions, suggesting rodents respond to large-scale factors (Reiter and Andersen 2008). These cycli-

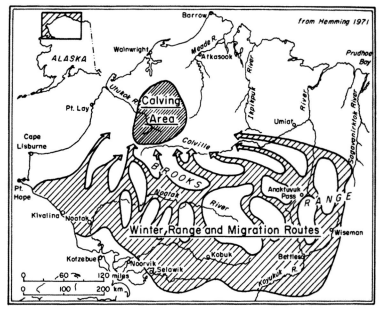

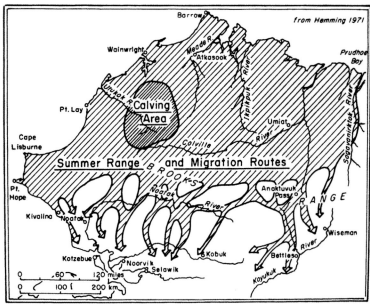

FIG. 26.8. The calving area, winter range, and summer range of the Western Arctic caribou herd. (From White and Trudell 1980.)

cal patterns may be shifting, perhaps in response to climate change (see Callaghan et al. 2004).

Musk ox are relics of the Pleistocene era that are visually dramatic on treeless Arctic landscapes; herds often create protective circles, with all individuals facing outward. Musk ox were hunted to extinction in Alaska but have been reintroduced, and populations have reestablished. They graze in both moist tundra and wet meadows. In the High Arctic, musk ox grazing can enhance moss growth and vascular plant productivity (Henry 1998).

Arctic caribou represent the last large-scale migrating herd mammal in North America. Early in the season, caribou migrate through moist and wet tundra for calving to exploit forage plants when most palatable and to avoid insect harassment. On Alaska's North Slope, four major herds exist. The Teshekpuk herd remains on the coastal plain in the winter, while

the other herds migrate south (Person et al. 2007). The Western Arctic herd near Atqasuk selectively grazes areas with high cover of deciduous shrubs and lichens, including moist graminoid tundra and lake margins (White and Trudell 1980) (Fig. 26.8). On high-centered polygons, they prefer floristically diverse wet troughs between polygons, perhaps because they can forage on flowers that generally have higher nutrient content than leaves or stems. As with musk ox, caribou grazing may stimulate plant productivity, creating positive feedbacks for the animals.

Predatory mammals include wolves (Canis lupus), fox, ermine, shrews (Sorex tundrensis) and wolverine (Gulo gulo). Populations are small, most likely because of food limitation. Fox and wolves follow their migratory prey and also shift distributions in response to small mammal population cycles. In Gates of the Arctic National Park, Alaska, Adams et al. (2008)

found that the wolf population had higher than expected emigration rates, but the population was robust to regulated harvest. Wolves may serve as important regulators of the Western Arctic caribou herd (Haskell and Ballard 2007). Omnivorous grizzly bears *(Ursus arctos horribilis)* also occur throughout the Arctic, but are smaller than individuals farther south because they lack protein in their diet. They rely mostly on ground squirrels, microtine rodents, berries, and sedges for food, and spend much of their time in tall willow riparian areas (McLoughlin et al. 2002).

Key Ecological Controls

Abiotic Factors

The most important ecological controls in Arctic wetlands are abiotic factors associated with the high northern latitudes, particularly very short growing seasons and low year-round temperatures. Many organisms adapt to such conditions with relatively short life cycles. Because of the permafrost, soil organisms (including plant roots) must tolerate freezing each winter, and metabolic activity is limited to the thawed active layer where nutrient availability is low. Wet-meadow sediments are anoxic for much of the summer. Because of these factors, growth rates are low in Arctic wetland plants, and, by extension, consumer populations are limited. Perhaps surprisingly, photosynthetic rates of Arctic wetland plants are comparable to those of temperate vegetation (Chapin and Shaver 1985), but limited growing seasons prevent them from accumulating larger amounts of biomass.

Disturbance and Succession

Disturbance, both natural and human caused, affects Arctic wetland communities. Successional sequences proceed slowly, with the longest time frames in response to glacier advance and retreat. Cryoturbation is the most frequent cause of small-scale disturbance. Frost-heaving varies with soil texture and moisture content. Areas of thermokarst occur where patches of ground ice thaw, causing slumping of the active layer and exposure of bare soil. These areas tend to be larger than frost boils, and may be increasing in occurrence as the climate warms. Succession can occur on these disturbed, exposed areas, with mosses first creeping in from the edges, stabilizing the substrate and facilitating germination by vascular plants (Gartner et al. 1986).

Succession also proceeds along riverbanks in riparian habitats as channels shift. Herbaceous species colonize first and trap sands and silts, eventually allowing *Salix* species to establish (Bliss and Cantlon 1957) (Fig. 26.9). Toward the coastal plain, a well-documented successional sequence occurs in thaw lakes over hundreds of years. Lakes drain, mosses establish, and then vascular wetland plants become common. Eventually the lakebed subdivides into low-centered polygons with ice wedges that eventually thaw, allowing polygons to coalesce to form a new thaw lake (Bliss and Peterson 1992).

Fire occurs in tundra wetlands, but until recently was mostly limited to western Alaska. Some moist tundra plant species, particularly the tussock-forming *E. vaginatum,* regrow well following fire (Racine et al. 1987), while others, such as lichens, take decades to recover. Fire causes permafrost to thaw, creat-

ing wetter soils and often increasing plant growth in the short term (Mackay 1995).

An extensive disturbance study was carried out in the R4D (response, resistance, resilience, and recovery from disturbance) project funded by the Department of Energy on the North Slope of Alaska to better understand the implications of oil and gas extraction (Oechel 1989; Reynolds and Tenhunen 1996). Although direct impacts of exploration for natural resources, pipeline construction, and related activities are limited in area, they may cause permanent changes (Walker et al. 1987). For example, vehicle tracks, left in moist tundra by the first vehicles to explore the North Slope in advance of the Alyeska Oil Pipeline, support different plant communities than surrounding tundra many years later (Chapin and Shaver 1981). Such disturbance can drive the community toward wet-meadow vegetation, with positive feedbacks maintaining standing water because increased water volume thaws more slowly.

Biotic Factors

Biotic variables have received less attention in Arctic wetlands than have abiotic ones. Recently, research on herbivory has increased. Detailed studies first conducted in coastal wet meadow at Barrow described the energetics and activity of small and large mammal herbivores (Batzli et al. 1980). Recent experiments conducted at Toolik Lake found that mammalian herbivores affect growth of vascular plants and lichens, particularly when soil nutrients are enhanced (Gough et al. 2007, 2008). In the High Arctic, musk ox herbivory in wet meadows may also stimulate plant growth. Studies of invertebrate herbivory are lacking (ACIA 2004).

Competition has also been understudied. In removal and transplant experiments, results suggest that moist tundra plants actively compete for nutrients and light (Hobbie et al. 1999; Gough 2006; Bret-Harte et al. 2008). Studies with labeled N indicate that moist tundra species preferentially take up different forms of nitrogen, including organic forms, allowing coexistence on a limited resource (McKane et al. 2002). Mosses compete with vascular plants, and there is intense competition between microbes and plants for soil nutrients soon after snow melts. Small mammals may exhibit niche partitioning, e.g., between collared lemmings and brown lemmings (Batzli et al. 1980).

In such a harsh environment, facilitation and mutualism might be expected to play an important role. Many Arctic vascular wetland plants are mycorrhizal, and mycorrhizae enhance N uptake, in some cases providing 80% of the nutritional needs of the plants (Hobbie and Hobbie 2006). Lichens, cyanobacteria, and vascular plants with root symbionts fix N in many tundra communities. Some studies indicate that Arctic vascular plants facilitate persistence of other species by ameliorating harsh environmental conditions such as wind abrasion and cold temperatures (ACIA 2004).

Conservation Concerns

Traditionally, conservation concerns have focused on tropical areas that harbor high species diversity. However, Post et al. (2009) point out that diversity of most groups is low in the Arctic, so there is little redundancy among species. The loss of

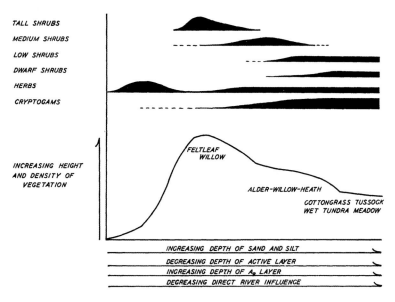

FIG. 26.9. Generalized summary of the relative importance of the various vegetation types in the successional sequence in an Alaskan riparian community as related to several edaphic factors. (From Bliss and Cantlon 1957.)

just one or two species may be catastrophic to Arctic ecosystems (and to native subsistence hunters). Alaska, Canada, and Greenland have set aside large wetland areas in preserves to protect them from human disturbance (Bliss 2000).

Climate Change

An indirect effect of human activities on tundra ecosystems is global climate change, and atmospheric warming in the Arctic has intensified in recent years (ACIA 2004; Anisimov et al. 2007). Changes vary regionally: e.g., permafrost is thawing in certain areas, but not others. If the boundary between discontinuous and continuous permafrost shifts, wetlands may be lost because soils drain better, but new wetlands might form where ponds and lakes drain (Pouse et al. 1997; Schindler and Smol 2006). In the High Arctic, a decrease in snowbanks may reduce water input and affect wetlands (Woo and Young 2006), and polygon wetlands may be negatively affected by changing geomorphology and vegetation (Ellis and Rochefort 2004).

ELEMENT CYCLING

A major concern with warming climate is the role of Arctic wetland soils as a C sink or a C source (Oechel et al. 1993); release of large quantities of CO_2 from wetland soils could exacerbate global warming, with subsequent effects on biota. The Arctic tundra has been a huge sink in the past, with recent estimates of the amount of organic C tied up in soils being even higher than previously thought (Ping et al. 2008). Much of the soil organic matter is available for mineralization, so if the active layer gets deeper, more C will be returned to the atmosphere via soil respiration (Weintraub and Schimel 2003; Mack et al. 2004; Dorrepaal et al. 2009). Cryoturbation can redistribute soil organic C as well, making it more available to respiring microbes (Ping et al. 2008).

C cycle responses to a warming climate will depend on mul-

tiple variables. Changes in precipitation or evapotranspiration may either offset or exacerbate effects of rising temperatures. If warming is accompanied by increases in precipitation, and soil moisture does not change, soils may not release more C. Oechel et al. (1998) found that an Alaskan wet sedge meadow was a net sink of CO_2 when soils were saturated but a source when soils dried. Wet tundra may be more of a sink than moist tundra during summer (Harazano et al. 2003; Nobrega and Grogan 2008), but processes outside of summer are not well understood. Late spring, early fall, and winter studies suggest that tundra wetlands are a significant source of CO_2 even when temperatures are extremely cold (Jones et al. 1999; Nobrega and Grogan 2007).

Nutrient cycling may increase in warmer soils, making N more available to plants and allowing enhanced photosynthesis to fix more of the CO_2 being released from soils (Fig. 26.4), limiting atmospheric increases. Empirical and modeling studies, however, suggest that this would be a short-term response, as plants become nutrient limited once again (McKane et al. 1997). Leaching of inorganic nitrogen could also limit plant access to N. Plant species composition (as related to C:N) also plays an important role in C cycling (Fig. 26.4). Plants that produce wood provide long-term storage of C, while herbaceous plants do not (Gough and Hobbie 2003; Hobbie et al. 2005).

Arctic wetlands are also sources of methane (CH_4), perhaps emitting a third of global CH_4 (Reeburgh 1996). Vascular plants release CH_4 through aerenchyma (King and Reeburgh 2002); mosses do not emit CH_4 in the same way. Thus, plant species composition is important in this process. CH_4 flux varies across the Arctic, so generalizations are difficult. Preliminary data indicate more CH_4 is released from wetlands in the southern Arctic and during summer. With increased temperatures, CH_4 efflux may increase if systems do not dry (ACIA 2004). With so many factors contributing to the function of Arctic wetland ecosystems, predicting flux of both CO_2 and CH_4 over large spatial scales and under changing environmental conditions is a major challenge.

PLANT PHENOLOGY AND SPECIES DISTRIBUTIONS

Shifts in vegetation phenology and community structure from warming temperatures (Crawford 2008), and longer growing seasons will affect regional biogeochemistry and consumer species. Plants with earlier phenologies may deny caribou calves food required for survival (Post et al. 2008). Such trophic mismatches may occur with other wetland organisms, including soil invertebrates that are crucial food sources for some birds (Tulp and Schekkerman 2001).

If the treeline moves north in response to warming (Suarez et al. 1999), ecosystem-level processes will be affected. In southwest Yukon, Danby and Hik (2007) found that historical treeline migration was affected by tree species, temperature, and local environmental conditions, particularly permafrost. Over the past 50 years, shrubs have increased in abundance across the Arctic, converting moist graminoid tundra to moist shrub tundra. Resulting shifts in surface albedo may cause additional feedbacks to warming (Tape et al. 2006).

ANIMAL POPULATIONS

Animal species may respond to warming directly by shifting geographic ranges or indirectly to changes in food sources, pathogens, or predators. Callaghan et al. (2004) reviewed declines in waterfowl populations in Arctic breeding grounds. Boreal forest insects are migrating into the tundra in some areas, and new plant pathogens have recently been implicated in large scale die-offs of boreal trees.

Declines of some large mammals have already been recorded in the Arctic. Arctic fox may be being displaced in the southern portion of its range by red fox (*Vulpes vulpes;* ACIA 2004). The grizzly bear population in Nunavut, Northwest Territories, has been shrinking (McLoughlin et al. 2003), but causes remain unclear. Reductions in caribou populations are also occurring (Vors and Boyce 2009). While major herds in Alaska appear to be relatively stable, those in eastern Canada and elsewhere in the Arctic are declining. Declines may be related to changing phenology of plants (food source) and insects (pests), as well as weather patterns. Vulnerability of caribou to predation may also be increasing, particularly in winter ranges. The recently formed CARMA (CircumArctic Rangifer Monitoring and Assessment; Gunn et al. 2009) is assembling datasets from disparate sources to better document current herd sizes and population changes. As caribou respond to changes in their environment brought about by climate warming, management plans (e.g., hunting quotas) may have to be altered.

FIRE

Fire in moist tundra regions of Alaska is now more common. Along with other, smaller fires on the North Slope in the last decade, the Anaktuvuk Fire in 2007 provides a startling reminder that conditions are changing. This fire burned for three months in moist graminoid tundra, encompassing an area > 100,000 ha (Jones et al. 2009). Previous studies (Bliss and Peterson 1992) suggest that some plant communities will recover quickly from burning. However, Joly et al. (2007) found that caribou avoided burned areas in northwestern Alaska, probably because of long-term negative effects of fire on lichens. Fires that occur at the tundra-forest transition may permit northern expansion of deciduous trees (Landhausser and Wein 1993). Follow-up studies of these areas allow us to predict how increasing fire may affect Arctic wetlands (Qui 2009).

Oil and Gas Development

Economically viable natural resources occur throughout the Arctic. As oil and gas development proceeds near Prudhoe Bay, Alaska, and in the Mackenzie Delta, Canada, concerns persist about long-term effects on wetland vegetation and fauna. Studies in wet meadows near Prudhoe Bay and moist tundra near Toolik Lake and in the Northwest Territories suggest that changes to drainage patterns and contaminant spread from road construction and other activities can be severe (Haag and Bliss 1974; Walker et al. 1987; Oechel 1989). Oil companies have improved some practices, employing winter snow and ice roads, for example, to minimize damage to tundra. Small sections of oil pipeline are belowground to allow wildlife to cross, but the presence of pipelines still affects animal movements (Cameron et al. 2005).

Some animal species probably benefit from oil and gas operations. Predatory birds perching on pipelines gain a better view of potential prey. Ravens successfully nest on oil field structures and raid local landfills for food (Powell and Backenstro 2009). At several North Slope sites, Liebezeit et al. (2009) found no ill effects of oil developments on shorebird nest survival, but passerine nest survival declined, possibly from predation

Cameron et al. (2005) found that caribou shifted calving grounds to avoid oil development, and used lower-quality forage areas. Female abundance and movement were lower at the Prudhoe Bay oil field complex than at other coastal meadows. However, Cronin et al. (1998) found no correlation between caribou distribution and oil and gas infrastructure; thus the overall effect of oil and gas extraction on caribou remains unclear.

Conclusions

Freshwater arctic wetlands of North America are some of our last true wilderness areas. These ecosystems are shaped by permafrost and its effects on soil hydrology. As elsewhere, tundra plants have adapted to wetland conditions, but must also complete growth and reproduction over very short summers. Migrating caribou and birds breeding on the tundra rely heavily on arctic wetlands for survival, as do resident small mammals and insects. Abundance of these species determines population size of predatory species. The most immediate threat to arctic wetlands and their associated biota is global warming. Water balance of the wetlands may be altered, releasing additional carbon from soils and creating a positive feedback for additional warming. Evidence is mounting that arctic flora and fauna are changing phenological patterns in response to warming, and geographic ranges may be shifting for some species. In addition, continued demand for fossil fuels and other resource extraction may alter wetland habitats irreversibly. More research is needed in these wetlands to understand and potentially offset detrimental effects on flora and fauna.

Acknowledgments

Many thanks to Gus Shaver for providing my initial opportunity to conduct research in Arctic Alaska. Carol Moulton provided extensive help with assembling the chapter, and Martha Raynolds graciously created the map for Fig. 26.1. Research funding by the National Science Foundation informed the writing of this chapter.

References

ACIA (Arctic Climate Impact Assessment). 2004. *Impacts of a warming Arctic: Arctic Climate Impact Assessment.* Cambridge: Cambridge Univ. Press.

Adams LG, Stephenson RO, et al. 2008. Population dynamics and harvest characteristics of wolves in the Central Brooks Range, Alaska. *Wildl. Monogr.* 170:1–25.

Alsos IG, Eidesen PB, et al. 2007. Frequent long-distance plant colonization in the changing Arctic. *Science* 316:1606–08.

Anisimov OA, Vaughn DG, et al. 2007. Polar regions (Arctic and Antarctic). In *Climate Change 2007: impacts, adaptation and vulnerability. Contribution of Working Group II to the Fourth Assessment Report of the Intergovernmental Panel on Climate Change,* Parry ML, Canziani OF, et al., editors. Cambridge: Cambridge Univ. Press, pp. 653–85.

Baskin CC, Baskin JM. 2001. *Seeds: ecology, biogeography, and evolution of dormancy and germination.* San Diego: Academic Press.

Batzli GO, Jung HJG. 1980. Nutritional ecology of microtine rodents: resource utilization near Atkasook, Alaska. *Arct. Alp. Res.* 12:483–99.

Batzli GO, White RG, et al. 1980. The herbivore-based trophic system. In *An Arctic ecosystem: the coastal tundra at Barrow, Alaska,* Brown J, Miller PC, et al., editors. Stroudsburg, PA: Dowden, Hutchinson and Ross, Inc., pp. 335–410.

Bhiry N, Robert EC. 2006. Reconstruction of changes in vegetation and trophic conditions of a palsa in a permafrost peatland, subarctic Quebec, Canada. *Ecoscience* 13:56–65.

Billings WD, Peterson KM, Shaver GR. 1978. Growth, turnover and respiration rates of roots and tillers in tundra graminoids. In *Vegetation and production ecology of an Alaskan Arctic tundra,* Tieszen LL, editor. New York: Springer-Verlag, pp. 415–34.

Bliss LC. 2000. Arctic tundra and polar desert biome. In *North American terrestrial vegetation,* Barbour MG, Billings WD, editors. New York: Cambridge Univ. Press, 1–40.

Bliss LC, Cantlon JE. 1957. Succession on river alluvium in northern Alaska. *Am. Midl. Nat.* 58:452–69.

Bliss LC, Matveyeva NV. 1992. Circumpolar arctic vegetation. In *Arctic ecosystems in a changing climate: an ecophysical perspective,* Chapin FS III, Jeffries RL, et al., editors. San Diego: Academic Press, pp. 59–90.

Bliss LC, Peterson KM. 1992. Plant succession, competition, and the physiological constraints of species in the Arctic. In *Arctic ecosystems in a changing climate: an ecophysical perspective,* Chapin FS III, Jeffries RL, et al., editors. San Diego: Academic Press, pp. 111–38.

Bockheim, JG, O'Brien JD, et al. 2003. Factors affecting the distribution of *Populus balsamifera* on the North Slope of Alaska, U.S.A. *Arct. Antarct. Alp. Res.* 35:331–40.

Boelman NT, Stielglitz M, et al. 2003. Response of NDVI, biomass, and ecosystem gas exchange to long-term warming and fertilization in wet sedge tundra. *Oecologia* 135:414–21.

Bret-Harte MS, Mack MC, et al. 2008. Plant functional types do not predict biomass responses to removal and fertilization in Alaskan tussock tundra. *J. Ecol.* 96:713–26.

Brown J, Everett KR, et al. 1980. The coastal tundra at Barrow. In *An Arctic ecosystem: the coastal tundra at Barrow, Alaska,* Brown J, Miller PC, et al., editors. Stroudsburg, PA: Dowden, Hutchinson and Ross, Inc., pp. 1–29.

Callaghan TV, Bjorn LO, et al. 2004. Responses to projected changes in climate and UV-B at the species level. *Ambio* 33:418–35.

Cameron RD, Smith WT, et al. 2005. Central Arctic caribou and petroleum development: distributional, nutritional and reproductive implications. *Arctic* 58:1–9.

Chapin FS III. 1989. The cost of tundra plant structures: evaluation of concepts and currencies. *Am. Nat.* 133:1–19.

Chapin FS, Shaver GR. 1981. Changes in soil properties and vegetation following disturbance of Alaskan Arctic tundra. *J. Appl. Ecol.* 18:605–17.

Chapin FS, Shaver GR. 1985. Arctic. In *Physiological ecology of North American plant communities,* Chabot BF, Mooney HA, editors. New York: Chapman and Hall, pp. 16–40.

Chapin FS, Fletcher N, et al. 1988. Productivity and nutrient cycling of Alaskan tundra: enhancement by flowing soil waters. *Ecology* 69:693–702.

Crawford RMM. 2008. *Plants at the margin: ecological limits and climate change.* Cambridge: Cambridge Univ. Press.

Cronin MA, Amstrup SC, et al. 1998. Caribou distribution during the post-calving period in relation to infrastructure in the Prudhoe Bay Oil Field, Alaska. *Arctic* 51:85–93.

Danby RK, Hik DS. 2007. Variability, contingency and rapid change in recent subarctic alpine tree line dynamics. *J. Ecol.* 95:352–63.

Danks HV. 2004. Seasonal adaptations in Arctic insects. *Integrat. Compar. Biol.* 44:85–94.

Dorrepaal E, Toet S, et al. 2009. Carbon respiration from subsurface peat accelerated by climate warming in the subarctic. *Nature* 460:616–20.

Dugan HA, Lamoureux SF, et al. 2009. Hydrological and sediment yield response to summer rainfall in a small high Arctic watershed. *Hydrol. Processes* 23:1514–26.

Edwards KA, McCulloch J, et al. 2006. Soil microbial and nutrient dynamics in a wet Arctic sedge meadow in late winter and early spring. *Soil Biol. Biochem.* 38:2843–51.

Ellis CJ, Rochefort L. 2004. Century-scale development of polygon-patterned tundra wetland, Bylot Island (73° N, 80°W). *Ecology* 85:963–78.

Epstein HE, Beringer J, et al. 2004. The nature of spatial transitions in the Arctic. *J. Biogeogr.* 31:1917–33.

Gartner BL, Chapin FS III, Shaver GR. 1986. Reproduction of *Eriophorum vaginatum* by seed in Alaskan tussock tundra. *J. Ecol.* 74:1–18.

Giblin AE, Nadelhoffer KJ, et al. 1991. Biogeochemical sequence diversity along a riverside toposequence in Arctic Alaska. *Ecol. Monogr.* 61:415–35.

Gough L. 2006. Neighbor effects on germination, survival, and growth in two Arctic tundra plant communities. *Ecography* 29:44–56.

Gough L, Hobbie SE. 2003. Responses of moist non-acidic Arctic tundra to altered environment: productivity, biomass, and species richness. *Oikos* 103:204–16.

Gough L, Ramsey EA, Johnson DR. 2007. Plant-herbivore interactions in Alaskan Arctic tundra change with soil nutrient availability. *Oikos* 116:407–18.

Gough L, Shaver GR, et al. 2000. Vascular plant species richness in Alaskan Arctic tundra: the importance of soil pH. *J. Ecol.* 88:54–66.

Gough L, Shrestha K, et al. 2008. Long-term mammalian herbivory and nutrient addition alter lichen community structure in Alaskan dry heath tundra. *Arct. Antarct. Alp. Res.* 40:65–73.

Gould WA, Walker MD. 1999. Plant communities and landscape diversity along a Canadian Arctic river. *J. Veg. Sci.* 10:537–48.

Gunn A, Russell D, et al. 2009. Facing a future of change: wild migratory caribou and reindeer. *Arctic* 62:iii–vi.

Haag RW, Bliss LC. 1974. Energy budget changes following surface disturbance to upland tundra. *J. Appl. Ecol.* 11:355–75.

Hamilton TD. 2003. Glacial geology of the Toolik Lake and Upper Kuparuk river region. Institute of Arctic Biology, Fairbanks, Alaska. Biological Papers of the University of Alaska, No. 26.

Harazano Y, Mano M, et al. 2003. Inter-annual carbon dioxide uptake of a wet sedge tundra ecosystem in the Arctic. *Tellus* 55B:215–31.

Haskell SP, Ballard WB. 2007. Modeling the Western Arctic caribou herd during a positive growth phase: potential effects of wolves and radiocollars. *J. Wildl. Manage.* 71:619–27.

Henry GHR. 1998. Environmental influences on the structure of sedge meadows in the Canadian High Arctic. *Plant Ecol.* 134:119–29.

Hobbie JE, Hobbie EA. 2006. N in symbiotic fungi and plants estimate nitrogen and carbon flux rates in Arctic tundra. *Ecology* 87:816–22.

Hobbie SE. 1996. Temperature and plant species control over litter decomposition in Alaskan tundra. *Eco. Monogr.* 66:503–22.

Hobbie SE, Gough L, Shaver GR. 2005. Species compositional differences on different-aged glacial landscapes drive contrasting responses of tundra to nutrient addition. *J. Ecol.* 93:770–82.

Hobbie SE, Shevtsova A, Chapin FS III. 1999. Plant responses to species removal and experimental warming in Alaskan tussock tundra. *Oikos* 84:417–34.

Joly K, Bente P, Dau J. 2007. Response of overwintering caribou to burned habitat in northwest Alaska. *Arctic* 60:401–10.

Jonasson S, Shaver GR1999. Within-stand nutrient cycling in Arctic and boreal wetlands. *Ecology* 80:2139–50.

Jones BM, Kolden CA, et al. 2009. Fire behavior, weather, and burn severity of the 2007 Anaktuvuk River Tundra Fire, North Slope, Alaska. *Arct. Antarct. Alp. Res.* 41:309–16.

Jones MH, Fahnestock JT, Welker JM. 1999. Early and late winter carbon dioxide efflux from Arctic tundra in the Kuparuk river watershed, Alaska, U.S.A. *Arct. Antarct. Alp. Res.* 31:187–90.

Kade A, Walker DA, Raynolds MK. 2005. Plant communities and soils in cyroturbated tundra along a bioclimate gradient in the Low Arctic, Alaska. *Phytocoenologia* 35:761–820.

Kane DL, Hinzman LD, et al. 1992. Arctic hydrology and climate change. In *Arctic ecosystems in a changing climate: an ecophysiological perspective,* Chapin FS III, Jeffries RL, et al., editors. San Diego: Academic Press, pp. 35–58.

King JY, Reeburgh WS. 2002. A pulse-labeling experiment to determine the contribution of recent plant photosynthesis to net methane emission in Arctic wet sedge tundra. *Soil Biol. Biochem.* 34:173–80.

Krebs CJ, Danell K, et al. 2003. Terrestrial trophic dynamics in the Canadian Arctic. *Can. J. Zool.* 81:827–44.

Landhausser SM, Wein RW. 1993. Postfire vegetation recovery and tree establishment at the Arctic treeline: climate-change-vegetation-response hypothesis. *J. Ecol.* 81:665–72.

Lecomte N, Gauther G, Giroux JF. 2009. A link between water availability and nesting success mediated by predator-prey interactions in the Arctic. *Ecology* 90:465–75.

Lecomte N, Careau V, et al. 2008. Predator behavior and predation risk in the heterogeneous Arctic environment. *J. Anim. Ecol.* 77:439–47.

Liebezeit JR, Kendall SJ, et al. 2009. Influence of human development and predators on nest survival of tundra birds, Arctic coastal plain, Alaska. *Ecol. Appl.* 19:1628–44.

Mack MC, Schuur EAG, et al. 2004. Ecosystem carbon storage in Arctic tundra reduced by long-term nutrient fertilization. *Nature* 431:440–43.

Mackay JR. 1995. Active layer changes (1968–1993) following the forest-tundra fire near Inuvik, N.W.T., Canada. *Arct. Alp. Res.* 27:323–36.

MacLean SF. 1980. The detritus-based trophic system. In *An Arctic ecosystem: the coastal tundra at Barrow, Alaska,* Brown J, Miller PC, et al., editors. Stroudsburg, PA: Dowden, Hutchinson and Ross, Inc., pp. 411–57.

MacLean SF, Fitzgerald BM, Pitelka FA. 1974. Population cycles in Arctic lemmings: winter reproduction and predation by weasels. *Arct. Alp. Res.* 6:1–12.

Martini IP, Jeffries RL, et al. 2009. Polar coastal wetlands: development, structure, and land use. In *Coastal wetlands: an integrated ecosystem approach,* Perillo GME, Wolanski, E et al., editors. New York: Elsevier, pp. 119–55.

McKane RB, Johnson LC, et al. 2002. Resource-based niches provide a basis for plant species diversity and dominance in Arctic tundra. *Nature* 415:68–71.

McKane RB, Rastetter EB, et al. 1997. Climatic effects on tundra carbon storage inferred from experimental data and a model. *Ecology* 78:1170–87.

McLoughlin PD, Case RL, et al. 2002. Hierarchical habitat selection by barren-ground grizzly bears in the central Canadian Arctic. *Oecologia* 132:102–08.

McLoughlin PD, Taylor MK, et al. 2003. Population variability of barren-ground grizzly bears in Nunavut and the Northwest Territories. *Arctic* 56:185–90.

Michaelson GJ, Ping CL, et al. 2008. Soils and frost boil ecosystems across the North American Arctic Transect. *J. Geophys. Res.* 113:1–11.

Munroe JS, Bockheim JG. 2001. Soil development in Low-Arctic tundra of the northern Brooks Range, Alaska, U.S.A. *Arct. Antarct. Alp. Res.* 33:78–87.

Nobrega S, Grogan P. 2007. Deeper snow enhances winter respiration from both plant-associated and bulk soil carbon pools in birch hummock tundra. *Ecosystems* 10:419–31.

Nobrega S, Grogan P. 2008. Landscape and ecosystem-level controls on net carbon dioxide exchange along a natural moisture gradient in Canadian Low Arctic tundra. *Ecosystems* 11:377–96.

Oberbauer SF, Dawson TE. 1992. Water relations of Arctic vascular plants. In *Arctic ecosystems in a changing climate: an ecophysiological perspective,* Chapin FS III, Jeffries RL, et al., editors. San Diego: Academic Press, pp. 259–80.

Oechel WC. 1989. Nutrient and water flux in a small Arctic watershed: an overview. *Holarct. Ecol.* 12:229–37.

Oechel WC, Vourlitis GL, et al. 1998. The effects of water table manipulation and elevated temperature on the net carbon dioxide flux of wet sedge tundra ecosystems. *Glob. Change Biol.* 4:77–90.

Oechel WC, Hastings SJ, et al. 1993. Recent change of Arctic tundra ecosystems from a net carbon dioxide sink to a source. *Nature* 361:520–23.

Ostendorf B, Reynolds JF. 1998. A model of Arctic tundra vegetation derived from topographic gradients. *Landscape Ecol.* 13:187–201.

Oswald WW, Brubaker LB, et al. In preparation. Late Quaternary environmental and ecological history of the Arctic Foothills, northern Alaska. In *A warming Arctic: ecological consequences for tundra, streams and lakes,* Hobbie J, editor. New York: Oxford Univ. Press.

Person BT, Prichard AK, et al. 2007. Distribution and movements of the Teshekpuk Caribou Herd 1990–2005: prior to oil and gas development. *Arctic* 60:238–50.

Pielou EC. 1994. *A naturalist's guide to the Arctic.* Chicago: Univ. Chicago Press.

Ping CL, Michaelson GJ, et al. 2008. High stocks of soil organic carbon in the North American Arctic region. *Nat. Geosci.* 1:615–19.

Pitelka FA. 1974. An avifaunal review for the Barrow region and North Slope of Arctic Alaska. *Arct. Alp. Res.* 6:161–84.

Post E, Forchhammer MC, et al. 2009. Ecological dynamics across the Arctic associated with recent climate change. *Science* 325:1355–58.

Post E, Pedersen C, et al. 2008. Warming, plant phenology and the spatial dimension of trophic mismatch for large herbivores. *Proc. Royal Soc. B* 275:2005–13.

Powell AN, Backenstro S. 2009. *Common ravens* (Corvus corax) *nesting on Alaska's North Slope oil fields.* Final Report OCS Study Minerals Management Service 2009–007, Univ. Alaska, Fairbanks.

Qui J. 2009. Arctic ecology: tundra's burning. *Nature* 461:34–36.

Quinton WL, Gray DM, Marsh P. 2000. Subsurface drainage from hummock-covered hillslopes in the Arctic tundra. *J. Hydrol.* 237:113–25.

Racine CH, Johnson LA, Viereck LA. 1987. Patterns of vegetation recovery after tundra fires in northwestern Alaska, U.S.A. *Arct. Alp. Res.* 19:461–69.

Reeburgh WS. 1996. "Soft spots" in the global methane budget. In *Microbial growth on C1 compounds,* Lidstrom ME, Tabita FR, editors. Boston: Kluwer Academic Publ., pp. 334–42.

Reiter ME, Anderson DE. 2008. Trends in abundance of collared lemmings near Cape Churchill, Manitoba, Canada. *J. Mammal.* 89:138–44.

Reynolds JF, Tenhunen JD. 1996. *Landscape function and disturbance in Arctic tundra.* New York: Springer-Verlag.

Robinson CH, Wookey PA. 1997. Microbial ecology, decomposition and nutrient cycling. In *Ecology of Arctic environments,* Woodin SJ, Marquis M, editors. Malden, MA: Blackwell Sciences Ltd., pp. 41–68.

Rouse WR, Douglas MSV, et al. 1997. Effects of climate change on the freshwaters of Arctic and subarctic North America. *Hydrol. Processes* 11:873–902.

Rupp T, Chapin FS III, Starfield AM. 2001. Modeling the influence of topographic barriers on treeline advance at the forest-tundra ecotone in northwestern Alaska. *Clim. Change* 48:399–416.

Ryden BE. 1981. Hydrology of northern tundra. In *Tundra ecosystems: a comparative analysis,* Bliss LC, Heal OW, Moore JJ, editors. Cambridge: Cambridge Univ. Press, pp. 115–37.

Schindler DW, Smol JP. 2006. Cumulative effects of climate warming and other human activities on freshwaters of Arctic and subarctic North America. *Ambio* 35:160–68.

Shaver GR, Chapin FS III. 1991. Production: biomass relationships and element cycling in contrasting Arctic vegetation types. *Ecol. Monogr.* 61:1–31.

Shaver GR, Billings WD, et al. 1992. Global change and the carbon balance of the Arctic ecosystem. *BioScience* 42:433–41.

Shaver GR, Bret-Harte MS, et al. 2001. Species composition interacts with fertilizer to control long-term change in tundra productivity. *Ecology* 82:3163–81.

Shaver GR, Johnson LC, et al. 1998. Biomass and carbon dioxide flux in wet sedge tundras: responses to nutrients, temperature and light. *Ecol. Monogr.* 68:75–97.

Sovada MA, Anthony RM, Batt BDJ. 2001. Predation on waterfowl in Arctic tundra and prairie breeding areas: a review. *Wildl. Soc. Bull.* 29:6–15.

Suarez F, Binkley D, et al. 1999. Expansion of forest stands into tundra in the Noatak National Preserve, northwest Alaska. *Ecoscience* 6:465–70.

Tape K, Sturm M, Racine R. 2006. The evidence for shrub expansion in northern Alaska and the Pan-Arctic. *Glob. Change Biol.* 12:686–705.

Tulp I, Schekkerman H. 2001. Has prey availability for Arctic birds advanced with climate change? Hindcasting the abundance of tundra arthropods using weather and seasonal variation. *Arctic* 61:48–60.

USFWS. 1994. *Status of Alaska wetlands.* Anchorage: USFWS.

Vors LS, Boyce MS. 2009. Global declines of caribou and reindeer. *Glob. Change Biol.* 15:2626–33.

Walker DA, Auerbach NA, et al. 1998. Energy and trace-gas fluxes across a soil pH boundary in the Arctic. *Nature* 394:469–73.

Walker DA, Raynolds MK, et al. 2005. The Circumpolar Arctic Vegetation map. *J. Veg. Sci.* 16:267–82.

Walker DA, Webber PJ, et al. 1987. Cumulative impacts of oil fields on northern Alaskan landscapes. *Science* 238:757–61.

Walker MD, Wahren CH, et al. 2006. Plant community responses to experimental warming across the tundra biome. *PNAS* 103:1342–46.

Weintraub MN, Schimel JP. 2003. Interactions between carbon and nitrogen mineralization and soil organic matter chemistry in Arctic tundra soils. *Ecosystems* 6:129–43.

White RG, Trudell J. 1980. Habitat preference and forage consumption by reindeer and caribou near Atkasook, Alaska. *Arct. Alp. Res.* 12:511–29.

Woo MK, Young KL. 2003. Hydrogeomorphology of patchy wetlands in the High Arctic, polar desert environment. *Wetlands* 23:291–309.

Woo MK, Young KL. 2006. High Arctic wetlands: their occurrence, hydrological characteristics and sustainability. *J. Hydrol.* 320:432–50.

INDEX

Composition: BookMatters

Text: 8/10.75 Stone Serif

Display: Akzidenz Grotesk

Prepress: Embassy Graphics

Printer and Binder: QuaLibre